Volume 97 • Number 3 • May 2026

SRL Seismological Research Letters

Focus Section
Myanmar-Tibet Earthquakes

SSA
Seismological Society of America

SRL Seismological Research Letters

Volume 97 • Number 3 • May 2026

Opinion

Ocean Acoustic Waves in Real-Time Tsunami Forecasting: Opportunities and Limitations 1571
Shuo Ma

On the Seismic Hazard Regulations for NPP Sites in Europe: A Controversial Case in Slovenia 1573
Livio Sirovich and Kurt Decker

Focus Section

Myanmar-Tingri Earthquakes
Guest Editors: Marie-Luce Chevalier, Wardah Fadil, Vineet Gahalaut, and Shengji Wei

Preface to the Focus Section on The 2025 M_w 7.7 Myanmar and M_w 7.1 Tingri Earthquakes: Multidisciplinary Insights into Seismogenesis, Hazard, and Community Resilience 1580
Marie-Luce Chevalier, Wardah Fadil, Vineet Gahalaut, and Shengji Wei

Aftershock Triggering Mechanism by the 7 January 2025 M_w 7.1 Tingri Earthquake 1582
Chong Yue, Danqing Dai, Xiaofan Li, Yue Wang, Yingfeng Zhang, Wen Yang, Yanyan Han, Chunyan Qu, and Lingyuan Meng

28 March 2025 Myanmar Earthquake: Strong Ground Motions, Macroseismic Intensity, Liquefaction, and ALOS-2 ScanSAR Remote Sensing Damage Observations 1595
Alejandro Cruz, Mohammad Ghasemi, Shaghayegh Karimzadeh, Sadra Karimzadeh, Aysegul Askan, Masashi Matsuoka, and Paulo B. Lourenço

On the Cover

In early 2025, two major earthquakes occurred in the broader Himalayan region. The first was the Mw 7.1 earthquake that occurred in Tingri, Tibet on 7 January and the second Mw 7.7 earthquake occurred in Mandalay, Myanmar, on 28 March. Both caused significant damage. The cover of this issue shows the Maha Myat Muni Pagoda in Mandalay, which collapsed due to the Myanmar earthquake. The focus section in this issue highlights recent multidisciplinary research on these two earthquakes, aiming to provide a better understanding not only of the earthquakes themselves but also of regional tectonics and seismic hazard.

Image credit: STRINGER/EPA-EFE/Shutterstock

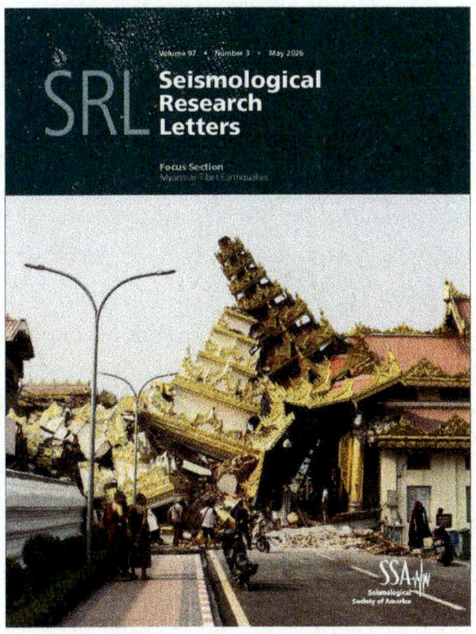

Asymmetric Y-Shaped Structural Rupture of the 2025 M_w 7.1 Tingri, Southern Tibet, Earthquake 1613
Ying Shi, Yongzhe Wang, Hua Pan, Kun Chen, Yuanzhi Liu, and Jiahao Zou

Coseismic Displacement Characteristics near the Epicenter of the M_w 7.7 Myanmar Earthquake on 28 March 2025: Insights from Beijing-3 High-Resolution Satellite Imagery Analysis 1628
Junjie Zou, Honglin He, Zhigang Shao, Wenqiao Li, Jianhua Huang, and Lu Gao

Spatiotemporal Evolution of Early Aftershocks Following the 2025 M_w 7.1 Dingri, Southern Tibet, Earthquake 1643
Ming Zhi, Qianhe Li, Dongdong Yao, Dun Wang, Fei Guo, and Li Sun

Mapping of Soil Liquefaction Induced by the 2025 M_w 7.8 Sagaing Earthquake in Myanmar Using High-Spatial-Resolution Images 1655
Guiming Hu, Renwei Xiong, Wenqiao Li, Peng Liang, Chaozhong Hu, Weiwei Wu, and Yueren Xu

The 2025 M_w 7.1 Tingri (South Tibet) Earthquake: Rupture of Normal Conjugate Optimally Oriented Faults, Shallow Coseismic Slip Deficit, and Early Afterslip 1667
Xiaoyu Zou and Yuri Fialko

Observed H/V Responses Across Thailand from the 2025 M_w 7.7 Myanmar Earthquake: Implications for Geologically Controlled Seismic Hazard 1681
Passakorn Pananont, Pansa Pholsonda, Patinya Pornsopin, Kevin Furlong, Koichi Hayashi, Songsak Muangnoi, and Kasian Prasertwongphilai

Surface Rupture and Slip Distribution of the 2025 M_w 7.7 Mandalay Earthquake and Updated Length Scaling of Supershear Earthquakes 1697
Nadine G. Reitman, Yu Wang, Yu-Ting Kuo, Catherine Hanagan, Alexandra E. Hatem, Christopher B. DuRoss, Chun-Chi Chen, Dara E. Goldberg, Harriet Zoe Yin, Richard W. Briggs, Jessica A. Thompson Jobe, Sylvia R. Nicovich, Emerson M. Lynch, Joseph Powell, William D. Barnhart, and Robert Schmitt

Coulomb Stress Transfer and Future Earthquake Hazard from the 2025 M_w 7.7 Myanmar Earthquake: Implications for the Sagaing Fault and Shan Plateau 1721
Tuo Shen, Weiwei Wu, Guojie Meng, Tai Liu, Lupeng Zhang, Jin Tang, and Xiwei Xu

Mailing & Subscription Information

Subscriptions to *Seismological Research Letters* (SRL): Information regarding institutional subscriptions can be found at https://www.seismosoc.org/publications/institutional-subscribers/. Members of the Seismological Society of American receive online access to SRL and may purchase a print subscription. For membership information visit https://www.seismosoc.org.

Seismological Research Letters (ISSN: 0895-0695) is published bimonthly in January, March, May, July, September, and November by the Seismological Society of America, 400 Evelyn Avenue, Suite 201, Albany, California 94706. Periodicals postage paid at Berkeley, California and at additional mailing offices.

Postmaster: Send address changes to Seismological Research Letters, 400 Evelyn Avenue, Suite 201, Albany, California 94706.

For information on submissions and instructions for authors, visit https://www.seismosoc.org/publications/srl. Communications regarding the journal apart from submission of manuscripts should be addressed to the Seismological Society of America at info@seismosoc.org.

Surface Rupture of the 2025 M_w 7.7 Mandalay, Myanmar, Earthquake: Insights from Field and Optical Remote Sensing Observations 1739
Soe Min, Thura Aung, Hiroyuki Tsutsumi, Wanna Htun, Chit Thet Mon, Lin Thu Aung, Kyaw Zin Win, Saw Myat Min, Ei Mhone Nathar Myo, Khaing Nyein Htay, Saw Ngwe Khaing, Myo Thant, Soe Thura Tun, and Yu Wang

Articles

The M 5.7 Parker Butte Earthquake near Yerington, Nevada: Anatomy of a Dual-Plane Rupture in the Walker Lane from High-Precision Relocated Earthquakes, InSAR, GPS, and Strong-Motion Data 1754
Kyren R. Bogolub, Daniel T. Trugman, Yu Jiang, William C. Hammond, Kenneth D. Smith, Rich D. Koehler, and Christie D. Rowe

Complex Multipatch Rupture and Aftershock Characteristics of the 2024 M_w 4.2 Buan, Korea, Earthquake Sequence 1767
Min-Seong Seo, Won-Young Kim, Sangwoo Han, Jun Yong Park, and YoungHee Kim

Early Warning Performance of FinDer, Virtual Seismologist, and eBEAR Systems in the 2024 M_L 7.2 Hualien, Taiwan, Earthquake 1782
Guan-Yi Song, Da-Yi Chen, Yih-Min Wu, Frédérick Massin, Maren Böse, and John Clinton

Frequency-Dependent Bilateral Rupture of the 2024 M_w 7.1 Wushi Earthquake, NW China: Insights from InSAR, Seismic Imaging, and Aftershock Relocation 1798
Bo Zhao, Yanlu Ma, and Xuejun Han

Adapting Hybrid CBR–RBF Models for Casualty and Emergency Supply Demand Forecasting in High-Altitude Regions: A Case Study of the 2022 Luding Earthquake 1812
Yiguo Zhou and Zhuojuan Xie

Evidence of Liquefaction-Induced Gradual Ground Tilt Settlement at Strong-Motion Stations 1827
Shengze Tian and M. Shahria Alam

Effects of Pore Pressure Change on Coulomb Stress Change and Initiation of Induced Seismicity in the Raton Basin, Colorado–New Mexico 1842
Fabiana Fuentes, Megan R. M. Brown, Manuel M. Mendoza, Shemin Ge, and Anne F. Sheehan

Forecasting Fluid-Induced Seismicity Using Machine Learning Time-Series Prediction 1853
Arthur Cuvier, Julie Maury, Hideo Aochi, and Hugo Breuillard

Detecting and Characterizing Swarm-Like Seismicity 1867
Luigi Passarelli, Gesa Petersen, Leila Mizrahi, and Simone Cesca

Analyzing Earthquake's Onset-Magnitude Correlation Using Modeled Source Time Functions of Recorded Earthquakes and Machine Learning 1881
Gopala Krishna Rodda and Yuval Tal

Identifying Vehicle Signals in Continuous Seismic Data Using Unsupervised Machine-Learning Techniques 1893
Chengping Chai, Omar Marcillo, Monica Maceira, Ryan Kerekes, and Bonnie Canion

Signal Enhancement of Distributed Acoustic Sensing Data Using a Spectral Subtraction–Based Approach 1905
Giulio Pascucci, Sonja Gaviano, Alice Pozzoli, and Francesco Grigoli

Fiber-Optic Sensing for Earthquake Hazards Research, Monitoring, and Early Warning 1919
Jeffrey J. McGuire, Andrew J. Barbour, Zack J. Spica, Verónica Rodríguez Tribaldos, Zhongwen Zhan, Bradley P. Lipovsky, Robert J. Mellors, Ettore Biondi, Clara Yoon, Martin Karrenbach, Adam T. Ringler, James Atterholt, Avinash Nayak, Theresa Sawi, Loïc Viens, Eileen R. Martin, Allen L. Husker, Paul Bodin, Morgan P. Moschetti, Qibin Shi, Nathaniel C. Miller, and Prisha Puri

Near-Surface High-Frequency Spectral Decay Kappa (κ) Model of *S* Waves in Western-Central Sichuan, China 1946
Pengfei Dang, Jie Cui, Bingyan Zhao, and Qifang Liu

Wavenumber Limitation of Medium in the Finite-Difference Modeling of Seismic-Wave Propagation: A Proof of Concept 1965
Jozef Kristek, Jaroslav Valovcan, Peter Moczo, Miriam Kristekova, Rune Mittet, and Martin Galis

Insights into ShakeAlert Earthquake Early Warning Alert Delivery by the MyShake Platform from Rapid Post-Event Analyses 1976
Savvas Marcou, Stephen Thompson, Angela I. Lux, Amy L. Williamson, Suresh Raman, Julien Marty, and Richard M. Allen

Searching for Seismic Precursors—The Barry Landslide Hazard 1990
Gabrielle K. Davy, Michael E. West, Ezgi Karasözen, and John J. Lyons

An Improved Method for Inverting the Spatiotemporal Stress Field Using Focal Mechanism Data and Its Application in Sichuan–Yunnan Region, China 2002
Xiangyun Guo and Zhenyue Li

Lower Crustal Density: Method and Uncertainty Quantification 2016
Yitan Wang, Raymond M. Russo, and Yuanhang Lin

Basin Geometry and Crustal Structure in and Around the Jianghan Basin of Central China: Implications for Geothermal Prospecting 2036
Rong Huang, Penglong Wei, Lei Liu, Fengxu Wang, Shaoqian Hu, Kaifeng Zhao, and Yinhe Luo

Long-Period Ground Motions from Dynamic Rupture Simulations of Large Earthquakes on the Creeping Hayward–Calaveras–Rodgers Creek Fault System 2050
Ruth A. Harris, Michael Barall, Grace A. Parker, and Evan T. Hirakawa

RMS and Hierarchical Agglomerative Clustering to Build Template Event Catalogs of Tectonic Tremors 2064
Gerardo Mendo-Pérez, Hiromichi Nagao, and Yoshikazu Terada

The Intensity Gap: A Global Analysis of Who Responds to the Crowdsourced "Did You Feel It?" System 2082
Elijah Knodel, David J. Wald, Vincent Quitoriano, and Sabine Loos

Environmental Effects on Broadband Seismic Noise: A Year-Long Assessment from Maitri Station, Dronning Maud Land, East Antarctica 2107
Satish Saha, Rahul Biswas, and Prakash Kumar

Lithosphere Tectonic Regionalization of China and Surrounding Regions from Unsupervised Learning Analysis of Surface-Wave Dispersion Data 2116
Jiao Yang, Han Zhang, Sidao Ni, Zefeng Li, and Xuewei Bao

Bedrock Offset Across the Wasatch Fault in Salt Lake City, Utah, from Teleseismic Converted Phases and Its Geologic Implications 2128
HyeJeong Kim, James C. Pechmann, Fan-Chi Lin, Adam P. McKean, and Christian L. Hardwick

Electronic Seismologist

PyGRT: An Efficient and Integrated Python Package for Computing Synthetic Seismograms in a Layered Half-Space Model 2138
Dengda Zhu, Jian Wang, Jinlai Hao, Shi Yao, Ya Xu, Tao Xu, and Zhenxing Yao

Ground-Motion Models at Your Fingertips: Easy, Rapid, and Flexible Analysis with eGSIM 2154
Riccardo Zaccarelli, Graeme Weatherill, Dino Bindi, and Fabrice Cotton

Historical Seismologist

Present to Past Reflection? Notes on the 1114/5 C.E. Earthquake Sequence After the February 2023 Türkiye Doublet 2167
Motti Zohar and Jefferson Williams

Data Mine

U.S. Geological Survey Geomagnetic Variometer Data: Capitalizing on Seismic Infrastructure 2179
Adam T. Ringler, Andrew Holcomb, Joshua E. Rigler, Spencer F. Wilbur, Christopher Balch, Corey Beutel, Brendan Geels, Jordan A. Guerra, Alan Horton, Edward Kromer, Kristen A. Lewis, Jeffrey J. Love, Yolando Root, Claudia K. Rossavik , Nicholas Shavers, John Spritzer, Tyler Storm, Alexandra N. Wernle, and David C. Wilson

SSA News and Notes 2191

Ocean Acoustic Waves in Real-Time Tsunami Forecasting: Opportunities and Limitations

OPEN ACCESS

Shuo Ma*[1]

Since the introduction of the tsunami earthquake concept by Kanamori (1972), it has been well recognized that some of the most tsunamigenic earthquakes radiate unusually weak high-frequency seismic energy (e.g., Lay *et al.*, 2012). Such events may be only weakly felt on land, yet they can generate devastating tsunamis tens of minutes later. This behavior is particularly well documented along the northern Japan Trench and presents a fundamental challenge for real-time tsunami early warning.

The 1896 Sanriku tsunami earthquake is a canonical example: despite minimal felt shaking, it produced a tsunami that killed approximately 22,000 people (Shuto *et al.*, 2007). A similar spatial pattern was observed during the 2011 M_w 9.1 Tohoku–Oki earthquake. Although that event generated large tsunamis overall, the largest runup—reaching nearly 40 m along the Sanriku Coast—occurred more than 100 km north of the epicenter (Kodaira *et al.*, 2021) and caused immense devastation. The inferred tsunami source region substantially overlapped the 1896 rupture area but was only weakly expressed in seismic and geodetic models (Lay, 2018; Uchida and Bürgmann, 2021), consistent with severely depleted high-frequency radiation.

Recent studies have shown that these anomalous observations can be explained by inelastic deformation of the shallow sedimentary wedge along the northern Japan Trench (Ma, 2023). In this framework, weak and unconsolidated sediments undergo inelastic deformation that produces large seafloor uplift without requiring large shallow slip on the plate interface, consistent with the differential bathymetry data north of 39° N for the 2011 Tohoku–Oki event (e.g., Kodaira *et al.*, 2021), while simultaneously dissipating energy and suppressing high-frequency seismic and acoustic radiation (Ma and Hirakawa, 2013). This mechanism provides a unified physical explanation for the coexistence of large tsunamis and weak high-frequency wavefields in this region.

Building on this idea, fully coupled simulations of dynamic rupture, ocean acoustic waves, and tsunami for both the 2011 Tohoku–Oki and 1896 Sanriku events (Du and Ma, 2025; Ma and Du, 2025) demonstrate that large tsunamis can occur even when ocean acoustic waves are weak. These results indicate that acoustic wave amplitudes do not scale reliably with tsunami size because the two are governed by fundamentally different characteristic periods and restoring forces: ocean acoustic waves arise from the elastic compressibility of the ocean whereas tsunamis are controlled by gravity. The absence of strong acoustic signals does not imply low tsunami hazard (e.g., Okal *et al.*, 2003; Wilson and Ma, 2021). Here, ocean acoustic waves refer to compressional and seismoacoustic pressure waves in the water column, with dominant periods of order 0.01–1 s and, in some cases, lower-frequency acoustic–gravity components extending to tens of seconds.

Against this physical background, recent computational efforts have explored real-time tsunami forecasting frameworks that assimilate ocean acoustic or pressure signals to infer evolving seafloor deformation. For example, Henneking *et al.* (2025) presented a high-performance computing approach that assimilates ocean-bottom pressure data for rapid inference. Although ocean-bottom pressure records contain both seismoacoustic signals and the tsunami-induced hydrostatic response, only the early, fast pressure fluctuations in the seconds-to-tens-of-seconds frequency band are available for real-time source inference prior to tsunami arrival. Accordingly, although this approach represents a significant computational achievement, its effectiveness for tsunami early warning depends on an implicit assumption that high-frequency seismoacoustic radiation provides reliable information about tsunami-effective seafloor deformation.

Tsunamis, however, are governed primarily by long-period or quasi-static seafloor displacement rather than by the detailed high-frequency characteristics of fault rupture. In events where high-frequency radiation is naturally depleted, such as tsunami earthquakes, the resulting acoustic signals may be too weak to provide reliable constraints on tsunami generation. In such cases, acoustic-based approaches may underestimate tsunami hazard or fail to resolve the developing source altogether (Wilson and Ma, 2021). These methods are therefore expected to perform best for earthquakes that generate strong acoustic radiation, such

1. San Diego State University, San Diego, California, U.S.A., https://orcid.org/0000-0002-9064-2765 (SM)

*Corresponding author: sma@sdsu.edu

Cite this article as Ma, S (2026). Ocean Acoustic Waves in Real-Time Tsunami Forecasting: Opportunities and Limitations, *Seismol. Res. Lett.*, **97**, 1571–1572, doi: 10.1785/0220250451.

as events dominated by rapid slip (Kozdon and Dunham, 2014; Lay *et al.*, 2019), although systematic testing across diverse rupture styles remains limited.

An additional practical consideration arises when acoustic waves are weak or propagate away from the source region. Under these conditions, the effective dimensionality of the inference problem collapses, and the governing physics reduce to long-period shallow-water behavior with far fewer spatiotemporal degrees of freedom. In this regime, large-scale 3D ocean modeling may offer limited additional constraint beyond that captured by simpler long-wave models (e.g., Tsushima *et al.*, 2009; Kubota *et al.*, 2021), given the lower spatiotemporal resolution of tsunami signals, particularly for rapid warning purposes. This is analogous to long-period seismic waves, which routinely provide robust estimates of seismic moment and thus a first-order constraint on tsunami potential, but limited spatial and temporal resolution restricts their ability to constrain the spatiotemporal evolution of tsunami-effective seafloor deformation in real time.

Together, these observations suggest that ocean acoustic signals by themselves do not provide a universally reliable basis for real-time tsunami early warning, particularly for tsunami earthquakes and large tsunamigenic earthquakes in sediment-rich subduction margins in which inelastic deformation may play a significant role. Although acoustic data may play a complementary role in some settings, such as locating high-frequency radiation sources, tsunami forecasting systems should explicitly account for the physical conditions under which such signals become information limited. Incorporating the essential physics of tsunami generation—including inelastic deformation—is critical to avoiding overconfidence in methods that are least sensitive to the most hazardous events.

Data and Resources

All data used in this article came from published sources listed in the references.

Declaration of Competing Interests

The author acknowledges that there are no conflicts of interest recorded.

Acknowledgments

The author is grateful to an anonymous reviewer for helpful comments. This work was supported by the National Science Foundation (Award Number EAR-2244703).

References

Du, Y., and S. Ma (2025). Wedge inelasticity and fully coupled models of dynamic rupture, ocean acoustic waves, and tsunami in the Japan Trench: The 1896 Sanriku earthquake, *J. Geophys. Res. Solid Earth* **130,** e2025JB032410, doi: 10.1029/2025JB032410.

Henneking, C., S. Venkat, V. Dobrev, J. Camier, T. Kolev, M. Fernando, A.-A. Gabriel, and O. Ghattas (2025). Real-time Bayesian inference at extreme scale: A digital twin for tsunami early warning applied to the Cascadia subduction zone, *Proc. of the International Conf. for High Performance Computing, Networking, Storage and Analysis (SC25)*, ACM, doi: 10.1145/3712285.3771787.

Kanamori, H. (1972). Mechanism of tsunami earthquakes, *Phys. Earth Planet. Int.* **6,** 346–359.

Kodaira, S., T. Iinuma, and K. Imai (2021). Investigating a tsunamigenic megathrust earthquake in the Japan Trench, *Science* **371,** eabe1169, doi: 10.1126/science.abe1169.

Kozdon, J. E., and E. M. Dunham (2014). Constraining shallow slip and tsunami excitation in megathrust ruptures using seismic and ocean acoustic waves recorded on ocean-bottom sensor networks, *Earth Planet. Sci. Lett.* **396,** 56–65, doi: 10.1016/j.epsl.2014.04.001.

Kubota, T., T. Saito, H. Tsushima, R. Hino, Y. Ohta, S. Suzuki, and D. Inazu (2021). Extracting near-field seismograms from ocean-bottom pressure gauges inside the focal area: Application to the 2011 M_w 9.1 Tohoku-Oki earthquake, *Geophys. Res. Lett.* **48,** e2020GL091664, doi: 10.1029/2020GL091664.

Lay, T. (2018). A review of the rupture characteristics of the 2011 Tohoku-Oki M_w 9.1 earthquake, *Tectonophysics* **733,** 4–36, doi: 10.1016/j.tecto.2017.09.022.

Lay, T., H. Kanamori, C. J. Ammon, H. Yue, K. D. Koper, A. R. Hutko, and E. E. Brodsky (2012). Depth-varying rupture properties of subduction zone megathrust faults, *J. Geophys. Res. Solid Earth* **117,** B04311, doi: 10.1029/2011JB009133.

Lay, T., C. Liu, and H. Kanamori (2019). Enhancing tsunami warning using P-wave coda, *J. Geophys. Res. Solid Earth* **124,** 10583–10609, doi: 10.1029/2019JB018221.

Ma, S. (2023). Wedge plasticity and a minimalist dynamic rupture model for the 2011 M_w 9.1 Tohoku-Oki earthquake and tsunami, *Tectonophysics* **869,** 230146, doi: 10.1016/j.tecto.2023.230146.

Ma, S., and Y. Du (2025). Wedge inelasticity and fully coupled models of dynamic rupture, ocean acoustic waves, and tsunami in the Japan Trench: The 2011 Tohoku-Oki earthquake, *Tectonophysics* **910,** 230831, doi: 10.1016/j.tecto.2025.230831.

Ma, S., and E. T. Hirakawa (2013). Dynamic wedge failure reveals anomalous energy radiation of shallow subduction earthquakes, *Earth Planet. Sci. Lett.* **375,** 113–122, doi: 10.1016/j.epsl.2013.05.016.

Okal, E. A., P.-J. Alasset, O. Hyvernaud, and F. Schindelé (2003). The deficient T waves of tsunami earthquakes, *Geophys. J. Int.* **152,** 416–432, doi: 10.1046/j.1365-246X.2003.01853.x.

Shuto, N., F. Imamura, S. Koshimura, K. Satake, and H. Matsutomi (2007). *Encyclopedia of Tsunami*, Asakura Publishing, Tokyo.

Tsushima, H., R. Hino, H. Fujimoto, Y. Tanioka, and F. Imamura (2009). Near-field tsunami forecasting from cabled ocean-bottom pressure data, *J. Geophys. Res. Solid Earth* **114,** B06309, doi: 10.1029/2008JB005988.

Uchida, N., and R. Bürgmann (2021). A decade of lessons learned from the 2011 Tohoku-Oki earthquake, *Rev. Geophys.* **59,** e2020RG000713, doi: 10.1029/2020RG000713.

Wilson, A., and S. Ma (2021). Wedge plasticity and fully coupled simulations of dynamic rupture and tsunami in the Cascadia subduction zone, *J. Geophys. Res. Solid Earth* **126,** e2020JB021627, doi: 10.1029/2020JB021627.

Manuscript received 26 December 2025
Published online 5 March 2026

On the Seismic Hazard Regulations for NPP Sites in Europe: A Controversial Case in Slovenia

OPEN ACCESS

Livio Sirovich*[1] and Kurt Decker[2]

Introduction

Unlike the United States, Europe lacks mandatory rules for the siting of all nuclear power plants (NPPs) and a regulatory body to monitor, for example, the technical quality of seismic hazard studies and to authorize the continuation of the activity of an existing NPP or permit a new construction. This situation stems from the same founding act of the European Union (EU).

We attract the reader's attention to seismic hazard studies of NPP sites in the EU and on some consequences of the lack of mandatory rules. The cases studied include the Krško-1 NPP and the planned, adjacent, Krško-2 plant, both in an area with medium–high seismicity in Slovenia.

The 2020 update of the European Seismic Hazard Model by Danciu *et al.* (2021, 2024) made the hazard curves available for a point 5 km southwest of the NPP (see Fig. 1a). The NPP is located just inside one of the areas of Slovenia with the maximum hazard ($0.8g < \text{PGA} < 0.9g$ with an exceedance probability of 0.01 in 50 yr; Fig. 1b). From the hazard curve, we can determine how the peak ground accelerations (PGAs) obviously increase as the probabilities decrease toward values today considered adequate for an existing NPP (0.005 in 50 yr according to Western European Nuclear Regulators Association [WENRA], 2021); even more stringent safety expectations apply to newly built plants (WENRA, 2013). The stress tests on Krško-1 (SNSA, 2011) predict possible accidents above a PGA of $0.8g$ (see subsequent paragraphs).

The site of Krško was chosen at the end of the 1960s, when the former Yugoslavia did not even have a seismic network. There were no probabilistic seismic-hazard analysis (PSHA) studies, nor were they performed for the new NPP. After independence (1991), wanting to close the plant, the first Slovenian government asked the National Institute of Italy for Oceanography and Experimental Geophysics (OGS) for scientific support, which appointed one of the authors (L. S.) as an OGS researcher.

Since the Maastricht Treaty of 1992 leaves the member states free to self-regulate in the matter, the role of the International Atomic Energy Agency (IAEA) remained that of its 1956 statute both for old and new NPPs: "to establish or adopt standards of safety […] that States can apply [but they] are not legally binding on Member States" (IAEA Safety Standards, 2022; pp. 2, 7, 9).

Writers have been dealing with the hazard of Krško for approximately 15 yr (Sirovich, 2012; Sirovich *et al.*, 2012, 2014) and had the opportunity to present the situation to the Italian Senate (see Data and Resources) and to the European Parliament. In Italy, various representatives have questioned the government on the subject, always receiving essentially the same answer, such as "[…] According to the Slovenian Agency for Nuclear Safety, stress tests confirm that the Krško power plant is among the safest in Europe." In 2015, the European Nuclear Safety Regulators Group (ENSREG) wrote that "the assessments found that the safety standards of nuclear power plants in Europe were generally high" (ENSREG, 2015; p. 1). However, when the EU was specifically questioned on the Krško plant, the competent Commissioner provided a much less reassuring assessment: "The stress tests carried out in 2011–2012 […] demonstrated that the seismic safety margins of the Krško power plant were sufficient" (European Parliament, 2016). Note the shift in language: from "among the safest in Europe" to "sufficient." The Krško problem is known in Brussels but has had no follow-up actions.

In the 1970s, the U.S. Nuclear Regulatory Commission (NRC) Regulatory Guide 1.60 was chosen for the earthquake resistance design of Krško-1 ($\text{PGA} = 0.3g$ to anchor the "Newmark/Hall" design spectra). Subsequent regulations required higher values. Now, as shown in Figure 1a, a PGA of $0.3g$ corresponds to a probability of almost 1 in 50 yr, a hazard level considered inadequate even for simple residential buildings. It was known that on 9 January 1917 a destructive earthquake of magnitude ~6 caused a macroseismic intensity VIII close to Krško, but almost nothing was known about seismogenic sources or capable faults (*sensu* IAEA Safety Standards, 2022) in the region.

1. Independent Scholar, https://orcid.org/0000-0003-2064-0884 (LS);
2. Department of Geology, University of Vienna, Vienna, Austria, https://orcid.org/0000-0001-6324-7164 (KD)
*Corresponding author: livio.sirovich@gmail.com

Cite this article as Sirovich, L., and K. Decker (2026). On the Seismic Hazard Regulations for NPP Sites in Europe: A Controversial Case in Slovenia, *Seismol. Res. Lett.*, **xx**, 1573–1579, doi: 10.1785/0220250329.

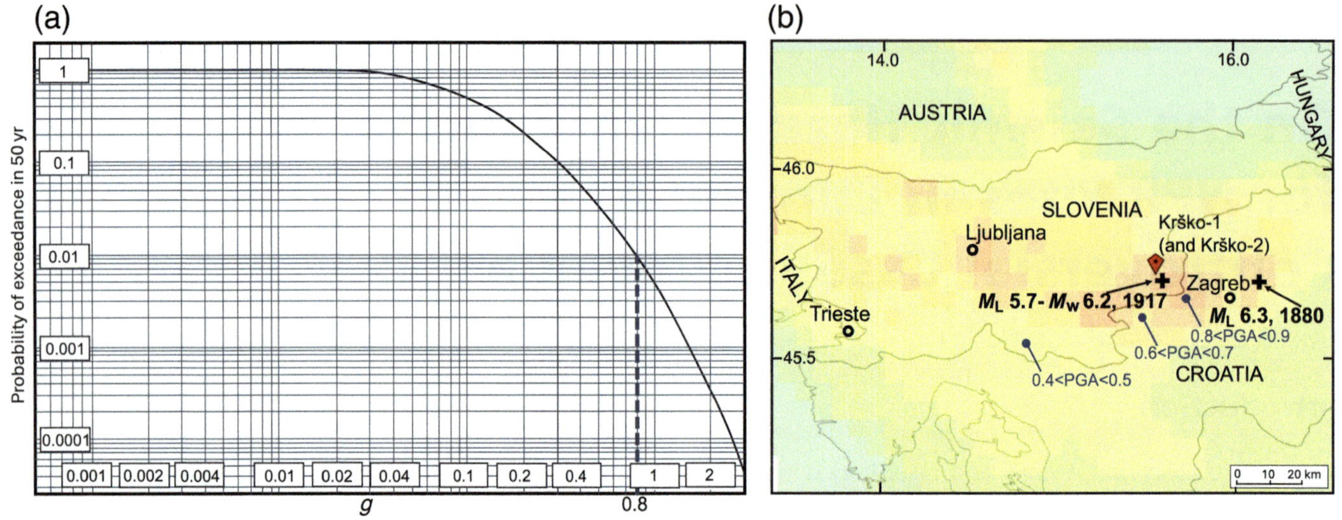

Figure 1. (a) Hazard curve of point (15.482° E; 45.900° N), 5 km southwest of the Krško nuclear power plant (NPP), from the 2020 update of the European Seismic Hazard Model (Copyright © 2020, ETH Zürich, produced under the Creative Commons Attribution 4.0 International License, CC BY; Danciu *et al.*, 2021, 2024; redrawn). (b) Peak ground acceleration (PGA; 5000-yr return period) from the 2020 update of the European Seismic Hazard Model (Danciu *et al.*, 2021, 2024, partim; Copyright © 2020, ETH Zürich, produced under the Creative Commons Attribution 4.0 International License, CC BY; redrawn; downloaded in August 2024, labels added). The lower vertex of the red symbol shows the Krško site; bold crosses: epicenters of the 1880 M_L 6.3 earthquake (Herak *et al.*, 2009) and of the 1917 M_L 5.7 (Ribarič, 1982)–M_w 6.2 (Grünthal *et al.*, 2013) earthquake; blue numbers guide you to the color legend (captions added).

The following points are discussed in this Letter: (1) the choice by the Slovenian Environmental Agency ARSO (for GEN Energija, see later) of macroseismic magnitude M_m for the 1917 earthquake instead of the local magnitude M_L, because here $M_m \ll M_L$; (2) the statement that a PGA of double 0.3g had been assumed for Krško-1 in the 1970s; and (3) the importance of capable and active faults for hazard assessment.

Magnitude of the 1917 Earthquake

Before the choice of the Krško site for the planned Krško-2 NPP, the 1917 earthquake was given a magnitude of 5.7–6.2 (e.g., M_L in Karnik, 1968, surface-wave magnitude MLH in Ribarič, 1982; moment magnitude M_w 6.2 in Grünthal *et al.*, 2013), which are disconcerting values for a nuclear site. In Grünthal *et al.* (2013), we read that the M_w 6.2 value for the 1917 earthquake was provided by ARSO to the Share European Earthquake Catalogue (SHEEC; Živćić, 1993).

However, once the Krško-2 project started, two M_m values (4.9 and 5.0) were proposed by an NPP consultant (Baumont, 2010a,b) and by a Slovenian researcher of ARSO (Cecić, 2018). Furthermore, the existence of Baumont (2010a,b) and the secrecy surrounding it came out only during the Klagenfurt international workshop on Krško, in which GEN Energija, owner of the NPP, participated (Decker, 2017; p.19). In fact, when the A.D. 567 to 2013 catalog, prepared for the new PSHA studies, was presented —and it was noticed that the 1917 M ~6 was missing from the shown map of epicenters—the speaker (M. Živčić, of ARSO, the same researcher who provided the M_w data to the SHEEC catalog) explained that "M 4.9 had been used for the 1917 earthquake, from a Baumont restricted report" (it was not specified what type of magnitude it was; ed.). It later turned out that Baumont used only macroseismic data (see Discussion and Conclusions).

At the time, the map of the epicenters of the 567 A.D. 2013 catalog could be downloaded from the ARSO website and later from a Slovenian government website (see Data and Resources), but today all the documents have been removed, and we do not have permission to show the figure. Therefore, we use SHEEC 1900–2006 (Grünthal *et al.*, 2013) at least for a partial comparison. As shown in Figure 2, (1) the Krško site is located within the most seismically active area of the region (in accordance with Fig. 1b), and (2) the downgrading of the magnitude of the 1917 earthquake to M_m 4.9 (according to Baumont, 2010a,b) eliminated the strongest historical earthquake in the region (see the blue circle).

Afterward, a book chapter (in Slovenian) appeared (Cecić, 2018), which seemed to confirm Baumont (2010a,b); in fact, M_m 5 was calculated from the average radii of the isoseismals using unpublished and unavailable formulas. However, this calculation was performed after having decreased most of the 140 intensities reported in Croatia by "half degree or by whole degree, and sometimes more" (Cecić, 2018, p. 177). Our general opinion is that, when a magnitude calculated from instrumental measurements is available, it should be preferred to the magnitude obtained only from macroseismic intensity values. We kept this opinion even when we proposed an innovative technique for estimating magnitudes through geophysical inversion of intensities (and magnitude has proven to be one of the most stable parameters obtained; Gentile *et al.*, 2004; p. 1747). Note that in a recent article Cecić herself did not even

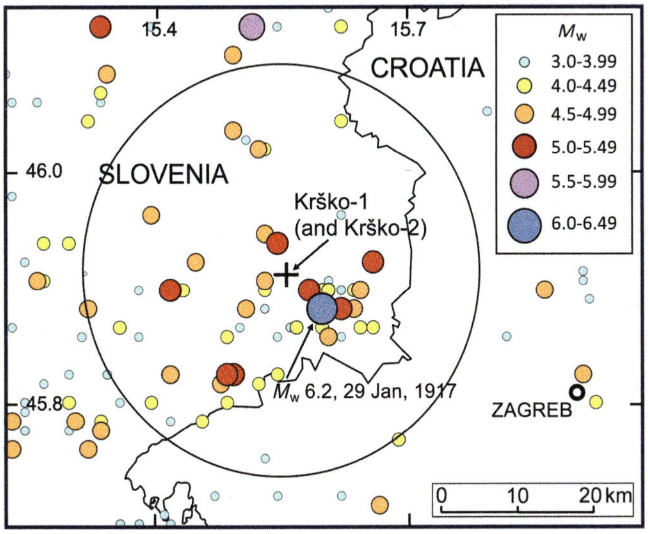

Figure 2. An excerpt from the Share European Earthquake Catalogue (SHEEC) 1900–2006 catalog (Grünthal *et al.*, 2013; moment magnitudes M_w). In the A.D. 567 to 2013 catalog, prepared by GEO-ZS and Paul C. Rizzo Associates, Inc., for the new probabilistic seismic-hazard analysis (PSHA) calculation for Krško-2, the 1917 earthquake (see the blue circle near the cross symbol that designates the location of the NPP) was downgraded to M_m 4.9.

mention the M_m value of 5, that she had obtained for the 1917 earthquake. In fact, in 2024, she wrote: "two historical earthquakes play an important role in the hazard calculation of the Krško NPP: 1880 (M_L 6.3, Herak *et al.*, 2009) and 1917 (M_{LH} 5.7, Ribarič 1982, who used eight stations)" (Pettenati *et al.*, 2024; p. 2). We conclude that the M_m values of 4.9 and 5.0 in 1917 should not have been included in the Krško-2 site hazard calculation.

In the 1970s, Was a PGA Double That of the NRC 1.60 Guide Adopted for Krško-1?

Even with mildly conservative assumptions and short catalogs, the PSHA studies of 1994 (Fajfar *et al.*, 1994) and 2004 (Geomatrix Consultants Inc., 2004) gave PGAs of 0.42*g* and 0.56*g*, respectively, for the Krško site on the free field. Is this still acceptable for existing NPPs? Is the site suitable for Krško-2? The position of the NPP operator (NEK) and its owner (GEN Energija) has always been that everything is OK with the project's PGA because 50 yr ago, the 0.3*g* PGA was applied not to the free field but at the foundation level (at −20 m depth) and that this allows the doubling to 0.6*g* for the free field (due to total reflection). However, this type of statement is usually made verbally in informal forums and in the mass media. There are few written statements in this regard to be found in technical texts that are available to the public. Incidentally, Geomatrix Consultants Inc. wrote that it took "numerous discussions of the Professional Board of NE Krško and the reconciliation of the consultants' opinions" to reach an agreement (Geomatrix Consultants Inc., 2004; p. 2.5–66).

Referring to the 0.42*g* and 0.56*g* values, the (in-house) 2011 stress test stated that "based on additional analysis [...], it was concluded that these values are similar to those obtained during the original design" (SNSA, 2011; pp. 1–2). Among attendees at the 2011 30th Congress of the Italian National Solid Earth Geophysics Group, GNGTS, there was a certain expectation for intervention by P. Fajfar of the University of Ljubljana, coauthor of the 1994 PSHA studies, because he wrote that the 0.3*g* of the NRC Regulatory Guide had been applied to the free field (Lapajne and Fajfar, 1997; p. 215). Instead, during the congressional session "Seismic Hazard of Complex Plants," P. Fajfar claimed that the 0.3*g* value had been applied at the foundation level of the excavation bottom (−20 m) and thus that the new PGA of 0.56*g* was compatible with the 0.3*g* of 1973 because of the total reflection from the topographic surface. However, no details on the modeling that supported this explanation were given.

At the end of the session, the press had scheduled an interview with only one of the two copresidents of the session, P. Fajfar (presented as a scientist and not as a consultant to the plant). Therefore, only his statements that everything was OK reached the public (see interviews in the newspapers Il Piccolo and Il Gazzettino, 17 November 2011). Afterward, for the proceedings of his session, P. Fajfar published an abstract mentioning an almost doubling of the PGA from −25 m to the free field, obtained with the Shake calculation code, but without any calculation details (Fajfar, 2011; slide number 16).

However, in a technical-popular report (Jamšek, 2024; p. 16), the GEN group has recently and officially reaffirmed their confidence in the doubling of the PGA from 0.3*g* to 0.6*g*. This report was made available at the end of September 2024 through a website specifically set up to inform Slovenian citizens in view of a national referendum on the construction of Krško-2 (referendum decided by the Slovenian Parliament on 11 October 2024, then annulled on 9 November 2024 following a new vote by the same Parliament after an appeal to the Constitutional Court).

Stress Tests

The NPP has always passed checks by the Slovenian Nuclear Regulator (SNSA, 2011, 2012). Unfortunately, only the PGA was chosen in communications to the public; thus, any detailed verification is impossible (think of the numerous NPP components important to safety). In the 2011 stress tests, we read that (1) "above a PGA of 0.8*g*, damage to the reactor core would be probable, with releases of radioactivity" and that (2) "sand liquefaction in the foundations cannot be excluded" (SNSA, 2011). As shown in Figure 1a, this value still corresponds to a rather high-exceedance probability in 50 yr (0.01).

Active Faults

The IAEA Safety Standards (2022; §5) states that "If a capable fault is identified in the site proximity of an existing nuclear installation, the site shall be deemed unsuitable if the safety of the nuclear installation cannot be demonstrated," and the situation is worse for a planned NPP: the "new site shall be considered unsuitable" (ibidem).

In 2000, for the first time, high-quality independent geophysical surveys were carried out on the Krško site and its surroundings under the framework of a European Commission technical assistance project (Persoglia, 2000); several buried structures likely to be active or capable faults were identified. For more than 20 yr, many geophysical campaigns were subsequently conducted under the direction of GEN Energija, mainly on possible capable faults. Little was done to better define some large primary active faults that affect the ground-shaking hazard. Paleoseismological research was initiated by a consortium of the Slovenian Geological Survey (GeoZS), the French Geological Survey (BRGM) and the French Institut de Radioprotection et de Sûreté Nucléaire (IRSN). However, in 2012, interpretative disputes arose between the French and Slovenians on the possible "capability" of some faults, deduced from trenches on the Libna hill, about 1–2 km north of the site. The French identified "clear evidence" of "coseismic and recurrent" fault offsets in the postglacial era (in the Holocene; Baize, 2017), confirming preliminary conclusions by Geomatrix Consultants Inc. (2004). However, in 2011, during the 30th GNGTS Congress, the Slovenian geologist "manager of the recent geological project in Krško for GeoZS" spoke out against the same 2004 estimates of Geomatrix. He announced that his group had performed a "new expertise that will reduce or even eliminate" some results by Geomatrix (the displacements of 1–10 m in the postglacial era at faults on the Libna hill, 6–2 km from the site). The new results "however, could not be made available to the conference" (Bavec, 2011) "and the client must also remain unknown" (M. Bavec, oral presentation, 30th GNGTS).

However, these assessments were contradicted by another—contemporary—study in an EU scientific context, carried out in part by the same people, coordinated by the same geologist in a UNESCO project, where we read: "This UNESCO report was focused on the paleoseismological study that was executed on the Libna hill, Krško Basin, including excavation, logging and interpretation of three paleoseismological trenches (the same as the other study; ed.) [the] survey revealed that all seismic deformation on Libna pre-dates the iron age" (Slovenian IGCP Committee, 2012).

At the end of 2012, interpretative differences became irreconcilable. On 9 January 2013, the general director of the IRSN (Jacques Repussard) wrote to his client (GEN Energija):

> *"this new and serious finding (of capable faults near the site; ed.) does not allow concluding in a favorable manner as regards the suitability of the Krško II sites (two study sites, adjacent to the existing NPP; ed.) for the implantation of a new nuclear power plant. (...) IRSN believes that GEN should reconsider revising its strategy for the Krško II project and further examine the possibility to search for an alternative site". "IRSN considers that it is of utmost importance that the possible implications on the safety of the existing plant of this fault capability, as well as its potential structural relationship to nearby faults be addressed without delay. I understood—continues Mr. Repussard—that GEN felt concerned about this issue and was willing indeed to inform Krško 1 plant operator (Nuklearna Elektrarna Krško - NEK) as well as the Slovenian Nuclear Safety Administration (NSA) about this finding. I would be very grateful if you could confirm that this has been actually done, since I do envisage drawing NSA's attention on this issue, considering the potential safety implications it may have at national and international level" (Repussard, 2013).*

In April 2013, the consortium dissolved, and Paul C. Rizzo Associates Inc. entered the field. These new consultants presented their preliminary technical position on the presence of any capable faults (mainly the Libna fault) near the site. They wrote that the current interpretation by IRSN was premature because there was no professional consensus even on the presence of the Libna fault on Libna Hill. They added that "the offset observed in the Libna Hill trench is either completely or partially related to mass wasting and karst development" and that the age of the observed offset "may have been pushed artificially younger due to bioturbation" (Paul C. Rizzo Associates Inc., 2013a).

The IAEA Safety Standards (2010, 2022) suggests calculating the maximum magnitudes for various seismogenic zones or structures. In 2012, a maximum potential magnitude of approximately 7.2 (including 1 standard deviation) was estimated for the entire Orlica fault (Sirovich *et al.*, 2012). For the northern segment of the same fault, Paul C. Rizzo Associates Inc. (2013b; its table 6) adopted maximum M_w 6.7 (highest weight) but also included M_w 7.0 (with low weight). Note that, after considering the two reference fault lengths, the estimates by Sirovich *et al.* (2012) and by Paul C. Rizzo Associates Inc. (2013b) substantially agree.

Finally, geological and paleoseismological investigations, performed to update the national seismic hazard map, confirm the existence of these likely active faults in the near region of the NPP: Artiče, <5 km from Krško; Orlica, <5 km from Krško; Dobrovec-Hrastnik fault system, approximately 10–20 km from Krško; Orehovec-Poštena vas, >7 km from Krško; and the eastern strand of the Dinaric fault system, approximately 25 km southwest of Krško with 1–2 mm slip per year (Atanackov *et al.*, 2021, fig. 10; Becker *et al.*, 2022). It appears that none of the mentioned faults have been adequately considered until now in existing seismic hazard models.

Discussion and Conclusions

It was not possible to see the "restricted" M_m calculation for the 1917 Krško earthquake by Baumont (2010a,b), despite many written requests and even a registered mail to GEN Energija d.o.o. Note that the secret is put simply on a characteristic of the region, something like keeping classified the width of a river over which a bridge should be built.

On 8 March 2017, Andrej Stritar, the then director of the Nuclear Safety Administration of Slovenia (which oversees the stress tests)—formerly the 2007–2011 chairperson of the ENSREG conference (which issues the standards for the stress tests themselves)—granted an interview with the Italian television network "La7" (journalist Lorenzo Caroselli in "Tagadà": see Data and Resources). To the question, "director, should we hope that a *M* 7 earthquake, as the experts predict, never occurs?," Stritar bangs his knuckles on the table and says: "knock on wood!"

The Krško-1 696 MWe (electric Megawatt) NPP entered service in 1983; its operation window has been extended to 2043, but it is expected to operate until 2063. For many years, the Slovenian government and GEN Energija have been studying the possibility of building a 1000–1650 MWe (electric Megawatt) Krško-2 alongside Krško-1, for an investment of 9.3–15.4 billion euros, and they seem determined to build the new plant, which would be operational for 60–80 yr.

For many years now it has also been known that the 2004 PSHA study would be updated in view of the construction of the new reactor. The new PSHA was expected by the end of 2025, but is now expected to end March 2027, with the construction decision to be made in 2028.

In our modest opinion, from the point of view of the seismic hazard, the in-house checks were not sufficient either to seriously evaluate the opportunity to continue the operation of Krško-1 for 60 or 80 yr or to inform the design of Krško-2. This is an indirect result of the 1992 Maastricht Treaty, which did not establish a body with the authority to check the quality of hazard studies and to issue and revoke permits. However, it is advisable not to contradict the IAEA's suggestions, even if they are not binding. In the United States, the NRC created by Congress in 1974 has the power to license and supervise NPPs, and their designers and operators must make natural hazard studies, measurements and monitoring data available to the public, though some reports might be restricted for security reasons.

The cost of decommissioning the Krško NPP would be roughly on the order of 1.5×10^{-2} of the gross domestic product (GDP) of tiny Slovenia (2.1 million inhabitants). (By comparison, it would represent approximately 3.1×10^{-4} of the GDP of France.) A rational way out should include the participation of the EU because the issue clearly is of common interest. Slovenia could be helped in determining another suitable site and/or the EU could partially bear the costs of decommissioning the current NPP.

Finally, the authors would like to point out that they and their past coauthors have never taken a position on the civil use of atomic energy.

Data and Resources

All the data and information used in this article were obtained from published and unpublished sources listed in the references. Senate of the Republic is available at https://bit.ly/4drychn. Map of the epicenters of the A.D. 567 to 2013 catalog could be downloaded from www.ursjv.gov.si/si/info/posamezne_zadeve/o_potresni_varnosti_nek/. Lorenzo Caroselli in "Tagadà" is available at https://bit.ly/3SOY7Y3. According to the Slovenian Agency for Nuclear Safety, stress tests confirm that the Krško power plant is among the safest in Europe can be found (in Italian) in the parliamentary records, for example here https://www.camera.it/leg17/410?idSeduta=0640&tipo=atti_indirizzo_controllo; see the replies to Members Prodani, Rizzetto, Pellegrino and Rosato. All websites were last accessed in March 2026.

Declaration of Competing Interests

The authors acknowledge that there are no conflicts of interest recorded.

Acknowledgments

The authors thank their coauthors of previous works; however, this letter is the total responsibility of the current authors. They thank NEK for having made chapter 2.5 (rev. 1) of Geomatrix Consultants Inc. (2004), available with the figures from rev. 14. Laurentiu Danciu kindly helped them connect the actual peak ground acceleration (PGA) values, given as a georeferenced shape file, to the informative color map of the 2020 update of the European Seismic Hazard Model (Danciu *et al.*, 2021, 2024). Mariano Garcia Fernandez provided suggestions that improved the article, Dario Slejko critically read this letter, and Ezio Faccioli critically reviewed it. Reviewer 2 made also accurate observations asking for some additional information which made the presentation clearer. The present letter is an extract from a more complete text, which can be requested from the authors.

References

Atanackov, J., P. Jamšek Rupink, J. Jež, B. Celaric, M. Novak, B. Milianič, J. A. Markeli, M. Bavec, and V. Kastelic (2021). Database of active faults in Slovenia: Compiling a new active fault database at the junction between the Alps, the Dinarides and the Pannonian Basin Tectonic Domains, *Front. Earth Sci.* **9,** 604388, doi: 10.3389/feart.2021.604388.

Baize, S. (2017). Active tectonics in the Krško Region and IRSN perspectives, *Fact Finding Workshop on the Active Tectonics of the Krško Region*,K. Decker (Editor). Rep-0612, Umweltbundesamt GmbH, Vienna, Austria, 13–14, available at https://www.umweltbundesamt.at/fileadmin/site/publikationen/rep0612.pdf (last accessed August 2025).

Baumont, D. (2010a). NPP II Krško (Slovenia) magnitude and depth estimates of historical earthquakes, *GG&S Project, Krško NPP-II, Task 4.4.2.b, Raport DEI/SARG/2010.029*, IRSN, France.

Baumont, D. (2010b). Unknown title, in *Geotechnical, Geological and Seismological Geological Survey of Slovenia l (GG&S) Evaluations for the New Nuclear Power Plant at the Krško Site (NPP Krško II)*, M. Bavec, J. Atanackov, S. Baize, D. Baumont, A. Bitri, B. Celarc, C. Gelis, P. Corboz, A. Gosar, and H. Jomard, *et al.* (Editors), Geological Survey of Slovenia, Ljubljana, 178 pp.

Bavec, M. (2011). Geologic setting of the Krško Basin, *Proc. of the 30th GNGTS 2011*, Session 2.1, 198–200.

Becker, O., K. Decker, L. Moschen, and G. Mraz (2022). *KKW Krsko/Slowenien Laufzeitverlängerung Umweltverträglichkeitsprüfung (NPP Krsko/Lowenia Lifetime extension environmental impact assessment),* Umweltbundesamt, Report REP-0810, Vienna, 142 pp.

Cecić, I. (2018). Potres pri Brežicah 29 januarja 1917 makroseizmične raziskave, in *Bilo je res grozljivo, bobnelo in grmelo je pod nami I,* J. Škofljanec (Editor), University of Ljubljana Press, Ljubljana, Slovenia, 582 pp. (in Slovenian).

Danciu, L., D. Giardini, G. Weatherill, R. Basili, S. Nandan, A. Rovida, C. Beauval, P.-Y. Bard, M. Pagani, C. G. Reyes, *et al.* (2024). The 2020 European Seismic Hazard Model: Overview and results, *Nat. Hazards Earth Syst. Sci.* **24,** 3049–3073, doi: 10.5194/nhess-24-3049-2024

Danciu, L., S. Nandan, C. Reyes, R. Basili, G. Weatherill, C. Beauval, A. Rovida, S. Vilanova, K. Sesetyan, P.-Y. Bard, *et al.* (2021). The 2020 update of the European Seismic Hazard Model: Model overview, *EFEHR Technical Rept. 001, v1.0.0,* available at http://hazard.efehr.org/en/hazard-data-access/hazard-maps/ (last accessed December 2025).

Decker, K (2017). Fact finding workshop on the active tectonics of the Krško Region, *Rep-0612,* Umweltbundesamt GmbH, Vienna, Austria, available at https://www.umweltbundesamt.at/fileadmin/site/publikationen/rep0612.pdf (last accessed August 2025).

ENSREG (2015). ENSREG statement on the progress in the implementation of post-FukushimaNational Action Plans (NAcPs), *HLG_p(2015-31)_146,* available at https://www.ensreg.eu/sites/default/files/attachments/hlg_p2015-31_146_ensreg_statement_nacp_final.pdf (last accessed December 2025).

European Parliament (2016) Parliament Questions, *P-006880/2016(ASW).* https://www.europarl.europa.eu/doceo/document/P-8-2016-006880-ASW_EN.html (last accessed December 2025).

Fajfar, P. (2011). Seismic hazard analysis of important structures in Slovenia, *Extended Abstracts 30th GNGTS Congress,* Session 2.1., Trieste, Italy, 207–208.

Fajfar, P., J. Lapajne, B. Aljinović, Z. Breška, J. Logar, D. Matičec, M. Poljak, E. Prelogović, U. Premru, V. Ribarič, *et al.* (1994). Probabilistic assessment of seismic hazard at Krško Nuclear Power Plant: Revision 1: Client, NPP Krško, FAGG, IKPIR, Ljubljana, Slovenia.

Gentile, F., F. Pettenati, and L. Sirovich (2004). Validation of the automatic nonlinear source inversion of the U.S. Geological Survey Intensities of the Whittier Narrows 1987 Earthquake, *Bull. Seismol. Soc. Am.* **94,** no. 5, 1737–1747.

Geomatrix Consultants Inc. (2004). Revised seismotectonic model of the Krško basin: Report PSR-NEK-2.7.1 (Revision 1, chapter 2.5), Geomatrix Consultants Inc., Oakland, California and University of Ljubljana, Slovenia and Environmental Agency of the Republic of Slovenia, Ljubljana, Slovenia: 2.5/1-2.5/153.

Grünthal, G., R. Wahlström, and D. Stromeyer (2013). The SHARE European Earthquake Catalogue (SHEEC) for the time period 1900-2006 and its comparison to European-Mediterranean Earthquake Catalogue (EMEC), *J. Seismol.* **17,** no. 4, 1339–1344.

Herak, D., M. Herak, and B. Tomljenović (2009). Seismicity and earthquake focal mechanisms in North-West Croatia, *Tectonophysics* **465,** 212–220, doi: 10.1016/j.tecto.2008.12.005.

IAEA Safety Standards (2010). Seismic hazards in site evaluation for nuclear installations, *Specific Safety Guide No. SSG-9,* Vienna, Austria, 76 pp.

IAEA Safety Standards (2022). Seismic Hazards in Site Evaluation for Nuclear Installations, *Specific Safety Guide No. SSG-9 (Rev. 1),* Vienna, Austria, 78 pp.

Jamšek, A. (Editor) (2024). Seismic safety of nuclear power plants, *Technical Rept. TS-TR-2024-016,* GEN Skupina, Ljubljana, Slovenia, 21 pp., available at https://jek2.si/studije-in-informacije-o-projektu-jek2/ (last accessed December 2025).

Karnik, V. (1968). Seismicity of the European Area, Part 1, Academia, Prague, Czech Republic , 364 pp.

Lapajne, J. K., and P. Fajfar (1997). Seismic hazard reassessment of an existing NPP in Slovenia, *Nuclear Eng. Design* **175,** 215–226.

Paul C. Rizzo Associates Inc. (2013a). Technical position paper, Libna Fault response to IRSN/Dir/2013-00010, *Project No. 12-4835,* Pittsburgh, Pennsylvania, 10 pp.

Paul C. Rizzo Associates Inc. (2013b). Probabilistic fault displacement hazard analysis Krško East and west sites proposed KršKo-2 (revision 1), *Project No. 11-4546,* Pittsburgh, Pennsylvania, 42 pp., 14 figs., 1 app.

Persoglia, S. (Editor) (2000). Geophysical research in the surrounding of the Krško NPP, *Final Report and Annexes, Contract No. 98-0286.00,* European Commission Directorate General IA Tacis Procurement Unit.

Pettenati, F., I. Jukić, L. Sirovich, I. Cecić, G. Costa, and P. Suhadolc (2024). The 1895 Ljubljana earthquake: Source parameters from inversion of macroseismic data, *J. Seismol.* **28,** 1–18, doi: 10.1007/s10950-023-10178-0.

Repussard, J. (2013). Letter of Jan. 9, 2013 from IRSN to GEN energija d.o.o, *Contract GG&S NPP KRSKO II, IRSN/DIR/2013-00010,* 5 pp., available at http://ursjv.arhiv-spletisc.gov.si/fileadmin/ujv.gov.si/pageuploads/si/medijsko-sredisce/dopisGen/p1.pdf (last accessed December 2025).

Ribarič, V. (1982). *Seizmičnost Slovenije,* Publikacije Seizmološkega zavoda SR Slovenije, Serija A, Št. 1-1, Ljubljana, Slovenia, 649 pp. (in Slovenian).

Sirovich, L. (2012). Riconsiderando la situazione sismica della centrale nucleare di Krško (Slovenia), *Workshop in Honor and Memory of Prof. Giuseppe Grandori,* Structural Engineering Department of the Politecnico di Milano, 5 November 2012, 429–440 (in Italian).

Sirovich, L., F. Pettenati, and M. Busetti (2012). The problem of earthquake-capable faults and maximum related magnitudes for two critical facilities in Italy and in Slovenia, *Proc. 33rd General Assembly of the European Seismological Commission ESC 2012,* 19–24 August, Moscow, Russia, Symp. NIS-3, 350 pp.

Sirovich, L., P. Suhadolc, G. Costa, and F. Pettenati (2014). A review of the seismotectonics and some considerations on the seismic hazard of the Krško NPP area (SE Slovenia), *Boll. Geof. Teor. Appl.* **55,** no. 1, 175–195, doi: 10.4430/bgta0103.

Slovenian IGCP Committee (2012). Report on 2011 IGCP activities in Slovenia, Ljubljana, Slovenia, 9 pp., available at https://doczz.net/doc/6896619/slovenian-igcp-committee-secretary--prof.-dr.-n (last accessed February 2026).

SNSA (2011). Slovenian national report on nuclear stress tests, Final Report, December 2011, 190 pp., available at https://www.ensreg.eu/sites/default/files/Slovenian%20Stress%20Test%20Final%20Report.pdf. (last accessed August 2025).

SNSA (2012). Slovenian Report for the 2nd Extraordinary Meeting of the Parties of the Convention on Nuclear Safety, April 2012, 58 pp., available at https://www.ensreg.eu/sites/default/files/Slovenian%20National%20Post%20Fukushima%20Action%20Plan.pdf (last accessed August 2025).

Western European Nuclear Regulators Association (WENRA) (2013). Report safety of new NPP designs, 52 pp., available at https://www.wenra.eu/publications (last accessed August 2025).

WENRA (2021). Report WENRA safety reference levels for existing reactors 2020, 58 pp., available at https://www.wenra.eu/publications (last accessed August 2025).

Živčić, M. (1993). Earthquake catalogue of Slovenia, The Seismology and Geology Office of the Environmental Agency of the Republic of Slovenia ARSO, Ljubljana, Slovenija (data file).

Manuscript received 24 September 2025
Published online 18 March 2026

Preface to the Focus Section on The 2025 M_w 7.7 Myanmar and M_w 7.1 Tingri Earthquakes: Multidisciplinary Insights into Seismogenesis, Hazard, and Community Resilience

Marie-Luce Chevalier[1], Wardah Fadil[2], Vineet Gahalaut[*3], and Shengji Wei[4]

The year 2025 was marked by two major earthquakes in the broader Himalayan region: the M_w 7.1 Tingri earthquake of 7 January in southern Tibet and the M_w 7.7 Myanmar earthquake of 28 March near Mandalay. Together, these events provide a rare opportunity to examine contrasting modes of continental deformation and seismic hazard across a vast and tectonically complex region.

The M_w 7.7 Myanmar earthquake ruptured the dextral Sagaing fault zone, one of Southeast Asia's most active plate-boundary faults, producing an exceptionally long surface rupture exceeding 400 km. The event caused widespread ground shaking, landslides, and infrastructure damage across Myanmar and neighboring countries, including the collapse of a high-rise building under construction in Bangkok. Its complex rupture dynamics, including evidence for supershear propagation, offer valuable insights into plate-boundary seismicity and fault interactions in an otherwise understudied region.

Approximately 1000 km to the northwest, the M_w 7.1 Tingri earthquake occurred ten years after the 2015 Gorkha earthquake, representing the first major event in decades north of the Himalayas. Rupturing a remote normal fault within the north–south-trending Xainza–Dinggye graben, the earthquake generated notable coseismic offsets and local damage despite its moderate magnitude. The event raised important questions regarding stress transfer to surrounding fault systems, including those in India and Nepal, and provides new constraints on deformation processes within the Tibetan plateau driven by India–Eurasia convergence.

This special issue of *Seismological Research Letters* brings together multidisciplinary contributions spanning seismology, geodesy, geology, remote sensing, and hazard assessment to advance understanding of these two earthquakes. Collectively, the studies highlight rapid scientific responses, integrated analytical approaches, and lessons essential for improving seismic hazard assessment and resilience in vulnerable regions. Overall, we received seven articles on the Myanmar earthquake and four articles on the Tingri earthquake.

Regarding the Myanmar earthquake, Cruz *et al.* (2026) offer a multidisciplinary assessment of the event, combining ground-motion analysis, macroseismic intensity mapping, liquefaction assessment, and Synthetic Aperture Radar (SAR)-based damage observations. It demonstrates the value of integrated datasets for rapid impact assessment and disaster response. Zou *et al.* (2026) analyze coseismic surface ruptures using high-resolution satellite imagery to quantify offsets and characterize rupture behavior. By explicitly incorporating both tectonic and nontectonic deformation, it provides a more comprehensive and practically relevant framework for seismic hazard assessment in a challenging field environment. Reitman *et al.* (2026) reported rupture characteristics using subpixel correlation and visual analysis of optical images. They report that the rupture length of the earthquake is much larger than that expected from an M_w 7.7 event, which may be due to bilateral supershear rupture on a simple and narrow fault with no stepovers. Min *et al.* (2026) combined postearthquake field measurements with optical satellite imagery to document the surface rupture. They found that offsets measured in the field are systematically ~1 m lower than satellite-derived values, attributed to distributed deformation within unconsolidated sediments in the very shallow parts of the fault. Shen *et al.* (2026) analyzed the long-term stress evolution of the Sagaing fault since 1897 using a multilayered viscoelastic model. They indicate that the 2025 earthquake significantly loaded the northern and southern tips of the rupture in addition to that along several adjacent faults and that the northern segment of the fault has a potential for future large earthquakes ($M_w \sim 7.3$–7.7). Hu *et al.* (2026) interpreted high-resolution satellite imagery to map coseismic soil liquefaction in the Central Myanmar basin, densely concentrated along river terraces and closely matching the rupture zone length along

1. Institute of Geology, Chinese Academy of Geological Sciences, Beijing, China; 2. University of Alberta, Edmonton, Alberta, Canada, https://orcid.org/0000-0002-8215-1210 (WF); 3. Wadia Institute of Himalayan Geology Dehradun and CSIR-National Geophysical Institute, Hyderabad, India, https://orcid.org/0000-0003-2514-4644 (VG); 4. Earth Observatory of Singapore, Singapore, https://orcid.org/0009-0009-9207-6216 (SW)

*Corresponding author: vkgahalaut@yahoo.com

Cite this article as Chevalier, M-Luce., W. Fadil, V. Gahalaut, and S. Wei (2026). Preface to the Focus Section on The 2025 M_w 7.7 Myanmar and M_w 7.1 Tingri Earthquakes: Multidisciplinary Insights into Seismogenesis, Hazard, and Community Resilience, *Seismol. Res. Lett.*, **97**, 1580–1581, doi: 10.1785/0220260141.

the coseismic surface rupture. Pananont *et al.* (2026) analyzed strong-motion records from 77 stations across Thailand to characterize nationwide site response behavior using horizontal-to-vertical spectral ratio-derived resonance periods and amplification patterns. They identified multiple Thai basins exhibiting long-period resonance, showing that deep basin structures across Thailand can amplify long-period seismic waves and must be accounted for in seismic hazard assessments.

Regarding the Tingri earthquake, Shi *et al.* (2026) developed a geodetically constrained fault rupture model for the earthquake using Interferometric Synthetic Aperture Radar (InSAR) observations. It reconstructs coseismic slip and rupture geometry and examines aftershocks and stress transfer to clarify the event's triggering relationship with the 2020 M_w 5.7 Tingri earthquake. Yue *et al.* (2026) also studied aftershock triggering by evaluating Coulomb stress changes. They found that coseismic slip triggered only a portion of the aftershocks and that poroelastic rebound was a more significant source of aftershocks. Zhi *et al.* (2026) apply matched-filter techniques and temporary seismic stations to improve detection of early aftershocks following the earthquake, revealing previously missed events and enhancing catalog completeness. Zou and Fialko (2026) show that the earthquake ruptured a conjugate pair of steeply dipping normal faults optimally oriented for failure. InSAR observations reveal a large shallow slip deficit, with postseismic deformation dominated by limited afterslip and shallow off-fault damage.

The articles in this special issue provide new, integrated insights into the rupture processes, deformation patterns, and hazard implications of the Myanmar and Tingri earthquakes. Satellite-based observations of crustal deformation (optical imagery and InSAR), and ground response to shaking provided constraints on rupture processes of both earthquakes. For the Myanmar earthquake, these along with field observations, reveal unusually long rupture length, likely linked to bilateral supershear propagation, along with widespread liquefaction and complex surface deformation, including significant shallow distributed strain that leads to discrepancies between field and remote measurements. Long-term modeling of stress evolution further highlights stress transfer to adjacent fault segments, increasing the likelihood of future large earthquakes, while regional studies demonstrate the importance of basin amplification for seismic hazard. For the Tingri earthquake, geodetic and seismological investigations revealed that aftershock evolution was also controlled by the poroelastic relaxation.

Data and Resources

There are no new data or resources to report for this article.

Declaration of Competing Interests

The authors acknowledge that there are no conflicts of interest recorded.

Acknowledgments

The authors are grateful to several reviewers for their thoughtful and constructive reviews on articles in this focus section. The *Seismological Research Letters* editorial team, Allison Bent and Miranda Bohl, are thanked for their guidance and support in compiling this focus section.

References

Cruz, A., M. Ghasemi, S. Karimzadeh, S. Karimzadeh, A. Askan, M. Matsuoka, and P. B. Laurenço (2026). 28 March 2025 Myanmar earthquake: Strong ground motions, macroseismic intensity, liquefaction and ALOS-2 ScanSAR remote-sensing damage observations, *Seismol. Res. Lett.*, doi: 10.1785/0220250258.

Hu, G., R, Xiong, W. Li, P. Liang, C. Hu, W. Wu, and Y. Xu (2026). Mapping of soil liquefaction induced by the 2025 Sagaing M_w 7.8 earthquake in Myanmar, using high-spatial-resolution images, *Seismol. Res. Lett.*, doi: 10.1785/0220250399.

Min, S., T. Aung, H. Tsutsumi, W. Htun, C. T. Mon, L. T. Aung, K. Z. Win, S. M. Min, K. N. Htay, S. N. Khaing, *et al.* (2026). Surface rupture of the 2025 M_w 7.7 Mandalay, Myanmar earthquake: Insights from field and optical remote sensing observations, *Seismol. Res. Lett.*

Pananont, P., P. Pholsonda, P. Pornsopin, K. Furlong, K. Hayashi, S. Muangnoi, and K. Prasertwongphilai (2026). Observed H/V responses across Thailand from the 2025 M_w 7.7 Myanmar earthquake: Implications for geological-controlled seismic hazard, *Seismol. Res. Lett.*, doi: 10.1785/0220250388.

Reitman, N. G., Y. Wang, Y. Kuo, C. Hanagan, A. E. Hatem, C. B. DuRoss, C. Chen, D. E. Goldberg, H. Z. Yin, R. W. Briggs, *et al.* (2026). Surface rupture and slip distribution of the 2025 M 7.7 Mandalay earthquake and updated length scaling of supershear earthquakes, *Seismol. Res. Lett.*, doi: 10.1785/0220250257.

Shen, T., W. Wu, G. Meng, T. Liu, L. Zhang, J. Tang, and X. Xu (2026). Coulomb stress transfer and future earthquake hazard from the 2025 M_w 7.7 Myanmar earthquake: Implications for the Sagaing fault and Shan plateau, *Seismol. Res. Lett.*, doi: 10.1785/0220250395.

Shi, Y., Y. Wang, H. Pan, K. Chen, Y. Liu, and J. Zou (2026). Asymetric Y-shaped structural rupture of the 2025 M_W 7.1 Tingri, southern Tibet earthquake, *Seismol. Res. Lett.*, 10.1785/0220250301.

Yue, C, D. Dai, X. Li, Y. Wang, Y. Zhang, W. Yang, Y. Han, C. Chu, and L. Meng (2026). Aftershock triggering mechanism by the M_W 7.1 Tingri earthquake, 7 January 2025, *Seismol. Res. Lett.*, doi: 10.1785/0220250091.

Zhi, M., Q. Li, D. Yao, D. Wang, F. Guo, and L. Sun (2026). Spatiotemporal evolution of early aftershocks following the 2025 M_W 7.1 Dingri, southern Tibet earthquake, *Seismol. Res. Lett.*, doi: 10.1785/0220250393.

Zou, J., H. He, Z. Shao, W. Li, J. Huang, and L. Gao (2026). Coseismic displacement characteristics near the epicenter of the M_w 7.7 Myanmar earthquake on March 28, 2025: Insights from BJ-3 high-resolution satellite imagery analysis, *Seismol. Res. Lett.*, doi: 10.1785/0220250397.

Zou, X., and Y. Fialko (2026). The 2025 M_w 7.1 Tingri (South Tibet) earthquake: Rupture of normal conjugate optimally oriented faults, shallow coseismic slip deficit, and early afterslip, *Seismol. Res. Lett.*, doi: 10.1785/0220250445

Manuscript received 23 March 2026
Published online 4 May 2026

Aftershock Triggering Mechanism by the 7 January 2025 M_w 7.1 Tingri Earthquake

Chong Yue[1,2], Danqing Dai[1], Xiaofan Li[1], Yue Wang[1], Yingfeng Zhang[2], Wen Yang[1], Yanyan Han[1], Chunyan Qu[*2], and Lingyuan Meng[1]

Abstract

The M_w 7.1 Tingri earthquake represents the largest normal-faulting event within the Lhasa block since 1952. This rupture occurred along the approximately north–south-trending Dengmocuo rift, which constitutes the seismogenic fault. The event provides an exceptional case study to examine aftershock distribution patterns and triggering mechanisms following large normal-fault earthquakes in the Tibetan plateau. We calculated Coulomb failure stress changes (ΔCFS) induced by coseismic slip and postseismic poroelastic rebound using a coseismic slip model inverted from Interferometric Synthetic Aperture Radar and strong-motion records. The earthquake rupture propagated ~40 km north of the mainshock hypocenter, with slip predominantly confined to the upper 10 km of the crust. Such ruptures typically produce stress loading at the fault's northern and southern termini while generating stress-shadow zones along the eastern and western flanks. Within this pattern, the main rupture zone spatially coincides with the stress-shadow zone, whereas adjacent regions constitute CFS loading zones. Postseismic fluid migration induces significant CFS loading within the main rupture zone, effectively compensating for coseismic stress shadows and subsequently triggering peripheral aftershocks. The triggering mechanisms of aftershocks vary significantly across different segments of the fault system. Coseismic slip accounts for only 44% of total aftershock triggering, whereas poroelastic rebound contributes a notably higher proportion, reaching up to 65%, particularly in the northern segment, where it peaks at 74%. This indicates that postseismic fluid migration has a significant impact on the occurrence of aftershocks in the main rupture zone.

Cite this article as Yue, C., D. Dai, X. Li, Y. Wang, Y. Zhang, W. Yang, Y. Han, C. Qu, and L. Meng (2025). Aftershock Triggering Mechanism by the 7 January 2025 M_w 7.1 Tingri Earthquake, *Seismol. Res. Lett.* **97**, 1582–1594, doi: 10.1785/0220250091.

Supplemental Material

Introduction

On 7 January 2025, an M_w 7.1 earthquake struck the southern segment of the Shenza-Dinggyê rifts (SZ-DGF) in XiZang Province, China (84.45° E, 28.5° N), causing extensive damage to local residents' lives and property. The earthquake occurred at a focal depth of 10 km, and the focal mechanism solution indicates that it is classified as a normal-fault earthquake. The moment magnitude reported by the U.S. Geological Survey (USGS) is M_w 7.1. The strike of nodal plane I is 349°, the dip is 42°, and the rake angle is −103°. The strike of nodal plane II is 187°, the dip is 49°, and the rake angle is −78°. The seismogenic fault associated with the M_w 7.1 Tingri earthquake is the Dengmocuo rift (DMCF), which is a west-dipping normal fault located in the southern section of the SZ-DGF, as illustrated in Figure 1a. The M_w 7.1 Tingri earthquake represents the largest normal-fault event within the Lhasa block since the M 8 Damxung earthquake on 18 November 1951 (with another M 7.5 aftershock occurring in 1952; Yang *et al.*, 2020; Yue *et al.*, 2025). The mainshock is situated at the intersection of the DMCF and the southern Tibetan detachment system (STDS). Several rifts are present on both sides of the DMCF. The west side features the west-dipping Quluo rift, and the east side includes the west-dipping Guojia rift and the east-dipping Dinggyê rift. In addition, the north-dipping STDS and an additional smaller west-dipping Cuoguo rift locate on the south side of the DMCF (Shao *et al.*, 2025; Shi *et al.*, 2025; Xu *et al.*, 2025). The complex fault structure complicates research efforts but also provides an excellent case study of rift interaction in southern Tibet.

Yao *et al.* (2025) compiled a preliminary catalog of early aftershocks following the Tingri earthquake using a nodal array around the seismogenic zone. This approach clearly delineated the intricate fault structures and provided reliable data for subsequent studies on the stress-triggering mechanisms of the

1. China Earthquake Networks Center, Beijing, China, https://orcid.org/0000-0003-2935-4462 (WY); 2. State Key Laboratory of Earthquake Dynamics and Forecasting, Institute of Geology, China Earthquake Administration, Beijing, China

*Corresponding author: dqchy@ies.ac.cn

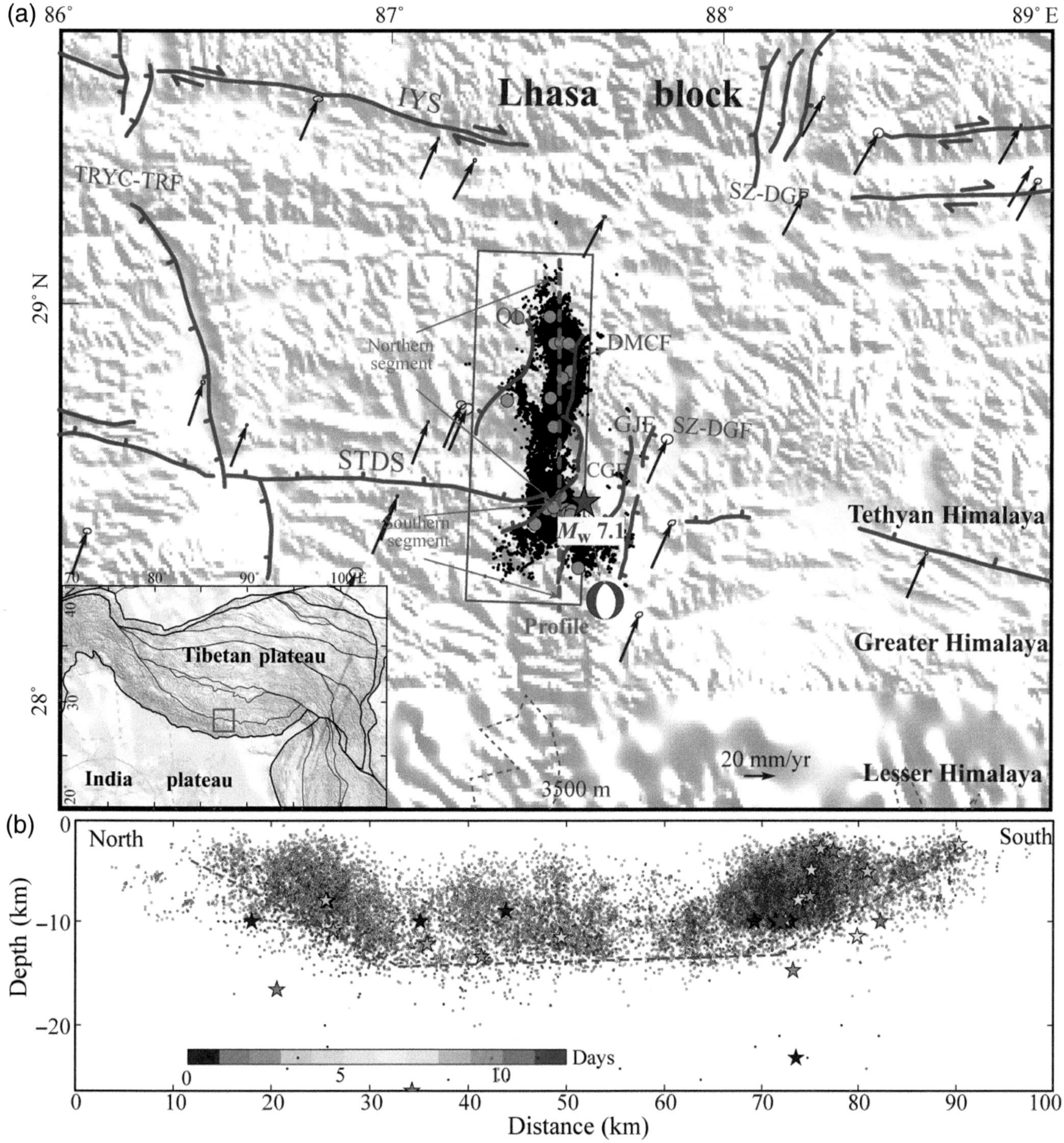

Figure 1. Tectonic setting and aftershocks distribution of the 2025 M_w 7.1 Tingri earthquake. (a) Tectonic setting surrounding the Tingri earthquake. The red rectangle indicates the location of the inverted slip model. The purple dashed line represents the position of the profile in Figure 1b. The red pentagram marks the epicenter of the M_w 7.1 Tingri earthquake. The black dots denote aftershocks (Yao *et al.*, 2025) with magnitudes below M_L 4.0, and the green dots indicate aftershocks with magnitudes above M_L 4.0 (as of 18 January). The red lines are active faults, and the blue arrows are Global Positioning System velocities (Wang and Shen, 2020). CGF, Cuoguo fault; DMCF, Dengmocuo fault; GJF, Guojia fault; IYS, Indus-Yarlung suture; STDS, southern Tibetan detachment system; SZ-DGF, Shenza-Dinggyê fault; QLF, Quluo fault; TRYC-TRF, TangraYumcuo-Tingri fault. (b) Distribution of aftershocks along the depth profile (Yao *et al.*, 2025). The colors of the dots ($<M_L$ 4.0) and pentagrams ($\geq M_L$ 4.0) indicate the time elapsed since the mainshock. The color version of this figure is available only in the electronic edition.

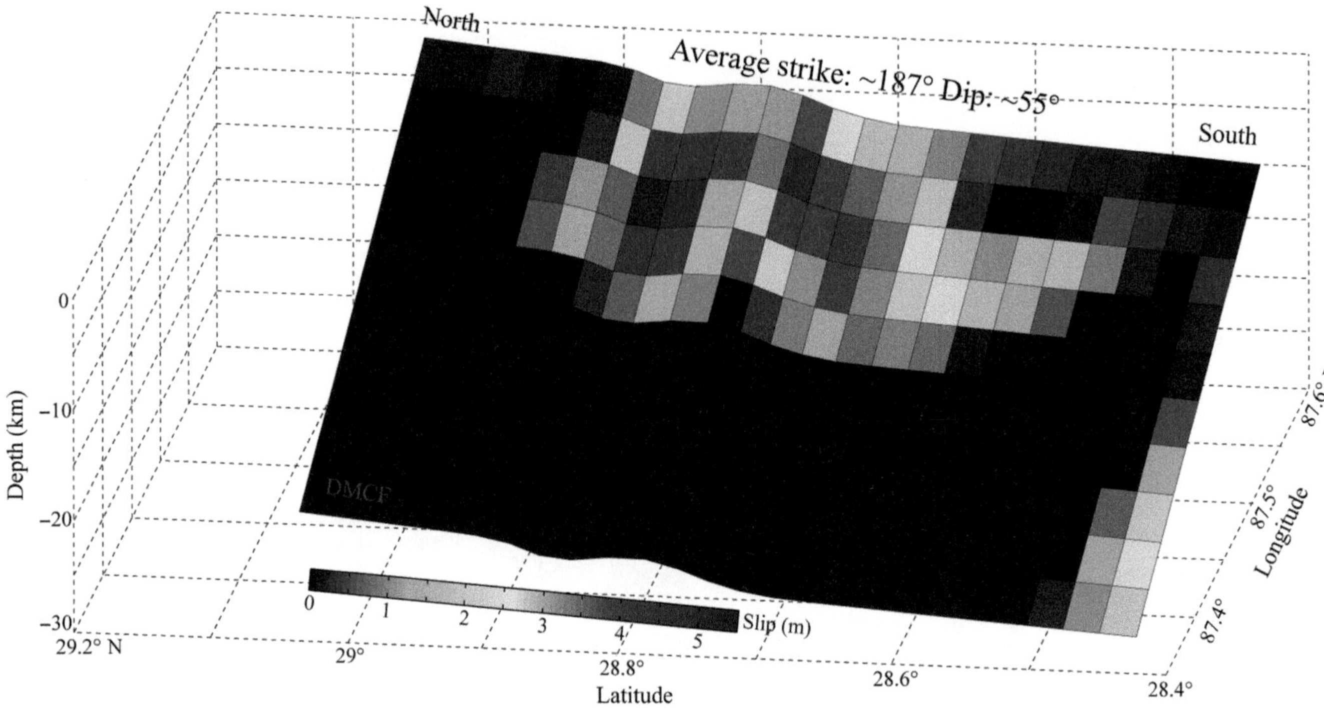

Figure 2. Coseismic slip distribution results of the Tingri earthquake (modified from Liu *et al.*, 2025). The color version of this figure is available only in the electronic edition.

Tingri earthquake. As of 18 January, a total of 25,393 relocated seismic events have been recorded using the double-difference positioning method (Waldhauser and Ellsworth, 2000), as illustrated in Figure 1. When projecting the aftershock sequence along the depth axis, we observed significant depth variations between the two ends and the middle segment. The aftershocks in the middle segment occurred at greater depths, and those at the northern and southern ends were shallower. The calculations of Coulomb failure stress changes (ΔCFS) indicate that both the source area and its surrounding regions experienced predominantly negative stress changes despite the occurrence of numerous aftershocks. Yin *et al.* (2025) attributed these aftershocks to postseismic afterslip. However, postseismic afterslip can persist for months or even years (Tian *et al.*, 2020; Hong and Liu, 2021; Yue *et al.*, 2024). However, the influence of poroelastic rebound, which significantly affects short-term stress changes, was not examined. Therefore, the mechanisms triggering aftershocks require further in-depth investigation.

To study the distribution characteristics and triggering mechanisms of the aftershocks associated with the M_w 7.1 Tingri earthquake, we constructed a layered half-space viscoelastic model in conjunction with a poroelastic rebound model. We calculated the ΔCFS induced by coseismic slip and postseismic poroelastic rebound using the coseismic slip model inverted by Interferometric Synthetic Aperture Radar (InSAR) data and strong-motion records.

Data and Method

Coseismic slip model

Field investigations and high-precision unmanned aerial vehicle aerial surveys of the Tingri earthquake rupture zone indicate a total rupture length of 36.5 km. The northern segment exhibits significant surface deformation, with maximum vertical displacements measuring 265 ± 27 cm (Shao *et al.*, 2025). Liu *et al.* (2025) inverted a coseismic slip model using Sentinel-1A Synthetic Aperture Radar (SAR) data (both ascending and descending tracks), ascending LuTan-1 SAR data, and local strong-motion records. This model reveals that the rupture is confined to the upper 10 km of the crust, featuring a peak slip of 4–5 m and near-surface vertical displacements of ~3 m (Fig. 2). The fault plane strikes at an average angle of 187°, with a westward dip and a relatively steep dip angle of 55°. The inverted slip distribution aligns closely with field measurements while explicitly accounting for heterogeneity in the strike direction. The fault model can effectively explain the observed results. Therefore, we use this validated model to compute the ΔCFS induced by coseismic slip and postseismic poroelastic rebound.

ΔCFS

In this article, we primarily calculate two types of ΔCFS induced by the Tingri earthquake. One is the static ΔCFS resulting from coseismic slip, and the other is the ΔCFS caused by the poroelastic rebound of the crust. The relaxation deformation of the viscoelastic lithosphere occurs over a relatively long timescale, which falls outside the scope of this study.

TABLE 1
Physical Parameters of the Model

No.	Depth (km)	V_P (km/s)	V_S (km/s)	Rho (kg/m^3)	Skempton Ratio	α	Hydraulic Diffusivity
1	0	5.847	3.422	2550	0.6	0.23	6.3
2	5	5.923	3.413	2550	0.6	0.23	1.0
3	10	5.998	3.404	2650	0.6	0.23	0.003
4	20	6.703	3.724	2700	0.6	0.23	0.003
5	30	6.267	3.83	2900	0.6	0.23	0.003
6	40	6.376	3.981	3050	0.6	0.23	0.003
7	50	7.729	4.276	3200	0.6	0.23	0.003
8	60	8.464	4.666	3300	0.6	0.23	0.003
9	70	8.191	4.646	3300	0.6	0.23	0.003
10	80	8.171	4.653	3300	0.6	0.23	0.003
11	100	8.085	4.699	3300	0.6	0.23	0.003

According to the Coulomb rupture criterion, the ΔCFS induced by an earthquake dislocation on a specific fault (Jaeger *et al.*, 1969) is given by the equation

$$\Delta \mathrm{CFS} = \Delta\tau + \mu(\Delta\sigma_n + \Delta P), \quad (1)$$

in which $\Delta\tau$ is the shear stress change (positive when the slip direction is along the fault), $\Delta\sigma_n$ is the normal stress change (positive for extension), ΔP is the pore-pressure change (positive for compression), and μ is the friction coefficient (ranges from 0 to 1). Equation (1) is often refined by determining the absolute change in shear stress on the fault plane (Harris, 1998), leading to the modified formula

$$\Delta \mathrm{CFS} = \Delta\tau + \mu'\Delta\sigma_n, \quad (2)$$

in which μ' is the effective friction coefficient, incorporating pore-fluid pressure (β') and media properties on the fault plane,

$$\mu' = \mu(1 - \beta'). \quad (3)$$

In general, the friction coefficient μ in laboratory is taken to be 0.85 (Byerlee, 1978), and μ' is usually taken to be 0.4 (Yue *et al.*, 2024, 2025) at moderate pore pressure ($\beta' = 0.5$). The effect of the friction coefficient on the CFS calculation is discussed in the following section.

Lithospheric stratification and physical parameters

A significant number of studies on lithospheric stratification and physical parameters have been conducted in the Tibetan plateau (Schulte-Pelkum *et al.*, 2005; Zhang and Klemperer, 2010; Li and Song, 2018; Li *et al.*, 2024). We developed a layered half-space viscoelastic model in conjunction with a poroelastic rebound model based on recent research findings (Table 1). The model extends to a total depth of 100 km, with the upper 0–30 km representing the elastic upper crust. The 30–60 km range corresponds to the viscoelastic lower crust, and the region below 60 km comprises the viscoelastic upper mantle (Li *et al.*, 2024). The density parameters are derived from the 3D crustal density results reported by Bai *et al.* (2013).

The specific parameters of the poroelastic rebound model are as follows: the bulk compressibilities are set at 1.03 for drained conditions and 1.20 for undrained conditions based on the *P*- and *S*-wave velocities. The Skempton ratio is 0.6, and the dimensionless effective stress coefficient (α) is 0.23 (Wang and Küumpel, 2003; Hong and Liu, 2021). Following the empirical formula proposed by Ingebritsen and Manning (2010) and Nespoli *et al.* (2018), we adopted nonuniform values of 6.3, 1.0, and 0.003 for the hydraulic diffusivity of soft sediment (~0.1 km), hard sediment (~5 km), and the upper crust (~10 km), respectively. The influence of the Skempton ratio and the dimensionless effective stress coefficient on the calculation of the CFS are discussed in the following section.

We used the PSGRN/PSCMP codes (Wang *et al.*, 2006) to calculate the coseismic static ΔCFS and the PEGRN/PECMP codes (Wang and Küumpel, 2003) to calculate the ΔCFS induced by poroelastic rebound.

Results and Discussion

Coseismic Coulomb stress change

We calculated the static coseismic ΔCFS on the rupture fault plane (the strike angle is 187°, the dip angle is 49°, and the slip angle is −78°) at depths of 5, 10, 15, and 20 km, respectively. The impact of the parameters related to the receiver fault is discussed in the following section.

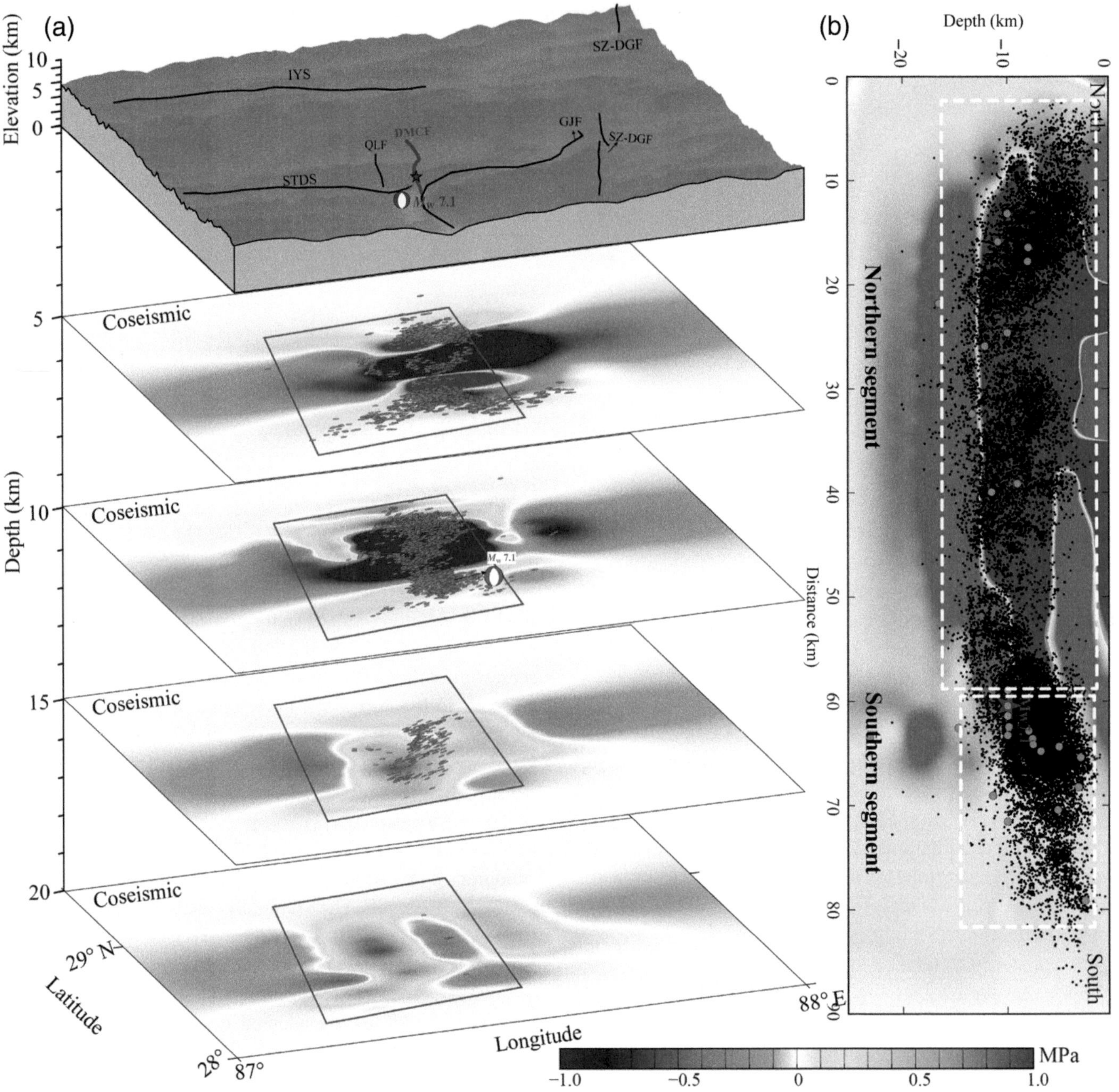

Figure 3. Static coseismic Coulomb failure stress change (ΔCFS) resulting from the M_w 7.1 Tingri earthquake. (a) The distribution of ΔCFS and aftershocks at depths of 5, 10, 15, and 20 km. The green dots denote aftershocks. The red rectangle indicates the location of the slip model. (b) The ΔCFS on the rupture fault plane. The red pentagram is the epicenter of the M_w 7.1 Tingri earthquake. The green dots denote aftershocks with magnitudes above M_L 4.0, and the black dots indicate aftershocks with magnitudes below M_L 4.0. The color version of this figure is available only in the electronic edition.

The analysis of ΔCFS across depth profiles reveals bilateral stress-shadow zones flanking the seismogenic fault (Fig. 3a). Consequently, aftershock clusters remain confined to the DMCF without lateral dispersion. Notably, pronounced CFS shadows occur at 5–10 km depths, indicating that this interval constitutes the primary coseismic rupture zone. As depth increases, CFS loading intensifies significantly, which is consistent with normal-faulting mechanics that amplify stress transfer at greater crustal levels.

The analysis of ΔCFS on the fault plane (Fig. 3b) reveals a distinct CFS shadow zone that extends from 10 to 60 km in distance and from 0 to 13 km in depth. This ΔCFS pattern indicates that the M_w 7.1 Tingri earthquake induced a shallow stress release along the DMCF, whereas the northern and southern ends reflect the stress-loading effect. Aftershocks were projected onto the fault plane and categorized into two segments. Numerous aftershocks occurred within the primary coseismic CFS shadow zone. Consequently, these earthquakes must be triggered by stresses other than coseismic static CFS. In contrast, the southern segment (60–90 km) displays shallower aftershock depths, with most aftershocks clustered within the CFS loading zone. The triggering effect of coseismic CFS may be particularly significant.

Poroelastic Rebound Coulomb Stress Change

We calculated the postseismic ΔCFS on the fault plane caused by poroelastic rebound approximately one month after the M_w 7.1 Tingri earthquake, with the results illustrated in Figure 4.

The rupture from the Tingri earthquake was primarily concentrated in northern segment, resulting in the earliest occurrence of shallow fluid migration within this segment, which generated a significant CFS loading effect (Fig. 4a). Consequently, abundant aftershocks occurred in this region despite the CFS shadow zone caused by the coseismic slip (Fig. 3b). The poroelastic CFS loading effect compensates for the influence of the coseismic CFS shadow zone. Over time, the extent of the CFS loading effect in northern segment gradually expanded into the southern segment. A comparison of aftershock onset times reveals that aftershocks are more frequent in the southern segment during a later timeframe (Fig. 4b,c), particularly with the occurrence of multiple aftershocks of magnitude greater than M_L 4.0. This suggests that postseismic fluid migration gradually extends into the regions of the southern segment over time, resulting in a pronounced CFS loading effect in these areas.

Coulomb stress effects of mainshocks on aftershocks

To further compare aftershock triggering by coseismic slip versus postseismic poroelastic rebound, we calculate the ΔCFS imparted by each mechanism on the aftershocks (Yao *et al.*, 2025) separately. Postseismic poroelastic rebound effects were evaluated using data recorded five days after the mainshock. The receiver fault parameters for aftershocks match those previously established: strike = 187°, dip = 49°, and rake = −78°. The statistical proportions and earthquakes are presented in Table 2 and Table S1, available in the supplemental material to this article, and the spatial distribution of triggered aftershocks is illustrated in Figures 5 and Figure S1.

The effectiveness of coseismic slip in triggering aftershocks demonstrates a significant dependence on depth. Triggering is minimal at intermediate depths (2.5–12.5 km) but substantial at both shallow (<2.5 km) and deeper (>12.5 km) levels (see Table 2, Fig. 5b). Notably, the Tingri earthquake generated main ruptures confined to 5–10 km, resulting in considerable stress release within this interval (Fig. 3b). Consequently, coseismic slip triggered only 31%–42% of aftershocks within this depth range. In contrast, the triggering proportions at shallow and deep depths reach 74%–85%. Overall, the contribution of coseismic slip to the triggering of aftershocks accounted for merely 44% along the entire fault system—less than half of the total. This is largely attributed to the occurrence of numerous aftershocks in the stress-shadow zone at depths of 5–10 km (see Fig. 5a, Fig. S1). This depth interval contains the highest concentration of aftershocks (n = 15,902), representing 63% of all recorded events.

In contrast, the spatial pattern of the poroelastic rebound's triggering effect on aftershocks resembles that of coseismic slip, with the exception of the 15–20 km depth interval. Notably, poroelastic rebound triggers a significantly higher proportion of aftershocks—reaching 65%—compared with coseismic slip (see Table 2, Fig. 5d). Specifically, within the 5–10 km depth range, poroelastic mechanisms account for 57%–69% of the triggered events. The primary rupture of the earthquake was concentrated in the northern segment of the DMCF. Although coseismic slip demonstrates comparable aftershock-triggering effectiveness across both northern and southern segments (refer to Table 2), poroelastic rebound exhibits markedly higher efficiency in the northern segment (74%) versus the southern segment (50%). This difference indicates that postseismic fluid migration significantly enhances the occurrence of aftershocks within the main rupture zone.

Stability of the results

Effective coefficients of friction and parameters of the receiver fault (e.g., strike, dip, and rake angles) can introduce uncertainties in CFS calculations (Yue *et al.*, 2024, 2025; Chen *et al.*, 2025). We compiled focal mechanism solutions (nodal plane II) for the Tingri earthquake from nine institutions and individual researchers (see Table 3). By integrating these solutions with our inverted fault-plane parameters, we systematically evaluated the sensitivity of the results to variations in receiver fault parameters and effective friction coefficients. For each of the 10 parameter sets, we calculated the minimum, maximum, and mean values, modifying only one variable per trial to isolate its effects. Figure 6a compares the results on the fault plane at 10 km with μ' of 0.2, 0.4, and 0.8, and Figure 6b–d demonstrates the dependencies on strike, dip, and slip angle at a fixed friction coefficient of 0.4. The Skempton ratio and the dimensionless effective stress coefficient play crucial roles in the distribution of the CFS in a poroelastic medium. We introduce another two sets of poroelastic models (refer to Table S2 for parameters) to compare the effects of the Skempton ratio and the dimensionless effective stress coefficient (see Fig. 6e). Figure 6f illustrates the percentage of aftershock triggering at depths of 9–11 km for several different parameter sets.

Frictional parameters and receiver fault geometry generate variability in ΔCFS across fault segments (Fig. 6a–d). In some segments, inverse correlations between parameter values and ΔCFS magnitudes are observed, but positive correlations predominate in others. This heterogeneity primarily reflects the

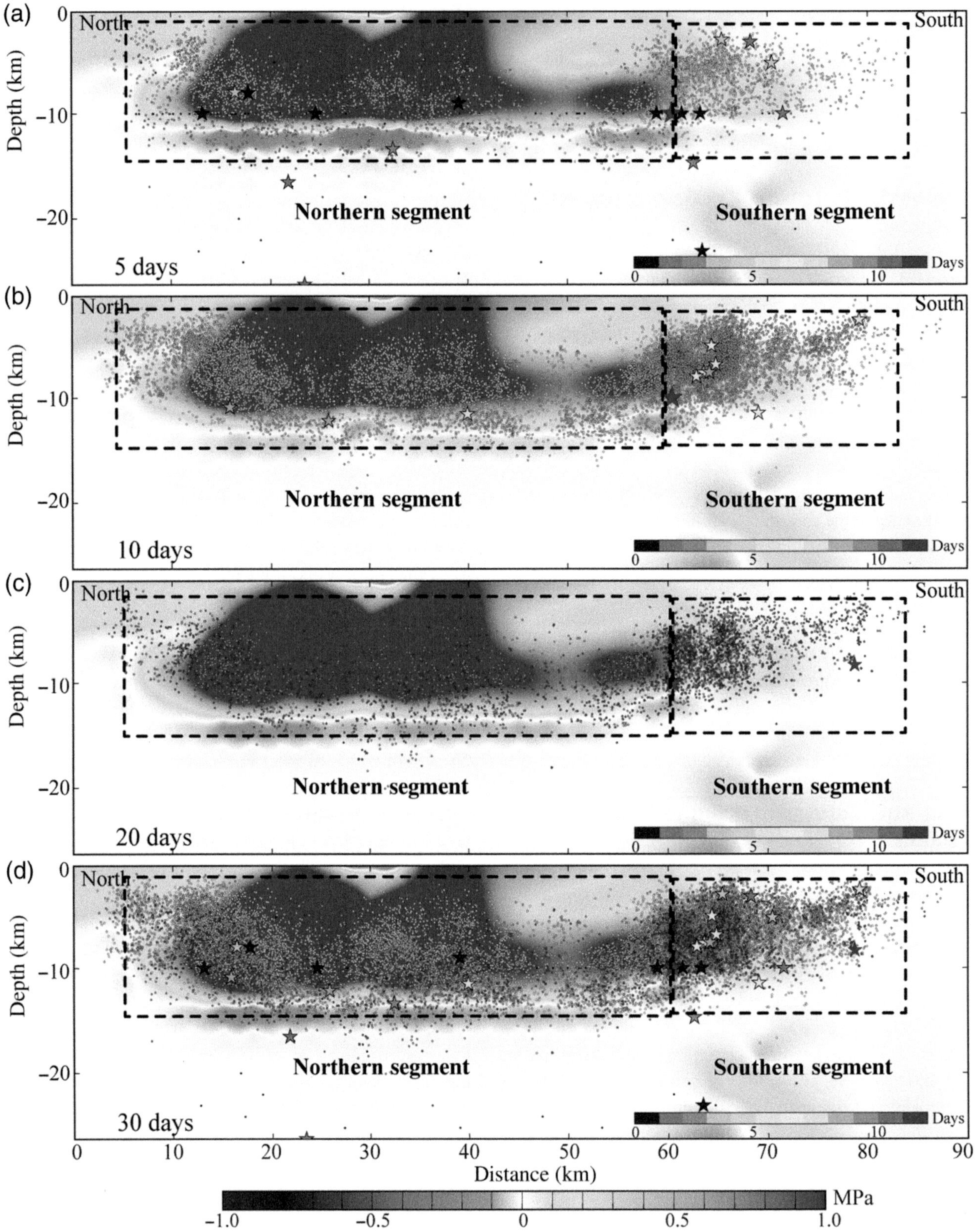

geometric complexities within the Tingri rupture zone. Although variations in parameters modulate ΔCFS amplitudes, they have a negligible effect on overall stress patterns. Notably, within the main rupture zone, parametric sensitivity is heightened, as evidenced by the pronounced peaks and

Figure 4. The ΔCFS caused by the poroelastic rebound of the crust. (a–d) The results at 5, 10, 20, and 30 days following the mainshock, respectively. The color version of this figure is available only in the electronic edition.

TABLE 2
Statistical Table of Coulomb Failure Stress Change (ΔCFS) for Aftershocks Under Two Mechanisms

Segment	Depth (km)	Co_Unload (%)	Co_Load (%)	Pore_Unload (%)	Pore_Load (%)	EQ Number
Entire fault	0–2.4	21	79	20	80	374
	2.5–4,.9	48	52	35	65	4,126
	5.0–7.4	69	31	43	57	8,702
	7.5–9.9	58	42	31	69	7,200
	10–12.4	44	56	29	71	3,626
	12.5–14.9	26	74	21	79	1,233
	15–20	15	85	41	59	110
	Total	**56**	**44**	**35**	**65**	25,371
Northern segment		**56**	**44**	**26**	**74**	15,726
Southern segment		**56**	**44**	**50**	**50**	9,645

Bold values indicate the relevant calculation results.

troughs shown in Figure 6a–d. Therefore, further in-depth research is still required regarding the selection of receiving fault parameters in the main rupture zone. This selection of parameters is more moderate and does not yield extreme computational results. Our model uses USGS nodal plane II parameters, in which the fault strike, dip, and rake align with the mean values. Conversely, increasing the Skempton ratio or dimensionless effective stress coefficients monotonically amplifies ΔCFS magnitudes without altering their distributions. Overall, the results of the calculations presented in this article are deemed reliable.

A comparative analysis of aftershock triggering proportions (Fig. 6f) reveals that the strike angle has the most significant influence, resulting in up to a 4% variation in triggered proportions. The rake angle demonstrates the second-greatest impact, accounting for a 3% variation. Both the dip angle and poroelastic model parameters contribute to 2% discrepancies. Notably, although the friction coefficient generates the largest ΔCFS perturbations on the fault plane, it has a minimal effect (1%) on aftershock triggering proportions. Therefore, assessing the impacts of normal-fault-type earthquakes on aftershock generation requires prioritizing the consideration of both strike and rake parameters.

Triggering mechanism of aftershocks

To further investigate the triggering mechanism of aftershocks, we analyzed the quantity and depth of aftershocks across various segments. We subdivided the northern segment into two parts: segment 1, which spans 0–25 km, and segment 2, which covers 25–60 km. The southern segment was designated as segment 3. We recorded the depth of aftershocks within each of the three segments. A total of 4,929 aftershocks occurred within 20 km of the upper crust in segment 1, with a mean depth of 7.1 km; 6,471 aftershocks occurred in segment 2 at a mean depth of 9.8 km; and 13,904 aftershocks occurred in segment 3 at a mean depth of 6.7 km (Fig. 7a). The aftershocks exhibit a central-deep, bilateral-shallow depth distribution, a pattern closely linked to the rupture mechanics of normal-fault earthquakes and Coulomb stress triggering.

Dynamic snapshots from the slip model reveal that segment 3 initiated the rupture; however, the primary coseismic slip concentrated in segments 1 and 2 (Fig. 7c). The inversion process of the coseismic slip model, using data recorded by strong-motion seismographs, is detailed in Figure S2. The M_w 7.1 Tingri earthquake represents a normal-fault event, characterized by the collapse deformation of the DMCF hanging wall relative to the footwall, with maximum vertical displacements reaching 2.5–3.0 m (Shao *et al.*, 2025; Shi *et al.*, 2025; Xu *et al.*, 2025). The deformation mode of the M_w 7.1 Tingri earthquake resembles the “seesaw model” depicted in the lower right corner of Figure 7b. The occurrence of the Tingri earthquake generates significant compressive stress on the seesaw, which is transmitted to the unruptured areas at both the northern and southern ends (the opposite side of the seesaw) through the elastic crust (akin to the seesaw itself). Coseismic CFS produces a pronounced loading effect at both the northern and southern ends as well as the base of the hanging wall. For the ΔCFS caused by poroelastic rebound, in addition to the recovery loading effect in the main rupture zone, postseismic fluid migration also generates a stress-loading effect that extends along the basement to the north and south. Because no significant subsidence occurred in segment 3, the fault rupture induced by fluid migration led to a higher number of aftershock events in this segment, with the number of aftershocks in this region being two to three times greater than in the other two regions during the same period (Fig. 4).

In summary, as a normal-fault earthquake, the central portion of the main rupture zone (segment 2) exhibits the most

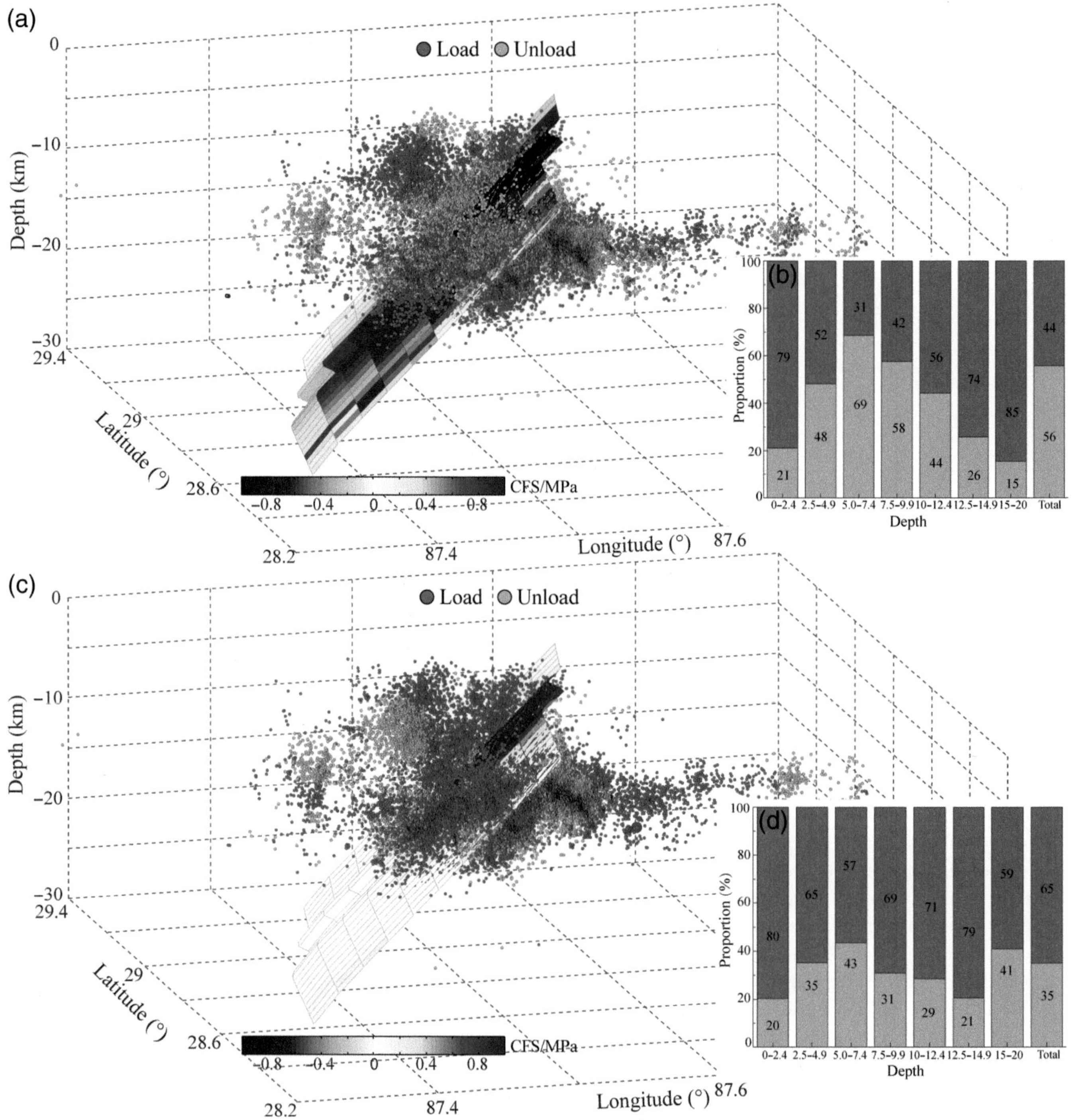

Figure 5. Results on the triggering effects of coseismic slip (a,b) and postseismic poroelastic rebound (c,d) on aftershocks. The color version of this figure is available only in the electronic edition.

significant seismic dismantling and subsidence. Aftershocks are triggered by the CFS resulting from both coseismic slip and poroelastic rebound of the crust. Notably, the coseismic CFS triggering effect is more pronounced and extends to greater depths, leading to deeper aftershock occurrences in this area, with an average depth of 9.8 km. Segments 1 and 3, located at the northern and southern ends of the rupture zone, are constrained by the elastic resistance of the upper crust, resulting in gradually diminishing vertical deformation. Postseismic fluid migration propagates outward from the main rupture zone toward both ends, generating CFS loading that effectively compensates for the coseismic CFS shadow zones. Consequently, aftershocks proliferated in these areas, exhibiting shallower focal depths (mean: 7.1 and 6.7 km, respectively) and a progressive shallowing trend in focal depths. Studies conducted after the 2015 Gorkha

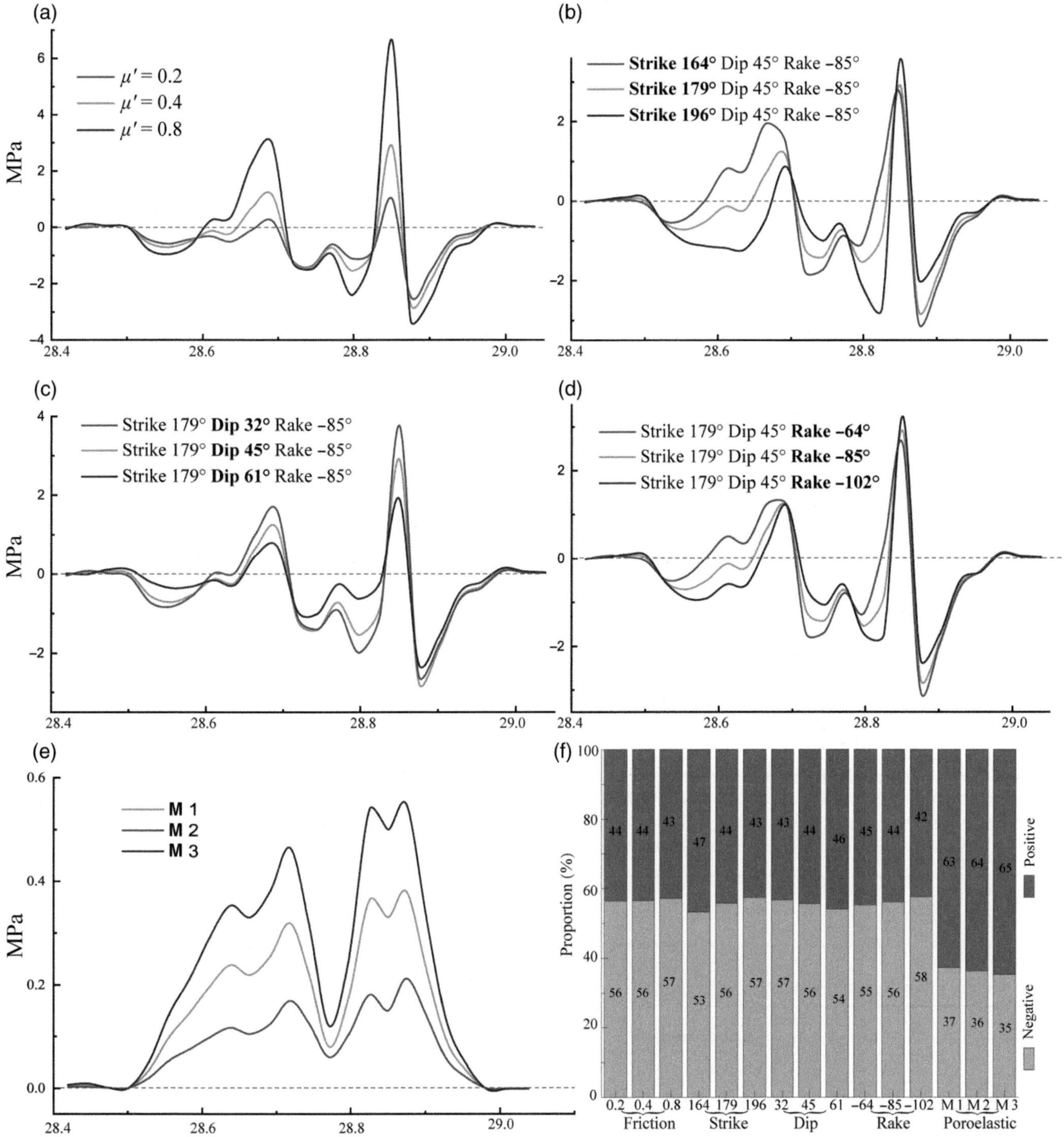

Figure 6. Influence of parameters on the results of coseismic and postseismic ΔCFS at 10 km. (a) Influence of effective friction coefficient. (b–d) Influence of strike angle, dip angle, and rake angle, respectively. (e) Influence of Skempton ratio and dimensionless effective stress coefficient. (f) Aftershock triggering proportions under different parameters. The color version of this figure is available only in the electronic edition.

earthquake indicate that fluid migration plays a crucial role in triggering both deep and shallow aftershocks of the mainshock, which also occur within the coseismic CFS shadow zone. The proportion of aftershocks triggered by poroelastic rebound is higher than that triggered by coseismic slip (Jamtveit *et al.*, 2018; Tung *et al.*, 2018). Calculations presented in this article demonstrate that a significant number of aftershocks occur within the same coseismic CFS shadow zone, and proportion of aftershocks triggered from postseismic fluid migration is 65%, which is significantly higher than the coseismic slip.

Conclusions

To investigate the distribution characteristics and triggering mechanisms of aftershocks following the M_w 7.1 Tingri

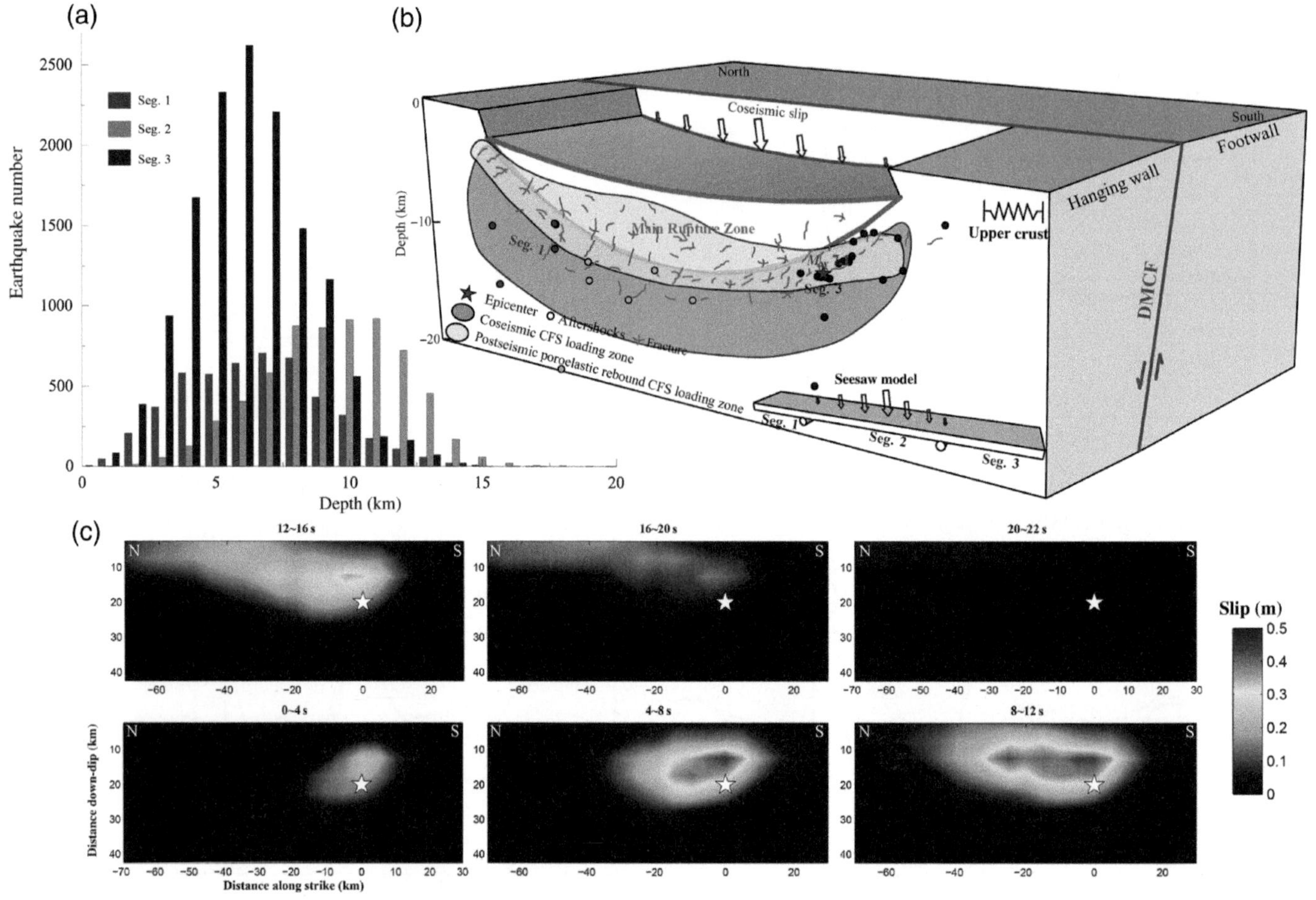

Figure 7. Depth statistics of aftershocks, the rupture process, and schematic diagrams of impact mechanisms. (a) Depth statistics of aftershocks across the three segments. (b) Schematic diagram depicting the impact mechanism of coseismic slip and poroelastic rebound on aftershocks in the different segments. (c) Snapshots of slip distribution every 5 s. The color version of this figure is available only in the electronic edition.

TABLE 3
Focal Mechanism Solutions of the Tingri Earthquake from Different Institutions and Individual Researchers

Source	Latitude	Longitude	Nodal Plane I			Nodal Plane II		
CENC	28.59	87.33	348	40	−100	181	51	−81
Zhang	28.49	87.47	346	49	−95	174	42	−85
Global CMT	28.56	87.47	356	42	−88	173	48	−92
USGS	28.573	87.375	349	42	−103	187	49	−78
IPGP	28.639	87.361	341	51	−113	196	44	−64
GFZ	28.57	87.41	0	49	−79	164	41	−102
SC4	28.53	87.40	342	29	−116	191	61	−76
AUST	28.603	87.402	355	50	−87	169	40	−94
GSRAS	28.62	87.46	353	45	−88	171	45	−92
Mean value	–	–	–	–	–	179	45	−85

Please see Data and Resources for the websites related to this table for: CENC, Zhang, Global Centroid Moment Tensor (Global CMT), U.S. Geological Survey (USGS), Institut de Physique du Globe de Paris (IPGP), GeoForschungsZentrums (GFZ), SC4, AUST, and GSRAS.

earthquake, we computed ΔCFS induced by coseismic slip and postseismic poroelastic rebound. These calculations used a coseismic slip model inverted from InSAR data and strong-motion records.

The normal-faulting earthquake along the DMCF establishes a coseismic ΔCFS pattern: stress loading dominates at the northern and southern ends of the seismogenic fault while stress shadows form on its eastern and western flanks. Rupture was concentrated within the upper 10 km, coinciding spatially with the main stress-shadow zone. Nevertheless, significant aftershock activity persisted within this depth range. Postseismic fluid migration generates substantial ΔCFS loading within the main rupture zone, effectively compensating coseismic stress shadows and triggering peripheral aftershocks.

The triggering efficacy of coseismic slip and poroelastic rebound exhibits a depth dependence: minimal at intermediate depths (2.5–12.5 km) but significantly enhanced at shallower (<2.5 km) and deeper (>12.5 km) depths. Mechanistic contributions to aftershock triggering diverge substantially across the fault system. Coseismic slip accounts for only 44% of total aftershock triggering, but poroelastic rebound contributes higher, reaching up to 65%. This contrast is most pronounced in the northern segment, where poroelastic effects dominate (74% contribution). These results demonstrate that postseismic fluid migration exerts a primary control on aftershock nucleation within the main rupture zone.

Data and Resources

In this article, some figures were made using the Generic Mapping Tools version 5.1.2. The PEGRN/PECMP codes (Wang and Küumpel, 2003) and PSGRN/PSCMP codes (Wang *et al.*, 2006) were used to calculate the Coulomb stress change. The coseismic slip model of the M_w 7.1 Tingri earthquake was cited from Liu *et al.* (2025). The aftershocks were cited from Yao *et al.* (2025). C. Yue supported conceptualization, writing of the original draft, and writing review and editing. D. Dai and Y. Zhang supported inversion of the slip model. Y. Wang, W. Yang, and Y. Han supported seismic relocation. X. Li, C. Qu, and L. Meng supported article revision. All authors have read and agreed to the published version of the article. This work was supported by the National Natural Science Foundation of China (52374103, 42474116). The websites for Table 3 are available as follows: CENC (https://www.cenc.ac.cn/cenc/tpxw/414670/index.html); Zhang (https://www.cea-igp.ac.cn/kydt/280883.html); Global Centroid Moment Tensor (Global CMT) (https://www.globalcmt.org); U.S. Geological Survey (USGS) (https://earthquake.usgs.gov/earthquakes/eventpage/us6000pi9w/moment-tensor); Institut de Physique du Globe de Paris (IPGP) (http://geoscope.ipgp.fr/index.php/en/catalog/earthquake-description?seis=us6000pi9w22212); GeoForschungs Zentrums (GFZ) (https://geofon.gfz.de/eqinfo/event.php?id=gfz2025albe); SC4 (https://www.emsc-csem.org/Earthquake_information/earthquake.php?id=1753287); AUST (https://earthquakes.ga.gov.au); and GSRAS (http://mseism.gsras.ru/EqInfo/RequestsHandler?cmd=toinfmsg&lang=en&imid=276). The supplemental material includes tables and figures mentioned in the main text. The link of the M_w 7.1 Tingri earthquake in the USGS is https://earthquake.usgs.gov/earthquakes/eventpage/us6000pi9w. All websites were last accessed in March 2025.

Declaration of Competing Interests

The authors acknowledge that there are no conflicts of interest recorded.

Acknowledgments

The authors thank Professor Rongjiang Wang for his help in the Coulomb stress calculation process. They also thank Professor Yong Zhang for his help in the inversion of the slip model, Yao *et al.* (2025) for the aftershocks relocation data, and Liu *et al.* (2025) for the coseismic slip model.

References

Bai, Z. M., S. Zhang, and C. Braitenberg (2013). Crustal density structure from 3D gravity modeling beneath Himalaya and Lhasa blocks, Tibet, *J. Asian Earth Sci.* **78,** no. 15, 301–317, doi: 10.1016/j.jseaes.2012.12.035.

Byerlee, J. (1978). Friction of rocks, *Pure Appl. Geophys.* **116,** 615–626.

Chen, F., D. Wang, S. Xu, B. Yan, J. Zhang, Y. Guo, D. Yao, J. Zhuang, G. Suárez, and P. Shearer (2025). Bi-segment fault rupture and long-lasting intraslab aftershock activity during the 2017 M_w 8.2 Tehuantepec, Mexico earthquake, *J. Geophys. Res.* **130,** e2024JB030699, doi: 10.1029/2024JB030699.

Harris, R. A. (1998). Introduction to special section: stress triggers, stress shadows, and implications for seismic hazard, *J. Geophys. Res.* **103,** no. B10, 24,347–24,358.

Hong, S., and M. Liu (2021). Postseismic deformation and afterslip evolution of the 2015 Gorkha earthquake constrained by InSAR and GPS observations, *J. Geophys. Res.* **126,** e2020JB020230, doi: 10.1029/2020JB020230.

Ingebritsen, S. E., and C. E. Manning (2010). Permeability of the continental crust: dynamic variations inferred from seismicity and metamorphism, *Geofluids* **10,** 193–205.

Jaeger, J. G., N. G. Cook, and W. R. W. Zimmerman (1969). Fundamental of Rock Mechanics, Blackwell Pob, New York.

Jamtveit, B., Y. Ben-Zion, F. Renard, and H. Austrheim (2018). Earthquake-induced transformation of the lower crust, *Nature* **556,** no. 7702, 487–491.

Li, J., S. Pei, Q. Sun, H. Liu, W. Liu, Q. Hua, and L. Li (2024). Oblique rifting in the southern Tibetan plateau revealed from 3-D high-resolution seismic travel-time tomography around the India–Eurasia continental collision zone, *J. Geophys. Res.* **129,** e2024JB029447, doi: 10.1029/2024JB029447.

Li, J. T., and X. D. Song (2018). Tearing of Indian mantle lithosphere from high-resolution seismic images and its implications for lithosphere coupling in southern Tibet, *Proc. Nat. Acad. Sci. Unit. States Am.* **115,** no. 33, 8296–8300.

Liu, Q., J. Hua, and Y. Zhang (2025). Geodetic observations and seismogenic structures of the 2025 M_w 7.0 Dingri earthquake: The largest normal faulting event in the southern Tibet rift, *Remote Sens.* **17,** 1096, doi: 10.3390/rs17061096.

Nespoli, M., M. E. Belardinelli, A. Gualandi, E. Serpelloni, and M. Bonafede (2018). Poroelasticity and fluid flow modeling for the 2012 Emilia-Romagna earthquakes: Hints from GPS and InSAR data, *Geofluids* **2018,** 4160570.

Schulte-Pelkum, V., G. Monsalve, A. Sheehan, M. R. Pandey, S. Sapkota, R. Bilham, and F. Wu (2005). Imaging the Indian subcontinent beneath the Himalaya, *Nature* **435,** no. 7046, 1222–1225, doi: 10.1038/nature03678.

Shao, Y. X., A. S. Wang, J. Liu, W. Wang, L. Han, and L. Xing (2025). Preliminary investigation on surface rupture and coseismic displacement of the January 7, 2025 Dingri earthquake in Xizang, *Chin. Sci. Bull.* doi: 10.3799/dqkx.2025.040 (Chinese with English abstract).

Shi, F., M. J. Liang, Q. X. Luo, J. X. Qiao, D. Zhang, X. Wang, W. X. Yi, J. W. Zhang, Y. F. Zhang, and H. P. Zhang (2025). Seismogenic fault and coseismic surace deformation of the Dingri M_S 6.8 earthquake in Tibet, China, *Seismol. Geol.* **47,** no. 1, 1–15 (Chinese with English abstract).

Tian, Z., J. T. Freymueller, and Z. Q. Yang (2020). Spatio-temporal variations of afterslip and viscoelastic relaxation following the M_W 7.8 Gorkha (Nepal) earthquake, *Earth Planet. Sci. Lett.* **532,** 116031, doi: 10.1016/j.epsl.2019.116031.

Tung, S., T. Masterlark, and T. Dovovan (2018). Transient poroelastic stress coupling between the 2015 M7.8 Gorkha, Nepal earthquake and its M7.3 aftershock, *Tectonophysics* **733,** 119–131.

Waldhauser, F., and W. Ellsworth (2000). A double-difference earthquake location algorithm: Method and application to the northern Hayward fault, California, *Bull. Seismol. Soc. Am.* **96,** no. 6, 1353–1368.

Wang, M., and Z.-K. Shen (2020). Present-day crustal deformation of continental China derived from GPS and its tectonic implications, *J. Geophys. Res.* **125,** e2019JB018774, doi: 10.1029/2019JB018774.

Wang, R., and H. J. Küumpel (2003). Poroelasticity: Efficient modeling of strongly coupled, slow deformation processes in multilayered half-space, *Geophysics* **68,** no. 2, 705–717, doi: 10.1190/1.1567241.

Wang, R. J., F. Lorenzo-Martin, and F. Roth (2006). PSGRN/PSCMP-A new code for calculating co- and postseismic deformation, geoid and gravity changes based on the viscoelastic-gravitational dislocation theory, *Comput. Geosci.* **32,** no. 4, 527–541.

Xu, X., S. Wang, J. Cheng, and X. Wu (2025). Shaking the Tibetan plateau Insights from the M_w 7.1 Dingri earthquake and its implications for active fault mapping and disaster mitigation, *Nat. Hazards* doi: 10.1038/s44304-025-00074-7.

Yang, G., Y. Tang, D. Lei, Q. Hu, and J. Wu (2020). Holocene activity and seismic hazard analysis of faults in Damxung, Tibet, *Acta Geophys.* doi: 10.1007/s11600-020-00426-z.

Yao, J., D. Yao, F. Chen, M. Zhi, L. Sun, and D. Wang (2025). A preliminary catalog of early aftershocks following the 7 January 2025 M_S 6.8 Dingri, Xizang earthquake, *J. Earth Sci.* doi: 10.1007/s12583-025-0210-9.

Yin, G. Y., H. Zhang, M. Q. Shi, S. H. An, and Y. L. Shi (2025). Coseismic deformation and Coulomb stress changes of the M_s 6.8 Dingri, Xizang 2 earthquake, *J. Earth Sci.* doi: 10.1007/s12583-025-0273-7.

Yue, C., C. Qu, X. Shan, D. Zhao, H. Chen, and Y. Wang (2024). Stress evolution of the Main Himalayan thrust fault Induced by the M_w 7.8 Gorkha earthquake, *Bull. Seismol. Soc. Am.* **114,** no. 3, 1639–1657.

Yue, C., C. Y. Qu, X. F. Li, L. Y. Meng, X. H. Jiang, and D. L. Wu (2025). Co- and postseismic stress transfer on different types of faults in southern Tibet by the 2015 M_w 7.8 Gorkha earthquake, *J. Struct. Geol.* **191,** 105336, doi: 10.1016/j.jsg.2024.105336.

Zhang, Z. J., and S. L. Klemperer (2010). Crustal structure of the Tethyan Himalaya, southern Tibet: New constraints from old wide-angle seismic data, *Geophys. J. Int.* **181,** 1247–1260.

Manuscript received 12 March 2025
Published online 2 September 2025

28 March 2025 Myanmar Earthquake: Strong Ground Motions, Macroseismic Intensity, Liquefaction, and ALOS-2 ScanSAR Remote Sensing Damage Observations

Alejandro Cruz[1,2], Mohammad Ghasemi[3], Shaghayegh Karimzadeh*[1], Sadra Karimzadeh[3,4], Aysegul Askan[5], Masashi Matsuoka[4], and Paulo B. Lourenço[1]

Abstract

On 28 March 2025, a devastating M 7.7 earthquake struck Myanmar along the right-lateral strike-slip Sagaing fault, followed by an M 6.7 aftershock twelve minutes later. This study presents a comprehensive assessment of the earthquake's effects through recorded strong ground motions, macroseismic intensity observations, secondary hazards including liquefaction, and remote sensing-based damage detection. The supershear rupture spanned ~460 km, with pronounced fault directivity effects resulting in high peak ground acceleration values of up to 0.57*g* recorded for the horizontal components and macroseismic intensities reaching modified Mercalli intensity = X in nearby cities. Analysis of acceleration time series and Fourier amplitude spectra at nearby recording stations revealed significant near-field effects and spectral exceedances over Myanmar National building code design levels, particularly in the short-period range, affecting mostly low-rise structures. Secondary hazard evaluation indicates widespread liquefaction, especially near the Irrawaddy River, supported by correlations between cumulative absolute velocity and liquefaction probability maps. Remote sensing analysis using multitemporal Advanced Land Observation Satellite-2 Synthetic Aperture Radar (SAR) coherence data identified severe building and road damage in urban centers. A differential coherence method, coupled with urban masking and OpenStreetMap road data, enabled spatial quantification of damage, revealing over 39,000 km of roads and 306 km^2 of buildings with moderate-to-heavy damage. The results provide critical insight into the earthquake's impact and demonstrate the joint evaluation of ground-motion analysis and SAR-based damage mapping for rapid seismic response.

Cite this article as Cruz, A., M. Ghasemi, S. Karimzadeh, S. Karimzadeh, A. Askan, M. Matsuoka, and P. B. Lourenço (2025). 28 March 2025 Myanmar Earthquake: Strong Ground Motions, Macroseismic Intensity, Liquefaction, and ALOS-2 ScanSAR Remote Sensing Damage Observations, *Seismol. Res. Lett.* **97**, 1595–1612, doi: 10.1785/0220250258.

Introduction

Myanmar is located in a seismically active region with earthquakes primarily resulting from two main causes, as shown in Figure 1: (1) the subduction of the northward-moving India plate beneath the Burma plate, transitioning to a collision zone in the north, along the Andaman megathrust at a rate of 2–3.5 cm/yr; and (2) the northward motion of the Burma plate, driven by seafloor spreading in the Andaman Sea, occurring at a rate of 2.5–3.0 cm/yr (Thein *et al.*, 2009). An earthquake of **M** 7.7 occurred in Myanmar on 28 March 2025, followed by a second event of **M** 6.7 twelve minutes later. The earthquakes occurred on the Sagaing fault, which lies between the Burma microplate and the Sunda plates as a main strike-slip fault system (e.g., Gögen *et al.*, 2024). The same fault caused destructive

1. Department of Civil Engineering, University of Minho, ISISE, ARISE, Guimarães, Portugal, https://orcid.org/0000-0002-5631-0548 (AC); https://orcid.org/0000-0003-3753-1676 (ShK); https://orcid.org/0000-0001-8459-0199 (PBL); 2. School of Civil Engineering and Geomatics, Universidad del Valle, G-7, Cali, Colombia; 3. Remote Sensing Laboratory, Department of Remote Sensing and GIS, University of Tabriz, Tabriz, Iran, https://orcid.org/0000-0002-6992-2893 (MG); https://orcid.org/0000-0002-5645-0188 (SaK); 4. Department of Architecture and Building Engineering, Institute of Science Tokyo, Tokyo, Japan, https://orcid.org/0000-0003-3061-5754 (MM); 5. Civil Engineering and Earthquake Studies Departments, Middle East Technical University, Ankara, Türkiye, https://orcid.org/0000-0003-4827-9058 (AA)

*Corresponding author: shaghkn@civil.uminho.pt

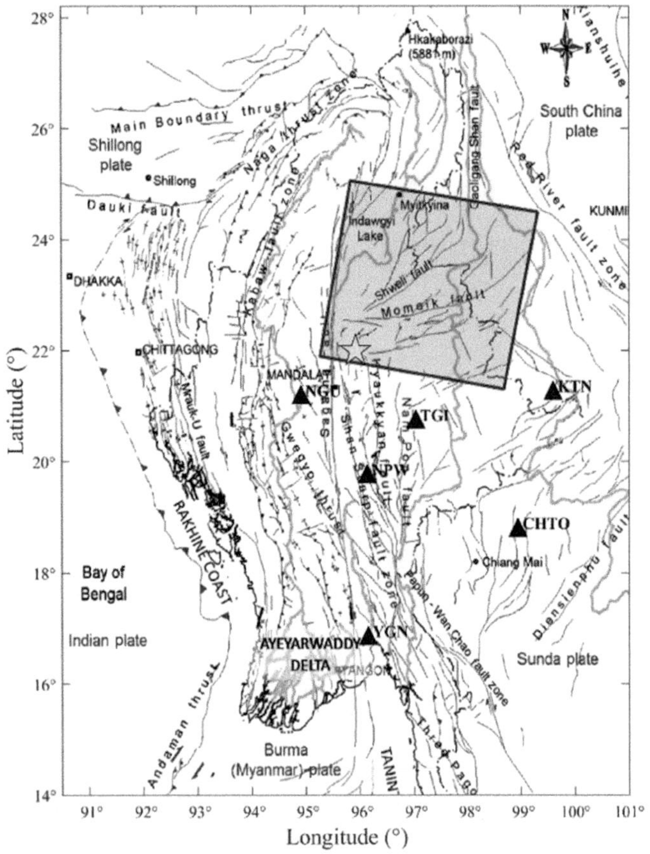

Figure 1. Tectonic map of Myanmar and nearby regions, highlighting major fault systems, plate boundaries, the epicenter of the 28 March 2025 **M** 7.7 earthquake (yellow star), seismic stations (blue triangles), together with the Advanced Land Observation Satellite (ALOS)-2 PALSAR-2 data footprint used in this study (red box). Base map taken from Thein *et al.* (2009). The color version of this figure is available only in the electronic edition.

events in the past, such as the 1930 **M** 7.3, 1946 **M** 7.7, and 1956 **M** 7.0 earthquakes. The 2025 **M** 7.7 event caused a supershear rupture of 460 km (Shahzada *et al.*, 2025).

With Advanced Land Observation Satellite (ALOS)-2 Synthetic Aperture Radar (SAR) data, extensive damage to the built environment during the 2025 Myanmar event in the cities of Mandalay, Sagaing, and Naypyidaw was observed due to near-field effects coupled with vulnerable building structures in the region. The ALOS-2 footprint covers a significant portion of central Myanmar (red area in Fig. 1), spanning from ~94° to 99° E longitude and 21° to 25° N latitude.

The macroseismic intensity values in the nearby urban centers reached modified Mercalli intensity (MMI) values of X. The directivity effects were clearly observed, including larger recorded peaks in the forward direction as well as a skyscraper collapsing in Bangkok, Thailand. This collapse may also be attributed to the soft soil conditions and potential basin effects (Qodri, 2018).

Given the scale of the event and the diversity of its impacts, a comprehensive assessment combining seismological data, macroseismic observations, secondary hazard mapping, and satellite-based damage detection is critical. This multidisciplinary study aims to document and analyze the ground-motion characteristics, evaluate the extent and nature of infrastructure damage, and investigate the geospatial patterns of secondary hazards, particularly liquefaction, using remote sensing techniques. The article presents ground-motion data and key insights from strong-motion records and macroseismic intensity. It also investigates secondary hazards, particularly liquefaction susceptibility and its spatial patterns, using geospatial indicators. Next, remote sensing analysis is conducted to map damage to roads and buildings using ALOS-2 SAR data. The study concludes by summarizing the main findings and their relevance for improving earthquake response and hazard mitigation strategies in the region.

Observations on Recorded Strong Ground Motions and Macroseismic Intensity Values

The mainshock was recorded at six strong ground motion stations within a 370 km rupture distance (R_{rup}) with rapidly varying peak ground-motion parameters (Fig. 2). Selected stations that recorded the 28 March 2025 **M** 7.7 Myanmar earthquake, including observed (Fig. 2a) peak ground acceleration (PGA), (Fig. 2b) peak ground velocity (PGV), (Fig. 2c) pseudospectral acceleration (PSA) (T = 0.2 s), and (Fig. 2d) PSA (T = 1.0 s). (The surface projection of the fault is also presented).

From the spatial distribution of the recorded data, it is observed that PGA, PGV, and PSA with 5% damping ratio values are lower north of the epicenter and much larger in the south. This observation is attributed to the fault directivity effects on the causative fault, which is the right-lateral strike-slip Sagaing fault segment. Despite the lack of data in the near field, it is observed that the maximum horizontal PGA reaches 0.57g at the closest station to the rupture with a corresponding short-period PSA value of almost 1.0g.

In this study, we present detailed information on the recorded strong ground motions at the six nearest stations with reliable data and assess the recorded motions (Table 1). The information includes station coordinates, rupture distance (R_{rup}), epicentral distance (R_{epi}), elevation, PGA, PGV, Housner intensity (HI), significant duration (D_{5-95}) within 5% and 95% of Arias intensity (I_A), and cumulative absolute velocity (CAV). The raw data are obtained from the Incorporated Research Institutions for Seismology website (Incorporated Research Institutions for Seismology [IRIS], 2025), baseline corrected, and filtered with a fourth-order Butterworth filter between 0.1 and 30 Hz. There is no precise information on the site classes or V_{S30} values of the stations; only general information about V_{S30} is discussed later in the secondary hazard section; however, the elevations of the

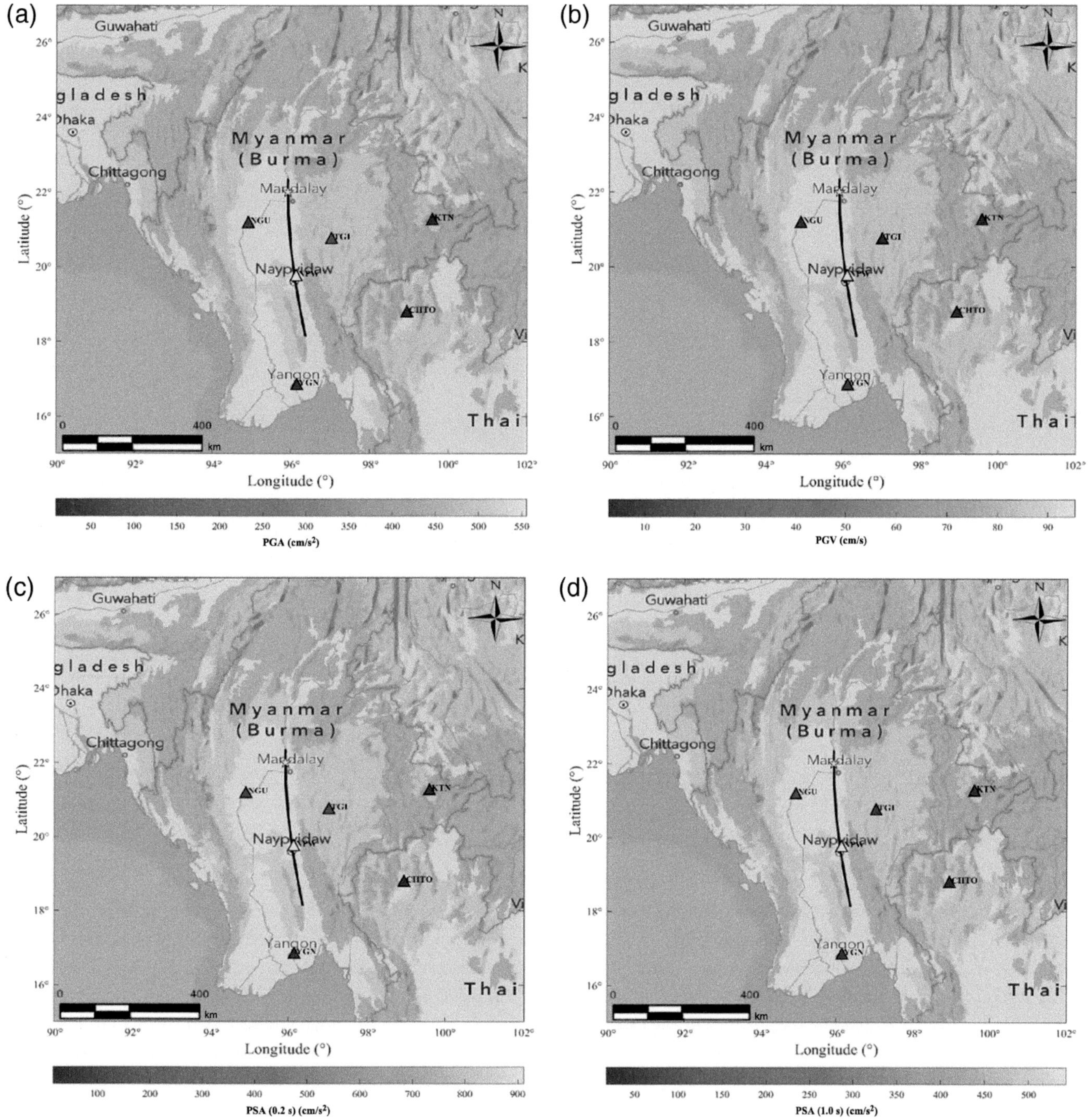

Figure 2. Selected stations that recorded the 28 March 2025 **M** 7.7 Myanmar earthquake, including observed (a) peak ground acceleration (PGA), (b) peak ground velocity (PGV), (c) pseudo-spectral acceleration (PSA) ($T = 0.2$ s), and (d) PSA ($T = 1.0$ s). (The surface projection of the fault is also presented). The color version of this figure is available only in the electronic edition.

stations on the tectonic map allow us to establish a framework. From Table 1, it is observed that the stations within close distances from the rupture located along the forward direction on low elevations experienced larger ground motions, whereas the farther stations and those on the mountain edge recorded much smaller motions.

We focus on the three closest stations to evaluate the acceleration time series and Fourier amplitude spectra (FAS) in Figures 3–5. On the same plots, we also compare the recorded response spectra (PSA) to the corresponding design spectra of Myanmar with 5% damping for a return period of 475 yr in the Myanmar National Building Code (MNBC) (2020). Among the recording stations, the NPW station is located at an R_{rup} of 2.75 km. The recorded PGA values in the horizontal directions are 511.5 cm/s^2 (east–west) and 603.45 cm/s^2 (north–south) with corresponding PGV values of 96.97 and 93.94 cm/s, respectively. The vertical component is almost

TABLE 1
Information on the Recorded Stations

Station	Latitude (°)	Longitude (°)	R_{rup} (km)	R_{epi} (km)	Elevation (m)	Channel	PGA (cm/s²)	PGV (cm/s)	HI (cm)	$D_{5–95}$ (s)	I_A (cm/s)	CAV (cm/s)
NPW	19.779° N	96.138° E	2.75	265.89	158	HNE	511.47	96.97	288.2	13.4	2.78	1625.12
						HNN	603.45	93.94	300.1	13.2	3.13	1621.48
						HNZ	1111.9	65.56	228.7	9.9	3.3	1351.84
TGI	20.768° N	97.034° E	Not available	192.29	1457.5	HHE	81.13	3.35	15.5	51.8	0.26	857.17
						HHN	73.95	2.63	14.6	49.0	0.2	754.29
						HHZ	41.75	3.01	12.6	42.7	0.05	340.57
NGU	21.206° N	94.917° E	113.95	147.15	70.4	HNE	45	6.2	31.1	65.7	0.096	588.60
						HNN	58.1	8.87	35.1	72.2	0.09	557.04
						HNZ	17.65	4.5	12.1	100.4	0.02	359.60
YGN	16.865° N	96.153° E	157.14	607.07	20	HNE	24.3	11.7	24.75	118.5	0.04	437.95
						HNN	14.7	7.8	18.08	118.1	0.04	499.16
						HNZ	19.5	3.7	15.24	120.8	0.01	256.51
CHTO	18.814° N	98.944° E	272.22	506.00	420	HN1	9.52	5.9	8.66	33.85	0.004	104.18
						HN2	8.21	3.97	9.26	34.97	0.004	114.77
						HNZ	12.9	4.44	10.83	33.41	0.005	118.65
KTN	21.286° N	99.590° E	370.59	416.70	832	HNE	10.63	2.54	12.18	87.31	0.015	267.78
						HNN	13.22	4.48	16.82	90.76	0.024	332.03
						HNZ	7.31	1.87	9.97	86.69	0.006	165.93

Channel, components of recorded ground motion: HH, high frequency and high sensitivity; HN, high gain, high-sampling rate; E, east–west direction; N, north–south direction; Z, vertical direction; 1, east–west direction; 2, north–south direction. CAV, cumulative absolute velocity; $D_{5–95}$, significant duration (time between 5% and 95% of Arias intensity); HI, Housner intensity; I_A, Arias intensity; PGA, peak ground acceleration; PGV, peak ground velocity; R_{epi}, epicentral distance; and R_{rup}, closest distance to rupture.

twice the horizontal component, attributed to the near-field source effects such as those observed in the 2023 Kahramanmaraş sequence (Altindal and Askan, 2024). At the NPW station, $D_{5–95}$ of the horizontal components is around 13 s at this station, HI is 288 cm and 300 cm in the east–west and north–south directions, respectively. Such high levels of HI usually correlate closely with structural damage (e.g., Askan *et al.*, 2022). At station NPW, there are strong near-field effects as observed in the form of velocity pulses, also consistent with the enhanced low-frequency content in the FAS.

The final observation is on the comparison of the acceleration response spectra (PSA) against the design spectra defined in the MNBC (2020) with 5% damping for a return period of 475 yr. As the station is located at a low elevation, we use the design spectra for sites C and D for the sake of comparison. It is noted that, according to the national building code MNBC (2020), the short-period site coefficient (*Fa*) is the same for site classes C and D, which explains the similarity of spectral values in the plateau. The difference between classes C and D appears in the long-period site coefficient (*Fv*), which controls velocity-dominated site effects.

It is observed that the recorded response spectra exceed the design spectra for both type C and D soils, up to periods of 0.3 s. This observation, coupled with the structural vulnerability, could have caused damage to the low-rise residential buildings. Within $T = 0.3–1.3$ s range, the recorded spectra are below the design spectra. For the longer periods, again, the recorded horizontal spectra exceed the corresponding design amplitudes.

Station TGI is located in the fault-normal direction, east of the Sagaing fault at an R_{epi} of 192.29 km. From the map, this station is at an elevation of 1457.5 m. As a result of the hard-rock conditions and increased distances, both PGA and PGV values are much lower than those recorded at the station NPW. The recorded PGA values are 81.13 cm/s^2 in the east–west and 73.95 cm/s^2 in the north–south directions. The vertical PGA is almost half of that of the horizontal ones. The PGV values are much lower, around 3 cm/s, for all components. $D_{5–95}$ for this station is around 50 s, whereas HI reaches 25 cm. The recorded response spectrum for this station is compared against the design spectra for rock and stiff soil conditions, sites B and C. It is observed that the recorded values are below both design spectra at all period ranges.

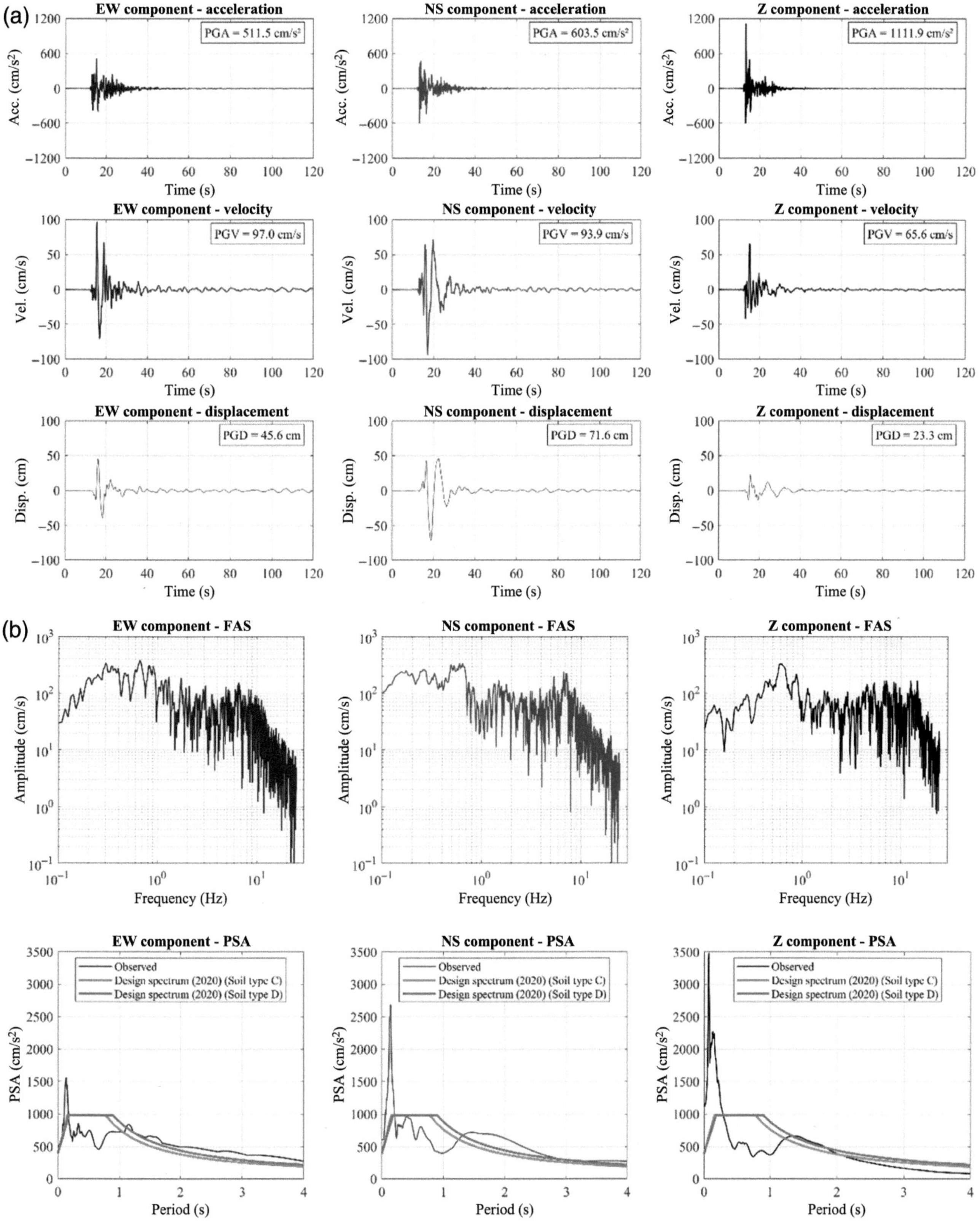

Finally, the station NGU is located at a lower elevation of 70.4 m and an R_{rup} distance of 113.95 km in the fault-normal direction, west of the Sagaing fault. The PGA values are recorded as 45.00 and 58.10 cm/s^2 for the east–west and north–south components, respectively. For the Z component,

Figure 3. Station NPW: (a) acceleration time series; (b) Fourier amplitude spectrum (FAS) and observed pseudoacceleration response spectra (PSA) compared with the code spectra. The color version of this figure is available only in the electronic edition.

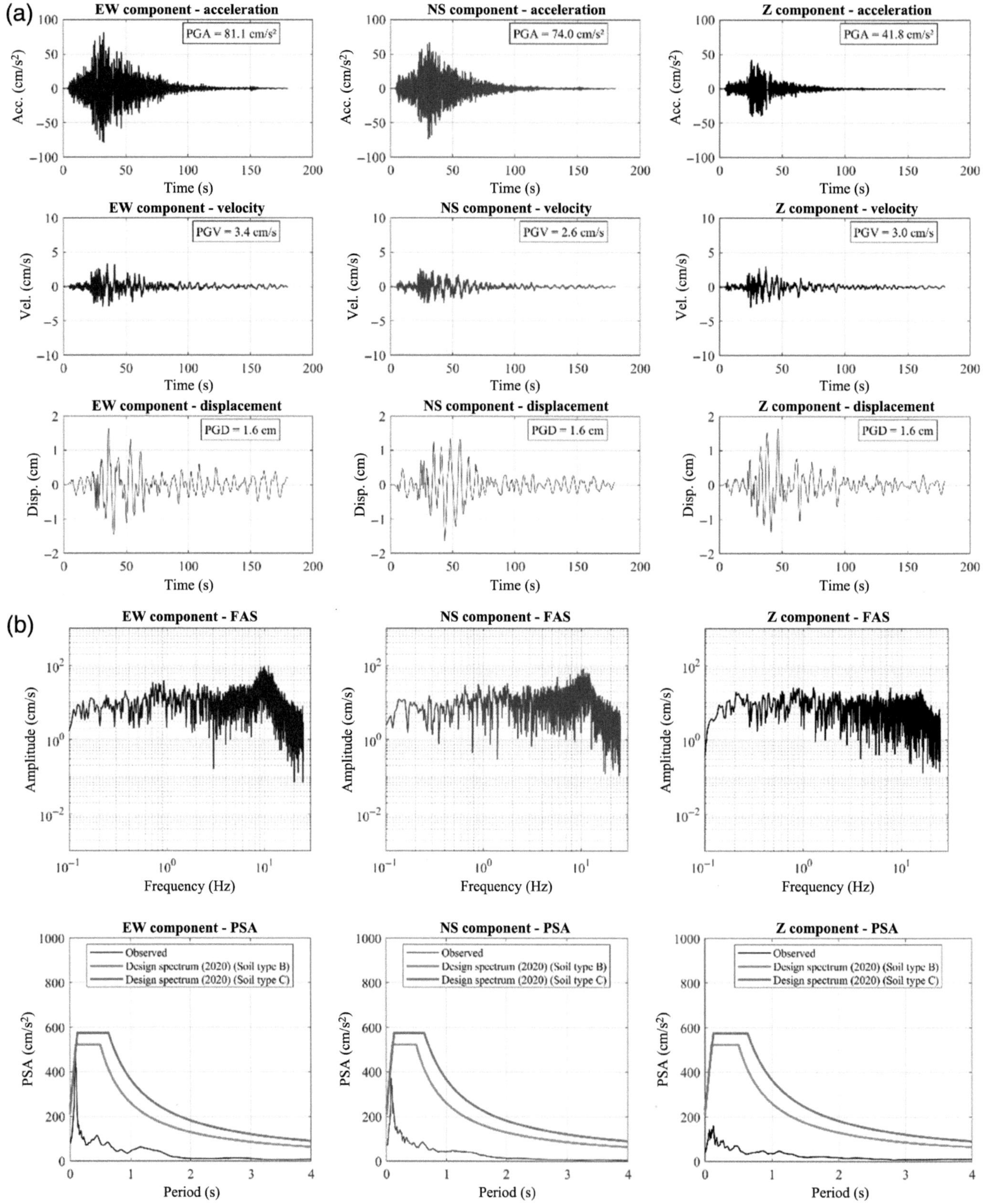

this value is much less, 17.65 cm/s^2. The PGV values are 6.20 and 8.87 cm/s for the corresponding horizontal directions. Although in the Z direction, it is almost half. The significant duration is longer at this station, reaching 65.70 and 72.20 s, mostly due to surface waves at this low elevation and longer

Figure 4. Station TGI (a) acceleration time series; (b) FAS and observed pseudoacceleration response spectra (PSA) compared with the code spectra. The color version of this figure is available only in the electronic edition.

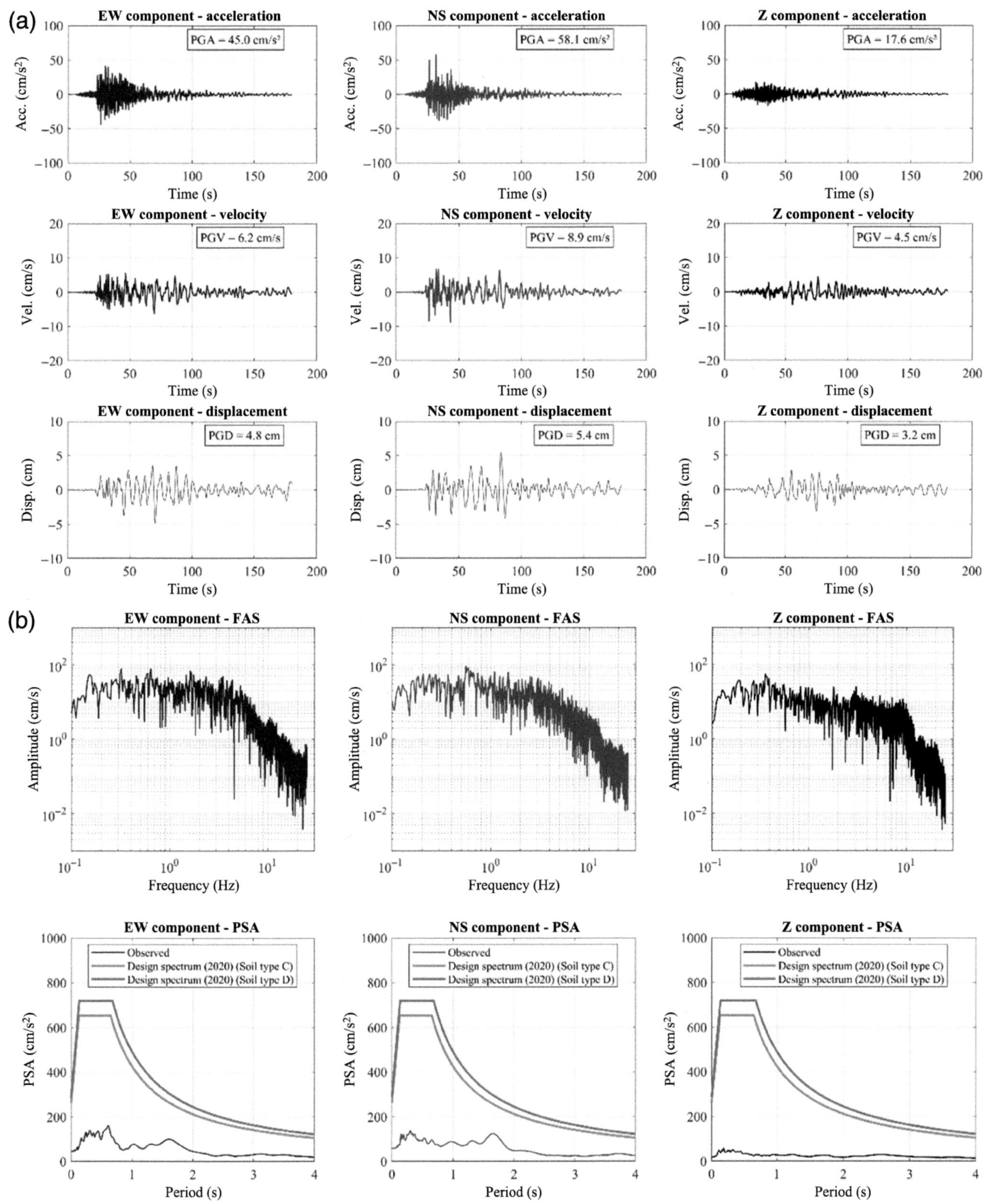

Figure 5. Station NGU: (a) acceleration time series; (b) FAS and observed pseudoacceleration response spectra (PSA) compared with the code spectra. The color version of this figure is available only in the electronic edition.

wavetrains, whereas it is even higher, 100.40 s, in the Z direction. In terms of HI, the value is around 35 cm for both horizontal directions, and in the Z direction, it reduces to 20 cm. When the response spectrum is compared with the design spectrum for site classes C and D, it is observed that the recorded motions are much lower than the design levels. This observation is consistent with the lack of severe damage in these areas.

For the three stations, CAV values in the three components are higher than 0.16 g.s (157 cm/s), which has been identified as a conservative threshold distinguishing damaging from nondamaging ground motions for well-designed and well-constructed buildings, as defined by the MMI scale (EPRI, Palo Alto and U.S. Department of Energy, 2006).

Figure 6a shows the spatial distribution of MMI as reported by the U.S. Geological Survey (USGS) (2025), as well as the MMI values at the selected stations in this study. It is observed that along the fault plane toward the south of the epicenter, the MMI values reach X+, consistent with the very heavy damage in that direction. The spatial distribution of the reported MMI values also confirms the strong directivity effects observed during the 28 March 2025 Myanmar event.

Next, in Figure 6b, we compare the MMI values reported in the DYFI system (USGS, 2025) against the MMI values at the stations obtained with conversions from corresponding recorded PGA and PGV values. For conversion, we use the relationships by Bilal and Askan (2014), which were developed based on PGA and PGV using data from masonry and reinforced-concrete structures in Türkiye affected by major earthquakes. As demonstrated in the studies by Erberik (2008a,b) and later applied and validated by Karimzadeh *et al.* (2018) for Erzincan, these models were successfully verified against observed damage in regions dominated by masonry and RC building typologies. To better represent the structural typologies, both PGA and PGV values were employed, capturing the behavior of rigid masonry and more flexible reinforced-concrete structures (Erberik, 2008a,b; Karimzadeh *et al.*, 2018). The computed MMI values from these conversions show good agreement with reported observations, with only minor deviations noted at the closest NPW station. Given that Myanmar exhibits similar construction typologies, we consider the adopted equations to be reliable within an expected range of uncertainties. Furthermore, comparison with reported data demonstrates consistent agreement, as illustrated in Figure 6b.

It is observed that the computed MMI values from PGA and PGV closely match the reported data, except for minor differences in MMI values at the closest NPW station.

Secondary Hazards

Secondary effects, such as tsunamis, landslides, liquefaction, and fire, account for ~25%–40% of total economic losses and fatalities associated with earthquakes worldwide (Gómez *et al.*, 2022). Liquefaction was a dominant secondary hazard in the studied earthquake, with substantial infrastructure damage consistently attributed to its effects in prior studies. In multiple sources, severe infrastructure damage is attributed to widespread liquefaction, especially in areas south of Mandalay, such as Inwa Town, near the Irrawaddy River (e.g., National Remote Sensing Centre, 2025), where there are local conditions, such as a shallow groundwater table, that contributed to soil instability (Wang *et al.*, 2025). Although field investigations confirmed the presence of liquefaction, this section evaluates the potential spatial extent of the phenomenon using U.S. Geological Survey (USGS, 2025) data and correlates it with various geospatial proxies. The estimated probability of liquefaction taken from USGS (2025) is based on the work of Allstadt *et al.* (2022), which is an adaptation of the model of Zhu *et al.* (2017). The model results carry substantial uncertainty because they depend on globally generalized predictor variables and ShakeMap-derived ground-motion intensities (Allstadt *et al.*, 2022), which may not fully capture local ground conditions or site-specific effects.

According to the data provided by the USGS (2025), the liquefaction probability due to this earthquake is estimated to be extensive in both severity and spatial extent. In this work, the analysis explores the relationships between geospatial proxies and the physical factors that influence liquefaction susceptibility in the Myanmar region (Fig. 7). For instance, V_{S30} serves as a proxy for soil density, as noted by Zhu *et al.* (2015), and it is a critical parameter in liquefaction analysis, as soil stiffness significantly influences liquefaction susceptibility. Higher V_{S30} values indicate stiffer soils, which are generally less prone to liquefaction compared to loose, softer soils (Yilmaz *et al.*, 2021; Cetin *et al.*, 2022). Figure 7a shows the V_{S30} distribution in the Myanmar region, based on USGS (2025) data.

As shown in Figure 7, liquefaction probability tends to be higher in areas classified as site classes E and D according to the National Earthquake Hazards Reduction Program (Building Seismic Safety Council [BSSC], 2020). The probability of liquefaction also appears elevated along the trace of the Sagaing fault. However, despite the widespread presence of softer soils in the central region, the estimated liquefaction probability is relatively low in that area, particularly on the western vertex of the Sagaing fault. In this area, the expected liquefaction probability is lower than 0.5%. This apparent anomaly may coincide with the spatial extent of geological unit TM, corresponding to the upper Pegu Group. This unit presents a north–south facies gradient that reflects a transition from nonmarine environments in the north to marine environments in the south. As a result, the deposits are characterized by thin-bedded fine to medium-grained sandstones interbedded with thick sequences of clays and siltstones, which exhibit various sedimentary structures (Ridd and Racey, 2015). The thick clay and silty layers within this geological unit are a key factor contributing to the low liquefaction susceptibility in this area. One notable observation is in Yangon City, which shows a high estimated liquefaction probability, aligning with previous findings that indicate greater vulnerability in the southern part of the city compared to the northern part (Htet *et al.*, 2018). These observations are consistent with the USGS

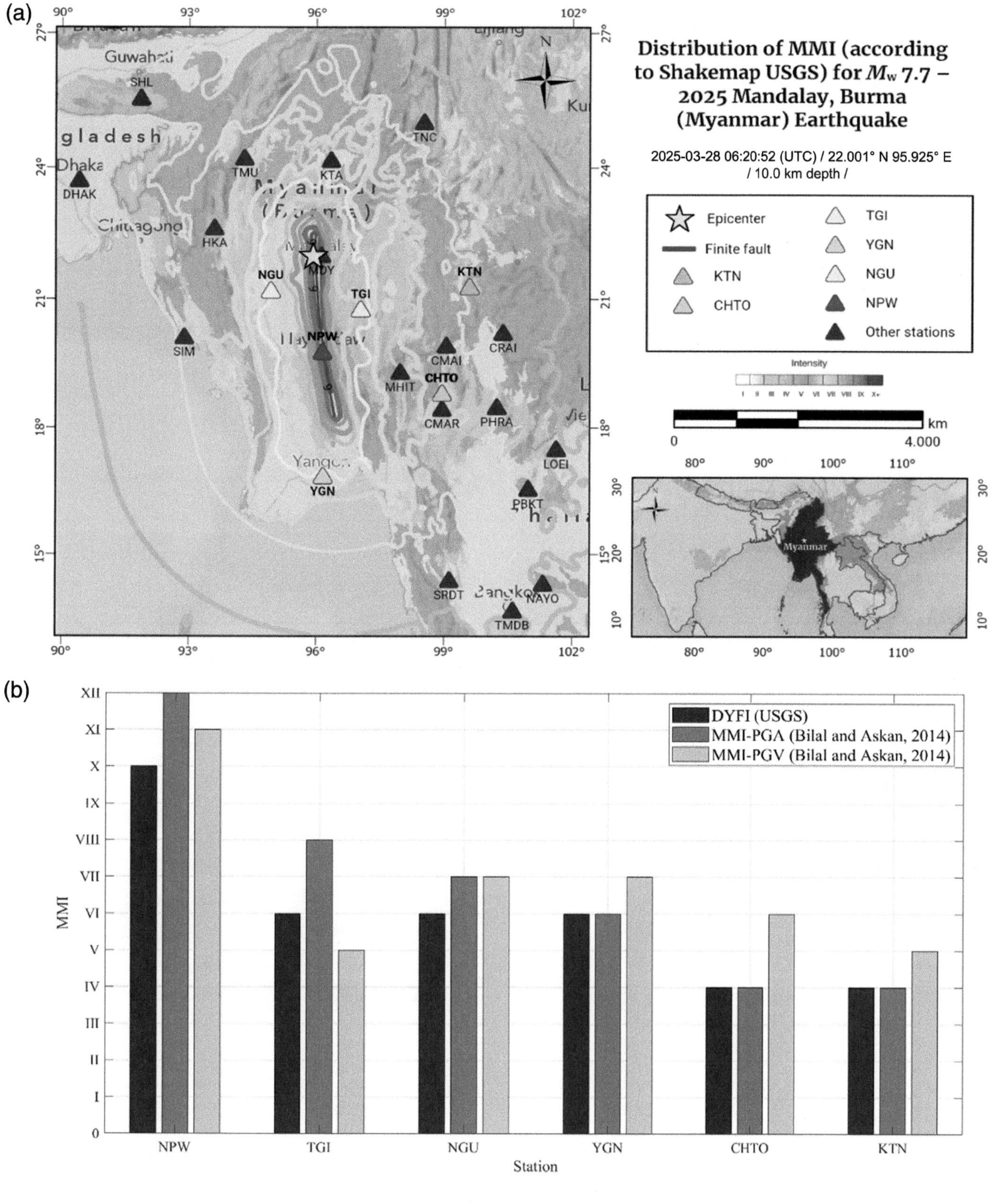

Figure 6. (a) Spatial distribution of modified Mercalli intensity (MMI) according to U.S. Geological Survey (USGS) (USGS, 2025) along with the causative fault and the recording stations on the location map of Myanmar; (b) MMI values according to the USGS—Did You Feel It? (DYFI) (USGS, 2025) and conversion equations of Bilal and Askan (2014). The color version of this figure is available only in the electronic edition.

liquefaction map (USGS, 2025) and documented field reports (e.g., National Remote Sensing Centre, 2025).

Another relevant proxy is PGA, which is directly related to earthquake-induced loading (Zhu *et al.*, 2015). However, the relationship between PGA and liquefaction occurrence (Fig. 7b) is not straightforward. Considering the recorded PGA values,

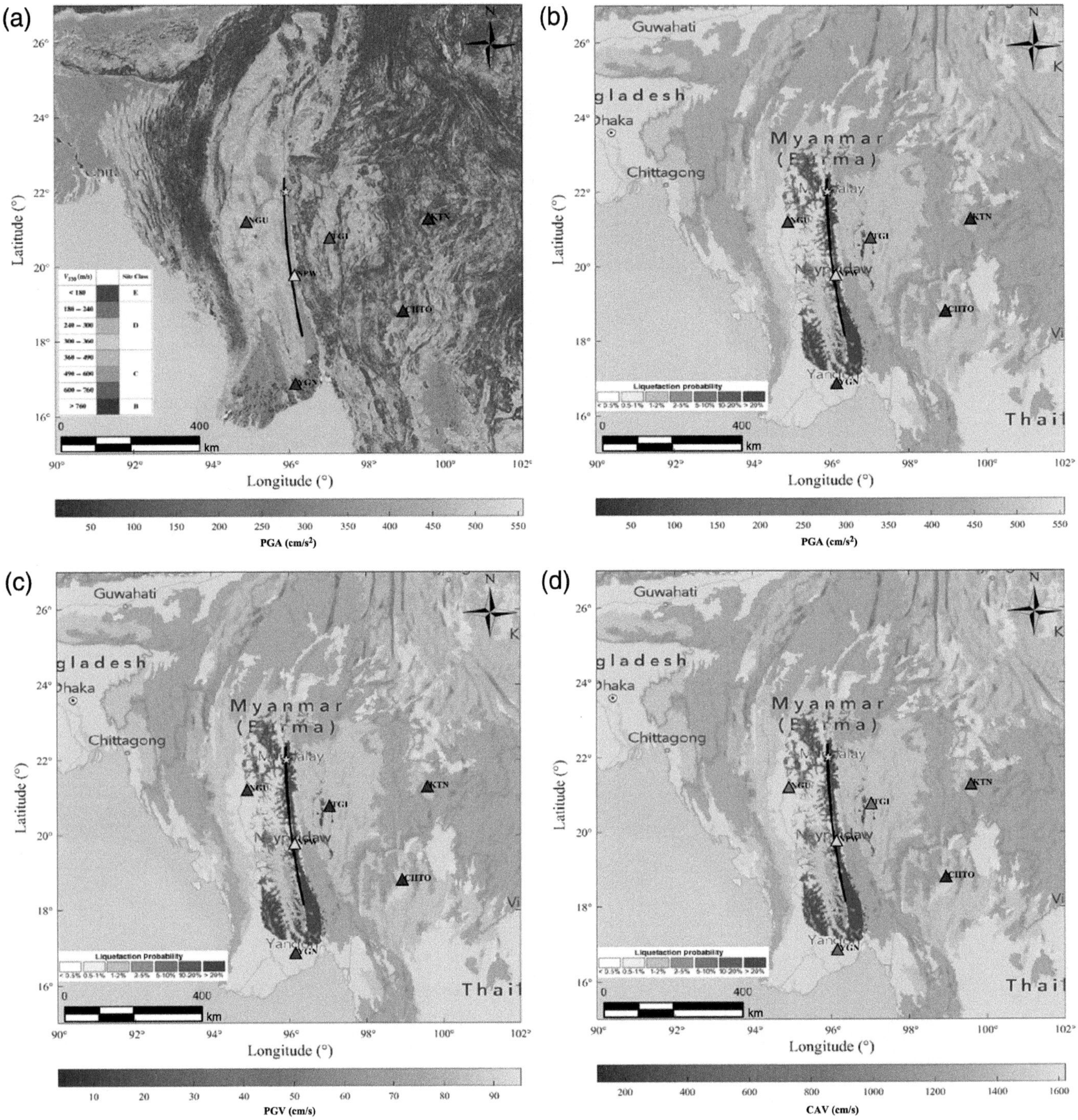

Figure 7. Geospatial proxies related to the probability of liquefaction in the Myanmar region: (a) V_{S30} map used as a proxy for soil stiffness; (b) estimated liquefaction probability map and the correlation with PGA; (c) estimated liquefaction probability map and the correlation with PGV; and (d) estimated liquefaction probability map and the correlation with cumulative absolute velocity (CAV). The color bars in each subplot represent the intensity of ground-motion parameters (PGA, PGV, and CAV) recorded at each station. The color version of this figure is available only in the electronic edition.

liquefaction probability is higher in areas located farther from the epicenter (close to Yangon City), where the observed PGA values are lower, as reported in Table 1. Near the NPW station, for example, the estimated liquefaction probability is high, which is consistent with literature suggesting that a minimum PGA of 0.10g can trigger liquefaction (Bozzoni *et al.*, 2021).

A similar analysis is conducted using recorded PGV values and liquefaction (Fig. 7c). The results are in agreement with those obtained with PGA and do not reveal a conclusive pattern. Furthermore, studies have shown that CAV, which is related to velocity, correlates well with liquefaction triggering at the site-specific scale (Kramer and Mitchell, 2006; Bray and Macedo, 2017). The recorded CAV values in Figure 7d show patterns that appear more consistent with the spatial distribution of the estimated liquefaction probability. This indicates that CAV may provide complementary insights into earthquake-induced loading in this context, although it should be interpreted cautiously, given that both CAV and the liquefaction probabilities are model-derived rather than direct field observations.

Finally, it is important to recognize the uncertainties in the USGS liquefaction model (USGS, 2025), particularly in the context of Myanmar. Fluvial deposits, variable groundwater conditions, and the absence of locally calibrated data strongly influence liquefaction occurrence. As a result, these limitations may lead to either underestimation or overestimation of the actual hazard.

Observation of Building and Road Damages Using SAR Remote Sensing

To assess the extent of damage in the affected area, three ALOS-2 SAR Single Look Complex (SLC) images in ScanSAR mode are used. Two preseismic and one postseismic images from descending orbits are acquired. The acquisition dates for the preseismic images are 16 January 2025 and 19 February 2025, whereas the acquisition date of the postseismic image is 30 March 2025. Although the temporal baselines of the images are not too short, their L-band (~24 cm) capabilities in tall vegetation areas, and large footprint coverage will be an ideal tool for a rapid and reliable Interferometric SAR (InSAR) analysis. SAR systems, with their distinct all-weather, day-and-night imaging capabilities, present a significant advantage for disaster monitoring, circumventing the limitations imposed by cloud cover or darkness that often impede optical remote sensing (Ghasemi *et al.*, 2021). Among SAR-based techniques, InSAR coherence analysis, which quantifies temporal surface changes through interferometric phase correlation measurements, has demonstrated significant potential for assessing earthquake-induced structural damage (Karimzadeh and Matsuoka, 2021). Coherence, which is the normalized complex correlation coefficient from two SAR images acquired at different times, is sensitive to physical changes on the ground surface (Ghasemi *et al.*, 2021). A significant reduction in coherence (decorrelation) directly indicates physical disturbances, such as ground deformation, structural damage, or vegetation changes, which are not completely observable in SAR intensity maps (Ghasemi *et al.*, 2021). Thus, the coherence is suitable enough for identifying earthquake-induced damages, ranging from building collapse to surface ruptures and road destruction (Ghasemi *et al.*, 2021).

In this section, we aim to provide a comprehensive and spatially explicit assessment of earthquake-induced damage to both built-up areas and essential linear infrastructure (i.e., roads) in the affected areas in Myanmar, after the 28 March 2025 earthquake. We employ a differential coherence analysis approach to precisely map and quantify damage patterns. Furthermore, we analyze backscattering characteristics (i.e., intensity) and their correlation to complement the coherence-based damage detection. The derived damage maps and quantitative assessments provide key insights to support emergency response, resource allocation, and post-disaster recovery using remote sensing.

For change detection and interferometric analysis, multiple SAR images must be co-registered to ensure identical spatial dimensions and pixel correspondence. To achieve precise pixel-to-pixel matching, one image is designated as the master image while subsequent acquisitions serve as slave images in the co-registration process. The ALOS-2 PALSAR-2 imaging geometry follows the standard side-looking SAR configuration, where the range coordinate represents the slant range distance from the sensor to the target, and the azimuth coordinate corresponds to the satellite's flight path direction. These radar coordinates differ fundamentally from conventional geographic coordinate systems, necessitating geometric transformation for cartographic applications (Tamkuan and Nagai, 2017; Ghasemi *et al.*, 2021). ALOS-2 PALSAR-2 images exhibit significant geometric distortions in the range direction, primarily attributed to topographic relief displacement and the inherent slant-range imaging geometry. These distortions manifest as foreshortening in areas facing the sensor, layover in steep terrain slopes toward the radar, and shadowing in areas blocked from radar illumination (Shimada *et al.*, 2014; Karimzadeh and Matsuoka, 2021).

Consequently, radiometric calibration and coordinate system transformation from radar geometry to geographic coordinates are essential preprocessing steps. The geometric rectification process employs a backward geocoding approach utilizing a digital elevation model (DEM) to establish the relationship between radar coordinates and ground positions. The transformation algorithm incorporates several key parameters, including Doppler centroid frequencies, radar pulse transmission timing, and precise orbital vectors describing sensor position and velocity, and the 3D coordinates of ground scatterers (Toutin, 2004). The range-Doppler terrain correction method is commonly applied for ALOS-2 PALSAR-2 data, where the DEM is used to simulate the SAR imaging geometry and correct for topographic distortions (Santoro *et al.*, 2015; Alaska Satellite Facility, 2024). SAR coherence approach evaluates the statistical correlation of radar backscatter characteristics at identical geographical locations across different temporal epochs, providing valuable insights into surface modification patterns (Rosen *et al.*, 2000).

The coherence parameter functions as a quantitative measure of surface temporal stability, where unity values indicate minimal changes between acquisitions, whereas diminished values reflect substantial surface modifications during the observation period (Dieter and Bamler, 1994; Touzi *et al.*,

1999). This characteristic renders coherence analysis particularly effective for rapid damage assessment and continuous change monitoring applications in seismic contexts (Hoffmann, 2007). The interferometric coherence (γ) between two temporally separated SAR acquisitions can be mathematically defined according to the following equation (Lee *et al.*, 1994; Seymour and Cumming, 1994):

$$\gamma = \frac{E\langle ab^* \rangle}{\sqrt{E\langle aa^* \rangle E\langle bb^* \rangle}}. \tag{1}$$

According to Karimzadeh and Matsuoka (2021), a and b represent the relatively complex values of the master and slave images, respectively, used in interferometric analysis. The asterisk (*) denotes the complex conjugates of the images. E represents the expectation operator. To isolate the pure phase changes caused by seismic activity, the authors remove the topographic phase using a 30-m DEM from the Shuttle Radar Topography Mission, whereas atmospheric noise is mitigated using established atmospheric models (Tamkuan and Nagai, 2017; Liu *et al.*, 2024).

Vegetated areas typically exhibit low coherence due to leaf growth and the random motion of tree foliage influenced by environmental factors such as wind. In contrast, urban environments maintain stable backscatter properties, as short-term effects like wind-induced movement are negligible. Consequently, higher coherence values are expected in urban regions (Karimzadeh and Matsuoka, 2021). In this study, we conducted a multitemporal coherence analysis using both ascending and descending ALOS-2 PALSAR-2 datasets to visualize the affected regions. The differential coherence method quantifies temporal stability by comparing preseismic and coseismic coherence maps for each acquisition geometry, as defined in the following equation:

$$\gamma_{\text{diff}} = \gamma_{\text{pre}} - \gamma_{\text{post}}. \tag{2}$$

Positive γ_{diff} values indicate coherence degradation likely caused by seismic-induced changes, whereas negative values may suggest increased coherence due to postevent stabilization or vegetation growth. A high coherence value indicates minimal surface change, whereas a low value reflects significant alterations (Karimzadeh *et al.*, 2022).

The study region (as shown in Fig. 1) is selected as the primary focus due to its documented seismic activity and the considerable impact sustained during the 28 March 2025 Myanmar earthquake. The study area's heterogeneous landscape, characterized by a mix of densely populated urban centers, sprawling rural areas, and varied topography, provides an ideal setting for a comprehensive evaluation of earthquake-induced damage across diverse land cover and infrastructure types.

Complementary datasets were employed to refine the analysis and constrain the investigation into anthropogenic structures. Global Urban Footprint generated from TerrraSAR-X data and SAR speckle divergence analysis was applied for urban masking. This mask allowed for the systematic exclusion of vegetated and purely rural regions, where coherence loss might be attributable to environmental factors rather than structural damage. In addition, road network data from OpenStreetMap (OSM) was integrated as vector layers. These layers served dual purposes: as essential spatial references for accurately locating and analyzing damage, and as specific indicators for identifying affected linear transportation infrastructure. The integration of OSM data significantly improved the precision of interpreting differential coherence losses along transportation corridors, facilitating a more targeted identification of damaged road segments.

All datasets were geometrically co-registered to the WGS 84/UTM zone 46 N coordinate system (covering Myanmar) and resampled to a 10-m spatial resolution for consistent coherence comparison and map visualization. ALOS-2 PALSAR-2 SLC images backscattering coefficients and interferometric coherence values revealed significant insights into the earthquake-induced damage patterns for both road networks and building structures within the study area.

Figure 8a,b presents the histograms and scatter plots illustrating the distribution and correlation of backscattering coefficients for the road segments and buildings, respectively. For road segments (Fig. 9a), the average preseismic backscattering coefficient is 72.46 (standard deviation = 3.65), which increased to 73.59 postseismically. The scatter plot correlating preseismic and coseismic backscattering for roads exhibited a coefficient of determination (R^2) of 0.60. This relatively high R^2 indicates a strong linear relationship between backscattering values before and after the event, suggesting that while changes occurred, a general trend in backscattering properties is maintained across road segments. Similarly, for buildings (Fig. 8b), the average preseismic backscattering is 69.28, increasing to 70.85 (standard deviation = 3.96) postseismically. The corresponding R^2 for building backscattering is 0.65, denoting a moderate-to-strong correlation. These observed increases in average backscattering, despite robust correlations, are not exclusively physical changes in the ground surface and infrastructure elements. Figure 8c provides the spatial representation of these backscattering coefficients, illustrating the intensity of radar returns (brighter pixels for higher backscattering) and areas of decorrelation.

Figure 9a,b illustrates the histograms and scatter plots of coherence values for the road segments and buildings, respectively. For road networks (Fig. 9a), the average preseismic coherence is 0.48 (standard deviation = 0.16), showing a slight decrease to 0.38 coseismically. The correlation between preseismic and coseismic coherence for roads yielded an R^2 of 0.29. Conversely, for building structures (Fig. 9b), the average preseismic coherence is 0.60, which slightly decreased to 0.49 coseismically (standard deviation = 0.17). Critically, the

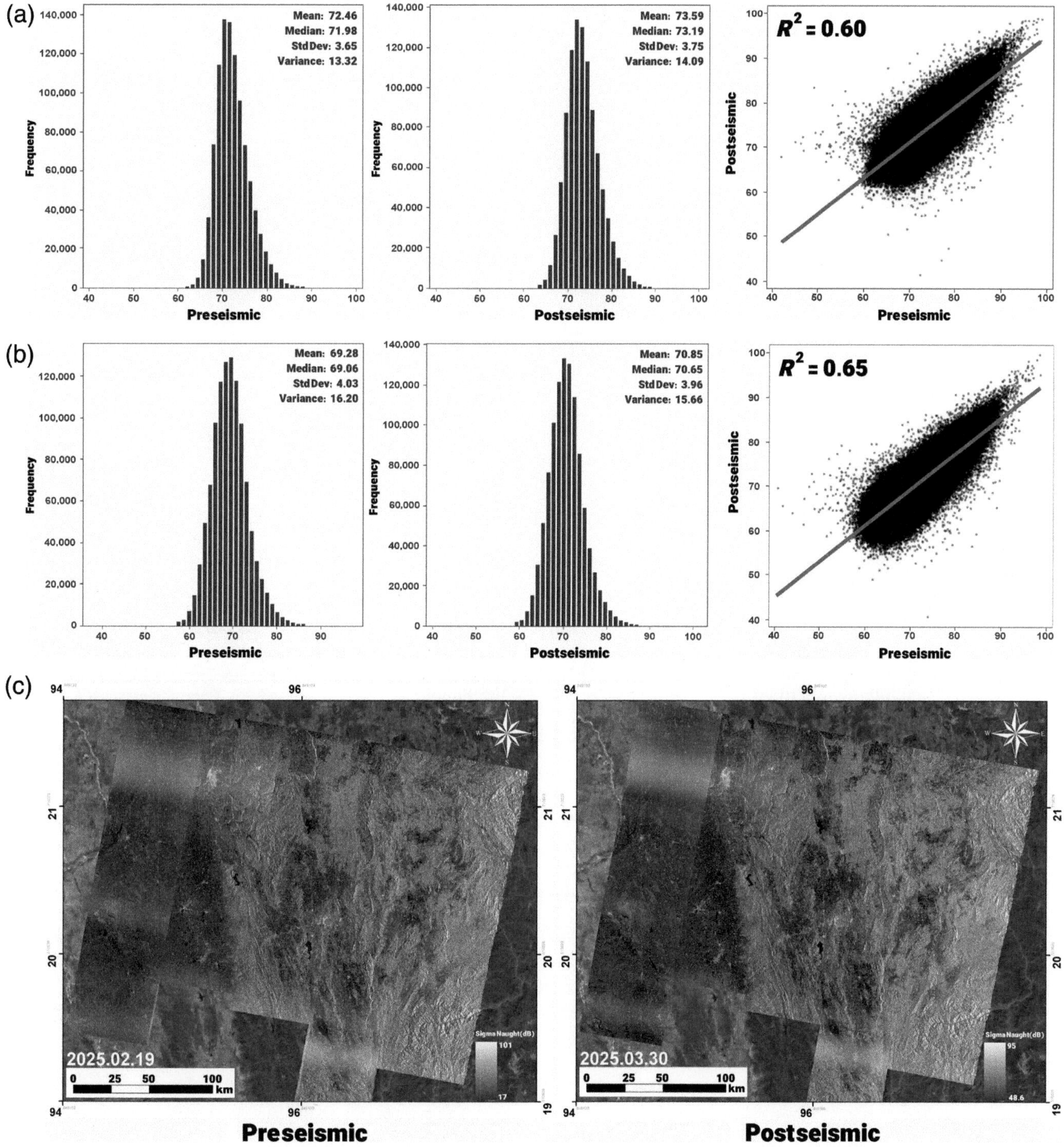

Figure 8. (a) Histogram of backscattering and the coefficient of determination (R^2) for the road network in the study area. (b) Histogram of backscattering and R^2 for the buildings in the study area. (c) Synthetic Aperture Radar (SAR) intensity images. The color version of this figure is available only in the electronic edition.

corresponding R^2 for building coherence is slightly higher at 0.39. These relatively low R^2 values for road segments and buildings are a direct indicator of substantial decorrelation between the preseismic and coseismic acquisitions, a hallmark of severe physical disturbance and damage to structures. They also suggest that the preseismic coherence values are poor predictors of coseismic coherence, primarily due to the widespread decorrelation induced by seismic activity. Finally, Figure 9c provides the spatial representation of coherence values, illustrating the intensity of radar returns (brighter pixels for higher backscattering) and areas of decorrelation.

Spatial Visualization of Building and Road Damage

The spatially explicit possible damage maps for roads (Fig. 10a) and buildings (Fig. 10b), generated through the differential

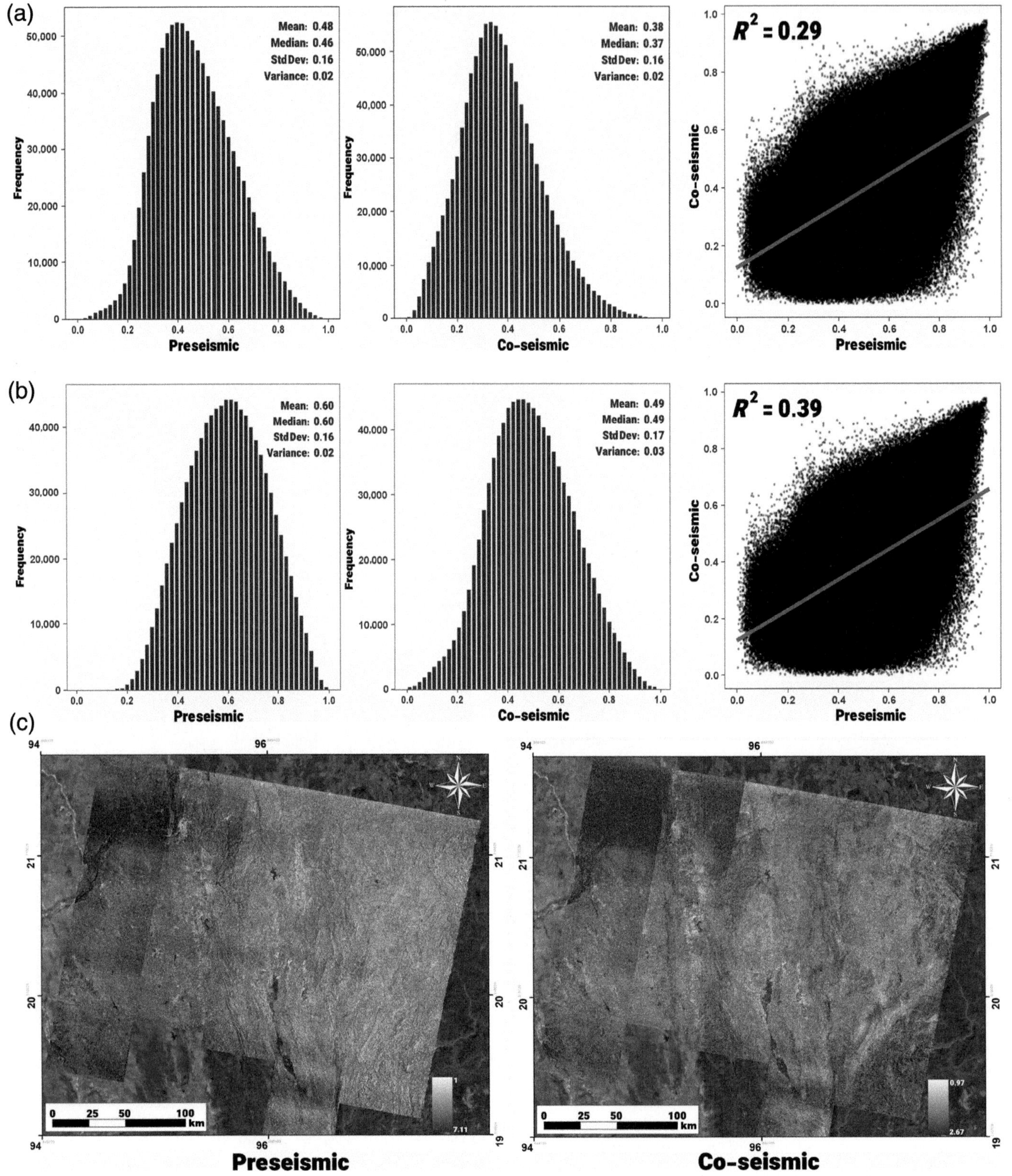

coherence analysis, further elucidate the extent and spatial distribution of earthquake-induced damage. Both maps utilize a consistent color scale, where green represents areas with no observable change, yellow signifies moderate damage, and red corresponds to heavy damage. By visually comparing Figure 10a (possible road damage) and Figure 10b (possible

Figure 9. (a) Histogram of coherence and the coefficient of determination (R^2) for the road network in the study area. (b) Histogram of coherence and R^2 for the buildings in the study area. (c) Preseismic coherence and coseismic coherence. The color version of this figure is available only in the electronic edition.

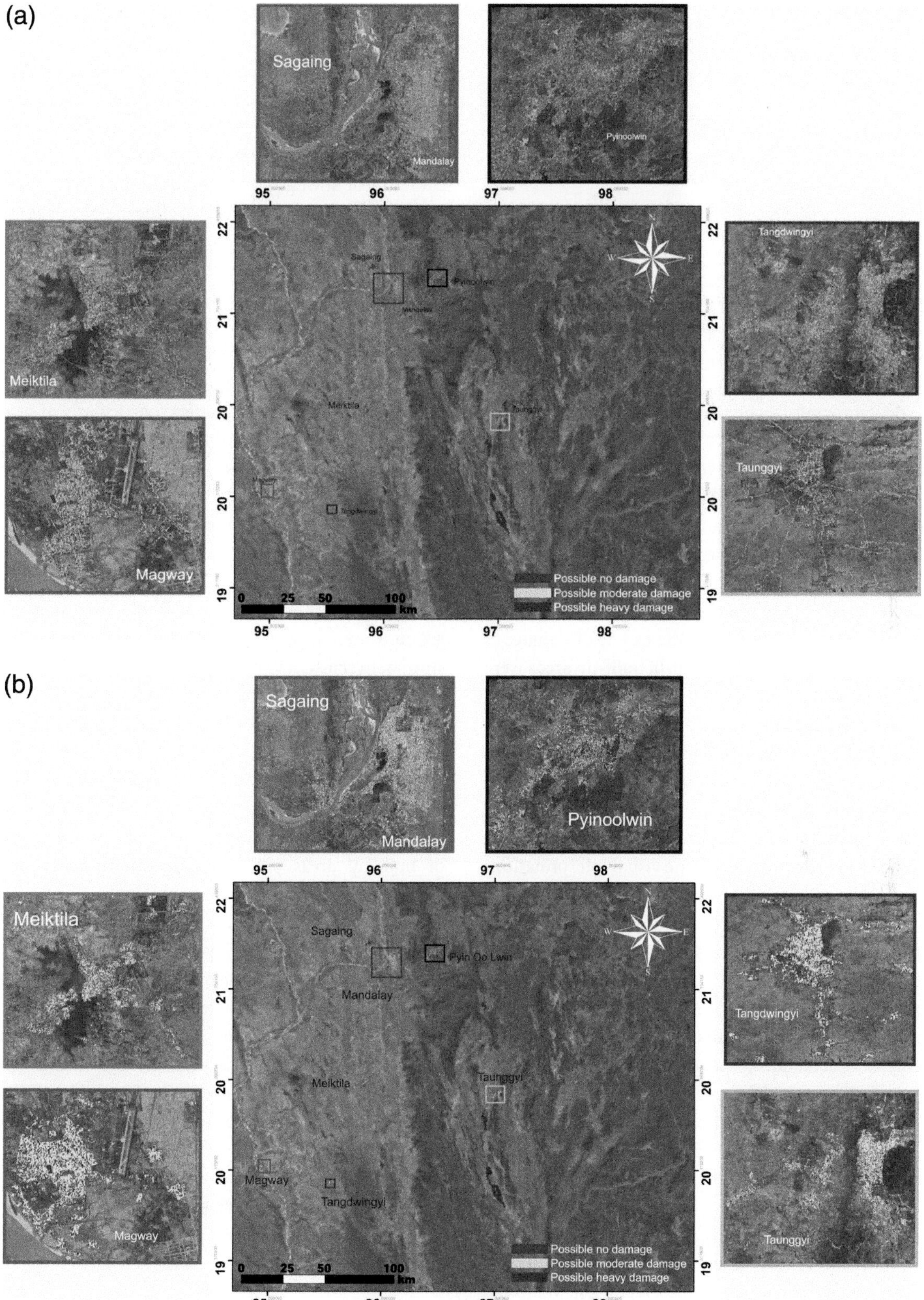

building damage), a pronounced spatial overlap of high-damage areas is observed. This overlap is particularly striking within the urban centers and densely populated regions, notably exemplified in the magnified insets. In these areas, both road networks and building structures exhibit extensive yellow

Figure 10. (a) Possible damage/change the map of the roads in the study area. (b) Possible damage/change the map of the buildings in the study area. The color version of this figure is available only in the electronic edition.

TABLE 2
Quantitative Summary of Earthquake-Induced Possible Damage to Roads and Buildings

Possible Damage	Road (km)	Building (km^2)
No damage	74,918	503.41
Moderate damage	35,019	205.12
Heavy damage	3,960	100.36

to red pixel classifications, indicating widespread and severe infrastructure damage. The linear patterns of damage visible in Figure 10a along road segments, coupled with the concentrated clusters of damaged buildings in Figure 10b, collectively confirm the devastating impact of the earthquake on the interconnected urban fabric.

Table 2 provides a comprehensive quantitative summary of the classified damage levels for both road networks and building structures within the study area. The analysis revealed that a substantial 3,960 km of roads sustained heavy damage, with an additional 35,019 km experiencing possible moderate damage. Conversely, 74,918 km of roads were categorized as having no observable damage. For buildings, the extent of damage is equally significant. A total of 100.36 km^2 of built-up areas were classified as possibly heavily damaged, and 205.12 km^2 as possibly moderately damaged. In contrast, 503.41 km^2 of buildings exhibited no discernible damage. The spatial distribution of the damaged areas from analyses of SAR data is observed to be consistent with the distribution of ground motions. These quantitative metrics, derived from the differential coherence analysis, corroborate the visual interpretations from the potential damage maps, providing approximate numerical values for the extent of earthquake-induced infrastructure devastation. The cumulative extent of severe and moderate damage highlights the critical need for large-scale recovery and reconstruction efforts. Although direct validation of the damage estimates was not feasible due to the absence of detailed ground observations, the coherence-based method employed here has been widely applied and validated in previous earthquakes (Karimzadeh and Mastuoka, 2017; Adriano *et al.*, 2018; Hasanlou *et al.*, 2021; Karimzadeh *et al.*, 2022), demonstrating its robustness for post-disaster damage mapping.

Although the SAR-based coherence analysis provides valuable insights into the spatial distribution of damage, several sources of uncertainty should be considered. First, temporal baselines between SAR acquisitions can pose decorrelation unrelated to structural damage, particularly when acquisition intervals are long. Second, vegetation dynamics, especially in periurban zones, may reduce coherence and complicate damage discrimination. Third, radar imaging geometry effects (layover, shadowing, and foreshortening) may obscure heavily affected structures in dense urban or mountainous regions. Finally, the lack of extensive field data limited our ability to directly validate the coherence-derived results.

Despite these limitations, the methodology has been extensively tested in prior seismic events and has consistently demonstrated reliable performance in identifying damaged areas. In this context, the observed agreement between the spatial distribution of strong ground motions and our coherence-based damage estimates provides confidence that the results presented in Table 2 represent a robust first-order approximation of actual damage patterns.

Conclusions

Analysis of the recorded seismic data from the 28 March 2025 Myanmar earthquake revealed strong directivity effects and high ground-motion parameters, particularly at near-field stations located in the forward rupture direction and on softer soil conditions. The recorded spectra at the near-field station exceeded the Myanmar National Building Code values for short periods, which may explain the widespread damage to low-rise buildings.

Liquefaction was one of the most prominent secondary hazards, especially in areas with soft soil conditions and shallow groundwater, such as near the Irrawaddy River. The relationship between CAV and estimated liquefaction probability appeared to be more consistent than PGA or PGV alone, indicating its potential as a better proxy for rapid postevent liquefaction assessment.

Through advanced SAR-based coherence analysis, we were able to detect and map extensive infrastructure damage. The results indicated that over 39,000 km of roads and 306 km^2 of built-up areas suffered moderate-to-heavy damage. The coherence-based damage mapping method proved particularly useful for highlighting changes in urban areas, with strong agreement between building and road damage zones, also consistent with the spatial distribution of ground motions.

Overall, this study underscores the importance of integrating strong-motion data, secondary hazard modeling, and remote sensing in postearthquake damage assessments. The insights gained can inform future emergency response planning and seismic risk mitigation strategies for Myanmar and other tectonically active regions.

Data and Resources

All data used in this article came from published sources listed in the references.

Declaration of Competing Interests

The authors acknowledge that there are no conflicts of interest recorded.

Acknowledgments

This work has been partly funded by the STAND4HERITAGE project that has received funding from the European Research Council (ERC) under the European Union's Horizon 2020 research and innovation program (Grant Agreement Number 833123), as an Advanced Grant. This work was partly financed by FCT/MCTES through national funds (PIDDAC) under the R&D Unit Institute for Sustainability and Innovation in Structural Engineering (ISISE), under reference UID/04029/Institute for Sustainability and Innovation in Structural Engineering (ISISE), and under the Associate Laboratory Advanced Production and Intelligent Systems ARISE under reference LA/P/0112/2020. This work is financed by national funds through FCT–Foundation for Science and Technology, under Grant Agreement 2022.12016.BD is attributed to the first author. The Advanced Land Observation Satellite (ALOS)-2 PALSAR-2 images are provided by the JAXA (Japan Aerospace Exploration Agency) working group. Sara Rengifo kindly provided technical assistance in preparing the base maps for three figures and contributed valuable geological insights. The authors also extend their sincere thanks to the two anonymous reviewers for their insightful comments and suggestions, which greatly improved the quality of this article.

References

Adriano, B., S. Koshimura, S. Karimzadeh, M. Matsuoka, and M. Koch (2018). Damage mapping after the 2017 Puebla earthquake in Mexico using high-resolution Alos2 Palsar2 data, *IGARSS 2018-2018 IEEE International Geoscience and Remote Sensing Symposium*, IEEE, 870–873, doi: 10.1109/IGARSS.2018.8517933.

Alaska Satellite Facility (2024). ALOS PALSAR—radiometric terrain correction, available at https://asf.alaska.edu/datasets/daac/alos-palsar-radiometric-terrain-correction/ (last accessed June 2025).

Allstadt, K. E., E. M. Thompson, R. W. Jibson, D. J. Wald, M. Hearne, E. J. Hunter, J. Fee, H. Schovanec, D. Slosky, and K. L. Haynie (2022). The US Geological Survey ground failure product: Near-real-time estimates of earthquake-triggered landslides and liquefaction, *Earthq. Spectra* **38,** no. 1, 5–36, doi: 10.1177/87552930211032685.

Altindal, A., and A. Askan (2024). Traditional seismic hazard analyses underestimate hazard levels when compared to observations from the 2023 Kahramanmaras earthquakes, *Commun. Earth Environ.* **5,** no. 1, 14, doi: 10.1038/s43247-023-01148-y.

Askan, A., Z. Gülerce, Z. Roumelioti, D. Sotiriadis, N. S. Melis, A. Altindal, B. Akbaş, E. Sopaci, S. Karimzadeh, I. Kalogeras, *et al.* (2022). The Samos Island (Aegean Sea) M 7.0 earthquake: Analysis and engineering implications of strong motion data, *Bull. Earthq. Eng.* **20,** no. 14, 7737–7762, doi: 10.1007/s10518-021-01251-5.

Bilal, M., and A. Askan (2014). Relationships between felt intensity and recorded ground-motion parameters for Turkey, *Bull. Seismol. Soc. Am.* **104,** no. 1, 484–496, doi: 10.1785/0120130093.

Bozzoni, F., R. Bonì, D. Conca, C. G. Lai, E. Zuccolo, and C. Meisina (2021). Megazonation of earthquake-induced soil liquefaction hazard in continental Europe, *Bull. Earthq. Eng.* **19,** no. 10, 4059–4082, doi: 10.1007/s10518-020-01008-6.

Bray, J. D., and J. Macedo (2017). 6th Ishihara lecture: Simplified procedure for estimating liquefaction-induced building settlement, *Soil Dynam. Earthq. Eng.* **102,** 215–231, doi: 10.1016/J.SOILDYN.2017.08.026.

Building Seismic Safety Council (BSSC) (2020). NEHRP (National Earthquake Hazards Reduction Program) recommended seismic provisions for new buildings and other structures, *FEMA P-2082-1*, Washington, D.C.

Cetin, K. O., S. Altun, A. Askan, M. Akgün, A. Sezer, C. Kıncal, Ö. C. Özdağ, Y. İpek, B. Unutmaz, Z. Gülerce, *et al.* (2022). The site effects in Izmir Bay of October 30 2020, M 7.0 Samos Earthquake, *Soil Dynam. Earthq. Eng.* **152,** 107,051, doi: 10.1016/j.soildyn.2021.107051.

Dieter, J., and R. Bamler (1994). Phase statistics of interferograms with applications to synthetic aperture radar, *Appl. Opt.* **33,** no. 20, 4361–4368.

EPRI, Palo Alto and U.S Department of Energy (2006). *Program on Technology Innovation: Use of Minimum CAV in Determining Effects of Small Magnitude Earthquakes on Seismic Hazard Analyses*, available at https://www.nrc.gov/docs/ML0603/ML060320738.pdf (last accessed June 2025).

Erberik, M. A. (2008a). Fragility-based assessment of typical mid-rise and low-rise RC buildings in Turkey, *Eng. Struct.* **30,** no. 5, 1360–1374, doi: 10.1016/j.engstruct.2007.07.016.

Erberik, M. A. (2008b). Generation of fragility curves for Turkish masonry buildings considering in-plane failure modes, *Earthq. Eng. Struct. Dynam.* **37,** no. 3, 387–405, doi: 10.1002/eqe.760.

Ghasemi, M., S. Karimzadeh, and B. Feizizadeh (2021). Urban classification using preserved information of high dimensional textural features of Sentinel-1 images in Tabriz, Iran, *Earth Sci. Inform.* **14,** no. 4, 1745–1762, doi: 10.1007/s12145-021-00617-2.

Gögen, B., S. Karimzadeh, and P. B. Lourenço (2024). Probabilistic seismic hazard analysis for Bagan (Myanmar), *Acta Geophys.* **72,** no. 4, 2193–2221, doi: 10.1007/s11600-023-01263-6.

Gómez, J. C., M. Pittore, N. Brinckmann, J. Lizarazo-Marriaga, S. Medina, N. Tarque, and F. Cotton (2022). Scenario-based multi-risk assessment from existing single-hazard vulnerability models. An application to consecutive earthquakes and tsunamis in Lima, Peru, *Nat. Hazards Earth Syst. Sci.* **23,** 2203–2228.

Hasanlou, M., R. Shah-Hosseini, S. T. Seydi, S. Karimzadeh, and M. Matsuoka (2021). Earthquake damage region detection by multitemporal coherence map analysis of radar and multispectral imagery, *Remote Sens.* **13,** no. 6, 1195, doi: 10.3390/rs13061195.

Hoffmann, J. (2007). Mapping damage during the Bam (Iran) earthquake using interferometric coherence, *Int. J. Remote Sens.* **28,** no. 6, 1199–1216, doi: 10.1080/01431160600928567.

Htet, W. P., M. Thant, and D. Arini (2018). Probability of liquefaction hazard map for Yangon City, Myanmar, doi: 10.1063/1.5047312.

Incorporated Research Institutions for Seismology (IRIS) (2025). IRIS Wilber-3: Find stations, available at https://ds.iris.edu/wilber3/find_stations/11952284 (last accessed June 2025).

Karimzadeh, S., and M. Mastuoka (2017). Building damage assessment using multisensor dual-polarized synthetic aperture radar data for the 2016 M 6.2 Amatrice earthquake, Italy, *Remote Sens.* **9,** no. 4, 330, doi: 10.3390/rs9040330.

Karimzadeh, S., and M. Matsuoka (2021). A preliminary damage assessment using dual path synthetic aperture radar analysis for the M 6.4 Petrinja earthquake (2020), Croatia, *Remote Sens.* **13,** no. 12, 2267, doi: 10.3390/rs13122267.

Karimzadeh, S., A. Askan, M. A. Erberik, and A. Yakut (2018). Seismic damage assessment based on regional synthetic ground motion dataset: A case study for Erzincan, Turkey, *Nat. Hazards* **92,** no. 3, 1371–1397, doi: 10.1007/s11069-018-3255-6.

Karimzadeh, S., M. Ghasemi, M. Matsuoka, K. Yagi, and A. C. Zulfikar (2022). A deep learning model for road damage detection after an earthquake based on synthetic aperture radar (SAR) and field datasets, *IEEE J. Sel. Top. Appl. Earth Obs. Remote Sens.* **15,** 5753–5765, doi: 10.1109/JSTARS.2022.3189875.

Kramer, S. L., and R. A. Mitchell (2006). Ground motion intensity measures for liquefaction hazard evaluation, *Earthq. Spectra* **22,** no. 2, 413–438, doi: 10.1193/1.2194970.

Lee, J.-S., K. W. Hoppel, S. A. Mango, and A. R. Miller (1994). Intensity and phase statistics of multilook polarimetric and interferometric SAR imagery, *IEEE Trans. Geosci. Remote Sens.* **32,** no. 5, 1017–1028, doi: 10.1109/36.312890.

Liu, H., C. Song, Z. Li, Z. Liu, L. Ta, X. Zhang, B. Chen, B. Han, and J. Peng (2024). A new method for the identification of earthquake-damaged buildings using sentinel-1 multitemporal coherence optimized by homogeneous SAR pixels and histogram matching, *IEEE J. Sel. Top. Appl. Earth Obs. Remote Sens.* **17,** 7124–7143, doi: 10.1109/JSTARS.2024.3377218.

Myanmar National Building Code (MNBC) (2020). Myanmar National Building Code-2020, Ministry of Construction, Nay Pyi Taw, Myanmar.

National Remote Sensing Centre (2025). Myanmar earthquake 2025: Damage assessment report, available at https://www.nrsc.gov.in/nrscnew/MyanmarEarthquake2025-main/index_earthquake.html (last accessed June 2025).

Qodri, M. F. (2018). Geophysical site investigation and ground response analysis of Bangkok subsoil due to earthquake, Chulalongkorn University, Bangkok, Thailand, doi: 10.58837/CHULA.THE.2018.133.

Ridd, M. F., and A. Racey (2015). *Chapter 4 Onshore Petroleum Geology of Myanmar: Central Burma Depression*, Vol. 45, Geological Society of London, 21–50, doi: 10.1144/M45.04.

Rosen, P. A., S. Hensley, I. R. Joughin, F. K. Li, S. N. Madsen, E. Rodriguez, and R. M. Goldstein (2000). Synthetic aperture radar interferometry, *Proc. IEEE* **88,** no. 3, 333–382, doi: 10.1109/5.838084.

Santoro, M., U. Wegmüller, C. Lamarche, S. Bontemps, P. Defourny, and O. Arino (2015). Strengths and weaknesses of multi-year Envisat ASAR backscatter measurements to map permanent open water bodies at global scale, *Remote Sens. Environ.* **171,** 185–201, doi: 10.1016/j.rse.2015.10.031.

Seymour, M. S., and I. G. Cumming (1994). Maximum likelihood estimation for SAR interferometry, *Proc. of IGARSS '94-1994 IEEE International Geoscience and Remote Sensing Symposium*, IEEE, 2272–2275, doi: 10.1109/IGARSS.1994.399711.

Shahzada, K., U. A. Noor, and Z.-D. Xu (2025). In the wake of the March 28, 2025 Myanmar earthquake: A detailed examination, *J. Dynam. Disasters* **1,** no. 2, 100,017, doi: 10.1016/j.jdd.2025.100017.

Shimada, M., T. Itoh, T. Motooka, M. Watanabe, T. Shiraishi, R. Thapa, and R. Lucas (2014). New global forest/non-forest maps from ALOS PALSAR data (2007–2010), *Remote Sens. Environ.* **155,** 13–31, doi: 10.1016/j.rse.2014.04.014.

Tamkuan, N., and M. Nagai (2017). Fusion of multi-temporal interferometric coherence and optical image data for the 2016 Kumamoto earthquake damage assessment, *ISPRS Int. J. Geo-Inform.* **6,** no. 7, 188, doi: 10.3390/ijgi6070188.

Thein, M., T. Myint, S. Thura Tun, and T. Lwin Swe (2009). Earthquake and tsunami hazard in Myanmar, *J. Earthq. Tsunami* **3,** 43–57.

Toutin, T. (2004). Review article: Geometric processing of remote sensing images: Models, algorithms and methods, *Int. J. Remote Sens.* **25,** no. 10, 1893–1924, doi: 10.1080/0143116031000101611.

Touzi, R., A. Lopes, J. Bruniquel, and P. W. Vachon (1999). Coherence estimation for SAR imagery, *IEEE Trans. Geosci. Remote Sens.* **37,** no. 1, 135–149, doi: 10.1109/36.739146.

U.S. Geological Survey (2025). M 7.7 - Myanmar region, *U.S. Geological Survey*, available at https://earthquake.usgs.gov/earthquakes/eventpage/us7000pn9s (last accessed June 2025).

Wang, T., Y. Zhou, J. Chen, X. Wang, H. Bi, and X. Wang (2025). Field survey of building damage at Mandalay during 2025 Myanmar M_w 7.7 earthquake, *Earthq. Eng. Eng. Vib.* doi: 10.1007/s11803-025-2325-5.

Yilmaz, C., V. Silva, and G. Weatherill (2021). Probabilistic framework for regional loss assessment due to earthquake-induced liquefaction including epistemic uncertainty, *Soil Dynam. Earthq. Eng.* **141,** 106,493, doi: 10.1016/J.SOILDYN.2020.106493.

Zhu, J., L. G. Baise, and E. M. Thompson (2017). An updated geospatial liquefaction model for global application, *Bull. Seismol. Soc. Am.* **107,** no. 3, 1365–1385, doi: 10.1785/0120160198.

Zhu, J., D. Daley, L. G. Baise, E. M. Thompson, D. J. Wald, and K. L. Knudsen (2015). A geospatial liquefaction model for rapid response and loss estimation, *Earthq. Spectra* **31,** no. 3, 1813–1837, doi: 10.1193/121912EQS353M.

Manuscript received 9 August 2025
Published online 20 October 2025

Asymmetric Y-Shaped Structural Rupture of the 2025 M_w 7.1 Tingri, Southern Tibet, Earthquake

Ying Shi[1,2], Yongzhe Wang*[1,2], Hua Pan[1,2], Kun Chen[1,2], Yuanzhi Liu[1,2], and Jiahao Zou[1,2]

Abstract

Understanding the seismogenic structures of large earthquakes is critical for constraining regional tectonic frameworks and improving future seismic hazard assessments. The 2025 M_w 7.1 Tingri earthquake in southern Tibet, China, a significant event following the 2020 M_w 5.7 earthquake, occurred at the junction of the Northern Himalaya and the Xainza-Dinggye fault system. To investigate the local structural complexities, we processed three Sentinel-1A Synthetic Aperture Radar (SAR) tracks (both ascending and descending) using Interferometric SAR (InSAR) and pixel offset tracking (POT) to derive the coseismic surface displacement field. The InSAR results reveal a maximum line-of-sight (LoS) displacement of −1.37 m, whereas the POT results identify two distinct fault ruptures associated with the 2025 event. By inverting the coseismic deformation field with an elastic half-space model, we obtained the fault rupture model, which shows that the 2025 earthquake ruptured an asymmetric, segmented Y-shaped fault system, with slip dominated by normal faulting and a peak slip magnitude of 4.9 m. The Coulomb stress change results further indicate that the 2025 earthquake rupture was primarily driven by the ongoing extensional tectonics of the regional rift system and may have been facilitated by static stress transfer from the 2020 Tingri earthquake. These results highlight the mechanical link between successive large events in complex fault systems and provide new constraints on the seismotectonic processes of the North Himalayan rift zone.

Cite this article as Shi, Y., Y. Wang, H. Pan, K. Chen, Y. Liu, and J. Zou (2026). Asymmetric Y-Shaped Structural Rupture of the 2025 M_w 7.1 Tingri, Southern Tibet, Earthquake, *Seismol. Res. Lett.* **97**, 1613–1627, doi: 10.1785/0220250301.

Supplemental Material

Introduction

According to the official report from the China Earthquake Networks Center (CENC), at 09:05 local time on 7 January 2025, an M_w 7.1 earthquake struck the Tingri County and adjacent areas in southern Tibet, China, with a focal depth of 10 km (Fig. 1). The epicentral distances from the mainshock to Tingri County, Lazi County, Xigaze City, and Lhasa City are 36, 67, 164, and 379 km, respectively. Field investigations confirmed the presence of surface ruptures (Liu *et al.*, 2025; Shi *et al.*, 2025; Xu *et al.*, 2025), and the maximum observed intensity reached IX (Chen *et al.*, 2025). Isoseismal contours show an elliptical pattern with major and minor axes of ~191 and ~152 km, respectively (Li, Sun, *et al.*, 2025). The earthquake caused widespread structural collapses, destroying more than 3000 households and resulting in significant casualties and economic losses.

The 2025 M_w 7.1 Tingri earthquake nucleated near Changsuo Town, Tingri County, within the seismically active southeastern segment of the Lazi fault zone, located in the Lhasa terrane of the Tibetan Plateau. This epicentral region lies at the structural intersection of the North Himalayan Thrust System and the Xainza-Dinggye fault (XDF) system, where ongoing India–Asia convergence derives complex crustal deformation. The southern Tibetan Plateau simultaneously accommodates north–south compression from the indentation of the Indian Plate and east–west extension driven by plateau uplift and crustal thickening, resulting in two principal fault orientations: sub-north–south and sub-east–west. Such intense deformation processes promoted persistent seismicity across the Lhasa block and adjacent fault zones, explaining the high-seismicity rate of the region. Consistent focal mechanism solutions reported by multiple agencies (Table 1) indicate a dominantly normal-faulting event with minor strike-slip components. This mechanism reflects a regional stress regime characterized by north-northwest–south-southeast compression and east-northeast–west-southwest extension, favoring normal faulting along roughly north–south-trending structures. The XDF zone remains one of the most seismically active systems in southern Tibet, have generated at least

1. Institute of Geophysics, China Earthquake Administration, Beijing, China, https://orcid.org/0000-0002-5115-0397 (YW); 2. Beijing Baijiatuan Earth Science National Observation and Research Station, Beijing, China

*Corresponding author: yzwang@cea-igp.ac.cn

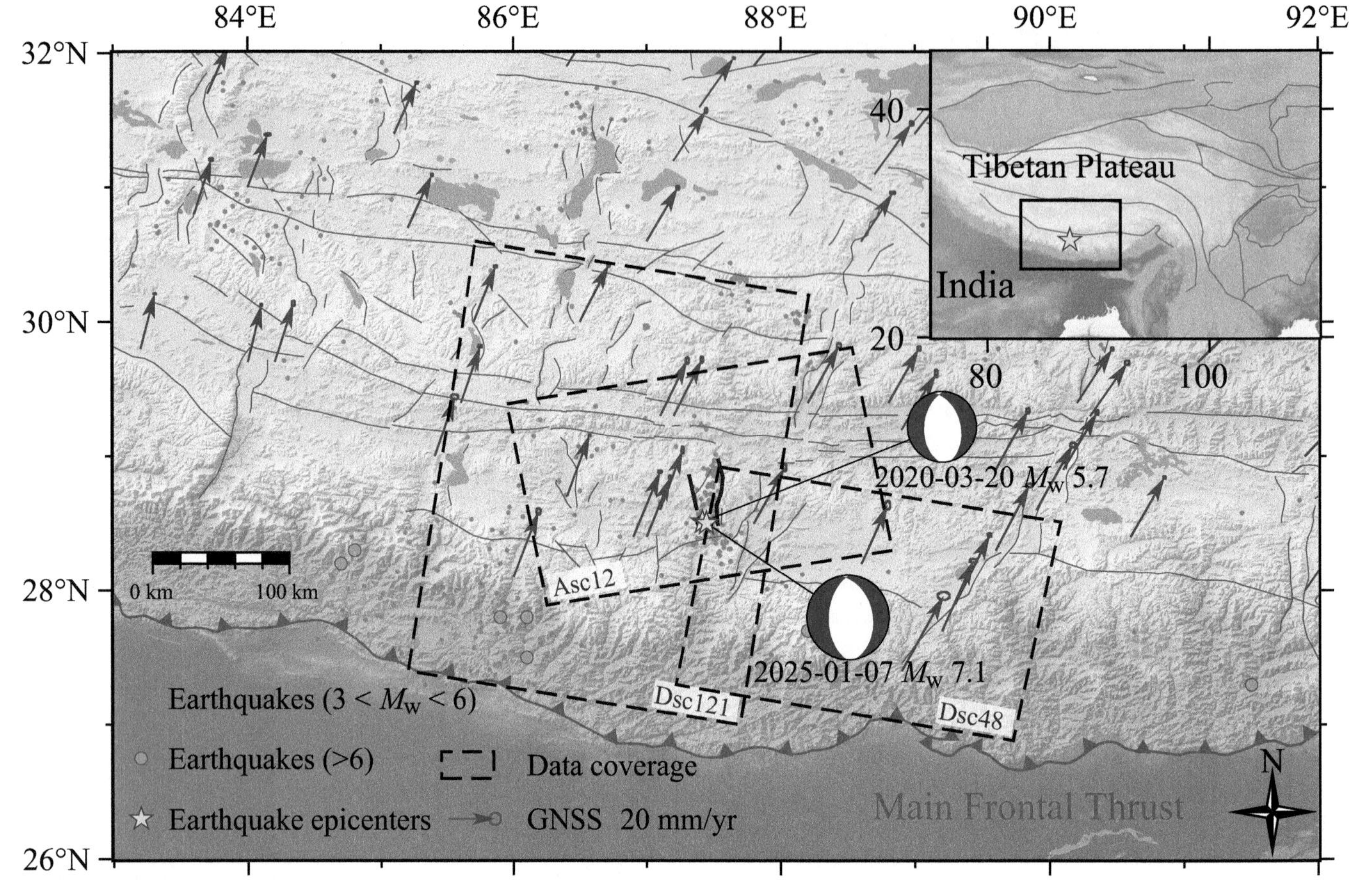

Figure 1. Seismotectonic background of the 7 January 2025 Tingri earthquake. Seismotectonic background of the 7 January 2025 Tingri earthquake. Regional horizontal velocity field, historical earthquake epicenters, and focal mechanism solutions across southern Tibet. The Global Navigation Satellite Systems (GNSS) interseismic velocities (gray arrows) are presented in the Eurasia-fixed reference frame and are sourced from Wang and Shen (2020). Active fault traces (gray lines) follow Deng *et al.* (2003) and Li *et al.* (2022). Focal mechanism solutions for the 2020 and 2025 Tingri earthquakes are taken from the Global Centroid Moment Tensor (Global CMT) catalog (see Data and Resources). Epicenters of events prior to 2020 (filled- brown circles) are provided by the China Earthquake Networks Center (CENC). The surface rupture lines identified in this study are marked with blue lines. Inset shows the geographical location of the 2025 Tingri epicenter area. The black rectangle outlines the map extent shown in the figure. The color version of this figure is available only in the electronic edition.

TABLE 1
Focal Mechanism Solutions of the 2025 Tingri Earthquake in Tibet Provided by Different Agencies

		Nodal Plane I/(°)			Nodal Plane II/(°)			
Moment Magnitude	**Centroid Depth (km)**	**Strike**	**Dip**	**Slip**	**Strike**	**Dip**	**Slip**	**Source of Information**
6.9	11.5	182	22	−64	334	71	−100	CENC
7.1	14	151	56	−116	12	41	−56	GFZ
7.1	11.5	187	49	−78	349	42	−103	USGS
7.1	12	173	48	−92	356	42	−88	Global CMT
7.2	14	196	44	−64	341	51	−113	IPGP
–	–	191	32	−67	344	60	−104	Zhang Yixiao

CENC, China Earthquake Networks Center; GFZ, GeoForschungsZentrum; Global CMT, Global Centroid Moment Tensor; IPGP, Institut de Physique du Globe de Paris; USGS, U.S. Geological Survey.

TABLE 2
Slip Model Based on Interferometric Radar Technology and the Number of Observed Fault Segments

References	Dip	Rake	Depth (km)	Seismic Moment (N)	Earthquake Magnitude (M_w)	Total Number of Fault Segments
Yang, Jin, *et al.* (2025)	55	−64.75	0–15	–	7.06	1
Wang *et al.* (2025)	40	–	1–6	–	7.1	1
Li, Wang, *et al.* (2025)	52.8	−95.75	0–14	6.43×10^{19}	7.17	1
Yu *et al.* (2025)	40.6	−82.81	0–10	–	7.1	1
Qiao *et al.* (2025)	65	−67	0–11	–	7.05	2
This research	Table S1	–	0–20	6.36×10^{19}	7.1	5

three earthquakes of magnitude greater than 5 in recent decades. Among these, the 2020 M_w 5.7 Tingri earthquake was the closest in both space and time to the 2025 earthquake, and source modeling identified a typical normal-faulting geometry (Wang *et al.*, 2021; Zubovich *et al.*, 2022).

Following the 2025 earthquake, several domestic and international research groups have rapidly published studies that constrain the seismic source geometry and rupture behavior using field observations and instrumental data. Nevertheless, near-field observations remain limited, restricting the accuracy of current source models. In addition, the high-relief terrain at elevations of 5300–5500 m, where the principal surface ruptures are exposed, makes detailed ground mapping extremely difficult (Kapp and Guynn, 2004; Chevalier *et al.*, 2020). During the past decades, Interferometric Synthetic Aperture Radar (InSAR) has emerged as a primary geodetic technique for characterizing earthquake deformation, particularly in remote or data-poor regions. Its ability to operate independently of ground stations and to perform consistent day–night, all-weather imaging makes it invaluable for studies of crustal deformation, active fault mapping, strain accumulation, aseismic creep detection, and slip-rate estimation (Daout *et al.*, 2019; Ou *et al.*, 2022; Zhang *et al.*, 2024). InSAR derives coseismic displacement along the satellite line-of-sight (LoS) by differencing phase measurements from sequential Synthetic Aperture Radar (SAR) acquisitions, typically achieving spatial resolutions of several tens of meters. Although Global Navigation Satellite Systems (GNSS) and seismic networks are sparse in western Tibet, the region is particularly favorable for InSAR owing to its abundant SAR data archives, high coherence, and relatively low atmospheric noise (Wright *et al.*, 2004; Wolff *et al.*, 2023). Compared with traditional point-based geodetic techniques, InSAR offers dense spatial coverage and has become an indispensable approach for monitoring static deformation through the seismic cycle (Massonnet *et al.*, 1993). Several preliminary source mechanism models were released soon after the 2025 event; however, most focused on a single-fault geometry. Precise aftershock relocations suggest that the rupture may have involved two distinct fault segments (Yang, Jin, *et al.*, 2025). Many studies overlooked the possible activation of a secondary fault west of the epicenter (Yang, Jin, *et al.*, 2025; Li, Wang, *et al*, 2025; Wang *et al.*, 2025; Yu *et al.*, 2025). Although Qiao *et al.* (2025) recognized two faults on either side of the epicenter, they did not incorporate the segmented characteristics of the rupture (Table 2). Because of the decoherence in near-field InSAR fringes, existing InSAR and pixel-offset tracking results suggest that neither a single-fault model nor a simple dual-fault model adequately reproduces the complex deformation pattern along the eastern segment of the main fault. Moreover, none of the previous investigations evaluated the potential role of static Coulomb stress transfer from the 2020 Tingri earthquake, which may have influenced rupture initiation in 2025.

Data were from the CENC, the GFZ Helmholtz Centre Potsdam (GFZ), the U.S. Geological Survey (USGS), the Global Centroid Moment Tensor (Global CMT) Project at Columbia University (Global CMT) and the Institut de Physique du Globe de Paris (IPGP). Zhang Yixiao was sourced at Zhang *et al.* (2025).

To clarify the seismogenic structure and source characteristics of the 2025 earthquake, and to evaluate stress perturbations imparted by the 2020 Tingri earthquake, we processed multitrack Sentinel-1A SAR data sets using conventional two-pass differential InSAR and pixel cross-correlation techniques to generate a high-coherence coseismic deformation field. The segmented fault-source model was then inverted using nonlinear and linear optimization methods constrained by the observed deformation. Subsequently, we analyzed the seismogenic structure of the 2025 earthquake, and carried out the analysis of stress disturbance by the 2020 Tingri earthquake through Coulomb stress change analysis. In addition, the surface rupture characteristics were interpreted by integrating fault kinematics, aftershock distribution, and field survey investigation results. The findings from this study provide new insights into the seismotectonic framework of southern Tibet and contribute to improving regional seismic hazard assessment.

Tectonic Setting and Historical Earthquakes

The Cenozoic collision between the Indian and Eurasian plates gave rise to the Tibetan Plateau, often referred to as the "roof of the world." Within this vast plateau, a series of north–south-trending rift systems has developed, delineating multiple graben valleys and fault-bounded basins. Collectively, these structures compose the South Tibet Rift System, a set of subparallel, laterally continuous, and tectonically active extensional faults (Armijo *et al.*, 1986; Yin and Harrison, 2000; Zhang *et al.*, 2004; Chevalier *et al.*, 2020; Dal Luca *et al.*, 2021; Wang *et al.*, 2021). Across the Tibetan Plateau, the rift system constitutes a principal locus of tectonic activity, accommodating significant extensional strain and hosting frequent seismic activity. The seismic regime is characterized by persistent low-magnitude activity punctuated by occasional large earthquakes (Armijo *et al.*, 1986; Tapponnier *et al.*, 2001; Kapp *et al.*, 2008). The 2025 earthquake occurred along the Xainza-Dinggye rift (XDR), which traverses the Yarlung Tsangpo suture zone and the southern Tibet detachment system (STDS; Huang *et al.*, 2024). The normal fault system associated with the rift extends for roughly 350 km in length and 50 km in width, striking approximately 15° northeast. From north to south, the rift can be subdivided into the Xainza segment, the Xietongmen segment, and the Dinggye segment. The Dinggye segment hosts several active faults, including the Guojia, Dinggye, Mabujia, and Dingmuco faults (Fig. 1; Kali *et al.*,2010; Xu, 2019; Chevalier *et al.*, 2025; Gao *et al.*, 2025; Wu *et al.*, 2025).

The 2025 earthquake occurred at the intersection of the XDR and the STDS, approximately east of central Tingri and close to the Dingmuco fault, which is one of the southwestern-dipping faults within the XDR. The topographic surface of the entire rift system is offset by multiple normal faults that bounded a series of grabens collectively accommodating approximately 9 mm/yr of east–west extension (Wu *et al.*, 2025). During the past 19 ± 5 ka, the Dingmuco fault has sustained a throw rate of 1.1 (+0.5, −0.2) mm/yr and an extensional rate of 1.1 ± 0.3 mm/yr (Chevalier *et al.*, 2025). GPS observations have indicated that the activity of this fault zone is closely correlated with the sustained northward motion of the Indian plate and the stress accumulation associated with its subduction. The seismic activity of this fault zone is high; over the last century, 10 earthquakes of magnitude ≥6 have occurred within 250 km of the 2025 epicenter, including the M_w 7.8 Nepal earthquake, located about 160 km to the southwest of Tingri. Following that event, stress loading and activity along the Dingmuco fault zone increased (Wang *et al.*, 2021). Based on fault dimensions and slip rates, Tian and Wu (2023) estimated a maximum potential magnitude of M_w 6.8–7.2 for this segment. Geodetic observations during the three years preceding the 2025 Tingri earthquake revealed persistent north–south shortening, enhanced east–west extension, and a progressive counter-clockwise rotation of the principal strain axis, all consistent with intensified normal-fault motion (Li, Wang, *et al.*, 2025). Field investigations also identified fault scarps up to ∼25 m high along the Dingmuco fault suggesting multiple large magnitude earthquakes (Wu *et al.*, 2025). Focal mechanism solutions reported by several agencies (Table 1) indicate that the 2025 rupture was dominated by normal faulting with a minor strike-slip component. This style reflects a tectonic stress regime characterized by north-northwest–south-southeast compression coupled with northeast-east–southwest-west extension, producing a strike-slip-influenced extensional field that favors normal faulting along approximately north–south-oriented structures.

Date and Methods

Data acquisition and processing

Since its launch, Sentinel-1A has played a crucial role in imaging deformation fields and constraining source-model parameters of large-magnitude earthquakes worldwide through high-quality radar observations. Its 12-day repeat cycle enables acquisition of closely spaced pre- and postevent images, thereby minimizing temporal decorrelation. Operating in interferometric wide mode with terrain observation by progressive scans, the sensor acquires three adjoining subswaths, providing a swath width of approximately 250 km. This wide coverage allows efficient observation of large-scale coseismic displacement fields (Shan *et al.*, 2017).

To fully characterize the surface displacement induced by the 2025 Tingri earthquake, Sentinel-1A short-time interval, short-baseline C band SAR scenes were processed in the open-source GMTSAR (InSAR processing system based on Generic Mapping Tools) framework (Sandwell *et al.*, 2011).

1. Precision orbit files downloaded from the European Space Agency (ESA) Copernicus website were used for the coregistration and topographic phase simulation.
2. A geoid-corrected 30 m × 30 m resolution digital elevation model (Shuttle Radar Topography Mission) was employed to simulate and subtract terrain-related phase (Farr *et al.*, 2007).
3. An 8:2 (range: azimuth) multilook ratio was imposed during image coregistration to produce a wrapped differential interferogram.
4. A nonlinear filter was employed to boost the signal-to-noise ratio (SNR) of the phase (Goldstein and Werner, 1998).
5. Statistical-cost, network-flow phase-unwrapping algorithm (SNAPHU) unwrapping was executed with a coherence mask of 0.1, excluding low coherence and water pixels (Chen and Zebker, 2002).
6. The online generic atmospheric correction online service for InSAR (GACOS, see Data and Resources) model was used to mitigate the potential atmospheric phase (Yu *et al.*, 2017).
7. The unwrapped interferometric phase was converted and geocoded into geographic coordinates, producing a detailed coseismic displacement field for further modeling (Shi *et al.*, 2023).

TABLE 3
SAR Data Information

Satellite Sensor	Flight Direction	Imaging Time (yyyy/mm/dd) First Image	Second Image	Fram	Path
Sentinel-1A	Ascending	2025/01/05	2025/01/17	89	T12
		2025/01/01	2025/01/13	493	T121
	Descending	2025/01/01	2025/01/13	499	
		2024/12/27	2025/01/08	494	T48
		2024/12/27	2025/01/08	499	

SAR, Synthetic Aperture Radar.

To capture the full extent of coseismic deformation, we employed Sentinel-1A data from three orbital tracks: one ascending (track 12) and two descending (tracks 121 and 48; Table 3). Track 48 provided focused coverage of the eastern epicentral zone, whereas the ~120 km rupture length exceeded the single-frame swath of a track 121. To overcome this limitation, two adjacent frames from the same descending orbit were mosaicked, enabling continuous coverage of the entire deformation field (Fig. 1).

Severe ground shaking and release of strong coseismic strain led to significant decorrelation near the surface rupture. To recover deformation signals in this low coherence, we applied pixel offset tracking (POT) to the single look complex images to estimate range-direction displacements. POT processing was carried out using the open-source GMTSAR software package. Initial coarse alignment of reference and secondary images was performed using satellite orbit and image metadata. Subsequently, the center pixel offset was computed to establish the baseline displacement vector between the image pair. This offset was then utilized to guide a pixel-wise correspondence search using a 32 × 32 window across both range and azimuth directions. We subsequently applied a moving-window median filter to the raw offset field, taking the median within each pixel neighborhood to suppress noise, mitigate artifacts associated with InSAR decorrelation (scatter loss), and improve the SNR. The POT measurements delineate the principal coseismic slip features of the 2025 Tingri earthquake and place tight constraints on the slip distribution along the Tingri rupture when interpreted jointly with InSAR displacement data (Lei *et al.*, 2021; Tong *et al.*, 2024).

Coseismic surface deformation

We analyzed the Sentinel-1A coseismic InSAR observations to outline the earthquake-induced surface rupture and quantify the magnitude of ground displacement. The derived displacements correspond to the satellite LoS motion. For earthquakes dominated by near-vertical normal or thrust faulting, vertical motion of the hanging wall and footwall produces a pronounced near-field vertical signal. For the 2025 Tingri strong earthquake, the coseismic deformation covered an area of approximately 100 km × 200 km, with the major axis of the deformation ellipse-oriented south–north. Opposite-sense displacements were observed on either side of the Dingmuco fault, and deformation gradients intensified toward the rupture zone. Descending track 121 and ascending track 12 together provided complete spatial coverage of the affected area. The far-field deformation exhibited smooth, gradual variations, whereas abrupt near-field discontinuities coincided with surface rupture traces confirmed by field investigations (Shi *et al.*, 2025). Strong interferometric decorrelation was also detected in the epicentral area. The overall deformation pattern clearly indicates a normal-faulting rupture along the Dingmuco fault, consistent with the regional extensional stress regime of southern Tibet.

Descending track 48 (Fig. 2a) captured deformation across the eastern segment of the rupture zone, in which the LoS motion reached a maximum of 0.78 m toward the satellite. Descending track 121 (Fig. 2e) provided complete epicentral coverage, recording uplift of 0.76 m on the eastern side of the main fault trace. In contrast, LoS subsidence dominated west of the principal rupture, attaining a maximum of −1.06 m. The ascending track 12 (Fig. 2l) exhibited a motion pattern opposite to that of the descending orbits, LoS subsidence occurred east of the fault and within ~10 km west of it, reaching a maximum drop of −1.37 m, whereas a localized uplift of 0.33 m was observed farther west. Because InSAR measures the projection of north–south, east–west, and vertical displacements onto the LoS and vertical motion contributes most to the LoS signal, the combined multitrack results indicate that surface motion was dominated by the subsidence. Collectively, these large-scale coseismic deformation patterns demonstrate a normal-fault rupture along the Dingmuco fault, consistent with the regional extensional regime of southern Tibet.

We applied POT to Sentinel-1A data from descending track 121 (Fig. 2i) and ascending track 12 (Fig. 2g) to resolve the geometry of the surface rupture. The POT-derived displacements exceeded LoS phase-derived measurements, indicating enhanced near-fault ground motion. The principal surface rupture was identified at the offset-field polarity reversal boundary. For descending track 121, positive offsets east of the rupture indicate eastward motion, whereas negative offsets west of the rupture correspond to westward motion. The ascending track 12 data reveal two kinematic domains: zones east and immediately west of the rupture display westward displacement, whereas displacement farther west reverses to eastward. Both viewing geometrics consistently indicate a tensional deformation pattern. Two separate rupture traces are evident in the POT fields (Fig. 2p), a western branch that does not clearly reach the surface, and an eastern primary rupture along the Dingmuco fault within XDR. The eastern rupture extends roughly 56 km, defining the main break of the event.

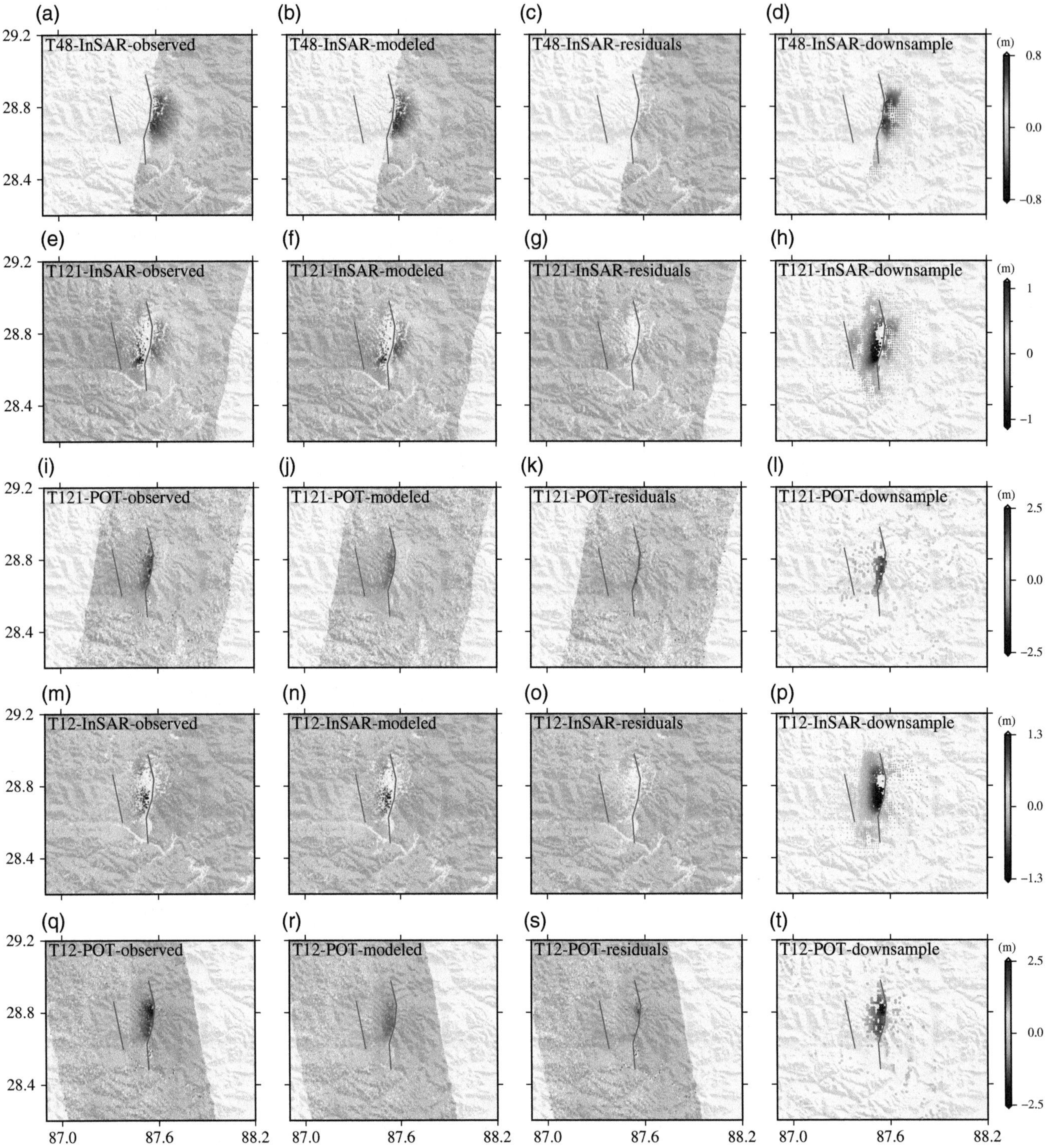

Figure 2. Observation and modeling of Interferometric Synthetic Aperture Radar (InSAR) line-of-sight (LoS) displacement data, residuals, and quadtree downsampled results. Each row presents, from left to right, the observed coseismic displacement, the model prediction, the residual, and the downsampled deformation field. (a–d) InSAR-derived LoS deformation for descending track 48, (e–h) InSAR-derived LoS deformation for descending track 121, (i–l) pixel offset tracking (POT)-derived range direction offsets for descending track 121, (m–p) InSAR-derived LoS deformation for ascending track 12, and (q–t) POT-derived range direction offsets for ascending track 12. The color version of this figure is available only in the electronic edition.

Integration of POT-derived offsets, mapped fault continuity, and prior structure data reveal that the Tingri earthquake rupture zone is strongly segmented. The main fault can be divided into four segments (Fig. 3), labeled S1–S4 from south to north. In addition, a western secondary fault S5 extends for approximately 30 km, located about 35 km west of the epicenter.

Fault modeling and slip distribution inversion

The inversion of fault rupture model is a fundamental approach to characterizing rupture and evaluating seismogenic structure.

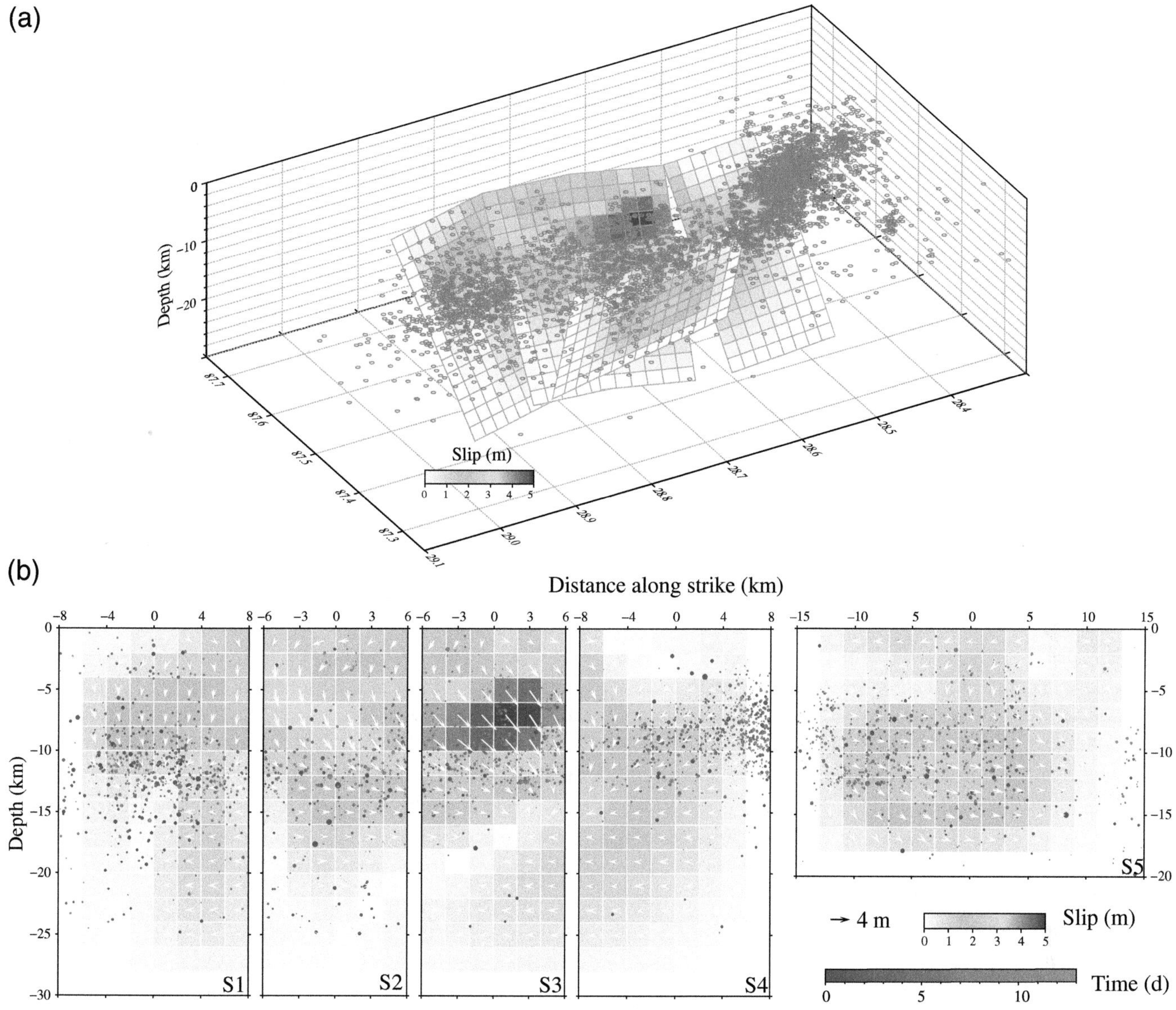

Figure 3. Coseismic slip models of the 2025 Tingri earthquake in a 3D view. (a) Three-dimensional source rupture model. The yellow pentagram indicates the mainshock location, and the blue circles represent the locations of aftershocks with a magnitude greater than M_w 3.5. (b) Two-dimensional slip distribution fault model marked with faults S1–S5. The colored dots represent the aftershocks, with the gradually varied color indicating the time elapsed since the mainshock and the size varying according to the magnitude. The arrows indicate the direction of fault slip, for which "Depth" refers to the direction along the fault's dip orientation. The color version of this figure is available only in the electronic edition.

The classical Okada dislocation model in a homogeneous elastic half-space provides the analytical relationship between fault-plane parameters and surface displacements (Okada, 1985). To optimize computational efficiency and minimize redundancy, we applied quadtree downsampling to the dense InSAR and POT deformation fields obtained from both descending and ascending Sentinel-1A tracks. Sampling points were retained in areas with strong spatial deformation gradients (Jónsson *et al.*, 2002), ensuring preservation of near-fault detail while reducing far-field error propagation. After downsampling, the number of observation points was 976 for track 48, 2107 for track 121, and 2088 for track 12. To enhance model constraints, POT-derived displacements were also incorporated into the inversion. Only data within the decorrelation zone were used, yielding 360 points from descending track 121 and 345 points from ascending track 12 (Fig. 2).The relative smaller modeled deformation near the fault, compared with the POT observations, likely results from a combination of factors: the limited precision and inherent uncertainty of POT measurements, underestimation of shallow slip in the inversion, neglect of inelastic deformation under elastic assumptions, and simplified fault geometry and material parameters. Moreover, the spatial smoothing applied during inversion may further attenuate localized deformation peaks (Xu *et al.*, 2025).

Prior to the slip distribution inversion, it was necessary to define the geometric parameters of fault. An initial geometric framework was constructed from the rupture trace length and position estimated using the POT-derived offsets, combined with the field-mapping constraints from preliminary observations. This framework was then integrated with the elastic half-space model to establish the mapping relationships between fault geometry and surface deformation. We then performed a nonlinear inversion of key geometric parameters including dip angle, width, strike slip, dip slip of both the main fault and western branch using the interior point method (Funning, 2005). This algorithm treats the fault location and length as prior constraints, reformulating the nonlinear inversion into a bounded optimization problem. This algorithm gradually minimizes the mismatch function along the "central path" within the feasible region until convergence to an optimal parameters set is achieved. Using this approach, we estimated the fault dip angles and their confidence intervals (see Fig. A1, available in the supplemental material to this article). The dip angles of faults S1–S4 were 61.8° ± 0.16°, and the dip angle of fault S5 was 78.37° ± 0.90°. The resulting geometric parameters (see Table S1) indicate that the western branch fault dips eastward, whereas the main fault dips westward.

To enhance the stability and reliability of the slip distribution inversion, we incorporated fault geometry and location parameters derived from nonlinear inversion, thereby linearizing the slip distribution inversion. By integrating rupture-trace information from POT with geometrically optimized parameters, the western branch fault was modeled as 30 km long and 20 km wide, and the main fault as 56 km long and 30 km wide, forming a comprehensive geometric framework for inversion. We constructed the Green's functions using the Okada (1985) elastic half-space formulation. For computational efficiency and adequate resolution in regions of strong deformation, the fault surfaces were discretized into uniform 2 km × 2 km subfaults, yielding 150 subfaults for the western branch fault and 420 subfaults for the eastern main fault. The coseismic slip distribution was then estimated through the constraint least-squares method. We used the inverse of optimal smoothing parameter α with a search range set between 0 and 6.5, and performed batch inversions incrementally with a step size of 0.1–1. This parameter balances the roughness of the model slip distribution with the fit to the sparse downsampled data. We selected $\alpha = 1.2$ (see Fig. A2) by the trade-off curve between the inversion residual (misfit) and the roughness (rough). The inverted source slip model is shown in Figure 3.

The preferred slip model successfully reproduced the observed deformation patterns, amplitudes, and kinematics in both InSAR and POT data sets, yielding minimal residuals (Fig. 2). The rupture was dominated by normal faulting with a minor sinistral strike-slip component. The seismogenic zone extends for approximately 56 km, closely matching the slip extent reported by Yang, Jin, *et al.* (2025). The eastern fault system (segments S1–S4) trends roughly north–south and dips westward. Rupture depth of the fault ranges from 0 to 20 km, with the maximum slip reaching 4.88 m, concentrated between 6 and 9 km depth. The secondary fault (F5), dipping eastward and oriented nearly north–south, was also identified west of the epicenter. This secondary fault extends about 30 km, ruptures from 0 to 20 km depth, and reaches a maximum slip of 2.85 m centered at 10–12 km depth. The location of the primary rupture zone (S1–S4) obtained from our inversion is well consistent with the main surface-rupture belt documented by Shi *et al.* (2025). However, their onsite investigation results reported maximum surface displacements of 2.5–3.0 m, whereas our model predicts 1.5–2.5 m at the corresponding sites. This shallow slip deficit likely reflects a combination of modeling limitations and the presence of thick sedimentary cover or distributed shallow deformation within the fault zone (Xu *et al.*, 2020). Variations in slip magnitude among the fault segments likely arise from differences in fault kinematics, lithological heterogeneity, and local structural complexities. To test the constraint ability of the InSAR observations on the rupture model inversion, we carried out the checkerboard test. The result of the test demonstrates that the simulated observations can retrieve a reliable source model (see Fig. A3).

The total geodetic moment tensor released by our preferred model is 6.36×10^{19} N · m (corresponding to M_w 7.1), slightly larger than the seismic one (4.75×10^{19} N · m, M_w 7.05) estimated by USGS (see Data and Resources). The main reason is that the InSAR observations of this event may include both coseismic and early postseismic deformation due to the temporal interval between SAR acquisitions; our preferred model incorporates coseismic slip and early afterslip, which may result in a slight overestimation of the total seismic moment. The early afterslip has been found in most of the previous studies and is difficult to distinguish by InSAR observations. (Tong *et al.*, 2010; Lindsey *et al.*, 2015).

Discussion

2025 Tingri earthquake ruptured an asymmetric Y-shaped structure

Each mainshock alters the stress distribution along the fault-stress decreases within the rupture zone but increases in the surrounding areas. Aftershocks occur within these stress-enhanced regions as strain energy is further released. Consequently, their spatial pattern often complements that of the mainshock rupture, providing important clues about the rupture process and fault geometry, as well as an independent check on the reliability of the slip model (Freed, 2005). According to the precise aftershocks relocations (Figs. 3 and 4; Yang, Wang, *et al.*, 2025), the 2025 Tingri mainshock was followed by an extensive aftershock sequence. By 20 January 2025, a total of 3830 events (M >1.4) had been recorded, including a significant M_w 5.0 aftershock on 13 January. Aftershocks migrated progressively from south to north, clustering on the western side of the Dingmuco fault and the eastern flank of the adjacent fault zones, the strikes of which parallel those of

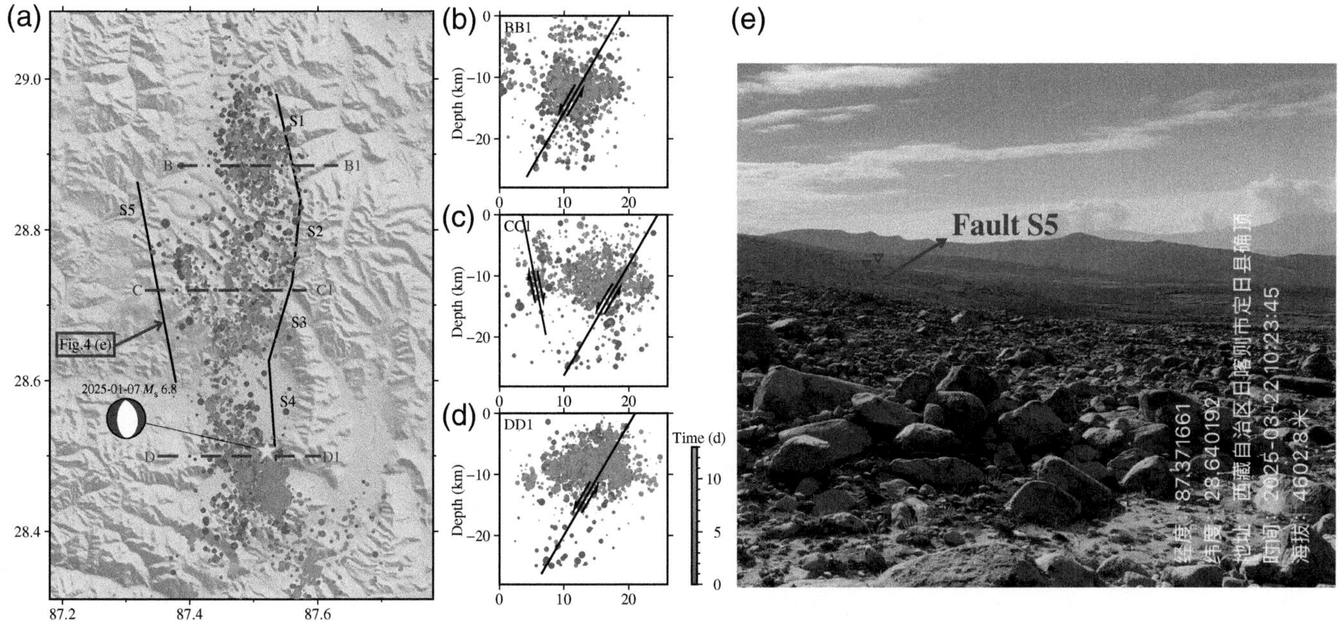

Figure 4. Spatiotemporal distribution of the aftershock sequence of the 2025 Tingri earthquake. Colored dots denote the epicenters of 3830 relocated aftershocks (Yang, Wang, *et al.*, 2025). The yellow star marks the location of the mainshock, and the yellow circles highlight aftershocks of M >3.5. Color gradation reflects the elapsed time since the mainshock. The black lines delineate the surface traces of faults. (a) Distribution of aftershocks and fault traces. (b–d) Cross-sectional distribution of seismic aftershocks. (e) Field photograph showing the surface rupture of the fault S5 section of the Tingri earthquake in 2025. The color version of this figure is available only in the electronic edition.

the main rupture. The distribution of aftershocks is primarily concentrated near the fault plane, occurring in a north–south orientation that spans approximately 60–70 km (Fig. 3). Hypocentral depths vary between 4 and 17 km, and three prominent aftershock clusters have been delineated. The northern cluster was characterized by multiple parallel fractures, the central cluster displayed distinct branching patterns, and the southern cluster, which was associated with the mainshock, accounted for most aftershocks exceeding a magnitude of 3.5. Overall, the spatial distribution of the main rupture is well complementary with the spatial distribution (Fig. 3), which demonstrates that our preferred rupture model is reliable and reasonable. Analysis of the spatial distribution of these aftershocks enables the assessment of the structural properties of the fault responsible for their generation (Pu and Li, 2023). To further assess the fault properties, three cross-sectional profiles (BB1, CC1, and DD1) were constructed through the aftershock clusters (Fig. 4), each extending 28 km. Profile CC1 intersects both rupture planes, and DD1 passes through the mainshock hypocenter. Aftershocks within 10 km of each trace were projected onto the cross sections according to hypocentral depth and along-profile distance. Each section reveals pronounced clustering along both fault flanks, with geometries that vary markedly among the different segments.

On the west of CC1, the secondary fault S5 branch of the mainshock rupture was identified. Although it did not rupture the surface obviously and produced only subtle near-fault deformation, it was recovered through POT analysis, and its presence was subsequently confirmed by field investigations (Fig. 4e). This east-dipping branch, situated roughly 20 km west of the main fault, diverges from the principal west-dipping rupture, forming a distinct Y-shaped structure. The Y-shaped geometry consists of a main fault and a secondary branch with similar strike orientations but opposing dips or low-angle intersections Y-shaped (Wang *et al.*, 2021). Previous work by Qiao *et al.* (2025) proposed that these two faults constitute a conjugate fault pair. Conjugate faults are typically strike-slip faults formed under a uniform stress field, intersecting at 60°–90° and exhibiting an "X"-shaped pattern with symmetrical slip (Zhang *et al.*, 1980). A well-known example is the San Andreas fault system in the United States, where both fault sets are simultaneously active and share the strain release (Savage and Burford, 1973; Wang *et al.*, 2022). However, the aftershocks derived from teleseismic waveform inversion and double-difference relocation reveal that the rupture branches from the main fault into two asymmetric limbs, forming a Y-shaped aftershock distribution (Fig. 4c). InSAR observations and the rupture model inverted from InSAR data further indicate a buried eastern-dipping fault lacking symmetric shear features, inconsistent with a conjugate fault model but consistent with a Y-shaped rupture pattern (Chen *et al.*, 2025; Yu *et al.*, 2025; Yang, Wang, *et al.*, 2025).

The multiprofile analysis of the 2025 event demonstrates a complex fault geometry involving both east- and west-dipping structures. In profile CC1 (Fig. 4), aftershocks cluster primarily between the two faults and are dominated by normal-fault mechanisms, coinciding with the region of the most intense coseismic and surface rupture. The opposing dips of the two faults create an acute intersection, reinforcing the Y-shaped structure pattern. Such fault configurations typically develop under multidirectional stress regimes or multiphase extensional deformation, for which the combined influence of gravity and crustal extension promotes tensile fracturing and the formation of shear branches. The main fault commonly generates upper-plate splays, giving rise to Y-shaped geometries (Zhu and Song, 1999). The 2020 M_w 5.7 Tingri earthquake ruptured a secondary fault within the same extensional system, forming part of the Y-shaped structure that characterizes the region. This geometric relationship, together with the observed stress interactions, indicates that the Tingri area is a stress-concentrated and seismically active zone prone to repeated moderate-to-large Y-shaped earthquakes (Wang *et al.*, 2021).

The cross-sectional aftershock distributions (Fig. 4b–d) reveal a complex seismogenic geometry, confirming that the 2025 Tingri event ruptured an asymmetric Y-shaped fault system. In contrast to mature, symmetric rift structures, the Tingri region exhibits indistinct graben topography and asymmetric fault slip, lacking large-scale subsidence or well-developed basins. These features indicate an incipient or transitional rift stage (Brune *et al.*, 2023). The geometric shapes of the two faults resemble grabenlike structures, and the Y-shaped fault associated with the 2025 Tingri earthquake may be related to the grabenlike structures in the southern part of the XDR valley. A graben-type fault combination consists of two faults with nearly parallel strike directions but opposite dip directions, separated by a single downthrown block, reflecting the fault combination pattern formed under tensional or torsional stress. The hallmark of a mature rift system typically includes symmetrical faults or fully developed sedimentary basins. The fracture patterns and local topography indicate that, compared with mature rift systems, this rift is bounded by S1 and S2–S5. The region lacks large-scale subsidence or basin formation, suggesting that the fault system is in its early developmental and formative stage. The rift may develop from initial faults or along boundary faults in its future evolution, indicating that the STDS is in an active developmental phase (Ziegler and Cloetingh, 2004).

Relationship between the 2020 M_w 5.7 Tingri and the 2025 M_w 7.1 Tingri earthquakes: Spatial and coulomb stress relationship

The occurrence of a large earthquake alters the stress field in the surrounding crust (Shan *et al.*, 2017). Coseismic rupture on a fault generates stress perturbations that are subsequently redistributed to adjacent structures. Static Coulomb failure stress changes (ΔCFS) on neighboring faults have been shown to either promote or inhibit subsequent seismic events (Yang *et al.*, 2019; Hu *et al.*, 2021). Consequently, ΔCFS analysis has become a standard tool for investigating aftershock behavior, remote triggering, and seismic hazard evolution. We computed the ΔCFS imparted by the 2020 M_w 5.7 Tingri earthquake onto the 2025 rupture surface using Coulomb version 3.4 (Toda *et al.*, 2011), under the assumption of a homogeneous elastic half-space. Consistent with previous findings, zones of positive ΔCFS correspond to enhanced failure potential, whereas negative ΔCFS values imply stress shadows. Hence, ΔCFS serves as the principal metric for evaluating potential triggering effects. The stress change was computed according to

$$\Delta \mathrm{CFS} = \Delta \tau_s + \mu \Delta \sigma_n, \tag{1}$$

in which $\Delta\tau_s$ is the shear stress perturbation acting along the slip vector of the receiver fault, and $\Delta\sigma_n$ is the normal stress change on the fault plane due to the preceding event.

The 2020 M_w 5.7 Tingri earthquake occurred approximately 18 km south of the 2025 rupture, implying that the earlier shock may have influenced the later event. Following the procedure of Wang *et al.* (2021), we reprocessed the InSAR data with stacking method to improve the coseismic deformation (Fig. 5). Furthermore, we determined the 2020 fault plane with a strike of 351.9° and a dip of 40.5°, and discretized into 15 × 10 subfaults over a 15 km × 10 km plane. Quadtree downsampled observations include 1078 InSAR data points on the track 121 orbit and 935 on track 12. The resulting slip model (Fig. 5) indicates no surface rupture, with a maximum slip of 0.8 m at a depth of 5 km, consistent with a pure normal-faulting mechanism.

To quantify the stress perturbation induced by the 2020 Tingri event, the 2025 preferred source model from this study was adopted as the receiver, and static ΔCFS were calculated (Fig. 5). Results indicate that the ΔCFS decreases progressively with depth, and that the 2020 earthquake imparted Coulomb stress loading at midcrustal level (4–20 km), exceeding the 0.01 MPa triggering threshold proposed by Harris (1998). The primary stress increase was concentrated along deep fault segments (10–20 km) and adjacent branch faults, thereby enhancing the likelihood of subsequent rupture. The initial rupture point of the mainshock occurred on the S4 fault (Yang, Wang, *et al.*, 2025). Although ΔCFS in the S4 fault zone increased, it did not exceed the critical rupture threshold of 0.01 MPa. Overall, these results suggest that the 2020 earthquake imposed additional stress loading on the fault system, which played a certain role in facilitating the fault rupture in 2025.

Seismogenic tectonics of the 2025 Tingri earthquake and its implications

Our preferred source model indicates that the seismogenic fault of the 2025 M_w 7.1 Tingri earthquake extends approximately 56 km, with a maximum slip of 4.88 m concentrated along the principal rupture-segment values consistent with Yang, Wang, *et al.* (2025). The inferred slip distribution is

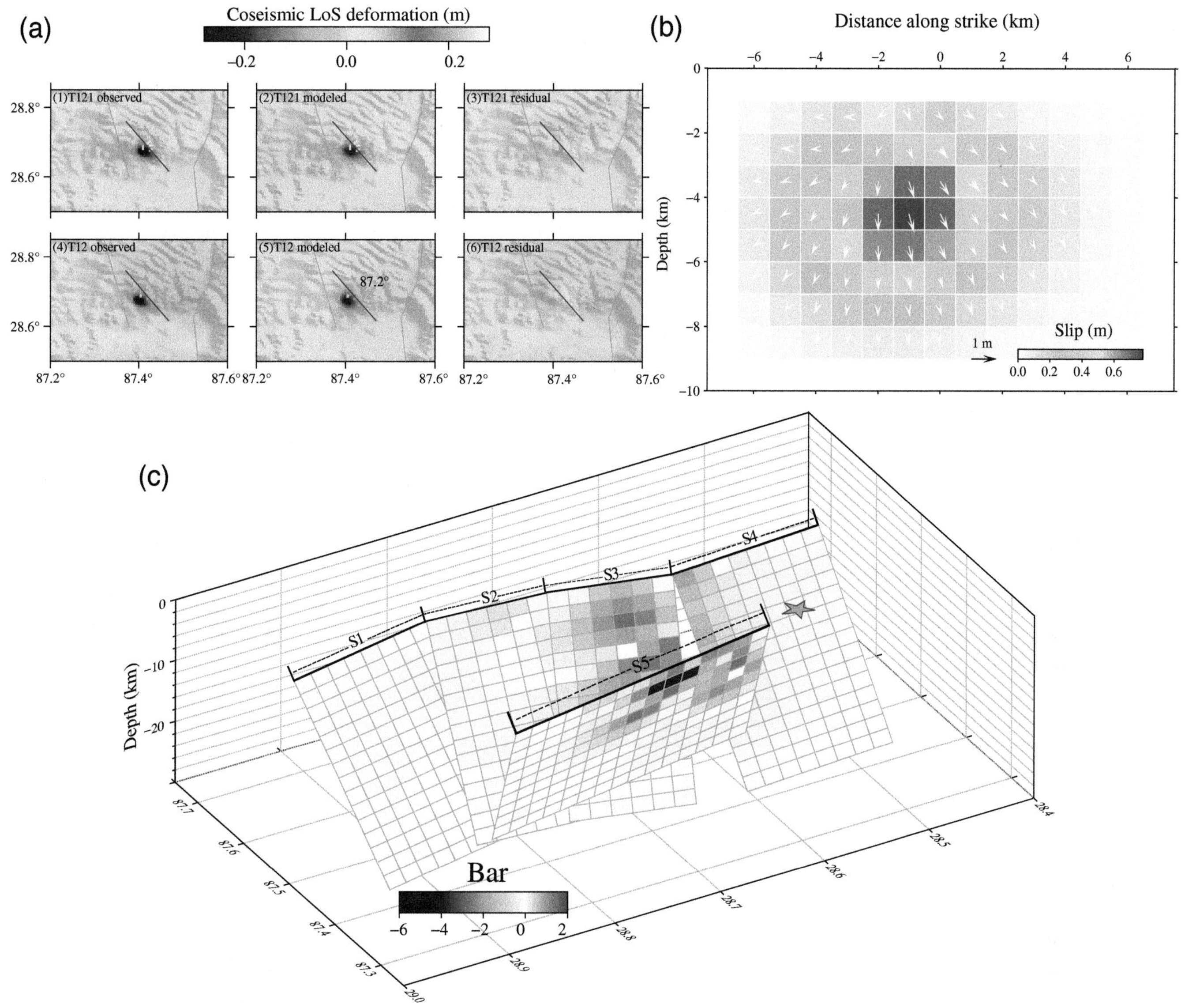

spatially concentrated and predominantly normal fault in character. However, field-based mapping reveals that the surface rupture trace is not linear but composed of multiple inflection points and curved sections with variable strike orientations, forming a geometrically complex, multisegmented fault network. In source modeling, incorporating fault segmentation better captures crustal stress heterogeneity, mechanical weakness zones, and realistic rupture dynamics. Thus, discrepancies between the true multisegment geometry and simplified planar models are critical to understanding the fault's mechanical behavior.

Figure 5. Fault model of the 2020 Tingri earthquake and associated 3D Coulomb stress changes model. (a1–a3) Descending track coseismic surface displacements-observed, modeled, and residual fields. (a4–a6) Ascending track coseismic surface displacements-observed, modeled, and residual fields. The red line denotes the seismic fault ruptured in 2020. (b) Two-dimensional slip distribution fault model. (c) Coulomb stress change distribution on the 2025 Tingri earthquake fault planes induced by the 2020 Tingri earthquake. The color version of this figure is available only in the electronic edition.

Normal faulting across southern Tibet arises from the interaction between compressional and extensional forces generated by the ongoing India–Eurasia collision, which produces a broad zone of tectonic stress and crustal deformation. During the incipient rift stage, the thick, ductile lower crust accommodated widespread faulting. As lithospheric thinning progressed, mantle upwelling and partial melting reduced lower-crustal viscosity, promoting brittle behavior and localized deformation (Bischoff and Flesch, 2018). Therefore, the rheological state of the lower crust plays a key role in fault initiation and slip localization. Laboratory experiments from the Baikal Rift (Corti *et al.*, 2011) demonstrate that rift asymmetry can arise from lateral variations in lithospheric strength, a process also applicable to southern Tibet. Geophysical imaging supports this interpretation: magnetotelluric and seismic studies have identified a low-velocity zone beneath southern Tibet, with its upper boundary at 15–20 km,

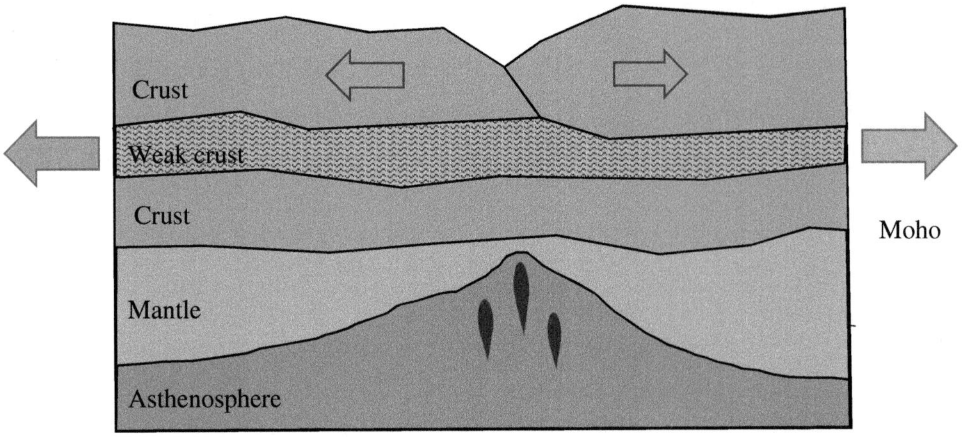

Figure 6. Cartoon illustration of rift formation model, which was revised according to Li *et al.* (2024), and shows the process of Xainza-Dinggye fault (XDF) formation. The formation of the rift valley occurs under a weak middle crust, resulting in a solid upper crust, and after the rift, the magma primarily moves vertically upward along the rift. The color version of this figure is available only in the electronic edition.

interpreted as partially molten lower crust (Brown *et al.*, 1996; Hetényi *et al.*, 2011). These findings suggest that the 2025 seismogenic fault evolved through an asymmetric fracturing process driven by rheological contrasts and mechanical heterogeneity associated with partial melt zone.

The XDF lies within the southern XDR, where the partially molten layer exhibits low viscosity relative to the overlying brittle upper crust. This rheological contrast may be a key factor in surface subsidence and crustal extension across the plateau. However, due to the limited melt fraction, crustal flow remains inhibited (Li *et al.*, 2024). Under the combined influence of north–south compression and gravitational potential energy, east–west extension induces elastic stretching of the weak middle crust, whereas the brittle upper crust fractures and forms normal faults (Williams and Wadge, 1998; Segall, 2010). At depth, tearing of the subducting Indian plate may facilitate magma upwelling, promoting overall crustal extension and the development of rift basins (Fig. 6). The 2025 Tingri earthquake nucleated above the low-velocity anomaly identified by Hetényi *et al.* (2011), implying that partial melt within the upper crust weakened the lithosphere and enabled asthenospheric material intrusion along pre-existing weak zones. This process, under gravitational equilibrium, induces upper-crustal subsidence and localized deformation. Taken together, these results suggest that as extensional stress and repeated seismic cycles continue, the intervening blocks between the immature fault segments will gradually subside, eventually developing into a mature rift system. The Y-shaped fault structure thus represents an evolving, immature configuration, prone to stress concentration and posing a heightened seismic hazard in southern Tibet.

The 2025 Tingri earthquake exhibits a rupture mechanism and strike orientation consistent with those of the 2020 M_w 5.7 event, indicating that both occurred within the same fault system. This relationship underscores the complex stress regime operating in southern Tibet and exposes limitations in current seismic risk mitigation strategies. Field investigations in the sedimentary zone near Dengmo Lake documented sand liquefaction, sand venting, and soft-soil subsidence associated with the earthquake (Xu *et al.*, 2025). These secondary effects highlight the vulnerability of unconsolidated deposits in the region to strong ground motion. To reduce future seismic risk, we recommend enhanced long-term monitoring of active fault systems and the establishment of a sustained InSAR-based deformation observation network, enabling continuous assessment of crustal activity and early identification of zones of accelerating strain accumulation.

Conclusions

The coseismic deformation fields of the 2025 M_w 7.1 Tingri earthquake were derived from ascending and descending Sentinel-1A SAR data using InSAR and POT techniques. By integrating surface-rupture observations, multitrack deformation fields, and field-survey constraints, we performed a joint inversion to obtain the source-slip model of the event. The maximum LoS displacement reached approximately −1.37 m, whereas POT results revealed the dominant east–west horizontal motion. The principal rupture zone, trending north–south, extends for about 56 km, and a secondary fault, approximately 30 km long, was also identified consistent with field evidence. The source rupture model indicates dominantly normal faulting, releasing a geodetic moment tensor of 6.36×10^{19} N · m, corresponding to M_w 7.1. Historical earthquakes in the same region exhibit comparable rupture mechanisms, reflecting a persistent east–west extensional stress regime in southern Tibet. Both the slip model and the aftershock distribution reveal that the eastern and western faults form an asymmetric Y-shaped structure with grabenlike geometry. The earthquake nucleated near the intersection of this Y-shaped system, a stress-concentrated zone that serves as a preferred site for rupture initiation. The graben system will persist and continue to influence future regional deformation and seismicity. Coulomb stress modeling further indicates that the 2020 M_w 5.7 Tingri earthquake imparted a positive stress load on the 2025 rupture plane, likely facilitating its failure. These results underscore the need for long-term geodetic monitoring and InSAR-based deformation surveillance to better assess the ongoing seismic hazard in this region.

Data and Resources

The Sentinel-1A Synthetic Aperture Radar (SAR) data are owned by the European Space Agency (ESA) and delivered by the Alaska Satellite Facility (ASF) service. All the figures were plotted with the Generic Mapping Tools (GMT; https://www.soest.hawaii.edu/gmt). The Global Centroid Moment Tensor (Global CMT) catalog search is available at https://www.globalcmt.org/CMTsearch.html. The generic atmospheric correction online service (GACOS) for Interferometric Synthetic Aperture Radar (InSAR) is available at http://www.gacos.net/. The 2005 M_w 7.1 Southern Tibetan Plateau earthquake is available at https://earthquake.usgs.gov/earthquakes/eventpage/us6000pi9w/moment-tensor. All websites were last accessed in September 2025. The supplemental material for this article includes additional figures and tables that provide supporting information for the main article, including the scatter plots and histograms of the nonlinear inversion results, the trade-off curve between data misfit and model roughness, the fault parameters obtained from the nonlinear source inversion, and checkerboard test results for the slip model resolution.

Declaration of Competing Interests

The authors acknowledge that there are no conflicts of interest recorded.

Acknowledgments

The authors are extremely grateful to Editor-in-Chief Allison Bent, Jeremy Maurer, and anonymous reviewers for their constructive comments. This work is supported by the Special Fund of the Institute of Geophysics, China Earthquake Administration, Grant Number DQJB225Y01.

References

Armijo, R., P. Tapponnier, J. L. Mercier, and T. L. Han (1986). Quaternary extension in Southern Tibet: Field observations and tectonic implications, *J. Geophys. Res.* **91,** no. B14, 13,803–13,872, doi: 10.1029/JB091iB14p13803.

Bischoff, S. H., and L. M. Flesch (2018). Normal faulting and viscous buckling in the Tibetan Plateau induced by a weak lower crust, *Nat. Commun.* **9,** no. 1, doi: 10.1038/s41467-018-07312-9.

Brown, L. D., W. J. Zhao, D. K. Nelson, M. Hauck, D. Alsdorf, A. Ross, M. Cogan, M. Clark, X. W. Liu, and J. K. Che (1996). Bright spots, structure, and magmatism in southern Tibet from INDEPTH seismic reflection profiling, *Science* **274,** no. 5293, 1688–1690, doi: 10.1126/science.274.5293.1688.

Brune, S., F. Kolawole, J.-A. Olive, D. S. Stamps, W. R. Buck, S. J. H. Buiter, T. Furman, and D. J. J. Shillington (2023). Geodynamics of continental rift initiation and evolution, *Nat. Rev. Earth Environ.* **4,** no. 4, 235–253, doi: 10.1038/s43017-023-00391-3.

Chen, C. W., and H. A. Zebker (2002). Phase unwrapping for large SAR interferograms: Statistical segmentation and generalized network models, *IEEE Trans. Geosci. Remote Sens.* **40,** no. 8, 1709–1719, doi: 10.1109/tgrs.2002.802453.

Chen, K., T. Yang, Y. Wang, X. Guo, Z. Zhang, X. Zhang, and R. Liu (2025). Quick output parameters related to the 7 January 2025 M6.8 earthquake in Dingri County, Tibet, *Prog. Earthq. Sci.* **55,** no. 3, 164–171 (in Chinese).

Chevalier, M. L., Z. Q. Fang, S. Q. Chen, J. W. Pan, H. B. Li, K. G. Wu, F. C. Liu, J. Y. Wang, and L. Ding (2025). Extension rate variations across the South Tibetan rifts-New data from the northern Xainza-Dinggye Graben, *Tectonophysics* **910,** no. 230824, doi: 10.1016/j.tecto.2025.230824.

Chevalier, M. L., P. Tapponnier, J. van der Woerd, P. H. Leloup, S. Wang, J. Pan, M. Bai, E. Kali, X. Liu, and H. Li (2020). Late quaternary extension rates across the Northern Half of the Yadong-Gulu Rift: Implication for east-west extension in Southern Tibet, *J. Geophys. Res.* **125,** no. 7, doi: 10.1029/2019JB019106.

Corti, G., E. Calignano, C. Petit, and F. Sani (2011). Controls of lithospheric structure and plate kinematics on rift architecture and evolution: An experimental modeling of the Baikal rift, *Tectonics* **30,** doi: 10.1029/2011tc002871.

Dal Luca, L., G. Hetenyi, J. Hubbard, and L. Bollinger (2021). Building the Himalaya from tectonic to earthquake scales, *Nat. Rev. Earth Environ.* **2,** no. 4, 251–268, doi: 10.1038/s43017-021-00143-1.

Daout, S., H. Sudhaus, T. Kausch, A. Steinberg, and B. Dini (2019). Interseismic and postseismic shallow creep of the North Qaidam thrust faults detected with a multitemporal InSAR analysis, *J. Geophys. Res.* **124,** no. 7, 7259–7279, doi: 10.1029/2019JB017692.

Deng, Q. D., P. Z. Zhang, Y. K. Ran, X. P. Yang, W. Min, and Q. Z. Chu (2003). Basic characteristics of active tectonics of China, *Sci. China Earth Sci.* **46,** no. 4, 356–372.

Farr, T. G., P. A. Rosen, E. Caro, R. Crippen, R. Duren, S. Hensley, M. Kobrick, M. Paller, E. Rodriguez, L. Roth, *et al.* (2007). The shuttle radar topography mission, *Rev. Geophys.* **45,** no. 2, doi: 10.1029/2005RG000183.

Freed, A. M. (2005). Earthquake triggering by static, dynamic, and postseismic stress transfer, *Annu. Rev. Earth Planet. Sci.* **33,** 335–367, doi: 10.1146/annurev.earth.33.092203.122505.

Funning, G. J. (2005). Source parameters of large shallow earthquakes in the Alpine-Himalayan belt from InSAR and waveform modelling, *Ph.D. thesis*, University of Oxford.

Gao, Y., Z. Wu, S. Han, and T. Tian (2025). Late Quaternary throw rate of the seismogenic fault (Dengmocuo fault) of the 2025 M_s 6.8 Dingri earthquake in Shigatse, *J. Seismol. Geol.* **47,** no. 3 (in Chinese).

Goldstein, R. M., and C. L. Werner (1998). Radar interferogram filtering for geophysical applications, *Geophys. Res. Lett.* **25,** 4035–4038.

Harris, R. A. (1998). Introduction to special section: Stress triggers, stress shadows, and implications for seismic hazard, *J. Geophys. Res.* **103,** no. B10, 24,347–24,358, doi: 10.1029/98JB01576.

Hetényi, G., J. Vergne, L. Bollinger, and R. Cattin (2011). Discontinuous low-velocity Zonesin southern Tibet question the viability of the channel flow model, *Geol. Soc.* **353,** no. 1, 99–108, doi: 10.1144/SP353.6.

Hu, J., J. Liu, Z. Li, J. Zhu, L. Wu, Q. Sun, and W. Wu (2021). Estimating three-dimensional coseismic deformations with the SM-VCE method based on heterogeneous SAR observations: Selection of homogeneous points and analysis of observation combinations, *Remote Sens. Environ.* **255,** doi: 10.1016/j.rse.2021.112298.

Huang, T., Z. Wu, S. Han, Y. Gao, and W. Bai (2024). The basic characteristics of active faults in the region of Xigaze, Tibet and the assessment of potential earthquake disaster risks, *Prog. Earthq. Sci.* **54,** no. 10, 696–711, doi: 10.19987/j.dzkxjz.2024-003 (in Chinese).

Jónsson, S., H. Zebker, P. Segall, and F. Amelung (2002). Fault slip distribution of the 1999 M_w 7.1 Hector Mine, California, earthquake, estimated from satellite radar and GPS measurements, *Bull. Seismol. Soc. Am.* **92,** no. 4, 1377–1389, doi: 10.1785/0120000922.

Kali, E., P. H. Leloup, N. Arnaud, G. Maheo, D. Liu, E. Boutonnet, J. Van der Woerd, X. Liu, L.-Z. Jing, and H. Li (2010). Exhumation history of the deepest central Himalayan rocks, Ama Drime range: Key pressure-temperature-deformation-time constraints on orogenic models, *Tectonics* **29,** doi: 10.1029/2009tc002551.

Kapp, P., and J. H. Guynn (2004). Indian punch rifts Tibet, *Geology* **32,** no. 11, 993–996, doi: 10.1130/g20689.1.

Kapp, P., M. Taylor, D. Stockli, and L. Ding (2008). Development of active low-angle normal fault systems during orogenic collapse: Insight from Tibet, *Geology* **36,** no. 1, 7–10, doi: 10.1130/g24054a.1.

Lei, Y., A. Gardner, and P. Agram (2021). Autonomous repeat image feature tracking (autoRIFT) and its application for tracking ice displacement, *Remote Sens.* **13,** no. 4, doi: 10.3390/rs13040749.

Li, D., X. Tian, X. Liang, and S. Nie (2024). Different formation modes of the north-south-trending rifts in Southern Tibet: Implications from ambient noise tomography, *Geophys. Res. Lett.* **51,** no. 9, doi: 10.1029/2024gl108254.

Li, K., P. Tapponnier, X. W. Xu, J. J. Ren, S. G. Wang, and J. X. Zhao (2022). Holocene slip rate along the Beng Co fault and dextral strike-slip extrusion of central eastern Tibet, *Tectonics* **41,** no. 8, doi: 10.1029/2022tc007230.

Li, Y., Y. Wang, Y. Shao, H. Shi, and T. Wang (2025). Seismogenic characteristics of the 2025 Dingri M_s 6.8 earthquake: Insights from GNSS observations, *Earthq. Res. Adv.* **25,** no. 1, 1–16, doi: 10.1016/j.eqrea.2025.100375 (in Chinese).

Li, Z., J. Sun, Z. Ji, M. Gao, J. Xie, and Y. Zhao (2025). Rapid simulation of acceleration waveform at Everest Seismic Station of Tibet Tingri M_s 6.8 earthquake on January 7, 2025, *Earth Sci.* **50,** no. 2, 798–804, doi: 10.3799/dqkx.2025.009 (in Chinese).

Lindsey, E. O., R. Natsuaki, X. H. Xu, M. Shimada, M. Hashimoto, D. Melgar, and D. T. Sandwell (2015). Line-of-sight displacement from ALOS-2 interferometry: M_w 7.8 Gorkha Earthquake and M_w 7.3 aftershock, *Geophys. Res. Lett.* **42**, no. 16, 6655–6661, doi: 10.1002/2015gl065385.

Liu, F., J. Pan, H. Li, S. Yang, K. Wu, Q. Su, S. Zhang, L. Chevalier Marie, and H. Lu (2025). Co-seismic surface rupture of the 2025 M_w 7.1 Tingri earthquake and potential seismic risk in southern Tibetan Plateau, *Acta Geol. Sin.* **99,** no. 3, 685–703, doi: 10.19762/j.cnki.dizhixuebao.2025069 (in Chinese).

Massonnet, D., M. Rossi, C. Carmona, F. Adragna, G. Peltzer, K. Feigl, and T. Rabaute (1993). The displacement field of the Landers earthquake mapped by Radar interferometry, *Nature* **364,** no. 6433, 138–142, doi: 10.1038/364138a0.

Okada, Y. (1985). Surface deformation due to shear and tensile faults in a half-space, *Bull. Seismol. Soc. Am.* **75,** no. 4, 1135–1154.

Ou, Q., S. Daout, J. R. Weiss, L. Shen, M. Lazecky, T. J. Wright, and B. E. Parsons (2022). Large-scale interseismic strain mapping of the NE Tibetan Plateau from Sentinel-1 interferometry, *J. Geophys. Res.* **127,** no. 6, doi: 10.1029/2022JB024176.

Pu, W., and Y. Li (2023). Evaluating structural failure probability during aftershocks based on spatiotemporal simulation of the regional earthquake sequence, *Eng. Struct.* **275,** 115267, doi: 10.1016/j.engstruct.2022.115267.

Qiao, X., Z. Lu, S. Yan, H. Shi, M. Zhi, and D. Zhao (2025). The 2025 M_w 7.0 Dingri Earthquake: Conjugate normal faulting of a Graben structure in the Southern Xainza-Dinggye Rift, *Geophys. Res. Lett.* **52,** no. 12, doi: 10.1029/2025gl116154.

Sandwell, D., R. Mellors, X. Tong, M. Wei, and P. Wessel (2011). GMTSAR: An InSAR processing system based on generic mapping tools, *Technical Report*, Scripps Institution of Oceanography, La Jolla, California.

Savage, J. C., and R. O. Burford (1973). Geodetic determination of relative plate motion in central California, *J. Geophys. Res.* **78,** no. 5, 832–845, doi: 10.1029/JB078i005p00832.

Segall, P. (2010). *Earthquake and Volcano Deformation*, Princeton University Press, Princeton, New Jersey.

Shan, X., C. Qu, W. Gong, D. Zhao, Y. Zhang, G. Zhang, X. Song, Y. Liu, and G. Zhang (2017). Coseismic deformation field of the Jiuzhaigou 7.0 earthquake from Sentinel-1A InSAR data and fault slip inversion, *Chin. J. Geophys.* **60,** no. 12, 4527–4536, doi: 10.6038/cjg20171201 (in Chinese).

Shi, F., M. Liang, Q. Luo, J. Qiao, D. Zhang, X. Wang, W. Yi, J. Zhang, Y. Zhang, H. Zhang, *et al.* (2025). Seismogenic fault and coseismic surface deformation of the Dingri M_s 6. 8 earthquake in Tibet, China. *Seismol. Geol.* **47,** no. 1, 1–15, doi: 10.3969/j.issn.0253-4967.2025.01.001 (in Chinese).

Shi, Y., Y. Wang, and Y. Bian (2023). Coseismic source model of the February 2023 M_w 6.8 Tajikistan earthquake from Sentinel-1A InSAR observations and its associated earthquake hazard, *Remote Sens.* **15,** no. 12, doi: 10.3390/rs15123010.

Tapponnier, P., Z. Q. Xu, F. Roger, B. Meyer, N. Arnaud, G. Wittlinger, and J. S. Yang (2001). Geology-Oblique stepwise rise and growth of the Tibet plateau, *Science* **294,** no. 5547, 1671–1677, doi: 10.1126/science.105978.

Tian, T., and Z. Wu (2023). Recent prehistoric major earthquake event of Dingmucuo Normal fault in the southern segment of Xainza-Dinggye Rift and its seismicgeological significance, *Geol. Rev.* **69,** no. S1, 53–55, doi: 10.16509/j.georeview.2023.s1.020 (in Chinese).

Toda, S., R. S. Stein, V. Sevilgen, and J. Lin (2011). Coulomb 3.3 Graphic-rich deformation and stress-change software for earthquake, tectonic, and volcano research and teaching-user guide, *U.S. Geol. Surv. Open-File Rept. 2011-1060*, 63 pp.

Tong, X., Y. Wang, and S. Chen (2024). Coseismic deformation of the 2023 Türkiye earthquake doublet from Sentinel-1 InSAR and implications for earthquake hazard, *Seismol. Res. Lett.* **95,** no. 2A, 574–583, doi: 10.1785/0220230282.

Tong, X. P., D. Sandwell, K. Luttrell, B. Brooks, M. Bevis, M. Shimada, J. Foster, R. Smalley, H. Parra, J. C. B. Soto, *et al.* (2010). The 2010 Maule, Chile earthquake: Downdip rupture limit revealed by space geodesy, *Geophys. Res. Lett.* **37**, no. 24, doi: 10.1029/2010gl045805.

Wang, M., and Z.-K. Shen (2020). Present-day crustal deformation of continental china derived from GPS and its tectonic implications, *J. Geophys. Res.* **125,** no. 2, doi: 10.1029/2019jb018774.

Wang, N., Y. Li, W. Shen, W. Jiang, Q. Li, and Q. Jiao (2025). Source parameters and rapid simulation of strong ground motion of the M_s 6.8 earthquake on January 7,2025 in Dingri (Tibet, China) derived from InSAR observation, *Geomat. Inform. Sci. Wuhan Univ.* **50,** no. 2, 404–411, doi: 10.13203/j.whugis20250022 (in Chinese).

Wang, Y., S. Chen, and K. Chen (2021). Source model and tectonic Implications of the 2020 Dingri M_w 5.7 earthquake constrained by InSAR data, *Earthquake* **41,** no. 1, 116–128, doi: 10.12196/j.issn.1000-3274.2021.01.009 (in Chinese).

Wang, Y., W. Feng, and P. Zhang (2022). Present deformation of 90° intersecting conjugate faults and mechancal implication to regional tectonics: A case study of 2019 $M_w \geq 6.4$ Philippines earthquake sequence, *Seismol. Geol.* **44,** no. 2, 313–332, doi: 10.3969/j.issn.0253-4967.2022.02.003 (in Chinese).

Williams, C. A., and G. Wadge (1998). The effects of topography on magma chamber deformation models: Application to Mt Etna and radar interferometry, *Geophys. Res. Lett.* **25,** no. 10, 1549–1552, doi: 10.1029/98gl01136.

Wolff, R., R. Hetzel, K. Hoelzer, I. Dunkl, Q. Xu, A. A. Anczkiewicz, and Z. Li (2023). Rift propagation in south Tibet controlled by underthrusting of India: A case study of the Tangra Yumco graben (south Tibet), *J. Geol. Soc.* **180,** no. 2, doi: 10.1144/jgs2022-090.

Wright, T. J., B. Parsons, P. C. England, and E. J. Fielding (2004). InSAR observations of low slip rates on the major faults of western Tibet, *Science* **305,** no. 5681, 236–239, doi: 10.1126/science.1096388.

Wu, K. G., M. L. Chevalier, J. W. Pan, F. C. Liu, S. H. Yang, S. Q. Zhang, Q. Su, and H. B. Li (2025). Recurrence of large earthquakes along the southern Xainza-Dinggye rift and comparison with the 7 January 2025, M_w 7.1 Tingri earthquake, southern Tibet, *Tectonophysics* **910,** no. 230827, doi: 10.1016/j.tecto.2025.230827.

Xu, X. (2019). *Late Quaternary Activity and its Environmental Effects of the N-S Trend Kharta Fault in Xainza-Dinggye Rift, Southern Tibet*, Academic Press, Beijing, China (in Chinese).

Xu, X., D. T. Sandwell, L. A. Ward, C. W. D. Milliner, B. R. Smith-Konter, P. Fang, and Y. Bock (2020). Surface deformation associated with fractures near the 2019 Ridgecrest earthquake sequence, *Science* **370,** no. 6516, 605–608, doi: 10.1126/science.abd1690.

Xu, Y., G. Fu, Z. Liang, G. Hu, X. Zhou, F. Shi, and Y. Yao (2025). Preliminary study on the characteristics of landslides and soil liquefaction triggered by the Dingri M_s 6.8 earthquake on January 7, 2025, Southern Tibetan Plateau, *Earth Sci.* **50,** no. 5, 1813–1829, doi: 10.3799/dqkx.2025.043 (in Chinese).

Yang, J., M. Jin, B. Ye, Z. Li, and Q. Li (2025). Source rupture mechanism and stress changes to the adjacent area of January 7, 2025, M_s 6.8 Dingri earthquake, Tibet China, *Seismol. Geol.* **47,** no. 1, 36–48, doi: 10.3969/j.issn.0253-4967.2025.01.003 (in Chinese).

Yang, T., S. Wang, L. Fang, W. Wang, S. Li, G. Xu, and F. Tanng (2025). Analysis of earthquake sequence and seismogenic structure of the 2025 M_s 6.8 Dingri earthquake in Tibetan Plateau, *Earth Sci.* **50,** no. 2, 1–17, doi: 10.3799/dqkx.2025.033 (in Chinese).

Yang, Y., Q. Chen, Q. Xu, G. Liu, and J. Hu (2019). Source model and Coulomb stress change of the 2015 M_w 7.8 Gorkha earthquake determined from improved inversion of geodetic surface deformation observations, *J. Geodes.* **93,** no. 3, 333–351, doi: 10.1007/s00190-018-1164-9.

Yin, A., and T. M. Harrison (2000). Geologic evolution of the Himalayan-Tibetan orogen, *Annu. Rev. Earth Planet. Sci.* **28,** 211–280, doi: 10.1146/annurev.earth.28.1.211.

Yu, C., N. T. Penna, and Z. Li (2017). Generation of real-time mode high-resolution water vapor fields from GPS observations, *J. Geophys. Res.* **122,** no. 3, 2008–2025, doi: 10.1002/2016jd025753.

Yu, S., S. Zhang, J. Luo, Z. Li, and J. Ding (2025). The tectonic significance of the M_w 7.1 earthquake source model in Tibet in 2025 constrained by InSAR data, *Remote Sens.* **17,** no. 5, doi: 10.3390/rs17050936.

Zhang, G., Q. Deng, and P. Jiang (1980). The implication of conjugate faulting in the earthquake brewing and originating process, *Seismol. Geol.* **2,** no. 1, 19–26.

Zhang, P., Z. Shen, M. Wang, W. J. Gan, R. Bürgmann, and P. Molnar (2004). Continuous deformation of the Tibetan Plateau from global positioning system data, *Geology* **32,** no. 9, 809–812, doi: 10.1130/g20554.1.

Zhang, Y., R. Liu, Z. Wang, and Z. Li (2025). Determination of radiated energy and energy-moment ratio for the 2025 Xizang Dingri 6.8 magnitude earthquake, *Earthq Sci.* **38,** 1–11, doi: 10.1016/j.eqs.2025.02.002.

Zhang, Y., S. Wimpenny, L. Dal Zilio, and X. Shan (2024). Strain partitioning and fault kinematics in the Northern Qilian Shan (NE Tibet) determined from Bayesian inference of geodetic data, *Geophys. Res. Lett.* **51,** no. 9, doi: 10.1029/2023gl107324.

Zhu, Z., and H. Song (1999). *Tectonic Geology*, China University of Geosciences Press, Wuhan, China (in Chinese).

Ziegler, P. A., and S. Cloetingh (2004). Dynamic processes controlling evolution of rifted basins, *Earth Sci. Rev.* **64,** nos. 1/2, 1–50, doi: 10.1016/s0012-8252(03)00041-2.

Zubovich, A., S. Metzger, T. Schone, J. Kley, O. Mosienko, C. Zech, B. Moldobekov, and A. Shsarshebaev (2022). Cyclic fault slip under the magnifier: Co- and postseismic response of the Pamir front to the 2015 M_w 7.2 Sarez, Central Pamir, earthquake, *Tectonics* **41,** no. 9, doi: 10.1029/2022tc007213.

Manuscript received 4 September 2025
Published online 8 January 2026

Coseismic Displacement Characteristics near the Epicenter of the M_W 7.7 Myanmar Earthquake on 28 March 2025: Insights from Beijing-3 High-Resolution Satellite Imagery Analysis

OPEN ACCESS

Junjie Zou*[1], Honglin He[2], Zhigang Shao[1], Wenqiao Li[1], Jianhua Huang[3], and Lu Gao[4]

Abstract

On 28 March 2025, an M_W 7.7 earthquake struck the Sagaing fault (SF) in Myanmar, causing severe casualties and infrastructure damage. Surface ruptures induced by this seismic event are crucial for analyzing the source rupture process and assessing seismic hazards. In this study, we focused on interpreting coseismic displacement distribution and deformation characteristics near Mandalay using high-resolution submeter satellite imagery (Beijing-3). The results reveal that coseismic deformation near the epicenter is clearly divided into tectonic (directional, concentrated, and narrow) and nontectonic (nondirectional, diffuse, and wide) types, both requiring consideration in seismic fortification. This seismic event exhibits typical right-lateral strike-slip motion, with the range of right-lateral displacement values spanning 0.4–5.3 m, an average coseismic displacement of 2.3 m within 35 km of the earthquake epicenter. The earthquake was a multisegment cascading rupture, and displacement in the northern SF segment shows a "bow-shaped" distribution, possibly controlled by fault geometric segmentation. Based on the coseismic surface rupture characteristics and displacement distribution, combined with historical earthquake data and high slip rates, we emphasize that future seismic hazard assessments should focus on the fault segments with a long elapsed time at both the northern and southern termini of the SF. This study enhances the understanding of earthquake hazards in Myanmar and highlights the utility of high-resolution remote sensing image interpretation for coseismic displacement analysis and hazard assessment.

Cite this article as Zou, J., H. He, Z. Shao, W. Li, J. Huang, and L. Gao (2026). Coseismic Displacement Characteristics near the Epicenter of the M_W 7.7 Myanmar Earthquake on 28 March 2025: Insights from Beijing-3 High-Resolution Satellite Imagery Analysis, *Seismol. Res. Lett.* **97**, 1628–1642, doi: 10.1785/0220250397.

Supplemental Material

Introduction

The ongoing convergence between the Indian and Eurasian plates drives intense tectonic deformation along the Himalaya–Burma Arc, a seismically active belt recognized as a global hotspot for earthquake hazard research because of its complex plate interactions and high population density (Panda *et al.*, 2020). On 28 March 2025 at 14:20 UTC + 06:30, a catastrophic earthquake struck central Myanmar, marking one of the most destructive seismic events in the region's modern history. The China Earthquake Networks Center initially reported a surface-wave magnitude (M_s) of 7.9 with a focal depth of 30 km, locating the epicenter at 21.85° N, 95.95° E—merely 20 km northeast of Mandalay, Myanmar's second-largest city, and ~300 km from the China–Myanmar border (Xinhua News Agency, 2025). Subsequent waveform inversion by the U.S. Geological Survey (USGS) and the China Earthquake Administration refined the moment magnitude (M_w) to 7.7, revealing a >400-km-long coseismic surface rupture zone (China Daily, 2025; U.S. Geological Survey [USGS], 2025). Preliminary postdisaster assessments documented >5000 fatalities, and economic losses equivalent to ~70% of Myanmar's 2024 gross domestic product, underscoring the event's devastating societal impact (Xinhua News Agency, 2025).

This earthquake occurred within a tectonically complex setting: Myanmar lies at the triple junction of the Indian, Eurasian, and Sunda plates, where the obliquely subducting

1. Institute of Earthquake Forecasting, China Earthquake Administration, Beijing, China; 2. State Key Laboratory of Earthquake Dynamics and Forecasting, Institute of Geology, China Earthquake Administration, Beijing, China; 3. Guangzhou Urban Planning and Design Survey Research Institute Co., Ltd., Guangzhou, China; 4. School of Resources and Civil Engineering, Northeastern University, Shenyang, China

*Corresponding author: junjiezou_ucas@126.com

Indian plate drives both crustal shortening (20–30 mm/a) and strike-slip deformation across the eastern Himalayan syntaxis (Panda *et al.*, 2020; Wang *et al.*, 2014). The primary structural controller of seismicity in this region is the Sagaing fault (SF), a 1200-km-long, right-lateral strike-slip system extending from northern Myanmar's Kachin State to the Gulf of Martaban in the south. As a key component of the Indo-Sunda transform boundary, the fault accommodates ~70% of the relative motion between the Indian and Sunda plates, with geodetically measured slip rates of 18–22 mm/a.

The 2025 earthquake occurred in a region with a well-documented history of large earthquakes. Historical seismic records indicate that the SF has produced at least six great earthquakes (**M** ≥ 7.0), including the 1912 M_s 8.0 Pyay earthquake and the 1946 M_s 7.5 Pegu earthquake, with the 2025 event rupturing a segment that had remained seismically quiescent for more than seven decades. Critically, this segment was previously identified as a high-risk "seismic rupture gap" in Coulomb stress analyses by Xiong *et al.* (2017), who emphasized long-term strain accumulation and heightened rupture potential based on 110 yr of seismic cycle data (Xiong *et al.*, 2017).

The 28 March 2025 Myanmar earthquake occurred at the high-risk "seismic rupture gap" characterized by the low level of background seismic activity. Surface ruptures induced by major earthquakes can be direct evidence of active fault slip, enabling the delineation of critical fault attributes such as deep geometric structures, rupture propagation patterns, and displacement distributions (Klinger *et al.*, 2005; Liu-Zeng *et al.*, 2009, 2010, 2012; Antoine *et al.*, 2022; Chen *et al.*, 2022; Wesnousky, 2006, 2008; Xu *et al.*, 2006; Oskin *et al.*, 2012; Rockwell and Klinger, 2013). Furthermore, the spatial extent and displacement variability of surface ruptures also furnish foundational data for quantifying empirical relationships between moment magnitude and surface rupture parameters, estimating earthquake recurrence intervals, and inverting for long-term fault-slip rates (Wells and Coppersmith, 1994; Pan *et al.*, 2022). Consequently, the systematic study of surface ruptures from major earthquakes not only facilitates a deeper comprehension of fundamental processes such as earthquake rupture dynamics but also serves as a cornerstone for conducting robust regional seismic hazard assessments (Wesnousky, 2006; Liu *et al.*, 2015; Liu-Zeng *et al.*, 2024; Yu *et al.*, 2024).

Currently, research on the seismic surface ruptures of the SF is scarce. The rupture extents of most historical earthquakes along this fault are mainly inferred from magnitude-fault rupture length empirical formulas and tectonic landforms (Curray, 2005; Hirakawa and Maung Maung, 2011; Wang *et al.*, 2011, 2014). Because of the long time elapsed, only rough estimates of the rupture ranges can be made for these historical earthquakes, and it is difficult to obtain detailed coseismic displacement distributions, especially the distribution characteristics near the epicenter. After the 2025 M_w 7.7 Myanmar earthquake, the risk of potential future major earthquakes in the region has become the focus of attention for both the public and the scientific community. Meanwhile, this earthquake also provides a good opportunity for researchers to conduct research on the coseismic displacement distribution and surface rupture patterns of a large intracontinental strike-slip fault.

After the occurrence of the Myanmar earthquake, many scholars have conducted research on this major earthquake using methods such as geodetic measurements, seismology, and geophysical inversion (Li, Jónsson, *et al.*, 2025; Li, Shan, *et al.*, 2025; Liang *et al.*, 2025; Wei *et al.*, 2025; Xu *et al.*, 2025). Optical imagery, Interferometric Synthetic Aperture Radar data, and rupture simulations revealed, on a large spatial scale, the 472 km surface rupture of the 2025 M_w 7.7 Myanmar with an average offset of 3.7 m, bilateral initiation, subshear propagation on the north side and two-stage propagation on the south side, as reported by Li, Shan, *et al.* (2025). Satellite synthetic aperture radar observations combined with seismic waveform backprojection indicate that the Myanmar huge earthquake breached the seismic gap, extended 160 km beyond it, and achieved a total rupture length of 460 km (Li, Jónsson, *et al.*, 2025; Yao *et al.*, 2025). Similarly, using holistic geodetic and seismic techniques, the recent study resolved the 2025 M_w 7.8 Myanmar earthquake's rupture dynamics and fault-zone structure and suggested that the thick fault zone—aided by fault geometry and basin structure—enabled prolonged supershear propagation (Wei *et al.*, 2025). The aforementioned previously conducted studies primarily focused on large spatial scales, emphasizing the inversion of coseismic rupture processes and investigation of their mechanisms. In contrast, this study focuses on a more refined analysis of coseismic rupture characteristics and coseismic displacement distribution at the spatial scale of the epicentral area. Based on clear differentiation of coseismic tectonic from nontectonic deformation and examination of seismic hazards (e.g., infrastructure damage) from this major earthquake, this study aims to assess future seismic hazard assessment in the region.

The study conducted detailed interpretation and measurement of surface ruptures and their displacement magnitudes based on 0.3 m high-resolution satellite imagery (Beijing-3, BJ-3), with linear features such as roads, bridges, and field ridges as markers, near the epicenter of the 2025 M_w 7.7 Myanmar earthquake. We compared the research results with two types of data from previous studies: observations from on-fault investigations, and large-displacement field data obtained via the pixel offset tracking (POT) technique. On this basis, we aimed to quantitatively reveal three key characteristics in the vicinity of the epicenter: the spatial distribution of surface ruptures, the features of displacement distribution, and the style of coseismic surface deformations. Furthermore, we analyzed the relationship between coseismic displacement in the near-fault area and distributed deformation in the area far from the fault.

Finally, the relationship between the 2025 M_w 7.7 earthquake and key tectonic elements (including fault-slip rates, historical major earthquakes, and seismic rupture gaps), as well as the tectonic significance of this earthquake in the context of regional dynamic mechanisms were studied.

Regional Tectonic Background

The regional tectonics of Myanmar is dominated by the convergence of the Myanmar plate and the collision of the Indian plate, resulting in a complex tectonic setting characterized by strike-slip faulting, subduction, and crustal deformation (Gardiner *et al.*, 2016). Characterized by oblique rather than orthogonal collision, the Indian plate advances northward at ~50 mm/a, generating intense shear stress that is primarily dissipated through large-scale strike-slip fault systems across mainland Southeast Asia. Among this active tectonics, the SF emerges as the primary seismogenic feature in central Myanmar, accommodating a substantial portion of regional tectonic strain (Fig. 1a). The 2025 earthquake's epicenter, situated near the Meiktila segment's northern margin, confirms activation of this long-recognized gap. Its shallow focal depth (~10 km) aligns with the SF's typical seismogenic zone (10–15 km), ensuring efficient transmission of seismic energy to the surface and amplifying ground shaking intensity—a characteristic feature of destructive earthquakes along this fault that also contributed to transboundary tremors felt >1000 km away in Bangkok (China Daily, 2025; USGS, 2025).

The SF is a ~1200 to 1400-km-long north–south-trending Holocene active fault dominated by right-lateral strike-slip motion, with a long-term horizontal slip rate of 18–20 mm/a, accounting for nearly half of the total crustal motion in the region. This elevated slip rate classifies it among the world's most dynamically active intracontinental faults (Wang *et al.*, 2011). Structurally segmented into the Sagaing, Meiktila, Nay Pyi Taw, Pyu, and Bago segments, the fault's geometry exerts critical control over the spatial distribution of seismicity and strain accumulation. Historical records indicate the SF has produced multiple $M_w \geq 7.0$ events since the twentieth century, with the most recent major rupture being the 1946 M_w 7.5 earthquake—establishing a ~70 yr interseismic interval prior to the 2025 seismic event. A pivotal framework for interpreting the 2025 earthquake is the concept of "seismic rupture gaps"—fault segments locked beyond typical recurrence intervals while accumulating rupture-ready strain. Geodetic and paleoseismic investigations, including work by Xiong *et al.* (2017), identified the Meiktila segment (northern-central SF) as a prominent such gap, which had not experienced $M_w \geq 7.0$ activity for 113 yr prior to 2025 despite a ~160 yr recurrence interval (Wang *et al.*, 2011, 2014). This prolonged locking facilitated substantial Coulomb stress buildup, which reached rupture threshold levels following decades of strain accumulation driven by plate motion (USGS, 2025).

Data and Method

The original datasets used in this study were postearthquake high-resolution satellite remote sensing data (BJ-3) with a spatial resolution of 0.3 m, acquired from the China Centre for Resources Satellite Data and Application and the High-Resolution Remote Sensing Earthquake Industry Centre of the China Earthquake Administration (Fig. 1b). Prior to interpreting surface ruptures, the high-resolution satellite images were subjected to geometric correction, image registration, and image fusion processes. To characterize the spatial distribution of surface ruptures induced by the 2025 M_w 7.7 Myanmar earthquake, a visual interpretation approach was used. Specifically, typical linear surface features intersected by surface ruptures—including roads, field ridges, and railways—were identified and marked as key reference markers. The coseismic surface displacement magnitudes along these linear features were then measured systematically, enabling the derivation of the spatial pattern of coseismic surface displacements along the rupture zone within the epicentral region (tens of kilometers around Mandalay). The uncertainty in coseismic displacement measurement mainly stem from interpretation biases caused by limited image resolution and depends on the delineation of the location and strike of surface ruptures, as well as the interpretation accuracy of the morphology and displacement relationships of linear features (e.g., gullies, roads, and field ridges) on both sides of the fault (Ren *et al.*, 2016). The lower the resolution, the more difficult it is to accurately capture rupture detail. In practice, we select the edges of the most identifiable linear markers for repeated measurements to reduce biases in restoring the original morphology of markers and provide the uncertainty of each coseismic offset with a precision of one decimal place. For linear features with a certain width (e.g., roads), measurements were conducted on both sides of the features.

We identified regularly linear markers that had undergone right-lateral offset along the coseismic surface rupture. Based on the geometric characteristics of these linear markers, we vectorized and extended them to the surface rupture trace, thereby obtaining the right-lateral offset of the linear markers on both sides of the coseismic surface rupture. To validate the reliability of the satellite-derived results, the results of this study were compared with the findings from previously conducted postearthquake field surveys. Finally, a comprehensive analysis was performed to examine the characteristics of surface ruptures in the epicentral region. This analysis integrated multiple complementary datasets and findings, including previous paleoseismic research on the SF (Liang *et al.*, 2025; Wei *et al.*, 2025; Xu *et al.*, 2025), a precisely located aftershock catalog, and displacement field data obtained via the POT technique from previous studies (Reitman *et al.*, 2025).

Results

We interpreted a total of 79 coseismic displacement measurement points along the SF within 35 km of the earthquake

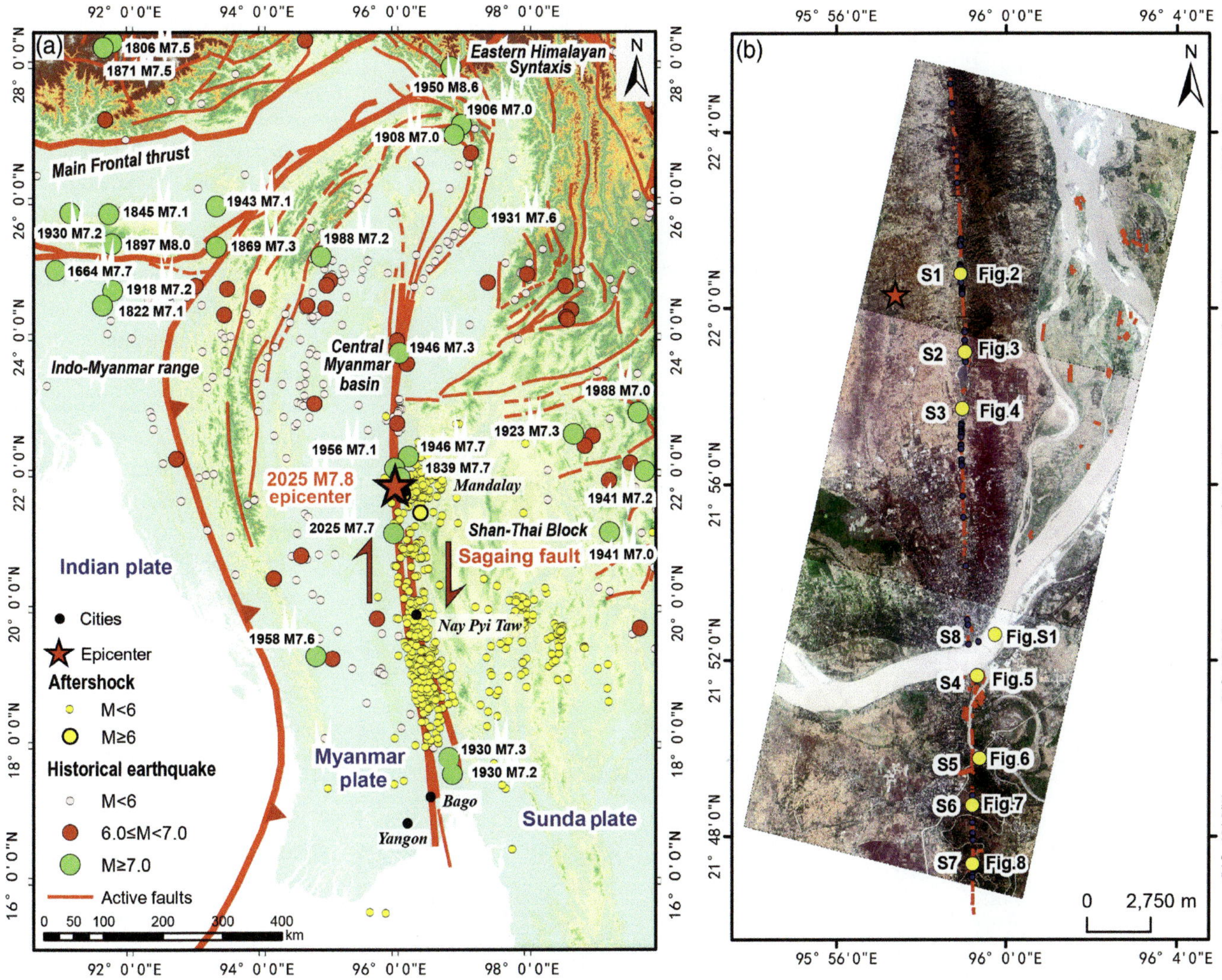

Figure 1. Tectonic map around Myanmar and distribution of study sites along the Sagaing fault (SF). (a) Fault geometry, kinematics, and historical earthquakes along the SF. The red five-pointed star denotes the 2025 M_w 7.7 Myanmar earthquake. Elevation data from the Shuttle Radar Topography Mission (SRTM) show active faults in the vicinity of Myanmar, which are indicated in red (Deng *et al.*, 2007). (b) Distribution of the target fault (SF), key study sites (S1–S8) represented by yellow dots, and displacement measurement points indicated by blue dots.

epicenter. To better characterize the surface rupture characteristics of the seismogenic fault, we selected four study sites each on the northern and southern banks of the Irrawaddy River for detailed analysis (Fig. 1b). Study site S1 is situated in 18 km north of the epicenter, with geographic coordinates: 22.01° N, 95.98° E. It lies within a rural landscape dominated by farmland and sparse vegetation. At study site S1, the fault exhibits a distinct surface rupture characterized by concentrated deformation, with a straight linear rupture trace that has displaced a series of field ridges (Fig. 2a). Surface ruptures associated with the seismogenic fault are clearly evident, and a field ridge offset of 1.8 ± 0.1 m was measured at this location using dashed yellow lines as measurement markers (Fig. 2b). Along the surface rupture trace, multiple field ridge offsets were observed, including 5.2 ± 0.2, 3.7 ± 0.1, and 2.5 ± 0.1 m (Fig. 2c), whereas field ridge offsets of 2.4 ± 0.1 and 3.4 ± 0.1 m were identified at another location of the rupture (Fig. 2d). In addition, field ridge offsets of 1.0 ± 0.1 and 2.4 ± 0.2 m were quantified within the rupture zone (Fig. 2e), and further field ridge offsets of 2.1 ± 0.2, 3.8 ± 0.2, and 4.6 ± 0.2 m were recorded along the extending surface rupture trace (Fig. 2f).

Study site S2 is located 15 km north of the epicenter, at geographic coordinates 21.98° N, 95.98° E. At this site, the surface rupture exhibits a high degree of linearity, with concentrated deformation, a narrow width, and no branching (Fig. 3a). Surface ruptures associated with the seismogenic fault are clearly evident, and a field ridge offset of 1.5 ± 0.1 m was measured here (Fig. 3b). Moving south along the surface rupture, two field ridge offsets (3.0 ± 0.2 and 3.4 ± 0.1 m) were observed (Fig. 3c), and offsets of 1.6 ± 0.1 and 2.1 ± 0.1 m were identified at another segment of the rupture (Fig. 3d). In addition, the surface rupture displaced multiple roads. Given that these

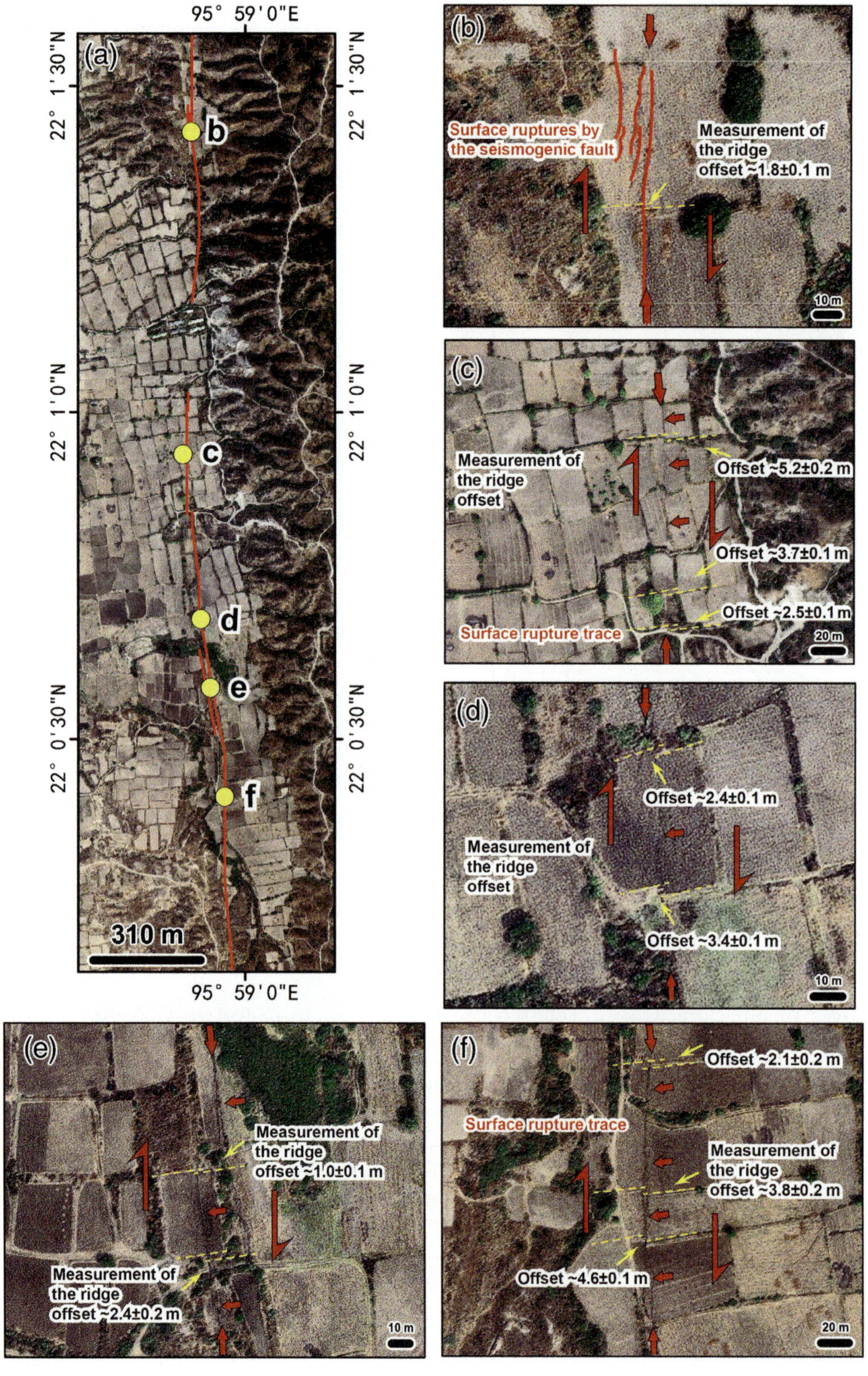

Figure 2. Interpretation of coseismic surface rupture and displacement characteristics at site S1. (a) Overview of the main surface rupture trace (red line) interpreted from Beijing-3 (BJ-3) satellite imagery, with yellow dots marking key sites where coseismic offsets were measured. (b–f) Detailed close-up views of surface ruptures, each showing seismogenic fault traces (red lines and arrows) and measured field ridge offsets.

roads have a certain width, displacement measurements were carried out on both sides of the roads, with coseismic offsets of 2.8 ± 0.1, 2.8 ± 0.2, and 3.8 ± 0.2 m, along the extending rupture trace (Fig. 3e,f).

Study site S3 is located 12 km north of the epicenter, at geographic coordinates 21.96° N, 95.98° E. Compared with the previous two study sites, the surface rupture trace is discontinuous, and no rupture was identifiable within Tamu Town or the reservoir (Fig. 4a). The surface rupture crosses the eastern side of the reservoir, exhibiting branching characteristics (Fig. 4b). As the surface rupture extends southward through Tamu Town, it displaced the road border by 1.4 ± 0.1 m on a mountain slope east of the town (Fig. 4c). South of Tamu Town, the coseismic surface rupture forms a slightly wide deformation zone with a width within 10 m, displacing four road borders from north to south with offsets of 1.3 ± 0.1, 2.2 ± 0.2, 1.4 ± 0.1, and 1.7 ± 0.1 m, respectively (Fig. 4d).

Overall, the aforementioned coseismic surface ruptures strike approximately north–south. In addition to these coseismic surface ruptures, the seismogenic fault exhibits nontectonic deformation at specific localities, such as study site S4 (21.86° N, 95.98° E). On the southern bank of the Irrawaddy River, an east–west-trending surface deformation zone, measuring ~400 m in length and 50 m in width, was identified; this zone formed as a consequence of ground shaking (Fig. 5a). At prominent riverbank promontories, directionless dense surface deformation zones and riverbank slope

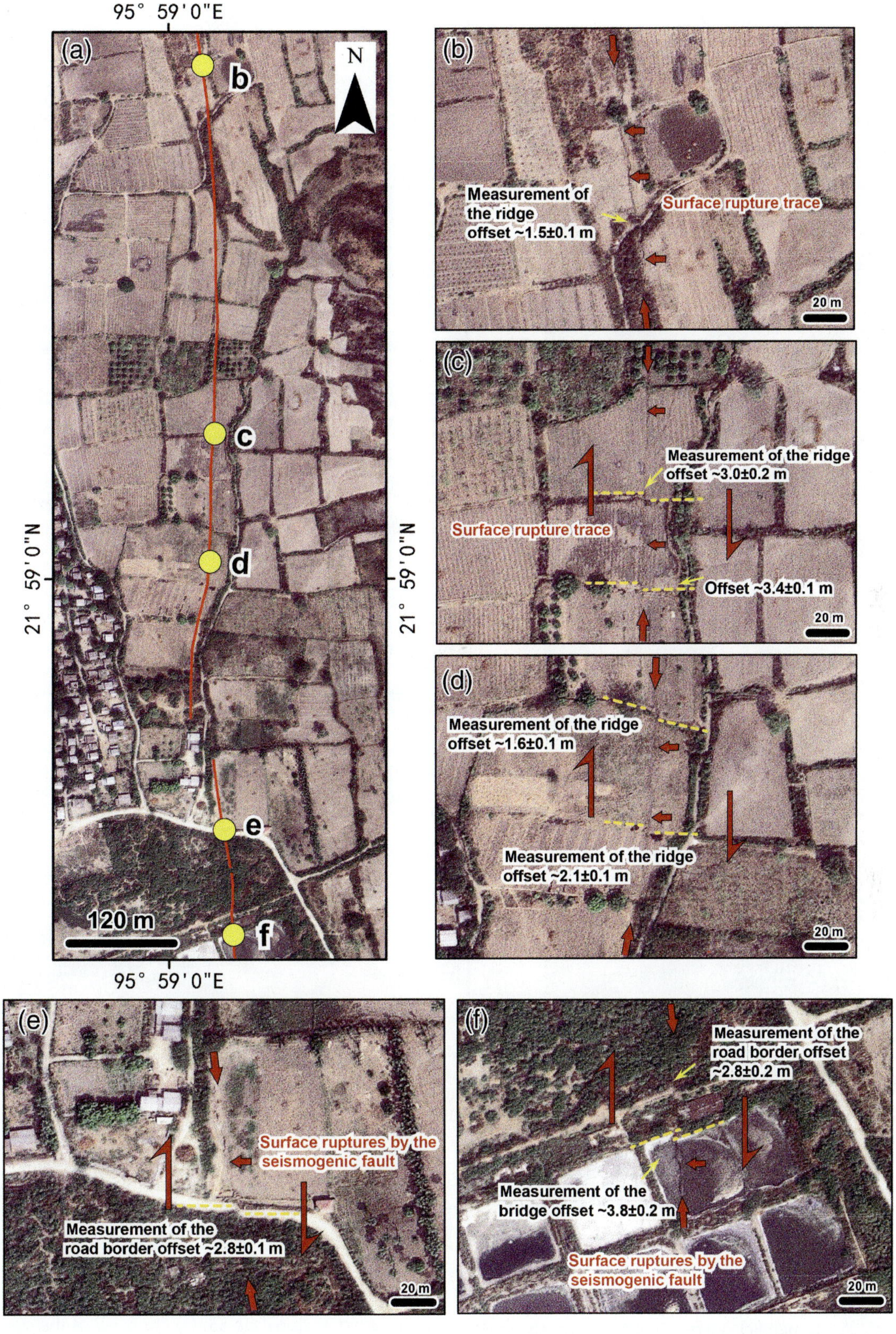

Figure 3. Interpretation of coseismic surface rupture and displacement characteristics at study site S2. (a) Overview of the main surface rupture trace (red line) interpreted from BJ-3 satellite imagery, with yellow dots marking key coseismic offset measurement points. (b–d) Detailed close-up views showing measured field ridge offsets. (e,f) Detailed close-up views of surface ruptures, showing measured road border offsets.

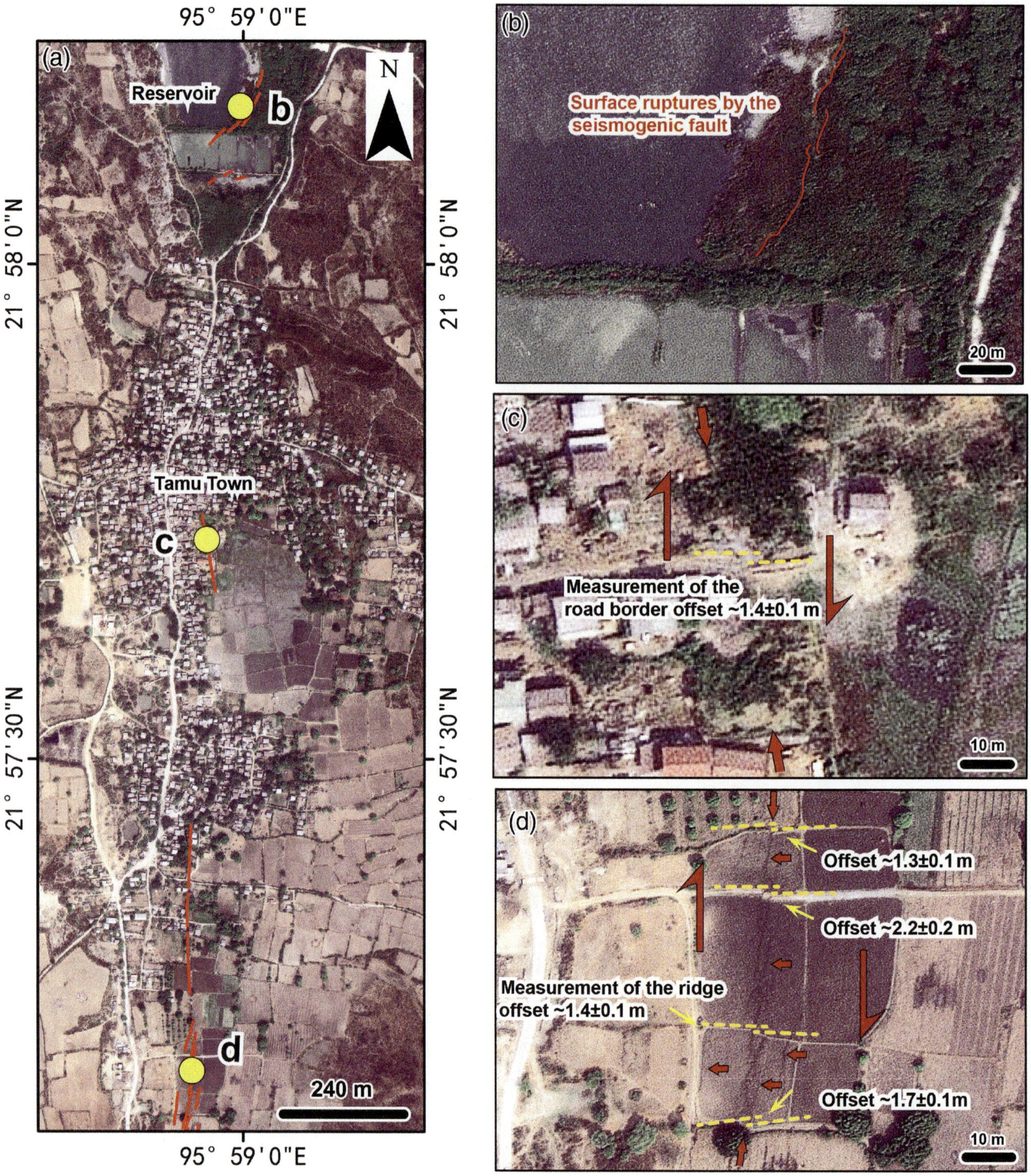

failures were recognized (Fig. 5b). Furthermore, near a damaged pagoda, several short, parallel surface cracks were observed, which, however, did not displace the adjacent roads or field ridges (Fig. 5c). Near a village, several short surface cracks were also identified; these cracks similarly failed to offset the marker features, with riverbank slope failures developed to their eastern side (Fig. 5d). These nontectonic deformations generally exhibit poor continuity as diffuse zones, with orientations inconsistent

Figure 4. Coseismic surface rupture geometry and displacement distribution at study site S3. (a) Overview of the surface rupture trace (red line) interpreted from high-resolution BJ-3 satellite imagery, with key coseismic displacement measurement points marked by yellow dots. (b) Detailed view of surface ruptures developed by the seismogenic fault near a dam. (c) Road border offset, with displacement direction indicated by red arrows. (d) Measured field ridge offsets indicated by dashed yellow lines.

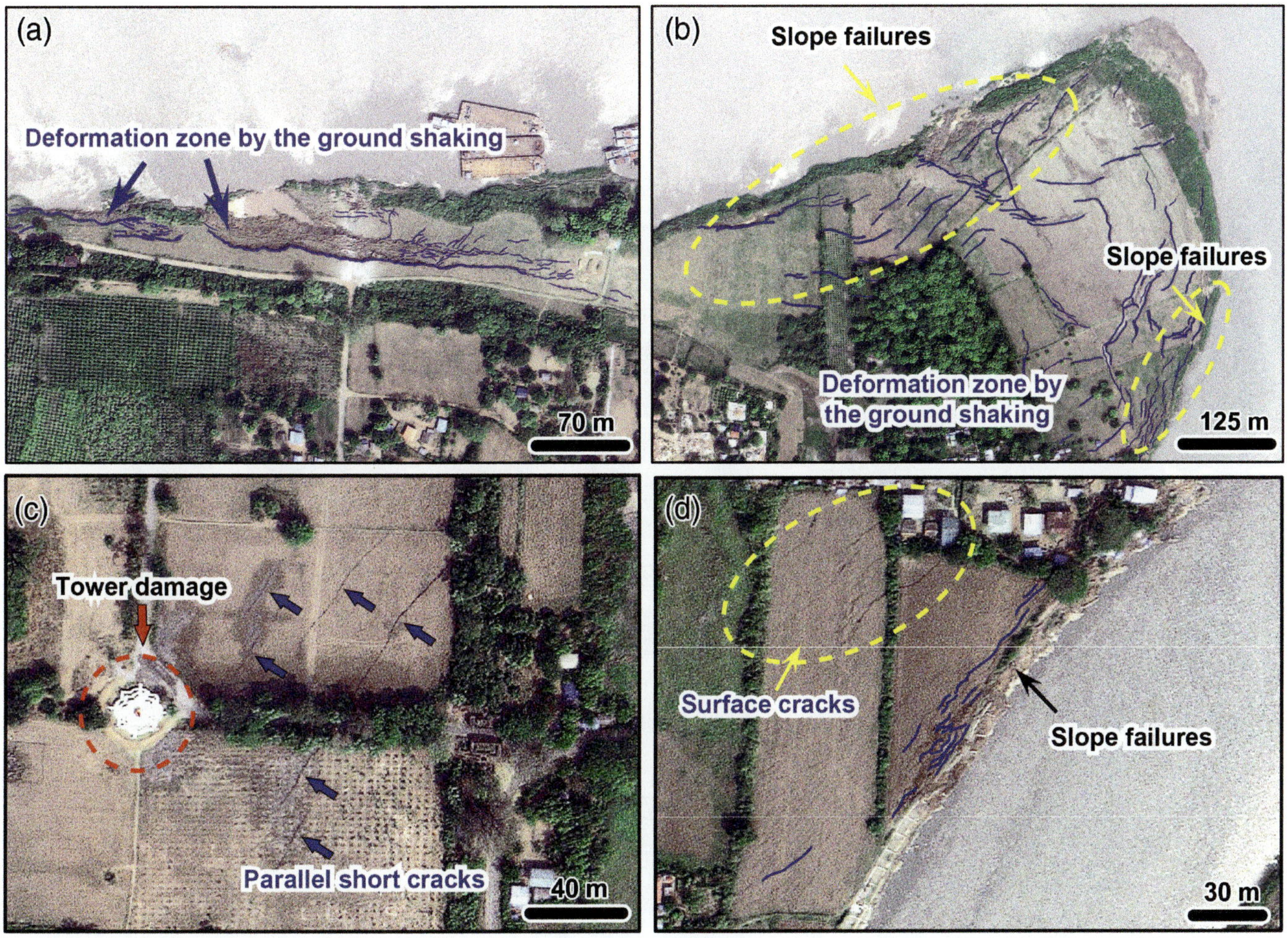

Figure 5. Nontectonic deformation features induced by the earthquake at study site S4. (a) Detailed view of a diffuse deformation zone developed by ground shaking, interpreted from high-resolution BJ-3 satellite imagery. (b) Detailed view of nondirectional dense surface deformation zones and riverbank slope failures. (c) Detailed view of short parallel surface cracks near a damaged pagoda. (d) Detailed view of dense surface cracks near a village, accompanied by riverbank slope failures.

with approximately north–south-trending fault and no displacement of marker features.

Study site S5 is located within the urban area of Kalaymyo Town on the southern bank of the Irrawaddy River. The area south of the town is covered by dense vegetation, with surface ruptures distributed discontinuously (Fig. 6a). Because of ground shaking, a bridge near the town was completely destroyed, and surface subsidence adjacent to the riverbank caused extensive building damage (Fig. 6b). Within the town, the surface ruptures exhibit a multibranch distribution with a northeast strike, forming a certain angle with the near north–south-trending main rupture zone. These ruptures show simple shear characteristics and offset a road by ~1.34 m (Fig. 6c). Several hundred meters away from the coseismic surface ruptures, ground shaking induced a diffuse deformation zone. This zone is 50–80 m wide, consisting of nearly dozens of parallel and discontinuous cracks, and caused damage to a road surface (Fig. 6d). Farther south, after the coseismic ruptures pass through a dense vegetation area, the near north–south-trending surface ruptures become distinct, showing a concentrated rupture pattern, and offset a road by ~2.62 m (Fig. 6e).

Study site S6 is located in a village near Kalaymyo Town, where the surface rupture trace generated by the seismogenic fault exhibits clear and continuous distribution, providing direct evidence of coseismic deformation (Fig. S1a). On the northern bank of an east–west-trending river, the fault displays prominent linear characteristics and has offset a field ridge by ~4.5 ± 0.1 m (Fig. S1b). Adjacent to the southern bank of the river, a large-scale diffuse deformation zone with east–west-trending discontinuous distribution has developed. Under the influence of ground shaking, this zone experienced slope instability and surface subsidence, leading to a large area of farmland sliding into the river (Fig. S1c). Farther south, the coseismic rupture traverses farmlands and roads, with its trace becoming increasingly distinct and presenting a concentrated rupture pattern (Fig. S1e). Notably, the fault shows obvious right-lateral strike-slip movement characteristics: it has offset a field ridge by 1.9 ± 0.1 m (Fig. S1d), a road by 1.9 ± 0.2 m (Fig. S1f), and two tracks by 1.3 ± 0.2 and 1.9 ± 0.2 m (Fig. S1g).

Figure 6. Coseismic offsets, nontectonic deformations, and earthquake-induced damages on the southern bank of the Irrawaddy River at study site S5. (a) Detailed view of the spatial distribution of study sites. (b–e) Along the surface rupture and deformation zones, interpreted from high-resolution BJ-3 satellite imagery. (b) Detailed view of surface subsidence, building collapse, and bridge damage, marked by dashed blue ellipses and rectangles. (c) Detailed view of coseismic surface ruptures developed by the seismogenic fault, with a measured road border offset shown in the inset. (d) Detailed view of road damage and a deformation zone induced by ground shaking. (e) Detailed view of a coseismic surface rupture with a measured road border offset.

At the southernmost end of the interpretation area in this study, a particularly typical coseismic surface rupture generated by the seismogenic fault was identified at study site S7. This surface rupture had a clear trace and a simple geometric structure and extended in a near north–south direction (Fig. S2a). When the coseismic surface rupture cut through a farmland, it offset a series of field ridges with measured offset values of 2.1 ± 0.1, 2.2 ± 0.2, 2.3 ± 0.1, 2.3 ± 0.1, 2.4 ± 0.2, and 2.6 ± 0.2 m (Fig. S2b). After traversing a small river, the surface rupture offset a road by 2.7 ± 0.2 m. In addition, northeast of the near north–south-trending main rupture zone, a diffuse deformation area was observed, consisting of randomly oriented cracks induced by ground shaking (Fig. S2c).

The aforementioned concentrated coseismic offsets and ground shaking–induced damage phenomena were concurrently observed near the Ava Bridge over the Irrawaddy River at study site S8 (Fig. S3a). On the northern bank of the river, a north–south-trending coseismic surface rupture zone offset a wide road. With the white centerline of the road as a reference marker, the measured offset was ~2.7 m (Fig. S3b). About 100 m east of the main rupture zone, a north-northeast-trending diffuse deformation area was identified, extending parallel to the riverbank (Fig. S3c). Meanwhile, ~500 m east of the main rupture zone, the well-known Ava Bridge sustained severe damage because of ground shaking (Fig. S3d), accompanied by a domino-style collapse (Fig. S3e).

Discussion

Coseismic tectonic and nontectonic deformation near the epicentral area

The characteristics of coseismic tectonic and nontectonic deformation near the epicenter are highly representative. Coseismic deformation of the SF shows distinct differences between tectonic and nontectonic types. Tectonic deformation is characterized by directionality and concentration: it is concentrated in a narrow zone of the main rupture, and its manifestations include offset linear features such as tracks, roads, and field ridges (e.g., Fig. 3). In remote sensing image interpretation, tectonic deformation appears as clear and continuous linear traces, trending near north–south with no chaotic textures.

In contrast, nontectonic deformation is characterized by diffuseness and nondirectionality, manifesting as wide diffuse deformation zones composed of dense discontinuous cracks, with widths typically ranging from tens to hundreds of meters (e.g., Fig. 5). These dense crack zones are induced by seismic shaking, inconsistent with the direction of the north–south-trending main rupture zone. They mostly develop in unconsolidated riverbank areas, often accompanied by surface subsidence, slope instability, and building damage. In remote sensing image interpretation, nontectonic deformation usually appears as chaotic crack clusters, forming a sharp contrast with the linear traces of tectonic deformation.

Considering the characteristics of coseismic deformation near the epicenter of the SF, infrastructure such as buildings and bridges should avoid the main rupture zone to prevent direct offset damage by the seismogenic fault during an earthquake. Meanwhile, infrastructure construction should also be avoided in areas such as riverbanks and unconsolidated soil layers to prevent damage in nontectonic deformation zones (e.g., surface subsidence and slope instability) induced by seismic shaking.

Along-fault distribution characteristics of coseismic offset near the epicenter

Early investigations of surface ruptures have observed high gradients in fault displacement along the strike across relatively short distances (Crone *et al.*, 1987). Subsequent studies have generally corroborated this finding, and it appears that substantial along-strike variations in on-fault displacement during large-scale rupture events are a common phenomenon (e.g., Zachariasen and Sieh, 1995; McGill and Rubin, 1999; Haeussler *et al.*, 2004; Gold *et al.*, 2013; Chen *et al.*, 2015). In this study, we similarly observed significant gradients in the along-strike lateral offset on the fault. Such offset gradients persist even within the 35 km range of the epicentral area. We measured 79 offset points on the fault within this 35 km range, with a maximum displacement value of 5.3 m, a minimum of 0.4 m, and an average of 2.3 m (Fig. 7a). The maximum offset on the fault is located at the epicenter, 15 km north of the Irrawaddy River. Centered on the microepicenter, offset values decrease significantly along the fault toward both the northern and southern directions. After reaching a low value at the Irrawaddy River, the coseismic offset in the southern direction shows an increasing trend (Fig. 7b).

This study reveals that the coseismic displacement distribution near the epicenter may be controlled by the geometric structure of the SF: north of the segment boundary, displacement values generally decay toward both sides from the epicenter—which serves as the location of the peak displacement value—showing a "bow-shaped" distribution (Fig. 7b). Previous studies, based on the geometric structure and activity of the fault and with the Irrawaddy River as the boundary, divided the fault into the Sagaing segment and the Meiktila segment (Wang *et al.*, 2014; Xu *et al.*, 2025). It is consistent with the understanding reflected by the geometric structure that the part of the fault north of the Irrawaddy River constitutes an independent fault segment. Such high displacement gradients may be related to shallow slip deficit, off-fault deformation, variations in the stress state associated with the prior earthquake, and even spatially variable slip at seismogenic depths (e.g., McGill and Rubin, 1999; Haeussler *et al.*, 2004), a conclusion that requires further discussion with additional data support.

Implications of coseismic offsets for magnitude-scaling relationships

The spatial distribution of surface rupture and displacement values can provide basic data support for characterizing the

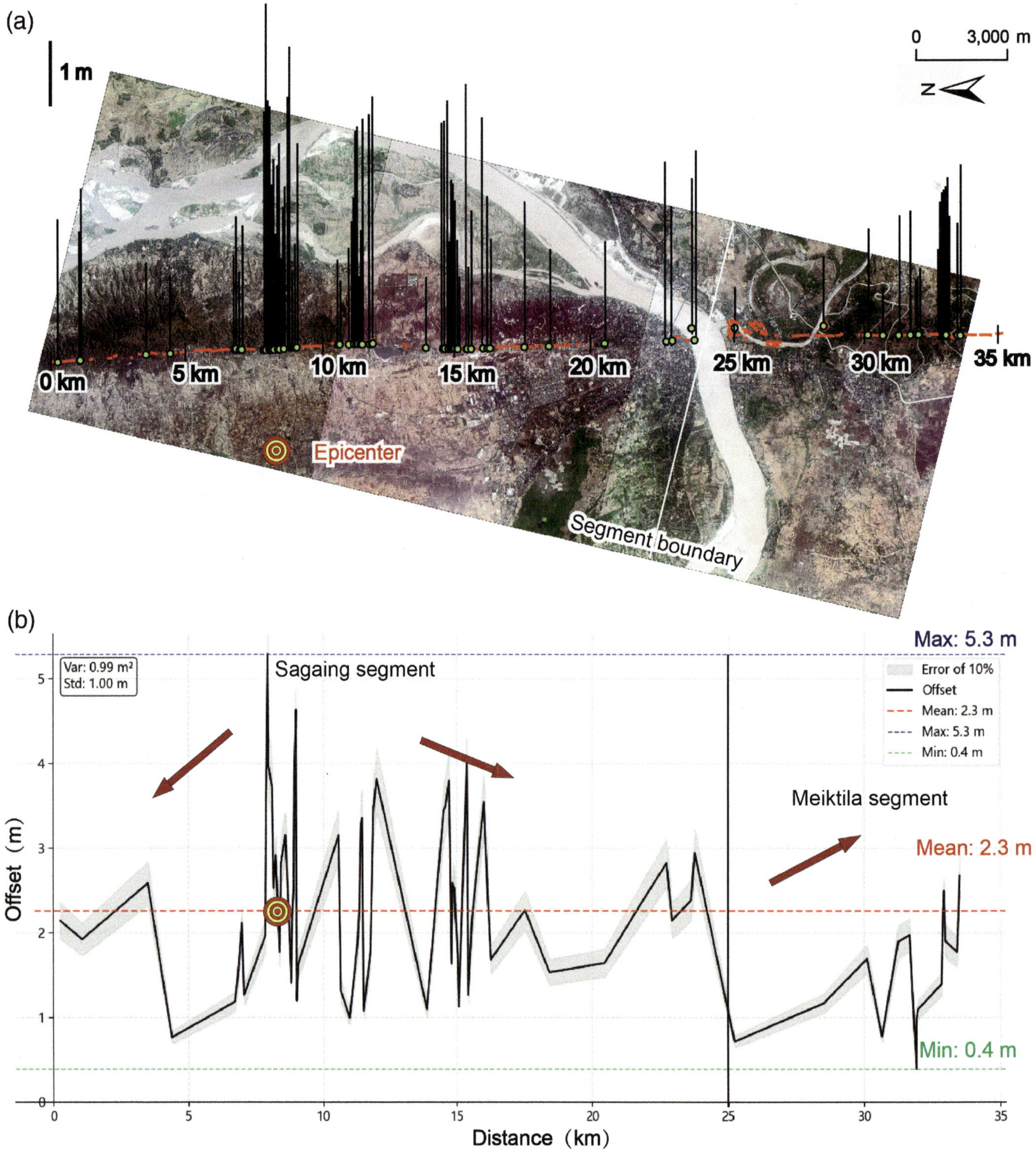

Figure 7. Distribution and statistical analysis of coseismic offsets. (a) Detailed view of the spatial distribution of measured offsets along the surface rupture trace-interpreted from high-resolution BJ-3 satellite imagery-with the epicenter marked by a red–yellow circle. (b) Detailed view of the statistical profile of offset variations with distance from the epicenter; the mean offset, maximum offset, and minimum offset are indicated by dashed red, blue, and green lines, respectively.

empirical relationships between moment magnitude (M_w) and surface rupture parameters. The length of surface rupture (L) and the displacement (D) on continental faults are two key parameters in the empirical relationship between various rupture parameters and magnitude (M; McCalpin, 1996). In this research, using the maximum coseismic displacement of 5.3 m and the average coseismic displacement of 2.3 m and applying the M–D empirical relationship for strike-slip faults (Wells and Coppersmith, 1994), we estimated the corresponding moment magnitudes to be M_w 7.4 in both cases, which is smaller than the instrumentally recorded M_w 7.7 (USGS, 2025). However, the result may only represent the rupture scenario within the epicentral area; accordingly, we need to take into account the whole rupture of the fault in a larger spatial scale. We compared our findings near the epicenter with the whole surface rupture results in other studies. Specifically, the maximum coseismic displacement of 5.5 m derived from the Sentinel satellite observation (Wei *et al.*, 2025) is in close agreement with our estimate of 5.3 m; by contrast, the whole-rupture average displacement of 3.7 m obtained via the POT technique (Li, Shan, *et al.*, 2025) is slightly higher than our epicentral measurement of 2.3 m. When using the maximum and average displacement values of the full surface rupture for calculations, the estimated magnitude falls within the range of M_w 7.4–7.6, generally consistent with the results obtained from epicentral vicinity data. In addition, we applied the *D–L* empirical relationship for strike-slip faults (Wells and Coppersmith, 1994) and used the maximum coseismic displacement and average coseismic displacement of the whole surface rupture to estimate the coseismic rupture length to be 250–280 km. These estimated lengths are much smaller than the rupture extent of >400 km obtained based on the POT technique, aftershock distribution and field investigations, which may be related to the fact that this earthquake belongs to a supershear multisegment cascading rupture (Liang *et al.*, 2025; Xu *et al.*, 2025). This also reminds us to pay attention to the applicability of traditional empirical statistical relationships to ultra-long-scale cascading ruptures.

Regional dynamic model and future seismic hazard assessment

The 2025 M_w 7.7 Myanmar earthquake represents the tectonic response of the SF to the convergence of the Indian and Eurasian plates. The driving forces controlling tectonic deformation in this region stem from three main sources: (1) the northward push of the Indian plate causes the southeastern extrusion of the Shan Plateau on the eastern block of the SF, (2) the oblique convergence of the Burma Arc leads to northeastern movement of the Indo-Burma ranges on the western block of the SF, and (3) the spreading of the Andaman Sea results in northward movement of the western block of the SF. The 1950 M 8 earthquake in the Eastern Syntaxis and the 2025 M_w 6.8 earthquake in Dingri County, Xigaze, Tibet both reflect the dynamic influence of the Indian plate, whereas a large earthquake in the Burma Arc in 1762 reflects the oblique compression of the Burma Arc (Fig. 8). In this Myanmar earthquake, investigating this dynamic issue can be effectively achieved by determining which of the eastern and western walls of the SF is the active or passive one. However, this requires support from kinematic data—specifically, identifying the absolute displacement magnitudes of the eastern and western blocks of the SF.

For the SF itself, identifying historical rupture gaps and fault segments with a long elapsed time (since their last earthquake) remains a robust method for determining future seismic hazard locations. At both the northern and southern ends (Sagaing and Bago) of the SF, there are fault segments with an elapsed time of nearly 100 yr (Fig. 8). Considering the high slip rate (18–20 mm/a) of the SF and the north–south-oriented coseismic Coulomb stress loading from this earthquake, the seismic hazard of these two segments (the Sagaing segment and its northern areas and the Bago segment and its southern areas) in the future merits attention.

Conclusion

Based on the interpretation of postearthquake high-resolution submeter satellite imagery (BJ-3), the coseismic displacement distribution and deformation characteristics in the epicentral area of large earthquakes can be rapidly and accurately obtained. The preliminary findings are as follows:

1. The 2025 M_w 7.7 Myanmar earthquake was a destructive event, with the SF identified as the seismogenic fault, exhibiting typical right-lateral strike-slip characteristics. Coseismic deformation can be clearly divided into two categories: tectonic and nontectonic deformation. Tectonic deformation is mainly manifested as seismic surface rupture zones that displaced linear ground features and geomorphic markers. In contrast, nontectonic deformation zones, triggered by seismic shaking, are wider and are usually composed of dense, short parallel cracks. Both deformation types need to be considered in seismic fortification.
2. The average coseismic displacement in the epicentral area is 2.3 m, with a peak value of 5.3 m located 15 km north of the Irrawaddy River. The seismogenic fault ruptured both the Sagaing segment and the Meiktila segment, representing a multisegment cascading rupture. Coseismic displacement in the Sagaing segment shows a typical "bow-shaped" distribution, with low-displacement values near the segment boundary. This indicates that the geometric segmentation of the SF may have a significant control on displacement distribution.
3. Comprehensive analysis combined with prior research reveals a mismatch between the earthquake's magnitude, coseismic displacement, and ultra-long rupture extent (>400 km), which deviates from the classical magnitude–displacement (*M–D*) and displacement–rupture length (*D–L*) relationships. This ultra-long rupture may be associated with multisegment cascading rupture.
4. From a regional geodynamic perspective, northward push of the Indian plate, oblique subduction of the Burma Arc, and spreading of the Andaman Sea may all contribute to stress loading on the SF. Integrating coseismic surface rupture characteristics, historical earthquake data, and the high slip rate, we emphasize that future seismic hazard assessments should

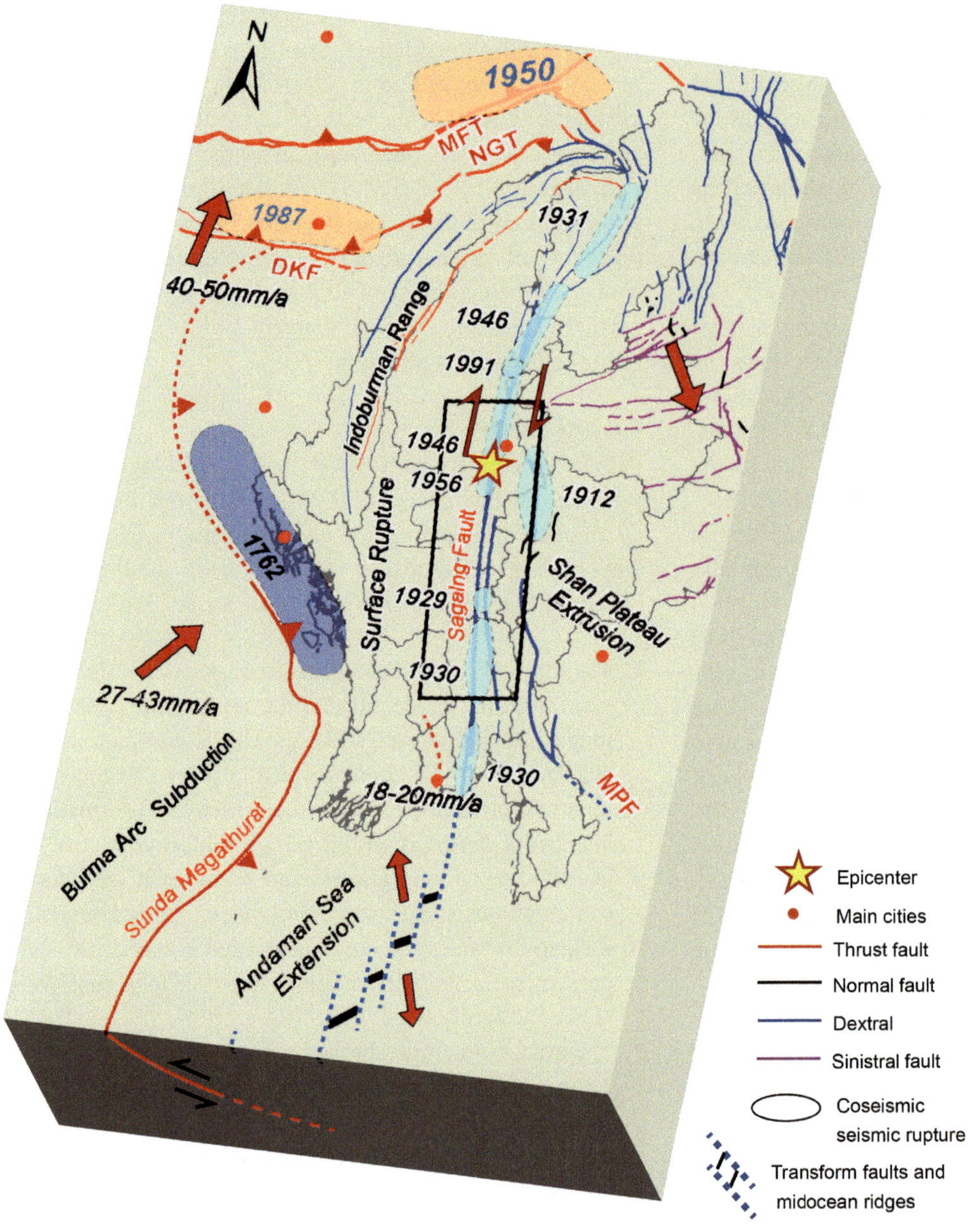

Figure 8. Diagram illustrating the regional seismogenic structure and dynamic model near the SF. Rupture zones of historical earthquakes are marked by blue shadows; the epicenter and rupture zone of the 2025 M_w 7.7 Myanmar earthquake by a yellow five-pointed star and a rectangular black box, respectively; and the direction of plate motion by red arrows. DKF, Dauki fault; MFT, Main Frontal thrust; MPF, Mae Ping fault; NGT, North Ganga thrust.

focus on the Sagaing and Bago segments at the termini of the SF.

Data and Resources

The seismic catalog is from U.S. Geological Survey (USGS) website (https://earthquake.usgs.gov/earthquakes/eventpage/us7000pn9s/executive, last accessed December 2025). The other data used in this article came from published sources listed in the references. The supplemental material includes three figures (Figs. S1–S3) that support the presentation in the main article. The high-resolution satellite images in this article are available via contact the corresponding author.

Declaration of Competing Interests

The authors acknowledge that there are no financial or personal relationships with other people or organizations that could inappropriately influence their work. This article has not been published or presented elsewhere in its entirety and is not under consideration by another journal.

Acknowledgments

This article is dedicated to commemorating. This research was supported by the National Science Foundation of China (Grant Numbers 42202255 and 42542206), the State Key Laboratory of Earthquake Dynamics (Grant Numbers LED2024B03 and LED2023B10), the Basic Research Fund from the Institute of Earthquake Forecasting, China Earthquake Administration (Grant Number CEAIEF20250207), the Active tectonic survey and data platform construction of the East Asian continental margin (Grant Number W-25-01), and the National Key Research and Development Program of China (Grant Numbers 2023YFC3012 2003-3 and 2023YFC30122001-2). The authors sincerely thank Adam Sproson for polishing the article. The authors are also grateful two reviewers, Guest Editor Marie-Luce Chevalier and Editor-in-Chief Allison Bent, for their constructive reviews and suggestions that greatly improved this article.

References

Antoine, S. L., Y. Klinger, A. Delorme, and R. D. Gold (2022). Off-fault deformation in regions of complex fault geometries: the 2013, Mw7.7, Baluchistan Rupture (Pakistan), *J. Geophys. Res.: Solid Earth* **127,** e2022JB024480, doi: 10.1029/2022JB024480.

Chen, G., Z. Li, X. Xu, H. Sun, G. Ha, P. Guo, P. Su, Z. Yuan, and T. Li (2022). Co-seismic surface deformation and late Quaternary accumulated displacement along the seismogenic fault of the 2021 Madoi M7.4 earthquake and their implications for regional tectonics, *Chin. J. Geophys.* **65,** 2984–3005 (in Chinese).

Chen, T., S. O. Akciz, K. W. Hudnut, D. Z. Zhang, and J. M. Stock (2015). Fault-slip distribution of the 1999 Mw 7.1 Hector Mine Earthquake, California, estimated from postearthquake airborne LiDAR data, *Bull. Seismol. Soc. Am.* **105,** no. 2a, 776–790.

China Daily (2025). Mandalay quake exposes hidden seismic risks, China Daily, available at https://www.chinadaily.com.cn/a/202504/09/WS67f5df7ba3104d9fd381e548.html (last accessed October 2025).

Crone, A. J., M. N. Machette, M. G. Bonilla, J. J. Lienkaemper, K. L. Pierce, W. E. Scott, and R. C. Bucknam (1987). Surface faulting accompanying the Borah Peak earthquake and segmentation of the lost river fault, central Idaho, *Bull. Seismol. Soc. Am.* **77,** nos. 739/770, NP731–NP732.

Curray, J. R. (2005). Tectonics and history of the Andaman Sea region, *J. Asian Earth Sci.* **25,** 187–232.

Deng, Q., Y. Ran, X. Yang, W. Min, and C. Qu (2007). *Map of Active Tectonics of China*, Seismology Press, Beijing, China (in Chinese).

Gardiner, N. J., L. J. Robb, C. K. Morley, M. P. Searle, P. A. Cawood, M. J. Whitehouse, C. L. Kirkland, N. M. Roberts, and T. A. Myint (2016). The tectonic and metallogenic framework of Myanmar: A Tethyan mineral system, *Ore Geol. Rev.* **79,** 26–45, doi: 10.1016/j.oregeorev.2016.04.024.

Gold, P. O., M. E. Oskin, A. J. Elliott, A. Hinojosa-Corona, M. H. Taylor, O. Kreylos, and E. Cowgill (2013). Coseismic slip variation assessed from terrestrial lidar scans of the El Mayor–Cucapah surface rupture, *Earth Planet. Sci. Lett.* **366,** 151–162.

Haeussler, P., D. P. Schwartz, T. E. Dawson, H. D. Stenner, J. J. Lienkaemper, B. Sherrod, F. R. Cinti, P. Montone, P. A. Craw, A. J. Crone, *et al.* (2004). Surface rupture and slip distribution of the Denal and Totschunda faults in the 3 November 2002 M 7.9 Earthquake, Alaska, *Bull. Seismol. Soc. Am.* **94,** S23–S52.

Hirakawa, N., and P. Maung Maung (2011). Two seismic gaps on the Sagaing Fault, Myanmar, derived from relocation of historical earthquakes since 1918, *Geophys. Res. Lett.* **38,** L01310, doi: 10.1029/2010GL046099.

Klinger, Y., X. Xu, P. Tapponnier, J. Van der Woerd, C. Lasserre, and G. King (2005). High-resolution satellite imagery mapping of the surface rupture and slip distribution of the Mw 7.8, 14 November 2001 Kokoxili earthquake, Kunlun Fault, Northern Xizang, China, *Bull. Seismol. Soc. Am.* **95,** 1970–1987.

Li, B., S. Jónsson, C. Suhendi, J. Liu, D. Li, A. Delorme, Y. Klinger, and P. M. Mai (2025). Seismic gap breached by the 2025 Mw 7.7 Mandalay (Myanmar) earthquake, *Nature Geosci.* **18,** 1287–1295.

Li, Y., X. Shan, C. Li, C. Huang, X. Wang, X. Xu, and H. Xiong (2025). Sustained supershear rupture during the 2025 Mandalay, Myanmar earthquake, *Commun. Earth Environ.* doi: 10.1038/s43247-025-02927-5.

Liang, P., Y. Xu, C. Hu, Q. Tian, L. Fang, A. Dou, R. Xiong, W. Wu, C. Xu, and F. Geng (2025). Surface rupture pattern and co-seismic displacement distribution of the 2025 Mw 7.7 Myanmar earthquake revealed by Chinese high-resolution satellite imagery, *Chin. Sci. Bull.* doi: 10.1360/CSB-2025-0672 (in Chinese).

Liu, J., C. Ji, J. Y. Zhang, P. Zhang, L. Zeng, Z. Li, and F. Wang (2015). Tectonic setting and general features of coseismic rupture of the 25 April, 2015 Mw7.8 Gorkha, Nepal earthquake, *Chin. Sci. Bull.* **60,** 2640–2655 (in Chinese).

Liu-Zeng, J., Z. Liu, X. Liu, C. Milliner, A. M. Rodriguez Padilla, S. Xu, J. P. Avouac, W. Yao, Y. Klinger, L. Han, *et al.* (2024). Fault orientation trumps fault maturity in controlling coseismic rupture characteristics of the 2021 Maduo Earthquake, *AGU Adv.* **5,** e2023AV001134, doi: 10.1029/2023AV001134.

Liu-Zeng, J., J. Sun, P. Wang, K. W. Hudnut, C. Ji, Z. Zhang, Q. Xu, and L. Wen (2012). Surface ruptures on the transverse Xiaoyudong fault: A significant segment boundary breached during the 2008 Wenchuan earthquake, China, *Tectonophysics* **580,** 218–241.

Liu-Zeng, J., L. Wen, J. Sun, Z. Zhang, G. Hu, X. Xing, L. Zeng, and Q. Xu (2010). Surficial slip and rupture geometry on the Beichuan Fault near Hongkou during the Mw 7.9 Wenchuan Earthquake, China, *Bull. Seismol. Soc. Am.* **100,** 2615–2650.

Liu-Zeng, J., Z. Zhang, L. Wen, P. Tapponnier, J. Sun, X. Xing, G. Hu, Q. Xu, L. Zeng, L. Ding, *et al.* (2009). Co-seismic ruptures of the 12 May 2008, Ms 8.0 Wenchuan earthquake, Sichuan: East–west crustal shortening on oblique, parallel thrusts along the eastern edge of Tibet, *Earth Planet. Sci. Lett.* **286,** 355–370.

McCalpin, J. (1996). *Paleoseismology*, Second Ed., Academic Press, San Diego, doi: 10.1016/S0074-6142(96)80070-2.

McGill, S. F., and C. M. Rubin (1999). Surficial slip distribution on the central Emerson fault during the June 28, 1992, Landers earthquake, California, *J. Geophys. Res.: Solid Earth* **104,** 4811–4833.

Oskin, M. E., J. R. Arrowsmith, A. H. Corona, A. J. Elliott, J. M. Fletcher, E. J. Fielding, P. O. Gold, J. J. G. Garcia, K. W. Hudnut, J. Liu-Zeng, *et al.* (2012). Near-field deformation from the El Mayor–Cucapah earthquake revealed by differential LIDAR, *Science* **335,** 702–705.

Pan, J., H. Li, M. L. Chevallier, P. Tapponnier, M. Bai, C. Li, F. Liu, D. Liu, K. Wu, P. Wang, *et al.* (2022). Co-seismic rupture of the 2021, M7.4 Maduo earthquake (northern Xizang): short-cutting of the Kunlun fault big bend, *Earth Planet. Sci. Lett.* **594,** 117703, doi: 10.1016/j.epsl.2022.117703.

Panda, D., B. Kundu, V. K. Gahalaut, and C. Rangin (2020). India-Sunda plate motion, crustal deformation, and seismic hazard in the Indo-Burmese Arc, *Tectonics* **39,** e2019TC006034, doi: 10.1029/2019TC006034.

Reitman, N. G., Y. Wang, Y. T. Kuo, C. E. Hanagan, A. E. Hatem, C. B. Duross, W. D. Barnhart, H. Z. Yin, R. Briggs, J. A. Jobe, *et al.* (2025). Remote surface rupture observations for the M7.7 2025 Mandalay, Burma (Myanmar) Earthquake, *U.S. Geol. Surv. Data Release*, doi: 10.5066/p1rymvwck.

Ren, Z., Z. Zhang, T. Chen, S. Yan, J. Yin, P. Zhang, W. Zheng, H. Zhang, and C. Li (2016). Clustering of offsets on the Haiyuan fault and their relationship to paleo earthquakes, *GSA Bull.* **128,** nos. 1/2, 3–18.

Rockwell, T. K., and Y. Klinger (2013). Surface rupture and slip distribution of the 1940 Imperial Valley earthquake, Imperial Fault, Southern California: implications for rupture segmentation and dynamics, *Bull. Seismol. Soc. Am.* **103,** 629–640.

U.S. Geological Survey (USGS) (2025). Earthquake recurrence patterns and forecasting challenges of major global active faults, *U.S. Geol. Surv. Rept.*, Washington, D.C.

Wang, Y., K. Sieh, T. Aung, S. Min, S. N. Khaing, and S. T. Tun (2011). Earthquakes and slip rate of the southern Sagaing Fault: Insights from an offset ancient fort wall, lower Burma (Myanmar), *Geophys. J. Int.* **185,** 49–64.

Wang, Y., K. Sieh, S. T. Tun, K. Y. Lai, and T. Myint (2014). Active tectonics and earthquake potential of the Myanmar region, *J. Geophys. Res.: Solid Earth* **119,** 3767–3822.

Wei, S., X. Wang, C. Li, H. Zeng, Z. Ma, Q. Shi, H. Chen, Y. Huang, M. Lyu, J. Liao, *et al.* (2025). Supershear Rupture sustained through a thick Fault Zone in the 2025 Mw 7.8 Mandalay Earthquake, *Science* **390,** no. 6772, 468–475.

Wells, D. L., and K. J. Coppersmith (1994). New empirical relationships among magnitude, rupture length, rupture width, rupture area, and surface displacement, *Bull. Seismol. Soc. Am.* **84,** 974–1002.

Wesnousky, S. G. (2006). Predicting the endpoints of earthquake ruptures, *Nature* **444,** 358–360.

Wesnousky, S. G. (2008). Displacement and geometrical characteristics of earthquake surface ruptures: issues and implications for seismic-hazard analysis and the process of earthquake rupture, *Bull. Seismol. Soc. Am.* **98,** 1609–1632.

Xinhua News Agency (2025). Why was the Myanmar earthquake so destructive? Xinhua News, available at https://www.news.cn/world/20250329/b4926bcf0bfe4d5789e342ca8c3d9d7f/c.html (last accessed October 2025).

Xiong, X., B. Shan, Y. Zhou, S. Wei, Y. Li, R. Wang, and Y. Zheng (2017). Coulomb stress transfer and accumulation on the Sagaing Fault, Myanmar, over the past 110 years and its implications for seismic hazard, *Geophys. Res. Lett.* **44,** no. 12, 6123–6131, doi: 10.1002/2017GL073452.

Xu, X., W. Kang, T. Wang, X. Zhang, Y. Liu, Y. Zhang, J. Zhao, K. Li, Q. Wang, J. Cheng, and J. Ren (2025). The Mw7.7 Myanmar earthquake: A continental longest surface-rupturing supershear cascading event, *Nat. Hazards* **2,** 73, doi: 10.1038/s44304-025-00125-z.

Xu, X., G. Yu, Y. Klinger, P. Tapponnier, and J. Van Der Woerd (2006). Reevaluation of surface rupture parameters and faulting segmentation of the 2001 Kunlunshan earthquake (Mw 7.8), northern Tibetan Plateau, China, *J. Geophys. Res.* **111,** 2004JB003488, doi: 10.1029/2004JB003488.

Yao, Q., C. Yu, and M. Zhou (2025). Bilateral supershear rupture of the 2025 Mw 7.7 Myanmar earthquake imaged by global P-wave and regional surface-wave back-projections, *Geophys. Res. Lett.* **52,** e2025GL116800, doi: 10.1029/2025GL116800.

Yu, J., Z. Ren, H. Zhang, C. Li, S. Wang, Z. Gong, X. Zhou, Y. Xu, P. Liang, and Z. Ma (2024). Surface rupture of the February 6, 2023 Mw7.5 Elbistan earthquake in Turkey, *Seismol. Geol.* **46,** 1263–1279 (in Chinese).

Zachariasen, J., and K. Sieh (1995). The transfer of slip between two en echelon strike-slip faults: A case study from the 1992 Landers earthquake, southern California, *J. Geophys. Res.: Solid Earth* **100,** 15,281–15,301.

Manuscript received 5 November 2025
Published online 17 March 2026

Spatiotemporal Evolution of Early Aftershocks Following the 2025 M_w 7.1 Dingri, Southern Tibet, Earthquake

Ming Zhi[1], Qianhe Li[2,3], Dongdong Yao*[3], Dun Wang[2], Fei Guo[1], and Li Sun[1]

Abstract

The spatial distribution and temporal evolution of early aftershocks provide valuable insights into understanding the stress transfer process following large mainshocks. Unfortunately, for poorly instrumented regions, due to the sparsity of seismic monitoring stations, and the difficulty in early aftershock detection, the early aftershock catalogs generally have relatively high magnitudes of completeness and large location uncertainties, which prevents accurate depiction of the spatiotemporal evolution of early aftershocks. The 2025 M_w 7.1 Dingri, southern Tibet, earthquake occurred in Dingri County, Rikaze City, the Tibet Autonomous region, China. Field investigations, together with finite-fault inversion and aftershock observations, suggest complex fault structure around the mainshock epicenter. We applied a matched-filter technique to detect early aftershocks following the Dingri earthquake. Using 3224 well-relocated aftershocks as templates, we scanned through continuous data of both permanent and temporary seismic stations within the first ~3 days. Compared to 1399 aftershocks and a magnitude of completeness ~2.5 reported by the China Earthquake Networks Center, 7179 aftershocks were detected, corresponding to fivefold more earthquakes. The newly detected catalog depicted the main fault geometry and highlighted the spatial variation of the early aftershock distribution.

Cite this article as Zhi, M., Q. Li, D. Yao, D. Wang, F. Guo, and L. Sun (2026). Spatiotemporal Evolution of Early Aftershocks Following the 2025 M_w 7.1 Dingri, Southern Tibet, Earthquake, *Seismol. Res. Lett.* **97**, 1643–1654, doi: 10.1785/0220250393.

Supplemental Material

Introduction

On 7 January 2025, an earthquake with moment magnitude (M_w) 7.1 (hereinafter the 2025 Dingri earthquake) struck the Tibet Autonomous Region, China, with its epicenter located at Dingri County (epicenter: 87.45° E, 28.50° N), according to the China Earthquake Networks Center (CENC). This catastrophic event claimed 126 lives and inflicted widespread structural collapse across the affected region (see Data and Resources). Field surveys documented a surface rupture extending approximately 36 km with complex along-strike rupture characteristics (Shao *et al.*, 2025). The observed maximum-seismic intensity reached IX based on the China Seismic intensity scale, roughly spanning an area of 411 km^2 (see Data and Resources).

The 2025 Dingri earthquake stands as the largest-magnitude seismically instrumented normal-faulting event in southern Tibet. Following the earthquake, numerous studies have been conducted to reveal the characteristics and mechanisms of the earthquake. Through field investigations, researchers systematically documented the geometry and displacement characteristics of surface ruptures (Shao *et al.*, 2025; Shi *et al.*, 2025). Based on focal mechanism and rupture process inversions, scholars further elucidated the rupture pattern and dynamic characteristics of the mainshock (Chen *et al.*, 2025; Xu *et al.*, 2025; Yang, Wang, *et al.*, 2025; Zhao *et al.*, 2025). Yang, Wen, *et al.* (2025) relocated aftershocks based on the CENC catalog to investigate the seismogenic structure. Wu *et al.* (2025) suggested that the seismogenic Dingmucuo fault (DMF) plays a significant role in the east–west extensional tectonics of southern Tibet. Yao *et al.* (2025) integrated the CENC catalog with temporary station data to obtain a high-precision aftershock catalog from 8 to 18 January, further revealing the spatial complexity of aftershock distribution along both strike and dip directions. Qiao *et al.* (2025) indicated that the inferred Interferometric Synthetic Aperture Radar (InSAR)-based slip model is consistent with relocated aftershocks, and Yue *et al.* (2025) proposed that the mechanisms of aftershock generation may vary along the strike of the fault system.

These aforementioned studies collectively indicate that the epicentral region features a complex fault system, including the

1. China Earthquake Networks Center, Beijing, China, https://orcid.org/0000-0002-5558-6809 (LS); 2. State Key Laboratory of Geological Processes and Mineral Resources, School of Earth Sciences, China University of Geosciences, Wuhan, China, https://orcid.org/0000-0002-9663-7895 (QL); https://orcid.org/0000-0001-6435-9168 (DW); 3. State Key Laboratory of Geological Processes and Mineral Resources, China University of Geosciences, Wuhan, China, https://orcid.org/0000-0002-2280-6617 (DY)

*Corresponding author: yaodongdong@cug.edu.cn

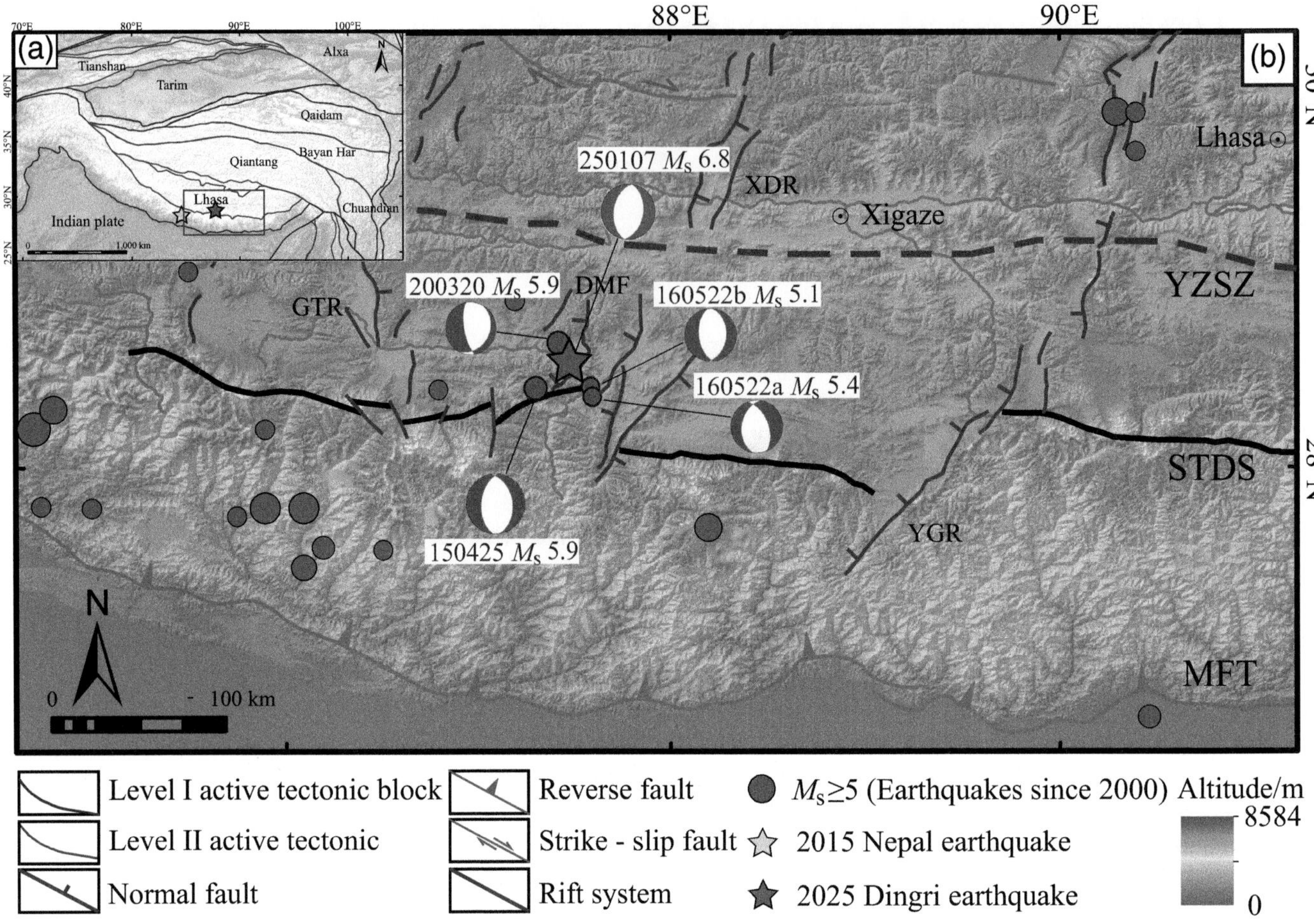

Figure 1. (a) Inset shows bigger tectonic context around the 2025 M_w 7.1 Dingri earthquake (red star). (b) Map showing the epicenter area. Background earthquakes were shown with blue circles (M_s > 5.0 since 2000), and focal solutions of four nearby earthquakes were plotted. DMF, Dingmucuo fault; GTR, Gangga-Tangra Yumco rift; MFT, Main Frontal thrust; STDS, South Tibet Detachment system fault; XDR, Xainza-Dingjie rift; YGR, Yadong–Gulu rift; YZSZ, Yarlung Zangbo suture zone. The color version of this figure is available only in the electronic edition.

approximately north–south-striking Xainza-Dingjie rift system (XDR) and the east–west-striking South Tibet Detachment system (STDS), which exhibit diverse strikes, dips, and slip mechanisms (Fig. 1). Although the mainshock rupture characteristic and underlying mechanism have been extensively investigated, simplified fault models have been used due to either limited resolvability of observation data or little available prior knowledge. Hence, a detailed imaging of the subsurface structure of the DMF and its activation pattern is still lacking.

The spatial distribution and temporal evolution of early aftershock sequences serve as a diagnostic tool for elucidating fault geometry and activation patterns (Felzer and Brodsky, 2006; Peng and Zhao, 2009; Wu *et al.*, 2017; Yao *et al.*, 2017; Zhu *et al.*, 2019). However, the epicentral region of this study is situated at an average elevation of approximately 5000 m and has sparse seismic station coverage. At the time of the mainshock, only two seismic stations (XZ.ZHF and XZ.ARZ, Fig. 2) were located within a 100 km radius, with the XZ.ZHF station experiencing postseismic data integrity issues. Although six stations were technically available within 200 km, four of these peripheral stations were positioned beyond 150 km from the epicenter (Fig. 2). This suboptimal station distribution imposed significant constraints on regional seismic monitoring capacity, resulting in a high detection threshold and large location uncertainties. In addition, the short recurrence intervals and overlapping waveforms of very early aftershocks, combined with the pronounced coda waves from the mainshock and larger aftershocks, further degrade the signal-to-noise ratio (SNR; Peng *et al.*, 2007), making it particularly difficult to identify smaller-magnitude events (Peng and Zhao, 2009).

Existing studies on this aftershock sequence contain data limitations in the very early postseismic stage: the CENC catalog is constrained by the high detection threshold and large location uncertainty due to the sparse permanent network, whereas the catalog of Yao *et al.* (2025) is limited by the deployment timeline of the temporary network. Given these deficiencies in early aftershock detection, we implemented the matched-filter technique (MFT; Peng and Zhao, 2009) to recover missing very early aftershocks within the first 3 days following the mainshock. We anticipate that our work will

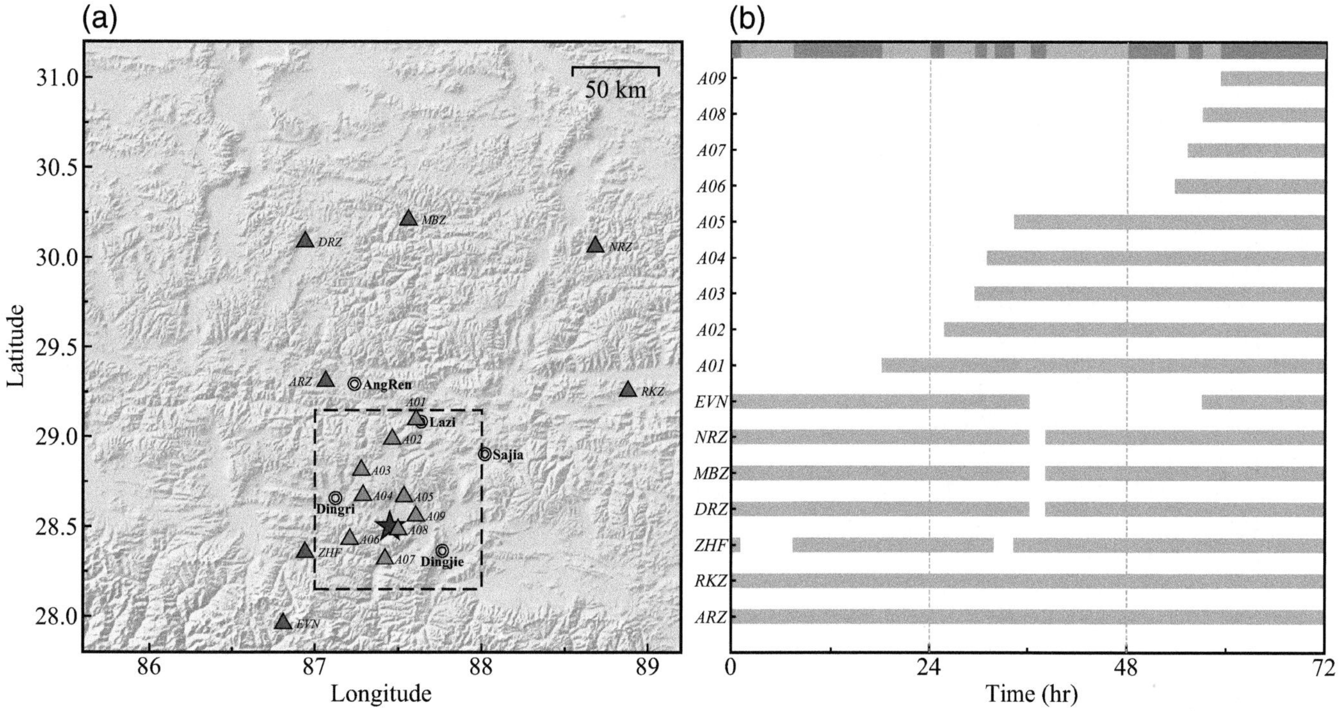

Figure 2. (a) Seismic station distribution and (b) data availability in the study area. (a) Permanent stations and temporary stations were shown with black and green triangles. The red star marks the epicenter. Dashed box outlined region plotted in Figure 3. (b) The availability of seismic data relative to 1 January 2025 00:00:00. The light- and dark-blue shaded bars indicate different segments of continuous data used in the MFT. The color version of this figure is available only in the electronic edition.

significantly lower the detection threshold and uncover very early aftershocks compared to standard catalogs. By analyzing the spatiotemporal evolution patterns of these detected early aftershocks, we aim to provide new and critical constraints for delineating the coseismic fault geometry and understanding the fault activation patterns.

Study Region

The Tibetan Plateau, resulting from the continuous collision between the Eurasian and Indian plates with northward underthrusting of the latter, has undergone prolonged crustal uplift. This colossal mountain system exhibits the most vigorous modern tectonic and seismic activity in China (Armijo *et al.*, 1986; Tapponnier *et al.*, 2001; Royden *et al.*, 2008; Styron *et al.*, 2015; Wang and Barbot, 2023).

Beyond north–south shortening, extensive east–west extensional structures have developed across the Himalayan, Lhasa, and Qiangtang terranes in the Tibetan Plateau. These are manifested as a series of north–south-trending rifts (the Southern Tibetan rift system [STRS]; Armijo *et al.*, 1989; Coleman and Hodges, 1995; Zhang and Ding, 2003; Kapp *et al.*, 2008). Although the formation mechanism of these rifts remains debated, the prevailing hypothesis attributes them to the transition from north–south compression to east–west extension during the ongoing India–Eurasia collision (Molnar and Tapponnier, 1978; Tapponnier *et al.*, 1986; Armijo *et al.*, 1989; England and Houseman, 1989; Yin, 2000; Styron *et al.*, 2011; Webb *et al.*, 2017; Pang *et al.*, 2018). As one of the most distinctive active tectonic domains in southern Tibet, this region is characterized by high-angle normal faults that generally exhibit significant seismogenic potential (Ha *et al.*, 2019; Gao *et al.*, 2024; Hu *et al.*, 2025).

Meanwhile, the STDS is a major east–west-striking, large-scale detachment fault system that parallels the Himalayan range (Burchfiel *et al.*, 1992; Carosi *et al.*, 1998; Liu *et al.*, 2004). In the Dingri region, the younger, ~350-km-long XDR of the STRS truncates and dextrally offsets the STDS by approximately 30 km (Zhang *et al.*, 2002; Kali *et al.*, 2010; Yang *et al.*, 2010; Tian and Wu, 2023). The seismogenic mechanism in this region likely involved the combined effects of both north–south compressional and east–west extensional stresses (Dewey, 1988; Chen *et al.*, 2004).

The epicenter of the 2025 Dingri earthquake is located adjacent to the DMF in the southern segment of the XDR. As the third major rift in the east-to-west sequence of the STRS, the XDR displays intense Quaternary activity (Burchfiel *et al.*, 1992; Kali *et al.*, 2010; Tian and Wu, 2023; Chevalier *et al.*, 2025; Wu *et al.*, 2025). At the southern terminus of the XDR, the fault system diverges into three parallel branches, with the westernmost DMF representing a Holocene active normal fault that strikes 5° N and extends approximately 60 km in length with a width varying between 30 and 300 m (Armijo *et al.*, 1989; Gao *et al.*, 2025; Wang *et al.*, 2025).

Notably, following the 25 April 2015 M_w 7.8 Nepal earthquake, seismic activity around the Dingri County was significantly

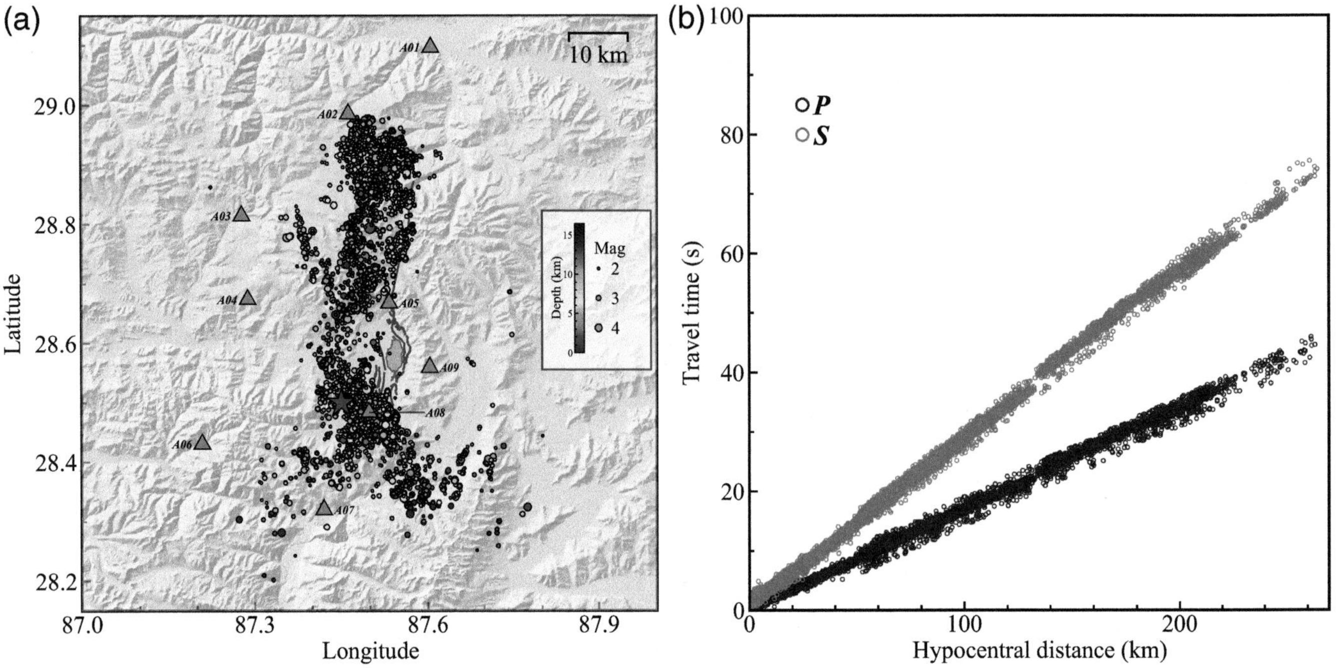

enhanced. The Nepal earthquake induced coseismic Coulomb stress increase in the Dingri area, likely triggered earthquakes in Dingri including an M_s 5.8 earthquake ~3 hr later (Liu *et al.*, 2015; Xiong *et al.*, 2015; Li *et al.*, 2017, 2025; Jin *et al.*, 2025). Prior to the most recent M_w 7.1 Dingri earthquake, the region had experienced four earthquakes with magnitudes $M_s \geq 5.0$, indicating high-regional stress levels (Fig. 1).

Figure 3. (a) Distribution of selected relocated candidate earthquakes and temporary stations. Earthquakes were color coded based on hypocentral depths and scaled with magnitudes. Red lines showed map surface trace of DMF. (b) Travel time versus hypocentral distance for predicted phase arrivals by PhaseNet. Blue and red circles are *P* and *S* phase picks, respectively. The color version of this figure is available only in the electronic edition.

Data and Method

Because the temporary seismic stations (A01–A09) were deployed one after another following the mainshock, the early aftershocks within the first 2–3 days were incomplete in the well-relocated catalog using the temporary seismic array (Yao *et al.*, 2025; Fig. S1, available in the supplemental material to this article). Hence, to uncover missing early aftershocks, we applied the MFT to detect earthquakes (Gibbons and Ringdal, 2006; Shelly *et al.*, 2007; Peng and Zhao, 2009). We used well-relocated aftershocks between 8 January 2025 and 18 January 2025 as templates, and scanned through continuous waveforms recorded by both temporary and permanent seismic stations within the first ~3 days following the mainshock (between 7 January 2025 00:00:00 and 10 January 2025 00:00:00 UTC; Fig. 2).

The template events were selected from the relocated aftershock catalog (Yao *et al.*, 2025). We selected templates using a fine spatial grid (0.01° × 0.01° × 1 km) mainly due to high aftershock rates and resulting candidate duplicate templates. A grid size of ~1 km horizontal and 1 km vertical is chosen empirically based on the location uncertainties. Given the stations used in template matching, a representative template within such fine grids would be adequate to match nearby aftershocks. We noted that earthquakes with different magnitudes might involve different source complexities. Hence, we utilized a magnitude-bin strategy to include earthquakes within the same spatial bin but spanning different magnitudes, and the event with the most phase picks was selected from each 0.5 magnitude bin. Through this method, a total number of 3703 template earthquakes with $M_L \geq 1.0$ were selected (see Data and Resources; Fig. 3a).

The event waveform was extracted from continuous data and PhaseNet (Zhu and Beroza, 2019) was first applied to automatically pick *P* and *S* phase arrivals for selected earthquakes. Theoretical *P* and *S* arrivals were calculated based on hypocentral distances and an assumed *P*- and *S*-wave velocity of 6.0 and 3.5 km/s, respectively. Predicted phase pick was saved if the travel difference relative to the theoretical arrivals was less than 2.5 s. If multiple predicted phases exist, the one closest to the theoretical arrivals was kept (Fig. 3b). To suppress cultural noise, a 2–12 Hz band-pass filter was applied to enhance the earthquake signal, similar to the filter used in Shelly (2020) for the 2019 Ridgecrest sequence. We then computed the SNR for candidate earthquakes. The SNR of a given channel was defined as the ratio between the cumulative energy of the signal window and the noise window. Among them, the signal window was defined as a 6-s-long window starting 1 s before and 5 s after the saved predicted *P* or *S* arrival for vertical or horizontal channels, respectively. Correspondingly, a 6-s-long window immediately before the signal window was used as the noise window. Only channels with SNRs above 5.0 were saved, and candidate earthquakes with at least seven saved channels were utilized as templates in MFT. Finally, we used 3224 templates in earthquake detection.

To improve the computational efficiency, both template and continuous data were downsampled to 40 Hz from the original 100 Hz. We then applied the template set to scan the continuous waveform data spanning the first 72 hr after the mainshock. We segmented the continuous data into distinct temporal intervals to account for the evolving seismic network configuration, which was due to data gaps at permanent stations and the staggered deployment of temporary stations. The boundaries between segments were determined based on changes in station operational status (specifically, the addition of a new station or loss of an existing one; see Fig. 2b). This approach ensured that, within each segment, all stations have the same data duration, thereby providing a uniform basis for matched-filter detection.

For each segment, the cross-correlation function (CCF) for every used channel of a template was computed using a sliding window. The CCFs from all used channels were shifted back to the template's origin time and then stacked to obtain the stacked CCF trace. When cross correlating a template with continuous data segments, we required a minimal number of seven channels, which guaranteed that detected earthquakes were reliable. A newly detected event was registered when the mean cross-correlation value (CCV) was above the mean value of the stacked trace plus 12 times its median absolute deviation (MAD; Yao *et al.*, 2020; Fig. 4). We then combined detections from all used templates and removed duplicated ones by saving the detected events with the highest CCV within every 3-s-long window.

Results and Discussions

The MFT detected 7179 seismic events within ~3 days after the mainshock. The local magnitudes of detected events were calculated based on the amplitude ratio between detected events and template events (see Data and Resources; Fig. 5a). Compared to 1399 events listed in the CENC standard catalog during the same period, the number of detected events increased by nearly five-fold, significantly enhancing the completeness of the early-stage aftershock catalog for the 2025 Dingri earthquake (Fig. 5a,b).

The Gutenberg–Richter (G-R) relationship (Gutenberg and Richter, 1944) is a commonly used method for evaluating the completeness of earthquake catalogs. In this study, the maximum-likelihood method was employed to analyze the seismic catalog (Wiemer and Wyss, 2000). Differences in the network's detection sensitivity were caused by the varying number and spatial distribution of operating stations across the temporal segments (Fig. 2b). To analyze the temporal evolution of the earthquake catalog while accounting for this effect, we computed the time-varying magnitude of completeness $M_c(t)$, using a window containing 700 events and a moving window of 100 events (Fig. 5c).

During the early postmainshock period, the large amplitude of coda waves substantially constrained detection capability, and sparse station coverage further elevated the actual detection threshold. The M_c was approximately 2.2 for the MFT catalog and 2.4 for the CENC catalog, reflecting the difficulty of identifying valid signals in high-noise environments and indicating that the MFT technique provided only limited improvement during this stage. As the interfering signals attenuated and aftershock rates decreased over time, at 24 hr after the mainshock, although the CENC catalog maintained an M_c of approximately 2.2, the MFT method achieved a substantially lower M_c of ~1.5 based on the same station configuration, demonstrating markedly enhanced detection capability. With the deployment of mobile stations and the continuous incorporation of additional seismic data, the M_c of both the MFT and CENC catalogs showed further improvement. The M_c of the CENC catalog stabilized around 2.0, whereas the MFT catalog progressively reached magnitudes as low as 1.0 when nearby temporary stations were included, demonstrating significant enhancement compared to the M_c values of both the CENC catalog and the earlier MFT catalog. This also reflects that denser station coverage can effectively lower the detection threshold of the MFT method.

Yao *et al.* (2025) combined the CENC catalog (covering approximately the first 30 hr postmainshock) with a machine-learning catalog using temporary station data to construct a high-resolution catalog (7 January 1:05 a.m. to 18 January 8:17 a.m. UTC). Their study reports that within the first 1.2 days, the magnitude of completeness is ~2.5, which gradually decreased to a value of ~1.0. Within 72 hr following the mainshock, this catalog detected approximately 3600 events (Fig. S1). In contrast, our MFT catalog achieved an M_c of ~1.5 within 24 hr postmainshock, and further decreased to ~1.0 after incorporating nearby temporary station data, detecting approximately twice the number of events. This comparison indicates that our MFT method obtains detection sensitivity comparable to later high-resolution catalogs at an earlier stage, thereby providing a distinct advantage in resolving the fine-scale spatiotemporal evolution of very early aftershocks.

The newly detected aftershock catalog reveals that the early aftershocks were generally distributed along a nearly north–south-trending zone (Fig. 6), with refined fault geometry when compared to Yao *et al.* (2025; Fig. S2 available in the supplemental material to this article). The aftershock sequence extends approximately 80 km in length and 10 km in width. The fault structure responsible for the 2025 Dingri earthquake exhibits significant complexity. Spatially, the aftershocks are distributed along the strike of the DMF and can be divided into northern, central, and southern segments. We highlighted the following main clusters: zone 1 in the northern segment, zone 2 in the southern segment, zone 3 on the western side of the central segment, and an extensive aftershock zone within the central

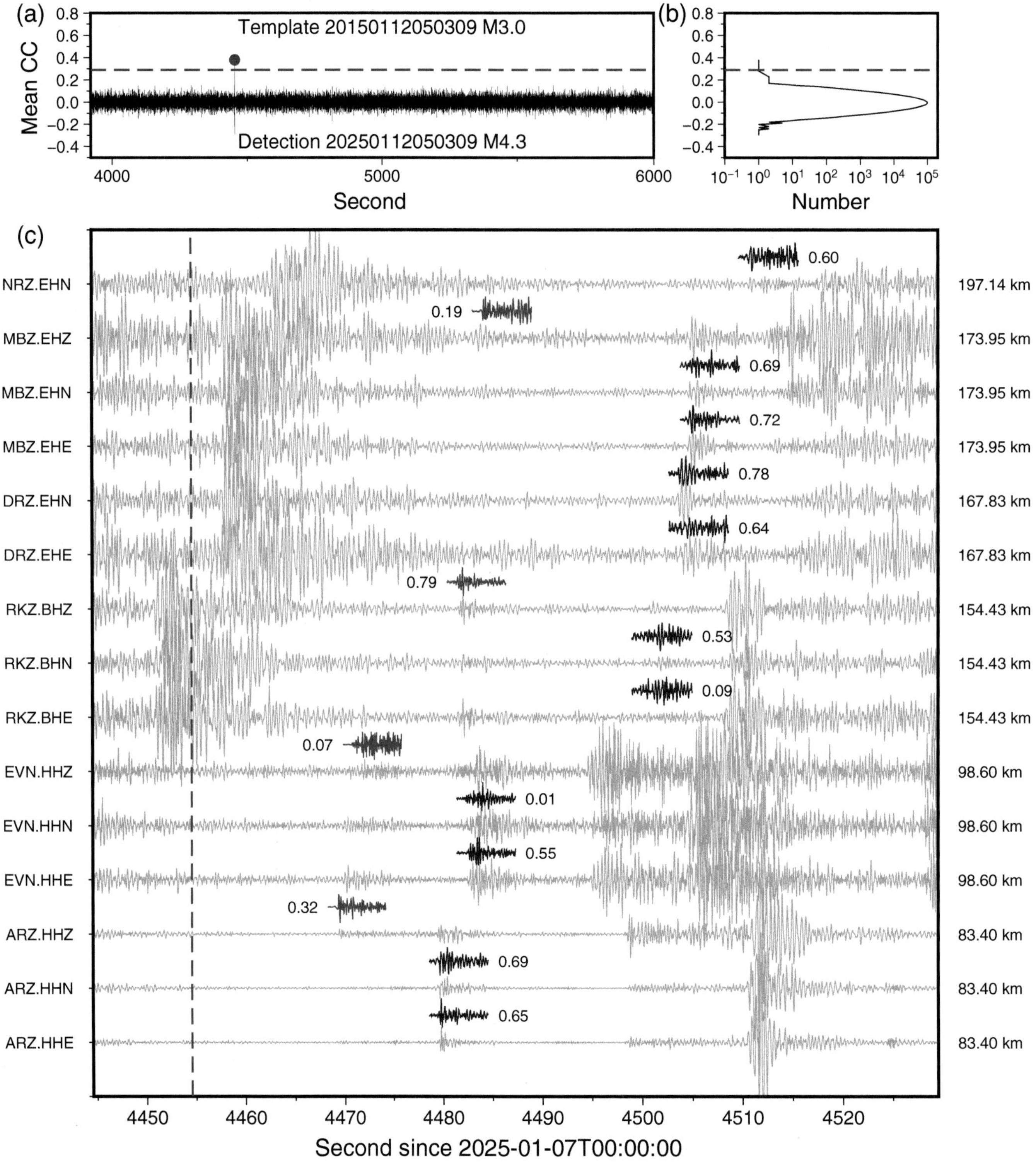

Figure 4. Example showing an early aftershock (~450 s after the mainshock) detected by MFT. (a) The stacked trace using an M_L 3.0 template 20250112050309, showing the distribution of mean cross-correlation (CC) value with time between 3900 and 6000 s relative to 7 January 2025 00:00:00. The positive detection (red circle) has a mean CC value of 0.384 and 15.7 × MAD (median absolute deviation). (b) Histogram of the mean CC values. (c) The gray waveform shows the detected event waveform, with time relative to 7 January 2025 00:00:00. Red-vertical dashed line marked the origin time of the detected event (7 January 2025 01:14:14.55 s). Red and blue waveforms showed the template waveforms of the M_L 3.0 template 20250112050309. Station and channel name, epicentral distance, and cross-correlation coefficient for corresponding channels were marked. The color version of this figure is available only in the electronic edition.

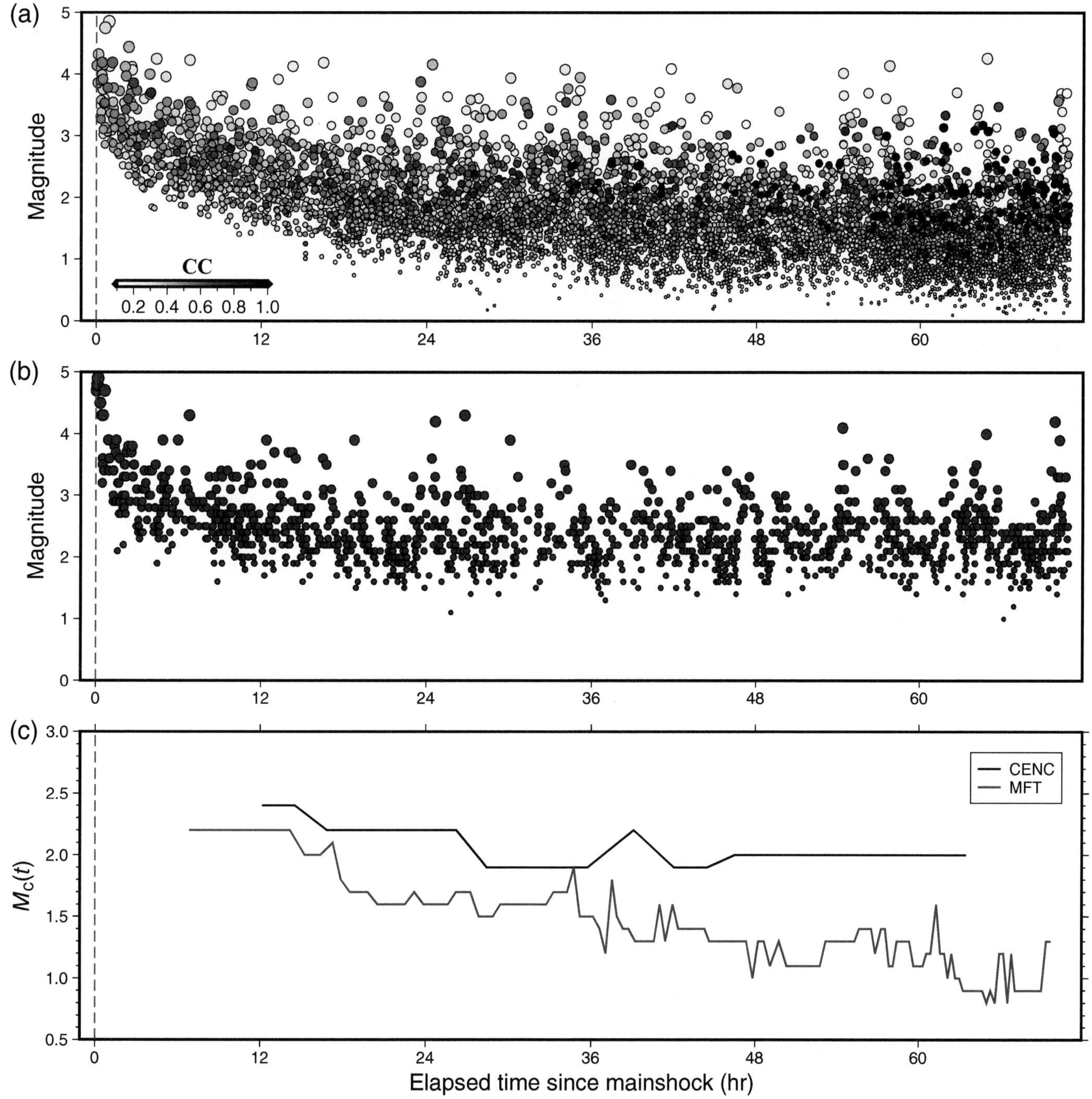

segment. Zones 1 and 2 exhibit high-seismic event densities. Zone 1 demonstrates a densely concentrated north–south-trending band with a relatively broad overall width, whereas zone 2 is characterized by a northwest-striking linear distribution with a southward-propagating trend over time, featuring a northeast-oriented branching segment at its terminus along with a northwest-extending section. In contrast, the central segment exhibits a relatively fewer number of seismic events, with distinct aftershock gaps observed immediately to the north of the epicenter (around the Dingmucuo Lake). On the western side of this segment, a small north-northwest-striking cluster is identified as zone 3.

Figure 5. Magnitude–time distribution of early aftershocks within the first 3 days following the Dingri mainshock. (a) MFT catalog, events were color coded by the mean CC values. (b) Earthquakes listed in China Earthquake Network Centers (CENC) catalog. (c) Time-evolving magnitude of completeness $M_c(t)$ for CENC and MFT earthquake catalogs, respectively. The color version of this figure is available only in the electronic edition.

The focal depths of the seismic sequence are predominantly concentrated within the range of 4–12 km, exhibiting a characteristic pattern of shallower depths in the northern and southern segments and greater depths in the central segment

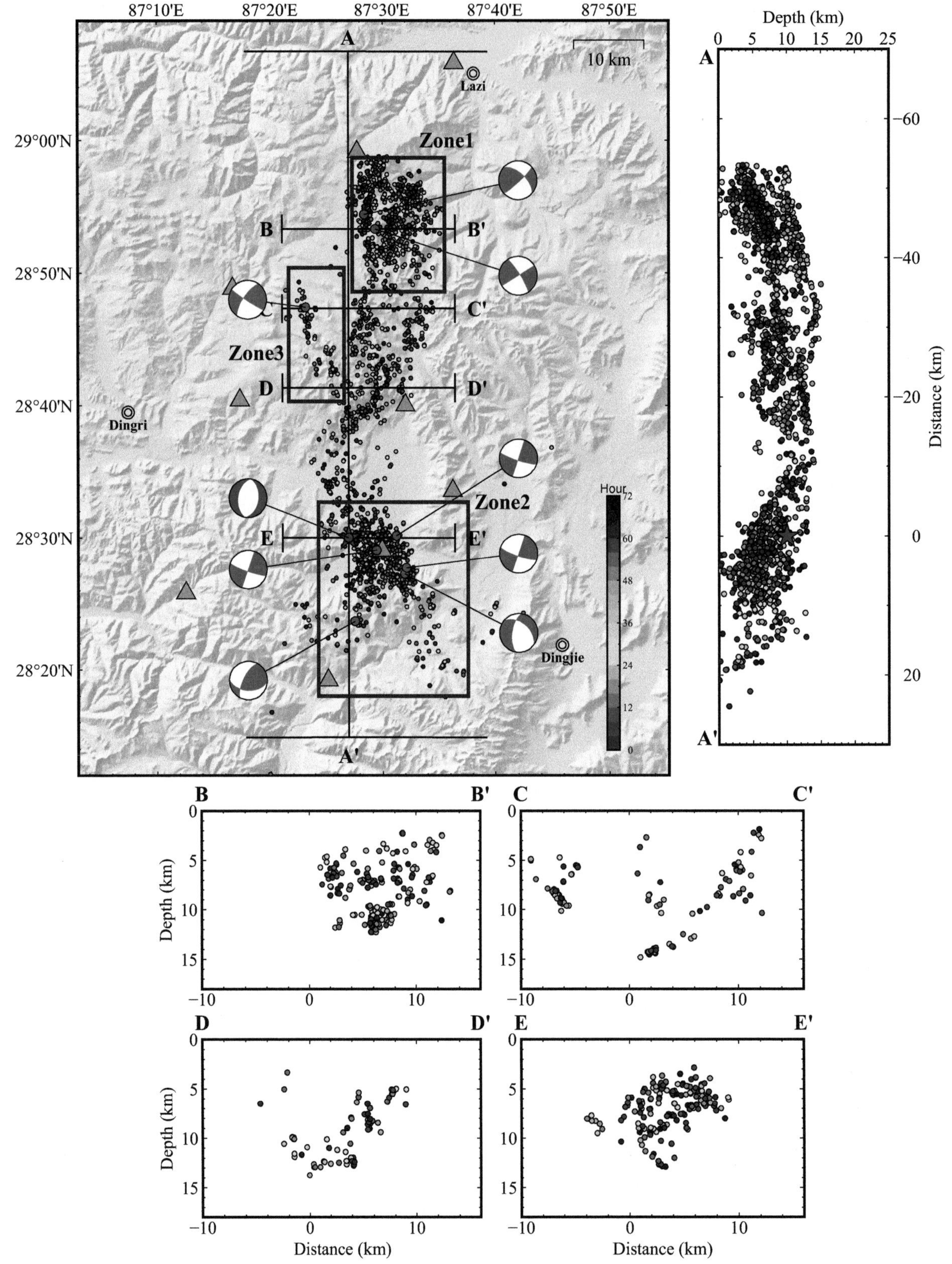

Figure 6. Spatiotemporal distribution of detected aftershocks (color coded based on elapsed time relative to the Dingri mainshock) and resolved focal mechanisms of $M_L \geq 4$ aftershocks. AA′ profile shows the depth distribution of aftershocks along the north–south direction. BB′, CC′, DD′, and EE′ profile marks the depth distribution of aftershocks along the east–west direction. The color version of this figure is available only in the electronic edition.

(AA′ profile in Fig. 6). Depth profiles reveal that the northern segment is primarily controlled by a west-dipping fault with a relatively steep dip angle, together with diffusive shallow deformation (BB′ profile in Fig. 6). The central segment exhibits a distinct structural pattern characterized by the coexistence of both west-dipping and east-dipping faults. The west-dipping fault and associated antithetic normal fault correspond to the Dingmucuo graben, whereas the east-dipping fault to the west aligns with a small north-northwest-striking cluster on the western side (CC′ profile in Fig. 6). This suggests that zone 3 may represent a secondary rupture zone influenced by buried faults. The geometry of this zone delineates a distinct belt-shaped pattern that emerged early in the postseismic period, which we interpret as evidence for coseismic rupture. This interpretation is consistent with the model proposed by Qiao *et al.* (2025) based on InSAR inversion. In comparison, the southern segment generally outlines a west-dipping master fault, together with a series of east-dipping subsidiary faults (EE′ profile in Fig. 6). This pattern aligns with the field investigation results of Shao *et al.* (2025), who identified multiple pre-existing, parallel east-dipping fault strands in the southern part of the region, which generated scarps with measurable coseismic displacement in this section.

Notably, the activity pattern in zone 2 exhibits distinct temporal evolution characteristics. Observations show that a dense earthquake cluster rapidly formed in this zone shortly after the mainshock. Subsequently, this cluster displayed a slow yet persistent trend of southward expansion. This southward migration was relatively subtle in the immediate postseismic period, with only a sparse, linear extension discernible by the third day. However, it became more pronounced in longer-term observational data (e.g., in the catalog up to 18 January 2025, from Yao *et al.*, 2025). A candidate mechanism proposed by Yue *et al.* (2025) suggests that poroelastic fluid migration contributes to the postseismic stress adjustment in this region. Their modeling further suggests that such fluid migration extends southward over time, generating a Coulomb stress loading effect, which is consistent with our observation of early aftershock migration in zone 2.

Combined with the overall seismicity distribution, the main seismogenic structure of this earthquake is identified as the west-dipping DMF. Xu *et al.* (2025) revealed that the maximum slip occurred within approximately 30 km north of the epicenter, whereas the southern region exhibited predominantly minor slip. From the newly detected catalog, the densely clustered aftershock activities are primarily distributed at both ends of the fault, whereas the central segment exhibits a lower number of events. This pattern suggests that the main rupture zone in the central segment released stress extensively, whereas the northern and southern segments underwent continuous postseismic stress adjustment (Yue *et al.*, 2025).

Earthquakes with magnitudes $M_L \geq 4.0$ were predominantly clustered in zones 1, 2, and 3. Fewer aftershocks of larger magnitudes were detected in the central segment, which exhibited the maximum coseismic slip during the main rupture. This distribution suggests that the extremities of the main rupture zone and the northwest-trending coseismic fault structures on the western side constitute the primary regions of postseismic stress instability. Zone 3 exhibits a relatively low number of aftershocks but demonstrates comparatively higher aftershock magnitudes. One plausible interpretation suggests that the complexity of the seismogenic structure impeded the propagation of the mainshock rupture in this area. The obstructed region may have subsequently released accumulated stress through high-magnitude aftershocks.

Following the Dingri earthquake, multiple institutions and researchers have provided focal mechanism solutions for the Dingri mainshock. The results indicate a normal-faulting mechanism with a left-lateral strike-slip component, exhibiting a dip angle of approximately 40°–50° and a westward dip direction (Chen *et al.*, 2025; Yang, Wang, *et al.*, 2025). To further investigate the fault kinematics, focal mechanism solutions were supplemented for earthquakes with $M_L \geq 4.0$, based on the early-stage aftershock catalog obtained through template matching. We utilized the frequency-domain *f-k* method (Zhu and Rivera, 2002) based on a horizontally layered model, along with the CRUST1.0 velocity model (Laske *et al.*, 2013), to compute empirical Green's functions. Waveform inversion was performed using the generalized cut and paste (gCAP) method (Zhu and Ben-Zion, 2013) for seismic stations located 80–400 km from the epicenter.

Focal mechanism solutions were robustly determined for eight aftershocks with relatively shallow focal depths (3.5–9.0 km; see Data and Resources). A key finding is that although normal-faulting mechanisms dominate the sequence, strike-slip earthquakes constitute a nonnegligible portion (Fig. 6). The co-occurrence of different rupture mechanisms within a single sequence provides critical insights into the complexity of stress release. Based on inversions of multiple data sets, Zhao *et al.* (2025) proposed that the mainshock rupture involved a geometrically complex, multisegment fault system rather than a single planar structure. The diverse mechanisms we observed along the same fault zone are consistent with a complex fault system. Therefore, the Dingri earthquake sequence exhibits a complex pattern dominated by normal faulting yet incorporating a significant strike-slip component. This diversity does not challenge the regional extensional setting but can be regarded as a direct manifestation of the internal complexity of the fault system during its postrupture adjustment, reflecting the complexity of stress release in the epicentral area.

Conclusions

This study used 3224 accurately relocated aftershocks through a dense temporary seismic array as earthquake templates. Using the MFT method, we scanned ~3 days of continuous postearthquake data from seven permanent stations and nine temporary stations within 300 km of the epicenter. The MFT catalog contains 7179 aftershocks, representing a nearly fivefold increase compared to the manually compiled CENC catalog, and significantly improved the magnitude of completeness. The MFT method significantly supplemented the early-stage seismic catalog of the Dingri earthquake, providing a foundation for further analysis of the spatiotemporal evolution of early aftershocks.

The aftershocks were predominantly distributed west of the DMF, exhibiting a nearly north–south-trending distribution. The aftershock sequence extends approximately 80 km in length and 10 km in width. The overall distribution demonstrates characteristics of a high-angle west-dipping DMF. The northern and southern segments of the aftershock sequence exhibit high-seismic density, indicating ongoing stress adjustment. A north-northwest-striking, east-dipping fault is present on the western side of the sequence, representing a secondary coseismic rupture zone influenced by other buried faults. In the southern region near the mainshock, aftershocks reveal the coexistence of the west-dipping main fault and east-dipping subsidiary faults, with early postseismic activity showing a slow but persistent southward migration. Focal mechanism solutions of $M_L \geq 4.0$ aftershocks reveal a considerable proportion of strike-slip events. The co-occurrence of different rupture mechanisms within the same sequence suggests the activation of a geometrically complex, multisegment fault system. Our high-resolution aftershock catalog delineates the rupture extent and outlines the detailed fault architecture. These findings provide direct observational constraints for refining models of fault interaction and for seismic hazard assessment in southern Tibet.

Data and Resources

The seismic data used in this study are archived in the China Earthquake Networks Center (CENC) and can be accessed upon request. The template and detected earthquake catalog, together with resolved focal solutions of $M_L \geq 4$ aftershocks can be downloaded from the Zenodo repository (https://zenodo.org/records/17505714). More information about the catastrophic events is available at https://yjt.xizang.gov.cn/sylmxqkx/105239.jhtml and www.cea.gov.cn/cea/xwzx/fzjzyw/5790712/index.html. Both websites were last accessed in February 2026. The supplemental material for this article includes Figures S1 and S2.

Declaration of Competing Interests

The authors acknowledge that there are no conflicts of interest recorded.

Acknowledgments

The China Earthquake Networks Center (CENC) and the Earthquake Agency of Tibet Autonomous Region provided the quick earthquake catalog and observation reports used in this study. Figures in this article were generated using the Generic Mapping Tool (GMT) software (Wessel *et al.*, 2013). The authors extend their sincere thanks to all of the authors. M. Z. is supported by the National Key Research and Development Program of China under Grant Number 2024YFC3012805. D. Y. is supported by the National Science Foundation of China (NSFC) Grant Number 42204062.

References

Armijo, R., P. Tapponnier, and T. L. Han (1989). Late Cenozoic right-lateral strike-slip faulting in southern Tibet, *J. Geophys. Res.: Solid Earth* **94,** no. B3, 2787–2838, doi: 10.1029/JB094iB03p02787.

Armijo, R., P. Tapponnier, J. L. Mercier, and T. L. Han (1986). Quaternary extension in southern Tibet: Field observations and tectonic implications, *J. Geophys. Res.: Solid Earth* **91,** no. B14, 13,803–13,872, doi: 10.1029/JB091iB14p13803.

Burchfiel, B. C., Z. L. Chen, K. V. Hodges, Y. P. Liu, L. H. Royden, C. R. Deng, and J. E. Xu (1992). *The South Tibetan Detachment System, Himalayan Orogen: Extension Contemporaneous with and Parallel to Shortening in a Collisional Mountain Belt*, Vol. 269, Geological Society of America, Boulder, Colorado, 1–41, doi: 10.1130/SPE269.

Carosi, R., B. Lombardo, G. Molli, G. Musumeci, and P. C. Pertusati (1998). The South Tibetan detachment system in the Rongbuk Valley, Everest region: Deformation features and geological implications, *J. Asian Earth Sci.* **16,** nos. 2/3, 299–311, doi: 10.1016/S0743-9547(98)00014-2.

Chen, H. L., Q. C. Wang, J. R. Gao, and J. Li (2025). Preliminary study on the seismogenic structure of the 2025 Xizang Dingri MS 6.8 earthquake sequence, *Seismol. Geol.* **47,** no. 3, 747–760, doi: 10.3969/j.issn.0253-4967.2025.03.20250021.

Chen, Q. Z., J. T. Freymueller, Q. Wang, Z. Q. Yang, C. J. Xu, and J. N. Liu (2004). A deforming block model for the present-day tectonics of Tibet, *J. Geophys. Res.: Solid Earth* **109,** no. B14, doi: 10.1029/2002JB002151.

Chevalier, M. L., Z. Q. Fang, S. Q. Chen, J. W. Pan, H. B. Li, K. G. Wu, F. C. Liu, J. Y. Wang, and L. Ding (2025). Extension rate variations across the South Tibetan rifts – New data from the northern Xainza-Dinggye Graben, *Tectonophysics* **910,** 230824, doi: 10.1016/j.tecto.2025.230824.

Coleman, M., and K. Hodges (1995). Evidence for Tibetan plateau uplift before 14 Myr ago from a new minimum age for east-west extension, *Nature* **374,** no. 6517, 49–52.

Dewey, J. F. (1988). Extensional collapse of orogens, *Tectonics* **7,** no. 6, 1123–1139, doi: 10.1029/TC007i006p01123.

England, P., and G. Houseman (1989), Extension during continental convergence, with application to the Tibetan Plateau, *J. Geophys. Res.* **94,** no. B12, 17,561–17,579.

Felzer, K. R., and E. E. Brodsky (2006). Decay of aftershock density with distance indicates triggering by dynamic stress, *Nature* **441,** no. 7094, 735–738.

Gao, Y., M. Li, Z. H. Wu, K. Q. Zhang, J. M. Zuo, T. T. Tian, and S. F. Wang (2024). Late quaternary normal faulting along the Western Boundary Fault of Peiku Co Graben in Southern Nyalam-Coqen Rift: Implications for extensional deformation in Southern Tibet and Seismic Hazard, *J. Struct. Geol.* **181,** 105087, doi: 10.1016/j.jsg.2024.105087.

Gao, Y., Z. H. Wu, S. Han, T. T. Tian, K. Q. Zhang, and S. F. Wang (2025). Late quaternary throw rate of the Seismogenic fault (Dengmecuo fault) of the 2025 MS 6.8 Dingri earthquake in Shigatse, *Seismol. Geol.* **47,** no. 3, 689–706, doi: 10.3969/j.issn.0253-4967.2025.03.20250034.

Gibbons, S. J., and F. Ringdal (2006). The detection of low magnitude seismic events using array-based waveform correlation, *Geophys. J. Int.* **165,** no. 1, 149–166, doi: 10.1111/j.1365-246X.2006.02865.x.

Gutenberg, B., and C. F. Richter (1944). Frequency of earthquake in California, *Bull. Seismol. Soc. Am.* **34,** no. 5, 185–188, doi: 10.1785/BSSA0340040185.

Ha, G. H., Z. H. Wu, H. L. Gai, and J. M. Zuo (2019). New discovery of surface rupture of large paleoearthquake along Northern Pagri-Duoqing Co Graben, Southern Yadong-Gulu Rift, *Acta Geol. Sin.* **93,** no. 4, 1135–1136, doi: 10.1111/1755-6724.13829.

Hu, G. M., Y. R. Xu, H. Liu, R. M. Yuan, and L. Y. Lu (2025). Estimation of the maximum magnitude of normal faults and seismic risk in the Southern Tibetan Rift Zones, *Earth Sci.* **50,** no. 5, 1794–1812, doi: 10.3799/dqkx.2025.055.

Jin, Z. T., M. Y. Zhou, J. C. Huang, and Y. G. Wan (2025). The stress triggering of the 2025 Dingri, Xizang, China MW6.8 earthquake by the 2015 Nepal MW7.8 and MW7.2 earthquakes, *Earth Sci.* **50,** no. 5, 1782–1793, doi: 10.3799/dqkx.2025.074.

Kali, E., P. H. Leloup, N. Arnaud, G. Mahéo, D. Y. Liu, E. Boutonnet, J. Van der Woerd, X. H. Liu, J. Liu-Zeng, and H. B. Li (2010). Exhumation history of the deepest central Himalayan rocks, Ama Drime range: Key pressure-temperature-deformation-time constraints on orogenic models, *Tectonics* **29,** no. 2, TC2014, doi: 10.1029/2009TC002551.

Kapp, P., M. Taylor, D. Stockli, and L. Ding (2008). Development of active low-angle normal fault systems during orogenic collapse: Insight from Tibet, *Geology* **36,** no. 1, 7–10, doi: 10.1130/G24054A.1.

Laske, G., G. Masters, Z. Ma, and M. Pasyanos (2013). Update on CRUST 1.0—A 1⊠?degree global model of Earth's crust, *EGU General Assembly 2013*, Vienna, Austria, 7–12 April 2013.

Li, L., D. D. Yao, X. F. Meng, Z. G. Peng, and B. S. Wang (2017). Increasing seismicity in Southern Tibet following the 2015 Mw 7.8 Gorkha, Nepal earthquake, *Tectonophysics* **714–715,** 62–70, doi: 10.1016/j.tecto.2016.08.008.

Li, Y., Y. B. Wang, Y. X. Shao, H. B. Shi, and T. Wang (2025). Seismogenic characteristics of the 2025 Dingri Ms 6.8 earthquake: Insights from GNSS observations, *Earthq. Res. Adv.* **5,** no. 4, 100375, doi: 10.1016/j.eqrea.2025.100375.

Liu, J., C. Ji, J. Y. Zhang, P. Z. Zhang, L. S. Zeng, Z. F. Li, and W. Wang (2015). Tectonic setting and general features of coseismic rupture of the 25 April 2015 Mw 7.8 Gorkha, Nepal earthquake, *Chin. Sci. Bull.* **60,** no. 27, 2640–2655, doi: 10.1360/N972015-00559.

Liu, Y., W. Siebel, J. Li, and X. C. Xiao (2004). Characteristics of the Main Central Thrust and Southern Tibetan Detachment in the Tingri Area, Southern Tibet, and ages of their activities, *Geol. Bull. China* **23,** no. 7, 636–644, doi: 10.12097/gbc.200407117.

Molnar, P., and P. Tapponnier (1978). Active tectonics of Tibet, *J. Geophys. Res.: Solid Earth* **83,** no. B11, 5361–5375, doi: 10.1029/JB083iB11p05361.

Pang, Y. J., H. Zhang, T. V. Gerya, J. Liao, H. H. Cheng, and Y. L. Shi (2018). The mechanism and dynamics of N-S rifting in southern Tibet: Insight from 3-D thermomechanical modeling, *J. Geophys. Res.: Solid Earth* **123,** no. 1, 859–877, doi: 10.1002/2017JB014011.

Peng, Z. G., and P. Zhao (2009). Migration of early aftershocks following the 2004 Parkfield earthquake, *Nature Geosci.* **2,** 877–881, doi: 10.1038/ngeo697.

Peng, Z. G., J. E. Vidale, M. Ishii, and A. Helmstetter (2007). Seismicity rate immediately before and after main shock rupture from high-frequency waveforms in Japan, *J. Geophys. Res.: Solid Earth* **112,** no. B3, doi: 10.1029/2006JB004386.

Qiao, X., Z. Lu, S. Y. Yan, H. T. Shi, M. Zhi, and D. Z. Zhao (2025). The 2025 MW7.0 Dingri earthquake: Conjugate normal faulting of a graben structure in the southern Xainza-Dinggye rift, *Geophys. Res. Lett.* **52,** e2025GL116154, doi: 10.1029/2025GL116154.

Royden, L. H., B. C. Burchfiel, and R. D. van der Hilst (2008). The geological evolution of the Tibetan Plateau, *Science* **321,** no. 5892, 1054–1058, doi: 10.1126/science.1155371.

Shao, Y. X., A. S. Wang, Z. J. Liu, W. X. Wang, L. F. Han, L. J. Xing, J. H. Xu, J. C. Wang, W. Q. Yao, H. X. Zhang, *et al.* (2025). Preliminary investigation on surface rupture and coseismic displacement of the January 7, 2025 Dingri earthquake in Xizang, *Earth Sci.* **50,** no. 5, 1677–1695, doi: 10.3799/dqkx.2025.040.

Shelly, D. R. (2020). A high-resolution seismic catalog for the initial 2019 Ridgecrest earthquake sequence: Foreshocks, aftershocks, and faulting complexity, *Seismol. Res. Lett.* **91,** no. 4, 1971–1978, doi: 10.1785/0220190309.

Shelly, D. R., G. C. Beroza, and S. Ide (2007). Complex evolution of transient slip derived from precise tremor locations in western Shikoku, Japan, *Geochem. Geophys. Geosys.* **8,** no. 10, Q10014, doi: 10.1029/2007GC001640.

Shi, F., M. J. Liang, Q. X. Luo, J. X. Qiao, D. Zhang, X. Wang, W. X. Yi, J. W. Zhang, Y. F. Zhang, H. P. Zhang, *et al.* (2025). Seismogenic fault and coseismic surface deformation of the Dingri MS6.8 Earthquake in Xizang, China, *Seismol. Geol.* **47,** no. 1, 1–15, doi: 10.3969/j.issn.0253-4967.2025.01.001.

Styron, R., M. Taylor, and K. Sundell (2015). Accelerated extension of Tibet linked to the Northward underthrusting of Indian Crust, *Nature Geosci.* **8,** no. 2, 131–134.

Styron, R. H., M. H. Taylor, and M. A. Murphy (2011). Oblique convergence, arc-parallel extension, and the role of strike-slip faulting in the High Himalaya, *Geosphere* **7,** no. 2, 582–596, doi: 10.1130/GES00606.1.

Tapponnier, P., G. Peltzer, and R. Armijo (1986). *On the Mechanics of the Collision Between India and Asia*, Geological Society, London, United Kingdom, Special Publications, Vol. 19, 113–157, doi: 10.1144/gsl.sp.1986.019.01.07.

Tapponnier, P., Z. Q. Xu, F. Roger, B. Meyer, N. Arnaud, G. Wittlinger, and J. S. Yang (2001). Oblique stepwise rise and growth of the Tibet Plateau, *Science* **294,** no. 5547, 1671–1677, doi: 10.1126/science.105978.

Tian, T. T., and Z. H. Wu (2023). Recent prehistoric major earthquake event of Dingmucuo Normal Fault in the Southern Segment of Shenzha-Dingjie Rift and its seismic geological significance, *Geol. Rev.* **69,** no. S1, 53–55.

Wang, D., L. C. Chen, Y. B. Li, H. Wang, Y. S. Jia, Y. Y. Gao, and K. Y. Xue (2025). Late quaternary activity of the Xietongmen to Dengmecuo segment along the Xainza-Dinggye Rift in Southern Qinghai-Xizang Plateau, *Seismol. Geol.* **47,** no. 3, 718–733, doi: 10.3969/j.issn.0253-4967.2025.03.20250012.

Wang, L. F., and S. Barbot (2023). Three-dimensional kinematics of the India-Eurasia collision, *Commun. Earth Environ.* **4,** no. 1, 164, doi: 10.1038/s43247-023-00815-4.

Webb, A. A. G., H. C. Guo, P. D. Clift, L. Husson, T. Müller, D. Costantino, A. Yin, Z. Q. Xu, H. Cao, and Q. Wang (2017). The Himalaya in 3D: Slab dynamics controlled mountain building and monsoon intensification, *Lithosphere* **9,** no. 4, 637–651, doi: 10.1130/L636.1.

Wessel, P., W. H. F. Smith, R. Scharroo, J. Luis, and F. Wobbe (2013). Generic mapping tools: Improved version released, *Eos Trans. AGU* **94,** no. 45, 409–410, doi: 10.1002/2013EO450001.

Wiemer, S., and M. Wyss (2000). Minimum magnitude of completeness in earthquake catalogs: Examples from Alaska, the western United States, and Japan, *Bull. Seismol. Soc. Am.* **90,** no. 4, 859–869, doi: 10.1785/0119990114.

Wu, J., D. D. Yao, X. F. Meng, Z. G. Peng, J. R. Su, and F. Long (2017). Spatial-temporal evolutions of early aftershocks following the 2013 Mw 6.6 Lushan earthquake in Sichuan, China, *J. Geophys. Res.: Solid Earth* **122,** no. 4, 2873–2889, doi: 10.1002/2016JB013706.

Wu, K. G., M. L. Chevalier, J. W. Pan, F. C. Liu, S. H. Yang, S. Q. Zhang, Q. Su, and H. B. Li (2025). Recurrence of large earthquakes along the southern Xainza-Dinggye rift and comparison with the 7 January 2025, Mw7.1 Tingri earthquake, southern Tibet, *Tectonophysics* **910,** 230827, doi: 10.1016/j.tecto.2025.230827.

Xiong, W., K. Tan, G. Liu, X. J. Qiao, and Z. S. Nie (2015). Coseismic and postseismic coulomb stress changes on surrounding major faults caused by the 2015 Nepal MW 7.9 Earthquake, *Chin. J. Geophys.* **58,** no. 11, 4305–4316, doi: 10.6038/cjg20151135.

Xu, Y. Y., B. B. Xu, C. Y. Xu, Z. G. Shao, and C. Z. Hu (2025). Joint inversion of the 2025 Dingri MS 6.8 earthquake rupture process based on teleseismic P waves, strong-motion and InSAR data, *Seismol. Geol.* **47,** no. 3, 734–746, doi: 10.3969/j.issn.0253-4967.2025.03.20250033.

Yang, J. Y., Y. M. Wen, C. J. Xu, and Q. F. Hu (2025). Complex multifault rupture during the 2016–2025 Dingri earthquakes, southern Tibetan Plateau, unraveled by multisource InSAR observations, *Seismol. Res. Lett.* **97,** no. 1, 28–37, doi: 10.1785/0220250095.

Yang, P. X., J. W. Ren, Z. W. Chen, and J. Zhang (2010). Tectonic geomorphology of the Northern Segment of Shenzha-Dingjie Graben Since Miocene in Middle Tibetan Plateau, *Earthquake* **30,** no. 3, 81–89.

Yang, T., S. G. Wang, L. H. Fang, W. L. Wang, S. Q. Li, G. Y. Xu, and F. T. Tang (2025). Analysis of earthquake sequence and seismogenic structure of the 2025 MS6.8 Dingri earthquake in Tibetan Plateau, *Earth Sci.* **50,** no. 5, 1721–1732.

Yao, D. D., Y. H. Huang, Z. G. Peng, and R. R. Castro (2020). Detailed investigation of the foreshock sequence of the 2010 Mw7.2 El Mayor-Cucapah earthquake, *J. Geophys. Res.: Solid Earth* **124,** e2019JB019076, doi: 10.1029/2019JB019076.

Yao, D. D., J. I. Walter, X. F. Meng, T. E. Hobbs, Z. Peng, A. V. Newman, S. Y. Schwartz, and M. Protti (2017). Detailed spatiotemporal evolution of microseismicity and repeating earthquakes following the 2012 Mw 7.6 Nicoya Earthquake, *J. Geophys. Res.: Solid Earth* **122,** 524–542, doi: 10.1002/2016JB013632.

Yao, J. Y., D. D. Yao, F. Chen, M. Zhi, L. Sun, and D. Wang (2025). A Preliminary catalog of early aftershocks following the 7 January 2025 MS 6.8 Dingri, Xizang earthquake, *J. Earth Sci.* **36,** no. 2, 856–860, doi: 10.1007/s12583-025-0210-9.

Yin, A. (2000). Mode of Cenozoic east-west extension in Tibet suggesting a common origin of rifts in Asia during the Indo-Asian collision. *J. Geophys. Res.: Solid Earth* **105,** no. B9, 21,745–21,759, doi: 10.1029/2000JB900168.

Yue, C., D. Q. Dai, X. F. Li, Y. Wang, Y. F. Zhang, W. Yang, Y. Y. Han, C. Y. Qu, and L. Y. Meng (2025). Aftershock triggering mechanism by the 7 January 2025 Mw 7.1 Tingri earthquake, *Seismol. Res. Lett.* doi: 10.1785/0220250091.

Zhang, J. J., and L. Ding (2003). East-West extension in Tibetan Plateau and its significance to tectonic evolution, *Chin. J. Geol.* **38,** no. 2, 179–189.

Zhang, J. J., L. Guo, and L. Ding (2002). Structural characteristics of the Central-Southern Segment of the Shenzha-Dingjie Normal Fault system and its relationship with the South Tibetan detachment system, *Chin. Sci. Bull.* **47,** no. 10, 738–743, doi: 10.1360/csb2002-47-10-738.

Zhao, X., Z. W. Xiao, W. Wang, and J. Li (2025). Along-strike variation of the unilateral rupture of the 2025 Mw7.1 Dingri, Xizang earthquake: One of the shallowest M7+ normal-faulting events on the Tibetan Plateau, *Geophys. Res. Lett.* **52,** e2025GL119397, doi: 10.1029/2025GL119397.

Zhu, L. J., Z. G. Peng, J. McClellan, C. Y. Li, D. D. Yao, Z. F. Li, and L. H. Fang (2019). Deep learning for seismic phase detection and picking in the aftershock zone of 2008 Mw7.9 Wenchuan Earthquake, *Phys. Earth Planet. In.* **293,** 106261, doi: 10.1016/j.pepi.2019.05.004.

Zhu, L. P., and Y. Ben-Zion (2013). Parametrization of general seismic potency and moment tensors for source inversion of seismic waveform data, *Geophys. J. Int.* **194,** no. 2, 839–843, doi: 10.1093/gji/ggt137.

Zhu, L. P., and L. A. Rivera (2002). A note on the dynamic and static displacements from a point source in multilayered media, *Geophys. J. Int.* **148,** no. 3, 619–627, doi: 10.1046/j.1365-246X.2002.01610.x.

Zhu, W. Q., and G. C. Beroza (2019). PhaseNet: A deep-neural-network-based seismic arrival-time picking method, *Geophys. J. Int.* **216,** no. 1, 261–273, doi: 10.1093/gji/ggy423.

Manuscript received 4 November 2025
Published online 23 March 2026

Mapping of Soil Liquefaction Induced by the 2025 M_w 7.8 Sagaing Earthquake in Myanmar Using High-Spatial-Resolution Images

Guiming Hu[1,2,3], Renwei Xiong[1,2], Wenqiao Li[1,2], Peng Liang[1,2], Chaozhong Hu[1,2,4], Weiwei Wu[1,2], and Yueren Xu*[1,2]

Abstract

Manual visual interpretation of high-resolution remote sensing imagery is a common method for analyzing coseismic secondary hazards, particularly in regions with limited fieldwork accessibility. We employed this method to interpret coseismic soil liquefaction from the 2025 M_w 7.8 Sagaing earthquake in Myanmar. We extracted earthquake induced over 10,000 soil liquefaction pits with a total area of ~200 km^2 in the Central Myanmar basin concentrated Naypyidaw and Mandalay. The dense liquefaction mainly located on lower terraces of Ayeyarwady River and related tributaries within the epicenter. For the spatial distribution, soil liquefaction had distinct segments, divided by density into northern (near epicenter) and southern (near Naypyidaw) parts, with the northern part being three times the southern part. Along the coseismic surface ruptures of strike-slip fault, the liquefaction zone length matched the rupture zone. Still, it was narrow along the riverbanks and within ~10–20 km of the rupture zone. These findings provide critical data for postearthquake rescue and for soil liquefaction associated with historical and/or paleoearthquakes along the Sagaing fault.

Cite this article as Hu, G., R. Xiong, W. Li, P. Liang, C. Hu, W. Wu, and Y. Xu (2026). Mapping of Soil Liquefaction Induced by the 2025 M_w 7.8 Sagaing Earthquake in Myanmar Using High-Spatial-Resolution Images, *Seismol. Res. Lett.* **97**, 1655–1666, doi: 10.1785/0220250399.

Supplemental Material

Introduction

Coseismic soil liquefaction frequently occurs during large earthquakes, specifically when the seismic magnitude exceeds M 6 (Ambraseys, 1988). As a secondary seismic hazard triggered by strong seismic shaking, soil liquefaction is defined as the phenomenon in which saturated, unconsolidated soils lose their shear strength under seismic loading and transition from a solid state to a liquid state once the stresses are removed (Seed and Idriss, 1971). This phenomenon is prevalent across low-altitude coastal zones and high-altitude plateau regions worldwide, both characterized by high groundwater tables and abundant sandy soils, such as the U.S. West Coast, the Mediterranean coastline, and the coastal/plain areas of Japan, New Zealand, and North China Plain (e.g., Seed *et al.*, 1991; Moss *et al.*, 2011; Wotherspoon *et al.*, 2012; Ishitsuka *et al.*, 2012; Quigley *et al.*, 2013; Liu-Zeng *et al.*, 2017; Pretell *et al.*, 2021; Guo *et al.*, 2023; Taftsoglou *et al.*, 2023; Wang *et al.*, 2023; Chen *et al.*, 2024; Liang *et al.*, 2025; Xu, Fu, *et al.*, 2025). Unlike coseismic surface ruptures that directly damage buildings, roads, and lifeline infrastructure which crosses active faults (e.g., the recent 2025 M_w 7.8 Sagaing earthquake, Myanmar, Fig. 1), soil liquefaction can still cause severe ground failures, resulting in enormous costs for postearthquake reconstruction, which typically includes the 2013 Christchurch earthquake, in New Zealand and the 1975 Haicheng earthquake, in northeast China (e.g., Fu and Tatsuoka, 1984; Cubrinovski *et al.*, 2011). Therefore, understanding the characteristics of modern seismically induced soil liquefaction are critical for mitigating the economic and social losses associated with this secondary disaster.

The M_w 7.8 Sagaing earthquake occurred on 28 March 2025 in central Myanmar, triggering widespread coseismic soil liquefaction, which has not yet been reported as a secondary hazard along the Sagaing fault previously (Fig. 2a; U.S. Geological Survey [USGS], 2025; see Data and Resources). The seismogenic structure, the right-lateral strike-slip Sagaing fault, is the primary boundary between the Burma and Sunda plates (Fig. 1b; e.g., Gahalaut and Gahalaut, 2007; Wang *et al.*, 2014). It

1. Key Laboratory of Earthquake Forecasting and Risk Assessment, Ministry of Emergency Management, Institute of Earthquake Forecasting, China Earthquake Administration, Beijing, China, https://orcid.org/0009-0002-9506-7090 (GH); https://orcid.org/0000-0001-5641-8041 (WW); https://orcid.org/0000-0001-7342-2210 (YX); 2. Key Laboratory of Earthquake Prediction, Institute of Earthquake Forecasting, China Earthquake Administration, Beijing, China; 3. China Institute of Engineering Physics (Institute of Fluid Physics), Mianyang, China; 4. College of Geoscience, China University of Petroleum, Beijing, China

*Corresponding author: xuyr@ief.ac.cn

(a)

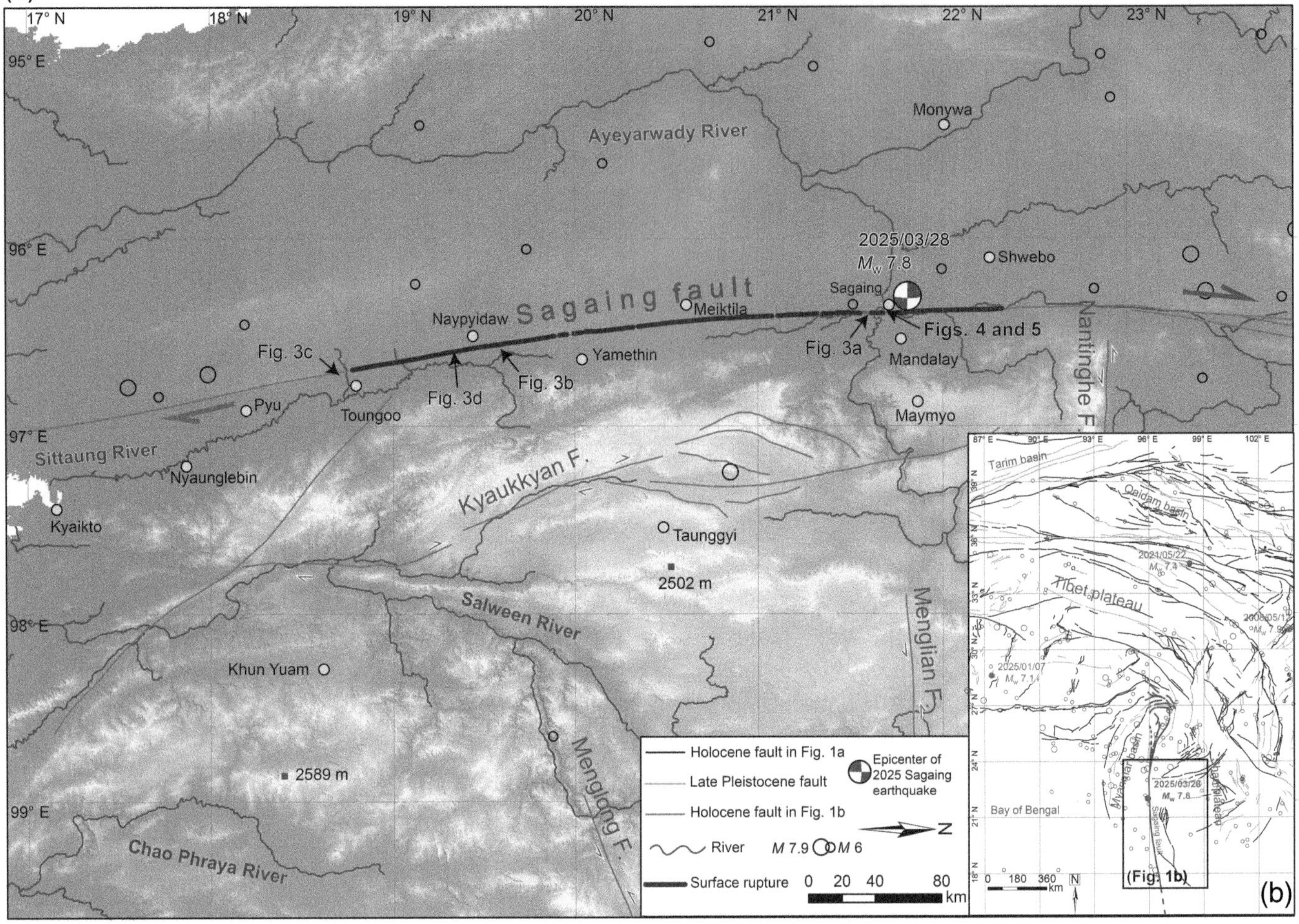

Figure 1. (a) Digital Elevation Model (DEM) of the study area showing tectonogeomorphic settings; the focal mechanism solution (focal mechanism plot) indicates the epicenter location of the 2025 M_W 7.8 Sagaing earthquake. The F is the abbreviation of fault. (b) Schematic map showing the locations of the Sagaing fault, the 2025 M_W 7.1 Tingri earthquake, and the 2021 M_W 7.4 Maduo earthquake; the rectangle indicates the location of the Sagaing fault. The color version of this figure is available only in the electronic edition.

accommodates northward motion of the Indian plate relative to the Sunda plate and defines the eastern margin of the Himalayan collision zone (Wang *et al.*, 2014; Shi *et al.*, 2018; Mallick *et al.*, 2019). The Sagaing fault strikes nearly north–south and extends >1200 km (Fig. 1b), with a well-documented history of strong earthquakes. Since 1900, it has produced 10 events with $M_W \geq 7.0$, including this mainshock (e.g., Wang *et al.*, 2014; Liang *et al.*, 2025). The general length of coseismic surface rupture of the 2025 earthquake spans ~460 km, with propagation dominated by supershear rupture movement (Antoine *et al.*, 2025; Goldberg *et al.*, 2025; Liang *et al.*, 2025; Melgar *et al.*, 2025; Wei *et al.*, 2025; Xu, Kang, *et al.*, 2025; Fig. 1c). The coseismic rupture zone targeted a long-recognized seismic gap (e.g., Wang *et al.*, 2014; Tin *et al.*, 2022), validating prior hazard assessments and highlighting the recurrent high seismic risk for the Sagaing fault. The peak ground acceleration (PGA) and peak ground velocity (PGV) data from the U.S. Geological Survey (USGS) show near-fault shaking exceeded 0.5*g* and 20 cm/s (Fig. 2a; USGS, 2025; see Data and Resources). This extreme ground motion caused extensive building collapse and fatalities, with felt shaking reported in neighboring regions, including Bangkok, Capital city of Thailand, and Ruili City, Yunnan Province, in Southwest China. The USGS predicts severe soil liquefaction risk along the Sagaing fault and coastal areas, and over 8000 km^2 and over 1 million people were exposed to these secondary hazards (Fig. 2a; USGS, 2025). Critically, soil liquefaction occurred in densely populated, urbanized regions, and this dataset advances understanding of coseismic liquefaction characteristics and effects along the Sagaing fault (Fig. 2a). However, field investigations in this region are constrained, further compounded by the large spatial extent of the soil liquefaction. High-resolution postearthquake aerial and satellite imagery has mitigated these limitations, providing robust support for remote sensing-based liquefaction interpretation.

Nowadays, remote sensing, utilizing high-resolution multisource aerial and satellite imagery, has become an auxiliary tool

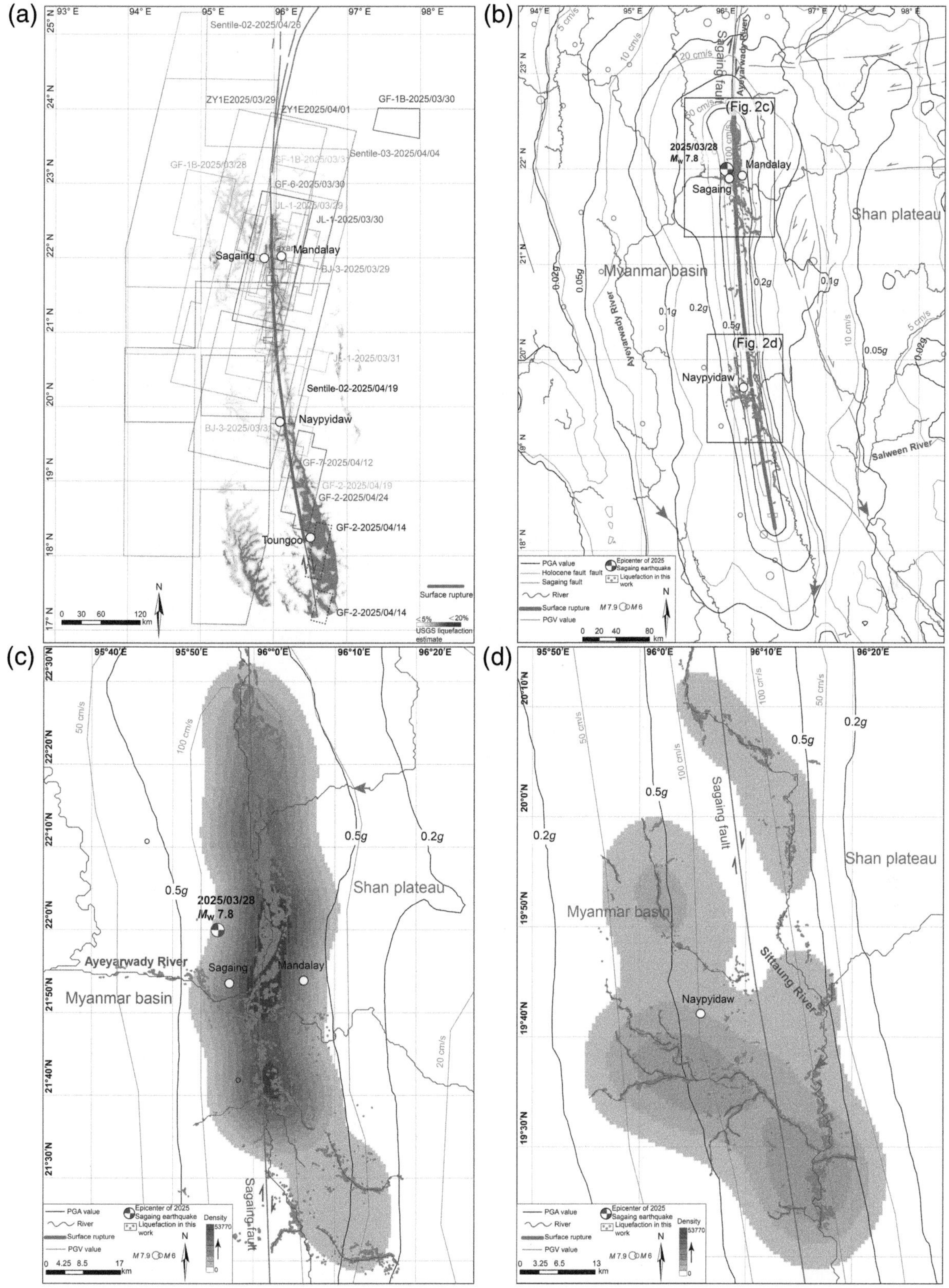

Figure 2. (a) Locations of high-resolution satellite images in the study area and soil liquefaction estimates from the U.S. Geological Survey (USGS). (b) Interpreted liquefaction sites (blue points); the two rectangles indicate the areas shown in panels (c) and (d). (c) Kernel density plot of soil liquefaction occurrences near the epicenter of the 2025 M_w 7.8 Sagaing earthquake. (d) Same as panel (c), but showing soil liquefaction around Naypyidaw. The color version of this figure is available only in the electronic edition.

Figure 3. Field investigation photos showing secondary seismic hazards caused by soil liquefaction: (a) unmanned aerial vehicle (UAV) image showing postseismic landscape, with visible earthquake-induced collapses, lateral spreads, and extensive soil liquefaction. (b) Photo showing sand blows, building foundation subsidence, and wall cracks due to severe soil liquefaction. (c) Road foundation failure and collapse caused by soil liquefaction. (d) Farmland damage caused by surface ruptures and soil liquefaction; persons in the images provide a scale reference. The color version of this figure is available only in the electronic edition.

for mapping the spatial characteristics of coseismic hazards (e.g., landslides, soil liquefaction, and surface ruptures) (e.g., Guo *et al.*, 2023; Xu, Fu, *et al.*, 2025). This approach offers a well-documented, rapid, and efficient method for assessing coseismic secondary hazards after earthquakes (e.g., Lu *et al.*, 2025; Xu, Fu, *et al.*, 2025). In this way, we characterize the spatial distribution of soil liquefaction induced by the 2025 M_w 7.8 Sagaing earthquake and investigate the triggering mechanisms of this liquefaction event. Our analysis combines high-resolution multisource aerial/satellite imagery with field data. It aims to improve the understanding of seismic secondary hazards in the central Myanmar basin and to establish a basis for quantifying the spatiotemporal patterns of historical and paleoseismic hazards along the Sagaing fault.

Methods

After the 2025 M_w 7.8 Sagaing earthquake, the China Earthquake Administration (CEA) guided postearthquake rescue/reconstruction and conducted field investigations of coseismic hazards (e.g., surface ruptures, soil liquefaction), collecting field evidence of soil liquefaction in Myanmar (Fig. 3). The USGS liquefaction estimates that the potential soil liquefaction extended far beyond the Sagaing fault (Fig. 2a); extreme liquefaction was concentrated in coastal areas of the southern fault segment (USGS, 2025). To validate these rough estimates and map the detailed coseismic soil liquefaction distribution, we combined with a limited field dataset, which enabled a systematic mapping of soil liquefaction.

Our satellite image datasets for coseismic liquefaction analysis of the 2025 M_w 7.8 Sagaing earthquake is dominated by high-spatial-resolution data from three primary sensors (Fig. 2a): BJ-3 (0.5 m spatial resolution, acquired on 29 and 30 March 2025, 1 and 2 days postearthquake, respectively), GF-2 (0.8 m spatial resolution, acquired on 14 and 24 April, 2025, 16 and 26 days postmainshock, respectively), and GF-1B (2 m spatial resolution, acquired on 30 and 31 March 2025, 1 and 2 days postearthquake, respectively), with additional high-spatial-resolution imagery including ZY1E (2.5 m, 29 March and 1 April 2025, 1 and 4 days postearthquake), Sentinel-3

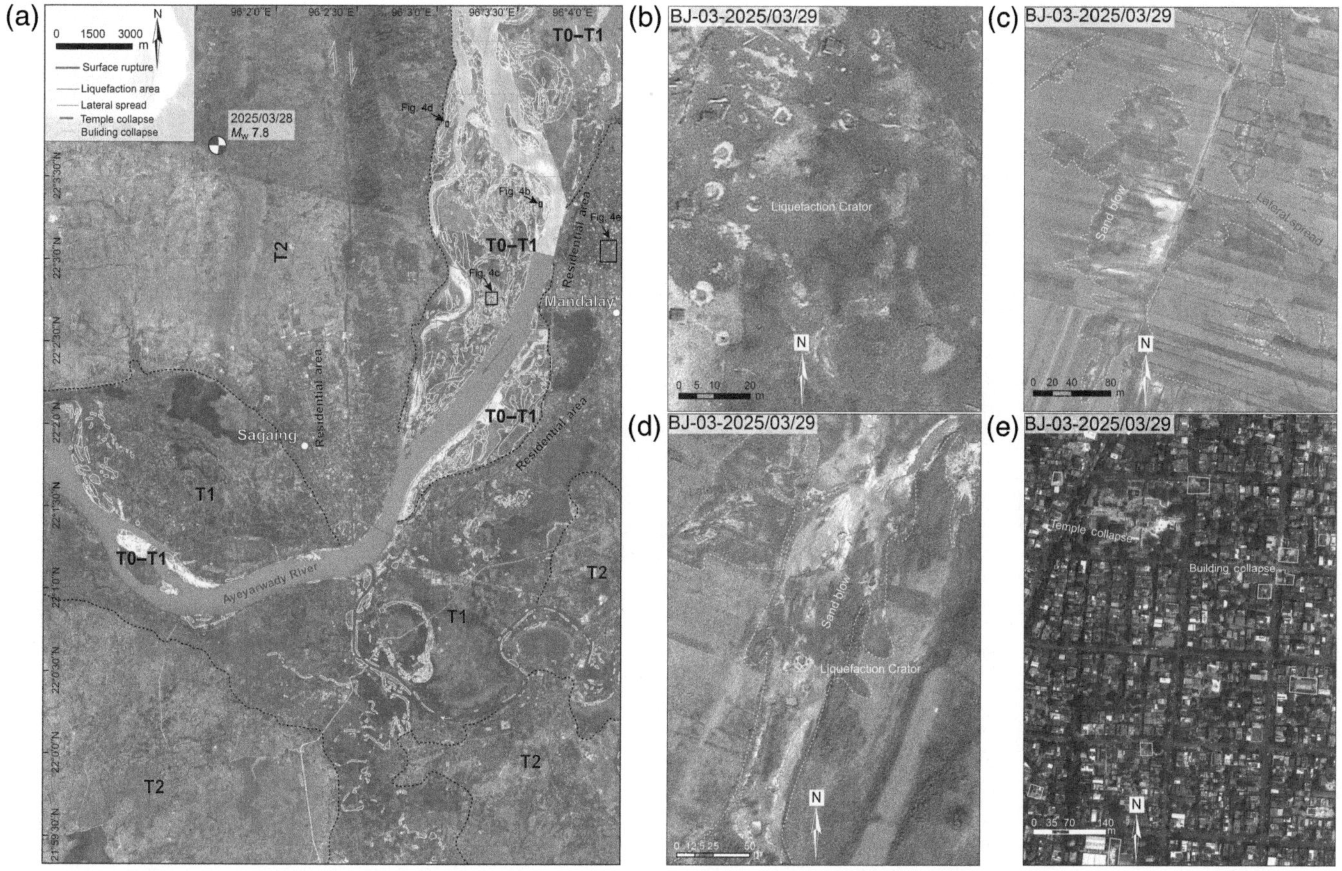

Figure 4. (a) Satellite image illustrating liquefaction distribution near the epicenter; soil liquefaction is widely and densely distributed along the T0–T1 river terraces of the Ayeyarwady River. (b,c) Enlarged views showing the morphology of soil liquefaction pits and lateral spreads. (d) Enlarged view showing damage to temples and buildings from the 2025 M_w 7.8 Sagaing earthquake. (e) Satellite imagery indicating building collapses and damage to temples caused by the earthquake. The color version of this figure is available only in the electronic edition.

(1 m, 4 April 2025, 7 days postearthquake), Sentinel-2 (1 m, 19 and 26 April 2025, 22 and 29 days postearthquake), JL-1 (1 m, 29–31 March 2025, 1–3 days postmainshock), GF-7 (0.65 m, 12 April 2025, 15 days postearthquake), and GF-6 (2 m, 30 March 2025, 2 days postearthquake); the epicentral region is fully covered by GF-1B and BJ-3 data acquired within three days postearthquake, areas with PGA > 0.5g and PGV > 20 cm/s are nearly entirely covered by very high-spatial-resolution imagery, and these datasets extend across our entire study area while nearly fully covering the epicentral region and areas along both sides of the fault (covered by GF-7, GF-2, GF-6, BJ-3, and JL-1, respectively), with satellite imagery broadly covering the soil liquefaction zone, estimated by the USGS except for partial coastal areas in the fault southern segment, which lack image coverage (Fig. 2a). Those high-resolution postseismic satellite images guarantee the reliability and accuracy of mapping interpretation.

Along the Sagaing fault, we employed manual visual interpretation to map coseismic soil liquefaction sites (e.g., Chini *et al.*, 2015; Zhao *et al.*, 2023; Lu *et al.*, 2025; Xu, Fu, *et al.*, 2025), and the results are checked by local field observations. With satellite imagery, that soil liquefaction features primarily manifested as sand blows, lateral spreads, sand volcanos, and occurrences along river valleys and lower river terraces (T0-T1; Figs. 3 and 4).

Along the Sagaing fault, we mapped coseismic soil liquefaction features through manual visual interpretation of satellite imagery (e.g., Chini *et al.*, 2015; Zhao *et al.*, 2023; Lu *et al.*, 2025; Xu, Fu, *et al.*, 2025), with field observations used to validate our interpretations. The identified liquefaction manifestations with satellite imagery primarily include sand blows, lateral spreads, and sand volcanoes, predominantly located along river valleys and on lower river terraces (T0–T1; Figs. 3 and 4). The liquefied sands, predominantly white to grayish-white, exhibit significant tonal contrast with surrounding sediments shown in postearthquake imageries (Figs. 3–5); in addition, individual liquefaction features generally exceed 10 m^2 in area, which facilitate their identification in satellite imageries with ~1 m spatial resolution. Because of the dense distribution and extensive coverage of liquefaction, these features were delineated as polygon shapes in ArcGIS software (Figs. 2b and 3–5). Subsequently, to characterize variations and analyze liquefaction impact, we generated a kernel density distribution map of coseismic liquefaction (Fig. 2c,d). For further analysis of soil liquefaction spatial distribution, we conducted buffer

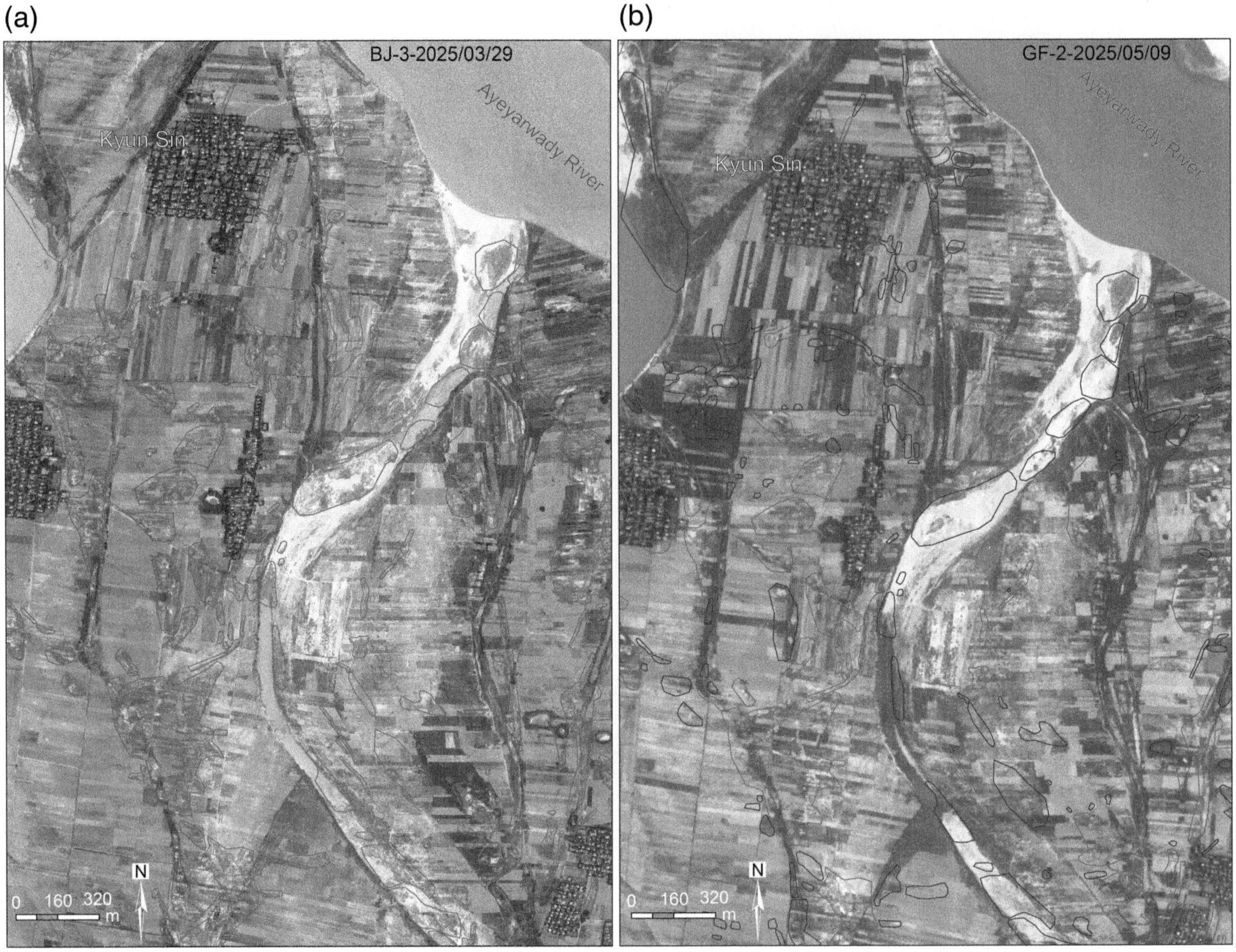

Figure 5. (a) Soil liquefaction distribution derived from a postseismic BJ-3 satellite image acquired one day after the earthquake. (b) Similar to panel (a), but from a postseismic GF-2 satellite image acquired 42 days after the earthquake. These two satellite images are used to highlight the importance of timely postearthquake liquefaction interpretation. The color version of this figure is available only in the electronic edition.

analysis: using coseismic surface ruptures as the central line, we created buffers at arbitrary 2.5 km intervals on both the eastern and western sides of the fault. We then summed the liquefaction area within each buffer and calculated the proportion of each buffer's liquefaction area relative to the total soil liquefaction area (Fig. 6). Based on these results, we analyzed the spatial characteristics and triggering mechanisms of soil liquefaction.

Results

Based on field investigations and satellite image interpretations, the 2025 M_w 7.8 Sagaing earthquake triggered extensive coseismic soil liquefaction in low terrains along river basins, composed by unconsolidated sands (Figs. 3–5). From the field photographic data and satellite imageries (Figs. 3 and 4), the liquefied sands are dominated by white and yellowish medium-coarse sands. The water table depth in areas with liquefaction observations is generally between 0.25 and 5 m (Fan *et al.*, 2013). Those fluvial geomorphological conditions are easily liquifiable during large earthquakes, by comparing soil liquefaction density with shaking and hydrogeologic features (Fig. 2b; e.g., Seed and Idriss, 1971; Seed *et al.*, 1991). The soil liquefaction observations and their secondary effects were primarily described as widespread liquefaction sand blows on roads, farmlands, and low river terraces (unconsolidated sands and low water table depth; Figs. 3 and 4b–d); earthquake-induced subsidence and lateral spreads developed along riverbanks (Fig. 3a); foundation failure and collapse in residential areas due to severe soil liquefaction (Fig. 3b); damage to road subgrades (Fig. 3c); and farmland destruction (Fig. 3a,d).

For the soil liquefaction features, sand blows mostly coincide in location with lateral spreads, forming a linear zonal distribution on both sides of the spreads (Figs. 3a and 4c). Gray-toned areas in satellite imagery indicate high water content of sand boils (Figs. 4b–d and 5a). Some soil liquefaction features exhibit stepped zones along both sides of surface

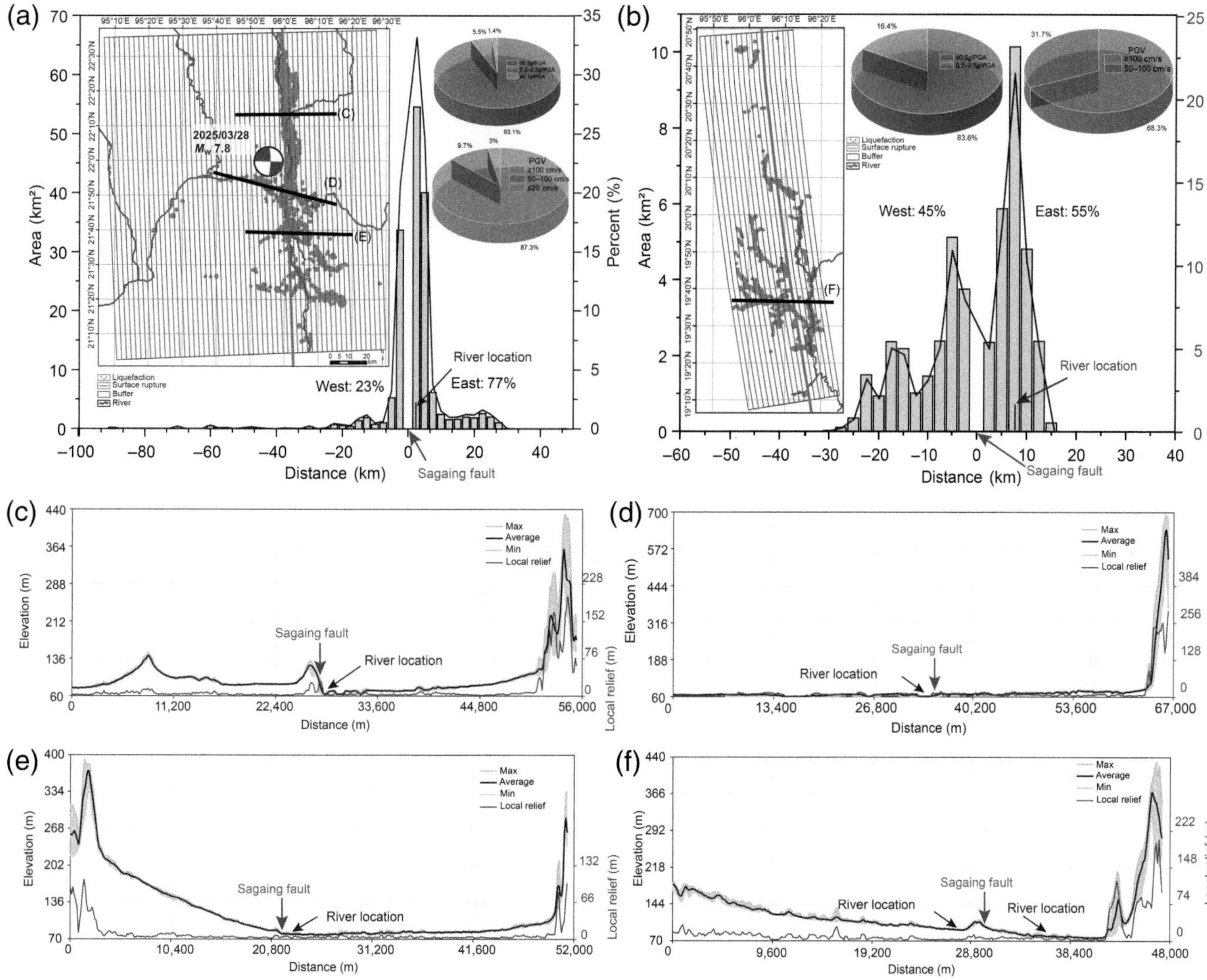

Figure 6. (a) Buffer analysis results showing the spatial distribution of soil liquefaction along the Sagaing fault and Rivers; the inset rectangle indicates the location of buffer zones near the epicenter, and the pie charts show the respective percentages of soil liquefaction under shaking levels of 0.5*g*, 0.2*g*, and 0.1*g* and 100, 50, 20 cm/s. respectively. The black bars indicate the locations of panels (c)–(e). (b) Similar to panel (a) but showing soil liquefaction around Naypyidaw. (c–f) Swath topographic profiles showing the geomorphic setting of the study area. The color version of this figure is available only in the electronic edition.

ruptures (Fig. 4d), whereas others appear as approximately circular "sand volcano" craters on surface (Fig. 4b,d).

By integrating satellite imagery and field verification, we identified 11,305 polygonal patches representing each soil liquefaction site, with a total liquefaction area exceeding 200 km^2 (Fig. 2b). Topographic profiles further show that soil liquefaction predominantly occurs at elevations of 60–100 m, corresponding to low T0–T1 river terraces with low water table depth (Figs. 4a and 6c–f), indicating that under strong ground motion, river systems, and geomorphic types jointly control the spatial pattern of soil liquefaction. The liquefaction zones are primarily located in the Ayeyarwady River basin near the epicenter of the M_w 7.8 Sagaing earthquake and Sittang River basin within the Myanmar basin, with a water divide separating these two river basins. Kernel density maps further reveal that the most densely distributed liquefaction area lies east of the epicenter, on the low terraces of the mainstem and tributaries of the Ayeyarwady River (marked in purple in Fig. 2c), accounting for 77% of the total soil liquefaction area (Fig. 6a). Around the Naypyidaw, the soil liquefaction area is smaller and more sparsely distributed (23% of the total area; Fig. 6b), mainly occurring on low river terraces along both sides of Sittang River. The soil liquefaction sites decrease rapidly with increasing distance from the rivers. This spatial distribution of liquefaction features in our study differs significantly from the USGS estimates overpredicting the spatial extent of liquefaction observations (Fig. 2a,b). Dense liquefaction in both regions is commonly observed at confluences where tributaries join the mainstems (Fig. 2c,d).

Buffer analysis reveals that liquefaction sites are strongly controlled by fault proximity, river morphology, and ground motion intensity. Around the Sagaing fault (Fig. 6), 77% of soil liquefaction occurs on the eastern side versus 23% on the western side, possibly related to distinct geology, elevation, and water table depth, with 96% of the total liquefaction area located within 5 km of the fault. Nearly all features fall within zones of PGA $\geq 0.2g$ and PGV $\geq$ 50 cm/s, whereas 93% and 87.3% are concentrated in areas with PGA $\geq 0.5g$ and PGV $\geq$ 100 cm/s, respectively (Fig. 6a). This distribution closely follows the main channel of the Ayeyarwady River: soil liquefaction extent declines sharply beyond 5 km from the river, with each subsequent 2.5 km interval containing less than 5 km^2 (under 5% of the total) in both area and occurrence count. In contrast, around Naypyidaw (Fig. 6f), liquefaction is more evenly split-55% east and 45% west of the fault-but exhibits distinct geomorphic controls: the western side extends ~25 km along Sittang River tributaries, whereas the eastern side is confined within 10 km of the main Sittang stem. Here, nearly all liquefaction also occurs in which PGA $\geq 0.2g$ and PGV $\geq$ 50 cm/s, with 84% and 68% falling in the higher-intensity zones (PGA $\geq 0.5g$, PGV $\geq$ 100 cm/s). Within the high-shaking zone (PGA $\geq 0.5g$, PGV $\geq$ 100 cm/s), liquefaction features display a zonal, planar pattern within an ~10–20 km width in the northern segment and ~10–25 km in the southern segment (Fig. 2b), concentrated near the epicenter and around Naypyidaw-two areas separated by a topographic water divide, underscoring the strong influence of terrain and drainage networks. The soil liquefaction zone spans approximately 400 km in length (Fig. 2b). The most severe soil liquefaction occurred at tributary-mainstem confluences near the epicenter, characterized by large individual sites ($\geq$10 m^2), high density (Fig. 2c), and diverse manifestations (sand blows, sand volcanoes, and lateral spreads; Figs. 4a and 6a), primarily confined to low terraces within ~10 km of rivers, forming narrow, and elongated zones (Fig. 6a). Although soil liquefaction density near Naypyidaw is lower, it similarly clusters at confluences (Figs. 2d and 6b), reinforcing the role of fluvial geomorphology in localizing liquefaction susceptibility.

Discussions

Uncertainty of mapping method of manual visual interpretation

This study conducted a preliminary investigation into the distribution characteristics and hazards of coseismic soil liquefaction triggered by the 2025 M_w 7.8 Sagaing earthquake, combining field reconnaissance and manual visual interpretation of multisource aerial remote sensing imagery. Thus, the results are highly dependent on the quality of multisource satellite remote sensing data, with data quality and the reliability of interpretation influenced by multiple factors.

On high-resolution remote sensing images, some materials appear similar to water-sand pits from soil liquefaction, potentially leading to misidentification of liquefaction sites. A typical example is cropping straw ash from on-farm burning by local residents (Fig. 3a). Although this interference resembles soil liquefaction features in imagery, key differences distinguish the two: these ash layers are primarily black or gray, with random planar distribution, distinct from liquefaction deposits, which have a white center surrounded by grayish-black water traces. In addition, the straw ash layers are limited in quantity, and no associated lateral spreads are observed. These characteristics enable easy differentiation of straw ash from liquefaction features in satellite imagery, thus having no impact on the accuracy of soil liquefaction interpretation.

Postearthquake weather conditions (e.g., heavy cloud cover, rainy seasons) can affect imaging quality. The earthquake occurred on 28 March 2025, just before the onset of the Southeast Asia rainy season; therefore, most remote sensing data were minimally affected by weather. However, partial cloud cover is evident in some data from southern coastal areas (e.g., GF-2 satellite data acquired on 14 April 2025). Although this may somewhat limit the completeness of the dataset, no evidence of soil liquefaction was observed in cloud-free areas where usable satellite imagery was available in this region.

Influence of postearthquake remote sensing image acquisition time on soil liquefaction identification

The completeness of manual visual interpretation of coseismic soil liquefaction also depends critically on the surface preservation time of liquefaction pits (i.e., materials vented to the surface) and the time interval between the earthquake and the acquisition of remote sensing imagery (Guo *et al.*, 2023).

The conditions to support long-term surface preservation of soil liquefaction features include low-intensity human modification, low vegetation cover, and low rainfall volume. In addition, the timely acquisition of high-resolution postearthquake imagery is essential for accurate interpretation. For the 2025 M_w 7.8 Sagaing earthquake (occurring in March 2025), field surveys confirmed that residents had not yet begun large-scale farming, preventing obstruction by crops. Except for built-up areas (cities and villages, where buildings block satellite visibility), liquefaction features remained highly exposed and clearly identifiable in farmlands and along roads. Most soil liquefaction sites are distributed on low river terraces (T0–T1). Although river floodplains (and thus liquefaction materials) are submerged during high-water periods, the Southeast Asia rainy season typically lasts from June to September but the March–May period is a low-rainfall period, making this window optimal for soil liquefaction interpretation using imagery (e.g., Misra and DiNapoli, 2014; Hu *et al.*, 2025).

The timeliness of postearthquake satellite data acquisition is a key factor of the interpretation reliability. Most of the remote sensing data used in this study were acquired within one-week postearthquakes (Fig. 2a). To visually demonstrate the importance of imagery timeliness and its direct impact on interpretation, we analyzed postearthquake imagery from different time periods in the most liquefaction-dense area (eastern epicenter, Ayeyarwady River segment). Figure 5a shows BJ-3 imagery acquired three days postearthquake: dense soil liquefaction features (numerous lateral spreads and sand blows) are visible along the Ayeyarwady River banks and in farmlands. On the imagery, sand-water pits appear as irregular polygons, characterized by grayish-black water traces and white liquefied sand, their distinct tone from surrounding materials enables easy identification. But, from Figure 5b, it shows GF-2 imagery of the exact location acquired 42 days postearthquake (9 May 2025; the BJ-3 satellite did not recover this area during this period). Although most soil liquefaction pits remained visible, the area of individual features had shrunk, and some had become obscured or even disappeared (indicated by blue color in the Fig. 5b). This may result from human modification, drying of sand-water pits (reducing surface visibility), or submergence by rising water levels in the Ayeyarwady River. Consequently, given that vented sand-water layers are easily disturbed and have short surface preservation times, the timely and efficient acquisition of postearthquake imagery is a critical factor for accurate soil liquefaction interpretation.

Comparison of USGS assessment map and our mapping result

As shown in Figure 2a,b, there are significant differences between the coseismic soil liquefaction distribution results derived from manual visual interpretation and those from the USGS results. These differences manifest likely in the following two aspects.

For the location of the most intensive liquefaction zones, and based on USGS inversion results using the Zhu *et al.* (2017) model, the most severe soil liquefaction triggered by the 2025 M_w 7.8 Sagaing earthquake was predicted to occur in southern coastal Myanmar, with a trend of increasing liquefaction severity toward the south along the fault (Fig. 2a; see Data and Resources). However, our results from high-resolution satellite image interpretation show an opposite pattern. As presented in Figure 2b–d, the most severe soil liquefaction is distributed on the low terraces of the Ayeyarwady River, east of the epicenter. The soil liquefaction area can be roughly divided into northern and southern segments: the total liquefaction area near the epicenter is approximately 165 km^2, whereas that near Naypyidaw in the south is approximately 48 km^2 (accounting for ~1/3 of the northern area). Thus, the most severe soil liquefaction pits are concentrated near the epicenter rather than in southern coastal regions. Furthermore, verification using GF-2 remote sensing imagery acquired 17 days postearthquake confirmed almost no traces of soil liquefaction in southern coastal areas (Fig. 2b). Besides, for the total liquefaction area and scale, USGS results allow a rough estimate that the area exposed to soil liquefaction exceeds 8000–9000 km^2 (Fig. 2a; see Data and Resources). Its estimates from the USGS cover most of the Central Myanmar basin, with a large proportion of the area distributed in regions with the PGA between 0.05 and 0.2g and generally over 150 km in width of soil liquefaction zone (Fig. 2a). But, the total liquefaction area interpreted from satellite imagery is approximately 210 km^2, markedly smaller than the USGS estimate, and is predominantly concentrated within a narrow range 10–20 km from the fault with the PGA $\geqq$ 0.2g and PGV $\geqq$ 100 cm/s (Fig. 2b–d).

The striking discrepancy between the two highlights a regional bias in the Global Geospatial Liquefaction Model (GGLM-2017) when applied to coseismic liquefaction, as previously documented by Rashidian and Baise (2020) and Asadi *et al.* (2024). To enhance the model's performance, updated liquefaction datasets—including paleoseismic, historical, and modern earthquake-induced cases—from the study region are urgently needed. Furthermore, either a region-specific prediction model should be developed to supersede GGLM-2017 (Rashidian and Baise, 2020; Asadi *et al.*, 2024), or the global model itself should be recalibrated using regionally updated parameters to improve its predictive accuracy.

Implications of the coseismic soil liquefaction from the M_w 7.9 Sagaing earthquake

The spatial pattern of soil liquefaction triggered by the 2025 M_w 7.9 Sagaing earthquake aligns closely with that observed in other major strike-slip earthquakes, such as the 2021 M_w 7.4 Maduo, the 2023 M_w 7.8 Türkiye, and M_w 7.5, the 1999 M_w 7.6 İzmit, and the 2010 M_w 7.0 Haiti events (Cetin *et al.*, 2002; Olson *et al.*, 2011; Wang *et al.*, 2023). In these cases, soil liquefaction is consistently confined to low-elevation river valleys intersected by surface ruptures. For instance, during the Maduo earthquake, soil liquefaction extended along ~150 km —approximately matching the rupture length—but was largely restricted to a narrow corridor (~1 km wide) adjacent to the fault trace (Wang *et al.*, 2023). This geometry reflects a distinct spatial signature of soil liquefaction associated with strike-slip faulting in intermontane basins, which we term strike-slip fault-type liquefaction in basins.

This pattern contrasts sharply with soil liquefaction induced by normal faults. The 2025 M_w 7.1 Tingri earthquake in the southern Tibetan rift system provides a representative example: its seismogenic structure, the Dengmecuo normal fault, lies within a graben basin (Xu, Fu, *et al.*, 2025). Although ~90% of the resulting liquefaction occurred near rivers and lakes within the Dengmecuo basin, ~10% was also observed in adjacent basins (Guojia and Dinggye basins)—areas controlled by separate faults (Guojia and Dinggye faults) and lacking surface rupture. Thus, soil liquefaction extended beyond the immediate zone of the primary seismogenic fault, suggesting a broader influence of regional hydrogeological connectivity. We refer to this as normal fault-type liquefaction in basins.

Thrust fault produces yet another distinct pattern. The 2008 M_w 7.9 Wenchuan earthquake exemplifies thrust fault-type liquefaction in basins: soil liquefaction was primarily distributed within the footwall-controlled Sichuan basin, forming an

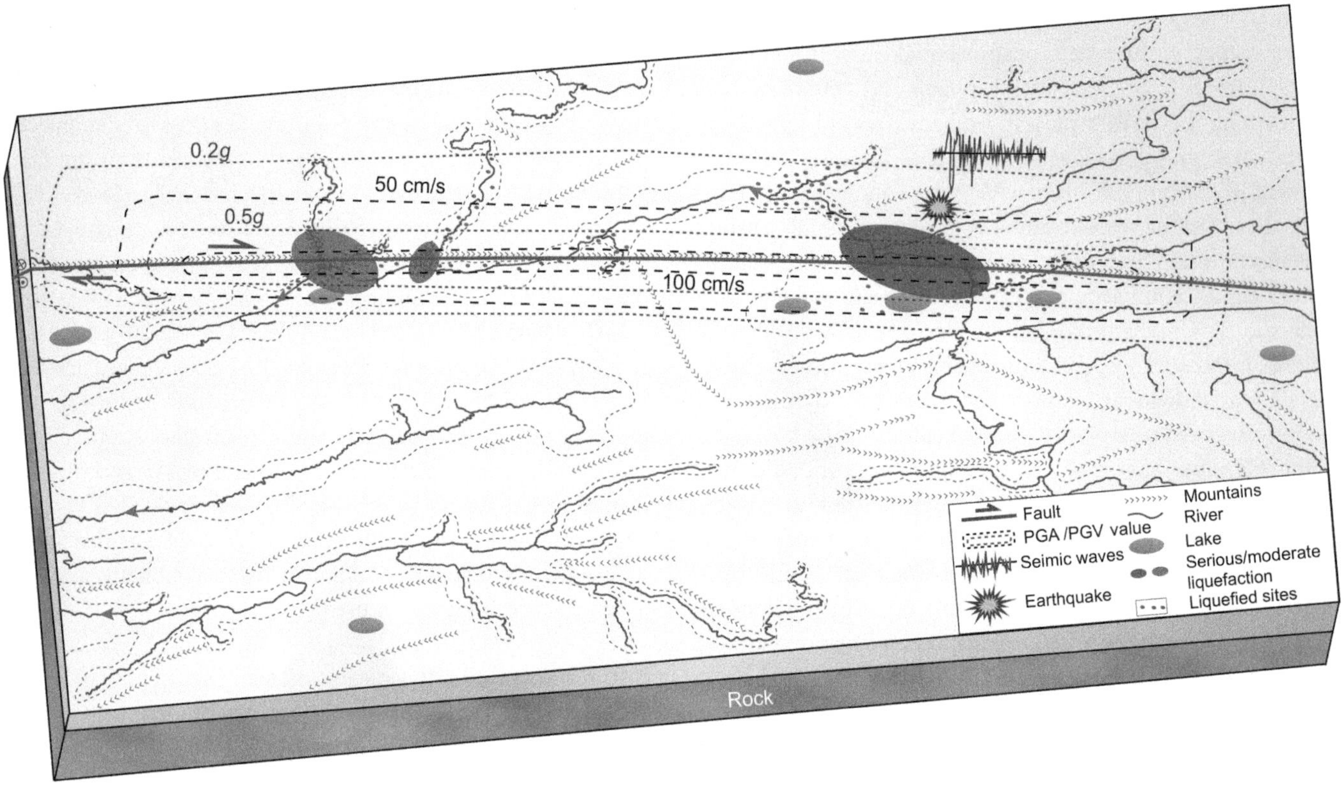

Figure 7. Schematic cartoon illustrating the spatial distribution and scenario of coseismic soil liquefaction along the Sagaing fault. Soil liquefaction is densely distributed within a narrow zone (in which peak ground acceleration [PGA] = 0.2g and peak ground velocity [PGV] = 100 cm/s) between the Shan plateau and Myanmar basin, with denser liquefaction areas near the epicenter. The color version of this figure is available only in the electronic edition.

elongated zone roughly parallel to the surface rupture (Chen *et al.*, 2009; Yuan *et al.*, 2009; Liu-Zeng *et al.*, 2017). However, the densest liquefaction occurred 20–40 km away from the main thrust fault, within a narrow (~20 km wide) belt influenced by blind faults and shallow groundwater conditions in the basin. This offset highlights the role of subsurface structural and hydrogeological controls in thrust settings.

Although this threefold classification may not encompass all global liquefaction scenarios, these cases demonstrate that hydrogeological factors exert a first-order control on the spatial architecture of coseismic soil liquefaction in tectonically active basins. From a tectonogeomorphic perspective, despite the presence of numerous rivers and alluvial–pluvial fans across the Central Myanmar basin and Shan plateau, strike-slip fault-induced liquefaction in the 2025 Sagaing earthquake was predominantly localized on low river terraces within a narrow zone (<5 km) with high PGA and PGV values (Fig. 7). This reflects three critical factors: (1) strong ground motion, (2) high groundwater tables, and (3) abundant, loosely compacted sandy deposits—all of which render these terraces highly susceptible to severe secondary hazards.

Critically, similar hydrogeological and geomorphic conditions exist along the northeast-trending active faults in southwestern Yunnan Province (Fig. 1b). These low terraces are densely populated and undergoing rapid urbanization. Given the demonstrated vulnerability to soil liquefaction during strike-slip earthquakes, proactive mitigation measures—such as foundation reinforcement and land-use planning—are urgently needed to reduce seismic risk in these areas.

Finally, the absence of soil liquefaction in the coastal lower Sittaung River region during the Sagaing earthquake stands in contrast to the extensive liquefaction observed during the 1976 M_s 7.8 Tangshan earthquake in China—even though both events involved right-lateral strike-slip faulting. In Tangshan, widespread soil liquefaction occurred across coastal plains under seismic intensities of VIII–IX (Guo *et al.*, 2011), facilitated by the flat topography of the North China Plain, thick unconsolidated sandy sediments, a dense river network, and a very shallow water table (typically <5 m depth). The short epicentral distance (~50–60 km) to the coast further amplified ground-shaking effects. Together, these comparisons underscore a key insight: within zones of high seismic intensity, the spatial extent and severity of liquefaction are ultimately governed not only by fault type, but also—and perhaps more decisively—by local hydrogeological and geomorphological conditions.

Conclusion

On 28 March 2025, an M_w 7.8 earthquake struck Myanmar, forming a length of ~400 km coseismic surface rupture, and triggering large-scale coseismic soil liquefaction. This secondary seismic hazard caused severe damage to local infrastructure. To rapidly assess the impact and spatial distribution of earthquake-induced soil liquefaction, we conducted a detailed manual visual interpretation of high-resolution satellite imagery. The reliability of the interpretation results was verified using field survey imagery.

We identified over 10,000 soil liquefaction pits, with a total liquefaction area ~200 km^2. In terms of spatial distribution, the earthquake-induced liquefaction zones can be divided into two regions based on density: the area near the epicenter and the area near Naypyidaw (on the southern segment of the fault). A water divide separates these two zones.

Soil liquefaction was distributed exclusively on low terraces along the Ayeyarwady River, Sittaung River, and their tributaries, around the surface ruptures. The ≧90% of liquefaction occurred within areas with a PGA of ≧0.5g and a PGV of ≧50 cm/s. The length of the total soil liquefaction area along the Sagaing fault is roughly equivalent to that of the surface rupture zone: most liquefaction extended within 10 km of both sides of the fault near the epicenter, and within ~10–20 km of both sides of the fault near Naypyidaw. Beyond the influence of strong ground motion from the strike-slip fault, this spatial pattern is also closely related to the local geomorphological setting and groundwater table depth.

Data and Resources

The seismic ShakeMap and liquefaction estimates are from the U.S. Geological Survey (USGS) (https://earthquake.usgs.gov/earthquakes/eventpage/us7000pn9s/pager). The USGS https://earthquake.usgs.gov/earthquakes/eventpage/us7000pn9s/executive and https://earthquake.usgs.gov/earthquakes/eventpage/us7000pn9s/map?shakeMapIntensity=false&ground-failure-liquefaction=true. The supplemental material for this article includes the soil liquefaction dataset, triggered by the 2025 M_w 7.5 Sagaing earthquake, and it has been publicly archived (https://zenodo.org/records/18059080). All websites were last accessed in December 2025.

Declaration of Competing Interests

The authors acknowledge that there are no conflicts of interest recorded.

Acknowledgments

The authors sincerely thank the editor and the two anonymous reviewers for their valuable suggestions that have greatly improved our article. This project was conducted under the funding of the Key Project of the Fundamental Research Funds for the Institute of Earthquake Forecasting, China Earthquake Administration (Numbers CEAIEF20240302 and CEAIEF20250101), and the National Natural Science Foundation of China (Number 42072248) to XYR and under the Young Scientists Fund of the National Natural Science Foundation of China (Number 42202212) to HGM, and Project of the National Key R&D Program (Number 2023YFC3012001-2) to LWQ.

References

Ambraseys, N. N. (1988). Engineering seismology: Earthquake engineering and structural dynamics, *Earthq. Eng. Struct. Dynam.* **17,** no. 1, 51–105.

Antoine, S. L., R. Shrestha, C. Milliner, K. Im, C. Rollins, K. Wang, K. Chen, and J. Avouac (2025). The 2025 M_w 7.7 Mandalay, Myanmar, earthquake reveals a complex earthquake cycle with clustering and variable segmentation on the Sagaing fault, *Proc. Natl. Acad. Sci. Unit. States Am.* **122,** no. 33, e2514378122.

Asadi, A., C. Sanon, E. Cakir, W. Zhan, H. Shirzadi, L. G. Baise, K. O. Cetin, and B. Moaveni (2024). Geospatial liquefaction modeling of the 2023 Türkiye earthquake sequence by an ensemble of global, continental, regional, and event-specific models, *Seismol. Res. Lett.* **95,** 697–719.

Cetin, K. O., T. L. Youd, R. B. Seed, J. D. Bray, R. Sancio, W. Lettis, M. T. Yilmaz, and H. T. Durgunoglu (2002). Liquefaction-induced ground deformations at Hotel Sapanca during Kocaeli (Izmit), Turkey earthquake, *Soil Dynam. Earthq. Eng.* **22,** 1083–1092.

Chen, L., J. Lei, and Y. Wang (2024). Liquefaction phenomena following the February 6th, 2023, Türkiye earthquakes: Observation and lessons, *Nat. Hazards* **120,** no. 12, 10,709–10,726.

Chen, L. W., X. M. Yuan, Z. Z. Cao, L. Q. Hou, R. Sun, L. Dong, W. M. Wang, F. C. Meng, and H. J. Chen (2009). Liquefaction macrophenomena in the great Wenchuan earthquake, *Earthq. Eng. Eng. Vib.* **8,** no. 2, 219–229.

Chini, M., M. Albano, M. Saroli, L. Pulvirenti, M. Moro, C. Bignami, E. Falcucci, S. Gori, G. Modoni, N. Pierdicca, *et al.* (2015). Coseismic liquefaction phenomenon analysis by COSMO-SkyMed: 2012 Emilia (Italy) earthquake, *Int. J. Appl. Earth Obs. Geoinf.* **39,** 65–78.

Cubrinovski, M., J. D. Bray, M. Taylor, S. Giorgini, B. Bradley, L. Wotherspoon, and J. Zupan (2011). Soil liquefaction effects in the Central Business district during the February 2011 Christchurch earthquake, *Seismol. Res. Lett.* **82,** no. 6, 893–904.

Fan, Y., H. Li, and G. Miguez-Macko (2013). Global patterns of groundwater table depth, *Science* **339,** 940–943.

Fu, S., and F. Tatsuoka (1984). Soil liquefaction during Haicheng and Tangshan earthquake in China: A review, *Soils Found.* **24,** no. 1, 11–29.

Gahalaut, V. K., and K. Gahalaut (2007). Burma plate motion, *J. Geophys. Res. Solid Earth* **112,** no. B10.

Goldberg, D. E., W. L. Yeck, C. E. Hanagan, J. Atterholt, H. Kehoe, N. G. Reitman, W. D. Barnhart, D. R. Shelly, A. E. Hatem, D. Wald, *et al.* (2025). Ultralong, supershear rupture of the 2025 M_w 7.7 Mandalay earthquake reveals unaccounted risk, *Science* **390,** no. 6772, 458–462.

Guo, H., W. L. Jiang, and X. S. Xie (2011). Late-Quaternary strong earthquakes on the seismogenic fault of the 1976 *Ms* 7.8 Tangshan earthquake, Hebei, as revealed by drilling and trenching, *Sci. China: Earth Sci.* **41,** no. 7, 1009–1028.

Guo, Y., Y. Xu, H. Li, L. Lu, W. Xu, and P. Liang (2023). Using Keyhole images to map soil liquefaction induced by the 1966 Xingtai *Ms* 6.8 and 7.2 earthquakes, North China, *Remote Sens.* **15,** no. 23, 5777.

Hu, Y., C. Cui, Z. Liu, and Y. Zhang (2025). Vegetation dynamics in Mainland southeast Asia: Climate and anthropogenic influences, *Land Use Policy* **153,** 107546.

Ishitsuka, K., T. Tsuji, and T. Matsuoka (2012). Detection and mapping of soil liquefaction in the 2011 Tohoku earthquake using SAR interferometry,*Earth Planets Space* **64,** no. 12, 1267–1276.

Liang, P., Y. Xu, C. Hu, Q. Tian, L. Fang, A. Dou, R. Xiong, W. Wu, C. Xu, and F. Geng (2025). Surface rupture pattern and coseismic displacement distribution of the 2025 M_w 7.7 Myanmar earthquake revealed by Chinese high-resolution satellite imagery, *Chin. Sci. Bull.* **50,** no. 17, 1813–1829 (in Chinese with English abstract).

Liu-Zeng, J., P. Wang, Z. Zhang, Z. Li, Z. Cao, J. Zhang, X. Yuan, W. Wang, and X. Xing (2017). Liquefaction in western Sichuan Basin during the 2008 M_w 7.9 Wenchuan earthquake, China, *Tectonophysics* **694,** 214–238.

Lu, L., Y. Xu, J. Tang, and G. Hu (2025). High-resolution satellite imagery analysis of coseismic landslides and liquefaction induced by the 2024 M_w 7.4 Hualien earthquake, Taiwan, China, *Earthq. Res. Adv.* **5,** no. 3, 100356.

Mallick, R., E. O. Lindsey, L. Feng, J. Hubbard, P. Banerjee, and E. M. Hill (2019). Active convergence of the India-Burma-Sunda plates revealed by a new continuous GPS Network, *J. Geophys. Res. Solid Earth* **124,** no. 3, 3155–3171.

Melgar, D., R. Weldon, Y. Wang, M. G. Bato, L. T. Aung, X. Shi, W. Wiwegwing, S. N. Khaing, S. Min, M. Thant, *et al.* (2025). Supershear source model of the 2025 M 7.8 Myanmar earthquake and paleoseismology of the Sagaing Fault: Regions of significant overlap with past earthquakes, *Seismica* **4,** no. 2, 1–15.

Misra, V., and S. DiNapoli (2014). The variability of the southeast Asian summer monsoon, *Int. J. Climatol.* **34,** 893–901.

Moss, R.E.S., R.E. Kayen, L.Y. Tong, S.Y. Liu, G.J. Cai, and J. Wu, (2011). Retesting of liquefaction and nonliquefaction case histories from the 1976 Tangshan earthquake, *J. Geotech. Geoenviron. Eng.* **137,** 334–343.

Olson, S. M., R. A. Green, S. Lasley, N. Martin, B. R. Cox, E. Rathje, J. Bachhuber, and J. French (2011). Documenting liquefaction and lateral spreading triggered by the 12 January 2010 Haiti earthquake, *Earthq. Spectra* **27,** 93–116.

Pretell, R., K. Ziotopoulou, and C. A. Davis (2021). Liquefaction and cyclic softening at Balboa Boulevard during the 1994 Northridge earthquake, *J. Geotech. Geoenviron. Eng.* **147,** no. 5, 05020014.

Quigley, M. C., S. Bastin, and B. A. Bradley (2013). Recurrent liquefaction in Christchurch, New Zealand, during the Canterbury earthquake sequence, *Geology* **41,** no. 4, 419–422.

Rashidian, V., and L. G. Baise (2020). Regional efficacy of a global geospatial liquefaction model, *Eng. Geol.* **272,** 105644.

Seed, H. B., and I. M. Idriss (1971). Simplified procedure for evaluating soil liquefaction potential, *J. Soil Mech. Found. Div.* **97,** no. 9, 1249–1273.

Seed, R. B., M. F. Riemer, and S. E. Dickenson (1991). Liquefaction of soils in the 1989 Loma Prieta earthquake, Missouri University of Science and Technology Scholars' Mine.

Shi, X., Y. Wang, K. Sieh, R. Weldon, L. Feng, C. Chan, and J. Liu-Zeng (2018). Fault slip and GPS velocities across the Shan plateau define a curved southwestward crustal motion around the eastern Himalayan Syntaxis, *J. Geophys. Res. Solid Earth* **123,** no. 3, 2502–2518.

Taftsoglou, M., S. Valkaniotis, G. Papathanassiou, and E. Karantanellis (2023). Satellite imagery for rapid detection of liquefaction surface manifestations: The case study of Türkiye-Syria 2023 earthquakes, *Remote Sens.* **15,** no. 16, 4190.

Tin, T. Z. H., T. Nishimura, M. Hashimoto, E. O. Lindsey, L. T. Aung, S. M. Min, and M. Thant (2022). Present-day crustal deformation and slip rate along the southern Sagaing fault in Myanmar by GNSS observation, *J. Asian Earth Sci.* **228,** 105125.

U.S. Geological Survey (2025). M7.7-2025 Mandalay, Burma (Myanmar) Earthquake, available at https://earthquake.usgs.gov/earthquakes/eventpage/us7000pn9s/pager (last accessed December 2025).

Wang, W., J. Liu-Zeng, Y. Shao, Z. Wang, L. Han, X. Shen, K. Qin, Y. Gao, W. Yao, G. Hu, *et al.* (2023). Mapping of soil liquefaction associated with the 2021 M_w 7.4 Maduo (Madoi) earthquake based on the UAV photogrammetry technology, *Remote Sens.* **15,** 1032.

Wang, Y., K. Sieh, S. T. Tun, K. Lai, and T. Myint (2014). Active tectonics and earthquake potential of the Myanmar region, *J. Geophys. Res. Solid Earth* **119,** no. 4, 3767–3822.

Wei, S., X. Wang, C. Li, H. Zeng, Z. Ma, Q. Shi, H. Chen, Y. Huang, M. Lyu, J. Liao, *et al.* (2025). Supershear rupture sustained through a thick fault zone in the 2025 M_w 7.8 Mandalay earthquake, *Science* **390,** no. 6772, 468–472.

Wotherspoon, L. M., M. J. Pender, and R. P. Orense (2012). Relationship between observed liquefaction at Kaiapoi following the 2010 Darfield earthquake and former channels of the Waimakariri River, *Eng. Geol.* **125,** 45–55.

Xu, X., W. Kang, T. Wang, X. Zhang, Y. Liu, Y. Zhang, J. Zhao, K. Li, Q. Wang, J. Cheng, *et al.* (2025). The M_w 7.7 Myanmar earthquake: A continental longest surface-rupturing supershear cascading event, *npj Nat. Hazards Earth Syst. Sci.* **2,** 73.

Xu, Y., G. Fu, Z. Liang, G. Hu, X. Zhou, F. Shi, and Y. Yao (2025). Preliminary study on the characteristics of landslides and soil liquefaction triggered by the Dingri M_s 6.8 earthquake on January 7, 2025, southern Tibetan plateau, *J. Earth Sci.*, doi: 10.1007/s12583-025-0308-0.

Yuan, X. M., Z. Z. Cao, R. Sun, L. W. Chen, S. J. Meng, L. Dong, W. M. Wang, F. C. Meng, H. J. Chen, J. Y. Zhang, *et al.* (2009). Preliminary research on liquefaction characteristic of Wenchuan 8.0 earthquake, *Chin. J. Rock Mech. Eng.* **28,** no. 7, 1288–1296 (in Chinese with English abstract).

Zhao, B., L. Su, Q. Xu, W. Li, C. Xu, and Y. Wang (2023). A review of recent earthquake-induced landslides on the Tibetan plateau, *Earth Sci. Rev.* **244,** 104534.

Zhu, J., L. G. Baise, and E. M. Thompson (2017). An updated geospatial liquefaction model for global application, *Bull. Seismol. Soc. Am.* **107,** 1365–1385.

Manuscript received 6 November 2025
Published online 25 March 2026

The 2025 M_w 7.1 Tingri (South Tibet) Earthquake: Rupture of Normal Conjugate Optimally Oriented Faults, Shallow Coseismic Slip Deficit, and Early Afterslip

OPEN ACCESS

Xiaoyu Zou[*1] and Yuri Fialko[1]

Abstract

On 7 January 2025, a magnitude 7.1 earthquake struck Tingri County in the south of the Tibetan Plateau, China, producing widespread damage in the Lhatse-Sa'gya-Tingri region and adjacent areas. The earthquake ruptured a pair of conjugate north-south striking normal faults in the Dengmecuo graben, and was the largest normal earthquake instrumentally recorded in the region. We use Interferometric Synthetic Aperture Radar observations from Sentinel-1A, Advanced Land Observation Satellite-2, and Lutan-1 satellites to investigate coseismic and early postseismic deformation due to the 2025 Tingri earthquake. We invert line-of-sight displacements and pixel offsets for the fault geometry and slip distribution using an iterative scheme that incorporates a 3D curved fault geometry and layered rigidity structure constrained by seismic tomography. The ruptured faults are modeled using a triangular mesh with a linear variation in slip between the nodes. The preferred model suggests average dip angles of 60°–70° for both the main (west-dipping) rupture and the subsidiary (east-dipping) conjugate fault, indicating optimal fault orientations consistent with Byerlee's law and coefficient of friction of 0.6–0.7. The best-fit model has a variance reduction of 91%, and an equivalent moment magnitude of 7.0. The modeled coseismic slip exhibits a large (~60%) shallow slip deficit, only a small fraction of which is relieved by shallow afterslip in the first ~8 months following the earthquake. The observed coseismic and postseismic deformation suggests velocity-strengthening friction, as well as extensive off-fault damage in the top several kilometers of the Earth's crust. Contributions from the early viscoelastic and poroelastic relaxation are found to be negligible. Continued geodetic observations will help quantify the evolving roles of afterslip and viscoelastic relaxation, provide tighter constraints on the effective rheology of the lower crust, and illuminate the mechanisms of the ongoing east–west extension in the southern Tibetan rift zone.

Cite this article as Zou, X., and Y. Fialko (2026). The 2025 M_w 7.1 Tingri (South Tibet) Earthquake: Rupture of Normal Conjugate Optimally Oriented Faults, Shallow Coseismic Slip Deficit, and Early Afterslip, *Seismol. Res. Lett.* **97**, 1667–1680, doi: 10.1785/0220250445.

Supplemental Material

Introduction

On 7 January 2025 at 01:05 UTC time, the moment magnitude (M_w) 7.1 earthquake struck Tingri County of the Tibet autonomous region, China, with an epicenter located at [28.604° N, 87.378° E] and a focal depth of 10 km (U.S. Geological Survey [USGS], 2025). The earthquake is the largest instrumentally recorded normal event in the southern Tibetan plateau, and the most destructive one since the 2015 M_w 7.8 Gorkha, Nepal, earthquake (e.g., Hall *et al.*, 2017; Wang and Fialko, 2018; Qi *et al.*, 2024). With an estimated intensity of IX, the 2025 Tingri (also referred to as Dingri) earthquake has devastated the Lhatse-Sa'gya-Tingri region, killing at least 126 people and destroying more than 3600 houses (e.g., Zhou and Li, 2025). The impact extended beyond China, with Bhutan, India, and Nepal also reporting casualties and property damage. Early reports using the Global Centroid Moment Tensor focal mechanism, satellite remote sensing data, and field observations showed that the earthquake ruptured a preexisting north–south-trending westward-dipping normal fault,

1. Institute of Geophysics and Planetary Physics, Scripps Institution of Oceanography, University of California San Diego, La Jolla, California, U.S.A., https://orcid.org/0009-0006-7283-5981 (XZ); https://orcid.org/0000-0002-6161-8467 (YF)

*Corresponding author: x3zou@ucsd.edu

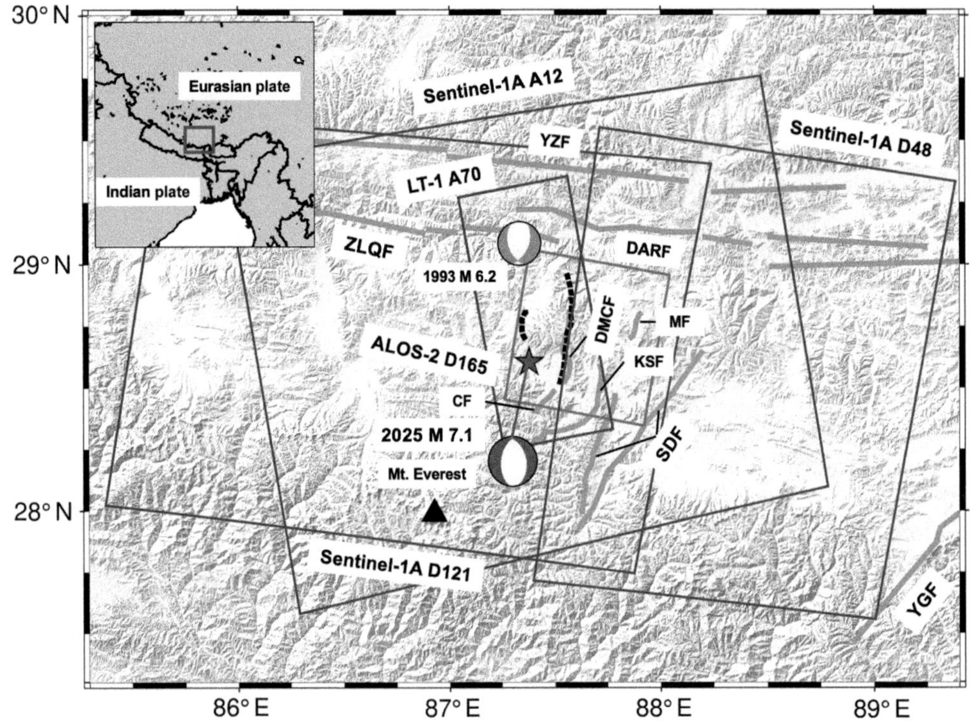

Figure 1. Regional map of the 2025 Tingri earthquake. The colored boxes denote the coverage area of the Interferometric Synthetic Aperture Radar (InSAR) data used in our study. The brown boxes indicate Sentinel-1A; the magenta box indicates Advanced Land Observation Satellite (ALOS)-2; the blue box indicates LT-1. The black dashed lines represent the fault traces of the main fault and the subfault inferred from the InSAR data. The red star is the earthquake epicenter of the Tingri earthquake, and the red focal mechanism plot represents its focal mechanism. The green focal mechanism plot represents the 1993 M_W 6.2 earthquake. The black triangle denotes the location of Mount Everest. The orange solid lines are mapped traces of major faults in the region. CF, Cuomai fault; DARF, Dajiling-Angren-Renbu fault; DMCF, Dengmecuo (Dingmucuo) fault; KSF, Kharta-Sangkar fault; MF, Mabja fault; SDF, Shenzha-Dingjie (Dinggye) fault; YGF, Yadong-Gulu fault; YZF, Yarlung Zangbo fault; and ZLQF, Zada-Lazi-Qiongdojiang fault. The location and names of the fault traces are inferred from Wu *et al.* (2024), Liu *et al.* (2025), and Wu *et al.* (2025). Fault naming and spellings may vary slightly among sources. The inset map in the top-left corner shows the location of the main map (red box), the Eurasian plate, and the Indian plate. The color version of this figure is available only in the electronic edition.

the Dengmecuo fault (DMCF; e.g., Kusky and Meng, 2025; Yu, Li, *et al.*, 2025; Zhou and Li, 2025). The DMCF is aligned with other major normal faults in the rift system of southern Tibet, including the nearby Shenzha-Dingjie fault system (Fig. 1). Several mechanisms have been proposed to drive the east–west extension of the Southern Tibet Rift System, including the gravitational spreading due to crustal thickening of the Tibetan plateau (e.g., Molnar *et al.*, 1993; Yang *et al.*, 2025), oblique convergence between the Eurasian and Indian plates (e.g., McCaffrey and Nabelek, 1998), and asthenospheric upwelling beneath the Eurasian plate (e.g., Pang *et al.*, 2018; Qiao *et al.*, 2025). Active extension within the southern Tibetan rift implies a considerable seismic hazard. Estimates of the slip-rate deficit based on Global Navigational Satellite System measurements suggested that normal faults in the region have the potential to generate earthquakes with magnitude 7 or greater (Li *et al.*, 2025).

Because the Dengmecuo fault was not associated with any notable seismic activity before the 2025 Tingri earthquake, its size, geometry, and slip history were largely unknown. Initial studies of the Tingri earthquake using seismic and Interferometric Synthetic Aperture Radar (InSAR) data revealed a predominantly normal slip on an ~50 km long westward-dipping fault (e.g., Chong *et al.*, 2025; Liu *et al.*, 2025; Qiao *et al.*, 2025; Yang *et al.*, 2025; Yu, Li, *et al.*, 2025). However, the reported dip angles vary considerably, from 41° (Yu, Zhang, *et al.*, 2025) to 49° (USGS, 2025) to 71° (Zhu *et al.*, 2025), possibly due to a limited resolving power and/or coverage of various data sets, inversion algorithms, or oversimplified model assumptions. Robust constraints on the orientation of active faults are of considerable interest as they can be used to constrain in situ fault strength (e.g., Collettini and Sibson, 2001; Scholz, 2019; Fialko, 2021; Zou *et al.*, 2023, p. 107). Most of the previous studies of the 2025 Tingri earthquake approximated the earthquake rupture as a planar fault in a homogeneous elastic half-space (e.g., Liu *et al.*, 2025; Yu, Li, *et al.*, 2025). Another major limitation was the lack of near-field data due to a strong decorrelation of the radar phase in Sentinel-1A (C-band) interferograms (e.g., Qiao *et al.*, 2025; Yu, Zhang, *et al.*, 2025). In this study, we combine interferometric phase measurements from Sentinel-1A satellite with those from the L-band Advanced Land Observation Satellite (ALOS)-2 and Lutan-1 (LT-1) satellites, as well as with pixel offset data to provide a full coverage of coseismic displacements from different lines of sight (LoS). We use these data to map the rupture trace and invert for the nonplanar subsurface fault geometry and slip distribution (e.g., Simons *et al.*, 2002; Furuya and Yasuda, 2011; Dutta *et al.*, 2021). Our coseismic slip models use Green's functions for a layered elastic half-space consistent with the local seismic velocity structure (e.g., Huang *et al.*, 2020; Tan *et al.*, 2023). We also include in our models a conjugate east-dipping fault to the west of the main rupture that was omitted in many previous studies. Finally, we present InSAR measurements of postseismic deformation that occurred during the first 8 months following the 2025 Tingri earthquake. A joint consideration of coseismic and postseismic deformation helps further reduce uncertainties in the rupture geometry and frictional properties of the host rocks (e.g., Lindsey and Fialko, 2016; Jin *et al.*, 2022).

Data and Methods

Analysis of satellite data

We use Synthetic Aperture Radar (SAR) data from Sentinel-1A (C-band, ascending track 12, descending track 48, and descending track 121), ALOS-2 (L-band, descending track 165, frame 3040), and LT-1 (L-band, ascending track 70) satellites. The spatial coverage, timespans, and perpendicular baselines of all input data are shown in Figure 1, and Figures S1–S3, and Tables S1 and S2, available in the supplemental material to this article. The Sentinel-1A and ALOS-2 data are processed using GMTSAR (Sandwell *et al.*, 2011). We remove the topographic phase using a digital elevation model from the Shuttle Radar Topography Mission (Farr *et al.*, 2007). The residual phase is filtered using a Gaussian filter with a wavelength of 300 m, and unwrapped using the residue-cut algorithm (Goldstein and Werner, 1998). Because the near-field radar phase in C-band is heavily decorrelated due to high displacement gradients and surface disruption, we compute pixel offsets for Sentinel-1A ascending track 12 and descending track 121, and ALOS-2 descending track 165. The pixel offset maps are quality checked, and obvious outliers and noisy areas are masked out. We only use the range offsets because the azimuth offsets have a low signal-to-noise ratio (SNR). The unwrapped radar phase from the LT-1 satellite is from a study by Yang *et al.* (2025).

We subsequently use Sentinel-1A range offsets and ALOS-2 and LT-1 interferograms to map the surface rupture. The data clearly show displacement discontinuities along two subparallel north–south-trending faults, a ~50 km long rupture near the 87.5° longitude ("main fault"), and a smaller rupture about 20 km to the west ("subfault"), see Figures 1 and Figures S1 and S2. We obtain rupture traces for both the main fault and the subfault by digitizing the respective displacement discontinuities, see black-dashed lines in Figure 1 and Figures S1 and S2.

Coseismic interferograms and pixel offsets may contain "ramps" due to long-wavelength variations in the troposphere, ionosphere, and/or imprecise orbit data or timing errors (e.g., Wang and Jónsson, 2014; Zhang *et al.*, 2019). We correct for such artifacts using an iterative procedure. First, we subtract the best-fit planar ramp from the original data. We then carry out a linear inversion of down-sampled data for the assumed initial fault geometry discretized using triangular dislocation elements in a homogeneous elastic half-space (Nikkhoo and Walter, 2015). We subtract model predictions from the data and use residuals to estimate the best-fit quadratic surface. The latter is subsequently subtracted from the data, and iterations continue. After the initial iteration, we down-sample the data using the gradient-based quad-tree algorithm and the current best-fit model to avoid oversampling of high-frequency noise (Wang and Fialko, 2015). Before detrending the residuals, we mask out the near-field data (~20 km on each side of the main fault trace) to minimize the influence of potential model-related errors. The deramping procedure typically converges after 2–3 iterations.

Inversions for fault geometry and slip distribution

The detrended LOS displacements and range offsets are used in joint inversions to estimate the subsurface fault geometry and slip distribution. We approximate each fault using a smooth curved surface that honors the fault trace. At the down-dip end, the surface follows a straight line that parallels the surface trace, but is offset horizontally according to the assumed dip angle. The curved surface is smoothly varying to satisfy both the top and bottom constraints on the rupture geometry. Based on the wavelength of the observed coseismic displacements and a few trial inversions, the main fault and the subfault are assumed to extend to depths of 25 and 7 km, respectively. The resulting curved fault surfaces are tessellated into a mesh consisting of triangular elements of variable size (see the supplemental material for details). The element size increases with depth to account for the depth-dependent model resolution (e.g., Fialko, 2004).

We use an improved and more realistic parameterization of fault slip that allows for linear (rather than piecewise constant) variations in slip between the mesh nodes (vertices of triangular elements). Given a triangular mesh representing the best-fit fault geometry (Fig. 2), we compute composite Green's functions for each node of the mesh using a superposition of point sources for all triangles that share the respective vertex (see Text S1 and Fig. S4). Green's functions for individual point sources (Wang *et al.*, 2006) are computed for a layered rigidity structure (Fig. S5) derived from the 3D shear-wave (V_S) velocity model (Huang *et al.*, 2020). The elastic moduli are found using the empirical relationship between the body-wave velocities and density (Brocher, 2005). We solve for the slip distribution u at the mesh vertices by minimizing the following functional,

$$F(u,\lambda) = \|Gu - d\|_2 + \lambda\|\nabla^2 u\|_2, \quad (1)$$

in which G is the matrix of composite Green's functions, d is the data vector, u is the unknown slip distribution at the nodes (including strike- and dip-slip components), $||\cdot||_2$ is the L2 norm, ∇^2 is a Laplacian operator, and λ is a smoothing parameter (Golub *et al.*, 1999) chosen based on the trade-off curve between the model roughness and data misfit (see Text S1 and

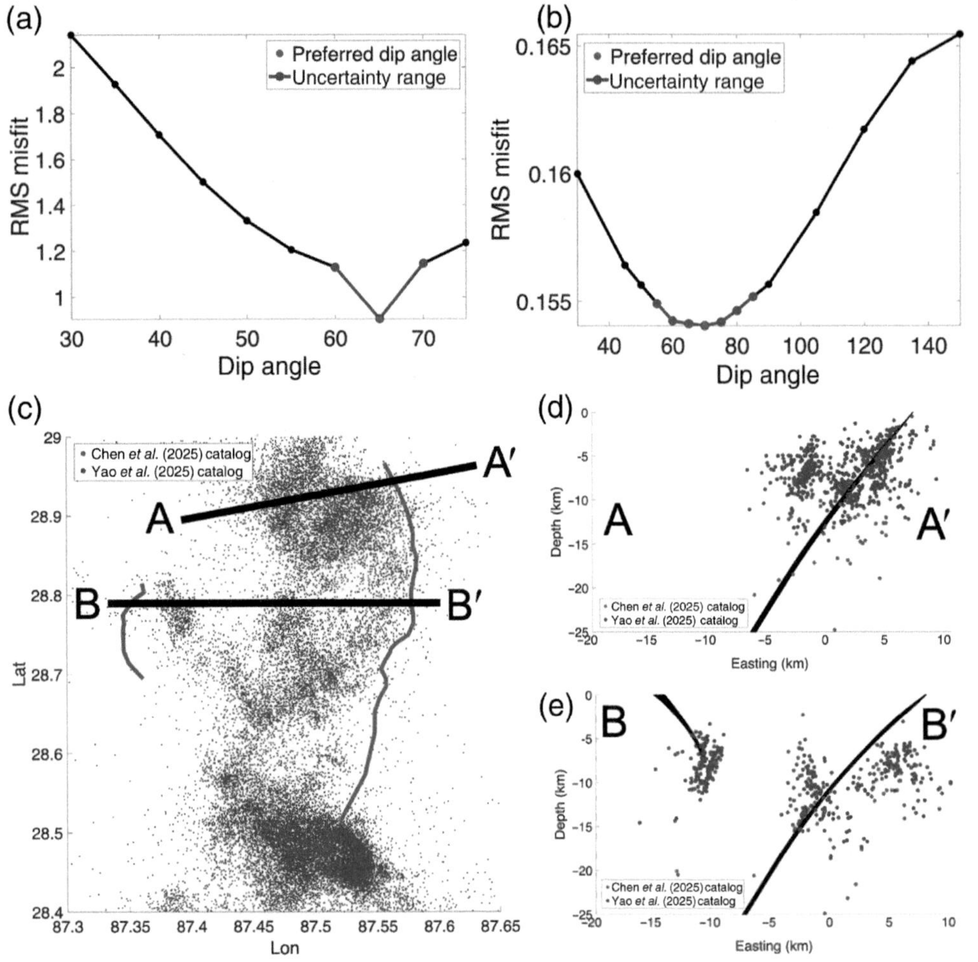

Figure 2. (a,b) Model misfit as a function of the assumed fault dip angle. Panel (a) is the main fault; panel (b) is the subfault. The red points represent the best fit (minimum root mean square [RMS] misfit). The blue points represent the estimated uncertainty range (20% and 10% of the difference between the maximum and minimum misfit for the main fault and subfault, respectively). Variations in the RMS misfit for the subfault are much smaller than those for the main fault because only a small fraction of the data are sensitive to slip on the subfault. (c) Fault traces and epicenters of precisely relocated aftershocks from Chen *et al.* (2025) and Yao *et al.* (2025) catalogs. (d,e) Cross sections from profiles A–A′ and B–B′, with best-fit fault geometries inferred from inversions of space geodetic data (panels a and b) and earthquake hypocenters from Chen *et al.* (2025) and Yao *et al.* (2025) catalogs. The color version of this figure is available only in the electronic edition.

Figs. S4–S7 for details). Because changes in radar range have limited sensitivity to meridional (north–south) displacements, the strike-slip component is less constrained compared with the dip-slip component. To suppress potential artifacts, we apply a stronger (by a factor of 3) smoothing to strike slip compared with dip slip.

We perform a grid search to find the best-fit dip angles of the two faults. To regularize the inversion, we first perform a grid search for the main fault alone. We vary the dip angle from 30° to 75° in 5° increments. For each assumed dip angle, we calculate the Green's functions for a new fault geometry and layered half-space and perform a least-squares linear inversion. We identify the best-fit dip angle based on the root mean square (RMS) of the residuals of all trial inversions. We then subtract the modeled contribution of the main fault from the data and invert the residuals for the best-fit dip angle of the subfault. The latter grid search is performed for a wider range of dip angles, 30°–150° (i.e., allowing for both eastward and westward dip), given no prior information on the attitude of the subfault. Only the datasets with sufficient coverage around the subfault are used in the respective grid search. Next, we use the inferred best-fit geometries to resample the data based on the model. The modeled contribution of the subfault is subtracted from the data, and the procedure is repeated to ensure that results are robust with respect to the data sampling.

Figure 2 shows the results of the grid search and the preferred fault geometries (see Fig. S8 for the initial round of grid search). For comparison, we also include precisely relocated aftershocks (Chen *et al.*, 2025; Yao *et al.*, 2025). Aftershock locations can be useful for constraining the 3D fault geometry at depth (e.g., Jin and Fialko, 2020; Jin *et al.*, 2023); however, in case of the Tingri earthquake aftershocks appear to form a diffuse cloud without an obvious localization around the main seismogenic rupture (Fig. 2c–e). Nevertheless, the overall trends of the aftershock hypocenters appear to be broadly consistent with the best-fit fault geometries inferred from inversions of space geodetic data (color dots and black meshes in Fig. 2d,e, respectively).

Early postseismic deformation

To investigate the early postseismic deformation, we processed data from Sentinel-1 tracks A12 and D121 spanning ~9 months after the mainshock (Fig. 1, Fig. S3). Our analysis focuses on the amplitude and spatial pattern of surface displacements. Using the first postseismic acquisition as a reference, we

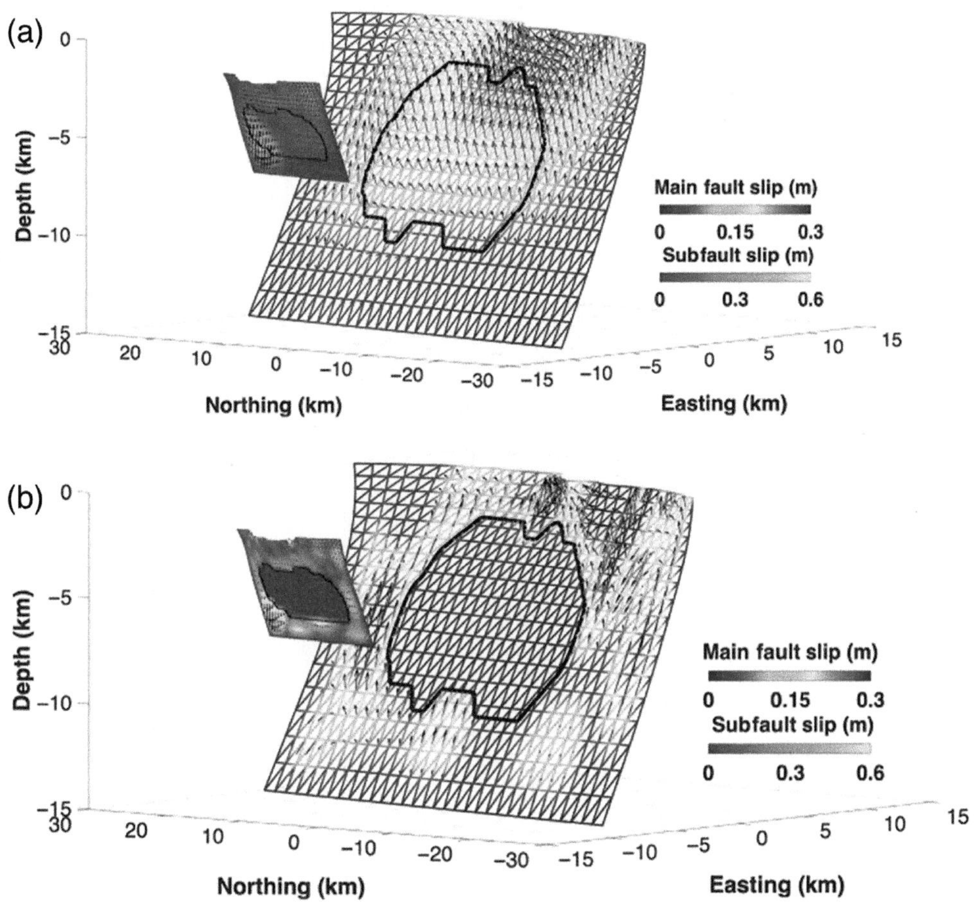

Figure 3. Kinematic inverse models of early afterslip. The black curvy lines represent the contour of the 50% peak coseismic slip for each fault. (a) Afterslip model with no constraint on the afterslip area. (b) Afterslip model with slip discouraged inside the 50% peak coseismic slip contour. For the main fault, the arrows represent the movement of the footwall; for the subfault, the arrows represent the movement of the hanging wall. The color version of this figure is available only in the electronic edition.

generated interferometric pairs with all subsequent acquisitions, for each track. We visually inspected the postseismic interferograms, and selected those that (1) are least affected by decorrelation and atmospheric noise, (2) maximize the time span, and (3) have a comparable time span for both tracks. Pairs that fit these criteria are listed in Table S2. To further increase the SNR, we stacked the identified long-term interferograms to produce averaged interferograms with time spans of ~8 months for each track. The resulting averaged interferograms are shown in Fig. S3. The postseismic interferograms reveal LoS displacements of several centimeters (Fig. S3), with a spatial pattern that is broadly consistent with the coseismic one (Fig. S1), suggestive of afterslip as a likely mechanism.

We estimate the distribution of afterslip using the same fault geometry and inversion procedure as for our preferred coseismic slip model. We limit the down-dip extent of the mesh to 15 km to prevent spurious deep slip as the SNR is poor further than ~20 km from the rupture trace (Fig. S3). Because kinematic inversions involve smoothing to reduce nonuniqueness, the inferred area of afterslip may considerably overlap with that of coseismic slip which may be unphysical (Barbot *et al.*, 2009; Lindsey and Fialko, 2016). To explore potential trade-offs between model smoothness and resolution, we perform several inversions subject to the following constraints: (1) a soft no-slip boundary condition (Jin and Fialko, 2020) at the side and bottom edges of the mesh; no a priori constraints on afterslip inside the model domain; (2) same as (1), but with a soft no-slip boundary condition on mesh elements that produced less than 50% of the peak coseismic slip; (3) same as (1), but with a soft no-slip boundary condition on mesh elements below the depth of 4 km; (4) same as (1), but with a soft no-slip boundary condition on mesh elements in the depth interval 3–11 km. The smoothness parameter of the afterslip model (1) is determined as usual, considering a trade-off between the model smoothness and misfit (Fig. S6). For models (2), (3), and (4), the smoothness parameters are chosen to produce the same variance reduction as for model (1). The resulting slip distributions are shown in Figure 3 and Figures S9 and S10.

For completeness, we also perform forward simulations of possible contributions due to viscoelastic and poroelastic deformation. We simulate viscoelastic relaxation using PSGRN-PSCMP software (Wang *et al.*, 2006), assuming the same layered rigidity structure as for the coseismic modeling. The rheology structure includes three layers: an elastic upper crust, a biviscous (Burgers) lower crust, and a Maxwell viscoelastic upper mantle, constrained by observations of postseismic deformation due to the 2015 M_w 7.8 Gorkha, Nepal, earthquake (Tian *et al.*, 2020). Because the effective thickness of the upper elastic layer is not well known, we perform calculations assuming elastic thicknesses of 15, 20, 25, and 30 km. In each simulation, we evaluate surface deformation over 3 time intervals: the initial 8 months after the mainshock, corresponding to the observation period (Fig. S3 and Table S2), one-half of the Maxwell relaxation time $\tau/2$, and full Maxwell

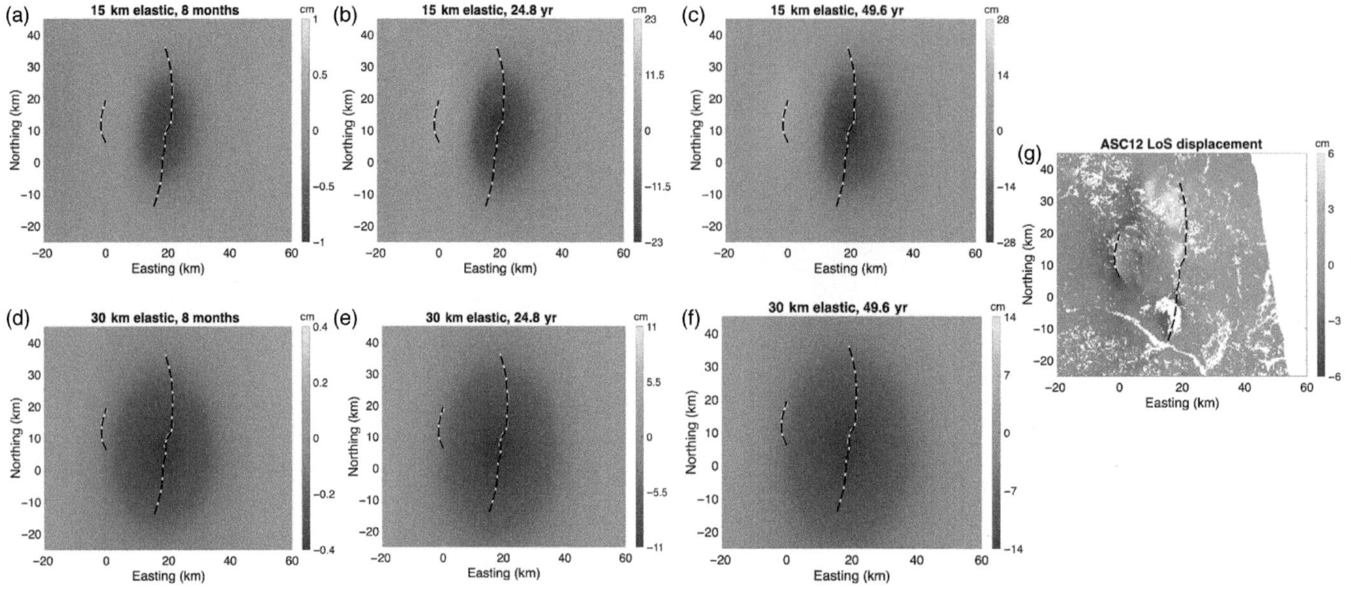

Figure 4. Forward models of viscoelastic relaxation: line-of-sight (LoS) displacements for Sentinel-1A ascending track 12. (a–c) 15 km elastic upper crust thickness, snapshots at 8 months, half Maxwell relaxation time, full Maxwell relaxation time. (d–f) 30 km elastic upper crust thickness, snapshots at 8 months, half Maxwell relaxation time, full Maxwell relaxation time. (g) Observed LoS displacements. The Maxwell relaxation time is calculated based on the regional rigidity and viscosity model of the upper mantle (Huang *et al.*, 2020; Tian *et al.*, 2020). The color version of this figure is available only in the electronic edition.

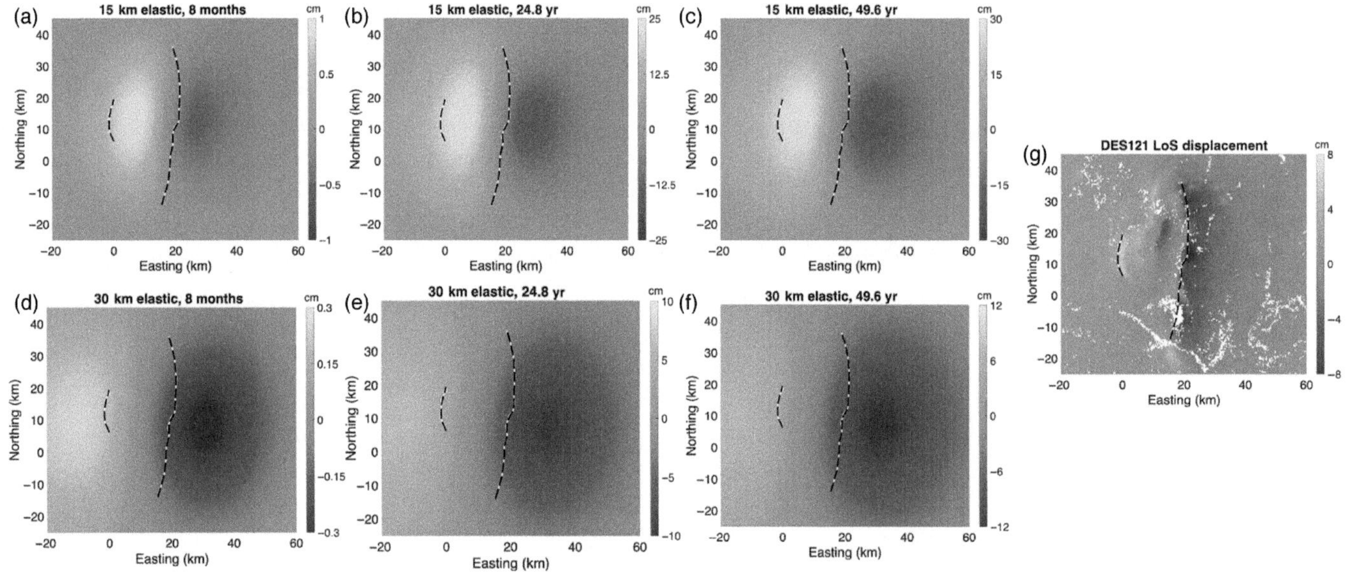

Figure 5. Forward models of viscoelastic relaxation: LoS displacements for Sentinel-1A descending track 121. (a–c) 15 km elastic upper crust thickness, snapshots at 8 months, half Maxwell relaxation time, full Maxwell relaxation time. (d–f) 30 km elastic upper crust thickness, snapshots at 8 months, half Maxwell relaxation time, full Maxwell relaxation time. (g) Observed LOS displacements. The Maxwell relaxation time is calculated based on the regional rigidity and viscosity model of the upper mantle (Huang *et al.*, 2020; Tian *et al.*, 2020). The color version of this figure is available only in the electronic edition.

relaxation time $\tau = \eta/\mu$, in which η is the dynamic viscosity, and μ is the shear modulus. The computed surface displacements projected on the respective LoS for each satellite track are shown in Figures 4 and 5 and Figures S11 and S12.

Results

Our preferred coseismic slip model (Fig. 6) gives rise to a 91% variance reduction of the input data. The 1σ of the residuals for each input data set is shown in Table 1. The model provides a

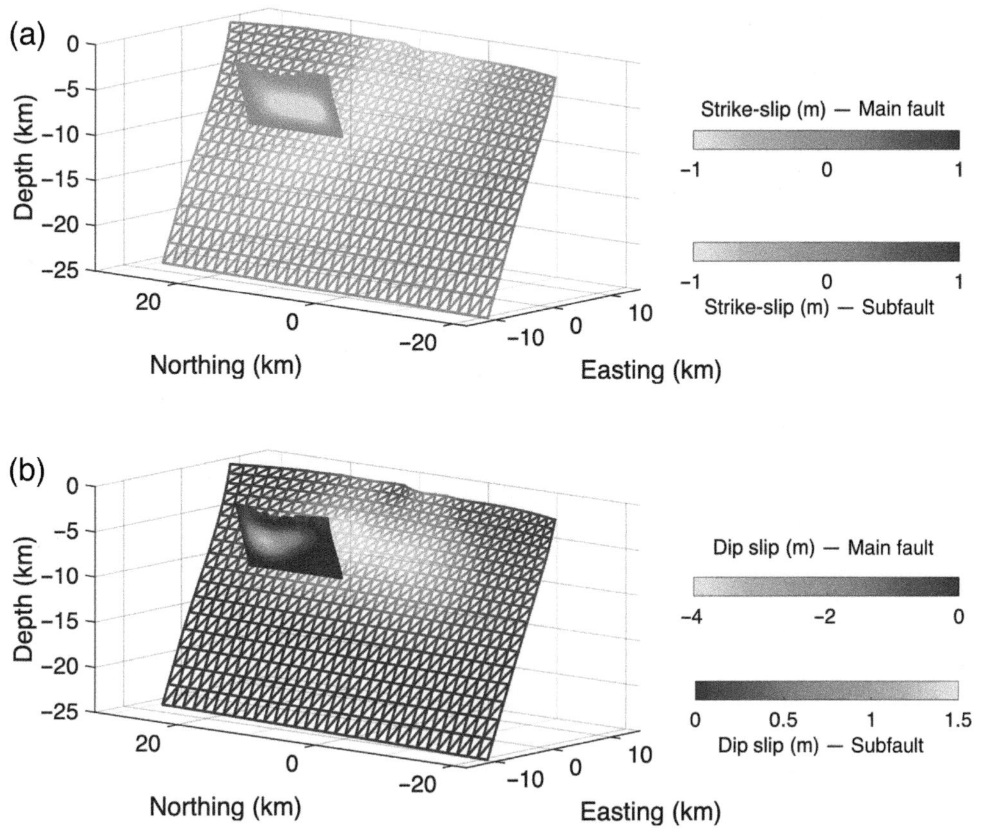

Figure 6. Preferred static slip model from geodetic inversion assuming a curved rupture geometry. (a) Strike slip; (b) dip slip. Left-lateral strike slip and west-side-down dip slip are deemed negative. The color version of this figure is available only in the electronic edition.

satisfactory fit to all datasets (Figs. 7 and 8). The estimated best-fit average dip angles are 65° ± 5° for the main fault and a 70° ± 15° for the subfault (Fig. 2a,b), which implies optimal orientations for the Mohr–Coulomb failure, assuming vertical orientation of the maximum compressive stress and the coefficient of friction of 0.6–0.7 (e.g., Anderson, 1951; Sibson, 1974; Byerlee, 1978). The fault attitudes inferred from inversions of geodetic data are in general agreement with the distribution of aftershocks (Fig. 2c–e), although the latter are too diffuse to provide robust constraints on the subsurface fault geometry. The moment magnitude calculated using our best-fit slip model (accounting for the depth-dependent shear modulus, Fig. S4) is 7.0, comparable with the seismically determined moment magnitudes using *W* phase (7.05, USGS, 2025) and centroid moment tensor (7.1, Ekström *et al.*, 2012), as well as previously published finite-fault models (e.g., Qiao *et al.*, 2025).

Coseismic offsets on the main fault are dominated by dip slip, with some component of left-lateral strike slip (Fig. 6). Maximum slip (~4.3 m) occurs at a relatively shallow depth of ~6 km. The conjugate subfault is also characterized by oblique slip, with a maximum slip of ~1.6 m at a depth of ~5 km (Fig. 6). The total slip amplitude decreases toward the surface, in agreement with field observations of fault scarps with offsets between 1 and 3 m (Wu *et al.*, 2025). The inferred strike-slip component has a lower resolution and higher uncertainty compared to the dip-slip component, especially for the secondary fault due to a lower SNR.

A decrease in coseismic slip toward the surface is further illustrated in Figure 9, which shows the total coseismic slip averaged along the strike of the main fault, for several depth intervals corresponding to the size of triangular elements (Fig. 6). The shallowest depth interval is constrained to have a constant slip, whereas the rest of the slip model allows for linear variations in slip between the nodes (see the supplemental material). As one can see from Figure 9, there is a large shallow coseismic slip deficit, with slip at the surface on average almost a factor of 3 smaller than the maximum slip in the middle of the seismogenic zone.

Kinematic inversions of postseismic InSAR data are indicative of the occurrence of early afterslip (Fig. 3). In unconstrained inversions, afterslip is maximum at the surface, but extends to depth of ~10 km, with a substantial spatial overlap

TABLE 1
1σ for the Residual of Each Track of Input Data (Unit: cm)

Satellite Track	1σ
Sentinel-1A ASC12 LoS	8.32
Sentinel-1A DES48 LoS	4.31
Sentinel-1A DES121 LoS	5.54
ALOS-2 DES165 LoS	8.19
LT-1 ASC70 LoS	21.01
Sentinel-1A ASC12 RNG	15.58
Sentinel-1A DES121 RNG	9.89
ALOS-2 DES165 RNG	13.91

ALOS, Advanced Land Observation Satellite; and LoS, line of sight.

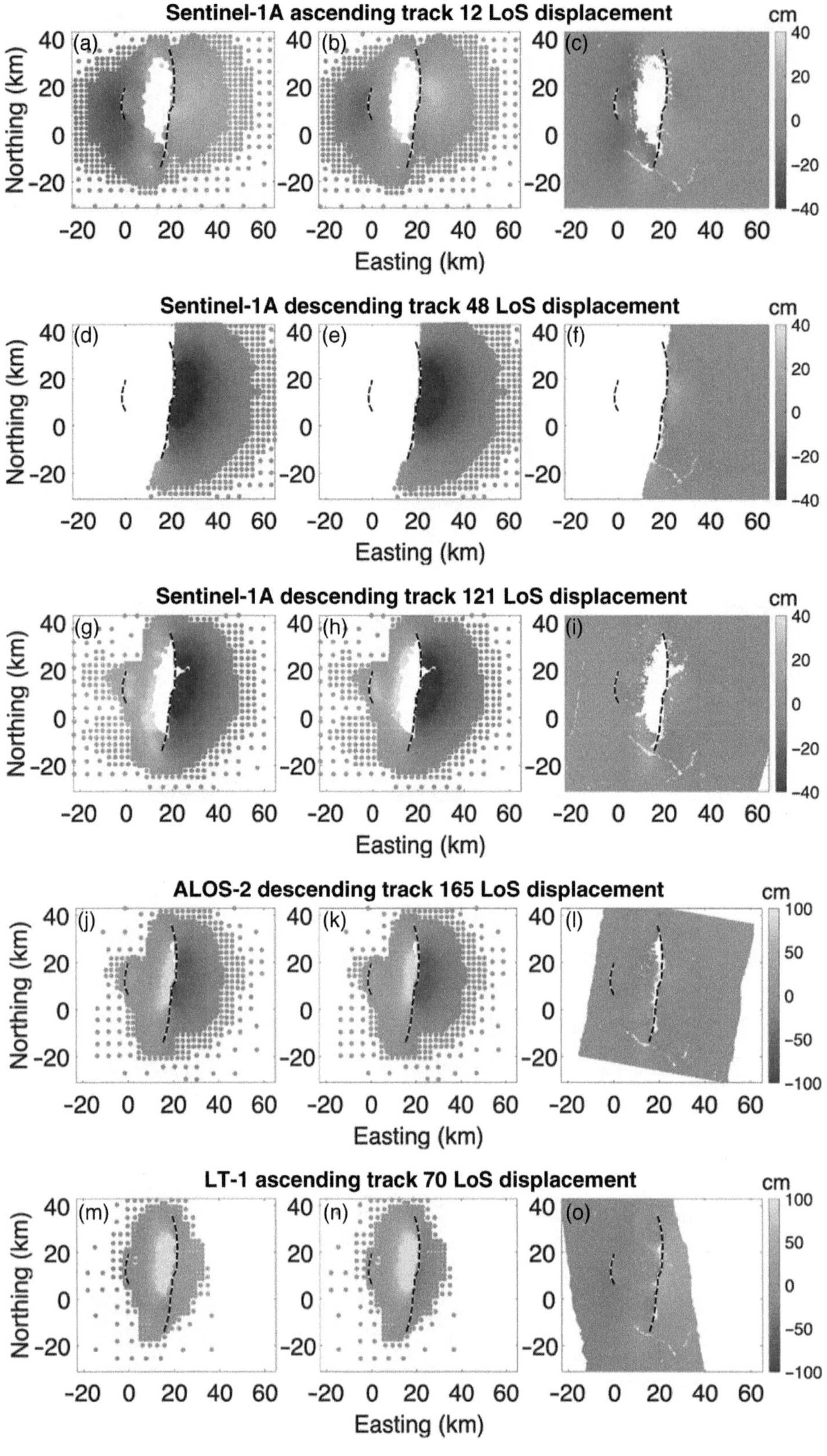

Figure 7. Subsampled input data (panels a, d, g, j, and m), model prediction (panels b, e, h, k, and n), and full-resolution residual (panels c, f, i, l, and o) for coseismic LoS displacements. The color version of this figure is available only in the electronic edition.

with the area of maximum coseismic slip, particularly on the main fault (Fig. 3a). Inversions in which afterslip is discouraged in the area of maximum coseismic slip show a concentration of afterslip on the periphery of the seismic rupture (Fig. 3b). Given that both models can explain the observed postseismic deformation with comparable misfits (Fig. 10), we interpret the overlap between the coseismic slip and afterslip as an artifact of the regularization constraint and limited model resolution at depth (Fialko and Kaneko, 2025).

Although our kinematic afterslip model is able to explain an overall pattern of the observed postseismic deformation, some systematic residuals are apparent (Fig. 10). These residuals may be due to atmospheric noise and unmodeled ground motion, for example, due to triggered slip on nearby unknown faults (e.g., Ma *et al.*, 2026), landslides, hydrologic effects, and so forth.

Forward models of viscoelastic relaxation assuming a simple 1D rheological structure predict LoS displacements that do not agree with observations either in amplitude or the spatial distribution (Figs. 4 and 5 and Figs. S11 and S12). In particular, the amplitudes of surface displacements predicted by viscoelastic models are about an order of magnitude smaller than the observed ones, assuming an effective elastic thickness of the upper crust of 15 km, and smaller still for thicker elastic layers. The amplitude of surface displacements due to viscoelastic relaxation over a given time period trades off with the assumed

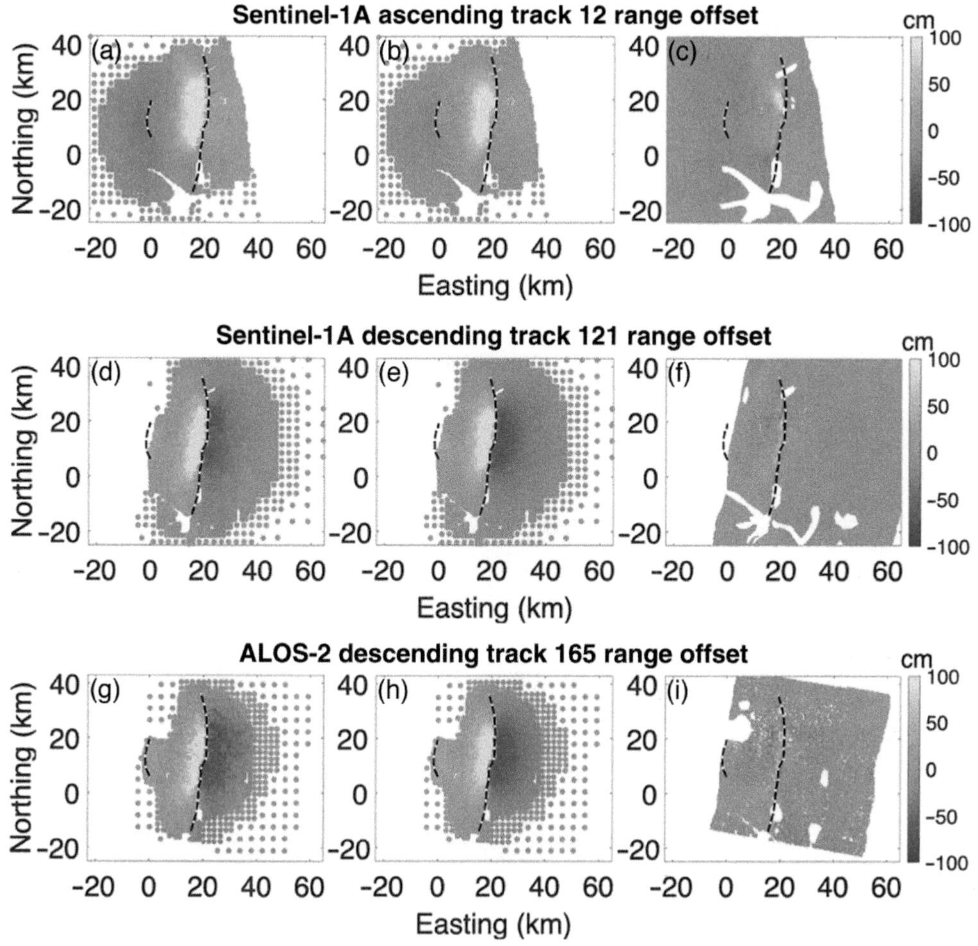

Figure 8. Subsampled input data (panels a, d, and g), model prediction (panels b, e, and h), and full-resolution residual (panels c, f, and i) for coseismic range offsets. The color version of this figure is available only in the electronic edition.

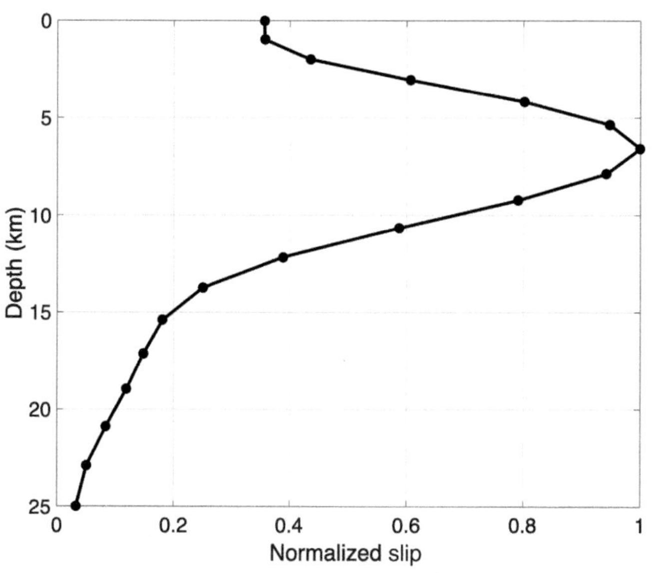

Figure 9. Coseismic slip on the main fault, averaged along-strike, and normalized by the maximum value (~4.3 m), as a function of depth.

effective viscosity, but the spatial pattern of surface displacements varies little in time. It follows that the contribution of viscoelastic relaxation to the observed deformation signal is negligible.

Poroelastic deformation in the limit of full relaxation (Fig. S13) predicts LoS displacements whose amplitude and polarity also do not exhibit much similarity with the observations, except perhaps locally near the rupture trace. Taken together, our results point to shallow afterslip as the dominant deformation mechanism in the first 8 months following the Tingri earthquake.

Discussion

Compared with previous studies that approximated the 2025 Tingri rupture using rectangular dislocations in a homogeneous elastic half-space (e.g., Liu *et al.*, 2025; Yu, Li, *et al.*, 2025), our finite-fault model features a more complex and realistic geometry that honors the curved fault trace at the Earth's surface, and variations in the effective elastic properties with depth. An accurate representation of the fault trace is important as small deviations of the modeled fault trace from the actual surface rupture can result in slivers of data points on the wrong side of the modeled fault, leading to biases in the shallow part of the slip model that in theory should be best resolved by the data. One solution is to simply mask out such data based on the expected sign (e.g., Jin and Fialko, 2021); however, adaptation of the more realistic fault geometry obviates the need for discarding potentially useful near-field data. The use of triangular elements ensures a continuous rupture surface without gaps and tears between the adjacent fault elements at depth, whereas linear base functions ensure a continuous slip distribution. Both features may prove important for dynamic rupture models.

The best-fit dip angles of 60°–70° inferred from our nonlinear inversions for the main fault and the conjugate subfault are consistent with optimal fault orientations predicted by the Mohr–Coulomb theory and Byerlee friction (e.g., Anderson, 1951; Collettini and Sibson, 2001; Scholz, 2019). Shallower dip angles reported in some previous studies (e.g., Chong

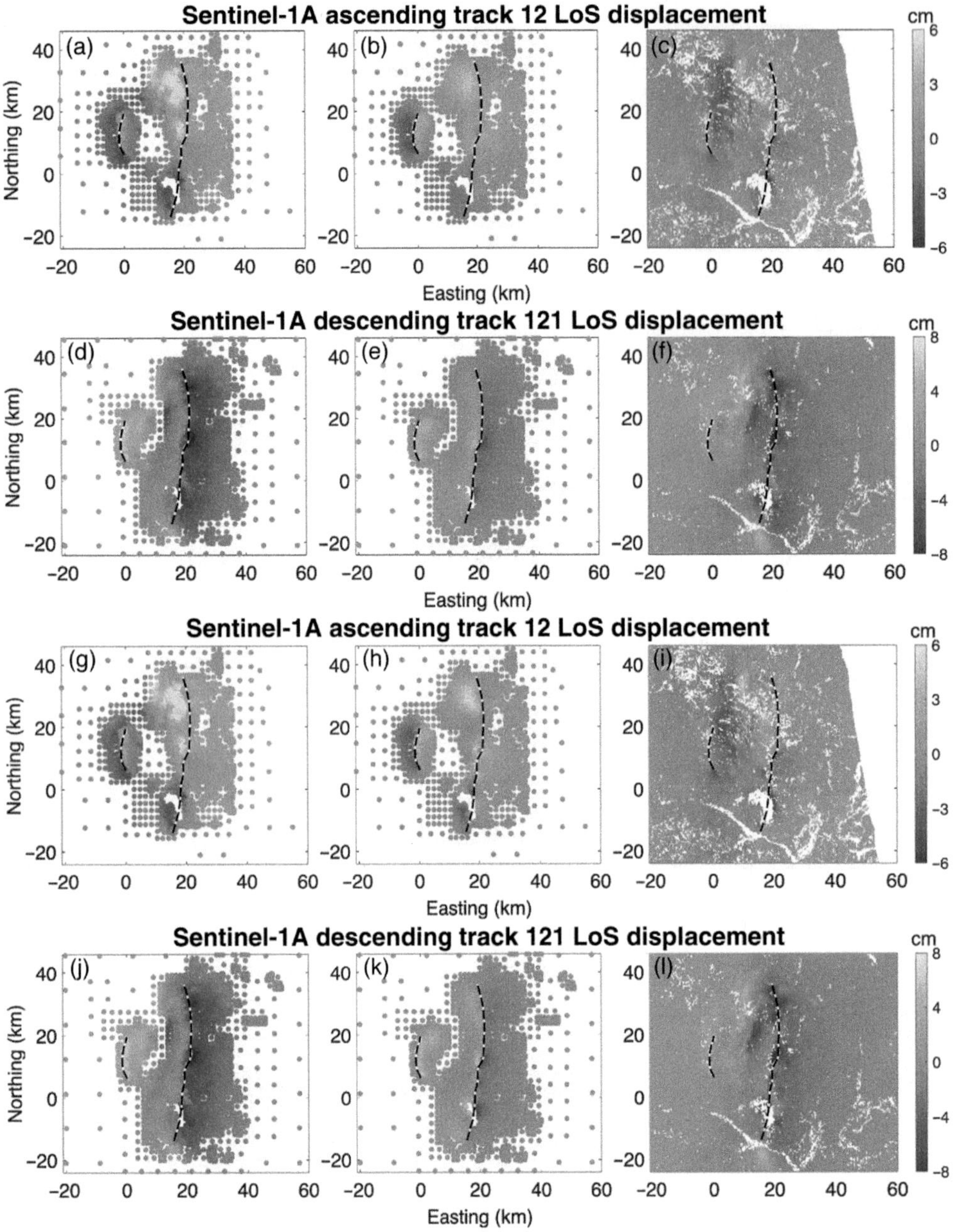

Figure 10. Subsampled input data (a,d,g,j), best-fit afterslip model (b,e,h,k), and full-resolution residual (c,f,i,l) for early postseismic deformation. (a–f) The afterslip model with no constraint on the afterslip area; (g–l) the afterslip model with slip discouraged inside the 50% peak coseismic slip contour. The color version of this figure is available only in the electronic edition.

et al., 2025; Yu, Zhang, *et al.*, 2025; Zhao *et al.*, 2025) could reflect biases due to incomplete data coverage, in particular on the western side of the main fault, which exhibits the largest coseismic displacements, but suffers from decorrelation in the C-band (Sentinel-1) interferograms. Our study mitigates this data gap using range offsets and L-band (ALOS-2 and LT-1) interferograms that remain correlated all the way to the rupture trace and additionally provide diverse lines of sight. Recent studies that used multiple high-quality data sets (Xu *et al.*, 2025; He *et al.*, 2026) have reported fault-dip angles similar to those suggested by our best-fit model.

Although faults are generally believed to initiate at optimal angles with respect to in situ principal stresses (e.g., Anderson, 1951; Scholz, 2019; Fialko, 2021), global compilations of earthquake focal mechanisms show a peak in dip angles of normal earthquakes around 45° (e.g., Jackson and White, 1989; Reston, 2020). Suboptimal fault orientations can be attributed to a progressive rotation away from the principal compression axis (e.g., Thatcher and Hill, 1991; Olive and Behn, 2014; Fialko and Jin, 2021). This would suggest that the Dengmecuo fault that produced the 2025 Tingri earthquake is still relatively young to have avoided a notable rotation, yet sufficiently mature to be able to generate major (magnitude 7+) earthquakes. Similar results were obtained for other major surface-rupturing normal earthquakes for which high-quality space-geodetic data are available (e.g., Kobayashi *et al.*, 2012). Wang *et al.* (2014) reported dip angles between 40° and 60° for several M_w 6 normal earthquakes in southern Tibet, and noted that dip angles inferred from inversions of InSAR and teleseismic data may differ by ~10°, especially if the nodal plane ambiguity is not resolved. A similar discrepancy is found between the dip angles suggested by our geodetic inversions (Fig. 2) and teleseismic data (USGS, 2025). This suggests that inferences of nonoptimal fault orientation based on earthquake focal mechanisms (Jackson and White, 1989; Reston, 2020) should be treated with caution.

The classic conjugate orientations of the main fault and the subfault suggest that the two faults form a graben structure in the southern Tibet rift zone. Their markedly different dimensions suggest they might represent an early-stage graben system that could evolve into a full graben in the future (Qiao *et al.*, 2025). Alternatively, Liu *et al.* (2025) proposed that the main fault defines a half-graben, and the subfault is a "branch rupture" on the opposite side of the Dengmecuo half-graben. Of interest is the slip sequence on the two faults. The earliest postearthquake SAR data (Table S1) indicate that slip on the subfault occurred either simultaneously or within hours following the mainshock. The absence of large aftershocks in the respective time interval and the fact that the subfault lies in the static stress shadow of the main fault (Chong *et al.*, 2025) suggest that the subfault could have been dynamically triggered and ruptured simultaneously with the mainshock (e.g., Yun *et al.*, 2025).

The high-quality observations of coseismic and postseismic deformation due to the 2025 Tingri earthquake provide an excellent opportunity to investigate contributions of on- and off-fault failure to surface displacements. Our analysis reveals a large (more than a factor of 2) ratio of slip at depth to slip at the surface (Figs. 6 and 9). Similar variations in slip with depth, termed shallow slip deficit (SSD), were inferred for several magnitude ~7 earthquakes on strike-slip faults (e.g., Fialko *et al.*, 2005; Jia *et al.*, 2023; Antoine *et al.*, 2024; Lindsey *et al.*, 2025; Milliner *et al.*, 2025). One should be careful to distinguish the shallow coseismic slip deficit (SCSD) from the SSD that was originally defined as the long-term shallow slip deficit (e.g., Fialko *et al.*, 2005; Jin and Fialko, 2020), and requires consideration of both coseismic slip and aseismic creep in the interseismic period. So far, no systematic analysis of SSD was performed for normal earthquakes that are large enough to saturate the seismogenic layer.

The reduced coseismic slip and robust afterslip at the Earth's surface (Figs. 3, 6, and 9) are indicative of velocity-strengthening frictional behavior of the shallow crust (e.g., Marone *et al.*, 1991; Scholz, 1998). However, a consideration of the magnitudes of the SCSD (>1 m) and early afterslip (< 10 cm) suggests that the latter may not be able to fully compensate for the former because the rates of afterslip are highest immediately after the earthquake, and rapidly decay with time (e.g., Marone *et al.*, 1991; Barbot *et al.*, 2009; Lindsey and Fialko, 2016). For the estimated slip rate of a few mm/yr and recurrence interval of less than 10^3 yr for the Dengmecuo fault (Wu *et al.*, 2025), shallow creep in the interseismic period is unlikely to account for the remaining deficit, given that the rate of shallow creep is typically a small fraction of the long-term fault-slip rate (e.g., Savage and Lisowski, 1993; Vavra *et al.*, 2023). We thus attribute an apparent SSD to the extensive off-fault damage due to dynamic stress perturbations (e.g., Fialko *et al.*, 2005; Dor *et al.*, 2006; Kaneko and Fialko, 2011). A similar combination of the shallow velocity-strengthening layer and off-fault damage was inferred for the 2021 M_w 7.4 Maduo earthquake in the north-eastern Tibetan plateau (e.g., Jin *et al.*, 2023).

The lack of a clear signal that might be attributable to viscoelastic relaxation in 8 months following the earthquake (Figs. 4 and 5, Figs. S11 and S12) is consistent with previous estimates of the lower bound on the short-term (transient) viscosity of the lower crust beneath Tibet of the order of 10^{18} Pa s (e.g., Ryder *et al.*, 2011; Wang and Fialko, 2018; Tian *et al.*, 2020). Continued space geodetic observations of the Tingri area will provide valuable constraints on the effective rheologic properties of the lower crust and upper mantle beneath the southern Tibet.

Conclusions

The 2025 M_w 7.1 Tingri earthquake is the largest instrumentally recorded normal earthquake in southern Tibet. We combined data from several SAR satellites, including Sentinel-1A, ALOS-2 and LT-1, to investigate coseismic and early postseismic deformation due to the Tingri earthquake, and derive a finite-fault model. We use a kinematic slip model that allows for complex curved rupture geometries, triangular tesellation, depth-dependent elastic moduli, and piecewise linear variation in slip components between the mesh nodes. Our best-fit static slip model indicates a 65° ± 5° dip angle for the westward-dipping main fault and a 70° ± 15° for the east-dipping conjugate subfault. These dip angles are in excellent agreement with predictions of the Mohr–Coulomb theory assuming Byerlee's law and coefficient of friction of 0.6–0.7. The main fault and the subfault form a conjugate pair that may define an incipient graben. The coseismic slip distribution is dominated by dip slip, with some component of left-lateral slip, and a maximum slip of approximately 4 m on the main fault, and 1.5 m on the subfault. The along-strike averaged slip suggests maximum slip at depth of 5–6 km, and an ~60% shallow coseismic slip deficit. Only a fraction of this deficit is compensated by afterslip in the first 8 months following the earthquake, implying significant off-fault damage, presumably due to strong dynamic stress perturbations. The early postseismic deformation is dominated by afterslip on the ruptured conjugate faults, with negligible contributions from viscoelastic or poroelastic relaxation. Our results improve understanding of coseismic and postseismic deformation processes in actively extended Earth's crust in the southern Tibet rift zone.

Data and Resources

The linear geodetic inversion code can be accessed at https://github.com/ZeyuJin/geodetic_inversion. The PSGRN-PSCMP software can be accessed at https://github.com/RongjiangWang/PSGRN-PSCMP_2020. The geodetic data and slip models are accessible via the Zenodo repository: https://zenodo.org/records/18022047. All websites were last accessed in December 2025. The supplemental texts, tables, and figures are in a separate supplemental material file. The supplemental material contains a text describing the geodetic inversion method for the static slip model (Text S1), two tables summarizing the Synthetic Aperture Radar datasets used in the coseismic and early postseismic slip modeling (Tables S1 and S2), figures showing the line of sight (LoS) and range-offset data used for coseismic and postseismic inversions (Figs. S1–S3), a figure illustrating the Laplacian weighting schemes used in the mesh regularization (Fig. S4), a figure showing the 1D layered rigidity model used to construct the hybrid Green's functions (Fig. S5), figures showing the roughness–misfit trade-off curves used to select the preferred model smoothness for the coseismic and unconstrained postseismic slip models (Figs. S6 and S7), a figure showing the initial dip-angle grid-search results for the main fault and subfault (Fig. S8), figures showing alternative afterslip models with slip restricted to shallow depths and to depths outside the 3–11 km interval (Figs. S9 and S10), figures showing forward models of viscoelastic relaxations projected into Sentinel-1 LoS directions assuming elastic crustal thickness from 15 km to 30 km in a 5 km increment (Figs. S11-S12), and forward models of poroelastic relaxation projected into the Sentinel-1 LoS directions (Fig. S13).

Declaration of Competing Interests

The authors acknowledge that there are no conflicts of interest recorded.

Acknowledgments

The authors thank Guest Editor M.-L. Chevalier, H. Wang, and an anonymous reviewer for comments and suggestions that improved this manuscript. Figures were produced using Generic Mapping Tools (GMT) (Wessel *et al.*, 2013) and Matlab.

References

Anderson, E. M. (1951). *The Dynamics of Faulting and Dike Formation with Application to Britain*, Oliver and Boyd, Edinburgh, 206 pp.

Antoine, S. L., Y. Klinger, K. Wang, and R. Bürgmann (2024). Coseismic shallow slip deficit accounted for by diffuse off-fault deformation, *Geophys. Res. Lett.* **51,** no. 24, e2024GL110798.

Barbot, S., Y. Fialko, and Y. Bock (2009). Postseismic deformation due to the M_w 6.0 2004 Parkfield earthquake: Stress-driven creep on a fault with spatially variable rate-and-state friction parameters, *J. Geophys. Res.* **114,** B07405.

Brocher, T. M. (2005). Empirical relations between elastic wavespeeds and density in the earth's crust, *Bull. Seismol. Soc. Am.* **95,** no. 6, 2081–2092.

Byerlee, J. (1978). Friction of rock, *Pure Appl. Geophys.* **116,** 615–626.

Chen, K., T. Yang, Y. Z. Wang, X. Y. Guo, J. Zhang, X. Zhang, and R. F. Liu (2025). Quick output parameters related to the 7 January 2025 M 6.8 earthquake in Dingri County, Shigatse City, Xizang, *Progr. Earthq. Sci.* **55,** no. 3, 164–171.

Chong, Y., D. Dai, X. Li, Y. Wang, Y. Zhang, W. Yang, Y. Han, C. Qu, and L. Meng (2025). Aftershock triggering mechanism by the 7 January 2025 M_w 7.1 Tingri earthquake, *Seismol. Res. Lett.*, 1–13.

Collettini, C., and R. H. Sibson (2001). Normal faults, normal friction? *Geology* **29,** 927–930.

Dor, O., Y. Ben-Zion, T. Rockwell, and J. Brune (2006). Pulverized rocks in the Mojave section of the San Andreas fault zone, *Earth Planet. Sci. Lett.* **245,** 642–654.

Dutta, R., S. Jónsson, and H. Vasyura-Bathke (2021). Simultaneous Bayesian estimation of non-planar fault geometry and spatially-variable slip, *J. Geophys. Res.*, e2020JB020441.

Ekström, G., M. Nettles, and A. Dziewoński (2012). The Global CMT project 2004–2010: Centroid-moment tensors for 13,017 earthquakes, *Phys. Earth Planet. Int.* **200,** 1–9.

Farr, T. G., P. A. Rosen, E. Caro, R. Crippen, R. Duren, S. Hensley, M. Kobrick, M. Paller, E. Rodriguez, L. Roth, *et al.* (2007). The shuttle radar topography mission, *Rev. Geophys.* **45,** no. 2.

Fialko, Y. (2004). Probing the mechanical properties of seismically active crust with space geodesy: Study of the co-seismic deformation due to the 1992 M_w7.3 Landers (southern California) earthquake, *J. Geophys. Res.* **109,** B03307, doi: 10.1029/2003JB002756.

Fialko, Y. (2021). Estimation of absolute stress in the hypocentral region of the 2019 Ridgecrest, California, earthquakes, *J. Geophys. Res.* **126,** e2021JB022000.

Fialko, Y., and Z. Jin (2021). Simple shear origin of the cross-faults ruptured in the 2019 Ridgecrest earthquake sequence, *Nature Geosci.* **14,** 513–518.

Fialko, Y., and Y. Kaneko (2025). On the effects of fault alignment on slip stability, *Nature* **642,** no. 8068, E19–E21.

Fialko, Y., D. Sandwell, M. Simons, and P. Rosen (2005). Three-dimensional deformation caused by the Bam, Iran, earthquake and the origin of shallow slip deficit, *Nature* **435,** 295–299.

Furuya, M., and T. Yasuda (2011). The 2008 Yutian normal faulting earthquake (M_w 7.1), NW Tibet: Non-planar fault modeling and implications for the Karakax fault, *Tectonophysics* **511,** nos. 3/4, 125–133.

Goldstein, R. M., and C. L. Werner (1998). Radar interferogram filtering for geophysical applications, *Geophys. Res. Lett.* **25,** no. 21, 4035–4038.

Golub, G. H., P. C. Hansen, and D. P. O'Leary (1999). Tikhonov regularization and total least squares, *SIAM J. Matrix Anal. Appl.* **21,** no. 1, 185–194.

Hall, M., A. Lee, C. Cartwright, S. Marahatta, J. Karki, and P. Simkhada (2017). The 2015 Nepal earthquake disaster: Lessons learned one year on, *Public Health* **145,** 39–44.

He, K., J. Cai, Y. Wen, and C. Xu (2026). Bipartite rupture in the 2025 dingri earthquake indicates normal conjugate faulting during orogenic collapse, *Commun. Earth Environ.*

Huang, S., H. Yao, Z. Lu, X. Tian, Y. Zheng, R. Wang, S. Luo, and J. Feng (2020). High-resolution 3-D shear wave velocity model of the Tibetan Plateau: Implications for custal deformation and porphyry Cu deposit formation, *J. Geophys. Res. Solid Earth* **125,** no. 7, e2019JB019215.

Jackson, J., and N. White (1989). Normal faulting in the upper continental crust: Observations from regions of active extension, *J. Struct. Geol.* **11,** no. 1, 15–36.

Jia, Z., Z. Jin, M. Marchandon, T. Ulrich, A.-A. Gabriel, W. Fan, P. Shearer, X. Zou, J. Rekoske, F. Bulut, *et al.* (2023). The complex dynamics of the 2023 Kahramanmaraş, Turkey, M_w 7.8-7.7 earthquake doublet, *Science* **381,** no. 6661, 985–990.

Jin, Z., and Y. Fialko (2020). Finite slip models of the 2019 Ridgecrest earthquake sequence constrained by space geodetic data and aftershock locations, *Bull. Seismol. Soc. Am.* **110,** 1660–1679.

Jin, Z., and Y. Fialko (2021). Coseismic and early postseismic deformation due to the 2021 M 7.4 Maduo (China) earthquake, *Geophys. Res. Lett.* **48,** e2021GL095213.

Jin, Z., Y. Fialko, H. Yang, and Y. Li (2023). Transient deformation excited by the 2021 M7.4 Maduo (China) earthquake: Evidence of a deep shear zone, *J. Geophys. Res.* **128,** e2023JB026643.

Jin, Z., Y. Fialko, A. Zubovich, and T. Schöne (2022). Lithospheric deformation due to the 2015 M 7.2 Sarez (Pamir) earthquake

constrained by 5 years of space geodetic observations. *J. Geophys. Res.* **127,** e2021JB022461.
Kaneko, Y., and Y. Fialko (2011). Shallow slip deficit due to large strike-slip earthquakes in dynamic rupture simulations with elasto-plastic off-fault response, *Geophys. J. Int.* **186,** 1389–1403.
Kobayashi, T., M. Tobita, M. Koarai, T. Okatani, A. Suzuki, Y. Noguchi, M. Yamanaka, and B. Miyahara (2012). InSAR-derived crustal deformation and fault models of normal faulting earthquake (M_j 7.0) in the Fukushima-Hamadori area, *Earth Planets Space* **64,** no. 12, 1209–1221.
Kusky, T. M., and J. Meng (2025). Perspectives on the M 7.1 2025 Southern Tibetan Plateau (Xizang) earthquake, *J. Earth Sci.* **36,** no. 2, 843–846.
Li, Y., X. Shan, C. Qu, G. Zhang, X. Wang, and H. Xiong (2025). Slip deficit rate and seismic potential on crustal faults in Tibet, *Geophys. Res. Lett.* **52,** no. 1, e2024GL112122.
Lindsey, E. O., and Y. Fialko (2016). Geodetic constraints on frictional properties and earthquake hazard in the Imperial Valley, southern California, *J. Geophys. Res.* **121,** 1097–1113.
Lindsey, E. O., Y.-T. Kuo, Y. Wang, M. Thant, and T. Z. H. Tin (2025). Mature fault mechanics revealed by the highly efficient 2025 Mandalay earthquake, *Nat. Commun.* **16,** no. 1, 10,937.
Liu, Q., J. Hua, Y. Zhang, W. Gong, J. Zang, G. Zhang, and H. Li (2025). Geodetic observations and seismogenic structures of the 2025 M_w 7.0 Dingri earthquake: The largest normal faulting event in the southern Tibet rift, *Remote Sens.* **17,** no. 6.
Ma, Z., C. Li, H. Zeng, H. Chen, M. Lyu, Y. Zhang, L. Dal Zilio, X. Shan, and S. Wei (2026). Deciphering stress perturbations throughout the 2025 M_w 7.1 Dingri, southern Xizang earthquake, *Nat. Commun.*
Marone, C., C. Scholz, and R. Bilham (1991). On the mechanics of earthquake afterslip, *J. Geophys. Res.* **96,** 8441–8452.
McCaffrey, R., and J. Nabelek (1998). Role of oblique convergence in the active deformation of the Himalayas and southern Tibet plateau, *Geology* **26,** no. 8, 691–694.
Milliner, C., J. Avouac, J. Dolan, and J. Hollingsworth (2025). Localization of inelastic strain with fault maturity and effects on earthquake characteristics, *Nature Geosci.* **18,** 793–800.
Molnar, P., P. England, and J. Martinod (1993). Mantle dynamics, uplift of the Tibetan Plateau, and the Indian Monsoon, *Rev. Geophys.* **31,** no. 4, 357–396.
Nikkhoo, M., and T. R. Walter (2015). Triangular dislocation: An analytical, artefact-free solution, *Geophys. J. Int.* **201,** no. 2, 1119–1141.
Olive, J.-A., and M. D. Behn (2014). Rapid rotation of normal faults due to flexural stresses: An explanation for the global distribution of normal fault dips, *J. Geophys. Res.* **119,** no. 4, 3722–3739.
Pang, Y., H. Zhang, T. V. Gerya, J. Liao, H. Cheng, and Y. Shi (2018). The mechanism and dynamics of N-S rifting in southern Tibet: Insight from 3-D thermomechanical modeling, *J. Geophys. Res. Solid Earth* **123,** no. 1, 859–877.
Qi, L., L. ChengTao, Z. Bin, H. Yong, W. YongGe, T. Kai, and D. Qing (2024). Estimated seismic source parameters for 2020 Dingri M_w 5.6 earthquake in Xizang and study on the stress triggering, *Chin. J. Geophys. (in Chinese)* **67,** no. 1, 172–188.
Qiao, X., Z. Lu, S. Yan, H. Shi, M. Zhi, and D. Zhao (2025). The 2025 M_W 7.0 Dingri earthquake: Conjugate normal faulting of a graben structure in the Southern Xainza-Dinggye rift, *Geophys. Res. Lett.* **52,** no. 12, e2025GL116154.
Reston, T. (2020). On the rotation and frictional lock-up of normal faults: Explaining the dip distribution of normal fault earthquakes and resolving the low-angle normal fault paradox, *Tectonophysics* **790,** 228550.
Ryder, I., R. Bürgmann, and F. Pollitz (2011). Lower crustal relaxation beneath the Tibetan plateau and Qaidam basin following the 2001 Kokoxili earthquake, *Geophys. J. Int.* **187,** no. 2, 613–630.
Sandwell, D., R. Mellors, X. Tong, M. Wei, and P. Wessel (2011). Open radar interferometry software for mapping surface deformation, *Eos Trans. AGU* **92,** no. 28, 234–234.
Savage, J., and M. Lisowski (1993). Inferred depth of creep on the Hayward fault, central California, *J. Geophys. Res.* **98,** 787–793.
Scholz, C. H. (1998). Earthquakes and friction laws, *Nature* **391,** 37.
Scholz, C. H. (2019). *The Mechanics of Earthquakes and Faulting*, New York, New York, Third Ed., 493 pp., Cambridge University Press.
Sibson, R. H. (1974). Frictional constraints on thrust, wrench and normal faults, *Nature* **249,** 542–544.
Simons, M., Y. Fialko, and L. Rivera (2002). Coseismic deformation from the 1999 M_w7.1 Hector Mine, California, earthquake, as inferred from InSAR and GPS observations, *Bull. Seismol. Soc. Am.* **92,** 1390–1402.
Tan, P., X. Liang, W. Li, and C. Wu (2023). Crustal structure of the Tibetan plateau and adjacent areas revealed from ambient noise tomography, *Gondwana Res.* **121,** 1–15.
Thatcher, W., and D. P. Hill (1991). Fault orientations in extensional and conjugate strike-slip environments and their implications, *Geology* **19,** 1116–1120.
Tian, Z., J. T. Freymueller, and Z. Yang (2020). Spatio-temporal variations of afterslip and viscoelastic relaxation following the M_w 7.8 Gorkha (Nepal) earthquake, *Earth Planet. Sci. Lett.* **532,** 116031.
U.S. Geological Survey (USGS) (2025). M 7.1-2025 Southern Tibetan plateau earthquake, https://earthquake.usgs.gov/earthquakes/eventpage/us6000pi9w/executive (last accessed November 2025).
Vavra, E. J., H. Qiu, B. Chi, P.-E. Share, A. Allam, M. Morzfeld, F. Vernon, Y. Ben-Zion, and Y. Fialko (2023). Active dipping interface of the southern San Andreas fault revealed by space geodetic and seismic imaging, *J. Geophys. Res.* **128,** e2023JB026811.
Wang, K., and Y. Fialko (2015). Slip model of the 2015 M_w 7.8 Gorkha (Nepal) earthquake from inversions of ALOS-2 and GPS data, *Geophys. Res. Lett.* **42,** 7452–7458.
Wang, K., and Y. Fialko (2018). Observations and modeling of co- and postseismic deformation due to the 2015 M_w 7.8 Gorkha (Nepal) earthquake, *J. Geophys. Res.* **123,** no. 1, 761–779.
Wang, T., and S. Jónsson (2014). Phase-ramp reduction in interseismic interferograms from pixel-offsets, *IEEE J. Sel. Top. Appl. Earth Obs. Remote Sens.* **7,** no. 5, 1709–1718.
Wang, R., F. Lorenzo-Martin, and F. Roth (2006). PSGRN/PSCMP-a new code for calculating co- and post-seismic deformation, geoid and gravity changes based on the viscoelastic-gravitational dislocation theory, *Comput. Geosci.* **32,** 527–541.
Wang, H., J. R. Elliott, T. J. Craig, T. J. Wright, J. Liu-Zeng, and A. Hooper (2014). Normal faulting sequence in the Pumqu-Xainza Rift constrained by InSAR and teleseismic body-wave seismology, *Geochem. Geophys. Geosyst.* **15,** no. 7, 2947–2963.

Wessel, P., W. H. F. Smith, R. Scharroo, J. Luis, and F. Wobbe (2013). Generic Mapping Tools: Improved version released, *Eos Trans. AGU* **94,** 409–410.

Wu, K., M.-L. Chevalier, J. Pan, F. Liu, S. Yang, S. Zhang, Q. Su, and H. Li (2025). Recurrence of large earthquakes along the southern Xainza-Dinggye rift and comparison with the 7 January 2025, M_w 7.1 Tingri earthquake, southern Tibet, *Tectonophysics* **910,** 230827.

Wu, X., X. Xu, G. Yu, J. Ren, X. Yang, G. Chen, C. Xu, K. Du, X. Huang, H. Yang, K. Li, and H. Hao (2024). The China active faults database (CAFD) and its web system, *Earth Syst. Sci. Data* **16,** no. 7, 3391–3417.

Xu, W., C. Bai, C. Huang, R. Bürgmann, B. Shan, X. Shan, Z. Chen, L. Xie, and F. Shi (2025). Northward rupture and early afterslip of two graben-bounding normal faults during the 2025 dingri earthquake of Tibet, *Commun. Earth Environ.*

Yang, J., Y. Wen, C. Xu, and Q. Hu (2025). Complex multifault rupture during the 2016–2025 Dingri earthquakes, southern Tibetan plateau, unraveled by, multisource InSAR observations, *Seismol. Res. Lett.*

Yao, J., D. Yao, F. Chen, M. Zhi, L. Sun, and D. Wang (2025). A preliminary catalog of early aftershocks following the 7 January 2025 M_s 6.8 Dingri, Xizang earthquake, *J. Earth Sci.* **36,** no. 2, 856–860.

Yu, C., Z. Li, X. Hu, C. Song, S. Li, H. Liu, J. Li, B. Han, Z. Liu, M. Liu, S. Zhu, X. Hao, Z. Li, and J. Peng (2025). Source parameters and induced Hazards of the 2025 M_w 7.1 Dingri earthquake on the southern Tibetan plateau (Xizhang), China, as revealed by imaging geodesy, *J. Earth Sci.* **36,** no. 2, 847–851.

Yu, S., S. Zhang, J. Luo, Z. Li, and J. Ding (2025). The tectonic significance of the M_w 7. 1 earthquake source model in Tibet in 2025 constrained by InSAR data, *Remote Sens.* **17,** no. 5, 936.

Yun, J., A.-A. Gabriel, D. A. May, and Y. Fialko (2025). Controls of dynamic and static stress changes and aseismic slip on delayed earthquake triggering: Application to the 2019 Ridgecrest earthquake sequence, *J. Geophys. Res.* **130,** no. 12, e2025JB031271.

Zhang, Y., H. Fattahi, and F. Amelung (2019). Small baseline Insar time series analysis: Unwrapping error correction and noise reduction, *Comput. Geosci.* **133,** 104331.

Zhao, X., Z. Xiao, W. Wang, and J. Li (2025). Along-strike variation of the unilateral rupture of the 2025 M_w 7.1 Dingri, Xizang earthquake: One of the shallowest m7+ normal-faulting events on the Tibetan plateau, *Geophys. Res. Lett.* **52,** no. 23, e2025GL119397.

Zhou, J., and L. Li (2025). An open access 90 m resolution VS30 data and map for areas affected by the January 2025 M6.8 Dingri Xizang, China earthquake, *Earthq. Sci.* **38,** no. 4, 1–7.

Zhu, J., B. Zhang, S. Yao, and Y. Cai (2025). Coseismic deformation, fault slip distribution, and stress changes of the 2025 MS 6.8 Dingri earthquake from Sentinel-1A InSAR observations, *Geosci.* **15,** no. 11, 421.

Zou, X., Y. Fialko, A. Dennehy, A. Cloninger, and S. J. Semnani (2023). High-angle active conjugate faults in the Anza-Borrego shear zone, southern California, *Geophys. Res. Lett.* **50,** e2023GL105783.

Manuscript received 23 December 2025
Published online 21 April 2026

Observed H/V Responses Across Thailand from the 2025 M_w 7.7 Myanmar Earthquake: Implications for Geologically Controlled Seismic Hazard

Passakorn Pananont*[1,2], Pansa Pholsonda[1], Patinya Pornsopin[2,3], Kevin Furlong[4], Koichi Hayashi[5], Songsak Muangnoi[1], and Kasian Prasertwongphilai[1]

Abstract

The 28 March 2025 M_w 7.7 Myanmar earthquake produced moderate-to-strong, long-period ground shaking across Thailand and offers a rare opportunity to evaluate nationwide site-response characteristics. Strong-motion data from 77 Thai Meteorological Department's seismic stations were analyzed using horizontal-to-vertical spectral ratio to determine fundamental resonance period (T_0) and amplification (H/V_{max}). Each geological province shows unique signatures in the ground-motion spectrum observed across the country. The northern intermontane basins exhibit a dual-mode resonance pattern ($T_0 \approx 0.7$–2.5 s) and short-period peaks ($T_0 < 0.6$ s) caused by both shallow-to-moderate alluvial sediments. The western fault valleys show sharp, short-period peaks caused by thin alluvial layers over hard bedrock, whereas the northeastern plateau shows both short-period peaks due to thin sediments and also behaves as a stable reference domain with flat, rocklike H/V curves. The central Thailand rift basin reveals sharp, short-period peaks ($T_0 \approx 0.2$–0.8 s) that indicate the presence of shallow-to-moderately deep sedimentary layers beneath the sites. The Bangkok basin shows broad, low-frequency amplification ($T_0 \approx 4$–7 s), a direct result of deep soft Quaternary sediments. The southern rift basins and coastal plains show mixed characteristics: sharp, short-period peaks ($T_0 = 0.2$–0.5 s) and dual or multipeaked H/V spectra ($T_0 = 1$–1.9 s), due to thin to moderate-to-thin sediment covers. For the first time, this study identifies long-period resonance ($T_0 > 4$ s) in multiple provincial basins beyond Bangkok (Chiang Mai, Lampang, Phrae, Pathum Thani, and Surat Thani provinces), indicating that deep sedimentary structures across Thailand can amplify long-period seismic waves that can affect tall and long structures such as high-rise buildings, bridges, and elevated expressways. These results provide the first observation for a countrywide frequency-dependent site response from a real earthquake event, which indicates that both short- and long-period site effects are equally important for seismic hazard evaluation in Thailand.

Cite this article as Pananont, P., P. Pholsonda, P. Pornsopin, K. Furlong, K. Hayashi, S. Muangnoi, and K. Prasertwongphilai (2026). Observed H/V Responses Across Thailand from the 2025 M_w 7.7 Myanmar Earthquake: Implications for Geologically Controlled Seismic Hazard, *Seismol. Res. Lett.* **97**, 1681–1696, doi: 10.1785/0220250388.

Supplemental Material

Introduction

Thailand is located within the central Indochina block of the Sunda plate, between the active Himalayan–India collision zone and a more stable intraplate region. Although no major destructive earthquakes have been recorded within Thailand throughout its history, large earthquakes occurring in neighboring countries to the north of Thailand, especially Myanmar and Lao PDR, can produce moderate-to-strong, long-period ground shaking within the country. The 28 March 2025 M_w 7.7 earthquake near Mandalay ruptured an ~475 km section of the Sagaing fault at a focal depth of approximately 10 km and exhibited supershear rupture behavior, thus producing enhanced near-fault ground motion and prolonged shaking durations (Peng *et al.*, 2025; U.S. Geological Survey [USGS], 2025; Xu *et al.*, 2025). Strong-

1. SEIS-SCOPE, Department of Earth Sciences, Faculty of Science, Kasetsart University, Bangkok, Thailand, https://orcid.org/0000-0001-9365-5046 (PP); https://orcid.org/0009-0003-3830-0447 (PP); https://orcid.org/0009-0002-5958-5376 (SM); 2. Earthquake Research Center of Thailand, National Research Council of Thailand, Thailand, https://orcid.org/0000-0003-3649-8480 (PP); 3. Thai Meteorological Department, Bangkok, Thailand; 4. Department of Geosciences, Pennsylvania State University, State College, Pennsylvania, U.S.A., https://orcid.org/0000-0002-2674-5110 (KF); 5. Disaster Prevention Research Institute, Kyoto University, Japan, https://orcid.org/0000-0001-5064-8874 (KH)

*Corresponding author: fscipkp@ku.ac.th

motion records from 77 Thai acceleration stations registered long-duration, low-frequency ground motion. These data allow us to thoroughly evaluate national-scale site response, basin resonance, and duration effects across Thailand.

Local site effects are one of the most important factors that control earthquake shaking intensity, which can increase earthquake damage. Variations in local geology, such as soft sediment thickness, basin geometry, and impedance contrast, can amplify the ground shaking by factors of 2–10 and can shift dominant frequencies (or periods) (Bard and Bouchon, 1985; Kawase, 1996). In Thailand, several large Quaternary basins lie beneath rapidly growing cities such as Bangkok, Chiang Mai, and Lampang. This makes it important to understand site responses for accurate seismic hazard assessment. Previous studies using ambient noise and geotechnical data in the Bangkok basin revealed a deep alluvial layer with the potential to generate long-period amplification (Poovarodom and Jirasakjamroonsri, 2016; Ornthammarath *et al.*, 2023). However, very few studies have calculated these resonance parameters using observed strong-motion earthquake records.

The horizontal-to-vertical spectral ratio (HVSR) method (i.e., Nakamura, 1989; Lermo and Chávez-García, 1993) is a practical tool to estimate fundamental resonance periods and relative amplification of a certain site. Although this technique has been frequently used in various places in Asia (i.e., Satoh *et al.*, 2001; Grutas and Yamanaka, 2012; Poovarodom *et al.*, 2017), its application to strong-motion earthquake data across southeast Asia has been limited. Therefore, the 2025 Myanmar earthquake provides a rare opportunity and valuable data set from which basin-scale site response can be extracted.

This study addresses three main objectives: (1) to classify the H/V spectral characteristics of acceleration data from the 28 March 2025 M_w 7.7 earthquake across Thailand; (2) to correlate resonance periods and amplification features with geological domains; and (3) to evaluate implications for national-scale seismic hazard and infrastructure design. By integrating both seismological and geological information, we aim to improve the understanding of the site response in Thailand's major urban centers. This work emphasizes the need for seismic hazard models that incorporate long-period site effects, especially in a country where large earthquakes are rare, but basin-scale site effects could amplify ground shaking and increase the level of damage from large and far-field earthquakes.

Geological Setting

Thailand's regional geology is dominated by the extrusion of continental crust, a tectonic consequence of the India–Eurasia collision (i.e., Metcalfe, 2013; Morley, 2002; Searle and Morley, 2011). The country is bounded by nearby major faults, including the Myanmar Sagaing fault to the west and the Red River fault of Vietnam to the northeast (i.e., Metcalfe, 2013; Morley and Racey, 2011; Searle and Morley, 2011). Tectonic activity in the region has produced Cenozoic extensional basins and uplifts across the country (Morley, 2002), resulting in variable sediment thickness, basin geometry, and near-surface seismic velocity structure. In this study, we simplify the geological setting of Thailand into five tectonic provinces as follows (Fig. 1).

Northern intermontane (NTI)

The NTI region consists of a chain of Neogene–Quaternary rift basins formed as fault-controlled half-grabens during distributed Cenozoic extension (Morley, 2002; Morley *et al.*, 2007). The Chiang Mai–Lamphun basin is approximately 100 km long, 30 km wide, and 1.3–2.3 km deep, containing Miocene fine-grained lacustrine sequences overlain by Quaternary sediments (Wattananikorn *et al.*, 1995; Morley and Racey, 2011). Similar basin systems exist at Lampang (Owen and Utha-Aroon, 1999), Chiang Rai (Mangkhemthong *et al.*, 2020), and near Mae Hong Son (Hisada *et al.*, 2004). These basins exhibit near-surface soft sediments typically associated with low shear-wave velocities in the basin center (i.e., Pornsopin *et al.*, 2024).

Western fault valleys (WFVs)

The WFVs in the western part of Thailand consist of narrow valleys with limited but variable thickness of sedimentary infill. Geophysical exploration in the Mae Sot basin indicates that the Cenozoic sediment thickness approaches approximately 2 km (Chaodumrong *et al.*, 1983). Valley floors are typically covered by thin Quaternary alluvium and colluvium sediments overlying metamorphic or granitic bedrock, resulting in strong lateral contrasts in lithology and structure along basin margins (Metcalfe, 2013).

Northeastern plateau (NEP)

The NEP is mostly underlain by Mesozoic continental clastic rocks of the Khorat Group, sitting on the Precambrian basement with very thin and discontinuous Quaternary sediment (Sattayarak, 1983). This region forms a relatively stable intracratonic platform with gentle structural warping and limited Neogene faulting (Morley and Racey, 2011).

Central Thailand rift basins and Bangkok basin (CRB-BST)

The Phitsanulok basin and related rift systems in central Thailand compose one of the largest onshore extensional basins, with sediment thicknesses exceeding 2–7 km (Morley *et al.*, 2011; Amonpantang and Wu, 2021). These basins consist of multiple half-graben segments filled with fluvial and lacustrine sediments and were influenced by strike-slip displacements along the Mae Ping–Three Pagodas fault system (Morley *et al.*, 2007; Morley and Racey, 2011). Farther south, subsurface rift depressions beneath the Ayutthaya–Suphan Buri–Kamphaeng Saen region contain thick syn-rift Cenozoic rocks that are composed of fine-grained lacustrine and fluvioalluvial sediments (O'Leary and Hill, 1989; Morley *et al.*, 2011). These basins are locally overlain by extensive Quaternary sediments. The

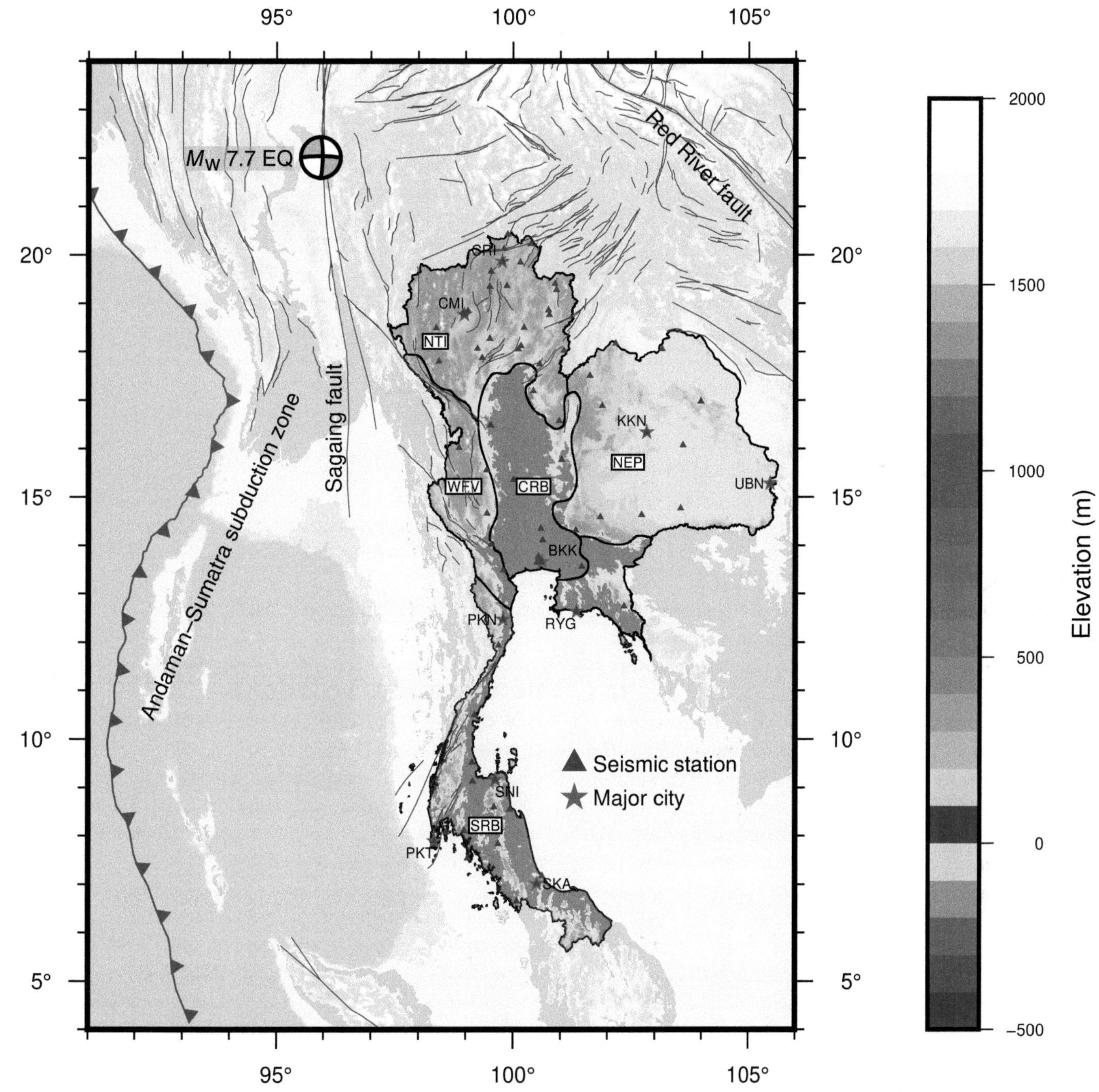

Figure 1. Tectonic and geographic setting of Thailand and surrounding regions. The red lines indicate active faults, including the Sagaing fault and the Red River fault, whereas the Andaman–Sumatra subduction zone (gray triangles) marks the convergent boundary between the Indo-Australian and Eurasian plates. The focal mechanism is at the epicenter of the M_w 7.7 Myanmar earthquake on 28 March 2025. The gray triangles denote the Thai seismic stations, and magenta stars indicate major cities. The shaded relief shows the topography and administrative boundaries of Thailand. Abbreviations of provinces shown in the map include: BKK, Bangkok; CMI, Chiang Mai; CRI, Chiang Rai; KKN, Khon Kaen; PKN, Prachuap Khiri Khan; PKT, Phuket; RYG, Rayong; SKA, Songkhla; SNI, Surat Thani; UBN, Ubon Ratchathani. Boundary of geologic domain are indicated: CRB-BKB, Central Thailand Rift basins and Bangkok basin; NEP, northeastern plateau; NTI, northern intermontane; SRB-CTP, southern rift basins and Coastal Plains; WFV, western fault valleys. The color version of this figure is available only in the electronic edition.

Bangkok basin, the major structural low in the region, is also filled with thick unconsolidated Quaternary sediments, including Holocene marine clay and deeper Pleistocene alluvial deposits (Phien-Wej *et al.*, 2006). The clay-rich deposits that dominate the upper tens of meters in the Bangkok area exhibit very low shear-wave velocities (Pananont *et al.*, 2025).

Southern rift basins and Coastal plains (SRB-CTP)

In southern Thailand, the Cenozoic extensional basins located in Surat Thani, Krabi, and Pattani consist of rock units with thick Paleogene–Neogene fluvio-deltaic sequences (Chaodumrong *et al.*, 1983). The overlying coastal plains consist of laterally extensive Quaternary marine and fluvial sediments that thicken toward the Gulf of Thailand (Dheeradilok, 1995).

Data Set and HVSR Analysis

The data set used in this study was obtained from triaxial accelerometers at 77 permanent seismic stations operated by the Thai Meteorological Department (TMD), which recorded the M_w 7.7 Mandalay earthquake on 28 March 2025. These recordings represent one of the most extensive high signal-to-noise, broadband strong-motion data sets ever collected in Thailand from a large regional event that spans the entire country. To evaluate local site effects, we analyzed earthquake waveforms using the HVSR method implemented in Geopsy software (Wathelet *et al.*, 2020), following standardized procedures established by the SESAME Project (Bard, 1999).

The H/V of the recorded ground motion was computed using the squared average of the horizontal components of the north–south and east–west. We selected waveform windows of approximately 9–12 min in length per station, covering the complete *P*–*S*–surface–coda-wave sequence of the mainshock. Each signal was windowed from approximately 15 s before *P*-wave arrival, subdivided into multiple overlapping segments of 40–150 s, and tapered using a cosine window (50% width) to minimize spectral leakage. Spectra were smoothed using a cosine smoothing function with a half-bandwidth of 50%, over a frequency range of 0.1–15 Hz, consistent with previous HVSR implementations for strong-motion data (i.e., Nakamura, 1989; Lermo and Chávez-García, 1993; Sylvette *et al.*, 2006). The processing flow is shown in Figure 2.

Unlike traditional microtremor H/V methods that rely on the diffuse-field assumption and ambient noise primarily composed of surface waves (Nakamura, 1989; Sánchez-Sesma *et al.*, 2011), the earthquake-based approach directly samples *S*- and surface-wave energy within the 0.1–10 Hz range, frequencies that control the dynamic response of both low-rise and tall structures. This enables a realistic characterization of basin resonance and frequency-dependent amplification under actual seismic loading conditions.

To verify the robustness of this approach, multiple validation tests were performed (Supplement S1–S4, Figs. S1–S4, available to this article). The removal of instrument response (S1) confirmed the robustness of our results. The H/V spectral shapes and fundamental resonance periods remained stable and nearly identical after correction, demonstrating clearly that the observed spectral peaks are not artifacts of the sensor transfer functions. Directional (S2), stability of H/V shape throughout the year (S3) and forward modeling (S4) analyses further established the stability and physical consistency of the observed peaks: synthetic H/V curves derived from independent 1D shear-wave velocity models reproduced the observed fundamental resonance periods (T_0) within 10%–20%. These tests confirm that event-based H/V ratios can provide reliable estimates of resonance periods and relative amplification across diverse geological settings.

Nevertheless, amplitude variations can still be influenced by factors such as source radiation, path attenuation, and 3D basin effects (SESAME Project Working Group, 2005). Consequently, this study emphasizes the resonance period because it is the most robust and reproducible measure of site response. We then interpret the H/V amplitude qualitatively, using it as an effective proxy for both the impedance contrast and the efficiency of surface wave trapping.

The H/V curves obtained were then classified into four types (Fig. 2):

Type A: long-period peak (criteria: $T_0 > 4$ s and $H/V_{max} > 2$).
Type B: dual/multipeak (criteria: $1 \le T_0 \le 4$ s and $H/V_{max} > 2$).
Type C: short-period sharp peak (criteria: $T_0 < 1$ s and $H/V_{max} > 2$).
Type D: flat/rock-like (criteria: $H/V_{max} < 2$).

Results and Discussions

H/V classification and regional geological correlation

Analysis of 77 TMD strong-motion stations from the 28 March 2025 M_w 7.7 Myanmar earthquake, based on four dominant spectral response types, shows that among all stations, type A accounts for ≈13%, type B ≈ 12%, type C ≈ 49%, and type D ≈ 26%. Spatially, type A dominates the Bangkok basin and lower Central Plain, in which thick Quaternary sediment generates long-period resonance (Kawase and Aki, 1989). Type B clusters in the NTI basins (Chiang Mai, Chiang Rai, and Nan). Type C typifies WFVs, whereas type D extends across the Khorat plateau and other crystalline provinces. This spatial classification reflects Thailand's geologic framework (Figs. 3 and 4).

NTI basins

Several stations (i.e., KOOA, CRAG, NANA, and MAES, Fig. 3) show sharp, short-period peaks ($T_0 = 0.1$–0.7 s; $H/V_{max} \approx$ 2–5). These suggest a strong impedance contrast between the shallow sediment and the underlying bedrock. This indicates that the ground motion at these sites was significantly amplified in the short-period range, potentially affecting low-rise structures. In addition, several stations (i.e., CMMT, UTTA, OMKO, and NAN, Fig. 3, Fig. S5) showed nearly flat spectra ($H/V \le 2$), behavior that corresponds to a rock site.

Stations MAEC, SANA, PAOA, LPGA, and PHEA showed dual or multipeaked H/V spectra ($T_0 = 1$–5 s and $T_1 = 0.3$–0.5 s; $H/V_{max} \approx 3$–7). The long-period peaks ($T_0 = 4$–5 s; $H/V_{max} \approx 4$–7) are clearly observed in Chiang Mai, Lampang,

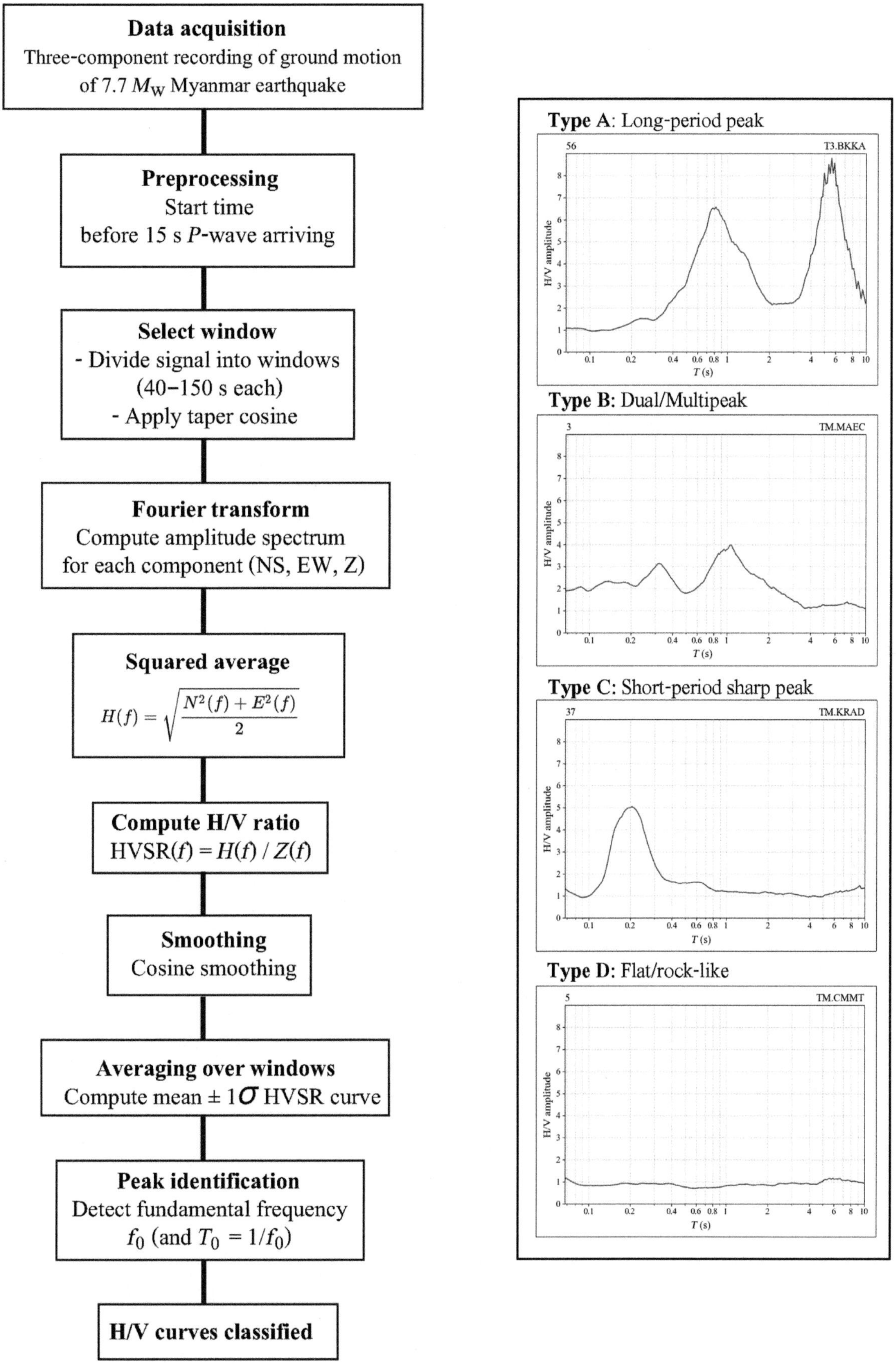

Figure 2. Processing workflow of the horizontal-to-vertical spectral ratio (HVSR) method and examples of H/V classification types. The color version of this figure is available only in the electronic edition.

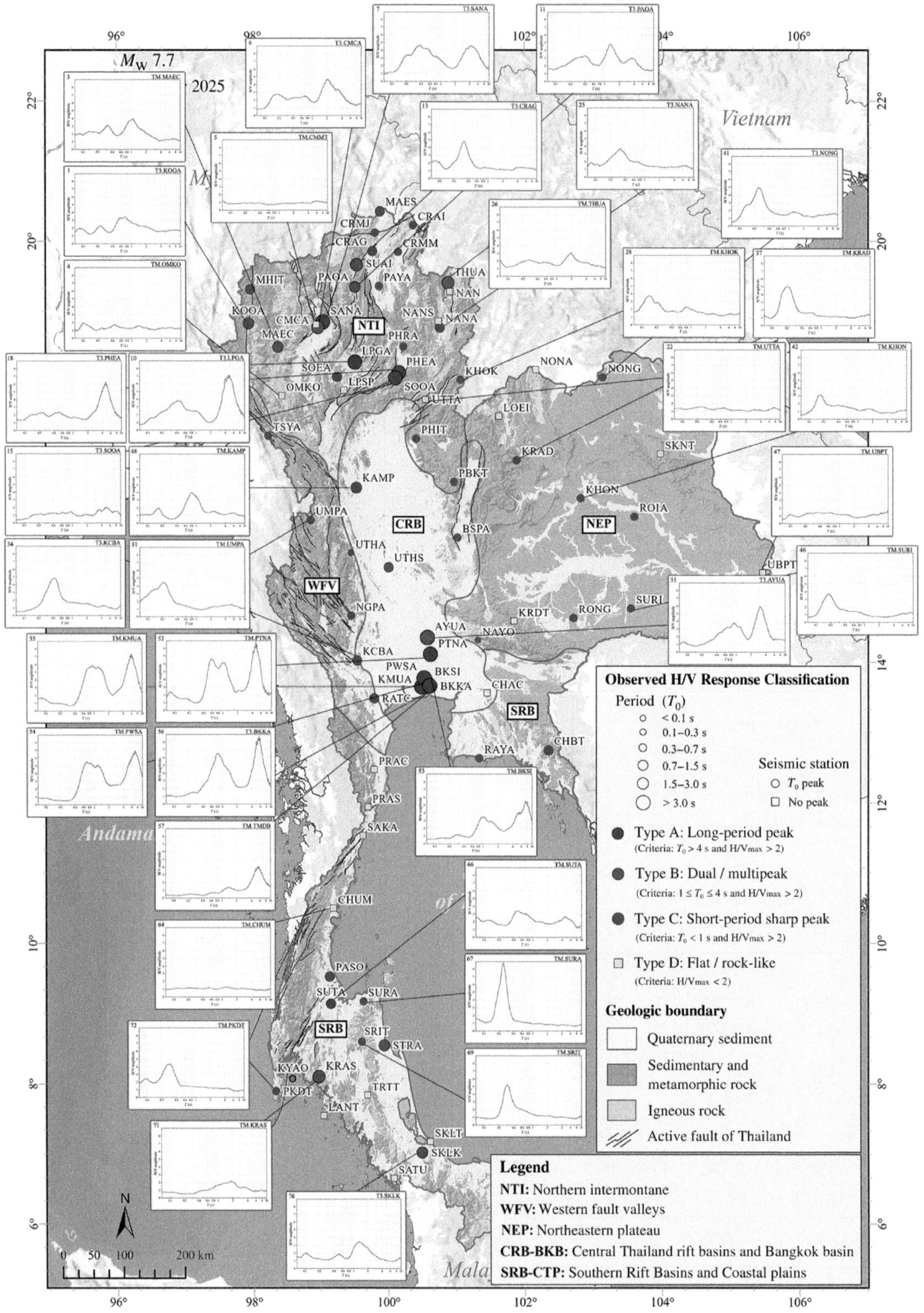

Figure 3. Observed H/V spectral ratio responses across Thailand from the 28 March 2025 M_w 7.7 Myanmar earthquake, overlaid on the country's simplified geological framework (Department of Mineral Resources [DMR], 2007). The circles denote seismic stations classified by resonance period (T_0) and amplification type: type A (red) = long-period peak ($T_0 > 4$ s, $H/V_{max} > 2$); type B (blue) = dual or multipeak ($1 \le T_0 \le 4$ s, $H/V_{max} > 2$); type C (purple) = short-period sharp peak ($T_0 < 1$ s, $H/V_{max} > 2$); and type D (gray) = flat or rocklike ($H/V_{max} < 2$). The shaded background, pale yellow, light brown, and pink colors represent Quaternary sediment, sedimentary–metamorphic, and igneous rock, respectively. Two principal resonance regimes are evident: (1) long-period amplification in deep basins such as Bangkok, Lampang, and Phrae, which threatens tall and flexible structures, and (2) short- to midperiod amplification in intermontane and rift basins (e.g., Chiang Mai, Nakhon Sawan, and Hat Yai), which increases shaking intensity for low- to midrise buildings. The color version of this figure is available only in the electronic edition.

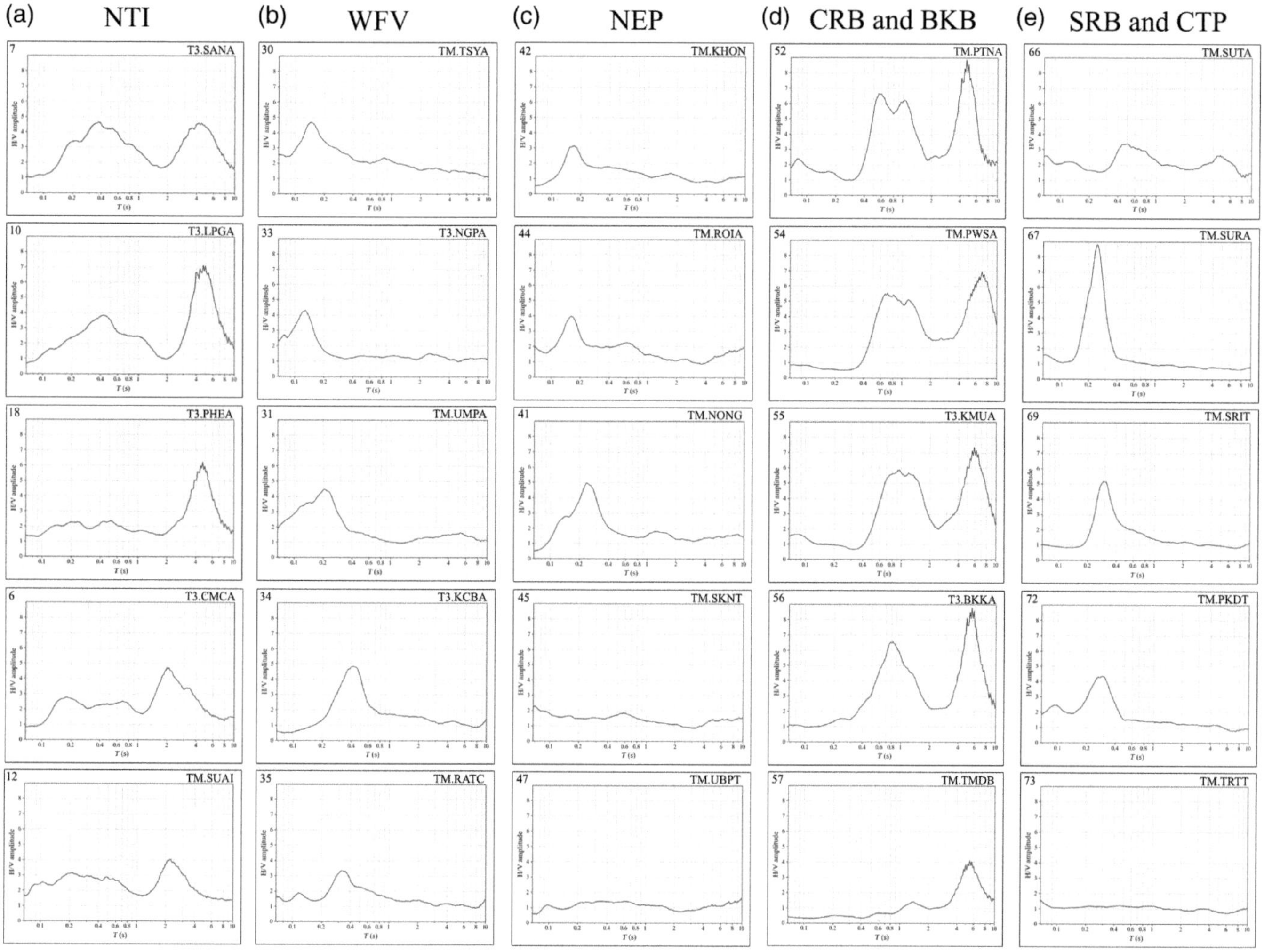

Figure 4. Example H/V spectra for representative geological domains. Each geologic domain is represented with H/V spectral ratios from five stations for its unique H/V characteristic. (a) NTI, northern intermontane; (b) WFV, western fault valleys; (c) NEP, northeastern plateau; (d) CRB-BKB, Central Thailand rift basins and Bangkok basin; and (e) SRB-CTP, southern rift basins and Coastal plains. The color version of this figure is available only in the electronic edition.

and Phrae provinces (SANA, LPGA, and PHEA, respectively, Figs. 3 and 4). This indicates a moderately deep basin, whereas the secondary shorter-period peaks are caused by shallow sediment layers. The observation of long-period response suggests that the ground motion at these sites can be significantly amplified in the long-period range, affecting both high-rise and long structures. These late-Cenozoic fault-bounded extensional basins display multimodal resonance, much like the complex behavior observed in the Kathmandu Valley (Poovarodom *et al.*, 2017). The amplification of midperiod energy, which overlaps with the natural period of midrise buildings with 8–15 stories ($T \approx 1$–2 s), as observed in stations MAEC, CMCA, and THUA (Fig. 3), is explained by the interference between shear-wave resonance and lateral velocity changes (Kawase and Aki, 1989).

WFVs

Stations TSYA, KCBA, NGPA, and UMPA (Fig. 3, Fig. S5) show sharp, short-period peaks ($T_0 = 0.2$–0.4 s; $H/V_{max} \approx 4$–5). This observed pattern is caused by the alluvial sediment lying on weathered bedrock, which produces strong impedance contrasts over short distances. Analytical and numerical models confirm that the basin-edge effects can locally double or triple shaking amplitudes (Bard and Bouchon, 1985; Kawase, 1996), posing a high risk to low- and midrise structures located near active faults along the Three Pagodas and Si Sawat fault systems in western Thailand.

NEP

Sharp, short-period peaks ($T_0 = 0.1$–0.2 s; $H/V_{max} \approx 3$–6) responses are observed throughout this region (i.e., KRAD, KHON, and NONG, Fig. 3), similar to observations in the WFVs. In addition, several stations (i.e., SKNT and UBPT, Fig. 3, Fig. S5) display nearly flat spectra ($H/V_{max} \leq 2$) with only a weak hump near 1 s. This behavior corresponds to a rock site, with high V_{S30} (i.e., more than 760 m/s). The absence of pronounced peaks indicates minimal impedance contrast, confirming the NEP as a regional rock reference zone suitable for ground-motion prediction equations calibration and site-to-rock normalization.

Central Thailand and Bangkok basin

Stations BKKA, BKSI, TMDB, PWSA, PTNA, and KMUA (Figs. 3 and 4) reveal broad, high-amplitude long-period peaks ($T_0 \approx 4$–7 s; $H/V_{max} \approx 4$–9) in the Lower Central plain and the Bangkok basin. These reflect several hundred meters in thickness of Quaternary–Neogene deposits infilling these Cenozoic basins (Phien-Wej *et al.*, 2006). Smooth midperiod secondary peaks near 1 Hz indicate shallow intrabasin layering. This H/V characteristic has been observed in deep basins such as the Jakarta basin (Cipta *et al.*, 2018) and the Los Angeles basin (Perton *et al.*, 2020).

Farther north, stations KAMP, UTHS, and BSPA (Fig. 3, Fig. S5) reveal sharp, short-period peaks ($T_0 = 0.2$–0.8 s; $H/V_{max} = 3$–4). These reflect shallow-to-moderately deep sediment layers, with the ground motion at these sites significantly amplified in the short-period range, potentially affecting low-rise structures.

Southern and Coastal plains

Stations STRA, KRAS, and SKLK (Fig. 3, Fig. S5) showed dual or multipeaked H/V spectra ($T_0 = 1$–1.9 s; $H/V_{max} = 2$–7) associated with several tens of meters of the Holocene marine–fluvial deposits (Dheeradilok, 1995). This characteristic of midperiod coastal amplifications could negatively affect ports, refineries, and coastal industrial corridors along both the Gulf of Thailand and the Andaman Sea. In addition, stations SRIT, SURA, and PKDT show sharp, short-period peaks ($T_0 = 0.2$–0.5 s; H/V = 2.5–9), which can pose a high risk to low- and midrise structures. We also observe a long-period peak ($T_0 = 4$–6 s; $H/V_{max} \approx 2.5$) in the eastern part of Surat Thani province (SUTA, Fig. 4), which suggests a deep basin, implying that the ground motion at this site can be moderately amplified in the long-period range and can affect high-rise and long structures such as those found in the Bangkok basin.

Long-Period Resonance Beyond the Bangkok Basin

H/V analysis of strong-motion records from the 28 March 2025 M_w 7.7 Myanmar earthquake throughout the country provides the first evidence of basin-controlled long-period amplification ($T_0 > 4$ s) occurring countrywide in several Thai basins, in addition to the Bangkok basin. Earlier studies documented long-period amplification only within the Bangkok basin (Ornthammarath *et al.*, 2023; Pananont *et al.*, 2025). In this work, unreported, clear low-frequency peaks have been identified at Chiang Mai (SANA), Lampang (LPGA), and Phrae (PHEA). Surat Thani (SUTA) also exhibits long-period resonance but has slightly lower H/V amplitude (Table 1; Figs. 3 and 5, Fig. S5). For example, station SANA shows an H/V amplitude nearly four times greater than that of the nearby rock reference site CMMT, indicating strong surface-wave excitation and efficient basin-scale trapping (i.e., Kawase and Aki, 1989).

To confirm the existence of basin-controlled long-period resonance across Thailand, we performed a comparative H/V analysis derived from multiple regional earthquakes. H/V curves at representative stations at different geological provinces (CRB/BKB, NTI, and SRB/CTP) were generated using strong-motion records from the 2025 M_w 7.7 Myanmar earthquake, the 2025 M_w 6.3 Sumatra earthquake, and the 2025 M_w 7.3 Philippines earthquake. The H/V curves of all stations consistently show high-amplitude peaks at $T_0 > 4$ s ($H/V_{max} = 1.8$–8) for all three earthquakes, despite having different source characteristics and path lengths (Fig. 5). This confirms that the observed long-period resonance is a site-controlled phenomenon strongly tied to the deep subsurface structure and basin geometry, rather than simply an artifact of a single earthquake's path or source (i.e., Lermo and Chávez-García, 1993; Parolai *et al.*, 2002).

The results extend this understanding to NTI basins (Chiang Mai, Lampang, and Phrae provinces) and southern coastal plains (Surat Thani province), demonstrating that multiple regional basins share similar long-period ground-shaking characteristics as the Bangkok basin. This places several rapid-growth Thai cities in the same category as other Asian megacities such as Taichung (Satoh *et al.*, 2001), Manila (Grutas and Yamanaka, 2012), and Kathmandu (Trevisani *et al.*, 2021). The observed 4–7 s resonance peaks correspond directly to the fundamental periods of high-rise structures (30–50 stories), long-span bridges, and elevated expressways (e.g., Federal Highway Administration [FHWA], 2014; and Pacific Earthquake Engineering Research Center [PEER], 2017). These findings identify new long-period ground-shaking vulnerability that was not previously included in national seismic hazard assessments of exposure to large regional earthquakes from nearby fault systems. This is especially true for the major cities in northern Thailand and the southern industrial corridor, that region where vertical urban growth has accelerated recently.

Population exposure and H/V response characteristics

The distribution of H/V spectral ratios across Thailand demonstrates a clear correlation between areas of moderate–high population density and amplified site response. Regions where the peak of H/V exceeds 2 are in major population centers situated on thick Quaternary and Cenozoic basins or fault-bounded alluvial plains (Fig. 6).

The Bangkok Metropolitan region and its suburbs (i.e., BKSI, BKKA, KMUA, and PSWA, Figs. 3 and 6) represent the most critical case, combining extremely high population density (>25,000 people/km^2) with broad, long-period amplification

TABLE 1

Summary of Observed Horizontal-to-Vertical (H/V) Response Characteristics and Resonance Classification (T_0-type) for Seismic Stations Across Thailand During the 28 March 2025 M_w 7.7 Myanmar Earthquake

No.	NET	Station Code	Region	LAT	LON	Sta. Elev.	R_{JB} (km)	R_{epi} (km)	Equip.	T_0	H/V(T_0)	T_1	H/V(T_1)	Type A–D
1	T3	KOOA	NTI	18.8309	97.9357	619	168	409	C	0.725	3.4444	0.227	2.2878	C
2	TM	MHIT	NTI	19.3148	97.9632	309	179	365	E	0.3545	2.4678	4.9779	1.6134	C
3	TM	MAEC	NTI	18.4969	98.3733	492	207	465	A	1.077	3.9766	0.321	3.1288	B
4	TM	OMKO	NTI	17.7985	98.4329	1141	218	534	F	No-peak	D			
5	TM	CMMT	NTI	18.8140	98.9444	403	272	473	E	No-peak	D			
6	T3	CMCA	NTI	18.7712	98.9694	307	274	478	C	1.996	4.7118	0.1776	2.7604	B
7	T3	SANA	NTI	18.8491	99.0454	314	283	477	C	4.2925	4.589	0.3724	4.6407	A
8	TM	SOEA	NTI	18.0659	99.2465	245	299	557	B	0.4319	2.5654	0.1006	2.3249	C
9	TM	LPSP	NTI	17.8754	99.3463	203	303	580	F	No-peak				D
10	T3	LPGA	NTI	18.2782	99.5066	244	326	557	C	4.738	7.1247	0.432	3.8246	A
11	TM	PAOA	NTI	19.3471	99.5068	543	340	475	A	1.312	4.7826	0.391	3.3071	B
12	TM	SUAI	NTI	19.6610	99.5345	477	348	456	B	2.2589	4.049	0.2111	3.1328	B
13	T3	CRAG	NTI	19.8596	99.7747	404	376	465	C	0.321	4.826	0.081	2.2877	C
14	TM	PAYA	NTI	19.3603	99.8692	444	378	504	E	0.1196	2.9307	5.23	1.9263	C
15	T3	SOOA	NTI	18.0505	100.1114	100	383	619	C	4.9779	2.0411	3.7014	1.7633	A
16	TM	CRMJ	NTI	20.1266	99.8094	435	384	454	F	0.2636	2.0711	0.1031	1.6551	C
17	T3	MAES	NTI	20.4276	99.8865	412	394	446	C	0.454	4.6244	4.086	1.7848	C
18	T3	PHEA	NTI	18.1272	100.1656	162	395	617	F	4.7381	6.216	0.5134	2.3463	A
19	TM	PHRA	NTI	18.4989	100.2293	186	403	594	E	0.1649	2.1724	0.3458	1.9781	C
20	TM	CRMM	NTI	19.8493	100.1538	383	415	500	F	0.1865	2.4793			C
21	TM	PHIT	NTI	17.1893	100.4165	146	439	711	E	0.1387	2.7799	0.2217	2.6443	C
22	TM	UTTA	NTI	17.7443	100.5541	121	441	676	E	No-peak				D
23	TM	CRAI	NTI	20.2289	100.3734	386	443	502	E	0.1457	5.4023	7.958	1.6933	C
24	TM	NANS	NTI	18.8636	100.7418	264	460	611	F	No-peak				D
25	T3	NANA	NTI	18.7672	100.7633	203	461	619	A	0.313	3.6518	0.081	1.862	C
26	TM	THUA	NTI	19.4085	100.8825	335	484	591	A	1.9965	3.0719	0.2636	2.0861	B
27	TM	NAN	NTI	19.2835	100.9116	295	485	600	E	No-peak				D
28	TM	KHOK	NTI	18.0265	101.0688	434	492	695	A	0.146	3.7498	0.762	2.2941	C
29	TM	PBKT	NTI	16.5733	100.9687	803	517	801	E	0.2217	4.9426			C

The table lists station codes, coordinates, geological domains, resonance periods (T_0), peak amplitudes (H/V_{max}), and assigned response types (A–D) based on frequency and amplitude criteria (please see the text). Stations with H/V_{max} > 2 denote strong site amplification associated with thick Quaternary sediments or fault-bounded basins, whereas those with T_0 > 2 s indicate potential long-period resonance affecting tall and flexible structures.

Equip., equipment; LAT, latitude; LON, longitude; NET, network; R_{epi}, epicentral distance; R_{JB}, Joyner–Boore distance; Sta. Elev., station elevation.

Region type indicated by: CRB-BKB, Central Thailand rift basins and Bangkok basin; NEP, northeastern plateau; NTI, northern intermontane; SRB-CTP, southern rift basins and Coastal plains; WFV, western fault valleys.

Equipment type indicated by: A, Güralp CMG-5 T + Affinity (1020000 count/m/s^2); B, Güralp 5TCDE (333660 count/m/s^2); C, Güralp Fortimus (1729600 count/m/s^2); D, Güralp Fortis + Minimus (409729 count/m/s^2); E, Güralp Fortis + Affinity (1020000 count/m/s^2); and F, CMG-5 TB (borehole) + Affinity (1020000 count/m/s^2).
(Continued next page.)

TABLE 1 (continued)

Summary of Observed Horizontal-to-Vertical (H/V) Response Characteristics and Resonance Classification (T_0-type) for Seismic Stations Across Thailand During the 28 March 2025 M_w 7.7 Myanmar Earthquake

No.	NET	Station Code	Region	LAT	LON	Sta. Elev.	R_{JB} (km)	R_{epi} (km)	Equip.	T_0	H/V(T_0)	T_1	H/V(T_1)	Type A–D
30	TM	TSYA	WFV	17.2275	98.2256	147	222	581	B	0.1457	4.6747	0.8413	2.3363	C
31	TM	UMPA	WFV	16.0257	98.8603	473	358	730	E	0.2059	4.4627	5.3607	1.6251	C
32	TM	UTHA	WFV	15.5586	99.4451	158	439	804	E	0.0767	3.1602			C
33	TM	NGPA	WFV	14.6624	99.4468	149	512	893	B	0.129	4.3008	0.079	2.6848	C
34	T3	KCBA	WFV	14.0223	99.5360	30	575	962	C	0.421	4.8297			C
35	TM	RATC	WFV	13.4898	99.7926	12	639	1027	F	0.3211	3.3381	0.1167	1.8588	C
36	TM	LOEI	NEP	17.5093	101.6244	305	557	777	E	No-peak				D
37	TM	KRAD	NEP	16.8838	101.8846	268	599	844	B	0.206	5.0338			C
38	TM	NONA	NEP	18.1751	102.1679	182	607	778	A	No-peak				D
39	TM	NAYO	NEP	14.3152	101.3209	130	681	1024	E	0.0846	3.2027			C
40	TM	KRDT	NEP	14.5905	101.8442	291	706	1031	E	No-peak				D
41	TM	NONG	NEP	18.0635	103.1457	175	711	872	E	0.239	4.9582	1.28	1.8054	C
42	TM	KHON	NEP	16.3378	102.8230	163	712	959	E	0.1732	3.123	0.3817	1.7745	C
43	TM	RONG	NEP	14.6328	102.7176	182	782	1086	A	0.1649	6.2238	0.4427	2.3967	C
44	TM	ROIA	NEP	16.0750	103.6046	158	800	1041	B	0.1609	3.9448	0.6103	2.2424	C
45	TM	SKNT	NEP	16.9742	103.9815	269	814	1012	E	No-peak				D
46	TM	SURI	NEP	14.7688	103.5529	163	852	1136	E	0.182	3.6785			C
47	TM	UBPT	NEP	15.2773	105.4695	120	1005	1252	E	No-peak				D
48	TM	KAMP	CRB-BKB	16.4864	99.5269	77	383	718	F	0.8207	3.9727	0.1649	1.9224	C
49	TM	UTHS	CRB-BKB	15.3536	100.0096	22	499	853	F	0.4111	4.2568	0.1422	2.4541	C
50	TM	BSPA	CRB-BKB	15.7781	101.0210	76	561	873	A	0.1531	3.2589	0.6905	3.0363	C
51	T3	AYUA	CRB-BKB	14.3521	100.5770	7	619	979	D	3.1138	5.9306	0.906	3.7885	B
52	TM	PTNA	CRB-BKB	14.1161	100.6203	2	621	1004	B	4.7381	8.8691	0.5667	6.6661	A
53	TM	BKSI	CRB-BKB	13.7263	100.5598	4	647	1039	F	7.3898	5.5736	1.025	3.4993	A
54	TM	PWSA	CRB-BKB	13.7775	100.5295	4	662	1033	A	7.0337	6.9784	0.7077	5.5217	A
55	TM	KMUA	CRB-BKB	13.6512	100.4942	3	670	1043	B	5.9172	7.3551	0.9518	5.8724	A
56	T3	BKKA	CRB-BKB	13.6640	100.6102	1	677	1047	D	5.6321	8.7791	0.8207	6.5717	A
57	TM	TMDB	CRB-BKB	13.6684	100.6068	1	677	1047	F	5.4947	4.1092	1.3785	1.3937	A
58	TM	CHAC	CRB-BKB	13.5675	101.4544	60	747	1102	F	No-peak				D

The table lists station codes, coordinates, geological domains, resonance periods (T_0), peak amplitudes (H/V_{max}), and assigned response types (A–D) based on frequency and amplitude criteria (please see the text). Stations with H/V_{max} > 2 denote strong site amplification associated with thick Quaternary sediments or fault-bounded basins, whereas those with T_0 > 2 s indicate potential long-period resonance affecting tall and flexible structures.

Equip., equipment; LAT, latitude; LON, longitude; NET, network; R_{epi}, epicentral distance; R_{JB}, Joyner–Boore distance; Sta. Elev., station elevation.

Region type indicated by: CRB-BKB, Central Thailand rift basins and Bangkok basin; NEP, northeastern plateau; NTI, northern intermontane; SRB-CTP, southern rift basins and Coastal plains; WFV, western fault valleys.

Equipment type indicated by: A, Güralp CMG-5 T + Affinity (1020000 count/m/s^2); B, Güralp 5TCDE (333660 count/m/s^2); C, Güralp Fortimus (1729600 count/m/s^2); D, Güralp Fortis + Minimus (409729 count/m/s^2); E, Güralp Fortis + Affinity (1020000 count/m/s^2); and F, CMG-5 TB (borehole) + Affinity (1020000 count/m/s^2).
(Continued next page.)

TABLE 1 (continued)

Summary of Observed Horizontal-to-Vertical (H/V) Response Characteristics and Resonance Classification (T_0-type) for Seismic Stations Across Thailand During the 28 March 2025 M_w 7.7 Myanmar Earthquake

No.	NET	Station Code	Region	LAT	LON	Sta. Elev.	R_{JB} (km)	R_{epi} (km)	Equip.	T_0	H/V(T_0)	T_1	H/V(T_1)	Type A–D
59	TM	PRAC	SRB-CTP	12.4726	99.7929	78	735	1132	E	No-peak				D
60	TM	PRAS	SRB-CTP	11.9385	99.6988	88	782	1184	F	No-peak				D
61	TM	SAKA	SRB-CTP	11.5332	99.6239	22	795	1224	A	No-peak				D
62	TM	RAYA	SRB-CTP	12.6338	101.3398	10	816	1186	A	0.233	4.0508	0.6572	2.5356	C
63	TM	CHBT	SRB-CTP	12.7441	102.3526	218	880	1231	E	0.4887	7.0151			C
64	TM	CHUM	SRB-CTP	10.4980	99.1885	9	908	1320	F	No-peak				D
65	TM	PASO	SRB-CTP	9.5220	99.1373	18	985	1423	F	0.4111	3.4629	0.1422	1.083	C
66	TM	SUTA	SRB-CTP	9.1336	99.1521	9	1027	1465	A	0.5009	3.3955	4.7381	2.6449	A
67	TM	SURA	SRB-CTP	9.1663	99.6295	19	1063	1475	E	0.2448	8.8078			C
68	TM	STRA	SRB-CTP	8.5460	99.9395	13	1115	1550	A	1.0000	6.9902	0.5262	5.3615	B
69	TM	SRIT	SRB-CTP	8.5955	99.6020	77	1122	1535	E	0.2982	5.1736			C
70	TM	KYAO	SRB-CTP	8.0743	98.5848	13	1149	1567	F	0.4427	2.5368	0.7254	1.5954	C
71	TM	KRAS	SRB-CTP	8.1035	98.9755	35	1155	1572	F	1.9003	2.1122	3.4371	1.3517	B
72	TM	PKDT	SRB-CTP	7.8920	98.3350	74	1164	1583	E	0.2982	4.335	0.0958	2.45	C
73	TM	TRTT	SRB-CTP	7.8362	99.6912	90	1204	1619	E	No-peak				D
74	TM	LANT	SRB-CTP	7.5448	99.0466	12	1217	1634	F	No-peak				D
75	TM	SKLT	SRB-CTP	7.1759	100.6157	11	1283	1716	E	No-peak				D
76	T3	SKLK	SRB-CTP	7.0177	100.4989	16	1295	1729	C	1.3121	3.4349	0.1057	1.9873	B
77	TM	SATU	SRB-CTP	6.6537	100.0833	7	1319	1756	F	No-peak				D
76	T3	SKLK	SRB-CTP	7.0177	100.4989	16	1295	1729	C	1.3121	3.4349	0.1057	1.9873	B

The table lists station codes, coordinates, geological domains, resonance periods (T_0), peak amplitudes (H/V_{max}), and assigned response types (A–D) based on frequency and amplitude criteria (please see the text). Stations with H/V_{max} > 2 denote strong site amplification associated with thick Quaternary sediments or fault-bounded basins, whereas those with T_0 > 2 s indicate potential long-period resonance affecting tall and flexible structures.

Equip., equipment; LAT, latitude; LON, longitude; NET, network; R_{epi}, epicentral distance; R_{JB}, Joyner–Boore distance; Sta. Elev., station elevation.

Region type indicated by: CRB-BKB, Central Thailand rift basins and Bangkok basin; NEP, northeastern plateau; NTI, northern intermontane; SRB-CTP, southern rift basins and Coastal plains; WFV, western fault valleys.

Equipment type indicated by: A, Güralp CMG-5 T + Affinity (1020000 count/m/s^2); B, Güralp 5TCDE (333660 count/m/s^2); C, Güralp Fortimus (1729600 count/m/s^2); D, Güralp Fortis + Minimus (409729 count/m/s^2); E, Güralp Fortis + Affinity (1020000 count/m/s^2); and F, CMG-5 TB (borehole) + Affinity (1020000 count/m/s^2).

($T_0 \approx$ 4–7 s; H/V_{max} up to 9). This response corresponds to the natural periods of mid- to high-rise buildings, long-span bridges, and elevated expressways. The findings indicate substantial vulnerability to long-duration shaking from large regional earthquakes that were well documented during the 2025 M_w 7.7 Myanmar earthquake (Pananont *et al.*, 2025). These long-period resonances ($T_0 > 4s$) are also observed in moderate population density cities (1000–3000 people/km^2) such as Chiang Mai, Lampang, and Phrae and Surat Thani (Figs. 3 and 6), which are now recognized in emerging northern and southern urban centers.

On the other hand, short- and midperiod amplification ($T_0 < 1.5$ s) is geographically widespread (Figs. 3 and 6), stemming from shallow soil contrasts that directly affect the 1–15 strong reinforced-concrete and masonry buildings, which constitute most of Thailand's housing and public infrastructure. In smaller cities such as Chiang Mai, Chiang Rai, Nakhon Sawan, Phitsanulok, Kanchanaburi, Hat Yai, and Surat Thani, these site effects can increase ground shaking by factors of two to five, raising the damage risk for common structures during moderate and large regional earthquakes. These results also reveal that while the high-consequence, long-period threat is confined to deep basins,

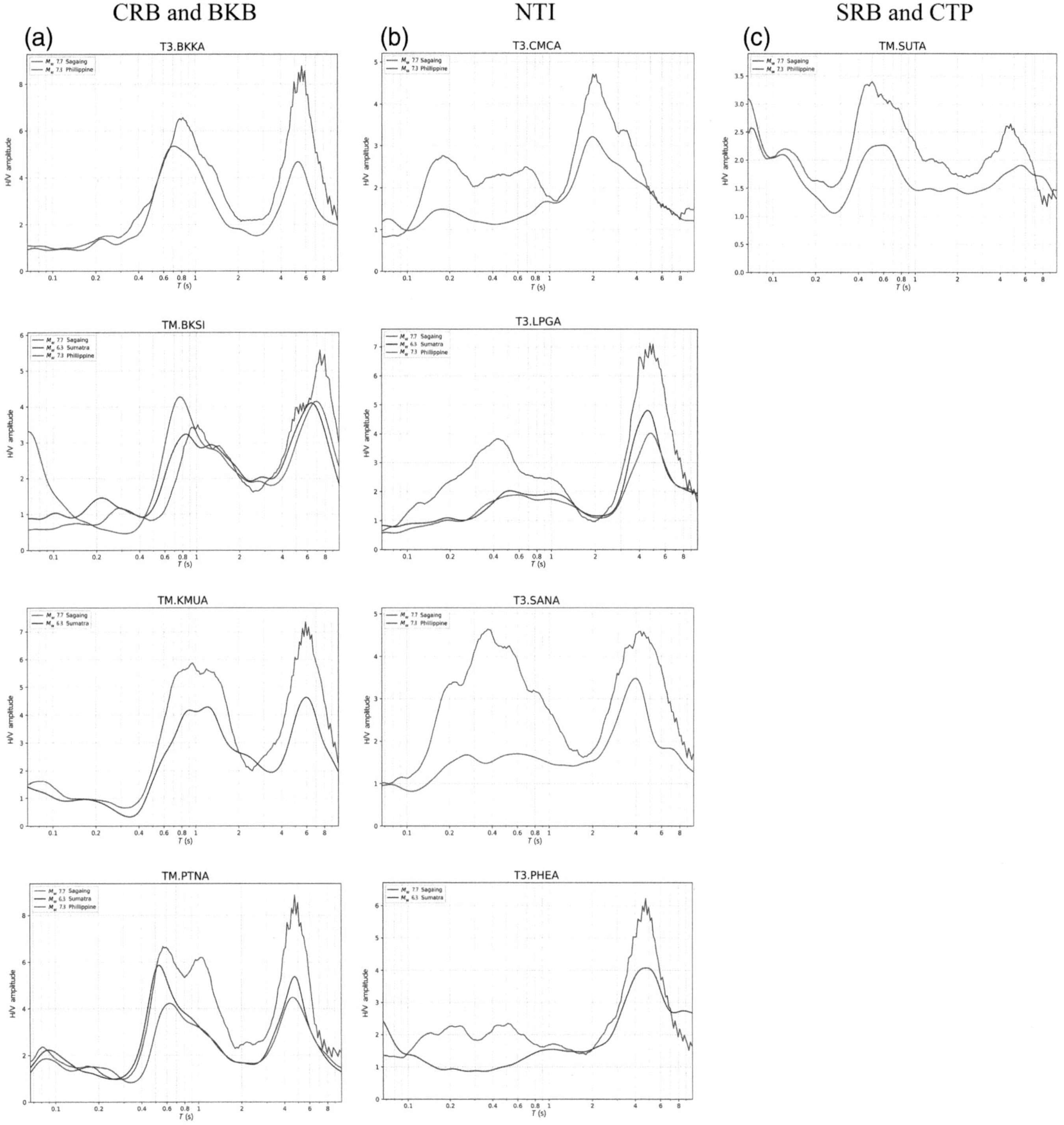

Figure 5. Prominent long-period peaks: type A = long-period peak ($T_0 > 4$ s, $H/V_{max} > 2$) are evident not only in Bangkok (BKKA, BKSI, KMUA, and PTNA) but also in northern basins (LPGA, SANA, and PHEA) and southern coastal plains (SUTA). The curves represent different earthquakes, including the M_w 7.7 Myanmar earthquake on 28 March 2025 (7.7 M_w; red line), the M_w 6.3 Sumatra earthquake on 5 May 2025 (6.3 M_w; blue line), and the 7.3 M_w Philippines earthquake on 10 October 2025 (7.3 M_w; green line). The color version of this figure is available only in the electronic edition.

the short-period amplification is nationwide and thus socially pervasive. Therefore, future hazard mitigations and national design codes and microzonation efforts need to integrate both short- and long-period site amplifications to minimize the earthquake hazard risk in all urban centers across Thailand.

Conclusions

This study offers the first nationwide picture of how Thailand's diverse geology shapes earthquake shaking. By analyzing HVSRs from strong-motion recordings of the 28 March

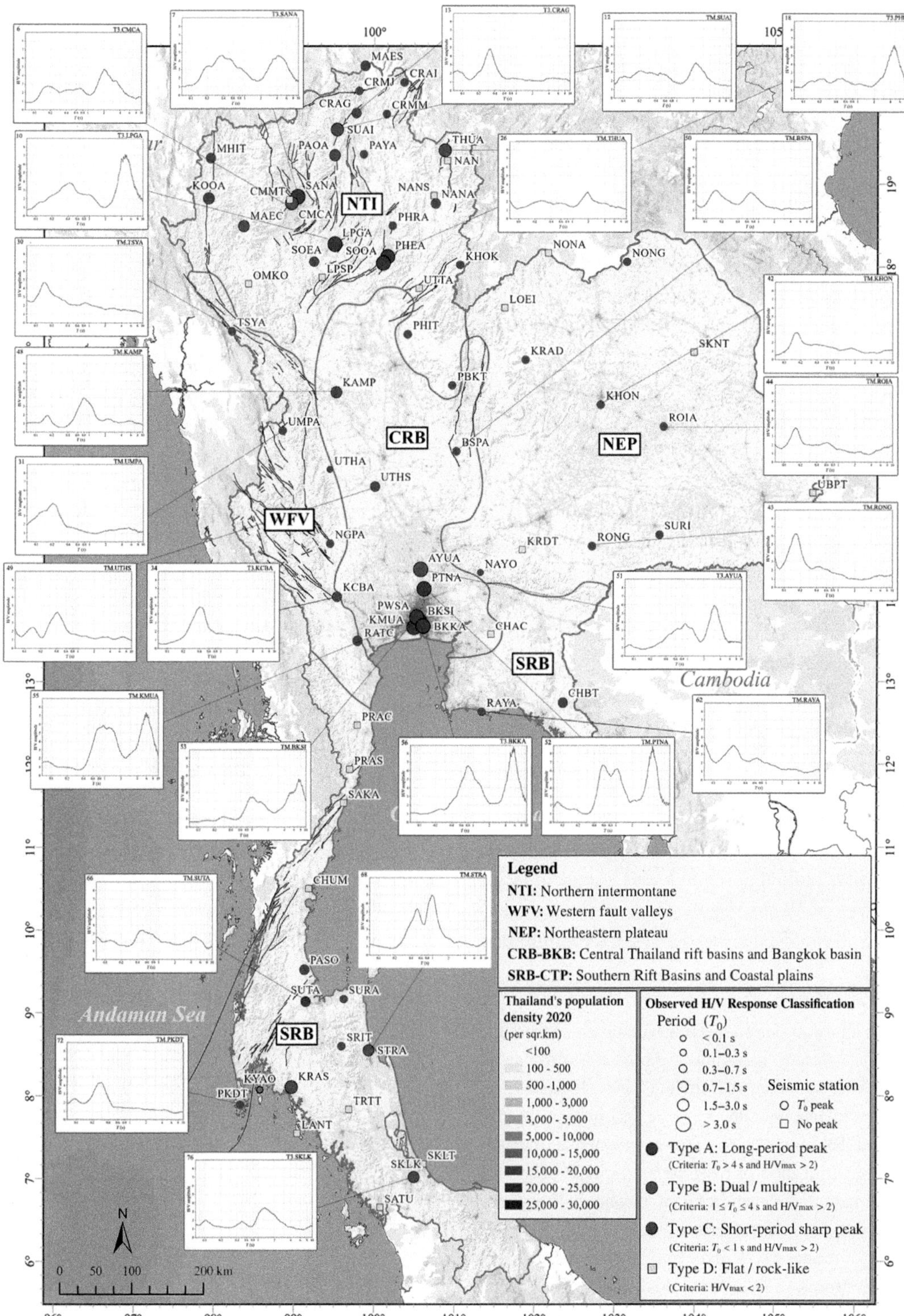

Figure 6. Spatial distribution of observed H/V spectral ratio responses across Thailand derived from strong-motion data of the 28 March 2025 M_w 7.7 Myanmar earthquake, overlaid with 2020's population density (Bondarenko *et al.*, 2025). Spatial distribution of H/V spectral classifications (types A–D) from 77 strong-motion stations overlaid on Thailand's 2020 population density map. The insets show representative H/V curves at selected sites. Although long-period peaks ($T_0 > 4$ s, red symbols) are limited to deep basins such as Bangkok, Chiang Mai, Lampang, and Phrae, the short-period ($T_0 < 1.5$ s, blue and purple symbols) amplification occurs predominantly across densely populated intermontane basins, western fault valleys, and coastal plains, regions containing most low- to midrise housing and industrial infrastructure. The integration of population distribution with spectral-type classification emphasizes how short-period resonance poses the most widespread hazard to Thailand's built environment, particularly within expanding urban corridors in the North, Central, and South. The color version of this figure is available only in the electronic edition.

2025 M_w 7.7 Myanmar earthquake, we show the ground resonance behavior during a large regional earthquake for the entire country.

Across the country, each geological province leaves a unique signature in the ground-shaking response. The Bangkok basin stands out for its broad, low-frequency amplification ($T_0 \approx$ 4–7s), a direct result of deep soft Quaternary sediments. In contrast, the NTI basins exhibit a dual-mode resonance pattern ($T_0 \approx 0.7$–2.5 s) and short-period peaks ($T_0 < 0.6$ s) caused by both shallow-to-moderate alluvial sediments. The WFVs show sharp, short-period peaks caused by thin alluvial layers over hard bedrock, whereas the NEP shows both short-period peaks due to thin sediments and behaves as a stable reference domain with flat, rocklike H/V curves.

A key finding from this work is that long-period resonance ($T_0 > 4$ s) is not exclusive to the Bangkok basin. Sites in Chiang Mai, Lampang, Phrae, and Surat Thani show similar long-period responses, suggesting that deep sedimentary basins across Thailand can sustain long-period ground shaking comparable with those in the Jakarta basin in Indonesia, the Kanto basin in Japan, and the Los Angeles basin in the United States. These long-period effects correspond with the vibration periods of tall buildings, bridges, and elevated expressways, structures that are increasingly common in Thailand's growing provincial cities.

The most prevalent seismic hazard across Thailand is the short- and midperiod amplification ($T_0 < 1.5$ s). This type of resonance poses a direct threat to most of the nation's structures, such as low- and midrise buildings, schools, and industrial facilities. Consequently, even moderate regional earthquakes can generate severe shaking and cause extensive damage to communities.

Data and Resources

Strong ground-motion data and station metadata are obtained from the Thai Meteorological Department. In addition, exported horizontal-to-vertical (H/V) results can be obtained from the Thai Meteorological Department at the following website: https://earthquake.tmd.go.th/shareeq/ (last accessed February 2026). The supplemental material for this article includes verification of instrument response effects on H/V spectral ratios, azimuthal dependence of resonance frequency robustness of seasonal horizontal-to-vertical spectral ratio (HVSR) measurements, forward modeling validation of H/V analysis, and results of H/V analysis from all 77 stations. Maps were made using the Generic Mapping Tools (GMT) version 6 (Wessel *et al.*, 2019). ObsPy was used for seismic records plots (Beyreuther *et al.*, 2010).

Declaration of Competing Interests

The authors acknowledge that there are no conflicts of interest recorded.

Acknowledgments

The authors thank the Thai Meteorological Department (TMD) for providing earthquake data used in this study. The authors also thank the National Research Council of Thailand (NRCT) for supporting this research through the project "Modeling of Tectonics System of Thailand to Evaluate Lithospheric Stress and Seismic Hazard" (Contract Numbers N25A650720 and N25A660575).

References

Amonpantang, P., and J. Wu (2021). Structural characterization of the Phitsanulok basin, onshore Thailand, and regional tectonic implications, *Mar. Pet. Geol.* **130,** 105110, doi: 10.1016/j.marpetgeo.2021.105110.

Bard, P.-Y. (1999). Microtremor measurements: A tool for site effect estimation? *Proc. 2nd Int. Symp. on the Effects of Surface Geology on Seismic Motion*, Yokohama, Japan, Vol. 3, 1251–1279.

Bard, P.-Y., and M. Bouchon (1985). The two-dimensional resonance of sediment-filled valleys, *Bull. Seismol. Soc. Am.* **75,** no. 2, 519–541, doi: 10.1785/BSSA0750020519.

Beyreuther, M., R. Barsch, L. Krischer, T. Megies, Y. Behr, and J. Wassermann (2010). ObsPy: A Python Toolbox for seismology, *Seismol. Res. Lett.* **81,** no. 3, 530–533, doi: 10.1785/gssrl.81.3.530.

Bondarenko, M., R. Priyatikanto, N. Tejedor-Garavito, W. Zhang, T. McKeen, A. Cunningham, T. Woods, J. Hilton, D. Cihan, B. Nosatiuk, *et al.* (2025). Constrained estimates of 2015-2030 total number of people per grid square at a resolution of 3 arc (approximately 100m at the equator) R2025A version v1, *Global Demographic Data Project - Funded by The Bill and Melinda Gates Foundation (INV-045237)*, WorldPop - School of Geography and Environmental Science, University of Southampton, doi: 10.5258/SOTON/WP00839.

Chaodumrong, P., S. Janmaha, V. Ukakimapan, S. Pradidtan, S. Snansieng, and N. Sae Leow (1983). A review of the Tertiary sedimentary rocks of Thailand, *Proc. of the Workshop on Stratigraphic Correlation of Thailand and Malaysia, Geological Society of Thailand*, Geological Society of Malaysia, Haad-Yai, Thailand, 8–10 September, 1983, Geological Society of Thailand and Geological Society of Malaysia, Bangkok, Thailand, 159–187.

Cipta, A., P. Cummins, J. Dettmer, E. Saygin, M. Irsyam, A. Rudyanto, and J. Murjaya (2018). Seismic velocity structure of the Jakarta basin, Indonesia, using trans-dimensional Bayesian inversion of horizontal-to-vertical spectral ratios, *Geophys. J. Int.* **215,** no. 1, 431–449, doi: 10.1093/gji/ggy289.

Department of Mineral Resources (DMR) (2007). Geological map of Thailand, scale 1:250,000, Available from Department of Mineral Resources, Thailand.

Dheeradilok, P. (1995). Quaternary coastal morphology and deposition in Thailand, *Quat. Int.* **26,** 49-54, doi: 10.1016/1040-6182(94)00045-7.

Federal Highway Administration (FHWA) (2014). LRFD seismic analysis and design of bridges reference manual, *Publication No. FHWA-NHI-130093*, U.S. Department of Transportation, Federal Highway Administration.

Grutas, R., and H. Yamanaka (2012). Shallow shear-wave velocity profiles and site response characteristics from microtremor array measurements in Metro Manila, the Philippines, *Explor. Geophys.* **43,** no. 4, 255–266, doi: 10.1071/EG12031.

Hisada, K.-I., M. Sugiyama, K. Ueno, P. Charusiri, and S. Arai (2004). Missing ophiolitic rocks along the Mae Yuam fault as the Gondwana–Tethys divide in north-west Thailand, *Isl. Arc* **13,** no. 1, 119–127, doi: 10.1111/j.1440-1738.2003.00412.x.

Kawase, H. (1996). The cause of the damage belt in Kobe: "The basin-edge effect," constructive interference of the direct S-wave with the basin-induced diffracted/Rayleigh waves, *Seismol. Res. Lett.* **67,** no. 5, 25–34, doi: 10.1785/gssrl.67.5.25.

Kawase, H., and K. Aki (1989). A study on the response of a soft basin for incident S, P, and Rayleigh waves with special reference to the long duration observed in Mexico City, *Bull. Seismol. Soc. Am.* **79,** no. 5, 1361–1382, doi: 10.1785/BSSA0790051361.

Lermo, J., and F. J. Chávez-García (1993). Site-effect evaluation using spectral ratios with only one station, *Bull. Seismol. Soc. Am.* **83,** no. 5, 1574–1594, doi: 10.1785/BSSA0830051574.

Mangkhemthong, N., C. K. Morley, S. Kanthiya, and S. Chaisri (2020). Geological model and development of the Cenozoic Wiang Pa Pao basin, Chiang Rai Province, northern Thailand, based on gravity data modelling and surface structural interpretation, *Tectonophysics* **786,** 228454, doi: 10.1016/j.tecto.2020.228454.

Metcalfe, I. (2013). Gondwana dispersion and Asian accretion: Tectonic and palaeogeographic evolution of eastern Tethys, *J. Asian Earth Sci.* **66,** 1–33, doi: 10.1016/j.jseaes.2012.12.020.

Morley, C. K. (2002). A tectonic model for the Tertiary evolution of strike-slip faults and rift basins in SE Asia, *Tectonophysics* **347,** 189–215, doi: 10.1016/S0040-1951(02)00061-6.

Morley, C. K., and A. Racey (2011). Tertiary stratigraphy, in *The Geology of Thailand*, M. F. Ridd, A. J. Barber, and M. J. Crow (Editors), Geological Society, London, Memoir 37, 223–270, doi: 10.1144/GOTH.10.

Morley, C. K., P. Charusiri, and I. M. Watkinson (2011). Structural geology of Thailand during the Cenozoic, in *The Geology of Thailand*, M. F. Ridd, A. J. Barber, and M. J. Crow (Editors), Geological Society of London, 273–334, doi: 10.1144/GOTH.1.

Morley, C. K., M. Smith, P. Charusiri, and S. Chantraprasert (2007). Evolution of deformation styles at a major restraining bend, constraints from cooling histories, Mae Ping fault zone, western Thailand, in *Tectonics of Strike-Slip Restraining and Releasing Bends*, W. D. Cunningham and P. Mann (Editors), Geological Society, London, Special Publications 290, 325–349, doi: 10.1144/SP290.12.

Nakamura, Y. (1989). A method for dynamic characteristics estimation of subsurface using microtremor on the ground surface, *Q. Rep. RTRI* **30,** no. 1, 25–33.

O'Leary, J., and G.S. Hill (1989). Tertiary basin development in the southern central plains, Thailand, *Proc. of the International Symposium on Intermontane Basins*, Department of Geology, Chiang Mai University, Chiang Mai, 30 January–2 February 1989, 254–264.

Ornthammarath, T., A. Jirasakjamroonsri, P. Pornsopin, R. Rupakhety, N. Poovarodom, P. Warnitchai, and T. T. T. Toe (2023). Preliminary analysis of amplified ground motion in Bangkok basin using HVSR curves from recent moderate to large earthquakes, *Geoenviron. Dis.* **10,** 28, doi: 10.1186/s40677-023-00259-0.

Owen, R., and C. Utha-Aroon (1999). Diatomaceous sedimentation in the Tertiary Lampang basin, northern Thailand, *J. Paleolimnol.* **22,** 81–95, doi: 10.1023/A:1008033813344.

Pacific Earthquake Engineering Research Center (PEER) (2017). Guidelines for performance-based seismic design of Tall Buildings, version 2.03, *PEER Tall Buildings Initiative (TBI)*, University of California, Berkeley, California.

Pananont, P., A. Naksawee, K. Hayashi, K. P. Furlong, P. Pornsopin, and S. Muangnoi (2025). Shear-wave velocity structure and site response analysis of the Bangkok basin for seismic hazard assessment, *Seismol. Res. Lett.*, doi: 10.1785/0220250142.

Parolai, S., P. Bormann, and C. Milkereit (2002). New relationships between Vs, thickness of sediments, and resonance frequency calculated by the H/V ratio of seismic noise for the Cologne area (Germany), *Bull. Seismol. Soc. Am.* **92,** 2521–2527, doi: 10.1785/0120010248.

Peng, Z., X. Lei, D. Wang, X. Si, P. Mach, Q. Zhong, C. Ding, Y. Deng, M. Qin, and S. Miao. (2025). Mainshock rupture properties, aftershock activities and remotely triggered seismicity associated with the 2025 M_w 7.7 Sagaing fault earthquake in Myanmar, *Earthq. Res. Adv.* **5,** no. 4, 100413, doi: 10.1016/j.eqrea.2025.100413.

Perton, M., Z. J. Spica, R. W. Clayton, and G. C. Beroza (2020). Shear wave structure of a transect of the Los Angeles basin from multimode surface waves and H/V spectral ratio analysis, *Geophys. J. Int.* **220,** 415–427, doi: 10.1093/gji/ggz458

Phien-Wej, N., P. H. Giao, and P. Nutalaya (2006). Land subsidence in Bangkok, Thailand, *Eng. Geol.* **82,** no. 4, 187–201, doi: 10.1016/j.enggeo.2005.10.004.

Poovarodom, N., and A. Jirasakjamroonsri (2016). Seismic site effects of soil amplifications in Bangkok, *J. Sci. Technol.* **21,** no. 3, 59–69.

Poovarodom, N., D. Chamlagain, A. Jirasakjamroonsri, and P. Warnitchai (2017). Site characteristics of Kathmandu Valley from array microtremor observations, *Earthq. Spectra* **33,** 85–93, doi: 10.1193/121516eqs234m.

Pornsopin, P., P. Pananont, K. P. Furlong, S. Chaila, C. Promsuk, C. Kamjudpai, and K. Phetkongsakul (2024). Seismic microzonation map of Chiang Mai basin, Thailand, *Trends Sci.* **21,** no. 3, doi: 10.48048/tis.2024.7370.

Sánchez-Sesma, F. J., M. Rodríguez, U. Iturrarán-Viveros, F. Luzón, M. Campillo, L. Margerin, A. García-Jerez, M. Suárez, M. A. Santoyo, and A. Rodríguez-Castellanos (2011). A theory for microtremor H/V spectral ratio: Application for a layered medium, *Geophys. J. Int.* **186,** no. 1, 221–225, doi: 10.1111/j.1365246X.2011.05064.x.

Satoh, T., H. Kawase, T. Iwata, S. Higaski, T. Sato, K. Irikura, and H. C. Huang (2001). S-wave velocity structure of Taichung basin, Taiwan estimated from array and single-station records of microtremors, *Bull. Seismol. Soc. Am.* **91,** 1267–1282, doi: 10.1785/0120000706.

Sattayarak, N. (1983). Review of the continental Mesozoic stratigraphy of Thailand, *Proceedings of the Workshop on Stratigraphic Correlation of Thailand and Malaysia*, Haad Yai, 8–10 September 1983, Geological Society of Malaysia (Tech. Paper 1), available at https://gsm.org.my/wp-content/uploads/gsm_file_1/SCTM_07.pdf (last accessed March 2026).

Searle, M. P., and C. K. Morley (2011). Tectonic and thermal evolution of Thailand in the regional context of SE Asia, in *The Geology of Thailand*, M. F. Ridd, A. J. Barber, and M. J. Crow (Editors), Geological Society, London, 539–571.

SESAME Project Working Group (2004). Guidelines for the implementation of the H/V spectral ratio technique on ambient vibrations measurements, processing and interpretation, *Technical Rept. SESAME European Research Project WP12—Deliverable D23.12*, available at https://sesame.geopsy.org/Papers/HV_User_Guidelines.pdf (last accessed October 2025).

Sylvette, B.-C., C. Cécile, B. Pierre-Yves, C. Fabrice, M. Peter, K. Jozef, and D. Fäh (2006) H/V ratio: A tool for site effects evaluation. Results from 1-D noise simulations, *Geophys. J. Int.* **67,** 827–837, doi: 10.1111/j.1365-246X.2006.03154.x.

Trevisani, S., F. Pettenati, S. Paudyal, and D. Sandron (2021). Mapping long-period soil resonances in the Kathmandu basin using microtremors, *Environ. Earth Sci.* **80,** 265, doi: 10.1007/s12665-021-09532-7.

U.S. Geological Survey (USGS) (2025). M 7.7 Mandalay, Burma (Myanmar) earthquake – Featured Story, available at https://www.usgs.gov/news/featured-story/m77-mandalay-burma-myanmar-earthquake (last accessed April 2025).

Wathelet, M., J.-L. Chatelain, C. Cornou, G. D. Giulio, B. Guillier, M. Ohrnberger, and A. Savvaidis (2020). Geopsy: A user-friendly open-source tool set for ambient vibration processing, *Seismol. Res. Lett.* **91,** no. 3, 1878–1889, doi: 10.1785/0220190360.

Wattananikorn, K., J. A. Beshir, and A. Nochaiwong (1995). Gravity interpretation of Chiang Mai basin, northern Thailand: Concentrating on Ban Thung Siew area, *J. Southeast Asian Earth Sci.* **12,** nos. 1/2, 53–64, doi: 10.1016/0743-9547(95)00022-4.

Wessel, P., J. F. Luis, L. Uieda, R. Scharroo, F. Wobbe, W. H. F. Smith, and D. Tian (2019) The Generic Mapping Tools version 6, *Geochem. Geophys. Geosys.* **20,** 5556–5564, doi: 10.1029/2019GC008515.

Xu, X., W. Kang, T. Wang, X. Zhang, Y. Liu, Y. Zhang, J. Zhao, K. Li, Q. Wang, J. Cheng, *et al.* (2025). The M_w 7.7 Myanmar earthquake: A continental longest surface-rupturing supershear cascading event, *npj Nat. Hazards* **2,** 73, doi: 10.1038/s44304-025-00125-z.

Manuscript received 3 November 2025
Published online 13 April 2026

Surface Rupture and Slip Distribution of the 2025 M_w 7.7 Mandalay Earthquake and Updated Length Scaling of Supershear Earthquakes

OPEN ACCESS

Nadine G. Reitman[*1], Yu Wang[2], Yu-Ting Kuo[3], Catherine Hanagan[4], Alexandra E. Hatem[1], Christopher B. DuRoss[1], Chun-Chi Chen[2], Dara E. Goldberg[1], Harriet Zoe Yin[1], Richard W. Briggs[1], Jessica A. Thompson Jobe[1], Sylvia R. Nicovich[1], Emerson M. Lynch[1], Joseph Powell[1], William D. Barnhart[5], and Robert Schmitt[1]

Abstract

The 2025 M_w 7.7 Mandalay, Burma (Myanmar), earthquake ruptured 475 km of the central Sagaing fault and is the longest continental strike-slip rupture on record. The observed rupture length is 1.6–4.7 times the value expected (100–300 km) from existing length–magnitude scaling relations for strike-slip earthquakes. The earthquake resulted from shallow dextral faulting and ruptured bilaterally with supershear speeds south of the epicenter, rupturing close to three major cities in Myanmar and exposing more than six million people to violent or extreme shaking. We report on the surface rupture character, length, and slip distribution based on subpixel correlation of Sentinel-2 (10 m) and Planet Dove (3 m) optical images and visual analysis of SkySat and WorldView (0.3–0.5 m) optical images. The earthquake had moderate surface slip (average = 3.3 m, maximum = 5.6 m, 25%–75%, range = 3.0–4.0 m), narrow deformation zone width (1–10 pixels in subpixel correlation and ≤ 190 m for the detailed surface rupture mapping), and simple fault geometry (no stepovers or large changes in strike, 87% of the rupture that was mapped in detail is single stranded). We attribute the extreme length of the Mandalay earthquake to supershear rupture speed, simple fault geometry, narrow down-dip width, and moderate surface slip. Based on a compilation of 25 supershear strike-slip earthquakes (M_w 6.5–8.6; 1979–2025), we find that the rupture length of supershear earthquakes does not fit empirical scaling relationships for strike-slip earthquakes that predict length from magnitude. A length–magnitude scaling relationship based on supershear earthquakes has a best fit of $\log_{10}$ (surface rupture length) = 0.89 M_w − 4.44, indicating that supershear earthquakes tend to be longer than their subshear counterparts for any given magnitude and thus may expose a greater population to shaking.

Cite this article as Reitman, N. G., Y. Wang, Y.-T. Kuo, C. Hanagan, A. E. Hatem, C. B. DuRoss, C.-C. Chen, D. E. Goldberg, H. Z. Yin, R. W. Briggs, *et al.* (2026). Surface Rupture and Slip Distribution of the 2025 M_w 7.7 Mandalay Earthquake and Updated Length Scaling of Supershear Earthquakes, *Seismol. Res. Lett.* **97**, 1697–1720, doi: 10.1785/0220250257.

Introduction

The moment magnitude (M_w) 7.7 Mandalay, Burma (Myanmar), earthquake occurred on a fast-slipping plate boundary fault (e.g., Wang *et al.*, 2014; Steckler *et al.*, 2016; Mallick *et al.*, 2019; Tin *et al.*, 2022; Lindsey *et al.*, 2023) in a known seismic gap (Hurukawa and Maung Maung, 2011; Wang *et al.*, 2014). However, one aspect of the rupture was unexpected: its extreme length. The earthquake ruptured 475 km of the central Sagaing fault (Goldberg *et al.*, 2025), making it the longest strike-slip surface rupture on record and 1.6–4.7 times longer than expected from existing surface rupture–length (SRL)–magnitude scaling relations for strike-slip earthquakes (Fig. 1; Wells and Coppersmith, 1994; Wesnousky, 2008; Blaser *et al.*, 2010; Leonard, 2014; Thingbaijam *et al.*, 2017; Brengman *et al.*,

1. U.S. Geological Survey, Geologic Hazards Science Center, Golden, Colorado, U.S.A., https://orcid.org/0000-0002-6730-2682 (NGR); https://orcid.org/0000-0001-7584-2235 (AEH); https://orcid.org/0000-0002-6963-7451 (CBD); https://orcid.org/0000-0002-0923-3180 (DEG); https://orcid.org/0000-0002-0670-6579 (HZY); https://orcid.org/0000-0001-8108-0046 (RWB); https://orcid.org/0000-0001-5574-4523 (JATJ); https://orcid.org/0000-0003-4280-4034 (SRN); https://orcid.org/0000-0003-1419-1373 (EML); https://orcid.org/0009-0004-8272-1043 (JP); https://orcid.org/0000-0001-8060-1954 (RS); 2. Department of Geosciences, National Taiwan University, Taipei, Taiwan, https://orcid.org/0000-0001-6798-2721 (YW); https://orcid.org/0009-0007-0456-2413 (C-CC); 3. Department of Earth and Environmental Sciences, National Chung Cheng University, Chiayi, Taiwan, https://orcid.org/0000-0002-0021-7280 (Y-TK); 4. U.S. Geological Survey, Earthquake Science Center, Moffett Field, California, U.S.A., https://orcid.org/0000-0002-2966-5175 (CH); 5. U.S. Geological Survey, Earthquake Hazards Program, Golden, Colorado, U.S.A., https://orcid.org/0000-0003-0498-1697 (WDB)

*Corresponding author: nreitman@usgs.gov

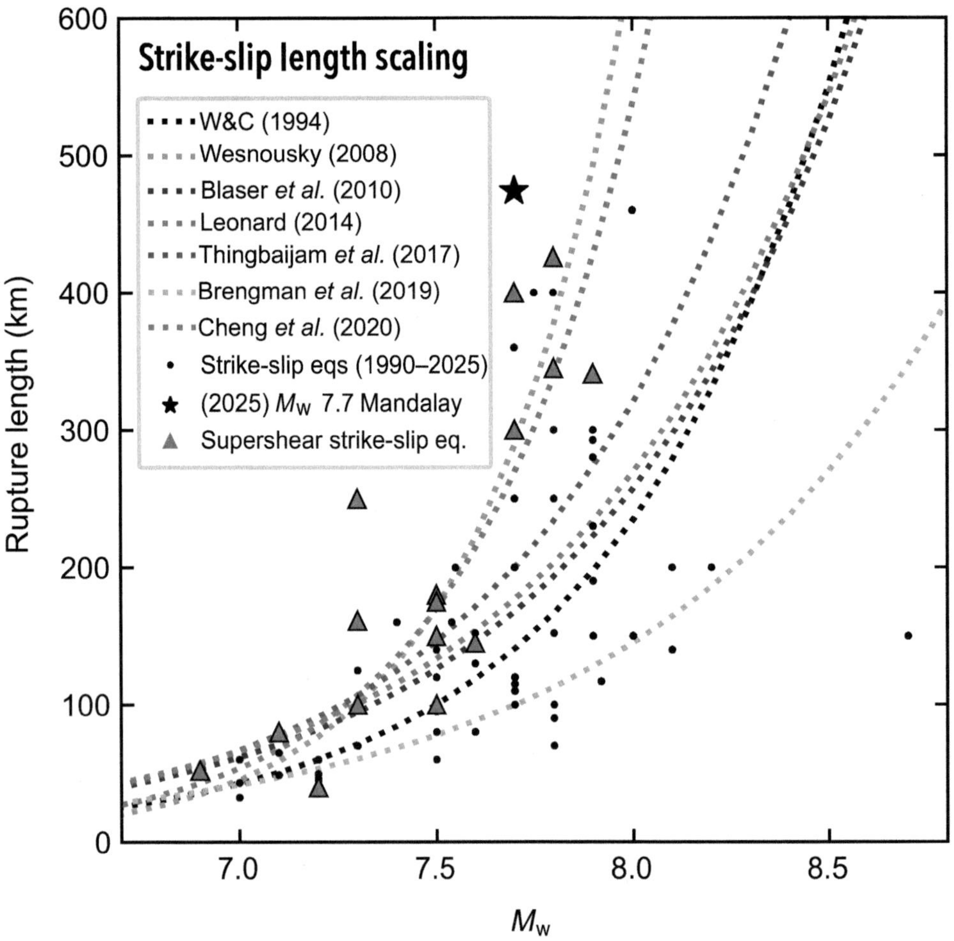

Figure 1. Length scaling of large strike-slip earthquakes. The black dots are strike-slip earthquakes (M_w 7.0–8.7) instrumentally recorded from 1990 to 2020 from Stirling *et al.* (2024) and $M_w \geq 7.5$ from 2020 to 2025 from the U.S. Geological Survey Comprehensive Catalog (U.S. Geological Survey, 2017). The combined dataset includes 64 entries and 44 unique earthquakes. An earthquake is included multiple times if there are different published interpretations of its magnitude or length. The gray triangles are supershear earthquakes from Bao *et al.* (2022), plus the 2021 Maduo and 2023 Pazarcık and Elbistan earthquakes. W&C (1994), Wells and Coppersmith (1994). The color version of this figure is available only in the electronic edition.

2019; Cheng *et al.*, 2019). The expected rupture length is one of the first pieces of information necessary for accurate U.S. Geological Survey (USGS) National Earthquake Information Center products such as ShakeMap (Wald *et al.*, 2022) and Prompt Assessment of Global Earthquakes for Response (PAGER), satellite tasking, and effective humanitarian response. However, in the first few minutes after an earthquake, there are not sufficient aftershocks to delineate the rupture length, and postearthquake satellite optical or radar data have not yet been acquired. Thus, scientists use empirical length–magnitude scaling relations based on the earthquake magnitude and tectonic setting to estimate rupture length.

Published length scaling relationships predict an M_w 7.7 strike-slip earthquake will produce a 100–300-km-long surface rupture (Fig. 1; Wells and Coppersmith, 1994; Wesnousky, 2008; Blaser *et al.*, 2010; Leonard, 2014; Thingbaijam *et al.*, 2017; Brengman *et al.*, 2019; Cheng *et al.*, 2019), but large strike-slip earthquakes (seismic moment, $M_0 \gtrsim 10^{20}$ N · m, length $\gtrsim$45 km, area > 537 km^2) are limited in down-dip width because the rupture approaches the seismogenic depth in the shallow crust (e.g., Hanks and Bakun, 2002, 2008; Leonard, 2010). This results in long strike-slip earthquakes that have larger length-to-width aspect ratios than dip-slip earthquakes (e.g., Leonard, 2010). However, the M_0–M_w scale developed by Hanks and Kanamori (1979) depends on a constant length-to-width aspect ratio in the M_0-area and M_0-length scaling relationships developed by Kanamori and Anderson (1975). Thus, whether M_0 length for large strike-slip earthquakes follows the same scaling relationships as dip-slip earthquakes and smaller strike-slip earthquakes has long been debated (e.g., Romanowicz, 1992; Scholz, 1994; Stirling *et al.*, 2002; Shaw and Wesnousky, 2008). Although much of the debate focuses on whether width-limited earthquake moment scales with width or length (e.g., Leonard, 2010), recent studies suggest that earthquake magnitude also scales with long-term fault slip rate (Anderson *et al.*, 2017, 2021). In addition, many of the longest strike-slip earthquakes on record have documented supershear rupture (rupture velocity faster than shear-wave velocity in the shallow crust, $\gtrsim$3.5 km/s; Fig. 1; Bao *et al.*, 2022), raising the question of whether these earthquakes fit established scaling relationships.

The surface rupture and surface-slip distribution of earthquakes are fundamental measurements that not only parameterize empirical earthquake scaling relationships but also inform humanitarian response and provide opportunities to learn about the physics of earthquake rupture processes. Here, we report on the surface rupture character, length, and displacement of the earthquake based on optical remote sensing observations and place the Mandalay rupture in context of other large strike-slip

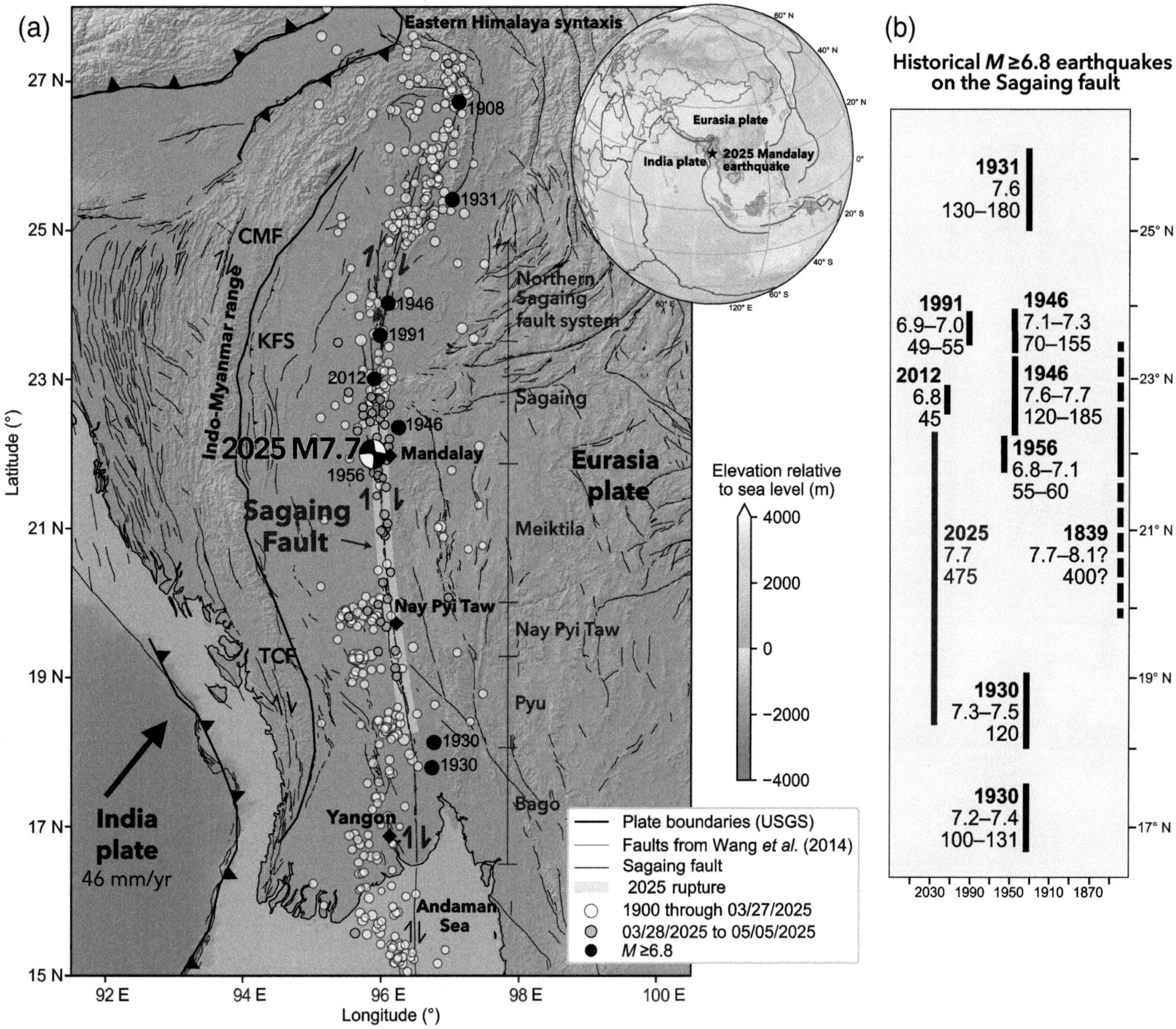

earthquakes and global scaling relationships to investigate the applicability of established scaling relationships for supershear strike-slip earthquakes.

Figure 2. (a) Regional tectonic context of the 2025 M_w 7.7 Mandalay earthquake. The earthquake ruptured ~475 km (yellow line) of the dextral Sagaing fault (thin blue lines) in central Myanmar. The 2025 earthquake occurred in a seismic gap observed to exist since at least 1900, as illustrated by shallow seismicity (<25 km depth) from 1900 through 27 March 2025 (white circles) and from 28 March 2025 to 5 May 2025 (orange circles). Earthquakes M ≥6.8 since 1900 shown as black circles (locations from Hurukawa and Maung Maung, 2011). Regional faults (gray lines) and Sagaing fault segments (blue) from Wang *et al.* (2014). Plate boundaries (black lines) from U.S. Geological Survey (USGS). Bathymetry and topography from the General Bathymetric Chart of the Oceans (GEBCO). CMF, Churachandpur-Mao fault; KFS, Kabaw fault system; TCF, Thahtay Chaung fault. (b) Historical ruptures along the Sagaing fault (modified from Wang *et al.*, 2014) illustrate the seismic gap filled by the 2025 earthquake. Magnitudes are M_w from U.S. Geological Survey (2017), Engdahl and Villaseñor (2002), and Wang *et al.* (2014). Lengths in kilometers are from Hurukawa and Maung Maung (2011) and Wang *et al.* (2014). 1839 Ava earthquake estimates are from Wang *et al.* (2014) and Wu (2022). The color version of this figure is available only in the electronic edition.

Seismotectonic Setting

Because India collides with Eurasia, the high Himalaya are built to the north, and oblique collision to the east occurs at a rate of ~46 mm/yr (Steckler *et al.*, 2016). Oblique collision is partitioned onto faults that accommodate convergence (12–24 mm/yr) and dextral strike slip (25–32 mm/yr) across Bangladesh, India, and Myanmar (Fig. 2a; e.g., Socquet *et al.*, 2006; Steckler *et al.*, 2016; Mallick *et al.*, 2019). The Sagaing fault accommodates the majority of dextral shear (20–23 mm/yr; Lindsey *et al.*, 2023) and spans ~1400 km (Wang *et al.*, 2014) through central Myanmar from the Andaman Sea spreading center in the south to the eastern Himalaya syntaxis in the north. The remainder of dextral slip is accommodated by the Churachandpur-Mao, Thahtay-Chaung, and other lower strain-rate faults in Myanmar and

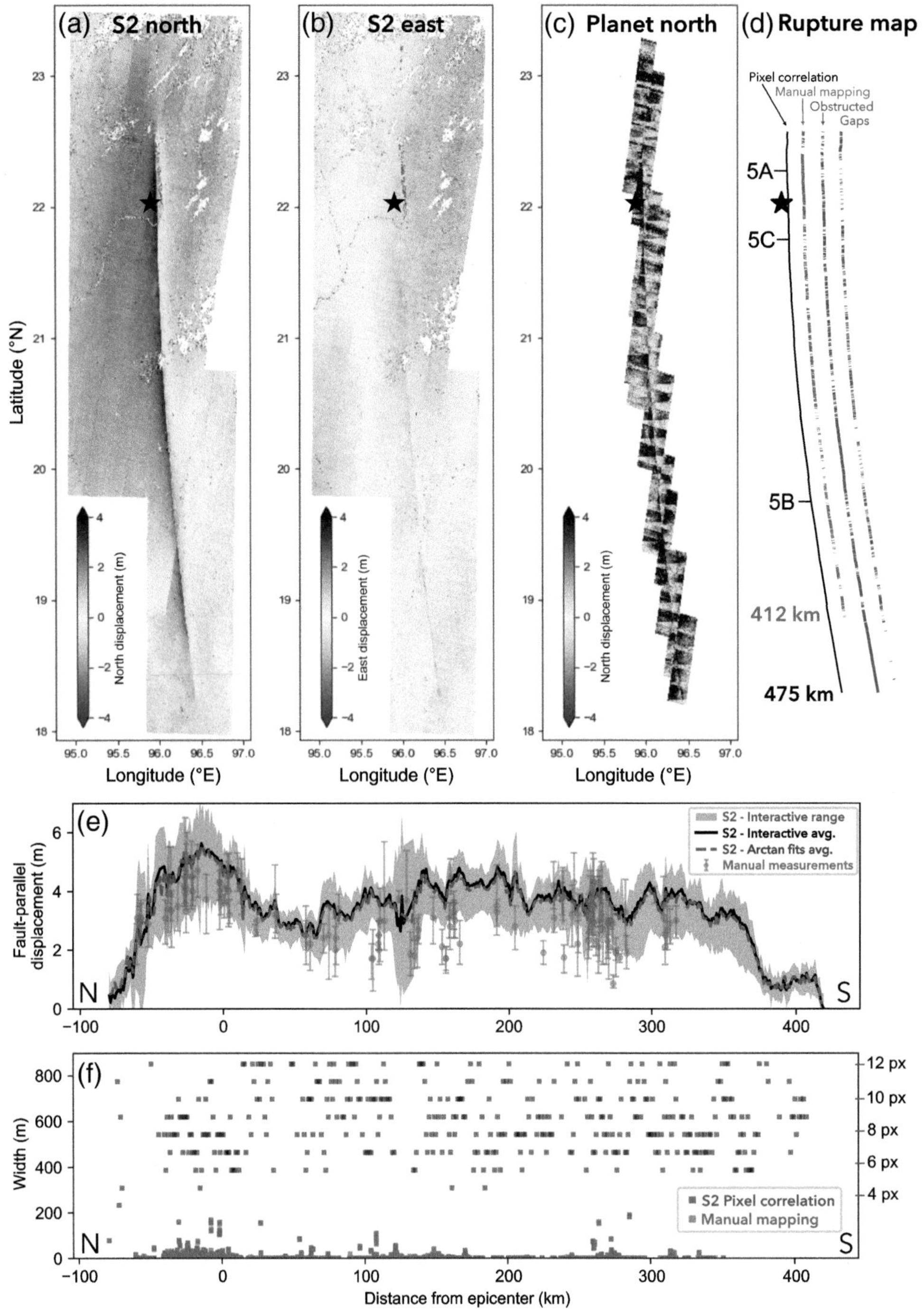

Figure 3. Subpixel correlation and surface slip distribution. Sentinel-2 (S2) pixel correlation results (~80 m resolution) in the (a) north–south and (b) east–west directions. North and east are positive. Black stars are earthquake epicenter. (c) North–south pixel correlation results from Planet Dove images (3 m resolution). (d) Rupture map from pixel correlation and visual analysis of high-resolution (≤0.5 m/pixel) optical satellite images. Full rupture length of 475 km (black text) is defined by optical pixel correlation, whereas rupture length of 412 km (blue text) is defined from visual surface rupture mapping. Locations of surface rupture examples shown in Figure 5 are marked. (e) Surface slip distribution from S2 correlation (black and green) and manual (blue) measurements. (f) Fault zone width derived from profiles through S2 pixel correlation results (gray squares) and manual mapping (blue circles). The color version of this figure is available only in the electronic edition.

the Indo-Myanmar Range (also known as the Indo-Burman Range; Fig. 2a; Wang *et al.*, 2014; Steckler *et al.*, 2016; Mallick *et al.*, 2019).

The 28 March 2025 M_w 7.7 Mandalay earthquake occurred at 12:51 p.m. local time (06:21 UTC) as a result of shallow faulting on the dextral Sagaing fault in central Myanmar (Fig. 2a), causing widespread destruction in Myanmar and Thailand and exposing more than six million people to violent or extreme shaking (USGS PAGER). The Sagaing fault is recognized for its potential for damaging earthquakes because of its location proximal to much of Myanmar's population, recognized seismic gap prior to the 2025 earthquake (e.g., Hurukawa and Maung Maung, 2011; Wang *et al.*, 2014), potential for supershear earthquakes (Robinson *et al.*, 2010), and role in accommodating a large portion of strain between India and Eurasia (e.g., Tin *et al.*, 2022; Lindsey *et al.*, 2023). The epicenter was located at 22.001° N, 95.925° E (USGS event ID us7000pn9s), within 15 km of the cities of Mandalay and Sagaing. The earthquake ruptured bilaterally to the north (65 km) and south (410 km), passing Myanmar's capital city of Nay Pyi Taw, with subshear speeds north of the epicenter and supershear speeds south of the epicenter (Goldberg *et al.*, 2025).

The Sagaing fault has hosted at least 10 earthquakes $M_w \geq 6.8$ since 1839 (Fig. 2b; Hurukawa and Maung Maung, 2011; Wang *et al.*, 2014). These large earthquakes and shallow seismicity $M_w \geq 4.0$ since 1900 (U.S. Geological Survey, 2017) highlight a seismic gap along the ~180-km-long Meiktila segment, from north of Nay Pyi Taw to south of Sagaing, that existed prior to the 2025 earthquake (Fig. 2). This region may have last ruptured in 1839 (Wang *et al.*, 2014) and forms the central part of the 2025 earthquake rupture. Wang *et al.* (2014) suggested that rupture of the 220-km-long Meiktila segment alone could produce an earthquake M_w 7.8–7.9 based on scaling relationships, again illustrating the extreme length of the 2025 M_w 7.7 Mandalay earthquake for its magnitude.

Data and Methods

Optical image subpixel correlation

We performed subpixel correlation of pre- and postearthquake optical satellite images from Sentinel-2 (S2) and Planet Dove. S2 images from track 46 cover approximately the northern two-thirds of the rupture with images collected on 25 and 30 March. Track 47 completed coverage of the rupture with images collected on 27 March and 1 April. We performed subpixel correlation using the red band (4) at 10 m resolution in COSI-Corr Python (Leprince *et al.*, 2007; Aati *et al.*, 2022) with a 64 m correlation window and an 8 m step size, for ~80 m resolution results in the north–south (NS) and east–west (EW) directions (Fig. 3a,b). Refer to Goldberg *et al.* (2025) for processing details. We used the S2 results to map the initial simple fault location and derive a surface slip distribution.

Planet Dove satellites cover most of the globe daily, providing high-temporal resolution optical images at ~3 m spatial resolution (Planet Team, 2025). Planet Dove images covered the rupture ~22 hr postearthquake, with a few gaps and clouds. We merged all pre-earthquake (26 and 28 March, $n = 47$) and postearthquake (30 and 31 March, $n = 61$) images and converted them to grayscale (0.2989 red, 0.5870 green, 0.1140 blue) before correlation. We performed subpixel correlation with MicMac (Rosu *et al.*, 2015; Rupnik *et al.*, 2017) using a nine-pixel correlation window, five-pixel search space, and SsResolOpt value of 1, for 3-m-resolution results in the NS and EW directions. The rupture is clearly delineated in the resulting images despite the noise, scene boundaries, differences in camera model and orbit, and patchy clouds at the southern end of the rupture (Fig. 3c). We used the Planet Dove results to generate a first approximation of earthquake rupture length and refine the simple fault location.

We calculate strain derivatives from the S2 subpixel correlation results using the following equations for curl (positive is anticlockwise rotation; equation 1; Zhou *et al.*, 2018), dilatation (positive is extension; equation 2; Zhou *et al.*, 2018; Materna and Maurer, 2023), and maximum shear strain ($\varepsilon_{\max}$; equation 3; Materna and Maurer, 2023):

$$\mathrm{Curl} = \partial \mathrm{NS}/\partial x - \partial \mathrm{EW}/\partial y, \quad (1)$$

$$\mathrm{Dilatation} = \varepsilon_{xx} + \varepsilon_{yy}, \quad (2)$$

$$\varepsilon_{\max} = 0.5 \times \sqrt{((\varepsilon_{xx} - \varepsilon_{yy})^2 + 4\varepsilon_{xy}^2)}, \quad (3)$$

in which ε_{xx} (east), ε_{yy} (north), and ε_{xy} (east–north) are

$$\varepsilon_{xx} = \partial \mathrm{EW}/\partial x, \quad (4)$$

$$\varepsilon_{yy} = \partial \mathrm{NS}/\partial y, \quad (5)$$

$$\varepsilon_{xy} = 0.5 \times (\partial \mathrm{NS}/\partial x + \partial \mathrm{EW}/\partial y). \quad (6)$$

Subpixel correlation displacement measurements

We measure the horizontal component of surface displacement from the S2 correlation results at 488 unique profiles along the rupture and extending past the rupture end points to the north and south. Each profile is oriented perpendicular to local fault strike and is 1-km wide and 12-km long (e.g., Fig. 4a). Horizontal displacement is measured by calculating the fault-perpendicular and fault-parallel components of deformation for each profile relative to local fault strike from the NS and EW S2 correlation results (Figs. 3 and 4).

We use both interactive and automated methods to quantify fault-parallel displacement and deformation zone width (Fig. 4). We compare the two approaches to determine the relative performance of the automatic methods to the more labor-intensive interactive methods. For the interactive methods, the fault zone boundaries for each profile are interactively selected by the user based on the gradient and average of the data in the profile (vertical lines in Fig. 4d). The fault-parallel horizontal displacement is calculated as the difference between data on either side of the fault zone. We then use four methods to calculate fault-parallel horizontal displacement and combine the results in a single preferred value with minimum and maximum uncertainty bounds as a proxy for how geologists calculate uncertainty of offset measurements in the field using multiple plausible projections of an offset feature (e.g., Gold *et al.*, 2015; DuRoss *et al.*, 2024). The four methods are (1) linear regression on either side of the fault zone excluding the fault zone and extending 1.5 km from the fault zone ("near-field regression") or (2) to the end of the profile ("far-field regression") and (3) mean of the data on either side of the fault zone excluding the fault zone and extending 1.5 km from the fault zone ("near-field mean") or (4) to the end of the profile ("far-field mean"). For each of the four methods, minimum and maximum displacements are calculated with 1-sigma uncertainty. The near-field regression offset values are more influenced by near-fault decorrelation from water bodies that parallel the Sagaing fault and are more variable than the other three methods, so we exclude them from the preferred slip distribution. The preferred displacement value for each profile is thus the average of the far-field regression, near-field mean, and far-field mean offset values. The uncertainty range for each profile is the minimum and maximum of the far-field regression, near-field mean, and far-field mean.

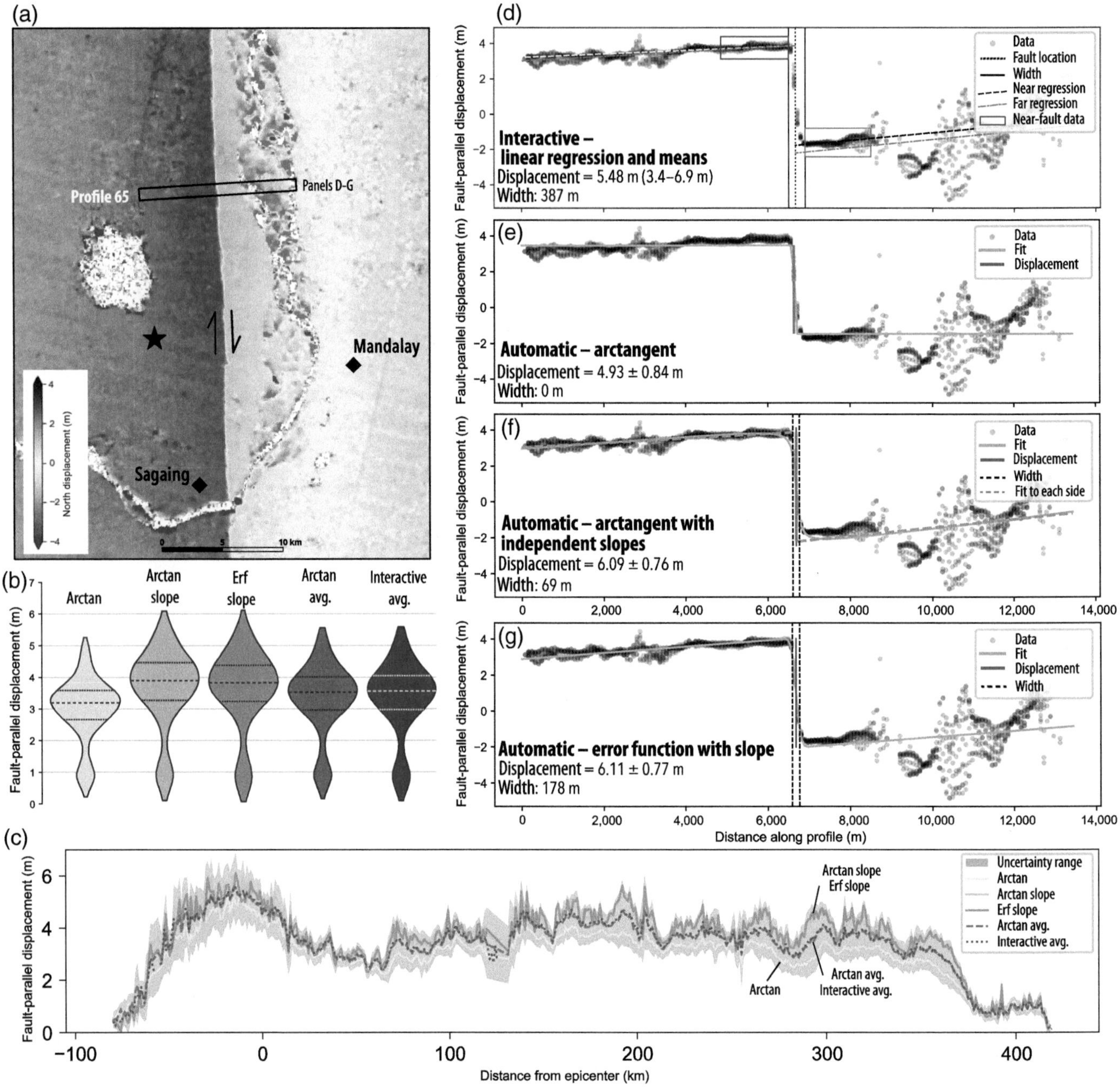

Figure 4. Surface displacement calculations from S2 correlation data. (a) S2 north–south subpixel correlation results with the earthquake epicenter (black star) and an example profile. Profiles are 12-km long and 1-km wide. (b) Violin plot of all measurements of fault-parallel horizontal displacement with the median (dashed lines) and 25th and 75th percentiles (dotted lines). (c) Fault-parallel horizontal displacement along the rupture. Arctangent (arctan) tends to underestimate displacement. Arctan with slope and error function (erf) with slope tend to overestimate displacement. The average of the two arctan methods (dashed line) is nearly identical to the average of the interactive measurement methods (dotted line). (d–f) Displacement calculations for profile 65 measured interactively (d), and by automatic arctan (e), automatic arctangent with independent slopes (f), and automatic erf with single slope (g). The color version of this figure is available only in the electronic edition.

For the automated methods, we calculate fault-parallel displacement by fitting different functional forms to the data. We use SciPy's "curve_fit" algorithm to fit arctangent functions (equation 7), arctangent functions with independent slopes (equation 8), and error functions (erfs) with a single slope (equation 9; Milliner *et al.*, 2024; Fig. 4e–g). The arctangent and arctangent with slope functions are, respectively,

$$y(x) = a \times \tan^{-1}(b \times (x - c)) + d, \tag{7}$$

$$y(x) = a \times \tan^{-1}(b \times (x - c)) + (x \geq c : m_1 \times (x - c), \quad x \leq c : m_2 \times (x - c)) + d, \tag{8}$$

in which $y(x)$ is the displacement at the x location along the profile, a is the amplitude, b is the steepness, c is the fault location along the profile, d is the intercept (vertical shift), and m is the slope (m_1 and m_2 are the upper and lower asymptotes). The arctangent with slope function (equation 8) allows independent slopes for each asymptote to better fit the data. For the arctangent function (equation 7), displacement is the amplitude (a) multiplied by pi. For the modified arctangent function, we define the fault zone width as $1/b$ and calculate displacement as the difference between the linear fit to each side of the profile excluding the fault zone and projected to the fault location, as with the interactive displacement calculations. We also use an erf (Milliner *et al.*, 2024) to evaluate how it performs relative to the arctangent functions:

$$y(x) = a + b/2 \times \mathrm{erf}((x - c)/(d \times \sqrt{(2)})) + m \times x, \quad (9)$$

in which $y(x)$ is the displacement at the x location along the profile, a is the intercept, b is the displacement, c is the fault location along the profile, d is the width, and m is the slope.

For both manual and automatic methods, we filter out high error displacement measurements defined by root mean square error (RMSE) >30% of the displacement value or RMSE >1.0 m, removing 3% of manual and 4% of automatic measurements. Calculating displacement using the automatic functions takes <1 min per function for 488 profiles versus multiple hours for manual fault zone delineation.

Fault mapping

We map a simple fault rupture trace at 1:250,000 scale from S2 and Planet Dove subpixel correlation results (Fig. 3d). The fault rupture is inferred, rather than directly observed, based on displacement discontinuities in the correlation datasets. The location of the simple rupture trace is adjusted to coincide with detailed surface rupture mapping from high-resolution optical images.

We map detailed surface rupture traces on high-resolution (0.3–0.5 m), postearthquake optical images from World View1, 2, 3 (2025 Maxar), BlackSky (2025 Maxar), and SkySat (2025 Planet Labs) satellites accessed via the U.S. Government (USG) Plus license. Mapping was completed at a scale of 1:1500 in which surface rupture is visible in the optical images (Figs. 3d and 5). The images were acquired 28 March–13 May 2025. The mapped rupture traces are interpreted as primary tectonic deformation and do not include shaking-related secondary deformation features such as landslides, liquefaction, and lateral spreading. Postearthquake images were compared with pre-earthquake high-resolution optical images from Google Earth and Bing to determine the presence of earthquake-related surface rupture.

We calculate surface rupture width automatically every 10 m along the rupture by measuring the distance between mapped surface rupture strands in an orientation perpendicular to local fault strike (Fig. 3f). We use a default value of 2 m for surface rupture width if only one fault strand exists. This value was selected by visual inspection of single-stranded rupture on the high-resolution (≤0.5 m) optical images. No value is recorded when the rupture is defined only from correlation results.

Manual displacement measurements

We measured 134 offset features manually on the high-resolution optical images (Figs. 3e and 5). Fault-parallel horizontal displacement measurements are of natural or cultural features right laterally offset by the rupture. We prioritize measurements when distinct and sublinear features (i.e., field or road edges, rows of trees or bushes, channels, and paths) cross a single-stranded rupture trace at high angle with clear pre-earthquake geometry, resulting in a set of more accurate offset measurements. Displacements were measured by projecting features observed in the satellite images into the fault rupture and then measuring the displacement parallel to the local rupture trend (e.g., Gold *et al.*, 2015; DuRoss *et al.*, 2024). Measurement uncertainty is based on minimum and maximum displacements resulting from alternate feature projections and for most measurements is at least twice the image pixel resolution (0.5 m). These offset measurements may not include additional centimeter-scale displacement along subparallel rupture branches not mappable at the pixel resolution of the satellite images (0.3–0.5 m).

Results

Rupture length

As defined by the S2 and Planet Dove subpixel correlation, the simplified fault trace (Fig. 3d; Reitman *et al.*, 2025) depicts an ~475-km-long rupture extending from 63 km north of Mandalay (22.541 N, 95.977 E) to 24 km south of Pyu (18.260 N, 96.427 E) along the Sagaing fault and rupturing all or part of the Sagaing, Meiktila, Nay Pyi Taw, and Pyu segments (Fig. 2; Wang *et al.*, 2014). Manual mapping confirms the northern rupture terminus, but the southern 65 km of the rupture are defined based on correlation alone because of clouds and forest obscuring the ground surface in the high-resolution images (Fig. 3d).

Rupture geometry

The rupture is linear and continuous at the resolution of the S2 correlation results (Fig. 3), with a lack of stepovers, splays, or substantial changes in strike. Average change in strike between each profile (1 km apart) is 0.2°. A total of 94.5% of measurements have <1° change in strike, and 99% of measurements have <5° change in strike. There are only three locations where the simple fault changes strike by >5°. However, the high-resolution images reveal a bit more variability. Manual mapping on optical images documents single, linear fault strands and places with multiple fault strands or minor splays (Fig. 5). Despite the clear expression of horizontal displacement in the optical correlation, only 25% (120 km) of the length of the simple fault trace is mapped in detail because of clouds, the built environment, water, or forest obscuring the ground (266 km, 56%) or lack of visible surface rupture at the resolution of the optical images

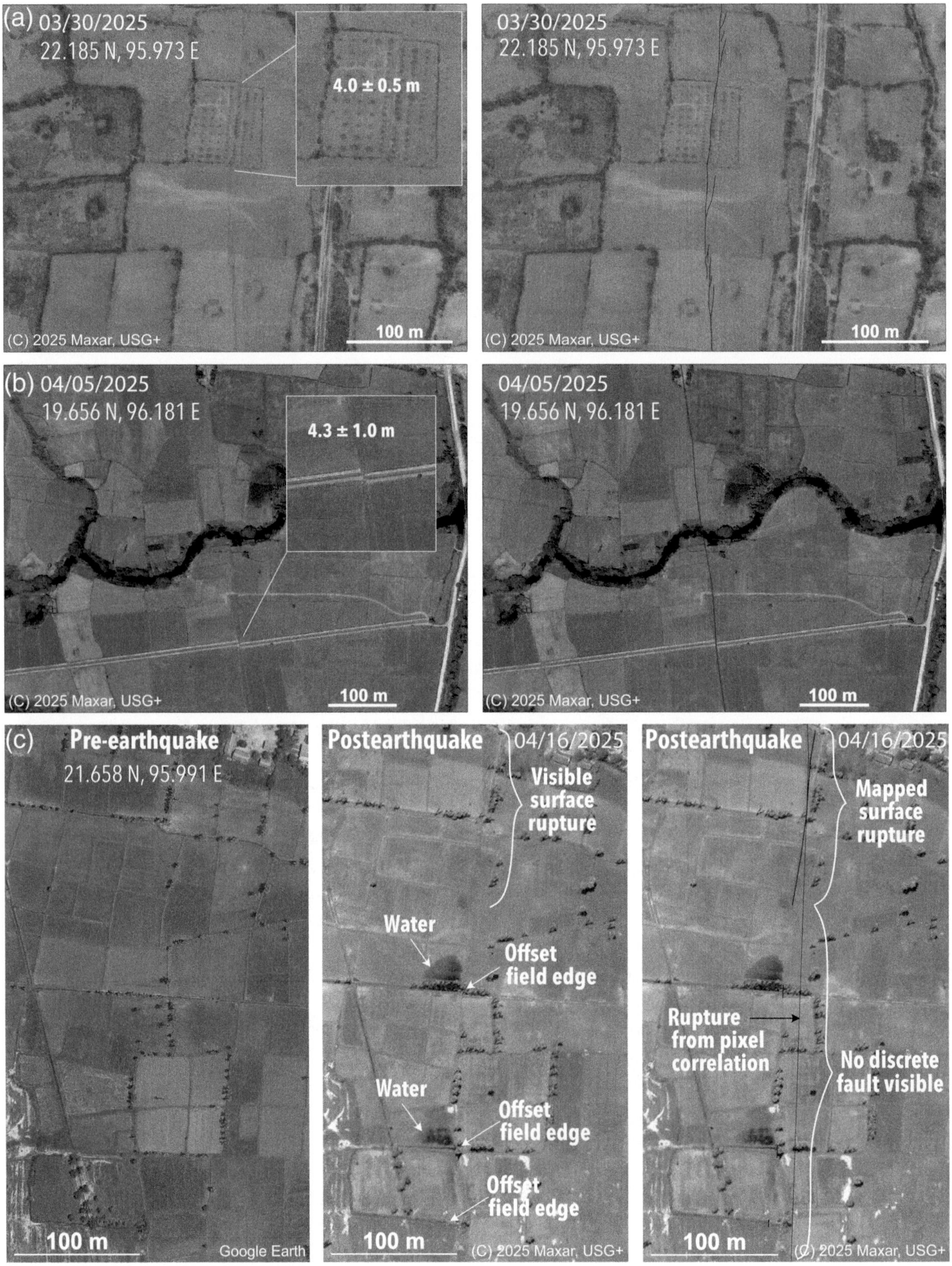

Figure 5. Manual mapping of surface faulting and offset features from WorldView (≤0.5 m/pixel) satellite images (2025 Maxar). (a,b) Uninterpreted (left) and interpreted (right) postearthquake images of surface rupture (blue lines) crossing fields and offsetting anthropogenic features such as an orchard, roads, and field edges. (c) Pre-earthquake (left) and postearthquake (center, right) images depict a location with visible surface rupture but no discrete fault observed in the image. The black line is the fault location from Sentinel-2 subpixel correlation. Locations of (a), (b), and (c) are shown in Figure 3d. USG, U.S. Government. The color version of this figure is available only in the electronic edition.

TABLE 1
Displacement Statistics from the Different Measurement Methods

Dataset	Count (Number)	Mean (m)	Std (m)	Minimum (m)	25% (m)	Median (m)	75% (m)	Maximum (m)
Interactive average	474	3.37	1.20	0.01	3.04	3.60	4.11	5.63
Arctan	469	2.98	1.01	0.22	2.66	3.20	3.59	5.25
Arctan with slopes	469	3.65	1.27	0.06	3.27	3.89	4.46	6.09
Arctan average*	469	3.32	1.13	0.16	2.97	3.53	4.01	5.56
Erf with slope	469	3.60	1.27	0.07	3.24	3.82	4.38	6.11
Manual	134	3.19	0.88	0.85	2.50	3.10	3.80	5.20

Arctan, arctangent; Erf, error function; Std, standard deviation.
*Arctan average is the preferred displacement dataset.

(91 km, 19%, e.g., Fig. 5c). Of the rupture mapped in detail, ~87% is single stranded at the resolution of the available images.

Surface slip distribution

Surface slip distribution from subpixel correlation interactive measurements, subpixel correlation automatic measurements, and manual measurements are all similar in pattern and amplitude (Figs. 3 and 4 and Table 1). However, subtle differences between the different measurement methods guide data use. The arctangent function systematically underestimates displacement relative to the interactive average, whereas the arctangent with independent slopes systematically overestimates displacement relative to the interactive average. The erf is nearly identical to the arctangent with slope and systematically overestimates displacement relative to the interactive average. All the automated functions systematically underestimate rupture zone width based on visual analysis and relative to interactive selection of the fault zone (Fig. 4e–g). Thus, we use the average of the two arctangent functions as the preferred automated displacement value (Table 1, Fig. 4, mean = 3.32 m, median = 3.53, and maximum = 5.56 m) because it is nearly identical to the average displacement measurements from interactive definition of the fault zone (Table 1 and Fig. 4b,c), automated, fast, and repeatable.

Surface slip along the Sagaing fault peaked at 5.6 m–15 km north of the epicenter and averages 3.3 m over the length of the rupture, with >300 km of surface slip >3.0 m. North and south of the epicenter are separate domains, with slip north of the epicenter ramping up, peaking, and ramping down over ~60 km, whereas south of the epicenter, slip is relatively constant for >300 km. Manual displacement measurements are unevenly distributed along strike (Fig. 3e), but they have similar characteristics (mean = 3.2 m, maximum = 5.2 m, and 25%–75% range of 2.5–3.8 m).

Using a 1-km moving average to compare manually measured and S2 correlation displacements where they are colocated, the correlation offsets are greater than the manual measurements by an average of 0.71 m (~30%), but correlation offsets are greater in only ~75% of comparisons (Fig. 3e). Of these, displacement from correlation is greater by 1.0 m on average. In the ~25% of comparisons in which manual offset measurements are greater, they are greater by 0.4 m on average. Of the manual offset measurements, 93% (124/134) are within uncertainty of the corresponding correlation measurements, underscoring the similarity between displacements measured manually and from subpixel correlation.

Fault zone width

Approximately 87% of the detailed rupture mapping is a single fault strand at the resolution (≤0.5 m) of the optical images. However, fault zone width is highly dependent on the dataset it is measured from because (1) the resolution of the dataset limits the resolving power of rupture width, and (2) different datasets capture displacement over different apertures, with subpixel correlation capturing far-field and distributed deformation and manual measurements from visible surface rupture measuring only localized, near-field, displacement mostly on the primary fault trace. From manual surface rupture mapping, the maximum surface rupture width is 190 m (Fig. 3f, blue circles), although there may be distributed cracking and other minor deformation not visible at the resolution of the satellite images (≤0.5 m). In comparison, estimating total deformation zone width from the S2 subpixel correlation fault-perpendicular profiles by interactively selecting the fault zone in each profile yields a median width of 700 m with a 25%–75% range of 550–850 m or 6–11 pixels, illustrating that width is controlled by the 80 m resolution of the correlation results (Fig. 3f, black squares). This demonstrates that extremely narrow rupture zones common to this earthquake cannot be reliably measured from swaths through coarse subpixel correlation fields.

Discussion

Mandalay earthquake kinematics

The 2025 M_w 7.7 Mandalay earthquake is the longest instrumentally recorded, continental strike-slip surface rupture. Comparable earthquakes include the 1906 M_w 7.9 San Francisco, United States, 2001 M_w 7.8 Kunlun (Kokoxili), China, and 2012 M_w 8.2 and 8.6 Sumatra earthquakes in the Indian Ocean. The longest estimated length for the 1906 San Francisco earthquake is 500 km from Song *et al.* (2008) based on a finite-fault model (FFM). However, in their model, slip goes to zero at ~450 km in the south (their figs. 4 and 6). The longest estimated length for the 2001 Kunlun earthquake is 450 km from Klinger *et al.* (2005) based on high-resolution satellite images and fieldwork in which they visited both rupture end points. The 2012 Sumatra earthquakes in the Indian Ocean are a complicated sequence of ruptures on intraplate oceanic transform faults distributed across a zone of at least four cross-cutting faults (Meng *et al.*, 2012; Yue *et al.*, 2012). Meng *et al.* (2012) model the M_w 8.2 with a length of 100 km and the M_w 8.6 with a length of 500 km, distributed across four orthogonal faults. From teleseismic back-projection, Yue *et al.* (2012) model the M_w 8.6 rupture as a series of ruptures on a "lattice" of sinistral and dextral strike-slip faults separated by up to a few hundred kilometers, with slip of 20–30 m and a down-dip width of >50 km. These large-magnitude earthquakes involve complex, multifault rupture of ≤200 km per fault, in contrast to the single fault activated in the Mandalay earthquake. Thus, the Mandalay earthquake is the longest recorded rupture on a single strike-slip fault.

The kinematics of the Mandalay rupture are simple. The long, continuous, straight rupture trace records little variation in fault geometry, rupture width, slip, or strain derivatives. Curl fluctuates around zero indicating little rotation. Dilatation is negative, indicating contraction consistent with regional tectonics (e.g., Socquet *et al.*, 2006) and geomorphic expression of the Sagaing fault. The greatest maximum shear strains are in the region of maximum slip north of the epicenter (Fig. 6b,c). Here, values exceed the theoretical maximum strain (0.005, 0.5%) that can be accommodated by elastic deformation in granite rock (Lockner, 1998), indicating inelastic deformation.

In the Mandalay earthquake, peak slip occurs north of the epicenter, where rupture speeds are subshear, and slip is more uniform south of the epicenter, where rupture speeds are supershear. Median displacement north of the epicenter is 1 m greater than south of the epicenter. Slip reaches a maximum of 5.6 m 15 km north of the epicenter and then monotonically declines to zero slip at the northern rupture terminus over ~50 km (Fig. 3e). In this region of maximum surface slip, dilatation is strongly negative, and maximum shear strain is above the elastic strain limit (Fig. 6b,c). In contrast, south of the epicenter slip is relatively constant at 3.5–4.0 m from ~50 km south of the epicenter for >300 km (Fig. 3e), dilatation is negative, and maximum shear-strain hovers around the elastic strain limit (Fig. 6b,d). Strain derivatives only deviate from their averages south of the epicenter in areas of noise within the correlation results (Fig. 6b,d). Slip variability (measured as the coefficient of variation, standard deviation/mean) along the rupture as a whole is ~35%, similar to other continental strike-slip fault ruptures (Reitman *et al.*, 2022), but slip is more variable north of the epicenter (~50%) than south of the epicenter (~30%).

Slip is largely localized on the primary fault trace, with minimal distributed deformation (defined as deformation 100 m–1 km from the primary fault trace) compared with other recent large strike-slip earthquakes with moderate slip such as Ridgecrest 7.1 (Antoine *et al.*, 2021; Gold *et al.*, 2021), Balochistan 2013 (Gold *et al.*, 2015), and Landers 1992 (Milliner *et al.*, 2015). The similarity between the manual and subpixel correlation displacement measurements may be partly attributed to the narrow rupture width because most slip is concentrated at the primary fault trace and thus is captured in the manual offset measurements. Although the mapped active traces of the Sagaing fault based on geomorphology indicate multiple parallel fault strands and splays have ruptured in the past (e.g., Wang *et al.*, 2014), no major splays or geometrical complexities are observed in this rupture at the scale of the S2 pixel correlation results.

The pervasively narrow deformation zone may imply a shallow rupture depth. The USGS FFM of the Mandalay earthquake (Goldberg *et al.*, 2025) has a maximum depth of 16 km and an average depth of 5.4 km for patches with at least 35 cm of slip (5% of maximum slip), with 75% of these patches <12-km depth. With a dip of 82°, the down-dip width is nearly identical to the depth. This modeled observation is consistent with slip occurring mostly above the locking depth of 10 and 16 km for the Sagaing and Meiktila sections, respectively, based on campaign and continuous Global Navigation Satellite System stations that span the fault (Tin *et al.*, 2022). In contrast, Fadil *et al.* (2023) suggest that the seismogenic depth is ≤20 km for the Sagaing section and shallows to the south based on the focal depth of earthquakes on the Sagaing fault, but only a few of these earthquakes occurred on the ruptured area of the 2025 event, indicating the shallow fault plane was highly coupled prior to the 2025 rupture.

These observations are consistent with the maturity and geomorphic expression of the Sagaing fault. Recent work dating a synkinematic basin along the northern portion of the fault indicates that dextral motion initiated 28–27 Ma (Morley and Arboit, 2019), supporting an estimated ~400 km of accumulated right-lateral slip based on offset ophiolite belts (Mitchell, 1993; Mitchell *et al.*, 2012). This is a similar order of magnitude to the long-term displacement of the San Andreas and Alpine faults. The present geomorphic expression of the Sagaing fault includes features typical of transpressive faulting, such as pressure ridges and positive flower structures (Fig. 6c). These features are especially clear in the northern half of the Meiktila segment, where a series of elongated hills are well aligned on the western side of the 2025 earthquake rupture.

In summary, the 2025 Mandalay earthquake was extremely long, with a simple rupture geometry, moderate slip, narrow deformation zone width, and narrow down-dip width. The epicenter roughly splits the slip domains, with maximum and

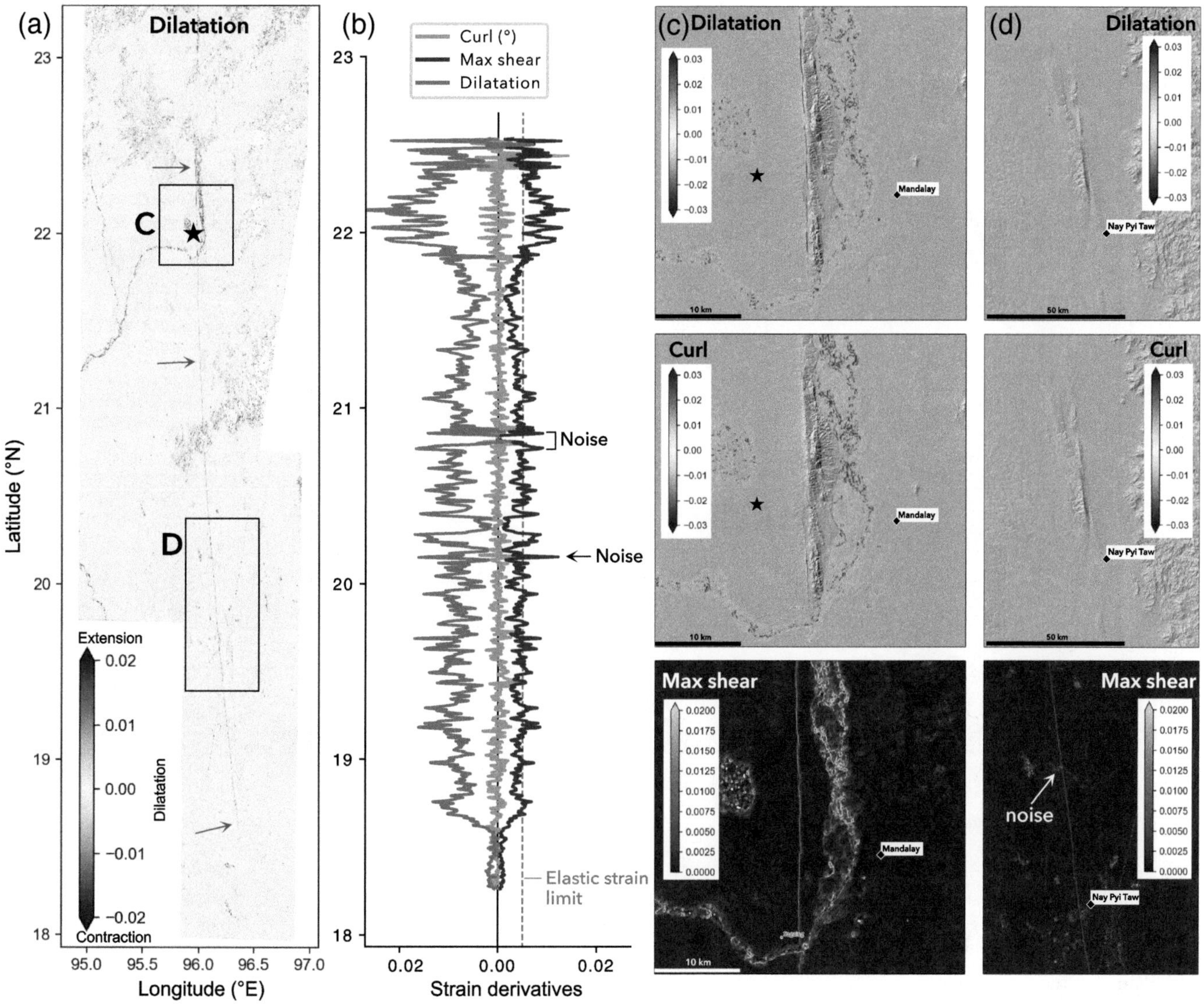

more variable surface slip and shear-strain north of epicenter where rupture speeds were subshear and more constant slip south of the epicenter where rupture speeds were supershear.

Length scaling of supershear earthquakes

At ~475-km length with an average of 3.3 m of surface slip and a maximum surface slip of 5.6 m, the Mandalay earthquake is extremely long with moderate slip compared with other large strike-slip earthquakes (Fig. 7). Large strike-slip earthquakes are limited in width as the width of the rupture area approaches the seismogenic depth (e.g., Leonard, 2010; Stafford (2014); Manighetti *et al.*, 2020). Because earthquake moment magnitude is dependent on rupture length, width, and displacement, if the fault is limited in the width dimension and crustal rigidity remains constant, then the earthquake must have either higher slip or longer length relative to its magnitude to accommodate the energy release. In contrast to the long Mandalay rupture, the 1855 M_w 8.2 Wairarapa, New Zealand, earthquake displays the opposite behavior. It has the largest surface slip of any recorded strike-slip earthquake (≤17–18 m; Rodgers and Little, 2006; Manighetti *et al.*, 2020) but a relatively short length of 120–150 km, implying a potentially deep fault width and/or a limit to rupture length. In addition, the Wairarapa fault has a history of ~13–16 m slip earthquakes (Rodgers and Little, 2006; Manighetti *et al.*, 2020), suggesting the large slip magnitude during the 1855 Wairarapa earthquake may be typical.

Figure 6. Strain derivatives calculated from Sentinel-2 correlation results illustrate the kinematics of the earthquake with primarily negative dilatation (contraction), minimal rotation (negative curl is clockwise), and deformation hovering around the elastic strain limit. (a) Dilatation. The star is the earthquake epicenter. Location of panels (c) and (d) shown with black boxes. The red arrows point to the Sagaing fault rupture. (b) Curl, dilatation, and maximum shear strain along strike of the surface rupture, extracted every 10 m and smoothed to 1-km spacing for visualization. (c,d) Dilatation, curl, and maximum shear strain in the location of maximum slip north of the epicenter (c) and south of the epicenter around Nay Pyi Taw (d). The color version of this figure is available only in the electronic edition.

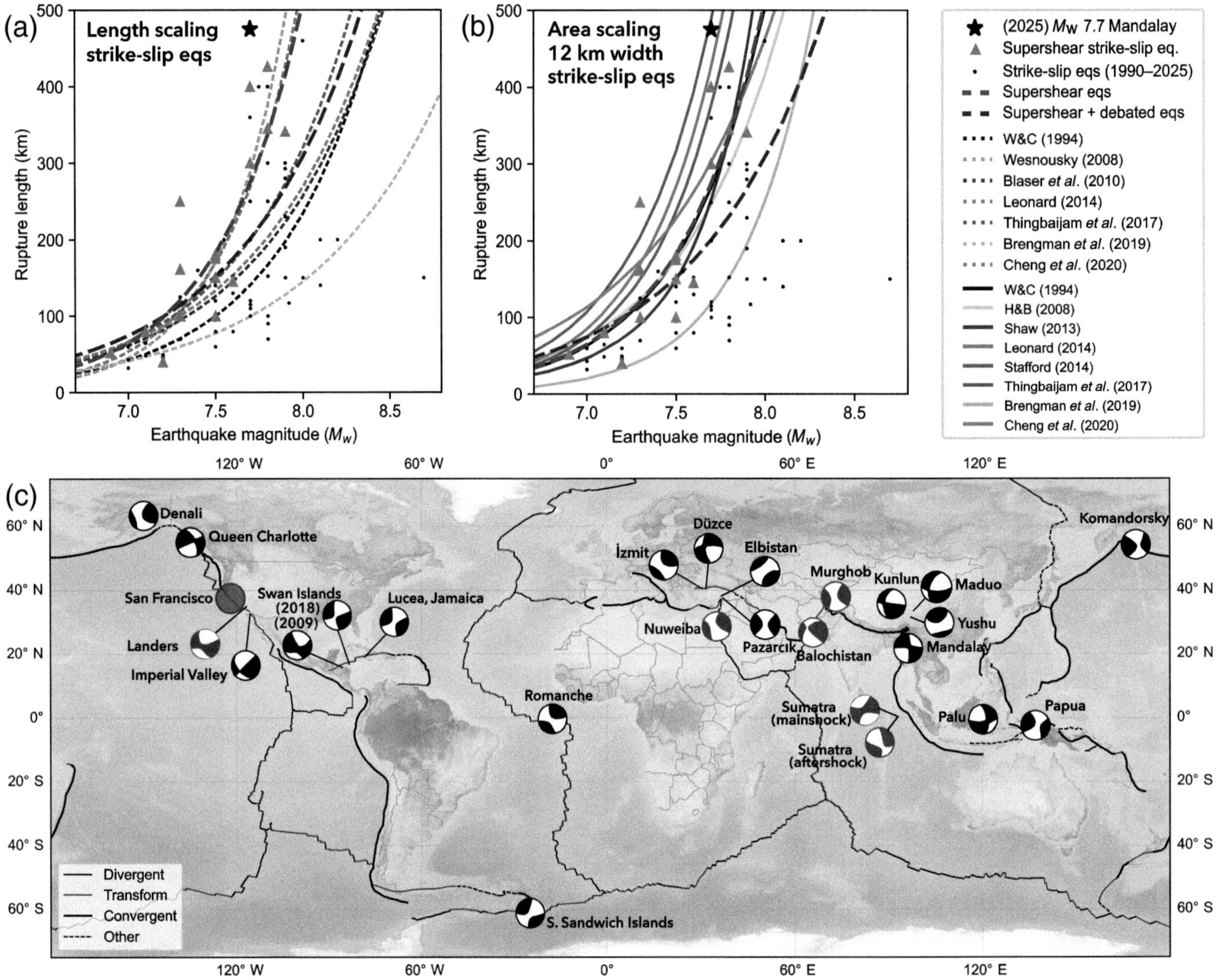

Figure 7. Published strike-slip earthquake scaling based on (a) length (dotted lines) and (b) area using a 12-km down-dip width (solid lines). In (a,b), dashed lines are relationships based on supershear earthquakes from this study, black dots are strike-slip earthquakes from 1990 to 2025 (as in Fig. 1), and gray triangles are supershear earthquakes, which are shown in black in (c). (c) Map of supershear (black) and debated supershear (maroon) earthquakes included in the analysis. Plate boundaries are from the USGS. W&C 1994, Wells and Coppersmith (1994); H&B 2008, Hanks and Bakun (2008). The color version of this figure is available only in the electronic edition.

What controls if a width-limited strike-slip fault tends to have greater length or slip than predicted by scaling relationships? One hypothesis is that geometrically simple faults have longer rupture length, and geometrically complex faults have greater slip for a given moment release because geometric complexity may be a limit on rupture length (e.g., Wesnousky, 2008; Bouchon *et al.*, 2010; Robinson *et al.*, 2010; Rodriguez Padilla *et al.*, 2024). DuRoss *et al.* (2024) calculated rupture complexity by comparing detailed surface rupture mapping length with simple rupture length. Of the faults they included in their comparison, the more complex ruptures are more likely to be subshear earthquakes (e.g., Hector Mine, El Mayor Cucapah, Kaikōura, and Ridgecrest 7.1), and some of the less complex ruptures are supershear earthquakes (e.g., Denali, Pazarcık). Although the number of earthquakes available to evaluate this hypothesis is small, it is consistent with the idea that faults that may have supershear rupture tend to be geometrically simple (e.g., Bouchon *et al.*, 2010; Robinson *et al.*, 2010).

Most published length–magnitude scaling relationships for strike-slip earthquakes fail to predict the SRL of some supershear strike-slip earthquakes (Fig. 7a). Area–magnitude scaling relationships that allow for width-limited ruptures better allow for the extreme length of supershear strike-slip earthquakes at narrow widths (e.g., 12 km; Fig. 7b), but down-dip width is more difficult to constrain than rupture length and often requires modeling of multiple geodetic datasets. The discrepancy between lengths of supershear earthquakes and empirical scaling relationships implies that supershear earthquakes may follow different scaling relations than large strike-slip earthquakes in general.

To test this hypothesis, we constructed length–magnitude scaling relationships based on two catalogs of (1) definitively supershear strike-slip earthquakes and (2) definitively plus debated supershear earthquakes (Fig. 7c; Tables 2 and 3). The definitively supershear catalog comprises 18 earthquakes: 14 from the Bao *et al.* (2022), 2021 Maduo (Tibet), 2023 Pazarcık and Elbistan (Türkiye), and 2025 Mandalay earthquakes. The larger catalog contains an additional seven earthquakes in which supershear behavior is debated (Bao *et al.*, 2022). The earthquakes are characterized as definitively supershear if they have an observed mach cone (Bao *et al.*, 2022) or any portion of the rupture reached supershear speeds in published studies. Only a portion of the rupture reached supershear speeds for most of the definitively supershear earthquakes.

We develop a scaling relationship based on length rather than area for two reasons: (1) down-dip width is more difficult to measure and define accurately than SRL, which is directly observable, and (2) down-dip width may vary substantially along the length of a rupture, as the modeled width does for the Mandalay earthquake (USGS FFM; Goldberg *et al.*, 2025). Most supershear earthquakes have estimated maximum widths of 15–20 km, but if they are similar to the Mandalay earthquake, they may have much smaller average widths. We use SRL rather than subsurface length because it can be directly observed, and SRL and subsurface rupture length are often similar for large earthquakes (e.g., Anderson *et al.*, 2021; Antoine *et al.*, 2024). We use geologic estimates of SRL when available and FFM inversion results to estimate SRL elsewhere. Like prior length scaling relationships (e.g., Wells and Coppersmith, 1994), we use the form

$$\log_{10}(\mathrm{SRL}) = a + b \times M_w, \quad (10)$$

in which SRL in kilometers and a and b are the intercept and slope, respectively, of a least-squares linear fit to $\log_{10}(\mathrm{SRL})$ and M_w.

The best-fit relationship for the definitively supershear dataset is $\log_{10}(\mathrm{SRL}) = 0.89M_w - 4.44$ (Fig. 8a; Table 3). For the supershear plus debated dataset, the best-fit relationship is $\log_{10}(\mathrm{SRL}) = 0.62M_w - 2.44$ (Fig. 8a; Table 3). The slope and intercept derived from the definitively plus debated supershear catalog are the same within uncertainty to most recent length–magnitude scaling relationships for strike-slip earthquakes (Fig. 7a; Table 3). However, the slope and intercept derived from the best fit to the definitively supershear catalog are significantly different from most recent length–magnitude scaling relationships (Fig. 7a; Table 3). Although the supershear scaling relationship is most similar to the Wesnousky (2008) and Leonard (2014) relationships (Fig. 7a), the residuals between the supershear earthquakes (red triangles in Fig. 8a) and all the length scaling relationships shown in Figure 7a are only significantly different from the Wells and Coppersmith (1994) and Brengman *et al.* (2019) residuals (Fig. 8b). Regardless, the supershear-specific scaling relationship has the highest R^2 value (0.77), lowest RMSE (0.089), and lowest mean and median residuals of all the strike-slip length scaling relationships (Fig. 8b, Table 3).

These results indicate that (1) supershear earthquakes may scale differently than other strike-slip earthquakes, and (2) some of the earthquakes in the "debated" dataset may not be supershear because they yield a regression similar to that for strike-slip earthquakes in general. Some of the earthquakes in the debated dataset are geometrically complex (e.g., Landers), further indicating they may not be supershear earthquakes, or such a small portion of the rupture was supershear that they do not follow supershear scaling relationships.

The uncertainties for both the relations presented here and published ones encompass nearly the entire plot area and thus do not provide meaningful boundaries on the minimum and maximum expected rupture lengths. Instead, we derive bounds on expected rupture length by considering multiple scaling relations. The length–scaling relationships in Figure 7a predict an M_w 7.7 strike-slip earthquake may have a rupture length of only 100–290 km, and the area-scaling relationships in Figure 7b with a 12-km width predict a rupture length of 50–490 km. Of the length–scaling relationships, the Wesnousky (2008) relationship based on 15 large strike-slip earthquakes and the Leonard (2014) relationship based on interplate strike-slip earthquakes are both similar to our supershear-specific scaling relationship. Based on our supershear-specific relation, Wesnousky (2008), and Leonard (2014), an M_w 7.7 strike-slip earthquake may have a rupture length of 270–290 km, still shorter than the Mandalay earthquake by a factor of ~1.75.

In practice, the different scaling of supershear earthquakes indicates that probabilistic seismic hazard models that include width-limited scaling for large strike-slip earthquakes may help to account for potential supershear earthquakes in seismic hazard estimates. Many published seismic hazard models do include the option of width-limited or bilinear scaling (e.g., Hanks and Bakun 2002, 2008; Stirling *et al.*, 2002, 2013, 2024; Yen and Ma, 2011; Cheng *et al.*, 2019), but the options in theory are not straightforward to put into practice. The 2023 USGS National Seismic Hazard Model considered the option of width-limited scaling (Shaw, 2023), but ultimately, all earthquakes are modeled with the same down-dip width (Field *et al.*, 2024), and at present, there is not an accepted way to assign the probability that faults will exhibit supershear rupture. Based on our findings, deterministic rapid postearthquake products may consider implementing a range of scaling relationships based on the tectonic setting and probable causative fault for large strike-slip earthquakes (e.g., USGS ShakeMap; Thompson and Worden, 2018).

Finally, the hypothesis that long, straight faults are more likely to have long rupture lengths for a given magnitude and shorter, more geometrically complex faults are more likely to have large slip for a given magnitude could benefit from further

TABLE 2
Supershear and Debated Supershear Strike-Slip Earthquakes

Earthquake	Event ID	Date (yyyy/mm/dd)	Magnitude (M_w)	Latitude (deg)	Longitude (deg)	Depth (km)	Supershear Confidence*	Supershear Sources†	Length (km)	Log_{10} (L)	Length Type	Length Source(s)
Imperial Valley	ci3352060	1979/10/15	6.5	32.667	−115.359	15.0	Yes	Archuleta (1984) and Spudich and Cranswick (1984)	31	1.48	Surface	Sharp *et al.* (1982) and Archuleta (1984)
İzmit	usp0009d4z	1999/08/17	7.6	40.748	29.864	17.0	Yes	Bouchon *et al.* (2001)	145	2.16	Surface	Barka *et al.* (2002)
Düzce	usp0009hev	1999/11/12	7.2	40.758	31.161	10.0	Yes	Bouchon *et al.* (2001)	40	1.60	Surface	Akyüz *et al.* (2002)
Kunlun (Kokoxili)	usp000asvm	2001/11/14	7.8	35.946	90.541	10.0	Yes	Bouchon and Vallée (2003) and Vallée and Dunham (2012)	426	2.63	Surface	Xu *et al.* (2006)
Denali	ak002e435qpj	2002/11/03	7.9	63.514	−147.453	4.2	Yes	Dunham and Archuleta (2004) and Ellsworth *et al.* (2004)	341	2.53	Surface	Haeussler *et al.* (2004)
Swan Islands, Honduras	usp000gxkj	2009/05/28	7.3	16.731	−86.217	19.0	Yes	Bao *et al.* (2022)	250	2.40	Depth/seismic and geodetic inversion	Graham *et al.* (2012)
Yushu (Qinghai)	usp000hbbt	2010/04/13	6.9	33.165	96.548	17.0	Yes	Wang and Mori (2012) and Zhang *et al.* (2010)	52	1.72	Depth/InSAR inversion	Li *et al.* (2011)
Papua, Indonesia	usp000he3f	2010/06/16	7.0	−2.174	136.543	18.0	Yes	Bao *et al.* (2022)	N/A	N/A	N/A	N/A
S. Sandwich Islands	usb000ief9	2013/07/15	7.3	−60.857	−25.070	11.0	Yes	Bao *et al.* (2022)	100	2.00	Surface	Estimated from USGS FFM for <2° longitude at 60° latitude
Queen Charlotte (Craig)	ak0138esnzr	2013/01/05	7.5	55.234	−134.800	8.7	Yes	Yue *et al.* (2013)	150	2.18	Depth/seismic and geodetic inversion	Yue *et al.* (2013)

Event ID, date, M_w, latitude, longitude, and depth from U.S. Geological Survey (USGS) Comprehensive Catalog. deg, degree; FFM, finite-fault model; L, length; N/A, not applicable.
*Supershear confidence was from Bao *et al.* (2022) except for Nuweiba, Maduo, Mandalay, Pazarcık, and Elbistan earthquakes.
†For "debated" entries, "/" separates studies supporting supershear from those that do not find supershear rupture speeds.
(Continued next page.)

TABLE 2 (continued)
Supershear and Debated Supershear Strike-Slip Earthquakes

Earthquake	Event ID	Date (yyyy/mm/dd)	Magnitude (M_w)	Latitude (deg)	Longitude (deg)	Depth (km)	Supershear Confidence*	Supershear Sources†	Length (km)	Log_{10} (L)	Length Type	Length Source(s)
Romanche	us20006uy6	2016/08/29	7.1	−0.047	−17.829	10.0	Yes	Hicks *et al.* (2020)	80	1.90	Depth/aftershocks	Hicks *et al.* (2020)
Komandorsky	us20009x42	2017/07/17	7.7	54.471	168.814	10.0	Yes	Kehoe and Kiser (2020)	400	2.60	Depth/seismic and geodetic inversion	Lay *et al.* (2020)
Palu	us1000h3p4	2018/09/28	7.5	−0.256	119.840	20.0	Yes	Bao *et al.* (2019)	180	2.26	Surface	Socquet *et al.* (2019)
Swan Islands, Honduras	us1000c2zy	2018/01/10	7.5	17.474	−83.519	19.0	Yes	Bao *et al.* (2022)	100	2.00	Surface	USGS FFM
Caribbean Sea (Lucea, Jamaica)	us60007idc	2020/01/28	7.7	19.421	−78.762	14.9	Yes	Tadapansawut *et al.* (2021)	300	2.48	Depth/inverted teleseismic *P* waves	Tadapansawut *et al.* (2021): 300–400 based on their model
Maduo	us7000e54r	2021/05/21	7.3	34.598	98.251	10.0	Yes	Zhang *et al.* (2022) and Lyu *et al.* (2022)	161	2.21	Surface	Yuan *et al.* (2022)
Pazarcık	us6000jllz	2023/02/06	7.8	37.226	37.014	10.0	Yes	Abdelmeguid *et al.* (2023), Jia *et al.* (2023), and Melgar *et al.* (2023)	345	2.54	Surface	Reitman *et al.* (2023)
Elbistan	us6000jlqa	2023/02/06	7.5	38.011	37.196	7.4	Yes	Abdelmeguid *et al.* (2023), Jia *et al.* (2023), and Melgar *et al.* (2023)	175	2.24	Surface	Reitman *et al.* (2023)
Mandalay	us7000pn9s	2025/03/28	7.7	22.011	95.936	10.0	Yes	Goldberg *et al.* (2025)	475	2.68	Surface	This study

Event ID, date, M_w, latitude, longitude, and depth from U.S. Geological Survey (USGS) Comprehensive Catalog. deg, degree; FFM, finite-fault model; L, length; N/A, not applicable.
*Supershear confidence was from Bao *et al.* (2022) except for Nuweiba, Maduo, Mandalay, Pazarcık, and Elbistan earthquakes.
†For "debated" entries, "/" separates studies supporting supershear from those that do not find supershear rupture speeds.
(Continued next page.)

TABLE 2 (continued)
Supershear and Debated Supershear Strike-Slip Earthquakes

Earthquake	Event ID	Date (yyyy/mm/dd)	Magnitude (M_w)	Latitude (deg)	Longitude (deg)	Depth (km)	Supershear Confidence*	Supershear Sources[†]	Length (km)	Log_{10} (L)	Length Type	Length Source(s)
San Francisco	official19060418131226300_12	1906/04/18	7.9	37.75	122.55	11.7	Debated	Song *et al.* (2008), Brune *et al.* (2022) / Wald *et al.* (1993)	475	2.68	Depth?/geodetic and seismic inversion	Song *et al.* (2008)
Landers	ci3031111	1992/06/28	7.3	34.200	−116.437	0.1	Debated	Olsen *et al.* (1997) / Wald and Heaton (1994)	85	1.93	surface	Sieh *et al.* (1993)
Nuweiba (Aqaba, Egypt)	usp0007788	1995/11/22	7.2	28.826	34.799	10.0	Debated	Li *et al.* (2025)/ Shamir *et al.* (2003)	80	1.90	Surface	Vasyura-Bathke *et al.* (2024) and 50–Shamir *et al.* (2003), but may extend under water
Murghob, Tajikistan (Sarez)	us100044k6	2015/12/07	7.2	38.211	72.780	22.0	Debated	Sangha *et al.* (2017) / Elliott *et al.* (2020)	79	1.90	Surface	Sangha *et al.* (2017)
Sumatra (mainshock)	official20120411083836720_20	2012/04/11	8.6	2.237	93.014	20.0	Debated	Wang *et al.* (2012) / Meng *et al.* (2012) and Yue *et al.* (2012)	500	2.70	Depth?/teleseismic back projection	Meng *et al.* (2012)
Sumatra (aftershock)	usp000jhjb	2012/04/11	8.2	0.802	92.463	25.1	Debated	Wang *et al.* (2016) / Yue *et al.* (2012)	100	2.00	Depth?/teleseismic back projection	Meng *et al.* (2012)
Balochistan	usb000jyiv	2013/09/24	7.7	26.951	65.501	15.0	Debated	Wang *et al.* (2016) / Avouac *et al.* (2014)	200	2.30	Surface	Gold *et al.* (2015)

Event ID, date, M_w, latitude, longitude, and depth from U.S. Geological Survey (USGS) Comprehensive Catalog. deg, degree; FFM, finite-fault model; L, length; N/A, not applicable.
*Supershear confidence was from Bao *et al.* (2022) except for Nuweiba, Maduo, Mandalay, Pazarcık, and Elbistan earthquakes.
[†]For "debated" entries, "/" separates studies supporting supershear from those that do not find supershear rupture speeds.

TABLE 3
Parameters for Strike-Slip Earthquake Scaling Relationships

Study	Mechanism	*a*	sa*	*b*	sb*	Form	*n*	Source Data	Source Data Characteristics	RMSE	R^2
Length Relationships											
Supershear (this study)	ss	−4.44	0.90	0.89	0.12	$\log_{10}(\mathrm{SRL}) = a + b \times M_w$	18	Geologic estimates of fault length	Definitively supershear earthquakes	0.089	0.767
Supershear and debated (this study)	ss	−2.44	0.66	0.62	0.09	$\log_{10}(\mathrm{SRL}) = a + b \times M_w$	25	Geologic estimates of fault length	Definitively and debated supershear earthquakes	0.103	0.691
Wells and Coppersmith (1994)	ss	−3.55	0.37	0.74	0.05	$\log_{10}(\mathrm{SRL}) = a + b \times M_w$	43	Fault dimensions from aftershocks		0.162	0.238
Wesnousky (2008)	ss	5.56	N/A	0.87	N/A	$M_w = a + b \times \log_{10}(L)$	15	Geologic estimates of fault length	Large continental earthquakes, geologic data	0.103	0.690
Blaser *et al.* (2010)	ss	−2.55	0.12	0.62	0.02	$\log(L) = a + b \times M_w$	128	Fault dimensions from aftershocks	Continental strike-slip, SRL	0.126	0.535
Leonard (2014)	ss	5.27	N/A	1.00	N/A	$M_w = a + b \times \log_{10}(L)$	§	Published datasets, aftershocks, geologic length	Interplate strike-slip earthquakes	0.093	0.749
Thingbaijam *et al.* (2017)	ss	−2.94	0.36	0.68	0.05	$\log_{10}(L) = a + b \times M_w$	§	Finite-fault rupture models		0.106	0.674
Brengman *et al.* 2019	ss	−2.17	0.95	0.54	0.14	$\log_{10}(L) = a + b \times M_w$	30	Geodetic inversions/models		0.213	−0.330
Cheng *et al.* (2019)	ss	−2.45	0.17	0.61	0.03	$\log_{10}(L) = a + b \times M_w$	56	Aftershocks, teleseismic waveforms	All M_w, all China >1900, SRL	0.119	0.584

A, area; const, constant; L, rupture length; N/A, not applicable; NGA, Next Generation Attenuation; RMSE, root mean square error; SRL, surface rupture length; sqrt, square root; ss, strike slip.
*sa and sb are the standard error on the a and b coefficients.
†The value is const, tuned to strike-slip faults. Other values are given in sa column.
‡The value is the beta parameter; other values are given in sb column.
§There is an unknown number of earthquakes.
(Continued next page.)

TABLE 3 (continued)
Parameters for Strike-Slip Earthquake Scaling Relationships

Study	Mechanism	*a*	sa*	*b*	sb*	Form	*n*	Source Data	Source Data Characteristics	RMSE	R^2
Area Relationships											
Wells and Coppersmith (1994)	ss	−3.42	0.18	0.90	0.03	$\log_{10}(A) = a + b \times M_w$	83	Fault dimensions from aftershocks			
Hanks and Bakun (2008)	ss	3.07	0.04	1.33	N/A	$M_w = a + b \times \log_{10}(A)$	26	W&C (1994) data and seven large ss earthquakes	Large continental ss earthquakes (area >537 km^2, M_w >6.7)		
Shaw (2009, 2013)	ss	3.07†	3.07, 3.98	6.9‡	6.9–7.7	$M_w = \log_{10}(A) + \frac{2}{3}\log_{10}(\max(1, \sqrt{(\frac{A}{width^2})}))/((1 + \max(1, \sqrt{(\frac{A}{(width^2)})} \times beta)))/2)) + const$	§	WGCEP03 database, Hanks and Bakun (2008) database	Large strike-slip faults (surface rupturing)		
Leonard 2014	ss	3.99	0.26	1.00	N/A	$M_w = a + b \times \log_{10}(A)$	§	Published datasets, aftershocks, geologic length	Interplate strike-slip earthquakes		
Stafford (2014)	ss	4.04	0.14	N/A	N/A	$M_w = \log_{10}(A) + a$	114	NGA-West 2 database	Earthquakes that rupture full seismogenic thickness		
Thingbaijam *et al.* (2017)	ss	−3.49	0.40	0.94	0.06	$\log_{10}(A) = a + b \times M_w$	§	Finite-fault rupture models			
Brengman *et al.* (2019)	ss	−2.23	1.42	0.64	0.21	$\log_{10}(A) = a + b \times M_w$	30	Geodetic inversions/models			
Cheng *et al.* (2019)	ss	1.86	N/A	1.64	N/A	$M_w = a + b \times \log_{10}(A)$	§	Aftershocks, teleseismic waveforms	M_w>6.7, all China >1900, SRL		

A, area; const, constant; L, rupture length; N/A, not applicable; NGA, Next Generation Attenuation; RMSE, root mean square error; SRL, surface rupture length; sqrt, square root; ss, strike slip.
*sa and sb are the standard error on the a and b coefficients.
†The value is const, tuned to strike-slip faults. Other values are given in sa column.
‡The value is the beta parameter; other values are given in sb column.
§There is an unknown number of earthquakes.

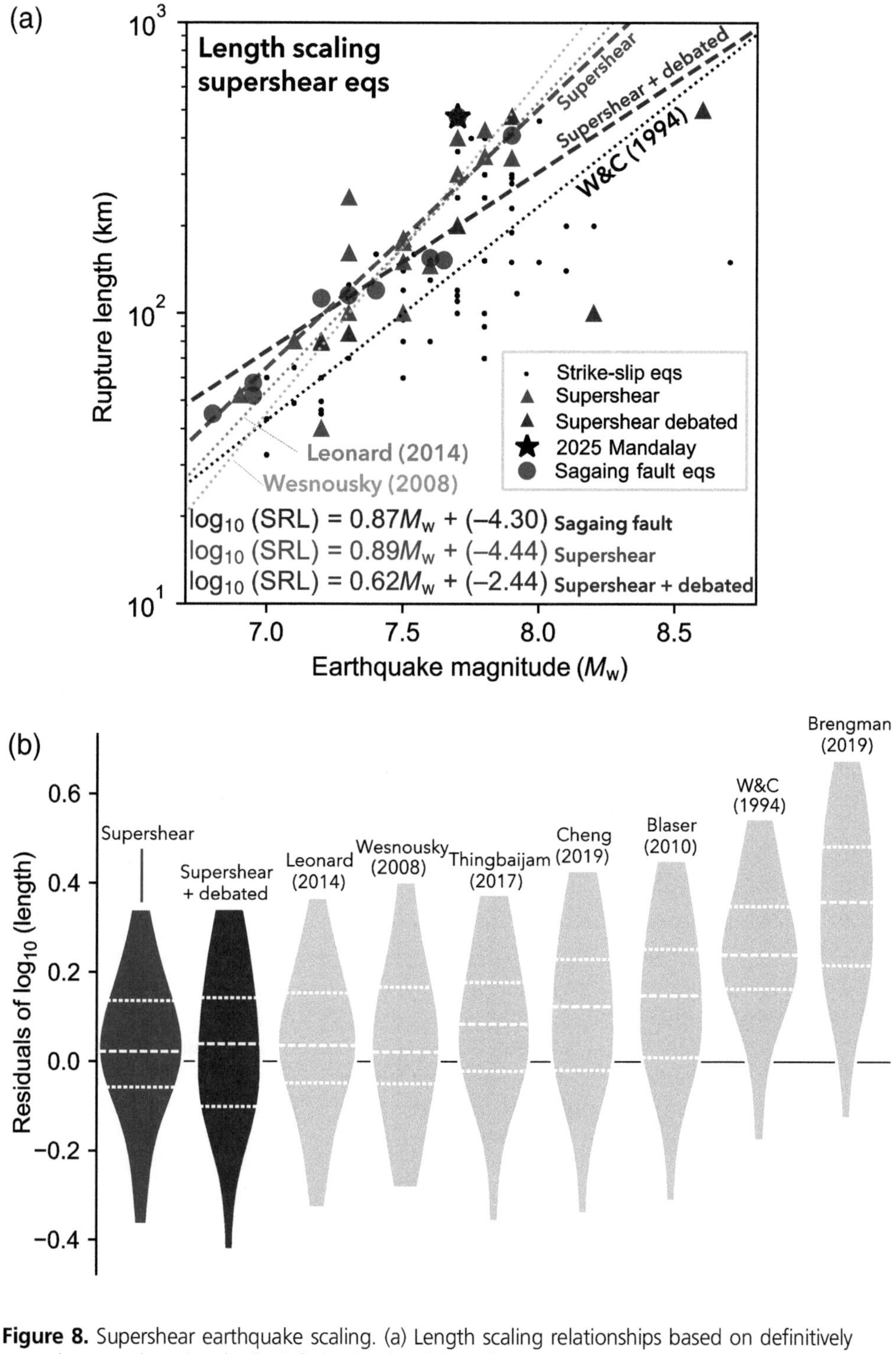

Figure 8. Supershear earthquake scaling. (a) Length scaling relationships based on definitively supershear earthquakes (red), definitively plus debated supershear earthquakes (maroon), and Sagaing fault historical earthquakes (blue). Supershear confidence from Bao *et al.* (2022). The Maduo, Mandalay, Pazarcık, and Elbistan earthquakes are included in the definitively supershear group. Parameters for the Sagaing fault earthquakes are shown in Figure 2b, here using the midpoint of the range from Figure 2b. (b) Violin plots of the residuals on $\log_{10}$ (surface rupture length [SRL]) of the supershear earthquakes, which appear as red triangles in (a) and the strike-slip length scaling relationships shown in Figure 7a and Table 3. Published scaling relationships (gray violins) are shown in order of decreasing R^2 value from left to right. Only Wells and Coppersmith (1994; W&C, 1994) and Brengman *et al.* (2019) residuals are significantly different than residuals for the supershear-specific relationship (red). Medians (dashed line) and interquartile range (dotted lines) are shown for each set of residuals. The color version of this figure is available only in the electronic edition.

investigation. If this relationship endures, it has implications for building along and around strike-slip faults to reduce losses from unexpectedly large slip or long earthquake ruptures.

Potential for repeated supershear behavior on the Sagaing fault

Plotting historical Sagaing fault earthquakes (lengths and magnitudes in Fig. 2b, averaged where there is a range) compared with global strike-slip earthquakes shows that Sagaing fault earthquakes tend to be long for their magnitudes compared with the compilation of global strike-slip earthquakes (Fig. 8a). A relation based on the 10 Sagaing fault historical earthquakes shown in Figure 2b, $\log_{10}(\mathrm{SRL}) = 0.87M_w - 4.30$, is most similar to the relation based on supershear earthquakes. Of the published scaling relationships, the Leonard (2014) and Wesnousky (2008) regressions are closest to the historical Sagaing fault earthquakes, but they underestimate lengths of the smaller-magnitude historical earthquakes. Thus, earthquakes on the Sagaing fault tend to be longer for their magnitude than predicted by most global scaling relationships. This does not necessarily indicate a history of supershear earthquakes on the Sagaing fault, but it does indicate that the Sagaing fault may be more likely to host long earthquakes because of its simple geometry, which could promote supershear behavior. For example, it is possible that the 1839 Ava earthquake (Fig. 8a; M 7.9, ~400 km) was a supershear event. The 1839 earthquake rupture does not have well-constrained end points or magnitude (Wang *et al.*, 2014; Wu, 2022), but the length could be similar to the Mandalay earthquake if it ruptured the entire Meiktila and Sagaing sections as hypothesized based on historical isoseismal intensity (Wang *et al.*, 2014; Wu, 2022). With a slip rate of 20–23 mm/yr (Lindsey *et al.*, 2023), 3.7–4.3 m of slip deficit may have accumulated between the 1839 and 2025 earthquakes, consistent with average surface slip in the 2025 earthquake, assuming no shallow slip deficit. From scaling relationships of Leonard (2014) and Wesnousky (2008) and average slip of 3.5–4.0 m based on offset geomorphic features, Wu (2022) estimated an M_w 7.7–8.1 earthquake, with M_w 7.9 preferred based on comparing historical intensity data. Alternatively, assuming a similar recurrence interval and slip to the 2025 earthquake and using a rupture length of 400 km and a down-dip width of 10–12 km, moment calculations predict an M_w 7.7–7.8 magnitude earthquake. The possibility that the 1839 earthquake had similar magnitude, long length, and moderate slip to the 2025 earthquake implies that this section of the Sagaing fault may have a history of supershear earthquakes.

Conclusion

The 2025 M_w 7.7 Mandalay earthquake is the longest strike-slip earthquake rupture in instrumental history at ~475 km. This exceptionally long rupture relative to its magnitude is attributed to its supershear rupture speed, simple fault geometry (zero stepovers or large changes in strike, 87% of the rupture mapped in detail is single stranded), narrow down-dip width (75% <12 km, USGS FFM), and moderate surface slip (average = 3.3 m, maximum = 5.6 m, 25%–75%, and range = 3.0–4.0 m). A global compilation of supershear earthquakes demonstrates that supershear strike-slip earthquakes are more likely than subshear earthquakes to have long lengths relative to their magnitudes and thus exhibit unique length–magnitude scaling. We present a length–magnitude scaling relationship for supershear strike-slip earthquakes, $\log_{10}(\mathrm{SRL}) = 0.89M_w - 4.44$, which offers an improved fit over established scaling relationships, but the length of the Mandalay earthquake remains atypical. The supershear-specific scaling relationship may be used to better forecast the length of strike-slip supershear earthquakes, which tend to be longer than their subshear counterparts for a given seismic moment.

Data and Resources

Data produced in this study are available from Reitman *et al.* (2025). The high-resolution optical images used for surface rupture mapping are available via https://hddsexplorer.usgs.gov (last accessed April 2025). Modified Copernicus Sentinel-2 data are processed by and available from the European Space Agency.

Declaration of Competing Interests

The authors acknowledge that there are no conflicts of interest recorded.

Acknowledgments

This study was supported by the U.S. Geological Survey Earthquake Hazards Program. Any use of trade, firm, or product names is for descriptive purposes only and does not imply endorsement by the U.S. Government.

References

Aati, S., C. Milliner, and J. P. Avouac (2022). A new approach for 2-D and 3-D precise measurements of ground deformation from optimized registration and correlation of optical images and ICA-based filtering of image geometry artifacts, *Remote Sens. Environ.* **277,** 113038, doi: 10.1016/j.rse.2022.113038.

Abdelmeguid, M., C. Zhao, E. Yalcinkaya, G. Gazetas, A. Elbanna, and A. Rosakis (2023). Dynamics of episodic supershear in the 2023 M7.8 Kahramanmaraş/Pazarcik earthquake, revealed by near-field records and computational modeling, *Commun. Earth Environ.* **4,** no. 1, 1–12, doi: 10.1038/s43247-023-01131-7.

Akyüz, H. S., R. Hartleb, A. Barka, E. Altunel, G. Sunal, B. Meyer, and R. Armijo (2002). Surface rupture and slip distribution of the 12 November 1999 Düzce earthquake (M 7.1), North Anatolian fault, Bolu, Turkey, *Bull. Seismol. Soc. Am.* **92,** no. 1, 61–66, doi: 10.1785/0120000840.

Anderson, J. G., G. P. Biasi, S. Angster, and S. G. Wesnousky (2021). Improved scaling relationships for seismic moment and average slip of strike-slip earthquakes incorporating fault-slip rate, fault width, and stress drop, *Bull. Seismol. Soc. Am.* **111,** no. 5, 2379–2392, doi: 10.1785/0120210113.

Anderson, J. G., G. P. Biasi, and S. G. Wesnousky (2017). Fault-scaling relationships depend on the average fault-slip rate, *Bull. Seismol. Soc. Am.* **107,** no. 6, 2561–2577, doi: 10.1785/0120160361.

Antoine, S. L., Y. Klinger, A. Delorme, K. Wang, R. Bürgmann, and R. D. Gold (2021). Diffuse deformation and surface faulting distribution from submetric image correlation along the 2019 Ridgecrest, California, ruptures, *Bull. Seismol. Soc. Am.* **111,** no. 5, 2275–2302, doi: 10.1785/0120210036.

Antoine, S. L., Y. Klinger, K. Wang, and R. Bürgmann (2024). Coseismic shallow slip deficit accounted for by diffuse off-fault deformation, *Geophys. Res. Lett.* **51,** no. 24, e2024GL110798, doi: 10.1029/2024GL110798.

Archuleta, R. J. (1984). Faulting model for the 1979 Imperial Valley earthquake, *J. Geophys. Res.* **89,** no. B6, 4559–4585, doi: 10.1029/JB089iB06p04559.

Avouac, J. P., F. Ayoub, S. Wei, J. P. Ampuero, L. Meng, S. Leprince, R. Jolivet, Z. Duputel, and D. Helmberger (2014). The 2013, M_w 7.7 Balochistan earthquake, energetic strike-slip reactivation of a thrust fault, *Earth Planet. Sci. Lett.* **391,** 128–134, doi: 10.1016/j.epsl.2014.01.036.

Bao, H., J. P. Ampuero, L. Meng, E. J. Fielding, C. Liang, C. W. D. Milliner, T. Feng, and H. Huang (2019). Early and persistent supershear rupture of the 2018 magnitude 7.5 Palu earthquake, *Nature Geosci.* **12,** no. 3, 200–205, doi: 10.1038/s41561-018-0297-z.

Bao, H., L. Xu, L. Meng, J. P. Ampuero, L. Gao, and H. Zhang (2022). Global frequency of oceanic and continental supershear earthquakes, *Nature Geosci.* **15,** no. 11, 942–949, doi: 10.1038/s41561-022-01055-5.

Barka, A., H. S. Akyüz, E. Altunel, G. Sunal, Z. Çakir, A. Dikbas, B. Yerli, R. Armijo, B. Meyer, J. B. De Chabalier, *et al.* (2002). The surface rupture and slip distribution of the 17 August 1999 İzmit earthquake (M 7.4), North Anatolian fault, *Bull. Seismol. Soc. Am.* **92,** no. 1, 43–60, doi: 10.1785/0120000841.

Blaser, L., F. Krüger, M. Ohrnberger, and F. Scherbaum (2010). Scaling relations of earthquake source parameter estimates with special focus on subduction environment, *Bull. Seismol. Soc. Am.* **100,** no. 6, 2914–2926, doi: 10.1785/0120100111.

Bouchon, M., and M. Vallée (2003). Observation of long supershear rupture during the magnitude 8.1 Kunlunshan earthquake, *Science* **301,** no. 5634, 824–826, doi: 10.1126/science.1086832.

Bouchon, M., M.-P. Bouin, H. Karabulut, M. N. Toksoz, M. Dietrich, and A. J. Rosakis (2001). How fast is rupture during an earthquake? New insights from the 1999 Turkey earthquakes, *Geophys. Res. Lett.* **28,** no. 14, 2723–2726.

Bouchon, M., H. Karabulut, M. P. Bouin, J. Schmittbuhl, M. Vallée, R. Archuleta, S. Das, F. Renard, and D. Marsan (2010). Faulting characteristics of supershear earthquakes, *Tectonophysics* **493,** nos. 3/4, 244–253, doi: 10.1016/j.tecto.2010.06.011.

Brengman, C. M. J., W. D. Barnhart, E. H. Mankin, and C. N. Miller (2019). Earthquake-scaling relationships from geodetically derived slip distributions, *Bull. Seismol. Soc. Am.* **109,** no. 5, 1701–1715, doi: 10.1785/0120190048.

Brune, R., J. G. Anderson, and J. N. Brune (2022). Unexpected directionality of failures in the 1906 San Francisco earthquake near Point Reyes station, *Seismol. Res. Lett.* **93,** no. 1, 91–99, doi: 10.1785/0220210062.

Cheng, J., Y. Rong, H. Magistrale, G. Chen, and X. Xu (2019). Earthquake rupture scaling relations for mainland China, *Seismol. Res. Lett.* **91,** no. 1, 248–261, doi: 10.1785/0220190129.

Dunham, E. M., and R. J. Archuleta (2004). Evidence for a supershear transient during the 2002 Denali fault earthquake, *Bull. Seismol. Soc. Am.* **94,** no. 6 SUPPL. B, 256–268, doi: 10.1785/0120040616.

Duross, C. B., N. G. Reitman, A. E. Hatem, H. B. Mason, G. Lavrentiadis, D. Asimaki, C. Milliner, M. Karakaş, and B. Seçen (2024). Are field observations of surface rupture useful? An example from the 2023 M_w 7.8 Pazarcık, Turkey (Türkiye), earthquake, *Seismol. Res. Lett.*, doi: 10.1785/0220240280.

Elliott, A., J. Elliott, J. Hollingsworth, G. Kulikova, B. Parsons, and R. Walker (2020). Satellite imaging of the 2015 M 7.2 earthquake in the Central Pamir, Tajikistan, elucidates a sequence of shallow strike-slip ruptures of the Sarez-Karakul fault, *Geophys. J. Int.* **221,** no. 3, 1696–1718, doi: 10.1093/GJI/GGAA090.

Ellsworth, W. L., M. Celebi, J. R. Evans, E. G. Jensen, R. Kayen, M. C. Metz, D. J. Nyman, J. W. Roddick, P. Spudich, and C. D. Stephens (2004). Near-field ground motion of the 2002 Denali fault, Alaska, earthquake recorded at pump station 10, *Earthq. Spectra* **20,** no. 3, 597–615, doi: 10.1193/1.1778172.

Engdahl, E. R., and A. Villaseñor (2002). 41—Global Seismicity: 1900–1999, in *International Handbook of Earthquake and Engineering Seismology, Part A*, W. H. K. Lee, H. Kanamori, P. C. Jennings, and C. Kisslinger (Editors), Vol. 81, Academic Press, London, United Kingdom, 665–690, doi: 10.1016/S0074-6142(02)80244-3.

Fadil, W., S. Wei, K. Bradley, Y. Wang, Y. He, E. Sandvol, B.-S. Huang, J. Hubbard, M. Thant, and Y. M. M. Htwe (2023). Active faults revealed and new constraints on their seismogenic depth from a high-resolution regional focal mechanism catalog in Myanmar (2016–2021), *Bull. Seismol. Soc. Am.* **113,** no. 2, 613–635, doi: 10.1785/0120220195.

Field, E. H., K. R. Milner, A. E. Hatem, P. M. Powers, F. F. Pollitz, A. L. Llenos, Y. Zeng, K. M. Johnson, B. E. Shaw, D. McPhillips, *et al.* (2024). The USGS 2023 Conterminous U.S. time-independent earthquake rupture forecast, *Bull. Seismol. Soc. Am.* **114,** no. 1, 523–571, doi: 10.1785/0120230120.

Gold, R. D., C. B. DuRoss, and W. D. Barnhart (2021). Coseismic surface displacement in the 2019 Ridgecrest earthquakes: Comparison of field measurements and optical image correlation results, *Geochem. Geophys. Geosys.* **22,** no. 3, 1–22, doi: 10.1029/2020GC009326.

Gold, R. D., N. G. Reitman, R. W. Briggs, W. D. Barnhart, G. P. Hayes, and E. Wilson (2015). On- and off-fault deformation associated with the September 2013 M_w 7.7 Balochistan earthquake: Implications for geologic slip rate measurements, *Tectonophysics* **660,** 65–78, doi: 10.1016/j.tecto.2015.08.019.

Goldberg, D. E., W. L. Yeck, C. E. Hanagan, J. Atterholt, H. Kehoe, N. G. Reitman, W. D. Barnhart, D. R. Shelly, A. E. Hatem, D. Wald, *et al.* (2025). Ultralong, supershear rupture of the 2025 M_w 7.7 Mandalay earthquake reveals unaccounted risk, *Science* **390,** 458–462, doi: 10.1126/science.ady3581.

Graham, S. E., C. Demets, H. R. Deshon, R. Rogers, M. R. Maradiaga, W. Strauch, K. Wiese, and D. Hernandez (2012). GPS and seismic constraints on the M = 7.3 2009 Swan Islands earthquake: Implications for stress changes along the Motagua fault and other nearby faults, *Geophys. J. Int.* **190,** no. 3, 1625–1639, doi: 10.1111/j.1365-246X.2012.05560.x.

Haeussler, P. J., D. P. Schwartz, T. E. Dawson, H. D. Stenner, J. J. Lienkaemper, B. L. Sherrod, F. R. Cinti, P. Montone, P. A. Craw, A. J. Crone, *et al.* (2004). Surface rupture and slip distribution of the Denali and Totschunda faults in the 3 November 2002 M 7.9 earthquake, Alaska, *Bull. Seismol. Soc. Am.* **94,** no. 6B, S23–S52, doi: 10.1785/0120040626.

Hanks, T. C., and W. H. Bakun (2002). A bilinear source-scaling model for M-log A observations of continental earthquakes, *Bull. Seismol. Soc. Am.* **92,** no. 5, 1841–1846, doi: 10.1785/0120010148.

Hanks, T. C., and W. H. Bakun (2008). M-log A observations for recent large earthquakes, *Bull. Seismol. Soc. Am.* **98,** no. 1, 490–494, doi: 10.1785/0120070174.

Hanks, T. C., and H. Kanamori (1979). A moment magnitude scale, *J. Geophys. Res.* **84,** no. B5, 2348–2350, doi: 10.1029/JB084iB05p02348.

Hicks, S. P., R. Okuwaki, A. Steinberg, C. A. Rychert, N. Harmon, R. E. Abercrombie, P. Bogiatzis, D. Schlaphorst, J. Zahradnik, J. M. Kendall, *et al.* (2020). Back-propagating supershear rupture in the 2016 M_w 7.1 Romanche transform fault earthquake, *Nature Geosci.* **13,** no. 9, 647–653, doi: 10.1038/s41561-020-0619-9.

Hurukawa, N., and P. Maung Maung (2011). Two seismic gaps on the Sagaing fault, Myanmar, derived from relocation of historical earthquakes since 1918, *Geophys. Res. Lett.* **38,** no. L01310, doi: 10.1029/2010GL046099.

Jia, Z., Z. Jin, M. Marchandon, T. Ulrich, A. A. Gabriel, W. Fan, P. Shearer, X. Zou, J. Rekoske, F. Bulut, *et al.* (2023). The complex dynamics of the 2023 Kahramanmaraş, Turkey, M_w 7.8-7.7 earthquake doublet, *Science* **381,** no. 6661, 985–990, doi: 10.1126/science.adi0685.

Kanamori, H., and D. L. Anderson (1975). Theoretical basis of some empirical relations in seismology, *Bull. Seismol. Soc. Am.* **65,** no. 5, 1073–1095.

Kehoe, H. L., and E. D. Kiser (2020). Evidence of a supershear transition across a fault stepover, *Geophys. Res. Lett.* **47,** no. 10, doi: 10.1029/2020GL087400.

Klinger, Y., X. Xu, P. Tapponnier, C. Lasserre, G. King, J. J. Van der Woerd, C. Lasserre, and G. King (2005). High-resolution satellite imagery mapping for the surface rupture and slip distribution of the $M_w \sim 7.8$, 14 November 2001 Kokoxili earthquake, Kunlun fault, northern Tibet, China, *Bull. Seismol. Soc. Am.* **95,** no. 5, 1970–1987, doi: 10.1785/0120040233.

Lay, T., L. Ye, Y. Bai, K. F. Cheung, H. Kanamori, J. Freymueller, G. M. Steblov, and M. G. Kogan (2017). Rupture along 400 km of the Bering fracture zone in the Komandorsky Islands earthquake (M_W 7.8) of 17 July 2017, *Geophys. Res. Lett.* **44,** no. 24, 12,161–12,169, doi: 10.1002/2017GL076148.

Leonard, M. (2010). Earthquake fault scaling: Self-consistent relating of rupture length, width, average displacement, and moment release, *Bull. Seismol. Soc. Am.* **100,** no. 5A, 1971–1988, doi: 10.1785/0120090189.

Leonard, M. (2014). Self-consistent earthquake fault-scaling relations: Update and extension to stable continental strike-slip faults, *Bull. Seismol. Soc. Am.* **104,** no. 6, 2953–2965, doi: 10.1785/0120140087.

Leprince, S., F. Ayoub, Y. Klingert, and J.-P. Avouac (2007). Co-registration of optically sensed images and correlation (COSI-Corr): An operational methodology for ground deformation measurements, *Geoscience and Remote Sensing Symposium*, 1943–1946.

Li, B., T. Ulrich, Gabriel, A.-A. Suhendi, C. Klinger, Y. Jonsson, and P. M. Mai (2025). Supershear rupture of the 1995 M_w 7.2 multi-segment Nuweiba earthquake in the Gulf of Aqaba, *Geophys. Res. Lett* **52,** no. 22, doi: 10.1029/2025GL117448.

Li, Z., J. R. Elliott, W. Feng, J. A. Jackson, B. E. Parsons, and R. J. Walters (2011). The 2010 M_W 6.8 Yushu (Qinghai, China) earthquake: Constraints provided by InSAR and body wave seismology, *J. Geophys. Res. Solid Earth* **116,** no. 10, 1–16, doi: 10.1029/2011JB008358.

Lindsey, E. O., Y. Wang, L. T. Aung, J. H. Chong, Q. Qiu, R. Mallick, L. Feng, P. S. Aung, T. Z. H. Tin, S. M. Min, *et al.* (2023). Active subduction and strain partitioning in western Myanmar revealed by a dense survey GNSS network, *Earth Planet. Sci. Lett.* **622,** 118384, doi: 10.1016/j.epsl.2023.118384.

Lockner, D. A. (1998). A generalized law for brittle deformation of Westerly granite, *J. Geophys. Res.* **103,** no. B3, 5107–5123, doi: 10.1029/97JB03211.

Lyu, M., K. Chen, C. Xue, N. Zang, W. Zhang, and G. Wei (2022). Overall subshear but locally supershear rupture of the 2021 Mw 7.4 Maduo earthquake from high-rate GNSS waveforms and three-dimensional InSAR deformation, *Tectonophysics* **839,** 229542, doi: 10.1016/j.tecto.2022.229542.

Mallick, R., E. O. Lindsey, L. Feng, J. Hubbard, P. Banerjee, and E. M. Hill (2019). Active convergence of the India-Burma-Sunda plates revealed by a new continuous GPS network, *J. Geophys. Res. Solid Earth* **124,** 3155–3171, doi: 10.1029/2018JB016480.

Manighetti, I., C. Perrin, Y. Gaudemer, S. Dominguez, N. Stewart, J. Malavieille, and S. Garambois (2020). Repeated giant earthquakes on the Wairarapa fault, New Zealand, revealed by lidar-based paleoseismology, *Sci. Rep.* **10,** no. 1, 1–11, doi: 10.1038/s41598-020-59229-3.

Materna, K., and J. Maurer (2023). Strain_2D (1.1.1), doi: 10.5066/P9JJW0DY.

Melgar, D., T. Taymaz, A. Ganas, B. W. Crowell, T. Öcalan, M. Kahraman, V. Tsironi, S. Valkaniotis, T. S. Irmak, T. Eken, *et al.* (2023). Sub- and super-shear ruptures during the 2023 M_w 7. 8 and M_w 7. 6 earthquake doublet in SE Türkiye, *Seismica*, doi: 10.26443/seismica.v2i3.387.

Meng, L., J. Stock, Z. Duputel, Y. Luo, and V. C. Tsai (2012). Earthquake in a maze: Compressional rupture branching during the 2012 M_w 8.6 Sumatra earthquake, *Science* 6–10, doi: 10.1785/0120050614.

Milliner, C., J. P. Avouac, and S. Aati (2024). Coseismic surface ruptures of 20 strike-slip earthquakes measured from geodetic imaging data, *Earthq. Spectra*, doi: 10.1177/87552930241280255.

Milliner, C. W. D., J. F. Dolan, J. Hollingsworth, S. S. Leprince, F. F. Ayoub, and C. G. Sammis (2015). Quantifying near-field and off-fault deformation patterns of the 1992 M_w 7.3 Landers earthquake, *Geochem. Geophys. Geosys.* **16,** no. 5, 1577–1598, doi: 10.1002/2014GC005693.

Mitchell, A., S. L. Chung, T. Oo, T. H. Lin, and C. H. Hung (2012). Zircon U-Pb ages in Myanmar: Magmatic-metamorphic events and the closure of a neo-Tethys ocean? *J. Asian Earth Sci.* **56,** 1–23, doi: 10.1016/j.jseaes.2012.04.019.

Mitchell, A. H. G. (1993). Cretaceous-Cenozoic tectonic events in the western Myanmar (Burma) - Assam region, *J. Geol. Soc. Lond.* **150,** no. 6, 1089–1102, doi: 10.1144/gsjgs.150.6.1089.

Morley, C. K., and F. Arboit (2019). Dating the onset of motion on the Sagaing fault: Evidence from detrital zircon and titanite U-Pb geochronology from the North Minwun Basin, Myanmar, *Geology* **47,** no. 6, 581–585, doi: 10.1130/G46321.1.

Olsen, K. B., R. Madariaga, and R. J. Archuleta (1997). Three-dimensional dynamic simulation of the 1992 Landers earthquake, *Science* **278,** 834–838.

Planet Team (2025) Planet application program interface: In space for life on earth, San Francisco, California, available at https://api.planet.com (last accessed April 2025).

Reitman, N. G., R. W. Briggs, W. D. Barnhart, A. E. Hatem, J. A. Thompson Jobe, C. B. DuRoss, R. D. Gold, J. D. Mejstrik, C. Collett, and R. D. Koehler, *et al.* (2023). Rapid surface rupture mapping from satellite data: The 2023 Kahramanmaraş, Turkey (Türkiye), earthquake sequence, *Seismic Rec.* **3,** no. 4, 289–298, doi: 10.1785/0320230029.

Reitman, N. G., K. J. Mueller, and G. E. Tucker (2022). Surface slip variability on strike-slip faults, *Earth Surf. Process. Landf.* **47,** no. 4, 908–935, doi: 10.1002/esp.5294.

Reitman, N. G., Y. Wang, Y. T. Kuo, C. E. Hanagan, A. E. Hatem, C. B. Duross, W. D. Barnhart, H. Z. Yin, R. Briggs, J. A. Jobe, *et al.* (2025). Remote surface rupture observations for the M 7.7 2025 Mandalay, Burma (Myanmar) earthquake, *U.S. Geol. Surv. Data Release*, doi: 10.5066/P1RYMWCK.

Robinson, D. P., S. Das, and M. P. Searle (2010). Earthquake fault superhighways, *Tectonophysics* **493,** nos. 3/4, 236–243, doi: 10.1016/j.tecto.2010.01.010.

Rodgers, D. W., and T. A. Little (2006). World's largest coseismic strike-slip offset: The 1855 rupture of the Wairarapa fault, New Zealand, and implications for displacement/length scaling of continental earthquakes, *J. Geophys. Res. Solid Earth* **111,** no. 12, 1–19, doi: 10.1029/2005JB004065.

Rodriguez Padilla, A. M., M. E. Oskin, E. E. Brodsky, K. Dascher-Cousineau, V. Herrera, and S. White (2024). The influence of fault geometrical complexity on surface rupture length, *Geophys. Res. Lett.* **51,** no. 20, doi: 10.1029/2024GL109957.

Romanowicz, B. (1992). Strike-slip earthquakes on quasi-vertical transcurrent faults: Inferences for general scaling relations, *Geophys. Res. Lett.* **19,** no. 5, 481–484, doi: 10.1063/1.3034822.

Rosu, A. M., M. Pierrot-Deseilligny, A. Delorme, R. Binet, and Y. Klinger (2015). Measurement of ground displacement from optical satellite image correlation using the free open-source software MicMac, *ISPRS J. Photogramm. Remote Sens.* **100,** 48–59, doi: 10.1016/j.isprsjprs.2014.03.002.

Rupnik, E., M. Daakir, and M. Pierrot Deseilligny (2017). MicMac – A free, open-source solution for photogrammetry, *Open Geospatial Data, Software and Standards,* **2,** no. 1, doi: 10.1186/s40965-017-0027-2.

Sangha, S., G. Peltzer, A. Zhang, L. Meng, C. Liang, P. Lundgren, and E. Fielding (2017). Fault geometry of 2015, M_w 7.2 Murghab, Tajikistan earthquake controls rupture propagation: Insights from InSAR and seismological data, *Earth Planet. Sci. Lett.* **462,** 132–141, doi: 10.1016/j.epsl.2017.01.018.

Scholz, C. H. (1994). A reappraisal of large earthquake scaling, *Bull. Seismol. Soc. Am.* **84,** no. 1, 215–218, doi: 10.1016/0148-9062(94)90076-0.

Shamir, G., G. Baer, and A. Hofstetter (2003). Three-dimensional elastic earthquake modelling based on integrated seismological and InSAR data: $M_w = 7.2$ Nuweiba earthquake, Gulf of Elat/Aqaba 1995 November, *Geophys. J. Int.* **154,** no. 3, 731–744, doi: 10.1046/j.1365-246X.2003.01978.x.

Sharp, R. V., J. J. Lienkaemper, M. G. Bonilla, D. B. Burke, B. F. Fox, D. G. Herd, D. M. Miller, D. M. Morton, D. J. Ponti, M. J. Rymer, *et al.* (1982). Surface faulting in the Central Imperial Valley, *U.S. Geol. Surv. Profess. Pap. The Imperial Valley, California, Earthquake of October 15, 1979,* 119–143.

Shaw, B. E. (2009). Constant stress drop from small to great earthquakes in magnitude-area scaling, *Bull. Seismol. Soc. Am.* **99,** no. 2A, 871–875, doi: 10.1785/0120080006.

Shaw, B. E. (2013). Earthquake surface slip-length data is fit by constant stress drop and is useful for seismic hazard analysis, *Bull. Seismol. Soc. Am.* **103,** no. 2A, 876–893, doi: 10.1785/0120110258.

Shaw, B. E. (2023). Magnitude and slip scaling relations for fault-based seismic hazard, *Bull. Seismol. Soc. Am.* **113,** no. 3, 924–947, doi: 10.1785/0120220144.

Shaw, B. E., and S. G. Wesnousky (2008). Slip-length scaling in large earthquakes: The role of deep-penetrating slip below the seismogenic layer, *Bull. Seismol. Soc. Am.* **98,** no. 4, 1633–1641, doi: 10.1785/0120070191.

Sieh, K., L. Jones, E. Hauksson, K. Hudnut, D. Eberhart-Phillips, T. Heaton, S. Hough, K. Hutton, H. Kanamori, A. Lilje, *et al.* (1993). Near-field investigations of the Landers earthquake sequence, April to July 1992, *Science* **260,** no. 5105, 171–176, doi: 10.1126/science.260.5105.171.

Socquet, A., J. Hollingsworth, E. Pathier, and M. Bouchon (2019). Evidence of supershear during the 2018 magnitude 7.5 Palu earthquake from space geodesy, *Nature Geosci.* **12,** no. 3, 192–199, doi: 10.1038/s41561-018-0296-0.

Socquet, A., C. Vigny, N. Chamot-Rooke, W. Simons, C. Rangin, and B. Ambrosius (2006). India and Sunda plates motion and deformation along their boundary in Myanmar determined by GPS, *J. Geophys. Res. Solid Earth* **111,** no. B5, 1–11, doi: 10.1029/2005JB003877.

Song, S. G., G. C. Beroza, and P. Segall (2008). A unified source model for the 1906 San Francisco earthquake, *Bull. Seismol. Soc. Am.* **98,** no. 2, 823–831, doi: 10.1785/0120060402.

Spudich, P., and E. Cranswick (1984). Direct observation of rupture propagation during the 1979 Imperial Valley earthquake using a short baseline accelerometer array, *Bull. Seismol. Soc. Am.* **74,** no. 6, 2083–2114.

Stafford, P. J. (2014). Source-scaling relationships for the simulation of rupture geometry within probabilistic seismic-hazard analysis, *Bull. Seismol. Soc. Am.* **104,** no. 4, 1620–1635, doi: 10.1785/0120130224.

Steckler, M.S., D.R. Mondal, S.H. Akhter, L. Seeber, L. Feng, J. Gale, E.M. Hill, and M. Howe (2016). Locked and loading megathrust linked to active subduction beneath the Indo-Burman Ranges, *Nature Geosci.* **9,** no. 8, 615–618, doi: 10.1038/ngeo2760.

Stirling, M., M. Fitzgerald, B. Shaw, and C. Ross (2024). New magnitude–area scaling relations for the New Zealand National Seismic Hazard Model 2022, *Bull. Seismol. Soc. Am.* **114,** no. 1, 137–149, doi: 10.1785/0120230114.

Stirling, M., T. Goded, K. Berryman, and N. Litchfield (2013). Selection of earthquake scaling relationships for seismic-hazard analysis, *Bull. Seismol. Soc. Am.* **103,** no. 6, 2993–3011, doi: 10.1785/0120130052.

Stirling, M., D. Rhoades, and K. Berryman (2002). Comparison of earthquake scaling relations derived from data of the instrumental and preinstrumental era, *Bull. Seismol. Soc. Am.* **92,** no. 2, 812–830, doi: 10.1785/0120000221.

Tadapansawut, T., R. Okuwaki, Y. Yagi, and S. Yamashita (2021). Rupture process of the 2020 Caribbean earthquake along the Oriente transform fault, involving supershear rupture and geometric complexity of fault, *Geophys. Res. Lett.* **48,** no. 1, 1–9, doi: 10.1029/2020GL090899.

Thingbaijam, K. K. S., P. M. Mai, and K. Goda (2017). New empirical earthquake source-scaling laws, *Bull. Seismol. Soc. Am.* **107,** no. 5, 2225–2246, doi: 10.1785/0120170017.

Thompson, E. M., and C. B. Worden (2018). Estimating rupture distances without a rupture, *Bull. Seismol. Soc. Am.* **108,** no. 1, 371–379, doi: 10.1785/0120170174.

Tin, T. Z. H., T. Nishimura, M. Hashimoto, E. O. Lindsey, L. T. Aung, S. M. Min, and M. Thant (2022). Present-day crustal deformation and slip rate along the southern Sagaing fault in Myanmar by GNSS observation, *J. Asian Earth Sci.* **228,** 105125, doi: 10.1016/j.jseaes.2022.105125.

U.S. Geological Survey (2017). Advanced National Seismic System (ANSS) Comprehensive Catalog of Earthquake Events and Products: Various, doi: 10.5066/F7MS3QZH.

Vallée, M., and E. M. Dunham (2012). Observation of far-field Mach waves generated by the 2001 Kokoxili supershear earthquake. *Geophys. Res. Lett.* **39,** no. 5, 1–5, doi: 10.1029/2011GL050725.

Vasyura-Bathke, H., A. Steinberg, F. Krüger, G. Feng, P. M. Mai, and S. Jónsson (2024). Discontinuous transtensional rupture during the M_w 7.2 1995 Gulf of Aqaba earthquake, *Seismica* **3,** no. 1, doi: 10.26443/seismica.v3i1.1135.

Wald, D. J., and T. H. Heaton (1994). Spatial and temporal distribution of slip for the 1992 Landers, California, earthquake, *Bull. Seismol. Soc. Am.* **84,** no. 3, 668–691, doi: 10.1785/bssa0840030668.

Wald, D. J., H. Kanamori, D. V. Helmberger, and T. H. Heaton (1993). Source study of the 1906 San Francisco earthquake, *Bull. Seismol. Soc. Am.* **83,** no. 4, 981–1019.

Wald, D. J., C. B. Worden, E. M. Thompson, and M. Hearne (2022). ShakeMap operations, policies, and procedures, *Earthq. Spectra* **38,** no. 1, 756–777, doi: 10.1177/87552930211030298.

Wang, D., and J. Mori (2012). The 2010 Qinghai, China, earthquake: A moderate earthquake with supershear rupture, *Bull. Seismol. Soc. Am.* **102,** no. 1, 301–308, doi: 10.1785/0120110034.

Wang, D., J. Mori, and K. Koketsu (2016). Fast rupture propagation for large strike-slip earthquakes, *Earth Planet. Sci. Lett.* **440,** 115–126, doi: 10.1016/j.epsl.2016.02.022.

Wang, D., J. Mori, and T. Uchide (2012). Supershear rupture on multiple faults for the M_w 8.6 off Northern Sumatra, Indonesia earthquake of April 11, 2012, *Geophys. Res. Lett.* **39,** no. 21, 6–10, doi: 10.1029/2012GL053622.

Wang, Y., K. E. Sieh, S. T. Tun, K. Y. Lai, and T. Myint (2014). Active tectonics and earthquake potential of the Myanmar region, *J. Geophys. Res. Solid Earth* **119,** 3767–3822, doi: 10.1002/2013JB010762.

Wells, D. L., and K. J. Coppersmith (1994). New empirical relationships among magnitude, rupture length, rupture width, rupture area, and surface displacement, *Bull. Seismol. Soc. Am.*, **84,** no. 4, 974–1002, doi: 10.1785/BSSA0840040974.

Wesnousky, S. G. (2008). Displacement and geometrical characteristics of earthquake surface ruptures: Issues and implications for seismic-hazard analysis and the process of earthquake rupture, *Bull. Seismol. Soc. Am.* **98,** no. 4, 1609–1632, doi: 10.1785/0120070111.

Wu, S.-H. (2022). Re-estimating the magnitude of 1839 Ava earthquake through geomorphic mapping and macroseismic records, central Myanmar, *Master's Thesis*, National Taiwan University, available at https://tdr.lib.ntu.edu.tw/jspui/handle/123456789/90872.

Xu, X., G. Yu, Y. Klinger, P. Tapponnier, and J. Van Der Woerd (2006). Reevaluation of surface rupture parameters and faulting segmentation of the 2001 Kunlunshan earthquake (M_w7.8), northern Tibetan plateau, China, *J. Geophys. Res. Solid Earth* **111,** no. 5, 1–16, doi: 10.1029/2004JB003488.

Yen, Y. T., and K. F. Ma (2011). Source-scaling relationship for M 4.6-8.9 earthquakes, specifically for earthquakes in the Collision zone of Taiwan, *Bull. Seismol. Soc. Am.* **101,** no. 2, 464–481, doi: 10.1785/0120100046.

Yuan, Z., T. Li, P. Su, H. Sun, G. Ha, P. Guo, G. Chen, and J. Thompson Jobe (2022). Large surface-rupture gaps and low surface fault slip of the 2021 M_w 7.4 Maduo earthquake along a low-activity strike-slip fault, Tibetan Plateau, *Geophys. Res. Lett.* **49,** no. 6, e2021GL096874, doi: 10.1029/2021GL096874.

Yue, H., T. Lay, J. T. Freymueller, K. Ding, L. Rivera, N. A. Ruppert, and K. D. Koper (2013). Supershear rupture of the 5 January 2013 Craig, Alaska (M_w 7.5) earthquake, *J. Geophys. Res. Solid Earth* **118,** no. 11, 5903–5919, doi: 10.1002/2013JB010594.

Yue, H., T. Lay, and K. D. Koper (2012). En échelon and orthogonal fault ruptures of the 11 April 2012 great intraplate earthquakes, *Nature* **490,** no. 7419, 245–249, doi: 10.1038/nature11492.

Zhang, X., W. Feng, H. Du, S. Samsonov, and L. Yi (2022). Supershear Rupture During the 2021 MW 7.4 Maduo, China, Earthquake, *Geophys. Res. Lett.* **49,** no. 6, e2022GL097984, doi: 10.1029/2022GL097984.

Zhang, Y., L. Xu, and Y. T. Chen (2010). Source process of the 2010 Yushu, Qinghai, earthquake, *Sci. China Earth Sci.* **53,** 1249–1251, doi: 10.1007/s11430-010-4045-5.

Zhou, Y., B. E. Parsons, and R. T. Walker (2018). Characterizing complex surface ruptures in the 2013 M_w 7.7 Balochistan earthquake using three-dimensional displacements, *J. Geophys. Res. Solid Earth* **123,** no. 11, 10,191–10,211, doi: 10.1029/2018JB016043.

Manuscript received 4 August 2025
Published online 21 April 2026

Coulomb Stress Transfer and Future Earthquake Hazard from the 2025 M_w 7.7 Myanmar Earthquake: Implications for the Sagaing Fault and Shan Plateau

Tuo Shen[1], Weiwei Wu*[1], Guojie Meng[1], Tai Liu[1], Lupeng Zhang[1], Jin Tang[2], and Xiwei Xu[3]

Abstract

On 28 March 2025, a major M_w 7.7 right-lateral strike-slip earthquake ruptured the Sagaing fault (SF) in Myanmar, causing significant casualties and infrastructure damage. The long-term stress evolution of the SF since 1897 has been strongly influenced by coseismic and postseismic Coulomb failure stress change (ΔCFS) associated with this event. These stress changes are evaluated using the PSGRN/PSCMP software combined with a multilayered viscoelastic model. Our results indicate that the earthquake significantly loaded the northern and southern tips of its rupture and several adjacent faults (e.g., the Kyaukme, Loi Kwi, Lancang, and southern Nantinghe faults), with ΔCFS increases exceeding the commonly used 10 kPa (0.1 bar) earthquake-triggering threshold in some areas. Postseismic viscoelastic relaxation is projected to further enhance stress accumulation in these regions over the coming decades. The exceptionally long coseismic rupture (~500 km) observed in this event significantly exceeds predictions from empirical magnitude-scaling relationships, highlighting the unique propensity for long, narrow ruptures on structurally mature fault zones. Comparisons among multiple coseismic slip models further show that models with larger magnitudes provide systematically better fits to far-field Global Navigation Satellite System observations, whereas smaller magnitude models fail to reproduce the observed deformation field. Furthermore, analysis of the historical earthquake sequence reveals persistent Coulomb stress accumulation on the northern segment of the SF, indicating a potential for future large earthquakes (M_w~7.3–7.7). This research provides critical insights into stress-triggering mechanisms and refines the seismic hazard assessment for central Myanmar.

Cite this article as Shen, T., W. Wu, G. Meng, T. Liu, L. Zhang, J. Tang, and X. Xu (2026). Coulomb Stress Transfer and Future Earthquake Hazard from the 2025 M_w 7.7 Myanmar Earthquake: Implications for the Sagaing Fault and Shan Plateau, *Seismol. Res. Lett.* **97**, 1721–1738, doi: 10.1785/0220250395.

Supplemental Material

Introduction

On 28 March 2025 at 06:20 LMT (00:50 UTC), an M_w 7.7 right-lateral strike-slip earthquake ruptured the central Sagaing fault (SF) near 22.01° N, 95.92° E at a focal depth of ~10 km (U.S. Geological Survey [USGS]: see Data and Resources) (Fig. 1). Ground shaking reached modified Mercalli intensity (MMI) values of X across Mandalay, Sagaing, and Naypyidaw, collapsing poorly constructed buildings and triggering landslides in surrounding hills (Cruz *et al.*, 2025). As of early May, state media and the World Health Organization report that over 3700 people were killed and approximately 5000 were injured, with hundreds still missing in remote townships. Field teams documented severe damage to critical infrastructure, including three major Chindwin River bridges, sections of the Mandalay–Myingyan highway, and key power substations, leaving tens of thousands without electricity or clean water for days.

The oblique convergence between the India and Sunda plates gives rise to a complex, transpressional plate boundary in western Myanmar, which accommodates strain through both subduction and strike-slip faulting (Tin *et al.*, 2022; Lindsey *et al.*, 2023). A major locus of dextral motion is the north–south-striking SF, a ~1200 km right-lateral strike-slip system that links the Andaman spreading center in the south to the eastern Himalayan syntaxis in the north (Wang *et al.*, 2014; Xiong *et al.*, 2017). Geodetic studies have shown a

1. Institute of Earthquake Forecasting, China Earthquake Administration, Key Laboratory of Earthquake Forecasting and Risk Assessment, Ministry of Emergency Management, Key Laboratory of Earthquake Forecasting, Beijing, China, https://orcid.org/0000-0003-4319-7248 (TS); https://orcid.org/0000-0001-5641-8041 (WW); https://orcid.org/0000-0002-4057-8435 (TL); 2. Petro China Research Institute of Petroleum Exploration and Development, Beijing, China; 3. School of Earth Sciences and Resources, China University of Geosciences, Beijing, China

*Corresponding author: wwei@ief.ac.cn

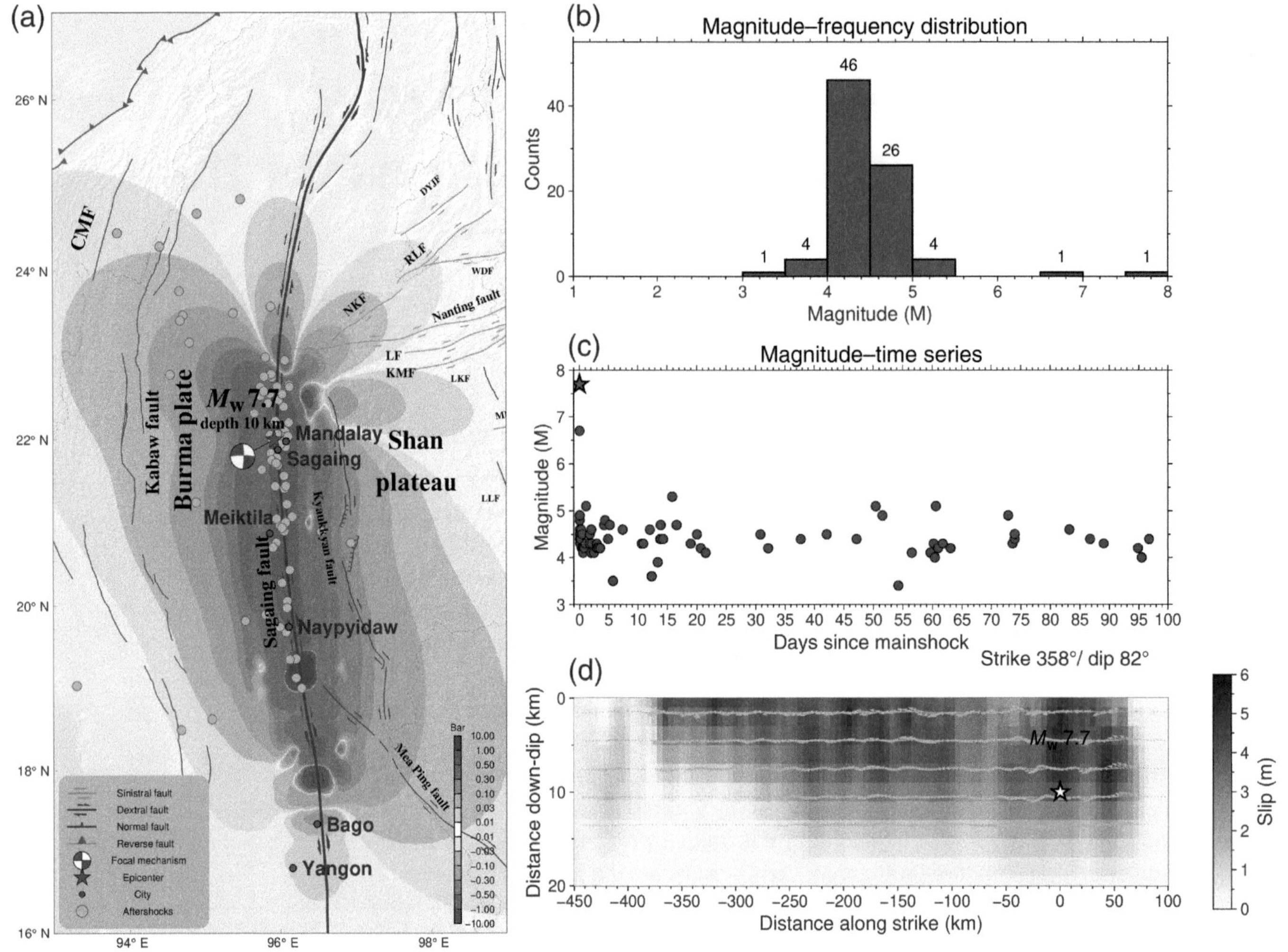

Figure 1. Coseismic Coulomb failure stress change (ΔCFS), aftershock distribution, frequency–magnitude statistics and slip profile of the 28 March 2025 M_w 7.7 Sagaing fault (SF) earthquake. (a) Map-view ΔCFS (bar color shading) model result from Li *et al.* (2025), where warm tones indicate positive ΔCFS (stress increase) and cool tones indicate negative ΔCFS (stress decrease), computed on a planar fault striking 358° and dipping 82° at 10 km depth, overlain by the 28 March mainshock focal mechanism (red focal mechanism plot) and subsequent M_w 3+ aftershocks (gray dots) (0–100 days) (U.S. Geological Survey [USGS]: see Data and Resources). Major regional faults are shown in orange (sinistral fault), green (Dextral fault), blue (normal fault), and red (reverse fault) lines. (b) Magnitude–frequency histogram of aftershocks (0–100 days). (c) Magnitude–time series of aftershocks since the mainshock (star at day 0). (d) Cross-sectional slip distribution (color scale in meters) along strike versus down-dip (Li *et al.*, 2025). Fault abbreviations: CMF, Churachandpur-Mao fault; DYJF, Dayingjiang fault; KMF, Kyaukme fault; LF, Lashio fault; LKF, Loi Kwi fault; LLF, Loi Lung fault; MLF, Menglian fault; NKF, Namkham fault; RLF, Ruili fault; and WDF, Wanding fault. The color version of this figure is available only in the electronic edition.

relatively uniform slip rate of 18–24 mm/yr along the central SF, with locking depths of 10–16 km (Vigny *et al.*, 2003; Maurin *et al.*, 2010; Tin *et al.*, 2022).

Since 1906, the SF has produced multiple 14 $M_w \geq 6.5$ earthquakes, including 11 $M_w > 7$ events in the past century, leaving notable seismic gaps in central and southern Myanmar (Hurukawa and Maung, 2011; Wang *et al.*, 2014) (Table 1). Coulomb failure stress change (ΔCFS) modeling effectively reveals the interactions among earthquakes along the SF. For instance, the positive ΔCFS lobes generated by historical rupture events closely coincide with the epicenters of subsequent earthquakes, whereas stress shadow zones correspond to relatively quiescent seismic activity (Xiong *et al.*, 2017). The 2025 Sagaing earthquake sequence provides an exceptional opportunity to investigate the evolution of ΔCFS using modern, densely recorded datasets, to assess its influence on aftershock migration, and to refine seismic hazard assessments for Myanmar's densely populated corridor (Lindsey *et al.*, 2023).

In this study, we employed the PSGRN/PSCMP toolkit (Wang *et al.*, 2006) to model coseismic and postseismic stress changes in a layered elastic–anelastic half-space (Fig. 2). By explicitly incorporating the 28 March 2025 M_w 7.7 Myanmar earthquake as a major modern event, we calculated both coseismic and postseismic (viscoelastic relaxation) ΔCFS components and evaluated their associated displacement fields. Our analysis systematically considers the combined influence

TABLE 1
M_w > 6.5 Earthquakes Along the Sagaing Fault and Surrounding Areas Since 1897

Year (mm/dd)	Latitude (°N)	Longitude (°E)	Strike	Dip	Rake	Length (km)	Width (km)	Slip (m)	Depth (km)	Magnitude	Location	References*
On Sagaing												
1906 (08/31)	27.46	97.04	355	80	180	66.68†	19.23†	0.75†	16	M_w 7.0	Nampak (Myanmar)	15, 16
1908 (12/12)	26.56	97.13	355	80	180	146.05†	25.97†	1.42†	20	M_w 7.5	Peru (Myanmar)	15, 16
1912 (05/23)	21	97.3	185	45	−90	108.34†	47.92†	2.07†	15	M_w 7.7	Maymyo (Myanmar)	10, 11, 16, 17
1929 (08/08)	19	96.5	180	87	176	66.68†	19.23†	0.75†	15	M_w 7.0	Nay Pyi Taw (Myanmar)	1, 7
1930 (05/05)	17.78	96.73	175	87	176	124.85†	24.46†	1.25†	35	M_s 7.4	Bago (Myanmar)	1, 8, 9, 10
1930 (12/03)	18.12	96.76	170	80	176	146.05†	25.97†	1.42†	10	M_s 7.5	Pyu (Myanmar)	1, 8, 9, 10
1931 (01/27)	25.41	97.02	188	85	179	199.85†	29.29†	1.84†	15	M_s 7.7	Kamaing (Myanmar)	1, 8, 9
1946 (09/12)	24.02	96.09	12	87	176	146.05†	25.97†	1.42†	15	M_b 7.5	Sagaing (Myanmar)	1, 8, 10
1946 (09/13)	22.35	96.24	12	87	176	233.78†	31.1†	2.09†	15	M_s 7.8	Sagaing (Myanmar)	1, 8, 10
1956 (07/16)	22.06	95.9	25	90	178	78†	20.42†	0.85†	34	M_w 7.1	Sagaing (Myanmar)	1, 8, 10
1991 (01/05)	23.59	95.97	2	65	171	57†	18.11†	0.66†	20	M_w 6.9	Mogok (Myanmar)	1, 8, 10
2003 (09/21)	19.91	95.63	8	80	180	35.61†	15.12†	0.45†	15.8	M_w 6.6	Taungdwingyi (Myanmar)	8, 16
2012 (11/11)	23	95.88	15	80	175	48.73	17.05	0.58	14	M_w 6.8	Shwebo (Myanmar)	1, 10
2025 (03/28)	22.001	95.925	1	82	−174	460	15	2.24	10	M_w 7.7	Sagaing (Myanmar)	11
Middle and far field												
1897 (06/12)	26	90.7	110	57	76	253.05†	87.4†	3.87†*	34	M_w 8.3	Assam	2, 3
1934 (01/15)	26.6	86.8	80	30	40	250	60	5.73†	20	M_w 8.3	Bihar–Nepal	4, 5, 6
1941 (06/26)	12.02	92.58	290	80	171	374.2†	37.25†	3.07†	20	M_w 8.1	Andaman	12
1950 (08/15)	28.38	96.72	293	16	107	330	90	16	37	M_w 8.7	Motuo	13, 14
2004 (12/26)	3.09	94.26	329	8	110	1500	150	19	28.6	M_w 9.0	Sumatra	11, 18, 19, 20
2008 (05/12)	32.52	105.43	231	35	138	315	40	8	12.8	M_w 7.9	Wenchuan	11, 21, 22, 23

*References: 1. Li *et al.* (2020), 2. Bilham and England (2001), 3. England and Bilham (2015), 4. Riesner *et al.* (2023), 5. Singh and Gupta (1980), 6. Sapkota *et al.* (2013), 7. Kundu and Gahalaut (2012), 8. Hurukawa and Maung (2011), 9. Tsutsumi and Sato (2009), 10. Wang *et al.* (2014), 11. NEIC, USGS, 12. Okal (2019), 13. Coudurier-Curveur *et al.* (2020), 14. Chen and Molnar (1977), 15. Maurin *et al.* (2010), 16. Xiong *et al.* (2017), 17. Holt *et al.* (1991), 18. Chlieh *et al.* (2007), 19. Banerjee *et al.* (2007), 20. Hoechner *et al.* (2008), 21. Xu *et al.* (2009), 22. Shen *et al.* (2009), 23. Toda *et al.* (2008). NEIC, National Earthquake Information Center; and USGS, U.S. Geological Survey.

†The rupture length and average slip are estimated based on the empirical scaling laws and relationships of Thingbaijam *et al.* (2017).

of near- and far-field earthquake interactions, allowing us to assess their cumulative contribution to stress loading along the SF (Shen *et al.*, 2026). Furthermore, we integrate depth-dependent coseismic and postseismic viscoelastic stress changes into a long-term Coulomb stress-evolution framework spanning from 1897 to the present, which is consistent with, yet extends beyond, earlier analyses of the SF (Xiong *et al.*, 2017). This integrated framework enables a more comprehensive evaluation of time-dependent stress redistribution associated with large continental strike-slip earthquakes. Based on comparisons with previous studies, we provide an updated assessment of the future seismic hazard potential of the SF and adjacent fault systems under the influence of the 2025 event.

Tectonic and Seismotectonic Setting

The Shan plateau, also known as the northern Indochina block or the Dian–Myanmar block, is situated at the southeastern margin of the Tibetan plateau where it intersects with the Indochina Peninsula. Located between the Red River fault and the Myanmar SF, the Shan plateau has played a critical role since the Oligocene in accommodating the lateral extrusion of the India–Eurasia plates and the tectonic evolution of the Sundaland region in Southeast Asia. Within the Shan plateau lies a left-lateral strike-slip fault system, including the Mae Chan, Nantinghe, Ruili, and Wanding faults, whereas a right-lateral strike-slip fault system, comprising the SF and Red River fault, bounds the plateau's eastern and western margins (see Fig. 3a) (Wang *et al.*, 2014; Shi *et al.*, 2018). The formation of these fault systems is controlled by multiple tectonic factors, such as southeastward extrusion of the Tibet plateau, lower crustal rheology, shallow-layer shearing due to Indian plate wedging, and asthenospheric drag (Tapponnier *et al.*, 1982; Clark *et al.*, 2005; Copley, 2008; Li *et al.*, 2019; Shen *et al.*, 2023).

Fault distributions within the Shan plateau reveal significant seismic activity, particularly along the western SF, which exhibits vigorous fault motion and frequent earthquakes, serving as a major conduit for regional stress release. The SF also defines the eastern margin of the Burma microplate, separating the Sunda block from the India–Burma wedge. GPS observations from a dense GNSS network reveal consistent right-lateral slip of 20–23 mm/yr along the SF (Tin *et al.*, 2022; Lindsey *et al.*, 2023), accommodating most of the ~35–40 mm/yr India–Sunda oblique convergence (Socquet *et al.*, 2006; DeMets *et al.*, 2010).

Geologic and morphotectonic studies document Miocene initiation of the SF, with total dextral displacement of 330–450 km since inception (Mitchell, 1993; Curray, 2005; Leloup *et al.*, 2007). Paleoseismic trenching and geochronology indicate Quaternary rupture recurrence intervals of 200–500 yr, punctuated by $M_w \geq 7$ events (Hurukawa and Maung, 2011; Wang *et al.*, 2014). Slip-rate variations along strike reflect changes in fault geometry and rheology: central Myanmar exhibits higher rates (~23 mm/yr) and deeper locking depths (~14 km) compared with the southern SF (~16 mm/yr; locking depth ~10 km) (Tin *et al.*, 2022).

Previous Coulomb stress studies on the SF (Xiong *et al.*, 2017) mapped positive ΔCFS lobes from major ruptures (e.g., 1906, 1930, and 1946 events) that coincided with subsequent earthquake clusters, and identified three stress-loaded gaps in the central and southern SF with elevated seismic hazard (Xiong *et al.*, 2017). However, such long-term reconstructions integrate only historic ruptures and neglect the continuous tectonic loading that steadily reloads the fault system. The 2025 M_w 7.7 mainshock, occurring near Mandalay in the central SF, provides a case to couple coseismic ΔCFS imparted to neighboring segments with interseismic recovery, offering a more complete picture of stress evolution and seismic potential across the SF.

By integrating coseismic and postseismic ΔCFS modeling with the study of Coulomb stress evolution on the SF, this research advances the understanding of static stress triggering mechanisms on the fault and refines the seismic hazard model for central Myanmar.

Methodology

Coulomb stress model

We compute the change in ΔCFS using the standard formulation (1): (Stein *et al.*, 1997; Jaeger *et al.*, 2007):

$$\Delta \text{CFS} = \Delta\tau + \mu' \Delta\sigma_N, \tag{1}$$

in which $\Delta\tau$ denotes the variation in shear stress on the receiver fault, $\Delta\sigma_N$ represents the change in normal stress (positive when extension increases), and μ' is the effective friction coefficient, which we set to 0.4 following King *et al.* (1994). To assess model robustness, we also perform sensitivity tests using alternative values of μ'. $\Delta\tau$ is positive in the slip direction of subsequent earthquakes (receiver fault), and $\Delta\sigma_N$ is positive when extensional stress increases. Positive ΔCFS values signify areas where earthquake occurrence is promoted, whereas negative values imply a delay in failure (Stein, 1999; Freed, 2005).

Multilayer lithosphere model

Our rheological framework incorporates a Burgers viscoelastic model to simulate postseismic relaxation. Based on the Crust1.0 seismic velocity model, we partition the lithosphere into four layers—upper crust, middle crust, lower crust, and lithospheric mantle—and assign each layer a density ρ, *P*-wave velocity (V_P), and *S*-wave velocity (V_S), as shown in Figure 2. The shear modulus G is derived from these properties via equation (2) (Aki and Richards, 2002).

$$G = \rho V_S^2 \approx \frac{1}{3}\rho V_P^2. \tag{2}$$

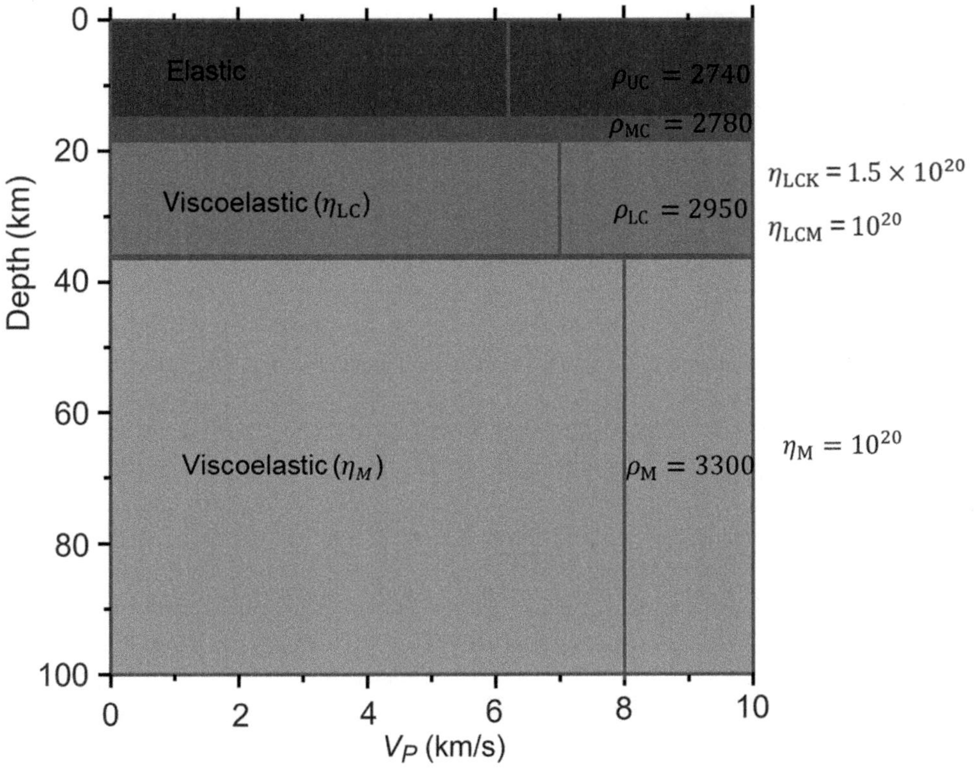

Figure 2. Rheological and seismic properties of the layered lithosphere model. The diagram illustrates an elastic upper crust underlain by a Burgers-type viscoelastic lower crust and a Maxwell viscoelastic mantle. Here, V_P denotes *P*-wave velocity, ρ is rock density, and η represents viscosity (with η_{LCK} for the Kelvin model and η_{LCM} for the Maxwell model of the Burgers model). All values are adopted from Laske *et al.* (2013) and Xiong *et al.* (2017). The color version of this figure is available only in the electronic edition.

Assuming a Poisson's ratio of 0.25. Seismicity depth distributions (Zhang *et al.*, 2002) guide our assumption that the uppermost 19 km of the crust behaves as purely elastic, whereas deeper crustal levels are represented by a Burgers viscoelastic rheology (Kelvin plus Maxwell body) with crustal viscosities η_{LCK} (Kelvin body) and η_{LCM} (Maxwell body) (Xiong *et al.*, 2017). The mantle is represented by a simple Maxwell body. The full set of rheological parameters is detailed in Figure 2 (Xiong *et al.*, 2017).

Source and receiver fault parameters

Table 1 summarizes the rupture characteristics of large near-to-far-field earthquakes used as stress sources since 1897, as well as earthquakes that occurred on the SF. The geometry and mechanical properties of the receiving faults are compiled from published fault databases and regional studies, with fault geometries primarily referenced from Styron and Pagani (2020) and Wu *et al.* (2024). Following Wang *et al.* (2014), most receiver faults are assigned a dip angle of 90°, consistent with their predominantly vertical strike-slip nature. We employ the PSGRN/PSCMP software (Wang *et al.*, 2006) to compute both coseismic stress transfer and time-dependent viscoelastic relaxation within a stratified elastic–inelastic half-space. Based on seismicity depth distributions showing that ~80% of earthquakes occur between 10 and 20 km depth, and considering that coseismic slip commonly peaks at midseismogenic depths (Mai and Thingbaijam, 2014), we adopt 10 km as the representative depth for all receiver faults. Accordingly, all ΔCFS calculations on horizontal planes and fault surfaces are evaluated at a depth of 10 km, representing the most seismically active portion of the crust (King *et al.*, 1994).

Result

Our analysis of the 2025 Sagaing earthquake sequence, summarized in Figure 1, reveals several characteristics. The coseismic ΔCFS were calculated using a finite-fault slip model derived from Li *et al.* (2025). To assess model dependence, additional ΔCFS calculations based on alternative slip distributions from Antoine *et al.* (2025) and the USGS are presented in Figures S1 and S2, available in the supplemental material to this article, respectively. The Coulomb stress distribution of the earthquake exhibits asymmetry, with a stress shadow extending southeastward. The Coulomb stress lobes evaluated at a depth of 10 km indicate that the primary loading zones are concentrated at the northern and southern ends of the rupture and on its northeastern side, with the northern end experiencing the maximum stress increase, whereas the central segment is dominated by stress reduction. A localized loading patch is also observed in the central–southern portion of the rupture, likely resulting from spatially heterogeneous coseismic slip at 10 km depth. Based on 100 days of aftershock records, most aftershocks remain concentrated within the source area, corresponding to regions of significant coseismic slip. The mainshock had a moment magnitude of 7.7 M_w; aside from a single 6.7 M_w aftershock, most aftershocks were below 5.5 M_w, with over 80% falling in the 4–5 M_w range. The coseismic slip distribution shows maximum slip on both sides of the source. Along-strike and dipping-slip profiles indicate that the maximum slip (~4 m) occurred at ~20 km depth, whereas shallower and deeper slip was smaller, reflecting differences in stress release and the layered rheology of the upper crust, which influence seismic radiation and surface motion distribution. The main rupture zone propagated bilaterally from the hypocenter, with a dominant southward extension of approximately 400 km and a minor northward extension of about 100 km (Fig. 1).

Effects of coseismic ΔCFS on faults in the Shan plateau

We find that coseismic loading is concentrated mainly on the northern and southern segments of the SF, with a petal-shaped stress lobing radiating from the epicenter (Fig. 3a). We compute coseismic ΔCFS based on the Li *et al.* (2025) finite-fault-slip model, whereas results using the Antoine and USGS models are provided in Figures S3 and S4 to assess model dependence. As shown in the Coulomb stress cross-section of the SF (Fig. 3c), within the coseismic rupture zone, stress unloading occurs only in limited areas at depths of 10–20 km, whereas the 20–30 km intervals are dominated by stress loading. Although the surface rupture propagated only ~100 km northward, much shorter than the ~400 km southward rupture, the coseismic Coulomb stress loading is greater on the northern side of the rupture zone. Regions experiencing stress increases exceeding 10 kPa, or within 1–10 kPa, extend more broadly along the northern segment than the southern segment of the SF.

In addition to the northern and southern segments, Coulomb stress increases were observed on the Kyaukme, Loi Kwi, Lancang, southern Nantinghe, Menglian, Jinghong, Wan Ha, Wuliangshan, and central Red River faults. In contrast, other fault zones primarily exhibited stress unloading. The stress-loading peaks were concentrated on the northern and southern SF segments, exceeding the 10 kPa hazard threshold (Reasenberg and Simpson, 1992; King *et al.*, 1994; Stein, 1999). Notably, stress increases near the source area, especially at the western end of the Nantinghe fault, the Kyaukkyan fault, and the northern end of the Mae Ping fault, and also surpasses this threshold.

Along the China–Myanmar border, the Kyaukme, Loi Kwi, southern Nantinghe, and Lancang faults experienced Coulomb stress increases of ~3 kPa, whereas the Menglian fault and eastern segment of the Wanding fault exhibited ~2 kPa increases (Fig. 3b). Chinese-territory faults, including the Jinghong, Wan Ha, Wuliangshan, and Red River faults, recorded modest loading of +0.3–0.8 kPa (Fig. 3b).

Overall, the 2025 M_w 7.7 Sagaing earthquake exerted a pronounced influence on the regional fault network, affecting multiple segments within Chinese territory.

Based on field investigations in Myanmar and the processing of Global Navigation Satellite System (GNSS) observations from stations along the China–Myanmar border in Yunnan Province, we compiled coseismic displacement measurements from two near-field GNSS stations located on opposite sides of the SF, together with 30 GNSS stations distributed across Yunnan Province (Table 2). The near-field stations recorded very large horizontal coseismic displacements exceeding 2 m, reflecting intense fault slip in the vicinity of the rupture. In contrast, GNSS stations in Yunnan exhibit much smaller coseismic displacements at the millimeter-to-centimeter scale, with the largest displacement of approximately 20 mm observed at the Yunnan Ruili (YNRL) station. Based on several recently published and high-quality studies on the Myanmar earthquake, we collected multiple published finite-fault-slip models and re-evaluated our results using these models. Specifically, we considered two kinematic rupture models proposed by Wei *et al.* (2025), Xu, Meng, *et al.* (2025), and Xu, Kang, *et al.* (2025) two geodetically derived static coseismic slip models based on Interferometric Synthetic Aperture Radar (InSAR) observations by Li *et al.* (2025) and Antoine *et al.* (2025), and two seismologically inverted coseismic slip models provided by Professor Zhang Yong (see Data and Resources) and the USGS (see Data and Resources). Using these six slip models, we simulate the coseismic displacement field to fit the observed GNSS displacements (Fig. 4).

Using the final fitting results (Fig. 4h), we quantitatively compared the performance of six published coseismic slip models against far-field GNSS observations within China. The root mean square (RMS) residuals, in ascending order, correspond to the Wei, Xu, Zhang, Li, Antoine, and USGS slip models, with values of 2.90, 3.28, 3.51, 4.24, 4.87, and 5.27 mm, respectively. These results indicate that the two kinematic rupture models provide the best fit to far-field GNSS data, followed by the seismologically derived coseismic slip model of Professor Zhang, whereas the static InSAR-based slip models yield comparatively larger misfits. The USGS model performs the worst among the six. This comparison suggests that coseismic slip models derived purely from near-field geodetic observations do not necessarily outperform other models when applied to far-field GNSS fitting. From classical elastic dislocation theory, the coseismic displacement at far-field observation points is primarily controlled by the total seismic moment (i.e., earthquake magnitude), rupture geometry, and the overall spatial distribution of slip on the fault plane, rather than by localized peak slip values.

Consistent with this trend, Figure 4h shows an inverse relationship between RMS misfit and seismic moment across the six models. The Wei and Xu models have the largest seismic moments and provide the best fits, whereas the USGS model has the smallest moment and the largest misfit. An exception is the Zhang model, which has the second-smallest seismic moment but yields a significantly better fit than the Li and Antoine models. As shown in Figure 4f,h, the Zhang model is characterized by the shortest rupture length but the largest rupture area, with slip concentrated farther north than in other models. Because most GNSS stations used in this study are located northeast of the rupture zone, this rupture geometry is associated with improved far-field fitting performance. Further comparisons among kinematic rupture models, static geodetic models, and seismologically derived models indicate that far-field GNSS observations are relatively

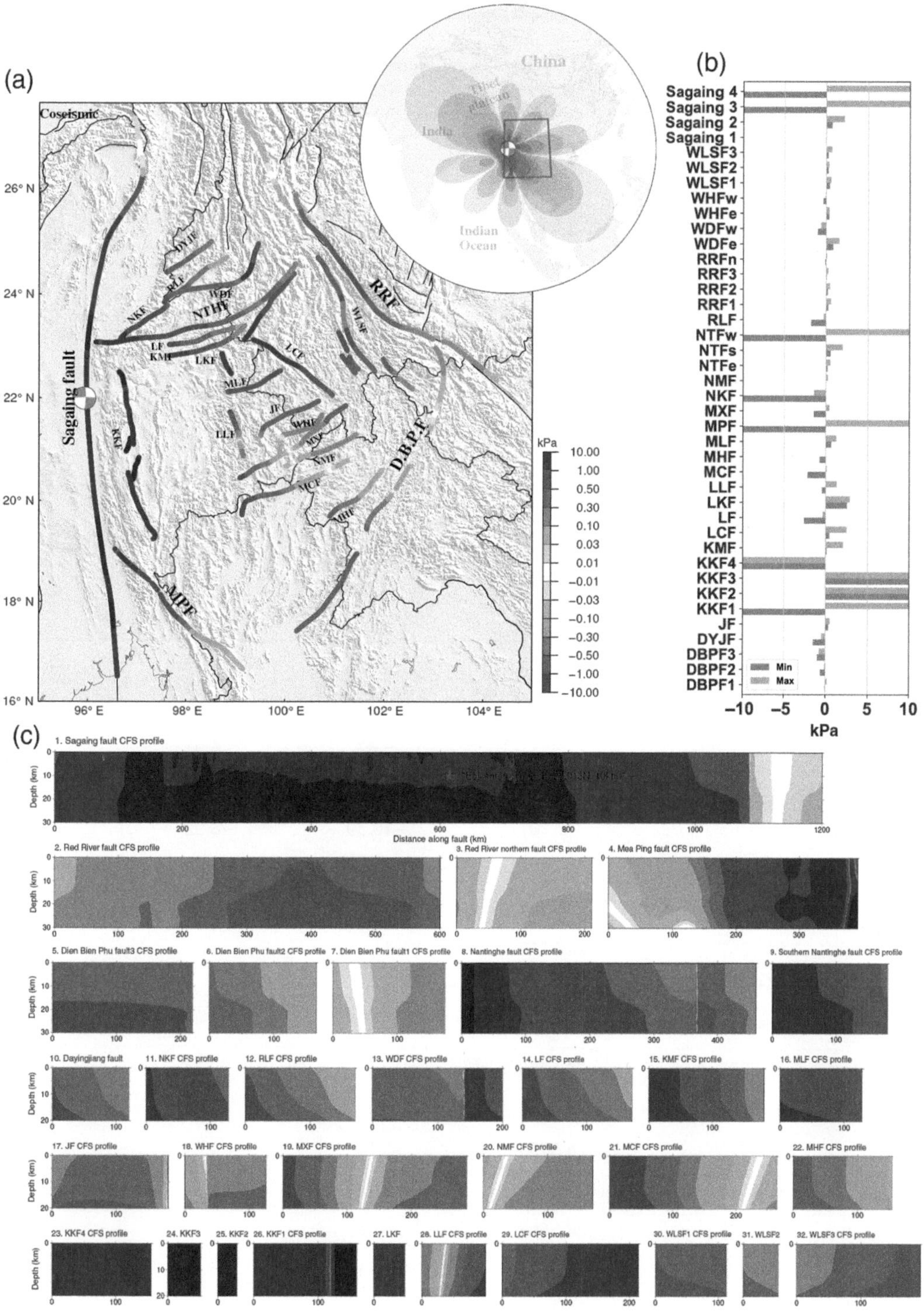

Figure 3. Coseismic ΔCFS on Shan plateau faults caused by the 2025 M_W 7.7 Sagaing earthquake, calculated using the coseismic slip model of Li *et al.* (2025). (a) Coseismic ΔCFS on the receiver faults at 10 km depth in the Shan plateau caused by the mainshock of the 2025 M_W 7.7 Sagaing earthquake. The focal mechanism (green focal mechanism plot) marks the Sagaing epicenter (USGS: see Data and Resources); the inset map at upper right shows the regional ΔCFS in surrounding plates, with the brown rectangle indicating the area shown in the main figure. (b) Segment-by-segment extremes of coseismic ΔCFS. For each receiving-fault segment (abbreviations along the *x* axis; see subsequently). Numbers following an abbreviation denote sub-segments of long faults. (c) Coseismic ΔCFS along the fault profiles in the Shan plateau caused by the 2025 M_W 7.7 Sagaing earthquake. Fault abbreviations: DYJF, Dayingjiang fault; JF, Jinghong fault; KKF, Kyaukkyan fault; KMF, Kyaukme fault; LCF, Lancangjiang fault; LF, Lashio fault; LKF, Loi Kwi fault; LLF, Loi Lung fault; MCF, Maechan fault; MHF, Muang Houn fault; MLF, Menglian fault; MXF—Mengxing fault; NKF, Namkham fault; NMF, Nam Ma fault; NTHF, Nantinghe fault; RLF, Ruili fault; WDF, Wanding fault; WHF, Wan Ha fault; WLSF, Wuliangshan fault. The major boundary faults in the study area include: D.B.P.F, Dien Bien Phu fault; MPF, Mea Ping fault; RRF, Red River fault; Sagaing fault. The color version of this figure is available only in the electronic edition.

TABLE 2
Coseismic GNSS Displacement Field of the 2025 M_w 7.7 Myanmar Earthquake Near the Sagaing Fault and in Yunnan Province, China

Site	Longitude	Latitude	*E* (mm)	*N* (mm)	E_err	N_err
Near-field points						
19	96.0927	20.4903	228.91	−2362.3	–	–
78	96.0266	19.9227	−197.52	894.5	–	–
Points in Yunnan China						
YNTC	98.4384	24.9546	−7.71	−8.74	1.1	0.74
YNRL	97.8453	24.0005	−12.32	−16.3	1.29	0.84
CYNL	99.3456	23.2718	−10.21	−9.1	1.08	0.8
LCNF	99.8128	22.2684	−9.27	−9.31	0.84	0.66
YNSM	101.0494	22.7406	−4.35	−4.54	0.83	0.63
YNLJ	100.0293	26.6956	−2.58	−4.55	1.45	0.75
YNJD	100.8808	24.4371	−8.25	−5.92	2.8	0.93
S185	100.1677	24.6621	−6.46	−6.38	1.48	0.67
S097	100.6291	25.9273	−4.39	−5.59	1.15	0.54
S175	100.5442	26.2565	−0.65	−3.35	1.48	0.71
S192	99.9311	23.953	−5.97	−6.91	1.39	0.61
YNML	103.3819	24.3963	−1.05	−3.01	0.85	0.59
YD04	99.0366	24.1101	−10.39	−8.92	1.11	0.77
YNMO	101.6704	23.4557	−3.14	−3.38	1.19	1.34
JGYZ	100.6345	23.1187	−3.61	−5.27	1.06	0.69
S196	98.925	24.3118	−11.41	−11.04	1.18	0.65
YNXP	101.9061	24.1024	−4.4	−5.92	1.62	0.76
YNYA	101.3274	25.7235	−1.06	−3.78	1.26	0.6
YD02	99.2957	24.1768	−8.52	−9.22	0.89	0.85
YDWM	99.6494	24.2344	−6.72	−7.49	1.23	0.77
YNCX	101.4928	25.0495	−3.15	−4.34	1.39	0.51
S197	99.1075	23.9167	−8.18	−8.97	0.91	0.64
YNLA	99.9536	22.5603	−5.06	−7.38	1.15	0.77
S095	100.3362	25.8644	−5.11	−5.52	1.53	0.52
YNTH	102.7514	24.1183	−1.91	−3.36	1.13	0.76
YD01	99.4619	24.1733	−9.01	−11.84	1.24	0.74
LCLB	99.6546	22.5453	−5.81	−8	0.73	0.64
LALP	102.1784	19.9091	2.25	−2.81	0.98	0.17
JHJN	100.8495	22.4822	−3.45	−5.26	0.86	0.93

GNSS, Global Navigation Satellite System.

insensitive to local peak slip amplitudes, but are more sensitive to the spatially averaged slip and the large-scale distribution of slip along strike and down-dip. For example, in the Li model, large-slip patches are located farther north and span a broader area, whereas in the Antoine model, slip is more evenly distributed along strike and concentrated at shallow depths, primarily within the upper 10 km (Figs. 4d,e, and 1, Fig. S1). These features are consistent with predictions from elastic dislocation theory.

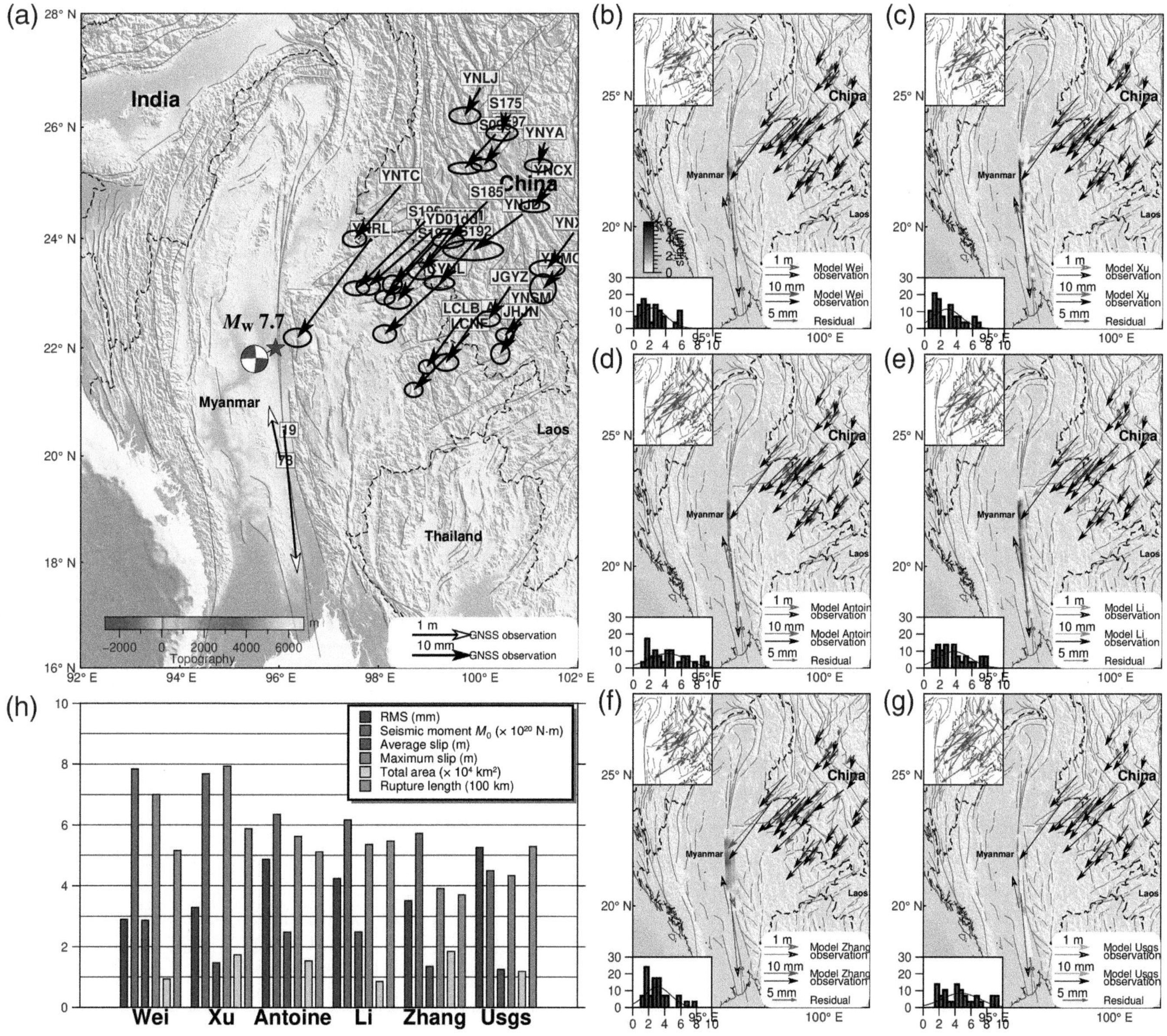

Figure 4. Coseismic GNSS observations and model comparisons for the 2025 M_W 7.7 Sagaing earthquake. (a) Near-field and far-field coseismic displacements recorded at 32 Global Navigation Satellite System (GNSS) stations following the 2025 Sagaing earthquake. Hollow arrows denote near-field GNSS displacements (plotted on a 1 m scale), whereas solid arrows indicate far-field displacements (plotted on a 10 mm scale). The red focal mechanism plot marks the epicenter, and the colored background shows topography. (b,c) Fits to the GNSS observations using kinematic rupture models derived from joint seismic and geodetic inversions by Wei *et al.* (2025) and Xu *et al.* (2025), respectively. The central colored patches indicate the corresponding coseismic slip distributions on the fault plane. Insets in the upper left show displacement residual vectors, and histograms in the lower left illustrate the statistical distribution of residual magnitudes. (d,e) Fits to the GNSS observations using geodetically derived static coseismic slip models from Antoine *et al.* (2025) and Li *et al.* (2025), respectively. The central panels display the static slip distributions, whereas the upper-left insets and lower-left histograms show displacement residual vectors and their distributions. (f,g) Fits to the GNSS observations using coseismic slip models inverted primarily from seismic data by Professor Zhang Yong (see Data and Resources) and USGS (see Data and Resources), respectively, with the same layout as in (b–e). (h) Comparison of model performance and source characteristics for the six slip models, including root mean square (RMS) misfit to GNSS observations, seismic moment, average slip, maximum slip, total rupture area, and rupture length. The color version of this figure is available only in the electronic edition.

Considering postseismic viscoelastic relaxation, The results show that the absolute values of Coulomb stress on the receiving faults increase progressively over time—at 5, 20, and 50 yr after the earthquake—regardless of whether the initial coseismic stress change was positive (loading) or negative (unloading) (Fig. 5; computed using the Li *et al.* (2025) finite-fault model; Antoine and USGS results shown in Figs. S5 and S6).

Notably, approximately 50 yr after the earthquake, the continued effects of postseismic viscoelastic relaxation have further increased the cumulative Coulomb stress along the Loi Kwi and Kyaukme faults, the southern segment of the Nantinghe fault, and the Lancang fault in the China–Myanmar border region, approaching the 10 kPa hazard threshold. Simultaneously, the midsection of the Red River fault, the Wuliangshan fault, the eastern segment of the Wanding fault, the Jinghong fault, and the Menglian fault also exhibit ongoing stress accumulation, reaching magnitudes of several kilopascals.

Accumulation of Coulomb stress on the SF since 1897

This multipanel figure presents the cumulative ΔCFS imparted to the SF and its immediate surroundings by successive large earthquakes since 1897 M_w 8.3 Assam event through 2025 M_w 7.7 Sagaing earthquake. Each subpanel (a–n) corresponds to a single historic or modern earthquake, with the star marking its epicenter along the fault trace. Together, these profiles illustrate how each rupture alternately loaded and unloaded different along-strike and depth portions of the fault (Fig. 6).

Since the 1897 Assam earthquake, the northern segment of the SF has begun accumulating Coulomb stress. Subsequent earthquakes in 1906 and 1908 occurred within the Coulomb stress-loading zones created by the preceding events. The 1912 earthquake, however, shifted to the southern segment of the SF. Later, the 1929 and 1930a earthquakes continued to occur within the stress-loading areas generated by prior events, while the 1930b earthquake further released residual stress along the southern fault segment. The 1931 earthquake mainly occurred within the stress-loading zone produced by the 1908 event on the SF.

The 1946a earthquake took place within the Coulomb stress-loading zone of the 1931 earthquake, though not within the main stress-accumulation region of the entire fault. In 1946, a doublet earthquake (1946a and 1946b) occurred with a mere three-minute interval, resulting in significant Coulomb stress accumulation on both the northern and southern segments of the SF. Subsequently, three earthquakes—M_w 7.1 in 1956, M_w 6.9 in 1991, and M_w 6.8 in 2012—occurred north of Mandalay and Sagaing region. From the perspective of Coulomb stress evolution, these events all took place in areas where stress had already been partially released, including the 2025 earthquake.

The M_w 6.6 earthquake in 2003 remains somewhat controversial, as its epicenter is located approximately 50 km from the trace of the SF, and there is currently insufficient evidence to confirm that it occurred on the fault; detailed studies are still limited (Wang *et al.*, 2014; Xiong *et al.*, 2017).

The rupture length of the 2025 Sagaing earthquake is approximately 500 km, extending ~100 km northward and ~400 km southward, essentially releasing the Coulomb stress accumulated on the southern segment since the 1946 doublet (Fig. 6n; computed using the Li *et al.* (2025) finite-fault model; Antoine and USGS results shown in Figs. S7 and S8). The detailed coseismic slip distribution of the 2025 event indicates that stress accumulated above the locked portion of the fault was largely released during the mainshock, whereas pronounced Coulomb stress loading developed beneath and adjacent to the principal slip zones. Beneath the main slip patches, the fault likely transitions into a creeping regime, where accumulated energy is expected to be dissipated shortly after the mainshock through afterslip and aftershocks (Villegas-Lanza *et al.*, 2016; Hu *et al.*, 2025). In contrast, Coulomb stress accumulated on the shallow locked regions flanking the rupture is more likely to be released by subsequent seismic events (Li *et al.*, 2021). However, Coulomb stress continues to accumulate along the northern segment within the study area. Since 1908, this area located in the northern segment of the SF, around 25° N latitude, has experienced multiple stress-loading events, including the M_w 7.7 earthquake in 1931, the M_w 7.5 and 7.8 doublet in 1946, and the recent M_w 7.7 event, all of which have further intensified stress accumulation in this loading zone. The current stress-loading zone is approximately 80 km in length; when considering interseismic stress accumulation connecting it to another northern stress-loading zone, the total loading belt can reach 150 ~200 km.

Based on empirical magnitude–rupture length relationships, a single 80 km stress-loading zone corresponds to a potential earthquake of $M_w \sim 7.3$; if the loading zone extends to 150 km, the potential magnitude could reach M_w 7.6; and if further extended to 200 km, the potential magnitude could reach $M_w \sim 7.7$ (Wells and Coppersmith, 1994; Thingbaijam *et al.*, 2017).

Discussion

Future seismic risk

Previous studies have identified a well-defined seismic gap along the SF, specifically the approximately 220 km long Meiktila segment located between ~22° and 23.5° N. Since the great 1839 Ava earthquake, this segment has remained unruptured, in stark contrast to the adjacent northern and southern segments, which experienced a series of large earthquakes with magnitudes ≥7 throughout the twentieth and early twenty-first centuries(Wang *et al.*, 2014). The 2025 earthquake, however, resulted in a complete rupture of the Meiktila segment (Fig. 7).

Prior studies indicate that the northern SF is characterized by strong seismic activity and pronounced structural

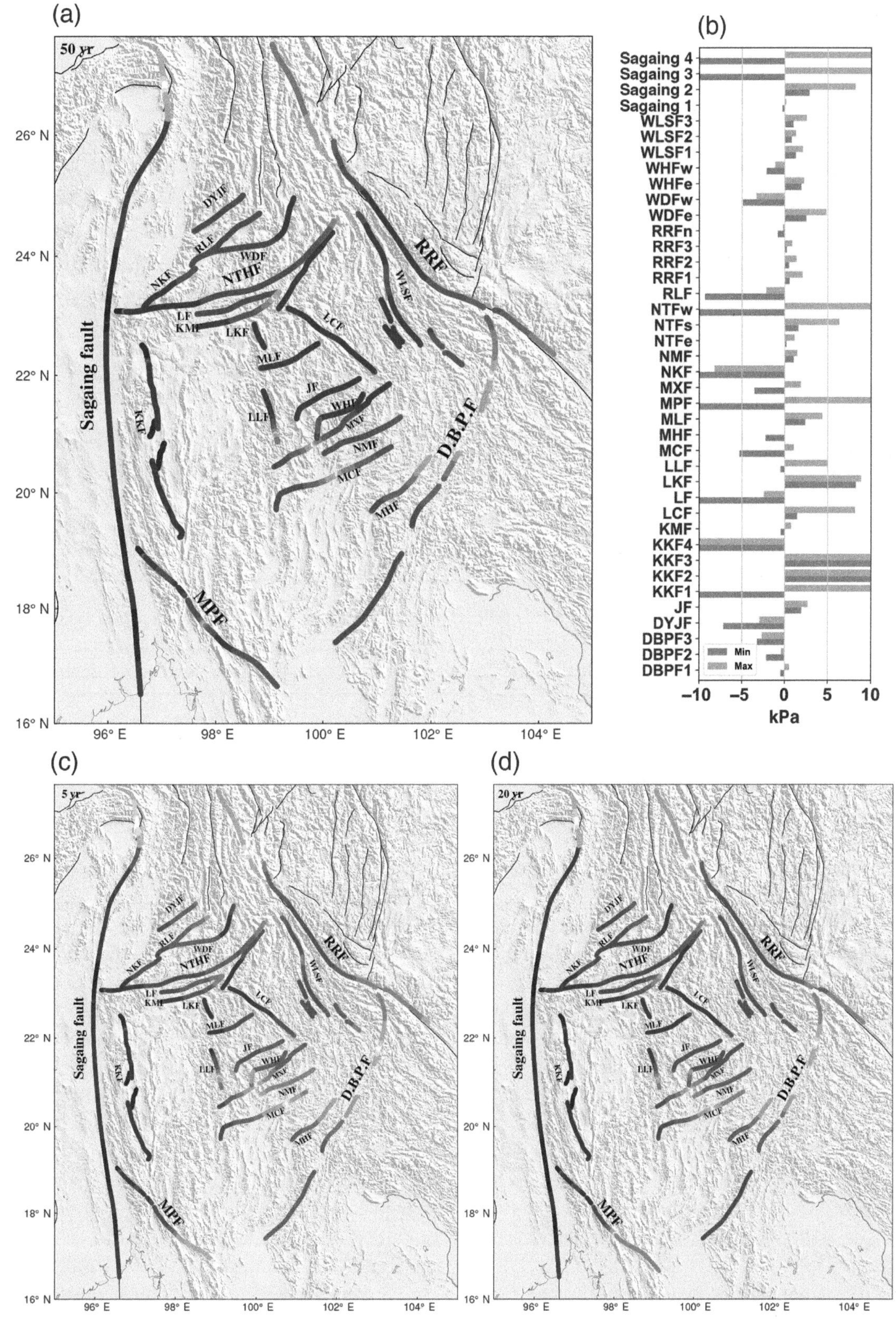

Figure 5. Time-dependent ΔCFS induced by the 2025 M_w 7.7 Sagaing earthquake under postseismic viscoelastic relaxation, based on the coseismic slip model of Li *et al.* (2025). (a) ΔCFS on each fault segment after 50 yr of viscoelastic relaxation. (b) Maximum ΔCFS on each fault segment after 50 yr, with the horizontal axis representing abbreviations of the receiving fault segments (see description subsequently), and subsegments of long faults numbered. (c) ΔCFS on each fault segment after 5 yr of viscoelastic relaxation. (d) ΔCFS on each fault segment after 20 yr of viscoelastic relaxation. Fault abbreviations are the same as in Figure 3. The color version of this figure is available only in the electronic edition.

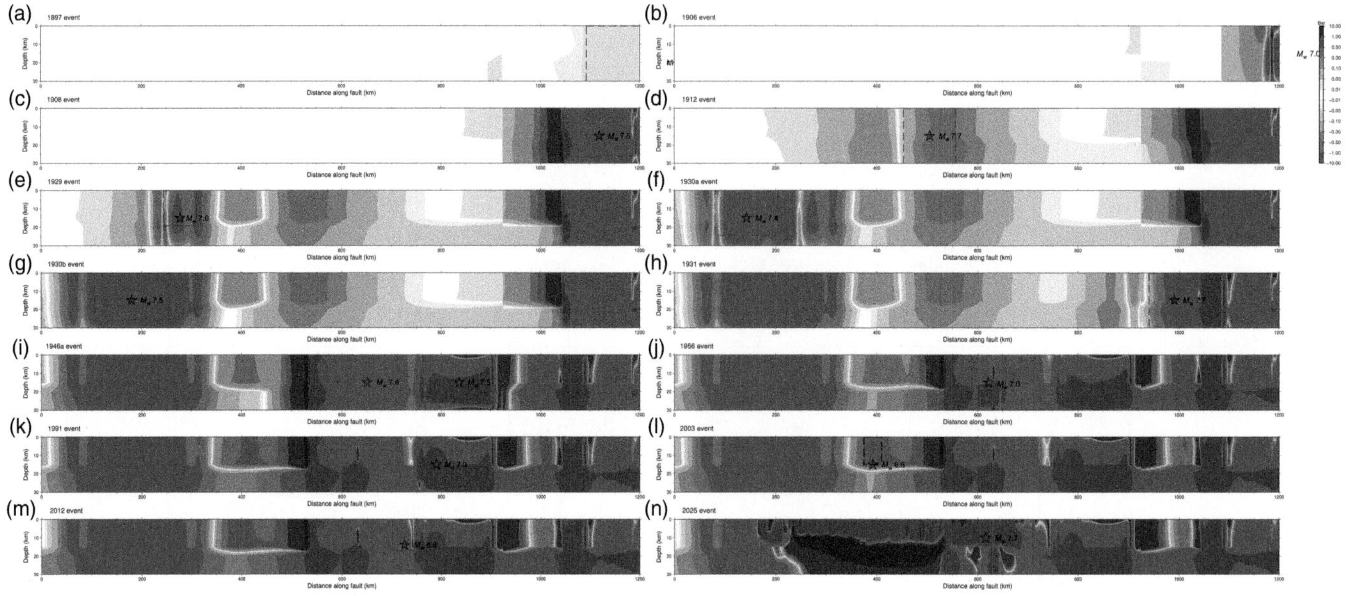

segmentation. North of ~23.5° N, strain is partitioned among multiple subparallel strands, with higher Late Quaternary slip rates on the eastern segments (In Daw–Mawlu–Kamaing–Mogang) than on the western strands (Tawma and Ban Mauk), and historical earthquakes (e.g., the 1931 M_w 7.6 and 1946 M_w 7.3 events) demonstrate that individual segments are capable of hosting large earthquakes despite uncertain rupture attribution due to the complex horsetail geometry (Pacheco and Sykes, 1992; Engdahl and Villaseñor, 2002; Maurin *et al.*, 2010). Notably, several northern segments have not experienced large earthquakes since 1931, forming a potential seismic gap between ~24° and 25° N, bounded by the inferred rupture zones of the 1931 and 1946 events (Wang *et al.*, 2014; Xiong *et al.*, 2017) (Fig. 7b).

Maurin *et al.* (2010) and Vigny *et al.* (2003) report that the SF slip rate is approximately 20 mm/yr; however, slip rates on the northern segments are lower. Some segments, such as the Ban Mauk segment, exhibit subdued geomorphic expression, suggesting relatively low activity. The northern segments may be characterized by shallow locking depths (only 5–7 km), implying slower strain accumulation and potentially longer earthquake recurrence intervals. Considering the geomorphology and structural complexity, the northern SF displays a "horsetail splay" configuration, with slip distributed across multiple branches. This slip partitioning reduces the slip rate on any single fault strand and prolongs the earthquake recurrence period.

A simplified recurrence interval model relates the long-term fault-slip rate (SR) to the average coseismic slip per characteristic event (D) as follows (Savage and Prescott, 1978):

$$T = \frac{D}{SR},$$

in which T is the recurrence interval (years), D is the average slip per event (m), and SR is the fault-slip rate (m/yr).

Figure 6. Coulomb stress evolution associated with 20 $M_w \geq 6.5$ earthquakes (Table 1) along and around the SF from 1897 to 2025 (five minor, middle, and far-field events with limited impact are excluded). The color scale on the right indicates ΔCFS (in bars; 1 bar = 100 kPa). In panels (a–n), the horizontal axis represents the along-strike distance of the Sagaing fault (0–1200 km from the southern end), and the vertical axis denotes depth within the elastic layer (0–40 km). The red stars mark the earthquake epicenters with corresponding M_w values, and red dashed boxes (where shown) outline the coseismic rupture zones. (The fault-slip model used for the 2025 Sagaing earthquake is based on Li *et al.*, 2025.) The color version of this figure is available only in the electronic edition.

Based on previous studies, an average slip rate of approximately 18 mm/yr is adopted. The average coseismic slip depends on the magnitude of the characteristic earthquake. Although no historical record exists for the current seismic gap, our earlier estimates suggest that for a potential M_w 7.3 event, the average slip would be about 1.1 m, whereas for M_w 7.7, it would be about 1.9 m. This yields a rough recurrence interval of 61–105 yr. If the 1931 earthquake did not rupture the seismic gap near ~25° N on the northern SF, the historical earthquake record would imply that a seismic gap has persisted on the northern segment since the 1839 Ava earthquake, corresponding to nearly 200 yr without a major rupture. If, instead, the 1931 earthquake ruptured the seismic gap around 25° N in the northern segment, and the slip rate in the northern section remains as high as currently estimated, then the northern segment would still be approaching its earthquake recurrence interval, indicating a high seismic hazard (Hurukawa and Maung, 2011). Therefore, the northern segment of the SF, where Coulomb stress accumulation persists, is likely within a high-risk zone for earthquake recurrence, consistent with multidisciplinary evidence from tectonic and seismological analyses.

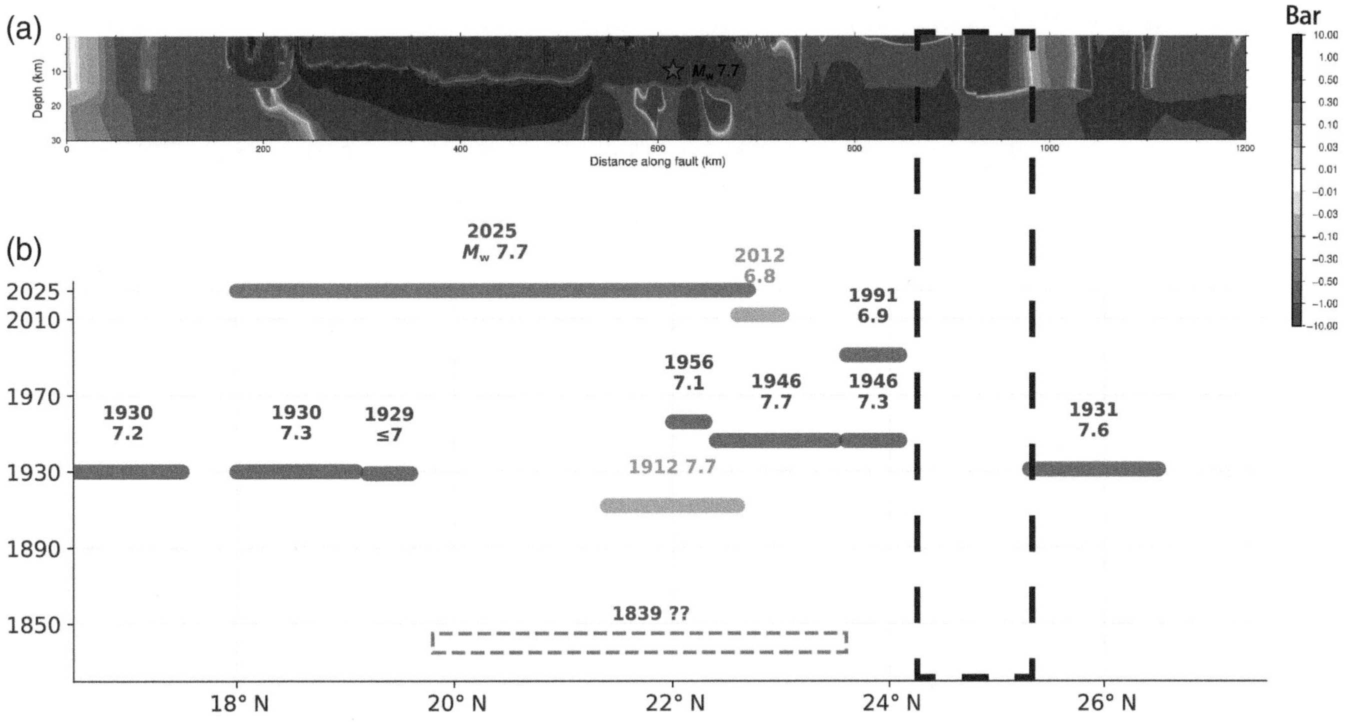

Figure 7. Cumulative ΔCFS and historical surface rupture zones along the Sagaing fault up to the present. (a) Distribution of cumulative ΔCFS changes along the Sagaing fault up to 2025 M_w 7.7 Myanmar earthquake. The color bar indicates the magnitude of ΔCFS (units: bar; 1 bar = 100 kPa), with red areas representing stress loading and blue areas representing stress unloading. The red rectangle outlines the coseismic rupture zone of the 2025 Myanmar earthquake, and the red star marks the mainshock epicenter. (b) Timeline and magnitudes of historical earthquakes along different segments of the Sagaing fault (Wang *et al.*, 2014; Xiong *et al.*, 2017). The color bar represents the confidence levels of earthquake events: red indicates the 2025 mainshock, green denotes significant historical earthquakes (some of which may not have occurred directly on the Sagaing fault). The red dashed box marks a possible suspected event interval around 1839. The horizontal axis represents latitude, and the vertical axis represents time (year), illustrating the spatial–temporal distribution of seismicity along the fault. The central black-dashed rectangle highlights the area of sustained Coulomb stress accumulation and a historical seismic gap analyzed in this study. The color version of this figure is available only in the electronic edition.

In addition, our results are broadly consistent with previous Coulomb stress studies in the Shan plateau region. Earlier work showed that stress transfer from large earthquakes along the SF produces positive ΔCFS lobes that often correlate with subsequent seismic activity (Xiong *et al.*, 2017). Recent studies of the 2025 M_w 7.7 Myanmar earthquake further suggests that several major faults along the China–Myanmar border region, including the Nantinghe, Menglian, Red River, Jinghong, and Lancang faults, experienced positive Coulomb stress changes, with both coseismic and postseismic viscoelastic models indicating increased seismic hazard in this fault system (Li *et al.*, 2026). Our results reveal a similar stress-transfer pattern, with significant increases in ΔCFS along the northern section of the Sagaing rupture. Notably, the largest cumulative stress loading occurs on the northern SF near ~25° N, consistent with a recently published study identifying this ~100 km long segment as the most strongly loaded section of the fault and a persistent seismic gap since the 1839 earthquake (He *et al.*, 2026).

Magnitude and coseismic rupture of the present earthquake

Based on the six-model comparison, models with larger magnitudes consistently provide better fits to far-field GNSS observations (Fig. 4). The Wei and Xu models have M_w values of 7.862 and 7.857, respectively, whereas the Zhang, Li, and Antoine models cluster around $M_w \sim 7.8$. In contrast, the USGS model has a smaller magnitude (M_w 7.70) and yields substantially poorer fits. Taken together, the near-field InSAR-based slip models, seismologically constrained rupture models, and our far-field GNSS fitting results suggest that the effective seismic moment of this event is more consistent with $M_w \gtrsim 7.8$ than with M_w 7.7.

Regarding surface rupture length, five of the six models exceed 500 km, with the Xu model reaching ~588 km. Even the shortest rupture model of Professor Zhang reaches ~370 km (Fig. 4h). These rupture lengths are significantly longer than those predicted by empirical scaling relationships for an M_w 7.7 earthquake (e.g., Wells and Coppersmith, 1994; Thingbaijam *et al.*, 2017). Historical earthquakes with magnitudes ≥ M_w 7.8 typically exhibit much shorter surface ruptures, such as the 2008 M_w 7.9 Wenchuan earthquake

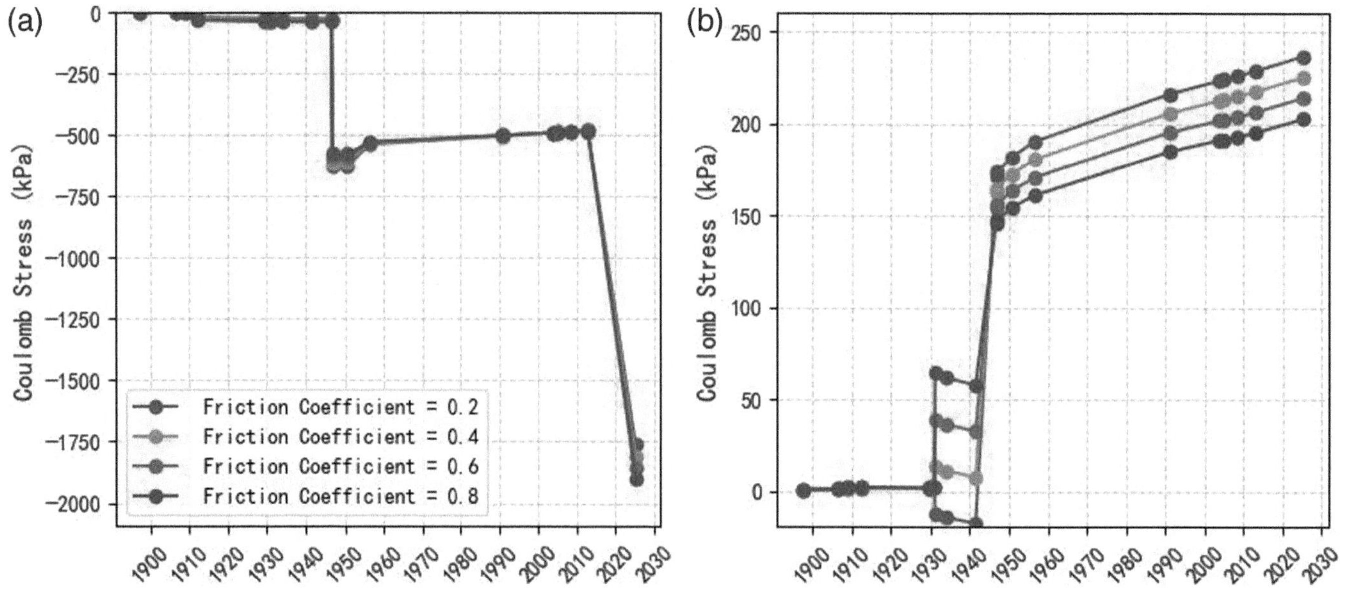

Figure 8. Influence of effective friction coefficients on the stability of Coulomb stress evolution results at different receiving points along the Sagaing fault. (a) Effects of varying effective friction coefficients on the Coulomb stress evolution at the epicenter of the 2025 M_w 7.7 Sagaing earthquake. (b) Influence of different effective friction coefficients on the Coulomb stress evolution in the northern Coulomb stress loading zone of the Sagaing fault (at a depth of 10 km). The red curve represents cumulative stress evolution with an effective friction coefficient of 0.8; the green curve corresponds to 0.6; the orange curve to 0.4; and the blue curve to 0.2. The color version of this figure is available only in the electronic edition.

(~280 km; Xu *et al.*, 2009) and the 2001 M_w 8.1 Kunlun earthquake (~420 km; Lin *et al.*, 2002; Xu *et al.*, 2002). These comparisons highlight the anomalously large rupture length of the 2025 Mandalay earthquake relative to its seismic moment.

Regarding the coseismic slip field and rupture length of the 2025 M_w 7.7 Mandalay earthquake, the traditional empirical scaling laws significantly overestimate the event parameters (Antoine *et al.*, 2025). According to global empirical scaling relationships, a strike-slip rupture approximately 500 km in length would typically correspond to an $M_w \sim 8.2$ earthquake with an average slip of about 9 m (Wells and Coppersmith, 1994; Thingbaijam *et al.*, 2017). However, the inferred average slip for this event is only 3.3–3.8 m, and the released seismic moment is substantially lower than predicted by these empirical relations. This discrepancy indicates that classical scaling laws are not directly applicable to ruptures characterized by an exceptionally long and narrow geometry (i.e., a very high length-to-width ratio), rather than implying an underestimation of the earthquake magnitude. Such behavior is consistent with ruptures occurring on structurally mature strike-slip faults (Wesnousky, 2008).

The fundamental reason for this unusually long coseismic rupture is likely related to the structural maturity of the SF zone (Antoine *et al.*, 2025; Xu *et al.*, 2025). Over the past approximately 13 million years, the fault has accumulated about 460 km of total displacement. The long-term strike-slip motion has acted like a "geological grinder," smoothing, straightening, and strengthening the fault, effectively removing most geometric barriers (such as bends or stepovers) that could impede rupture propagation (Manighetti *et al.*, 2007). This simple and robust fault geometry not only allowed the rupture to cascade unimpeded over 465 km, but also created favorable energy conditions that enabled sustained supershear rupture, ultimately producing the longest strike-slip surface rupture ever recorded within a continental interior (Bouchon *et al.*, 2010; Xu *et al.*, 2025).

In summary, the 2025 Mandalay earthquake represents an end-member rupture style involving an exceptionally long, low-slip rupture on a structurally mature strike-slip fault. Far-field GNSS observations consistently favor larger-magnitude models, highlighting the limitations of classical scaling laws and rupture models assuming typical geometries, and suggesting that the effective seismic moment of this event is more consistent with $M_w \gtrsim 7.8$ than with M_w 7.7.

Result stability

The effective friction coefficient (μ) is a key parameter in calculating variations in ΔCFS. As indicated in equation (1), μ directly influences the estimation of normal stress. Figure 8 illustrates that different choices of μ can lead to variations of less than 10% in the resulting ΔCFS on the receiver fault planes. Previous research has shown that μ may vary with fault type: reverse faults typically exhibit higher values around 0.8, normal faults around 0.6, and strike-slip faults generally between 0.2 and 0.4 (Xiong *et al.*, 2010). Since most faults in the study area display strike-slip characteristics, a friction coefficient within the range of 0.2–0.4 is more suitable. In general, a value of $\mu = 0.4$ is widely adopted in ΔCFS calculations (Parsons *et al.*, 1999). Sensitivity tests in previous studies indicate that changing μ from 0.2–0.4 to 0.4–0.6 results in stress variations of roughly 10%, suggesting that the influence of μ is relatively minor (Xiong *et al.*, 2017). Therefore, a friction coefficient of 0.4 is adopted in this study.

Figure 8 further illustrates that, at the epicenter of the 2025 M_w 7.7 Sagaing earthquake, the cumulative Coulomb stress before the event was approximately −1750 kPa, indicating a significant stress drop. This large unloading may be due to a high slip rate and shallow locking depth near the epicenter, suggesting that the interseismic Coulomb stress loading, unaccounted for here, could have been substantial enough to trigger a major earthquake when combined (Tin *et al.*, 2022).

In contrast, the cumulative Coulomb stress in the northern segment of the SF has already exceeded 200 kPa even without considering interseismic loading, which is well above the commonly recognized threshold for seismic triggering. When the high interseismic loading associated with the SF's rapid strike-slip rate is included, it further confirms that the northern segment of the fault possesses a very high potential for future earthquake occurrence.

Within the timescale considered in this study (approximately 100 yr), variations in the selected viscosity parameters exert only a minor influence on the spatial pattern of ΔCFS and on the triggering relationships among the earthquake sequence. This finding is consistent with the results of Verdecchia and Carena (2015) in the California–Nevada border region, where they also observed that changes in viscosity do not significantly alter the spatial characteristics of ΔCFS or the interaction patterns between events. The viscoelastic model adopted here follows Xiong *et al.* (2017), in which the effects of viscosity parameters were systematically examined and evaluated.

Conclusion

This study systematically analyses the coseismic and postseismic stress changes associated with the 2025 M_w 7.7 Sagaing earthquake, integrated with the stress evolution of the historical earthquake sequence along the SF, leading to the following key conclusions:

1. Significant ΔCFS: The 2025 Myanmar earthquake induced notable Coulomb stress increases along the northern and southern segments of the SF, as well as on several adjacent faults. In some areas, ΔCFS exceeded 10 kPa, indicating an elevated probability of future seismic events. Approximately 50 yr postearthquake, continued viscoelastic relaxation has further enhanced cumulative Coulomb stress near the China–Myanmar border region, particularly along the Loi Kwi fault, Kyaukme fault, southern segment of the Nantinghe fault, and the Lancang fault, approaching the 10 kPa hazard threshold. Concurrently, the midsection of the Red River fault, Wuliangshan fault, eastern segment of the Wanding fault, Jinghong fault, and Menglian fault exhibit persistent stress accumulation at the scale of several kilopascals.
2. Unusual rupture characteristics: The 2025 Myanmar earthquake produced an exceptionally long coseismic rupture of ~500 km, far exceeding predictions from traditional empirical scaling laws for an M_w 7.7 strike-slip event. This represents an end-member rupture style, characterized by a long, narrow rupture geometry with relatively low average slip on a structurally mature strike-slip fault. The prolonged slip history of the SF likely smoothed geometric barriers, facilitating long-distance, largely unimpeded rupture propagation. Comparisons among multiple coseismic slip models show that larger-magnitude models systematically provide better fits to far-field GNSS observations, whereas smaller magnitude models fail to reproduce the observed deformation. Together with near-field InSAR constraints and the anomalously large rupture length, these results underscore the limitations of applying classical scaling laws and rupture models assuming typical geometries to structurally mature fault systems.
3. High seismic potential in the northern segment: The northern segment of the SF (approximately 24° N–25° N) has historically lacked major earthquakes, representing a surface rupture gap and an area of ongoing Coulomb stress accumulation. This segment possesses the potential to generate earthquakes of $M_w \sim 7.3$–7.7 and thus warrants focused monitoring and hazard assessment.

In summary, the SF and its surrounding region continue to face high seismic risk. Enhanced geophysical and geodetic monitoring, combined with ongoing studies of fault behavior, is crucial for improving the accuracy of seismic hazard assessments and mitigating risk in Myanmar's densely populated corridor.

Data and Resources

The catalog of modern earthquakes was obtained from China Earthquake Networks Center (http://data.earthquake.cn/), the Global Centroid Moment Tensor Project (Global CMT, https://www.globalcmt.org/), the International Seismological Centre (Online Bulletin, doi: 10.31905/D808B830), and U.S. Geological Survey (https://earthquake.usgs.gov/ and https://www.usgs.gov/). Active faults within the region are from Styron and Pagani (2020) and Wu *et al.* (2024). The focal mechanism solutions were obtained from the Global CMT. Some plots were generated using the Generic Mapping Tools version 6.4.0 (Wessel *et al.*, 2013). The inverted coseismic slip models are available at https://pku-geophysics-source.group/htmls/20250328062056Myanmar.html. All websites were last accessed in April 2026.

Declaration of Competing Interests

The authors acknowledge that there are no conflicts of interest recorded.

Acknowledgments

This work is financially supported by the Basic Scientific Research Fund of the Institute of Earthquake Forecasting, China Earthquake

Administration (Grant Numbers CEAIEF202302013, CEAIEF20260206, CEAIEF20220404, and CEAIEF20240201), the National Key R&D Program of China (2019YFE0108900), and the National Natural Science Foundation of China (42374009, 41874024, and 42304008).

References

Aki, K., and P. G. Richards (2002). *Quantitative Seismology*, Second Edition, University Science Books, Mill Valley, California.

Antoine, S. L., R. Shrestha, C. Milliner, K. Im, C. Rollins, K. Wang, K. Chen, and J.-P. Avouac (2025). The 2025 M_w 7.7 Mandalay, Myanmar, earthquake reveals a complex earthquake cycle with clustering and variable segmentation on the Sagaing fault, *Proc. Natl. Acad. Sci. Unit. States Am.* **122,** no. 33, 2017, doi: 10.1073/pnas.2514378122.

Banerjee, P., F. Pollitz, B. Nagarajan, and R. Bürgmann (2007). Coseismic slip distributions of the 26 December 2004 Sumatra-Andaman and 28 March 2005 Nias earthquakes from GPS static offsets, *Bull. Seismol. Soc. Am.* **97**, no. 1A, 86–102, doi: 10.1785/0120050609.

Bilham, R., and P. England (2001). Plateau "pop-up" in the great 1897 Assam earthquake, *Nature* **410**, no. 6830, 806–809, doi: 10.1038/35071057.

Bouchon, M., H. Karabulut, M. P. Bouin, J. Schmittbuhl, M. Vallée, R. Archuleta, S. Das, F. Renard, and D. Marsan (2010). Faulting characteristics of supershear earthquakes, *Tectonophysics* **493,** nos. 3/4, 244–253, doi: 10.1016/j.tecto.2010.06.011.

Chen, W., and P. Molnar (1977). Seismic moments of major earthquakes and the average rate of slip in central Asia, *J. Geophys. Res.* **82,** no. 20, 2945–2969, doi: 10.1029/JB082i020p02945.

Chlieh, M., J.-P. Avouac, V. Hjorleifsdottir, T.-R. A. Song, C. Ji, K. Sieh, A. Sladen, H. Hebert, L. Prawirodirdjo, Y. Bock, *et al.* (2007). Coseismic slip and afterslip of the great Mw 9.15 Sumatra-Andaman earthquake of 2004, *Bull. Seismol. Soc. Am.* **97**, no. 1A, 152–173, doi: 10.1785/0120050631.

Clark, M. K., J. W. M. Bush, and L. H. Royden (2005). Dynamic topography produced by lower crustal flow against rheological strength heterogeneities bordering the Tibetan plateau, *Geophys. J. Int.* **162,** no. 2, 575–590, doi: 10.1111/j.1365-246X.2005.02580.x.

Copley, A. (2008). Kinematics and dynamics of the southeastern margin of the Tibetan plateau, *Geophys. J. Int.* **174,** no. 3, 1081–1100, doi: 10.1111/j.1365-246X.2008.03853.x.

Coudurier-Curveur, A., P. Tapponnier, E. Okal, J. Van der Woerd, E. Kali, S. Choudhury, S. Baruah, M. Etchebes, and Ç. Karakaş (2020). A composite rupture model for the great 1950 Assam earthquake across the cusp of the East Himalayan Syntaxis, *Earth Planet. Sci. Lett.* **531**, 1–13, doi: 10.1016/j.epsl.2019.115928.

Cruz, A., M. Ghasemi, S. Karimzadeh, S. Karimzadeh, A. Askan, M. Matsuoka, and P.B. Lourenço (2025). 28 March 2025 Myanmar earthquake: Strong ground motions, macroseismic intensity, liquefaction, and ALOS-2 ScanSAR remote sensing damage observations, *Seismol. Res. Lett.*, doi: 10.1785/0220250258.

Curray, J. R. (2005). Tectonics and history of the Andaman Sea region, *J. Asian Earth Sci.* **25,** no. 1, 187–232, doi: 10.1016/j.jseaes.2004.09.001.

DeMets, C., R. G. Gordon, and D. F. Argus (2010). Geologically current plate motions, *Geophys. J. Int.* **181,** no. 1, 1–80, doi: 10.1111/j.1365-246X.2009.04491.x.

Engdahl, E. R., and A. Villaseñor (2002). Global Seismicity: 1900^1999, *Int. Handb. Earthq. Eng. Seismol.* 81A, 665–690.

England, P., and R. Bilham (2015). The Shillong Plateau and the great 1897 Assam earthquake, *Tectonics* **34**, no. 9, 1792–1812, doi: 10.1002/2015TC003902.

Freed, A. M. (2005). Earthquake triggering by static, dynamic, and postseismic stress transfer, *Annu. Rev. Earth Planet. Sci.* **33,** 335–367, doi: 10.1146/annurev.earth.33.092203.122505.

He, L., R. Salman, B. Marfito, G. Feng, H. Jiang, W. Wang, Z. Xiong, K. Sun, Y. Wang, and S. H. Yun (2026). Coulomb pre-stress changes modulate coseismic rupture kinematics of the 2025 M_w 7.7 Myanmar earthquake revealed by space geodesy, *Geophys. Res. Lett.* **53,** no. 3, doi: 10.1029/2025GL120587.

Hoechner, A., A. Y. Babeyko, and S. V. Sobolev (2008). Enhanced GPS inversion technique applied to the 2004 Sumatra earthquake and tsunami, *Geophys. Res. Lett.* **35**, no. 8, 10–14, doi: 10.1029/2007GL033133.

Holt, W. E., J. F. Ni, T. C. Wallace, and A. J. Haines (1991). The active tectonics of the eastern Himalayan syntaxis and surrounding regions, *J. Geophys. Res. Solid Earth* **96,** no. B9, 14,595–14,632, doi: 10.1029/91JB01021.

Hu, Q., H. Liang, H. Li, X. Shan, and G. Zhang (2025). Aftershock spatiotemporal activity and coseismic slip model of the 2022 M_w 6.7 Luding earthquake: Fault geometry structures and complex rupture characteristics, *Remote Sens.* **17,** no. 1, doi: 10.3390/rs17010070.

Hurukawa, N., and P. M. Maung (2011). Two seismic gaps on the Sagaing fault, Myanmar, derived from relocation of historical earthquakes since 1918, *Geophys. Res. Lett.* **38,** no. 1, 1–5, doi: 10.1029/2010GL046099.

Jaeger, J. C., N. G. Cook, and R. Zimmerman (2007). *Fundamentals of Rock Mechanics*, Blackwell.

King, G. C. P., R. S. Stein, and J. Lin (1994). Static stress changes and the triggering of earthquakes, *Bull. Seismol. Soc. Am.* **84,** no. 3, 935–953, doi: 10.1016/0148-9062(95)94484-2.

Kundu, B., and V. K. Gahalaut (2012). Earthquake occurrence processes in the Indo-Burmese wedge and Sagaing fault region, *Tectonophysics* **524–525,** 135–146, doi: 10.1016/j.tecto.2011.12.031.

Laske, G., G. Masters, Z. Ma, and M. E. Pasyanos (2013). Update on CRUST1.0 - A 1-degree global model of Earth's crust.

Leloup, P. H., P. Tapponnier, R. Lacassin, and M. P. Searle (2007). Discussion on the role of the Red River shear zone, Yunnan and Vietnam, in the continental extrusion of SE Asia, *J. Geol. Soc. Lond.* **164**, no. 6, 1253–1260, doi: 10.1144/0016-76492007-065.

Li, Y., M. Liu, Y. Li, and L. Chen (2019). Active crustal deformation in southeastern Tibetan plateau: The kinematics and dynamics, *Earth Planet. Sci. Lett.* **523,** doi: 10.1016/j.epsl.2019.07.010.

Li, Y., J. Nocquet, X. Shan, and X. Song (2021). Geodetic observations of shallow creep on the Laohushan-Haiyuan fault, northeastern Tibet, *J. Geophys. Res. Solid Earth* **126,** no. 6, 1–18, doi: 10.1029/2020JB021576.

Li, Y., X. Shan, C. Li, C. Huang, X. Wang, X. Xu, and H. Xiong (2025). Sustained supershear rupture during the 2025 Mandalay, Myanmar earthquake, *Commun. Earth Environ.* **6,** no. 1, 1030, doi: 10.1038/s43247-025-02927-5.

Li, Y., Z. Shao, F. Shi, and L. Chen (2020). Stress evolution on active faults in the southwestern Yunnan region, southeastern Tibetan plateau, and implications for seismic hazard, *J. Asian Earth Sci.* **200,** no. 1, 104470, doi: 10.1016/j.jseaes.2020.104470.

Li, Y., C. Yang, X. Hu, J. Yuan, R. Yao, and H. Li (2026). Coulomb stress transfer from the 2025 M_W 7.7 Myanmar earthquake to active faults in southwestern Yunnan, China: Implications for seismic hazard, *Earthq. Res. Adv.* **6,** no. 1, 100397, doi: 10.1016/j.eqrea.2025.100397.

Lin, A., B. Fu, J. Guo, Q. Zeng, G. Dang, W. He, and Y. Zhao (2002). Co-seismic strike-slip and rupture length produced by the 2001 Ms 8.1 Central Kunlun earthquake, *Science* **296,** no. 5575, 2015–2017, doi: 10.1126/science.1070879.

Lindsey, E. O., Y. Wang, L. T. Aung, J. H. Chong, Q. Qiu, R. Mallick, L. Feng, P. S. Aung, T. Z. H. Tin, S. M. Min, *et al.* (2023). Active subduction and strain partitioning in western Myanmar revealed by a dense survey GNSS network, *Earth Planet. Sci. Lett.* **622,** 118384, doi: 10.1016/j.epsl.2023.118384.

Mai, P. M., and K. K. S. Thingbaijam (2014). SRCMOD: An online database of finite-fault rupture models, *Seismol. Res. Lett.* **85,** no. 6, 1348–1357, doi: 10.1785/0220140077.

Manighetti, I., M. Campillo, S. Bouley, and F. Cotton (2007). Earthquake scaling, fault segmentation, and structural maturity, *Earth Planet. Sci. Lett.* **253,** nos. 3/4, 429–438, doi: 10.1016/j.epsl.2006.11.004.

Maurin, T., F. Masson, C. Rangin, U. T. Min, and P. Collard (2010). First global positioning system results in northern Myanmar: Constant and localized slip rate along the Sagaing fault, *Geology* **38,** no. 7, 591–594, doi: 10.1130/G30872.1.

Mitchell, A. H. G. (1993). Cretaceous-Cenozoic tectonic events in the western Myanmar (Burma)- Assam region, *J. Geol. Soc.* **150,** no. 6, 1089–1102, doi: 10.1144/gsjgs.150.6.1089.

Okal, E. A. (2019). The Large Andaman Islands Earthquake of 26 June 1941: Why No Significant Tsunami?, *Pure Appl. Geophys.* **176,** no. 7, 2869–2886, doi: 10.1007/s00024-018-2082-8.

Pacheco, J. F., and L. R. Sykes (1992). Seismic moment catalog of large shallow earthquakes, 1900 to 1989, *Bull. Seismol. Soc. Am.* **82,** no. 3, 1306–1349, doi: 10.1785/BSSA0820031306.

Parsons, T., R. S. Stein, R. W. Simpson, and P. A. Reasenberg (1999). Stress sensitivity of fault seismicity: A comparison between limited-offset oblique and major strike-slip faults, *J. Geophys. Res. Solid Earth* **104,** no. B9, 20183–20202, doi: 10.1029/1999jb900056.

Reasenberg, P. A., and R. W. Simpson (1992). Response of regional seismicity to the static stress change produced by the Loma Prieta earthquake, *Science* **255,** no. 5052, 1687–1690, doi: 10.1126/science.255.5052.1687.

Riesner, M., L. Bollinger, M. Rizza, Y. Klinger, Ç. Karakaş, S. N. Sapkota, C. Shah, C. Guérin, and P. Tapponnier (2023). Surface rupture and landscape response in the middle of the great Mw 8.3 1934 earthquake mesoseismal area: Khutti Khola site, *Sci. Rep.* **13,** no. 1, 1–13, doi: 10.1038/s41598-023-30697-7.

Sapkota, S. N., L. Bollinger, Y. Klinger, P. Tapponnier, Y. Gaudemer, and D. Tiwari (2013). Primary surface ruptures of the great Himalayan earthquakes in 1934 and 1255, *Nat. Geosci.* **6,** no. 1, 71–76, doi: 10.1038/ngeo1669.

Savage, J. C., and W. H. Prescott (1978). Asthenosphere readjustment and the earthquake cycle, *J. Geophys. Res. Solid Earth* **83,** no. B7, 3369–3376, doi: 10.1029/jb083ib07p03369.

Singh, D. D., and H. K. Gupta (1980). Source dynamics of two great earthquakes of the Indian subcontinent: The Bihar-Nepal earthquake of January 15, 1934 and the Quetta earthquake of May 30, 1935, *Bull. Seismol. Soc. Am.* **70,** no. 3, 757–773, doi: 10.1785/BSSA0700030757.

Shen, T., G. Meng, T. Liu, W. Wu, J. Tang, and C. Wei (2026). Tectonophysics Coulomb stress evolution on the major faults of the Shan plateau and adjacent tectonic regions due to the large earthquakes in the middle and far fields, *Tectonophysics* **926,** no. 63, 231134, doi: 10.1016/j.tecto.2026.231134.

Shen, T., X. Xu, S. Zhou, P. Tapponnier, L. Chen, Y. Li, E. A. Rogozhin, J. Tang, X. Tan, W. Kang, *et al.* (2023). Role of the Ruoergai subblock in tectonic partitioning on the eastern margin of Tibet, *Eng. Geol.* **315,** no. II, 107042, doi: 10.1016/j.enggeo.2023.107042.

Shen, Z., J. Sun, P. Zhang, Y. Wan, M. Wang, R. Bürgmann, Y. Zeng, W. Gan, H. Liao, and Q. Wang (2009). Slip maxima at fault junctions and rupturing of barriers during the 2008 Wenchuan earthquake, *Nat. Geosci.* **2,** no. 10, 718–724, doi: 10.1038/ngeo636.

Shi, X., Y. Wang, K. Sieh, R. Weldon, L. Feng, C. Chan, and J. Liu-Zeng (2018). Fault slip and GPS velocities across the Shan plateau define a curved southwestward crustal motion around the eastern Himalayan syntaxis, *J. Geophys. Res. Solid Earth* **123,** no. 3, 2502–2518, doi: 10.1002/2017JB015206.

Socquet, A., C. Vigny, N. Chamot-Rooke, W. Simons, C. Rangin, and B. Ambrosius (2006). India and Sunda plates motion and deformation along their boundary in Myanmar determined by GPS, *J. Geophys. Res. Solid Earth* **111,** no. 5, 1–11, doi: 10.1029/2005JB003877.

Stein, R. S. (1999). The role of stress transfer in earthquake occurrence, *Nature* **402,** no. 6762, 605–609, doi: 10.1038/45144.

Stein, R. S., A. A. Barka, and J. H. Dieterich (1997). Progressive failure on the North Anatolian fault since 1939 by earthquake stress triggering, *Geophys. J. Int.* 594–604.

Styron, R., and M. Pagani (2020). The GEM Global active faults database, *Earthq. Spectra* **36,** no. 1_suppl, 160–180, doi: 10.1177/8755293020944182.

Tapponnier, P., G. Peltzer, A. Y. Le Dain, R. Armijo, and P. Cobbold (1982). Propagating extrusion tectonics in Asia: New insights from simple experiments with plasticine, *Geology* **10,** no. 12, 611.

Thingbaijam, K. K. S., P. M. Mai, and K. Goda (2017). New empirical earthquake source-scaling laws, *Bull. Seismol. Soc. Am.* **107,** no. 5, 2225–2246, doi: 10.1785/0120170017.

Tin, T. Z. H., T. Nishimura, M. Hashimoto, E. O. Lindsey, L. T. Aung, S. M. Min, and M. Thant (2022). Present-day crustal deformation and slip rate along the southern Sagaing fault in Myanmar by GNSS observation, *J. Asian Earth Sci.* 228, no. doi: 10.1016/j.jseaes.2022.105125.

Toda, S., J. Lin, M. Meghraoui, and R. S. Stein (2008). 12 May 2008 M = 7.9 Wenchuan, China, earthquake calculated to increase failure stress and seismicity rate on three major fault systems, *Geophys. Res. Lett.* **35,** no. 17, 1–6, doi: 10.1029/2008GL034903.

Tsutsumi, H., and T. Sato (2009). Tectonic geomorphology of the southernmost Sagaing fault and surface rupture associated with the May 1930 Pegu (Bago) earthquake, Myanmar, *Bull. Seismol. Soc. Am.*, **99,** no. 4, 2155–2168, doi: 10.1785/0120080113.

Verdecchia, A., and S. Carena (2015). One hundred and fifty years of Coulomb stress history along the California-Nevada border, USA, *Tectonics* **34,** no. 2, 213–231, doi: 10.1002/2014TC003746.

Vigny, C., A. Socquet, C. Rangin, N. Chamot-Rooke, M. Pubellier, M. Bouin, G. Bertrand, and M. Becker (2003). Present-day crustal deformation around Sagaing fault, Myanmar, *J. Geophys. Res. Solid Earth* **108,** no. B11, doi: 10.1029/2002jb001999.

Villegas-Lanza, J. C., J. M. Nocquet, F. Rolandone, M. Vallee, H. Tavera, F. Bondoux, T. Tran, X. Martin, and M. Chlieh (2016). A mixed seismic-aseismic stress release episode in the Andean subduction zone, *Nature Geosci.* **9,** no. 2, 150–154, doi: 10.1038/ngeo2620.

Wang, R., F. Lorenzo-Martín, and F. Roth (2006). PSGRN/PSCMP - A new code for calculating co- and post-seismic deformation, geoid and gravity changes based on the viscoelastic-gravitational dislocation theory, *Comput. Geosci.* **32,** no. 4, 527–541, doi: 10.1016/j.cageo.2005.08.006.

Wang, Y., K. Sieh, S. T. Tun, K. Lai, and T. Myint (2014). Active tectonics and earthquake potential of the Myanmar region, *J. Geophys. Res. Solid Earth* **119,** no. 4, 3767–3822, doi: 10.1002/2013JB010762.

Wei, S., X. Wang, C. Li, H. Zeng, Z. Ma, Q. Shi, H. Chen, Y. Huang, M. Lyu, J. Liao, *et al.* (2025). Supershear rupture sustained through a thick fault zone in the 2025 M_w 7.8 Mandalay earthquake, *Science* **390,** no. 6772, 468–475, doi: 10.1126/science.adz2101.

Wells, D. L., and K. J. Coppersmith (1994). New empirical relationships among magnitude, rupture length, rupture width, rupture area, and surface displacement, *Bull. Seismol. Soc. Am.* **84,** no. 4, 974–1002.

Wesnousky, S. G. (2008). Displacement and geometrical characteristics of earthquake surface ruptures: Issues and implications for seismic-hazard analysis and the process of earthquake rupture, *Bull. Seismol. Soc. Am.* **98,** no. 4, 1609–1632, doi: 10.1785/0120070111.

Wessel, P., W. Smith, R. Scharroo, J. Luis, and F. Wobbe (2013). Generic mapping tools: Improved version released, *Eos Trans. AGU* **94,** no. 45, 409–410, doi: 10.1029/95EO00198.

Wu, X., X. Xu, G. Yu, J. Ren, X. Yang, G. Chen, C. Xu, K. Du, X. Huang, H. Yang, *et al.* (2024). The China Active Faults Database (CAFD) and its web system, *Earth Syst. Sci. Data* **16,** no. 7, 3391–3417, doi: 10.5194/essd-16-3391-2024.

Xiong, X., B. Shan, Y. Zheng, and R. Wang (2010). Stress transfer and its implication for earthquake hazard on the Kunlun fault, Tibet, *Tectonophysics* **482,** nos. 1/4, 216–225, doi: 10.1016/j.tecto.2009.07.020.

Xiong, X., B. Shan, Y. M. Zhou, S. J. Wei, Y. D. Li, R. J. Wang, and Y. Zheng (2017). Coulomb stress transfer and accumulation on the Sagaing fault, Myanmar, over the past 110 years and its implications for seismic hazard, *Geophys. Res. Lett.* **44,** no. 10, 4781–4789, doi: 10.1002/2017GL072770.

Xu, L., L. Meng, Z. Yunjun, Y. Yang, Y. Wang, C. Hu, H. Weng, W. Xu, E. Su, and C. Ji (2025). Bimaterial effect and favorable energy ratio enabled supershear rupture in the 2025 Mandalay earthquake, *Science* **390,** no. 6772, 476–481, doi: 10.1126/science.ady6100.

Xu, X., W. Chen, W. Ma, G. Yu, and G. Chen (2002). Surface rupture of the kunlunshan earthquake (M_s 8.1), northern Tibetan plateau, China, *Seismol. Res. Lett.* **73,** no. 6, 884–892, doi: 10.1785/gssrl.73.6.884.

Xu, X., W. Kang, T. Wang, X. Zhang, Y. Liu, Y. Zhang, J. Zhao, K. Li, Q. Wang, J. Cheng, *et al.* (2025). Author correction: The M_w 7.7 Myanmar earthquake: A continental longest surface-rupturing supershear cascading event, *npj Nat. Hazards* **2,** no. 1, 1–12, doi: 10.1038/s44304-025-00140-0.

Xu, X., X. Wen, G. Yu, G. Chen, Y. Klinger, J. Hubbard, and J. Shaw (2009). Coseismic reverse- and oblique-slip surface faulting generated by the 2008 M_w 7.9 Wenchuan earthquake, China, *Geology* **37,** no. 6, 515–518, doi: 10.1130/G25462A.1.

Zhang, G., S. Wang, L. Li, X. Zhang, and H. Ma (2002). Focal depth research of earthquakes in Mainland China: Implication for tectonics, *Chin. Sci. Bull.* **47,** no. 12, 969–974, doi: 10.1007/BF02907562.

Manuscript received 4 November 2025
Published online 27 April 2026

Surface Rupture of the 2025 M_w 7.7 Mandalay, Myanmar, Earthquake: Insights from Field and Optical Remote Sensing Observations

Soe Min[1], Thura Aung[2], Hiroyuki Tsutsumi[3], Wanna Htun[2], Chit Thet Mon[4], Lin Thu Aung[5], Kyaw Zin Win[2], Saw Myat Min[6], Ei Mhone Nathar Myo[6], Khaing Nyein Htay[2], Saw Ngwe Khaing[7], Myo Thant[8,9], Soe Thura Tun[2], and Yu Wang[*6]

Abstract

We document coseismic right-lateral offsets of the 2025 M_w 7.7 Mandalay earthquake in Myanmar using post-quake field surveys and optical remote sensing data. Both results confirm that the 2025 Mandalay earthquake generated a surface rupture exceeding 470 km in length, extending from the central to southern section of the Sagaing fault. Our investigation confirmed the presence of a continuous, narrow rupture, with coseismic slip peaking at ~4.6 m across the rupture, and ~6.2 m from optical satellite imagery in the northern Sagaing Hills. Although the slip distribution measured in the field shows a pattern similar to that derived from optical satellite data, comparison of field measurements against remote sensing observations reveals a systematic ~1 m deficit along most parts of the rupture. This difference suggests that a substantial portion of displacement was accommodated by distributed deformation within unconsolidated Quaternary alluvial deposits in the very shallow part of the fault. This interpretation is further supported by a highly localized offset along the fault section that cuts through metamorphic rocks with minimal overlying sediments in the Sagaing Hills. Since the southernmost segment of the Sagaing fault, which last ruptured in May 1930, is the principal remaining unruptured section, we highlight the seismic hazard potential for densely populated southern Myanmar, necessitating urgent paleoseismological work and seismic risk assessment.

Cite this article as Min, S., T. Aung, H. Tsutsumi, W. Htun, C. T. Mon, L. Thu Aung, K. Z. Win, S. M. Min, E. M. N. Myo, K. N. Htay, *et al.* (2026). Surface Rupture of the 2025 M_w 7.7 Mandalay, Myanmar, Earthquake: Insights from Field and Optical Remote Sensing Observations, *Seismol. Res. Lett.* **97**, 1739–1753, doi: 10.1785/0220250443.

Supplemental Material

Introduction

On 28 March 2025, an M_w 7.7 earthquake struck central Myanmar, causing significant damage and intense ground shaking across mainland Southeast Asia. The mainshock's epicenter was located approximately 30 km northwest of Mandalay, with many aftershocks clustered near Mandalay and Naypyitaw (U.S. Geological Survey [USGS], 2025) (Fig. 1a,b). The mainshock, which is among the largest strike-slip events recorded in Mainland Southeast Asia since the beginning of the twentieth century (Wang *et al.*, 2014), was caused by the rupture of the central and southern part of the plate-boundary Sagaing fault. The Sagaing fault is the transform boundary between the Burma and Sunda plates, accommodating 20–24 mm/yr dextral motion (Fig. 1a) (Vigny *et al.*, 2003; Socquet *et al.*, 2006; Maurin *et al.*, 2010; Tha Zin Htet *et al.*, 2022; Lindsey *et al.*, 2023).

Preliminary remote sensing investigations suggest a remarkable ~470-km-long surface rupture (e.g., Antoine *et al.*, 2025; Hirano *et al.*, 2025; Li *et al.*, 2025; Lindsey *et al.*, 2025; Melgar *et al.*, 2025; Reitman *et al.*, 2025, 2026; Wei *et al.*, 2025; Xu *et al.*, 2025;). The rupture extended beyond a well-known seismic gap on the central section of the Sagaing fault, the Meiktila segment, which had not experienced a major earthquake since 1839 (Fig. 1a) (Hurukawa and Maung, 2011;

1. Department of Geology, Banmaw University, Myanmar; 2. Myanmar Earthquake Committee, Myanmar, https://orcid.org/0000-0002-7207-1911 (STT);
3. Department of Environmental Systems Science, Doshisha University, Japan; 4. Key Laboratory of Planetary Science and Frontier Technology, Institute of Geology and Geophysics, Chinese Academy of Sciences, China; 5. Earth Observatory of Singapore, Nanyang Technological University, Singapore, https://orcid.org/0000-0003-4022-1791 (LTA); 6. Department of Geosciences, National Taiwan University, Taiwan, https://orcid.org/0000-0001-6798-2721 (YW); 7. Department of Geology, Hinthada University, Myanmar, https://orcid.org/0009-0009-5116-2556 (SNK);
8. Myanmar Institute of Earth and Planetary Sciences, Myanmar, https://orcid.org/0000-0002-5484-0609 (MT); 9. Department of Geology, University of Yangon, Myanmar

*Corresponding author: wangyu79@ntu.edu.tw

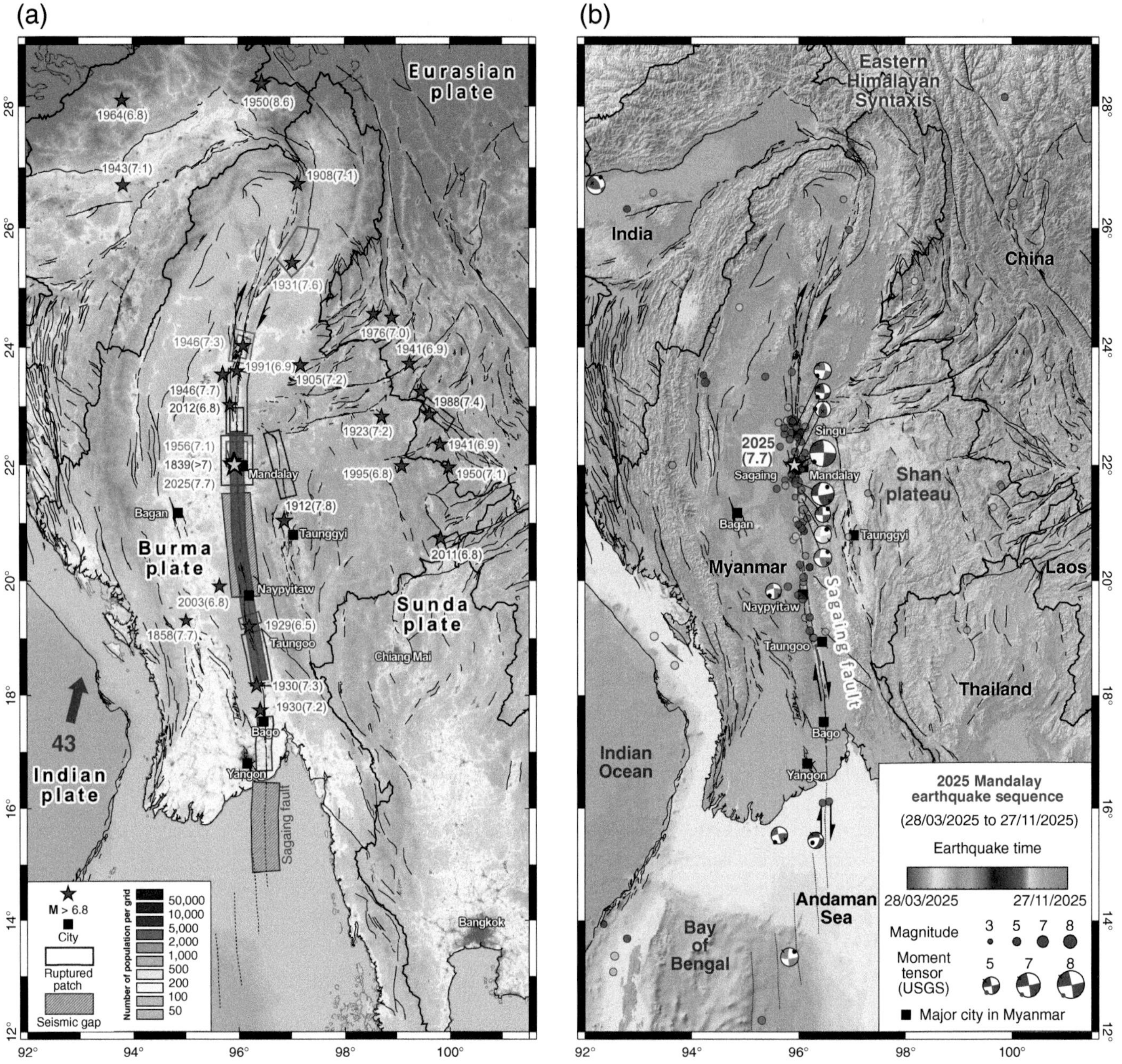

Figure 1. Historical earthquakes and the 2025 Mandalay earthquake sequence along the Sagaing fault. (a) Significant earthquakes and their rupture extents in Myanmar since the beginning of the twentieth century. The plate-boundary Sagaing fault, located between the Sunda and Burma plates, is a major seismogenic source in Southeast Asia. The fault has generated a series of magnitude 7+ earthquakes since the beginning of the twentieth century and is responsible for the 2025 Mandalay earthquake in central Myanmar. Previous analysis indicated two major seismic gaps along the fault: one in central Myanmar, between Mandalay and Naypyitaw, and the other south of Bago, offshore southern Myanmar. The purple-colored boxes indicate seismic gaps defined from the historical earthquake record; other colored boxes represent the approximate rupture extents associated with historical earthquakes. The red stars indicate the epicenters of damaging earthquakes from the global earthquake catalog, and the yellow star marks the epicenter of the 2025 Mandalay earthquake. The solid colored rectangle shows the section ruptured during the 2025 Mandalay earthquake. (b) The earthquake sequence and the surface rupture of the 2025 Mandalay earthquake. Most of the aftershocks occurred near the northern and southern parts of the rupture. Focal mechanisms and earthquake catalog are obtained from the U.S. Geological Survey. The color version of this figure is available only in the electronic edition.

Wang *et al.*, 2014; Tun and Watkinson, 2017). The 2025 Mandalay earthquake (also referred to as the 2025 Sagaing earthquake) caused substantial damage in cities including Mandalay, Sagaing, and Naypyitaw due to both intense ground motion and surface rupture. Its impact extended beyond Myanmar's borders, causing a high-rise building to collapse in Bangkok, Thailand, approximately 1000 km from the earthquake's epicenter (Laosunthara *et al.*, 2025; Ornthammarath *et al.*, 2025). Despite the earthquake's broad impact, much of the earthquake's damage occurred in areas of Myanmar's internal conflict, making comprehensive post-quake field investigations challenging and risky.

Despite these difficulties, several teams of Myanmar geologists conducted postquake field investigations within a few weeks after the earthquake to document coseismic surface rupture and offsets along the Sagaing fault. In this article, we present key findings from these field investigations and supplement them with satellite-based optical remote sensing observations. Insights gained have significant implications for disaster preparedness, not only for Southeast Asia, but also for any region that could be affected by future ruptures on major continental transform faults, such as the San Andreas fault in California and the North Anatolian fault in Türkiye.

Geological Setting

Myanmar occupies the eastern boundary of the Himalayan collision between the Indian and Sunda plates (Le Dain *et al.*, 1984; Tapponnier *et al.*, 1986; Socquet *et al.*, 2006; Racey and Ridd, 2015) (Fig. 1a,b). Ongoing oblique collision between these plates is primarily accommodated by two major plate-boundary faults: the Arakan (Rakhine) megathrust offshore western Myanmar and Bangladesh, and the Sagaing fault near the western margin of the Shan plateau (Fig. 1a) (Socquet *et al.*, 2006; Wang *et al.*, 2013; 2014; Lindsey *et al.*, 2023). The active Sagaing fault is a prominent dextral strike-slip fault that defines the boundary between the Burma and Sunda plates (Maung, 1987; Vigny *et al.*, 2003; Tun and Watkinson, 2017). The fault extends over 1200 km, from the Andaman Sea in the south to the eastern Himalayan Syntax is to the north (Curray, 2005). Modern geodetic analyses suggest the fault accommodates 20–24 mm/yr of right-lateral motion, with a significant interseismic locking at least along its central and southern sections (Vigny *et al.*, 2003; Socquet *et al.*, 2006; Maurin *et al.*, 2010; Tha Zin Htet *et al.*, 2022; Lindsey *et al.*, 2023). Global Navigation Satellite System (GNSS) transects across the Sagaing and Meiktila sections suggest the locking depth varies between 10 and 16 km, and seismicity before the 2025 earthquake indicates the fault is subvertical, dipping slightly eastward in the area north of Sagaing and Mandalay (Mon *et al.*, 2020). Farther south, locking depth reaches at least 10 km (i.e., Bago segment), with its fault plane plausibly dipping westward underneath the Bago-Yoma Range (Fig. 2a) (Tha Zin Htet *et al.*, 2022).

Geologically, the Sagaing fault traverses a diverse range of lithologies, including Quaternary alluvial deposits (i.e., Irrawaddy Formation; Bender *et al.*, 1983; Tun, Wang, *et al.*, 2014) (Fig. 2a). The fault separates Cenozoic sedimentary rocks in the Central Myanmar belt to the west from metamorphic rocks and Paleozoic sedimentary rocks in the Shan plateau to the east (Chhibber and Ramamirtham, 1934; Bender *et al.*, 1983; Tun, Wang, *et al.*, 2014) (Fig. 2a). North of Sagaing, the fault crops out along the western margin of the metamorphic Sagaing Hills, an elongated tectonic ridge west of the Ayeyarwady River, marking the contact between the Mogok metamorphic rocks and post-Miocene sedimentary rocks (Tun and Watkinson, 2017). South of Sagaing, the fault cuts through late-Quaternary alluvial sediments of the Ayeyarwady River and its tributaries, with high groundwater levels close to their modern channels and lowlands. Farther south, the fault forms the eastern flank of the Bago-Yoma Range, which is mainly composed of the Miocene Pegu Formation, characterized by shallow marine sandstone and shale (Fig. 2a). The southernmost part of the Sagaing fault (mainly the Bago segment) cuts across Sitong (Sittang) Delta sediments before reaching the Andaman Sea, offsetting a series of beach ridges close to the coastline (Tsutsumi and Sato, 2009).

Despite complex lithological conditions along the central and southern sections of the Sagaing fault, its trace remains smooth and continuous, with few stepovers and bends. Wang *et al.* (2014) subdivided the fault into several segments based on tectonic geomorphic features, such as fault splays, bends, and potential stepovers, and estimated potential earthquake magnitudes for each segment. The early twentieth century's earthquake record appears to support the idea that these segments could act as independent seismogenic sources; however, the 2025 Mandalay earthquake clearly demonstrated that many of these segment boundaries are not strong enough to always arrest rupture propagation during a major earthquake.

Before the 2025 earthquake, significant earthquakes occurred along the Sagaing fault including the 1930 Bago and Pyu earthquakes (Coggin Brown *et al.*, 1931), the 1931 Kami earthquake (Chhibber and Ramamirtham, 1934), the 1946 Sagaing earthquakes, and smaller 1956, 1991, and 2012 earthquakes (Hurukawa and Maung, 2011; Mon *et al.*, 2020) (Fig. 1a). These events formed two seismic clusters along the fault, leaving a significant seismic gap between Mandalay and Naypyitaw (Hurukawa and Maung, 2011; Wang *et al.*, 2014; Tun and Watkinson, 2017). The last major rupture event in this gap, the Meiktila segment, is believed to have occurred in 1839, devastating cities and towns near Mandalay, causing widespread shaking across mainland Southeast Asia (Oldham, 1883). The magnitude of the 1839 earthquake, however, remains poorly constrained due to its occurrence before modern seismological observations.

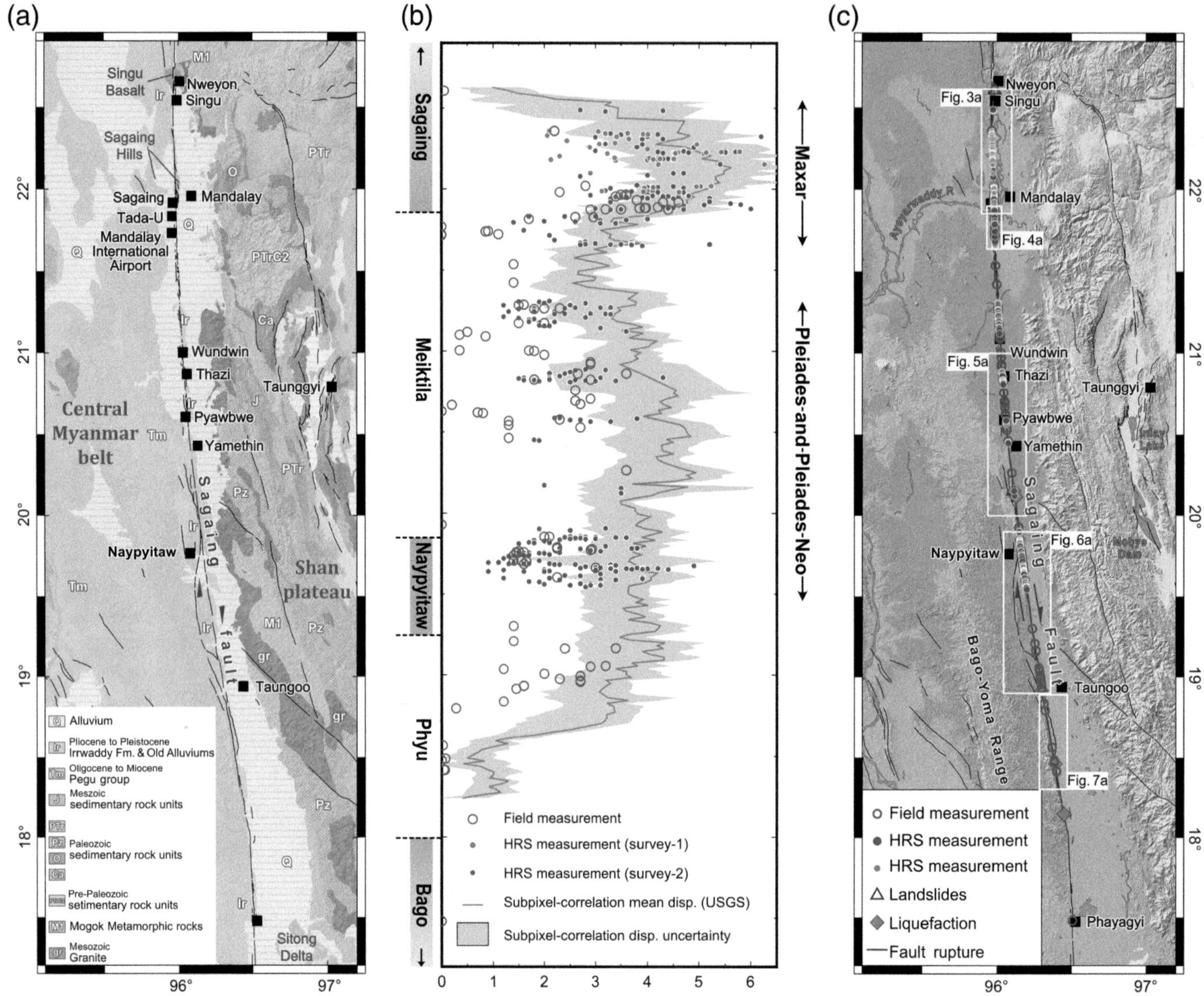

Figure 2. (a) Geological map around the central and southern sections of the Sagaing fault from Tun, Maung, *et al.* (2014). Major cities and towns are marked by black rectangles. (b) Dextral offsets measured from high-resolution optical satellite (HRS) imagery and in the field by this study. The gray band line is the offset estimated from subpixel correlation of the Sentinel-2 data (Reitman *et al.*, 2025, 2026). Segment boundaries from Wang *et al.* (2014) are marked along the left side of the figure. The extent of optical satellite imagery used in this study is marked along the right side of the figure. (c) Field-surveyed locations and HRS observation points along the Sagaing fault. The color version of this figure is available only in the electronic edition.

Postquake investigation

Several teams of Myanmar geologists investigated the surface rupture of the 2025 Mandalay earthquake from 29 March to 23 April 2025, before the onset of the monsoon season. Because of security concerns and ongoing conflicts in Myanmar, the spatial extent of our field investigation was limited to sections accessible by car or motorcycle, and to where the risk is manageable (Fig. 2b,c). We also include social media reports from residents and travelers to enhance the spatial coverage of our data, especially in areas near the northern end of the rupture. In general, outside the areas near Sagaing and Naypyitaw, population density is low along the rupture trace except for several areas along National Highway Number 1 (i.e., the Road to Mandalay), including Wundwin, Thazi, Pyawbwe, Shwedar, and Tada-U between Naypyitaw and Sagaing (Fig. 2a,c). Many of these towns were heavily damaged by the earthquake.

Because of security concerns and limited access to suitable vehicles and survey instruments, most field measurements were made with a compass and tape measures. These measurements were later validated using field photos. The rupture location was recorded using a handheld GNSS or smartphone's GNSS applications, with typical location uncertainty of less than 5 m under open-sky conditions.

We also analyzed high-resolution optical satellite (HRS) imagery to map surface rupture and measure right-lateral offsets (Fig. 2b). Unlike field-based measurements, which provide both vertical and horizontal offsets along the rupture, measurements from HRS imagery provide horizontal offsets without information on their vertical deformation. For the area north of Mandalay International Airport (MDL), we interpreted Maxar's HRS imagery, available on Google Earth Pro, to map the rupture and offset. South of the Mandalay International Airport, we interpreted Airbus's Pleiades (50-cm resolution) and Pleiades Neo (30-cm resolution) imagery to measure the offset along the fault rupture indicated by the Copernicus Sentinel-2's subpixel correlation result (Reitman *et al.*, 2025). Precision of offsets measured from satellite imagery is estimated to be ±0.5 m. The most significant advantage of satellite imagery over field measurements is that we can measure the offset using a longer baseline of once-straight features, thereby including off-fault deformation. We visited more than 100 field locations and obtained over 300 offset measurements from HRS imagery (Fig. 2b,c, Tables S1 and S2). We describe the characteristics of surface rupture during the 2025 Mandalay earthquake from north to south.

Results

Characteristics of the 2025 Mandalay earthquake surface rupture

Surface rupture of the 2025 Mandalay earthquake can be roughly subdivided into five subsections based on their characteristics: (1) Singu to Sagaing City, (2) Ava (Inwa), at the southern bank of the Ayeyarwady (Irrawaddy) River, to southeast of the Mandalay International Airport (MDL), (3) Wundwin to Naypyitaw, (4) Naypyitaw to Taungoo, and (5) from Taungoo to the southern termini of the 2025 surface rupture (Fig. 2c). Except for sections between Ava (Inwa) and the Mandalay International Airport, and south of Taungoo, both field measurements and HRS observations indicate that fault offsets exceeded 3 m along the rupture.

Singu to Sagaing City

The northern termination of the 2025 rupture is located north of Singu, approximately 67 km north of the mainshock epicenter (Fig. 2a). The rupture appeared primarily along the western margin of the Sagaing Hills, transecting the Ayeyarwady River in the north, and extending into the area where the Sagaing fault ruptured during the 2012 Thabeikkyin earthquake (Tun and Watkinson, 2017) (Fig. 3a). Although field investigation is critical in the area near the northern termination of the 2025 surface rupture, the Singu area was under intense conflict, posing significant security concerns. We therefore utilized records sent by local travelers to locate the surface rupture near Singu.

Photos provided by local travelers show clear evidence of surface rupture, including mole tracks and Riedel shears, near Singu (Fig. 3b,c), where the rupture is not clearly visible in HRS imagery (Reitman *et al.*, 2025). North of Singu, local witness accounts suggest that the 2025 rupture overlaps with the southernmost rupture of the 2012 M_w 6.8 Thabeikkyin earthquake (Tun and Watkinson, 2017). Similar to the 2012 surface rupture, the 2025 surface ruptures trend north–south, occurring east of Khuleinn Lake, north of the Kule Village (Fig. 3a). Features associated with the surface rupture include en-échelon Riedel shears and tension cracks, and 0.3 to 1 m wide mole tracks found along the trail (Fig. 3b,c). Villagers also reported several earthquake-induced landslides along the ridge composed of Singu Basalt (Fig. S1, available in the supplemental material to this article). Although no field photos are available to document surface rupture farther north, the 2025 Mandalay earthquake surface rupture may have continued for another few kilometers from the northernmost reported location, into the Singu Basalt area (Fig. 2a).

South of Singu, the 2025 rupture is distinct and easily mapped from HRS imagery on the sandbanks of the Ayeyarwady River (Reitman *et al.*, 2025). The surface rupture can also be mapped in the field along the western margin of the Sagaing Hills south of the Yelemaw. Between Yelemaw and Sagaing, the main rupture trace identified in the field matches the rupture mapped from HRS imagery (Fig. 3a). In Yelemaw Village, photos contributed by local travelers suggest that the rupture offset fences and trails, with an estimated offset of 2.1 and 2.2 m (Fig. 3d, Fig. S2). The reported dextral offset is less than the measurement from HRS imagery (3.1 m; Reitman *et al.*, 2025) (Fig. 2b), suggesting some distributed near-fault deformation occurred across the main rupture at this location. South of the village, the main rupture trace appeared on alluvium, just west of the metamorphic Sagaing Hills. Parallel to the main rupture trace, we also observed secondary en-échelon cracks developed at the base of the Sagaing Hills, including at the trench site described by Melgar *et al.* (2025) (Fig. 3). Although the main trace ruptured through the trench site with clear right-lateral offsets along the previously mapped fault scarp, another secondary trace, mainly en-échelon cracks, developed at the base of the hill without clear offsets. In other places, offsets across these secondary ruptures are also unmeasurable from HRS imagery, suggesting most of the deformation is concentrated on the main fault rupture.

Measurements from field photos and HRS imagery suggest that the amount of dextral offset quickly increased from approximately 2 m in Yelemaw to more than 5 m at the latitude of 22.15° N, where the measurements from HRS are comparable with the ground displacement estimated from Sentinel-2's subpixel correlation result (Reitman *et al.*, 2025). The largest offset we measured from HRS imagery exceeded 6 m along the Sagaing Hills (Fig. 2b), even larger than the ground displacement estimated from the Sentinel-2's subpixel correlation result (Fig. 2b). The rupture formed a narrow deformation zone (i.e., <5 m) along the western flank of the Sagaing Hills and appeared along the west side of the linear valley between Yae Khar Lake and Sagaing (Fig. 3a). Several witness accounts from villagers near Yae Khar Lake suggest that strong ground motion propagated from south to north, followed by surface rupture.

Figure 3. (a) Map of surface rupture between Singu and Sagaing. "M" marks the trench site location (Melgar *et al.*, 2025). (b,c) Surface rupture and mole track found in the area north of Singu, with ~0.5 m dextral offset estimated from the opening of the ground crack. (d) Offset fence and road in the Yelemaw Village, showing ~2.1 m dextral offset. (e) Offset brick wall in the Kyauk Tha Village south of the Yae Khar Lake. (f,g) Fault offset within the Sagaing area. E, east; N, north; S, south; W, west. The color version of this figure is available only in the electronic edition.

The 2025 surface rupture can be easily traced in the City of Sagaing from HRS imagery and in the field, as the fault offset many roads and buildings in the city. The rupture primarily follows the fault trace mapped before the earthquake (Wang *et al.*, 2014), with field-measured dextral offsets exceeding 3 m, slightly smaller than the subpixel correlation result (Fig. 2b). Most of the collapsed buildings in Sagaing, especially those located near the northern bank of the Ayeyarwady River, were located on the rupture. The damage and casualties quickly decreased away from the surface rupture, according to a resident interviewed after the earthquake.

Inwa to Mandalay International Airport

The rupture becomes less traceable just south of the Ayeyarwady River, in the vicinity of Inwa (Ava), where the palace was destroyed during the 1839 earthquake (Oldham, 1883) (Fig. 4a). Subpixel correlation results from Reitman *et al.* (2026) also show reduced dextral offset (<4 m) along this fault section. Except for a few locations along the fault section transecting the floodplain of the Ayeyarwady River and its tributaries (Fig. 2b), most field measurements and HRS measurements are at least ~1 m smaller than the subpixel correlation result. Extensive riverbank failure and liquefaction are also observed on the floodplain, particularly along the riverbank (Fig. 4a,b). These riverbank failures and ground cracks associated with liquefaction are disoriented without a systemic pattern, and can be

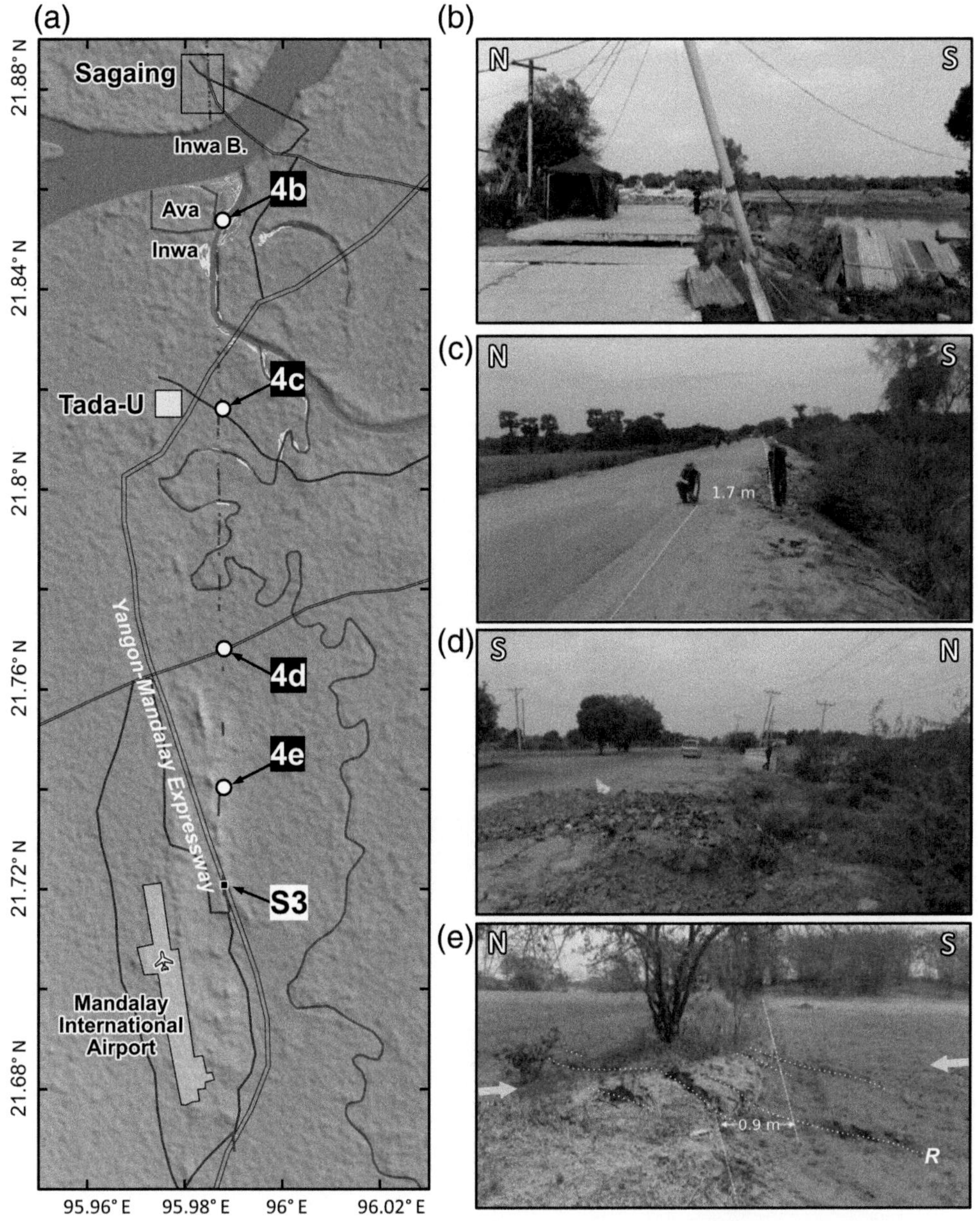

Figure 4. (a) Surface rupture between Inwa and the Mandalay International Airport. (b) Large-scale riverbank failure due to liquefaction east of Inwa. (c) 1.7 m road offset near Tada-U. (d) Ground ruptures with unmeasurable offset across the road between Tada-U and the Mandalay International Airport. (e) Offset of paddy field boundary northeast of the Mandalay International Airport, showing a wide deformation zone of the main rupture trace. The color version of this figure is available only in the electronic edition.

easily distinguished from the fault rupture, especially in the area just east of the Ava (Inwa) Palace.

Many mapped surface ruptures showed a clear north-north-east–south-southwest-trending en-échelon Riedel shear pattern, without mole tracks developed along the fault. Except for a short section northeast of Tada-U (Tadaoo), and a fault section southeast of the Mandalay International Airport, where we found dextral offsets of 3 m or more in the field and from HRS imagery, the offset is less measurable along most of this section, suggesting that the dextral offset is distributed off the main rupture. Most of the measured dextral offsets are smaller than 1.7 m (Fig. 4c), and are accompanied by significant surface warping across the main fault rupture, forming a deformation zone of at least 10 m or wider (Fig. 4e).

Although the offset is less measurable in the field, the surface rupture found in the field is well developed between Tada-U and the Mandalay International Airport (MDL), along the eastern margin of pressure ridges formed by the Sagaing fault (Wang *et al.*, 2014) (Fig. S3). Although we could only map en-échelon ground fractures without observing any clear offset along most of this fault section, subpixel correlation shows more than 3 m of dextral offset (Reitman *et al.*, 2026). This difference suggests that there is a broadly distributed ground deformation near the ground surface along this section of the fault. The damage to the residential buildings in this section was also less significant than in Sagaing. In some cases, even poorly built fences and brick walls showed no damage near the fault. These observations support our hypothesis that either the main surface rupture did not fully propagate to the surface or that the rupture formed a much more diffuse deformation zone due to the presence of a thick, water-saturated alluvial deposit from the Ayeyarwady River system.

Wundwin to Naypyitaw

Surface rupture and offsets become distinct and continuous again, approximately 20 km south of Mandalay International Airport, where the rupture passes through Shwe Taung (north of Wundwin), Thazi, Pyawbwe, and the hilly area north of Naypyitaw (Figs. 2 and 5a). This area is politically stable and conveniently located near National

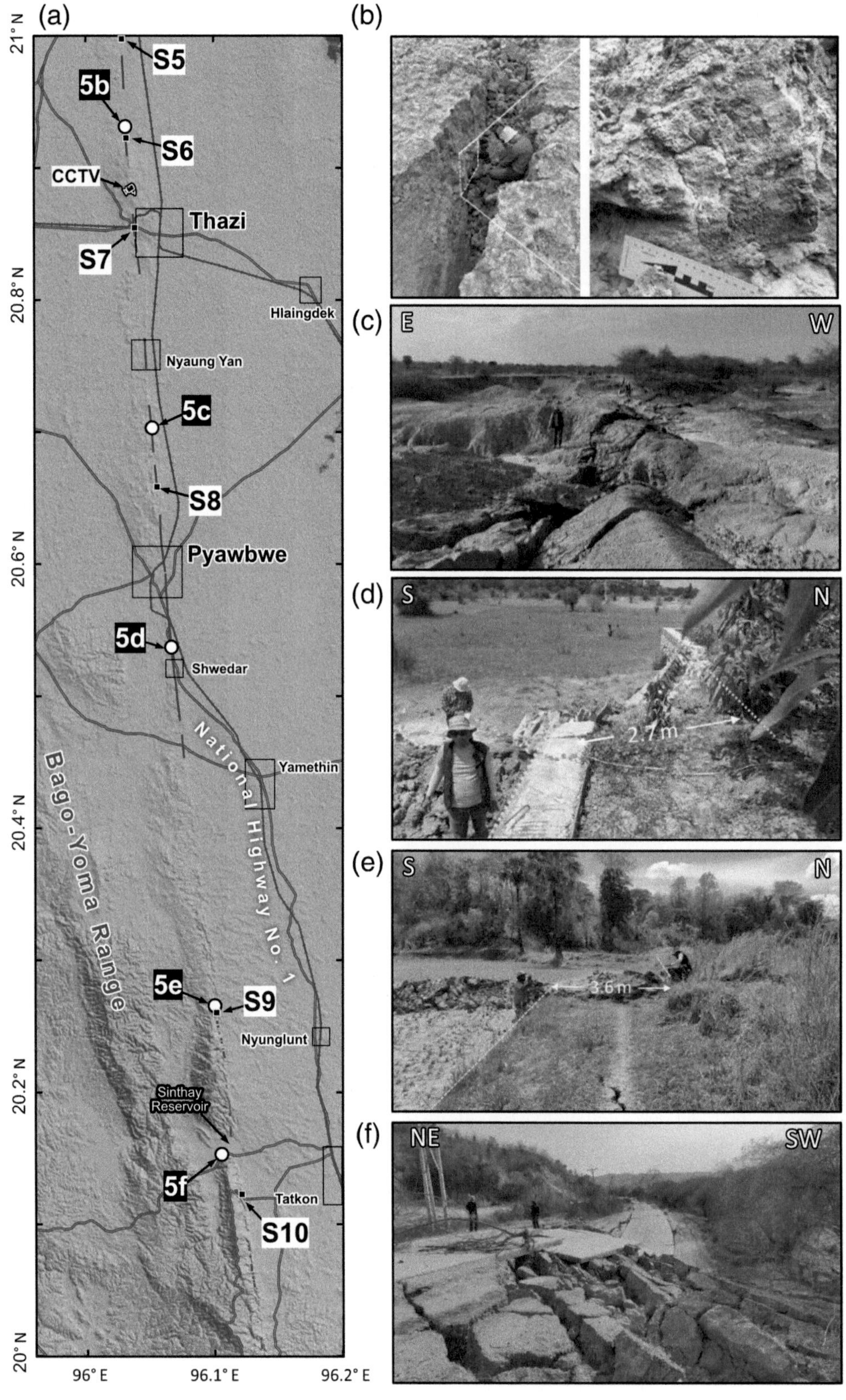

Figure 5. (a) Surface rupture between Thazi and the area north of Naypyitaw. (b) Paddy field boundary offset, northwest (NW) of Muslin Cemetery, Thazi. (c) Surface ruptures west of Inn Ga Net, north of Pyawbwe. (d) Retaining wall offset, just north of Shwedar. (e) Paddy field offset, just west of Inn Gauk Village, west of Nyunglunt. (f) A large earthquake-induced landslide on the road just west of the Sinthay Reservoir. NE, northeast; SW, southwest. The color version of this figure is available only in the electronic edition.

Highway No. 1, and has therefore been well surveyed by multiple teams (e.g., Gürboğa *et al.*, 2025). The largest dextral offset measured in the field is ~4 m, comparable with the ground deformation estimated from subpixel correlation (Reitman *et al.*, 2025, 2026) (Fig. 2b). The 4 m offset is also larger than the offset estimated from CCTV footage located in a solar farm north of Thazi (2.5 ± 0.5 m) (Kearse and Kaneko, 2025). Mole tracks, large-scale en-échelon Riedel shears, and fault scarps are also visible along this section of the fault trace (Fig. 5b–e, Figs. S4–S8). Large open fractures with slickenlines on the vertical fault plane are also commonly observed in this region, exhibiting nearly pure dextral motion with pitch angles ranging from 0° to 3° (Fig. 5b).

Except for the pressure ridge in Thazi (Fig. S7), most ruptures appeared along the eastern margin of pressure ridges, offsetting a series of buildings, roads, bridges, field boundaries, and channels, and forming mole tracks 1–1.5 m high at several places along the fault (Fig. 5c–e). In many places we surveyed, the width of the fault rupture is significantly narrower than that of the adjacent section to the north, with the width of the primary deformation zone ranging from 2 to 4 m (Fig. S9). Although our field measurements show a range of dextral offset along this section, the largest measured dextral cross-fault offset is comparable with that observed from HRS imagery, confirming the appearance of a narrow deformation zone along this section of the rupture (Fig. 2b).

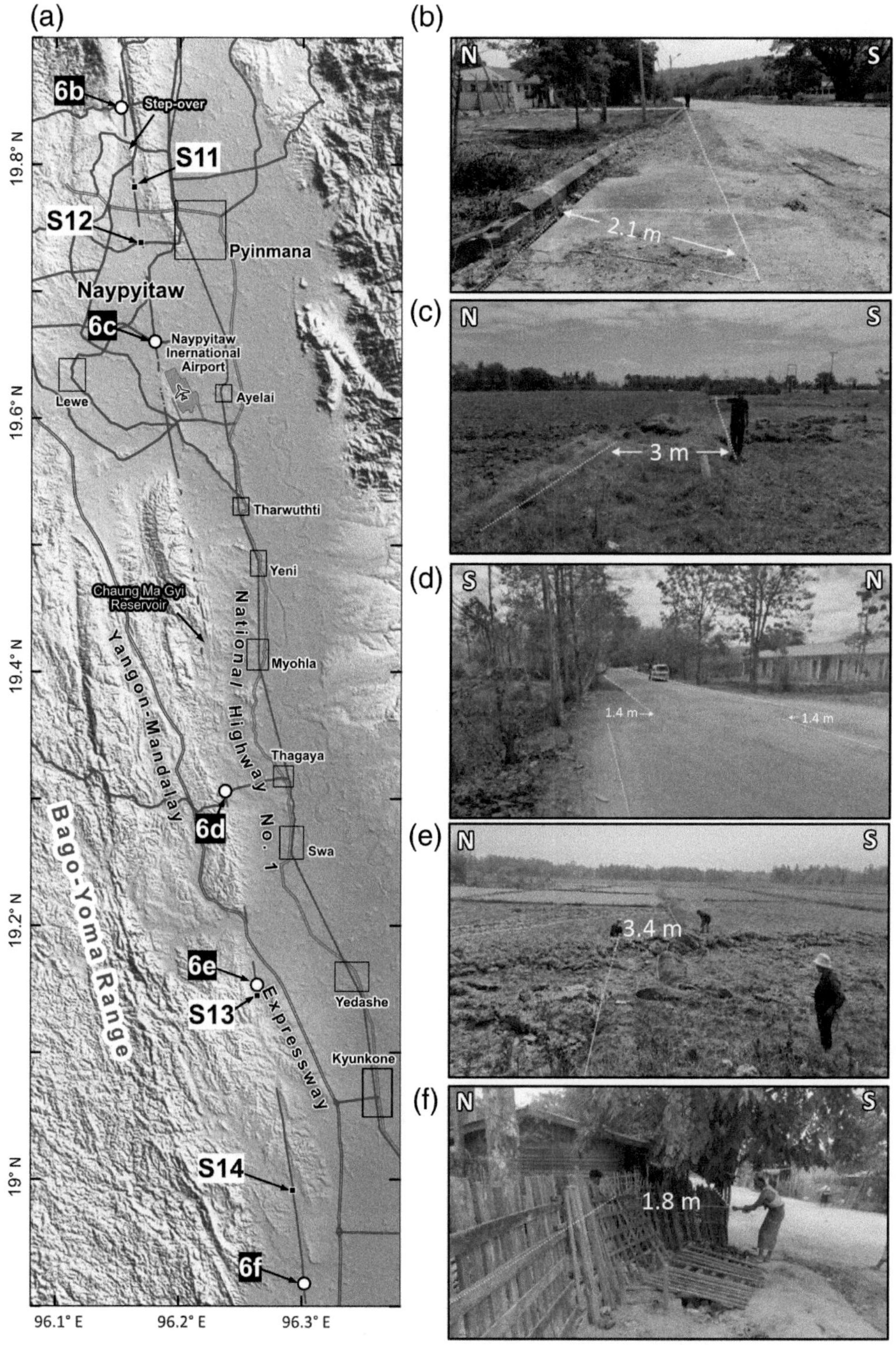

Figure 6. (a) Surface rupture between Naypyitaw and Taungoo. The red lines are surface ruptures surveyed in the field (b) 2.1 m offset near the step-over on the Sagaing fault. (c) 3 m offset found northwest of the Naypyitaw International Airport. (d) 1.4 m dextral offset found west of Thagaya. (e) Mole track and dextral offset west of Kone Myint Thar Village, just west of the Yangon-Mandalay Expressway. (f) Displaced fences across the fault rupture in Bogone Village, west of Taungoo. The color version of this figure is available only in the electronic edition.

South of Pyawbwe, surface rupture extended into the hilly area along the eastern flank of the Bogo-Yoma Range, which is primarily composed of the Irrawaddy Formation (Fig. 2a). Here, we identified distinct surface ruptures and offsets only in a few places in the river valley (Fig. 5e), and fault rupture is difficult to map on the hillside. Along the rupture on the hillside, landslides are common (Fig. 5f), and liquefaction is observed in the alluvial plain adjacent to the fault (Fig. S10). The fault rupture crosses the southwestern end of the Sinthay Reservoir (Fig. 5a), which was breached during the earthquake. Field investigations and remote sensing observations indicate that the surface rupture is southwest of the dam breach location, and did not directly cause the breach; instead, liquefaction and structural failure during strong ground motion were likely responsible (e.g., Fig. S10).

Naypyitaw to Taungoo

From Naypyitaw to Taungoo, the fault transects two sedimentary basins east of the Bago-Yoma Range. The northern part is the Naypyitaw basin, where Myanmar's capital has been located since 2006, and the southern part is the basin west of Taungoo, one of Myanmar's ancient capital cities. Both basins are filled by alluvial deposits from the Bago-Yoma Range (Fig. 6a). Buildings and infrastructures in the Naypyitaw basin, as well as in the foothill area west of the fault, were severely damaged by ground motion and surface ruptures. The maximum offset recorded in the field ranges from 1.2 to 2.9 m across the fault, and the vertical offset along the main fault scarp facing westward reaches 0.3–0.4 m (Fig. S11).

West of Pyinmana, we observe that the 2025 surface rupture formed a 1-km-wide left stepover at the northernmost end of the Naypyitaw basin, where the basin's geomorphology transitions from a triangle-shaped to a linear valley along the Sagaing fault (Fig. 6a). The location of the step-over matches the location of a north-northwest–south-southeast-trending pressure ridge on the Sagaing fault, and the surface rupture is dominated by east–west (EW)-trending compressive surface fractures. Many buildings and infrastructure in this area were damaged by the EW fractures, indicating the distributed nature of deformation around this stepover.

South of this 1-km-wide stepover, rupture formed a continuous trace that passed through the center of the basin, largely following the trace mapped before 2010 (Fig. S12) to the western margin of the Naypyitaw International Airport (Fig. 6a). The maximum dextral offset we measured in the field is 3.0 m, with a west-facing scarp reaching 0.3–0.4 m in height. South of the Naypyitaw basin, the rupture appears along the easternmost edge of the foothills, approximately 300 m east of the previously mapped trace (Wang *et al.*, 2014; Tun and Watkinson, 2017). Because of security concerns and dense vegetation cover, we were unable to map the rupture in detail; however, most of our mapping is consistent with the rupture mapped from HRS imagery, except for west of Myohla (Fig. 6a), where a secondary trace appeared approximately 200 m west of the main rupture (Fig. 6a). Surprisingly, both the main and secondary surface ruptures across the Chaung Ma Gyi Reservoir Dam northwest of Myohla without causing the dam to fail catastrophically (Fig. 6a).

Another secondary trace was found west of the main rupture in the northwestern part of the Naypyitaw basin, between the alluvium and the foothill of the Bago-Yoma Range (Fig. 6a). The rupture primarily follows a previously mapped fault trace that splays out from the main Sagaing fault, along the western edge of basin (Wang *et al.*, 2014; Tun and Watkinson 2017), damaging the concrete road. Although the damage pattern suggests the rupture developed along one of Naypyitaw's major roads, fault ruptures have been identified at only two locations. The lack of observable offset suggests the dextral slip is likely minor along this secondary rupture (i.e., <0.5 m).

Farther south, the rupture enters another basin west of Taungoo (Fig. 2a,c), with a distinct surface rupture in the open paddy field where the fault trace was clearly mapped in the field before 2010 (Figs. S13 and S14). Dextral offset measured in this area is between 1.8 and 3.4 m, and the width of its primary deformation zone is 5–10 m. The maximum fault scarp height is 0.3–0.5 m, facing westward. Similar to the section north of Naypyitaw, slickenlines are also observed on the vertical fault plane, indicating nearly pure dextral motion with pitch angle ranging from 0° to 17° (Fig. S13).

South of Taungoo

Field investigation becomes challenging in the area south of Taungoo due to dense vegetation and limited accessibility (Fig. 2c). Surface ruptures are less distinct compared with those in the sections to the north (Fig. S15). Most ruptures appeared along the main boundary between the Bago-Yoma Range and its eastern foothills (Fig. 7a), following a fault trace previously mapped from aerial photo and satellite imagery (Wang *et al.*, 2011, 2014; Tun and Watkinson, 2017). Although our field survey locations are sparsely distributed, our measurements suggest that dextral slip changed from ~1.2 m near Baw Di Gone to ~0.3 m, ~4.7 km south of Baw Di Gone (Figs. 2b and 7). Surface ruptures are primarily en-échelon Riedel shears south of Baw Di Gone, with the deformation zone ranging from 0.5 to 7 m in width. The amount of dextral slip decreased southward and became unmeasurable southeast of the Kun Chaung Reservoir (Fig. 7a). Minor surface fractures and tension cracks in paddy fields can be traced farther south, extending to the area west of Phyu (Fig. 7a,e, Figs. S15 and S16).

The Sentinel-2's subpixel correlation result from Reitman *et al.* (2026) suggests the rupture continued for another ~23 km south of our southernmost surveyed location, where the surface rupture in the field is barely measurable. Close to the Phyu area, the cross-fault right-lateral displacement estimated from Sentinel-2's subpixel correlation result is around 1 m, 0.7–0.8 m higher than our field survey results. This suggests that the majority of the ground displacement is absorbed by warping and distributed near the surface rupture, especially near the southern end of the 2025 surface rupture. We did not observe the surface rupture south of 18.15° N (Figs. S17 and S18). However, sand blows and minor surface cracks associated with liquefaction are visible along the previously mapped fault trace.

Discussion

Slip distribution and fault segmentation

Our field-based survey and offset estimated from HRS imagery show a similar slip pattern during the 2025 Mandalay earthquake (Fig. 2b). Dextral slip peaked in the Sagaing Hills area, north of the mainshock epicenter, with right-lateral offset exceeding 4.6 m in the field, and more than 6 m estimated from HRS imagery (Fig. 2b). South of 22° N, the field-measured right-lateral offset drops to less than 2.5 m, and the subpixel correlation slip decreases to approximately 3 m, forming a saddle in the 2025 slip distribution. The slip then gradually increases southward to 21° N, where field survey results and remote sensing measurements indicate that right-lateral slip across the rupture reaches 3.5–4 m, forming a stable slip plateau between 21° and 19° N. Farther south, right-lateral slip on the fault decreased dramatically, from more than 3 m to approximately 1 m in the subpixel correlation data, and from ~3 m to less than 0.5 m in the field-based results (Fig. 2b).

Although the pattern of field-measured fault slip is similar to the slip pattern derived from remote sensing data, the amount of slip measured in the field is usually more than 1 m less than that estimated from the satellite imagery. This suggests that in most

Figure 7. (a) Surface rupture between Taungoo and Phyu (Pyu), near the southern end of the 2025 rupture. (b) ~1.2 m dextral offset west of Oaktwin. (c) Mole track and slight track offset found on the 2025 rupture trace. (d) ~0.2 m offset across the ground crack near Phyu. (e) A small opening crack near Phyu, close to the southernmost part of the rupture trace, was identified in the field. The color version of this figure is available only in the electronic edition.

parts of the fault, at least ~1 m of fault slip is accommodated by distributed deformation off the main rupture close to the surface. Such near-fault deformation can be observed in optical satellite imagery near Sagaing and Naypyitaw, where the offset estimated from features very close to the fault is generally less than that estimated from features extending farther from the fault (i.e., 50 m). In some extreme cases, the difference between subpixel correlation and field-based measurements can exceed 3 m, indicating that most deformation is distributed off the main fault near the surface. Based on the change in rupture pattern observed in the field and the geological mapping along the fault, we suggest that the water-saturated Quaternary Irrawaddy Formation and overlying unconsolidated alluvial deposits played a significant role in controlling the pattern and degree of off-fault deformation. The difference between the HRS measurement and the subpixel correlation result is generally smaller than the difference between the field measurement and the subpixel correlation result. Since measurement from HRS imagery determines the offset using a longer baseline of once-straight offset features (e.g., 10–50 m from the rupture), this difference suggests a large portion of the off-fault deformation is likely accommodated by the distributed deformation close to the fault, rather than farther away from the fault rupture. Similar observations were made in many recent surface-rupturing earthquakes, including the 2011 Tarlay earthquake in Myanmar (Tun, Wang, *et al.* 2014), the 2013 Balochistan earthquake in Pakistan (Gold *et al.*, 2015), the 2018 Hualien earthquake (Kuo *et al.*, 2018), and the 2022 Guanshan–Chihshang earthquakes in Taiwan (Wang *et al.*, 2024).

In the northernmost rupture section, where the fault had over 5 m of slip at the surface, we suggest that it is spatially correlated with the presence of metamorphic rocks along the Sagaing ridge. The high strength of the metamorphic rock and the rheological contrast between the fault gouge and the metamorphic country rocks near the surface could cause slip to be concentrated on the main fault rupture (Kaneko and Fialko,

2011), and therefore decrease the difference between the subpixel correlation result, HRS observation, and field-based measurements (Fig. 2b). The high strength of the bedrock may also enhance fault coupling near the surface, allowing more strain to accumulate during the interseismic period near the shallow part of the fault.

Another key observation is that the earthquake rupture propagated through multiple fault segments, resulting in surface rupture exceeding 450 km in length. Previous studies suggest that the central and southern part of the Sagaing fault can be subdivided into four to five different segments, corresponding to different earthquakes and surface ruptures that occurred during the first half of the twentieth century (Tsutsumi and Sato, 2009; Wang *et al.*, 2011, 2014; Tun and Watkinson, 2017). The 2025 Mandalay earthquake demonstrated that these segment boundaries can be breached during a major earthquake like the 2025 event, with the fault-slip pattern changing from one segment to another (i.e., from the Sagaing to Meiktila segment, north and south of Sagaing City, Fig. 2). Similar multiple-segment ruptures are seen on other strike-slip fault systems, including the San Andreas and the North Antonian faults. For example, Sieh *et al.* (1989) suggest a variable rupture length of the San Andreas fault in southern California over the past two millennia, indicating that the segment boundary along the San Andreas fault does not always arrest the rupture. Another study by Rockwell *et al.* (2015) on the southernmost section of the San Andreas fault suggests a similar scenario: some major rupture events may terminate at the fault stepover, while others may propagate through it, forming a much longer rupture in the paleoseismological records. Kondo *et al.* (2005) also suggest that the 180-km-long rupture of the 1944 Bolu-Gerede earthquake on the North Antonian fault involved five fault segments, defined by fault-slip distribution, fault stepovers, and bends.

The 2025 rupture on the Sagaing fault and the 1944 rupture on the North Antonian fault share many similarities, including being extremely linear, with no major fault discontinuities, and having maximum coseismic slip exceeding 5 m across the fault. In both cases, the steps found along these ruptures are less than 5 km in width, allowing the coseismic rupture to easily propagate through these fault steps (Wesnousky, 2006; Nissen *et al.*, 2016). Although historical earthquake records indeed show that several events occurred along the southern half of the rupture, including the M_w 6.5 Swa earthquake in 1929 and the M_w 7.3 Pyu earthquake in 1930, slip accumulated on the fault plane in the past 100 yr, and the residual strain from previous events along the Sagaing fault's southern segments seems to be enough to drive the fault rupture during the 2025 earthquake, making the rupture breaching into these fault sections during the earthquake.

The lack of accumulated slip since the 2012 earthquake is likely to have stopped the rupture north of Singu, even though part of the 2012 fault patch reruptured during the 2025 earthquake. The maximum dextral slip of the 2012 Thabeikkyin earthquake was approximately 1 m near the northern part of its 45-km-long surface rupture extending from Singu to Thabeikkyin (Tun and Watkinson, 2017). If the 2012 earthquake released most of the slip accumulated before the 2012 event, the slip accumulated between 2012 and 2025 near Singu is approximately 0.3 m, assuming the fault returned to its fully coupled state quickly after the 2012 earthquake. The submeter slip accumulation on the shallow fault plane may not be sufficient to drive the 2025 cascading rupture; thus, the 2025 rupture stopped in the 2012 ruptured section. A similar condition may be responsible for its southern rupture termination, where the Sagaing fault ruptured during the December 1930 earthquake. The model from Lindsey *et al.* (2025) suggests that fault slip decreased dramatically when the rupture entered the high-intensity zone of the December 1930 earthquake and gradually tapered farther south. Based on these observations, as well as the historical earthquake pattern, we therefore suggest that the stress condition in the northern and southern parts of the rupture controlled the slip distribution and rupture length of the 2025 earthquake.

Future seismic hazard on the Sagaing fault

The twentieth-century rupture history and the rupture extent of the 2025 Mandalay earthquake suggest that the section that remains largely unruptured is the southernmost part of the fault (i.e., Bago segment; Hurukawa and Maung, 2011; Wang *et al.*, 2011, 2014; Tun and Watkinson, 2017). The segment is close to the densely populated City of Yangon (Fig. 1a). The last known surface-rupturing event was the 1930 M_w 7.2 Bago earthquake, which caused significant destruction and damage in Bago and Yangon (Coggin Brown *et al.*, 1931). Tsutsumi and Sato (2009) estimated the coseismic displacement of the Bago earthquake to be ~3 m, based on a geomorphological survey of offset field boundaries conducted ~70 yr after the earthquake. This implies a mean recurrence interval for an event similar to the 1930 earthquake is ~150 yr, assuming the 2 cm/yr average slip rate of the Sagaing fault from the GNSS study (Vigny *et al.*, 2003). Earthquakes from fault sections north and south of the 1930 Bago earthquake rupture are not well documented, but Wang *et al.* (2011) speculate that these sections may be responsible for the damaging earthquakes that occurred in 1888 and 1768. The global seismic catalog also showed that no earthquake with a magnitude larger than 5 occurred along the southern section of the Sagaing fault after the 1930 Bago earthquake. Even after the 2025 Mandalay earthquake, no aftershocks are recorded along this section of the fault in global and regional catalogs (Fig. 1b), suggesting that the fault plane remains highly coupled and that significant slip potential has accumulated on the fault. Although it is difficult to forecast the magnitude and timing of the next earthquake along the Sagaing fault, the dense population living in southern Myanmar, combined with the long quiescence of background seismicity and the plausible slip loaded on the fault plane, leads us to be concerned about the seismic hazard and risks in southern Myanmar in the near future. Assessment of the seismic safety of residential buildings and infrastructures in Yangon and Bago, along with detailed paleoseismological investigations, is therefore crucial for mitigating future seismic hazard.

Conclusions

The 2025 M_w 7.7 Mandalay earthquake produced a striking, 470-km-long dextral surface rupture along the central and southern Sagaing fault. Our field investigations confirmed that the rupture breached the long-recognized seismic gap between Mandalay and Naypyitaw, propagating into other previously defined fault segments in the south. The slip distribution from our field survey shows a pattern similar to that derived from remote sensing analyses, with more than 4.5 m right-lateral offset occurring in the northern part of the rupture, and 3–4 m mean surface fault slip along the southern part of the rupture, separated by a low slip region in between.

Compared with the fault displacement derived from remote sensing data, the field-measured fault offset is ~1 m smaller along the entire rupture. This is likely caused by distributed deformation in the less-consolidated sediments in the shallow part of the Earth along the ruptured fault. In contrast, the high slip in the northern part of the fault, as well as the similarity between field measurements and remote sensing observations, can be attributed to the exposure of high-strength bedrock along the Sagaing ridge.

The 2025 rupture, combined with the history of twentieth-century events, leaves the southernmost section of the Sagaing fault, from the Bago segment to the offshore section of the fault, including the segment that ruptured in the 1930 Bago earthquake, as the primary remaining portion of the fault that has not experienced recent ruptures in southern Myanmar (Figs. 1 and 2). The long quiescence of seismicity and the lack of 2025 aftershocks highlight the seismic hazard potential in the densely populated region of southern Myanmar, including the major urban centers of Yangon and Bago, and an urgent regional seismic risk assessment is needed along this segment.

Data and Resources

Earthquake epicenters and moment tensor solutions plotted in this study were collected from the U.S. Geological Survey catalog (USGS) (https://earthquake.usgs.gov/earthquakes/search/, last accessed November 2025). Maxar's WorldView imagery was accessed via Google Earth Pro, and Pleiades and Pleiades Neo images were obtained from Airbus. Fault offset estimated from the Sentinel-2's subpixel correlation result is obtained from the USGS (doi: 10.5066/P1RYMWCK). The supplemental material for this article includes the location and additional photos of the field investigation, and the offset estimation from the optical satellite imagery.

Declaration of Competing Interests

The authors acknowledge that there are no conflicts of interest recorded.

Acknowledgments

The authors thank Kerry Sieh for his kind support and suggestions after the 2025 Mandalay (Sagaing) earthquake. The authors also thank all the help and contributions from residents in the earthquake-affected areas and from the Myanmar geologists' community, even under the harsh conditions after the earthquake. The authors are greatly indebted to Aye Lwin, Khun San Aung, and all those who provided various forms of support during the field survey. Comments and suggestions from the editor and reviewers, and the editing from Ray Weldon, greatly improved the quality of this article. The research is supported by the National Science and Technology Council (113-2116-M-002 -028 - and 114-2116-M-002 -002 -) to Y.W. This work comprises the Myanmar Institute of Earth and Planetary Sciences Contribution Number 01/2026.

References

Antoine, S. L., R. Shrestha, C. Milliner, K. Im, C. Rollins, K. Wang, K. Chen, and J.-P. Avouac (2025). The 2025 M_w 7.7 Mandalay, Myanmar, earthquake reveals a complex earthquake cycle with clustering and variable segmentation on the Sagaing fault, *Proc. Natl. Acad. Sci. Unit. States Am.* **122,** e2514378122, doi: 10.1073/pnas.2514378122.

Bender, F. (1983). *Geology of Burma*, Gebrüder Borntraeger, Berlin, Stuttgart.

Chhibber, H. L., and R. Ramamirtham (1934). *The Geology of Burma*, MacMillan, London.

Coggin Brown, J., P. Leicester, and H. L. Chhibber (1931). A preliminary note on the Pegu earthquake of May 5th, 1930, *Rec. Geol. Surv. India* **LXV,** 221–284.

Curray, J. R. (2005). Tectonics and history of the Andaman Sea region, *J. Asian Earth Sci.* **25,** 187–232, doi: 10.1016/j.jseaes.2004.09.001.

Gold, R. D., N. G. Reitman, R. W. Briggs, W. D. Barnhart, G. P. Hayes, and E. Wilson (2015). On- and off-fault deformation associated with the September 2013 M_w 7.7 Balochistan earthquake: Implications for geologic slip rate measurements, *Tectonophysics* **660,** 65–78, doi: 10.1016/j.tecto.2015.08.019.

Gürboğa, Ş., F. C. Çomut, S. Lyu, M. Motagh, K. S. Thu, and M. Karadağlar (2025). Heterogeneous rupturing and barrier mechanism during the 2025 M_w 7.7 Myanmar earthquake, *Sci. Rep.* **15,** 41144, doi: 10.1038/s41598-025-25026-z.

Hirano, S., R. Doke, and T. Maeda (2025). Supershear-subshear-supershear rupture sequence during the 2025 Mandalay earthquake in Myanmar, *Seismica* **4,** doi: 10.26443/seismica.v4i2.1785.

Hurukawa, N., and P. M. Maung (2011). Two seismic gaps on the Sagaing fault, Myanmar, derived from relocation of historical earthquakes since 1918, *Geophys. Res. Lett.* **38,** L01310, doi: 10.1029/2010GL046099.

Kaneko, Y., and Y. Fialko (2011). Shallow slip deficit due to large strike-slip earthquakes in dynamic rupture simulations with elasto-plastic off-fault response, *Geophys. J. Int.* **186,** 1389–1403, doi: 10.1111/j.1365-246X.2011.05117.x.

Kearse, J., and Y. Kaneko (2025). Curved fault slip captured by CCTV video during the 2025 M_w 7.7 Myanmar earthquake, *The Seism. Rec.* **5,** 281–288, doi: 10.1785/0320250024.

Kondo, H., Y. Awata, O. m. Emre, A. Doğan, S. Özalp, F. Tokay, C. Yıldırım, T. Yoshioka, and K. Okumura (2005). Slip distribution, fault geometry, and fault segmentation of the 1944 Bolu-Gerede earthquake rupture, North Anatolian fault, Turkey, *Bull. Seismol. Soc. Am.* **95,** 1234–1249, doi: 10.1785/0120040194.

Kuo, Y. T., Y. Wang, J. Hollingsworth, S. Y. Huang, R. Y. Chuang, C. H. Lu, Y. C. Hsu, H. Tung, J. Y. Yen, and C. P. Chang (2018). Shallow fault rupture of the Milun fault in the 2018 M_w 6.4 Hualien earthquake: A high-resolution approach from optical correlation of Pléiades Satellite Imagery, *Seismol. Res. Lett.* **90,** 97–107, doi: 10.1785/0220180227.

Laosunthara, A., K. Krutphong, N. Leelawat, W. Wararuksajja, N. Sukulthanasorn, A. Suppasri, R. Thongthip, and C. Chintanapakdee (2025). Initial observations and immediate lessons learned from Thailand's response to the 2025 Mandalay earthquake, *Int. J. Disaster Risk Reduction*, 105675, doi: 10.1016/j.ijdrr.2025.105675.

Le Dain, A. Y., P. Tapponnier, and P. Molnar (1984). Active faulting and tectonics of Burma and surrounding regions, *J. Geophys. Res.* **89,** 453, doi: 10.1029/JB089iB01p00453.

Li, B., S. Jónsson, C. Suhendi, J. Liu, D. Li, A. Delorme, Y. Klinger, and P. M. Mai (2025). Seismic gap breached by the 2025 M_w 7.7 Mandalay (Myanmar) earthquake, *Nature Geosci.* **18,** 1287–1295, doi: 10.1038/s41561-025-01861-7.

Lindsey, E. O., Y.-T. Kuo, Y. Wang, M. Thant, and T. Z. H. Tin (2025). Mature fault mechanics revealed by the highly efficient 2025 Mandalay earthquake, *Nat. Commun.* **16** 10937, doi: 10.1038/s41467-025-65942-2.

Lindsey, E. O., Y. Wang, L. T. Aung, J.-H. Chong, Q. Qiu, R. Mallick, L. Feng, P. S. Aung, T. Z. H. Tin, S. M. Min, *et al.* (2023). Active subduction and strain partitioning in western Myanmar revealed by a dense survey GNSS network, *Earth Planet. Sci. Lett.* **622,** 118384, doi: 10.1016/j.epsl.2023.118384.

Maung, H. M. (1987). Transcurrent movements in the Burma–Andaman Sea region, *Geology* **15,** 911–912, doi: 10.1130/0091-7613(1987)15%3C911:TMITBS%3E2.0.CO;2.

Maurin, T., F. Masson, C. Rangin, U. T. Min, and P. Collard (2010). First global positioning system results in northern Myanmar: Constant and localized slip rate along the Sagaing fault, *Geology* **38,** 591–594, doi: 10.1130/G30872.1.

Melgar, D., R. Weldon, Y. Wang, M. G. Bato, L. T. Aung, X. Shi, W. Wiwegwin, S. N. Khaing, S. Min, and M. Thant (2025). Supershear source model of the 2025 M 7. 8 Myanmar earthquake and paleoseismology of the Sagaing fault: Regions of significant overlap with past earthquakes, *Seismica* **4,** doi: 10.26443/seismica.v4i2.1771.

Mon, C. T., X. Gong, Y. Wen, M. Jiang, Q.-F. Chen, M. Zhang, G. Hou, M. Thant, K. Sein, and Y. He (2020). Insight into major active faults in Central Myanmar and the related geodynamic sources, *Geophys. Res. Lett.* **47,** e2019GL086236, doi: 10.1029/2019GL086236.

Nissen, E., J. R. Elliott, R. A. Sloan, T. J. Craig, G. J. Funning, A. Hutko, B. E. Parsons, and T. J. Wright (2016). Limitations of rupture forecasting exposed by instantaneously triggered earthquake doublet, *Nature Geosci.* **9,** 330–336, doi: 10.1038/ngeo2653.

Oldham, T. (1883). A catalogue of Indian earthquakes, *Mem. Geol. Surv. India* **19,** 163–215.

Ornthammarath, T., P. Warnitchai, Y. Maruyama, P. Pornsopin, and F. Yamazaki (2025). Far-field ground motion characteristics of the Bangkok basin, Thailand, in the 2025 M_w 7.7 Mandalay earthquake: Initial insights, *Bull. Earthq. Eng.* 1–26, doi: 10.1007/s10518-025-02295-7.

Racey, A., and M. F. Ridd (2015). Chapter 8 Petroleum geology of the Tanintharyi region, Myanmar, in *Geological Society*, London, Memoirs, 83–91, doi: 10.1144/M45.08.

Reitman, N. G., Y. Wang, Y.-T. Kuo, C. Hanagan, A. E. Hatem, C. B. DuRoss, C.-C. Chen, W. D. Barnhart, H. Z. Yin, R. W. Briggs, *et al.* (2025). Remote surface rupture observations for the M 7.7 2025 Mandalay, Burma (Myanmar) earthquake (2025), *U.S. Geol. Surv. Data Release*, doi: 10.5066/P1RYMWCK.

Reitman, N. G., Y. Wang, Y.-T. Kuo, C. Hanagan, A. E. Hatem, C. B. DuRoss, C.-C. Chen, D. E. Goldberg, H. Z. Yin, R. W. Briggs, *et al.* (2026). Surface rupture and slip distribution of the 2025 M7.7 Mandalay earthquake and updated length scaling of supershear earthquakes, *Seismol. Res. Lett.* doi: 10.1785/0220250257.

Rockwell, T. K., T. E. Dawson, J. Young Ben-Horin, and G. Seitz (2015). A 21-event, 4,000-year history of surface ruptures in the Anza seismic gap, San Jacinto fault, and implications for long-term earthquake production on a major plate boundary fault, *Pure Appl. Geophys.* **172,** 1143–1165, doi: 10.1007/s00024-014-0955-z.

Sieh, K., M. Stuiver, and D. Brillinger (1989). A more precise chronology of earthquakes produced by the San Andreas fault in southern California, *J. Geophys. Res.: Solid Earth* **94,** 603–623, doi: 10.1029/JB094iB01p00603.

Socquet, A., C. Vigny, N. Chamot-Rooke, W. Simons, C. Rangin, and B. Ambrosius (2006). India and Sunda plates motion and deformation along their boundary in Myanmar determined by GPS, *J. Geophys. Res.: Solid Earth* **111,** B05406, doi: 10.1029/2005JB003877.

Tapponnier, P., G. Peltzer, and R. Armijo (1986). On the mechanics of the collision between India and Asia, *Geol. Soc. London, Spec. Publ.* **19,** 113–157, doi: 10.1144/GSL.SP.1986.019.01.07.

Tha Zin Htet, T., T. Nishimura, M. Hashimoto, E. O. Lindsey, L. T. Aung, S. M. Min, and M. Thant (2022). Present-day crustal deformation and slip rate along the southern Sagaing fault in Myanmar by GNSS observation, *J. Asian Earth Sci.* **228,** 105125, doi: 10.1016/j.jseaes.2022.105125.

Tsutsumi, H., and T. Sato (2009). Tectonic geomorphology of the southernmost Sagaing fault and surface rupture associated with the May 1930 Pegu (Bago) earthquake, Myanmar, *Bull. Seismol. Soc. Am.* **99,** 2155–2168, doi: 10.1785/0120080113.

Tun, S. T., T. Maung, H. Nyunt, and S. Kyaing (2014). *Geological Map of Myanmar, 2014,* Myanmar Geosciences Society.

Tun, S. T., Y. Wang, S. N. Khaing, M. Thant, N. Htay, Y. M. M. Htwe, T. Myint, and K. Sieh (2014). Surface ruptures of the M_w 6.8 March 2011 Tarlay earthquake, eastern Myanmar, *Bull. Seismol. Soc. Am.* **104,** 2915–2932, doi: 10.1785/0120130321.

Tun, S. T., and I. M. Watkinson (2017). Chapter 19 The Sagaing fault, Myanmar, *inGeological Society*, Memoirs, London, 413–441, doi: 10.1144/M48.19.

U.S. Geological Survey (2025). M 7.7-2025 Mandalay, Burma (Myanmar) earthquake, available at https://earthquake.usgs.gov/

earthquakes/eventpage/us7000pn9s/executive (last accessed February 2026).

Vigny, C., A. Socquet, C. Rangin, N. Chamotrooke, M. Pubellier, M. N. Bouin, G. Bertrand, and M. Becker (2003). Present-day crustal deformation around Sagaing fault, Myanmar, *J. Geophys. Res: Solid Earth* **108,** 2533, doi: 10.1029/2002JB001999.

Wang, Y., J. B. H. Shyu, K. Sieh, H.-W. Chiang, C.-C. Wang, T. Aung, Y.-n. N. Lin, C.-C. Shen, S. Min, O. Than, *et al.* (2013). Permanent upper plate deformation in western Myanmar during the great 1762 earthquake: Implications for neotectonic behavior of the northern Sunda megathrust, *J. Geophys. Res.: Solid Earth* **118,** 1277–1303, doi: 10.1002/jgrb.50121.

Wang, Y., K. Sieh, T. Aung, S. Min, S. N. Khaing, and S. T. Tun (2011). Earthquakes and slip rate of the southern Sagaing fault: Insights from an offset ancient fort wall, lower Burma (Myanmar), *Geophys. J. Int.* **185,** 49–64, doi: 10.1111/j.1365-246X.2010.04918.x.

Wang, Y., K. Sieh, S. T. Tun, K.-Y. Lai, and T. Myint (2014). Active tectonics and earthquake potential of the Myanmar region, *J. Geophys. Res.: Solid Earth* **119,** 3767–3822, doi: 10.1002/2013JB010762.

Wang, Y., S.-H. Wu, H. L. B. Chou, Y.-Y. Li, W. S. Cheng, A. Ho, J.-M. Chen, S.-C. Liu, C.-Y. Hsieh, S. Duan, *et al.* (2024). Surface ruptures of the 2022 Guanshan-Chihshang earthquakes in central Longitudinal Valley area, eastern Taiwan, *Terr. Atmos. Ocean. Sci.* **35,** 16, doi: 10.1007/s44195-024-00077-3.

Wei, S., X. Wang, C. Li, H. Zeng, Z. Ma, Q. Shi, H. Chen, Y. Huang, M. Lyu, and J. Liao (2025). Supershear rupture sustained through a thick fault zone in the 2025 Mw 7.8 Mandalay earthquake, *Science* **390,** 468–475, doi: 10.1126/science.adz2101.

Wesnousky, S. G. (2006). Predicting the endpoints of earthquake ruptures, *Nature* **444,** 358–360, doi: 10.1038/nature05275.

Xu, X., W. Kang, T. Wang, X. Zhang, Y. Liu, Y. Zhang, J. Zhao, K. Li, Q. Wang, J. Cheng, and J. Ren (2025). The M_w 7.7 Myanmar earthquake: A continental longest surface-rupturing supershear cascading event, *npj Nat. Hazards* **2,** 73, doi: 10.1038/s44304-025-00125-z.

Manuscript received 23 December 2025
Published online 29 April 2026

The M 5.7 Parker Butte Earthquake near Yerington, Nevada: Anatomy of a Dual-Plane Rupture in the Walker Lane from High-Precision Relocated Earthquakes, InSAR, GPS, and Strong-Motion Data

Kyren R. Bogolub*[1], Daniel T. Trugman[1], Yu Jiang[1], William C. Hammond[2], Kenneth D. Smith[1], Rich D. Koehler[2], and Christie D. Rowe[1]

Abstract

On 9 December 2024, at 3:08 p.m. local time, the M_w 5.7 Parker Butte earthquake occurred about 24 km north-northeast of Yerington, Nevada. From 1 December 2024 to 10 May 2025, we cataloged 1301 earthquakes, including seven events $M_L > 3.5$. We use high-precision earthquake relocation, Interferometric Synthetic Aperture Radar (InSAR) data, Global Positioning System (GPS) data, and strong-motion data to explore the tectonic context and spatiotemporal evolution of this sequence. The high-precision relocations of the sequence reveal a main cluster of earthquakes that form a planar feature which can be fit with a plane striking N62°E and dipping 85° SE. Events that are not in the main cluster are primarily 5–10 km to the southeast and are more scattered, but some smaller linear clusters can be identified. We used InSAR and GPS data to model fault geometry and slip. From this analysis, we found that the ground deformation can be fit with a single fault 12 km long × 8 km wide with a strike of N61.5°E ± 1.0°, dipping 73° ± 1.5° southeast and slip up to ~50 cm, concentrated between depths of 2.5 and 7 km, consistent with an M_w 5.7 rupture. However, a better fit is found by adding a second fault plane. The second fault strikes N24.5°W and was detected as a displacement discontinuity in descending InSAR scenes, correlating to minor surface fracturing observed in the field, but had low aftershock activity. The GPS observations of interseismic deformation before the event show similar directions of principal strain accumulation and strain release in the mainshock moment tensor. Ground-motion measurements from the mainshock strong-motion data are generally in agreement with existing active crustal ground-motion models for the western United States. The sequence provided a valuable dataset for examining faulting rupture patterns in the Walker Lane Shear Zone.

Cite this article as Bogolub, K. R., D. T. Trugman, Y. Jiang, W. C. Hammond, K. D. Smith, R. D. Koehler, and C. D. Rowe (2025). The M 5.7 Parker Butte Earthquake near Yerington, Nevada: Anatomy of a Dual-Plane Rupture in the Walker Lane from High-Precision Relocated Earthquakes, InSAR, GPS, and Strong-Motion Data, *Seismol. Res. Lett.* **97**, 1754–1766, doi: 10.1785/0220250203.

Supplemental Material

Introduction

The mainshock of the Parker Butte sequence (M_L 5.74, M_w 5.71, Fig. 1) occurred on Monday, 9 December 2024, at about 3:08 p.m. local time (23:08:31 UTC) and 24 km north-northeast of Yerington, Nevada. The mainshock produced very strong (modified Mercalli intensity [MMI] VII) shaking close to the rupture (within ~20 km distance) and was widely felt in Carson City and Reno, Nevada (MMI IV), with numerous felt reports as far west as Sacramento, California (MMI III, ~200 km distance). Residents of eastern California (though not Nevada) received a ShakeAlert notification, with the system accurately locating and estimating the size of the event despite its out-of-network location. The mainshock was preceded by a sequence of foreshocks in the week leading up to the event, including an M_w 3.8 event on 4 December. Over a 1000 aftershocks occurred in the following six months, including an M_w 4.2 that occurred about an hour and a half after the mainshock. The sequence did not occur on any previously mapped fault, and the immediate

1. Nevada Seismological Laboratory, Nevada Geosciences, University of Nevada, Reno, Nevada, U.S.A., https://orcid.org/0000-0003-0605-8142 (KRB); https://orcid.org/0000-0002-9296-4223 (DTT); https://orcid.org/0000-0002-6238-9141 (YJ); https://orcid.org/0000-0002-9208-3960 (CDR); 2. Nevada Geodetic Laboratory, Nevada Bureau of Mines and Geology, Nevada Geosciences, University of Nevada, Reno, Nevada, U.S.A., https://orcid.org/0000-0001-7367-9489 (WCH); https://orcid.org/0000-0003-0777-6939 (RDK)

*Corresponding author: kbogolub@unr.edu

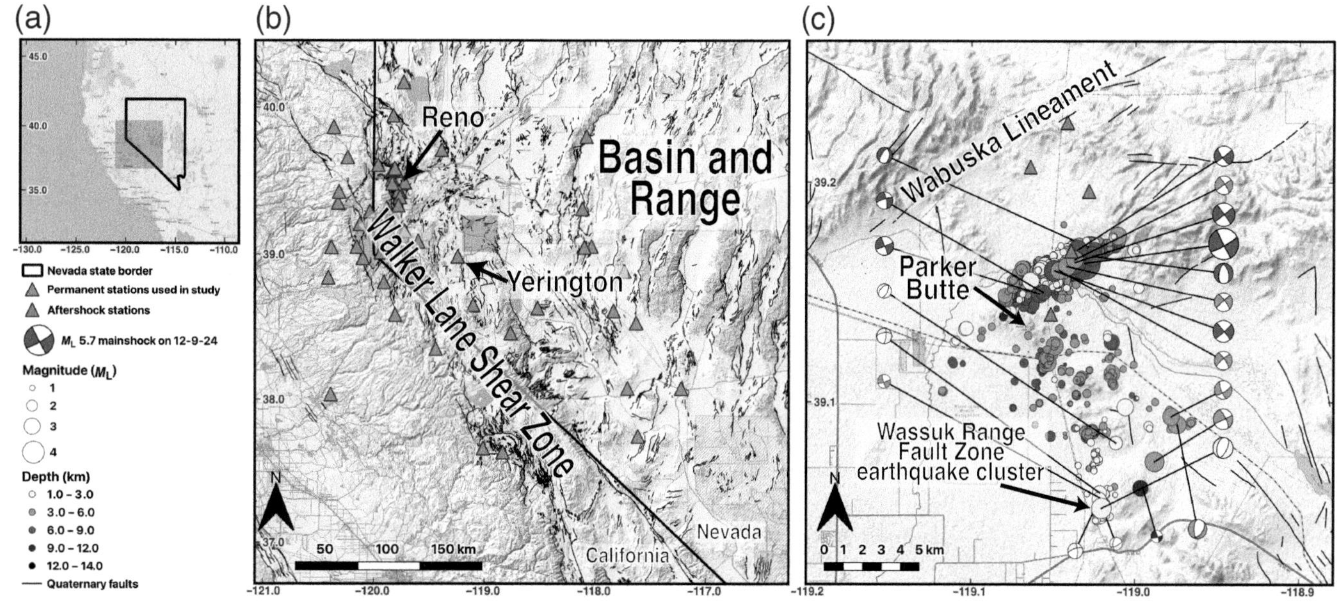

Figure 1. (a) Regional map showing Nevada's location within the western United States. Red-shaded box shows footprint of map in panel (b). (b) Tectonic overview of study area. Red shaded box shows footprint of study is map in panel (c). (c) Map of study area, which includes relocated seismicity with moment tensors and focal mechanisms. The 9 December mainshock is included with its NonLinLoc location. The moment tensors are plotted in a vertical line on the right side. The focal mechanisms are plotted on the left and bottom. Additional areas of interest discussed in the Introduction and Discussion sections of text are labeled. The color version of this figure is available only in the electronic edition.

area has been relatively quiet seismically in the past few decades, with only 86 earthquakes of M_L 1.5 and above located within a 15 km radius of the mainshock epicenter, between 1 January 2000 and 31 November 2024, per the Nevada Seismological Laboratory (NSL) catalog. The NSL installed five temporary seismic stations, the first installed on 10 December 2024 and the final station installed on 4 February 2025, to monitor aftershocks.

Large and potentially damaging normal and strike-slip earthquakes are a regular occurrence in western Nevada (Ryall, 1977; dePolo *et al.*, 1997; Anderson and Miyata, 2006; Anderson *et al.*, 2019; Trugman, 2024), which is within the seismically active tectonic zone of the Walker Lane (Hearn and Humphreys, 1998; Cashman and Fontaine, 2000; Faulds *et al.*, 2005; Wesnousky, 2005a; Busby, 2013), with the Central Nevada Seismic Belt and Basin and Range to the east (VanWormer and Ryall, 1980; Bell *et al.*, 2004; Caskey, 2004; Wesnousky *et al.*, 2005). West-central Nevada experienced a suite of large earthquakes in the 1900s, including the 1915 M_{Wg} 7.3 Pleasant Valley earthquake (Jones, 1915), the 1932 M_{Wg} 7.1 Cedar Mountain earthquake (Gianella and Callaghan, 1934), and the 1954 M_w 6.6, M_w 7.0, M_{Wg} 7.1, M_{Wg} 6.9 Rainbow Mountain and Dixie Valley sequences (Ryall and Malone, 1971). More recently, the 1994 M_w 5.9 Double Spring Flat earthquake (Ichinose *et al.*, 1998), 2020 M_w 6.5 Monte Cristo earthquake (Koehler *et al.*, 2021; Liu *et al.*, 2021; Ruhl *et al.*, 2021; Kariche, 2022), and 2021 M_w 6.0 Antelope Valley earthquake (Pollitz *et al.*, 2022; Trugman, Brune, *et al.*, 2023; Wang *et al.*, 2023) caused significant shaking across western Nevada. Because of the population density near Reno, Carson City, and Lake Tahoe, even slightly smaller local events like the 2008 M_w 5.0 Mogul (Anderson *et al.*, 2009; dePolo, 2011), 2013 M_w 4.2 Spanish Springs (Trugman and Shearer, 2017), 2015 M_w 4.4 Thomas Creek (Anderson and Biasi, 2016), 2020 M_w 4.5 Carson City, and the 1966 M_w 5.4 and 2021 M_w 4.7 Truckee earthquakes, can be widely felt and impactful.

The Parker Butte sequence provided a unique opportunity to conduct a detailed examination of a Walker Lane earthquake sequence and its relationship to active tectonics. Using high-precision relocations and fault-slip modeling from Interferometric Synthetic Aperture Radar (InSAR) and Global Positioning System (GPS) data, we estimated the location and geometry of the source fault for the mainshock, a previously unmapped structure. We also had ample strong and weak motion data that was useful to calculate ground intensity metrics such as peak ground acceleration (PGA), peak ground velocity (PGV), and response spectral acceleration (SA) to compare to PGA, PGV, and SA values predicted by existing western U.S. ground-motion models (GMMs). The results represent a comprehensive assessment of ground motions that complement limited reconnaissance estimates calculated for sites where secondary shaking effects were observed (Koehler *et al.*, 2025) during the rapid earthquake response.

Data and Methods

Earthquake relocations

We used 1301 analyst-reviewed events in the NSL catalog from 1 December 2024 to 10 May 2025 (Fig. 1), for our initial locations. Twelve of these events were foreshocks to the M_w 5.71

event. We analyzed events using all available data, so later events included more pick times because they were recorded on more of the temporary aftershock stations. The initial NSL locations were refined with NonLinLoc (Lomax *et al.*, 2000, 2009), which uses a probabilistic sampling technique to estimate hypocenter locations and uncertainties. The travel-time grids used in this procedure are station- and phase-specific and thus can account for station elevations, which is important for earthquakes recorded in mountainous western Nevada. We tested three 1D velocity models commonly used in the Walker Lane region for these locations. For each model, we plotted a histogram of the residual travel times for each event, as well as compared the root mean squared (rms) residual for all the events located with each model. We ultimately selected the velocity model used by Trugman, Brune, *et al.* (2023) in the final set of relocations because it had the lowest rms of the three velocity models.

For our final set of relocations, we used GrowClust3D.jl (Trugman, Chamberlain, *et al.*, 2023), a high-precision double-difference relocation algorithm that uses differential travel times derived from cross correlation between event pairs. The double-difference relocation method implicitly takes advantage of the more accurately located, later events (which were recorded on more of the temporary stations) to improve the locations of the earlier events (which were recorded on fewer, or none, of the temporary stations). In particular, the method optimizes the relative positions of events based on precise, correlation-based differential travel times measured on the subset of stations that recorded both earlier and later events. Of the 1301 events in the original catalog, we were able to relocate 1244 using a cross-correlation coefficient threshold of 0.65. It is common for larger earthquakes not to cross-correlate well with nearby events due to the complexity of their waveforms. One of the events we were not able to relocate was the 9 December M_w 5.7 mainshock. The body-wave arrivals for this event were far more emergent than the subsequent events, and therefore, the waveforms did not adequately correlate with those from any other event.

Plane fitting

We fit a plane to a subset of the final relocations to approximate the strike and dip of the fault that ruptured in the mainshock and the majority of aftershocks (Fig. 2). To find the subset, we excluded events that were judged to be off plane (by visual inspection) from the main northeast-trending cluster of earthquakes that included the mainshock. We used a grid search with half-degree steps over the full range of possible strikes and dips and minimized the mean distance of all the earthquake hypocenters from each possible plane.

Moment tensors and focal mechanisms

For moderate-to-large earthquakes (generally, mid-magnitude 3 and above), it is possible to directly invert long-period

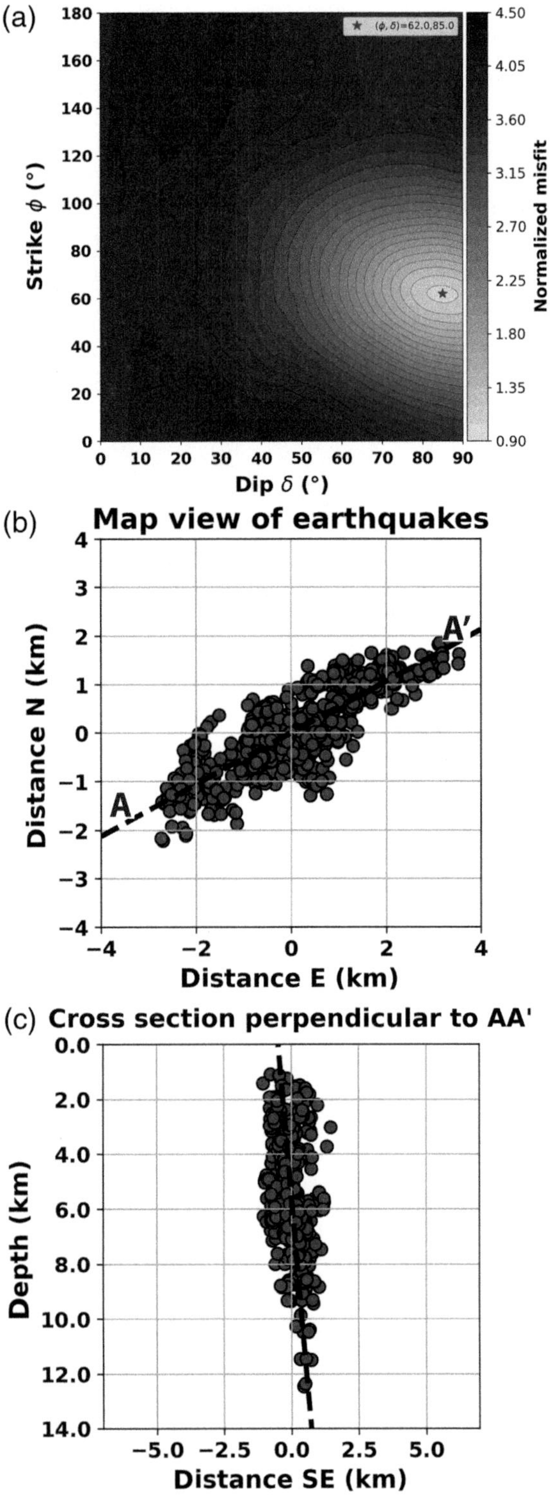

Figure 2. (a) Mainshock plane-fitting grid-search results. (b) Seismicity during study period used in plane fitting in map view, with axis indicating distance E and distance N in kilometers from the point 39.17, −119.04. Dashed line shows AA′ and is drawn at a strike angle of N62°E. (c) Cross section of seismicity during study period used in plane fitting projected onto line perpendicular to AA′. Dashed lines in panels (b) and (c) show the plane with the best fit, a strike of N62°E and dip 85° southeast. The color version of this figure is available only in the electronic edition.

(10–100 s) waveforms for a moment tensor solution. We applied the moment tensor inversion (MTINV) algorithm (Ichinose *et al.*, 2003) to all events in the sequence with local magnitude M_L 3.3 and greater. Some of the smaller events do not have sufficient signal-to-noise ratios at long periods to allow for a stable solution, but we were still able to obtain moment magnitudes and moment tensor solutions for 11 events in total, including all 9 events larger than M_L 3.4.

We generated *P*-wave first-motion focal mechanisms for an additional nine of the events. To generate the focal mechanisms, we used the Python package SKHASH (Skoumal *et al.*, 2024). SKHASH (based on the HASH algorithm of Hardebeck, 2002) is a grid-search method in which a set of acceptable mechanisms is developed with Monte Carlo perturbations in the hypocentral location and velocity model; the set of acceptable mechanisms can be averaged to find a preferred solution. We parameterized the grid-search method to look over 2° intervals across the possible angles on the focal sphere for the principal axes of the source mechanism and ran 100 Monte Carlo perturbations to hypocentral location. We excluded the closest stations, the temporary aftershock stations, from the focal mechanism calculations due to the large uncertainties in takeoff angle imposed by coupled uncertainties in the velocity model and hypocenter depth. We did not generate focal mechanisms for any of the nine events for which we generated moment tensor solutions. Thus, we have source mechanism estimates (moment tensor or first-motion mechanism) for 21 unique events in total (Fig. 1).

InSAR and GPS data and modeling

We imaged the coseismic ground surface displacement caused by the 2024 Parker Butte earthquake using InSAR. We used one ascending track (T64) and one descending track (T144) from the Sentinel-1 Synthetic Aperture Radar (SAR) images acquired by the European Space Agency between November 2024 and January 2025. For each track, we acquired three pre-event and three post-event SAR images (see Table S1, available in the supplemental material for details), allowing us to generate multiple interferograms to improve signal quality. We processed the SAR images using a geocoded single-look complex processor (Zebker, 2017). We generated 18 multi-looked interferograms (to reduce phase noise) with 30 m pixel spacing. The phase unwrapping process is done by the Statistical-Cost Network-Flow Algorithm for phase unwrapping (Chen and Zebker, 2001). See the supplemental material for the 18 SAR interferograms (Figs. S1 and S2) with details listed in Table S1. Figure 3a,b shows the stacked unwrapped interferograms for both ascending and descending tracks. The maximum surface deformation in the satellite line-of-sight direction is up to approximately 4 cm.

We estimated coseismic displacements at 55 GPS stations (red and blue triangles in Fig. 4) located within ~114 km of the mainshock epicenter. The stations are a combination of semicontinuous from the MAGNET GPS network (Blewitt *et al.*, 2009) and regional continuous stations from various agencies, including the National Science Foundation (NSF) Network of the Americas and Nevada GPS Network in Washoe County. The GPS data were processed by the Nevada Geodetic Laboratory (Blewitt *et al.*, 2018) with the GipsyX software from the Jet Propulsion Laboratory (Bertiger *et al.*, 2020). East-, north-, and up-component time series from stations within 114 km were differenced with those from stations outside 114 km to remove the effects of signals and noise common across the regional network. Coseismic displacement was estimated by solving for a trend and amplitude of a Heaviside function in the differenced time series using robust median-based methods that are insensitive to outlier data. Near-field GPS displacement at station P130 (13.5 km from epicenter) was 6.8 ± 1.8 mm south-southwest and at station YER1 (23.5 km from epicenter) was 6.0 ± 1.7 mm north-northeast. These motions are consistent in azimuth with the P and T axes of first motion measured by the seismic data (Fig. 1), suggesting that they represent surface deformation associated with slip on the source plane. More details of the station locations and offsets are provided in Table S2.

We integrated SAR interferograms and GPS data to retrieve fault geometry and fault-slip distribution. First, we estimated fault geometry by performing a nonlinear inversion of InSAR and GPS data, assuming a uniform-slip rectangular dislocation model based on the Okada (1985) elastic half-space model. We utilized a geodetic inversion package, Geodetic Bayesian Inversion Software (GBIS; Bagnardi and Hooper, 2018), which applies a Markov chain Monte Carlo approach to explore the posterior distribution of fault parameters, to search for optimal sets of fault geometries.

Second, we refined the fault slip distribution based on the GBIS-derived fault geometry. We extended the fault plane to a 12-km-long and 8-km-wide fault plane, where depth ranged from 0 to 8 km. The discretized fault includes 165 patches, with patch size varying from 0.5 km at the surface to 1 km at depth = 8 km. We applied Laplacian smoothing constraints to regularize the slip distribution and suppress noise-induced artifacts. We used both ascending and descending InSAR displacements and horizontal GPS offsets to jointly constrain the strike-slip and dip-slip components of slip.

Magnitude corrections

For the duration of the study period, the NSL catalog magnitude estimates are local magnitude (M_L) found by measuring synthetic Wood–Anderson displacement amplitudes at different qualifying stations and adjusting for distance using the correction table of Richter (1958). Trugman (2024) recently derived a new distance correction formulation that has the advantage of being a continuous function that is specific to Nevada earthquakes and better resolves magnitude information from near-source stations. Here, we applied the Trugman

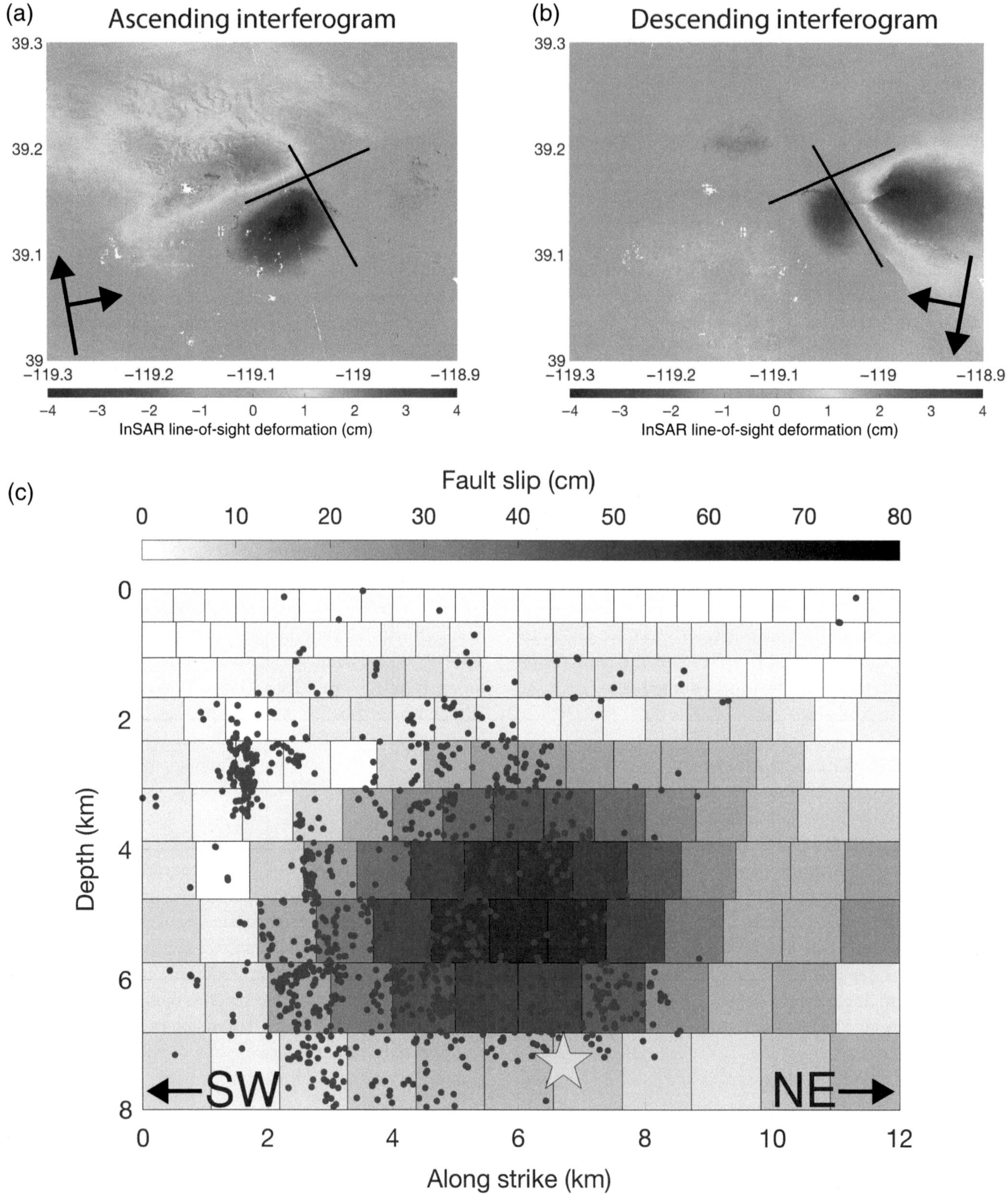

Figure 3. (a,b) Surface displacement observations for the 2024 Parker Butte earthquake. The ascending and descending interferometric phases are a stacked of interferograms in Figures S1 and S2, respectively. Short arrows show satellite look direction and long arrows show flight direction. Red color indicates movement toward the satellite. Black lines show the surface traces for the two fault planes defined in the two-plane solution to fit the Interferometric Synthetic Aperture Radar (InSAR) and Global Positioning System (GPS) data. (c) Fault-slip model for the 2024 Parker Butte earthquake assuming a single fault plane. The strike angle is N61.5°E and the dip angle is 73° southeast. Red dots show the relocated seismicity, and the yellow star shows the mainshock, projected onto the fault plane. The color version of this figure is available only in the electronic edition.

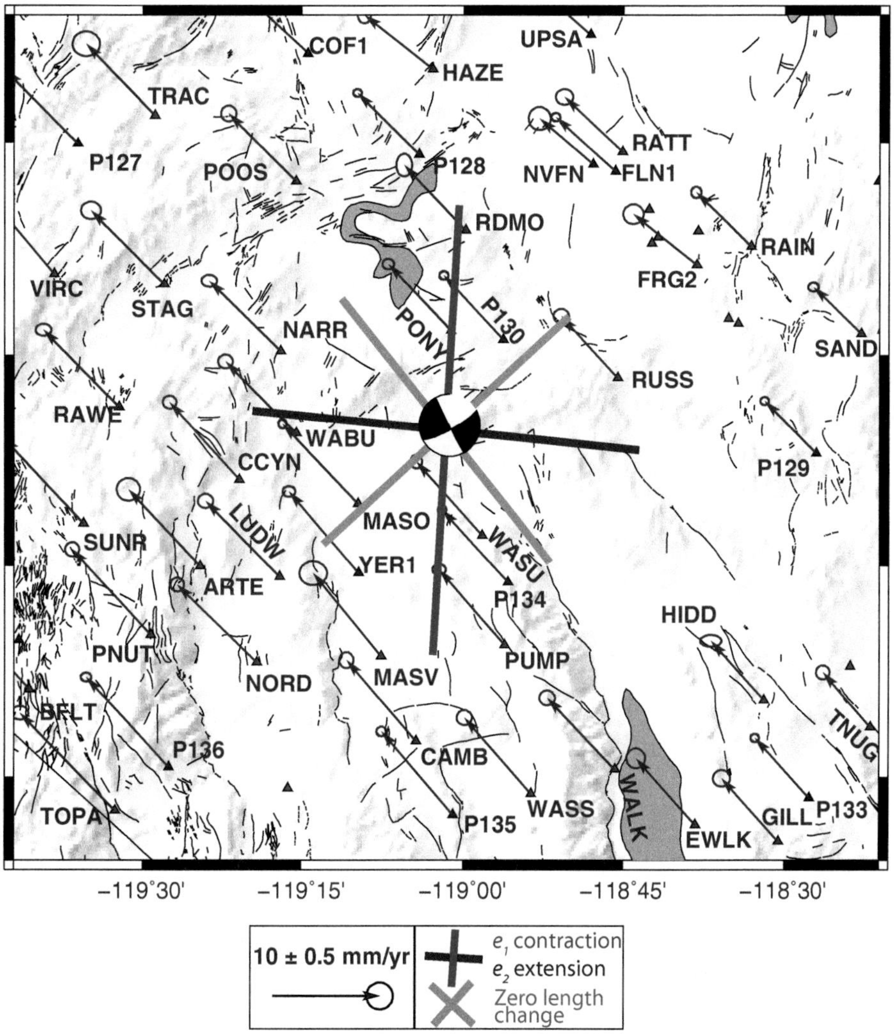

Figure 4. Interseismic velocities with respect to stable North America measured at GPS stations (blue vectors with 95% confidence uncertainty ellipses). Principal axis of extension (e_1: blue bar) and principal axis of contraction (e_2: red bar) are derived from the velocities. Continuous (MAGNET) station locations are given by blue and red triangles, respectively, four character station IDs are annotated next to stations. Azimuths of zero length change are given by gray bars. Moment tensor is from Figure 1. Alignment of extension and contraction directions with T and P axes of the mainshock suggests consistency between tectonic strain accumulation and seismic moment release. The color version of this figure is available only in the electronic edition.

(2024) formulation alongside updated distance information from the relocated hypocenters to revise the M_L estimates for the Parker Butte catalog. In most cases, the revisions are relatively small (<0.1 magnitude unit) but provide enhanced accuracy, especially for nearby stations. We did not consider station-specific corrections for this work because each station records data only from a limited range of azimuth corresponding to earthquakes in the sequence.

Ground-motion analysis

The Parker Butte mainshock provides a valuable dataset to understand the characteristics of strong ground motion, which is important for preparing for future large earthquakes that could impact the population centers of the central Walker Lane. We used the gmprocess software package (Thompson *et al.*, 2024) to calculate ground-motion intensity metrics: PGV, PGA, and SA at different periods for the Parker Butte mainshock. We compared the observed ground motions to model predictions from the average of the four active crustal GMMs used for hazard estimation in the western U.S. (Abrahamson *et al.*, 2014; Boore *et al.*, 2014; Campbell and Bozorgnia, 2014; Chiou and Youngs, 2014; Moschetti *et al.*, 2024). For the model predictions, we assumed the rupture geometry defined by the moment tensor solution to compute the rupture and Joyner–Boore distances to the site, and test various site conditions to understand their effect on the model residuals.

Results

In our relocated catalog, most of the events form a northeast-trending linear feature with scattered events to the southeast, shown in Figure 1. Although only a few of the events fall directly on visible InSAR lineaments (where there are abrupt changes in the direction of surface deformation, approximately where the surface traces of the modeled fault planes are drawn in Fig. 3), many of them plot in areas that correspond to some surface displacement, particularly in the hills southeast of Parker Butte. The main cluster of events can be fit with a plane, which strikes N62°E and dips 85° to the southeast (Fig. 2). This is consistent with most of the focal mechanisms in the cluster (Fig. 1), which have left-lateral strike-slip nodal planes that strike ~70° N to 80° E and have near vertical dips. There is also good agreement with the moment tensor solutions (Fig. 1), which, again, primarily have a left-lateral strike-slip nodal plane, striking from ~50° N to 75° E with near-vertical dips. Two of the events in this main cluster indicate normal faulting (one focal mechanism and one moment tensor).

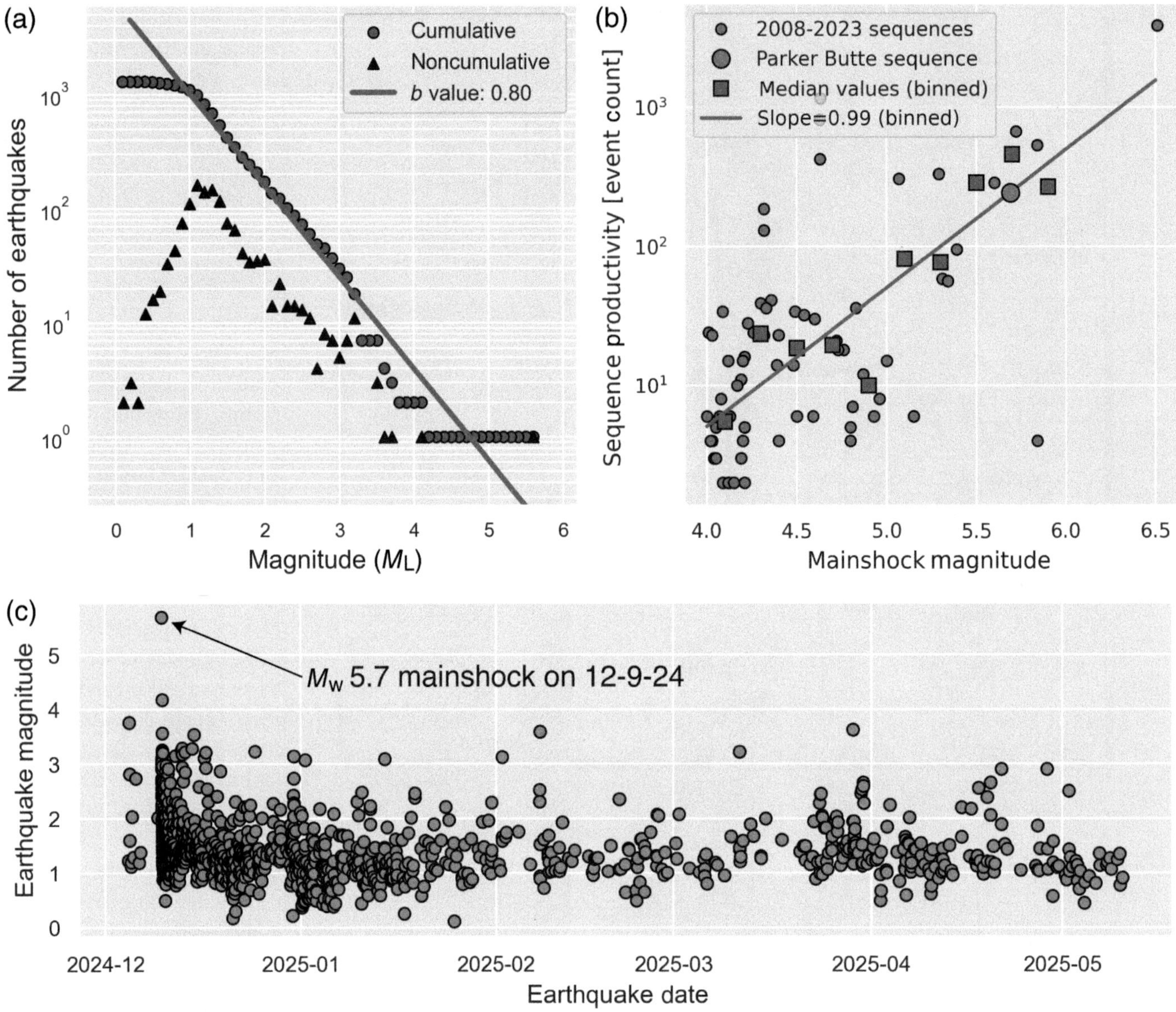

Figure 5. Statistical seismicity analysis. (a) Frequency–magnitude distribution along with the line of best fit for a Gutenberg–Richter distribution. (b) Earthquake productivity of the Parker Butte sequence in comparison to other Nevada sequences. The red line shows a linear fit to the median of binned values (red squares). (c) Earthquake magnitudes plotted with respect to time. The color version of this figure is available only in the electronic edition.

They both have a more northerly strike and are less steeply dipping than the strike-slip mechanisms in the cluster, suggesting some complexity in the faulting structure. Focal mechanisms and moment tensors for events outside the main cluster primarily reflect a strike-slip geometry with a few normal rakes.

Earthquake statistics for the Parker Butte sequence from 1 December 2024 to 10 May 2025, with corrected magnitudes, are shown in Figure 5. Figure 5a shows the frequency–magnitude distribution along with a line of best fit for a Gutenberg–Richter distribution. We determined the *b* value of the catalog using the maximum-likelihood estimation method (Aki, 1965). To determine what magnitude of completeness to use, we calculated the *b* value for multiple test values for magnitude of completeness (Fig. S5) and found a point of stability in the *b* value estimate, which we select as an appropriate magnitude of completeness for the catalog (Cao and Gao, 2002). The sequence has a magnitude of completeness of 1.2 and a *b* value of 0.80 ± 0.03. From visual inspection of the frequency–magnitude distribution, it is not clear that an exponential distribution adequately describes the earthquakes recorded to date in the sequence, which would limit the applicability of the *b* value calculations in this context.

Figure 5b shows the productivity of the Parker Butte sequence (Trugman and Ben-Zion, 2023) in relation to other recent Nevada sequences reported by Trugman (2024), using a cutoff magnitude of 1.8 for consistency across datasets. The Parker Butte sequence falls almost perfectly onto the magnitude scaling line fit to the preceding Nevada sequences, meaning it is not unusual in terms of productivity as compared to others in Nevada, though slightly more productive than the western U.S. average (Trugman and Ben-Zion, 2023). Because the sequence is ongoing at present writing, the productivity may be underestimated.

Figure 5c shows the earthquake magnitudes plotted with respect to date to show the relative frequency and magnitudes of the events over time, including the foreshocks in the week prior to the mainshock. As expected, there is a general reduction in magnitude and frequency of events, but the sequence is ongoing and has produced occasional M_L 3+ events after the six-month study period of this report. The reported frequency of events with magnitudes below the magnitude of completeness is slightly biased by staffing availability because only events that were manually located and reviewed by a seismic analyst are included.

Based on the uniform slip model inversion, the strike angle of the fault plane is N61.5°E ± 1.0°, which agrees well with the strike of N62°E estimated from fitting a plane through the aftershock cluster. The retrieved dip angle is 73° ± 1.5° southeast, which is gentler than the dip angle inferred from seismicity plane fitting analysis (85° southeast). Figure 3c shows the distributed slip model derived using the GBIS-estimated fault geometry. The fault dimension is approximately 8–10 km long and 5 km down-dip extent. This estimation is consistent with the fault dimension of 8 km × 6 km estimated from the aftershock distribution. The posterior distributions of model parameters by jointly inverting InSAR and GPS data are shown in Tables S3 and S4, and Figure S6 presents the modeled InSAR and GPS observations and the residuals.

The maximum fault slip reaches ~50 cm, and most of the slip is concentrated between depths of 2.5 and 7 km, consistent with the depth range of the relocated seismicity and supporting the reliability of the InSAR-derived model. Assuming a shear modulus of 32 GPa, the geodetic moment is 4.4×10^{17} N · m, equivalent to an M_w 5.7 event. This is consistent with the seismic moment magnitude (M_w 5.7), suggesting that most of the moment was radiated seismically. The seismicity extends from 2 to 10 km depth, whereas there is no significant slip below 7 km, which might be related to the limited ability for InSAR to resolve slip at greater depths. However, inclusion of the GPS data in the medium- to far-field compensates for the weakness that the InSAR data have at longer wavelengths, suggesting that the bottom of the slip patch is adequately resolved. We also consider the scenario where the fault geometry is steeper, as suggested by seismological observations. Assuming a fault dip angle of 90°, as shown in Figure S7, the fault-slip distribution pattern does not change significantly, but the data misfit reduction significantly decreases from 88% to 76% compared to the model with a dip angle of 73° southeast. Figures S8 and S9 show the observed and modeled GPS and InSAR displacements for dip angles of 73° southeast and 90°, respectively.

In addition to the northeast–southwest-striking main fault plane (plane I), both InSAR and field observations reveal surface fractures aligned along a northwest–southeast orientation, indicating the presence of a secondary fault (Koehler *et al.*, 2025). We therefore incorporated a second, northwest–southeast-striking fault plane into the inversion framework (plane II). The strike and location of this fault were inferred from surface fracture mapping (Koehler *et al.*, 2025), and the initial dip angle was assumed to be vertical (90°). We performed a new geodetic inversion using this two-fault model, allowing both fault planes to slip independently. To evaluate sensitivity to the assumed dip of the northwest–southeast-striking fault, we tested four additional dip scenarios: dipping 70°/80° eastward and 70°/80° westward, as shown in Table S4. The resulting slip distributions showed increased misfit reduction compared to a one-plane model (Table S4), but no significant differences between the different dip assumptions as shown in Figure S10, suggesting the inversion results are robust with respect to reasonable dip uncertainties. The modeling of InSAR and GPS data, as well as the misfit reduction, can be found in Figures S11–S15 and Table S4.

We calculated Coulomb stress changes to investigate potential interaction between the two fault planes. Using the slip distribution from the northeast–southwest-striking fault (plane I), we computed the Coulomb stress change on the northwest–southeast-striking fault (plane II), assuming a friction coefficient of 0.6. Figure S16 shows the resulting Coulomb stress transfer based on the distributed fault slip in Figure S10. The stress change on plane II is positive (0.1–0.3 MPa) at depths of 0–3 km, and negative (−0.3 to −0.1 MPa) at depths of 3–7 km. This stress pattern is consistent with the geodetic modeled slip distribution on plane II, where fault slip is concentrated at depths of 3–7 km and small, but not zero, above 3 km. These findings suggest that slip on the northeast–southwest-striking main fault promoted failure at depth on the northwest–southeast-striking plane, while limiting shallow slip on the same fault.

To assess the possibility that aseismic slip on the northwest-striking fault triggered the mainshock on the northeast-striking fault (Koehler *et al.*, 2025), we tested the alternative scenario in which the stress change resulting from the slip from plane II was responsible for positive Coulomb stress change on plane I, using the slip distribution on plane II allowed from the GPS-InSAR joint inversion for the two-fault model (Fig. S10). The results are shown in Figure S17. Although the resulting Coulomb stress change on plane I is positive, it is lower (~0.2 MPa) and localized near the intersection of the two planes. Thus, a slip on plane I triggered by stress change transferred from plane II is only favored if plane II is dipping west. In contrast, slip on plane II triggered by stress transferred from plane I is robust to the geometric arrangement of the two planes. This result suggests that it is more likely that aseismic slip on plane II was triggered by the mainshock slip on plane I, rather than the reverse.

Overall, the recorded ground motions for the Parker Butte mainshock (Fig. 6) are broadly consistent with the level and variability anticipated by the GMMs. The PGV data show

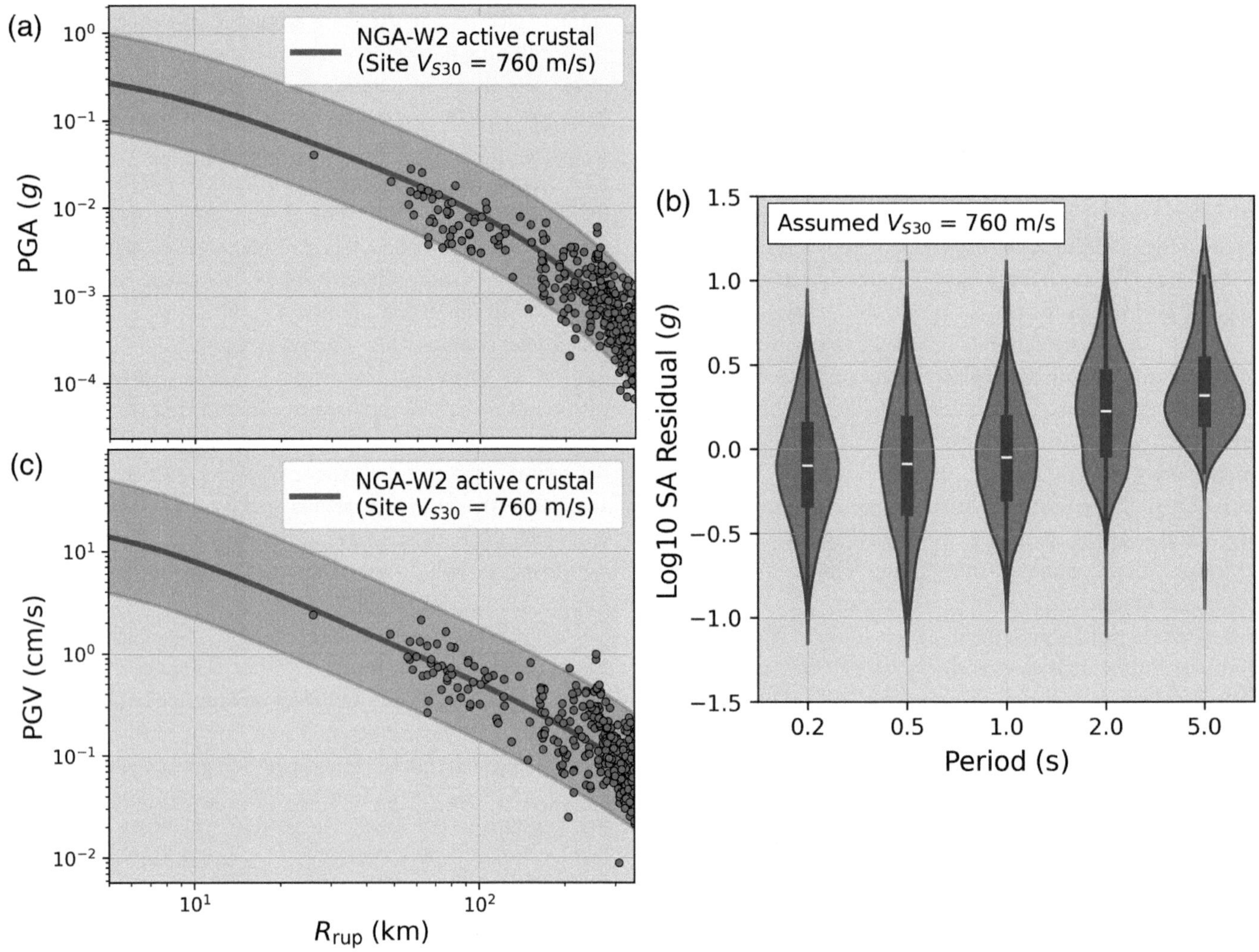

Figure 6. Mainshock ground-motion analysis. (a,c) Observed (blue dot) and predicted (red-shaded region) peak ground acceleration (PGA) and peak ground velocity (PGV), respectively. The solid line shows the median prediction of the composite ground-motion model, and the shaded area represents a two-standard-deviation interval (in log units) surrounding the median prediction. (b) Spectral acceleration (SA) residual between the observed and predicted ground motions as a function of period. NGA-W2, Next Generation Attenuation-West2 Project. The color version of this figure is available only in the electronic edition.

nearly zero bias with respect to the GMMs (assuming a neutral site condition), whereas the PGA data show a subtle negative bias (PGA data are lower than the GMM median prediction) for the same site condition. This trend suggests a frequency dependence of the GMM residuals, which can be examined in greater detail via the residual distributions for different SA periods (Fig. 6c). The residuals at short periods (<1.0 s) are near-zero, though slightly negative on average, but increase to values greater than zero at long periods.

Alignment of tectonic interseismic strain accumulation with sudden coseismic strain release is expected in the earthquake cycle. We compared interseismic deformation to the strain release in the mainshock by estimating the directions and magnitudes of the principal components of the horizontal tensor strain rate in the Central Walker Lane median interannual difference adjusted for skewness (MIDAS) velocity field (Blewitt *et al.*, 2016). We selected 14 stations having 6 or more years of data within 34 km of the epicenter and estimated the strain rate on a sphere (Savage *et al.*, 2001). We found that the principal axis of interseismic extension (azimuth of $\dot{e}_1$) is close to the T axis of the mainshock moment tensor, and the axis of principal contraction (azimuth of $\dot{e}_2$) is close to the P axis (Fig. 4). The alignment between directions of coseismic and interseismic extension and contraction suggests consistency between strain accumulation and release. Although the alignment is not exact, this is the expected outcome because it is typical for there to be a diversity of moment tensors and focal mechanisms associated with a single given stress field.

From the geodetic network, we estimate the shear strain rate ($\dot{e}_1 - \dot{e}_2$) to be $56.8 \pm 6.0 \times 10^{-9}$/yr and the dilatation rate ($\dot{e}_1 + \dot{e}_2$) to be $3.5 \pm 6.0 \times 10^{-9}$/yr. Thus, the deformation is mostly shear strain with low dilatation, consistent with the level and style of strain rates throughout the northern

Walker Lane (Hammond and Thatcher, 2007) and consistent with the strike-slip mechanism on both planes. To compare to the fault strike, we estimated the directions of zero length change from the strain rate tensor; these are the azimuths that we would expect faults to strike inside a pure shear field to release accumulating strain. We use the formula of Holt and Haines (1993) to estimate these azimuths (gray bars in Fig. 4). The azimuth closest to the inferred fault strike (N47.7°E) is misaligned with the strike of the fault (N61.5°E, Table S3) by ~13.8°. This misalignment is inconsistent with the assumption of pure strike slip, and consistent with the presence of a dip-slip component of the mainshock that is ~18% of the total slip on the primary rupture plane.

Although the horizontal dilatation rate (area growth vs. contraction) is not significantly different than zero when focusing on GPS stations near the epicenter, it is positive. Widening the zone over which we estimate the dilatation rate to include more stations (96) within 80 km of the Parker Butte epicenter reduces uncertainties substantially: $\dot{e}_1 + \dot{e}_2 = 4.7 \pm 0.9 \times 10^{-9}$/yr, making the dilatation rate significant. Although less specifically resolved to the Parker Butte epicentral location compared to the shear strain rate, we can say that the earthquake occurred within a tectonic domain exhibiting significant transtension. Positive dilatation is compatible with regional geologic and geodetic observations of crustal extension (Wesnousky, 2005b; Kreemer and Hammond, 2007), and with the component of normal slip on the mainshock. Positive dilation could be a contributing factor (along with other structural factors) to the recent occurrence of dual-fault ruptures in other parts of the Walker Lane and Eastern California Shear Zone, such as Superstition Hills, Nine Mile Ranch, Ridgecrest, and Monte Cristo Range, all of which were preceded by positive interseismic dilatation.

Discussion

The pattern of seismicity and fault-slip modeling analysis has indicated the presence of a previously unmapped, nearly vertical (73°–85° S), left-lateral strike-slip fault trending ~N60°E. The northeast–southwest-trending Wabuska Lineament, which is composed of active faults that accommodate left-lateral motion (Li *et al.*, 2017), is approximately 7 km north of and parallel to the Parker Butte mainshock plane. Orthogonal northeast–southwest-striking left-lateral and northwest–southeast-striking right-lateral strike-slip faulting is common in the Walker Lane (Wesnousky, 2005a,b). In the case of Parker Butte, the two-plane fault-slip modeling and corresponding Coulomb stress change analysis suggest that the mainshock plane (northeast–southwest striking) ruptured first, leading to a coseismic stress transfer to a northwest–southeast-striking plane, which is visible on the descending track interferogram (Fig. 3b) and where surface fracturing was confirmed in the field (Koehler *et al.*, 2025). Several sequences in the region have consisted of a rupture on a northeast–southwest-striking plane followed by a rupture on a northwest–southeast-striking plane, including the 1986 Chalfant sequence (Smith, 2000), the 1987 Superstition Hills sequence (Magistrale *et al.*, 1989), the 2016 Nine Mile Ranch sequence (Hatch-Ibarra *et al.*, 2022), the 2019 Ridgecrest sequence (Ross *et al.*, 2019), and the 2020 Monte Cristo sequence (Koehler *et al.*, 2021; Ruhl *et al.*, 2021). However, we have yet to identify an obvious single earthquake event in the aftershock sequence that qualifies as the "second rupture" on the northwest–southeast-striking plane. InSAR, as well as field observations made the morning of 16 December, constrain the timing of the northwest-striking surface fracture (and therefore timing of the "second rupture") to the time window 8–16 December. Although there are several candidate M 3 events in the vicinity, these are unlikely to be large enough to cause the visible surface fracturing or geodetically modeled slip. It is thus possible that moment release on the northwest-striking fault was dominantly aseismic. The roles of dynamic stressing and/or postseismic creep and relaxation in driving aseismic slip on the northwest-striking fault remain enigmatic.

Further adding to the complexity, the distribution of earthquakes to the southeast of the mainshock cluster includes multiple short, linear clusters, mostly unassociated with mapped faults. One shallow cluster in the southernmost part of the sequence (Fig. 1) is collocated with a mapped fault with normal slip sense that is associated with the Wassuk Range fault zone (Adams and Sawyer, 1999; Dong *et al.*, 2014). There are a limited number of focal mechanisms for this subcluster, but most of them have a component of normal slip to them. It is also worth noting that this shallow southern cluster is one of the more recent areas of activity in the sequences, with most of the events occurring after February 2025. Questions remain about the detailed geometry of this network of faults and how stress transfers triggered localized clusters around the sequence.

The ground motions of the Parker Butte are largely consistent with existing active crustal GMMs for the western United States (Fig. 6). This is encouraging for future application of these GMMs in Nevada because the models were trained using ground-motion recordings compiled almost exclusively from outside of the state. However, the period dependence of the SA residuals (Fig. 6c) suggests that there are slight but measurable differences in ground-motion characteristics of Nevada earthquakes compared to the records used in the GMM development. In future work, systematic analysis of ground motions from earthquakes throughout the state could reveal the physical cause underlying these trends and potential means of adapting GMMs to account for them.

Data and Resources

The Nevada Seismological Laboratory (NSL) earthquake catalog may be found on the NSL website (http://www.seismo.unr.edu/, last accessed May 2025) or in the U.S. Geological Survey (USGS) Comprehensive Catalog (ComCat; https://earthquake.usgs.gov/data/comcat/, last accessed May 2025) to which the NSL is an authoritative contributor. The earthquake catalog, with both NonLinLoc and GrowClust locations, that was developed in this study, is available on Zenodo at doi: 10.5281/

zenodo.15644553. Waveforms and seismic metadata are available in the Incorporated Research Institutions for Seismology (IRIS). NonLinLoc and GrowClust3D.jl software are both publicly available on GitHub at https://github.com/ut-beg-texnet/NonLinLoc (last accessed January 2024) and https://github.com/dttrugman/GrowClust3D.jl (last accessed December 2024). Continuous Global Positioning System (GPS) station data were accessed from the National Science Foundation (NSF) Geodetic Facility for the Advancement of Geoscience (GAGE) data archive operated by EarthScope Consortium (NSF Award 1724509; https://www.earthscope.org/nota/, last accessed May 2025) and the Nevada GPS Network managed by the State of Utah's Automated Geographic Reference Center in the Department of Technology Services (https://nevadagps.utah.gov/, last accessed May 2025). MAGNET GPS data are distributed by the Nevada Geodetic Laboratory (available at https://geodesy.unr.edu/magnet.php, last accessed May 2025). The supplemental material includes data tables with information on GPS and Interferometric Synthetic Aperture Radar (InSAR) data, unstacked interferograms, details on fault geometry and slip modeling, and stability analysis on the *b* value of the catalog.

Declaration of Competing Interests

The authors acknowledge that there are no conflicts of interest recorded.

Acknowledgments

The authors would like to thank the U.S. Geological Survey (USGS) for providing the rapid deployment kits to study the aftershock sequences. Collection of seismic data in the Nevada Seismological Laboratory's (NSL) seismic network, including the temporary network of aftershock kits, was supported by the USGS Advanced National Seismic System (ANSS) cooperative agreement G25AC00163. D. T. T. and Y. J. acknowledge support for this study from National Aeronautics and Space Administration (NASA) Earth Surface and Interiors Award 80NSSC24K0736, National Science Foundation (NSF) Awards EAR-2121666 and EAR-2231705, and Nevada Division of Emergency Management Award HMGP DR-4523-08-08P. Collection of Global Positioning System (GPS) data in the MAGNET GPS network was supported by the USGS Geodetic Networks program under cooperative agreement G25AC00183. GPS data processing at the Nevada Geodetic Laboratory was supported by NASA Grant 80NSSC22K0463. The authors thank Tom Rennie, Bill Savran, Will Honjas, Andrew Rosenberg-Main, Brandon Bell, Ryan Brandani, Jackson Mendelsohn, Matt Barnard, Ian Scoggin, Austin Armstrong, Quinn O'Neil, Hannah Martin, and Avigyan Chatterjee. The authors would also like to thank two anonymous reviewers whose valuable feedback helped them improve the quality and clarity of this report, and Editor-in-Chief Allison Bent.

References

Abrahamson, N. A., W. J. Silva, and R. Kamai (2014). Summary of the ASK14 ground motion relation for active crustal regions, *Earthq. Spectra* **30,** no. 3, 1025–1055, doi: 10.1193/070913EQS198M.

Adams, K., and T. L. Sawyer (1999). Fault number 1300, Wassuk Range fault zone, in Quaternary fault and fold database of the United States, available at https://earthquakes.usgs.gov/hazards/qfaults (last accessed May 2025).

Aki, K. (1965). Maximum likelihood estimate of b in the formula log N= a-bM and its confidence limits, *Bull. Earthq. Res. Inst. Tokyo Univ.* **43,** 237–239.

Anderson, J. G., and G. P. Biasi (2016). Some observations based on the strong-motion accelerograms from the Thomas Creek, Nevada, earthquake of 23 December 2015, *Seismol. Res. Lett.* **88,** no. 1, 6–12, doi: 10.1785/0220160015.

Anderson, J. G., and Y. Miyata (2006). Ranking STATES BY SEISMIC Activity, *Seismol. Res. Lett.* **77,** no. 6, 672–676, doi: 10.1785/gssrl.77.6.672.

Anderson, J. G., R. D. Koehler, R. Abercrombie, S. K. Ahdi, S. Angster, J. Bormann, J. N. Brune, S. M. Dee, C. dePolo, S. E. Dickenson, *et al.* (2019). A seismic hazards overview of the urban regions of Nevada: Recent advancements and research directions, *Seismol. Res. Lett.* **90,** no. 4, 1577–1583, doi: 10.1785/0220180357.

Anderson, J. G., I. Tibuleac, A. Anooshehpoor, G. Biasi, K. Smith, and D. von Seggern (2009). Exceptional ground motions recorded during the 26 April 2008 Mw 5.0 earthquake in Mogul, Nevada, *Bull. Seismol. Soc. Am.* **99,** no. 6, 3475–3486, doi: 10.1785/0120080352.

Bagnardi, M., and A. Hooper (2018). Inversion of surface deformation data for rapid estimates of source parameters and uncertainties: A Bayesian approach, *Geochem. Geophys. Geosys.* **19,** no. 7, 2194–2211, doi: 10.1029/2018GC007585.

Bell, J. W., S. J. Caskey, A. R. Ramelli, and L. Guerrieri (2004). Pattern and rates of faulting in the Central Nevada Seismic Belt, and paleoseismic evidence for prior Beltlike behavior, *Bull. Seismol. Soc. Am.* **94,** no. 4, 1229–1254, doi: 10.1785/012003226.

Bertiger, W., Y. Bar-Sever, A. Dorsey, B. Haines, N. Harvey, D. Hemberger, M. Heflin, W. Lu, M. Miller, A. W. Moore, *et al.* (2020). GipsyX/RTGx, a new tool set for space geodetic operations and research, *Adv. Space Res.* **66,** no. 3, 469–489, doi: 10.1016/j.asr.2020.04.015.

Blewitt, G., W. Hammond, and C. Kreemer (2018). Harnessing the GPS data explosion for interdisciplinary science, *Eos* **99,** doi: 10.1029/2018EO104623.

Blewitt, G., W. C. Hammond, and C. Kreemer (2009). Geodetic observation of contemporary deformation in the northern Walker Lane: 1. Semipermanent GPS strategy, in *Late Cenozoic Structure and Evolution of the Great Basin-Sierra Nevada Transition*, J. S. Oldow and P. H. Cashman (Editors), Geological Society of America, Boulder, Colorado, doi: 10.1130/2009.2447(01).

Blewitt, G., C. Kreemer, W. C. Hammond, and J. Gazeaux (2016). MIDAS robust trend estimator for accurate GPS station velocities without step detection, *J. Geophys. Res.* **121,** no. 3, 2054–2068, doi: 10.1002/2015JB012552.

Boore, D. M., J. P. Stewart, E. Seyhan, and G. M. Atkinson (2014). NGA-West2 equations for predicting PGA, PGV, and 5% damped PSA for shallow crustal earthquakes, *Earthq. Spectra* **30,** no. 3, 1057–1085, doi: 10.1193/070113EQS184M.

Busby, C. J. (2013). Birth of a plate boundary at ca. 12 Ma in the Ancestral Cascades arc, Walker Lane belt of California and Nevada, *Geosphere* **9,** no. 5, 1147–1160, doi: 10.1130/GES00928.1.

Campbell, K. W., and Y. Bozorgnia (2014). NGA-West2 ground motion model for the average horizontal components of PGA, PGV, and 5% damped linear acceleration response spectra, *Earthq. Spectra* **30,** no. 3, 1087–1115, doi: 10.1193/062913EQS175M.

Cao, A., and S. S. Gao (2002). Temporal variation of seismic b-values beneath northeastern Japan island arc, *Geophys. Res. Lett.* **29,** no. 9, doi: 10.1029/2001GL013775.

Cashman, P. H., and S. A. Fontaine (2000). Strain partitioning in the northern Walker Lane, western Nevada and northeastern California, *Tectonophysics* **326,** no. 1, 111–130, doi: 10.1016/S0040-1951(00)00149-9.

Caskey, S. J. (2004). Historic surface faulting and paleoseismicity in the area of the 1954 rainbow mountain-stillwater earthquake sequence, Central Nevada, *Bull. Seismol. Soc. Am.* **94,** no. 4, 1255–1275, doi: 10.1785/012003012.

Chen, C. W., and H. A. Zebker (2001). Two-dimensional phase unwrapping with use of statistical models for cost functions in nonlinear optimization, *J. Opt. Soc. Am. A* **18,** no. 2, 338, doi: 10.1364/JOSAA.18.000338.

Chiou, B. S.-J., and R. R. Youngs (2014). Update of the Chiou and Youngs NGA Model for the average horizontal component of peak ground motion and response spectra, *Earthq. Spectra* **30,** no. 3, 1117–1153, doi: 10.1193/072813EQS219M.

dePolo, C. M. (2011). Observations and reported effects of the February–April, 2008 Mogul-Somersett, Nevada earthquake sequence, *Open-File Rept. 11-5*, Nevada Bureau of Mines and Geology, Reno, Nevada, 33 pp.

dePolo, C. M., J. G. Anderson, D. M. dePolo, and J. G. Price (1997). Earthquake occurrence in the Reno-Carson City Urban Corridor, *Seismol. Res. Lett.* **68,** no. 3, 401–412, doi: 10.1785/gssrl.68.3.401.

Dong, S., G. Ucarkus, S. G. Wesnousky, J. Maloney, G. Kent, N. Driscoll, and R. Baskin (2014). Strike-slip faulting along the Wassuk Range of the northern Walker Lane, Nevada, *Geosphere* **10,** no. 1, 40–48, doi: 10.1130/GES00912.1.

Faulds, J. E., C. D. Henry, and N. H. Hinz (2005). Kinematics of the northern Walker Lane: An incipient transform fault along the Pacific–North American plate boundary, *Geology* **33,** no. 6, 505–508, doi: 10.1130/G21274.1.

Gianella, V. P., and E. Callaghan (1934). The Cedar Mountain, Nevada, earthquake of December 20, 1932, *Bull. Seismol. Soc. Am.* **24,** no. 4, 345–384, doi: 10.1785/BSSA0240040345.

Hammond, W. C., and W. Thatcher (2007). Crustal deformation across the Sierra Nevada, northern Walker Lane, Basin and Range transition, western United States measured with GPS, 2000–2004, *J. Geophys. Res.* **112,** no. B5, 2006JB004625, doi: 10.1029/2006JB004625.

Hardebeck, J. L. (2002). A new method for determining first-motion focal mechanisms, *Bull. Seismol. Soc. Am.* **92,** no. 6, 2264–2276, doi: 10.1785/0120010200.

Hatch-Ibarra, R. L., R. E. Abercrombie, C. J. Ruhl, K. D. Smith, W. C. Hammond, and I. K. Pierce (2022). The 2016 Nine Mile Ranch earthquakes: Hazard and tectonic implications of orthogonal conjugate faulting in the Walker Lane, *Bull. Seismol. Soc. Am.* **112,** no. 3, 1727–1741, doi: 10.1785/0120210149.

Hearn, E. H., and E. D. Humphreys (1998). Kinematics of the southern Walker Lane Belt and motion of the Sierra Nevada block, California, *J. Geophys. Res.* **103,** no. B11, 27,033–27,049, doi: 10.1029/98JB01390.

Holt, W. E., and A. J. Haines (1993). Velocity fields in deforming Asia from the inversion of earthquake-released strains, *Tectonics* **12,** no. 1, 1–20, doi: 10.1029/92TC00658.

Ichinose, G. A., J. G. Anderson, K. D. Smith, and Y. Zeng (2003). Source parameters of Eastern California and Western Nevada earthquakes from regional moment tensor inversion, *Bull. Seismol. Soc. Am.* **93,** no. 1, 61–84, doi: 10.1785/0120020063.

Ichinose, G. A., K. D. Smith, and J. G. Anderson (1998). Moment tensor solutions of the 1994 to 1996 Double Spring Flat, Nevada, earthquake sequence and implications for local tectonic models, *Bull. Seismol. Soc. Am.* **88,** no. 6, 1363–1378.

Jones, J. C. (1915). The pleasant valley, Nevada, earthquake of October 2, 1915, *Bull. Seismol. Soc. Am.* **5,** no. 4, 190–205, doi: 10.1785/BSSA0050040190.

Kariche, J. (2022). The 2020 Monte Cristo (Nevada) earthquake sequence: Stress Transfer in the context of conjugate strike-slip faults, *Tectonics* **41,** no. 3, e2020TC006506, doi: 10.1029/2020TC006506.

Koehler, R. D., S. Dee, A. Elliott, A. Hatem, A. Pickering, I. Pierce, and G. Seitz (2021). Field Response and surface-rupture characteristics of the 2020 M 6.5 Monte Cristo Range Earthquake, Central Walker Lane, Nevada, *Seismol. Res. Lett.* **92,** no. 2A, 823–839, doi: 10.1785/0220200371.

Koehler, R. D., C. D. Rowe, D. R. Vlaha, S. Masoch, N. Wagoner, Y. Jiang, D. T. Trugman, K. Bogolub, W. C. Hammond, A. Crandall-Bear, *et al.* (2025). The 9 December 2024 M5.7 Parker Butte earthquake: Orthogonal surface fracturing and associated ground disturbances near Yerington, Nevada, central Walker Lane, *Seismica* **4,** no. 2 (in press).

Kreemer, C., and W. C. Hammond (2007). Geodetic constraints on areal changes in the Pacific-North America plate boundary zone; what controls basin and range extension? *Geology (Boulder)* **35,** no. 10, 943–946, doi: 10.1130/G23868A.1.

Li, X., W. Huang, I. K. D. Pierce, S. J. Angster, and S. G. Wesnousky (2017). Characterizing the Quaternary expression of active faulting along the Olinghouse, Carson, and Wabuska lineaments of the Walker Lane, *Geosphere* **13,** no. 6, 2119–2136, doi: 10.1130/GES01483.1.

Liu, C., T. Lay, F. F. Pollitz, J. Xu, and X. Xiong (2021). Seismic and geodetic analysis of rupture characteristics of the 2020 Mw 6.5 Monte Cristo Range, Nevada, earthquake, *Bull. Seismol. Soc. Am.* **111,** no. 6, 3226–3236, doi: 10.1785/0120200327.

Lomax, A., A. Michelini, and A. Curtis (2009). Earthquake location, direct, global-search methods, in *Encyclopedia of Complexity and Systems Science*,R. A. Meyers (Editor), Springer, New York, New York, 1–33, doi: 10.1007/978-3-642-27737-5_150-2.

Lomax, A., J. Virieux, P. Volant, and C. Berge-Thierry (2000). Probabilistic earthquake location in 3D and layered models, in *Advances in Seismic Event Location*,C. H. Thurber and N. Rabinowitz (Editors), Modern Approaches in Geophysics, Springer, Dordrecht, The Netherlands, 101–134, doi: 10.1007/978-94-015-9536-0_5.

Magistrale, H., L. Jones, and H. Kanamori (1989). The Superstition Hills, California, earthquakes of 24 November 1987, *Bull. Seismol. Soc. Am.* **79,** no. 2, 239–251, doi: 10.1785/BSSA0790020239.

Moschetti, M. P., B. T. Aagaard, S. K. Ahdi, J. Altekruse, O. S. Boyd, A. D. Frankel, J. Herrick, M. D. Petersen, P. M. Powers, S. Rezaeian, *et al.* (2024). The 2023 US National Seismic Hazard Model: Ground-motion characterization for the conterminous United States, *Earthq. Spectra* **40,** no. 2, 1158–1190, doi: 10.1177/87552930231223995.

Okada, Y. (1985). Surface deformation due to shear and tensile faults in a half-space, *Bull. Seismol. Soc. Am.* **75,** no. 4, 1135–1154.

Pollitz, F. F., C. W. Wicks, and W. C. Hammond (2022). Kinematic slip model of the 2021 M 6.0 Antelope Valley, California, earthquake, *Seism. Record* **2,** no. 1, 20–28, doi: 10.1785/0320210043.

Richter, C. F. (1958). *Elementary Seismology*, W. H. Freeman, San Francisco, California.

Ross, Z. E., B. Idini, Z. Jia, O. L. Stephenson, M. Zhong, X. Wang, Z. Zhan, M. Simons, E. J. Fielding, S.-H. Yun, *et al.* (2019). Hierarchical interlocked orthogonal faulting in the 2019 Ridgecrest earthquake sequence, *Science* **366,** no. 6463, 346–351, doi: 10.1126/science.aaz0109.

Ruhl, C. J., E. A. Morton, J. M. Bormann, R. Hatch-Ibarra, G. Ichinose, and K. D. Smith (2021). Complex fault geometry of the 2020 Mww 6.5 Monte Cristo Range, Nevada, earthquake sequence, *Seismol. Res. Lett.* **92,** no. 3, 1876–1890, doi: 10.1785/0220200345.

Ryall, A. (1977). Earthquake hazard in the Nevada region, *Bull. Seismol. Soc. Am.* **67,** no. 2, 517–532, doi: 10.1785/BSSA0670020517.

Ryall, A., and S. D. Malone (1971). Earthquake distribution and mechanism of faulting in the Rainbow Mountain-Dixie Valley-Fairview Peak Area, central Nevada, *J. Geophys. Res.J. Geophys. Res.* **76,** no. 29, 7241–7248, doi: 10.1029/JB076i029p07241.

Savage, J. C., W. Gan, and J. L. Svarc (2001). Strain accumulation and rotation in the Eastern California Shear Zone, *J. Geophys. Res.* **106,** no. B10, 21,995–22,007, doi: 10.1029/2000JB000127.

Skoumal, R. J., J. L. Hardebeck, and P. M. Shearer (2024). SKHASH: A python package for computing earthquake focal mechanisms, *Seismol. Res. Lett.* **95,** no. 4, 2519–2526, doi: 10.1785/0220230329.

Smith, K. D. (2000). Faulting in the 1986 Chalfant, California, sequence: Local tectonics and earthquake source parameters, *Bull. Seismol. Soc. Am.* **90,** no. 4, 813–831, doi: 10.1785/0119990129.

Thompson, E. M., M. Hearne, B. T. Aagaard, J. M. Rekoske, C. B. Worden, M. P. Moschetti, H. E. Hunsinger, G. C. Ferragut, G. A. Parker, J. A. Smith, *et al.* (2024). Automated, near real-time ground-motion processing at the U.S. Geological Survey, *Seismol. Res. Lett.* **96,** no. 1, 538–553, doi: 10.1785/0220240021.

Trugman, D. T. (2024). A high-precision earthquake catalog for Nevada, *Seismol. Res. Lett.* **95,** no. 6, 3737–3745, doi: 10.1785/0220240106.

Trugman, D. T., and Y. Ben-Zion (2023). Coherent spatial variations in the productivity of earthquake sequences in California and Nevada, *Seism. Record* **3,** no. 4, 322–331, doi: 10.1785/0320230039.

Trugman, D. T., and P. M. Shearer (2017). GrowClust: A hierarchical clustering algorithm for relative earthquake relocation, with application to the Spanish Springs and Sheldon, Nevada, earthquake sequences, *Seismol. Res. Lett.* **88,** no. 2A, 379–391, doi: 10.1785/0220160188.

Trugman, D. T., J. Brune, K. D. Smith, J. N. Louie, and G. M. Kent (2023). The rocks that did not fall: A multidisciplinary analysis of near-source ground motions from an active normal fault, *AGU Adv.* **4,** no. 2, e2023AV000885, doi: 10.1029/2023AV000885.

Trugman, D. T., C. J. Chamberlain, A. Savvaidis, and A. Lomax (2023). GrowClust3D.jl: A Julia package for the relative relocation of earthquake hypocenters using 3D velocity models, *Seismol. Res. Lett.* **94,** no. 1, 443–456, doi: 10.1785/0220220193.

VanWormer, J. D., and A. S. Ryall (1980). Sierra Nevada-Great Basin boundary zone: Earthquake hazard related to structure, active tectonic processes, and anomalous patterns of earthquake occurrence, *Bull. Seismol. Soc. Am.* **70,** no. 5, 1557–1572.

Wang, K., D. S. Dreger, R. Burgmann, and T. Taira (2023). Finite-source model of the 8 July 2021 M 6.0 Antelope Valley, California, earthquake, *Seismol. Res. Lett.* **94,** no. 3, 1352–1366, doi: 10.1785/0220220262.

Wesnousky, S. G. (2005a). Active faulting in the Walker Lane, *Tectonics* **24,** no. 3, doi: 10.1029/2004TC001645.

Wesnousky, S. G. (2005b). The San Andreas and Walker Lane fault systems, western North America: Transpression, transtension, cumulative slip and the structural evolution of a major transform plate boundary, *J. Struct. Geol.* **27,** no. 8, 1505–1512, doi: 10.1016/j.jsg.2005.01.015.

Wesnousky, S. G., A. D. Barron, R. W. Briggs, S. J. Caskey, S. Kumar, and L. Owen (2005). Paleoseismic transect across the northern Great Basin, *J. Geophys. Res.* **110,** no. B5, 2004JB003283, doi: 10.1029/2004JB003283.

Zebker, H. A. (2017). User-friendly InSAR data products: Fast and simple timeseries processing, *IEEE Geosci. Remote Sens. Lett.* **14,** no. 11, 2122–2126, doi: 10.1109/LGRS.2017.2753580.

Manuscript received 23 June 2025
Published online 15 October 2025

Complex Multipatch Rupture and Aftershock Characteristics of the 2024 M_w 4.2 Buan, Korea, Earthquake Sequence

OPEN ACCESS

Min-Seong Seo[1], Won-Young Kim[2], Sangwoo Han[1], Jun Yong Park[1], and YoungHee Kim[*1]

Abstract

Moderate-magnitude earthquakes in stable continental regions (SCRs) can pose significant hazards, yet their rupture processes remain poorly understood due to sparse instrumentation and their infrequent occurrence. The 2024 M_w 4.2 Buan, Korea, earthquake, and its aftershock sequence were exceptionally well recorded by a local seismic network, providing a rare opportunity to investigate the rupture process of a moderate-magnitude earthquake in an SCR. Focal mechanisms and high-precision relocations reveal multiple fault strands activated during the eight-month-long sequence. Using an aftershock as an empirical Green's function, we retrieve relative source time functions of the mainshock, which are subsequently used to construct a detailed slip model. We apply two different rupture modeling approaches: a two-patch modeling with elliptical subfaults and a linear slip inversion. Both approaches consistently reveal two spatially distinct, high-stress-drop patches that ruptured sequentially, with a short temporal overlap, indicating notable rupture complexity. Furthermore, both on-fault and off-fault aftershocks appear to have been triggered by static stress increases associated with the mainshock rupture.

Cite this article as Seo, M.-S., W.-Y. Kim, S. Han, J. Y. Park, and Y. Kim (2025). Complex Multipatch Rupture and Aftershock Characteristics of the 2024 M_w 4.2 Buan, Korea, Earthquake Sequence, *Seismol. Res. Lett.* **97**, 1767–1781, doi: 10.1785/0220250261.

Supplemental Material

Introduction

On 11 June 2024, an M_w 4.2 earthquake struck near Buan, in the southwestern part of the Korean Peninsula (KP; Fig. 1a). The mainshock was widely felt across South Korea, with a peak ground acceleration of 0.13*g* recorded at the nearest station, PUAA ($\Delta = 3.4$ km, Az. = 350°). This earthquake was the largest in southwestern Korea since the 1980s, when reliable earthquake catalogs first became available for the region. A foreshock of M_L 0.5 preceded the mainshock by about 28 min, followed by 36 aftershocks through 13 February 2025, according to the Korea Meteorological Administration (KMA). Southern KP lies within a stable continental region (SCR) and is characterized by negligible tectonic strain rates and low seismicity (Fig. 1a; Jin *et al.*, 2006; Lee *et al.*, 2022). This earthquake was well recorded by stations with good coverage, providing an opportunity to address several questions about the rupture processes of such a moderate-sized earthquake in an SCR setting.

The rupture process of moderate-size earthquakes in SCRs remains poorly understood, primarily due to limited seismic station coverage and the infrequent occurrence of such events. However, in recent years, improved seismic networks with adequate station coverage have enabled detailed studies that reveal features such as complex slip distributions (e.g., Pennington, Chang, *et al.*, 2022; Neves *et al.*, 2024), multiple subevents (Horton *et al.*, 2015; Meng *et al.*, 2021), and unusually high stress drops compared to global averages (e.g., Viegas *et al.*, 2010; Boyd *et al.*, 2017). Specific case studies from SCRs globally clearly demonstrate these recurring features, including rupture complexity and high stress drops. For example, in Eastern North America, the 2011 M_w 5.8 Mineral, Virginia, earthquake exhibited a complex rupture comprising three subevents (Chapman, 2013; Hartzell *et al.*, 2013) and stress drops of 25–67 MPa (Hartzell *et al.*, 2013; Wu and Chapman, 2017). In Europe, the 2019 M_w 4.9 Le Teil earthquake in southeastern France showed a heterogeneous slip distribution, rupturing at least three asperities (Godano *et al.*, 2025). In southern KP, the 2016 M_w 5.4 Gyeongju earthquake ruptured on multiple slip patches, with an average stress drop of 23 MPa (Uchide and Song, 2018). Dynamic rupture simulations further indicate that both high stress drop and elevated fracture energy were needed

1. School of Earth and Environmental Sciences, Seoul National University, Seoul, Republic of Korea, https://orcid.org/0000-0001-7043-8938 (M-SS); https://orcid.org/0000-0001-5832-7127 (SH); https://orcid.org/0000-0003-2244-0210 (JYP); https://orcid.org/0000-0002-1111-632X (YHK); 2. Lamont-Doherty Earth Observatory of Columbia University, Palisades, New York, U.S.A., https://orcid.org/0000-0002-0005-9681 (W-YK)

*Corresponding author: younghkim@snu.ac.kr

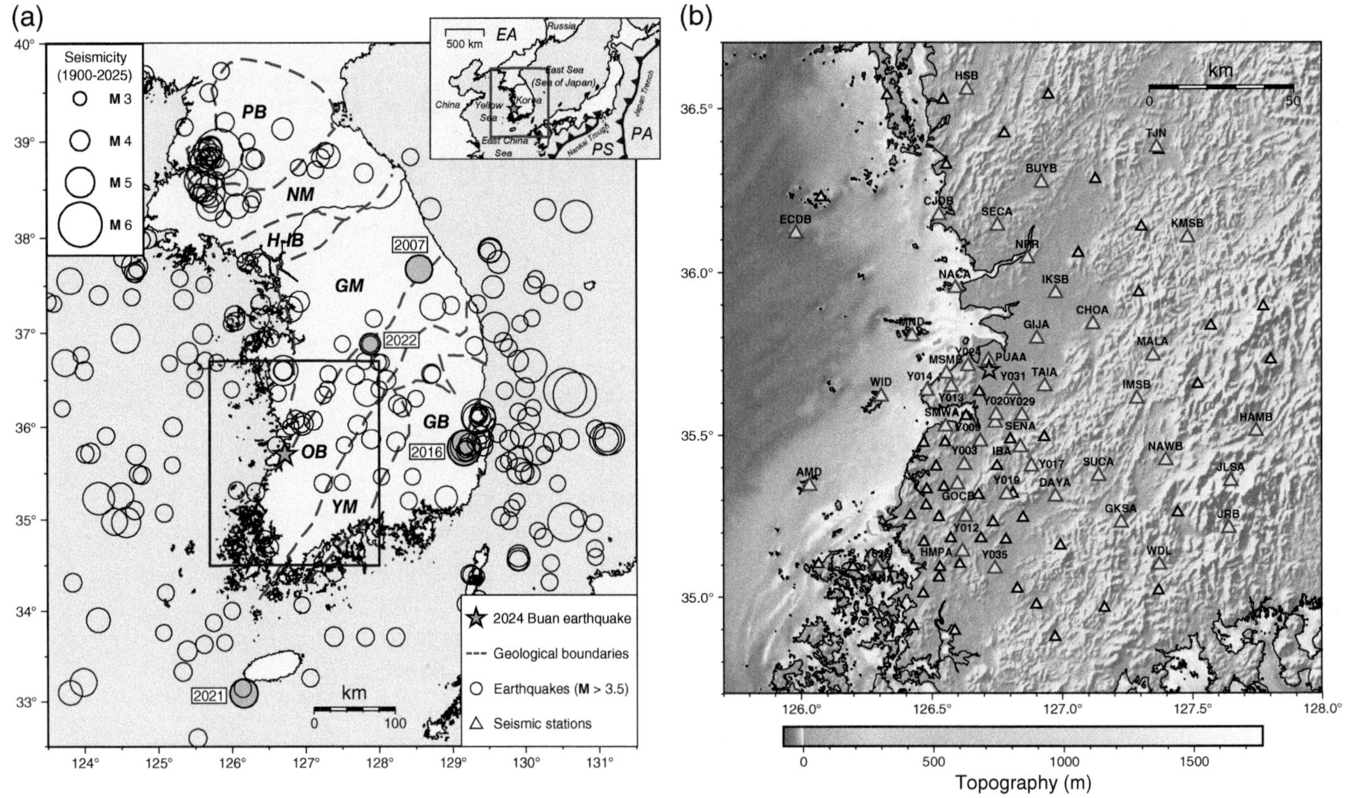

Figure 1. (a) Seismicity and geological boundaries of the Korean Peninsula (KP). Epicenters of shallow earthquakes (magnitudes ≥ 3.5) that occurred between 1900 and 2025 are shown. The cyan star marks the hypocenter of the 2024 Buan mainshock. Green-filled circles denote the epicenters of notable events, including the 2007 Odaesan, 2016 Gyeongju, 2021 Jeju Island, and 2022 Goesan earthquakes. Geological unit boundaries are shown as red-dashed lines (Kee *et al.*, 2019). Major geologic units of the KP are abbreviated as follows: GB, Gyeongsang basin; GM, Gyeonggi massif; H-IB, Hongseong–Imjingang belt; NM, Nangrim massif; OB, Ogcheon fold belt; PB, Pyeongnam basin; and YM, Yeongnam massif. The inset map shows the tectonic setting of East Asia, with the study area outlined in red. Plate abbreviations: EA, Eurasian plate; PA, Pacific plate; PS, Philippine Sea plate. (b) Distribution of seismic stations used in this study, overlaid on regional topography and bathymetry. Yellow triangles indicate the locations of seismic stations; those used in the slip inversion are outlined in red. The color version of this figure is available only in the electronic edition.

to reproduce observed near-source ground motions (Song and Duan, 2024). More recently, the 2022 M_w 3.8 Goesan earthquake and its foreshock (M_w 3.5) exhibited unusually high stress drops of 107 and 84 MPa, respectively, based on corner-frequency analysis and aftershock spatial distributions (Kim *et al.*, 2023). Even with limited station coverage, the 2007 M_w 4.6 Odaesan earthquake showed signs of rupture complexity (Kim *et al.*, 2010). Similarly, the 2021 M_w 4.9 offshore Jeju Island earthquake involved at least two nucleation phases followed by two major subevents, as inferred from both local and regional waveforms (Han, Kim, Lim, *et al.*, 2024).

Although these recent studies suggest that rupture complexity and high stress drop are recurring features of moderate-size earthquakes in SCR, such characteristics are not universal. For instance, the 2024 M_w 4.8 Tewksbury, New Jersey, earthquake exhibited a relatively simple rupture and a range of stress drop from 6.6 MPa (Han, Kim, Park, *et al.*, 2024) to a moderate 20 MPa (Beaucé *et al.*, 2025). Similarly, the 2022 M_w 3.8 Goesan earthquake showed no clear evidence of rupture complexity or directivity (Kim *et al.*, 2023). Such variability may reflect differences in source properties, but could also result from limitations in data quality and station coverage. Most previous studies have relied on regional or teleseismic data because local station density has typically been low near the epicenters of unexpected events. This has limited the resolution of rupture models, particularly in the fault dip direction, where local body waves provide superior sensitivity. Some studies have utilized single-station waveform analyses to constrain rupture directivity (Yao *et al.*, 2025). However, these approaches remain limited in their ability to resolve the fine kinematic details of rupture processes. Consequently, despite these advances, systematic analyses of moderate-size SCR earthquakes recorded by dense local networks are still rare, leaving the diversity of rupture behaviors largely unexplored. Therefore, to better assess rupture diversity in SCR settings, it is essential to examine more events with dense local seismic recordings.

In contrast to many past moderate-sized earthquakes in KP, the 2024 Buan earthquake sequence was well recorded by

TABLE 1
Focal Mechanisms of Major (M≥2) Events

		Nodal Plane 1			Nodal Plane 2			*P* Axis	*T* Axis
ID	M_w	Strike (°)	Dip (°)	Rake (°)	Strike (°)	Dip (°)	Rake (°)	*tr/pl* (°)	*tr/pl* (°)
2*	4.23	220	73	−160	124	71	−18	82/26	352/1
17*	2.93	201	32	144	322	72	63	72/22	198/55
29†	2.37	212	73	−166	118	77	−17	74/22	165/2
38†	2.38	225	70	−173	133	83	−20	87/19	180/9

*Seismic moments and focal mechanisms are derived from waveform modeling.
†Seismic moments are obtained from spectral fitting, and focal mechanisms are from *P*-wave first motions.

nearby permanent stations with sufficient azimuthal coverage, enabling a high-resolution rupture model for a complex mainshock. In this study, we first determine the focal mechanisms of significant earthquakes and delineate the geometry of the fault system by high-precision hypocenter relocations. We then retrieve relative source time functions (RSTFs) at stations with broad azimuthal coverage to infer the mainshock rupture process. We successfully model the complex mainshock rupture as two elliptical patches using the RSTFs, which eliminates path and site effects from the observed records. Finally, we discuss the underlying physical mechanisms of the observed rupture complexity and its role in aftershock triggering in a complex fault system with multiple segments.

11 June 2024 Buan, Korea, Earthquake Sequence

To characterize the fault geometry and clarify its spatial relationship with aftershocks, we first determine focal mechanisms and relocate events with high precision. We utilize waveform data from over 300 stations in South Korea, equipped with broadband, short-period, and strong-motion sensors. Given the high station density in the epicentral region, we selected stations situated within about 100 km, ensuring optimal azimuthal coverage and good signal quality (see Data and Resources).

Focal mechanisms

We constrain the focal mechanisms for the mainshock and three $M_L \geq 2$ aftershocks (events 17, 29, and 38; Table 1). For the mainshock and event 17, we model waveforms and invert for focal mechanisms. The double-couple focal mechanism and seismic moment are determined through a grid search over strike, dip, and rake angles. Synthetics are calculated with a two-layer crustal velocity model for the KP (Kim and Kim, 1983), using the frequency–wavenumber integration method (Saikia, 1994). Both observed and synthetic waveforms are band-pass filtered between 0.03 and 0.1 Hz for the mainshock and 0.08–0.25 Hz for event 17. Focal depths are constrained by fitting the synthetics computed at 1 km depth intervals and selecting the depth that minimizes waveform misfit (Fig. S1, available in the supplemental material to this article).

The M_w 4.23 mainshock exhibits a strike-slip mechanism, with nodal planes striking northeast–southwest (NE–SW; 220°) and west-northwest–east-southeast (WNW–ESE; 124°), both with steep dips (~70°; Fig. S1a). The best-fitting focal depth is 9 (±1) km for the mainshock (Fig. S1a). Event 17, with M_w 2.93, is the largest aftershock in the sequence and occurred about six hours after the mainshock. This event shows a thrust faulting mechanism (Fig. S1b). Its north-northeast-south-southwest (NNE–SSW; 201°)-trending nodal plane dips shallowly at 32°, whereas the NW–SE (322°)-trending nodal plane dips steeply at 72°. The best-fitting focal depth is 8 (±1) km, slightly shallower than the mainshock (Fig. S1b).

For the smaller events 29 and 38 (both M_w 2.4), the low long-period energy precludes reliable waveform modeling. Instead, we rely on *P*-wave first motions to invert for the focal mechanism using FOCMEC (FOCal MEChanism determinations; Snoke, 2003). *P* polarity measurements with adequate azimuthal coverage enable focal mechanism solutions with high confidence (Fig. S1c). Both events show well-constrained strike-slip mechanisms with double-couple nodal planes oriented NE–SW and NW–SE, consistent with the mainshock. This suggests that events 29 and 38 likely ruptured on planar structures parallel to the mainshock, whereas event 17 occurred on a structurally distinct segment. The focal mechanisms of the four events are listed in Table 1.

Fault geometry from the precise location of the earthquake sequence

To delineate the fault planes activated during the sequence, we locate earthquakes that occurred between 11 June 2024 and 20 March 2025. In addition to the 38 events reported by KMA, we apply a matched-filter technique to detect smaller events for which waveforms resemble those of template events cataloged by KMA. We detect 47 additional events with magnitudes ranging from −1.03 to 0.98 (Table S1). The magnitude of each detected event is estimated by measuring its peak amplitude

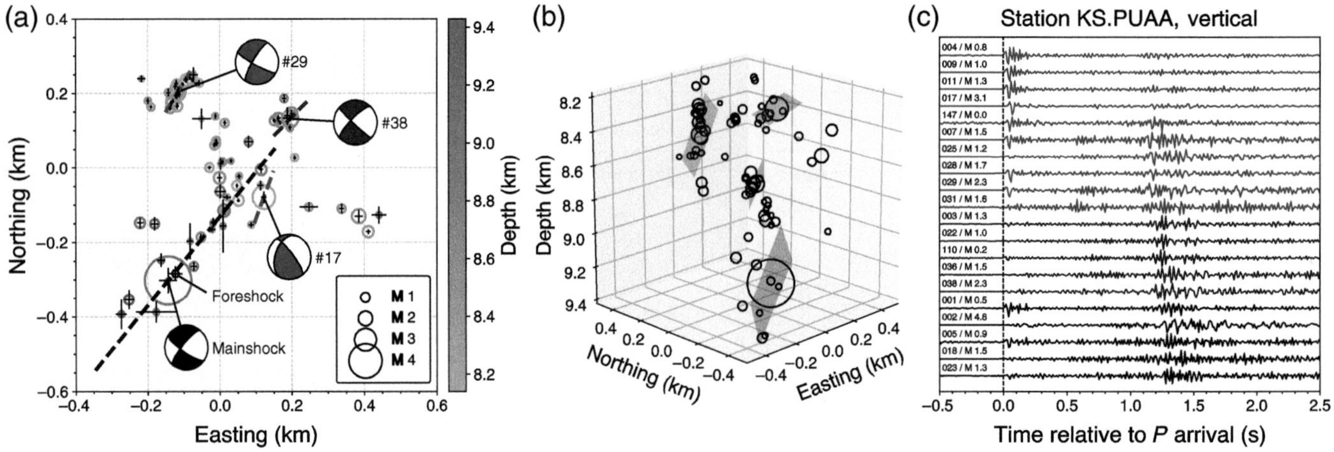

Figure 2. (a) Map view of 74 earthquakes relocated using the double-difference algorithm. Events are color-coded by focal depth, with the foreshock marked by an orange hexagon. Event depths have been shifted relative to the mainshock depth determined by HYPOINVERSE (Table S1). Error bars correspond to 95% confidence intervals derived from the bootstrap resampling. Focal mechanisms of **M** ≥ 2 events are shown (Table 1), with inferred fault strikes indicated by colored dashed lines. Segmented fault planes of the mainshock, derived from the elliptical patch inversion (Table 2), are indicated by black-dashed lines. (b) Three-dimensional view of the relocated events and the fault planes associated with four **M** ≥ 2 events. Strike and dip angles of each plane are based on the focal mechanism solutions. (c) Unfiltered vertical-component waveforms recorded at station PUAA for five representative events, each selected from a different fault-plane cluster. Waveform colors correspond to the fault planes shown in panel (b). The color version of this figure is available only in the electronic edition.

ratio relative to the best-matching template event, determined by the highest cross-correlation coefficient (Cc).

Absolute locations are first determined using HYPOINVERSE (Klein, 2002) with manually picked *P*- and *S*-wave arrivals. Although the events are broadly distributed in the NE–SW direction, horizontal location uncertainties (0.1–1.4 km; Table S1) limit detailed geometric interpretation of the fault structure. Therefore, we refine the locations using the double-difference relocation code HypoDD (Waldhauser and Ellsworth, 2000). Differential travel times of *P* and *S* phases are measured by waveform cross correlation within a narrow time window of 0.1 s (from −0.03 to +0.07 s relative to *P* or *S* arrivals), after band-pass filtering between 2 and 25 Hz. We apply cutoff Cc thresholds of 0.8 for *P* and 0.9 for *S* phases, ultimately relocating a total of 74 events (Fig. 2a).

The relocated hypocenters, combined with focal mechanisms of $M_L \geq 2$ events, reveal several clusters (i.e., fault segments; Fig. 2). A prominent NE–SW-trending seismicity at ~9 km depth aligns with the 220°-striking nodal plane of the mainshock. This cluster extends ~500 m both laterally and vertically (Fig. 2b). Notably, the location of the only foreshock (event 1) coincides with the mainshock hypocenter, possibly indicating a short-term nucleation process (e.g., Kim *et al.*, 2010; Gomberg, 2018). Event 38 (M_w 2.4), which occurred eight months after the mainshock, is also aligned along the mainshock strike direction (Fig. 2a), but is offset by ~200 m when viewed from the depth section (Fig. 2b). Given its similar focal mechanism to the mainshock (Table 1), event 38 likely ruptured on a planar, shallower NE–SW-trending segment, hosting a cluster of closely spaced aftershocks.

We identify two shallow, spatially distinct aftershock clusters associated with events 17 and 29. Their focal depths are ~1 km shallower than that of the mainshock, indicating that they occurred on isolated fault segments (Fig. 2b). A cluster near event 17 exhibits high-waveform similarities at the nearest station PUAA (Δ = 3.4 km, Az. = 350°), characterized by large *P-to-S* amplitude ratios, suggesting consistent focal mechanisms (Fig. 2c). These events define a fault segment gently dipping to the northwest, consistent with the NNE–SSW-trending nodal plane (strike = 201°) of event 17. Meanwhile, the cluster associated with event 29 clearly delineates a ~100-m-long NE–SW-trending subvertical segment, consistent with the 212°-striking nodal plane of event 29. Although event 29 (M_w 2.4) is relatively small compared to the mainshock (M_w 4.2) or event 17 (M_w 2.9), this cluster is the most seismically productive during the sequence, possibly reflecting variations in fault properties or triggering mechanisms that influenced segment-specific seismicity.

Mainshock Rupture Process

Observed *S* waves on transverse component records (*SH* phase) around the epicenter show azimuthal variation; in particular, the pulse duration of the *SH* phase varies with station azimuth as shown in Figure 3. For the stations located near the strike direction (220°) (Fig. 3a–c), the mainshock *SH* phases show notable complexity, for which a second pulse (S_2) arrives 0.2–0.3 s after the first pulse (S_1). However, this second pulse is absent in event 38, indicating that this feature is unlikely to be

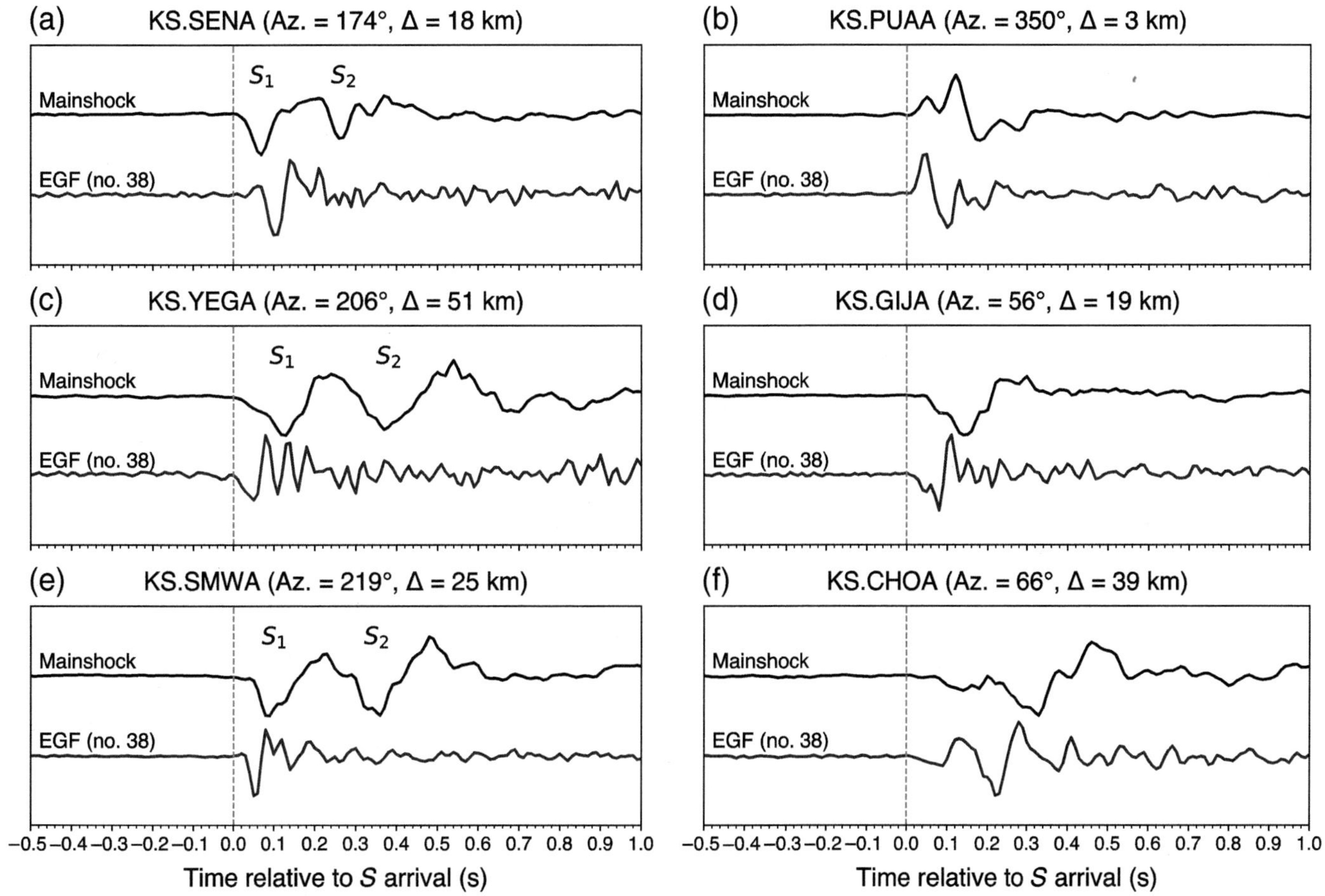

Figure 3. High-pass filtered (1 Hz) transverse-component velocity waveforms for the mainshock (black) and empirical Green's function (EGF) events (blue) are shown for (a,c,e) forward-strike stations and (b,d,f) backward-strike stations. All waveforms are aligned at the *S*-wave arrival. For the forward-strike stations, two distinct subevent signals are annotated as S_1 and S_2. Note that the S_2 signal appears only in the mainshock waveforms at the forward-strike stations. The color version of this figure is available only in the electronic edition.

path or site effects but rather reflects source-related complexity. On the other hand, for stations in the opposite directions (Fig. 3d–f), signals are much shorter and simpler, comparable to those of event 38. These observations suggest a complex source process involving rupture directivity. Such azimuthal variation has been observed for other moderate-sized earthquakes in the KP in recent years, including the 12 September 2016 M_w 5.4 Gyeongju earthquake in southeastern Korea (Uchide and Song, 2018) and the 16 December 2021 M_w 4.9 offshore Jeju Island earthquake (Han, Kim, Lim, *et al.*, 2024). Boatwright (2007) also reported directivity in small earthquakes ($3.5 < \mathbf{M} < 4.1$) in San Ramon, California.

To unravel the complexity of the source, we employ a method for kinematic inversion of the rupture process based on the elliptical subfault approximation developed by Vallée and Bouchon (2004). They applied their method to two well-known large earthquakes ($M_w > 7$) using teleseismic body and surface waves to determine the main features of the earthquake rupture in terms of one- and two-patch models. Di Carli *et al.* (2010) and Twardzik *et al.* (2012) employed the method for large earthquakes (2000 M_w 6.7, Tottori, Japan; 2004 M_w 6.0, Parkfield, California) using near-field strong-motion records.

In this study, we employ the same method for the moderate-size 2024 M_w 4.2 Buan earthquake, utilizing the empirical Green's function (EGF) approach to eliminate path and site effects from the observed seismic records at local distances (up to ~100 km). RSTFs retrieved from stations at various distances and azimuths are then used to retrieve the main features of the mainshock rupture.

RSTFs from EGF deconvolution

We employ the EGF method to retrieve the RSTFs of the mainshock (Mori and Frankel, 1990). Event 38 is selected as the EGF event, which is located ~600 m northeast of the mainshock hypocenter (Fig. 2a) with a similar focal mechanism as the mainshock (Table 1). It also exhibits a sufficiently large signal-to-noise ratio at stations up to 100 km from the epicenter. Although other aftershocks were also tested as EGF candidates and yielded similar RSTFs (Fig. S2), event 38 produced the most RSTFs that satisfied the quality criteria.

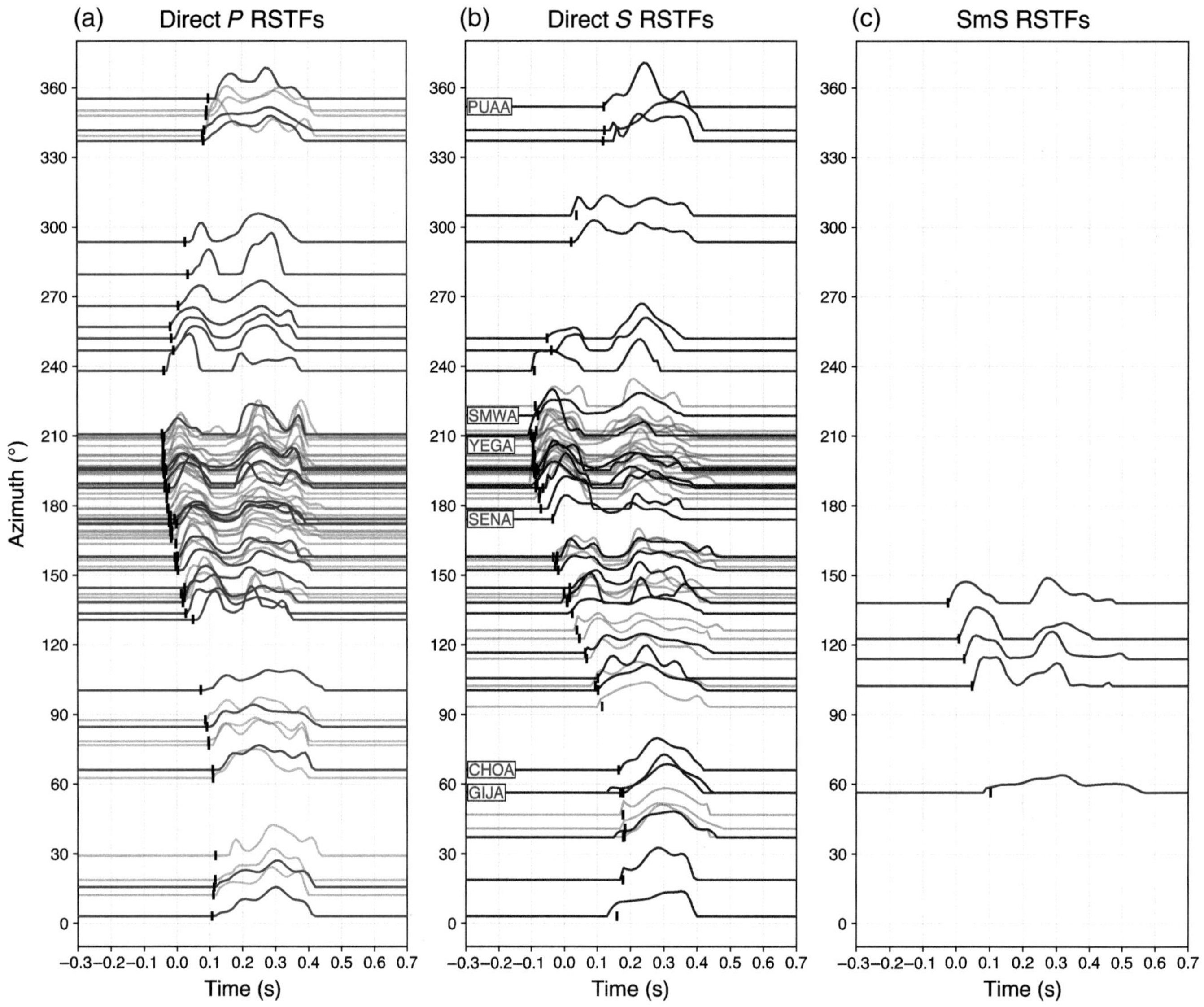

Figure 4. Relative source time functions (RSTFs) obtained from the mainshock–EGF pair for (a) direct *P*, (b) direct *S*, and (c) *SmS* phases that meet the quality criteria. The RSTFs are aligned by station azimuth and normalized by seismic moment. Those selected for constructing the slip model are shown with dark-colored lines, whereas others are shown with light-colored lines. Black vertical bars mark theoretical differential times, calculated based on the relative location between the mainshock and the EGF event. The RSTFs for stations shown in Figure 3 are annotated. The color version of this figure is available only in the electronic edition.

We follow the method of Han, Kim, Lim, *et al.* (2024) to retrieve the RSTF with waveforms windowed from 0.5 s before to 1.0 s after the *P* or *S* arrivals, and filtered at 1–10 Hz prior to deconvolution. The mainshock and EGF waveforms are aligned within a common time window starting from origin times. The projected Landweber deconvolution method with positivity and causality constraints is applied (Bertero *et al.*, 1997; Lanza *et al.*, 1999). In addition to direct *P* and *S* phases, we utilize the Moho-reflected *S* phase (*SmS*) at five stations at distances of 70–100 km. The use of *SmS* phase for source analysis was suggested by Song and Helmberger (1996) and Saikia and Helmberger (1997), but has been rarely used. Incorporating *SmS* RSTFs can enhance the resolution of the rupture model because the direct phases are primarily upgoing, whereas the *SmS* phases are downgoing from the source.

To ensure good-quality RSTFs, we require the variance reduction (VR) between the observed and synthetics—obtained by convolving the EGF with the RSTF—to exceed 70% (e.g., Meng *et al.*, 2020; Fig. S3). We further exclude RSTFs from stations near radiation nodes of *P* and *SH* phases. After quality control, we obtain RSTFs from 73 *P*, 65 *SH*, and 5 *SmS* phases as plotted in Figure 4. The RSTFs show systematic azimuthal variations in start time and duration. The sinusoidal start-time variations reflect differences in hypocentral locations. The variations in duration indicate typical rupture directivity, with rupture propagating toward the northeast (~40°) and exhibiting shorter durations, whereas durations are longer

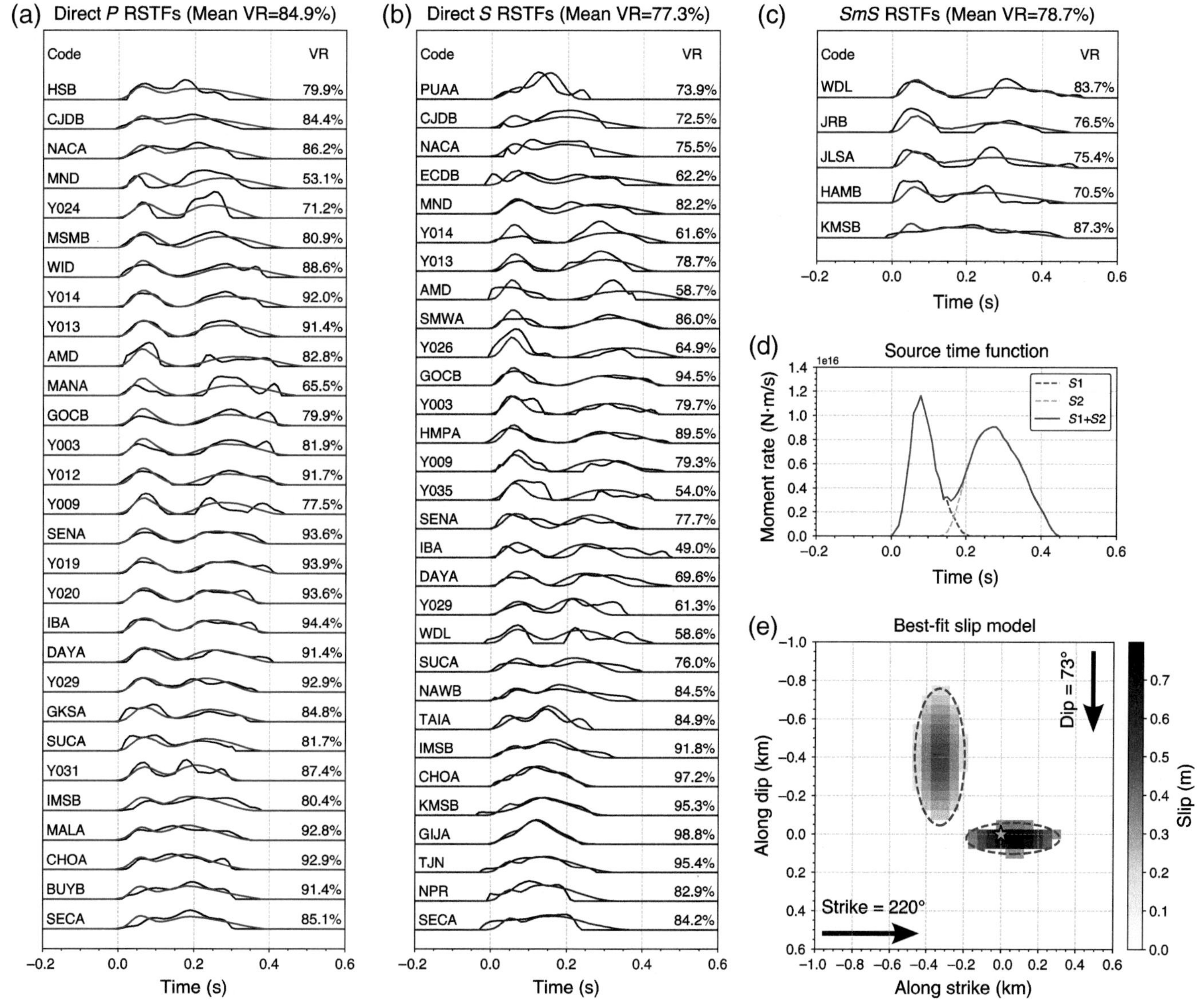

Figure 5. Comparisons between observed and synthetic apparent STFs (ASTFs) forward modeled from the best-fit elliptical patch model, shown for (a) direct *P*, (b) direct *S*, and (c) *SmS* phases. All ASTFs are aligned at their origin times ($t = 0.0$ s) and normalized by seismic moment. Variance reductions (VRs) between observed and synthetic ASTFs at individual stations are indicated. (d) Source time function representing the overall rupture process. Contributions from the first patch (S_1) and second patch (S_2) are plotted as green and yellow dashed lines, respectively. (e) The best-fit two elliptical patch model plotted on the mainshock fault plane. The cyan star denotes the hypocenter. The color version of this figure is available only in the electronic edition.

in the rear (southwest, ~220°). The inferred rupture direction is consistent with the NE–SW-striking nodal plane of the mainshock focal mechanism and the trend of the aftershock distribution (Fig. 2). In addition, the RSTFs from stations along the azimuth of ~120° start to show a second source pulse, which persists up to ~300° (Fig. 4). This indicates a rupture involving at least two subevents and suggests a complex rupture process of the mainshock.

Mainshock rupture modeling: Elliptical subfault inversion

Motivated by the observation of double-pulse RSTFs at stations with azimuths between 120° and 300° (Fig. 4), we explore a kinematic rupture model composed of two elliptical patches to fit the RSTFs (Vallée and Bouchon, 2004). Although we have high-quality RSTFs with adequate station coverage (Fig. 1b), the distribution is uneven due to the offshore region in the west and high station density in the south. To mitigate potential bias in rupture modeling from this uneven spatial distribution, we bin the RSTFs into 15° intervals of azimuth (0°–360°) and take-off angle (45°–165°), resulting in 29, 30, and 5 groups for *P*, *SH*, and *SmS* phases, respectively. From each group, we select the RSTF with the highest VR for inversion.

We assume that the final slip distribution can be represented as a combination of two elliptical patches. We then

TABLE 2
Summary of the Elliptical Patch Model for the Mainshock

Model Parameter	a_1 (km)	b_1 (km)	x_1 (km)	y_1 (km)	a_2 (km)	b_2 (km)	x_2 (km)	y_2 (km)	s_1^{max}/s_2^{max}	V_r (km/s)
Best-fit value	0.250	0.080	0.065	0.022	0.134	0.356	−0.329	−0.402	1.687	2.176
Uncertainty range*	(0.128, 0.341)	(0.038, 0.180)	(−0.016, 0.114)	(−0.038, 0.061)	(0.072, 0.273)	(0.257, 0.433)	(−0.417, −0.283)	(−0.417, −0.283)	(1.250, 2.414)	(2.088, 2.429)

*The uncertainty range denotes the minimum and maximum values for each model parameter such that the misfit is less than 1.1 times the global minimum misfit.

search for the optimal sizes and locations of the two ellipses by forward modeling synthetic apparent STFs (ASTFs) that best match the observed RSTFs. In detail, we search for 10 parameters, which are the centers ($x_1,y_1;x_2,y_2$) and the major and minor axes of the two ellipses ($a_1,b_1;a_2,b_2$), the ratio of maximum slip of the two patches (s_1^{max}/s_2^{max}), and the rupture speed (V_r). Within each ellipse, the slip distribution is assumed to follow a Gaussian distribution $s(x,y) = s^{max} \exp[-(\frac{x^2}{a^2} + \frac{y^2}{b^2})]$. Moreover, we assume that the major and minor axes of the ellipses are parallel to the strike and dip of the fault plane. The rupture front is assumed to propagate from the hypocenter at a constant speed.

To forward model the RSTFs, one needs to specify the subfault grid size as well as the duration of the triangular slip-rate function corresponding to each subfault (or rise time t_r). The grid size is set to 50 m in both strike and dip directions, and t_r is set to 0.06 s based on the empirical scaling relationship derived by Somerville *et al.* (1999). We test the sensitivity of both the grid size and t_r on the solution and find that the best-fit solution is robust to variations in these parameters (see Fig. S4).

The best-fit model is searched via the neighborhood algorithm (NA; Sambridge, 1999), which allows an efficient search in the high-dimensional model space through Voronoi cell partitioning. Although NA does not guarantee exhaustive sampling as a full grid search would, it has been successfully applied in a variety of rupture modeling studies (e.g., Vallée and Bouchon, 2004; Twardzik *et al.*, 2012). Moreover, NA generates an ensemble of solutions with comparable misfits, enabling uncertainty quantification. The misfit between synthetic and observed RSTFs is defined as the sum of least-squares misfits for direct *P*, direct *S*, and *SmS* phases: $\sum_j [\frac{1}{N_j} \sum_i^{N_j} \frac{||\text{obs}_i - \text{syn}_i||^2}{||\text{obs}_i||^2}]$, in which *i* and *j* index stations and phases, respectively. The misfit definition enables better modeling of the relatively few *SmS* RSTFs, while maintaining good fits to the direct phases.

The best-fit model successfully reproduces the observed azimuthal variations in RSTF shape and duration, with average VRs of 84.9%, 77.3%, and 78.7% for direct *P*, direct *S*, and *SmS* phases, respectively (Fig. 5a–c). The final average source time function exhibits two distinct pulses in moment rate, spanning ~0.45 s (Fig. 5d). The model includes two clearly separated slip patches in which the first patch (S_1) is located near the hypocenter, whereas the second patch (S_2) is located in the northeast, up-dip direction (Fig. 5e). The distance between the two patches is ~100 m. To estimate uncertainties of the model parameters, we select an ensemble of models with misfits less than 1.1 times the global minimum. Uncertainty bounds for each model parameter are given by their minimum and maximum values in Table 2.

Linear slip inversion

To cross-validate the results from the elliptical subfault inversion, we perform a linear slip inversion following the approach of Dreger (1994). This approach models the apparent RSTFs using a 2D rupture propagating on a predefined fault plane at a constant rupture speed. We use 50 m × 50 m subfaults, consistent with the elliptical inversion. Considering the small number of available *SmS* RSTFs, we apply a weighting factor of six to the *SmS* phases relative to *P* and *S* phases, following the same weighting scheme used in the elliptical inversion. A nonnegative least-squares inversion is performed for each V_r and t_r pair, and the optimal combination is selected based on the maximum VR. The regularization parameter is set to $\lambda = 500$ based on *L*-curve analysis (Mendoza and Hartzell, 2013). The optimal rupture model yields $V_r = 0.62V_S$ and $t_r = 0.05$ s. The resulting slip distribution shows two high-slip regions that are spatially correlated with the elliptical patches in the two-patch model (Fig. 6). The higher VR achieved in this model compared to the elliptical inversion likely reflects the greater modeling flexibility afforded by the unconstrained linear model (see Fig. S5). However, relatively weak slip patches observed in peripheral subfaults may be poorly resolved, possibly due to non-uniqueness inherent in the inversion process (Beresnev, 2003; Pennington, Uchide, and Chen, 2022).

An anticorrelation between high-slip regions and on-fault aftershock density is commonly observed in finite-fault inversion studies (e.g., Wössner *et al.*, 2006; Ross *et al.*, 2017), and is also evident in our case. Aftershocks within 100 m of the mainshock fault tend to cluster near the edges of the high-slip patches (Fig. 6), possibly indicating failure of unbroken barriers due to elevated coseismic stress (Das and Henry, 2003). Notably, some aftershocks also occurred between the two slip patches, which would be difficult to reconcile if the mainshock had ruptured a single large, continuous fault area.

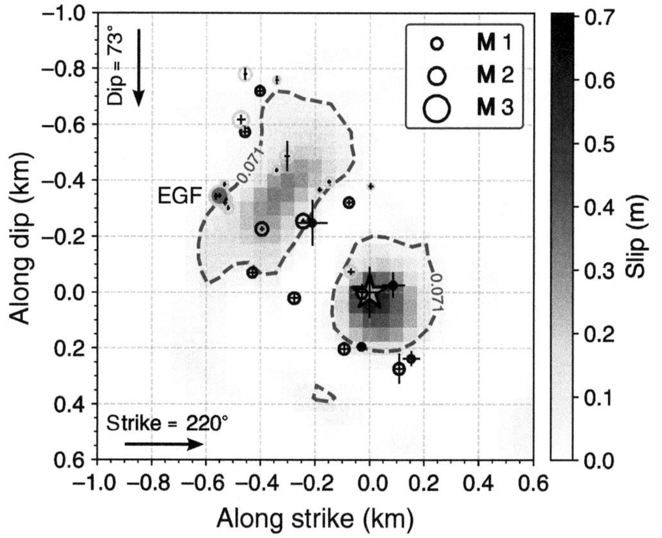

Figure 6. Slip distribution from the linear inversion. Contours indicating 10% of the peak slip are shown as green-dashed lines. The mainshock hypocenter (cyan star), foreshock (orange hexagon), and near-fault aftershocks (open circles) are projected onto the mainshock fault plane. The EGF event (event 38) is shown as a filled-magenta circle. Black circles represent aftershocks within 100 m of the mainshock fault, whereas gray circles denote those within 300 m. Error bars represent 95% confidence intervals derived from bootstrap resampling. The color version of this figure is available only in the electronic edition.

Discussion

Robustness and limitations of the two-patch rupture model

The key feature of the mainshock rupture process revealed by our analysis is substantial slip on two spatially distinct patches that ruptured sequentially, with a short-temporal overlap of approximately 0.05 s (Fig. 5d,e). Although we cannot exclude the possibility that a small amount of slip exists between the two patches—potentially forming a connecting zone not captured in the elliptical subfault inversion—the linear inversion, which imposes no assumptions about the number of patches, also reveals two clearly separated high-slip regions (Fig. 6). This consistency implies that the spatial separation between the two slip patches is likely a well-resolved and robust feature of the rupture model. We further attempted to model the RSTFs using three elliptical patches by adding an additional patch and found that the third patch is located within S_2, representing a localized high-slip region (Fig. S6). Although the average VR slightly improves, the third patch does not introduce a new rupture episode, supporting that the two-patch model sufficiently captures the essential features of the RSTF shapes.

In this study, we incorporate *SmS* phases alongside direct *P* and *S* phases to enhance rupture model resolution. To evaluate their contribution, we repeat both elliptical and linear inversions using only direct phase RSTFs. These inversions consistently show that the second patch is poorly constrained (Fig. S7), indicating limited resolution in the dip direction when relying solely on phases with upgoing take-off angles. We also conduct inversions using only stations with 180° azimuthal coverage (Fig. S8), applying an aspect ratio penalty in the elliptical inversion to avoid overly elongated patches. In three out of four configurations, at least one *SmS* phase is included. We find that even with reduced azimuthal coverage, the relative positions of the two high-slip patches are reasonably recovered. However, excluding *SmS* phases causes the second patch to be poorly resolved in both size and location. Comparison of direct *S* and *SmS* RSTFs at azimuths 90°–150° (Fig. 4) shows that *SmS* RSTFs display double-pulse shapes with longer durations (~0.5 s), whereas direct *S* RSTFs are simpler and shorter (~0.3 to 0.4 s), reflecting the up-dip location and upward rupture propagation of S_2, captured by the different sensitivities of the upgoing (*S*) and downgoing (*SmS*) phases. These results demonstrate that *SmS* phases substantially improve rupture model resolution for small-to-moderate events, particularly under limited station coverage such as for offshore earthquakes. Other downgoing phases, such as *PmP* or *Pn*, could be explored in future studies to provide similar constraints.

In addition to slip distribution, we resolve a rupture speed of $0.63V_S$ (Table 2), which is lower than the $0.7–0.8V_S$ typically reported for large global earthquakes (Geller, 1976; Vera *et al.*, 2024), or the commonly assumed $0.9V_S$ used in stress-drop estimation based on simple circular crack models (Madariaga, 1976). Guo *et al.* (2023) systematically investigated $M_w \geq 6$ shallow strike-slip events and found that rupture speed correlates inversely with fault maturity. In this context, the slow rupture of the Buan event may similarly reflect rupture on an immature fault within a slowly deforming SCR (e.g., Pennington, Chang, *et al.*, 2022; Žilić *et al.*, 2025). However, the uncertainty range derived from our NA solution ensemble ($0.60–0.70V_S$) indicates that a wide range of rupture speeds can also explain the observed RSTFs with similarly low misfits. Importantly, both the elliptical and linear inversions assume a constant rupture speed across the entire rupture. In other words, a single rupture speed is used to simultaneously match both the azimuthal variation in RSTF pulse widths and the azimuth-dependent timing of the two subevents. In reality, the rupture speed may vary significantly, as shown in dynamic rupture simulations (Li *et al.*, 2023; Gallovič *et al.*, 2025). Given the short-rupture duration (~0.45 s; Fig. 5d) and the inherent non-uniqueness of finite-source inversions, introducing a variable rupture speed is unlikely to yield meaningful improvements for this event.

Complex rupture and high stress drop in a stable continental crust

To date, only a handful of earthquakes in the KP have been investigated with detailed rupture models (Abdel-Fattah *et al.*, 2014; Uchide and Song, 2018; Cho *et al.*, 2023; Han, Kim, Lim, *et al.*, 2024). These studies suggest that complex ruptures may be relatively common even among moderate-sized events in the region. For instance, Han, Kim, Lim, *et al.* (2024) used RSTF modeling to show that the 2021 M_w 4.9 offshore Jeju Island earthquake involved sequential rupture of two distinct slip patches over ~1.2 s. Interestingly, these two subevents were separated by a ~0.2 s pause, allowing us to constrain the rupture speeds of each patch. Their results revealed distinct rupture directivities and speeds between the patches, implying substantial heterogeneity in rupture dynamics along the short fault (~2 km). Although the overall rupture duration of the 2024 Buan mainshock was much shorter, its rupture pattern closely resembles that of the 2021 Jeju Island earthquake. Specifically, S_1 ruptured bilaterally with some asymmetry, whereas S_2 propagated northeastward and up-dip (Fig. 6). A key difference is that in the 2024 Buan event, S_2 followed S_1 almost instantaneously, whereas in the 2021 Jeju event, the two subevents were separated by a ~0.2 s pause. This contrast in timing suggests different triggering mechanisms: although the Jeju event rupture may have involved static stress transfer between the two patches (Ellsworth and Bulut, 2018; Han, Kim, Lim, *et al.*, 2024), the short-temporal overlap (~0.05 s) in the Buan event indicates that the second rupture began before the first had fully terminated. This close temporal overlap indicates a substantial role of transient dynamic stress in triggering S_2, although distinguishing contributions of dynamic and static stress changes remains challenging (Belardinelli *et al.*, 1999; Antonioli *et al.*, 2002). Alternatively, the event may represent a single rupture episode, as the timing between patch failures is consistent with a reasonable rupture speed.

Another noteworthy feature of the Buan rupture model is the locally elevated stress drops in both slip patches. Using the analytical solution for elliptical cracks (Eshelby, 1957; Kaneko and Shearer, 2015), we estimate the stress drop for each patch, with uncertainty bounds derived from the NA solution ensemble (Fig. S9a). Despite large uncertainties, the inferred stress drops are substantially high: 227 (74–741) MPa for S_1 and 82 (20–270) MPa for S_2. These estimates show a strong positive correlation, which arises naturally from the positively correlated rupture areas of the two patches (Fig. S9b). Approximating the total rupture area using the minimum-area ellipse encompassing both patches, we obtain an average stress drop of ~15 MPa. Although this value is much lower than the stress drops of individual patches, it aligns well with previously reported average stress-drop estimates for other moderate-size earthquakes in the KP (e.g., Kim *et al.*, 2010; Uchide and Song, 2018).

Stress drops that are locally high but low on average have also been reported for **M** 2–4 earthquakes in Northern California using finite-fault modeling (Dreger *et al.*, 2007; Taira *et al.*, 2015). Despite the contrasting tectonic environments, the 2016 Gyeongju earthquake sequence in southeastern Korea exhibited comparable behavior, with stress drops of up to 62 MPa for the mainshock (M_w 5.4) and 43 MPa for the largest foreshock (M_w 5.0), whereas the average values were significantly lower at 23 and 15 MPa, respectively (Uchide and Song, 2018). The 2024 Buan earthquake also exhibited two spatially separated high-slip patches with locally elevated stress drops up to ~230 and ~80 MPa, whereas the average stress drop was rather low at ~15 MPa. These observations suggest that localized zones of high stress drop may not be limited to specific tectonic environments, but can occur in both active and stable crustal settings, thereby influencing rupture initiation and propagation (Day *et al.*, 1998; Li *et al.*, 2023).

Aftershock triggering in a complex fault network

The relocated 2024 Buan earthquake sequence reveals that at least two shallow and spatially distinct fault planes are activated during the sequence (Fig. 2b). The focal mechanisms of the largest events in each segment are well constrained (Table 1), which enables an assessment of whether these aftershocks were triggered by stress changes imparted by the mainshock rupture. We conduct Coulomb stress transfer analysis using the Coulomb 3.3 software (Toda *et al.*, 2011). We first built the mainshock source model composed of two rectangular patches based on the best-fitting elliptical patch model (Table 2). We then calculate shear ($\Delta\tau$) and normal ($\Delta\sigma$) stress changes on the receiver fault planes (Fig. 7). The Coulomb failure stress change (ΔCFS) is then calculated as $\Delta CFS = \Delta\tau + \mu\Delta\sigma$, in which μ is the effective friction coefficient. We assume a commonly adopted value of $\mu = 0.6$ (Soh *et al.*, 2018). A positive ΔCFS on the receiver fault indicates that slip is promoted, whereas a negative ΔCFS suggests that slip is inhibited.

For both events 17 and 29, we calculate the ΔCFS imparted by the mainshock, assuming the NE–SW- or NNE–SSW-trending nodal planes as receiver faults. The results show clearly positive ΔCFS values, which are +4.1 MPa for event 17 and +1.0 MPa for event 29 (Fig. 7). Aftershocks associated with each fault segment also exhibit good spatial correlation with regions of positive ΔCFS, suggesting that seismicity on these structures was primarily influenced by the mainshock rupture, although secondary triggering by aftershocks cannot be ruled out (Marsan and Lengline, 2008). Notably, the down-dip extent of seismicity on the event 29 fault coincides with the boundary of the positive ΔCFS region, suggesting that deeper seismicity may have been inhibited by the surrounding stress shadow zone (Fig. 7d). To test the robustness of our results against the choice of slip model, we repeat the calculations with the linear inversion slip model and find that the overall pattern is consistent (Fig. S10).

Fault plane of the largest aftershock

According to our relocation results (Fig. 2), the Buan earthquake sequence predominantly ruptured along NE–SW- or NNE–SSW-striking fault planes. However, the fault-plane geometry of the largest aftershock (event 17) remains uncertain, as the

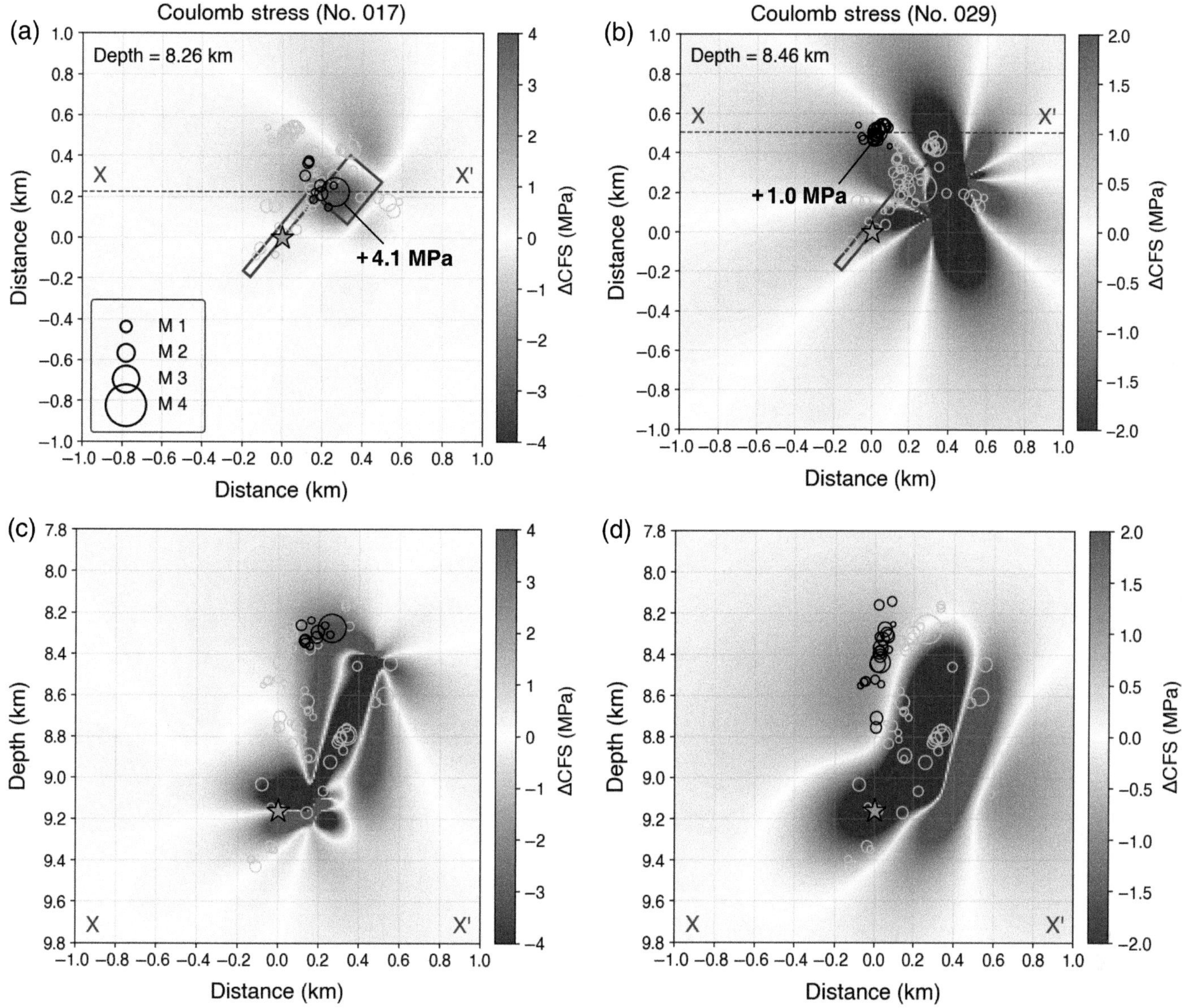

Figure 7. (a) Coulomb failure stress change (ΔCFS) calculated for the receiver fault of event 17, assuming (strike, dip, rake) = (201°, 32°, 144°) at 8.26 km depth. The input mainshock source model is shown as the brown rectangles, and the mainshock hypocenter is shown as a cyan star. Events associated with the target fault plane are shown as black circles, whereas other events are shown as gray circles. (b) Same as panel (a), but for the receiver fault of event 29, assuming (strike, dip, rake) = (212°, 73°, −166°) at 8.46 km depth. (c) Cross section of ΔCFS along the X–X′ line in panel (a). (d) Cross-section of ΔCFS along the X–X′ line in panel (b). The color version of this figure is available only in the electronic edition.

spatial distribution of epicenters does not clearly delineate the strike direction, likely due to its pronounced reverse-faulting component. Han and Kim (2025), based on their independent relocation of events during the first two days of the Buan sequence, suggested that event 17 may have ruptured a NW–SE-striking fault. They further evaluated its rupture potential using a quasi-dynamic simulation based on rate-and-state friction and found that unrealistically low friction ($\mu < 0.2$) would be required for rupture nucleation under the regional stress field.

To provide independent constraints on the fault-plane geometry, we analyze the rupture directivity and spatial extent of event 17 using the second-degree moment inversion approach (McGuire, 2004; Meng *et al.*, 2020; Guo *et al.*, 2025). This method has proven effective in resolving fault-plane ambiguities, particularly for small- to moderate-size earthquakes (**M** ≤ 5). Following the EGF deconvolution procedure applied to the mainshock (see the Mainshock rupture process section), we calculate RSTFs with VR ≥ 70% for the *P*, *S*, and *SmS* phases. We select event 11 (M_L 1.3) as the EGF event based on its spatial proximity and waveform similarity to event 17, yielding a total of 23 *P*, 59 *S*, and 4 *SmS* RSTFs (Fig. S11).

Given the apparent characteristic durations (τ_c) measured from the RSTFs (Silver, 1983; McGuire, 2004), we invert for the rupture duration, rupture area, and directivity vector using the

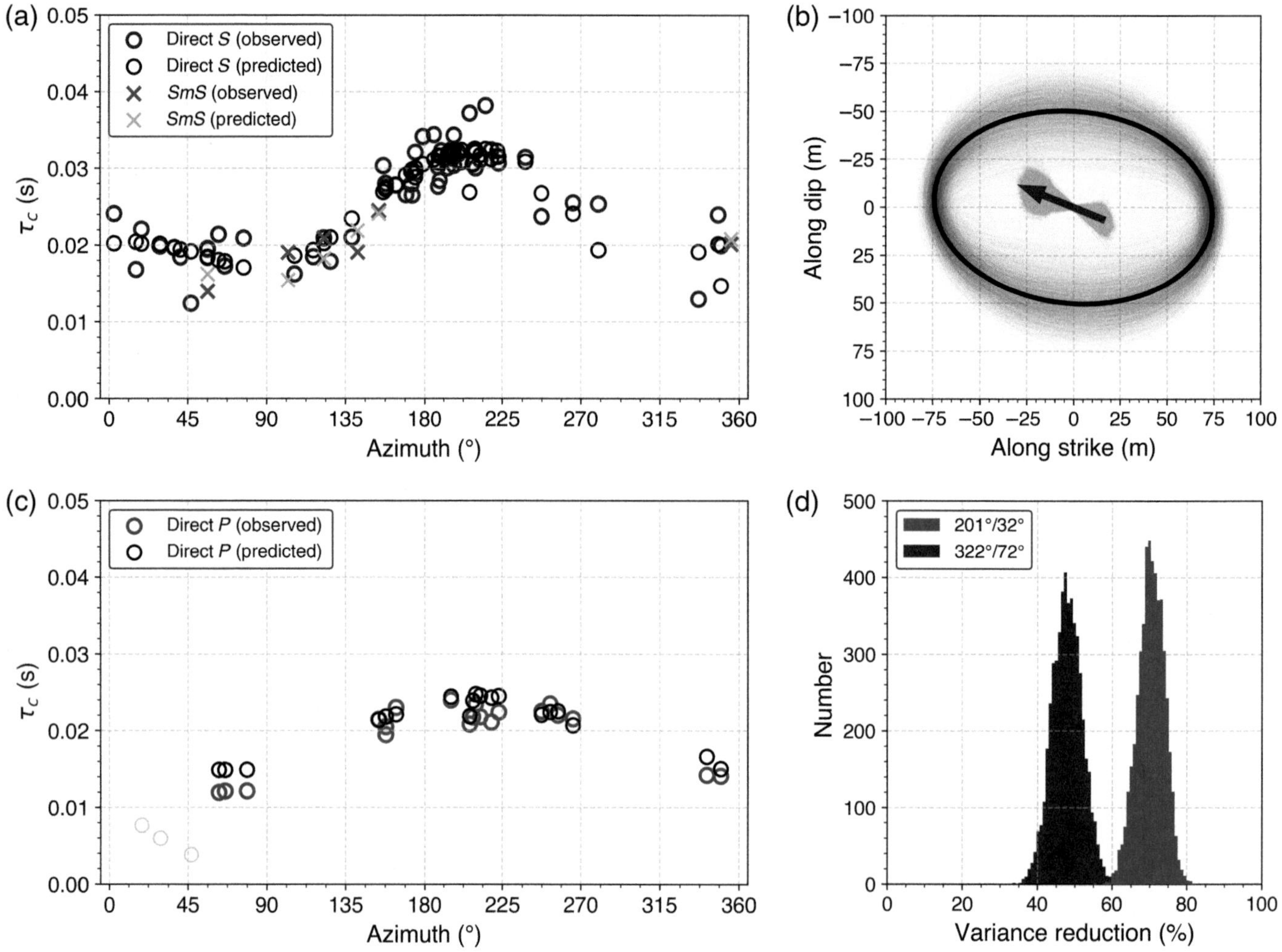

second-degree moment method. To ensure physically meaningful solutions (i.e., positive rupture duration and area), we formulate the inversion as a nonnegative least-squares problem and solve it using a convex optimization framework (Diamond and Boyd, 2016). We perform separate inversions for the two candidate nodal planes and select the one with the lower misfit as the preferred fault plane. To assess uncertainty and significance, we perform 5000 bootstrap inversions by adding Gaussian noise to the apparent τ_c values, sampled from $N(0,\sigma)$, in which σ is the root-mean-square misfit of the original inversion.

The inversion strongly favors the NNE–SSW-oriented nodal plane as the actual fault plane, achieving a significantly higher VR (82%) compared to the NW–SE plane (55%). The close match between the predicted and observed τ_c values (Fig. 8a,b) indicates that the solution is well constrained. The rupture dimension is approximately 150 m × 100 m, with rupture propagating dominantly toward an azimuth of ~40° (Fig. 8c; Table S2). Furthermore, bootstrap results show consistently high-VR values for the NNE–SSW plane (Fig. 8d). Therefore, we interpret the NNE–SSW-trending nodal plane as the actual rupture plane for event 17.

Figure 8. (a) Characteristic durations (τ_c) from *S*-wave RSTFs plotted as a function of station azimuth. Observed values are shown as blue-open circles (direct *S*) and red crosses (*SmS*), whereas predicted durations are shown as black-open circles (direct *S*) and orange crosses (*SmS*). (b) Best-fitting second moment ellipse (black), with semimajor and semi-minor axes representing L_c and W_c, and centroid directivity vector (blue arrow) scaled by $v_0 \times \tau_c$. Gray ellipses and light-blue arrows indicate the ensemble of solutions derived from 5000 inversions with added random noise. (c) τ_c values from *P*-wave RSTFs plotted by azimuth. Observed and predicted durations for direct *P* phases are shown as green and black open circles, respectively. Light-colored open circles indicate measurements from very short RSTFs with limited resolution, which were excluded from the inversion. (d) Histograms of VRs for the two nodal planes, derived from the 5000 inversion ensembles with added random noise. The color version of this figure is available only in the electronic edition.

Conclusions

We analyze the rupture process of the 2024 M_w 4.2 Buan earthquake by constructing a kinematic rupture model that consists of two elliptical patches using EGF-derived RSTFs. The model reveals a complex rupture involving two spatially distinct slip patches that rupture sequentially with a short temporal overlap. The estimated stress drops for the two patches are locally high, approximately 230 and 80 MPa, whereas the average stress drop is about 15 MPa, consistent with estimates from previous moderate-size events in the southern KP. The rupture predominantly propagated in the northeastward and up-dip directions, consistent with the NE–SW alignment of the aftershocks. Both on- and off-fault aftershocks appear to have been triggered by stress transfer from the mainshock; on-fault aftershocks are located near the edges of the high-slip regions, whereas off-fault clusters coincide with areas of positive Coulomb stress changes. These findings demonstrate that even moderate-sized earthquakes in SCRs exhibit complex rupture processes, heterogeneous stress drops, and systematic aftershock triggering governed by fault geometry and stress interaction.

Data and Resources

Waveform data of the Korea Meteorological Administration (KMA) were downloaded from the National Earthquake Comprehensive Information System website (https://necis.kma.go.kr) upon registration; data from the Korea Institute of Geoscience and Mineral Resources (KIGAM) are accessible from the Geo Big Data Open Platform of KIGAM (https://data.kigam.re.kr/quake/data) upon registration; data of the Korea Institute of Nuclear Safety were acquired through personal communication and are not publicly accessible. Seismic data were processed using the Seismic Analysis Code (SAC) version 101.6a (https://ds.iris.edu/ds/nodes/dmc/software/downloads/sac/; Goldstein and Snoke, 2005) and ObsPy version 1.4.0 (https://docs.obspy.org/archive/1.4.0/; Beyreuther *et al.*, 2010). First-motion focal mechanisms were determined using FOCMEC (http://ds.iris.edu/pub/programs/focmec/; Snoke, 2003). Absolute earthquake locations were determined using HYPOINVERSE-2000 (https://www.usgs.gov/software/hypoinverse-earthquake-location; Klein, 2002), and double-difference relocations were performed using HypoDD version 1.3 (~https://www.ldeo.columbia.edu/~felixw/hypoDD.html; Waldhauser and Ellsworth, 2000). The neighborhood algorithm (NA) was implemented using the Python library neighpy (https://neighpy.readthedocs.io/en/latest/). Coulomb stress analysis was conducted using Coulomb 3.3 software (https://temblor.net/coulomb/; Toda *et al.*, 2011). Second moment inversion analysis was conducted based on a Python script modified from an openly available MATLAB toolbox (https://www.seismosoc.org/Publications/SRL/SRL_88/srl_88-2A_mcguire-esupp/; McGuire, 2017). Figures were created using Matplotlib version 3.7.1 (https://matplotlib.org/3.7.1/; Hunter, 2007) and Inkscape version 1.1 (https://inkscape.org/release/inkscape-1.1/). Maps were created using PyGMT version 0.10.0 (https://www.pygmt.org/v0.10.0/; Uieda *et al.*, 2021), a Python library based on Generic Mapping Tools (GMT) version 6 (https://www.generic-mapping-tools.org/; Wessel *et al.*, 2019). Codes used for performing rupture modeling are available from the corresponding author upon request. All websites were last accessed in July 2025. The supplemental material for this article includes 11 figures and 2 tables.

Declaration of Competing Interests

The authors acknowledge that there are no conflicts of interest recorded.

Acknowledgments

This research was supported by the Korea Meteorological Administration (KMA) Research and Development Program (Grant Number RS-2025-02313103) and the National Research Foundation (NRF) of Korea (Grant Number RS-2022-NR070842). W.-Y. Kim also acknowledges support from the Brain Pool Program through the NRF, funded by the Ministry of Science and ICT through the NRF of Korea (Grant Number RS-2024-00444848). Authors acknowledge the Korea Institute of Nuclear Safety for granting permission to use the waveform data. The authors thank the editor and the associate editor for support to this work, and appreciate two anonymous reviewers for their constructive comments.

References

Abdel-Fattah, A. K., K. Y. Kim, M. S. Fnais, and A. M. Al-Amri (2014). Source process and tectonic implication of the January 20, 2007 Odaesan earthquake, South Korea, *Phys. Earth Planet. In.* **229,** 72–81, doi: 10.1016/j.pepi.2014.01.006.

Antonioli, A. M., S. D. Cocco, and C. Henry (2002). Dynamic stress triggering during the great 25 March 1998 Antarctic Plate earthquake, *Bull. Seismol. Soc. Am.* **92,** no. 3, 896–903.

Beaucé, E., F. Waldhauser, D. Schaff, W.-Y. Kim, and F. Kolawole (2025). The 5 April 2024 M_w 4.8 Tewksbury, New Jersey aftershock sequence resolved with machine- learning-enhanced detection methods, *Geophys. Res. Lett.* **52,** no. 12, doi: 10.1029/2024GL113598.

Belardinelli, M. E., M. Cocco, O. Coutant, and F. Cotton (1999). Redistribution of dynamic stress during coseismic ruptures: Evidence for fault interaction and earthquake triggering, *J. Geophys. Res.* **104,** no. B7, 14,925–14,945.

Beresnev, I. A. (2003). Uncertainties in finite-fault slip inversions: To what extent to believe? (a critical review), *Bull. Seismol. Soc. Am.* **93,** no. 6, 2445–2458.

Bertero, M., D. Bindi, P. Boccacci, M. Cattaneo, C. Eva, and V. Lanza (1997). Application of the projected Landweber method to the estimation of the source time function in seismology, *Inverse Probl.* **13,** no. 2, 465–486.

Beyreuther, M., R. Barsch, L. Krischer, T. Megies, Y. Behr, and J. Wassermann (2010). ObsPy: A Python toolbox for seismology, *Seismol. Res. Lett.* **81,** no. 3, 530–533.

Boatwright, J. (2007). The persistence of directivity in small earthquakes, *Bull. Seismol. Soc. Am.* **97,** no. 6, 1850–1861.

Boyd, O. S., D. E. McNamara, S. Hartzell, and G. Choy (2017). Influence of lithostatic stress on earthquake stress drops in North America, *Bull. Seismol. Soc. Am.* **107,** no. 2, 856–868.

Chapman, M. C. (2013). On the rupture process of the 23 August 2011 Virginia earthquake, *Bull. Seismol. Soc. Am.* **103,** no. 2A, 613–628.

Cho, E., J.-U. Woo, J. Rhie, T.-S. Kang, and S. Y. Baag (2023). Rupture process of the 2017 M_w 5.5 Pohang, South Korea, Earthquake via an Empirical Green's function method, *Bull. Seismol. Soc. Am.* **113,** no. 2, 592–603.

Das, S., and C. Henry (2003). Spatial relation between main earthquake slip and its aftershock distribution, *Rev. Geophys.* **41,** no. 3, doi: 10.1029/2002RG000119.

Day, S. M., G. Yu, and D. J. Wald (1998). Dynamic stress changes during earthquake rupture, *Bull. Seismol. Soc. Am.* **88,** no. 2, 512–522.

Di Carli, S., C. François-Holden, S. Peyrat, and R. Madariaga (2010). Dynamic inversion of the 2000 Tottori earthquake based on elliptical subfault approximations, *J. Geophys. Res.* **115,** no. B12, doi: 10.1029/2009JB006358.

Diamond, S., and S. Boyd (2016). CVXPY: A Python-embedded modeling language for convex optimization, *J. Mach. Learn. Res.* **17,** no. 83, 1–5.

Dreger, D., R. M. Nadeau, and A. Chung (2007). Repeating earthquake finite source models: Strong asperities revealed on the San Andreas Fault, *Geophys. Res. Lett.* **34,** no. 23, doi: 10.1029/2007GL031353.

Dreger, D. S. (1994). Empirical Green's function study of the January 17, 1994 Northridge, California earthquake, *Geophys. Res. Lett.* **21,** no. 24, 2633–2636.

Ellsworth, W. L., and F. Bulut (2018). Nucleation of the 1999 Izmit earthquake by a triggered cascade of foreshocks, *Nat. Geosci.* **11,** no. 7, 531–535.

Eshelby, J. D. (1957). The determination of the elastic field of an ellipsoidal inclusion, and related problems, *Proc. Math. Phys. Sci.* **241,** no. 1226, 376–396.

Gallovič, F., V. Plicka, L. Valentová, E. Sokos, and J. Zahradník (2025). Complex dynamic rupture of an M_w 5.8 intermediate-depth earthquake in the Hellenic slab, *Geophys. Res. Lett.* **52,** no. 7, doi: 10.1029/2024GL113649.

Geller, R. J. (1976). Scaling relations for earthquake source parameters and magnitudes, *Bull. Seismol. Soc. Am.* **66,** no. 5, 1501–1523.

Godano, M., C. Larroque, B. Delouis, J.-P. Ampuero, F. Arzu, F. Courboulex, A. Deschamps, M. van den Ende, S. Baize, and J.-F. Ritz (2025). Back to the source: Connecting the seismological observations of Le Teil earthquake (M_w 4.9, 2019/11/11, France) to the local geology, *J. Geophys. Res.* **130,** no. 9, doi: 10.1029/2025JB031133.

Goldstein, P. A. U. L., and A. Snoke (2005). SAC availability for the IRIS community, *Incorporated Research Institutions for Seismology Data Management Center Electronic Newsletter*, available at https://seiscode.iris.washington.edu/projects/sac (last accessed August 2025).

Gomberg, J. (2018). Unsettled earthquake nucleation, *Nat. Geosci.* **11,** no. 7, 463–464.

Guo, H., J. W. Atterholt, J. J. McGuire, and C. Thurber (2025). Evidence for low effective stress within the crust of the subducted Gorda plate from the 2022 December M_w 6.4 Ferndale earthquake sequence, *Seismol. Res. Lett.* **96,** no. 3, 1504–1520.

Guo, H., T. Lay, and E. E. Brodsky (2023). Seismological indicators of geologically inferred fault maturity, *J. Geophys. Res.* **128,** no. 10, doi: 10.1029/2023JB027096.

Han, J., and S. Kim (2025). The 2024 M_L 4.8 Buan earthquake sequence and aligned multiple clusters in the southwestern Korean Peninsula, *Geosci. J.* 1–15, doi: 10.1007/s12303-025-00048-x.

Han, S., W.-Y. Kim, H. Lim, Y. O. Son, M.-S. Seo, J. Y. Park, and Y. Kim (2024). Resolving multi-stage rupture process of the 2021 M_w 4.9 Offshore Jeju Island earthquake from relative source time functions, *Geophys. Res. Lett.* **51,** no. 3, doi: 10.1029/2023GL106059.

Han, S., W.-Y. Kim, J. Y. Park, M.-S. Seo, and Y. Kim (2024). Rupture Model of the 5 April 2024 Tewksbury, New Jersey, earthquake based on regional Lg-wave data, *Seism. Record* **4,** no. 3, 214–222.

Hartzell, S., C. Mendoza, and Y. Zeng (2013). Rupture model of the 2011 Mineral, Virginia, earthquake from teleseismic and regional waveforms, *Geophys. Res. Lett.* **40,** no. 21, 5665–5670.

Horton, J. W., M. C. Chapman, and R. A. Green (2015). The 2011 Mineral, Virginia, earthquake, and its significance for seismic hazards in eastern North America— Overview and synthesis, in *The 2011 Mineral, Virginia, Earthquake, and its Significance for Seismic Hazards in Eastern North America*, M. Horton Jr., C. Chapman, and R. A. Green (Editors), Geological Society of America, Boulder, Colorado, Special Paper 509, 1–25, doi: 10.1130/2015.2509(01).

Hunter, J. D. (2007). Matplotlib: A 2D graphics environment, *Comput. Sci. Eng.* **9,** no. 03, 90–95.

Jin, S., Z. C. Li, and P. H. Park (2006). Seismicity and GPS constraints on crustal deformation in the southern part of the Korean Peninsula, *Geosci. J.* **10,** no. 4, 491–497.

Kaneko, Y., and P. M. Shearer (2015). Variability of seismic source spectra, estimated stress drop, and radiated energy, derived from cohesive-zone models of symmetrical and asymmetrical circular and elliptical ruptures, *J. Geophys. Res.* **120,** no. 2, 1053–1079.

Kee, W.-S., S. Kim, H. Kim, P. Hong, C. Kwon, H.-J. Lee, D.-L. Cho, H. Hoh, K.-Y. Song, and U. Byun (2019). Geologic Map of Korea (1:1,000,000), Korea Institute of Geoscience and Mineral Resources, doi: 10.22747/data.20220816.4826.

Kim, S. J., and S. G. Kim (1983). A study on the crustal structure of South Korea by using seismic waves, *Econ. Environ. Geol.* **16,** no. 1, 51–61.

Kim, W.-Y., H. Choi, and M. Noh (2010). The 20 January 2007 Odaesan, Korea, earthquake sequence: Reactivation of a buried strike-slip fault? *Bull. Seismol. Soc. Am.* **100,** no. 3, 1120–1137.

Kim, W.-Y., M.-S. Seo, J. Y. Park, S. Han, Y. O. Son, and Y. Kim (2023). The 28 October 2022 M_w 3.8 Goesan earthquake sequence in Central Korea: Stress drop, aftershock triggering, and fault interaction, *Bull. Seismol. Soc. Am.* **113,** no. 6, 2416–2431.

Klein, F. W. (2002). User's guide to HYPOINVERSE-2000, a Fortran program to solve for earthquake locations and magnitudes, *Open-File Rept. 02-171.*

Lanza, V., D. Spallarossa, M. Cattaneo, D. Bindi, and P. Augliera (1999). Source parameters of small events using constrained deconvolution with empirical Green's functions, *Geophys. J. Int.* **137,** no. 3, 651–662.

Lee, S., A. Saxena, J. H. Song, J. Rhie, and E. Choi (2022). Contributions from lithospheric and upper-mantle heterogeneities to upper crustal seismicity in the Korean Peninsula, *Geophys. J. Int.* **229,** no. 2, 1175–1192.

Li, J., T. Kim, N. Lapusta, E. Biondi, and Z. Zhan (2023). The break of earthquake asperities imaged by distributed acoustic sensing, *Nature* **620,** no. 7975, 800–806.

Madariaga, R. (1976). Dynamics of an expanding circular fault, *Bull. Seismol. Soc. Am.* **66,** no. 3, 639–666.

Marsan, D., and O. Lengline (2008). Extending earthquakes' reach through cascading, *Science* **319,** no. 5866, 1076–1079.

McGuire, J. J. (2004). Estimating finite source properties of small earthquake ruptures, *Bull. Seismol. Soc. Am.* **94,** no. 2, 377–393.

McGuire, J. J. (2017). A MATLAB toolbox for estimating the second moments of earthquake ruptures, *Seismol. Res. Lett.* **88,** no. 2A, 371–378.

Mendoza, C., and S. Hartzell (2013). Finite-fault source inversion using teleseismic P waves: Simple parameterization and rapid analysis, *Bull. Seismol. Soc. Am.* **103,** no. 2A, 834–844.

Meng, H., J. J. McGuire, and Y. Ben-Zion (2020). Semiautomated estimates of directivity and related source properties of small to moderate Southern California earthquakes using second seismic moments, *J. Geophys. Res.* **125,** no. 4, doi: 10.1029/2019JB018566.

Meng, Q., S. Ni, and Z. Peng (2021). Complex source behaviors and spatiotemporal evolution of seismicity during the 2015–2016 earthquake sequence in Cushing, Oklahoma, *J. Geophys. Res.* **126,** no. 6, doi: 10.1029/2021JB022168.

Mori, J., and A. Frankel (1990). Source parameters for small events associated with the 1986 North Palm Springs, California, earthquake determined using empirical Green functions, *Bull. Seismol. Soc. Am.* **80,** no. 2, 278–295.

Neves, M., L. Y. Chuang, W. Li, Z. Peng, P. M. Figueiredo, and S. Ni (2024). Complex rupture dynamics of the extremely shallow August 2020 M5. 1 Sparta, North Carolina earthquake, *Commun. Earth Environ.* **5,** no. 1, doi: 10.1038/s43247-024-01316-8.

Pennington, C. N., H. Chang, J. L. Rubinstein, R. E. Abercrombie, N. Nakata, T. Uchide, and E. S. Cochran (2022). Quantifying the sensitivity of microearthquake slip inversions to station distribution using a dense nodal array, *Bull. Seismol. Soc. Am.* **112,** no. 3, 1252–1270.

Pennington, C. N., T. Uchide, and X. Chen (2022). Slip characteristics of induced earthquakes: Insights from the 2015 M_w 4.0 Guthrie, Oklahoma earthquake, *J. Geophys. Res.* **127,** no. 5, doi: 10.1029/2021JB023564.

Ross, Z. E., H. Kanamori, and E. Hauksson (2017). Anomalously large complete stress drop during the 2016 M_w 5.2 Borrego Springs earthquake inferred by waveform modeling and near-source aftershock deficit, *Geophys. Res. Lett.* **44,** no. 12, 5994–6001.

Saikia, C. K. (1994). Modified frequency-wavenumber algorithm for regional seismograms using Filon's quadrature: Modelling of *Lg* waves in eastern North America, *Geophys. J. Int.* **118,** no. 1, 142–158.

Saikia, C. K., and D. V. Helmberger (1997). Approximation of rupture directivity in regional phases using upgoing and downgoing wave fields, *Bull. Seismol. Soc. Am.* **87,** no. 4, 987–998.

Sambridge, M. (1999). Geophysical inversion with a neighbourhood algorithm—I. Searching a parameter space, *Geophys. J. Int.* **138,** no. 2, 479–494.

Silver, P. (1983). Retrieval of source-extent parameters and the interpretation of corner frequency, *Bull. Seismol. Soc. Am.* **73,** no. 6A, 1499–1511.

Snoke, J. A. (2003). FOCMEC: FOCal MEChanism determinations, in *International Handbook of Earthquake and Engineering Seismology, Part B*, W. H. K. Lee, H. Kanamori, P. C. Jennings, and C. Kisslinger (Editors), Academic Press, London, United Kingdom, 1629–1630.

Soh, I., C. Chang, J. Lee, T.-K. Hong, and E. S. Park (2018). Tectonic stress orientations and magnitudes, and friction of faults, deduced from earthquake focal mechanism inversions over the Korean Peninsula, *Geophys. J. Int.* **213,** no. 2, 1360–1373.

Somerville, P., K. Irikura, R. Graves, S. Sawada, D. Wald, N. Abrahamson, Y. Iwasaki, T. Kagawa, N. Smith, and A. Kowada (1999). Characterizing crustal earthquake slip models for the prediction of strong ground motion, *Seismol. Res. Lett.* **70,** no. 1, 59–80.

Song, S. G., and B. Duan (2024). Dynamic rupture models of the 2016 M_L 5.8 Gyeongju, South Korea, earthquake, constrained by a Kinematic rupture model and seismic waveform data, *Bull. Seismol. Soc. Am.* **114,** no. 2, 710–725.

Song, X. J., and D. V. Helmberger (1996). Source estimation of finite faults from broadband regional networks, *Bull. Seismol. Soc. Am.* **86,** no. 3, 797–804.

Taira, T. A., D. S. Dreger, and R. M. Nadeau (2015). Rupture process for micro-earthquakes inferred from borehole seismic recordings, *Int. J. Earth Sci.* **104,** 1499–1510, doi: 10.1007/s00531-015-1217-8.

Toda, S., R. S. Stein, V. Sevilgen, and J. Lin (2011). Coulomb 3.3 Graphic-rich deformation and stress-change software for earthquake, tectonic, and volcano research and teaching—User guide, *U.S. Geol. Surv. Open-File Rept. 2011-1060*, 63 pp.

Twardzik, C., R. Madariaga, S. Das, and S. Custódio (2012). Robust features of the source process for the 2004 Parkfield, California, earthquake from strong-motion seismograms, *Geophys. J. Int.* **191,** no. 3, 1245–1254.

Uchide, T., and S. G. Song (2018). Fault rupture model of the 2016 Gyeongju, South Korea, earthquake and its implication for the underground fault system, *Geophys. Res. Lett.* **45,** no. 5, 2257–2264.

Uieda, L., D. Tian, W. J. Leong, L. Toney, W. Schlitzer, M. Grund, D. Newton, M. Ziebarth, M. Jones, and P. Wessel (2021). PyGMT: A Python interface for the Generic Mapping Tools (v0.9.0), *Zenodo*, doi: 10.5281/zenodo.8303186.

Vallée, M., and M. Bouchon (2004). Imaging coseismic rupture in far field by slip patches, *Geophys. J. Int.* **156,** no. 3, 615–630.

Vera, F., F. Tilmann, and J. Saul (2024). A decade of short-period earthquake rupture histories from multi-array back-projection, *J. Geophys. Res.* **129,** no. 2, doi: 10.1029/2023JB027260.

Viegas, G., R. E. Abercrombie, and W.-Y. Kim (2010). The 2002 M5 Au Sable Forks, NY, earthquake sequence: Source scaling relationships and energy budget, *J. Geophys. Res.* **115,** no. B7, doi: 10.1029/2009JB006799.

Waldhauser, F., and W. L. Ellsworth (2000). A double-difference earthquake location algorithm: Method and application to the northern Hayward fault, California, *Bull. Seismol. Soc. Am.* **90,** no. 6, 1353–1368.

Wessel, P., J. F. Luis, L. Uieda, R. Scharroo, F. Wobbe, W. H. F. Smith, and D. Tian (2019). The generic mapping tools version 6. *Geochem. Geophys. Geosys.* **20,** no. 11, 5556–5564.

Wössner, J., D. Schorlemmer, S. Wiemer, and P. M. Mai (2006). Spatial correlation of aftershock locations and on-fault main shock properties, *J. Geophys. Res.* **111,** no. B8, doi: 10.1029/2005JB003961.

Wu, Q., and M. Chapman (2017). Stress-drop estimates and source scaling of the 2011 Mineral, Virginia, mainshock and aftershocks, *Bull. Seismol. Soc. Am.* **107,** no. 6, 2703–2720.

Yao, S., Z. Yang, and H. Yang (2025). Determination of rupture directivity of the 2024 Feidong M4.7 earthquake using Single Near-Source Station, *Earthq. Sci.* **38,** no. 5, 399–407.

Žilić, I., M. Causse, M. Vallée, and S. Markušić (2025). High stress drop and slow rupture during the 2020 M_w 6.4 intraplate Petrinja Earthquake, Croatia, *J. Geophys. Res.: Solid Earth* **130,** no. 1, doi: 10.1029/2024JB029107.

Manuscript received 7 August 2025
Published online 11 December 2025

Early Warning Performance of FinDer, Virtual Seismologist, and eBEAR Systems in the 2024 M_L 7.2 Hualien, Taiwan, Earthquake

Guan-Yi Song*[1,2], Da-Yi Chen[1], Yih-Min Wu[2], Frédérick Massin[3], Maren Böse[3], and John Clinton[3]

Abstract

Public earthquake early warning (EEW) in Taiwan has been operating for more than a decade with a single point-source algorithm, existing Earthworm-Based Earthquake Alarm Reporting (eBEAR). For large earthquakes with finite rupture, point-source EEW algorithms will fail to accurately predict ground motion for all affected regions, even when the magnitude is correctly estimated. Further, single-algorithm EEW systems are more likely to fail than those that operate multiple independent algorithms. Since mid-2023, the Central Weather Administration (CWA) has been testing the Swiss Seismological Service (SED) at ETH Zurich SeisComP EEW system, developed at the Swiss Seismological Service at ETH Zürich, to explore the benefits of integrating Finite-fault rupture Detector (FinDer) and virtual seismologist (VS) using the SeisComP platform. This study aims to evaluate whether combining line-source and point-source models can overcome limitations observed in the existing EEW strategy, particularly during large earthquakes. During the recent M_L 7.2 earthquake on 3 April 2024, in Hualien County, the original eBEAR faced challenges with its alert updating mechanism, issuing high-level Public Warning System alerts to only 12 counties and cities, notably missing five highly populated northern areas, including the capital, Taipei. To address this issue, CWA lowered the magnitude change threshold for updating alerts from 0.5 to 0.1 magnitude units. This adjustment improved the responsiveness of initial alerts; however, its point-source assumption still resulted in limited spatial coverage. In contrast, FinDer accurately captured rupture geometry and achieved the highest accuracy in ground-motion prediction as well as broader spatial alert coverage. Although the VS algorithm initially suffered from a configuration issue, the offline-corrected version yielded results similar to eBEAR, reflecting shared limitations of point-source methods. Our results demonstrate the complementary characteristics of point-source and finite-fault models in EEW applications. We suggest that integrating rapid point-source methods such as eBEAR or VS with finite-fault approaches like FinDer may significantly enhance both ground-motion prediction and reliability of EEW systems in future large earthquakes.

Cite this article as Song, G.-Y., D.-Y. Chen, Y.-M. Wu, F. Massin, M. Böse, and J. Clinton (2026). Early Warning Performance of FinDer, Virtual Seismologist, and eBEAR Systems in the 2024 M_L 7.2 Hualien, Taiwan, Earthquake, *Seismol. Res. Lett.* **XX**, 1782–1797, doi: 10.1785/0220250187.

Supplemental Material

Introduction

Taiwan is located at the convergent boundary between the Eurasian and Philippine Sea plates, making it highly susceptible to destructive earthquakes. earthquake early warning (EEW) is a critical component of Taiwan's disaster mitigation strategies, particularly given the frequency and magnitude of seismic events affecting the region. Currently, the Central Weather Administration's (CWA) operational EEW infrastructure primarily employs point-source algorithms. The Central Weather Bureau was renamed to the CWA in September 2023. Although

1. Central Weather Administration, Taipei, Taiwan, https://orcid.org/0000-0002-7308-9080 (G-YS); 2. Department of Geosciences, National Taiwan University, Taipei, Taiwan, https://orcid.org/0000-0003-4542-1741 (Y-MW); 3. ETHZ-SED, Swiss Seismological Service, Zürich, Switzerland, https://orcid.org/0000-0002-7532-5139 (FM); https://orcid.org/0000-0003-4639-719X (MB); https://orcid.org/0000-0001-8626-2703 (JC)

*Corresponding author: taipei83109@cwa.gov.tw, taipei83109@gmail.com computationally efficient and well-suited for rapid initial alerts, these methods treat the earthquake source as a single point, which may inadequately represent the spatial complexity of large fault ruptures. As a result, these methods may underestimate the magnitude, shaking intensity, and affected area during large seismic events, particularly those involving significant rupture propagation and heterogeneous energy release.

To address these limitations, various approaches have been proposed, including the integration of real-time Global Navigation Satellite Systems data for enhancing magnitude estimation (Ruhl *et al.*, 2017) and finite-fault source modeling. In anticipation of future large-magnitude earthquakes, CWA proactively began integrating ETHZ-SED SeisComP EEW (ESE) algorithms in 2023 through collaboration with ETH Zürich. These included the Finite-fault rupture Detector (FinDer), a line-source algorithm capable of tracking fault rupture geometry in real time, and the virtual seismologist (VS), a globally established point-source-based method. Although FinDer captures the evolving spatial characteristics of the fault rupture, VS provides rapid magnitude and location estimates based on early waveforms, offering complementary strengths. Both algorithms were implemented within the SeisComP framework and operated in parallel with the existing Earthworm-Based Earthquake Alarm Reporting (eBEAR) system in a preoperational testing stage. However, a systematic comparison of these algorithms during real-time conditions of large earthquakes, especially within Taiwan's operational infrastructure, has not yet been thoroughly explored.

On 3 April 2024, at 07:58:09 local time (UTC + 8), an M_L 7.2 (M_w 7.4) earthquake struck Hualien County, resulting from reverse faulting along the boundary between the Eurasian and Philippine Sea plates (CWA, 2024; U.S. Geological Survey, 2024). This information is detailed in the CWA earthquake report, shown in Figure 1a (see Data and Resources). The maximum peak ground acceleration (PGA) for this event was observed as 1102 cm/s^2 at station ETL in Taroko at 33 km epicentral distance, whereas the maximum peak ground velocity (PGV) recorded at the EHP station in Hoping at 52 km was 84 cm/s.

The earthquake caused significant damage and casualties, with 18 fatalities and 1147 injuries reported, as well as 90 red-tagged and 92 yellow-tagged buildings classified as structurally damaged (Fig. 1b). In Taiwan's seismic intensity scale, adopted by the CWA since 2020, a two-parameter approach is used: PGA informs intensities from 0 to 4, whereas PGV is applied for intensities of 5 lower and above (Hsu, 1979; Wu *et al.*, 2003; CWA, 2019; Table 1). Figure 1b shows that nearly all damaged buildings and casualties were located in areas with PGV-based intensity, corresponding to CWA intensity 5 and higher.

Because the largest earthquake in Taiwan since the 1999 Chi-Chi event, and coinciding with the deployment of new EEW algorithms, the 2024 Hualien earthquake offered an unprecedented opportunity to evaluate the real-time performance of eBEAR, FinDer, and VS under real-world conditions.

This study aims to evaluate whether the integration of the ESE algorithms can effectively enhance the capabilities of the CWA's existing eBEAR system. Our analysis focuses on several key performance metrics, including hypocenter location accuracy, magnitude estimation, alert coverage, alert timeliness, and PGA prediction accuracy for the eBEAR, VS, and FinDer systems during the 2024 Hualien earthquake. Through this comparison, we seek to identify the relative strengths, limitations, and adequate range of application for each approach.

Data and Methods

eBEAR system and EEW alerting criteria at the time of the 2024 Hualien earthquake

In 1986, an M_w 7.4 earthquake struck off the eastern coast of Taiwan. Apart from causing damage in the nearby Hualien County, it also resulted in significant seismic disasters in the Taipei basin, over 100 km north of the epicenter. This earthquake marked the beginning of Taiwan's development of an EEW system, and significant progress has been made since then (Wu *et al.*, 1998, 1999; Wu and Teng, 2002; Hsiao, 2007, Hsiao *et al.*, 2009; Chen *et al.*, 2015, 2019).

With the efforts of predecessors in developing EEW technology and algorithms, coupled with the installation of a dense network of real-time stations, the CWA has established the eBEAR system, also known as the CWA EEW system (Chen *et al.*, 2015). The system focuses on three main stages: data acquisition, processing, and alerting. It relies solely on *P*-wave arrivals for earthquake location, employing the short-term average/long-term average (STA/LTA) method to ensure accurate detection and quality assessment while mitigating excessive picks by implementing a 20 s pause after each detection. The subsequent step involves collecting *P*-wave arrival times and using Geiger's method (Geiger, 1912) and the effective epicenter method (Teng *et al.*, 1997) to determine the hypocenter. After the initial pick is made, the displacement amplitude from each pick is used to estimate the magnitude. The system updates this amplitude by expanding the *P*-wave time window from 2 to 9 s after the initial pick time to improve efficiency and accuracy. The same regression equations are applied across different time windows to compute the magnitude (M_{pd}), which is based on peak displacement (Pd) and hypocentral distance (Chen *et al.*, 2019). For intensity estimation, CWA set up 47 reference points, equipped with real-time seismic stations, across 22 counties and cities in Taiwan (Fig. 2). The selection criteria for these reference points prioritize densely populated areas, with additional consideration given to counties or cities with spatially elongated shapes. Once the EEW system has generated the hypocenter and magnitude information, the epicentral distances to the 47 reference points are calculated, and PGA values are estimated using the ground-motion prediction equation (GMPE) of Hsiao (2007).

Establishing thresholds for public alerting is crucial for the EEW system. If the magnitude or PGA thresholds are set too

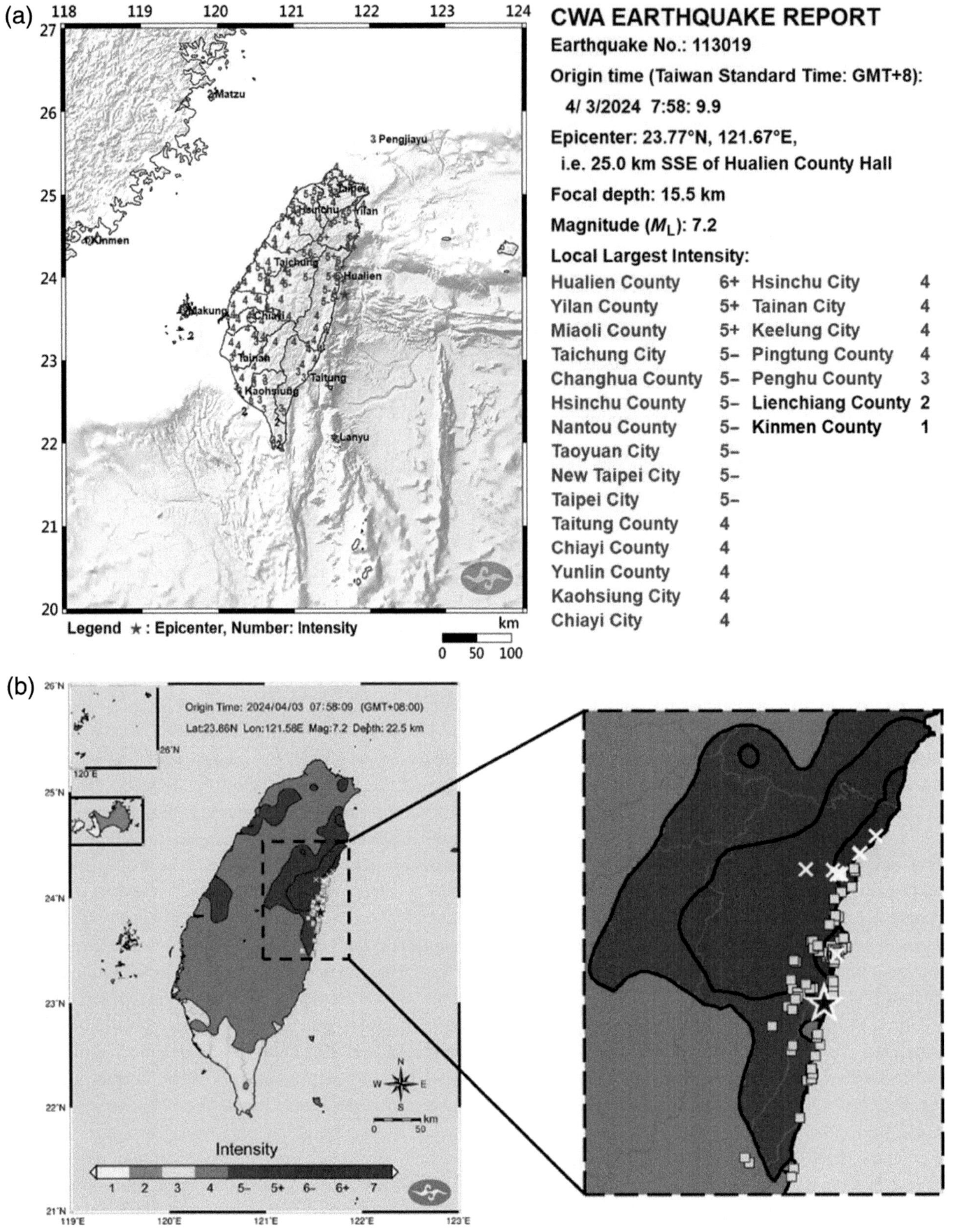

Figure 1. (a) Central Weather Administration (CWA) earthquake report for the 3 April 2024 M_L 7.2 Hualien earthquake. The red star indicates the epicenter. The numbers give the seismic intensity at each location. (b) The distribution of CWA intensities and disasters illustrates a strong correlation between high-intensity areas and the locations of damaged buildings (yellow squares) and fatalities (white X marks). This map shows that nearly all damaged buildings and casualties are located in areas with peak ground velocity (PGV)-based intensity (CWA intensity 5 or higher), highlighting the relationship between PGV intensity and the severity of structural damage and casualties, thus supporting the effectiveness of using PGV to assess earthquake impact. GMT, Generic Mapping Tools. The color version of this figure is available only in the electronic edition.

TABLE 1
Central Weather Administration (CWA) Intensity Scale

Intensity	**0**	**1**	**2**	**3**	**4**	**5−**	**5+**	**6−**	**6+**	**7**
PGA (cm/s^2)	<0.8	**0.8–2.5**	**2.5–8.0**	**8.0–25**	**25–80**	80–140	140–250	250–440	440–800	≥800
PGV (cm/s)	<0.2	0.2–0.7	0.7–1.9	1.9–5.7	5.7–15	**15–30**	**30–50**	**50–80**	**80–140**	≥140

Since 2020, the CWA considers both peak ground acceleration (PGA) and peak ground velocity (PGV) to calculate seismic intensity in earthquake reports. The bold text in the table indicates the current ranges adopted by the CWA intensity scale. PGA is used for intensities ranging from 0 to 4, whereas PGV is utilized for intensities from 5 to 7.

low, an excessive number of alerts could be created, which eventually may result in alert fatigue in the public. Conversely, if the thresholds are set too high, alerts may be missed and prevent people from taking action. According to surveys conducted in the aftermath of the 1999 Chi-Chi earthquake, damage primarily occurred when PGA reached or exceeded 80 cm/s^2 (CWA intensity 5; Wu *et al.*, 2003, 2004). This PGA value provides an important reference for setting thresholds. However, relying solely on PGA is insufficient, as the magnitude of the earthquake also plays a significant role in determining potential damage, because high-PGA values are also often observed in smaller magnitude events (Wu *et al.*, 2003). Based on the aforementioned considerations, potential system errors, and user needs, CWA implemented two magnitude thresholds at 4.5 and 5.0, and two PGA thresholds at 8 cm/s^2 (CWA intensity 3) and 25 cm/s^2 (CWA intensity 4). These thresholds are used for three communication channels that meet different needs (Table 2). Since 2014, the eBEAR system has been providing EEW messages via internet-based notification software to a limited number of dedicated users, including schools and government agencies, using low magnitude and intensity thresholds of 4.5 and 3, respectively. Since 2016, eBEAR has expanded to include both television broadcasts and the Public Warning System (PWS) to reach the general public (Wu *et al.*, 2021). TV broadcasts use magnitude and intensity thresholds of 5.0 and 3, respectively. The PWS plays a crucial role in ensuring that people receive timely earthquake information, especially during significant seismic events. It is utilized by the Taiwanese government infrastructure to deliver presidential alert messages directly to mobile phones via cell broadcast, sending alerts for the most significant ground shaking, using the highest magnitude and PGA thresholds (magnitude 5.0, intensity 4). Because cell broadcast has the broadest reach, it is the primary channel for delivering earthquake alerts to the Taiwanese public.

For the 2024 Hualien earthquake, the results generated by the eBEAR system (hereafter referred to as original eBEAR) met all the thresholds for the three mentioned channels and successfully provided EEW messages to the public (Fig. 3). It issued a first PWS report (M_{pd} 6.2) just 8 s after the event origin time, followed by a second report (M_{pd} 6.8) at 14 s. The system provided PWS alerts to 12 counties and cities across Taiwan. At the same time, the original eBEAR system also issued alerts to 19 of the 22 counties and cities across Taiwan, including the capital city Taipei, through TV broadcasts and the internet. However, due to the magnitude update threshold being set at 0.5 (for all three dissemination channels), requiring at least an M_{pd} 7.3 for an alert update, all subsequent internal reports with M_{pd} between 6.8 and 7.2 were not distributed to the public. Despite these reports indicating that estimated PGA values would exceed 25 cm/s^2 at many reference points in northern Taiwan, including Taipei, the residents in these areas did not receive PWS alerts. To address this issue, the CWA adjusted and tested the update mechanism after the Hualien mainshock, implementing the modified eBEAR system (a CWA operational policy change, not an experimental setting in this study). This modification reduces the alert issuance threshold from 0.5 to 0.1, thus enabling rapid alerts whenever additional areas meet the PGA threshold. The original and modified eBEAR systems must be identical in terms of EEW performance; the only difference is in the frequency of their published alert updates.

ESE System

SeisComP is a popular, widely used earthquake monitoring software, known for being free, open-source, and providing a complete earthquake data processing workflow (Helmholtz Centre Potsdam GFZ German Research Centre for Geosciences and gempa GmbH, 2008; SeisComP Documentation, 2024b). Developed by the ETHZ-SED team on the SeisComP platform, the ESE system (Massin *et al.*, 2021) incorporates the VS (Cua, 2005; Cua and Heaton, 2007; Cua *et al.*, 2009) point-source and the FinDer (Böse *et al.*, 2012, 2015, 2018, 2023) algorithms. Currently, the ESE system is employed across Central America, and VS is providing operational EEW alerts to the region (Porras *et al.*, 2021; Massin *et al.*, 2022). ESE is also undergoing real-time testing in Switzerland. The FinDer algorithm is one of the two seismic algorithms that comprise the ShakeAlert

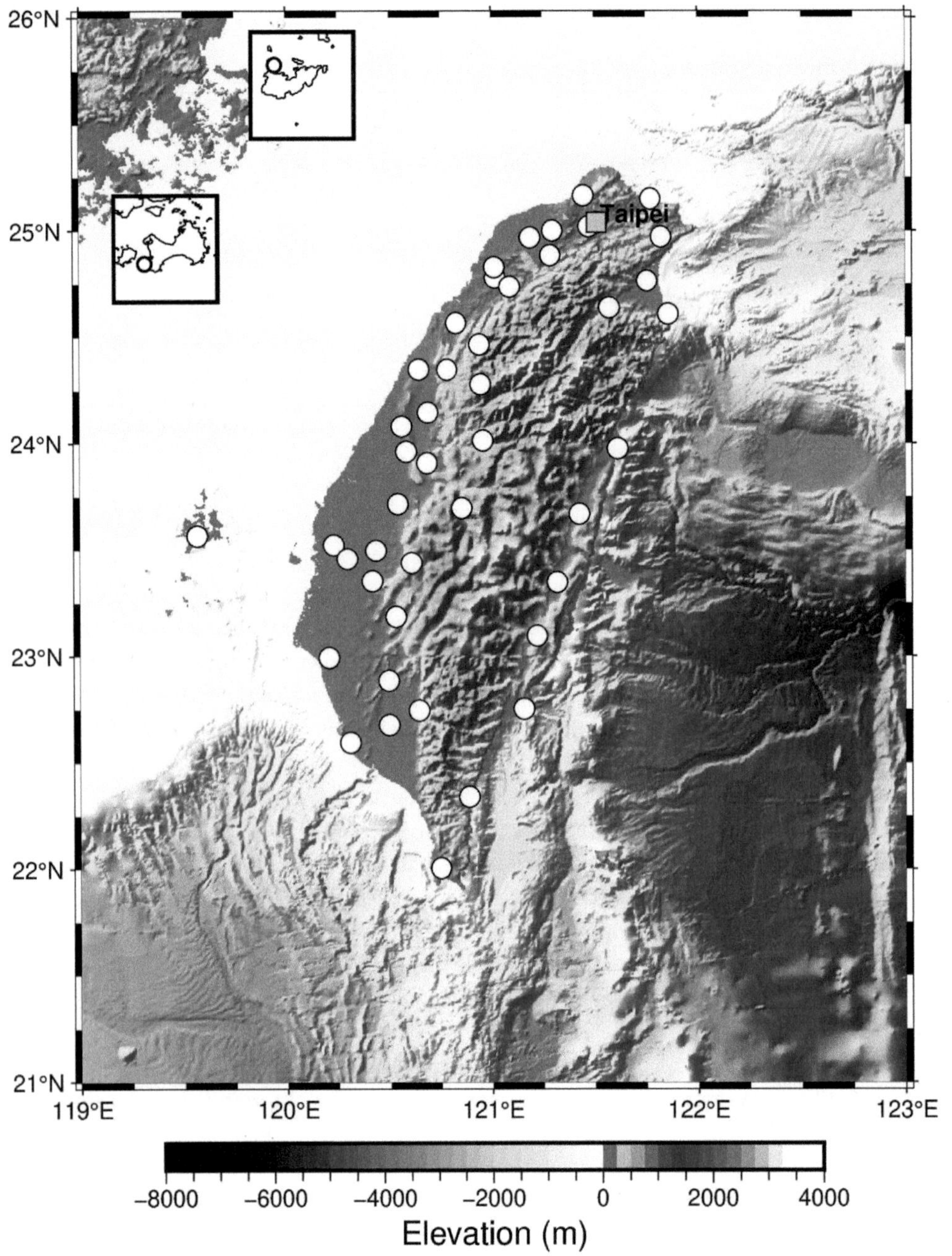

Figure 2. Forty-seven reference points used in the Earthworm-Based Earthquake Alarm Reporting (eBEAR) system. The white circles indicate locations used by the earthquake early warning (EEW) system to estimate peak ground acceleration (PGA). The capital, Taipei City, is highlighted with a yellow square for spatial reference. Once the predicted PGA at a reference point exceeds specified thresholds, a local alert is declared. Insets show the two offshore counties of Taiwan, Lienchiang County (upper) and Kinmen County (lower). The color version of this figure is available only in the electronic edition.

system operating along the U.S. West Coast (Kohler *et al.*, 2020) and is being real-time and offline tested in other regions (see Böse *et al.*, 2023, for an overview). ESE includes complete documentation and mature software. Using ESE, CWA can introduce new EEW algorithms that may complement the traditional point-source method used in the eBEAR system to estimate earthquake location and magnitude.

The ESE system consists of three data processing steps (Fig. 4), including real-time data import, earthquake localization, and magnitude estimation. The system imports real-time seismic signals from a SeedLink server (see Data and Resources), which in Taiwan operates downstream of an Earthworm Ringserver (see Data and Resources). In CWA, earthquake detection in VS is performed using the *scautopick* module, which is based on the STA/LTA and Akaike information criterion pickers, alongside the *scanloc* associator (Scanloc Documentation, 2024a; Grigoli *et al.*, 2018).

The *scanloc* module estimates the preliminary location of an earthquake using *P*- or *S*-wave phases from at least four picks and the Density-Based Spatial Clustering of Applications with Noise (Ester *et al.*, 1996). The VS magnitude estimation module *scvsmag* predicts the final magnitude from each station using envelopes from *scenvelope* and origins from *scanloc* using a ratio of Pd and acceleration envelope values. A first magnitude estimate is made for each station once 1 s of data is available after pick time, and estimates continue to be updated every second as later data arrives. VS and *scfinder* use the same ground-motion envelopes, based on the maximal absolute amplitude reached over consecutive 1 s signal windows from the vertical and the combined horizontal components. Unlike the point-source eBEAR system and VS algorithm, *scfinder* integrates envelope amplitude information (processed internally) with the FinDer library to infer the length and strike of finite-fault ruptures based on the spatial amplitude distribution at stations across the seismic network. *scfinder* does not rely on external picks and locations. FinDer is particularly useful for earthquakes with M_L greater than 6.0 because the

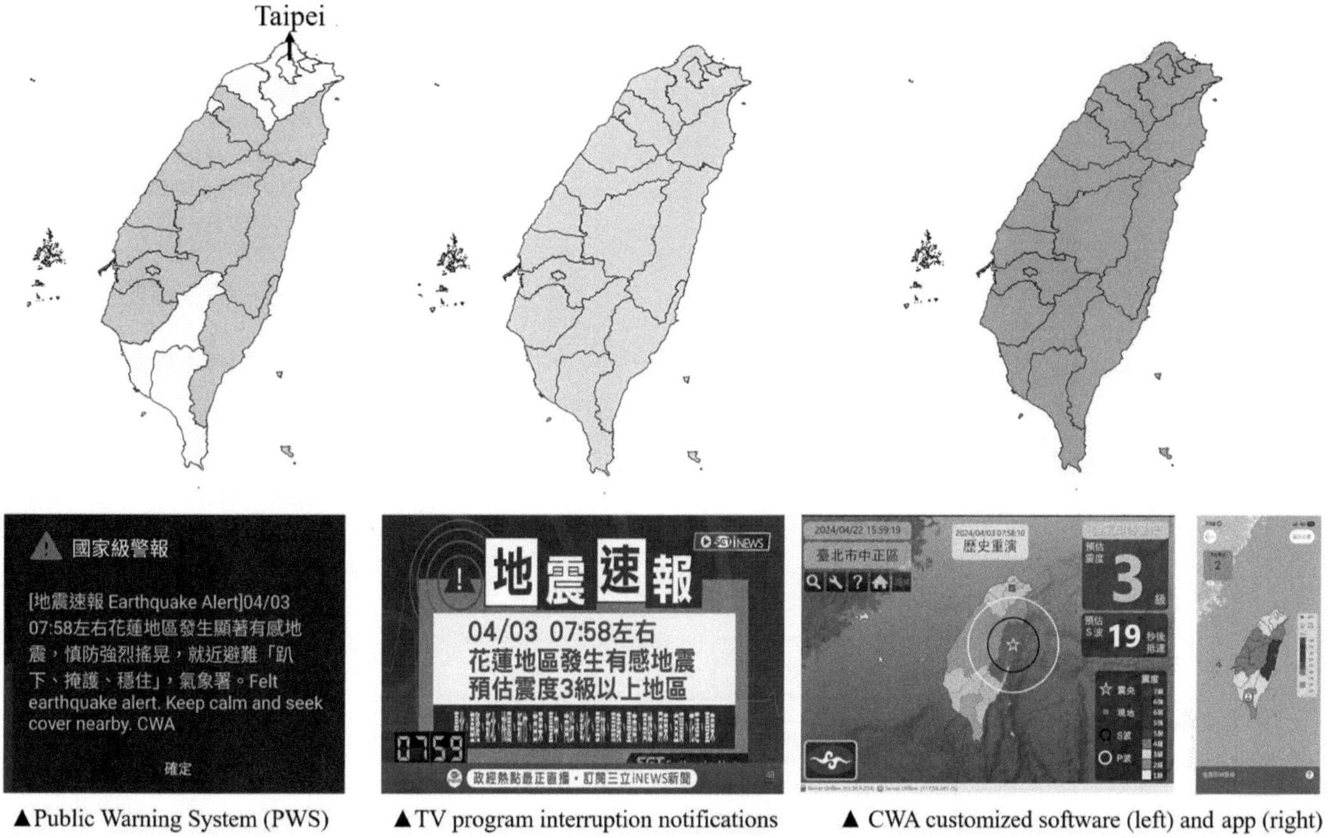

Figure 3. Areas alerted by eBEAR through Public Warning System (PWS) (light blue), television (yellow), and CWA app and software (pink) after the 2024 Hualien mainshock. The eBEAR system provided PWS services to 12 counties and cities across Taiwan and alerted 19 counties and cities through TV broadcasts and the internet. The color version of this figure is available only in the electronic edition.

algorithm provides important information on rupture characteristics, such as rupture length and orientation, that enhances subsequent PGA forecasts. Once the location, fault rupture position, and magnitude information are obtained from the ESE system, CWA's GMPE can be used to estimate the PGA at each reference point, similar to the eBEAR system, but with consideration of fault rupture extent determined by FinDer.

Real-time seismic data

The real-time stations used by the eBEAR system comprise 661 stations sourced from the CWA Seismographic Network (CWASN), Taiwan Strong Motion Instrumentation Program Network (TSMIP), Broadband Array in Taiwan for Seismology (BATS)—all networks use network code TW (Institute of Earth Sciences, Academia Sinica, Taiwan, 1996; Central Weather Administration [CWA, Taiwan], 2012), with a station density of approximately 55 km^2 per station. This high density ensures comprehensive coverage and enhances the system's ability to provide accurate and timely earthquake monitoring and response. The CWASN and TSMIP are both managed by CWA. The primary task of the CWASN is to monitor small-to-medium-size earthquakes, whereas the TSMIP focuses on monitoring medium-to-large events. CWASN comprises 193 stations equipped with various instruments, including force balance accelerometer (FBA), short-period (SP), and broadband (BB) instruments. Of these, 86 borehole stations are equipped with both FBA and BB instruments. In addition, there are nine cable-based

TABLE 2
Thresholds and Actions for Three Dissemination Channels

Magnitude	PGA (cm/s^2)	Action
5.0	25	Issue alert messages through PWS via cell broadcast to affected county or city residents
5.0	8	Interrupt programs on 12 television channels to display alerted areas
4.5	8	Provide EEW message via internet to government agencies, schools, and app users

This table gives the thresholds for magnitude and peak ground acceleration (PGA), along with the corresponding actions taken by the Earthworm-Based Earthquake Alarm Reporting (eBEAR) system, including (1) the Public Warning System (PWS), (2) television broadcasts, and (3) internet services such as government agencies, schools, and app users, in response to seismic events. EEW, earthquake early warning.

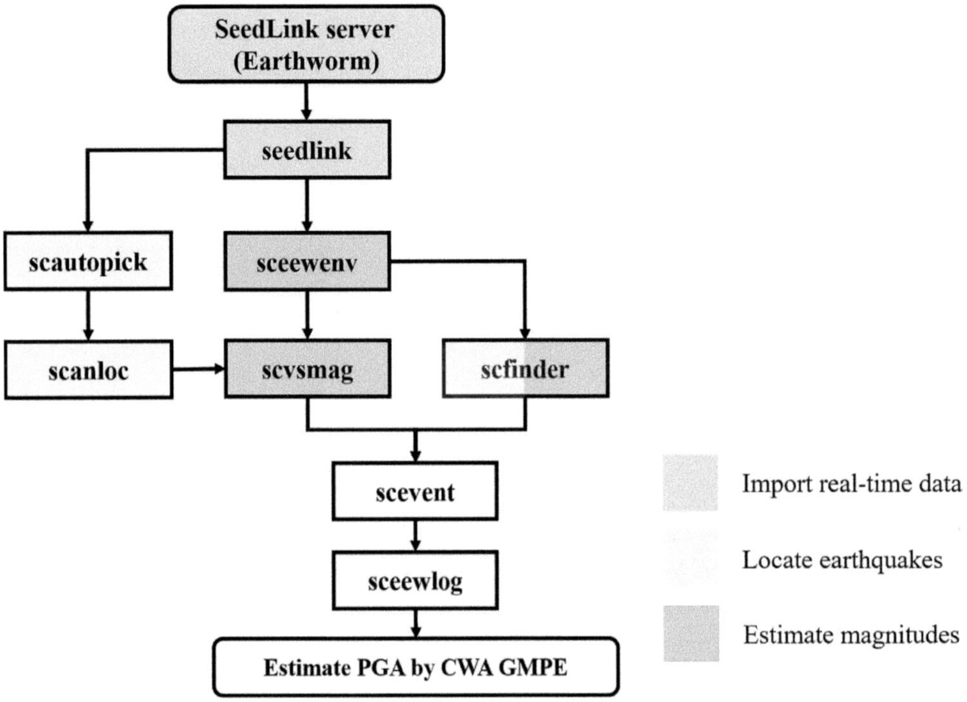

Figure 4. Flowchart of the ETHZ-SED SeisComP EEW (ESE) system. It consists of three data processing steps: importing real-time data (blue), locating earthquakes (yellow), and estimating magnitudes (red). Once the location (for virtual seismologist [VS], hypocenter; for Finite-fault rupture Detector [FinDer], line source) and magnitude information are obtained from the ESE system, the CWA ground-motion prediction equation (GMPE) is used to estimate the PGA at each reference point (Fig. 2). The color version of this figure is available only in the electronic edition.

ocean-bottom seismometer (OBS) stations located in the Pacific Ocean off the eastern side of Taiwan, which are equipped with FBA and SP instruments. In contrast, the TSMIP consists of 577 stations equipped with FBA instruments.

For the eBEAR system, the dense TSMIP stations enable rapid estimation of earthquake parameters and timely issuance of alerts. Although 159 CWASN stations overlap with TSMIP, the remaining 25 land stations, 9 OBS stations, and 44 BATS BB stations collectively strengthen earthquake detection coverage beyond the strong-motion network, significantly improving detection capability for offshore events and in regions where TSMIP coverage is relatively sparse, as well as enhancing location accuracy.

Because ESE is currently in a testing phase, it uses a simpler instrument configuration. Considering its primary purpose of providing EEW messages for medium-to-large earthquakes, the VS and FinDer algorithms use the 577 real-time stations from TSMIP. However, to enhance the precision of earthquake localization (*scanloc*), VS also incorporates signals from nine OBS stations (Fig. 5b). FinDer does not currently use OBS signals, since it initially targets large onshore earthquakes. The OBS accelerometers may be included in FinDer in the next phase of work (Fig. 5c).

Real-time performance of FinDer, VS, and eBEAR system during the 2024 M_L 7.2 Hualien earthquake

Location results. The CWA determined the epicenter of the 2024 Hualien earthquake is in Hualien County (Fig. 1a). In this study, all real-time EEW results are reported using the time when earthquake parameters are generated by each system, which inherently includes both network transmission delays and computational processing time. Figure 6a shows the temporal changes in the discrepancies between the locations estimated by VS, FinDer, and the modified eBEAR system compared to the CWA hypocenter.

The VS algorithm is designed to operate on an origin that includes associated phase picks for magnitude estimation. Under correct configuration, VS should always prioritize the latest *scanloc* origin to ensure results are consistent with its intended workflow. However, in real-time during the Hualien mainshock, due to an incorrect ESE system configuration, VS initially used the hypocenter determined by *scanloc* for the first 2 s, but then switched to the centroid determined by FinDer, which did not include associated phase picks. From 8 s after the earthquake onward, VS and FinDer consistently reported the same location. The discrepancy between the final CWA origin and reported hypocenters (*scanloc*) and centroids (FinDer) ranges from 15 to 21 km. In addition, the FinDer centroids show a slight northward shift relative to the CWA epicenter, possibly influenced by the direction of fault rupture during the earthquake.

The final FinDer line-source model agrees well with the aftershock distribution of the Hualien earthquake (Fig. 6b) and the U.S. Geological Survey (USGS) finite-fault model (Fig. 6c), suggesting a predominantly unilateral rupture propagation toward the northern direction. An animation showing the full evolution of the FinDer source models is given in the supplemental material available to this article.

In contrast, the location discrepancies between the modified eBEAR and final CWA origins range from 2 to 22 km, and in general, its hypocenter estimates are closer to the CWA earthquake report than those of VS and FinDer. In the initial

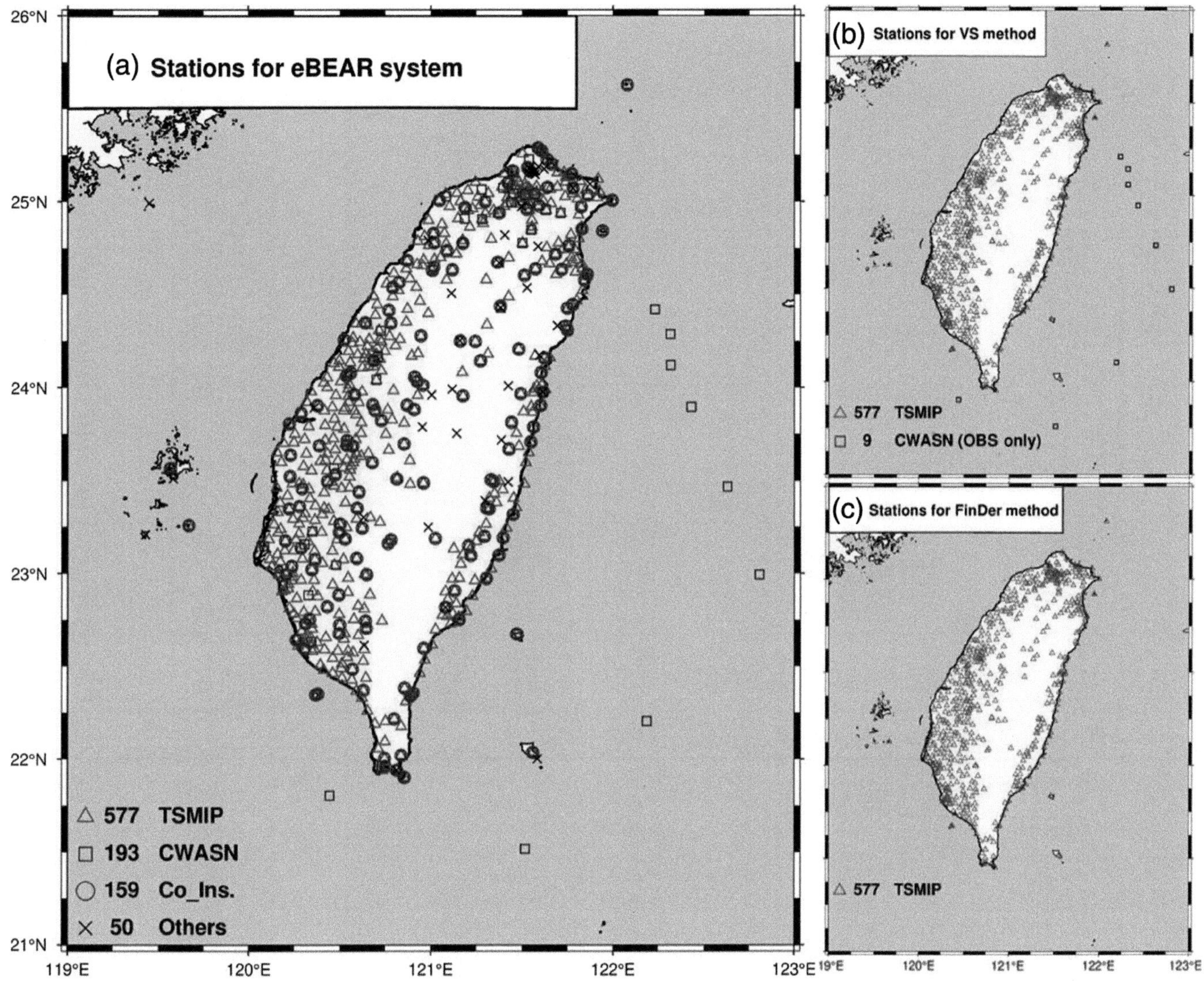

estimates, larger discrepancies of around 15–22 km occur approximately 8 s after the origin time, but most discrepancies fall between 2 and 16 km.

Figure 5. (a) Distribution of stations utilized by the eBEAR system, with data sourced from CWA Seismographic Network (CWASN, blue squares, 193 stations), Taiwan Strong Motion Instrumentation Program Network (TSMIP, red triangles, 577 stations), and other networks (black crosses, 50 stations). Notably, 159 surface strong-motion instruments (green circles) are collocated between CWASN and TSMIP, and are counted in both network totals, bringing the combined total to 661 stations. (b) Distribution of stations utilized by the VS algorithm, primarily using TSMIP (red triangles, 577 stations) together with the nine ocean-bottom seismometer (OBS)-only stations from CWASN (blue squares). (c) Distribution of stations utilized by the FinDer algorithm, using only TSMIP (red triangles, 577 stations). The color version of this figure is available only in the electronic edition.

Magnitude determination. Figure 7a shows the evolution of magnitude estimates from the VS and FinDer algorithms and the eBEAR system for the 2024 Hualien earthquake. The modified eBEAR system estimated a magnitude of approximately 6.4 in its first report 8 s after the origin time. Between 10 and 22 s, the magnitude was estimated as 7.0, and finally, at 44 s, at around 7.2. VS provides magnitude estimates using all available data from each triggered station, with updates provided for 30 s after the first alert. The first VS magnitude estimate, 7 s after the origin time, used a *scanloc* origin, reporting a significant underestimate of 3.9, reflecting the use of only 1 s of data after the *P* pick. Between 10 and 20 s, the VS estimated magnitude ranged between 6.0 and 7.0. During this time, VS also began using the centroid location calculated by FinDer. Finally, at around 27 s, the VS magnitude estimation converges to 7.5, which is very close to the M_w 7.4 reported by USGS (see Data and Resources). FinDer generated its first report 8 s after origin time, with an initial magnitude of 4.1. Between 10 and 20 s FinDer magnitudes reached 6.4 and 6.9 between 20 and 30 s. Finally, the FinDer magnitudes converged to 7.0 at 37 s after origin. Overall, the final magnitude from VS is similar to the USGS solution, whereas the modified eBEAR is similar to

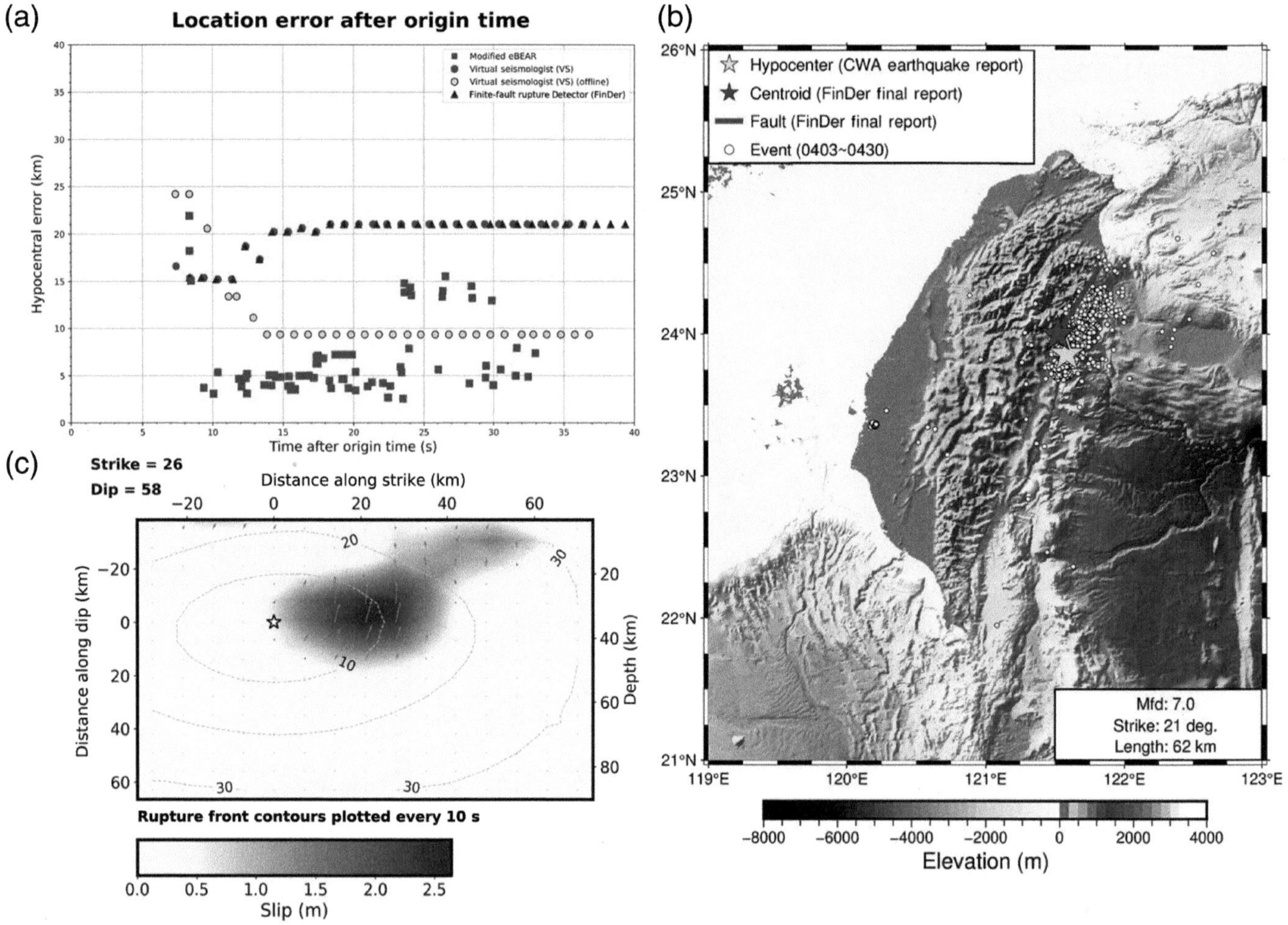

Figure 6. (a) Location discrepancies with respect to the final CWA location for the modified eBEAR system (green squares), VS (red circles), VS (offline, pink circles with thick borders), and FinDer (blue triangles). Initially, VS utilized hypocenter information from *scanloc*, but from 8 s after the earthquake started to misuse FinDer's centroid for magnitude estimation. The location discrepancy ranges from approximately 15 to 21 km for VS and FinDer, and from about 2 to 22 km for the eBEAR system (with the largest errors for the initial solutions). After the configuration was corrected, the location discrepancy for VS (offline) was initially large, ranging from 11 to 25 km, but it stabilized within 10 km after 13 s. (b) Distribution of earthquakes reported by CWA from 3 to 30 April 2024 (white circles). The locations of the earthquakes extended northward from the mainshock. Both the fault rupture length and direction estimated by FinDer (red line) align well with this distribution, suggesting a primarily northward (unilateral) rupture propagation of the mainshock. In addition, the centroid location estimated by FinDer (red star) may be influenced by this northward energy propagation, resulting in its position being further north compared to the mainshock location reported by CWA (yellow star). (c) Cross section of slip distribution (see Data and Resources). The results from panels (a) and (b) suggest a similar observation with the cross section of slip distribution. See animation in the supplemental material for full FinDer line source evolution. The color version of this figure is available only in the electronic edition.

CWA. The final FinDer magnitude, which is estimated empirically from the length of its line-source model and its fixed 10 km depth assumption for the rupture location, is slightly lower than M_L 7.2 of the CWA earthquake report (with a depth of 22.5 km). Before 15 s after origin time, the estimated magnitude from the modified eBEAR system is higher than that from VS and FinDer. After 15 s, the magnitude estimated by VS is the highest and close to the USGS M_w 7.4, whereas the modified eBEAR magnitude is closer to the CWA reported M_L 7.2.

Result validation. To verify the impact of the VS misconfiguration, we ran a full waveform playback with a correct configuration to ensure VS used hypocenters from *scanloc* instead of the FinDer centroid. Figures 6 and 7 show the magnitude and location evolution from VS for this offline playback. We observe that although the location discrepancy of VS (offline) results is initially large, ranging from 11 to 25 km, it stabilizes within 10 km after 13s. As for the magnitude of VS (offline), it reaches 5.8 after the first report. Subsequently, the magnitude increased more slowly compared to the real-time results, likely due to the use of many more stations with larger epicentral distances and only short-time windows of event data. Compared to the original real-time performance, the offline results show a slower and

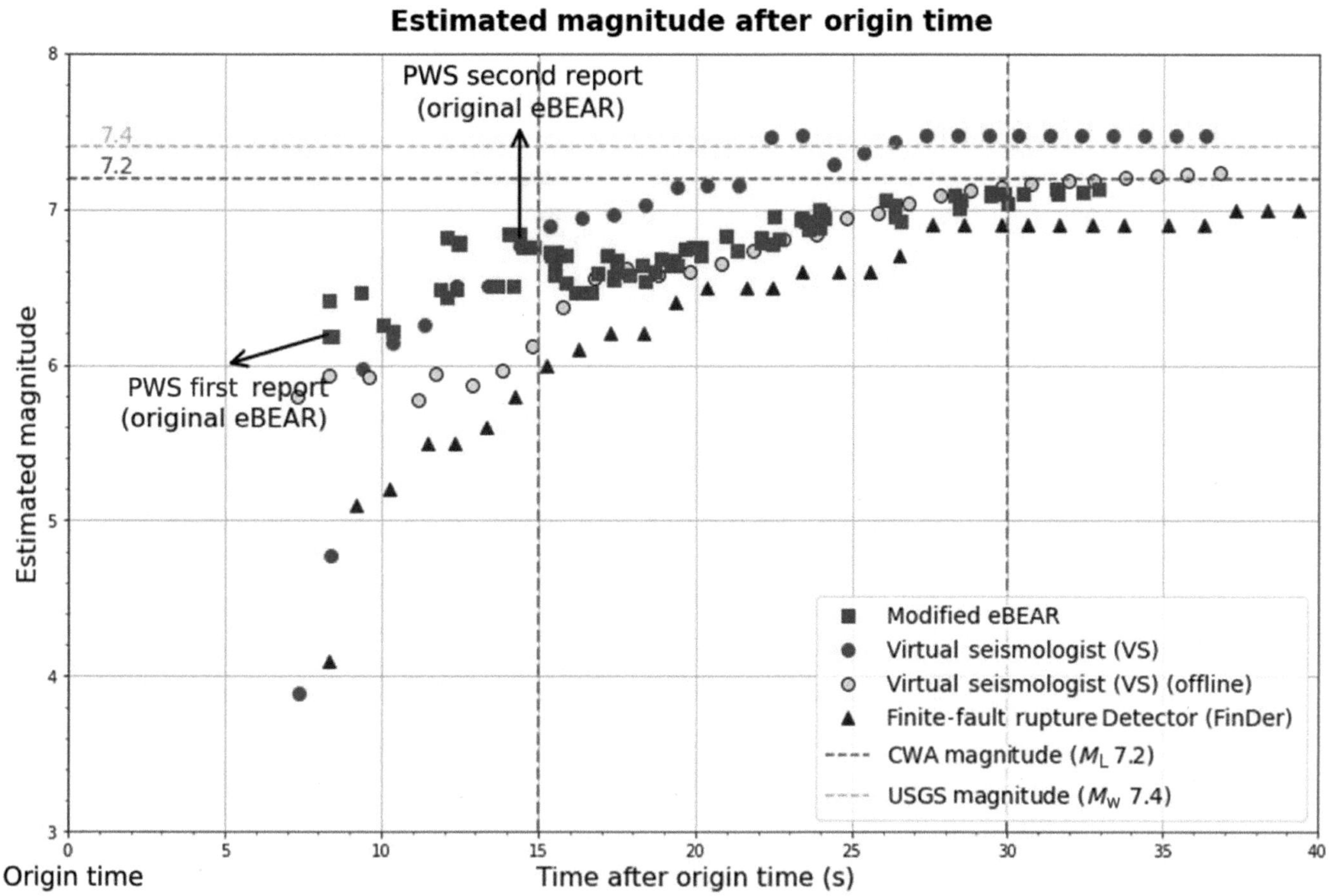

Figure 7. Temporal evolution of estimated magnitudes by the modified eBEAR system (green squares), VS (red circles) and FinDer (blue triangles), VS (offline, pink circles with thick borders), and offline FinDer (light-blue triangles). The original eBEAR system was limited by its magnitude update mechanism, only using M_{pd} 6.2 and 6.8 for this event. After adjustments, the modified eBEAR system can utilize all the results represented by the green squares in the figure. Overall, within the 15 s after the origin time, the estimated magnitude from the modified eBEAR system is higher than that from VS and FinDer. After 15 s, the magnitude estimated by VS is the highest and close to the U.S. Geological Survey (USGS) reported M_w 7.4, whereas the modified eBEAR system's estimated magnitude follows, being closer to the CWA reported M_L 7.2. FinDer's magnitude, on the other hand, is lower than both the VS and modified eBEAR systems. Following the ESE configuration corrections, the VS (offline) closely tracked the modified eBEAR magnitude evolution, though it remained slightly lower until after 27 s, at which point it surpassed eBEAR, reaching a final magnitude slightly above 7.2. The color version of this figure is available only in the electronic edition.

slightly lower evolution trend. This is likely related to the absence of a centroid with rupture direction that led to a smaller magnitude evolution in VS (offline), making it closer to the eBEAR results. Overall, VS (offline) closely tracks the eBEAR magnitude evolution, though it remained slightly lower until after 27 s, at which point it rises above eBEAR to a final magnitude slightly above 7.2. This phenomenon suggests that the location algorithm settings in VS are highly configurable, which can result in a range of performance, potentially contributing to variations in the results.

Implications of EEW Algorithm Characteristics on PWS Coverage and Timeliness

In this discussion section, we evaluate and interpret how the modified eBEAR, VS, and FinDer would have performed in issuing PWS alerts during the 2024 Hualien earthquake, under the CWA's latest operational policy of reducing the alert publication threshold from 0.5 to 0.1 magnitude units. The goal is to compare the systems in terms of both spatial coverage (number of counties and cities alerted) and alert timeliness. Figure 8a,b illustrates the temporal evolution and cumulative distribution of PWS alerts for each algorithm. Because each new solution in PWS adds to the existing alerts and no alert retraction is possible, the number of alerted counties and cities is inherently cumulative. The supplemental material includes further visualizations of the real-time source progression and predicted PGA values across 47 reference points.

Within the first 14 s of the earthquake, the modified eBEAR system, which benefited from relatively higher initial magnitude estimates, would be able to rapidly issue alerts for 12 counties and cities. By 26 s, FinDer would have issued alerts for

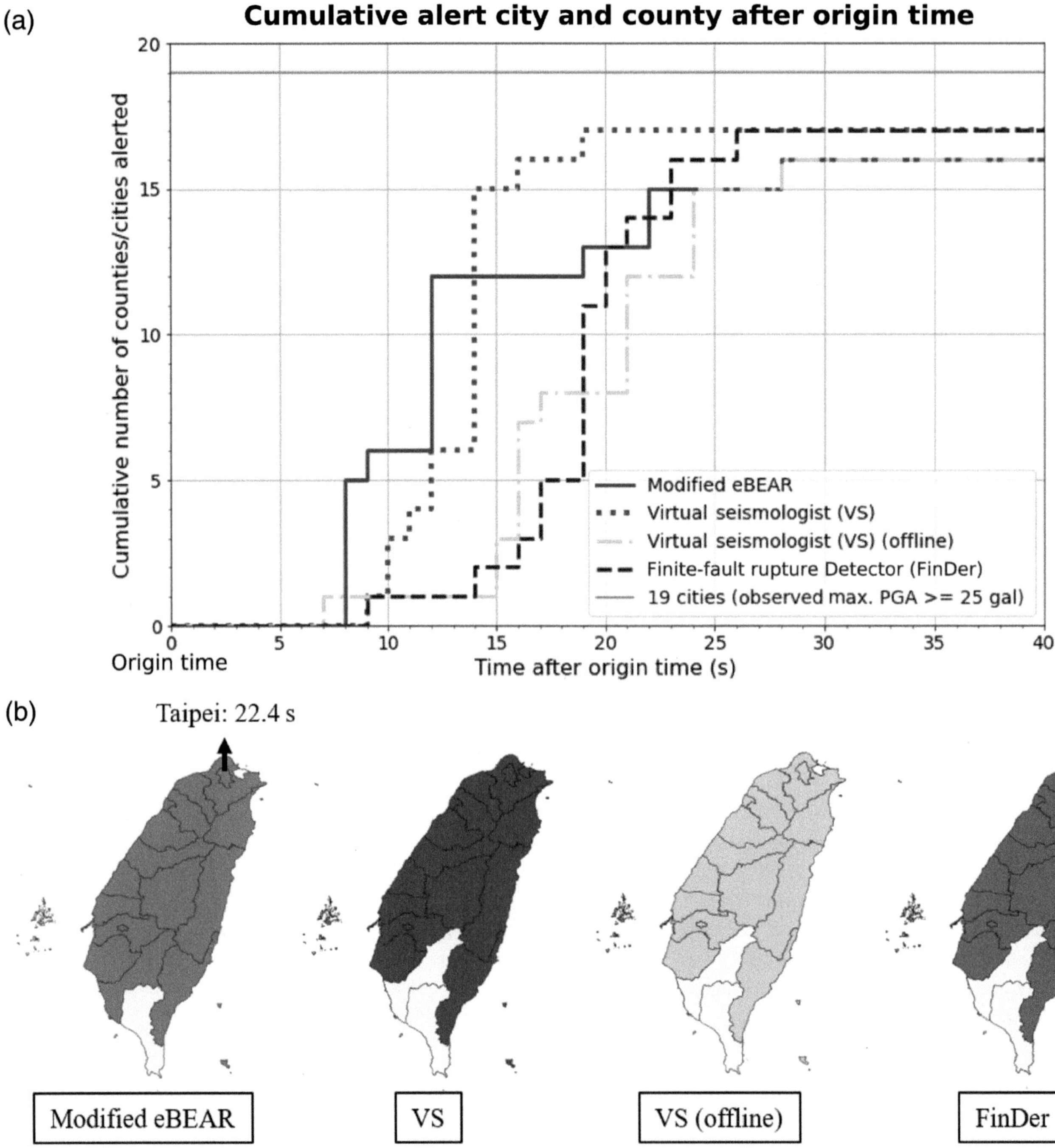

Figure 8. (a) Cumulative number of counties and cities alerted by three methods during the 2024 Hualien earthquake. Green-solid, red-dotted, pink-dashed–dotted, and blue-dashed lines represent modified eBEAR, VS, VS (offline), and FinDer, respectively. The modified eBEAR system issues alerts for 16 areas within 8–28 s, whereas VS and FinDer would have issued alerts for 17 areas within 9–19 and 9–26 s, respectively. For the VS (offline), alerts are issued for 16 areas between 7 and 28 s. (b) The PWS alert distribution in counties and cities for eBEAR, VS, VS (offline), and FinDer, based on reports from each system that first met the PWS sending criteria, until the cumulative distribution of alerts reached saturation for assessing the cumulative number of counties and cities alerted by each method. It shows that FinDer would have been able to send appropriate PWS alerts to more counties and cities than eBEAR. As for VS, due to the adjustment of the hypocenter location, the number of counties and cities receiving alerts decreased from 17 to 16, so whether it could provide the most appropriate alerts should be viewed conservatively. See the animations in supplemental material for the complete source evolution of eBEAR, VS, and FinDer, along with their estimated PGA. The color version of this figure is available only in the electronic edition.

17 counties and cities, whereas eBEAR reached 16 counties and cities by 28 s. Although the modified eBEAR demonstrated strong early-warning capability, its final coverage was constrained by its point-source model, resulting in one county in northern Taiwan not receiving an alert. In contrast, although FinDer tended to estimate magnitudes more conservatively, its ability to capture rupture geometry, including the strike direction and fault length, would enable it to achieve broader spatial coverage of alerts. As a result, FinDer would have successfully issued alerts to all northern counties and cities, effectively compensating for the spatial limitations of point-source methods. This finding underscores the operational value of incorporating finite-fault models into EEW systems, particularly for large earthquakes with complex rupture dynamics.

In its real-time configuration, VS adopted the centroid location output from FinDer, which was slightly north of the actual epicenter. This led to a magnitude overestimation and underestimated distances to northern sites, resulting in inflated PGA values and broader initial alert zones. To isolate this effect, we re-evaluated the VS results using offline-corrected location and magnitude inputs. In this revised scenario, the number of PWS alerted counties and cities decreased to 16, and the alerts would have been issued later. This reduction in coverage is primarily due to the corrected epicenter location being farther south, which is closer to the actual epicenter. Because VS uses a point-source model, similar to modified eBEAR, it failed to issue alerts for one northern county, similar to what was observed with the modified eBEAR. Nevertheless, the similarity in alert coverage also suggests that VS, even with similar assumptions, can serve as a redundant backup for eBEAR system, providing an additional source of alerts that may help reinforce system robustness in future implementations.

This comparison illustrates a core limitation of point-source EEW systems. Although both the modified eBEAR and offline VS results plateaued at 16 counties and cities, FinDer, with its finite-fault sensitivity, successfully reached 17, providing complete northern Taiwan coverage and surpassing point-source models in spatial responsiveness. Our findings affirm that FinDer's finite-fault characterization offers a valuable supplement to existing methodologies.

According to the observed intensity distribution (Fig. 1a), 19 counties and cities experienced CWA intensity 4 or higher. In this event, even the best-performing system under current thresholds, FinDer, fell short of full coverage primarily due to the limitations of the GMPE model. Nevertheless, a hybrid EEW approach combining the rapid onset of eBEAR with the spatial source characterization of FinDer may still offer a notable improvement over current single-algorithm configurations and provide a more robust solution for national alerting strategies. VS shows promise under real-time operation but would benefit from further validation across additional events to address configuration sensitivities.

Recent studies outside Taiwan have proposed various algorithm integration methods, such as weighted parameter averaging (Kohler *et al.*, 2020), solution matching with observed ground motions (Jozinović *et al.*, 2024), and waveform envelope fitting (Minson *et al.*, 2017). In contrast, our approach evaluates individual algorithms under a consistent framework to emphasize their complementary strengths rather than fusing outputs. This modular strategy promotes system redundancy and adaptability, reducing both missed and false alerts.

To summarize, our results suggest that a multialgorithm EEW framework, in which point- and line-source systems operate in parallel, can significantly improve the spatial and temporal effectiveness of Taiwan's public warning infrastructure. Such integration enhances overall system resilience and ensures more timely and comprehensive alerts for future large earthquakes.

Impact of EEW Algorithm Characteristics on PWS Accuracy and Warning Time

The previous section was based on CWA's current PWS policy, which issues alerts when the estimated PGA exceeds 25 cm/s^2 at any reference point within a district. However, this district-based approach may overlook local variations, particularly in elongated or topographically complex regions. To further discuss the practical implications of these limitations, we adopt a point-based evaluation to provide a more precise picture of alert performance, particularly in terms of accuracy and warning timeliness. Therefore, in this section, we evaluate the effectiveness of the three EEW algorithms by analyzing their performance at the level of individual reference points, rather than aggregated administrative districts.

When evaluating overall alert accuracy, defined as the combined rate of correct alerts and correct no-alerts, FinDer demonstrates the best performance at 95.75%, followed by VS at 91.49%, VS (offline) at 89.14%, and the modified eBEAR system at 85.11% (Fig. 9a). Only VS would have issued two false alerts, primarily due to the use of FinDer's centroid location, which led to an overestimation of magnitude and consequently higher predicted PGA values at two reference points. However, when using corrected source parameters, VS (offline) eliminated all false alerts, indicating improved performance in controlling false alarms. At the same time, the southward correction of the epicenter, combined with the simplified point-source assumption, results in a slightly increased missed alert rate in the VS (offline) configuration.

A similar pattern was observed with the modified eBEAR system, which also employs a point-source model. It missed alerts at seven reference points, including three in the southern region and four in northern Taiwan. These findings suggest that point-source models tend to underestimate shaking intensity at locations farther from the epicenter, particularly during large earthquakes involving significant rupture extent.

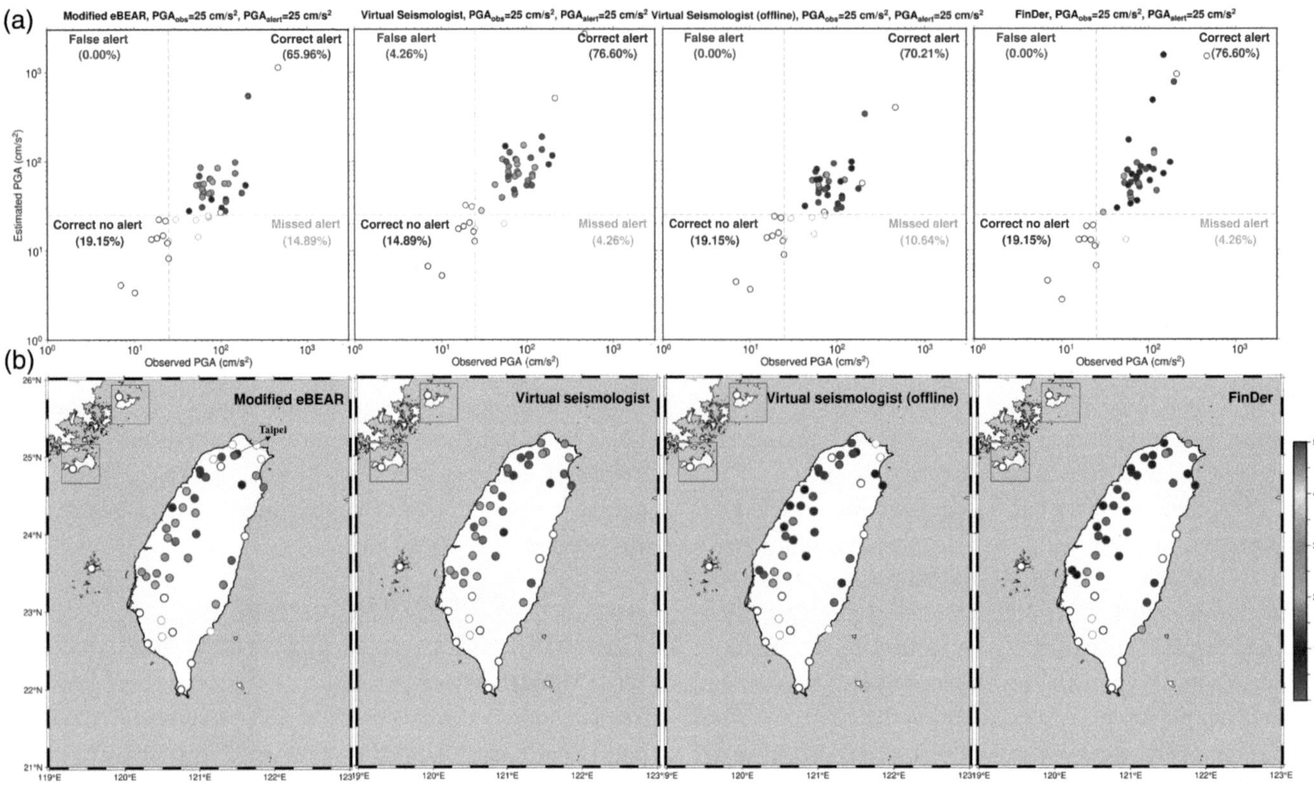

Figure 9. (a) Confusion matrix for the modified eBEAR system, VS, VS (offline), and FinDer. The circles on the figure show the distribution of data based on the estimated PGA results from 47 reference points compared to observed PGA. Correct alerts are shown as solid green-bordered circles. A solid center indicates the presence of a warning time. Correct no alerts, missed alerts, and false alerts are represented by blue-bordered, yellow-bordered, and red-bordered circles, respectively. In terms of alert accuracy, FinDer's rate of 95.75% exceeds that of VS (91.49%), VS (offline) (89.14%), and modified eBEAR (85.11%). (b) The VS method generally provided the longest warning times; however, the VS (offline) results showed shorter warning times due to the southward correction of the hypocenter and slower magnitude evolution. In Taipei, the warning times for each method were as follows: modified eBEAR: 11.2 s, VS: 19.3 s, VS (offline) 8.9 s, and FinDer 14.4 s. Overall, the modified eBEAR system provided longer warning times at 24 reference points compared to FinDer, whereas FinDer outperformed modified eBEAR at right reference points, including Taipei City. Inset shows the two offshore counties of Taiwan, Lienchiang County (upper) and Kinmen County (lower). The color version of this figure is available only in the electronic edition.

In contrast, FinDer, with its line-source model, not only achieves the highest overall alert accuracy but also avoids both false alerts and widespread missed alerts. This demonstrates that the clear advantage of incorporating fault geometry into ground-motion prediction. Our findings highlight the practical value of finite-fault modeling in improving both the precision and spatial coverage of EEW systems. Based on both accuracy statistics and physical-model considerations, we suggest that integrating finite-fault modeling into EEW systems, particularly as a complement to point-source algorithms like eBEAR, can provide more stable and effective alerts during future large-magnitude earthquakes.

Warning time, defined as the interval between the issuance of a PWS alert (including all latencies) and the moment when the observed PGA reaches 25 cm/s^2, is shown in Figure 9. This metric reflects whether a system can deliver timely alerts before damaging shaking arrives, thereby allowing individuals, vehicles, and critical facilities to initiate emergency responses.

Among the three algorithms evaluated, the modified eBEAR and FinDer systems demonstrated complementary strengths in terms of warning time performance. The modified eBEAR system produced longer warning times at 24 of the 47 reference points, whereas FinDer provided longer lead times at 7 sites. For example, in Taipei, FinDer achieved a warning time of 14.4 s, compared to 11.2 s for the modified eBEAR system. This indicates that FinDer, by tracking the rupture front and incorporating finite-fault geometry, was able to recognize directional propagation and anticipate shaking earlier in certain regions. Although the modified eBEAR system offered broader temporal coverage of alerts, its performance was limited by the physical constraints of point-source modeling. These results imply that combining both systems could yield more comprehensive warning coverage, particularly in areas such as Taipei where FinDer exhibited superior timeliness.

The VS algorithm generally provides the longest warning times during the 2024 Hualien earthquake. However, when location and magnitude inputs are corrected in the VS (offline) configuration, the warning times are noticeably shorter. This reduction can be attributed to two main factors: the southward adjustment of the hypocenter, which increased the distance to northern reference points, and the slower evolution of magnitude estimates, likely influenced by the magnitude scaling relationships originally developed from Southern California data (VS; Cua, 2005; Cua and Heaton, 2007; Cua *et al.*, 2009). These findings suggest that although the VS system is capable of producing timely alerts, its performance is highly sensitive to the accuracy of source parameters and the simplifications inherent in point-source assumptions. Therefore, further back testing with additional earthquake cases is necessary, and it may also be important to modify the magnitude model to better reflect the seismic characteristics of Taiwan.

Finally, we observe the presence of blind zones, defined as locations where alerts were issued only after the observed PGA surpassed the 25 cm/s^2 threshold (marked with white circles and green borders in Fig. 9). Although these instances were rare and mostly limited to sites very close to the epicenter for FinDer, the modified eBEAR system displayed a more unexpected pattern. One of its blind zones appeared in Taoyuan City (see Fig. 9b), approximately 120 km from the epicenter. This delay stemmed from the system's late calculation at that site, occurring 42 s after origin time when the estimated magnitude approached 7.2. A similar delay was also observed in the VS (offline) output. These occurrences highlight the importance of both algorithm responsiveness and spatial sensitivity. Enhancing EEW effectiveness may therefore require not only faster magnitude convergence but also more robust modeling of rupture propagation and spatial energy distribution.

Our results suggest that integrating point- and line-source methods offers distinct advantages. Although point-source algorithms like eBEAR can initiate alerts rapidly, line-source models such as FinDer can extend coverage and improve warning times, in particular in regions affected by unilateral rupture propagation and strong directivity effects. A hybrid approach may provide the most effective and reliable alerts during future large-magnitude earthquakes.

Conclusions

For the 2024 Hualien earthquake, shortcomings were observed in the CWA EEW system. PWS alerts from CWA should have been sent to residents of 19 counties and cities in Taiwan, including Taipei. Initial eBEAR alerts were sent for M_{pd} 6.2, and although eBEAR magnitude estimates were raised to M_{pd} 6.8, subsequent alerts were not updated; the system in place at the time only updates if the magnitude increased by 0.5 or more magnitude units. Hence, only 12 counties and cities were alerted, of which Taipei was crucially missing, and if the final magnitude had been used, 16 counties, including Taipei, would have been alerted. To address this issue, the CWA decided to lower the magnitude threshold for triggering alert updates to 0.1 magnitude unit change shortly after the earthquake occurred. This adjustment makes the system more responsive and flexible, allowing a broader range of EEW reports to be evaluated and used in alert decisions.

At the time of the earthquake, the CWA was conducting real-time testing of both the VS and FinDer algorithms using the ESE system. Among the three algorithms, the modified eBEAR system provided higher initial magnitude estimates, allowing it to issue a first alert within 8 s of origin time. However, FinDer offered broader and more consistent spatial coverage of alerts, despite providing more conservative magnitude estimates. Because FinDer provides finite-fault information, such as rupture strike and length, it can provide an improved accuracy in ground-motion prediction, and would ultimately issue alerts to 17 counties within 26 s, one county more than the eBEAR system. Although VS provides longer warning times during real-time operation, the offline reconstruction, based on the corrected hypocenter location, achieved coverage comparable to eBEAR, reflecting a consistent limitation of point-source models in representing the full rupture extent of large earthquakes. Nonetheless, the similar spatial PWS alert coverage between VS and eBEAR suggests that VS can function as a valuable redundant component, providing confirmatory alerts that strengthen the overall reliability of the EEW system. In addition, the comparison between the VS and VS (offline) also underscores the system's sensitivity to input parameters. The relatively slow evolution of magnitude estimates in VS may be linked to its calibration on Californian earthquakes. This suggests that recalibrating the model with Taiwan's seismic data, along with further validation using additional earthquake cases, may be important to enhance its stability and reliability. Similarly, ground-motion templates used by FinDer should be calibrated with Taiwanese ground-motion models.

To implement these calibrations and further assess the robustness of hybrid EEW strategies, extended offline testing using a broader set of historical Taiwan earthquakes is planned. These tests will include events of varying rupture styles, such as bilateral, deep, and offshore earthquakes, to evaluate algorithm performance under diverse source characteristics. For VS, this process will involve refining magnitude scaling relationships and evaluating performance across different source depths and epicentral locations. In general, FinDer is capable of characterizing both unilateral and bilateral ruptures, and its templates could be regionalized using Taiwan-specific ground-motion models to improve regional performance. The outcomes of these tests will also guide the design of a hybrid EEW integration framework, potentially drawing on approaches such as the decision module described by Jozinović *et al.* (2024), to combine the strengths of point-source and finite-fault algorithms in a unified operational setting.

When evaluating performance at the 47 EEW reference points across the country that are used to determine the spatial extent of EEW alerts, FinDer demonstrated strong advantages. It provided the highest overall alert accuracy (95.75%) compared to VS (91.49%), VS (offline) (89.14%), and the modified eBEAR system (85.11%). FinDer performed particularly well in regions farther from the epicenter, where point-source methods struggled to capture the full extent of rupture. In terms of warning times, eBEAR generally outperformed FinDer at most locations. However, FinDer offered earlier PWS alerts at select sites, including Taipei, suggesting that combining the two systems could yield complementary benefits.

In summary, this study demonstrates that hybrid EEW architectures that integrate both point-source and finite-fault models can provide practical benefits for Taiwan. In particular, it highlights the operational value of incorporating finite-fault information into EEW strategies. The ability of FinDer to provide a line-source complements the rapid initial response of point-source algorithms like eBEAR, particularly during large earthquakes with complex rupture characteristics. Further, such a hybrid approach provides a more comprehensive and reliable framework for EEW. As EEW systems continue to evolve, the integration of multiple algorithms with complementary strengths will be essential to improving national preparedness and enhancing public safety.

Data and Resources

The real-time waveforms used in this study were obtained from the Central Weather Administration (CWA) Seismographic Network (CWASN), Taiwan Strong Motion Instrumentation Program Network (TSMIP) Network of CWA and Broadband Array in Taiwan for Seismology (BATS) of Institute of Earth Sciences (IES), Academia Sinica. The SeisComP software and *scanloc* were provided by gempa GmbH. The virtual seismologist (VS), Finite-fault rupture Detector (FinDer), and other modules of the ETHZ-SED SeisComP Early Warning System were supplied by the Swiss Seismological Service (SED) at ETH Zürich. The Generic Mapping Tools (GMT) software (Wessel *et al.*, 2019) was used for plotting some of the figures. The information about M_w 7.4 Hualien City, Taiwan, earthquake is available at https://earthquake.usgs.gov/earthquakes/eventpage/us7000m9g4/executive (last accessed July 2024). The information about the CWA seismological center is available at https://scweb.cwa.gov.tw/en-us/earthquake/data (last accessed November 2024). The SeedLink server is available at http://docs.fdsn.org/projects/seedlink. The Earthworm Ringserver is available at https://github.com/EarthScope/ringserver/wiki. The supplemental material for this article includes video S1, which demonstrates the evolution of modified Earthworm-Based Earthquake Alarm Reporting (eBEAR), VS, and FinDer, along with the estimated peak ground acceleration (PGA) at the 47 earthquake early warning (EEW) reference points. The video S1 can be accessed at the following links: video S1a (modified eBEAR): https://cloud.seismosoc.org/s/wz3Pm2sDi2f4zPz, video S1b (VS): https://cloud.seismosoc.org/s/7PZrNLsNk5W7ak2, and video S1c (FinDer): https://cloud.seismosoc.org/s/ELDGBHR9axdqDby.

Declaration for Competing Interests

The authors acknowledge that there are no conflicts of interest recorded.

Acknowledgments

The authors would like to express their sincere gratitude to gempa GmbH and the Helmholtz-Centre Potsdam-German Research Centre for Geosciences (GFZ) for supplying the SeisComP software. In addition, the authors extend their thanks to the National Fire Agency of Taiwan for providing accurate casualty data and to the Hualien County Government for supplying locations of damaged buildings. The authors also appreciate the Generic Mapping Tools (GMT) software developed by Wessel *et al.* (2019), which was used for plotting some of the figures. These resources and support have been invaluable to the success of their research, and the authors extend their heartfelt thanks. The authors also thank the reviewers and the editors for their valuable comments and suggestions that helped improve this study.

References

Böse, M., J. Andrews, R. Hartog, and C. Felizardo (2023). Performance and next generation development of the Finite-Fault Rupture Detector (FinDer) within the United States West Coast ShakeAlert warning system, *Bull. Seismol. Soc. Am.* **113,** no. 2, 648–663, doi: 10.1785/0120220183.

Böse, M., C. Felizardo, and T. H. Heaton (2015). Finite-Fault Rupture Detector (FinDer): Going real-time in Californian ShakeAlert warning system, *Seismol. Res. Lett.* **86,** no. 6, 1692–1704, doi: 10.1785/0220150154.

Böse, M., T. H. Heaton, and E. Hauksson (2012). Real-time Finite Fault Rupture Detector (FinDer) for large earthquakes, *Geophys. J. Int.* **191,** no. 2, 803–812.

Böse, M., D. Smith, C. Felizardo, M.-A. Meier, T. H. Heaton, and J. F. Clinton (2018). FinDer v.2: Improved real-time ground-motion predictions for M2-M9 with seismic finite-source characterization, *Geophys. J. Int.* **212,** no. 1, 725–742, doi: 10.1093/gji/ggx430.

Central Weather Administration (CWA). (2024). Earthquake report, Central Weather Administration, available at https://scweb.cwa.gov.tw/en-us/earthquake/data (last accessed November 2024).

Central Weather Administration (CWA, Taiwan) (2012). Central Weather Administration Seismographic Network [Data set], *International Federation of Digital Seismograph Networks*, doi: 10.7914/SN/T5.

Central Weather Administration (CWA, Taiwan) (2019). Operational guidelines for the release of earthquake, Reports by the Central Weather Administration, Ministry of Transportation and Communications (in Chinese).

Chen, D. Y., T.-L. Lin, H.-C. Hsu, Y.-C. Hsu, and N.-C. Hsiao (2019). An approach to improve the performance of the earthquake early warning system for the 2018 Hualien earthquake in Taiwan, *Terr. Atmos. Ocean. Sci.* **30,** 423–433, doi: 10.3319/TAO.2018.12.23.02.

Chen, D.-Y., N.-C. Hsiao, and Y.-M. Wu (2015). The Earthworm based earthquake alarm reporting system in Taiwan, *Bull. Seismol. Soc. Am.* **105,** 568–579, doi: 10.1785/0120140147.

Cua, G. (2005). Creating the virtual seismologist: Developments in ground motion characterization and seismic early warning, *Ph.D. Thesis*, California Institute of Technology, Pasadena, California, doi: 10.7907/M926-J956.

Cua, G., and T. Heaton (2007). The Virtual Seismologist (VS) method: A Bayesian approach to earthquake early warning, in *Seismic Early Warning*, P. Gasparini, G. Manfredi, and J. Zschau (Editors), 85–132, Springer, Heidelberg, Germany.

Cua, G., M. Fischer, T. Heaton, and S. Wiemer (2009). Real-time performance of the Virtual Seismologist earthquake early warning algorithm in southern California, *Seismol. Res. Lett.* **80,** 740–747, doi: 10.1785/gssrl.80.5.740.

Ester, M., H.-P. Kriegel, J. Sander, and X. Xu (1996). A density-based algorithm for discovering clusters in large spatial databases with noise, *KDD'96*, Vol. 96, 226–231.

Geiger, L. (1912). Probability method for the determination of earthquake epicenters from the arrival time only, *Bull. St. Louis Univ.* **8,** 60–71.

Grigoli, F., L. Scarabello, M. Böse, B. Weber, S. Wiemer, and J. F. Clinton (2018). Pick- and waveform-based techniques for real-time detection of induced seismicity, *Geophys. J. Int.* **213,** no. 2, 868–884, doi: 10.1093/gji/ggy019.

Helmholtz-Centre Potsdam - GFZ German Research Centre for Geosciences, and GEMPA GmbH (2008). The SeisComP seismological software package, *GFZ Data Services*, doi: 10.5880/GFZ.2.4.2020.003.

Hsiao, N. C. (2007). The application of real-time strong-motion observations on the earthquake early warning in Taiwan, *Ph.D. Thesis*, Institute of Geophysics, National Central University, Taiwan, 178 pp.

Hsiao, N. C., Y. M. Wu, T. C. Shin, L. Zhao, and T. L. Teng (2009). Development of earthquake early warning system in Taiwan, *Geophys. Res. Lett.* **36,** L00B02, doi: 10.1029/2008GL036596.

Hsu, M. T. (1979). *Seismology*, Lee-Ming Culture Publication Company, Taipei, Taiwan, 16–26 (in Chinese).

Institute of Earth Sciences, Academia Sinica, Taiwan (1996). Broadband array in Taiwan for seismology, *Other/Seismic Network*, Institute of Earth Sciences, Academia Sinica, Taiwan, doi: 10.7914/SN/TW.

Jozinović, D., J. Clinton, F. Massin, M. Böse, and C. Cauzzi (2024). Realtime selection of optimal source parameters using ground motion envelopes, *Seismica* **3,** no. 1, doi: 10.26443/seismica.v3i1.1142.

Kohler, M., D. Smith, J. Andrews, A. Chung, R. Hartog, I. Henson, D. Given, R. Groot, and S. Guiwits (2020). Earthquake early warning ShakeAlert 2.0: Public rollout, *Seismol. Res. Lett.* **91,** doi: 10.1785/0220190245.

Massin, F., M. Böse, B. E. Burgoa, J. F. Clinton, G. Marroquin, C. Munoz, B. Orihuela, M. Protti, W. Strauch, and R. Yani (2022). Towards national public earthquake early warning systems across Central America, *AGU Fall Meeting Abstracts*, Vol. 2022, NH34B-01 pp.

Massin, F., J. F. Clinton, and M. Böse (2021). Status of earthquake early warning in Switzerland. Lausanne, Switzerland, *Front. Earth Sci.* **9,** 707654, doi: 10.3389/feart.2021.707654.

Minson, S. E., S. Wu, J. L. Beck, and T. H. Heaton (2017). Combining multiple earthquake models in real time for earthquake early warning, *Bull. Seismol. Soc. Am.* **107,** no. 4, 1868–1882, doi: 10.1785/0120160331.

Porras, J., F. Massin, M. Arroyo-Solórzano, I. Arroyo, L. Linkimer, M. Böse, and J. Clinton (2021). Preliminary results of an earthquake early warning system in Costa Rica, *Front. Earth Sci.* **9,** doi: 10.3389/feart.2021.700843.

Ruhl, C. J., D. Melgar, R. Grapenthin, and R. M. Allen (2017). The value of real-time GNSS to earthquake early warning, *Geophys. Res. Lett.* **44,** 8311–8319, doi: 10.1002/2017GL074502.

Scanloc Documentation (2024a). Scanloc documentation, available at https://docs.gempa.de/scanloc/current/ (last accessed May 2024).

SeisComP Documentation (2024b). SeisComP documentation, available at https://www.seiscomp.de/doc/ (last accessed May 2024).

Teng, T., L. Wu, T.-C. Shin, Y.-B. Tsai, and W. H. K. Lee (1997). One minute after: Strong-motion map, effective epicenter, and effective magnitude, *Bull. Seismol. Soc. Am.* **87,** 1209–1219.

U.S. Geological Survey (2024). M 7.4-15 km S of Hualien City, Taiwan, available at https://earthquake.usgs.gov/earthquakes/eventpage/us7000m9g4/executive (last accessed July 2024).

Wessel, P., J. F. Luis, L. Uieda, R. Scharroo, F. Wobbe, W. H. F. Smith, and D. Tian (2019). The Generic Mapping Tools Version 6, *Geochem. Geophys. Geosyst.* **20,** no. 11, 5556–5564, doi: 10.1029/2019GC008515.

Wu, Y. M., and T. L. Teng (2002). A virtual sub-network approach to earthquake early warning, *Bull. Seismol. Soc. Am.* **92,** 2008–2018.

Wu, Y. M., J. K. Chung, T. C. Shin, N. C. Hsiao, Y. B. Tsai, W. H. K. Lee, and T. L. Teng (1999). Development of an integrated seismic early warning system in Taiwan, *Terr. Atmos. Ocean. Sci.* **10,** 719–736

Wu, Y. M., N. C. Hsiao, and T. L. Teng (2004). Relationships between strong ground motion peak values and seismic loss during the 1999 Chi-Chi, Taiwan earthquake, *Nat. Hazards* **32,** 357–373.

Wu, Y. M., T. C. Shin, and Y. B. Tsai (1998). Quick and reliable determination of magnitude for seismic early warning, *Bull. Seismol. Soc. Am.* **88,** 1254–1259.

Wu, Y. M., T. L. Teng, T. C. Shin, and N. C. Hsiao (2003). Relationship between peak ground acceleration, peak ground velocity, and intensity in Taiwan, *Bull. Seismol. Soc. Am.* **93,** 386–396

Wu, Y.-M., H. Mittal, D.-Y. Chen, T.-Y. Hsu, and P.-Y. Lin (2021). Earthquake early warning systems in Taiwan: Current status, *J. Geol. Soc. India* **97,** no. 12, 1525–1532, doi: 10.1007/s12594-021-1909-6.

Manuscript received 8 June 2025
Published online 5 November 2025

Frequency-Dependent Bilateral Rupture of the 2024 M_w 7.1 Wushi Earthquake, NW China: Insights from InSAR, Seismic Imaging, and Aftershock Relocation

Bo Zhao[1], Yanlu Ma*[1], and Xuejun Han[1]

Abstract

The 2024 M_w 7.1 Wushi earthquake at the Tianshan-Tarim collisional boundary in northwest China was characterized by a frequency-dependent bilateral rupture process. By integrating Differential Interferometric Synthetic Aperture Radar (D-InSAR), finite-fault inversion (FFI), backprojection (BP), and aftershock relocation, we unravel the spatiotemporal complexity of rupture across distinct frequency bands. D-InSAR resolved two main asperities on the reactivated Kuqi-Maidan fault system, with maximum coseismic slips of 1.61 m (east-northeast direction) and 2.19 m (west-southwest direction). FFI of near-field microelectromechanical systems data (< 0.5 Hz) revealed temporally staggered earthquake rupture initiation: the east-northeast-directed rupture nucleated immediately, peaking at 5–6 s, whereas the west-southwest-directed rupture commenced ~6 s later with a slower rupture velocity. BP analysis of *S*-wave radiation demonstrated frequency-dependent rupture directivity: high-frequency (> 1 Hz) rupture branch propagated east-northeast with a velocity of ~3.45 km/s into the deeper Tianshan orogenic structures, contrasting with west-southwest-oriented low-frequency (0.5–1 Hz) front (~3.05 km/s) migrating toward shallow structural depths. Relocated aftershocks confirm alignment of clusters with rupture segments corresponding to the asperities. Our multidisciplinary approach reconciles static and kinematic models, providing new insights into intracontinental earthquake mechanisms in active collision settings.

Cite this article as Zhao, B., Y. Ma, and X. Han (2025). Frequency-Dependent Bilateral Rupture of the 2024 M_w 7.1 Wushi Earthquake, NW China: Insights from InSAR, Seismic Imaging, and Aftershock Relocation, *Seismol. Res. Lett.* **97**, 1798–1811, doi: 10.1785/0220250132.

Supplemental Material

Introduction

The Xinjiang region, located in Central Asia, is one of the most seismically active and tectonically complex areas globally. This region is shaped by the ongoing convergence of the Eurasian and Indian plates, which has driven dynamic crustal deformation since the Cenozoic era (Gao *et al.*, 1998; Xiao *et al.*, 2013). Its prominent geological features include the Tianshan Mountains and the Tarim basin, which exhibit contrasting mechanical behaviors due to their distinct crustal architectures. The Tianshan orogen comprises a collage of Paleozoic oceanic and arc remnants (Windley *et al.*, 1990), whereas the Tarim basin is a stable craton with thick Phanerozoic sedimentary sequences overlying Precambrian basement (Lu *et al.*, 2008). The transition between these units is marked by a north-dipping Late Paleozoic subduction zone (Zhang *et al.*, 1996), forming a critical tectonic boundary that accommodates intense intracontinental compression.

Geodynamically, the region's seismicity is closely tied to the reactivation of pre-existing structures under persistent plate convergence, leading to distributed crustal shortening and uplift (Thompson *et al.*, 2002). Recent geophysical studies reveal significant lateral variations in crustal thickness, with Moho depths increasing sharply from ~45 km beneath the Tarim basin to ~60 km beneath the Tianshan Mountains (Lu *et al.*, 2008). As illustrated in Figure 1, Global Positioning System-derived velocity fields (Zhao *et al.*, 2015) and digital elevation model data confirm active north–south shortening and crustal thickening across the Tianshan orogen. Moreover, this northward-thickening crust reflects long-term subduction and underthrusting of the Tarim lithosphere beneath the Tianshan, generating spatially heterogeneous stress regimes and deformation patterns.

On 22 January 2024, an M_w 7.1 earthquake struck Wushi County (78.63° E, 41.26° N) at a depth of ~22 km, near the junction of the Kuqi and Maidan faults. The earthquake has resulted in three fatalities and five injuries. The maximum

1. China Earthquake Networks Center, Beijing, China

*Corresponding author: mayanlu@hotmail.com

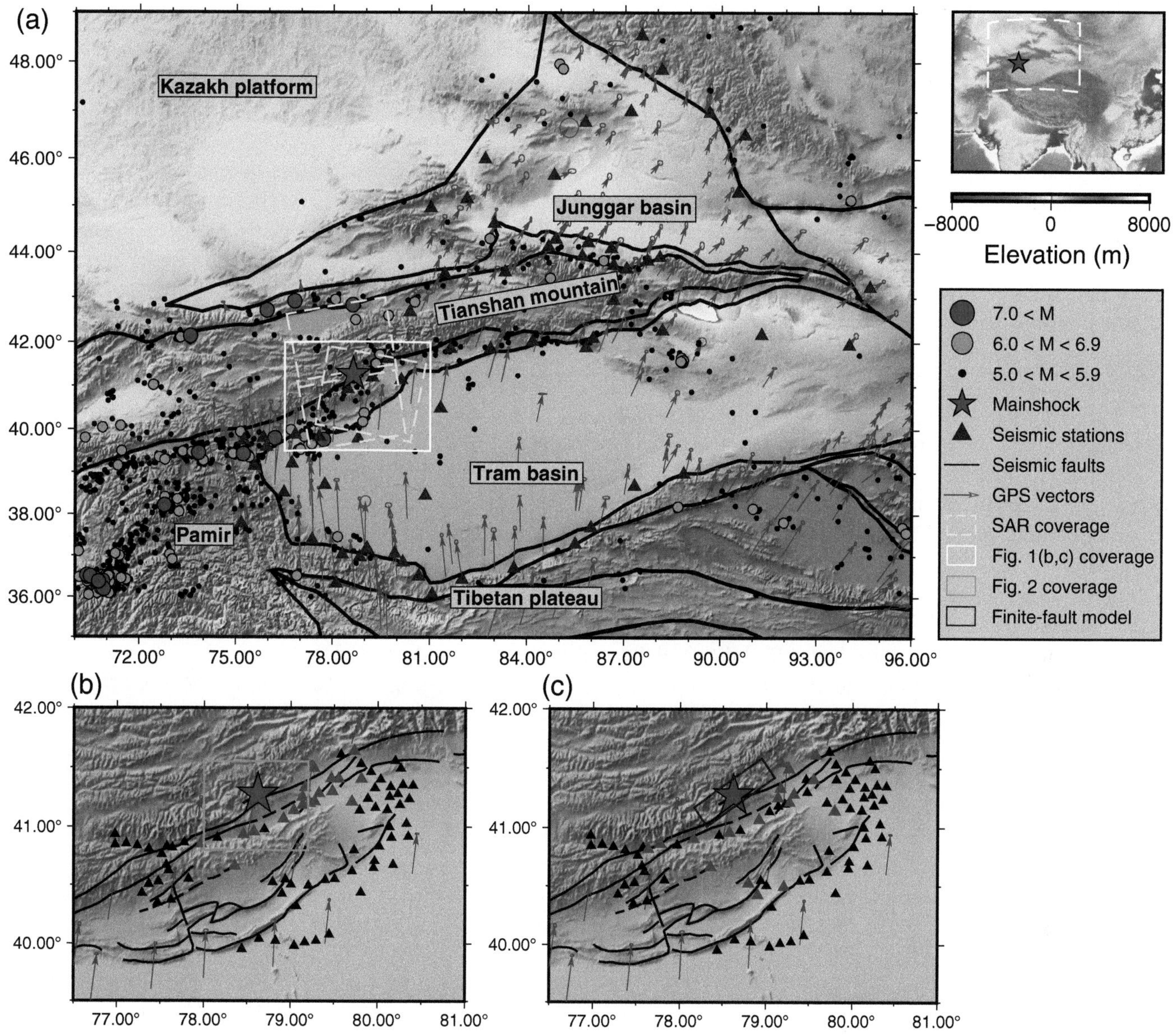

Figure 1. Tectonic fork, seismicity, and topography of the Xinjiang region and surroundings. (a) Seismicity, elevation, and tectonic units map. The red pentagon represents the M_w 7.1 Wushi mainshock in Xinjiang. The black, green, and red dots indicate historical earthquakes. The blue triangles represent broadband seismometers used for aftershock location. The yellow box shows the coverage area of Interferometric Synthetic Aperture Radar (InSAR) imagery. The red arrows indicate Global Positioning System (GPS) velocity vectors (indicating crustal horizontal motion direction and rate). (b,c) Distribution of microelectro-mechanical system (MEMS) intensity meter stations (triangles). The red triangles in (b) denote stations used for backprojection (BP) studies. The red triangles in (c) denote stations used for finite-fault inversion (FFI) studies. Black triangles denote stations not used in the finite fault inversion. The color version of this figure is available only in the electronic edition.

intensity recorded was IX-degree (9 degrees), with the IX-degree (9 degrees) intensity area spanning 252 square kilometers. Within this zone, 70% of buildings sustained damage. This event, located at the transition zone between the Tarim basin and Tianshan Mountains, provides a unique opportunity to investigate rupture dynamics in a region characterized by crustal heterogeneity and complex fault geometries. Focal mechanism solutions from the U.S. Geological Survey (USGS) indicate a northwest-dipping fault (strike: 235°, dip: 45°, and rake: 42°), aligning with the tectonic stress field dominated by northeast–southwest compression. Historical seismic activity records indicate that multiple strong earthquakes have occurred along this tectonic boundary, including the 1902 M_w 7.7 (M_w 8.3 Richter) Atushi earthquake, the 1961 M_w 7.0 Kashgar earthquake, and more than a dozen earthquakes of M_w 6.0 or greater. The focal mechanisms of these historical events are predominantly thrust type, with fault strikes primarily oriented east–west and northeast–southwest, which aligns well with the regional tectonic characteristics.

Studies on the aftershock sequence migration of the Wushi earthquake (Wang *et al.*, 2025) have revealed that the aftershocks are primarily distributed near the Midan fault. However, another fault—the Kulun fault—exists in the southern part of the seismogenic belt, and aftershocks in the southwestern region are spatially closer to the Kulun fault. Thus, the confirmation of the seismogenic fault for this earthquake still requires further investigation. In addition, current published results (Qiu *et al.*, 2024; Zheng *et al.*, 2024; Thompson *et al.*, 2025; Yang *et al.*, 2025) indicate that the maximum slip on the fault plane ranges from 1.0 to 3.3 m, with a relatively deep rupture depth (~5–25 km). This contradicts the surface rupture survey results from the seismogenic area (Zhang *et al.*, 2024; Chen *et al.*, 2025). Notably, studies on the inversion of kinematic parameters and source imaging of the Wushi earthquake rupture based on near-field data remain insufficient.

Building on advancements in geodetic, seismic, and kinematic methodologies, this study integrates Differential Interferometric Synthetic Aperture Radar (D-InSAR), finite-fault inversion (FFI), backprojection (BP) analysis, and 3D aftershock relocation to comprehensively unravel the spatio-temporal characteristics of the complex rupture. D-InSAR, a cornerstone in coseismic deformation mapping since its landmark application to the 1992 Landers earthquake (Massonnet *et al.*, 1993), enables high-resolution constraints on static slip distribution; modern refinements—such as atmospheric corrections via Generic Atmospheric Correction Online Service (GACOS) (Yu *et al.*, 2018) and multi-orbit data fusion—have further enhanced its reliability, though it inherently lacks temporal resolution. Complementing this, FFI reconstructs low-frequency rupture kinematics (<0.5 Hz) using broadband network waveforms (as demonstrated in regions like the Hellenic arc; Gallovič and Zahradník, 2011), yet it struggles to resolve high-frequency radiation critical for directivity analysis—a gap addressed by BP methods. Originally developed for teleseismic *P* waves (Ishii *et al.*, 2005), BP has evolved to leverage near-field *S* waves from dense networks (Evangelidis and Kao, 2014; Mesimeri *et al.*, 2020), enabling high-frequency (1–10 Hz) rupture tracking with improved spatial fidelity. Finally, precise aftershock relocation using 3D velocity models (e.g., USTClitho1.0; Xin *et al.*, 2019) bridges seismicity patterns to fault geometry, validating source models derived from independent datasets. Specifically, this study applies D-InSAR to invert static slip between the Kuqi and Maidan faults, uses locally dense microelectromechanical systems (MEMS) accelerometer data for FFI to constrain low-frequency rupture evolution, employs BP of near-field *S* waves from dense MEMS arrays to characterize high-frequency radiation directivity, and leverages 3D aftershock relocation to refine subsurface fault segmentation. By comprehensively comparing the static deformation field (e.g., InSAR observations), dynamic nucleation processes of the hypocenter (based on high-frequency rupture information from FFI and BP), and spatiotemporal migration patterns of aftershocks, this study systematically elucidates the geometric complexity of the seismogenic fault, energy partitioning mechanisms during rupture, and multiscale interactions within the deep seismic source zone. Our findings reconcile static and kinematic rupture models, offering new insights into intracontinental earthquake mechanics in collision zones.

D-InSAR Coseismic Deformation Analysis

We processed Sentinel-1A C-band Interferometric Wide Swath (IW) data (wavelength: 0.055 m; Copernicus Programme) from ascending orbit (track 56; 14–26 January 2024) and descending orbit (track 136; 20 January 2024–25 February 2024) to generate coseismic line-of-sight (LoS) displacement fields. Satellite coverage is shown by yellow boxes in Figure 1a. Topographic phase contributions were removed using the ASTER Global Digital Elevation Model V003 (resolution: 30 m; NASA/METI).

Data processing was performed using GMTSAR v6.3 (Sandwell *et al.*, 2011), with key steps as follows: (1) Multilooking: applied a range-azimuth ratio of 16:4 to reduce speckle noise; (2) Filtering: implemented a Gaussian filter (cutoff wavelength: 200 m) to suppress phase noise; (3) Atmospheric correction: mitigated phase delays using the GACOS (Yu *et al.*, 2018); (4) Phase unwrapping: completed using the statistical-cost, network-flow algorithm (Chen and Zebker, 2000) with minimum gradient cost threshold; (5) Geocoding: projected final LoS displacement to WGS84 UTM zone 44N coordinates with 30 m resolution.

The ascending (track 56) and descending (track 136) interferograms (Fig. 2a,b) reveal two distinct deformation lobes, with maximum LoS displacements of −0.19 m (subsidence) and +0.79 m (uplift), respectively (profiles in Fig. 2c,d). These deformation patterns indicate a northwest-dipping fault plane. Three types of fault models are defined in this study: (1) a single-planar fault model (Fig. S3c) constructed from the focal mechanism solution provided by the USGS (strike: 235°, dip: 45°, and rake: 42°), with the surface trace of its fault plane marked in green in Figure 2h; (2) a single-planar model (Fig. S3d) with the dip angle adjusted to 75°, whereas all other parameters remain consistent with model (1); (3) a two-segment fault model (Fig. 2h, Fig. S3e,f), where the shallow segment of the fault plane has a dip angle of 75° and the deep segment has a dip angle of 45°. The geometric structure of the fault plane (particularly the dip angle) was constrained based on the results of aftershock relocation.

Slip inversion using a steepest descent method (Wang *et al.*, 2009) discretized the fault plane into 2 km × 2 km subfaults, resolving two asperities (Fig. 2h): (1) East-northeast asperity:

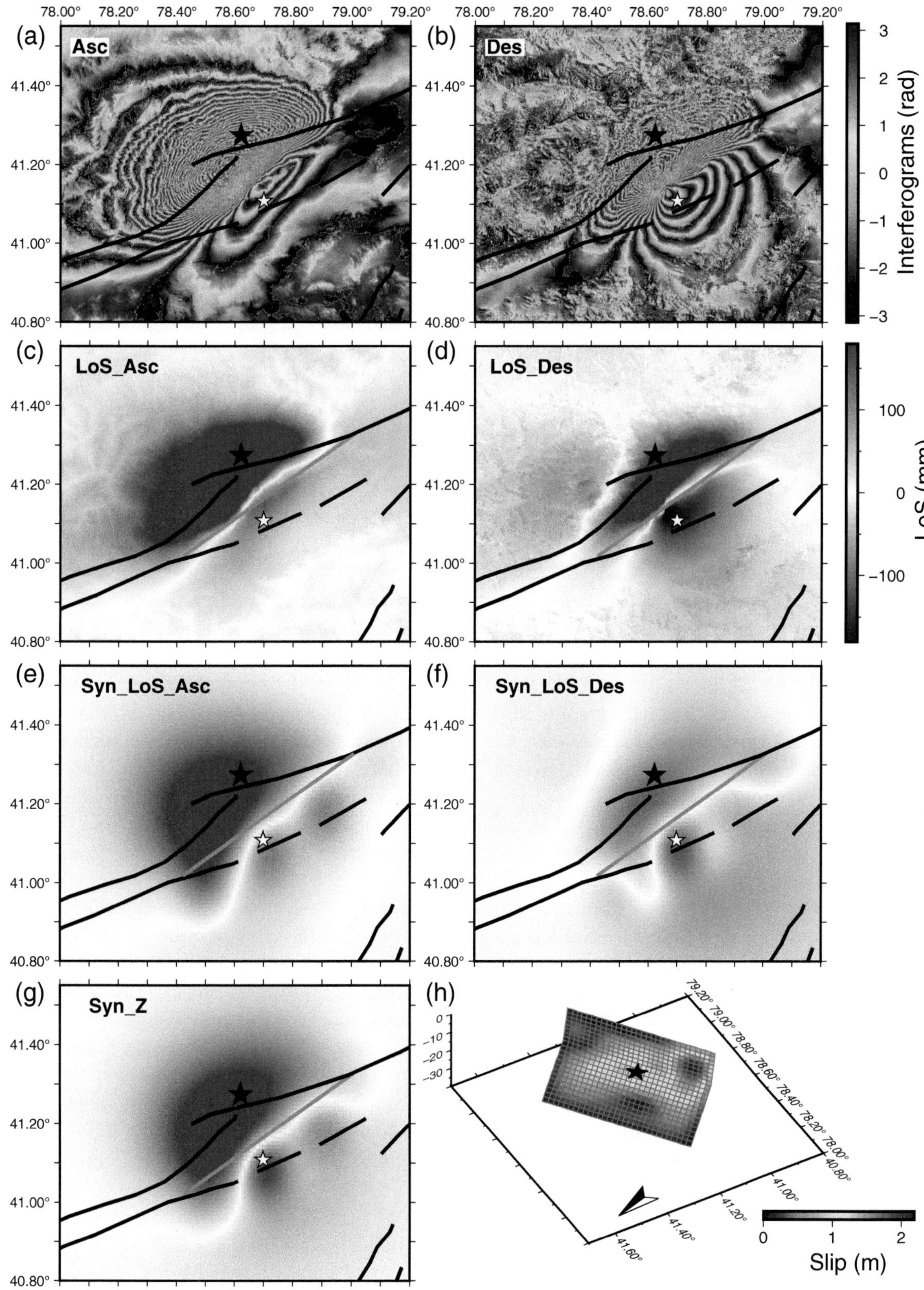

Figure 2. Differential Interferometric Synthetic Aperture Radar (D-InSAR) measurements of coseismic deformation and fault-slip distribution. (a,b) Interferometric phase (ascending and descending tracks). (c,d) Line-of-sight (LoS) displacement (ascending and descending tracks). (e) Ascending track LoS displacement. (f) Descending track LoS displacement. (g) Vertical displacement. (h) Static slip distribution on the fault plane. The black pentagrams in (a)–(g) indicate the location of the mainshock, and white pentagrams in (a)–(g) denote the location of the M_w 5.7 aftershock on 29 January 2024. The green line in (c)–(g) represents the surface trace of the finite-fault model. The color version of this figure is available only in the electronic edition.

maximum slip of 1.61 m at ~15 km depth, corresponding to a seismic moment 2.4×10^{19} N · m (M_w 6.85); (2) West-southwest asperity: maximum slip of 2.19 m at ~10 km depth, corresponding to a seismic moment 2.3×10^{19} N · m (M_w 6.84). The total seismic moment reached 4.71×10^{19} N · m (M_w 7.0), with an average slip of 0.67 m and stress drop ranging from 1.36 MPa (average) to 6.35 MPa (peak).

Forward modeling with CPS v.3.3.0 (Herrmann, 2013) demonstrated strong agreement between synthetic and observed LoS displacements (Fig. 2e–g). Although D-InSAR accurately constrained the static slip distribution, the temporal rupture process, including delayed west-southwest nucleation and frequency-dependent directivity, is further analyzed through FFI and BP methods in the following sections.

FFI Analysis of Near-Field MEMS Accelerometer Data

The FFI was conducted using the LinSlipInv algorithm (Gallovič and Zahradník, 2011; Gallovič *et al.*, 2014), a robust tool validated for kinematic rupture modeling in tectonically complex regions. Near-field acceleration waveforms were retrieved from 18 MEMS accelerometers deployed within 100 km epicentral distance (Fig. 1c). Data quality control included manual waveforms screening with criteria of signal-to-noise ratio (SNR) >5 dB in the 0.05–0.5 Hz band and baseline stability verification. Preprocessing included mean removal, linear trend correction, and application of a fourth-order Butterworth band-pass filter (0.1–0.5 Hz) to both observed and synthetic waveforms.

Similar to the two-segment model inverted from InSAR, the FFI model also consists of two segments. The dip angle of the shallow portion of the fault plane is 75°, whereas that of the deep portion is 45°. The fault plane (80 km × 40 km) was discretized into 200 subfaults (4 km × 4 km). The inversion utilized a multitime-window approach with six overlapping triangular source time functions (STFs) per subfault, allowing rupture propagation at variable velocities. Regularization parameters (slip smoothing and moment minimization) were optimized via L-curve analysis to balance model complexity and waveform fit.

The FFI resolved a seismic moment of 6.432×10^{19} N · m (M_w 7.1), showing 26% deviation compared with the static moment derived from D-InSAR. Slip distribution reveals two asperities (Fig. 3): (1) East-northeast asperity: peak slip of 0.87 m, nucleating near the hypocenter and propagating unilaterally east-northeast; (2) West-southwest asperity: delayed slip initiation ($\Delta t = 7$ s), achieving 1.53 m slip and up-dip propagating toward the surface.

Temporal snapshots (Fig. 4) highlight asynchronous bilateral rupture: east-northeastward unilateral rupture dominates the 0–6 s, succeeded by bilateral partitioning. West-southwest-directed rupture initiates after 6 s with reduced slip rates, likely influenced by shallow structural barriers.

BP Analysis of High-Frequency Rupture Propagation

To resolve the high-frequency (1–10 Hz) rupture kinematics, we applied the source-scanning BP algorithm (Kao and Shan, 2004, 2007) to *S*-wave waveforms recorded by regional MEM accelerometers (Fig. 1b). Three-component waveforms from 83 MEMS stations within an epicentral distance of 1°(about 110 km) were preprocessed through sequential steps: (1) removal of mean values and linear trends, (2) rotating to radial–transverse–vertical (R–T–Z) coordinates, and (3) band-pass filtering (1–10 Hz, fourth-order Butterworth). Following waveform amplitude normalization, we manually picked *S*-wave arrivals and retained 20 stations with high SNR > 5 dB on transverse components for BP stacking (Fig. S1, available in the supplemental material to this article). Theoretical travel times were calculated using the USTClitho1.0 3D velocity model (Xin *et al.*, 2019) to account for lateral heterogeneities in crustal velocity structure (Fig. S2).

The USGS-determined fault plane was discretized into a rectangular grid of 120 × 100 nodes with 0.5 km × 0.5 km spatial resolution. Time corrections were determined by aligning observed and theoretical *S*-wave arrival times at the relocated hypocenter (78.621° E, 41.274° N; 21.0 km depth) and applied to all grid points. Energy stacking utilized a square-root stacking approach (Rost and Thomas, 2002) with 0.5 s sliding windows over 15 s of post-nucleation, consistent with the mainshock's half-duration (~8 s). Synthetic tests (Appendix 1) and bootstrap uncertainty analyses (Appendix 2) confirmed the algorithm's robustness and constrained potential localization errors. The BP results of the far-field data can be found in Appendix 3.

BP results revealed east-northeast-directed rupture propagation dominated by 1–10 Hz radiation energy (Figs. 5 and 6b,d). The spatiotemporal energy distribution exhibited three phases: (1) Initial phase (0–3 s): westward rupture at ~2.36 km/s near 20 km depth; (2) Transition phase (3–5 s): eastward acceleration to ~3.26 km/s; (3) Mature phase (5–15 s): sustained east-northeast propagation at ~3.45 km/s with shallow dip.

Peak energy released at 3–6 s (Fig. 6e), spatially correlated with the east-northeast asperity resolved by D-InSAR and FFI. Frequency-dependent partitioning was investigated through sub-band BP analysis (0.5–1 Hz and 1–10 Hz): (1) East-northeast branch: dominated at 1–10 Hz, rupture propagation (~3.45 km/s) penetrating deeper Tianshan crust (Fig. 6b,d); (2) West-southwest branch: dominated at 0.5–1 Hz, initial deep rupture (~2.14 km/s, 0–3 s) transitioning to west-southwest-directed propagation (~3.05 km/s, 3–11 s) at shallower depths (Figs. 6a,c and 7).

This frequency-dependent bilateral rupture reconciles with FFI and D-InSAR: high-frequency east-northeast slip correlates with deep asperities, whereas low-frequency west-southwest rupture aligns with near-surface slip. The east-northeast branch is also obtained by the BP stacking of teleseismic waveforms (see in Appendix 3).

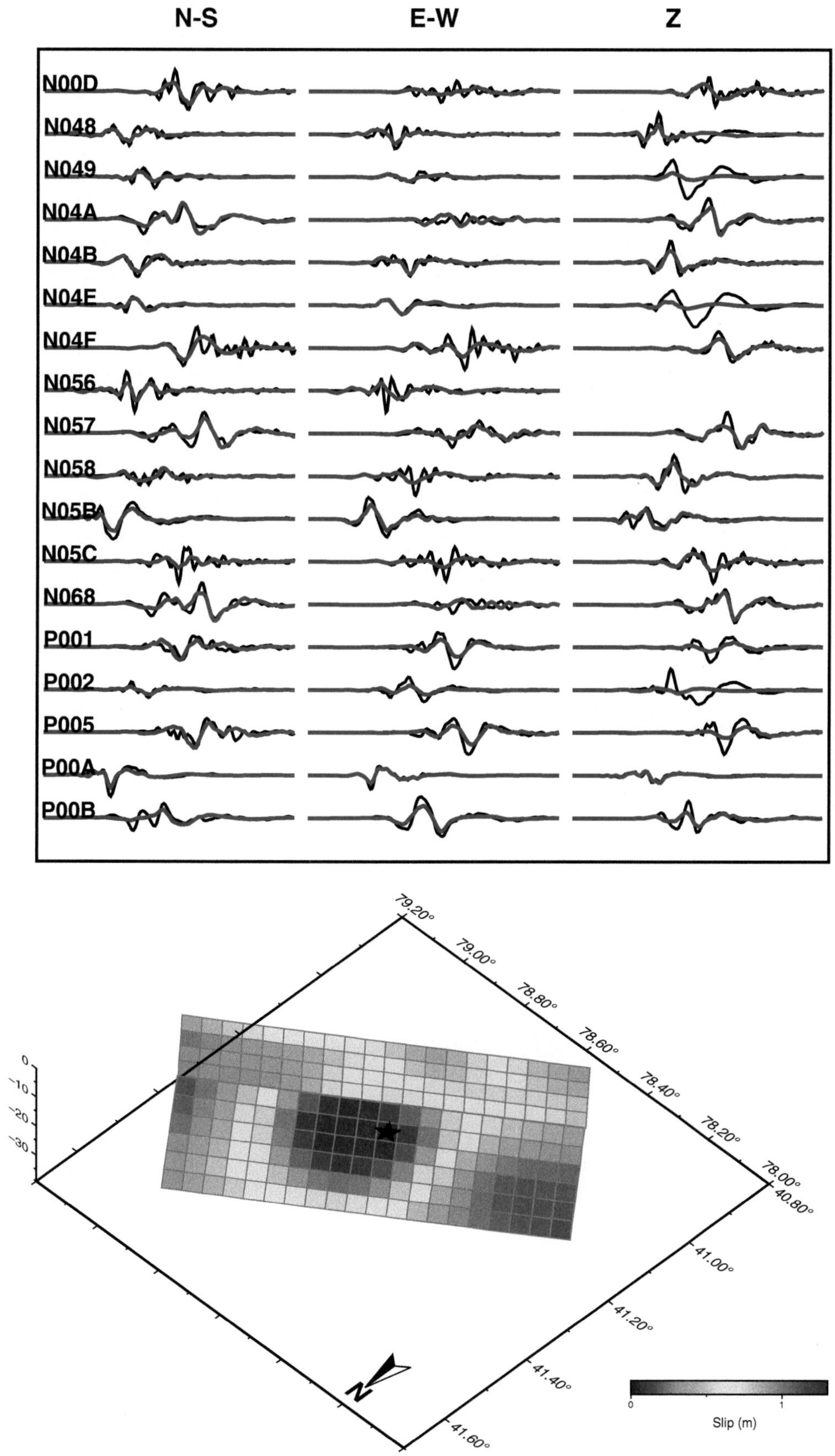

Figure 3. FFI results. The top panel is the comparison of observed (red) and synthetic (black) waveforms. The bottom panel illustrates the slip distribution on the fault plane. E–W, east–west; N–S, north–south; Z, vertical. The color version of this figure is available only in the electronic edition.

Aftershock Relocation

High-precision relocation of the 2024 M_w 7.1 Wushi earthquake sequence was performed using three-component broadband waveforms recorded by the Xinjiang Regional Seismic Network (China Earthquake Networks Center) (Fig. 1a) and the USTClitho1.0 3D velocity model (Xin *et al.*, 2019). The relocation workflow combined absolute and relative techniques to optimize hypocenter accuracy. First, absolute relocations were computed via the equal differential time (EDT) method (Zhou, 1994; Font *et al.*, 2004; Lomax *et al.*, 2014), which reduces origin dependence by minimizing differential travel-time residuals between phase pairs and uses the 3D velocity model to calculate theoretical travel times. Subsequently, relative relocation was integrated by incorporating double-difference (DD) travel-time residuals with the EDT objective function. Hypocenters were refined using a nonlinear grid-search algorithm, with the travel-time DDs calculated using the 3D velocity model. Cross-validation was then performed via HypoDD (Waldhauser and Ellsworth, 2000), which calculates travel-time differences using 1D velocity models.

The relocated mainshock hypocenter (78.621° E, 41.274° N; depth 21 km) anchors a northeast–southwest-trending aftershock sequence extending ~70 km along strike (Fig. 8a). Depth profiles reveal a northwestward-dipping geometry (Fig. 8b,c), consistent with the USGS-determined fault-plane solution. The aftershock distribution exhibits two distinct spatial clusters: (1) The east-

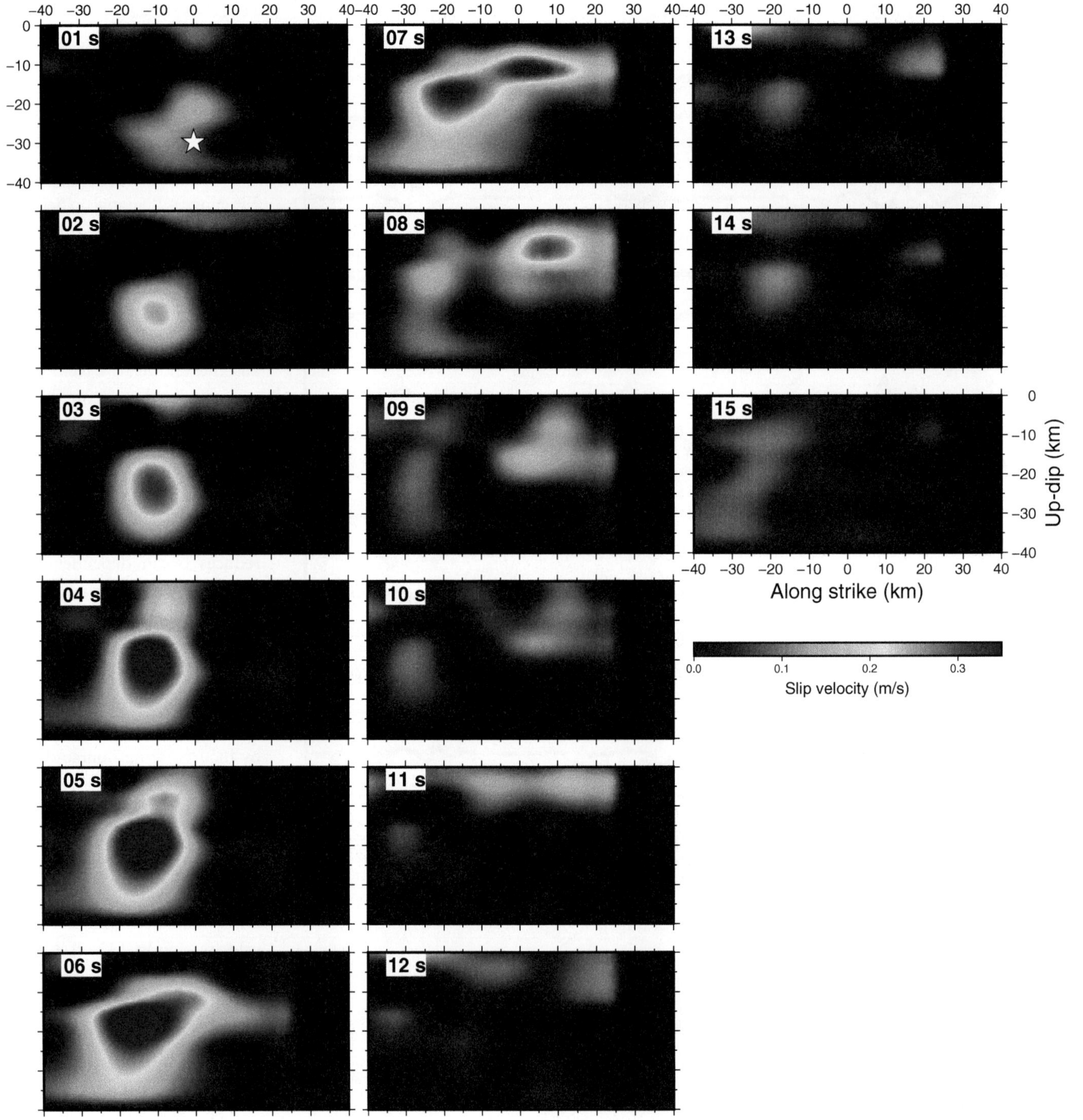

Figure 4. Spatiotemporal snapshots of dynamic slip velocity on the fault plane (1–15 s). The color version of this figure is available only in the electronic edition.

northeast cluster (centroid depth ~13 km) displays diffuse spatial characteristics, correlating with the deeper coseismic asperity identified in both D-InSAR and FFI analyses; (2) The west-southwest cluster (centroid depth ~9 km) shows tight spatial clustering that coincides with the shallow slip zone resolved by FFI analysis.

The pronounced aftershock concentration in the west-southwest direction (Fig. 9c), coupled with significant afterslip observed in D-InSAR data (Fig. 9a), provides compelling evidence for west-southwest-directed rupture propagation (Fig. 9b) during the mainshock. These observations suggest the west-southwest segment represents a distinct rupture branch that likely reached the fault termination, triggering both the concentrated aftershock activity and subsequent afterslip. The spatial correlation between the shallow slip zone, aftershock hypocenters, afterslip distribution, and high-frequency rupture tracks strongly supports the existence of the two geometrically distinct rupture branches.

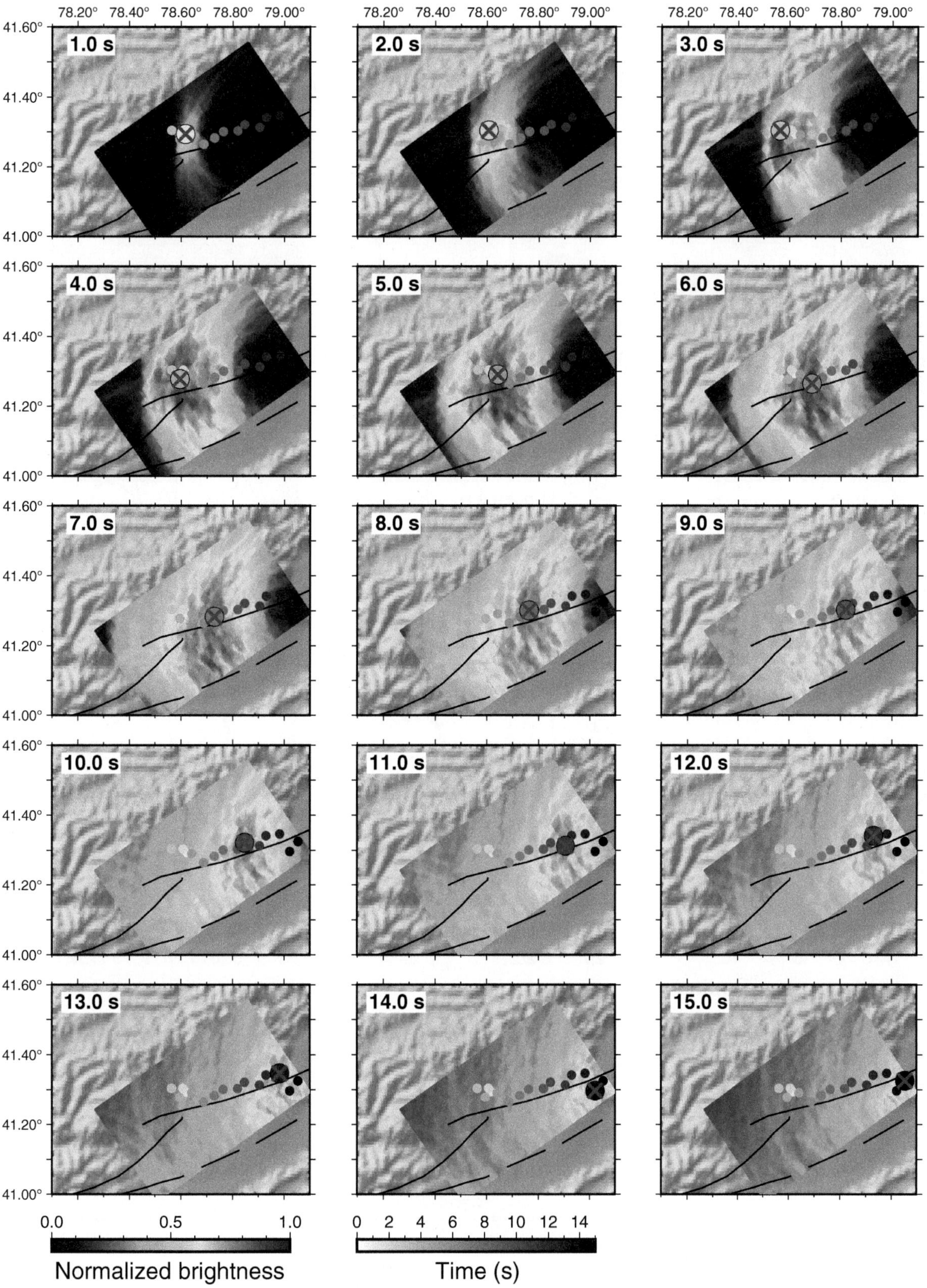

Figure 5. Spatiotemporal snapshots of normalized brightness values for 1–10 Hz energy (1–15 s). The brightness values correspond to the amplitude of near-field waveform BP stacking. Gradient gray circular markers trace the temporal evolution of the maximum brightness locations, and the red × symbol denotes the position of the peak normalized brightness value at the current timestep. The color version of this figure is available only in the electronic edition.

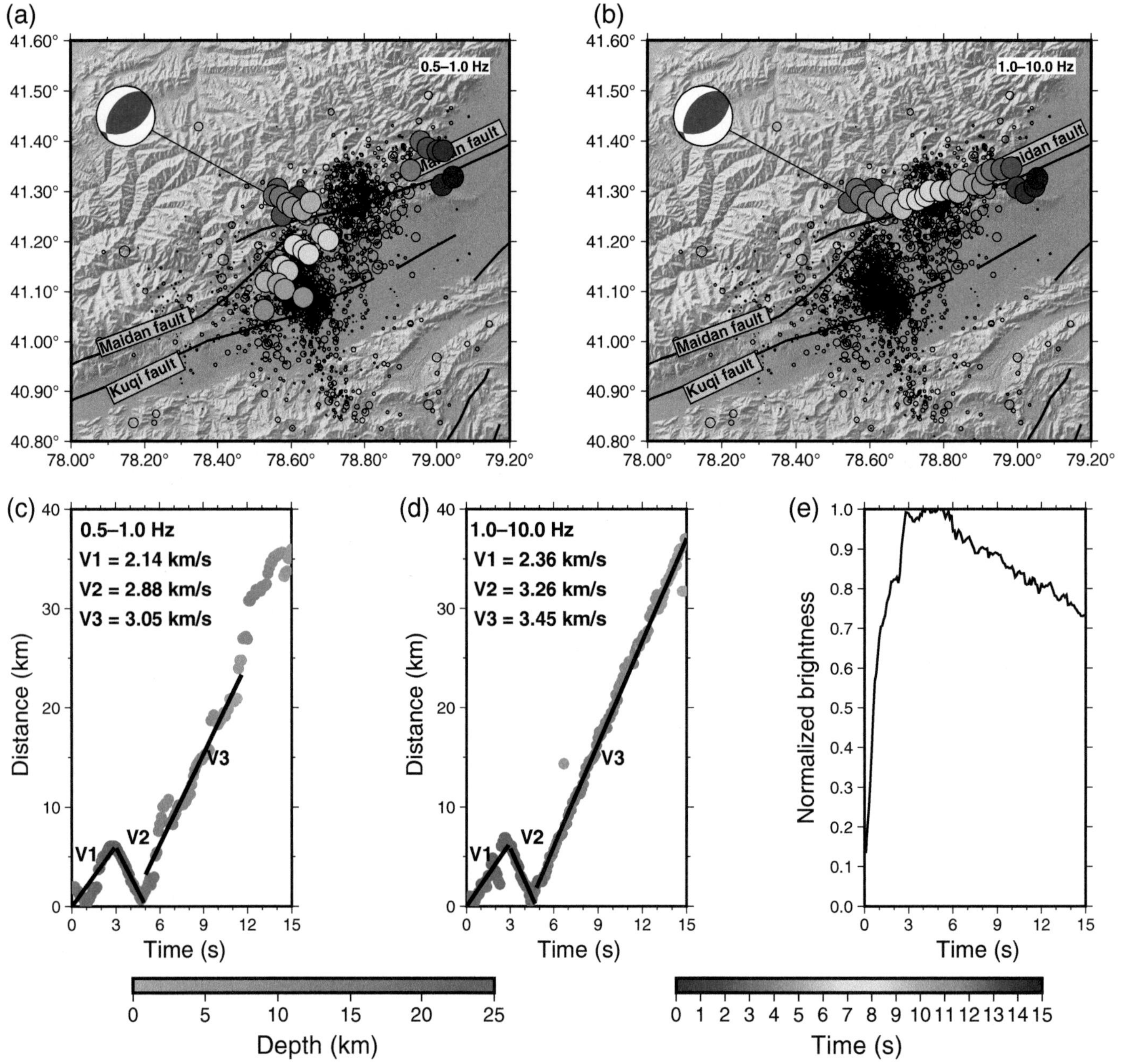

Figure 6. BP stacking results for different frequency energies. (a, b) BP stacking results for different frequencies. Colored dots represent the positions of maximum normalized energy brightness at different times. (c,d) Relationship between rupture energy location and rupture time. (e) Temporal variation of normalized brightness. The color version of this figure is available only in the electronic edition.

Discussion

Our analysis of aftershock distributions reveals a northwest-dipping seismicity trend that steepens progressively toward shallower depths (Fig. 8, Fig. S3a,b). To investigate this geometric complexity, we conducted a systematic evaluation of fault dip angles through InSAR modeling, testing values ranging from 45° to 75° (Fig. S3c,d). These tests demonstrate a clear relationship between dip angle and slip distribution, with increasing dip angles correlating with shallower slip concentrations.

This finding motivated the development of a two-segment fault model that better accounts for the observed rupture characteristics. The model maintains consistent strike orientation between segments while incorporating distinct dip angles (45° versus 75°) and rake values. This configuration successfully reconciles the presence of two spatially separated asperities at different depth levels, providing a more physically realistic representation of the fault geometry than single-plane solutions.

Our InSAR-derived slip model reveals two distinct asperities with contrasting depth distributions: the east-northeast asperity exhibits deeper slip concentrations (15–25 km), whereas the west-southwest asperity shows shallower slip

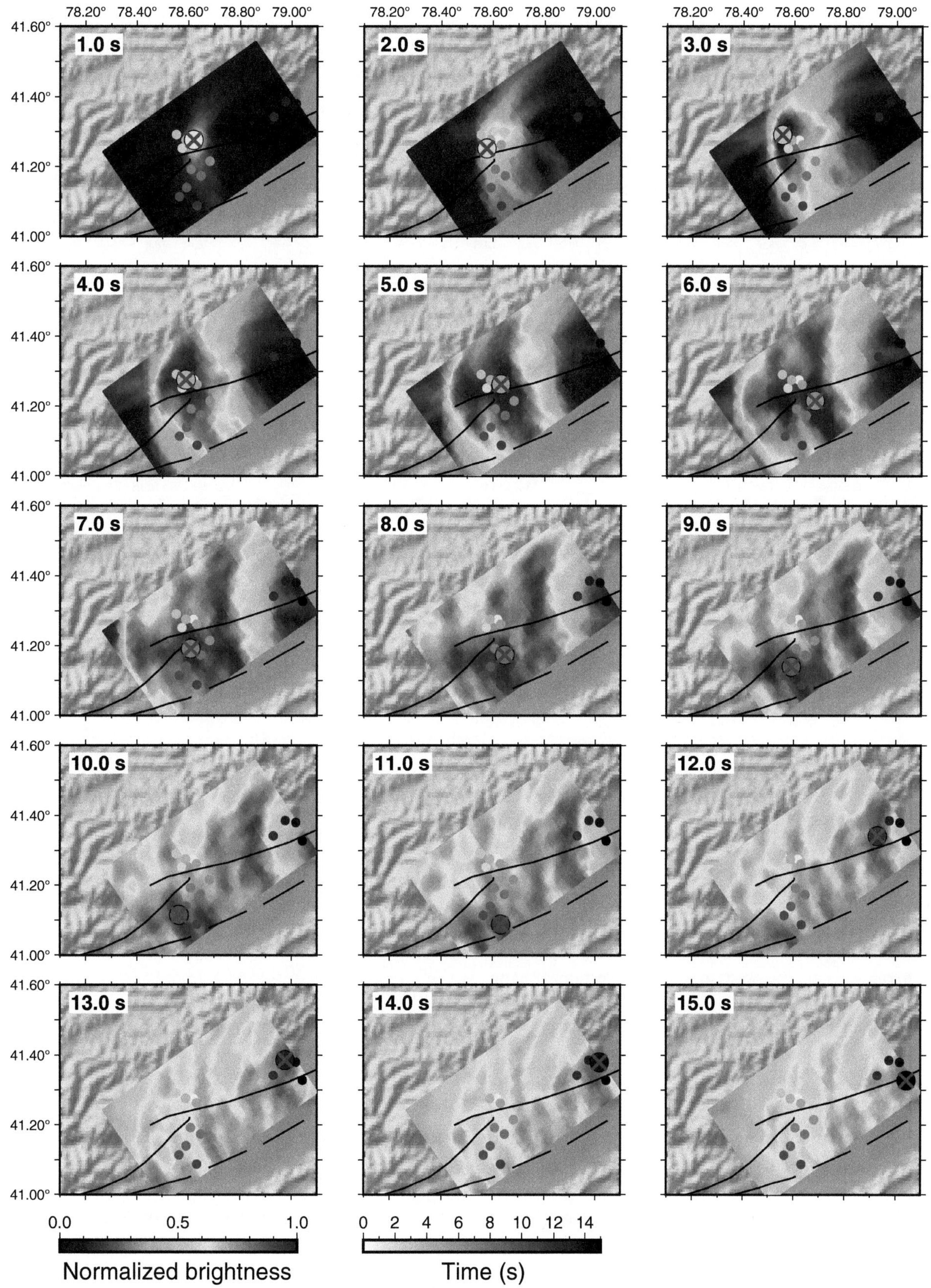

Figure 7. Spatiotemporal snapshots of normalized brightness values for 0.5–1.0 Hz energy (1–15 s). The brightness values correspond to the amplitude of near-field waveform BP stacking. Gradient gray circular markers trace the temporal evolution of the maximum brightness locations, and the red × symbol denotes the position of the peak normalized brightness value at the current timestep. The color version of this figure is available only in the electronic edition.

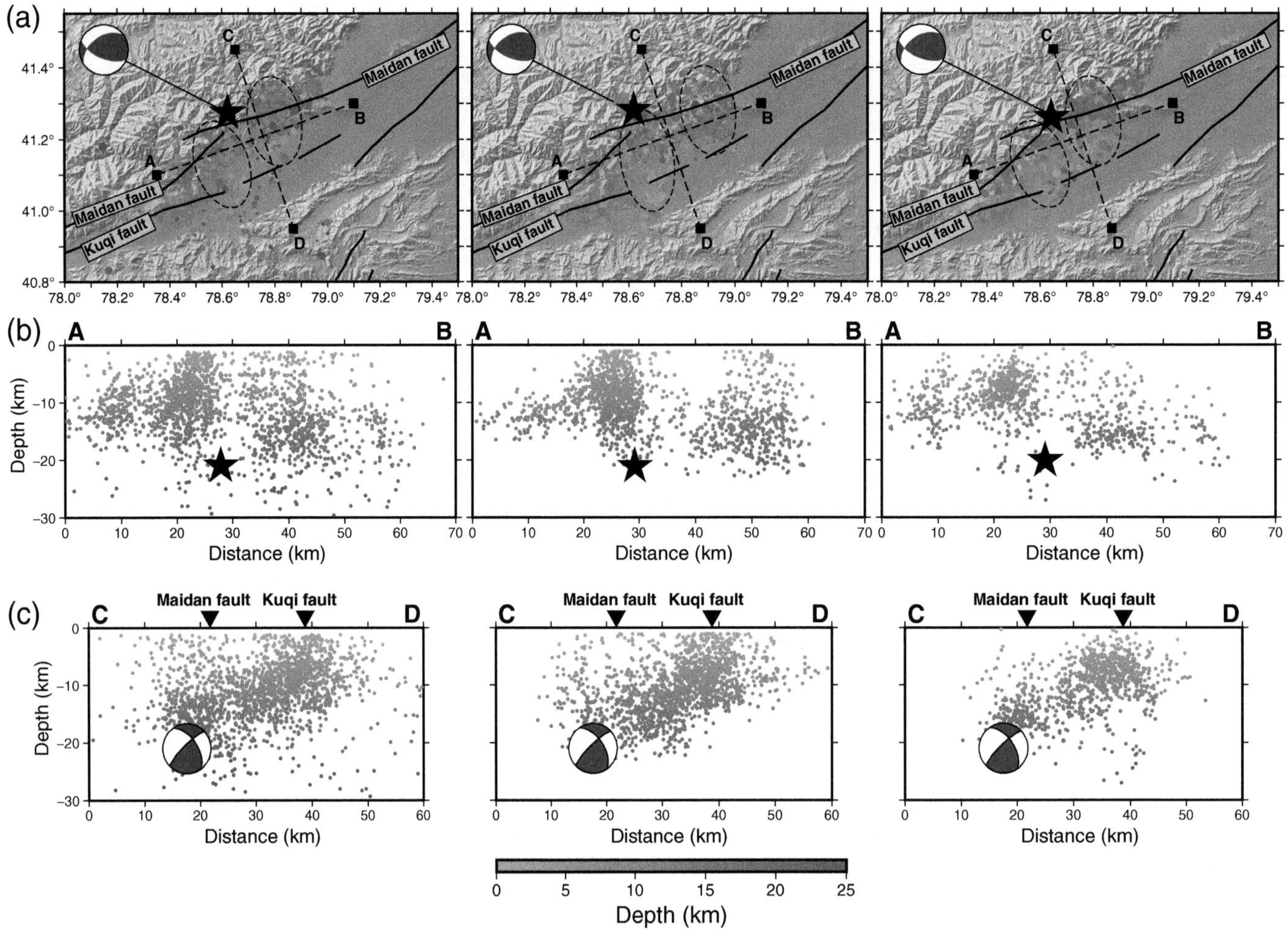

Figure 8. (a) Epicenter distribution of the aftershock sequence. The dashed lines A–B and C–D indicate the locations of the depth profiles. From left to right, the results are based on absolute location using a 3D velocity model, relative location, and HypoDD. The black pentagram marks the location of the mainshock, and the focal mechanism plot represents the focal mechanism of the mainshock. (b,c) Depth profiles of the seismic sources. The black inverted triangles indicate the surface projection of the fault. The color version of this figure is available only in the electronic edition.

(<10 km) that may extend to the surface (Fig. 2h, Fig. S3e,f). Although the deeper east-northeast asperity aligns with previous studies (Qiu *et al.*, 2024; Zheng *et al.*, 2024; Yang *et al.*, 2025), the shallow west-southwest asperity presents an important discrepancy. Notably, this shallow slip feature is consistently resolved in both our InSAR and FFI analyses (Figs. 2 and 3), and is further supported by field observations of surface ruptures in the west-southwest direction (Zhang *et al.*, 2024; Chen *et al.*, 2025).

Our study reveals a notable discrepancy in slip distribution between InSAR and FFI analyses regarding the relative strength of the two primary asperities (Figs. 2 and 3). The InSAR results indicate stronger slip in the shallower west-southwest asperity, whereas FFI analysis shows maximum slip occurring in the deeper east-northeast asperity. This divergence likely stems from fundamental differences in the temporal sampling of each method. The FFI incorporates waveform recordings limited to the first 100 s following rupture initiation, capturing primarily coseismic slip. In contrast, the InSAR solution combines data from both ascending (4 days post-event) and descending (34 days post-event) orbits, thereby incorporating contributions from postseismic deformation, including afterslip and larger aftershocks (e.g., the M_w 5.7 event on 29 January 2024; white star in Fig. 2 and Fig. S3a).

A systematic along-strike offset of 12–15 km is observed between the west-southwest-directed slip distributions derived from InSAR and FFI analyses (Fig. 9a,b), with the InSAR-resolved slip maximum displaced farther west-southwest relative to the FFI-inferred shallow slip concentration. This spatial offset correlates strongly with aftershock distribution patterns, exhibiting maximum seismicity density precisely within the FFI-resolved slip zone and reduced aftershock activity in the InSAR-identified slip area (Fig. 9c). These observations indicate that while the FFI solution predominantly captures primary coseismic slip that directly triggered aftershocks on both sides of the rupture zone, the InSAR measurements

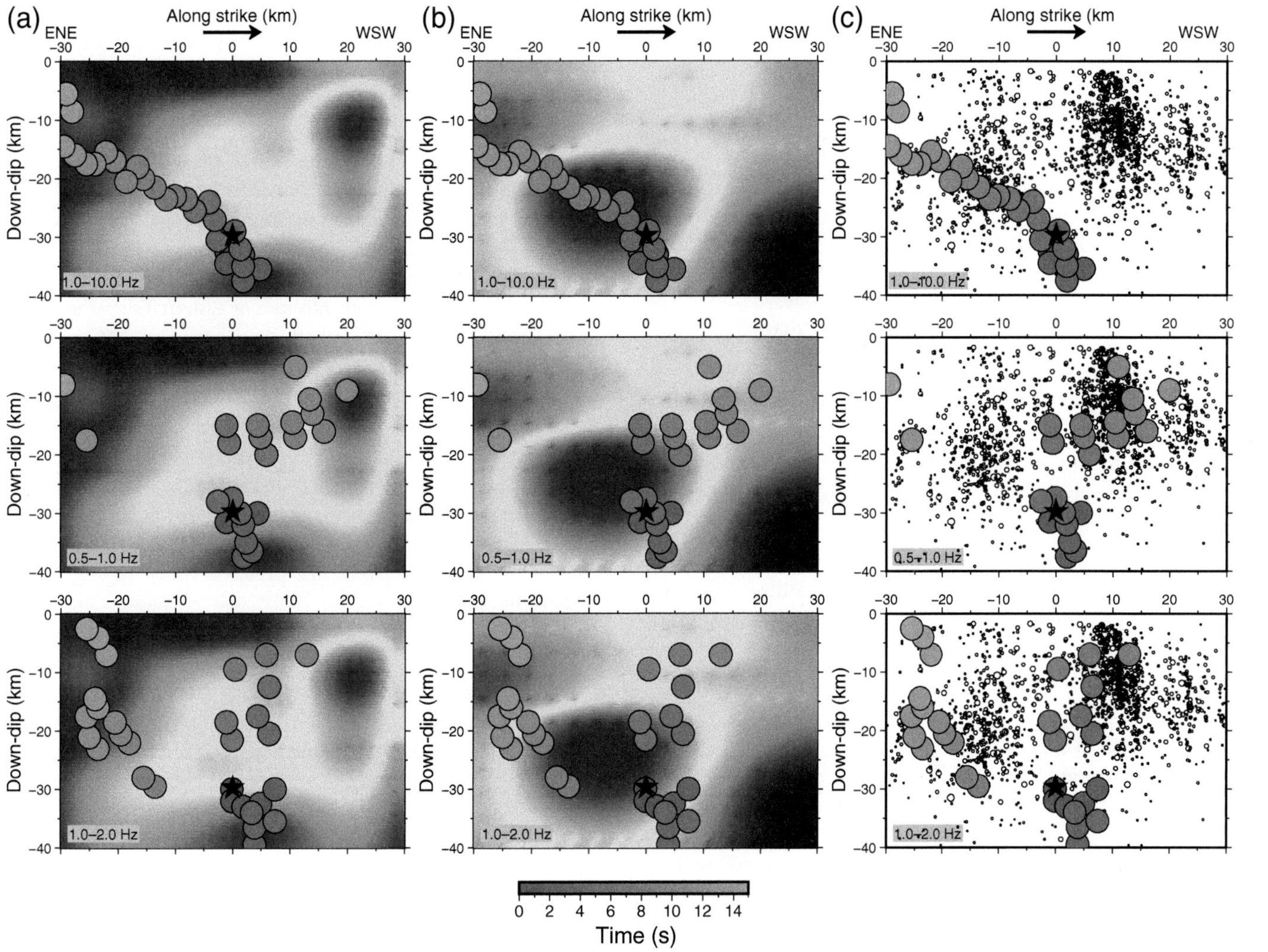

Figure 9. (a) Comparison of InSAR slip inversion and BP results. (b) Comparison of FFI and BP results. (c) Comparison of aftershock distribution and BP results. The top, middle, and bottom panels show BP results for energy at 1–10 Hz, 0.5–1.0 Hz, and 1–2.0 Hz, respectively. The color version of this figure is available only in the electronic edition.

additionally incorporate substantial shallow crustal postseismic deformation, including distributed afterslip in peripheral regions surrounding the main rupture area.

The temporal evolution of rupture propagation exhibits remarkable consistency between FFI and BP analyses (Figs. 4–7). Both methods indicate that the east-northeast asperity dominated the initial rupture phase (0–6 s), with FFI slip velocity snapshots (Fig. 4) and BP energy distributions (Figs. 5 and 7) showing spatial coherence in high-amplitude regions during this interval. The rupture bifurcation becomes apparent at ~6 s, coinciding with the initiation of the west-southwest asperity rupture. This temporal separation enables clear discrimination of the two rupture branches through frequency-dependent BP analysis of *SH* waveforms because the subevents exhibit distinct dominant frequency characteristics: high-frequency (>1 Hz) radiation predominates from the east-northeast asperity, whereas the west-southwest rupture generates stronger low-frequency (0.5–1 Hz) energy.

Conclusion

Through multidisciplinary integration of D-InSAR, FFI, BP, and aftershock relocation, we resolve a complex rupture process exhibiting bilateral slip propagation and frequency-dependent seismic energy radiation.

1. Coseismic slip inversions derived from D-InSAR reveal distinct rupture asperities propagating east-northeast and west-southwest, separated spatially by the mainshock hypocenter. This bilateral slip pattern is consistent with the temporally staged rupture sequence resolved through FFI.
2. FFI resolves a temporally staggered rupture sequence: East-northeast-directed rupture nucleated at the hypocenter (0 s), achieving peak slip magnitudes at 5–6 s, whereas west-southwest-directed rupture initiated 6 s later with reduced propagation velocity. The delayed west-southwest rupture nucleation likely reflects stress heterogeneities

controlled by pre-existing structural barriers, suggesting that inherited tectonic boundaries dynamically modulate rupture propagation.
3. BP analysis demonstrates frequency-dependent rupture directivity: High-frequency *S*-wave energy (1–10 Hz) predominates in the east-northeast direction, propagating at ~3.45 km/s into the deeper Tianshan orogenic crust, whereas low-frequency radiation (0.5–1 Hz) dominates the west-southwest direction with slower rupture velocities (~3.05 km/s) and shallow slip penetration toward the surface.
4. Aftershock segmentation implications: Relocated aftershocks cluster into two distinct groups along the east-northeast–west-southwest structural trend, spatially correlated with the mainshock's bilateral asperities and rupture segmentation. The east-northeast cluster exhibits deeper hypocenters (mean depth: ~13 km) compared to the west-southwest cluster (~9 km), supporting slip partitioning along geometrically distinct fault strands. This segmentation implies dynamic bifurcation of rupture into pre-existing structures, potentially reactivating secondary faults within the Kuqi-Maidan fault system.

Data and Resources

Strong-motion records and phase data were provided by the National Earthquake Data Center, available at https://data.earthquake.cn. The Sentinel-1 Synthetic Aperture Radar (SAR) data used in this study were copyrighted by the European Space Agency and are available at https://dataspace.copernicus.eu. Both websites were last accessed in February 2024. All figures were made using the Generic Mapping Tools (GMT). The supplemental material for this article includes Appendix 1–3, Figures S1–S8, and Table S1.

Declaration of Competing Interests

The authors acknowledge that there are no conflicts of interest recorded.

Acknowledgments

The Sentinel-1 Synthetic Aperture Radar was provided by the European Space Agency. The strong-motion records and phase data were provided by the National Earthquake Data Center. The authors thank the editor and two anonymous reviewers for their helpful suggestions that helped improve this work. This work was supported by the Science and Technology Basic Resources Survey Special Project (Grant 2023FY101504), National Natural Science Foundation of China (Grant 41774063), Science for Earthquake Resilience (Grant XH21044), and National Key R&D Program of China (Grant 2021YFC3000705). The authors thank the developers of Generic Mapping Tools (GMT; Wessel and Smith, 1998) and GMTSAR (Sandwell *et al.*, 2011).

References

Chen, C. W., and H. A. Zebker (2000). Network approaches to two-dimensional phase unwrapping: Intractability and two new algorithms, *J. Opt. Soc. Am. A* **17,** no. 3, 401–414, doi: 10.1364/josaa.17.000401.

Chen, Z., G. Liu, Q. Li, W. Chen, X. Zhao, M. Li, L. Tao, X. Qiao, and Z. Nie (2025). InSAR coseismic deformation and seismogenic structure of the 2024 M_W 7.0 Wushi earthquake, *Seismol. Geol.* **47,** no. 2, 429–447, doi: 10.3969/j.issn.0253-4967.2025.02.20240142.

Evangelidis, C. P., and H. Kao (2014). High-frequency source imaging of the 2011 October 23 Van (eastern Turkey) earthquake by back-projection of strong motion waveforms, *Geophys. J. Int.* **196,** no. 2, 1060–1072, doi: 10.1093/gji/ggt437.

Font, Y., H. Kao, S. Lallemand, C. S. Liu, and L. Y. Chiao (2004). Hypocentre determination offshore of eastern Taiwan using the maximum intersection method, *Geophys. J. Int.* **158,** 655–675, doi: 10.1111/j.1365-246X.2004.02317.x.

Gallovie, F., and J. Zahradnik (2011). Toward understanding slip-inversion uncertainty and artifacts: 2. Singular value analysis, *J. Geophys. Res.* **116,** B02309, doi: 10.1029/2010JB007814.

Gallovie, F., W. Imperatori, and P. M. Mai (2014). Effects of three-dimensional crustal structure and smoothing constraint on earthquake slip inversions: Case study of the M_w 6.3 2009 L'Aquila earthquake, *J. Geophys. Res.* **120,** 428–449, doi: 10.1002/2014JB011650.

Gao, J., M. Li, X. Xiao, Y. Tang, and G. P. He (1998). Paleozoic tectonic evolution of the Tianshan orogen, northwestern China, *Tectonophysics* **287,** 213–231, doi: 10.1016/S0040-1951(98)80070-X.

Herrmann, R. B. (2013). Computer programs in seismology: An evolving tool for instruction and research, *Seismol. Res. Lett.* **84,** 1081–1088, doi: 10.1785/0220110096.

Ishii, M., P. M. Shearer, H. Houston, and J. E. Vidale (2005). Extent, duration and speed of the 2004 Sumatra-Andaman earthquake imaged by the Hi-Net array, *Nature* **435,** no. 7044, 933–936, doi: 10.1038/nature03675.

Kao, H., and S. J. Shan (2004). The source-scanning algorithm: Mapping the distribution of seismic sources in time and space, *Geophys. J. Int.* **157,** no. 2, 589–594, doi: 10.1111/j.1365-246X.2004.02276.x.

Kao, H., and S. J. Shan (2007). Rapid identification of earthquake rupture plane using source-scanning algorithm, *Geophys. J. Int.* **168,** no. 3, 1011–1020, doi: 10.1111/j.1365-246X.2006.03271.x.

Lomax, A., A. Michelini, and A. Curtis (2014). Earthquake location, direct, Global-search methods, in R. Meyers (Editors), *Encyclopedia of Complexity and Systems Science*, Springer, New York, New York, doi: 10.1007/978-3-642-27737-5_150-2.

Lu, S. N., H. K. Li, C. L. Zhang, and G. H. Niu (2008). Geological and geochronological evidences for the Precambrian evolution of the Tarim craton and surrounding continental fragments, *Precambrian Res.* **160,** 94–107, doi: 10.1016/j.precamres.2007.04.025.

Massonnet, D., M. Rossi, C. Carmona, F. Adragna, G. Peltzer, K. Feigl, and T. Rabaute (1993). The displacement field of the Landers earthquake mapped by radar interferometry, *Nature* **364,** no. 6433, 138–142, doi: 10.1038/364138a0.

Mesimeri, M., H. Zhang, and K. L. Pankow (2020). Backprojection Imaging of the 2020 M_w 5.5 Magna, Utah, earthquake using a local dense strong-motion network, *Seismol. Res. Lett.* **92,** no. 2A, 640–646, doi: 10.1785/0220200326.

Qiu, J., J. Sun, and L. Ji (2024). The 2024 M_w 7.1 Wushi earthquake: A thrust and strike-slip event unveiling the seismic mechanisms of the South Tian Shan's thick-skin tectonics, *Remote Sens.* **16,** 2937, doi: 10.3390/rs16162937.

Rost, S., and C. Thomas (2002). Array seismology: Methods and applications, *Rev. Geophys.* **40,** no. 3, 2-1-2-27, doi: 10.1029/2000RG000100.

Sandwell, D., R. Mellors, X. Tong, M. Wei, and P. Wessel (2011). Open radar interferometry software for mapping surface deformation, *Eos. Trans. AGU* **92,** no. 28, doi: 10.1029/2011EO280002.

Thompson, J. J. A., C. E. Hanagan, A. E. Hatem, W. D. Barnhart, D. E. Goldberg, and W. L. Yeck (2025). Surface rupture from an aftershock: Remote observations from the January 2024 Wushi (Aykol), China, earthquakes, *Seismol. Res. Lett.* 1–21, doi: 10.1785/0220240347.

Thompson, S. C., R. J. Weldon, C. M. Rubin, K. Abdrakhmatov, P. Molnar, and G. W. Berger (2002). Late Quaternary slip rates across the central Tien Shan, Kyrgyzstan, central Asia, *J. Geophys. Res.* **107,** no. B9, 2203, doi: 10.1029/2001jb000596.

Waldhauser, F., and L. W. Ellsworth (2000). A double-difference earthquake location algorithm: Method and application to the northern Hayward fault, California, *Bull. Seismol. Soc. Am.* **90,** no. 6, 1353–1368, doi: 10.1785/0120000006.

Windley, B. F., M. B. Allen, C. Zhang, Z. Y. Zhao, and G. R. Wang (1990). Paleozoic accretion and Cenozoic redeformation of the Chinese Tien Shan Range, Central Asia, *Geology* **18,** 128–131, doi: 10.1130/0091-7613(1990)018<0128:PAACRO>2.3.CO;2.

Wang, L., R. Wang, F. Roth, B. Enescu, S. Hainzl, and S. Ergintav (2009). Afterslip and viscoelastic relaxation following the 1999 M 7.4 Izmit earthquake from GPS measurements, *Geophys. J. Int.* **178,** no. 3, 1220–1237, doi: 10.1111/j.1365-246X.2009.04228.x.

Wang, X., C. Wu, J. Liu, K. Zang, H. Yuan, Z. Gao, J. Zhang, and Y. Ma (2025). Earthquake sequence relocation and seismogenic structure of the 2024 M_S 7.1 Wushi earthquake on January 23, 2024, Xinjiang, *Seismol. Geol.* **47,** no. 2, 488–506, doi: 10.3969/j.issn.0253-4967.2025.02.20240153.

Wessel, P., and W. H. F. Smith (1998). New, improved version of Generic Mapping Tools released, *Eos Trans. AGU* **79,** no. 47, 579, doi: 10.1016/j.gr.2012.01.012.

Xiao, W., B. F. Windley, M. B. Allen, and C. Han (2013). Paleozoic multiple accretionary and collisional tectonics of the Chinese Tianshan orogenic collage, *Gond. Res.* **23,** 1316–1341, doi: 10.1016/j.gr.2012.01.012.

Xin, H., H. Zhang, M. Kang, R. He, L. Gao, and J. Gao (2019). High-resolution lithospheric velocity structure of continental China by double-difference seismic travel-time tomography, *Seismol. Res. Lett.* **90,** no. 1, 229–241, doi: 10.1785/0220180209.

Yang, J. Y., Y. M. Wen, C. J. Xu, and W. W. Jia (2025). Coseismic deformation and slip distribution of the January 2024 Xinjiang Wushi *MS*7.1 earthquake revealed by InSAR observations, *Chin. J. Geophys.* **68,** no. 7, 2531–2542, doi: 10.6038/cjg2024S0116.

Yu, C., Z. Li, N. T. Penna, and P. Crippa (2018). Generic atmospheric correction model for Interferometric Synthetic Aperture Radar observations, *J. Geophys. Res.* **123,** no. 10, 9202–9222, doi: 10.1029/2017JB015305.

Zhang, B., L. Qian, T. Li, J. Chen, J. Xu, Y. Yao, L. Fang, C. Xie, J. Chen, G. Liu, *et al.* (2024). Geological disaster and surface ruptures of January 23, 2024 M_S 7.1 Wushi earthquake, Xinjiang, China, *Seismol. Geol.* **46,** no. 1, 220–234, doi: 10.3969/j.issn.0253-4967.2024.01.013.

Zhang, P. Z., Q. D. Deng, and X. P. Yang (1996). Late Cenozoic tectonic deformation and mechanism along the Tianshan Mountain, northwestern China, *Earthq. Res. China* **12,** 127–140.

Zhao, B., Y. Huang, C. Zhang, W. Wang, K. Tan, and R. Du (2015). Crustal deformation on the Chinese mainland during 1998-2014 based on GPS data, *Geod. Geodyn.* **6,** no. 1, 7–15, doi: 10.1016/j.geog.2014.12.006.

Zheng, R., R. Zou, R. Dong, Z. Fang, and Q. Wang (2024). The 2024 M_w 7.0 Wushi earthquake in southern Tianshan convergent zone: Finite-fault model for the coseismic rupture and aftershock, *Seismol. Res. Lett.* **96,** 816–827, doi: 10.1785/0220240126.

Zhou, H. (1994). Rapid three-dimensional hypocentral determination using a master station method, *J. Geophys. Res.* **99,** no. B8, 15,439–15,455, doi: 10.1029/94JB00934.

Manuscript received 30 April 2025
Published online 24 October 2025

Adapting Hybrid CBR–RBF Models for Casualty and Emergency Supply Demand Forecasting in High-Altitude Regions: A Case Study of the 2022 Luding Earthquake

Yiguo Zhou[1] and Zhuojuan Xie*[1]

Abstract

Earthquakes frequently occur worldwide and cause extensive damage. Effective emergency response is crucial, and accurate forecasting of emergency supply needs is essential for efficient disaster relief operations. This study proposes an emergency supply demand prediction model for high-altitude regions by combining case-based reasoning (CBR) with a radial basis function (RBF) neural network. Building on previous research into factors influencing earthquake casualties, we identified six key parameters, namely, the magnitude, seismic intensity, seismic fortification intensity, affected population, population density, and the number of damaged houses. After evaluating various machine learning models, the RBF neural network was found to have the highest accuracy in predicting earthquake casualties. Then, the model was integrated with CBR to further estimate emergency supply demand, with regional adjustments made according to the geological structures and specific supply needs of the western Sichuan plateau. To enhance practical usability, a graphical user interface was developed, enabling users to input earthquake parameters and obtain predictions of casualties and supply requirements. This research provides a valuable decision-support tool for earthquake emergency response in high-altitude regions and offers methodological insights for emergency supply demand prediction in other complex environments.

Cite this article as Zhou, Y., and Z. Xie (2025). Adapting Hybrid CBR–RBF Models for Casualty and Emergency Supply Demand Forecasting in High-Altitude Regions: A Case Study of the 2022 Luding Earthquake, *Seismol. Res. Lett.* **97**, 1812–1826, doi: 10.1785/0220250188.

Introduction

Earthquakes rank among the most devastating natural disasters globally. While they accounted for only 7.8% of all natural disasters over the past 20 yr, earthquakes were responsible for 56% of disaster-related deaths and 23% of economic losses Jaiswal and Wald (2020). Emergency rescue operations are vital for minimizing losses and protecting human lives and property. Accurate forecasting of emergency supply needs is foundational to achieving effective response, enabling timely procurement, efficient allocation of supplies, cost control, rapid mobilization, and reduced casualties.

Initial approaches to earthquake relief supply forecasting relied on empirical and judgment-based methods such as fuzzy comprehensive evaluation, analytic hierarchy processes, and domino effect analysis. However, these traditional methods often fall short in large-scale, high-casualty scenarios. With advancements in artificial intelligence, big data, and machine learning, researchers have proposed a range of predictive models. These models typically fall into two categories.

The first is the direct prediction method, which establishes a demand forecasting model directly based on disaster-related impact factors or historical case data. For example, Xia (2010), Zhao (2011), Liu *et al.* (2013), and Zeng *et al.* (2015) applied multiple regression, support vector machines (SVM), and backpropagation (BP) neural networks, respectively, to forecast tent demand. Similarly, Chao and Wang (2015), Guo (2017), Mohammadi *et al.* (2014), Zhu *et al.* (2020), Pinthong (2022), and Miyauchi (2023) employed methods such as case-based reasoning (CBR), time-series models, genetic algorithm-adaptive particle swarm optimization-radial basis function neural networks (GA-APSO-RBF), and convolutional neural networks (CNN) to predict demand for medical equipment, engineering vehicles, and daily necessities after earthquakes. However, the accuracy of direct prediction methods is limited by the selection of impact factors and the availability of case data, and the resulting models often focus on a single type of

1. National Institute of Natural Hazards, Ministry of Emergency Management of the People's Republic of China, Beijing, China, https://orcid.org/0000-0002-4055-6973 (ZX)

*Corresponding author: 3377242@qq.com

supply. The second is the indirect prediction method, which first forecasts intermediate variables such as casualties, and then estimates supply demand based on the quantitative relationship between casualties and emergency supplies. For instance, Aghamohammadi *et al.* (2013), Li *et al.* (2013), Liu (2015), Xi and Zhao (2015), Hu *et al.* (2019), Fan (2020), Chang *et al.* (2022), Geng and Hou (2023), and Sun (2023) predicted earthquake casualties or casualty rates using models such as the metabolism-based GM(1,1), particle swarm optimization-backpropagation neural networks (PSO-BP) neural networks, and grey Markov chain models, and then inferred demand for medical and basic living supplies.

Although these methods improve the scientific rigor of prediction to some extent, most existing studies focus primarily on conventional supplies (e.g., tents, water, food, and medicines) and rarely consider regional differences. In particular, systematic modeling of emergency supplies specific to high-altitude regions remains scarce. This gap is especially evident in western China's plateau regions, such as the Qinghai–Tibet plateau and its eastern margins, where tectonic collisions are complex, topographic relief is extreme, and strong earthquakes occur frequently with large-scale destruction. Statistics show that since 1900, numerous earthquakes above magnitude 6 have struck this region, with the Longmenshan, Xianshuihe, and Bayan Har faults being seismically active zones (Wang *et al.*, 2001; Deng *et al.*, 2014). Postearthquake challenges in plateau regions—such as transportation blockages, communication failures, and difficulties in material delivery—pose higher requirements for timeliness and precision in emergency response and material supply systems. Moreover, residents' unique physiological needs in high-altitude environments make the structure and types of emergency supplies significantly different from those in lowland regions. However, most existing supply demand models do not specifically address plateau conditions, which greatly limits their applicability in high-altitude earthquake relief.

In response, this study proposes a hybrid prediction model that integrates CBR with a radial basis function (RBF) neural network. The model first predicts earthquake casualties (deaths and injuries), and then estimates emergency supply demand accordingly. It is optimized for the specific rescue needs of high-altitude regions, incorporating plateau-specific materials such as portable oxygen equipment and altitude sickness medicines into the prediction framework. Using the 2022 Sichuan Luding earthquake as a case study, the model's applicability and effectiveness in complex terrain and high-altitude environments are demonstrated. Furthermore, a graphical user interface (GUI) was developed to enhance usability and operability.

Data

Definitions of factors affecting casualty numbers

In indirect emergency supply demand forecasting, casualty prediction is a crucial step for determining supply needs and selecting the right factors for casualty estimation is fundamental for achieving accurate earthquake casualty forecasting. Earthquake casualties are the result of a complex interplay of multiple factors. Including too many factors can cause information overlap, making it difficult for neural networks to converge. In this study, we selected six representative parameters that are relatively complete and easy to obtain based on historical data and the principles of data availability. These factors include the earthquake magnitude, seismic intensity, seismic fortification intensity, population density, house damage level, and the affected population.

The earthquake magnitude is a measure of the seismic energy released during an earthquake. The energy released can help estimate the extent of the affected area, which in turn influences the number of casualties. The data used in this study are based on the surface-wave magnitude (M_s).

The seismic intensity is a measure of the level of destruction caused by the earthquake to the surface and building structures in a specific region. According to China's seismic intensity classification standards, in this study, the seismic intensity was divided into 12 levels.

The seismic fortification intensity refers to the seismic intensity used in local earthquake-resistant building design codes. The fortification intensity directly affects the resilience of buildings in the region and consequently the number of casualties. The information on the seismic fortification intensity used in this study was derived from China's building seismic design standards.

The population density is an estimate of the population density in the earthquake-affected areas based on national statistics. Generally, areas with higher population densities are likely to experience higher casualty rates during an earthquake. The population density for the year of the disaster can be obtained from the national statistical yearbook.

The house damage level refers to the numbers of houses that have been completely destroyed, severely damaged, and moderately damaged. This factor directly affects the number of casualties as building collapses are one of the leading causes of death and injury during earthquakes.

The affected population represents all the people who have been directly or indirectly affected by the disaster. Generally, this can be estimated by consulting national administrative divisions and population databases.

Data sources

The dataset used in this study consists of 12 earthquakes of magnitude 6.0 or above that occurred in Mainland China between 1976 and 2024, each with relatively comprehensive parameter values and significant numbers of casualties. Because of the limited availability of earthquakes with complete data, some events were included at the county level, resulting in a total of 42 samples. Earthquake source locations, magnitudes, and related parameters were obtained from the

China Earthquake Networks Center (CENC), whereas casualty numbers and house damage data were collected from official postdisaster statistical compilations (Compilation of Seismic Disaster Loss Assessment in Mainland China, 2001–2005; 2006–2010), public postdisaster assessment reports, as well as news reports and academic literature (see Data and Resources). The detailed parameter values are presented in Table 1, and the spatial distributions of the epicenters and sample locations are shown in Figure 1.

Correlation and multicollinearity analysis of variables

We used Python 3.9.13 to preprocess the data and perform feature analysis. First, the six variables were standardized using the "StandardScaler" to obtain Z-scores. Then, a Pearson correlation heatmap was generated to visually display the linear relationships among the variables. As shown in Figure 2, the highest correlation coefficient between any two factors is only 0.59 (between population density and affected population), whereas the rest are all below 0.5, indicating generally weak correlations among the variables. Magnitude shows a weak positive correlation with intensity (0.27) and a negative correlation with seismic fortification intensity (−0.41). House damage is positively correlated with intensity (0.37), suggesting that building vulnerability increases with seismic intensity.

In addition, we used the "variance_inflation_factor" function to calculate the VIF value of each feature to assess multicollinearity among the influencing factors. The results in Table 2 show that all VIF values are well below the commonly used threshold of 5 (the highest being only 2.05), indicating no significant multicollinearity among the variables. Therefore, all variables can be retained for subsequent modeling.

Methodology

CBR can leverage past earthquake data to predict future events, offering an intuitive and easily interpretable reasoning process. However, its accuracy is limited by the availability of historical cases and often declines for new or unseen scenarios. To overcome this, models that automatically capture the relationships between earthquake characteristics and casualties are needed. Machine learning approaches, such as RBF neural networks, BP neural networks, and random forests, can meet this demand. In this study, we compared their predictive performances to identify the most suitable model.

Method description

CBR. CBR is an analogical reasoning method that solves new problems by leveraging past experiences (cases). The working principle of CBR can be summarized in four main steps.

Retrieval: This step involves computing the similarity between the current problem and existing cases in the case database using a certain similarity metric. The most similar case is then retrieved. In this study, the Euclidean distance was used to conduct the similarity measurement. It can be expressed as follows:

$$\text{Distance}(A,B) = \sqrt{\sum_{i=1}^{n}(a_i - b_i)^2}. \quad (1)$$

Reuse: In this step, the solution part of the retrieved case is extracted and used as the initial proposed solution to the current problem. Revision: The differences between the current problem and the retrieved case are analyzed, and the preliminary solution is adjusted according to the specific characteristics of the current problem. Retainment: The current problem and the revised solution are stored as a new case in the case database for future use.

Machine learning methods. Artificial neural network (ANN) is a computational model inspired by biological neural systems, designed to process complex data patterns by simulating the functions of biological neurons. Its basic structure includes at least three layers: an input layer, one or more hidden layers, and an output layer. Common types of ANNs include the BP neural network and the RBF neural network.

BP neural network is a multilayer feedforward network consisting of an input layer, one or more hidden layers, and an output layer. Its learning process involves two stages: forward propagation and error BP. During forward propagation, input signals are transmitted from the input layer to the hidden layer and then to the output layer. During error BP, the network error is propagated backward through the hidden and input layers, and the weights and thresholds are adjusted to minimize the error.

RBF neural network is a feedforward network with three layers: input, hidden, and output. The mapping in an RBF network consists of two parts: a nonlinear transformation from the input layer to the hidden layer, and a linear weighted transformation from the hidden layer to the output layer.

SVM is a supervised learning algorithm. Its core idea is to find an optimal decision boundary (hyperplane) that maximizes the margin between data points of different classes and identifies the support vectors—points lying on the boundary of the maximum margin. When new data are input, the prediction is obtained by computing the weighted sum of kernel function values between the new data and all support vectors.

Random forest (RF) is an ensemble learning algorithm that improves prediction performance by constructing multiple decision trees and aggregating their results. During training, randomness is introduced using bootstrap sampling to select training samples with replacement. Each decision tree is built using the selected samples and feature subsets until stopping criteria are met. For new input data, each tree predicts based on its feature subset, and the final prediction is obtained by averaging the predictions from all trees.

TABLE 1

Data on Magnitude, Seismic Intensity, and Time for the Sample Earthquakes, and Fortification Intensity, Population Density, Damaged Houses, as well as the Casualty Numbers

Sample	Time	Location	Magnitude (M_s)	Intensity	Seismic Fortification Intensity	Affected Population	Population Density	Damaged Houses	Deaths	Injuries
1	28 July 1976 at 03:42 a.m.	Tangshan City, Hebei Province	7.8	XI	VI	544,000	269.6	530,0000	242,769	164,851
2	6 November at 09:03 p.m.	Lancang County, Yunnan Province	7.6	IX	VII	430,944	49	81,161	643	3,585
3	6 November 1988 at 09:03 p.m.	Gengma County, Yunnan Province	7.6	IX	VII	160,278	42	31,253	12	254
4	6 November 1988 at 09:03 p.m.	Cangyuan County, Yunnan Province	7.6	VIII	VI	119,833	49	21,783	75	713
5	19 November 1998 at 07:31 p.m.	Ninglang County, Yunnan Province	6.2	VIII	VII	12,7870	37	17,500	5	208
6	24 February 2003 at 10:03 a.m.	Qiemo-Bachu, Xinjiang Uygur autonomous region	6.8	IX	VIII	510,000	44.74	42,000	268	4,853
7	12 May 2008 at 02:28 p.m.	Wenchuan County, Sichuan Province	8.0	XI	VII	145,600	36	32,749	23,781	34,583
8	12 May 2008 at 02:28 p.m.	Beichuan County, Sichuan Province	8.0	XI	VII	161,000	56	51,623	16,668	26,916
9	12 May 2008 at 02:28 p.m.	Mianzhu City, Sichuan Province	8.0	X	VII	513,579	412	133,800	11,375	37,208
10	12 May 2008 at 02:28 p.m.	Shifang City, Sichuan Province	8.0	X	VII	412,000	499	102,200	6,122	33,075
11	12 May 2008 at 02:28 p.m.	Qingchuan County, Sichuan Province	8.0	X	VII	250,000	78	64,760	4,821	15,789
12	12 May 2008 at 02:28 p.m.	An County, Sichuan Province	8.0	IX	VII	510,000	363	103,953	3,295	88,623
13	12 May 2008 at 02:28 p.m.	Dujiangyan City, Sichuan Province	8.0	IX	VII	597,000	504	69,949	3,231	10,560
14	12 May 2008 at 02:28 p.m.	Pingwu County, Sichuan Province	8.0	IX	VII	187,000	32	74,140	5,661	32,191
15	12 May 2008 at 02:28 p.m.	Pengzhou City, Sichuan Province	8.0	IX	VII	597,000	555	644,000	991	5,775
16	12 May 2008 at 02:28 p.m.	Jiangyou City, Sichuan Province	8.0	VIII	VII	870,000	320	200,000	437	19,278
17	12 May 2008 at 02:28 p.m.	Zitong County, Sichuan Province	8.0	VIII	VI	312,807	21,7	16,517	25	2,489
18	12 May 2008 at 02:28 p.m.	Youxian District, Mianyang City, Sichuan Province	8.0	VIII	VI	450,000	556	112,987	85	482
19	12 May 2008 at 02:28 p.m.	Xiaojin County, Sichuan Province	8.0	VIII	VII	79,982	14	12,888	27	452
20	12 May 2008 at 02:28 p.m.	Fucheng District, Mianyang City, Sichuan Province	8.0	VIII	VI	545,465	1,100	38,298	86	2,038
21	12 May 2008 at 02:28 p.m.	Luojiang District, Mianyang City, Sichuan Province	8.0	VIII	VI	203,000	546	24,596	19	307
22	12 May 2008 at 02:28 p.m.	Heishui County, Sichuan Province	8.0	VIII	VII	61,984	16	8,517	94	15

(Continued next page.)

TABLE 1 (continued)
Data on Magnitude, Seismic Intensity, and Time for the Sample Earthquakes, and Fortification Intensity, Population Density, Damaged Houses, as well as the Casualty Numbers

Sample	Time	Location	Magnitude (M_s)	Intensity	Seismic Fortification Intensity	Affected Population	Population Density	Damaged Houses	Deaths	Injuries
23	12 May 2008 at 02:28 p.m.	Chongzhou City, Sichuan Province	8.0	VIII	VII	321,600	614	15,020	82	8,775
24	12 May 2008 at 02:28 p.m.	Santai County, Sichuan Province	8.0	VIII	VI	1,427,000	553	88,401	43	887
25	12 May 2008 at 02:28 p.m.	Yanting County, Sichuan Province	8.0	VIII	VI	258,975	366	164,917	15	1,936
26	12 May 2008 at 02:28 p.m.	Zhongjiang County, Sichuan Province	8.0	VIII	VI	1,130,000	691	41,082	24	423
27	12 May 2008 at 02:28 p.m.	Dayi County, Sichuan Province	8.0	VIII	VII	516,000	389	8,142	13	417
28	12 May 2008 at 02:28 p.m.	Ningqiang County, Sichuan Province	8.0	VIII	VI	40,000	105	22,700	11	1,078
29	30 August 2008 at 04:30 p.m.	Huili County, Sichuan Province	6.1	VIII	VII	103,054	101	36,500	30	359
30	30 August 2008 at 04:30 p.m.	Renhe District, Panzhihua City, Sichuan Province	6.1	VIII	VII	130,311	121	7,455	5	145
31	14 April 2010 at 07:49 a.m.	Shiqu County, Qinghai Province	7.1	VI	VII	20,865	4.12	4,173	78	234
32	14 April 2010 at 07:49 a.m.	Dege County, Qinghai Province	7.1	VI	VII	42,300	7.85	94	81	286
33	14 April 2010 at 07:49 a.m.	Baiyu County, Qinghai Province	7.1	VI	VII	820	9.09	209	7	4
34	14 April 2010 at 07:49 a.m.	Ganzi County, Qinghai Province	7.1	IX	VII	246,842	10	192,100	2,698	12,135
35	20 April 2013 at 08:02 a.m.	Lushan County, Sichuan Province	7.0	IX	VII	122,235	102.62	46,550	117	5,537
36	20 April 2013 at 08:02 a.m.	Baoxing County, Sichuan Province	7.0	IX	VII	58,954	18.93	21,479	26	2,500
37	20 April 2013 at 08:02 a.m.	Mingshan District, Ya'an City, Sichuan Province	7.0	IX	VII	155,157	64.9	55,631	5	811
38	20 April 2013 at 08:02 a.m.	Yingjing County, Sichuan Province	7.0	IX	VII	279,903	455.67	90,403	2	607
39	22 July 2013 at 07:45 a.m.	Dingxi City, Gansu Province	6.6	VIII	VII	477,400	122.9	84,300	95	868
40	8 August 2017 at 09:19 p.m.	Jiuzhaigou County, Sichuan Province	7.0	IX	VII	176,429	11	73,671	25	525
41	1 June 2022 at 05:00 p.m.	Lushan County, Sichuan Province	6.1	VIII	VII	13,081	101.18	1,753	4	42
42	18 December 2023 at 11:00 p.m.	Jishishan County, Linxia Hui Autonomous Prefecture, Gansu Province	6.2	VIII	VII	772,000	57.88	148,000	151	983

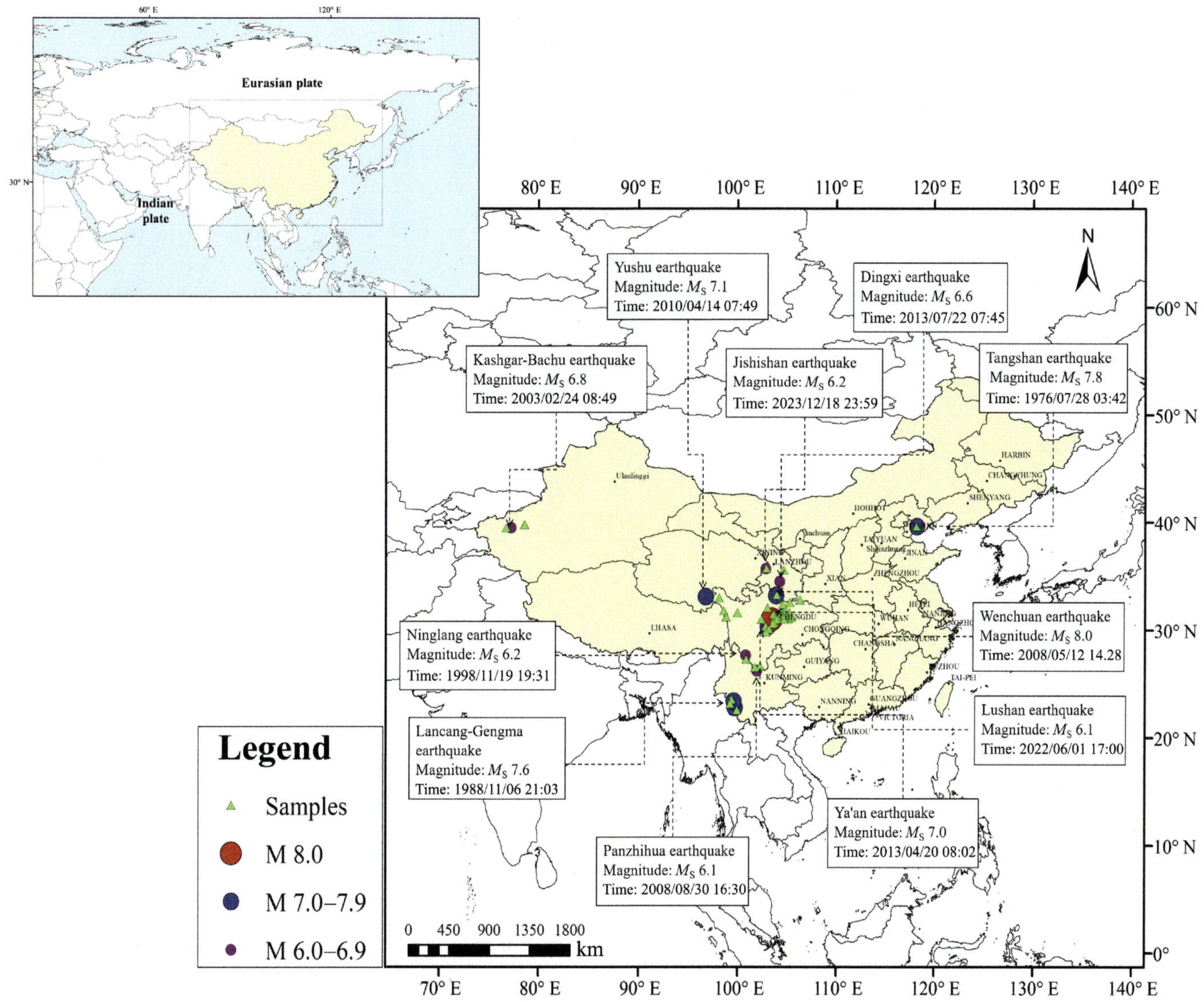

Figure 1. Distribution of epicenters and sample locations.

Performance analysis and comparison of models

To ensure the robustness of the predictions, this study adopted a systematic data preprocessing and modeling workflow. First, the dataset was randomly split into training and testing sets in an 8:2 ratio, with the training set used for model training and hyperparameter optimization, and the testing set for evaluating model generalization performance. During data preprocessing, outliers were first detected and removed based on the Mahalanobis distance, followed by feature selection guided by correlation analysis. For standardization, a robust median absolute deviation (MAD)-based scaling was applied to reduce the influence of outliers.

During model training, BP neural network, RBF neural network, support vector regression, and RF models were constructed. Hyperparameters were optimized using MATLAB's grid search combined with fivefold cross validation. Model performance was comprehensively evaluated using the coefficient of determination (R^2), mean absolute error (MAE), root mean square error (rmse), and the 95% confidence interval of R^2.

The R^2 value measures the proportion of the variance in the target variable that can be explained by the model. The formulae for calculating the R^2value are as follows:

$$R^2 = 1 - \frac{SS_{\text{res}}}{SS_{\text{tot}}}, \tag{2}$$

$$SS_{\text{res}} = \sum_{i=1}^{n} (y_i - \hat{y}_i)^2, \tag{3}$$

$$SS_{\text{tot}} = \sum_{i=1}^{n} (y_i - \bar{y})^2. \tag{4}$$

The R^2 value quantifies the proportion of variance in the target variable that the model can explain, with values ranging from 0

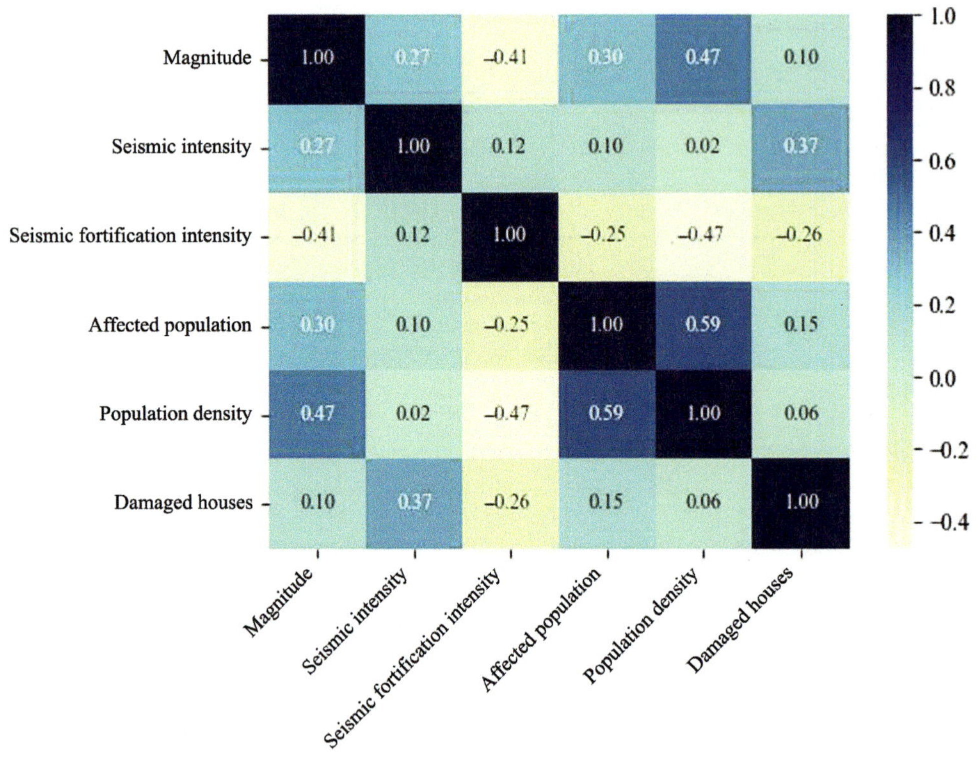

Figure 2. Correlation heatmap.

to 1. A higher R^2 indicates a better model fit and stronger explanatory power for the variance in the dependent variable. As shown in Figure 3, the RBF neural network demonstrated the best performance in predicting deaths, achieving an R^2 of 0.6812. This value indicates that ~68% of the variance in death numbers can be explained by the model, which is substantially higher than the BP neural network ($R^2 = 0.4921$), SVM ($R^2 = 0.5581$), and RF ($R^2 = 0.5842$). For injury prediction, the RBF model again achieved the highest R^2 of 0.5823, indicating a better ability to capture the underlying patterns in the injury data compared to the other models.

The MAE is a commonly used metric that measures the average absolute difference between predicted and actual values. It is calculated as follows:

$$\mathrm{MAE} = \frac{1}{n}\sum_{i=1}^{n}(y_i - \hat{y}_i). \quad (5)$$

The rmse is another error metric that reflects the magnitude of the difference between the predicted and actual values. It is calculated by taking the square root of the average of the squared differences:

$$\mathrm{Rmse} = \sqrt{\frac{1}{n}\sum_{i=1}^{n}(y_i - \hat{y}_i)^2}. \quad (6)$$

Lower MAE and rmse values indicate smaller differences between the predictions and actual outcomes, implying a higher model accuracy. In terms of prediction errors, the RBF model had an MAE of 0.5116 and rmse of 0.7581 for death prediction, and an MAE of 0.5746 and rmse of 0.9275 for injury prediction, all lower than the other three algorithms.

Although the RBF model showed the best predictive accuracy, its 95% confidence intervals were relatively wide (death prediction: [0.4690, 0.8935]; injury prediction: [0.3356, 0.8290]), indicating some prediction uncertainty. Nevertheless, considering overall accuracy, the RBF neural network outperformed the other three models. The BP neural network performed the worst, whereas SVM and RF showed intermediate performance between BP and RBF. Therefore, the RBF neural network was selected as the method for the integrated prediction approach.

TABLE 2
Variance Inflation Factors (VIF) of Influencing Factors

Feature	VIF
Population density	2.045329
Seismic fortification intensity	1.698588
Magnitude	1.596495
Affected population	1.582847
Seismic intensity	1.463978
House damage level	1.372123

Integration of RBF neural network and CBR method

Based on the model comparison in the previous section, we integrated the RBF neural network with the CBR method. In the integration process, the role of case similarity is first considered. When similarity is high, the current earthquake scenario closely matches historical cases in the case base, and CBR can effectively leverage past experience to produce more reliable predictions, thus deserving a higher weight. Conversely, when similarity is low, the current scenario differs significantly from historical cases, reducing the applicability of CBR, and the strong generalization ability of the RBF neural network should be relied upon, thereby increasing its weight.

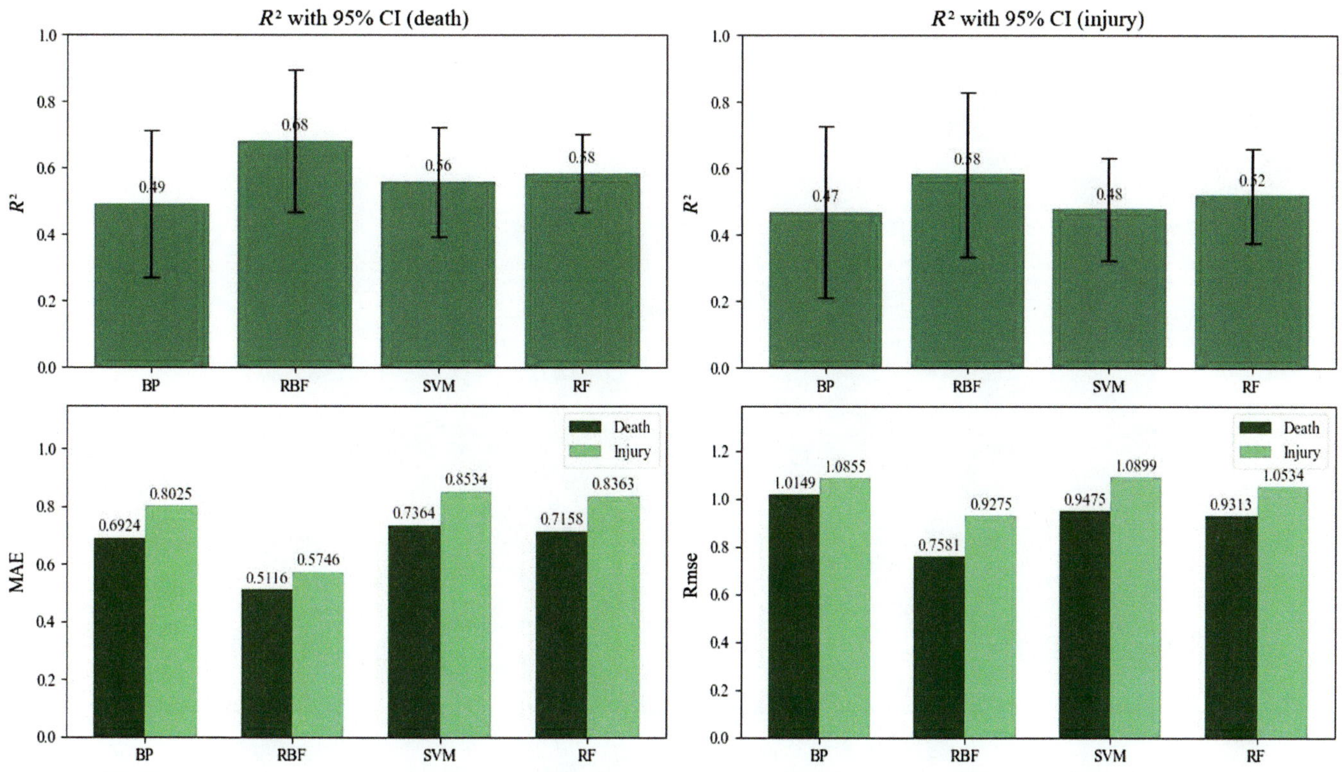

Figure 3. Predictive performance metrics for each model. BP, backpropagation; CI, confidence interval; MAE, mean absolute error; RBF, radial basis function; RF, random forest; Rmse, root mean square error; SVM, support vector machines.

To achieve this dynamic weighting, a Sigmoid function is used to map case similarity to the CBR weight, whereas the RBF weight is defined complementarily, enabling the integration of CBR and RBF:

$$\omega_{\mathrm{CBR}}(S) = \frac{1}{1 + e^{-a(S-b)}} \qquad \omega_{\mathrm{RBF}} = 1 - \omega_{\mathrm{CBR}}. \tag{7}$$

Where parameter a controls the steepness of the weight change, parameter b determines the center point of the weight transition, and S represents the case similarity.

During the training stage, the data were split into training and validation sets in an 8:2 ratio. The RBF neural network parameters were trained on the training set, and the CBR case base was constructed. In the validation set, the similarity S between each sample and the case base was calculated, and the RBF prediction was obtained. The objective function was defined as the minimization of the MSE on the validation set:

$$L(a,b) = \frac{1}{N}\sum_{i=1}^{N}(y_i - \hat{y}_i(a,b))^2. \tag{8}$$

Here, N is the number of samples in the validation set, y_i is the true value of the ith sample, and $\hat{y}_i(a,b)$ is the integrated prediction based on parameters a and b. Through grid search, the optimal parameter combination was found to be $a = 1$ and $b = 0.3$. This dynamic weighting strategy fully leverages the experiential advantage of CBR in high-similarity scenarios and the generalization advantage of the RBF neural network in low-similarity scenarios, thereby improving the overall accuracy and adaptability of casualty predictions under earthquake scenarios. The flowchart of the integration method is shown in Figure 4.

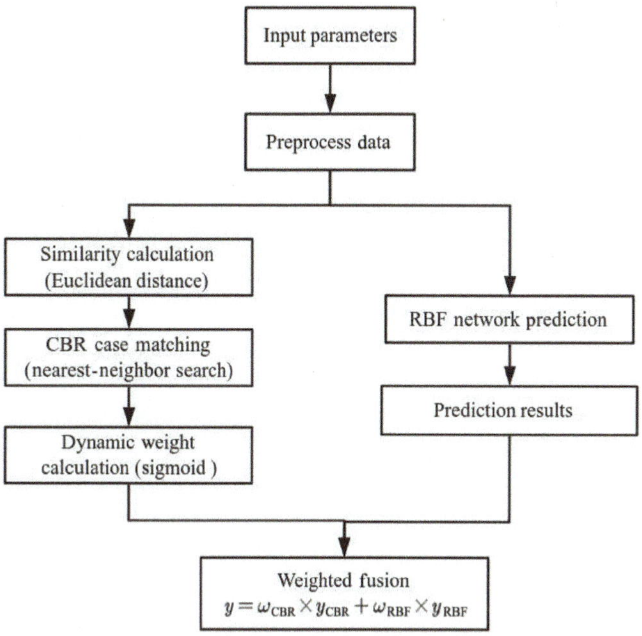

Figure 4. Flowchart of CBR–RBF neural network integration. CBR, case-based reasoning.

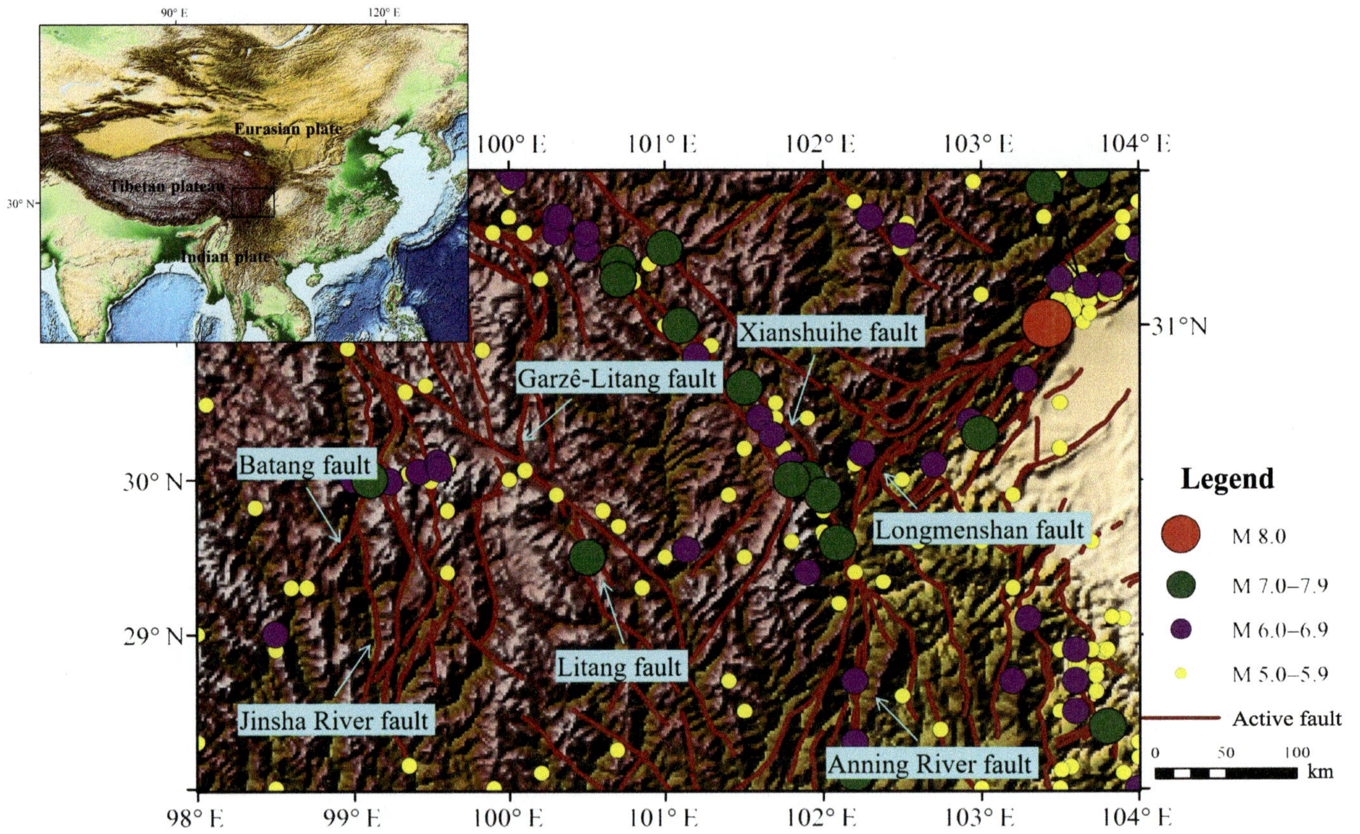

Figure 5. Major faults and the distribution of the earthquakes within the study area.

Model Application in Western Sichuan

Tectonic background and geological features of western Sichuan

The Western Sichuan region (28–32° N, 98–104° E) is located on the eastern edge of the Qinghai–Tibet plateau, where three major tectonic blocks, namely, the Sichuan–Yunnan, Bayan Har, and South China blocks, converge. This region is characterized by prominent neotectonic activity, numerous active high-slip-rate faults, and frequent destructive earthquakes by Xu *et al.* (2005).

Several groups of active seismogenic faults are well developed in western Sichuan. The main ones include the northwest–southeast-oriented (~N45° W) Xianshuihe fault zone, the nearly north–south-oriented (N–S) Jinshajiang fault zone, and the northeast–southwest-oriented (~N45°E) Longmenshan fault zone.

The Xianshuihe fault zone consists of secondary faults such as the Luhuo fault, Daofu fault, and Qianning fault and extends for a distance of ~300 km. It is primarily characterized by left-lateral strike-slip motion and plays a dominant role in controlling seismic activity across the western Sichuan plateau. Historically, it has generated multiple major earthquakes, including the 1973 M_s 7.6 Luhuo earthquake.

The Jinshajiang fault zone is an active fault system that has been active since the Cenozoic. It includes parallel faults such as the Jinshajiang Main fault and Batang fault, which have experienced multiple phases of activity from the Cenozoic to the Holocene. This zone is dominated by right-lateral strike-slip motion and forms a significant boundary between the Sichuan–Yunnan block and the South China block.

The Longmenshan fault zone comprises three main faults: the Houshan fault, the Central fault, and the Qianshan fault. It primarily features thrusting motion and is the frontal fault zone of the eastward extrusion of the Qinghai–Tibet plateau. It was responsible for the 2008 M_s 8.0 Wenchuan earthquake.

Because of the influence of these active fault systems, earthquakes are frequent in western Sichuan. Because the earliest recorded destructive earthquake in 23 B.C.E., the study area has experienced a total of 156 earthquakes with magnitudes of M_s 5.0–5.9, 44 earthquakes with magnitudes of M_s 6.0–6.9, 16 earthquakes with magnitudes of M_s 7.0–7.9, and one earthquake with a magnitude of M_s 8.0. The spatial distribution of these events is shown in Figure 5.

In addition to tectonic activity, the region's geological structure is highly complex and exhibits distinct regional characteristics. Western Sichuan is located in the transitional zone between the northern Hengduan Mountains and the Sichuan basin, and it has a general topographic gradient sloping from north to south. Based on the elevation, river incision depth, and surface morphology, the region can be divided into three terrain types: plateau hills, alpine plains, and alpine gorges Qin *et al.* (2021). The area is also rich in river systems, and major rivers such as the Jinsha River, Yalong River, and Dadu River flow from west to east. The region is subject to intense glacial and fluvial geological processes. Neotectonic movement and plateau uplift make the region prone to secondary geological hazards such as landslides, collapses, debris flows, and earthquakes. The complex terrain and geological conditions pose significant challenges for postearthquake emergency rescue and relief efforts.

Characteristics of emergency supply demand in western Sichuan

The emergency supply demand is inherently uncertain, diverse, and dynamic. Because the timing, location, magnitude, and damage extent of earthquakes are difficult to predict accurately, the types of required emergency supplies are highly variable, and the quantities are often uncertain. In the early stages of an earthquake, due to limited access to information, supply needs must be dynamically adjusted in response to the evolving disaster situation. In addition, the importance of different types of emergency supplies varies depending on the phase of the disaster response.

In western Sichuan, the complexity of the terrain and geological conditions adds unique challenges to emergency supply demand. Many parts of the region are high-altitude mountainous areas with weak transportation infrastructure, making the delivery and distribution of emergency supplies extremely difficult and inefficient. Therefore, it is necessary to reserve portable, lightweight, and easy-to-transport materials for such areas. Moreover, due to the cold climate and low oxygen concentration at high altitudes, emergency supplies must be adapted to plateau environments. These supplies include specialized medical equipment for high-altitude use, oxygen cylinders, thermal supplies, and medications for altitude sickness.

According to China's classification standards for emergency supplies (GB/T 38565-2020, 2020), supplies are categorized into three types: basic life support supplies, emergency equipment and associated supplies, and engineering materials and mechanical processing equipment. Standards like Chinese earthquake intensity scale (national standard; GB/T 17742-2020, 2020; specifications for the construction of emergency material storage depots, DB42/T 2151-2023, 2023) provide per capita benchmarks for daily-use supplies, whereas high-altitude or oxygen-deficient environment specifications are found in the Code for Earthquake Emergency Response (GB/T 38565-2020, 2020). In this study, the specific per capita demand for basic life support supplies includes 0.25 tents, 4 L of drinking water, 250 g of compressed biscuits, 0.01 emergency lights, 0.075 g of water purification tablets, 0.25 g of antialtitude sickness medicine, 1 cotton jacket, 0.1 oxygen cylinders, and 0.05 portable oxygen generators.

Case study

To illustrate the application of the model, we analyzed the emergency supply demand following the magnitude 6.8 earthquake in Luding County, Ganzi Tibetan Autonomous Prefecture, Sichuan Province, at 12:52 p.m. on 5 September 2022. The two areas with the greatest casualties, that is, Luding County in Ganzi Prefecture and Shimian County in Ya'an City, were selected for analysis using our newly developed earthquake casualty prediction model based on a combination of CBR and RBF neural networks, along with the emergency supply demand estimation formula.

We begin by discussing the model input parameters. According to Figure 6, that is, the seismic intensity map of the Luding earthquake, the maximum observed intensity reached IX (9) on the Chinese seismic intensity scale. Therefore, the seismic intensity input for the model was set to IX. Regarding the seismic fortification intensity, we referred to the Seismic Ground-Motion Parameter Zonation Map of China and relevant national standards. Before the earthquake, both Luding County and Shimian County had a seismic fortification intensity rating of VIII.

Because it is difficult to obtain the number of collapsed houses and affected population in the early stage of an earthquake, we estimated these values based on the resident population and registered households at the time. According to the 2021 Statistical Bulletin of National Economic and Social Development of Luding County, there were 27,788 registered households and a total population of 86,234 at year-end. According to the 2021 Ya'an Statistical Yearbook, Shimian County had 39,891 households and a resident population of 120,383. Luding County comprises nine towns, with a population density of ~39 persons/km^2, whereas Shimian County has a population density of about 32 persons/km^2. Because areas with seismic intensity VI or higher almost entirely cover Luding and Shimian counties, the total resident population was used as the affected population input.

The number of collapsed houses was estimated by treating the total number of households in the region as the total number of houses, and then applying the building vulnerability matrix and seismic fortification intensity. The formula is as follows:

$$N = H \times \sum_{j} (p_j \times r_j(I,F)), \quad (9)$$

in which H is the total number of houses in the area, p_j is the proportion of building type j, and $r_j(I,F)$ is the collapse rate of building type j under seismic intensity I and fortification level F. Using this method, ~2507 houses collapsed in Luding County and 2130 houses in Shimian County.

The influencing factors of each county were input into the trained model to predict casualty numbers. The results show that the predicted deaths were 84 in Luding County (actual: 55) and 84 in Shimian County (actual: 38). For injuries, the predictions were 900 in Luding County (actual: 170) and 906 in Shimian County (actual: 78). Although there is some deviation

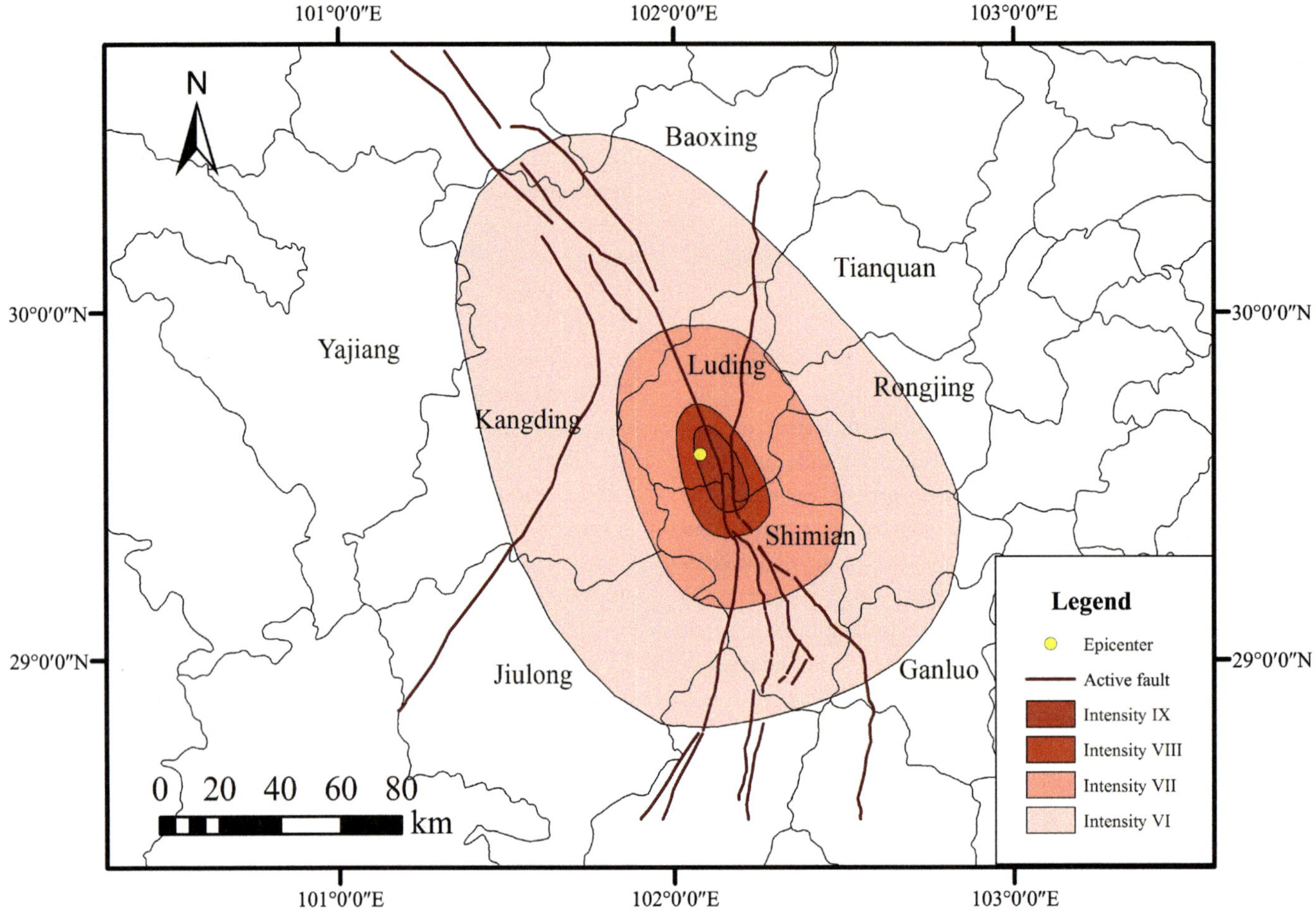

Figure 6. Intensity map of the 6.8 earthquake in Sichuan Luding.

from the observed values, the predictions are generally consistent in terms of order of magnitude.

It should be noted that earthquake casualties are determined by multiple factors, including building vulnerability, population exposure, and rescue efficiency. Their complexity leads to considerable uncertainty in predictions. Numerous studies, both in China and internationally, indicate that even advanced models such as the U.S. Geological Survey (USGS) PAGER system or the China Earthquake Administration's rapid postdisaster reporting system can only ensure reliability at the order-of-magnitude level shortly after an earthquake, and cannot provide precise numerical values. Therefore, the model predictions in this study, being consistent in order of magnitude with the actual situation, are sufficient to support rapid postearthquake response. For emergency supply demand, knowing the order of magnitude of casualties is enough to guide decisions on supply storage and allocation, ensuring the practical value of the prediction method.

The overestimation of injury numbers may be attributed to two main factors: first, differences in statistical criteria, because the predictions may include minor injuries, whereas actual statistics often count only more severe cases; second, secondary disasters in this earthquake were mainly small- to medium-scale, high-altitude landslides that were relatively concentrated, causing limited impact on densely populated areas and thus lower actual casualties. In the future, the model can be further improved through methods such as ensemble calibration.

Based on these casualty predictions and their correspondence with specific emergency supplies, we further predicted the supply demand. The detailed quantities of materials are listed in Table 3.

Packaging of the Model

In this study, the RBF–CBR adaptive fusion prediction model was developed using Python. The trained model is saved in .pkl format. In the event of an earthquake, users only need to load the trained fusion model and input the earthquake feature parameters to quickly predict casualties and emergency supply demand. However, requiring emergency responders to have programming skills is impractical. Therefore, a GUI was built using Python's Tkinter, which directly calls the casualty prediction and emergency resource calculation functions, enabling real-time display of prediction results and automatic computation of supply demand.

Figure 7 shows the user interface of the earthquake casualty prediction and emergency supply demand system. The interface adopts a two-column layout: the left column is the parameter

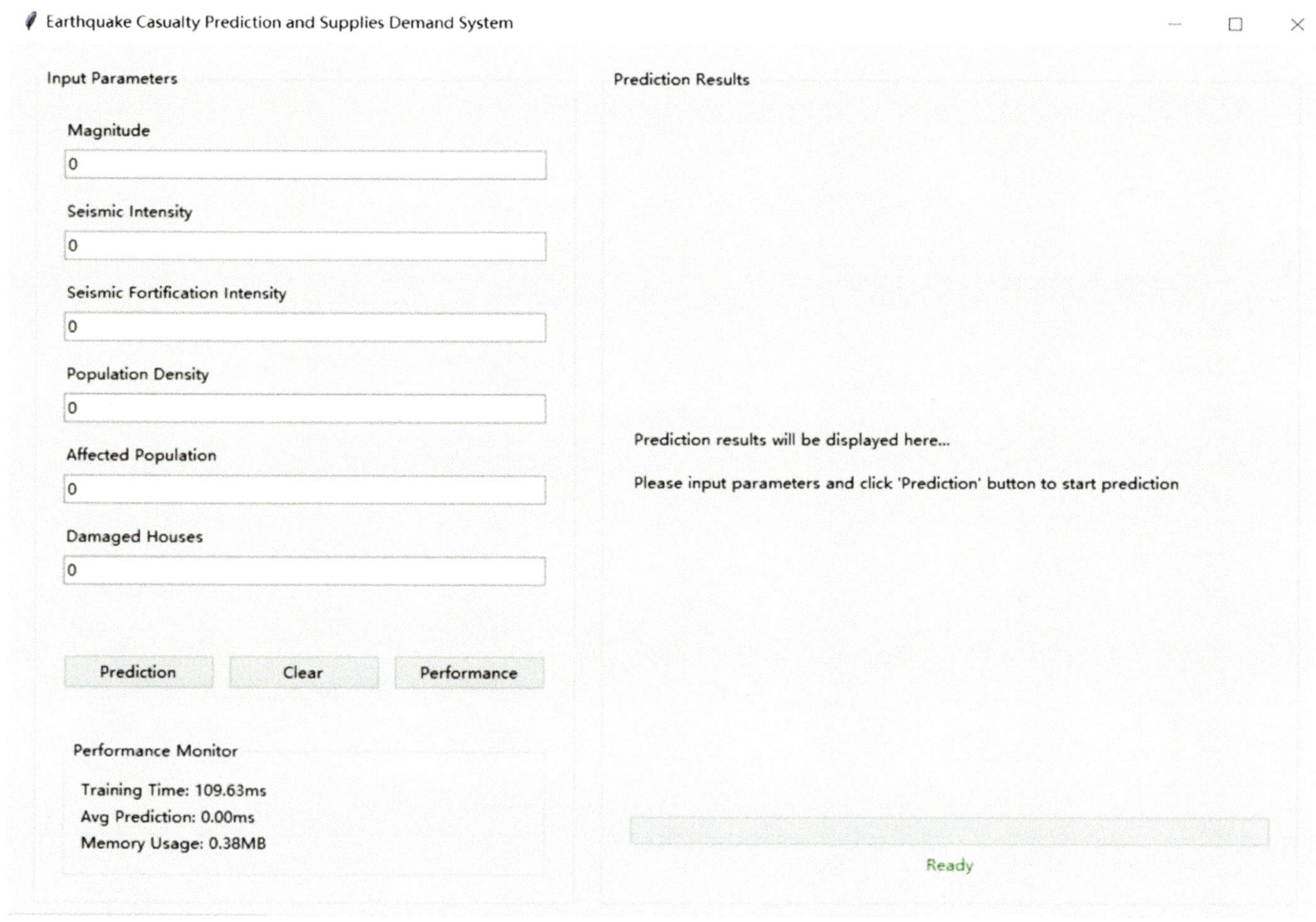

Figure 7. User interface for emergency resources demand prediction software.

input area with buttons for prediction, clearing, and performance viewing, whereas the right column displays prediction results, including casualty numbers and detailed emergency supply requirements. The system also integrates a real-time performance monitoring panel, showing key metrics such as model training time, average prediction time, and memory usage.

For demonstration, we used Shimian County as an example. After entering the six key earthquake parameters (magnitude, intensity, fortification intensity, population density, affected population, and collapsed houses) in the input area, the user clicks the "Prediction" button, as shown in Figure 8a. The system performs the prediction based on the input data; when the progress bar turns fully green and displays "complete" the prediction is finished, and the right column shows the predicted potential casualties and the detailed quantities of nine categories of emergency supplies, as illustrated in Figure 8b. Clicking the "Performance" button outputs key performance metrics. For the prediction of Shimian County, the model training time was 100.02 ms, average prediction time 1 ms, and memory usage 0.42 MB, as shown in Figure 8c.

With this software system, emergency responders can quickly predict casualties and emergency supply needs based

TABLE 3
Model's Predictions for the Emergency Material Demand in Luding County, Ganzi Prefecture, and Shimian County, Ya'an City

County	Tents (Units)	Drinking Water (L)	Compressed Biscuits (kg)	Water Purification Tablets (g)	Antialtitude Sickness Medicine (g)	Cotton Jackets (Pieces)	Oxygen Cylinders (Units)	Portable Oxygen Generators (Units)	Emergency Lights (Units)
Luding County	21,538	344,602	215,37.6	6,462	21,538	8,616	8,616	4,308	862
Shimian County	30,075	481,196	300,74.7	9,023	30,075	12,030	12,030	6,015	1,203

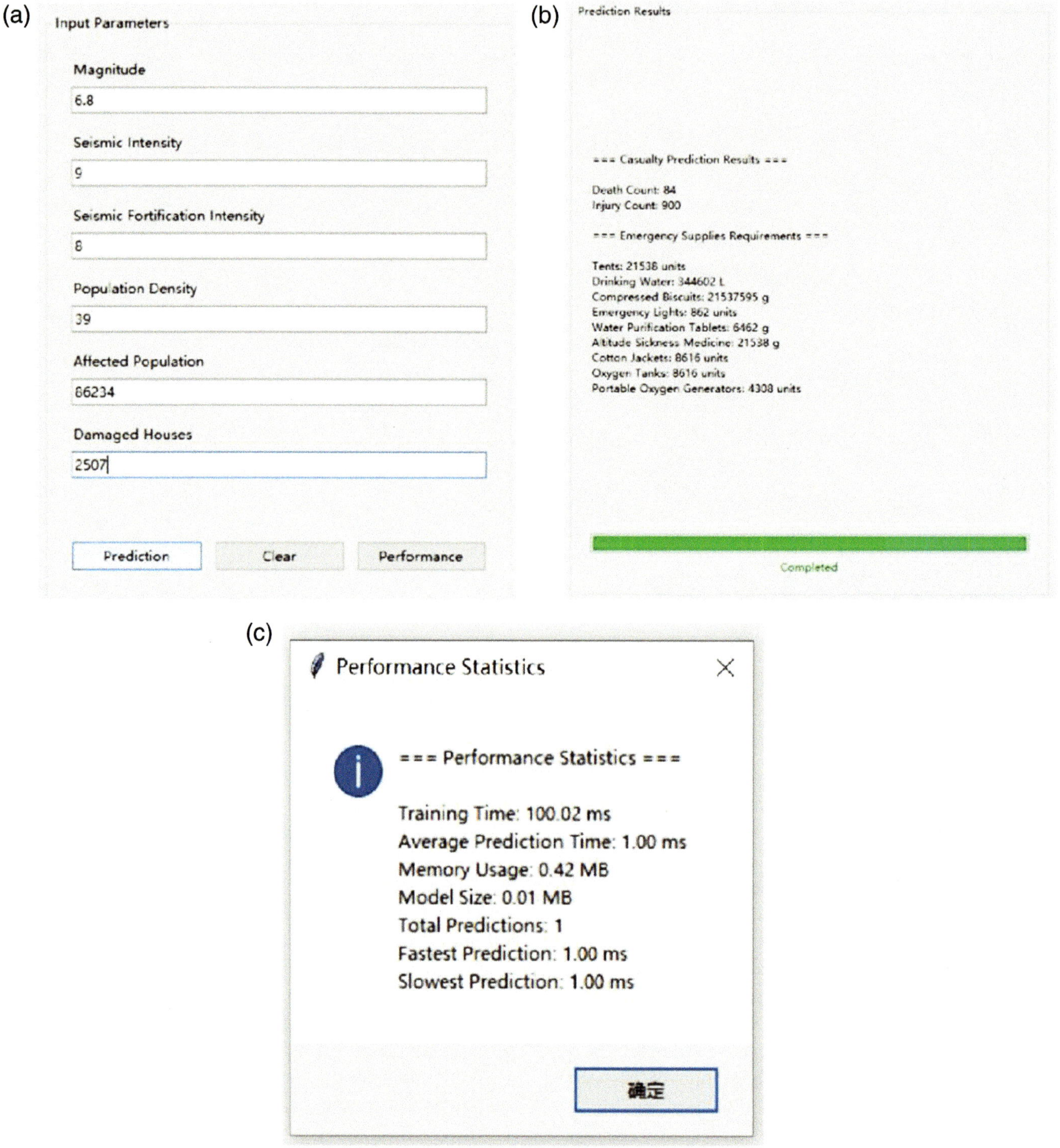

Figure 8. User interface function Display.

on incident parameters without any programming skills, lowering the barrier to model use. Furthermore, by converting the prediction model to TensorFlow Lite or ONNX format, it can be integrated into mobile applications for cross-platform deployment.

Conclusions

The main findings and contributions of this study are as follows:

1. Methodological integration: We proposed an earthquake emergency supply demand prediction method that integrates RBF neural networks with CBR, establishing the link between earthquake features, casualty numbers, and supply demand. This enables rapid inference from disaster characteristics to

required quantities, providing a new technical approach for emergency decision-making.
2. Regional adaptation innovation: By considering the unique geological and material demand characteristics of the western Sichuan plateau, the model can reasonably predict some supply needs in high-altitude areas, offering a reference for emergency supply planning in similarly complex terrains.
3. Practical tool development: A GUI was developed using Python Tkinter, allowing nontechnical personnel to use the prediction model easily, enhancing its practicality and potential for wider adoption.

Although this study can rapidly predict certain emergency supply demands after an earthquake, all predictive models inherently carry uncertainty and error. The accuracy of the RBF neural network depends on the quality, diversity, and comprehensiveness of the training samples, as well as its generalization capability across historical earthquake events. In real-world scenarios, due to the complexity and variability of earthquakes, prediction errors may still occur, particularly in estimating injury numbers. Moreover, the current study is based on a dataset of only 42 samples, which may further constrain the model's generalization to other high-altitude earthquake scenarios.

Future research could focus on several directions to enhance model performance and applicability:

1. Distinguishing the feature factors required for predicting deaths versus injuries, and developing multipath prediction models to improve accuracy. Injury numbers could be further classified into minor, moderate, and severe categories, enabling more targeted allocation of different types of emergency materials.
2. Continuously expanding the case database and introducing a dynamic updating mechanism to improve the model's adaptability in real disaster scenarios. Data augmentation techniques, such as generating synthetic cases based on scenario simulations, and transfer learning approaches, including pretraining models on larger datasets from nonhigh-altitude earthquakes and fine-tuning them for plateau regions, could be employed to mitigate the limitations of small sample sizes.
3. At the application level, integrating the model with national and local disaster emergency management systems (e.g., the Ministry of Emergency Management or local earthquake emergency command centers) can serve as a decision-support tool for real-time emergency dispatch. Methods such as transfer learning, domain adaptation, and federated learning could also be explored to further improve the model's generalization under data-limited conditions and for cross-regional applications.

Overall, this study provides a novel and practical approach for predicting emergency supply demand following earthquakes, offering scientific support for policymakers and emergency management agencies in disaster preparedness and rapid response, with strong practical significance and potential for broader application.

Data and Resources

2008 Sichuan Yearbook is available at http://tjj.sc.gov.cn/tjnj/cs/2008/chinese/dir/chinesemenu.htm. 2010 Qinghai Statistical Yearbook is available at http://tjj.qinghai.gov.cn/nj/2010/lefte.htm. 2013 Ya'an Yearbook is available at https://tjj.yaan.gov.cn/xinwen/show/61cd8ad2-eb3d-4ce3-9054-28735dba441d.html. The data to China Earthquake Networks Center are available at http://data.earthquake.cn/. Yushu Earthquake Post-Disaster Reconstruction Baseline Assessment Report is available at https://www.docin.com/p-124660550.html. Some Chinese dissertations (e.g., Guo, 2012) are only available in the CNKI Dissertations Database and do not have a registered DOI. Therefore, we provide complete bibliographic information (author, title, university, year, and database source) to ensure traceability. China Earthquake Administration, Division of Earthquake Disaster Emergency Rescue. Compilation of Earthquake Disaster Loss Assessment in Mainland China (2001–2005) [M]. Beijing: Seismological Press, 2010. China Earthquake Administration, Division of Earthquake Disaster Emergency Rescue. Compilation of Earthquake Disaster Loss Assessment in Mainland China (2006–2010) [M]. Beijing: Seismological Press, 2015. Guo Jinfeng. Research on Emergency Supplies Demand Forecasting Method for Large-Scale Earthquakes [D]. Tianjin: Tianjin University, 2012. Available from CNKI Dissertations Database. The code, graphical user interface (GUI), and dataset used in this study have been uploaded to Zenodo and are publicly accessible via doi: 10.5281/zenodo.16945538. Access to the trained model and GUI is provided to enhance transparency and reproducibility. All websites were last accessed in May 2025.

Declaration of Competing Interests

The authors acknowledge that there are no conflicts of interest recorded.

Acknowledgments

The authors are grateful to the Seismological Press for providing the data. This research was sponsored by research grants from National Institute of Natural Hazards, Ministry of Emergency Management of China (Grant Number: ZDJ2025-36) and the National Key Research and Development Program of China (2017YFC1500400).

References

Aghamohammadi, H., M. S. Mesgari, A. Mansourian, and D. Molaei (2013). Seismic human loss estimation for an earthquake disaster using neural network, *Int. J. Environ. Sci. Technol.* **10,** no. 5, 931–939.

Chang, D., Y. Wang, and R. Fan (2022). Forecast of large earthquake emergency supplies demand based on PSO-BP neural network, *Tehnički Vjesnik* **29,** no. 2, 561–571.

Chao, Y., and Q. R. Wang (2015). Emergency material demand prediction based on fuzzy rough set case-based reasoning, *Trans. Sci. Technol. Econ.* **17,** no. 5, 1–4.

DB42/T 2151-2023 (2023). Specifications for the construction of emergency material storage depots, Hubei Province Market Supervision Administration.

Deng, Q., S. Cheng, J. Ma, and P. Du (2014). Seismic activities and earthquake potential in the Tibetan Plateau, *Chin. J. Geophys.* **57,** no. 5, 678–697.

Fan, R. (2020). Research on large-scale earthquake emergency material demand forecasting based on PSO-BP neural network, Beijing Jiaotong University, doi: 10.26944/d.cnki.gbfju.2020.001371.

GB/T 17742-2020 (2020). Chinese earthquake intensity scale (national standard), General Administration of Quality Supervision, Inspection and Quarantine of the People's Republic of China, Beijing, China.

Geng, S., and H. Hou (2021). Demand stratification and prediction of evacuees after earthquakes, *Sustainability* **13,** no. 16, 8837.

Guo, J. F. (2012). *Research on Emergency Material Demand Forecasting Methods for Large Earthquakes*, Tianjin University, Tianjin, China.

Guo, X. M. (2017). *Research on Emergency Material Demand Forecasting Based on Case-Based Reasoning*, Lanzhou Jiaotong University, Lanzhou, China.

Hu, Z. J., Y. Q. Liu, and J. Li (2019). Dynamic demand forecasting of flood disaster emergency materials based on improved GM(1,1), *J. Sys. Simul.* **31,** no. 4, 702–709, doi: 10.16182/j.issn1004731x.-joss.17-0112.

Jaiswal, K. S., and D. J. Wald (2020). Global occurrence models for human and economic losses due to earthquakes (1967–2018) considering exposed GDP and population, *Nat. Hazards* **102,** no. 3, 1231–1254.

Li, L. L., J. Zhang, and B. Zeng (2013). Large-scale earthquake emergency rescue material demand prediction based on metabolism GM(1,1) model, *World Sci. Technol. Res. Develop.* **35,** no. 3, 430–433, 442.

Liu, D. Y., C. F. Zhu, and W. Ding (2013). Research on emergency material demand forecasting method based on similar case reasoning, *J. Lanzhou Jiaotong Univ.* **32,** no. 4, 119–123.

Liu, Z. (2015). *Research on Disaster Relief Material Demand Simulation and Scheduling*, Beijing University of Posts and Telecommunications, Beijing, China.

Miyauchi, T. (2023). Bipartite graph convolutional network for emergency medical resource demand prediction, *IEEE Transact. Medical Inf.* **21,** no. 4, 567–579.

Mohammadi, R., S. Ghomi, and F. Zeinali (2014). A new hybrid evolutionary based RBF networks method for forecasting time series: A case study of forecasting emergency supply demand time series, *Eng. Appl. Artif. Int.* **36,** 204–214.

Pinthong, N. (2022). Air ambulance resource prediction using random forest, *J. Emerg. Med. Serv.* **45,** no. 3, 123–135.

Qin, Y. L., J. L. Wu, H. Y. Zhan, C. L. Xiong, C. Jia, X. Z. Bai, M. Z. Li, W. H. Wu, and Y. F. Xu (2021). Discussion on the correlation between active faults and geological disaster distribution in the Ganzi area, western Sichuan province, China, *Seismol. Geol. Stud.* **27,** no. 3, doi: 10.12090/j.issn.1006-6616.2021.27.03.042.

Standardization Administration of China. GB/T 38565-2020 (2020). *Code for Earthquake Emergency Response[S]*, Standards Press of China, Beijing, China.

Sun, S. X. (2023). Research on emergency material demand prediction for major earthquake disasters, Disaster Prevention Technology Institute, doi: 10.27899/d.cnki.gfzkj.2023.000035.

Wang, Q., P. Zhang, J. T. Freymueller, R. Bilham, K. M. Larson, X. Lai, Z. Wang, W. Fan, Z. Liu, Z. Ge, *et al.* (2001). Regional earthquakes in northern Tibetan plateau: Implications for lithospheric strength in Tibet, *Geophys. Res. Lett.* **28,** no. 22, 4387–4390, doi: 10.1029/2001GL013014.

Xi, C., and L. Zhao (2015). Demand forecast of emergency supplies based on grey model, *Int. Conf. on Advances in Mechanical Engineering and Industrial Informatics*, Wuhan, China, University of Geosciences, 1357–1361.

Xia, P. (2010). *Research on Emergency Material Allocation Problem Based on Demand Analysis in Disaster Emergency Logistics*, Beijing Jiaotong University, Beijing, China.

Xu, X. W., P. Z. Zhang, X. Z. Wen, Z. L. Qin, G. H. Chen, and A. L. Zhu (2005). Basic characteristics of active tectonics in western Sichuan and its adjacent areas and the recurrence model of strong earthquakes, *Earthq. Geol.* **27,** no. 3, 446–461.

Zeng, B., W. Meng, S. Liu, C. Li, and J. Cui (2015). Prediction modeling method of grey isomerism data for calamity emergency material demand, *Chin. J. Manage. Sci.* **23,** no. 8, 84–91, doi: 10.16381/j.cnki.issn1003-207x.2015.08.010.

Zhao, T. (2011). *Optimization Research on Emergency Relief Material Distribution System for Sudden Natural Disasters in China*, Dalian Maritime University, Dalian, China.

Zhu, X., Y. Wang, D. Regan, and B. Sun (2020). A quantitative study on crucial food supplies after the 2011 Tohoku earthquake based on time series analysis, *Int. J. Environ. Res. Publ. Heal.* **17,** no. 19, 1–13.

Manuscript received 9 June 2025
Published online 3 November 2025

Evidence of Liquefaction-Induced Gradual Ground Tilt Settlement at Strong-Motion Stations

Shengze Tian[1] and M. Shahria Alam[*1]

Abstract

We analyzed strong-motion recordings, which were reportedly related to potential development of soil liquefaction during the 2011 M_w 9.0 Tohoku earthquake and the 2011 M_w 6.2 Christchurch earthquake. Besides visual inspection of recorded accelerograms, their Stockwell spectrograms, and their integrated velocities, the corrected ground displacements, obtained using the baseline correction method with physics-based correction patterns, were carefully analyzed. We found that soil liquefaction could be one possible cause of the nonlinearly drifted integrated velocities by triggering gradual ground tilt settlement of the concrete instrument pad that holds an accelerometer. Tilt settlement may be less pronounced for strong-motion stations with larger instrument pads. With such an explanation, the baseline correction method proposed for linearly detrended accelerograms was applied to calculate ground displacements using recorded accelerograms from the 2023 M_w 7.8 Kahramanmaraş earthquake. The calculated coseismic displacements are generally consistent with geodetic measurements.

Cite this article as Tian, S., and M. S. Alam (2025). Evidence of Liquefaction-Induced Gradual Ground Tilt Settlement at Strong-Motion Stations, *Seismol. Res. Lett.* **97**, 1827–1841, doi: 10.1785/0220240387.

Supplemental Material

Introduction

Seismometry and inclinometry are two independent branches in seismological research. Sometimes, instruments used to measure translational recordings are used in tilt measurements. Translational recordings are affected by ground tilt, and tilt recordings are affected by translational recordings (Graizer, 2006). Thus, it is challenging to separate them apart in a robust and trustworthy way. At teleseismic distances, the rotational component of ground motion is of the order of 10^{-8} to 10^{-6}, which is relatively low compared with the translational component. Ground tilts in the near field can be high. For example, during the 1994 M_w 6.7 Northridge earthquake, the residual tilt extracted from the strong-motion record at the Pacoima dam-upper left Abutment reached 3.1° in the N45° E direction, whereas tilts at most stations were well less than 0.5° (Graizer, 2006).

Obtaining ground displacements from strong-motion recordings remains an open problem. One big part is that ground rotations (particularly ground tilts) may contaminate the translational recordings of accelerometers. Up till now, trustworthy and robust ground rotational recordings are still very rare (Zembaty *et al.*, 2016). The integrated ground velocity typically exhibits a linear drift at long times, usually after the strongest portion of ground shaking. Getting rid of the velocity drift trend is a promising direction, which leads to empirical baseline correction methods (Graizer, 1979; Iwan *et al.*, 1985; Boore, 2001; Wu and Wu, 2007; Wang *et al.*, 2011; Tian, Gardoni, Li, and Yuan, 2019; Tian and Alam, 2024). However, without robust ground rotational recordings, the accuracy of such ground-displacement calculations may not be guaranteed without validation from geodetic measurements (Melgar *et al.*, 2013). In practice, nonlinearly drifted integrated velocities may be observed, indicating abnormal tilt patterns (Boore, 2001; Wang *et al.*, 2011). This further complicates the calculation of ground displacements (Graizer, 2005).

In our study, we focus on strong-motion seismology. Because of the difficulty in obtaining ground rotational recordings, ground tilts with unknown shapes have not been well presented in the past. There are two reasons for that. First, filtering of recorded accelerations has been the common practice. For example, the Pacific Earthquake Engineering Research Center uses a fourth-order band-pass Butterworth filter to process recorded ground accelerations (Darragh *et al.*, 2004). This would remove the unusual gradual ground tilt, which theoretically exists in the lower-frequency range (Graizer, 2006). Second, most empirical baseline correction methods are mathematical or statistical improvements on immature understandings (see

1. Applied Lab for Advanced Materials and Structures (ALAMS), School of Engineering, The University of British Columbia, Kelowna, Canada, https://orcid.org/0000-0002-9092-1473 (MSA)

*Corresponding author: shahria.alam@ubc.ca

Graizer, 2010, 2021; Tian, Gardoni, Li, and Yuan, 2019). These discourage inferences of ground tilt from accelerograms.

A seismic station often houses a triaxial accelerometer and a recorder to measure ground motions. Typically, the accelerometer is mounted on the surface of a concrete block, which is embedded in the ground at a certain depth (usually less than 2 m). The size and the design of the concrete block may vary (Gorini *et al.*, 2010; Tün *et al.*, 2016; Alver *et al.*, 2017). Seismic stations can be deployed in free-field or on engineered structures, including buildings and bridges. Free-field stations are usually located away from structures, and their recordings are generally considered to represent the actual ground movement. This is largely true for seismic stations situated on solid rocks or firm ground. It would be a different story if liquefaction occurs, where ground-motion recordings reflect soil–structure interactions.

Evidence of earthquake-induced soil liquefaction is usually identified by surface manifestations (Andrus and Stokoe, 2000). The susceptibility and triggering of soil liquefaction are studied with field testing of nearby soil characteristics (Youd and Idriss, 2001). When the overlying nonliquefiable crust is thick enough, sand boils may not develop even if liquefaction in depth does occur. If the liquefied layer is too thin, it will not produce enough pore water pressure to cause sand boils to develop. On the other hand, sand boils may occur in thick and shallow layers of liquefiable soil even if the high degree of softening and weakening commonly associated with initial liquefaction does not happen (Ishihara, 1985). As a result, the presence of sand boils is neither a strictly necessary nor a sufficient indicator of the occurrence of liquefaction (Kramer *et al.*, 2016).

Over the years, strong-motion stations have been widely deployed. By analyzing the recordings, we may detect the occurrence of soil liquefaction where no surface manifestation was identified in the field surveys (for instance, during the 2011 M_w 6.2 Christchurch earthquake, see Bradley and Cubrinovski, 2011; Wotherspoon *et al.*, 2015). It may also help when the evidence of surface manifestations gets washed away by a subsequent tsunami (e.g., during the 2011 M_w 9.0 Tohoku earthquake; see Greenfield, 2017). The identification of soil liquefaction using recorded ground motions relies on the detection of the deamplification of high-frequency components as well as dilation-related acceleration pulses. In this process, the Stockwell spectrogram may help determine liquefaction triggering time (Kramer *et al.*, 2015). The Stockwell, or S-, transform (Stockwell *et al.*, 1996) uses a moving window of frequency-dependent width to achieve a balanced time–frequency resolution (Kramer *et al.*, 2016). However, the manifestation of these liquefaction-induced characteristics may depend on the degree of soil liquefaction. It was also found that soil liquefaction can be quite local, that ground-motion recordings may not exhibit signs of liquefaction, though surface manifestation existed in the vicinity (Kramer *et al.*, 2015; Özener *et al.*, 2020). This means that for the detection of soil liquefaction based on strong-motion recordings, nearby surface manifestation is neither a strictly necessary nor a sufficient indicator. With the development of advanced constitutive models of liquefiable soils, numerical analysis has been engaged in the interpretations of liquefaction triggering case histories, which greatly benefits our understanding of soil liquefaction (Kramer *et al.*, 2018). This can be particularly important for historical case studies, such as the Wildfire Liquefaction Array in the 1987 Elmore Ranch and Superstition Hills earthquakes, about which extensive discussions have been conducted regarding the performance of pore pressure transducers (Kramer and Greenfield, 2019). It should be noted that, without the acknowledgement of the false-positive and false-negative errors, correlations based on surface manifestations of soil liquefaction and strong-motion recordings may not be robust (Zhan and Chen, 2021).

Obtaining ground tilt from recorded accelerograms can be difficult. As shown by Graizer (2006), this can be achieved by applying low-frequency filtering to the horizontal accelerograms at a cutoff frequency determined by the horizontal-to-vertical ratio of the Fourier amplitude spectra. However, for near-field strong-motion records exhibiting permanent ground displacements, misinterpretation may occur because this component can be confused with ground tilt.

Though the fact that ground tilt may contaminate translational recordings is well recognized, effectively incorporating this effect into baseline correction methods remains a significant challenge. To address this, we assume that ground tilt can be seen as the ground rotational displacement, which accumulates during the strongest portion of ground shaking. Following the assumption that ground displacement follows a ramp function (Wu and Wu, 2007) or a step function (Wang *et al.*, 2011), we assume that the trend of ground tilt shall, in general, follow the shape of the cumulative energy of accelerograms (Tian, Gardoni, Li, and Yuan, 2019; Tian, Gardoni, and Yuan, 2019). A tilt correction pattern can first be applied to eliminate the effect of ground tilt. With analysis of recordings from the non-tilt shake table tests, a cumulative correction pattern is then applied to eliminate the cumulative integrated velocity error.

In this article, the baseline correction method with physics-based correction patterns (Tian, Gardoni, Li, and Yuan, 2019; Tian, Gardoni, and Yuan, 2019) is first introduced. Then, we present two types of abnormal velocity drift patterns, which were identified to be related to the occurrence of soil liquefaction based on case histories from the 2011 M_w 9.0 Tohoku earthquake and the 2011 M_w 6.2 Christchurch earthquake. The nonlinear velocity drifts were also identified in case histories from the 2023 M_w 7.8 Kahramanmaraş earthquake. Furthermore, to obtain the coseismic ground displacements, the baseline correction method designed for linearly detrended accelerograms (Tian and Alam, 2024) was applied to deal with the effect of gradual ground tilt settlement.

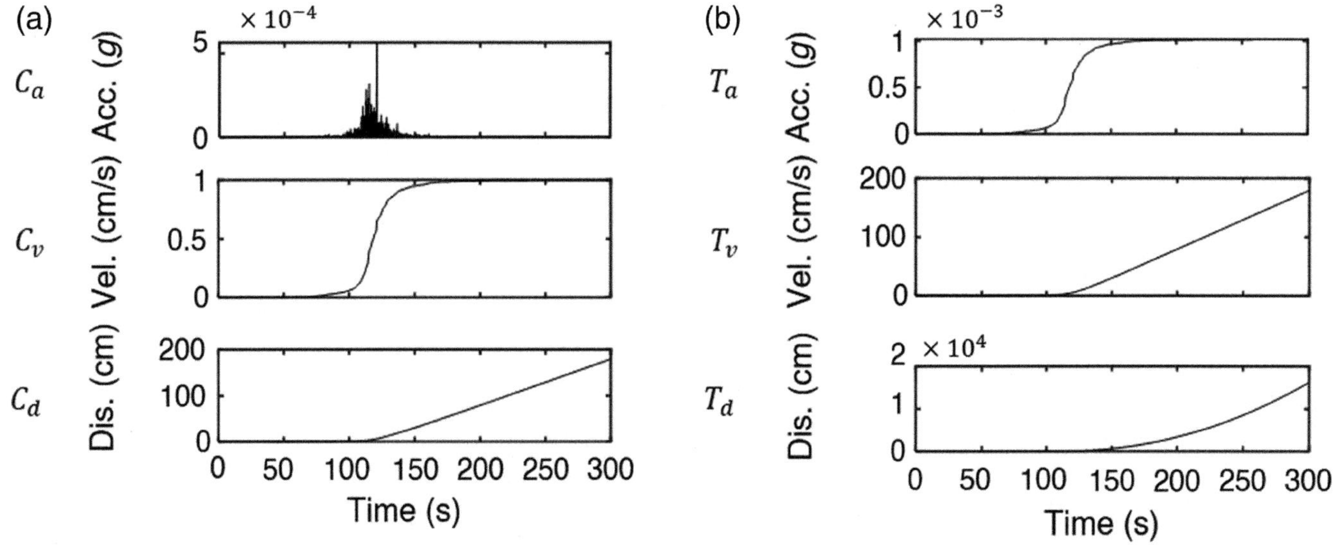

Figure 1. Normalized correction patterns. (a) Normalized cumulative correction pattern C. Here, C_a, C_v, and C_d are the acceleration, velocity, and displacement of the normalized cumulative correction pattern, respectively. (b) Normalized tilt correction pattern T. Here, T_a, T_v, and T_d are the acceleration, velocity, and displacement of the normalized tilt correction pattern, respectively. Here, normalize means that the maximum velocity of the cumulative correction pattern is 1 cm/s and the maximum acceleration of the tilt correction pattern is 1 gal.

Baseline Correction of Ground Motions with Physics-Based Correction Patterns

The difficulty of baseline correction for recorded accelerograms lies in finding a robust and smooth fit to the drifted integrated velocity. It is commonly assumed that baseline drifts in accelerograms are triggered by strong shaking, and these drifts shall become steady after a certain threshold (Iwan *et al.*, 1985). This assumption is physically meaningful as ground dislocations usually complete in a short period of time. Fitting an integrated velocity can be done by assuming a two-step baseline shift within an accelerogram (Iwan *et al.*, 1985) or using a polynomial function (Graizer, 1979). However, both methods and the subsequent improvements rely on determining specific time points. And the results may not be trustworthy because of the sensitivity of those time points (Boore and Bommer, 2005). Therefore, geodetic measurements, such as Global Positioning System (GPS) data, are needed for cross validation (Melgar *et al.*, 2013). It is widely acknowledged that the problem of baseline shift shall remain unsolved without ground rotational recordings (Nigbor, 1994; Trifunac and Todorovska, 2001).

As addressed by Graizer (1979, 2006, 2010, 2021), it is fundamental to understand the physics behind the phenomenon of baseline shift, where ground tilt plays an important role. To bring state-of-the-art understandings into practice, we introduced the idea of using physics-based correction patterns to correct recorded accelerograms (Tian, Gardoni, Li, and Yuan, 2019; Tian, Gardoni, and Yuan, 2019; Tian and Alam, 2024). To illustrate the baseline correction procedure, we use the north–south (NS) component at Kiban–Kyoshin (KiK)-net station IBRH20, which recorded the 2011 M_w 9.0 Tohoku earthquake as an example. The normalized cumulative correction pattern and the tilt correction pattern are shown in Figure 1. After eliminating the initial system offset, the acceleration is squared and integrated to obtain the cumulative velocity. This cumulative velocity is then normalized to C_v, of which the maximum velocity is 1 cm/s. We then assume that ground tilt follows the trend of C_v. This means that ground tilt forms during the strongest portion of ground shaking. And we let the maximum acceleration of T_a be 1 gal.

The step results of the correction process are shown in Figure 2. We may observe that the integrated velocity exhibits a linear drift at long times, as shown in Figure 2a. This may indicate the existence of a stable baseline shift in the accelerogram. Such a shift could be the result of a permanent ground tilt, which can be calculated using the tilt correction pattern shown in Figure 1b. After the elimination of ground tilt, the integrated velocity now contains only the cumulative velocity error, as shown in Figure 2b. This cumulative velocity error is then eliminated using the cumulative correction pattern shown in Figure 1a. The corrected ground motion is shown in Figure 2c. We may find that the integrated velocity has no drifts, and the integrated displacement exhibits a physically meaningful waveform, with a permanent displacement of about 16 cm (to the north). Because the shapes of the tilt correction pattern and cumulative correction pattern are fixed, we only need one time point t_r for the fitting calculation of the permanent ground tilt and the cumulative velocity error. As a result, the selection of the time point t_r shall not greatly affect the correction results. In fact, the sensitivity of the time point t_r may be used to check the stability of the correction performance (Tian, Gardoni, Li, and Yuan, 2019; Tian, Gardoni, and Yuan, 2019).

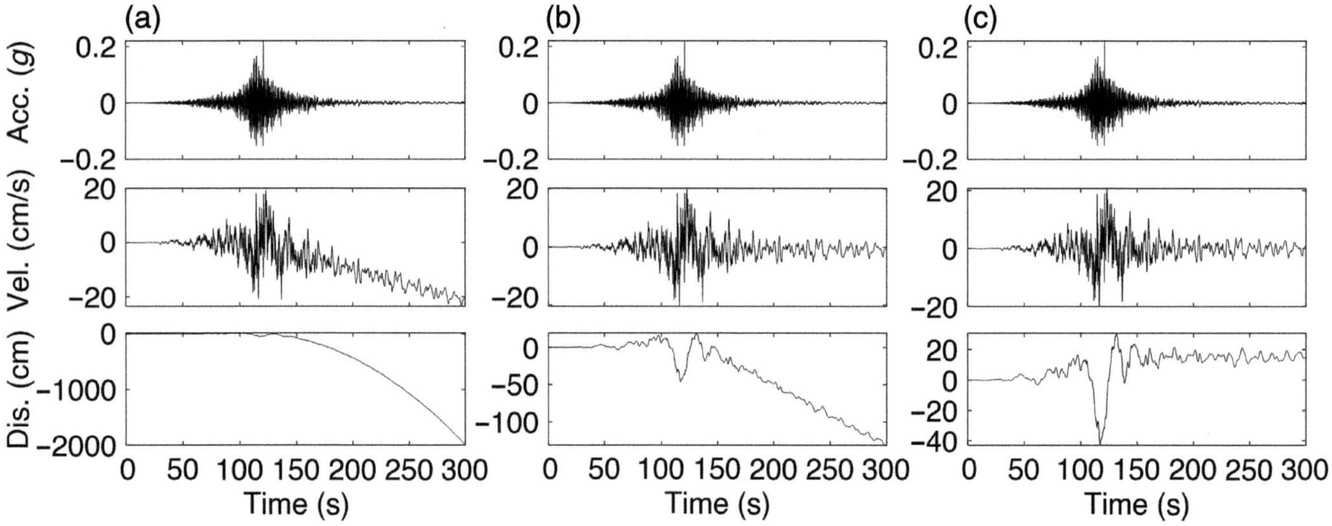

Figure 2. Step results of baseline correction for the north–south (NS) component at Kiban–Kyoshin (KiK)-net station IBRH20. (a) Raw recording, the integrated velocity, and the integrated displacement. (b) Ground motion after the elimination of ground tilt. (c) Ground motion after the elimination of the cumulative velocity errors. Here, the time point t_r is set at 170 s.

It is noted that the success of the proposed baseline correction method relies on the assumption that ground tilt forms during the strongest portion of ground shaking. If ground rotation is complex during the strongest portion of ground shaking, the recovered ground displacement may deviate from the true value, though the displacement waveforms can sometimes be physically reasonable (Tian, Gardoni, Li, and Yuan, 2019). In addition, if ground tilt abnormalities exist outside the strongest portion of ground shaking, baseline correction will become more difficult. Wang *et al.* (2011) pointed out that the nonlinearly drifted integrated velocity in the long times can be solved by assuming that the velocity is quadratically drifted, meaning that we may assume a linear drift in the accelerogram. With this assumption, the proposed baseline correction method for linearly detrended accelerograms can be applied (Tian and Alam, 2024), where a jerk correction pattern is introduced to preprocess the accelerograms before the implementation of the tilt correction pattern and the cumulative correction pattern.

Results and Discussion

We present two types of possible nonlinearly drifted integrated velocities associated with soil liquefaction. A schematic demonstration of potential ground tilt responses due to soil liquefaction is shown in Figure 3. Ground deformations typically form during the strongest portion of ground shaking and remain stable afterward. As demonstrated by Graizer (2006, 2010, 2021), ground tilt plays a dominant role in affecting translational ground motion recordings. A typical ground tilt shall follow the trend of the lower-frequency component of translational recordings (Graizer, 2006). Here, the typical ground tilt shown in Figure 3 follows the tilt correction pattern shown in Figure 1b. The residual value usually results from a permanent ground tilt. The permanent ground tilt is usually small (Graizer, 2006). Analysis of strong-motion records associated with soil liquefaction reveals that nonlinearly drifted integrated velocities may reflect the evolution of ground tilt, which can extend beyond the strongest portion of ground shaking. Depending on the severity of soil liquefaction and the possible responses of strong-motion stations, such gradual ground tilt may terminate at different times. As shown in Figure 3, with reference to the typical permanent ground tilt, type I refers to the case where a gradual ground tilt persists until the end of the recording, and type II terminates at an earlier time point.

Because the accelerometer is mounted on the surface of a rigid concrete block, the identified gradual ground tilt indicates tilting of the concrete instrument pad. Soil liquefaction may induce a loss of bearing capacity of the concrete block, leading to tilt settlement. This is similar to the tilting of buildings with basements

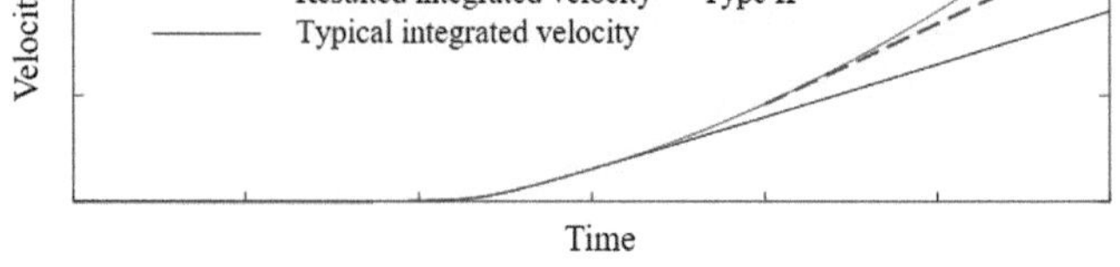

Figure 3. Potential ground tilts and the resulted integrated velocities due to soil liquefaction. The color version of this figure is available only in the electronic edition.

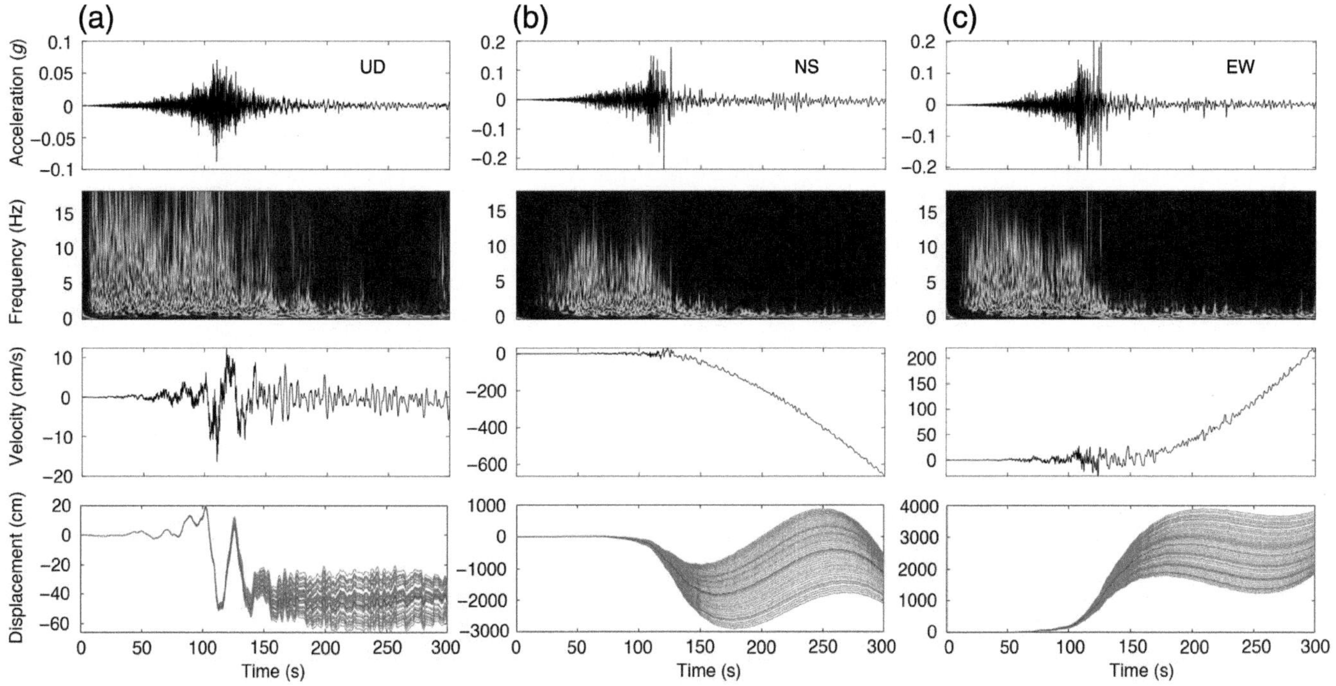

Figure 4. Recorded accelerograms, their respective normalized Stockwell spectrograms, integrated velocities, and integrated ground displacements from baseline corrected accelerograms in the up–down (UD) (a), north–south (NS) (b), and east–west (EW) (c) directions at Kyoshin network (K-NET) station CHB024. The selected time point t_r is in the range of 150–200 s with a 1 s time interval. The gray lines in the displacements are the ones associated with each time point t_r. The red line is the one closest to the mean residual displacement. The color version of this figure is available only in the electronic edition.

observed during liquefaction (Hughes and Madabhushi, 2019). As shown by Wang *et al.* (2011), the recovery of ground displacements using borehole recordings was better than that using surface recordings. This suggests that borehole sensors are less affected by ground tilt than surface ones, likely due to reduced soil amplification effect. Moreover, the fact that ground-displacement calculations can be well performed for the majority of surface recordings suggests that ground tilts at most surface strong-motion stations can be considered typical (Wang *et al.*, 2011; Tian, Gardoni, Li, and Yuan, 2019; Tian, Gardoni, and Yuan, 2019). In return, if such nonlinearly drifted velocities were identified, one possible cause would be the occurrence of soil liquefaction.

2011 M_w 9.0 Tohoku earthquake

Several stations from the Strong-Motion Seismograph Network (Kyoshin network [K-NET] and KiK-net) were reportedly related to soil liquefaction during the 2011 M_w 9.0 Tohoku earthquake (Cox *et al.*, 2013; Greenfield, 2017), with identified surface manifestations in the vicinity or around the sites.

K-NET strong-motion station CHB024 was reported to experience severe liquefaction, with large sand boils in the vicinity and around the station (Geotechnical Extreme Events Reconnaissance [GEER] Association, 2011). As shown in Figure 4b,c, the NS and EW recordings exhibit distinct drops in high-frequency components from 110 to 130 s. After 130 s, the Stockwell spectrograms show that low-frequency components dominate the accelerograms. We may also identify acceleration pulses at long times, which may be a sign of cyclic mobility. Based on field investigation and the identified characteristics of recorded accelerograms, we can conclude that liquefaction occurred at this site during the earthquake.

From the perspective of baseline correction, we may first notice nonlinear velocity drifts in the NS and EW directions. Such nonlinearities exist in the long times till the end. As a result, they can be classified as a type I response, as shown in Figure 3. This phenomenon differs from the typical linear velocity drift at long times due to potential permanent ground tilt (Boore, 2001; Boore and Bommer, 2005; Graizer, 2006). The nonlinearly drifted velocity indicates that the recorded accelerogram may contain at least a first-order drifted acceleration, rather than a permanent baseline shift. This suggests that the concrete block on which the seismometer was mounted experienced gradual ground tilt settlement due to soil liquefaction. Nonlinear velocity drift has been identified in other earthquake recordings; however, its underlying cause has yet to be determined. Wang *et al.* (2011) identified this phenomenon at station 51JYC (31.96° N, 104.98° E) from the 2008 Wenchuan earthquake. Boore (2001) also mentioned that he did see some cases in records from California earthquakes that exhibited nonlinear trends in velocities.

Because the nonlinear velocity drift is different from the typical linear velocity drift, corrected ground displacements

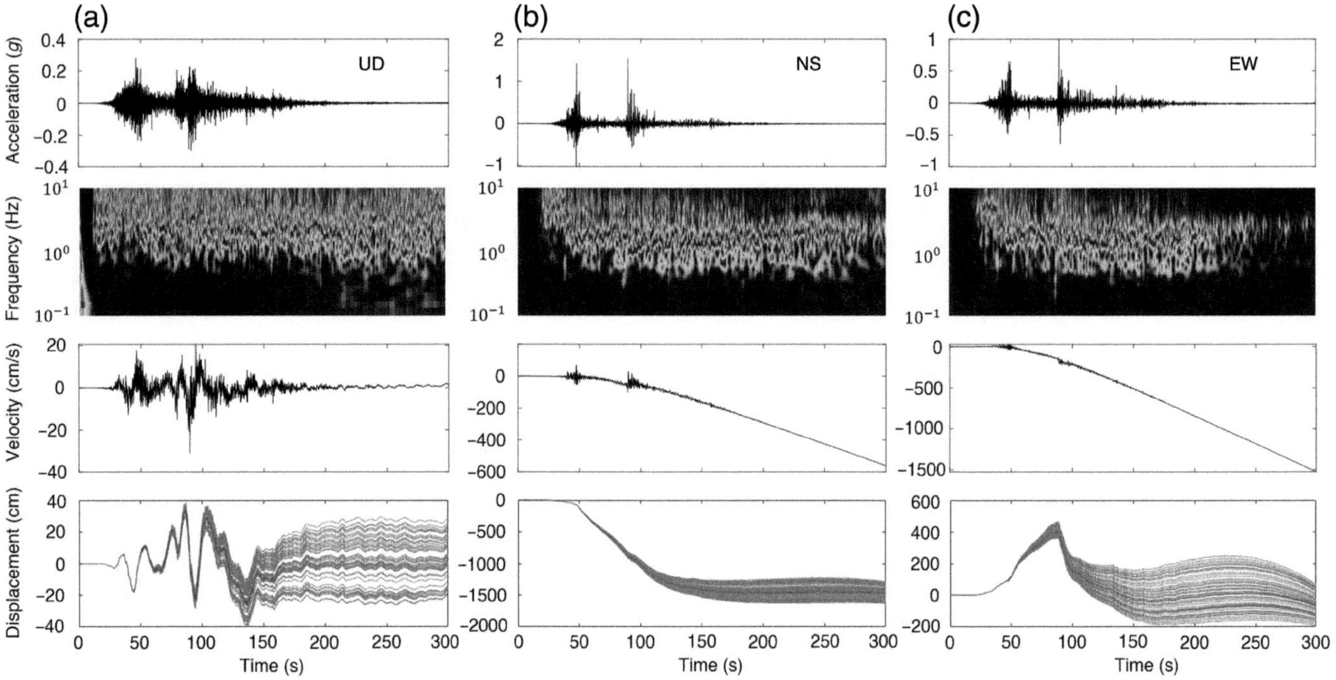

Figure 5. Recorded accelerograms, their respective normalized Stockwell spectrograms, integrated velocities, and integrated ground displacements from baseline corrected accelerograms in the UD (a), NS (b), and EW (c) directions at K-NET station MYG013. The selected time point t_r is in the range of 150–200 s with a 1 s time interval. The gray lines in the displacements are the ones associated with each time point t_r. The red line is the one closest to the mean residual displacement. The color version of this figure is available only in the electronic edition.

obtained using existing baseline correction methods may result in unphysical waveforms (Graizer, 2005). The recovered ground displacements shown in Figure 4 are derived using the baseline correction method of Tian, Gardoni, Li, and Yuan (2019), as introduced in the previous section. As shown in Figure 4b,c, the corrected ground displacements for the horizontal components exhibit nonlinear waveforms at long times. Apparently, the nonlinear waveforms at long times are not physically meaningful. On the other hand, we may observe in this specific example that the vertical recording does not exhibit the typical characteristics of soil liquefaction like the horizontal ones do, and the result of baseline correction is generally acceptable. One possible reason is that vertical recording is much less sensitive (approximately one order of magnitude less) to ground tilt (Graizer, 2006). Based on numerical analyses, Yang (2004) showed that the transfer function for vertical motions at liquefiable sites is likely independent of the intensity of input motions, with no reduction in amplitude under strong shaking. This may indicate that vertical ground-motion recordings are less sensitive to soil liquefaction compared to horizontal ones, which may be greatly deamplified due to the softening of soil shear stiffness. Such differences in the vertical and horizontal components may, in turn, help detect the occurrence of soil liquefaction (Kostadinov and Yamazaki, 2001).

K-NET station MYG013 was reported to experience soil liquefaction around the station, along with possible settlement of the instrument pad (Geotechnical Extreme Events Reconnaissance [GEER] Association, 2011; Greenfield, 2017). As shown in Figure 5, the accelerograms in all three directions do not visually exhibit obvious signs of lower-frequency dominancy. The Stockwell spectrograms in the two horizontal directions (NS and EW) show clear frequency drops at 39 and 47 s (see Fig. 6). Greenfield (2017) pointed out that the first drop in 39 s could be due to the transition from *P* wave to *S* wave, and the frequency drop in 47 s could be the triggering time of soil liquefaction. However, finding such subtle signs in the spectrograms practically is not an easy task by visual inspection. Figure 6 zooms in to show the details within the 30–70 s time range. We may find that the accelerograms exhibit more obvious signs of acceleration pulses after 47 s. These acceleration spikes may be presumably caused by the liquefied soil dilating in response to large shear strains as strong shaking continued (Greenfield, 2017).

Unlike the nonlinearly drifted integrated velocities at station CHB024 shown in Figure 4, the integrated velocities at station MYG013 were visually linear at long times (after around 150 s). However, we may find that the velocities in the two horizontal directions show nonlinear drifts between 100 and 150 s. From the Stockwell spectrogram in the NS direction, we may find that the fundamental frequency increases over time. As indicated by Greenfield (2017), this means that the liquefied soils drained and stiffened as the amplitude of the shaking diminished. The linearly drifted velocity at long times

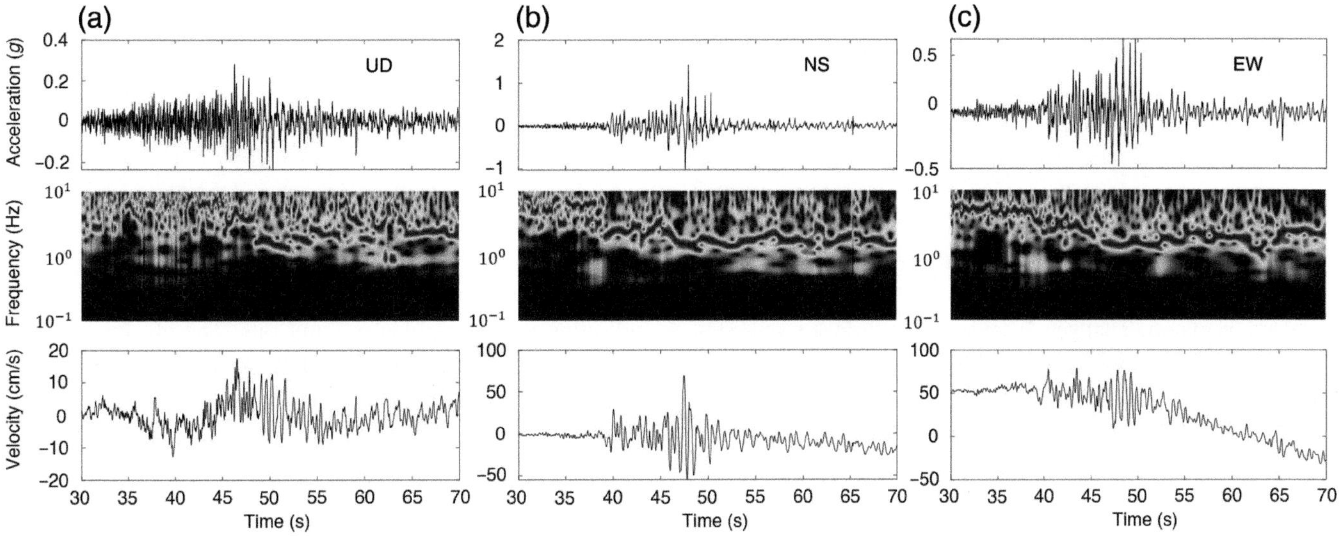

Figure 6. Acceleration time histories, normalized Stockwell spectra, and integrated velocities near the potential onset of liquefaction in the UD (a), NS (b), and EW (c) directions at K-NET station MYG013. The color version of this figure is available only in the electronic edition.

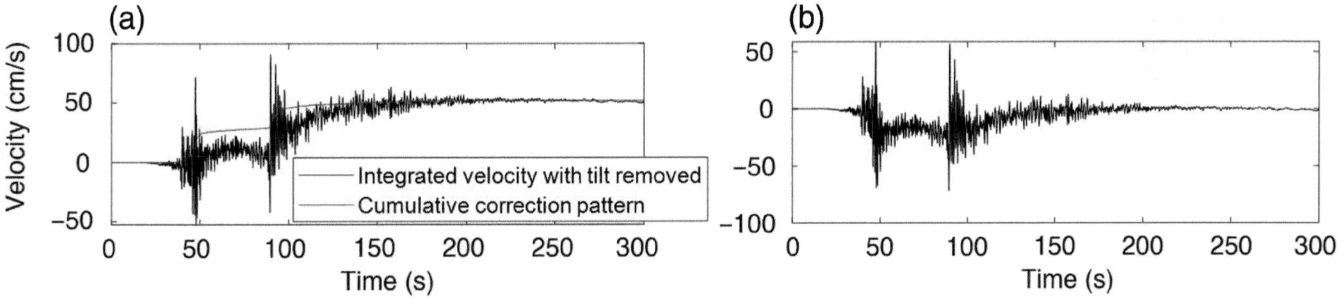

Figure 7. Correction process of the accelerogram in the NS direction. (a) The comparison of the integrated velocity after the implementation of the tilt correction pattern and the cumulative correction pattern. (b) The corrected velocity after the implementation of the cumulative correction pattern. The color version of this figure is available only in the electronic edition.

may indicate that the tilt settlement of the concrete instrument pad has become stable due to these changes.

We take the accelerogram in the NS direction as an example. The baseline correction process is shown in Figure 7. Figure 7a shows that the cumulative correction pattern differs from the integrated velocity in two parts. The first part is within 50–80 s, in which the cumulative correction pattern is on a plateau above the processed velocity. The second part occurs within 100–150 s, during which we can identify that the processed velocity exhibits a nonlinear velocity drift, whereas the cumulative velocity pattern has reached its steady plateau. This can be classified as a type II gradual ground tilt, as shown in Figure 3. In this case, the gradual ground tilt terminates at around 150 s. Because of a lack of ground rotational recordings, ground tilt within the strongest portion of ground shaking can only be partly compensated by the cumulative correction pattern (Tian, Gardoni, Li, and Yuan, 2019). Nevertheless, the nonlinear velocity drift in the second part suggests that the development of ground tilt extended beyond the strongest portion of ground shaking. This is in accordance with the identified settlement of the instrument pad caused by soil liquefaction (Greenfield, 2017). As a result, the waveforms of the corrected ground displacements shown in Figure 5 are not physically meaningful in the two horizontal directions. The vertical ground motion, however, is less sensitive to ground tilt or soil liquefaction.

The site at KiK-net station IBRH20 (140.7323° E, 35.8284° N) was characterized as moderate liquefaction, with sand boils in the vicinity on three sides but not directly around the station (Cox *et al.*, 2013). Figure S1, available in the supplemental material to this article, shows the accelerograms in three directions, their respective Stockwell spectrograms, the integrated velocities, and the integrated ground displacements, all with the implementation of our baseline correction method discussed previously. On the one hand, we may find that there are no distinct drops of high-frequency components with a visual inspection of the accelerograms and the respective Stockwell spectrograms (Kramer *et al.*, 2015). Though surface manifestations of soil liquefaction were evident in the vicinity, it would be a false-positive characterization of recorded accelerograms at station IBRH20 (Özener *et al.*, 2020). This suggests that soil liquefaction may be relatively local and that surface manifestations of liquefaction may not validate the occurrence of liquefaction at nearby sites.

On the other hand, we may find that the integrated velocities exhibit typical linear drifts at long times in the two horizontal (NS and EW) directions. Applying the proposed baseline correction method described previously, we may find that the corrected ground displacements are generally acceptable, of which the waveforms conform to an ideal ramp-function (Wu and Wu, 2007) or a step-function (Wang *et al.*, 2011). This suggests that ground tilts at this strong-motion station did not exhibit abnormalities that would distort the ground-displacement calculations.

K-NET station MYG010 was deployed on a flat surface, which was 2–3 m above the Port of Ishinomaki waterfront to the south. This site was flooded by the subsequent tsunami, and as a result, potential surficial evidence of soil liquefaction was obscured. However, evidence of soil liquefaction close to the station, as well as soil liquefaction induced by the M_w 7.1 aftershock on 7 April, suggests that this site could have been liquefied during the 2011 M_w 9.0 Tohoku earthquake (Greenfield, 2017).

Based on the normalized Stockwell spectrogram (in the NS direction) shown in Figure S2, a frequency drop is observed at ~46 s. After 46 s, high-frequency components reappeared and dropped occasionally. This differs from the Stockwell spectrograms at site CHB024, in which lower-frequency components dominate after the initiation of soil liquefaction, occurring around 110 s. It is also different from the spectrograms at site MYG013, where higher-frequency components appear occasionally due to dilation-related acceleration pulses. This suggests that the effect of soil liquefaction at station MYG010 may be less phenomenal than those at stations CHB024 and MYG013. One potential reason could be the unsaturated clayed sand (2.5 m thick) at site MYG010, whereas soil liquefaction was expected to occur at depths ranging from 2.5 to 15 m (Greenfield, 2017). According to the integrated velocities and corrected displacement waveforms, we may find that the gradual tilt settlement was not evident at site MYG010, where ground tilt became stable roughly after 150 s. However, the variation in the recovered ground displacements in the vertical direction appears more pronounced compared to the horizontal ones, indicating the potential complexity of the ground tilting process. This is different from those shown at stations CHB024 and MYG013. This suggests that soil liquefaction may have occurred during this earthquake, although the typical characteristics of soil liquefaction were not obvious.

We also present recorded accelerograms at station MYG010 from the 7 April M_w 7.1 aftershock in Figure S3. It may be found that the peak ground accelerations at station MYG010 were equivalent for the M_w 9.0 mainshock and the M_w 7.1 aftershock, whereas the duration of ground shaking from the aftershock was much shorter. We may find that the slopes of the velocity drifts in the long times were much smaller in the aftershock event, indicating smaller residual ground tilts. The obtained ground displacements in the EW and vertical directions exhibit slightly abnormal waveforms, indicating the development of potential abnormal ground tilt. However, we may find the ground displacement at station MYG010 was much smaller in the aftershock event. In the phase of strong ground shaking, high-frequency components did not show obvious disappearance from 15 to 70 s. As a result, based on visual inspection of the accelerograms and their Stockwell spectrograms, it is not sufficient to confirm the development of soil liquefaction during the M_w 7.1 aftershock. In conclusion, although extensive sand boils were identified in the vicinity for both the mainshock and the aftershock, the degree of soil liquefaction at the strong-motion station MYG010 was less apparent.

Unfortunately, there are no direct tilt measurements of strong-motion stations at liquefied sites. Because translational recordings and tilt recordings affect each other, separating them in a physically meaningful way remains a challenge. As a result, the precise ground tilt during the strongest portion of ground shaking and the possible gradual tilt settlement in long times remain unclear.

According to the differential equations for strong-motion accelerometers under small oscillations, the residual values in horizontal recordings can be attributed to permanent ground tilt (Graizer, 2006). The residual ground tilt calculated using this theory was close to the measured residual ground tilt at the strong-motion station at Pacoima dam–upper left Abutment for the 1994 Northridge earthquake. In addition, with recordings from the nontilt 2D shake table tests, we identified cumulated integrated velocities rather than linearly drifted ones (Tian, Gardoni, Li, and Yuan, 2019). This finding, in turn, validates the assumption that the linear velocity drift at long times usually results from permanent ground tilt. As indicated by Graizer (2006), if the recorded level of long-period motion is significantly higher in the horizontal components, this could possibly be due to ground tilts. Under this theory, the nonlinearly drifted velocity at long times might be attributed to abnormal ground tilt. In the future, shake table tests of strong-motion stations on liquefiable soils may be one possible solution to verify this assumption.

2011 M_w 6.2 Christchurch earthquake

Instrument pads for strong-motion stations in Christchurch, New Zealand, were different from typical free-field ones.

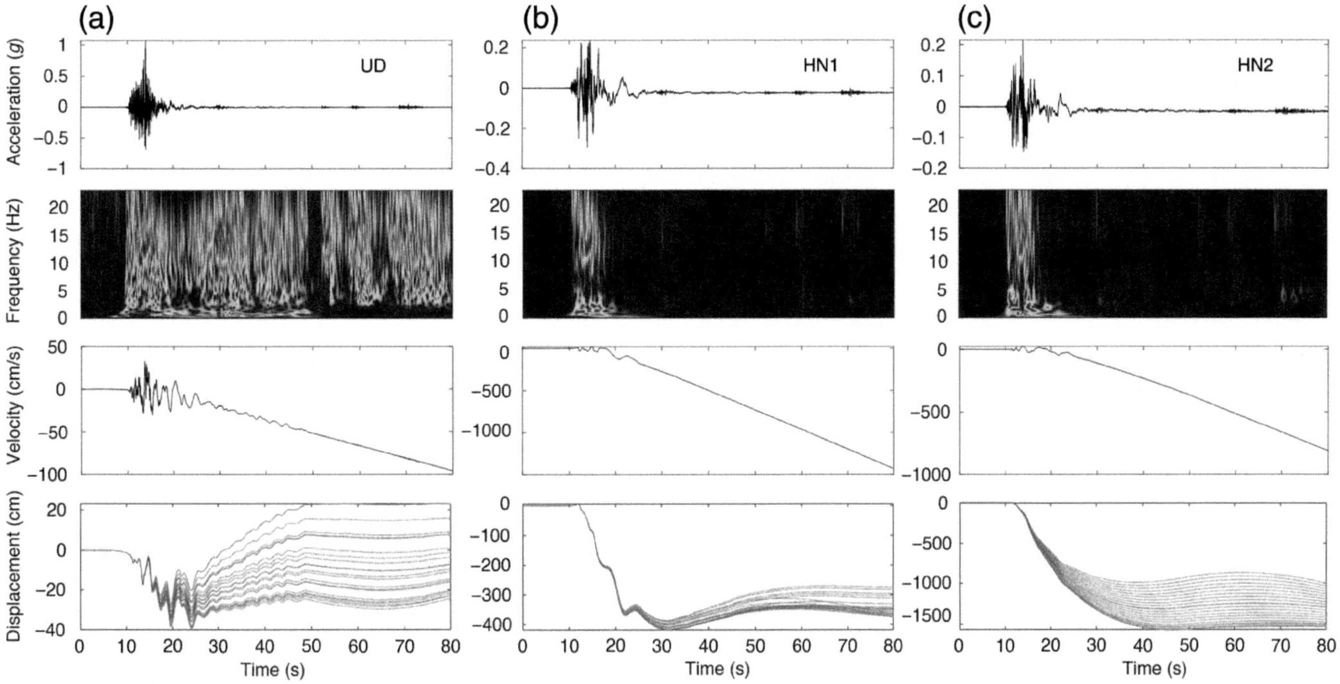

Figure 8. Recorded accelerograms, their respective normalized Stockwell spectrograms, integrated velocities, and integrated ground displacements from baseline corrected accelerograms in the UD (a), HN1 (b), and HN2 (c) directions at strong-motion station HPSC. The selected time point t_r is in the range of 30–50 s with a 1 s time interval. The gray lines in the displacements are the ones associated with each time point t_r. The red line is the one closest to the mean residual displacement. The color version of this figure is available only in the electronic edition.

Take station HPSC (43.50157144 S, 172.7021909 E) as an example. Situated by the Avon River, station HPSC was housed in a single story concrete masonry building with a shallow concrete pad foundation of about 4 × 8 m, and is attached to a larger embedded concrete structure (~7 × 7 m) that is part of the pumping station (Wotherspoon *et al.*, 2013). Surface manifestation of severe soil liquefaction was identified at the ground surface. The site suffered damage from considerable buoyancy uplift, rotation, and lateral spreading. The pump station itself underwent substantial rotation during the 2010 Darfield and 2011 Christchurch earthquakes (Mirza, 2013), and the tilt observed represents the cumulative effects of both events.

As shown in Figure 8, clear shifts of acceleration baselines in two horizontal directions may be noticed in the accelerograms. According to equations for small oscillations of the pendulum type seismometers (Graizer, 2010), the permanent tilt angles can be estimated to be 1.24° and 0.89°, respectively, for HN1 and HN2 directions. It may also be noticed in the horizontal accelerograms that long-period components became dominant after the strongest portion of ground shaking. This may be reflected in the Stockwell spectrograms, in which we may find clear frequency drops at around 15 s in the horizontal recordings. Though integrated velocities exhibit linear drifts in the long times by visual inspection, the unphysical waveforms of corrected displacements suggest that there may exist abnormal tilt settlement after the strongest portion of ground shaking. This weakened tilt settlement may be related to the size effect of the larger instrument pad, similar to the response of buildings with a larger basement (Hughes and Madabhushi, 2019).

Based on the corrected displacements shown in Figure 8a, it appears that there is a transition at ~48 s, indicating an abrupt change in the accelerogram around this time point. This can also be observed from the correction process shown in Figure 9. A nearly linear drift in the integrated velocity is evident from 30 to 50 s in Figure 9a, and the cumulative correction pattern deviates from the trend of the integrated velocity. Under this situation, truncating the accelerograms (keeping the first 48 s) may lead to reasonable correction results with the typical two-step baseline correction methods because of the nearly linear velocity drift.

It should be noted that, according to analysis on liquefaction potential (Wotherspoon *et al.*, 2013), only a single thin layer was found to have a factor of safety less than one throughout the soil profile. This result does not correlate well with the observance of surface manifestations of severe soil liquefaction in a wide area. It was assumed that one potential reason could be the presence of initial shear stresses in the soil profile, given its proximity to the Avon River.

2023 M_w 7.8 Kahramanmaraş earthquake

Soil liquefaction has been widely identified during the 2023 M_w 7.8 and 7.6 Türkiye earthquake doublet (Ozkula *et al.*, 2023; Taftsoglou *et al.*, 2023; Cetin *et al.*, 2024; Demir *et al.*, 2024). However, field investigations on strong-motion stations in relation to soil liquefaction have not yet been released. In

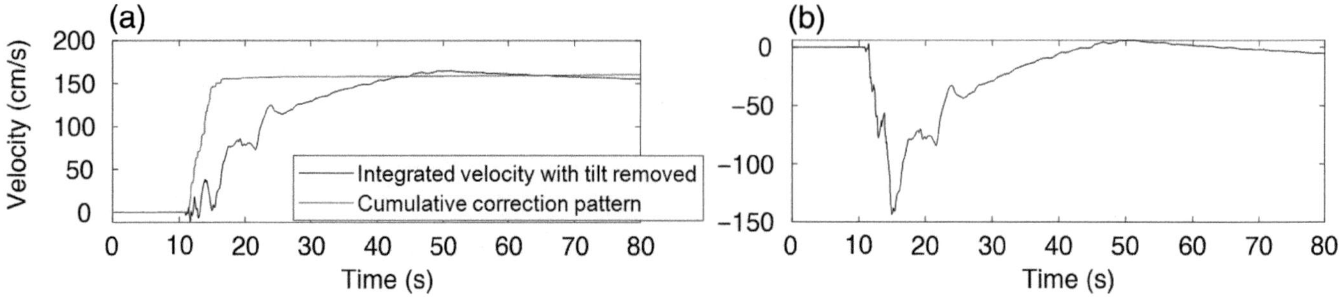

Figure 9. Correction process of the accelerogram in the HN2 direction. (a) The integrated velocity after the implementation of the tilt correction pattern. (b) The corrected velocity after the implementation of the cumulative correction pattern. The selected time point t_r is 40 s. The color version of this figure is available only in the electronic edition.

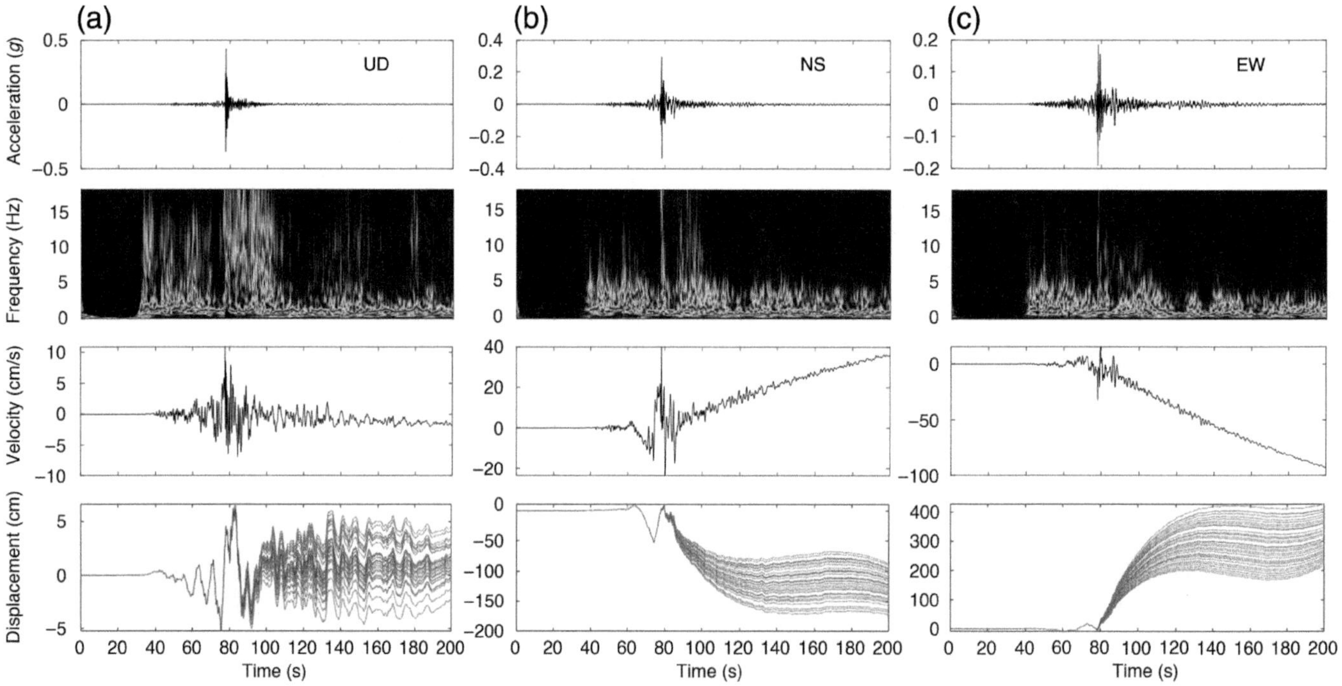

Figure 10. Recorded accelerograms, their respective normalized Stockwell spectrograms, integrated velocities, and integrated ground displacements from baseline corrected accelerograms in the UD (a), NS (b), and EW (c) directions at strong-motion station TK_2308. The selected time point t_r is in the range of 100–130 s with a 1 s time interval. The gray lines in the displacements are the ones associated with each time point t_r. The red line is the one closest to the mean residual displacement. The color version of this figure is available only in the electronic edition.

processing recorded accelerograms from the 2023 M_w 7.8 Kahramanmaraş earthquake, we identified the presence of gradual ground tilt settlement, similar to those identified in the 2011 M_w 9.0 Tohoku earthquake and the 2011 M_w 6.2 Christchurch earthquake, which might indicate potential occurrence of soil liquefaction. Recorded accelerograms at strong-motion stations 2308 and 2708 of the Turkish National Strong-Motion Network (TK) are demonstrated in this article.

Station TK_2308 was situated on the west shore of the Hazar Lake. According to the U.S. Geological Survey (USGS) liquefaction hazard map (see Data and Resources), it is a liquefaction-prone area, which had developed soil liquefaction at nearby sites in the past, for example, during the 2020 M_w 6.7 earthquake in Elazig (Çetin *et al.*, 2020). Figure 10 shows the recorded accelerograms at station TK_2308, along with their respective Stockwell spectrograms, the integrated velocities, and the corrected ground displacements. Visual inspection of the accelerograms and the spectrograms suggests that soil liquefaction likely occurred at around 82 s, where we may find frequency drops in the two horizontal components. We may also find that the integrated velocities in the two horizontal directions exhibit nonlinear drifts at long times, similar to

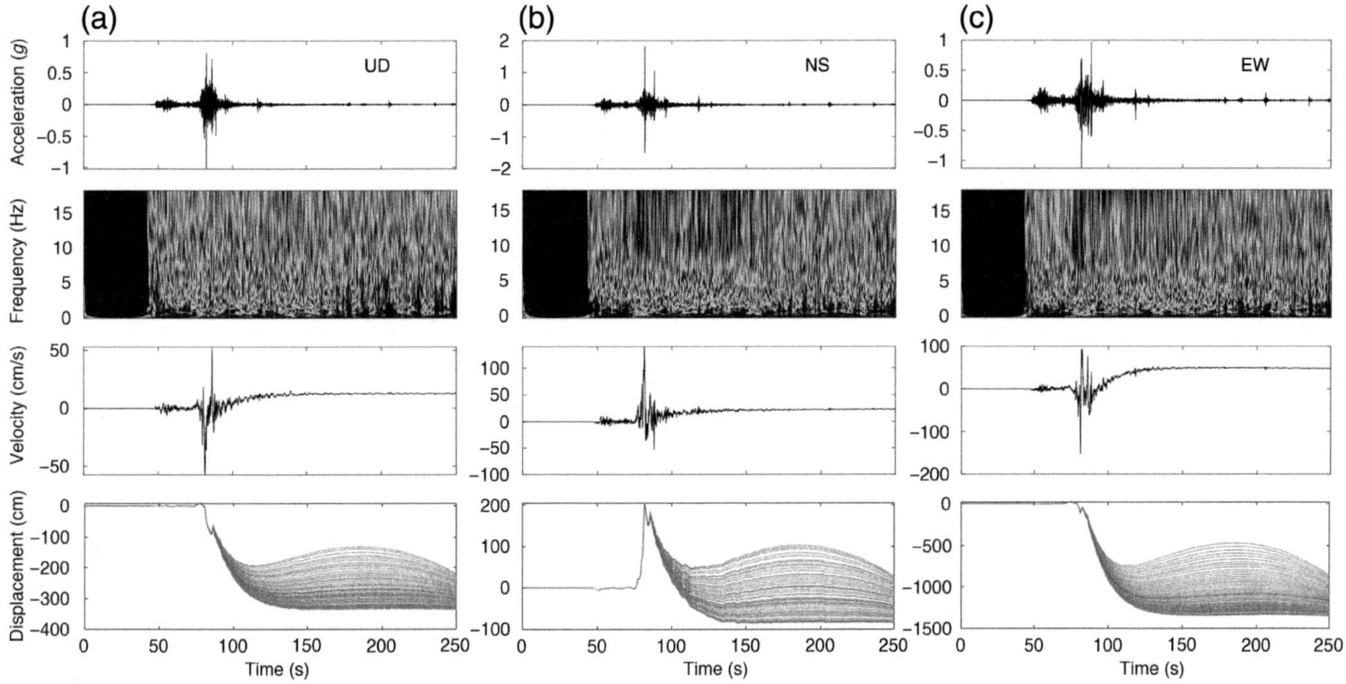

Figure 11. Recorded accelerograms, their respective normalized Stockwell spectrograms, integrated velocities, and integrated ground displacements from baseline corrected accelerograms in the UD (a), NS (b), and EW (c) directions at strong-motion station TK_2708. The selected time point t_r is in the range of 90–140 s with a 1 s time interval. The gray lines in the displacements are the ones associated with each time point t_r. The red line is the one closest to the mean residual displacement. The color version of this figure is available only in the electronic edition.

those at station CHB024 during the 2011 M_w 9.0 Tohoku earthquake. Those nonlinear velocity drifts are evident after the strongest portion of ground shaking, which extend to the end of the recording, suggesting that ground tilt settlement at this site likely continued for a long time. This can be classified as type I gradual ground tilt, as shown in Figure 3.

As shown in Figure 11, for ground motions at strong-motion station TK_2708, we may find that the integrated velocities exhibit nonlinear drifts after the strongest portion of ground shaking. But unlike those extended to the end of the recording, as were at station TK_2308, the integrated velocities became stable after around 150 s. This suggests that tilt settlement at this site only lasted for a short period of time and became stable thereafter. This can be classified as type II gradual ground tilt, as shown in Figure 3. The phenomenon at station TK_2708 is similar to that observed at K-NET station MYG013 during the 2011 M_w 9.0 Tohoku earthquake.

We can observe in Figure 11 that the Stockwell spectrograms of the horizontal accelerograms exhibit frequency drops at ~76 s. This might indicate the time of the *S*-wave arrival. It should be noted that the M_w 7.8 earthquake started from the previously unmapped Nurdagi–Pazarcık fault, which ruptured northward and initiated the east Anatolian fault bilaterally (Melgar *et al.*, 2023). As a result, depending on the location of strong-motion stations, recorded ground motions can be complex. Neither the accelerograms nor the spectrograms show clear evidence of the reduction of high-frequency components due to potential soil liquefaction. According to geotechnical surveys, the minimum shear-wave velocities are greater than 400 m/s, as determined by both multichannel analysis of surface waves and refraction microtremor techniques. And V_{S30} at this site was measured to be 523 m/s with MASW. According to Andrus *et al.* (2004), soil liquefaction is believed not to develop with such high shear-wave velocities. Therefore, geotechnical efforts shall be given to the investigation of liquefaction potential at strong-motion stations for the 2023 Türkiye earthquake doublet.

To deal with accelerograms at potentially liquefied sites, the baseline correction method proposed for linearly detrended accelerograms (Tian and Alam, 2024) is applied in this study. The jerk correction pattern is introduced to remove the linear trend in the accelerogram due to the potential gradual tilt settlement before the implementation of the tilt correction pattern and the cumulative correction pattern. With this method, we may find in Figure 12 that the waveforms of the integrated ground displacements from corrected accelerations at station TK_2308 are physically meaningful. The situation is different for station TK_2708, where gradual tilt settlement only lasts until 150 s. As a result, it is reasonable to truncate recorded accelerograms and perform baseline corrections on the truncated ones. Thus, we keep the first 120 s of recordings at station TK_2708. We may observe in Figure 13 that corrected ground displacements, which take into consideration the gradual tilt settlement, are physically meaningful in terms of the waveform shapes.

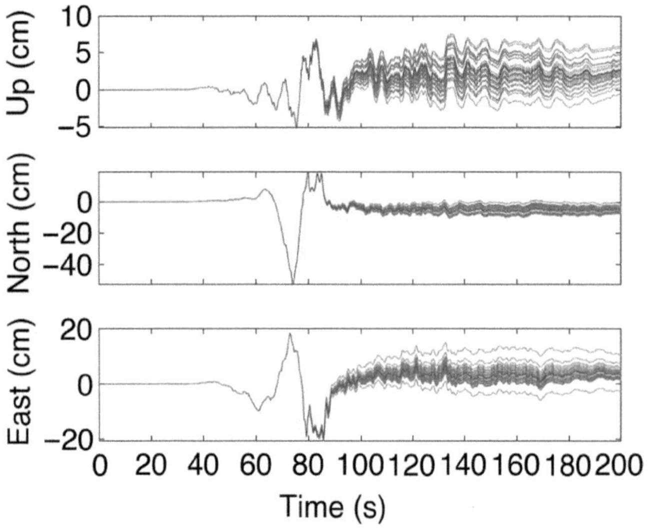

Figure 12. Integrated ground displacements at station TK_2308. The recoveries are obtained with the proposed baseline correction method in Tian and Alam (2024). Our selected time points are in the range of 100–130 s with a 1 s time interval. The red lines are the ones closest to the mean residual displacements. The means of the recovered residual displacements are 2.49, −4.93, and 3.41 cm, respectively. And the standard deviations are 1.45, 1.85, and 2.20 cm, respectively. The color version of this figure is available only in the electronic edition.

Seventy-one (71) strong-motion stations along the east Anatolian fault were analyzed. We marked the two types of velocity drift patterns in Figure 14, along with the obtained horizontal coseismic ground displacements using our baseline correction method. The displacement time histories for the NS and EW directions are shown in Figures S4 and S5, respectively. We may find that the phenomenon of nonlinear velocity drift can be found on both sides of the fault, especially at near-fault stations. We may also find that the distribution of these stations, which exhibit nonlinear velocity drifts, is well correlated with liquefaction-prone areas provided by USGS (see Data and Resources). It also correlates well with identified soil liquefaction manifestations using satellite imagery (Taftsoglou *et al.*, 2023). Their results are generally consistent with the mapped identified liquefaction-prone areas by USGS. As shown in Figure 14, the recovered ground displacements are generally consistent with the detected ground deformations based on Advanced Land Observation Satellite (ALOS)-2 data shown in the base-colored map. In addition, the corrected displacements are consistent with measurements from continuous GPS stations wherever available. The results indicate a left-lateral movement of the east Anatolian fault. The derived displacements in a relatively large region have the potential to be used to determine the centroid moment tensor as well as in the application of fault inversion (Melgar *et al.*, 2012, 2023; Chen *et al.*, 2024). Because the number of continuous GPS stations in this region is somewhat limited, recovered ground

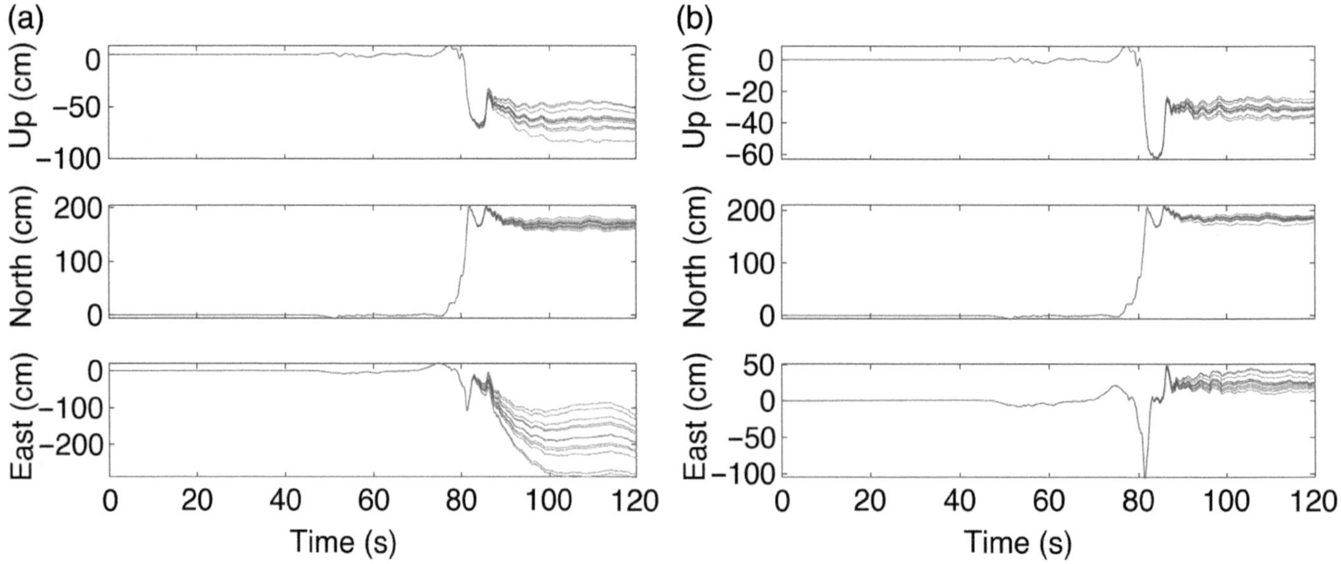

Figure 13. Integrated ground displacements of accelerograms at station TK_2708. Here, the total time length is set as 120 s. (a) Results from the baseline correction method, which does not consider the linear acceleration drift. The mean recovered residual displacements are −64.84, 168.78, and −199.22 cm, respectively, and the standard deviations are 9.24, 5.13, and 55.89 cm, respectively. (b) Results from baseline correction that takes into consideration the linear acceleration drift. The mean recovered residual displacements are −31.28, 184.83, and 26.35 cm, respectively, and the standard deviations are 3.44, 3.60, and 7.78 cm, respectively. The selected time range for the calculation is 90–100 s for both (a) and (b). The color version of this figure is available only in the electronic edition.

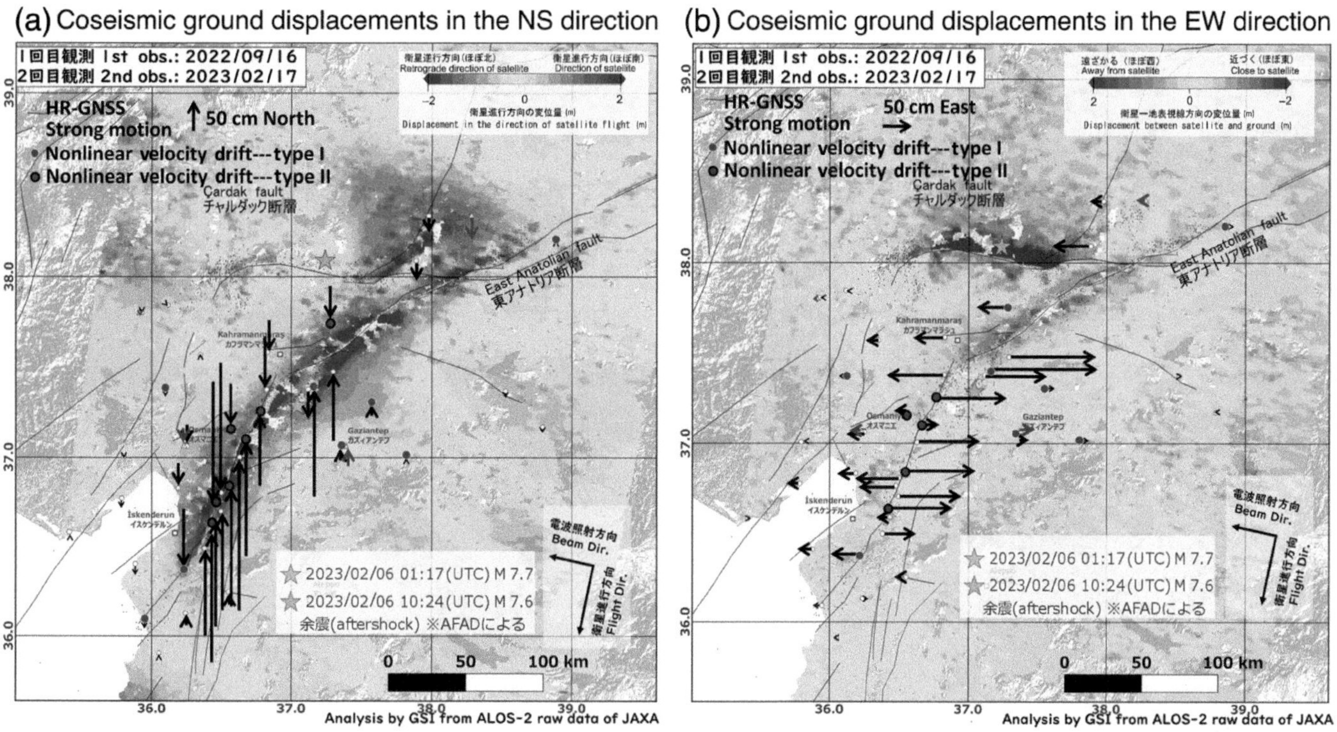

Figure 14. Residual ground displacements in the NS (a) and EW (b) directions. The two types of nonlinear velocity drift patterns are also identified in the figures using solid red circles. The colored base map shows ground deformations for the M_w 7.8 and 7.6 earthquake doublet (adapted from GSI Japan, see Data and Resources), using a pixel offset method. The epicenter and aftershock distribution are from the Disaster and Emergency Management Authority (AFAD) catalog. The fault lines are based on Styron *et al.* (2020). ALOS, Advanced Land Observation Satellite; GNSS, Global Navigation Satellite System. The color version of this figure is available only in the electronic edition.

displacements from recorded accelerograms may serve as an additional data set to help better understand this earthquake.

Conclusion

In this study, by analyzing case histories, which were reportedly related to potential soil liquefaction from the 2011 M_w 9.0 Tohoku earthquake and the M_w 6.2 Christchurch earthquake, we found the existence of nonlinearly drifted integrated velocities, which were marked by Wang *et al.* (2011) in the 2008 M_w 7.9 Wenchuan earthquake and Boore (2001) in the California earthquakes. This study provides one possible explanation for the abnormal integrated velocity drifts. We demonstrate that gradual ground tilt settlement may occur after the strongest portion of ground shaking, resulting from potential soil liquefaction. The settlement may be identified by recognizing the existence of nonlinearly drifted integrated velocities and may also be inferred from the waveforms of corrected displacements using our baseline correction method. If soil liquefaction occurs at the site of a strong-motion station, it is possible that the concrete block supporting the accelerometer may lose its bearing capacity and exhibit abnormal ground tilts. Depending on the intensity of soil liquefaction, durations of such gradual tilt settlements may vary. It should be noted that the analysis in this study is based solely on recorded accelerograms, which lack validation from direct measurements of ground tilts. Shake table tests and numerical analysis of strong-motion stations at liquefiable sites may help us better understand the mechanisms and processes of such gradual tilt settlements.

Based on the analysis of 71 strong-motion stations that recorded the 2023 M_w 7.8 Kahramanmaraş earthquake, we find that the distribution of strong-motion stations exhibiting nonlinearly integrated velocity drifts was well correlated with liquefaction-prone areas. With the identified cause of the nonlinearly drifted integrated velocities, the baseline correction method, which was designed for linearly detrended accelerograms, can be used for ground-displacement calculations. We show that the calculated coseismic displacements for the 2023 M_w 7.8 Kahramanmaraş earthquake are in good agreement with geodetic measurements.

The study in this article may serve as an additional characterization of ground motions, complementing the visual inspection of recorded accelerograms and the time–frequency distributions. The unique aspect of baseline correction of accelerograms is that it provides information related to ground tilts, which enriches our understanding of recorded ground motions.

Data and Resources

This study uses strong-motion data from the Strong-Motion Seismic Networks of Japan (data are available at http://www.kyoshin.bosai.go

.jp/, last accessed May 2024), Strong-Motion Database of New Zealand (data are available at https://www.geonet.org.nz/, last accessed May 2024), and the Disaster and Emergency Management Authority (AFAD) (https://tadas.afad.gov.tr/map, last accessed May 2023). For the 2023 Kahramanmaraş earthquake, the Interferometric Synthetic Aperture Radar (InSAR) results of crustal deformation detected by Advanced Land Observation Satellite (ALOS)-2 data can be obtained from the Geospatial Information Authority of Japan (https://www.gsi.go.jp/cais/topic20230206-e_Turkey.html, last accessed May 2023). Soil liquefaction-prone areas can be found on the U.S. Geological Survey (USGS) earthquake event webpage (https://earthquake.usgs.gov/earthquakes/eventpage/us6000jllz, last accessed May 2023). The supplemental material figures for the case studies of strong-motion recordings as well as recovered ground-displacement waveforms for the 2023 M_w 7.8 Kahramanmaraş earthquake.

Declaration of Competing Interests

The authors acknowledge that there are no conflicts of interest recorded.

Acknowledgments

The financial contributions of Mitacs and Kon Kast Products were critical to conducting this research and have been gratefully acknowledged.

References

Alver, F., Ö. Kılıçarslan, K. Kuterdem, M. Türkoğlu, and M. D. Şentürk (2017). Seismic Monitoring at the Turkish National Seismic Network (TNSN), *Summ. Bull. Int. Seismol. Cent.* **53,** 41–58.

Andrus, R. D., and K. H. Stokoe II (2000). Liquefaction resistance of soils from shear-wave velocity, *J. Geotech. Geoenviron. Eng.* **126,** no. 11, 1015–1025.

Andrus, R. D., K. H. Stokoe, and C H. Hsein Juang (2004). Guide for shear-wave-based liquefaction potential evaluation, *Earthq. Spectra* **20,** no. 2, 285–308.

Boore, D. M. (2001). Effect of baseline corrections on displacements and response spectra for several recordings of the 1999 Chi-Chi, Taiwan, earthquake, *Bull. Seismol. Soc. Am.* **91,** no. 5, 1199–1211, doi: 10.1785/0120000703.

Boore, D. M., and J. J. Bommer (2005). Processing of strong-motion accelerograms: Needs, options and consequences, *Soil Dynam. Earthq. Eng.* **25,** no. 2, 93–115, doi: 10.1016/j.soildyn.2004.10.007.

Bradley, B. A., and M. Cubrinovski (2011). Near-source strong ground motions observed in the 22 February 2011 Christchurch earthquake, *Seismol. Res. Lett.* **82,** no. 6, 853–865.

Çetin, K. Ö., M. Ilgaç, G. Can, E. Çakır, and B. Söylemez (2020). Preliminary report on engineering and geological effects of the January 24, 2020 Magnitude 6.7 earthquake in Elazi⊠, Turkey, doi: 10.17603/ds2-9jz1-e287.

Cetin, K. O., B. Soylemez, H. Guzel, and E. Cakir (2024). Soil liquefaction sites following the February 6, 2023, Kahramanmaraş-Türkiye earthquake sequence, *Bull. Earthq. Eng.* **23,** 921–944.

Chen, K., G. Wei, C. Milliner, L. Dal Zilio, C. Liang, and J. P. Avouac (2024). Super-shear ruptures steered by pre-stress heterogeneities during the 2023 Kahramanmaraş earthquake doublet, *Nat. Commun.* **15,** no. 1, 7004.

Cox, B. R., R. W. Boulanger, K. Tokimatsu, C. M. Wood, A. Abe, S. Ashford, J. Donahue, K. Ishihara, R. Kayen, K. Katsumata, *et al.* (2013). Liquefaction at strong motion stations and in Urayasu City during the 2011 Tohoku-Oki earthquake, *Earthq. Spectra* **29,** no. 1_suppl, 55–80.

Darragh, B., W. A. L. T. Silva, and N. I. C. K. Gregor (2004). Strong motion record processing for the PEER center, *Proc. of COSMOS Invited Workshop on Strong-Motion Record Processing*, Richmond, California, 26–27.

Demir, A., E. Celebi, H. Ozturk, Z. Ozcan, A. Ozocak, E. Bol, S. Sert, F. Z. Sahin, E. Arslan, Z. Yaman Dere, *et al.* (2024). Destructive impact of successive high magnitude earthquakes occurred in Türkiye's Kahramanmaraş on February 6, 2023, *Bull. Earthq. Eng.* **23,** 893–919.

Geotechnical Extreme Events Reconnaissance (GEER) Association (2011). Geotechnical effects of the M_w 9.0 Tohoku, Japan, earthquake of March 11, 2011, *EERI Special Earthquake Report*, Earthquake Engineering Research Institute, 12 pp.

Gorini, A., M. Nicoletti, P. Marsan, R. Bianconi, R. De Nardis, L. Filippi, S. Marcucci, F. Palma, and E. Zambonelli (2010). The Italian strong motion network, *Bull. Earthq. Eng.* **8,** 1075–1090.

Graizer, V. (2006). Tilts in strong ground motion, *Bull. Seismol. Soc. Am.* **96,** no. 6, 2090–2102, doi: 10.1785/0120060065.

Graizer, V. (2010). Strong motion recordings and residual displacements: What are we actually recording in strong motion seismology? *Seismol. Res. Lett.* **81,** no. 4, 635–639, doi: 10.1785/gssrl.81.4.635.

Graizer, V. (2021). Comment on "dynamic tilt correction using direct rotational motion measurements" by Felix Bernauer, Joachim Wassermann, and Heiner Igel, *Seismol. Res. Lett.* **92,** no. 3, 2081–2086.

Graizer, V. M. (1979). Determination of the true ground displacement by using strong motion records, *Izvestiya Phys. Solid Earth* **15,** no. 12, 875–885.

Graizer, V. M. (2005). Effect of tilt on strong motion data processing, *Soil Dynam. Earthq. Eng.* **25,** 197–204.

Greenfield, M. W. (2017). Effects of long-duration ground motions on liquefaction hazards, *Doctoral dissertation*, University of Washington.

Hughes, F. E., and S. P. G. Madabhushi (2019). Liquefaction induced displacement and rotation of structures with wide basements, *Soil Dynam. Earthq. Eng.* **120,** 75–84.

Ishihara, K. (1985). Stability of natural deposits during earthquakes, *Proc. of the 11th Int. Conf. on Soil Mechanics and Foundation Engineering*, Vol. 1, San Francisco, 321–376.

Iwan, W. D., M. A. Moser, and C. Y. Peng (1985). Some observations on strong-motion earthquake measurement using a digital accelerograph, *Bull. Seismol. Soc. Am.* **75,** no. 5, 1225–1246.

Kostadinov, M. V., and F. Yamazaki (2001). Detection of soil liquefaction from strong motion records, *Earthq. Eng. Struct. Dynam.* **30,** no. 2, 173–193.

Kramer, S. L., B. Asl Astaneh, P. Ozener, and S. S. Sideras (2015). Effects of liquefaction on ground surface motions, in *Perspectives on Earthquake Geotechnical Engineering. Geotechnical, Geological and Earthquake Engineering*, A. Ansal and M. Sakr (Editors), Vol. 37, Springer, Cham, Switzerland, 285–309.

Kramer, S. L., and M. W. Greenfield (2019). The use of numerical analysis in the interpretation of liquefaction case histories, in *Earthquake*

Geotechnical Engineering for Protection and Development of Environment and Constructions, F. Silvestri and N. Moraci (Editors), CRC Press, London, 173–188.

Kramer, S. L., S. S. Sideras, and M. W. Greenfield (2016). The timing of liquefaction and its utility in liquefaction hazard evaluation, *Soil Dynam. Earthq. Eng.* **91,** 133–146.

Kramer, S. L., S. S. Sideras, M. W. Greenfield, and B. Hushmand (2018). Liquefaction, ground motions, and pore pressures at the Wildlife Liquefaction Array in the 1987 Superstition Hills earthquake, *Geotechnical Earthquake Engineering and Soil Dynamics V*, 384–402.

Melgar, D., Y. Bock, and B. W. Crowell (2012). Real-time centroid moment tensor determination for large earthquakes from local and regional displacement records, *Geophys. J. Int.* **188,** no. 2, 703–718, doi: 10.1002/jgrb.50135.

Melgar, D., Y. Bock, D. Sanchez, B. W. Crowell, *et al.* (2013). On robust and reliable automated baseline corrections for strong motion seismology, *J. Geophys. Res.* **118,** no. 3, 1177–1187.

Melgar, D., T. Taymaz, A. Ganas, B. W. Crowell, T. Öcalan, M. Kahraman, V. Tsironi, S. Yolsal-Çevikbil, S. Valkaniotis, T. S. Irmak, *et al.* (2023). Sub-and super-shear ruptures during the 2023 M_w 7.8 and M_w 7.6 earthquake doublet in SE Türkiye, *Seismica*, doi: 10.26443/seismica.v2i3.387.

Mirza, A. (2013). Pump Station and Pressure Main No.128, *Water New Zealand's 55th Annual Conference and Expo*, 16–18 October 2013, Hamilton, New Zealand.

Nigbor, R. L. (1994). Six-degree-of-freedom ground-motion measurement, *Bull. Seismol. Soc. Am.* **84,** no. 5, 1665–1669.

Özener, P. T., M. W. Greenfield, S. S. Sideras, and S. L. Kramer (2020). Identification of time of liquefaction triggering, *Soil Dynam. Earthq. Eng.* **128,** 105,895.

Ozkula, G., R. K. Dowell, T. Baser, J. L. Lin, O. A. Numanoglu, O. Ilhan, C. G. Olgun, C. W. Huang, and T. D. Uludag (2023). Field reconnaissance and observations from the February 6, 2023, Turkey earthquake sequence, *Nat. Hazards* **119,** no. 1, 663–700.

Stockwell, R. G., L. Mansinha, and R. P. Lowe (1996). Localization of the complex spectrum: The S transform, *IEEE Trans. Signal Process.* **44,** no. 4, 998–1001.

Styron, R., and M. Pagani (2020). The GEM global active faults database, *Earthq. Spectra* **36,** no. 1_suppl, 160–180, doi: 10.1177/8755293020944182.

Taftsoglou, M., S. Valkaniotis, G. Papathanassiou, and E. Karantanellis (2023). Satellite imagery for rapid detection of liquefaction surface manifestations: The case study of Türkiye–Syria 2023 earthquakes, *Remote Sens.* **15,** no. 17, 4190.

Tian, S., and M. S. Alam (2024). Baseline correction of ground motions for linearly detrended accelerograms, *Bull. Seismol. Soc. Am.* doi: 10.1785/0120230162.

Tian, S., P. Gardoni, H. Li, and W. Yuan (2019). Baseline correction of ground motions with physics-based correction patterns, *Geophys. J. Int.* **217,** no. 1, 668–681.

Tian, S., P. Gardoni, and W. Yuan (2019). Coseismic deformation of the 6 February 2018 M_w 6.2 Hualien earthquake based on strong-motion recordings, *Seismol. Res. Lett.* **90,** no. 1, 108–117.

Trifunac, M. D., and M. I. Todorovska (2001). A note on the useable dynamic range of accelerographs recording translation, *Soil Dynam. Earthq. Eng.* **21,** no. 4, 275–286.

Tün, M., E. Pekkan, S. Mutlu, and Y. Güney (2016). AnaNet: A new weak/strong-motion network for metropolitan Eskisehir And Bursa, West Anatolia, Turkey, *International Workshop on Earthquakes in North Iceland*, Husavik, North Iceland, 31 May to 3 June 2016.

Wang, R., B. Schurr, C. Milkereit, Z. Shao, and M. Jin (2011). An improved automatic scheme for empirical baseline correction of digital strong-motion records, *Bull. Seismol. Soc. Am.* **101,** no. 5, 2029–2044, doi: 10.1785/0120110039.

Wotherspoon, L. M., R. Orense, B. Bradley, B. R. Cox, C. Wood, and R. A. Green (2013). Geotechnical characterization of Christchurch strong motion stations, *New Zealand Earthquake Commission* 195.

Wotherspoon, L. M., R. P. Orense, R. A. Green, B. A. Bradley, B. R. Cox, and C. M. Wood (2015). Assessment of liquefaction evaluation procedures and severity index frameworks at Christchurch strong motion stations, *Soil Dynam. Earthq. Eng.* **79,** 335–346.

Wu, Y. M., and C. F. Wu (2007). Approximate recovery of coseismic deformation from Taiwan strong-motion records, *J. Seismol.* **11,** no. 2, 159–170, doi: 10.1007/s10950-006-9043-x.

Yang, J. (2004). Reappraisal of vertical motion effects on soil liquefaction, *Geotechnique* **54,** no. 10, 671–676.

Youd, T. L., and I. M. Idriss (2001). Liquefaction resistance of soils: Summary report from the 1996 NCEER and 1998 NCEER/NSF workshops on evaluation of liquefaction resistance of soils, *J. Geotech. Geoenviron. Eng.* **127,** no. 4, 297–313.

Zembaty, Z., G. Mutke, D. Nawrocki, and P. Bobra (2016). Rotational ground-motion records from induced seismic events, *Seismol. Res. Lett.* **88,** no. 1, 13–22, doi: 10.1785/0220160131.

Zhan, W., and Q. Chen (2021). Accelerogram-based method for quick assessment of liquefaction occurrence, *J. Geotech. Geoenviron. Eng.* **147,** no. 8, 04,021,060.

Manuscript received 30 September 2024
Published online 29 October 2025

Effects of Pore Pressure Change on Coulomb Stress Change and Initiation of Induced Seismicity in the Raton Basin, Colorado–New Mexico

Fabiana Fuentes[1,2], Megan R. M. Brown*[3], Manuel M. Mendoza[1,4], Shemin Ge[1], and Anne F. Sheehan[1,4]

Abstract

We investigate the effect of pore pressure on Coulomb static stress calculations of induced earthquakes in the Raton basin on the Colorado–New Mexico border. Change in Coulomb static stress (ΔCSS) on faults can bring the area closer or further from failure. Wastewater injection in the basin began in 1994, and multiple sequences of induced seismicity have occurred, especially since 2001. Overall Coulomb static stress includes the pore pressure increase from wastewater injection and Coulomb static stress transfer from induced earthquakes. We use three models to account for these two components: (1) constant apparent friction model in which pore pressure effect is folded into friction coefficient; (2) isotropic model in which pore pressure is computed as a function of volumetric strain; and (3) diffusion model in which pore pressure is obtained from a groundwater diffusion model. These three models are used to calculate the ΔCSS caused in part by M_w 4.0 or larger earthquakes that occurred prior to the largest M_w 5.3 event in 2011. The differences in modeled results clearly show that pore pressure is an important causal mechanism for initiating seismicity. In particular, the diffusion model best explains the locations of the seismicity. Model results indicate that deliberate inclusion of pore pressure in ΔCSS calculations is necessary; oversimplification of the pore pressure component can significantly change the distribution and value of ΔCSS in model results.

Cite this article as Fuentes, F., M. R. M. Brown, M. M. Mendoza, S. Ge, and A. F. Sheehan (2025). Effects of Pore Pressure Change on Coulomb Stress Change and Initiation of Induced Seismicity in the Raton Basin, Colorado–New Mexico, *Seismol. Res. Lett.* **97**, 1842–1852, doi: 10.1785/0220250148.

Supplemental Material

Introduction

Seismicity occurrence and wastewater injection activity

The Raton basin, located in southern Colorado and northern New Mexico, has been a focus of study to understand the relationship between increased seismicity and anthropogenic stress related to oil and gas development (Fig. 1). Seismicity in the Raton basin began increasing in 2001 and multiple lines of evidence indicate that most of the earthquake sequences were induced by wastewater injection perturbations in the subsurface (Rubinstein *et al.*, 2014; Nakai *et al.*, 2017). Seismicity in the Raton basin was relatively low from 1972 to July 2001 during which only one event greater than moment magnitude (M_w) 4.0 occurred. Between August 2001 and 2024, more than 15 events with M_w greater than 4.0 were recorded in the Raton basin (Fig. S1, available in the supplemental material to this article). This earthquake sequence included the largest event recorded in the basin, an M_w 5.3 earthquake in 2011. The increase in seismicity corresponds spatially and temporally with increased wastewater injection rates in the Raton basin. Oil and gas extraction generates large volumes of wastewater that is then injected into the subsurface (Figs. S2 and S3).

The increase in seismicity in the central United States (e.g., Colorado, New Mexico, Oklahoma, Texas) was caused by the rapid increase in injection associated with oil and gas production (e.g., Ellsworth, 2013; Keranen *et al.*, 2014). Previous studies focused on understanding the seismicity pattern (Rubinstein *et al.*, 2014; Nakai *et al.*, 2017; Glasgow *et al.*, 2021) and the mechanisms that could be contributing to

1. Department of Geological Sciences, University of Colorado Boulder, Boulder, Colorado, U.S.A., https://orcid.org/0000-0002-9022-5056 (MMM); https://orcid.org/0000-0002-0960-1609 (SG); https://orcid.org/0000-0002-9629-1687 (AFS); 2. Now at LRE Water, Denver, Colorado, U.S.A.; 3. Department of Earth, Atmosphere, and Environment, Northern Illinois University, DeKalb, Illinois, U.S.A., https://orcid.org/0000-0002-6523-927X (MRMB); 4. Cooperative Institute for Research in Environmental Sciences, University of Colorado Boulder, Boulder, Colorado, U.S.A.

*Corresponding author: mbrown18@niu.edu

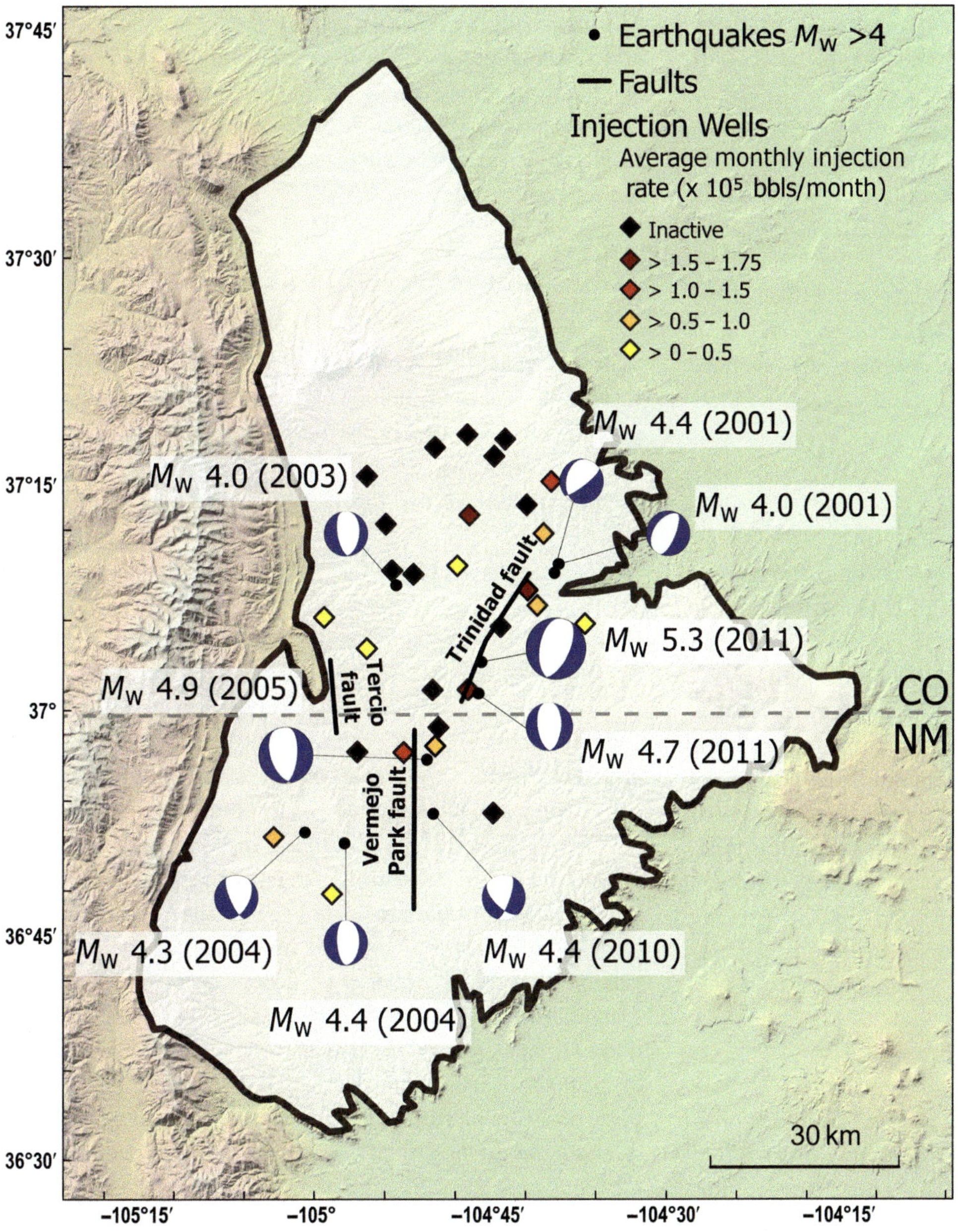

Figure 1. Locations and focal mechanisms of earthquakes sequences with M_W greater than or equal to 4.0 within the Raton basin between 2001 and 2011. The black solid lines represent the three fault systems active during 2001–2023. Plotted epicenters correspond to seismic events analyzed in this study. The diamond symbols indicate wastewater injection wells, and their colors indicate the average monthly injection rate through August 2001 (COGCC, 2023; New Mexico Oil Conservation Division, NMOCD, 2023).

inducing seismicity, from the perspective of increased pore pressure and poroelasticity (Ge and Saar, 2022; Stokes *et al.*, 2023; Chambers *et al.*, 2024; Hill *et al.*, 2024). Proposed models suggest the injection of fluids increases pore pressure, which can initiate seismicity by reducing the effective normal stress on critically stressed faults. Goebel and Brodsky (2018) suggested that poroelastic stress may be a causal mechanism for induced seismicity that is far from the injection source. Furthermore, earthquakes can modify the stress state of nearby faults, leading to either an increase or decrease in seismic activity, and can be quantified by studying the interactions between them (King *et al.*, 1994). The static stress theory assumes that aftershocks can be triggered by the mainshock that causes the Coulomb stress increase at aftershock locations (Toda *et al.*, 1998; Lin and Stein, 2004).

Objectives

To better understand the distribution and triggering mechanisms of the increased seismicity observed in the Raton basin from 2001 to 2011, this study combines Coulomb static stress changes and pore pressure effects to assess stress variations, aftershock locations, and cumulative stress buildup in the basin over 10 yr of seismic activity for earthquakes of magnitudes greater than 4.0. By integrating these mechanisms, we can effectively evaluate the spatial evolution of postseismic stress changes, enabling improved forecasting of aftershock patterns and seismic hazards.

The primary objectives are to explain the potential for triggered seismicity, the locations of aftershocks, and quantify the stress changes imparted by the earlier earthquakes on the surrounding fault network. In addition, we incorporate pore pressure changes from volumetric strain and consider the spatiotemporal evolution of pore pressure diffusion from wastewater injection (Stokes *et al.*, 2023) into our analysis.

Materials and Methods

Methods

In this study, we model the Coulomb static stress changes (ΔCSS) (Toda *et al.*, 2011) resulting from the earthquake sequences in the Raton basin between 2001 and 2011 (Table S1). The methodology employed involves the following steps:

1. Modeling the Coulomb stress changes resulting from the earthquake sequences in the Raton basin between 2001 and 2011 (prior to the largest event).
2. Incorporating pore pressure changes due to volumetric strain into calculating Coulomb stress change.
3. Incorporating the spatiotemporal evolution of pore pressure from wastewater injection (Stokes *et al.*, 2023) into calculating Coulomb stress change.
4. Quantifying the stress changes imparted by the earlier earthquakes on the surrounding fault systems.
5. Utilizing the modeled Coulomb stress changes to evaluate the potential for triggered seismicity and explain the locations of observed aftershocks.

Coulomb static stress change modeling

Coulomb static stress change occurs as a result of slip along a source fault and can promote or inhibit potential earthquake triggering (King *et al.*, 1994; Toda *et al.*, 1998) based on changes in shear and normal stresses on the fault plane. Positive values of the Coulomb stress change promote rupture, and negative values inhibit rupture. Coulomb static stress change can be quantified on faults surrounding the earthquake slip zone, particularly on receiver faults or optimally oriented faults. Coulomb static stress change on a receiver fault is independent of the regional stress regime; rather, it depends on fault geometry, slip sense, and friction coefficient (King *et al.*, 1994). The general equation for calculating ΔCSS corresponds to (Stein, 1999)

$$\Delta \mathrm{CSS} = \Delta\tau_s + \mu(\Delta\sigma_n + \Delta p), \quad (1)$$

in which $\Delta\tau_s$ is the change in shear stress (positive in the direction of fault slip), μ is the friction coefficient, usually values range from 0.6 to 0.8 (Harris, 1998), $\Delta\sigma_n$ is the change in normal stress (positive if the fault is unclamped), and Δp is the pore pressure change within the fault. Experimental observation suggests that in many cases, changes in pore pressure in rocks and soils are determined by changes in the mean stress (Skempton, 1954).

For a homogeneous isotropic poroelastic medium, the relation between stress changes and pore pressure under undrained conditions is given by (Rice and Cleary, 1976; Roeloffs, 1996)

$$\Delta p = -\frac{B\Delta\sigma_{kk}}{3}, \quad (2)$$

in which B is the Skempton's coefficient $0 \le B < 1$, $\Delta\sigma_{kk}$ is the summation over the diagonal elements of the stress tensor (Rice and Cleary, 1976), and $\Delta\sigma_{kk}/3$ corresponds to the mean stress. The sign convention dictates that positive stress represents tension, whereas negative stress represents compression. Skempton's coefficient is a ratio that describes how pore pressure changes based on a change in externally applied stress and often ranges in value from 0.5 to 0.9 (Cocco and Rice, 2002; Zhang *et al.*, 2009). Using the Skempton's coefficient, Cocco and Rice (2002) incorporated pore pressure into Coulomb stress as shown in equation (3) that is termed as the isotropic model:

$$\Delta \mathrm{CSS} = \Delta\tau_s + \mu\left(\Delta\sigma_n + \frac{B\Delta\sigma_{kk}}{3}\right). \quad (3)$$

It is assumed (e.g., King *et al.*, 1994; Harris, 1998; Cocco and Rice, 2002) that in Coulomb static stress analysis the change in pore pressure becomes proportional to the fault-normal stress $\Delta p = -B\Delta\sigma_n$ when $\sigma_{xx} = \sigma_{yy} = \sigma_{zz}$ (Rice, 1992), which leads to the definition of the apparent friction model defined by

$$\Delta \mathrm{CSS} = \Delta\tau_s + \mu'(\Delta\sigma_n), \quad (4)$$

in which the apparent friction coefficient corresponds to $\mu' = \mu(1 - B)$. The apparent friction coefficient ranges between 0 and 1, and 0.4 is a proposed value (King *et al.*, 1994). According to Beeler *et al.* (2000), the widely employed apparent friction coefficient model exhibits a considerable dependency on the assumed value of the apparent friction coefficient. Consequently, this model may present a misleading perspective when estimating stress changes. A comparison between the isotropic model and the apparent friction coefficient model revealed significant differences in the calculated values of the ΔCSS (Beeler *et al.*, 2000; Cocco and Rice, 2002).

Fluid injection increases pore pressure, reducing the effective normal stress and thereby increasing the Coulomb stress toward failure promotion (Hsieh and Bredehoeft, 1981). Small pore pressure perturbations can enable slip along critically stressed pre-existing faults. We incorporate dynamic, semi-transient pore pressure change from injection into Coulomb stress change modeling. This enables a more comprehensive analysis by integrating the mechanical influences of fault strength and fluid pressure effects on the stress changes. We define the following as the diffusion model:

$$\Delta \mathrm{CSS} = \Delta\tau_s + \mu\left(\Delta\sigma_n + \frac{B\Delta\sigma_{kk}}{3} + \Delta p_s\right), \quad (5)$$

in which Δp_s correspond to the pore pressure change from injection.

The isotropic model (equation 3) and the apparent friction model (equation 4) incorporate pore pressure based on the mean stress due to slip on the source fault, that is, a compression will increase pore pressure. The value of pore pressure change is related to stress through the Skempton's coefficient. The diffusion model (equation 5) explicitly includes the pore pressure generated from wastewater injection in addition to the pore pressure generated from stress caused by fault slip.

TABLE 1
Estimates of Magnitude and Fault Parameters

Event Date (yyyy/mm/dd)	Magnitude (M_w)	Length (km)	Width (km)	Average Displacement (m)
2011/08/23	5.3	4.20	3.96	0.20
2011/08/22	4.7	1.71	2.05	0.12
2010/01/18	4.0	0.60	0.96	0.06
2005/08/10	4.9	2.31	2.56	0.14
2004/08/01	4.3	0.94	1.33	0.08
2004/03/22	4.4	1.09	1.48	0.09
2003/09/13	4.0	0.60	0.96	0.06
2001/09/05	4.4	1.09	1.48	0.09
2001/09/04	4.0	0.60	0.96	0.06

Fault parameters: Average slip and rupture length given magnitude

Coulomb static stress transfer to specified faults is influenced by key parameters (King *et al.*, 1994): earthquake source parameters, coefficient of friction, receiver fault geometry, and slip direction of the receiver fault. Some fault parameters can be obtained with reasonable detail from well-constrained recorded earthquakes. We use relocated earthquakes (Rubinstein *et al.*, 2014) and their focal mechanism solutions (Herrmann, 2020). We calculate the average displacement for the nine earthquakes using the empirical relationships of Wells and Coppersmith (1994) that relate magnitude, average displacement, and rupture length. We model them as predominantly normal faulting events (Table 1).

Coulomb static stress change calculation

Coulomb stress change was modeled utilizing the U.S. Geological Survey Coulomb 3.3 software (Lin and Stein, 2004; Toda *et al.*, 2005, 2011). This modeling approach assumes an elastic half-space with uniform isotropic elastic properties, based on the theoretical framework developed by Okada (1985). The software considers the constant apparent friction model for fluid pressure influences on the calculated stress changes. To account for the influence of pore-fluid pressure on fault slip, we incorporated the isotropic model, which provides a more distinct representation of poroelasticity than the constant apparent friction model. Cocco and Rice (2002) suggest that the apparent friction and the isotropic models yield variations in the spatial patterns. Beeler *et al.* (2000) quantified these variations and found considerable differences across diverse fault types. Most importantly, we integrated the pore pressure distribution resulting from fluid injection into the diffusion model. The pore pressure distribution is extracted from a 3D pore pressure diffusion model (Stokes *et al.*, 2023), which models pore pressure change based on injection across the basin starting in 1994, calculated at 3 km below ground surface. Their model employed a diffusivity range of 0.01–1.0 m^2/s. In our models, we used the pore pressure change results that were modeled with a diffusivity of 1.0 m^2/s, which corresponds to the high end of the diffusivity range.

The three Coulomb stress change models take pore pressure into effect in different ways:

1. For the apparent friction model (equation 4) the effective coefficient of friction used is $\mu' = 0.4$ as proposed by King *et al.* (1994), which accounts for the effect of fluid pressure generated by static strain.
2. For the isotropic model (equation 3), the static friction coefficient used is $\mu = 0.75$, and the Skempton coefficient corresponds to $B = 0.47$ (Zhang *et al.*, 2009).
3. For the diffusion model (equation 5), we incorporated the pore pressure distributions resulting from the fluid injection. Specifically, we utilized the modeled pore pressure data (Stokes *et al.*, 2023) for three distinct time periods: September 2001, August 2005, and August 2011, corresponding to the cumulative Coulomb stress change for those respective periods.

Coulomb stress changes on specified receiver fault planes

We assess ΔCSS on specified receiver fault planes. Their fault geometry and slip direction corresponds to the input parameters. To further examine whether the events triggered subsequent seismicity, we calculated the Coulomb stress change using a 0.1 m × 0.1 m grid over a 45 km × 45 km domain. We quantify the ΔCSS on the Trinidad and Vermejo Park faults following the 2001–2011 earthquake sequences. Through ΔCSS modeling, we elucidate how these 2001–2011 earthquake sequences, before the largest magnitude event, impacted the specified faults of interest (Vermejo Park and Trinidad) by promoting or inhibiting potential future seismicity. A dip-slip normal source fault is used for each earthquake event, following the Aki and Richards (2009) strike/dip/rake convention. Coulomb static stress changes are evaluated at a depth of 3 km below ground surface, corresponding to the chosen hypocenter depth of the earthquakes, which represents the average depth of seismicity.

Seismicity and faults zones in the Raton basin

Injection-induced seismicity in the Raton basin increased shortly after widespread wastewater injection began in 1999 and has continued to the present. The observed seismicity is localized within the Precambrian crystalline basement, at an average depth of 3–4 km below ground surface (Nakai *et al.*, 2017; Herrmann, 2020; Stokes *et al.*, 2023). The Raton basin lies within an east–west extensional stress field associated with the Rio Grande rift system (Lundstern and Zoback, 2020). The northeast-striking normal faulting observed in the region is consistent with this extensional regime.

Three prominent north–south-trending normal fault zones have exhibited considerable seismicity (Rubinstein *et al.*, 2014; Nakai *et al.*, 2017): (1) the Trinidad fault zone, (2) the Vermejo Park fault zone, and (3) the Tercio fault zone (Fig. 1, Table S1). These fault zones have exhibited temporal variations in seismicity rates since the start of injection. A total of nine earthquakes ($M_w > 4$) occurred within the basin during this period (Fig. 1), culminating to the largest event to date (M_w 5.3) in 2011. Another important characteristic is that the observed decline in wastewater injection rates coincided with decreasing seismicity after peak injection activity from 2001 to 2011 (Colorado Oil and Gas Conservation Commission; COGCC, 2023; New Mexico Oil Conservation Division; NMOCD, 2023).

Trinidad fault

The Trinidad fault is a complex northeast–southwest-striking normal fault consisting of two segments: northern Trinidad and southern Trinidad. Seismic activity began on the northern fault segment in August 2001. A combination of high-rate injection wells likely triggered this sequence by increasing pore pressure in the fault zone (Stokes *et al.*, 2023). A foreshock of M_w 4.0 occurred on 4 September 2001, followed by an M_w 4.4 mainshock the next day. Aftershock locations migrated southward along the northern Trinidad segment. After the 2001 sequence, the Trinidad fault remained relatively quiescent until 22 August 2011, when an M_w 4.7 foreshock struck the southern Trinidad segment. Hours later, on 23 August 2011, the largest recorded earthquake in the Raton basin to date occurred, with a magnitude of M_w 5.3 (Rubinstein *et al.*, 2014; Glasgow *et al.*, 2023). This event was widely felt across Trinidad, Colorado, and northern New Mexico. Glasgow *et al.* (2023) provide a detailed study of the seismicity associated with the 2011 mainshock including the complexity of the foreshocks and aftershocks. Here, we focus on only the events that are greater than M_w 4.0.

Injections near the Trinidad fault experienced a significant decrease after 2011, likely contributing to the declining seismicity rate from 2012 to 2024. Overall, seismicity rates on the Trinidad fault have exhibited temporal variations (e.g., Glasgow *et al.*, 2023), with major activity occurring between 2001 and 2011, likely influenced by the injection rates at the nearby wells.

Vermejo Park fault

The Vermejo Park fault (Fig. 1) is a complex roughly north–south-striking normal fault that extends approximately 22 km (Nakai *et al.*, 2017; Wang *et al.*, 2024). Seismic activity in this area began in January 2002 and has remained consistently high since then. Prior to the M_w 4.9 mainshock in August 2005, more than six earthquakes with magnitudes greater than 3.0 were recorded within the fault zone (Rubinstein *et al.*, 2014). Because of the sparse seismic network coverage at that time, the exact locations and depths of the early-stage seismic events remain uncertain. However, the 2008–2010 earthquake catalog from Nakai *et al.* (2017) shows numerous events along the Vermejo Park fault zone, with an average depth of approximately 5 km. The Vermejo Park fault is an active system with the highest observed seismicity rate in the basin between 2005 (when seismicity began on the fault) and 2024. Wang *et al.* (2024) use YX array that began recording in 2016 and a deployment of a nodal array during the summer of 2018 to further detail the complexity of this fault zone based on events between 2016 and 2020.

Tercio fault

The Tercio fault is a north-northwest–south-southeast-striking normal fault that extends roughly 10 km (Nakai *et al.*, 2017). The seismicity catalog by Nakai *et al.* (2017) from 2008 to 2010 shows high concentrations of seismic events occurring at an average depth of approximately 4 km. Most events within the Tercio fault indicate northwest-striking normal faults (Glasgow *et al.*, 2021). The Tercio fault, which is the last of the three fault zones to become active in 2004, is over 10 km from the highest historical injection in central Raton basin. Spatiotemporal changes in injection on a regional scale likely caused the delay in activity. Even though total injection started decreasing in the basin in 2011, the Tercio fault zone became the most seismically active during 2016 and 2017 with several events of $M_w > 4$. Pore pressure diffusion continues with lower rates of injection and after injection stops (Yeo *et al.*, 2020; Hill *et al.*, 2024).

Results and Discussion

The results from three different ΔCSS models differ in how pore pressure was incorporated into the calculation: the apparent friction model (equation 4), the isotropic model (equation 3), and the diffusion model (equation 5).

2001–2004 earthquake sequence

The northern Trinidad fault segment experienced a foreshock of M_w 4.0 on 4 September 2001. We computed ΔCSS on the northern Trinidad fault (Fig. 2); the red lobes represent areas where the ΔCSS has increased, indicating elevated likelihood of future seismic activity in those regions. In contrast, the purple/blue regions correspond to the area where a decrease in ΔCSS is observed. This decrease suggests a delay of seismicity in those areas over time. The apparent friction model (Fig. 2a) exhibits how the earthquake raised the stress at the future mainshock location, represented by the white star. In Figure 2b, the isotropic model exhibits an increase in the distribution of ΔCSS in the off-fault lobes, emphasizing the role of pore pressure in earthquake failure processes compared to the apparent friction model. The location of the mainshock

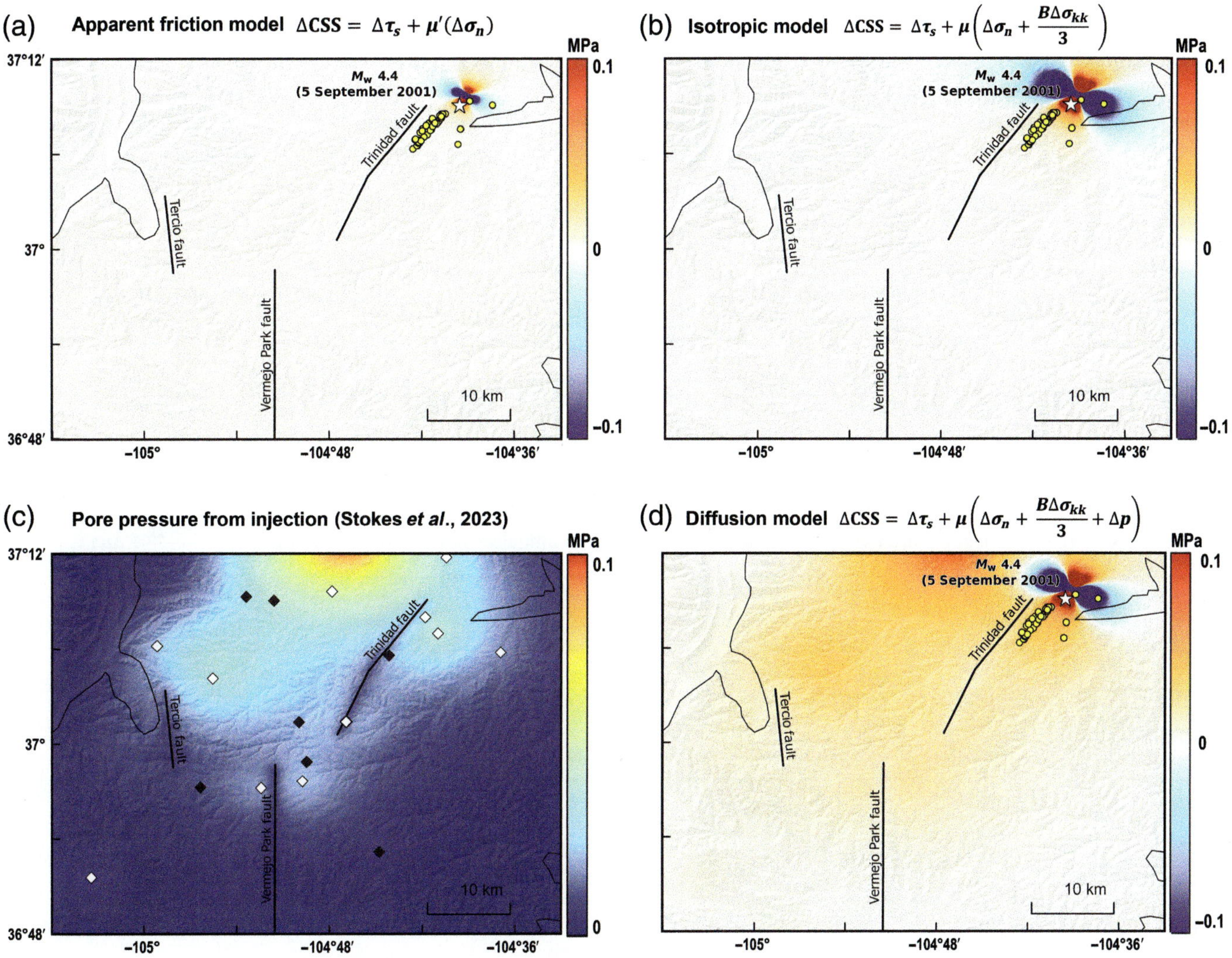

(M_w 4.4) is well correlated with the areas of elevated positive ΔCSS, where the stress increase ranges from 0.04 to 0.08 MPa. In addition, the aftershock locations along the Trinidad fault can be explained by the isotropic model because it raised the stress distribution along the fault.

Pore pressure change for September 2001 (Fig. 2c), modeled from fluid injection during this period (Stokes *et al.*, 2023), was then incorporated into the diffusion model (Fig. 2d). The ΔCSS calculated by the diffusion model significantly modifies the ΔCSS distribution, across the Trinidad fault, west of the fault, and onto the northern part of the Vermejo Park fault. The diffusion model suggests that the initial M_w 4.0 event potentially triggered the M_w 4.4 mainshock where ΔCSS > 0.08 MPa. Furthermore, it is proposed that the initial M_w 4.0 earthquake sequence in 2001 was likely triggered by increased pore pressure due to injection (Stokes *et al.*, 2023). These three models show significant variations in the spatial distribution of ΔCSS as a result of different approaches for incorporating pore pressures. Overall, an examination of the spatial distribution revealed correlations between areas experiencing positive increase in ΔCSS and the progression of seismicity. It is pertinent to note, however, that a limited number of aftershock events occurred within zones exhibiting a decreased ΔCSS.

Figure 2. Coulomb static stress change (ΔCSS) imparted by the M_w 4.0 event (4 September 2001) on the Trinidad fault (strike/dip/rake: 53/71/–73). The white star denotes the future M_w 4.4 mainshock location; yellow dots show aftershock distribution. (a) Constant apparent friction model. (b) Isotropic model. (c) Pore pressure model results in September 2001; the white diamonds indicate active injection wells through 2001; the black diamonds indicate inactive injection wells (Stokes *et al.*, 2023). (d) Diffusion model including pore pressure from injection.

Two years after the occurrences of the magnitude 4.0 and 4.4 earthquakes on the northern Trinidad fault segment in 2001, an M_w 4.0 earthquake occurred on 13 September 2003 (Figs. 1 and 3) approximately 20 km west of the Trinidad fault. Stokes *et al.* (2023) suggest that the 2003 event might have been attributed to an escalation in pore-fluid pressure from injection. After 2001, pore pressure increases became more evident due to the rise in wastewater injection rates. The 2003 event

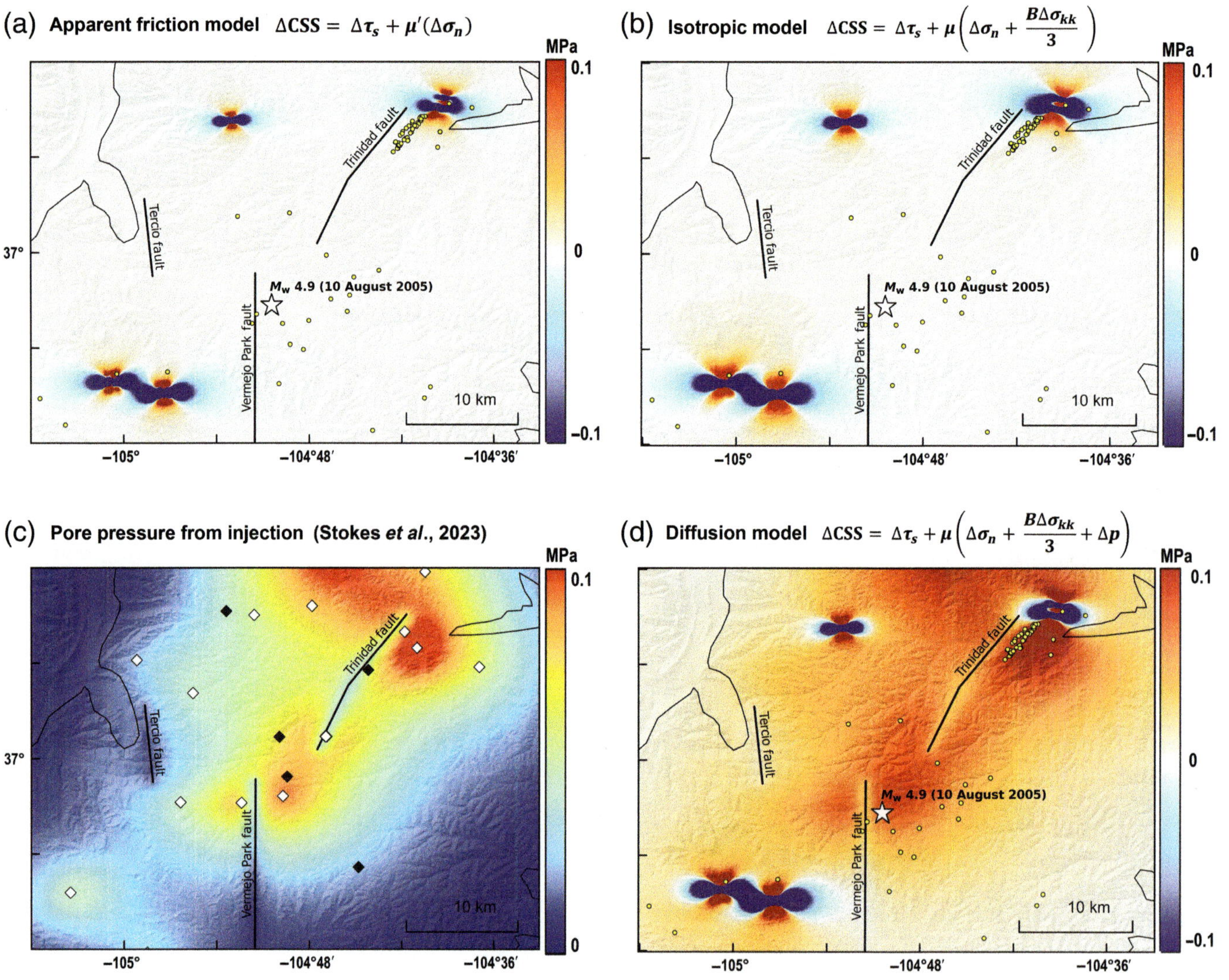

Figure 3. Coulomb static stress change (ΔCSS) imparted by the 2001–2004 sequence on the Vermejo Park fault (strike/dip/rake: 5/53/−74). (a) ΔCSS distribution for the apparent friction model. (b) ΔCSS distribution for the isotropic model. (c) Modeled pore pressure change in August 2004; the white diamonds indicate injection wells active through 2004; the black diamonds indicate inactive injection wells (Stokes *et al.*, 2023). (d) ΔCSS distribution for the diffusion model.

was followed by a sequence of two earthquakes in March and August 2004, with magnitudes of 4.4 and 4.3, respectively. The 2004 events were located approximately 30 km southwest of the 2003 event and approximately 10 km south of the Tercio fault and 8 km west of the Vermejo Park fault (Fig. 1).

To analyze the stress changes imparted by the 2001–2004 events and explain the location of the M_w 4.9 mainshock in 2005, we computed the Coulomb stress change on the Vermejo Park fault (Fig. 3). The apparent friction model (Fig. 3a) does not demonstrate a discernable spatial correlation between these events attributable to ΔCSS. The isotropic model (Fig. 3b) illustrates a spatial increase of ΔCSS (red lobes) into the Tercio fault zone and into the northern Trinidad fault. Modeled pore pressure change (Fig. 3c) for August 2004 (Stokes *et al.*, 2023) is incorporated into the calculations within the diffusion model (Fig. 3d). The increase in ΔCSS is strongly influenced by the pore pressure, rather than being only influenced by the earlier and sparse earthquakes. The diffusion model shows an increase in ΔCSS > 0.04 MPa across the Trinidad fault and northern Vermejo Park fault (Fig. 3d).

2001–2005 earthquake sequence

We next explored the cumulative ΔCSS from 2001 to 2005 and its impact on the Trinidad fault, which experienced M_w 4.7 and 5.3 earthquakes in 2011. There are significant differences in ΔCSS among the three models (Fig. 4). The apparent friction model (Fig. 4a) exhibits a slight positive increase in ΔCSS on the southern Trinidad fault segment. The isotropic model (Fig. 4b) shows greater ΔCSS over broader regions and an increase exceeding 0.02 MPa across the Trinidad fault. The modeled pore pressure change from injection for August

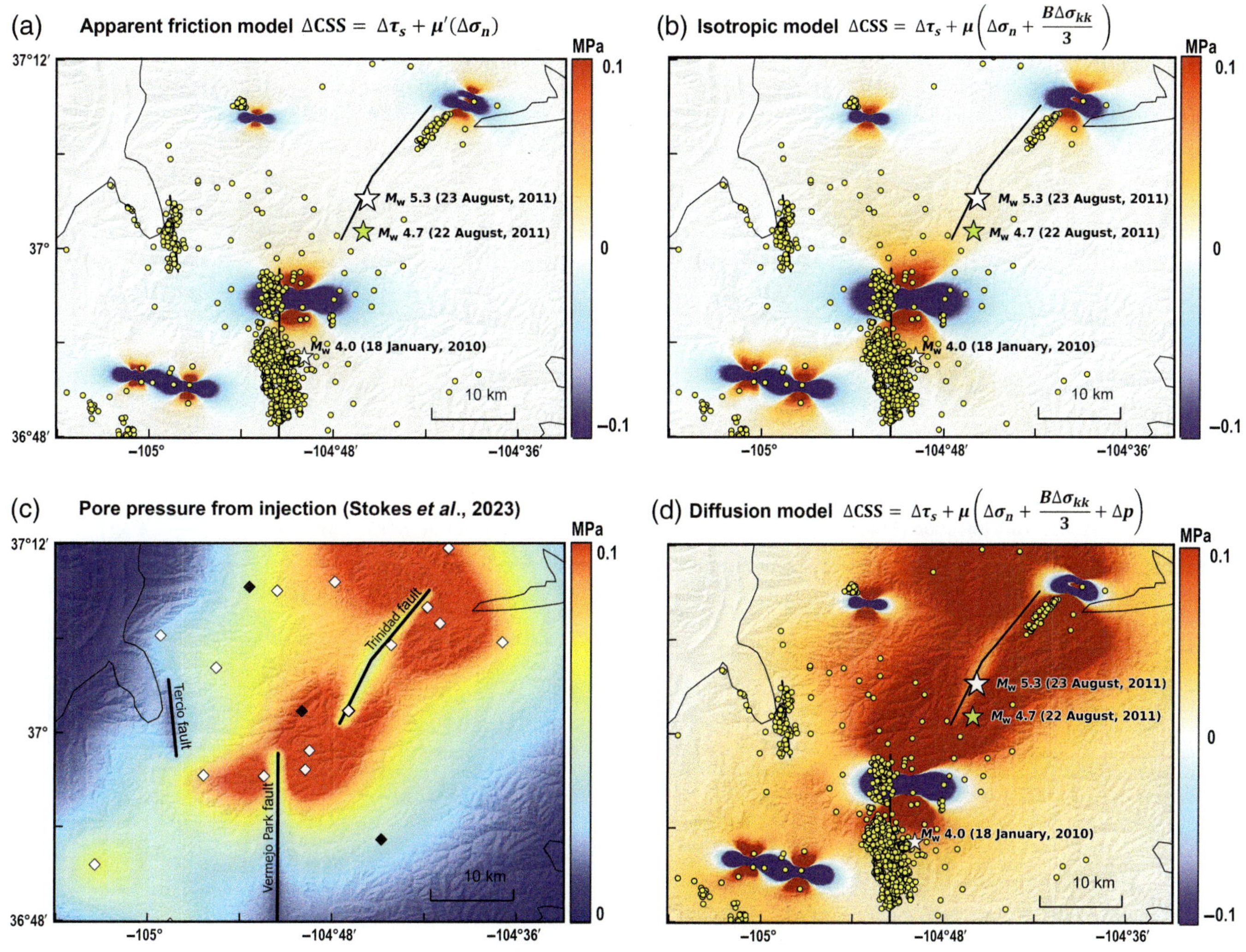

Figure 4. Coulomb static stress change (ΔCSS) imparted by the 2001–2005 sequence on the Trinidad fault (strike/dip/rake: 25°/50°/−80°). (a) ΔCSS distribution for the apparent friction model. (b) ΔCSS distribution for the isotropic model. (c) Modeled pore pressure change in August 2005; the white diamonds indicate active injection wells through 2005; the black diamonds indicate inactive injection wells (Stokes *et al.*, 2023). (d) ΔCSS distribution for the diffusion model.

2004 is shown in Figure 3c (Stokes *et al.*, 2023). The diffusion model (Fig. 4d) shows that the Vermejo Park fault experienced ΔCSS increase ranging from 0.05 to 0.1 MPa, reaching 0.06 MPa at the 2010 M_w 4.0 earthquake location. Notably, the Trinidad fault was subjected to a higher ΔCSS increase exceeding 0.07 MPa. The observed stress increase exceeds the 0.01 MPa threshold, which is considered sufficient to trigger seismicity (Reasenberg and Simpson, 1992; Stein, 1999). Moreover, Figure 4d illustrates a notable increase of ΔCSS toward the Tercio fault area, suggesting an explanation for the observed seismic activity in this area, particularly for seismic activity after 2006 (Rubinstein *et al.*, 2014), which can also be attributed to the augmented pore pressure.

The isotropic model and, more evidently, the diffusion model suggest that the early seismic events in the basin are likely connected to the 2010 and 2011 earthquake events, potentially explaining the location of the future M_w 4.0 event in 2010 and the M_w 4.7 and 5.3 earthquakes in 2011. Consequently, these ΔCSS models suggest that the earthquakes and the associated pore pressure have increased the likelihood of future rupture on the Trinidad fault more significantly than on the Vermejo Park fault. Furthermore, the models can effectively show the effect of pore pressure and the change in the distribution of ΔCSS across the faults and within the basin (Figs. S4 and S5).

2011 sequence in Central Raton basin

The 2011 sequence is considered an extension of the 2001 sequence on the southern segment of the Trinidad fault. On 22 August 2011, an M_w 4.7 earthquake ruptured along the southern Trinidad fault segment. The next day, an M_w 5.3 mainshock occurred, exhibiting normal faulting on a southeast-dipping fault plane. The focal mechanism solution for this

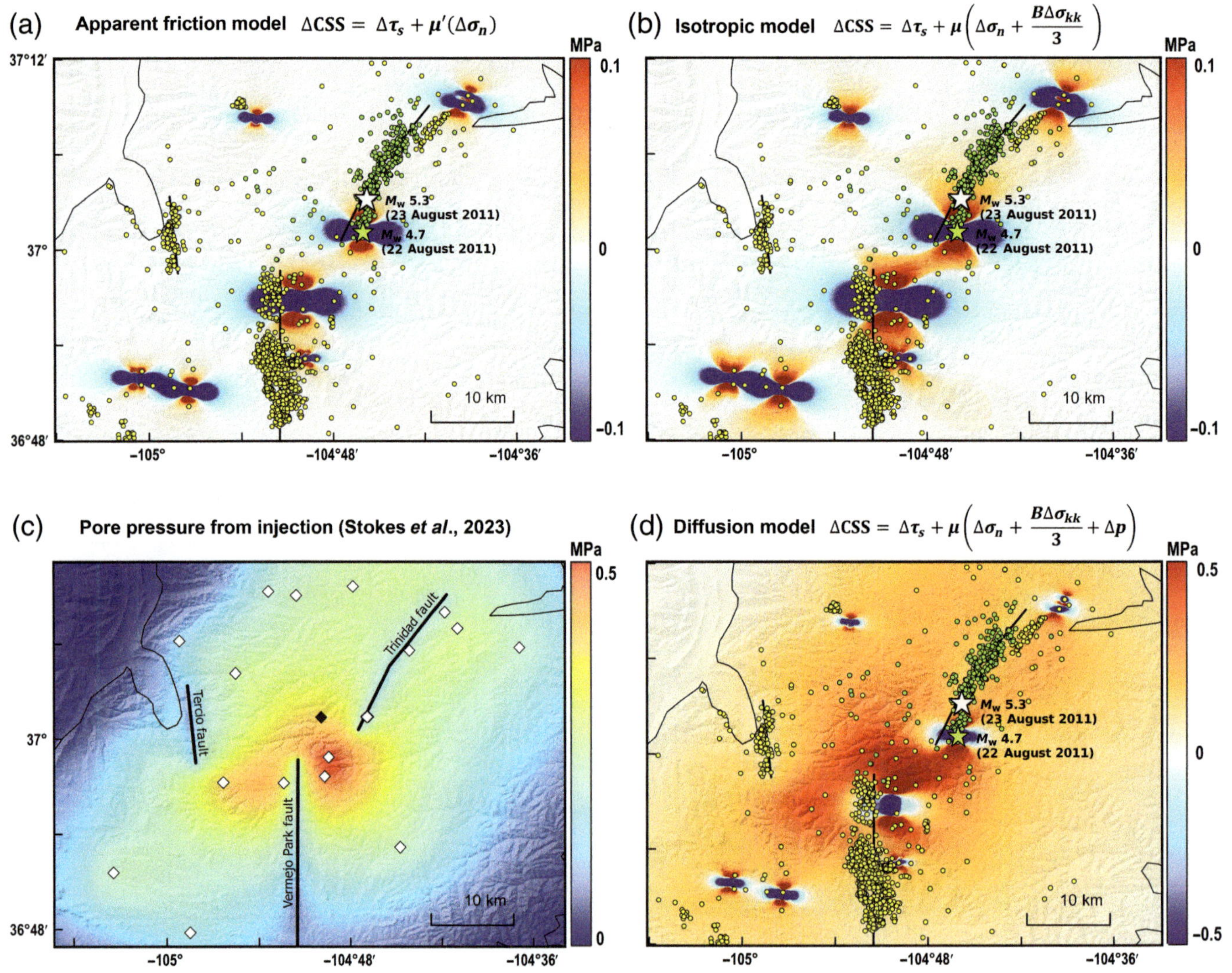

Figure 5. Coulomb static stress change (ΔCSS) imparted by the 2001–2011 sequence on the Trinidad fault (strike/dip/rake: 25°/50°/−80°). The white star denotes the future M_w 5.3 event location; the green dots show aftershock distribution attributed to the M_w 4.7. (a) ΔCSS distribution for the apparent friction model. (b) ΔCSS distribution for the isotropic model. (c) Modeled pore pressure change in August 2011; the white diamonds indicate active injection wells through 2011; the black diamonds indicate inactive injection wells (Stokes *et al.*, 2023). (d) Diffusion model of ΔCSS, showing a significant increase in stress, ΔCSS > 0.3 MPa, along the Trinidad fault.

event was similar to the 2001 Trinidad earthquake (Meremonte *et al.*, 2002). The increase in ΔCSS caused by the M_w 4.7 earthquake played a significant role in the occurrence of the M_w 5.3 event, as evidenced by the increase in stress of approximately 0.1 MPa (Fig. 5).

The increase in the ΔCSS was more pronounced toward the Trinidad fault and the area between the Trinidad and Vermejo Park faults, whereas a decrease was observed in the east–west directions at each source event (Fig. 5a,b). The diffusion model, which incorporated modeled pore pressure change (Fig. 5c) for August 2011 (Stokes *et al.*, 2023), shows that the seismic activity was predominantly concentrated in areas of positive ΔCSS, where the ΔCSS exceeded 0.05 MPa in the isotropic model (Fig. 5b) and 0.3 MPa in the diffusion model (Fig. 5d). Figures S6 and S7 show the spatial distribution of Coulomb stress change along the strike direction of the Trinidad fault and Vermejo Park fault from 2001 to 2011.

There were approximately 495 aftershocks (Rubinstein *et al.*, 2014) that occurred following the 2011 events within a 10 km radius. The diffusion model revealed that over 92% of the aftershocks occurred in regions where ΔCSS > 0.01 MPa. The percentage of aftershocks in regions where ΔCSS > 0.01 MPa was 88% with the isotropic model and 44% with the apparent friction model.

The cumulative results of pore pressure diffusion and stress transfer from the greater than M_w 4.0 events between 2001 and 2011 (Fig. 4d) indicate that a majority of the area modeled remains in an increased state of stress. Fault complexity indicated by in-depth studies of many small events (Glasgow *et al.*, 2023; Wang *et al.*, 2024) could affect the calculated ΔCSS caused by the earthquakes. Modeled results show that the August 2005 M_w 4.9 event reduced total ΔCSS in the northern section of the Vermejo Park fault (Fig. 4d). The fault remains active largely in the southern area where modeled results show increased ΔCSS; however, seismicity still occurs in the northern section. Interestingly, because pore pressure diffusion continues (Fig. 5d), the area of reduced stress decreases in the northern section of the Vermejo Park fault. Because the pore pressure diffusion is only included through 2011, increased pore pressure from continued diffusion likely decreases the area of reduced stress. Fault complexity limitations in the Coulomb static stress modeling could explain discrepancies between modeled areas and actively seismic areas; continued pore pressure diffusion likely also plays a role. The changes in pore pressures estimated by the modeling of Hill *et al.* (2024) show the area of the Vermejo Park fault with pore pressure changes between 0.05 and 0.10 MPa by 2016. This is consistent with the importance that we find in including pore pressure diffusion in modeling ΔCSS and a mechanism that will counteract decreases caused by previous earthquakes.

Conclusions

Seismic activity in the northern Trinidad fault zone began in 2001, subsequently migrating to the Vermejo Park fault zone in 2005, and into the Tercio fault zone in 2006. The spatiotemporal pattern of seismicity agrees with modeled Coulomb stress change that incorporated pore pressure increases caused by wastewater injection in the Raton basin between 2001 and 2011.

Incorporating dynamic, semitransient pore pressure change into the Coulomb stress change model significantly alters the ΔCSS distribution. Among the three different models of incorporating pore pressure, the diffusion model produces the ΔCSS values that best explain the majority of the observed seismicity. This model combines earthquake–earthquake interaction with the effects of the pore pressure changes resulting from wastewater injection. Incorporating semitransient pore pressure changes into the Coulomb stress calculations could improve seismic hazard monitoring and assessment.

The results of this study suggest that early seismic activity and the pore pressure buildup from injection were sufficient to initiate seismicity on the Vermejo Park fault and the Trinidad fault. The M_w 4.4 (2001), M_w 4.4 (2010), and M_w 4.7 and M_w 5.3 (2011) earthquakes occurred in areas of elevated positive ΔCSS. The largest event was likely triggered and facilitated by ΔCSS from earlier event interactions and the pore pressure increase resulting from wastewater injection (Stokes *et al.*, 2023), with a ΔCSS > 0.3 MPa.

Finally, our findings emphasize the importance of incorporating pore pressure effects when modeling stress interactions, especially in regions with significant fluid injection activities. Neglecting or oversimplifying pore pressure effects from injection activities can lead to underestimation of seismic risk and potential triggering mechanisms.

Data and Resources

The Nakai *et al.* (2017) earthquake catalog was retrieved from the Supporting Information of the Nakai *et al.* (2017) article. The Rubinstein *et al.* (2014) catalog was received from Justin Rubinstein but is reported to have been incorporated into the U.S. Geological Survey (USGS) ComCat catalog. An open-source software called Coulomb 3.3 (Toda *et al.*, 2011) was used to model Coulomb stress changes and can be obtained from https://pubs.usgs.gov/of/2011/1060/. Modeled pore pressure data were retrieved from Stokes *et al.* (2023) and supplementary information. Wastewater injection data for the wells located in the Colorado portion of the basin were retrieved from COGCC (2023; https://cogcc.state.co.us/data.html). Wastewater injection data for the wells located in the New Mexico portion of the basin were retrieved from NMOCD (2023; https://wwwapps.emnrd.nm.gov/OCD/OCDPermitting/Data/Wells.aspx). All websites were last accessed in January 2023. The supplemental material includes figures and tables of additional data and results.

Declaration of Competing Interests

The authors acknowledge that there are no conflicts of interest recorded.

Acknowledgments

The authors thank the two anonymous reviewers for the insightful suggestions. Funding for this research was provided in part by the United States Department of Energy Grant DE-SC0020222.

References

Aki, K., and P. G. Richards (2009). *Quantitative Seismology*, Second Ed., corrected printing, University Science Books, Sausalito, California.

Beeler, N. M., R. W. Simpson, S. H. Hickman, and D. A. Lockner (2000). Pore fluid pressure, apparent friction, and Coulomb failure, *J. Geophys. Res.* **105,** no. B11, 25533–25542, doi: 10.1029/2000JB900119.

Chambers, C. R., M. R. M. Brown, S. M. Stokes, S. Ge, E. A. Menezes, K. F. Tiampo, and A. F. Sheehan (2024). Surface deformation and seismicity linked to fluid injection in the Raton basin, *Groundwater* **62,** no. 5, doi: 10.1111/gwat.13393.

Cocco, M., and J. R. Rice (2002). Pore pressure and poroelasticity effects in Coulomb stress analysis of earthquake interactions, *J. Geophys. Res.* **107**, no. B2, ESE 2-1–ESE 2-17, doi: 10.1029/2000JB000138.

COGCC (2023). Colorado oil and gas conservation commission, available at https://ecmc.colorado.gov/data-maps/cogis-database (last accessed January 2023).

Ellsworth, W. L. (2013). Injection-induced earthquakes, *Science* **341,** no. 6142, 1,225,942, doi: 10.1126/science.1225942.

Ge, S., and M. O. Saar (2022). Review: Induced seismicity during geoenergy development—A hydromechanical perspective, *J. Geophys. Res.* **127**, no. 3, e2021JB023141, doi: 10.1029/2021JB023141.

Glasgow, M., B. Schmandt, and S. L. Bilek (2023). Cascading multisegment rupture in an injection-induced earthquake sequence with a M_w 5.3 mainshock, *Earth Planet. Sci. Lett.* **620,** 118,335, doi: 10.1016/j.epsl.2023.118335.

Glasgow, M., B. Schmandt, R. Wang, M. Zhang, S. L. Bilek, and E. Kiser (2021). Raton Basin induced seismicity is hosted by networks of short basement faults and mimics tectonic earthquake statistics,

J. Geophys. Res. **126,** no. 11, e2021JB022839, doi: 10.1029/2021JB022839.

Goebel, T. H. W., and E. E. Brodsky (2018). The spatial footprint of injection wells in a global compilation of induced earthquake sequences, *Science* **361,** 899–904, doi: 10.1126/science.aat5449.

Harris, R. A. (1998). Introduction to special section: Stress triggers, stress shadows, and implications for seismic hazard, *J. Geophys. Res.* **103,** no. B10, 24,347–24,358, doi: 10.1029/98JB01576.

Herrmann, R. B. (2020). North America moment tensor 1995–2020, St. Louis University, available at http://www.eas.slu.edu/eqc/eqc_mt/MECH.NA/ (last accessed July 2023).

Hill, R. G., M. Weingarten, C. Langenbruch, and Y. Fialko (2024). Mitigation and optimization of induced seismicity using physics-based forecasting, *J. Geophys. Res.* **129,** doi: 10.1029/2024JB028759.

Hsieh, P. A., and J. D. Bredehoeft (1981). A reservoir analysis of the Denver earthquakes: A case of induced seismicity, *J. Geophys. Res.* **86,** no. B2, 903–920, doi: 10.1029/JB086iB02p00903.

Keranen, K. M., M. Weingarten, G. A. Abers, B. A. Bekins, and S. Ge (2014). Sharp increase in central Oklahoma seismicity since 2008 induced by massive wastewater injection, *Science* **345,** no. 6195, 448–451, doi: 10.1126/science.1255802.

King, G., R. Stein, and J. Lin (1994). Static stress changes and the triggering of earthquakes, *Bull. Seismol. Soc. Am.* **84,** 935–953.

Lin, J., and R. S. Stein (2004). Stress triggering in thrust and subduction earthquakes and stress interaction between the southern San Andreas and nearby thrust and strike-slip faults, *J. Geophys. Res.* **109,** no. B2, doi: 10.1029/2003JB002607.

Lundstern, J.-E., and M. D. Zoback (2020). Multiscale variations of the crustal stress field throughout North America, *Nat. Commun.* **11,** no. 1, doi: 10.1038/s41467-020-15841-5.

Meremonte, M. E., J. C. Lahr, A. D. Frankel, J. W. Dewey, A. J. Crone, D. E. Overturf, D. L. Carver, and W. T. Bice (2002). The investigation of an earthquake swarm near Trinidad, Colorado, August, and October 2001, *U.S. Geol. Surv. Open-File Rept. 02-0073*, available at https://pubs.usgs.gov/of/2002/ofr-02-0073/ofr-02-0073.html (last accessed March 2024).

Nakai, J. S., A. F. Sheehan, and S. L. Bilek (2017). Seismicity of the Rocky Mountains and Rio Grande Rift from the EarthScope transportable array and CREST temporary seismic networks, 2008–2010, *J. Geophys. Res.* **122,** no. 3, 2173–2192, doi: 10.1002/2016JB013389.

NMOCD (2023). New Mexico oil conservation division, OCD Permitting - Wells, available at https://wwwapps.emnrd.nm.gov/OCD/OCDPermitting/Data/Wells.aspx (last accessed January 2023).

Okada, Y. (1985). Surface deformation due to shear and tensile faults in a half-space, *Bull. Seismol. Soc. Am.* **75,** no. 4, 1135–1154, doi: 10.1785/BSSA0750041135.

Reasenberg, P. A., and R. W. Simpson (1992). Response of regional seismicity to the static stress change produced by the Loma Prieta earthquake, *Science* **255,** no. 5052, 1687–1690, doi: 10.1126/science.255.5052.1687.

Rice, J. R. (1992). Fault stress states, pore pressure distributions, and the weakness of the San Andreas fault, in *International Geophysics*, B. Evans and T.-f. Wong (Editors), Vol. 51, Academic Press, London, 475–503, doi: 10.1016/S0074-6142(08)62835-1.

Rice, J. R., and M. Cleary (1976). Some basic stress diffusion solutions for fluid-saturated elastic porous media with compressible constituents, *Rev. Geophys.* **14,** 227–241.

Roeloffs, E.A. (1996) Poroelastic techniques in the study of earthquake-related hydrologic phenomena, *Adv. Geophys.* **36,** 135–195.

Rubinstein, J. L., W. L. Ellsworth, A. McGarr, and H. M. Benz (2014). The 2001-present induced earthquake sequence in the Raton basin of northern New Mexico and southern Colorado, *Bull. Seismol. Soc. Am.* **104,** no. 5, 2162–2181, doi: 10.1785/0120140009.

Skempton, A. W. (1954). The pore-pressure coefficients *A* and *B*, *Géotechnique* **4,** no. 4, 143–147, doi: 10.1680/geot.1954.4.4.143.

Stein, R. S. (1999). The role of stress transfer in earthquake occurrence, *Nature* **402,** no. 6762, 605–609, doi: 10.1038/45144.

Stokes, S. M., S. Ge, M. R. M. Brown, E. A. Menezes, A. F. Sheehan, and K. F. Tiampo (2023). Pore pressure diffusion and onset of induced seismicity, *J. Geophys. Res.* **128,** no. 3, e2022JB026012, doi: 10.1029/2022JB026012.

Toda, S., R. S. Stein, P. A. Reasenberg, J. H. Dieterich, and A. Yoshida (1998). Stress transferred by the 1995 Mw = 6.9 Kobe, Japan, shock: Effect on aftershocks and future earthquake probabilities, *J. Geophys. Res.* **103,** no. B10, 24,543–24,565, doi: 10.1029/98JB00765.

Toda, S., R. S. Stein, K. Richards-Dinger, and S. B. Bozkurt (2005). Forecasting the evolution of seismicity in southern California: Animations built on earthquake stress transfer, *J. Geophys. Res.* **110,** no. B5, doi: 10.1029/2004JB003415.

Toda, S., R. S. Stein, V. Sevilgen, and J. Lin (2011). Coulomb 3.3 Graphic-rich deformation and stress-change software for earthquake, tectonic, and volcano research and teaching—User guide, *U.S. Geol. Surv. Open-File Rept. 2011-1060*, 63 pp.

Wang, R., E.A. Onyango, B. Schmandt, and L. Worthington (2024). Injection-induced basement seismicity beneath the Raton basin: Constraints from refined fault architectures and basin structure, *Phil. Trans. Roy. Soc. Lond. A.* **382,** 20230181, doi: 10.1098/rsta.2023.0181.

Wells, D. L., and K. J. Coppersmith (1994). New empirical relationships among magnitude, rupture length, rupture width, rupture area, and surface displacement, *Bull. Seismol. Soc. Am.* **84,** no. 4, 974–1002, doi: 10.1785/BSSA0840040974.

Yeo, I.W., M. R. M. Brown, S. Ge, and K. K. Lee (2020). Causal mechanism of injection-induced earthquakes through the M_w 5.5 Pohang earthquake case study, *Nature* **11,** 2614, doi: 10.1038/s41467-020-16408-0.

Zhang, Y., F. Huang, and G. Lai (2009). Research on Skempton's coefficient B based on the observation of groundwater of Changping station, *Earthq. Science* **22,** no. 6, 631–638, doi: 10.1007/s11589-009-0631-z.

Manuscript received 8 May 2025
Published online 2 December 2025

Forecasting Fluid-Induced Seismicity Using Machine Learning Time-Series Prediction

Arthur Cuvier*[1], Julie Maury[1], Hideo Aochi[1], and Hugo Breuillard[1]

Abstract

Seismicity induced by fluid injection (enhanced geothermal systems [EGSs], waste water disposal, and CO_2 storage) remains a significant risk to communities and industry because it may cause structural damage and economic losses. In some cases, this can lead to the immediate shutdown of the project, as observed at the Pohang geothermal site in South Korea (2017), after inducing a magnitude 5.5 earthquake. Consequently, it is crucial to develop new strategies to anticipate and mitigate the seismic risk posed by these operations. In this work, we present an innovative machine learning-based approach to forecast the seismicity induced by fluid injection into the ground. It leverages a time series of various injection parameters, such as injected volume, flow rate, and wellhead pressure, to capture their relationship with the seismicity rate. Once our model is trained, we forecast the future number of induced earthquakes on a fixed timescale of interest. We apply this strategy to two case studies that have caused induced seismicity at different spatial and temporal scales. First, we investigate the relationship between the massive wastewater injection in Oklahoma since 2006 and the increase in seismicity. Capturing this relationship with linear regression, it is then possible to forecast the seismicity caused by any future hypothetical injection scenario. Second, we study the seismicity induced during the hydraulic stimulation of the Soultz-sous-Forêts (France) EGS in 2005. Using a gradient boosting model, we predict the seismicity over the next 24 hr, relying solely on injection parameters. Our results show that, while model selection should account for site complexity, machine learning can effectively predict seismicity rates using injection parameters, even with limited training data. This work paves the way for real-time applications, such as predicting microseismicity during ongoing operations at the Rittershoffen EGS site, 6 km from Soultz-sous-Forêts.

Cite this article as Cuvier, A., J. Maury, H. Aochi, and H. Breuillard (2025). Forecasting Fluid-Induced Seismicity Using Machine Learning Time-Series Prediction, *Seismol. Res. Lett.* **97**, 1853–1866, doi: 10.1785/0220250210.

Supplemental Material

Introduction

Induced seismicity refers to earthquakes caused by human activities, resulting from anthropogenic stress changes in the rockmass that reactivate pre-existing faults or fractures. Often, induced earthquakes are observed during subsurface industrial activities involving fluid injection into the ground, such as geothermal energy production (Lu, 2018), hydraulic fracturing (Smith and Montgomery, 2015), wastewater injection (Warner and Lehr, 1977), and carbon storage (Bickle, 2009). Although most of the induced seismicity is composed of microseismicity, some events can reach higher magnitudes, like observed in Vendenheim, France (2021), Pohang, South Korea (2017), or Oklahoma (2016), with magnitudes of 3.9, 5.5, and 5.8, respectively (Yeck *et al.*, 2017; Ellsworth *et al.*, 2019; Fiori *et al.*, 2023). The energy released by these high-intensity induced earthquakes represents a significant concern for the public, may damage infrastructures, and can result in substantial economic losses (Giardini, 2009; Hong *et al.*, 2022). Because subsurface industrial activities will certainly continue in the future, it is then essential to (1) have a better comprehension of the relation between fluid injection and the associated seismic response and (2) develop strategies to control and mitigate the risk posed by induced seismicity.

To address the challenge posed by fluid-induced earthquakes, several strategies have been developed to characterize, monitor, or control this seismicity. These include analysis of the microseismic response (Stork *et al.*, 2015; Aochi *et al.*, 2021; Rajesh and Gupta, 2021; Jacquemond *et al.*, 2024), estimation of the next maximum magnitude (Hallo *et al.*, 2014; McGarr, 2014; Van der Elst *et al.*, 2016), and good practice

1. BRGM, Orléans, France, https://orcid.org/0000-0003-2383-3665 (AC); https://orcid.org/0000-0002-4132-5819 (JM); https://orcid.org/0000-0001-9405-9596 (HA); https://orcid.org/0000-0003-4187-7303 (HB)

*Corresponding author: a.cuvier@brgm.fr

guidelines during injection operations (Baisch *et al.*, 2019; Ineris and BRGM, 2023). Although these approaches provide crucial information, it does not allow for quantifying the future level of seismic activity induced during a given operation. In this context, significant advances were made in the development of models to forecast induced seismicity, using physics and/or statistical information (Gaucher *et al.*, 2015). Although physics-based models may successfully capture the seismic response to fluid injection, they are often complicated to generalize to different sites because they require advanced knowledge on mechanical and geometrical features, like the characterization of the reservoir, local geology, soil porosity/permeability, as well as fault location (Langenbruch and Zoback, 2016; Langenbruch *et al.*, 2018; Qin *et al.*, 2022). In addition, physical models can rarely be directly transposed to a different site. This disadvantage could be overcome by the statistical approaches, designed to predict the future seismicity rate using only operational parameters like injection pressure or flow rate (Bachmann *et al.*, 2011; Mena *et al.*, 2013). Given the complex relationship between operational parameters and seismic response, statistical approaches may be combined with artificial intelligence-based tools because they provide an effective and well-suited method for predicting seismicity rate under varying operational conditions.

The last decades have been marked by the emergence of machine learning applied widely in various fields of seismology (Kong *et al.*, 2019; Münchmeyer *et al.*, 2022; Woollam *et al.*, 2022; Kubo *et al.*, 2024). Key findings include event detection/discrimination (Meier *et al.*, 2019), estimations of earthquake location (Mousavi and Beroza, 2019; Shi *et al.*, 2022), and automatic arrival-time picking (Zhu and Beroza, 2019; Münchmeyer *et al.*, 2022), which have shown improved performance compared to traditional methods (Allen, 1982; Havskov *et al.*, 2012). In the context of induced seismicity, machine learning applications show promising potential to capture smaller events (Ma and Chen, 2022; Shi *et al.*, 2024), predict artificial labquakes (Rouet-Leduc *et al.*, 2017; He *et al.*, 2020), or forecast the maximum magnitude observed during hydraulic fracturing (Li *et al.*, 2023). Although induced seismicity arises from complex interactions between operational parameters and geological features like fault properties and reservoir characteristics, machine learning offers an opportunity to capture these nonlinear and multivariate relationships. Consequently, recent advancements in artificial intelligence must be considered as a unique opportunity to monitor and predict anthropogenic earthquakes (see the work of Li *et al.*, 2025, for a full review of applications).

In this work, we analyze the temporal variations of injection parameters and leverage machine learning techniques (linear regression and gradient boosting method [GBM]) to capture the associated seismic response. Because seismicity rate is often found to be directly related to measured injection parameters such as flow rate and pressure (Calò *et al.*, 2014; Qin *et al.*, 2022), we focus on predicting seismicity rate rather than the maximum magnitude, which is more commonly associated with the total injected volume (McGarr, 2014). Once trained, our model stands out for its ability to perform a prediction without using past values of the seismicity. The remainder of this article is structured as follows. In the second section, we present our approach to forecast the induced seismicity caused by massive wastewater injections in Oklahoma since 2010. The Prediction of induced seismicity over local temporal/spatial scales: Case study of the Soultz-sous-Forets EGS section describes our proposed strategy to predict the seismicity induced during a stimulation of the Soultz-sous-Forêts enhanced geothermal system (EGS). Finally, some technical aspects of our machine learning approach, along with the study's conclusions, are discussed in the Discussion and Conclusion section.

Prediction of Induced Seismicity Over Large Temporal/Spatial Scales: Case Study of Wastewater Injection in Oklahoma

Data presentation

We investigate the sharp increase of seismicity in Oklahoma during the past decades, which has been mostly associated with wastewater injection (Langenbruch and Zoback, 2016; Hincks *et al.*, 2018; Rajesh and Gupta, 2021). This seismicity is mainly concentrated in the central/northern region of Oklahoma, as shown in Figure 1a, where the orange circles indicate the earthquake locations. Consequently, we focus on a study area, bounded by longitude [−98.7°, −96.7°] and latitude [35.1°, 36.9°], represented by the red dashed rectangle. This area contains around 73% of the seismicity from 2006 to 2025, corresponding to 23,280 earthquakes over a total number of 32,034 events. The earthquakes analyzed in this study are limited to those with a moment magnitude greater than 1.8 because the development of the seismic network in Oklahoma has led to a difference in the sensitivity of microseismicity over time. Although this value falls just below the dataset's magnitude of completeness ($M_c = 2.15$), our experience reveals that a 1.8 threshold leads to slightly higher correlation between injected volume and seismicity rate (gain of 5%). More statistical information about our seismic catalog can be found in Table 1.

Figure 1b presents the seismicity rate as a time series (black curve) from January 2006 to December 2024. For each day in this time period, we define the seismicity rate as the number of earthquakes detected within the next 30 days (i.e., monthly seismicity rate). The seismicity rate is characterized by values consistently near zero before 2010 and a sharp increase up to 900 earthquakes per month in 2015. In addition to the seismicity rate, Figure 1b also presents the monthly volume of wastewater injected underground, represented by the blue time series. For each month, the injected volume used in this work is defined by the total injected volume among all wells in our study area. For each day, the injected volume time series

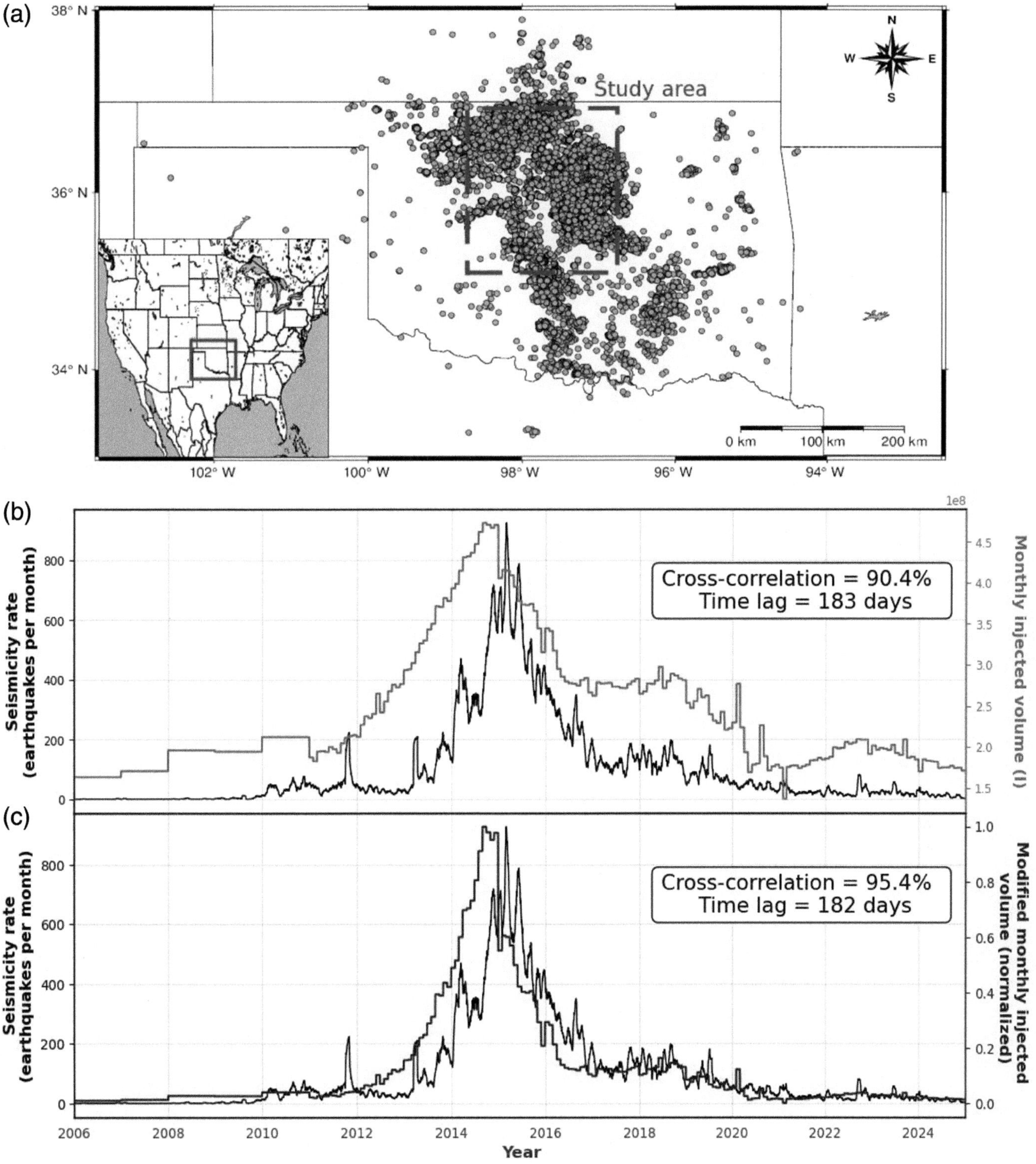

Figure 1. (a) Observed seismicity in Oklahoma between 2006 and 2025 ($M_w > 1.8$). (b) Correlation between the monthly seismicity rate (black) and injected volume (blue). (c) Same as (b) with the modified monthly injected volume (see the text for the definition). Seismic and injection datasets are reported by the Oklahoma Geological Survey and the Oklahoma Corporation Commission, respectively (see Data and Resources for more information). The color version of this figure is available only in the electronic edition.

is supposed to be constant, fixed at the values given by the associated month. This operation allows for obtaining the same sampling rate between the injected volume and the seismicity rate time series. It is important to note that the injected volume time series is constant for each year before 2011 in Figure 1b because injection data were not available on a monthly basis at that time. Because (1) our injection dataset is limited to data prior to 31 December 2024 and (2) we aim to investigate the

TABLE 1
Additional Information on the Seismic Datasets Used in Our Case Studies: M_w for Oklahoma and M_L for Soultz-sous-Forêt (EOST and GEIE-EMC, 2018)

Case Study	Duration	Number of Events	Area of the Seismicity	*b* Value	M_{max}	M_c	M_{mean}
Oklahoma	19 yr	23,280	3.2×10^{10} m^2	1.30	5.8	2.15	1.60
Soultz-sous-Forêts stimulation (2005)	2 months	2,352	2.4×10^{6} m^2	0.66	2.3	−0.75	−0.37

relationship between the injection and the seismicity, we consider the seismicity after 1 January 2025 as future, unknown information.

The monthly injected volume shows similar variations to the seismicity rate, as emphasized by their (maximum) cross-correlation score of 90.4% in Figure 1b. However, this score is only obtained after shifting the injection time series exactly 183 days toward the future. This time lag probably corresponds to the delay between the injection of fluid into the ground and the seismic response, which may be controlled by the hydraulic diffusivity of the medium (Langenbruch and Zoback, 2016; Schoenball and Ellsworth, 2017). Although a time lag is observed, the important cross-correlation score confirms that the volume of fluid injected under the ground is the main feature controlling the seismicity in our study area. In the following, we will use a slightly modified version of the monthly injected volume, represented by the blue curve in Figure 1c. It is obtained by raising the original injection time series to a certain power *p*, in order to maximize its cross-correlation score with respect to the seismicity rate. This optimization problem is solved using the SciPy Python library Virtanen *et al.* (2020) and results in $p = 3.8$. This operation increases the cross-correlation score from 90.4% to 95.4% with almost no change in the time lag, as shown in Figure 1b,c. Although this transformation clearly improves the correlation, it should be noted that there is no direct physical justification for raising the injection volume to this specific power. It should therefore be interpreted as an empirical adjustment that captures the nonlinear relationship between injected volume and seismicity rate. To assess the robustness of this approach, a sensitivity analysis over a range of *p* values is performed, evaluating how the final prediction error varies (see Fig. S1).

Methodology

We now present our strategy to forecast the seismicity rate using the information provided by the injected volume. We use a machine learning approach, particularly well-suited to processing and extracting information from large datasets. Because the injection/seismicity relation is characterized by a large cross-correlation score (see Fig. 1c), we select a linear regression model (Montgomery *et al.*, 2021). In the following, the time series we aim to forecast (i.e., seismicity rate) will be called "Target series," and a "Covariate" will designate another time series providing useful information for the prediction (i.e., injected volume). It should be noted that a min–max normalization is performed on both covariate and target time series before applying the linear regression.

The linear regression aims to minimize the following loss function:

$$\frac{1}{T}\sum_{t=0}^{T}(y'_t - y_t)^2, \tag{1}$$

in which y'_t is the predicted seismicity rate and y_t the observed value for each day $t \in [0,T]$. Because Figure 1c highlighted a time lag of 182 days between the covariate and the target value, it is then decisive to include this period for the prediction. Consequently, we define the predicted value y'_t as a linear expression depending on the past 365 days of the injected volume time series $(x_{t-365},..,x_{t-1})$. Then, for each time *t*, the predicted value y'_t is defined by

$$y'_t = \sum_{i=t-365}^{t-1} w_i x_i + c, \tag{2}$$

in which $(w_{t-365},..,w_{t-1})$ and *c* are coefficients fixed by the regression model. To do so, the model analyses a time period containing enough information to capture the seismicity/injection relation (training phase). Then, it is possible to validate our model by ensuring a good approximation of the predictions with respect to the observations during another time period (validation phase). It is important to note that our model does not require any information on past values of the seismicity rate to perform a prediction, which represents a considerable advantage in comparison to other time-series prediction techniques.

Results

We now apply the linear regression model to the hydraulic and seismic time series recorded in Oklahoma from 1 January 2006 to 31 December 2024. Our time series is split on 1 January 2016, defining the date that separates our training and validation periods. This choice is motivated by the need to train our model over a significant amount of time, including the seismicity and injection peaks, but also to validate our approach during a period with large variations of the target value.

Figure 2a presents the forecasting results (orange curve), obtained by iterating the prediction over each point included

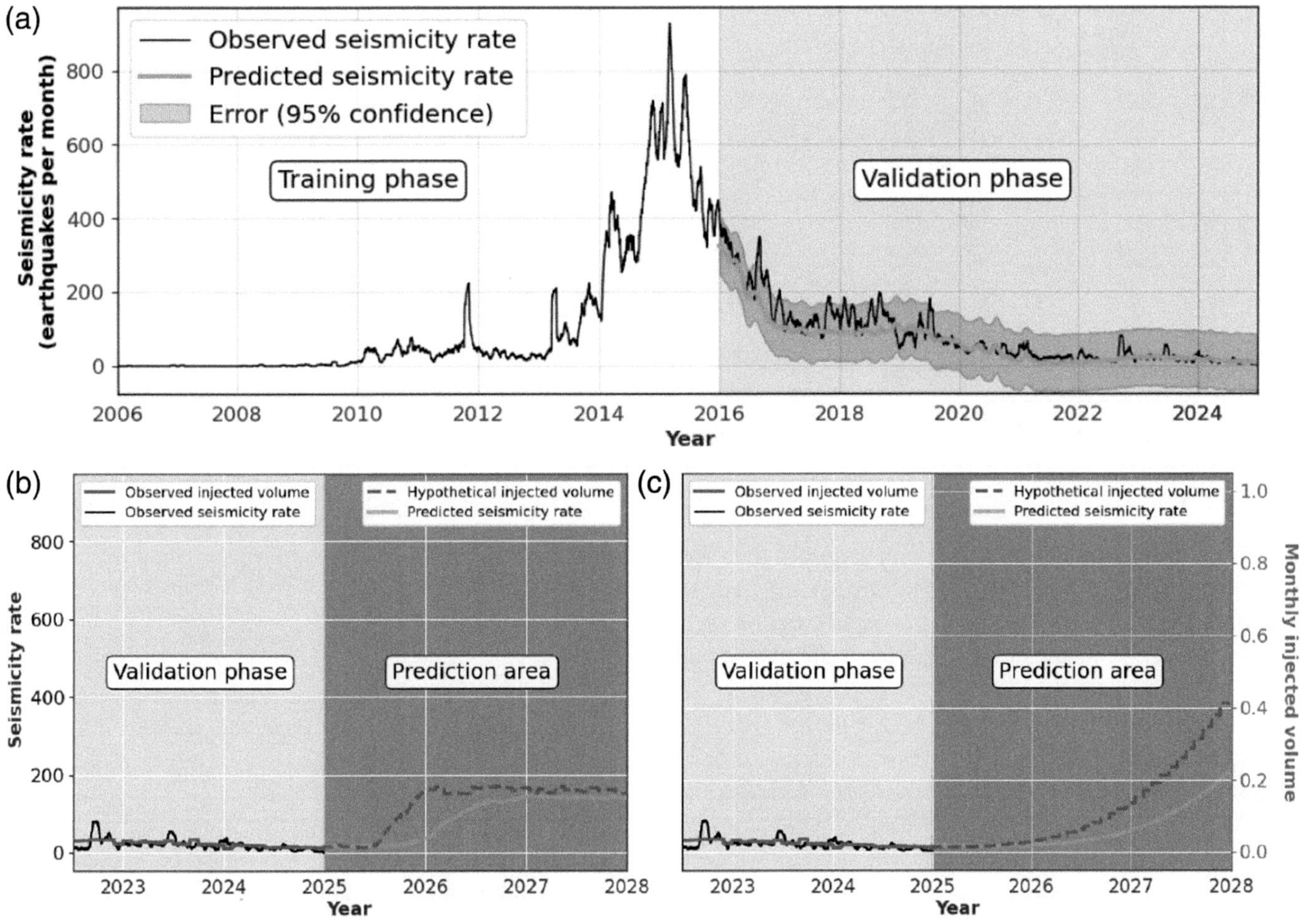

Figure 2. (a) Comparison between the observed seismicity rate and our predictions during the validation phase (light gray area). (b,c) Seismicity prediction for different hypothetical future injection scenarios from 1 January 2025 to 31 December 2027. The color version of this figure is available only in the electronic edition.

in the validation phase, represented by the light gray area. Our prediction shows a very good match compared to the observed seismicity rate (black curve), with a mean absolute error (MAE) of 21.7 earthquakes per month. This is particularly remarkable given that the seismicity rate varies from 400 to almost 0 during the validation phase. The error can be characterized by a confidence interval around the predictions of our model and represented by the orange area in Figure 2a. It is defined by translating the predicted time series by a constant value (75.7 earthquakes per month), such that the obtained interval contains exactly 95% of the observed seismicity rate. In a practical application case, this error interval may be used to quantify the prediction uncertainty in a 95% confidence interval. Although our results proved that our model is able to forecast the future seismicity trend, we note that it is less accurate with rapid variations of the target value, as shown, for example, around the beginning of 2018 in Figure 2a. This could be the consequence of the relative simplicity of our model, using only the injection time series to predict the seismicity rate, which also depends on many other parameters like the variation of the seismic network over time, the presence of mainshocks/aftershocks sequences, or various physical/geological information. It is also important to note that the quality of the prediction naturally depends on the location of the study area, from which both seismic and injection data are extracted. Further details regarding the importance of the study area and the injection wells' locations can be found in Figures S2 and S3, respectively.

Because our model is now trained and validated, we can then forecast the seismicity induced by any hypothetical future injection scenario. Figure 2b,c presents two injection scenarios, from the beginning of 2025 to the end of 2028 (dark gray areas). It is important to note that the injected volume before 1 January 2025 (validation phase) corresponds to actual observed data when the injection after this date is a synthetic signal. The first scenario (b) presents a linear increase in the injection in 2025, while the other (c) is characterized by a steady rise. Synthetic fluctuations are introduced in both cases to simulate variability. In each scenario, our models forecast the seismic response, the trend for which depends strongly

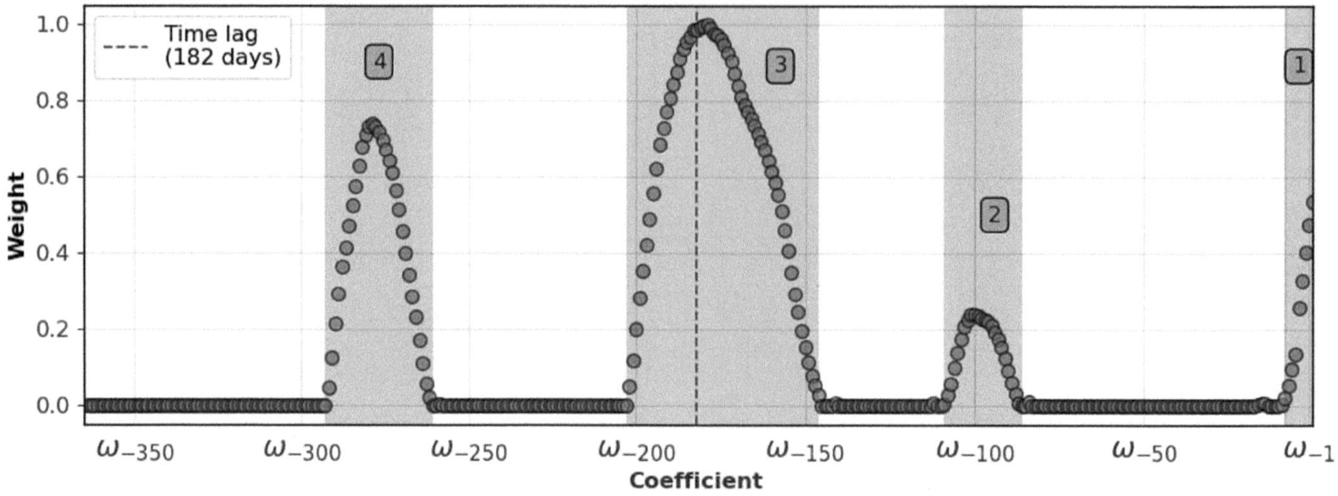

Figure 3. Weights of the 365 coefficients ω_i, fixed by the linear regression model. The indices of each coefficient range from −1 to −365, representing the number of days preceding time $t = 0$, when the prediction is performed. Each coefficient is defined by its weight, representing its importance in equation (2). The color version of this figure is available only in the electronic edition.

on the injected volume time series, with a certain time lag. Finally, the ability of our approach to forecast the number of earthquakes using only a given injection scenario presents a strong practical interest in controlling and monitoring the future seismicity rate.

Features importance

The regression model presented in this section forecasts the next value of the seismicity rate using data from the past year of the injection time series. The relation between seismicity and past injection is characterized by the weights of the coefficients ω_i, defined in equation (2), with i ranging from −1 to −365 (respectively 1 and 365 days before the value we aim to forecast). Figure 3 presents the relative importance of these coefficients, values for which are fixed by the regression model after the training phase. We note important differences between the coefficient weights, reaching high values during four continuous periods: $[\omega_{-1},\omega_{-9}]$, $[\omega_{-85},\omega_{-109}]$, $[\omega_{-145},\omega_{-203}]$, and $[\omega_{-260},\omega_{-293}]$ (see the blue areas). Because the coefficient values are nearly zero elsewhere, the final prediction relies almost entirely on the injection values during these four periods. The high values observed during the $[\omega_{-1},\omega_{-9}]$ interval indicates that the final prediction is influenced by the amount of injection in the near past, within 9 days of injection. The $[\omega_{-145},\omega_{-203}]$ interval stands out from the others because it contains the most positive coefficients and reaches the highest values. In addition, its maximum is reached at ω_{-180}, which almost corresponds to the time lag of 182 days, defined in Figure 1c. This reveals that, for our model, the most useful information about past injection turns out to be very close to this time lag. Such correspondence confirms the importance of the cross-correlation study performed in the Data Presentation section. It will then be interesting to generalize this cross-correlation strategy because the $[\omega_{-85},\omega_{-109}]$ and $[\omega_{-260},\omega_{-293}]$ may correspond to the location of local maximums.

From a physical point of view, the four lag periods may correspond to the characteristic timescales of fluid transfer between the injection wells and the seismogenic faults. The most dominant period $[\omega_{-145},\omega_{-203}]$ may be linked to the overall seismic response of the region (covering around 40,000 km^2), where the seismogenic faults are embedded deeper than the geological layer of the fluid injection (Keranen *et al.*, 2014). The shorter periods $[\omega_{-1},\omega_{-9}]$ and $[\omega_{-85},\omega_{-109}]$ may correspond to local responses, which can also occur when seismicity is already activated in the surroundings of the wells. The shortest reaction $[\omega_{-1},\omega_{-9}]$ may be possible; however, we note that the used injection data are only monthly reported, and there is no resolution to discuss in detail. Laterally, it has been reported that the seismic migration is reported until 50 km away, so that the longest timescale $[\omega_{-260},\omega_{-293}]$ may reflect this distance (Goebel *et al.*, 2017). Finally, Aochi *et al.* (2021) reported that the attenuation timescale of the seismicity after the peak is about one year, so it may also correspond to such a timescale of deceleration.

Prediction of Induced Seismicity Over Local Temporal/Spatial Scales: Case Study of the Soultz-sous-Forêts EGS

Data presentation

Since 1986, an EGS has been developed at Soultz-sous-Forêts (Alsace, France) in the Upper Rhine graben region (Koelbel and Genter, 2017). Within the framework of this project, five deep wells have been drilled between 1986 and 2004: EPS-1, GPK1, GPK2, GPK3, and GPK4, at depths ranging from 3600 to 5000 m. Soultz-sous-Forêts was a research site before transitioning to a commercial exploitation in 2016 (Genter

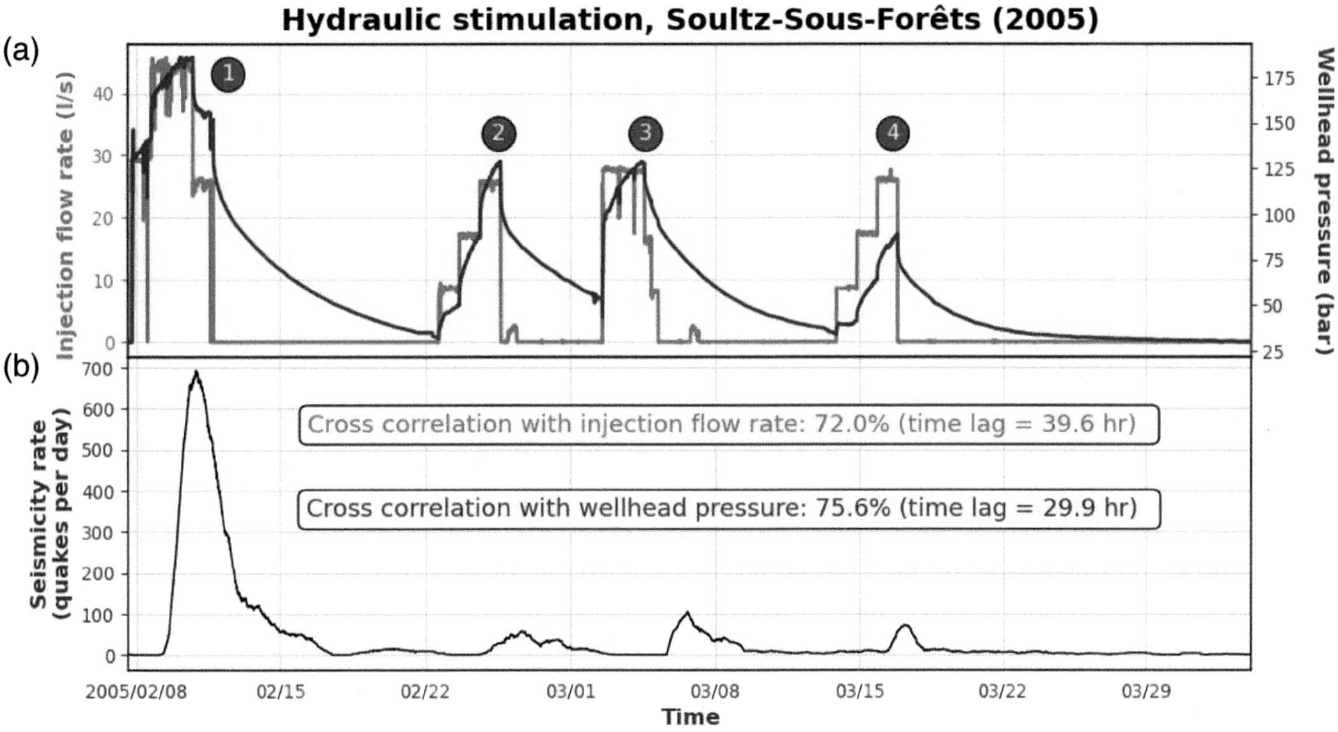

Figure 4. (a) Injection flow rate and wellhead pressure time series, measured during the 2005 Soultz-sous-Forêts stimulation (blue and purple curves, respectively), both increasing during the four injection phases (1, 2, 3, and 4). (b) Number of observed events per hour ($M_L > -0.75$). The color version of this figure is available only in the electronic edition.

et al., 2010). To improve the hydraulic properties of the reservoir and test the efficiency of different methods, several stimulation schemes have been applied between 1993 and 2010. Hydraulic, thermic, and chemical stimulation cycles have been tested while monitoring hydraulic properties at the wellhead and induced seismicity. Hydraulic stimulation is a commonly used operation in geothermal projects, which often leads to an increase in seismicity, as previously observed on different sites (Majer *et al.*, 2007; Zang *et al.*, 2014). To monitor the Soultz-sous-Forêts induced seismicity, different seismic networks were installed, recording several thousand earthquakes for each stimulation (Charléty *et al.*, 2007; Cuenot *et al.*, 2008; Dorbath *et al.*, 2009). In this work, we focus on the 2005 stimulation cycle, from 7 February to 5 April. It is composed of a hydraulic stimulation, followed by a step rate injection, a chemical stimulation, and ending with another step rate injection (the duration of each of these four operations ranges from 65 to 72 hr). These operations are all separated by a few days to evaluate their associated seismic response. In the following, we will simply refer to this stimulation cycle as the 2005 stimulation of Soultz-sous-Forêts (EOST and GEIE-EMC, 2018). During this stimulation, a total of 3709 events were observed over 2 months (see Table 1 for more information about the earthquake catalog). From this dataset, we consider only the events with a local magnitude exceeding −0.75 (i.e., the magnitude of completeness of this catalog), resulting in 2352 selected events.

Figure 4a presents two injection parameters measured during the Soultz-sous-Forêts 2005 stimulation. It includes the injection flow rate (l/s) and the wellhead pressure (bar), displayed in blue and purple, respectively, both sampled every 5 min. These time series show similar variations, particularly during the four injection phases (1, 2, 3, and 4 in Fig. 4a), characterized by a simultaneous increase in the injection. Figure 4b presents the seismicity rate time series during the stimulation. We define the seismicity rate as the number of earthquakes observed in the next 24 hr. The sampling rate is fixed every 5 min to ease the comparison with the injection parameters. We observe similar variations between the injection parameters and the seismicity, especially during the four injection phases, where the three time series increase simultaneously. These similarities are highlighted by the high cross-correlation values with the seismicity rate: 72.0% and 75.6% for the injection flow rate and the wellhead pressure, respectively. However, as in the Oklahoma case study, these correlation values are only reached after shifting the injection parameters in the future by 39.6 hr for the flow rate and 29.9 hr for the wellhead pressure. This time lag corresponds to the delay between the injection of fluid into the ground and the seismic response, which may be caused by the Kaiser effect (Kaiser, 1950; Lavrov, 2003), already observed during fluid injection operations (Dorbath *et al.*, 2009; Kwiatek *et al.*, 2014; Baisch *et al.*,

2015). Such a delay may also be attributed to the hydraulic diffusion properties of the subsurface. Finally, it is important to note that although other injection parameters are available (cumulated injected volume, fluid temperature, ...), we decided to only use the injection flow rate and the wellhead pressure because they present the highest cross-correlation values with the seismicity rate.

Methodology

Similar to the Oklahoma case study, we propose a time-series analysis strategy to forecast the seismicity rate (target value), using both injection flow and wellhead pressure as covariates. First of all, we proceed to a min–max normalization of these time series, to avoid, in particular, biasing our approach by integrating covariates with large amplitude differences, as shown in Figure 4a. Because the relation between the injection parameters and the seismicity rate is more complex than the one observed in the Oklahoma case study (i.e., nonlinear), we use a GBM to perform the prediction of the seismicity rate (Friedman, 2001). The GBM is a powerful machine learning technique that has demonstrated its ability in the field of time-series prediction on a wide range of applications (Körner *et al.*, 2018; Cinto *et al.*, 2020; Hartanto *et al.*, 2023; Song and Chen, 2024). It relies on the construction of "decision trees" to capture the relation between the covariates and the target value. In our work, a decision tree consists of a sequence of conditions on the covariates' amplitudes, allowing us to forecast the target value by learning simple decision rules inferred from the injection parameters. Because Figure 4 shows that the target value is positively correlated with the covariates, this would imply that a rise in the injection parameters will result in an increase in the predicted seismicity rate. The GBM combines several decision trees (also named "weak learners") to build a strong model able to perform accurate predictions. Because each decision tree is integrated sequentially, the model improves over time, and each new model corrects the errors of the previous ones. One can refer to Natekin and Knoll (2013) for more information about the GBM. More specifically, the model used in this work is the light gradient boosting method (LGBM), a slightly modified version of the GBM, which is known to speed up computation times by up to 20 times while achieving almost the same accuracy (Ke *et al.*, 2017). This is carried out with two data processing techniques, named "Exclusive Feature Bundling" and "Gradient-based One-Side Sampling," allowing for to reduction of the number of features by discarding the ones containing redundant or little information.

Our model forecasts the next point in the seismicity rate time series—representing the total number of earthquakes in the upcoming 24 hr—by leveraging covariates' past information from the previous 48 hr. This value is consistent with both time lags presented in Figure 4b: 39.6 and 29.9 hr for the injection flow rate and the wellhead pressure, respectively. Indeed, our model benefits from the information captured over both time lags by processing covariates from the previous 48 hr. To estimate the quality of a given prediction, our model aims to minimize the mean square error loss function, defined by equation (1). As is common in machine learning models, the LGBM requires a training phase to capture the relation between the injection parameters and the associated seismic response. During the training phase, the LGBM constructs its decision trees, which, once combined, result in a strong predictive model. Once the model is trained, it is then possible to perform a prediction of the seismicity rate and compare it with the observed values during the validation phase. It is important to mention that we integrate a third covariate into our model, defined by the multiplication of the injection flow rate by the wellhead pressure (see Fig. S4, presenting the features' importance). The hyperparameters of the LGBM were selected using a GridSearch strategy (Andonie, 2019) to minimize the MAE, resulting in 200 decision trees, 13 leaves, and a learning rate of 0.1 (see Natekin and Knoll, 2013, for more information about these hyperparameters).

Results

Figure 5 presents the forecasting results of the LGBM model compared to the observed seismicity rate, represented by the orange and black time series, respectively. We note the time periods defining the training phase: from 7 to 24 February (white area), and the validation phase: from 24 February to 5 April (light gray area). It is important to point out that the proportion of the training phase is surprisingly low compared to the validation period. Indeed, the training period covers only around 30.9% of the total stimulation, which is unusual in machine learning. This choice reflects the challenge posed by the short duration of the stimulation, with the need to extract as much information as possible in a short period of time. In this particular case, this allows us to perform a prediction during the three seismic swarms included in the validation phase (2, 3, and 4 in Fig. 5).

The forecasting results provided by the LGBM are a good estimation of the observed seismicity rate during the validation phase. Indeed, we observe three significant increases in the predicted seismicity, all corresponding to the locations of the seismic swarms included in the validation phase. In addition, these increases reveal similar variations and duration with the observed seismicity rate. For example, the third seismic swarm is characterized by a sharp rise of seismicity, followed by a steady, almost linear decrease, which is similar to our predictions (despite an early start). On the other hand, our predictions are also reliable outside the seismic swarms, as shown, for example, in the last two weeks of prediction, with values close to zero, once again in agreement with the observed seismicity. Over the total validation phase, our predictions are characterized by an MAE of 15.7 quakes per hour.

Although our model is able to predict the trend of the future seismicity rate, some minor inaccuracies are present, for

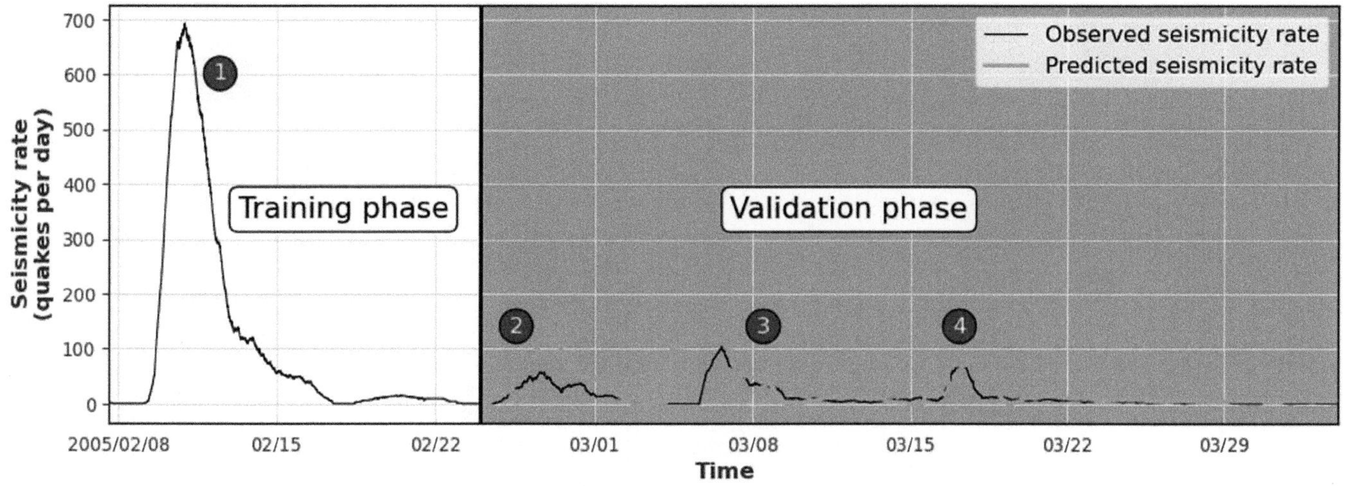

Figure 5. Forecasting results of the seismicity rate during the Soultz-sous-Forêt stimulation in 2005. The time period is divided into two sections: the training and the validation phases, represented by the white and light gray areas, respectively. The prediction results are obtained with a light gradient boosting method and are represented by the orange curve during the validation phase. The color version of this figure is available only in the electronic edition.

example, with the forecasting of the fourth seismic swarm, which was predicted around one day later. A similar time shift was also observed for the third seismic swarm, for which the rise of the predicted seismicity starts around one day before the actual observed values. This is due to the fact that the seismic response time delay differs slightly between the training period and the validation phase.

Influence of training duration on forecasting performance

The duration of the training phase is of great importance in machine learning because it directly affects the model's ability to learn meaningful patterns and generalize effectively to other datasets. Because stimulations are generally limited to several weeks, it is then crucial to be able to extract as much information as possible during a reduced amount of time. To investigate this aspect, we present in Figure 6 the forecasting results for different training and validation periods (see the caption for the exact dates). Figure 6a shows an extremely reduced training phase of around 3 days. This short training period does not contain enough information to train our model and only includes high values of both injection parameters, as shown in Figure 4a. Consequently, our model has low prediction accuracy, especially during the periods when almost no seismicity is observed. However, we note increases in the target time series during the four seismic swarms (1, 2, 3, and 4 in Fig. 6), which indicates that the model understands the positive correlation between injection parameters and seismicity. Figure 6b presents a larger training phase of approximately 10 days, including the first seismic swarm. We observe a clear improvement of the prediction, highlighted by an MAE of 21.5 quakes/day compared to the previous forecasting with an MAE of 65.5 (a). This improvement concerns the three seismic swarms included during the validation period, but also better predictions outside these areas, when almost no seismicity is observed, for example, after 22 March. Concerning the last three examples, Figure 6c–e, the training area expands up to a total duration of approximately 24 (c), 31 (d), and 38 days (e). We observe that increasing the length of the training area results in a significant decrease of the MAE, from 65.5 (a) to 4.2 (e). Although this gain in performance is certainly due to the accumulation of information assimilated by our model, it is also important to note that the MAE is computed over different time intervals with decreasing seismic activity, which may influence the evaluation.

Discussion and Conclusion

In this work, we investigated the potential of machine learning to forecast fluid-induced seismicity using operational time series from two distinct case studies. Our results show that machine learning models can exploit information from the injection parameters, such as injection flow rate and wellhead pressure, to forecast the variations of the future seismicity. Time-series prediction reveals to be particularly well-suited because it allows for capturing long- and/or short-term dependencies between covariates and target value. As demonstrated by the applications in Oklahoma and Soultz-sous-Forêt, our strategy can be applied to various injection scenarios at different spatial and temporal scales. These findings open the door to several aspects that require further discussion.

An important aspect that needs to be discussed concerns the application of our time-series forecasting strategy in real time. Because real-time applications often have to deal with a limited volume of information, this question is directly related to the minimum amount of data required to train the model. When

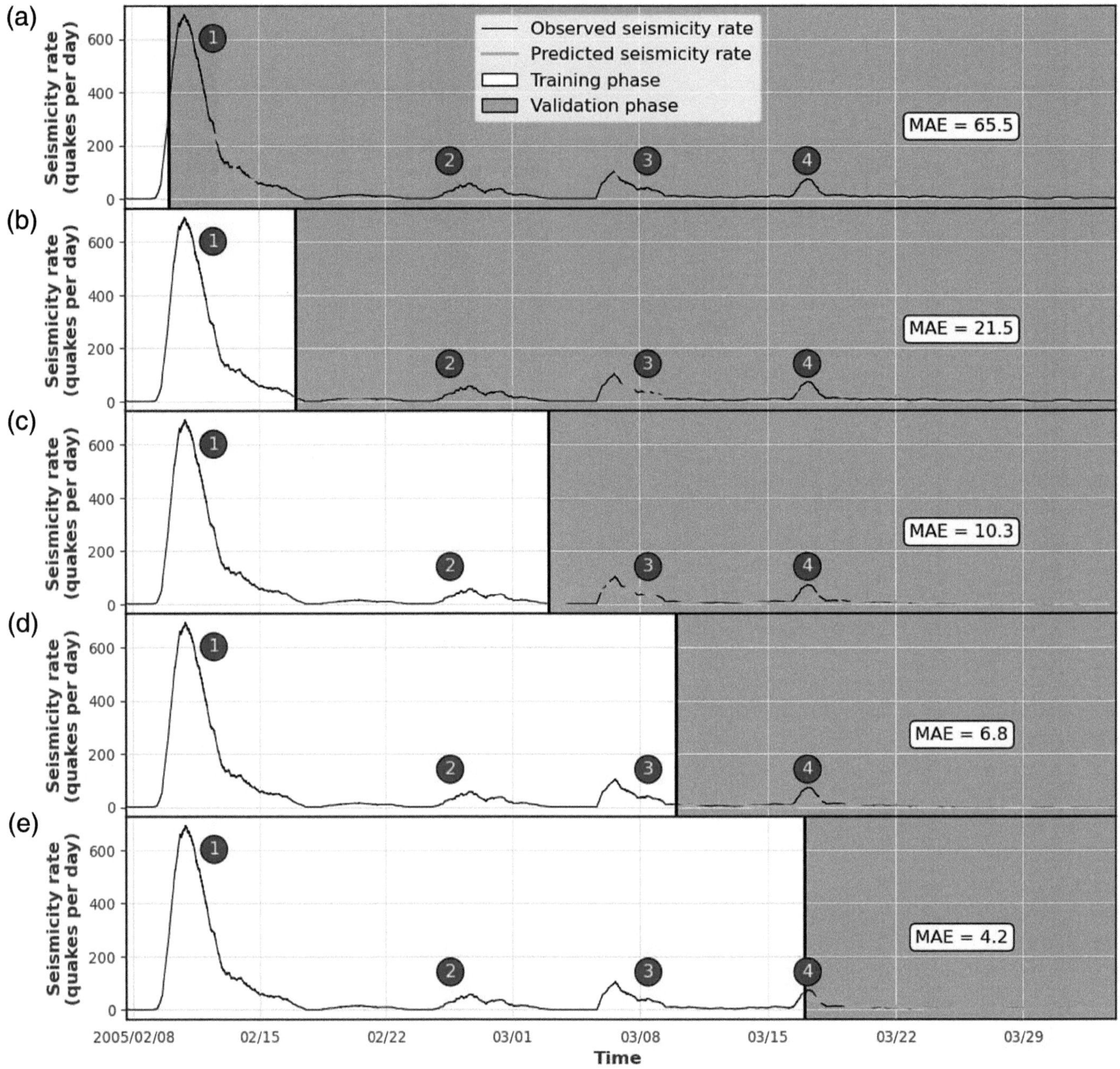

Figure 6. Forecasting results during the 2005 Soultz-sous-Forêt stimulation. Each prediction is carried out using different durations for the training phase: 3 days (a), 10 days (b), 24 days (c), 31 days (d), and 38 days (e). The prediction results are obtained with a light gradient boosting method and are represented by orange curves during the validation phase. The mean absolute error (MAE) between predicted and observed seismicity rate (black curves) is displayed in each case. The color version of this figure is available only in the electronic edition.

this issue was investigated on the particular case study of Soultz-sous-Forêt (Fig. 6), the ideal training duration depends, in general, on parameters like the seismic response to injection or the time lag. In addition, it is also essential for the model to train during periods containing "valuable information." For example, our experience showed that training our model from 2006 to 2011 in Oklahoma resulted in a poor quality of prediction as both time series are close to zero (see Fig. 1). Extending this period up to 2015 leads to a significant increase in the forecasting accuracy because it includes valuable information, with significant increases in injected volume and seismicity rate (see Fig. S5). However, the example of Soultz-sous-Forêts shows that even with a training period limited to 10 days, the increase in seismicity rate observed in the data can be reproduced in the validation phase. This suggests that with further development, it may be possible to use a machine learning algorithm to predict seismicity rate in real time during a stimulation after a short training phase. This would yield only first-order information and no detailed analysis, but may be sufficient to react in case of unplanned seismicity.

Another challenge for real-time applications lies in the duration of past information used by the model to perform the prediction, which is fixed in this study, at 48 hr for Soultz-sous-Forêt and 365 days for Oklahoma. We choose this duration according to time lags, computed by cross-correlations on the whole time series, when only partial datasets will be available during ongoing operations. Consequently, cross-correlation applied to incomplete time series may lead to uncertainty regarding the time-lag linking seismicity to injection parameters. As a precautionary measure, we recommend selecting a significantly higher duration value than the time lag to ensure that the model uses as much valuable information as possible. This recommendation is justified by the unique ability of machine learning to extract only the information that is useful for prediction and reject the rest, as already observed in Figure 3. In real-time applications, a central difficulty also lies in selecting an appropriate machine learning model. This requires comparing different predictions to select the model that minimizes the MAE with respect to the observed data (see Fig. S6).

Particular attention should also be given to the selection of the input parameters, which play a decisive role in the final prediction. In this study, our predictions were performed using the injected volume in Oklahoma and a combination of flow rate and wellhead pressure time series in Soultz-sous-Forêts. This final selection is the result of testing many combinations of the different available injection parameters. These parameters include fluid temperature and/or pressure measurements from nearby wells to minimize the MAE during the validation phase. Because the selection of input parameters represents an essential aspect of our approach, we recommend that this comparative analysis be carried out systematically. On the other hand, we also found that feeding the model with irrelevant parameters could deteriorate the prediction accuracy. For example, adding covariates that have proven to be weakly correlated with the seismicity rate, like the temperature time series or completely irrelevant like a synthetic random Gaussian noise, leads to worse predictions. Consequently, retaining only essential parameters provides the best results while preserving the relative simplicity of the model.

Although our method shows promising results, it also faces some limitations that should be discussed. Among these limitations is the influence of earthquake aftershocks triggered by high-magnitude events that reactivate faults. Such a phenomenon was observed in November 2011 in Oklahoma, when an earthquake of magnitude M_w 5.7 triggered thousands of events (Keranen *et al.*, 2012). This rise of events is visible in Figure 1 and altered the capture of the injection/seismicity relation during the training phase. This issue could be solved by applying the declustering technique of the epidemic-type aftershock sequence model to build a catalog that excludes earthquake aftershocks (Console *et al.*, 2010). Another limitation of our method lies in the lack of information about the magnitudes of the events we aim to forecast. Although we agree that such a prediction presents a clear interest, forecasting the number of induced earthquakes higher than a given magnitude remains a complex task. However, it is important to note that we observed similar variations between the seismicity rate and the mean level of magnitude in Oklahoma.

The study presented in this article paves the way for several perspectives. Concerning the improvement of prediction accuracy, we might consider integrating geological and/or physical information like earthquake hypocenters, fault locations, or spatialized pore pressure estimation derived from modelization. However, this type of model is time-consuming, so such a strategy would be useful for long-term analysis of seismicity. Although not perfect, the correlation found between injection parameters and seismicity rate shows that, at first order, there is no need for a physical model to predict it. Performance could also be improved by leveraging past information from one site to train the model and then applying it to perform the predictions on another. Although such a strategy would be promising to overcome, for example, the amount of data required for the training phase, its practical use is challenging. Indeed, our experience showed that the seismic response differs for each fluid injection site: different geologies, depth wells, and fault locations. In addition, we also observed variations in the seismic response time lag during the second stimulation of the GPK4 well in Soultz-sous-Fôrets. Finally, a promising challenge would be to apply our strategy to the prediction of microseismicity within ongoing geothermal operations, like the EGS site located in Rittershoffen (Upper Rhine Graben, France).

Data and Resources

The seismicity catalog is obtained and available from the Oklahoma Geological Survey (OGS, https://ogsweb.ou.edu/eq_catalog). The injected volumes are reported monthly for each well via the Oklahoma Corporation Commission (OCC), Oil and Gas Division (https://oklahoma.gov/occ/divisions/oil-gas/oil-gas-data.html). All hydraulic and seismic data (waveforms and earthquake catalogs) of the Soultz-sous-Forêts stimulations used in this study are available in the CDGP (Data Center for Deep Geothermal Energy) at https://cdgp.u-strasbg.fr/ (EOST and GEIE-EMC, 2018). An Authentication, Authorization, and Accounting Infrastructure (AAAI) ensures that data distribution respects the intellectual property rights (IPR) of the owner. As such, data can be provided, after registration and entering the user's affiliation (i.e., academic, industrial, ...), either automatically or after approval by the data owner. All websites were last accessed in October 2025. The supplemental material to this article includes information concerning the influence of the p parameter as well as the study area on the final prediction in Oklahoma, the location of the injection wells, features importance of the light gradient boosting method (LGBM), the forecasting results for different training/validation phases, and performance comparison of several machine learning models.

Declaration of Competing Interests

The authors acknowledge that there are no conflicts of interest recorded.

Acknowledgments

This project is funded by ANR-AIS (ANR-22-FAI2-0008). The work presented in this study was done with a Python program (Van Rossum, 2007) using, in particular, the NumPy (Harris *et al.*, 2020), SciPy (Virtanen *et al.*, 2020), and ObsPy (Beyreuther *et al.*, 2010) libraries. The figures presented in this study were generated with the Matplotlib library (Ari and Ustazhanov, 2014). The time-series data processing as well as the forecasting machine learning methods were both carried out using the DARTS library (Herzen *et al.*, 2022).

References

Allen, R. (1982). Automatic phase pickers: Their present use and future prospects, *Bull. Seismol. Soc. Am.* **72,** no. 6B, S225–S242.

Andonie, R. (2019). Hyperparameter optimization in learning systems, *J. Membr. Comput.* **1,** no. 4, 279–291.

Aochi, H., J. Maury, and T. Le Guenan (2021). How do statistical parameters of induced seismicity correlate with fluid injection? Case of Oklahoma, *Bull. Seismol. Soc. Am.* **92,** no. 4, 2573–2590.

Ari, N., and M. Ustazhanov (2014). Matplotlib in python, *2014 11th International Conference on Electronics, Computer and Computation (ICECCO)*, IEEE, 1–6.

Bachmann, C. E., S. Wiemer, J. Woessner, and S. Hainzl (2011). Statistical analysis of the induced Basel 2006 earthquake sequence: Introducing a probability-based monitoring approach for enhanced geothermal systems, *Geophys. J. Int.* **186,** no. 2, 793–807.

Baisch, S., C. Koch, and A. Muntendam-Bos (2019). Traffic light systems: To what extent can induced seismicity be controlled? *Seismol. Res. Lett.* **90,** no. 3, 1145–1154.

Baisch, S., E. Rothert, H. Stang, R. Vörös, C. Koch, and A. McMahon (2015). Continued geothermal reservoir stimulation experiments in the cooper basin (Australia), *Bull. Seismol. Soc. Am.* **105,** no. 1, 198–209.

Beyreuther, M., R. Barsch, L. Krischer, T. Megies, Y. Behr, and J. Wassermann (2010). Obspy: A python toolbox for seismology, *Seismol. Res. Lett.* **81,** no. 3, 530–533.

Bickle, M. J. (2009). Geological carbon storage, *Nature Geosci.* **2,** no. 12, 815–818.

Calò, M., C. Dorbath, and M. Frogneux (2014). Injection tests at the EGS reservoir of Soultz-sous-Forêts. Seismic response of the GPK4 stimulations, *Geothermics* **52,** 50–58.

Charléty, J., N. Cuenot, L. Dorbath, C. Dorbath, H. Haessler, and M. Frogneux (2007). Large earthquakes during hydraulic stimulations at the geothermal site of Soultz-sous-Forêts, *Int. J. Rock Mech. Min. Sci.* **44,** no. 8, 1091–1105.

Cinto, T., A. Gradvohl, G. Coelho, and A. Da Silva (2020). Solar flare forecasting using time series and extreme gradient boosting ensembles, *Sol. Phys.* **295,** no. 7, 93.

Console, R., D. Jackson, and Y. Kagan (2010). Using the etas model for catalog declustering and seismic background assessment, *Pure Appl. Geophys.* **167,** no. 6, 819–830.

Cuenot, N., C. Dorbath, and L. Dorbath (2008). Analysis of the microseismicity induced by fluid injections at the EGS site of Soultz-sous-Forêts (Alsace, France): Implications for the characterization of the geothermal reservoir properties, *Pure Appl. Geophys.* **165,** no. 5, 797–828.

Dorbath, L., N. Cuenot, A. Genter, and M. Frogneux (2009). Seismic response of the fractured and faulted granite of Soultz-sous-Forêts (France) to 5 km deep massive water injections, *Geophys. J. Int.* **177,** no. 2, 653–675.

Ellsworth, W. L., D. Giardini, J. Townend, S. Ge, and T. Shimamoto (2019). Triggering of the Pohang, Korea, earthquake (m_w 5.5) by enhanced geothermal system stimulation, *Seismol. Res. Lett.* **90,** no. 5, 1844–1858.

EOST and GEIE-EMC (2018). Episode: 2005 stimulation Soultz-sous-Forêts, *EOST-CDGP*, doi: 10.25577/ssfs2005.

Fiori, R., J. Vergne, J. Schmittbuhl, and D. Zigone (2023). Monitoring induced microseismicity in an urban context using very small seismic arrays: The case study of the Vendenheim EGS project, *Geophysics* **88,** no. 5, WB71–WB87.

Friedman, J. H. (2001). Greedy function approximation: A gradient boosting machine, *Ann. Stat.* **29,** 1189–1232.

Gaucher, E., M. Schoenball, O. Heidbach, A. Zang, P. A. Fokker, J.-D. van Wees, and T. Kohl (2015). Induced seismicity in geothermal reservoirs: A review of forecasting approaches, *Renew. Sustain. Energy Rev.* **52,** 1473–1490.

Genter, A., K. Evans, N. Cuenot, D. Fritsch, and B. Sanjuan (2010). Contribution of the exploration of deep crystalline fractured reservoir of Soultz to the knowledge of enhanced geothermal systems (EGS), *C.R. Geosci.* **342,** nos. 7/8, 502–516.

Giardini, D. (2009). Geothermal quake risks must be faced, *Nature* **462,** no. 7275, 848–849.

Goebel, T., M. Weingarten, X. Chen, J. Haffener, and E. Brodsky (2017). The 2016 m_w 5. 1 Fairview, Oklahoma earthquakes: Evidence for long-range poroelastic triggering at > 40 km from fluid disposal wells, *Earth Planet. Sci. Lett.* **472,** 50–61.

Hallo, M., I. Oprsal, L. Eisner, and M. Y. Ali (2014). Prediction of magnitude of the largest potentially induced seismic event, *J. Seismol.* **18,** 421–431.

Harris, C. R., K. J. Millman, S. J. Van Der Walt, R. Gommers, P. Virtanen, D. Cournapeau, E. Wieser, J. Taylor, S. Berg, N. J. Smith, *et al.* (2020). Array programming with NumPy, *Nature* **585,** no. 7825, 357–362.

Hartanto, A. D., Y. N. Kholik, and Y. Pristyanto (2023). Stock price time series data forecasting using the light gradient boosting machine (LightGBM) model, *JOIV: Int. J. Inform. Vis.* **7,** no. 4, 2270–2279.

Havskov, J., P. Bormann, and J. Schweitzer (2012). Seismic source location, *New Manual of Seismological Observatory Practice 2 (NMSOP-2)*, Deutsches GeoForschungsZentrum GFZ, pp. 1–36.

He, M., Q. Li, and X. Li (2020). Injection-induced seismic risk management using machine learning methodology–a perspective study, *Front. Earth Sci.* **8,** 227.

Herzen, J., F. Lässig, S. G. Piazzetta, T. Neuer, L. Tafti, G. Raille, T. Van Pottelbergh, M. Pasieka, A. Skrodzki, N. Huguenin, *et al.* (2022). Darts: User-friendly modern machine learning for time series, *J. Machine Learn. Res.* **23,** no. 124, 1–6.

Hincks, T., W. Aspinall, R. Cooke, and T. Gernon (2018). Oklahoma's induced seismicity strongly linked to wastewater injection depth, *Science* **359,** no. 6381, 1251–1255.

Hong, J., H. Jo, D. Seo, and S. You (2022). Impact of induced seismicity on the housing market: Evidence from Pohang, *Buildings* **12,** no. 3, 286.

Ineris and BRGM (2023). Good practices guide for managing induced seismicity by deep geothermal operations, available at https://www

.ineris.fr/sites/default/files/contribution/Documents/Guide%20geothermie_Ineris-BRGM_anglais%20%28ID%202821990%29.pdf (last accessed November 2025).

Jacquemond, L., J. Letort, F. Cotton, M. Causse, J. Grasso, G. Senechal, J. Ammirati, B. Derode, F. Grimaud, H. Pauchet, *et al.* (2024). Analysing 50 yr of the Lacq induced seismicity (southwestern, France) highlights the role of fluid injection, *Geophys. J. Int.* **238,** no. 1, 214–234.

Kaiser, J. (1950). An investigation into the occurrence of noises in tensile tests, or a study of acoustic phenomena in tensile tests, *Doctor of Philosophy*, Technical University of Munich, Munich, Germany.

Ke, G., Q. Meng, T. Finley, T. Wang, W. Chen, W. Ma, Q. Ye, and T.-Y. Liu (2017). Lightgbm: A highly efficient gradient boosting decision tree, *Advances in Neural Information Processing Systems*, Vol. 30.

Keranen, K., H. Savage, G. Abers, and E. Cochran (2012). Fluid injection triggering of 2011 earthquake sequence in Oklahoma, *AGU Fall Meeting Abstracts*, Vol. 2012, S34A–03 pp.

Keranen, K. M., M. Weingarten, G. A. Abers, B. A. Bekins, and S. Ge (2014). Sharp increase in central Oklahoma seismicity since 2008 induced by massive wastewater injection, *Science* **345,** no. 6195, 448–451.

Koelbel, T., and A. Genter (2017). Enhanced geothermal systems: The Soultz-Sous-Forêts project, in *Towards 100% Renewable Energy: Techniques, Costs and Regional Case-Studies*, T. M. Letcher (Editor), Springer, Amsterdam, The Netherlands, 243–248.

Kong, Q., D. T. Trugman, Z. E. Ross, M. J. Bianco, B. J. Meade, and P. Gerstoft (2019). Machine learning in seismology: Turning data into insights, *Seismol. Res. Lett.* **90,** no. 1, 3–14.

Körner, P., R. Kronenberg, S. Genzel, and C. Bernhofer (2018). Introducing gradient boosting as a universal gap filling tool for meteorological time series, *Meteorol. Z.* **27,** no. 5, 369–376.

Kubo, H., M. Naoi, and M. Kano (2024). Recent advances in earthquake seismology using machine learning, *Earth Planets Space* **76,** no. 1, 36.

Kwiatek, G., F. Bulut, M. Bohnhoff, and G. Dresen (2014). High-resolution analysis of seismicity induced at Berlin geothermal field, El Salvador, *Geothermics* **52,** 98–111.

Langenbruch, C., and M. D. Zoback (2016). How will induced seismicity in Oklahoma respond to decreased saltwater injection rates? *Sci. Adv.* **2,** no. 11, e1601542, doi: 10.1126/sciadv.1601542.

Langenbruch, C., M. Weingarten, and M. D. Zoback (2018). Physics-based forecasting of man-made earthquake hazards in Oklahoma and Kansas, *Nat. Commun.* **9,** no. 1, 3946.

Lavrov, A. (2003). The Kaiser effect in rocks: Principles and stress estimation techniques, *Int. J. Rock Mech. Min. Sci.* **40,** no. 2, 151–171.

Li, J., H. Zhai, C. Jiang, Z. Wang, P. Wang, X. Chang, Y. Zhang, Y. Wei, and Z. Si (2025). Application of artificial intelligence technology in the study of anthropogenic earthquakes: A review, *Artif. Intell. Rev.* **58,** no. 5, 1–42.

Li, Z., D. W. Eaton, and J. Davidsen (2023). Physics-informed deep learning to forecast m max during hydraulic fracturing, *Sci. Rep.* **13,** no. 1, 13,133.

Lu, S.-M. (2018). A global review of enhanced geothermal system (EGS), *Renew. Sustain. Energy Rev.* **81,** 2902–2921.

Ma, X., and T. Chen (2022). Small seismic events in Oklahoma detected and located by machine learning-based models, *Bull. Seismol. Soc. Am.* **112,** no. 6, 2859–2869.

Majer, E. L., R. Baria, M. Stark, S. Oates, J. Bommer, B. Smith, and H. Asanuma (2007). Induced seismicity associated with enhanced geothermal systems, *Geothermics* **36,** no. 3, 185–222.

McGarr, A. (2014). Maximum magnitude earthquakes induced by fluid injection, *J. Geophys. Res.* **119,** no. 2, 1008–1019.

Meier, M.-A., Z. E. Ross, A. Ramachandran, A. Balakrishna, S. Nair, P. Kundzicz, Z. Li, J. Andrews, E. Hauksson, and Y. Yue (2019). Reliable real-time seismic signal/noise discrimination with machine learning, *J. Geophys. Res.* **124,** no. 1, 788–800.

Mena, B., S. Wiemer, and C. Bachmann (2013). Building robust models to forecast the induced seismicity related to geothermal reservoir enhancement, *Bull. Seismol. Soc. Am.* **103,** no. 1, 383–393.

Montgomery, D. C., E. A. Peck, and G. G. Vining (2021). *Introduction to Linear Regression Analysis*, John Wiley & Sons, Hoboken, New Jersey.

Mousavi, S. M., and G. C. Beroza (2019). Bayesian-deep-learning estimation of earthquake location from single-station observations, arXiv preprint arXiv:1912.01144.

Münchmeyer, J., J. Woollam, A. Rietbrock, F. Tilmann, D. Lange, T. Bornstein, T. Diehl, C. Giunchi, F. Haslinger, D. Jozinović, *et al.* (2022). Which picker fits my data? A quantitative evaluation of deep learning based seismic pickers, *J. Geophys. Res.* **127,** no. 1, e2021JB023499, doi: 10.1029/2021JB023499.

Natekin, A., and A. Knoll (2013). Gradient boosting machines, a tutorial, *Front. Neurorobot.* **7,** 21.

Qin, Y., T. Chen, X. Ma, and X. Chen (2022). Forecasting induced seismicity in Oklahoma using machine learning methods, *Sci. Rep.* **12,** no. 1, 9319.

Rajesh, R., and H. K. Gupta (2021). Characterization of injection-induced seismicity at north central Oklahoma, USA, *J. Seismol.* **25,** 327–337.

Rouet-Leduc, B., C. Hulbert, N. Lubbers, K. Barros, C. J. Humphreys, and P. A. Johnson (2017). Machine learning predicts laboratory earthquakes, *Geophys. Res. Lett.* **44,** no. 18, 9276–9282.

Schoenball, M., and W. L. Ellsworth (2017). A systematic assessment of the spatiotemporal evolution of fault activation through induced seismicity in Oklahoma and Southern Kansas, *J. Geophys. Res.* **122,** no. 12, 10–189.

Shi, P., F. Grigoli, F. Lanza, G. C. Beroza, L. Scarabello, and S. Wiemer (2022). Malmi: An automated earthquake detection and location workflow based on machine learning and waveform migration, *Bull. Seismol. Soc. Am.* **93,** no. 5, 2467–2483.

Shi, P., M.-A. Meier, L. Villiger, K. Tuinstra, P. A. Selvadurai, F. Lanza, S. Yuan, A. Obermann, M. Mesimeri, J. Münchmeyer, *et al.* (2024). From Labquakes to megathrusts: Scaling deep learning based pickers over 15 orders of magnitude, *J. Geophys. Res.* **1,** no. 4, e2024JH000220, doi: 10.1029/2024JH000220.

Smith, M. B., and C. Montgomery (2015). *Hydraulic Fracturing*, CRC Press, Boca Raton, Florida.

Song, X., and Z. S. Chen (2024). Enhancing financial time series forecasting in the shipping market: A hybrid approach with light gradient boosting machine, *Eng. Appl. Artif. Intell.* **136,** 108,942.

Stork, A. L., J. P. Verdon, and J.-M. Kendall (2015). The microseismic response at the in Salah carbon capture and storage (ccs) site, *Int. J. Greenhouse Gas Control* **32,** 159–171.

Van der Elst, N. J., M. T. Page, D. A. Weiser, T. H. Goebel, and S. M. Hosseini (2016). Induced earthquake magnitudes are as large as (statistically) expected, *J. Geophys. Res.* **121,** no. 6, 4575–4590.

Van Rossum, G. (2007). Python programming language, *USENIX Annual Technical Conference*, Vol. 41, Santa Clara, California, 1–36.

Virtanen, P., R. Gommers, T. E. Oliphant, M. Haberland, T. Reddy, D. Cournapeau, E. Burovski, P. Peterson, W. Weckesser, J. Bright, *et al.* (2020). Scipy 1.0: Fundamental algorithms for scientific computing in python, *Nat. Methods* **17,** no. 3, 261–272.

Warner, D. L., and J. H. Lehr (1977). An introduction to the technology of subsurface wastewater injection, Vol. 1, Municipal Environmental Research Laboratory, Office of Research and Development, available at &https://nepis.epa.gov/Exe/ZyNET.exe/20012ME9.txt?ZyActionD=ZyDocument&Client;=EPA&Index;=1976%20Thru%201980&Docs;=&Query;=introduction%20technology%20subsurface%20wastewater%20injection&Time;=&EndTime;=&SearchMethod;=2&TocRestrict;=n&Toc;=&TocEntry;=&QField;=&QFieldYear;=&QFieldMonth;=&QFieldDay;=&UseQField;=&IntQFieldOp;=0&ExtQFieldOp;=0&XmlQuery;=&File;=D%3A%5CZYFILES%5CINDEX%20DATA%5C76THRU80%5CTXT%5C00000008%5C20012ME9.txt&User;=ANONYMOUS&Password;=anonymous&SortMethod;=h%7C-&MaximumDocuments;=15&FuzzyDegree;=0&ImageQuality;=r85g16/r85g16/x150y150g16/i500&Display;=hpfr&DefSeekPage;=&SearchBack;=ZyActionL&Back;=ZyActionS&BackDesc;=Results%20page&MaximumPages;=1&ZyEntry;=1 (last accessed October 2025).

Woollam, J., J. Münchmeyer, F. Tilmann, A. Rietbrock, D. Lange, T. Bornstein, T. Diehl, C. Giunchi, F. Haslinger, D. Jozinović, *et al.* (2022). Seisbench—A toolbox for machine learning in seismology, *Bull. Seismol. Soc. Am.* **93,** no. 3, 1695–1709.

Yeck, W. L., G. P. Hayes, D. E. McNamara, J. L. Rubinstein, W. D. Barnhart, P. S. Earle, and H. M. Benz (2017). Oklahoma experiences largest earthquake during ongoing regional wastewater injection hazard mitigation efforts, *Geophys. Res. Lett.* **44,** no. 2, 711–717.

Zang, A., V. Oye, P. Jousset, N. Deichmann, R. Gritto, A. McGarr, E. Majer, and D. Bruhn (2014). Analysis of induced seismicity in geothermal reservoirs–An overview, *Geothermics* **52,** 6–21.

Zhu, W., and G. C. Beroza (2019). Phasenet: A deep-neural-network-based seismic arrival-time picking method, *Geophys. J. Int.* **216,** no. 1, 261–273.

Manuscript received 27 June 2025
Published online 21 November 2025

Detecting and Characterizing Swarm-Like Seismicity

OPEN ACCESS

Luigi Passarelli*[1], Gesa Petersen[2], Leila Mizrahi[3], and Simone Cesca[2]

Abstract

Swarm-like seismicity manifests as earthquake clusters driven by aseismic transients. The investigation of the mechanisms behind their occurrence is generally based on automatic detection and characterization of swarm-like clusters. In this study, we investigate four different (de-)clustering algorithms to identify earthquake clusters, and then classify these clusters as either swarm-like or mainshock–aftershocks sequences. The classification uses the clusters' distribution of seismic moment over time, quantified by standardized central moments. Synthetic catalogs from an epidemic-type aftershock sequence model are used to establish confidence bounds for swarm classification. The workflow is applied to the swarm-dominated regions Húsavík–Flatey fault, Iceland, and Pollino range, Italy. Our workflow effectively detects/classifies earthquake clusters, but their inherent variability in duration and seismic moment release can bias automated swarm/mainshock–aftershocks labeling. The results provide benchmarks for future swarm-like seismicity analyses, highlighting the importance of a posteriori careful inspection of clusters to understand the underlying physical mechanisms.

Cite this article as Passarelli, L., G. Petersen, L. Mizrahi, and S. Cesca (2025). Detecting and Characterizing Swarm-Like Seismicity, *Seismol. Res. Lett.* **97**, 1867–1880, doi: 10.1785/0220250204.

Supplemental Material

Introduction

The intriguing nature of swarm-like seismicity lies in its spatiotemporal and magnitude scaling properties, which are inconsistent with the empirical laws governing mainshock–aftershocks sequences, such as the Gutenberg–Richter, Omori–Utsu, and Båth relationships (Hill, 1977; Hainzl *et al.*, 2013; Marsan *et al.*, 2013). In contrast to tectonically driven mainshock–aftershocks clusters, the genesis of earthquake swarms has been attributed to a diverse range of aseismic transient phenomena, including fluid pressurization, aseismic slip events, and magmatic stress perturbations in volcanic regions (Hensch *et al.*, 2008; Roland and McGuire, 2009; Passarelli *et al.*, 2021; Sirorattanakul *et al.*, 2022; Danré *et al.*, 2024; Essing *et al.*, 2025). Given that the spatial, temporal, and magnitude attributes of earthquakes within swarm-like clusters are dictated by the underlying causative mechanisms (Ross *et al.*, 2020; Cesca *et al.*, 2023; Danré *et al.*, 2024), a robust characterization of earthquake swarms is essential for advancing our understanding of their source processes (Zhang and Shearer, 2016; Mesimeri *et al.*, 2019; Ross and Cochran, 2021; Ruch *et al.*, 2021; Ventura-Valentín and Brudzinski, 2022; Yoshida *et al.*, 2023) and the rheological state of the host crust in which they occur (Holtkamp and Brudzinski, 2011; Nakajima, 2022; Petersen *et al.*, 2025).

A defining characteristic of swarm-like clusters is their deviation from the typical mainshock–aftershocks pattern; the largest magnitude event does not usually initiate the sequence, instead, the majority of seismic moment is released later in the sequence (Mogi, 1963; Utsu, 2002; Lohman and McGuire, 2007; Chen and Shearer, 2011). In addition, hypocentral migration is common in swarm clusters, and the total rupture area illuminated by the swarm earthquakes can surpass that of a single event with equivalent seismic moment (Passarelli *et al.*, 2018; Fischer and Hainzl, 2021). These distinguishing features effectively differentiate swarm-like from mainshock–aftershocks clusters, facilitating swarm detection and characterization in earthquake catalogs at local, regional, and global scales (Chen and Shearer, 2011; Holtkamp *et al.*, 2011; Mesimeri *et al.*, 2019; Peng *et al.*, 2021). Nonetheless, in regions characterized by moderate-to-high seismicity, accurately identifying and classifying earthquake clusters remains a significant challenge (Chen and Shearer, 2011; Mesimeri *et al.*, 2019).

Two primary strategies are employed to identify swarm-like clusters within earthquake catalogs: (1) spatial–temporal and magnitude clustering analysis detects anomalous high rates of seismicity, followed by the characterization of these clusters based on seismic moment release over time within the sequence (Vidale and Shearer, 2006; Roland and McGuire, 2009; Jacobs

1. INGV Istituto Nazionale di Geofisica e Vulcanologia, Sezione di Bologna, Bologna, Italy, https://orcid.org/0000-0001-8995-8765 (LP); 2. GFZ German Research Centre for Geosciences, Potsdam, Germany, https://orcid.org/0000-0002-7138-0499 (GP); https://orcid.org/0000-0001-9419-3904 (SC); 3. SED Swiss Seismological Service, ETH Zürich, Zürich, Switzerland, https://orcid.org/0000-0002-5262-3168 (LM)

*Corresponding author: luigi.passarelli@ingv.it

et al., 2013; Zhang and Shearer, 2016; Ross *et al.*, 2017; Passarelli *et al.*, 2018; Pesicek *et al.*, 2018; Mesimeri *et al.*, 2019; Ross and Cochran, 2021; Schneider *et al.*, 2023); and (2) seismicity models, such as the epidemic-type aftershock sequence (ETAS) model, are used to identify swarm-like clusters as deviations from expected background and/or aftershock rates (Hainzl and Ogata, 2005; Llenos *et al.*, 2009; Marsan *et al.*, 2013, 2023; Peng *et al.*, 2021). These algorithms vary in automation level and accuracy in extracting and assessing the swarm-like characteristics of earthquake clusters—a crucial aspect for further analyzing individual swarm-like earthquakes and/or building up large swarm databases to eventually identify their causative mechanisms (Holtkamp and Brudzinski, 2011; Holtkamp *et al.*, 2011; Danré *et al.*, 2022).

In this study, we employ the first approach using a two-step detection and characterization workflow. Initially, earthquake clusters are identified through four established and widely used declustering algorithms. Subsequently, each cluster is fully characterized as either swarm-like or a mainshock–aftershocks sequence by analyzing the shape and tail behavior of its seismic moment distribution over time. This analysis is conducted using standardized central moments, average moment-weighted time, skewness, and kurtosis. The cluster detection and characterization workflow is applied to two regions known for swarm-like activity: the Húsavík–Flatey fault (HFF) in northern Iceland and the Pollino range in southern Italy. Concurrently, a comprehensive parametric study is conducted to determine the optimal range of these parameters to define swarm-like clusters, utilizing earthquake catalogs simulated using an ETAS model, which contain numerous swarm-like and mainshock–aftershocks clusters. The results indicate systematic differences among the detection algorithms and establish confidence bounds for classifying earthquake clusters as either swarm-like or mainshock–aftershocks sequences.

Detecting Earthquake Clusters

Declustering algorithms are statistical tools designed to separate independent (background) earthquakes from dependent events, such as foreshocks and aftershocks (van Stiphout *et al.*, 2011, 2012; Mizrahi *et al.*, 2021; Zaliapin and Ben-Zion, 2021). The primary goal of declustering is to robustly identify and remove foreshocks and aftershocks to produce a catalog of background earthquakes (van Stiphout *et al.*, 2012). However, declustering algorithms have also been proven effective at detecting swarm-like clusters, often categorized as "anomalous" seismicity rates in background seismicity (Passarelli *et al.*, 2018; Peng *et al.*, 2021; Zaliapin and Ben-Zion, 2021; Spassiani *et al.*, 2025). From the range of available declustering algorithms (van Stiphout *et al.*, 2012), we utilize four distinct and widely adopted declustering algorithms to detect earthquake clusters that we subsequently characterize in terms of earthquake moment released in time. We selected the following algorithms: Gardner and Knopoff (GK) (Gardner and Knopoff, 1974), Reasenberg (RES) (Reasenberg, 1985), and the Zaliapin and Ben-Zion algorithm (ZAL) (Zaliapin and Ben-Zion, 2013, 2020), and deployed a density-based clustering with a space–time distance metric (Davis and Frohlich, 1991a,b) implemented within the algorithm DBScan (DBS) (Ester *et al.*, 1996).

These algorithms use different definitions to identify earthquake clusters. The GK algorithm iterates through the catalog ordered by magnitude, starting with the largest magnitude event. For each such main event, the algorithm defines all events within a magnitude-dependent space–time window around it to be dependent events, that is, fore- and aftershocks (Knopoff and Gardner, 1972; Gardner and Knopoff, 1974). As a default, the foreshock time window has the same length as the aftershock time window, and the spatial window extends in a circle around the mainshock epicenter. The RES algorithm links earthquakes to clusters according to local proximity of events in space and time (Reasenberg, 1985). The space extension of the interaction zone is given by the earthquake moment assuming a circular crack model (Reasenberg, 1985; Molchan and Dmitrieva, 1992), whereas the time extension is derived by the Omori–Utsu law with exponent equal to one (Molchan and Dmitrieva, 1992; van Stiphout *et al.*, 2012). In contrast to the GK algorithm, RES links clusters iteratively; hence, higher-order aftershocks are considered. The ZAL algorithm uses a nearest neighbor approach in the space–time–magnitude domain to distinguish between clustered and background earthquakes. This approach relies on a metric that combines interevent distance, interevent time, and magnitude, and classifies nearest neighbor event pairs as related or unrelated based on a statistically derived nearest neighbor distance threshold (Zaliapin and Ben-Zion, 2013). DBS is a clustering method based on DBScan (Ester *et al.*, 1996). It groups earthquakes that are close together in space and time using a metric that combines interevent distances and interevent times (Frohlich and Davis, 1990). The algorithm is magnitude independent and does not include any a priori physical assumptions on the characteristics of seismic sequences.

We use standard parameters for the declustering algorithms (van Stiphout *et al.*, 2012), except for DBS, for which the standard approach developed for regional seismicity (Davis and Frohlich, 1991b) proved unsuitable for local earthquake clusters within a few kilometers and lasting only a few days. For interested readers, a brief description of the algorithms' parameters is provided in the supplemental material, available to this article. For an introduction into declustering and standard parameterization, see also van Stiphout *et al.* (2012). Throughout the article, we only consider earthquake clusters containing at least 30 earthquakes, setting a cutoff to avoid overinterpreting statistical characteristics of even smaller event clusters.

Characterizing Swarm-Like Seismicity

Swarm-like and mainshock–aftershocks clusters differ in the timing of their largest seismic moment release. Unlike swarm-like sequences, mainshock–aftershocks sequences are typically dominated by the energy of the mainshock that initiates the sequence, unless large aftershocks occur later and increase the complexity of the sequence. This distinction has been used to differentiate earthquake clusters based on the shape and tail behavior of the seismic moment release in time $F(t)$ through centralized moment analysis (Roland and McGuire, 2009; Chen and Shearer, 2011; Zhang and Shearer, 2016; Passarelli *et al.*, 2018; Valenzuela-Malebrán *et al.*, 2020; Lanza *et al.*, 2022).

For a given cluster, $F(t) = \int_{t_0}^{t} m_0(t')dt'$ represents the probability density function of the moment release over time by earthquakes (Roland and McGuire, 2009; Chen and Shearer, 2011). Here, t_0 is the start time of the sequence and $m_0(t')$ is the seismic moment released at time t', normalized by the cumulative seismic moment of all earthquakes in the cluster, such that $\lim_{t\to\infty} F(t) = 1$. To compare different clusters, earthquake origin times t_i are shifted by $-t_0$ and normalized by the mean origin time of the cluster. When seismic moments are unavailable, they can be derived from standard scaling relationships (e.g., Hanks and Kanamori, 1979).

$F(t)$ can be described by the average origin time weighted by the seismic moment, that is, centroid time, and the third and fourth discrete central moments. These parameters indicate when the majority of the seismic moment is released and describe the shape and tail behavior of the distribution, respectively.

The centroid time t_c is defined as

$$t_c = \frac{\sum_{i=1}^{N} t_i \times m_0(t_i)}{\sum_{i=1}^{N} m_0(t_i)}, \quad (1)$$

in which $t_i,\ldots t_N$ are the occurrence times of events in the cluster. t_c quantifies when the majority of seismic moment is released during the cluster and $m_0(t_i)$ is the normalized seismic moment release by the earthquake occurring at t_i. Recalling that the central moments of the distribution are $\mu_n = \sum_{i=1}^{N}(t_i - t_c)^n \times m_0(t_i)$, and $\sigma = \sqrt{\mu_2}$ is the standard deviation, the standardized third moment or skewness, and the standardized fourth moment or kurtosis are informative on the shape of the distribution and the presence of outliers (Forbes *et al.*, 2010). They are defined as

$$\text{Skewness}: S = \frac{\mu_3}{\sigma^3} = \frac{\sum_{i=1}^{N}(t_i - t_c)^3 \times m_0(t_i)}{[\sum_{i=1}^{N}(t_i - t_c)^2 \times m_0(t_i)]^{\frac{3}{2}}}, \quad (2)$$

$$\text{Kurtosis}: K = \frac{\mu_4}{\sigma^4} = \frac{\sum_{i=1}^{N}(t_i - t_c)^4 \times m_0(t_i)}{[\sum_{i=1}^{N}(t_i - t_c)^2 \times m_0(t_i)]^2}. \quad (3)$$

Skewness describes the shape of the distribution: it is zero for a nearly symmetric distribution, positive for right-skewed distributions (i.e., with a tail extending to the right), and negative for left-skewed distributions (i.e., with a tail extending to the left). Mainshock–aftershocks clusters, characterized by a concentration of energy release at the sequence's onset, typically exhibit large positive skewness. Conversely, swarm-like sequences are expected to have zero or negative skewness, suggesting that the dominant seismic moment release occurs later in the cluster's evolution. Kurtosis provides information about the presence of outliers in the distribution's tails. The term $(t_i - t_c)^4 \times m_0(t_i)$ becomes large for earthquakes occurring more than one standard deviation from t_c. Therefore, high kurtosis values indicate either a significant portion of seismic moment release in the tail of $F(t)$ or a concentration of $F(t)$'s mass around t_c with occasional outliers. As a side note, kurtosis and skewness exhibit a positive power-law scaling relationship (Mesimeri *et al.*, 2019), a property that we do not explore further in this work.

To additionally characterize the moment release in each cluster, we use the positive magnitude difference ΔM (Mesimeri *et al.*, 2019; Petersen and Pankow, 2023):

$$\Delta M = M_1 - M_2, \quad (4)$$

in which M_1 is the magnitude of the largest earthquake, and M_2 is the second largest one regardless of its temporal occurrence within the cluster. We refer to the previously listed parameters in equations (1)–(4) as swarmy parameters because we will utilize them to characterize the swarmy behavior of each detected cluster of earthquakes. We do not use t_{max} (Roland and McGuire, 2009; Chen and Shearer, 2011; Mesimeri *et al.*, 2019), that is, the time of the largest earthquake in a cluster. Although small values of t_{max} are indicative of more mainshock–aftershocks clusters (Chen and Shearer, 2011), the centroid time (equation 1) conveys more information about the majority of the seismic moment release over time.

Earthquake Cluster Characterization via Synthetic Catalogs

Analyses of the "swarminess" of earthquake clusters, detected in instrumental catalogs, have focused on skewness alone or a combined assessment of skewness and kurtosis together. Published studies have used a range of skewness values, typically ≤8, to identify earthquake swarms in real catalogs (Roland and McGuire, 2009; Chen and Shearer, 2011; Zhang and Shearer, 2016; Passarelli *et al.*, 2018; Valenzuela-Malebrán *et al.*, 2020; Lanza *et al.*, 2022). When combined with kurtosis, the proposed ranges are generally smaller, that is, [−3.5,3.5] for skewness and ≤20 for kurtosis (Mesimeri *et al.*, 2019). Although these values of skewness and kurtosis are commonly used, their sensitivity to robustly classify the nature of earthquake clusters has not been thoroughly investigated. We address this gap by performing a detailed analysis of the range of variation of skewness, kurtosis, centroid time, and magnitude difference (equations 1–4) on numerous synthetic catalogs containing earthquake swarm clusters.

We use the ETAS model (Ogata, 1988) as described and implemented in Mizrahi *et al.* (2021, 2023) with both temporal and spatial aftershocks decay kernels to simulate earthquake catalogs and incorporate swarm-like clusters by employing a time-dependent background rate. The model's aftershock parameters are derived from the optimization of an ETAS time-dependent model (Hainzl *et al.*, 2013; Marsan *et al.*, 2013) of the long-lasting swarm-like sequence in the Pollino region (Passarelli *et al.*, 2015). The resulting aftershock's parameters are unbiased with respect to the transient forcing (Hainzl *et al.*, 2013) (see supplemental material and Mizrahi *et al.* (2021) for a full specification of the applied ETAS model). A key advantage of using synthetic ETAS catalogs is that we know the genealogy of each earthquake: whether it is a generation zero (gen0) background earthquake, or swarm background earthquake, or a generation n aftershock. In our simulations, each earthquake can trigger aftershocks according to the earthquake–earthquake-triggering framework of ETAS.

We generate synthetic catalogs as follows: (1) many individual short-duration swarm-like sequences embedded in longer seismicity catalogs; and (2) four 30-year catalogs simulated with varying background rates. We refer thereafter to (1) as the individual simulation set and to (2) as the catalog simulation set. Consequently, we first group earthquakes into mainshock–aftershocks and swarm clusters according to the model output, with the specification explained in the next section. We then assess their characteristics using the swarmy parameters statistics (equations 1–4) for both individual and catalog simulation sets. In addition, we apply the full detection–characterization workflow to the four synthetic catalogs only.

ETAS individual simulation set

In the individual simulation set, a single swarm-like cluster, with durations of 14, 60, and 365 days, is simulated with a total number of events that is tenfold that of the background seismicity, which is set to 0.5 events/day for a minimum magnitude of 2. We simulate this swarm-like cluster in the middle of a longer seismicity catalog that extends ±20 times the swarm duration, resulting in synthetic catalogs with total durations of 574, 2,460, and 14,965 days, or 1.5, 6.7, and 41 yr (Fig. S3). We assumed that the background rate during swarms changes in three different shapes according to a normal, a triangular, and a uniform distribution (see supplemental material and Fig. S3). We generated 50 catalogs for the nine distinct combinations of duration and shape of the background rate of swarm clusters, totaling 450 synthetic catalogs. Seismicity is simulated in a spatial domain of $1° \times 1°$ latitude/longitude.

We defined swarm clusters (SWCLs) as all earthquakes occurring within the imposed swarm duration, that is, the gen0 background swarm earthquakes, all their generations of aftershocks, and any other background earthquakes or aftershocks within that timeframe. We chose this cluster selection criterion as the most straightforward from a visual cluster detection in earthquake catalogs (Fig. S3). As mainshock–aftershocks clusters (MACLs), we selected only the gen0 background earthquake with >30 aftershocks (i.e., magnitude$\in$[4.2,6.1]) plus their n generations of aftershocks. On the resulting 450 SWCLs and 4003 MACLs, we have calculated the swarmy parameters of equations (1)–(4) (Fig. 1a,b), and we refer this cluster selection as cluster group 1.

In general, centroid times, skewness, and kurtosis are correlated quantities (Fig. 1a,b) because skewness and kurtosis alone have a parabolic correlation (Fig. S4 and Mesimeri *et al.*, 2019). Generally, SWCLs have most of their seismic moment released later in the sequence (large centroid times) and thus tend to have low skewness and kurtosis, whereas MACLs with early moment release show high skewness and kurtosis (Fig. 1a, b). The magnitude difference (equation 4) weakly correlates with other parameters, and large magnitude differences pertain to small centroid times, and large skewness and kurtosis are typical of "classical" mainshock–aftershocks sequences. Furthermore, the shape of the seismicity rate (i.e., normal, triangular, or uniform) change during simulated swarms has no impact on these parameters (Fig. 1a,b).

The 450 SWCLs highlight a clear variational range of centroid time, skewness, and kurtosis statistics, with centroid time $t_c = 0.98(0.24,1.87)$, skewness $0.08(-7.83,9.90)$, and kurtosis $3.33(1.13,123.79)$, expressed as median (minimum, maximum). The range of values of skewness is compatible with previous inferences (Roland and McGuire, 2009, i.e.), whereas the kurtosis shows a larger variability than previously estimated (Mesimeri *et al.*, 2019). Skewness versus centroid time of SWCLs shows a negative linear trend (Fig. 1a, inset) as expected for progressively more left-skewed seismic moment–time distribution, whereas kurtosis seems not correlated to centroid time for SWCLs (Fig. 1b, inset), showing a large scatter because it is a quantity sensitive to outliers.

The majority (93%) of MACLs exhibit swarmy parameter values distinct from those of SWCLs (Fig. 1a,b), characterized by short centroid times and large magnitude differences. These are typical MACLs for which the seismic moment release is concentrated early in time, resulting in a sharply right-skewed distribution with the tail characterized by occasional large aftershocks resulting in high kurtosis values. However, 7% of MACLs overlap with SWCLs. These MACLs differ from the classical MACLs in that they contain aftershocks with magnitudes close to or even greater than the initial mainshock (small-magnitude differences) that trigger secondary aftershock chains.

To assess how the cluster selection criteria affected the swarm parameter values, we tested different groupings. We redefined MACLs to include only the gen0 mainshocks and their first-generation aftershocks, and SWCLs to consist solely of the gen0 background swarm events, thereafter cluster group 2. The results remained consistent with the previous grouping (Fig. S5a,b). However, we observed in this case that 2% of MACLs have centroid times exceeding the maximum centroid times of SWCLs (Fig. S5a,b). Upon closer inspection, these MACLs are clusters in which the largest "first-generation" aftershock is triggered

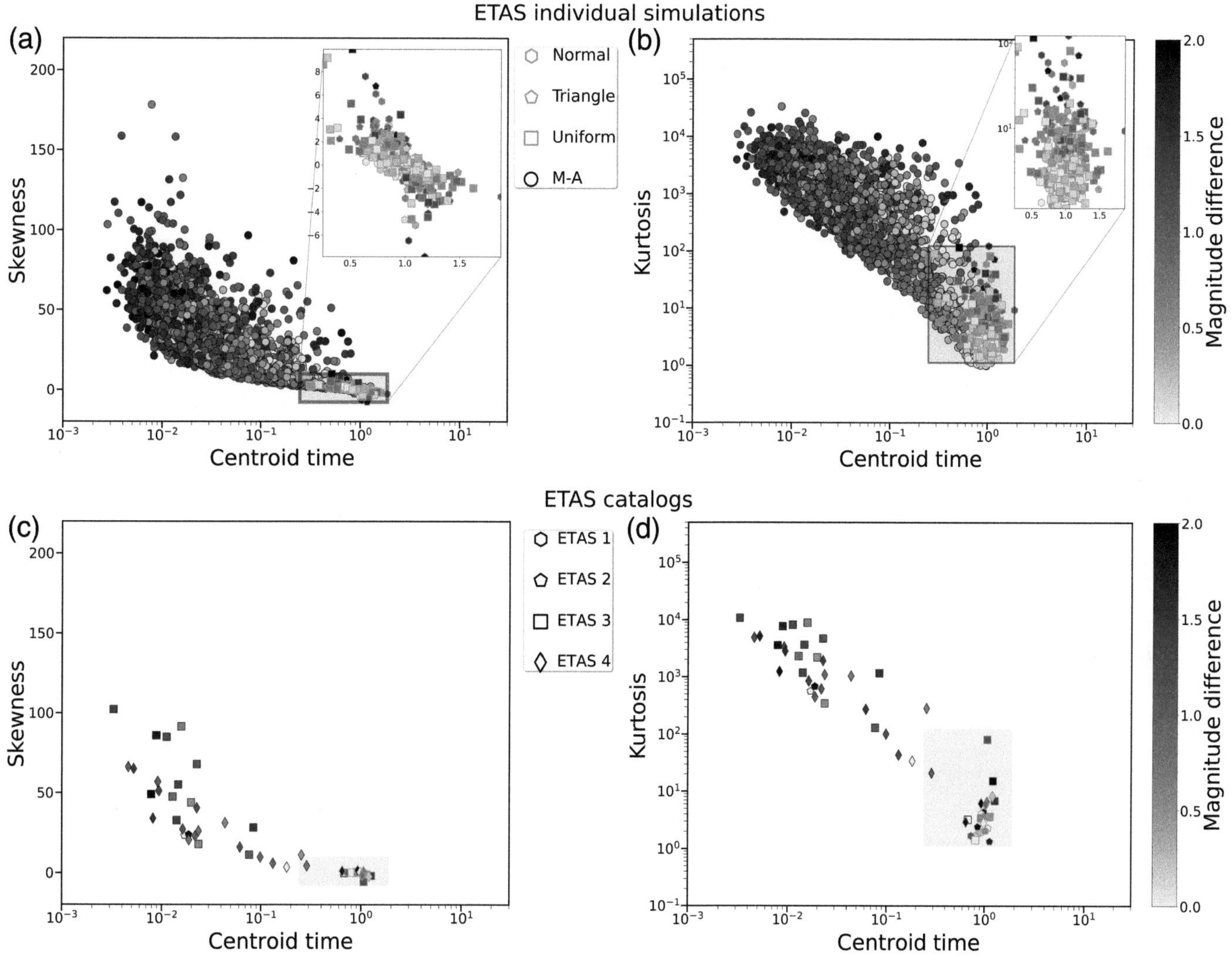

Figure 1. Variational range of the swarmy parameters for epidemic-type aftershock sequence (ETAS) simulated clusters. (a) Skewness versus centroid time and color-coded magnitude difference. The symbols indicate the shape of the simulated swarm clusters (SWCLs), as in the legend circles, are mainshock–aftershocks clusters (MACLs). The insets magnify the maximum and minimum values of swarmy parameters for SWCLs. (b) Same as panel (a), but for kurtosis versus centroid time. (c) Same as panel (a), and (d) same as panel (b) for the four ETAS 1–ETAS 4 simulated catalogs. Clusters in ETAS 1 to ETAS 4 are highlighted with different symbols. The shaded regions are the minimum and maximum values of swarmy parameters (see text). In all panels, SWCLs are highlighted with an orange outline. The color version of this figure is available only in the electronic edition.

very late in the sequence (Fig. S6). We also examined grouping SWCLs as gen0 background events and all their generation aftershocks, whereas MACLs as gen0 aftershocks plus all their generation aftershocks. In this scenario, both skewness and kurtosis for SWCLs became high, with 56% of their values falling outside the reference range (Fig. S7a,b) and thus being classified as MACLs. Notably, when including aftershocks of gen0 swarm events, named *cluster group 3*, the duration of these SWCLs increases significantly (Fig. S8) compared with other groupings previously used, causing them to resemble MACLs. However, when the aftershock decay is artificially truncated at the 80th percentile of the origin time distribution (Ross *et al.*, 2017; Petersen and Pankow, 2023), SWCLs are correctly classified as swarm-like clusters rather than mainshock–aftershock ones (Fig. S9).

We also tested the sensitivity of the swarmy parameters' statistics to a different parameterization of the ETAS model. To do this, we simulated 450 additional seismicity catalogs using a spatiotemporal ETAS model with aftershock parameters calibrated on the California catalog, which has a branching ratio of ~0.9 (Mizrahi *et al.*, 2021). Each of these synthetic catalogs contains only a single swarm-like sequence, simulated with the same characteristics described earlier. We calculated the swarm parameters for cluster group 1, finding $t_c = 1.01$ (0.32,2.04), skewness −0.10(−16.85,6.03), and kurtosis 3.21 (1.05,965.86). These values largely overlap with the previously inferred range (Fig. S10). The general range of parameters used to define swarm-like sequences appears to be minimally affected by the ETAS parameterization. Although small discrepancies exist in the extreme values of skewness and kurtosis, these are attributed to a few outliers (Fig. S10 compared with Fig. S7). We repeated the calculation of the swarm parameters for cluster groups 2 and 3, and the results were similar to those previously discussed (Fig. S10 compared with Fig. S5a,b).

Our results highlight two important considerations when using swarm parameter statistics. First, this method can effectively classify compact swarm-like clusters that occur with seismicity rates much larger than background, as demonstrated by our tests across various SWCL durations. However, for SWCLs with a very long fading phase with minor seismic moment release, the time–seismic moment distribution can become bi- or multimodal (Pfister *et al.*, 2013), leading to high skewness and kurtosis values and misclassifying SWCLs as mainshock–aftershocks ones. Second, applying our approach to characterize swarms, even in a controlled environment with numerous ETAS cluster realizations, reveals that some MACLs can be misclassified as swarm-like when large aftershocks occur later on during the sequence. Therefore, the proposed metrics represent a continuum rather than a sharp separation between cluster types. Thus, automatic cluster analysis should be conducted cautiously, potentially requiring manual inspection of each sequence (Passarelli *et al.*, 2018; Ventura-Valentín and Brudzinski, 2022).

ETAS catalog simulation set

For this simulation set, we created four simulated earthquake catalogs, each 30 year long, and named them ETAS1, ETAS2, ETAS3, and ETAS4 with the same set of aftershock parameters of the ETAS model in the previous section and calibrated on the Pollino swarm-like sequence as in Passarelli *et al.* (2015). Each of these 30-year catalogs included six swarm-like clusters, three of them lasting 30 days, and three lasting 14 days, with a background seismicity rate of five events per day. Outside of the swarm-like clusters, background seismicity rate (Fig. S11) was set 100 times lower (i.e., 0.05 events/day) for ETAS1 and ETAS2, and 10 times lower (0.5 events/day) in ETAS3 and ETAS4, which also spread out over a larger region (see Fig. S11). We used a minimum magnitude of 2 in all simulations.

To select SWCLs and MACLs, we use the same assumptions as in cluster group 1 (i.e., gen0 swarm events plus all other events over the swarm duration and gen0 mainshock events plus all aftershocks) and calculate the swarmy parameters on a total of 33 MACLs—with mainshock magnitudes $M \in [4.4, 5.9]$—and 24 SWCLs (Fig. 1c,d). Please note in Figure 1c,d that ETAS1 catalog has no generation zero mainshock events that passed our cluster selection criteria of 30 aftershocks. Mimicking real catalogs, fewer SWCLs and MACLs show distinct separation in the swarmy parameters' space, and all SWCLs fall in the range previously determined, that is, $t_c \in [0.64, 1.27]$, $S \in [-5.55, 1.51]$, and $K \in [1.34, 81.43]$. When varying the overall cluster composition as discussed before, as in cluster groups 2 and 3 (Figs. S5c,d and S7c,d), we consistently see that SWCLs that include all generation aftershocks (i.e., cluster group 3) lasting for years result in a misclassification of SWCLs into MACLs (Fig. S7c,d).

We applied the detection–characterization workflow to each of the ETAS1 through ETAS4 catalogs. However, in this section, we will mainly focus on the findings from the ETAS2 catalog, as illustrated in Figure 2. The ETAS2 has a low background rate, and the six swarms are spatially and temporally distinct, making it an ideal catalog for testing our workflow. The full set of results for the remaining catalogs can be found in Figures S12–S14, with more intricacies that we discuss later. All simulated clusters (Fig. 2c, A clusters) are detected by the declustering algorithms (Fig. 2c, B–E clusters). However, ZAL and GK find two additional clusters, whereas DBS and RES only one more (nonlabeled in Fig. 2c, additionally refer to Figs. S12b and S13b).

The number of events identified within each SWCL by the declustering algorithms (B1–B6, C1–C6, D1–D6, and E1–E6 in Fig. 2c) exceeds the number of events in the simulated swarms (A1–A6 in Fig. 2c). This is because these algorithms employ time kernels designed to capture the long decay of aftershock sequences that goes beyond the finite duration of the simulated SWCLs. ZAL and GK methods typically identify larger clusters, whereas DBS and RES produce clusters more similar in size to the simulated swarms. Despite this difference in cluster size, the swarmy parameters appear to be largely unaffected because we observe a good agreement in the small skewness values and the late centroid times between the simulated and the detected SWCLs (Fig. 2d,e). The effect of a long time window to gather aftershocks by the declustering methods can be seen in the systematically higher value of kurtosis with respect to the simulated clustering (Fig. 2d,e).

Moreover, the ZAL algorithm tends to misclassify SWCLs as MACLs, producing systematically larger values of skewness and kurtosis and small centroid times (Fig. 2d,e, Fig. S14). The GK algorithm, which uses a look-back window to identify foreshocks, tends instead to produce more symmetric clusters in terms of time–seismic moment release (Fig. 2d,e, Fig. S14). This biases the swarmy parameter statistics toward larger centroid times ~ 1 and smaller skewness and kurtosis, with a tendency to classify clusters as swarm-like ones (Fig. 2d,e, Fig. S14). In contrast, the RES and DBS algorithms effectively identify SWCLs, correctly classifying them as such (Fig. 2d,e), making them more suitable for swarm-like detection. These features are even more pronounced in catalogs with a high background seismicity rate (ETAS3 and ETAS4 in Fig. S14).

Detecting and Classifying Clusters in Real Catalogs

To rigorously evaluate the performance and reliability of our proposed cluster detection and characterization workflow, we apply it to real earthquake catalogs in which swarm-like seismicity has been previously identified and documented in the literature, that is, the swarm activity along the westernmost

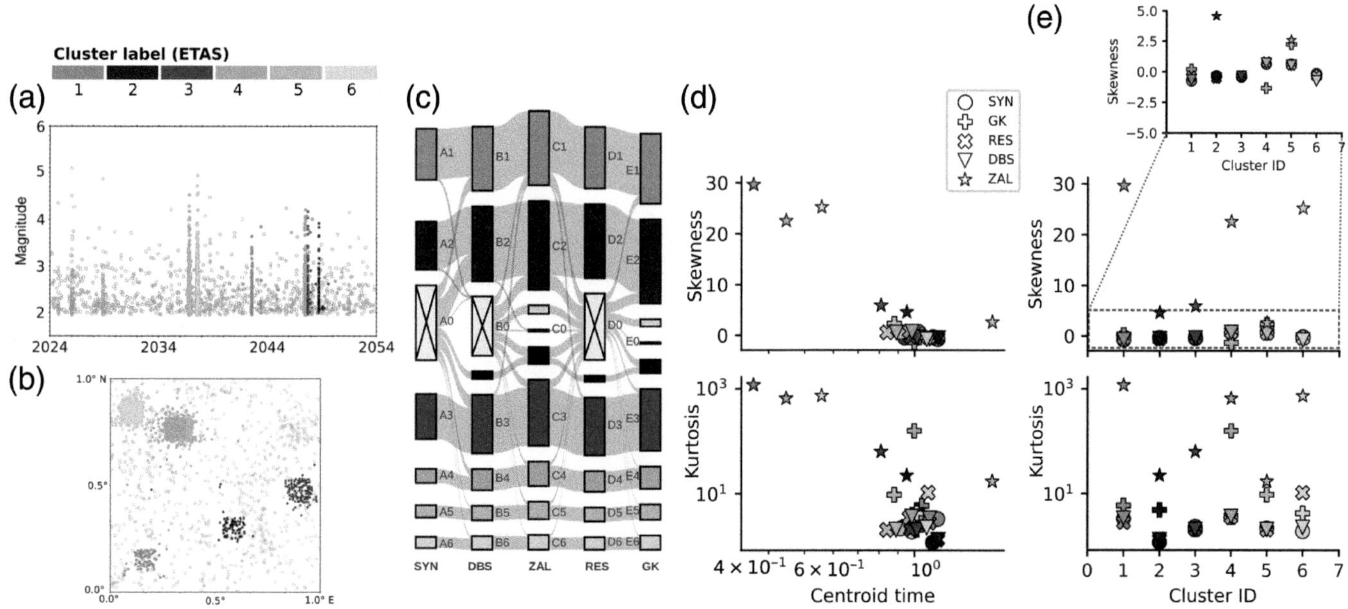

Figure 2. Result of cluster detection–characterization workflow applied to ETAS 2. Color-coded are the six clusters reported in panel (a) as seismicity over time versus magnitude, and in panel (b) as a map view. (c) The flow diagram depicts a comparison of simulated swarm clusters (SYN A1–A6) to the swarm clusters detected by the declustering algorithms DBS (B1–B6), ZAL (C1–C6), RES (D1–D6), and GK (E1–E6). The colored bars and gray bandwidths are proportional to the number of shared events connected through lines. Unlabeled bars correspond to additionally found small clusters, bars identified with 0 are events common across the clusters, so that the total number of events belonging to clusters is conserved. (d,e) The skewness and the kurtosis versus centroid time or cluster label/ID, respectively. The circles are simulated clusters of the model, and other symbols are clusters detected by declustering algorithms. DBS, DBScan algorithm; GK, Gardner and Knopoff algorithm; RES, Reasenberg algorithm; SYN, synthetic; ZAL, Zaliapin and Ben-Zion algorithm. The color version of this figure is available only in the electronic edition.

portion of the HFF, northern Iceland, and the Pollino range, southern Italy 2010–2014 swarm-like sequence (Passarelli *et al.*, 2015; Cheloni *et al.*, 2017; Passarelli *et al.*, 2018; Napolitano *et al.*, 2020).

The two benchmark case studies exhibit distinct swarm characteristics: HFF features spatially and temporally separated swarm-like activity along a 30 km fault segment, whereas Pollino displays repeatedly activating, localized swarm-like clusters within a 10 km region. These examples are crucial for evaluating our method's ability to accurately detect and characterize SWCLs in swarm-dominated catalogs. Analyzing these two cases, even under seemingly favorable conditions, is vital for understanding our workflow's strengths and limitations when swarms are the primary clustering phenomenon, providing key insights into its practical utility for regions where the nature of seismicity might be less clear.

North Iceland: HFF

HFF is a ridge-transform fault with right-lateral kinematics bridging the onshore North volcanic zone to the offshore Eyjafjarðaráll rift and Kolbeinsey ridge (Metzger and Jonsson, 2014). This ~100-km-long fault exhibits segmentation in terms of seismic moment release. The southeastern two-thirds of the fault are characterized by microseismicity, likely due to a stress shadow from the compression induced by the Krafla rifting episode, whereas the northwesternmost portion experienced nearly continuous swarm-like seismicity from 1995 to 2015 (Maccaferri *et al.*, 2013).

Along this 30 km fault segment, earthquakes clustered on six major earthquake swarms, which further composed a total of 16 shorter subswarms (gray bands in Fig. 3a) (Passarelli *et al.*, 2018). Interestingly, swarm activity developed complementarily along the fault, with later clusters not overlapping with areas previously activated by earlier swarms (Passarelli *et al.*, 2018). These SWCLs were statistically identified by applying the beta statistics approach to a Reasenberg declustered catalog (Matthews and Reasenberg, 1988) to identify anomalies in the background rate. Swarms were further manually analyzed using the original catalog for their clustering properties and source processes. Each of the 16 subswarms exhibited a skewness value within a range of [−2,8] (Passarelli *et al.*, 2018).

We applied the four declustering algorithms to the seismicity that occurred from 1997 to 2015 along the HFF for earthquakes above the completeness magnitude 1.5 (Passarelli *et al.*, 2018). We obtained that GK detects 10 clusters, RES and DBS detect 14 clusters each, and ZAL 15 clusters (Fig. 3). In general, all declustering algorithms detect clusters within the previously identified earthquake swarm periods except for the June/July 2004 swarm (gray bars in Fig. 3). The largest and most complex

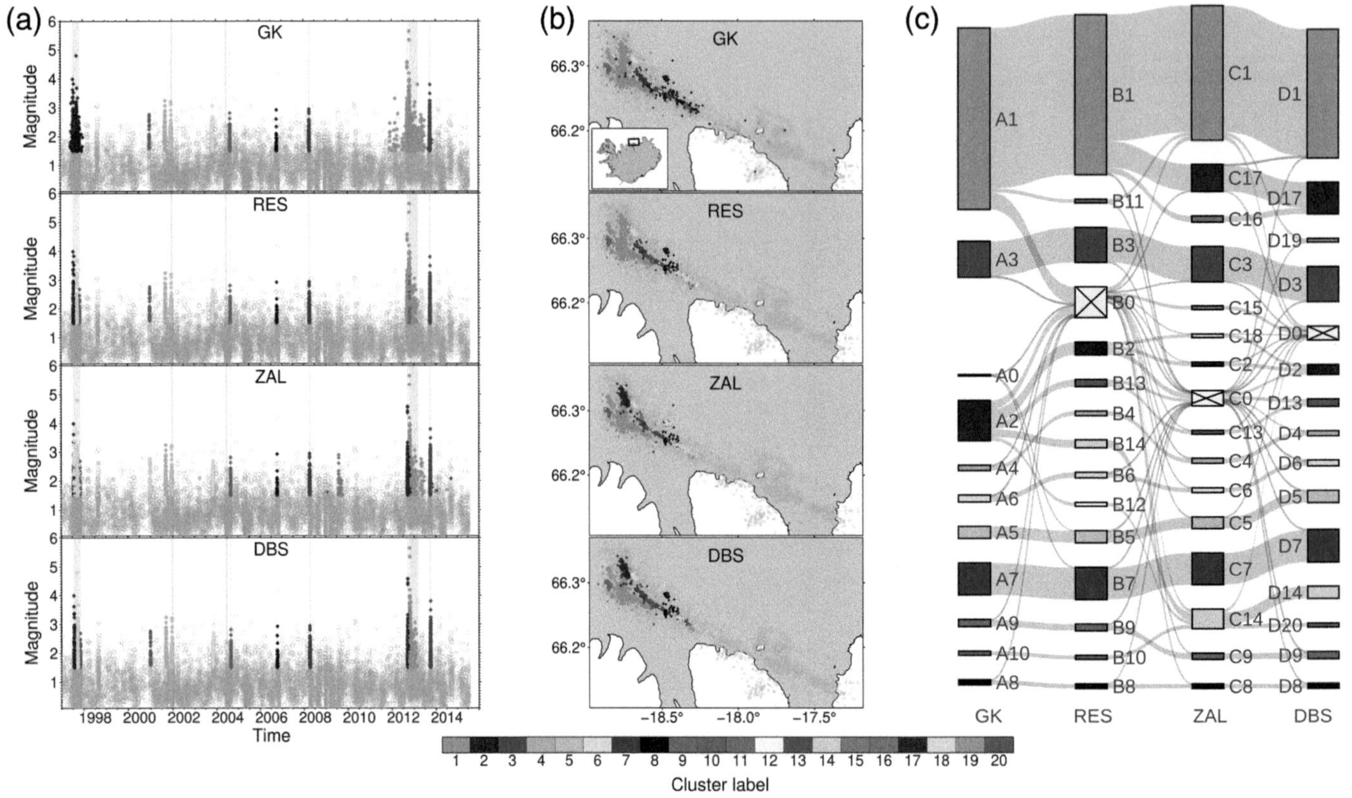

Figure 3. Result of the four different swarm-detection workflows applied to seismicity along Húsavík–Flatey fault (1997–2015). (a) Seismicity over time, gray bars are swarms and subswarms detected in a previous study (Passarelli *et al.*, 2018). (b) In-map view and (c) comparison of clusters obtained by the declustering algorithms. The same color indicates the same sequence across the four algorithms. The color version of this figure is available only in the electronic edition.

cluster of activity, spanning Fall 2012 to Winter 2013, is detected as one large cluster by GK (A1), whereas RES (B1 and B11), ZAL (C1, C16, and C17), and DBS (D1, D16, and D19) split it in two or three clusters, respectively (Fig. 3), and produce detections compatible with the three subswarms previously identified (Passarelli *et al.*, 2018). The 1997 long and complex swarm phase, composed by eight distinct subswarms (Passarelli *et al.*, 2018), is identified as one single cluster by GK (A2), whereas RES splits it into four (B2, B12, B13, and B14), ZAL in four (C2, C13, C14, and C18), and DBS in three (D2, D13, and D14) (Fig. 3). None of the algorithms can identify the eight subswarms that it is composed of according to the previous manual analysis (Passarelli *et al.*, 2018). Furthermore, due to its long-range temporal interactions kernel (Zaliapin and Ben-Zion, 2020), the ZAL algorithm identifies cluster C14 as extending from 1997 to the end of 2000 C.E., whereas the 2000 cluster is detected as independent by the other algorithms (A10, B10, and D20) (Fig. 3c). The 1997 and 2012–2013 examples illustrate how challenging it is for the four declustering algorithms to separate clusters close both in time and space.

When instead clusters are spatially and temporally separated, all the algorithms consistently identify clusters well, such as clusters labeled 3, 5, 7, and 9, showing a good match with the previously identified swarms (gray bars in Fig. 3). Moreover, the algorithms identify additional clusters (A-D4, A-D6, A-D8, A-B10, and C15) that are not in the published database of HFF swarms (Passarelli *et al.*, 2018). These newly identified clusters are likely due to the present application of declustering to the full catalog, whereas they may have been overlooked by the previous study because they detected clusters as anomalies in the background rate obtained through the beta statistics approach (Passarelli *et al.*, 2018).

The results of the cluster characterization are reported in Figure 4a–d. The majority of clusters across algorithms are classified as swarms, exhibiting a large centroid time of about >0.5, skewness below 10, and kurtosis below 125, as a range of values inferred for SWCLs in ETAS individual simulations; magnitude differences do not show any correlation with these other swarm parameters. The clusters detected by GK are all classified as SWCLs, confirming this algorithm's tendency to produce more symmetric clusters in terms of moment release. All the clusters detected by the RES algorithm are classified as swarms, except for B12—a cluster that is part of the long swarm sequence of 1997 C.E. (Fig. 3). Only two clusters from DBS fall outside the range of swarm parameters to be classified as swarms, whereas ZAL confirms its tendency to produce more MACLs because 8 out of 14 clusters are classified as such. The new cluster detections (A-D4, A-D6, A-D8, A-B10, and C15) are all classified as SWCLs.

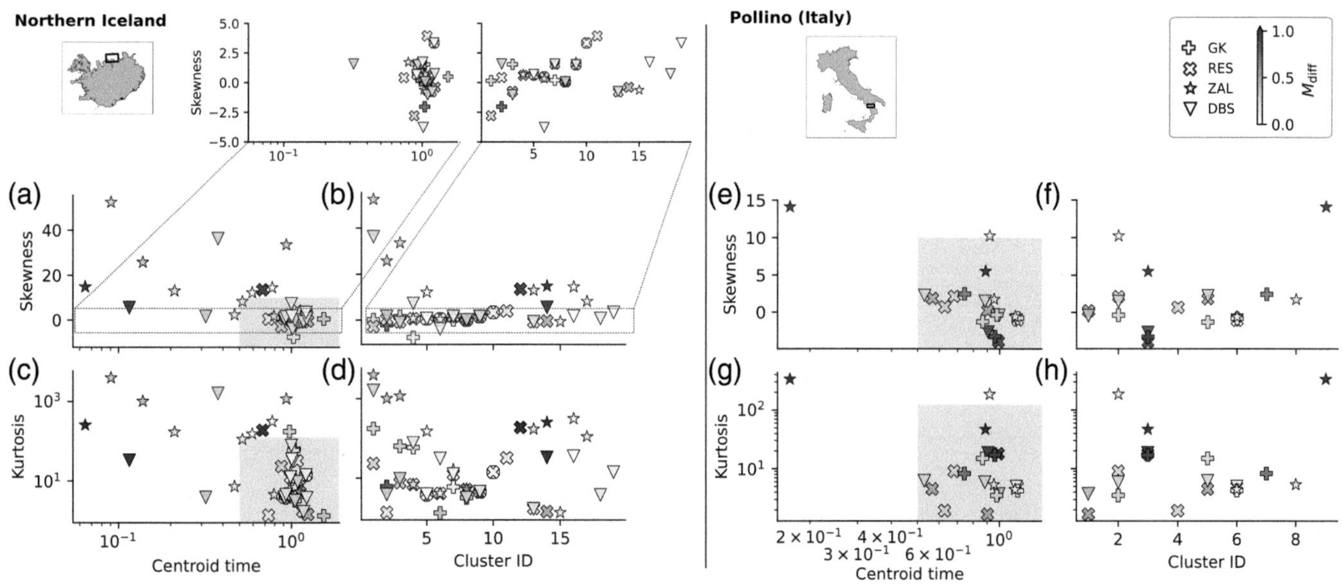

Figure 4. Skewness and kurtosis of the seismic sequences in Northern Iceland (left) and Pollino, Italy (right) were computed for the sequences detected by the four different methods (symbols) as shown in Figures 3 and 5. Skewness and Kurtosis are shown over centroid time (a,c,e,g) and over cluster identification number (b,d,f,h) for a simpler comparison. The color of the symbols reflects the magnitude difference between the largest and the second-largest event in each sequence. The gray-shaded area marks the swarmy parameter thresholds (skewness <10, kurtosis <125, and centroid time >0.5). The color version of this figure is available only in the electronic edition.

Southern Italy: Pollino Range

The Pollino region experienced a prolonged period of earthquake swarm activity along its westernmost fault system from Fall 2010 to Summer 2014 (Cheloni *et al.*, 2017; Napolitano *et al.*, 2020; Cirillo *et al.*, 2021). During Summer 2012 and Spring 2013, a slow-slip event has been detected as a part of the sequence (Cheloni *et al.*, 2017). An isolated swarm also occurred in the easternmost part of the region in Fall 2016 (ISIDe Working Group, 2007) (Fig. 5). The extensive 2010–2014 sequence has been thoroughly investigated for its clustering characteristics, revealing seven distinct phases in which the rate of earthquakes gradually increased and then decreased (Passarelli *et al.*, 2015; Cirillo *et al.*, 2021). Although all other phases align with typical swarm-like behavior, the cluster that began with a magnitude 4.2 earthquake in May 2012 is consistent with a mainshock–aftershocks sequence (Passarelli *et al.*, 2015). Situated within a complex pull-apart basin bounded by two mountain ranges (Fig. 5), the whole sequences repeatedly activated two spatially close clusters with radii of 5 and 10 km, respectively (Cirillo *et al.*, 2021). The spatial tightness of these clusters makes the cluster detection challenging.

The detection algorithms applied to the 2005–2018 Pollino earthquake catalog above the completeness magnitude 1.5 (Passarelli *et al.*, 2015) results in five clusters detected by ZAL, GK, and DBS, and six by RES. RES and DBS successfully detect the initial burst-like cluster of Fall 2010 that started the sequence (A1 and B1 in Fig. 5), whereas ZAL identifies it as a longer lasting cluster extending from Fall 2010 to early 2011 (D8 in Fig. 5). The largest period of activity spans from Spring 2012 to Spring 2013 and coincides with the geodetically detected slow-slip event (Cheloni *et al.*, 2017). During this period, RES, DBS, and GK effectively detect the sequence in time, but they do not separate the eastern and western clusters (A3, B3, and C3 in Fig. 5), which belong to two different fault sets (Cirillo *et al.*, 2021). In contrast, ZAL instead identifies a single, long-lasting sequence spanning from 2011 to 2017 belonging to the western cluster (D3 in Fig. 5). However, ZAL is unique to separately detect the May 2012 sequence (D9 in Fig. 5). Only RES (A5), DBS (B5), and GK (C5) successfully detect the Summer 2014 cluster, whereas all algorithms effectively identify the spatially separated 2016 cluster (A-D6) that struck the easternmost part of the Pollino region (Fig. 5).

As shown in Figure 4e–h, all detected clusters are classified as swarms due to their centroid times >0.5, skewness <10, and kurtosis <125, as a range of values inferred for SWCLs in ETAS individual simulations. Clusters labeled 3 have the smallest value of skewness and kurtosis for RES, DBS, and GK, whereas ZAL shows slightly larger values due to the longer duration (Fig. 4f,h). ZAL's D2 cluster is misclassified as a mainshock–aftershocks cluster (Fig. 4e–h), whereas D9 cluster, with the smallest centroid time and the largest skewness and kurtosis, is correctly classified as a mainshock–aftershocks cluster (Fig. 4), representing the aftershock sequence following the magnitude 4.2 earthquake of May 2012 (Passarelli *et al.*, 2015). Apart from ZAL's algorithm, the other three algorithms show strong consistency in both cluster detection and classification, with minimal variation in their swarm-like parameters.

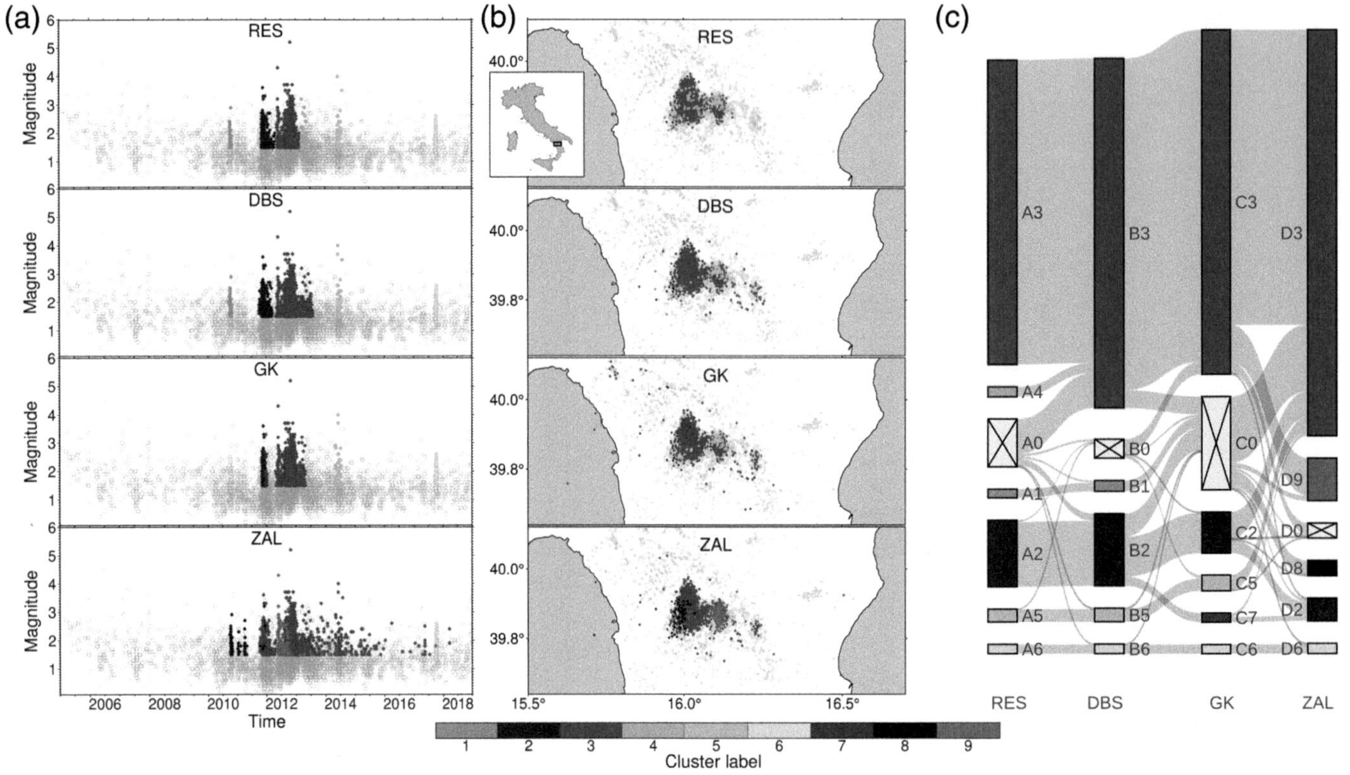

Figure 5. Result of the four different swarm-detection workflows applied to seismicity in the Pollino Range region, Italy. (a) Seismicity over time, (b) in map view, and (c) comparison of obtained clusters. The same color indicates the same sequence across the four algorithms. The color version of this figure is available only in the electronic edition.

Even in these consistent results, the magnitude difference seems to add little information to the SWCL classification (Fig. 4e–h).

Discussion and Conclusion

We show that using the centroid time, skewness, and kurtosis of the seismic moment release distribution over time provides simple yet effective statistics for distinguishing between swarm-like and mainshock–aftershocks-like earthquake clusters. Previous successful studies have used only skewness or a combination of skewness and kurtosis to classify swarm-like clusters in real earthquake catalogs (Roland and McGuire, 2009; Chen and Shearer, 2011; Passarelli *et al.*, 2018; Mesimeri *et al.*, 2019; Lanza *et al.*, 2022). However, by leveraging the stochastic variability of the ETAS model on a large sample size, we obtained a range of values for centroid time, skewness, and kurtosis that confidently allows a better discrimination between SWCLs and MACLs.

The swarmy parameters effectively classify swarm-like clusters in which earthquakes' bursts occur over a finite period of time (compact clusters) with a substantial increase in the seismicity rate yielding to centroid times >0.5, skewness <10, and kurtosis <125 (Fig. 1). These values indicate a quasi-symmetric distribution of seismic moment release over time with thin tails, meaning most of the seismic moment is released around the centroid time. Conversely, neither the shape of the seismicity rate change during swarms nor the magnitude difference (equation 4) appears to significantly aid in classifying swarm-like clusters (Fig. 1a,b). Instead, for clusters in which most seismic moment is released early and the seismicity rate fadeout is long, the proposed statistic tends to consistently classify such clusters as mainshock–aftershocks sequences (Figs. 1 and 4, Figs. S8 and S9). We additionally remark that the values of swarmy parameters for swarm-like classification can have larger extremes, as demonstrated by our additional tests on both the individual simulation set and natural seismicity. Therefore, the usual binary classification of MACLs versus SWCLs needs to be handled with care, as discussed at the end of this section.

Swarmy parameters correctly classify most mainshock–aftershocks clusters with centroid time, skewness, and kurtosis values falling far outside the typical range for swarms (Fig. 1). In these cases, the large magnitude difference (~2) indicates clusters dominated by the mainshock's magnitude, with aftershocks contributing minimally to the seismic moment release. However, MACLs with extended durations can be misclassified as swarm-like sequences, particularly when long-lasting aftershock sequences include a late, large-magnitude aftershock that releases a significant portion of the total seismic moment of the sequence (Fig. 1, Fig. S6). Those clusters result in a bi- or multimodal distribution of seismic moment release over time, making the application of swarm-like parameter statistics unreliable (Fig. S6). Cluster duration and seismicity rate are important factors to consider when applying swarmy parameter statistics for cluster classification to avoid biased results.

We used well-established declustering algorithms to detect clusters, rather than to discard them by seeking an optimal background seismicity rate. The cluster detection in ETAS1-4 catalogs demonstrates that all the declustering algorithms, despite not being designed for swarm detection, can effectively identify clusters with simulated swarm-like behavior in addition to MACLs (Fig. 2, Figs. S12 and S13). Specifically, the clusters produced by RES and DBS algorithms are correctly classified as swarm-like clusters, whereas GK tends to produce quasi-symmetric clusters with fat tails (larger kurtosis) that are always classified as swarm-like (Fig. 2, Fig. S14). ZAL effectively detects swarm-like clusters that are almost always classified as mainshock–aftershocks sequences given their large skewness and kurtosis values (Fig. 2, Fig. S14). Moreover, the observed discrepancies in the start and end or durations of the clusters, which in turn result in discrepancies of swarmy parameters, stress the importance of carefully revisiting the full catalog after the detection state to evaluate the duration based on the background rates.

The success of applying cluster detection to real-world catalogs dominated by swarm-like clusters depends on the spatial and temporal separation of those clusters. In our case studies, the total number of detected clusters is similar to previous detection by statistical and/or manual analyses (Passarelli *et al.*, 2015, 2018). Standard declustering performs well when earthquake clusters are clearly separated in space and time, as seen in the HFF case (Fig. 3). This indicates that these algorithms can be effective swarm detectors also in real seismicity catalogs. However, their performance deteriorates when distinguishing between multiple earthquake bursts over short periods in sustained swarm-like sequences, such as the 1997 swarm along the HFF (Fig. 3), or in cases with repeated activity over months and years that results in clusters tight in space and time, as observed in the 2010–2014 Pollino Range case (Figs. 3 and 5). We purportedly used the standard formulation of the space kernel of the declustering algorithm. However, their capacity to detect a swarm tightly in space may improve by choosing an optimized parameterization of their space kernel function. Using a larger variability of (de-)clustering parameters for the same catalog, it is in general possible to further investigate the sequences to understand if they are in fact composed of many bursts of seismicity or show more continuous activity (e.g., Petersen and Pankow, 2023).

Generally, using established declustering algorithms to detect swarm-like seismicity has proven to be an effective and simple method for identifying swarm-like clusters, although with the limitations and biases previously discussed. These algorithms often identify clusters with high kurtosis because they are designed to detect aftershocks over extended time windows. In our applications, DBS and RES appear more effective at detecting swarm-like clusters and less biased in their classification compared to ZAL and GK.

Analyzing earthquake clusters with swarmy parameter statistics provides an additional way to monitor the overall evolution of earthquake sequences in terms of seismic moment release, complementing other cluster classification techniques based solely on seismicity rate changes (Jacobs *et al.*, 2013; Marsan *et al.*, 2023). Although it is important to recognize that swarm-like and mainshock–aftershock sequences represent the end members of a continuum in earthquake cluster characteristics, nature can be more complex. Hybrid or complex sequences have been observed, including multiplets, mainshocks-triggering extended swarm-like aftershock activity that does not follow Omori–Utsu law, or swarm-like sequences composed of numerous small mainshock–aftershock sequences (Lanza *et al.*, 2022; Ventura-Valentín and Brudzinski, 2022; Petersen and Pankow, 2023; Xiang and Marsan, 2025). In such cases, the automatic application of swarm parameters' statistics may provide an unclear classification or even misclassify the sequence type. When an earthquake cluster falls within the swarm-like range of values we found, we suggest this is a sufficient but not a necessary condition to be classified as a swarm-like sequence. Therefore, we stress the importance and recommend that automated detection and characterization workflows, particularly for regional-scale applications, include a posteriori manual supervision to verify the nature of each earthquake cluster. Furthermore, we suggest complementing the cluster analysis by examining the migration properties of earthquake clusters because these are more indicative of transient-driven swarm-like seismicity, although generalized algorithms for estimating the earthquake's migration properties are lacking.

Data and Resources

The Pollino catalog is available at https://terremoti.ingv.it/en (last accessed December 2022) (ISIDe Working Group, 2007): we queried all earthquakes in a 30 km radius around Castrovillari town in the earthquake bulletin search criteria. The Húsavík–Flatey fault (HFF) catalog is available upon request to the authors. Reasenberg (RES) and Gardner and Knopoff (GK) algorithms are available in OpenQuake engine (Pagani *et al.*, 2014; Silva *et al.*, 2014). Zaliapin and Ben-Zion algorithm (ZAL) code is available upon request to the authors. For the DBScan clustering (Ester *et al.*, 1996), we used the implementation in scikit learn (https://scikit-learn.org/stable/modules/generated/sklearn.cluster.DBSCAN.html, last accessed December 2024) (Pedregosa *et al.*, 2011). Software packages Pyrocko (Heimann *et al.*, 2017), NumPy (https://numpy.org, last accessed October 2024) (Harris *et al.*, 2020), SciPy (https://docs.scipy.org/doc, last accessed October 2024), GMT (Wessel *et al.*, 2013), and Matplotlib (Hunter, 2007), were used for data processing and plotting. Plotly (Plotly Technologies Inc., 2015) was used to generate the flow diagrams (https://plotly.com/python/sankey-diagram, last accessed October 2024), as used and implemented in Petersen *et al.* (2021). The supplemental material includes: a detailed description of the declustering algorithms; a detailed description of the epidemic-type aftershock sequence (ETAS) model used to simulate synthetic catalogs; Figures S1–S14 that complement the main article.

Declaration of Competing Interests

The authors acknowledge that there are no conflicts of interest recorded.

Acknowledgments

The authors thank the associate editor and two anonymous reviewers for their constructive feedback, which greatly improved the quality of this article. L. P. acknowledges funding from CETPartnership, the Clean Energy Transition Partnership under the 2023 joint call for research proposals, cofunded by the European Commission (GA N°101069750) and with the funding organizations detailed on https://cetpartnership.eu/funding-agencies-and-call-modules and by the INGV Departmental Strategic Project "Progetto Centro Italia DL50 - Monitoraggio sismico."

References

Cesca, S., M. Metz, P. Büyükakpınar, and T. Dahm (2023). The energetic 2022 seismic unrest related to magma intrusion at the north mid-Atlantic ridge, *Geophys. Res. Lett.* **50,** no. 13, e2023GL102782.

Cheloni, D., N. D'Agostino, G. Selvaggi, A. Avallone, G. Fornaro, R. Giuliani, D. Reale, E. Sansosti, and P. Tizzani (2017). Aseismic transient during the 2010–2014 seismic swarm: Evidence for longer recurrence of m ≥6.5 earthquakes in the Pollino gap (southern Italy)? *Sci. Rep.* **7,** no. 1, 576.

Chen, X., and P. M. Shearer (2011). Comprehensive analysis of earthquake source spectra and swarms in the Salton trough, California, *J. Geophys. Res.* **116,** no. B9.

Cirillo, D., C. Totaro, G. Lavecchia, B. Orecchio, R. de Nardis, D. Presti, F. Ferrarini, S. Bello, and F. Brozzetti (2021). Structural complexities and tectonic barriers controlling recent seismic activity of the Pollino area (Calabria-Lucania, southern Italy)–Constraints from stress inversion and 3d fault model building, *Solid Earth Discuss.* **2021,** 1–45.

Danré, P., L. De Barros, and F. Cappa (2022). Inferring fluid volume during earthquake swarms using seismic catalogues, *Geophys. J. Int.* **232,** no. 2, 829–841.

Danré, P., L. De Barros, F. Cappa, and L. Passarelli (2024). Parallel dynamics of slow slips and fluid-induced seismic swarms, *Nat. Commun.* **15,** no. 1, 8943.

Davis, S. D., and C. Frohlich (1991a). Single-link cluster analysis of earthquake aftershocks: Decay laws and regional variations, *J. Geophys. Res.* **96,** no. B4, 6335–6350.

Davis, S. D., and C. Frohlich (1991b). Single-link cluster analysis, synthetic earthquake catalogues, and aftershock identification, *Geophys. J. Int.* **104,** no. 2, 289–306.

Essing, D., A. Hellbrück, and V. Schlindwein (2025). Magmatic activity at the slowest spreading rates: Insights from a high-resolution earthquake catalog obtained from Gakkel ridge deep (Arctic Ocean), *Seismica* **4,** no. 1.

Ester, M., H.-P. Kriegel, J. Sander, X. Xu, *et al.* (1996). A density-based algorithm for discovering clusters in large spatial databases with noise, in *Kdd*, Vol. 96(34), pp. 226–231.

Fischer, T., and S. Hainzl (2021). The growth of earthquake clusters, *Front. Earth Sci.* **9,** 638,336.

Forbes, C., M. Evans, N. Hastings, and B. Peacock (2010). *Terms and Symbols*, Chapter 2, John Wiley & Sons, Ltd, pp. 3–14.

Frohlich, C., and S. D. Davis (1990). Single-link cluster analysis as a method to evaluate spatial and temporal properties of earthquake catalogues, *Geophys. J. Int.* **100,** no. 1, 19–32.

Gardner, J., and L. Knopoff (1974). Is the sequence of earthquakes in southern California, with aftershocks removed, Poissonian? *Bull. Seismol. Soc. Am.* **64,** no. 5, 1363–1367.

Hainzl, S., and Y. Ogata (2005). Detecting fluid signals in seismicity data through statistical earthquake modeling, *J. Geophys. Res.* **110,** no. B5.

Hainzl, S., O. Zakharova, and D. Marsan (2013). Impact of aseismic transients on the estimation of aftershock productivity parameters, *Bull. Seismol. Soc. Am.* **103,** no. 3, 1723–1732.

Hanks, T. C., and H. Kanamori (1979). A moment magnitude scale, *J. Geophys. Res.* **84,** no. B5, 2348–2350.

Harris, C. R., K. J. Millman, S. J. van der Walt, R. Gommers, P. Virtanen, D. Cournapeau, E. Wieser, J. Taylor, S. Berg, N. J. Smith, *et al.* (2020). Array programming with NumPy, *Nature* **585,** no. 7825, 357–362.

Heimann, S., M. Kriegerowski, M. Isken, S. Cesca, S. Daout, F. Grigoli, C. Juretzek, T. Megies, N. Nooshiri, A. Steinberg, *et al.* (2017). Pyrocko-An open-source seismology toolbox and library, V. 0.3. GFZ Data Services, doi: 10.5880/GFZ.2.1.2017.001.

Hensch, M., C. Riedel, J. Reinhardt, T. Dahm, and The NICE-People (2008). Hypocenter migration of fluid-induced earthquake swarms in the Tjörnes fracture zone (north Iceland), *Tectonophysics* **447,** nos. 1/4, 80–94.

Hill, D. P. (1977). A model for earthquake swarms, *J. Geophys. Res. (1896-1977)* **82,** no. 8, 1347–1352.

Holtkamp, S., and M. Brudzinski (2011). Earthquake swarms in circum-pacific subduction zones, *Earth Planet. Sci. Lett.* **305,** nos. 1/2, 215–225.

Holtkamp, S., M. Pritchard, and R. Lohman (2011). Earthquake swarms in South America, *Geophys. J. Int.* **187,** no. 1, 128–146.

Hunter, J. D. (2007). Matplotlib: A 2D graphics environment, *Comput. Sci. Eng.* **9,** no. 3, 90–95.

ISIDe Working Group (2007). Italian Seismological Instrumental and Parametric Database (ISIDe) (Version 1), doi: 10.13127/ISIDE.

Jacobs, K. M., E. G. C. Smith, M. K. Savage, and J. Zhuang (2013). Cumulative rate analysis (curate): A clustering algorithm for swarm dominated catalogs, *J. Geophys. Res.* **118,** no. 2, 553–569.

Knopoff, L., and J. Gardner (1972). Higher seismic activity during local night on the raw worldwide earthquake catalogue, *Geophys. J. Int.* **28,** no. 3, 311–313.

Lanza, F., D. C. Roman, J. A. Power, C. H. Thurber, and T. Hudson (2022). Complex magmatic-tectonic interactions during the 2020 Makushin volcano, Alaska, earthquake swarm, *Earth Planet. Sci. Lett.* **587,** 117,538.

Llenos, A. L., J. J. McGuire, and Y. Ogata (2009). Modeling seismic swarms triggered by aseismic transients, *Earth Planet. Sci. Lett.* **281,** nos. 1/2, 59–69.

Lohman, R. B., and J. J. McGuire (2007). Earthquake swarms driven by aseismic creep in the Salton trough, California, *J. Geophys. Res.* **112,** no. B4.

Maccaferri, F., E. Rivalta, L. Passarelli, and S. Jonsson (2013). The stress shadow induced by the 1975–1984 Krafla rifting episode, *J. Geophys. Res.* **118,** no. 3, 1109–1121.

Marsan, D., E. Prono, and A. Helmstetter (2013). Monitoring aseismic forcing in fault zones using earthquake time series, *Bull. Seismol. Soc. Am.* **103,** no. 1, 169–179.

Marsan, D., T. Reverso, and A. Socquet (2023). Earthquake swarms along the Chilean subduction zone, 2003–2020, *Geophys. J. Int.* **235,** no. 3, 2758–2777.

Matthews, M. V., and P. A. Reasenberg (1988). Statistical methods for investigating quiescence and other temporal seismicity patterns, *Pure Appl. Geophys.* **126,** no. 2, 357–372.

Mesimeri, M., V. Karakostas, E. Papadimitriou, and G. Tsaklidis (2019). Characteristics of earthquake clusters: Application to western Corinth gulf (Greece), *Tectonophysics* **767,** 228,160.

Metzger, S., and S. Jonsson (2014). Plate boundary deformation in north Iceland during 1992–2009 revealed by INSAR time-series analysis and GPS, *Tectonophysics* **634,** 127–138.

Mizrahi, L., S. Nandan, and S. Wiemer (2021). The effect of declustering on the size distribution of mainshocks, *Bull. Seismol. Soc. Am.* **92,** no. 4, 2333–2342.

Mizrahi, L., N. Schmid, and M. Han (2023). lmizrahi/etas: Etas. Zenodo, doi: 10.5281/zenodo.7584575.

Mogi, K. (1963). Experimental study on the mechanism of the earthquake occurrences of volcanic origin, *Bull. Volcanol.* **26,** 197–208.

Molchan, G., and O. Dmitrieva (1992). Aftershock identification: Methods and new approaches, *Geophys. J. Int.* **109,** no. 3, 501–516.

Nakajima, J. (2022). Crustal structure beneath earthquake swarm in the Noto peninsula, Japan, *Earth Planets Space* **74,** no. 1, 160.

Napolitano, F., D. Galluzzo, A. Gervasi, R. Scarpa, and M. La Rocca (2020). Fault imaging at Mt Pollino (Italy) from relative location of microearthquakes, *Geophys. J. Int.* **224,** no. 1, 637–648.

Ogata, Y. (1988). Statistical models for earthquake occurrences and residual analysis for point processes, *J. Am. Stat. Assoc.* **83,** no. 401, 9–27.

Pagani, M., D. Monelli, G. Weatherill, L. Danciu, H. Crowley, V. Silva, P. Henshaw, L. Butler, M. Nastasi, L. Panzeri, *et al.* (2014). Openquake engine: An open hazard (and risk) software for the global earthquake model, *Seismol. Res. Lett.* **85,** no. 3, 692–702.

Passarelli, L., S. Hainzl, S. Cesca, F. Maccaferri, M. Mucciarelli, D. Roessler, F. Corbi, T. Dahm, and E. Rivalta (2015). Aseismic transient driving the swarm-like seismic sequence in the Pollino range, southern Italy, *Geophys. J. Int.* **201,** no. 3, 1553–1567.

Passarelli, L., E. Rivalta, S. Jónsson, M. Hensch, S. Metzger, S. S. Jakobsdóttir, F. Maccaferri, F. Corbi, and T. Dahm (2018). Scaling and spatial complementarity of tectonic earthquake swarms, *Earth Planet. Sci. Lett.* **482,** 62–70.

Passarelli, L., P. A. Selvadurai, E. Rivalta, and S. Jónsson (2021). The source scaling and seismic productivity of slow slip transients, *Sci. Adv.* **7,** no. 32, eabg9718.

Pedregosa, F., G. Varoquaux, A. Gramfort, V. Michel, B. Thirion, O. Grisel, M. Blondel, P. Prettenhofer, R. Weiss, V. Dubourg, *et al.* (2011). Scikit-learn: Machine learning in Python, *J. Machine Learn. Res* **12,** 2825–2830.

Peng, W., D. Marsan, K. H. Chen, and E. Pathier (2021). Earthquake swarms in Taiwan: A composite declustering method for detection and their spatial characteristics, *Earth Planet. Sci. Lett.* **574,** 117,160.

Pesicek, J. D., J. J. Wellik, S. G. Prejean, and S. E. Ogburn (2018). Prevalence of seismic rate anomalies preceding volcanic eruptions in Alaska, *Front. Earth Sci.* **6,** 100.

Petersen, G., and K. Pankow (2023). Small-magnitude seismic swarms in Central Utah (US): Interactions of regional tectonics, local structures and hydrothermal systems, *Geochem. Geophys. Geosyst.* **24,** no. 7, e2023GC010867.

Petersen, G. M., L. J. Hofman, J. Kummerow, and S. Cesca (2025). Microseismicity in the large-n swath-d network: Revealing seismic sequences and active faults in the eastern Alps, *J. Geophys. Res.* **130,** no. 2, e2024JB030516.

Petersen, G. M., P. Niemz, S. Cesca, V. Mouslopoulou, and G. Bocchini (2021). Clusty, the waveform-based network similarity clustering toolbox: Concept and application to image complex faulting offshore Zakynthos (Greece), *Geophys. J. Int.* **224,** no. 3, 2044–2059.

Pfister, R., K. A. Schwarz, M. Janczyk, R. Dale, and J. B. Freeman (2013). Good things peak in pairs: A note on the bimodality coefficient, *Front. Psychol.* **4,** 700.

Plotly Technologies Inc. (2015). Collaborative data science, available at https://plot.ly (last accessed June 2024).

Reasenberg, P. (1985). Second-order moment of central California seismicity, 1969–1982, *J. Geophys. Res.* **90,** no. B7, 5479–5495.

Roland, E., and J. J. McGuire (2009). Earthquake swarms on transform faults, *Geophys. J. Int.* **178,** no. 3, 1677–1690.

Ross, Z. E., and E. S. Cochran (2021). Evidence for latent crustal fluid injection transients in southern California from long-duration earthquake swarms, *Geophys. Res. Lett.* **48,** no. 12, e2021GL092465. e2021GL092465 2021GL092465.

Ross, Z. E., E. S. Cochran, D. T. Trugman, and J. D. Smith (2020). 3d fault architecture controls the dynamism of earthquake swarms, *Science* **368,** no. 6497, 1357–1361.

Ross, Z. E., C. Rollins, E. S. Cochran, E. Hauksson, J.-P. Avouac, and Y. Ben-Zion (2017). Aftershocks driven by afterslip and fluid pressure sweeping through a fault-fracture mesh, *Geophys. Res. Lett.* **44,** no. 16, 8260–8267.

Ruch, J., D. Keir, L. Passarelli, D. Di Giacomo, G. Ogubazghi, and S. Jónsson (2021). Revealing 60 years of earthquake swarms in the southern red sea, afar and the Gulf of Aden, *Front. Earth Sci.* **9,** 664,673.

Schneider, M., H. Flury, P. Guttorp, and A. Wright (2023). Earthquake catalog processing and swarm identification for the Pacific Northwest, *Seismol. Res. Lett.* **94,** no. 5, 2500–2513.

Silva, V., H. Crowley, M. Pagani, D. Monelli, and R. Pinho (2014). Development of the Openquake engine, the global earthquake model's open-source software for seismic risk assessment, *Nat. Hazards* **72,** 1409–1427.

Sirorattanakul, K., Z. E. Ross, M. Khoshmanesh, E. S. Cochran, M. Acosta, and J.-P. Avouac (2022). The 2020 Westmorland, California earthquake swarm as aftershocks of a slow slip event sustained by fluid flow, *J. Geophys. Res.* **127,** no. 11, e2022JB024693.

Spassiani, I., S. Gentili, R. Console, M. Murru, M. Taroni, and G. Falcone (2025). Reconciling the irreconcilable: Window-based versus stochastic declustering algorithms, *Geophys. J. Int.* **240,** no. 2, 1009–1027.

Utsu, T. (2002). Statistical features of seismicity, in *International Handbook of Earthquake and Engineering Seismology, Part A*, W. H. Lee, H. Kanamori, P. C. Jennings, and C. Kisslinger (Editors), Vol. 81, International Geophysics, Academic Press, pp. 719–732.

Valenzuela-Malebrán, C., S. Cesca, S. Ruiz, L. Passarelli, F. Leyton, S. Hainzl, B. Potin, and T. Dahm (2020). Seismicity clusters in central Chile: Investigating the role of repeating earthquakes and swarms in a subduction region, *Geophys. J. Int.* **224,** no. 3, 2028–2043.

van Stiphout, T., D. Schorlemmer, and S. Wiemer (2011). The effect of uncertainties on estimates of background seismicity rate, *Bull. Seismol. Soc. Am.* **101,** no. 2, 482–494.

van Stiphout, T., J. Zhuang, and D. Marsan (2012). Seismicity declustering, *Community Online Resource for Statistical Seismicity Analysis*, doi: 10.5078/corssa52382934.

Ventura-Valentín, W., and M. R. Brudzinski (2022). Characterization of swarm and mainshock–aftershock behavior in Puerto Rico, *Bull. Seismol. Soc. Am.* **93,** no. 2A, 641–652.

Vidale, J. E., and P. M. Shearer (2006). A survey of 71 earthquake bursts across southern California: Exploring the role of pore fluid pressure fluctuations and aseismic slip as drivers, *J. Geophys. Res.* **111,** no. B5.

Wessel, P., W. H. Smith, R. Scharroo, J. Luis, and F. Wobbe (2013). Generic mapping tools: Improved version released, *Eos Trans. AGU* **94,** no. 45, 409–410.

Xiang, L., and D. Marsan (2025). Characterizing seismic swarm activity in the aftershock zone of the 2016 Amatrice-Norcia seismic sequence, *J. Geophys. Res.* **130,** no. 6, e2024JB029651.

Yoshida, K., N. Uchida, Y. Matsumoto, M. Orimo, T. Okada, S. Hirahara, S. Kimura, and R. Hino (2023). Updip fluid flow in the crust of the northeastern Noto peninsula, Japan, triggered the 2023 m_w 6.2 Suzu earthquake during swarm activity, *Geophys. Res. Lett.* **50,** no. 21, e2023GL106023. e2023GL106023 2023GL106023.

Zaliapin, I., and Y. Ben-Zion (2013). Earthquake clusters in southern California I: Identification and stability, *J. Geophys. Res.* **118,** no. 6, 2847–2864.

Zaliapin, I., and Y. Ben-Zion (2020). Earthquake declustering using the nearest-neighbor approach in space-time-magnitude domain, *J. Geophys. Res.* **125,** no. 4, e2018JB017120. e2018JB017120 2018JB017120.

Zaliapin, I., and Y. Ben-Zion (2021). Perspectives on clustering and declustering of earthquakes, *Seismol. Res. Lett.* **93,** no 1, 386–401.

Zhang, Q., and P. M. Shearer (2016). A new method to identify earthquake swarms applied to seismicity near the San Jacinto fault, California, *Geophys. J. Int.* **205,** no. 2, 995–1005.

Manuscript received 23 June 2025
Published online 18 November 2025

Analyzing Earthquake's Onset-Magnitude Correlation Using Modeled Source Time Functions of Recorded Earthquakes and Machine Learning

Gopala Krishna Rodda*[1] and Yuval Tal[1]

Abstract

Predicting an earthquake's final magnitude from its initial characteristics is of fundamental importance for earthquake physics and practical applications such as early warning systems. However, past research presents conflicting views on using initial rupture characteristics for magnitude estimation. This study explores a novel hybrid convolutional neural network–recurrent neural network (CNN-RNN) model for magnitude prediction using only the first two seconds of source time functions (STFs) that were derived from finite-fault inversion of the earthquakes present in the U.S. Geological Survey database consisting of 228 events. Moment magnitude predictions from the CNN-RNN algorithm yield promising results, with a correlation coefficient of 0.71 and a mean absolute error of 0.21 magnitude units for the testing dataset, for which most magnitudes range between 6.75 and 8.25. For most earthquakes, the model exhibits strong performance for both fractional durations less than 1/10 and between 1/10 and 1/3. This suggests that for this dataset, a relationship, although complex, exists between the initial stages of an earthquake, as captured by the STF, and its final size. Furthermore, the analysis using 1–3 s reveals that a 2 s STF window is sufficient for the model to capture the relevant features for prediction. To advance the understanding of earthquake dynamics and improve early warning systems, future studies should investigate a broader magnitude range and more diverse STFs from methodological advances to reduce potential acausal artifacts introduced by source inversion regularization.

Cite this article as Rodda, G. K., and Y. Tal (2025). Analyzing Earthquake's Onset-Magnitude Correlation Using Modeled Source Time Functions of Recorded Earthquakes and Machine Learning, *Seismol. Res. Lett.* **97**, 1881–1892, doi: 10.1785/0220240161.

Supplemental Material

Introduction

A fundamental question in earthquake mechanics hinges on the potential relationship between the early stages of an earthquake, its "onset," and its final size, expressed as moment magnitude (M_w). Accurately and rapidly estimating the moment magnitude within the first few seconds of the observed *P* wave could enable timely warnings for regions facing potential damage (Olson and Allen, 2005; Allen and Melgar, 2019). However, if earthquake early warning systems require observing a significant portion of the rupture to estimate magnitude, warnings might be delayed for larger events (Minson *et al.*, 2018; Trugman *et al.*, 2019).

Decades of research have yielded contrasting viewpoints about the relationship between earthquake onset and final size. On one hand, several studies suggested early differentiation between small and large events (Ellsworth and Beroza, 1995; Colombelli *et al.*, 2014; Melgar and Hayes, 2019), implying magnitude prediction using initial rupture characteristics. On the other hand, other studies concluded that earthquakes start similarly and grow to different sizes owing to favorable rupture conditions (Mori and Kanamori, 1996; Kilb and Gomberg, 1999; Meier *et al.*, 2016; Ide, 2019), emphasizing challenges in early magnitude prediction.

Source time functions (STFs), extracted from the deconvolution of teleseismic records, provide valuable insights into earthquake source properties. They are available for numerous global earthquakes and accessible through databases such as SCARDEC (Seismic source ChAracteristics Retrieved from DEConvolvolving teleseismic body waves—Vallée and Douet, 2016) and the ones of U.S. Geological Survey (USGS; Hayes, 2017) and Ye16 (Ye *et al.*, 2016). Danré *et al.* (2019) analyzed the STFs in the SCARDEC dataset and their constituent

1. Department of Earth and Environmental Sciences, Ben-Gurion University of the Negev, Beer Sheva, Israel, https://orcid.org/0000-0003-3987-3338 (GKR); https://orcid.org/0000-0001-7308-9294 (YT)

*Corresponding author: gopalakr@post.bgu.ac.il

subevents, revealing that larger earthquakes contain more subevents than smaller ones. Although not advocating for complete earthquake determinism, the authors propose that subevent properties hold information for early magnitude estimation. By analyzing the first subevent, it might be possible to statistically infer the number and size of subsequent ones, aiding in early warning systems.

Examining the growth rates of these STFs, recent studies based on STFs have reached conflicting conclusions regarding early size prediction (Meier *et al.*, 2017; Melgar and Hayes, 2019). Both studies analyzed large STF datasets using consistent methods. Meier *et al.* (2017) found no difference in early growth rates for large earthquakes ($M_w > 7$), although their study was primarily limited to subduction zone earthquakes. On the other hand, Melgar and Hayes (2019) reported significantly faster acceleration for larger events. Both the studies (Meier *et al.*, 2017; Melgar and Hayes, 2019) analyzed STF datasets from SCARDEC, USGS, and Ye16. Building on contrasting findings, Meier *et al.* (2021) investigated the different conclusions from these two STF-based studies and reported a new nomenclature to facilitate discussions about earthquake rupture predictability and determinism. This nomenclature classifies predictability based on the portion of the rupture duration required for accurate magnitude estimates: strong predictability (observations that span less than 1/10 of the source duration), moderate predictability (1/10 to 1/3 of the rupture), weak predictability (1/3 to 1/2 of the rupture), and no predictability (requires the entire rupture). Meier *et al.* (2021) further reported that conclusions drawn by Melgar and Hayes (2019) suffer from the selection bias toward events with unusually long durations and by erroneous estimates of STF growth made when the STF is already decaying. A much weaker correlation was reported between the initial characteristics of the STF and the final magnitude for the events of similar duration. Moreover, they discussed additional issues related to the resolution of the teleseismic source inversions that can affect the correlation, such as phase-arrival-time uncertainties, magnitude-dependent band-pass filters applied before the STF inversion for $M_w < 7.0$ events, and the depletion of high frequencies in teleseismic records.

Münchmeyer *et al.* (2022) analyzed the STF datasets aforementioned and reported that there are no definitive signs of such predictability using either STFs or broadband teleseismic *P* waveforms. This indicates that reliable final magnitude estimation based on these data sources may only be possible after the peak moment release, posing challenges for early warning systems seeking real-time magnitude predictions. Reinforcing the notion of weak predictability, Wang *et al.* (2022) analyzed data from the K-NET strong-motion network and China Strong-Motion Networks Center and concluded that earthquake ruptures exhibit limited determinism. Their findings suggest that although earthquakes may initiate similarly, they diverge significantly as the rupture progresses.

This study sheds light on the correlation between early STF growth and earthquake magnitude by analyzing the USGS STF dataset with machine learning algorithms. We use a novel hybrid convolutional neural network–recurrent neural network (CNN-RNN) model to estimate the moment magnitude from just the first two seconds of the STF, significantly shortening the observation window compared to conventional methods. CNNs excel at extracting spatial features from data, which is ideal for processing the intricate patterns within the initial STF. RNNs, adept at handling sequential data, effectively capture the temporal evolution of the earthquake's early stages. The hybrid model combines these capabilities to explore the possible correlation between the onset of the earthquake and its final magnitude. The input STF data are carefully curated to mitigate potential biases and to generalize the potential correlation across diverse earthquake scenarios and validating the model's performance.

Data

If a correlation between early STF growth and earthquake magnitude exists, identifying an optimal machine learning algorithm (hybrid CNN-RNN model) that can estimate the final moment magnitude of an earthquake from the first few seconds of its STF requires a robust and diverse dataset to train and validate the algorithm, preventing overfitting and ensuring generalizability. This study initially considered the STFs from the USGS (Hayes, 2017), Ye16 (Ye *et al.*, 2016), and SCARDEC (Vallée and Douet, 2016) databases for investigating the earthquake onset and magnitude correlation in field-recorded earthquakes.

The USGS and Ye16 STF datasets are based on finite-fault slip inversion, whereas the SCARDEC dataset is based on a spatial point-source mechanism. The USGS database consists of 257 STF records from 1990 to 2024. After eliminating a few STFs with a sampling interval of 4 and 0.4 s, the number of available events in the USGS dataset is reduced to 228 (182 and 46 records with native sampling intervals of 0.2 and 0.01 s, respectively). Body waves used in source inversion for the USGS STF database are band-pass filtered in the range ~1 to 200 s (Hayes, 2017), and the finer native sampling rate can help capture higher frequency content in the rupture process. The SCARDEC database (native sampling interval of 0.07 s) currently covers nearly 3950 earthquakes recorded between 1992 and 2021 with magnitudes ranging from 5.8 to 9.02 (see Data and Resources), whereas the Ye16 dataset contains 120 STFs for earthquakes recorded between 1990 and 2016, with magnitudes ranging from 6.8 to 9.0. Our preliminary analysis revealed limitations in the SCARDEC and Ye16 datasets. The STFs from the SCARDEC database for events with moment magnitudes below 7 assume a power-law relationship between source duration and seismic moment, which introduces an inherent bias in the input STF data. The remaining SCARDEC data exhibit a narrow range of magnitudes

(7–7.5, Fig. S1d, available in the supplemental material to this article), hindering the model's generalizability. The Ye16 dataset has a sampling interval of 0.5 s, which is too coarse for the 2 s STF window used in this study. Therefore, we focus on the USGS dataset in this study. For completeness, results, including the two other datasets, are presented in the supplemental material.

We employ the following preprocessing steps to ensure a balanced dataset of diverse magnitudes and source duration for optimal training and evaluation of the CNN-RNN model. To avoid any potential bias, STF record is considered to be triggered when it first crosses the value 1×10^{17} N · m/s. In the present analysis, STF threshold criteria (1×10^{17} N · m/s) are applied first and then STFs are resampled to 64 Hz for uniformity. Source duration is defined in this article as the duration corresponding to 95% of the final seismic moment. Assuming this threshold as the peak value of a triangle STF shape and 2 s half-duration, this corresponds to a moment magnitude of 5.47. Figure 1a presents sample STFs from USGS dataset for several of the earthquakes.

Before using the CNN-RNN models against the STF input, we examine the potential correlation between simpler measures of early STF growth, such as the average moment acceleration (AMA) over 2 s (Fig. 1b) and the accumulated seismic moment (M_{t2}) at 2 s (Fig. 1c), and M_w. Because the size of the USGS dataset available for this study is small, to assess the reliability of the reported correlation coefficients, a 95% confidence interval (CI) was calculated using Fisher's z-transformation, a method commonly employed to account for the nonnormal distribution of Pearson's correlation (Bonett and Wright, 2000). The correlation coefficients are reported along with the associated CIs wherever relevant in the remainder of this study. Both parameters (AMA and M_{t2}) show a weak correlation, with correlation values of 0.37 and 0.28, respectively. This lack of straightforward correlation underscores one of the key motivations behind employing machine learning techniques: to discover potential, more complex, relationships between the early portion of the STF (e.g., the first 2 s) and the final moment magnitude. Figure 1d presents the variation of the final moment magnitude against the starting STF value $\dot{M}_0$, showing no apparent relationship between the corresponding parameters. The lack of any strong correlation between the starting STF characteristics (either starting STF, AMA, or 2 s seismic moment) and the final moment magnitude further shows that there is no inherent bias in the dataset considered for training and optimizing the machine learning algorithm.

Figure 2 presents the histogram of the durations and moment magnitudes of the USGS dataset, revealing a well-defined distribution for both source duration and the associated moment magnitude. The source duration spans from 6.75 to 130 s, and the moment magnitude ranges from 5.98 to 8.4, with the exception of the 2004 Sumatra earthquake, which had a magnitude of 9.1 and a duration of 505 s.

Machine Learning Model Considered

The present article makes use of the hybrid deep CNN-RNN architecture (Wang *et al.*, 2016) for predicting the final moment magnitude of the earthquake from the observations of the first 2 s of the STF. To ensure compatibility with the CNN-RNN model's input requirements, the STFs are resampled to a uniform size. This involves resampling the data to a frequency of 64 Hz, resulting in 128 data points for a 2 s STF window. To fully harness the valuable information encoded within STFs and optimize the capabilities of the hybrid CNN-RNN model, the input beyond a single STF channel is employed here.

Input channels considered

A three-channel input representation that captures distinct aspects of STF is considered here. Logarithmic cumulative STF is chosen as channel 1. For channel 2 (standard normalized STF) and channel 3 (standard normalized STF slope [time derivative]), a standard normalization technique is applied. This involves, for each data point within the first 2 s of the STF or STF slope, subtracting the mean of that 2 s segment and then dividing by the standard deviation of that same 2 s segment. Although normalization (in channels 2 and 3) scales absolute amplitude, it preserves the relative amplitude information, such as the shape and temporal evolution of the STF. This enables the machine learning model to learn characteristic patterns independent of absolute signal strength, enhancing its robustness and generalizability across diverse earthquake sizes. In contrast, channel 1, the logarithmic cumulative STF, retains absolute amplitude information as it is not normalized.

Channel 1: Logarithmic cumulative STF. Final moment magnitude is directly related to the logarithm of the final seismic moment. Keeping this in mind, the natural logarithm of the cumulative STF, which highlights the early energy release patterns, is selected as the first input channel. This transformation mitigates potential biases arising from earthquakes with exceptionally large magnitudes that might dominate the signal.

Channel 2: Standard normalized STF. This channel preserves the relative STF shape and amplitude information, crucial for capturing characteristic features such as peak values, rise times, and durations. Standard normalization (using the respective mean and standard deviation) ensures consistency across different earthquakes, meaning the normalization process brings the STFs from various events to a comparable scale, allowing the hybrid CNN-RNN model to learn patterns independent of varying signal amplitudes.

Channel 3: Standard normalized STF slope. This channel introduces the rate of change in STF amplitude, highlighting acceleration, and deceleration phases during earthquake rupture. Normalization (using the respective mean and standard deviation) facilitates the comparison of slope

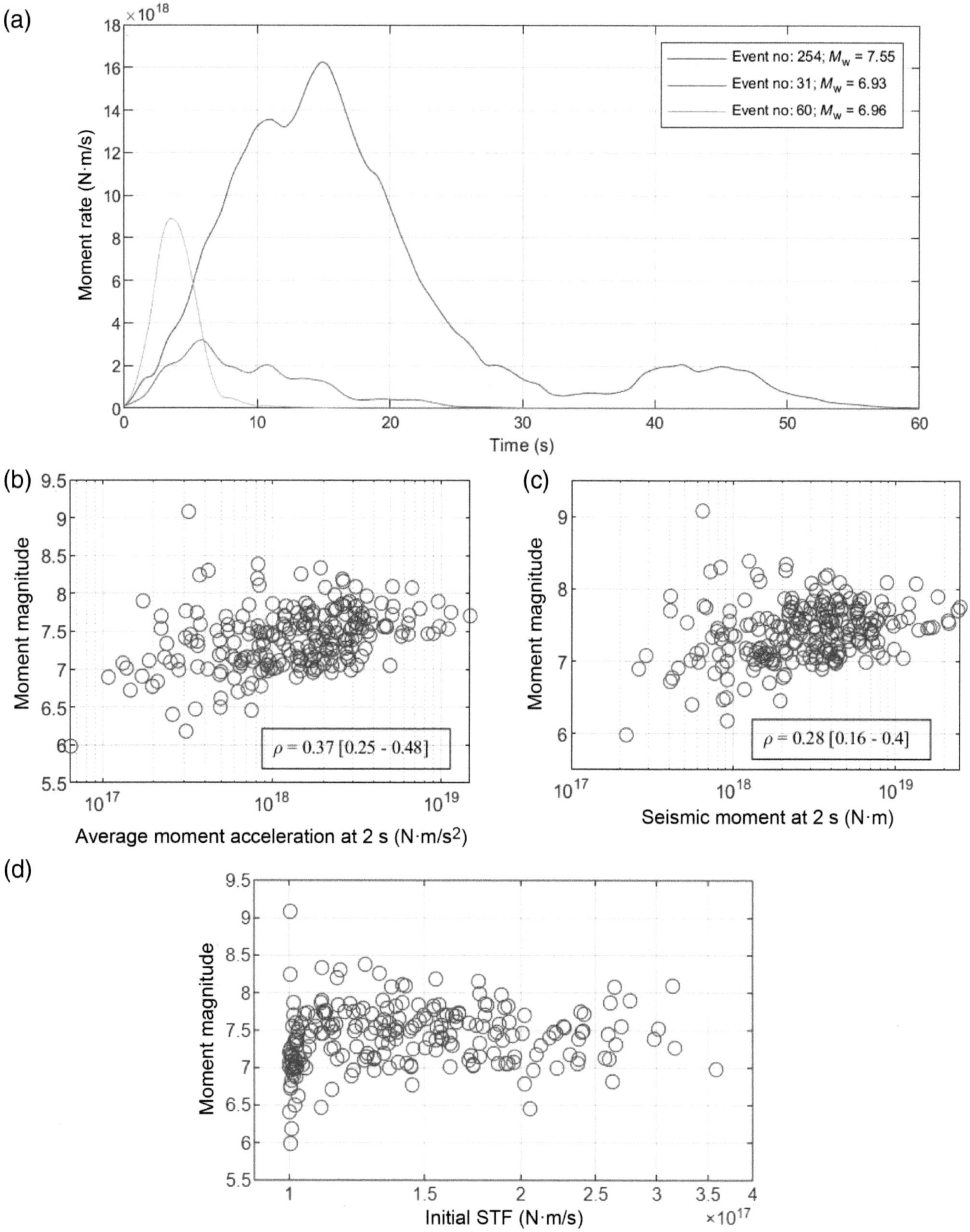

Figure 1. Exploring the correlation between the initial characteristics of the source time function (STF) and final moment magnitude. (a) Sample STFs from U.S. Geological Survey (USGS) database, (b) M_w versus average moment acceleration (AMA) at 2 s and correlation values, (c) M_w versus seismic moment at 2 s and correlation values. A weak correlation is observed in panels (b) and (c), and (d) M_w versus initial STF value after triggering: no observed correlation suggesting no bias in the data. The color version of this figure is available only in the electronic edition.

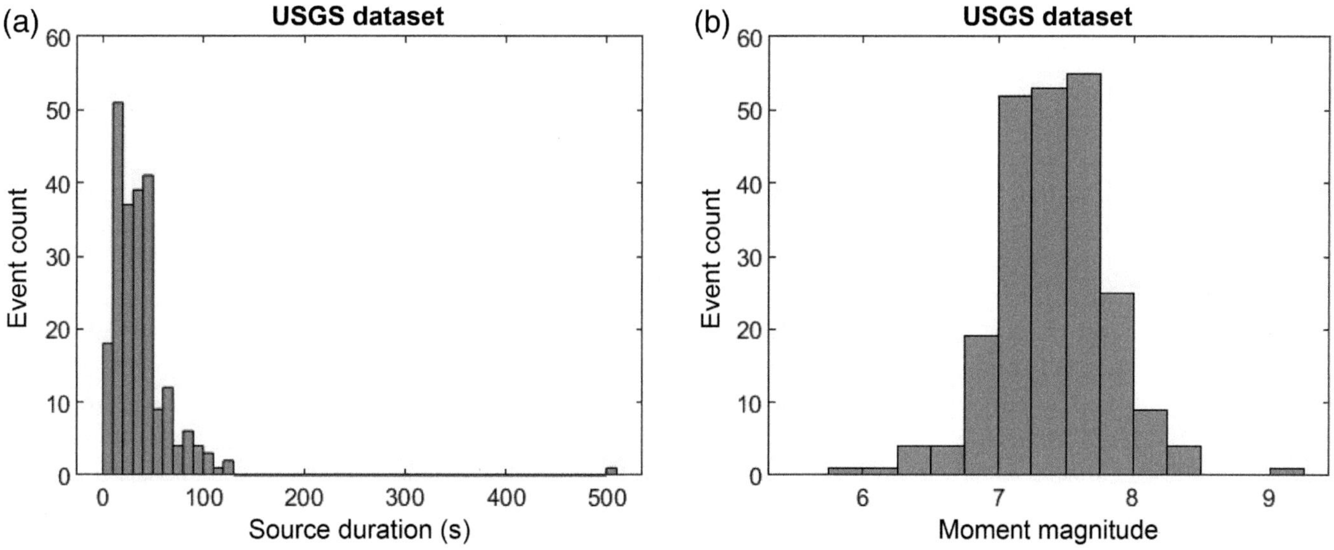

Figure 2. Statistics of the modeled source characteristics for the earthquakes in USGS finite-source database: (a) histogram of the source duration and (b) histogram (in steps of 0.25) for the final moment magnitude M_w. The color version of this figure is available only in the electronic edition.

characteristics across diverse events. By incorporating slope information, the hybrid CNN-RNN model gains sensitivity to subtle variations in rupture dynamics that might not be evident in the STF amplitude alone.

This enriched input empowers the model to extract deeper insights and potentially achieve more accurate magnitude estimation, compared to reliance on a single STF channel. A sample of the three-channel input is presented in Figure S3.

Architecture of the CNN model

The considered hybrid CNN-RNN model, meticulously chosen to uncover hidden details within STFs and to produce accurate magnitude predictions, features a series of carefully crafted layers:

1. **Batch normalization at the start**: immediately following the three-channel input layer, batch normalization (Ioffe and Szegedy, 2015) is strategically employed to establish a stable foundation for the learning process. This technique effectively normalizes the input data, ensuring consistent distribution, and mitigating potential internal covariate shifts during training.
2. **Convolutional cascade**: the core of the model comprises four convolutional blocks. Each block includes a convolutional layer. These layers are designed to extract hierarchical spatial features from the input data. This is followed by batch normalization layers that maintain stability and consistency within each layer's activations. Swish activation functions (Ramachandran *et al.*, 2017) introduce nonlinearity, enabling the model to capture intricate patterns within STF data. Average pooling layers downsample the feature maps, reducing spatial dimensions while preserving essential information and enhancing computational efficiency.
3. **Final convolution layer**: a singular 1×1 convolutional layer, equipped with swish activation, condenses the extracted features into a compact representation.
4. **Gated recurrent unit (GRU) for the RNN**: this layer, adept at handling sequential data, processes the time-dependent evolution of the extracted features from the CNN. By utilizing GRUs (Cho *et al.*, 2014), it captures the temporal variations within the initial stages of the earthquake rupture, providing valuable insights into the earthquake's development.
5. **Fully connected layers**: three fully connected layers, each accompanied by 0.25 dropout and layer normalization, further process and refine the condensed features.
6. **Custom activation**: a customized activation function, scaled (a factor of 10) sigmoid activation, is employed here to align with the specific requirements of bounded earthquake magnitude estimation (0–10) for the final moment magnitude prediction.

This hybrid CNN-RNN model and the associated kernel sizes, and fully connected sizes are presented in Table S1 in detail. To guide the model's learning process, mean absolute error (MAE) is chosen as the loss function, directly measuring the average size of errors between predicted and true magnitudes. Adam optimization (Kingma and Ba, 2017), known for its adaptability and effectiveness in diverse deep learning scenarios, is chosen for estimating the optimal model parameters.

The following hyperparameters are identified by the grid-search algorithm:

1. Initial learning rate: 1×10^{-2} [1×10^{-4}, 3×10^{-4}, 1×10^{-3}, 3×10^{-3}, 1×10^{-2}].
2. Piecewise learning rate drops 50% per 20 epochs.

3. Early stopping: 20 epochs.
4. Minibatch size: 32 [8, 16, 32, 64].
5. L2 regularization: 1×10^{-3} [1×10^{-4}, 1×10^{-3}, 1×10^{-2}].

Data Partitioning

The final dataset assembled for training and evaluation with the machine learning model consists of a total of 228 records. To ensure the model learns from a diverse and representative sample of earthquakes, we employ stratified sampling during the data-splitting process. This technique involves dividing the available STF data into categories based on moment magnitude bins (5.75–9.25 in steps of 0.25), and source duration bins (ranging from 6.75 to 510 s). Following this categorization, we split the data into training (52%, 118), validation (10%, 23), and testing (38%, 87 records) sets. This stratified sampling approach ensures that each partition of the data (training, validation, and testing) contains a proportional representation of earthquakes from all duration bins and moment magnitudes, preventing biases toward specific earthquake characteristics.

Results

An assessment of the moment magnitudes predicted by the CNN-RNN model against the target moment magnitudes for the testing dataset is presented in Figure 3, suggesting that for most events in the USGS dataset, the final magnitude can be estimated from the initial STF evolution. A clear positive correlation ($\rho = 0.71$) is observed between the predicted and target moment magnitude (Fig. 3a), demonstrating the model's ability to extract the correlation between STF characteristics during the first 2 s and final magnitude. Considering the overall target magnitude range of 6–8.5, and most of the events in the range of 6.75–8.25, the low MAE of 0.2 magnitude units underscores the CNN-RNN model's effectiveness in approximating actual magnitudes. Figure 3a overlays an ideal equality line ($y = x$) and ±0.25 error bounds (dashed lines) to provide a visual reference for assessing the accuracy of the model's predictions. The majority of data points cluster near the equality line, indicating strong alignment between predicted and target magnitudes. This demonstrates that the model's ability to capture the underlying relationship between STFs and earthquake magnitudes. Because the dataset available for the analysis is small (87 in the testing dataset), to assess the reliability of the reported correlation coefficient ($\rho = 0.71$), a 95% CI was also considered for this assessment. The resulting interval [0.59, 0.80] indicates that the true population correlation is expected to fall within these bounds. This supports the statistical significance of the observed relationship. Furthermore, a bootstrapping analysis was performed on the testing dataset. This involved creating 1000 resampled datasets by drawing samples with replacement from the original 87 testing records. For each of these 1000 resampled datasets, the correlation coefficient between the predicted and target moment magnitudes was calculated. The histogram of these 1000 bootstrap correlation coefficients is presented in Figure 3b, with a median value of 0.72. This median correlation coefficient (Fig. 3b, $\rho = 0.72$) confirms the statistical significance and stability of the correlation. To further assess the statistical significance of this observed correlation, a permutation test was performed. This involves randomly permuting the predicted moment magnitudes while keeping the target magnitudes fixed, thereby destroying any inherent correlation. The correlation coefficient was calculated for each permuted dataset, and this process was repeated 10,000 times to generate a null distribution of correlation coefficients under the assumption of no correlation. The observed correlation coefficient ($\rho = 0.71$) was found to be highly statistically significant when compared against this null distribution (Fig. 3c). This further confirms the statistical significance and stability of the observed correlation.

Figure 3d presents the results representing the accuracy of the CNN-RNN model's predictions, with particular attention to the relationship between fractional duration (=2 s/source duration) and absolute error. In line with the nomenclature defined in Meier *et al.* (2021), events falling in 0–1/10 and 1/10–1/3 are highlighted in different colors. The USGS dataset lacks any events with fractional durations exceeding 1/3, as the minimum source duration is 8 s in testing and 6.75 s in overall dataset. Although it would be interesting to investigate whether the median absolute error or MAE decreases with increasing fractional duration (as shorter events provide more relative information), the limited range of fractional durations in the testing dataset prevents us from drawing any definitive conclusions. Figure 3d illustrates the mean and standard deviation of the absolute error for events categorized into 0–1/10 and 1/10–1/3 fractional duration windows. The observation that the mean (and standard deviation) of the absolute error is lower for the 0–1/10 window compared to the 1/10–1/3 window can likely be attributed to the larger number of training data available for the shorter (0–1/10) fractional duration window (80 vs. 38). Figure 3e complements the scatter plot by presenting a histogram of the absolute error. Here, it becomes evident that nearly 70% (59 out of 87) of the predictions fall within a narrow range of 0.25 error, further solidifying the model's ability to deliver precise estimations.

To further assess the model's performance, Figure 4 presents a selection of STFs of seismic events from Figure 3a, incorporating both accurate predictions (Fig. 4a–d) and less successful ones (Fig. 4e–g). As observed in Figure 4a,b, the STFs exhibit varying characteristics—source durations. Despite these differences, the CNN-RNN model predicts their moment magnitudes. Figure 4c,d shows an example of the CNN-RNN model's strength. STF evolution over the first two seconds looks different, but the final moment magnitude is nearly the same. Unlike traditional methods relying on predefined static parameters such as peak amplitude or average acceleration at a fixed time, the CNN-RNN model, especially

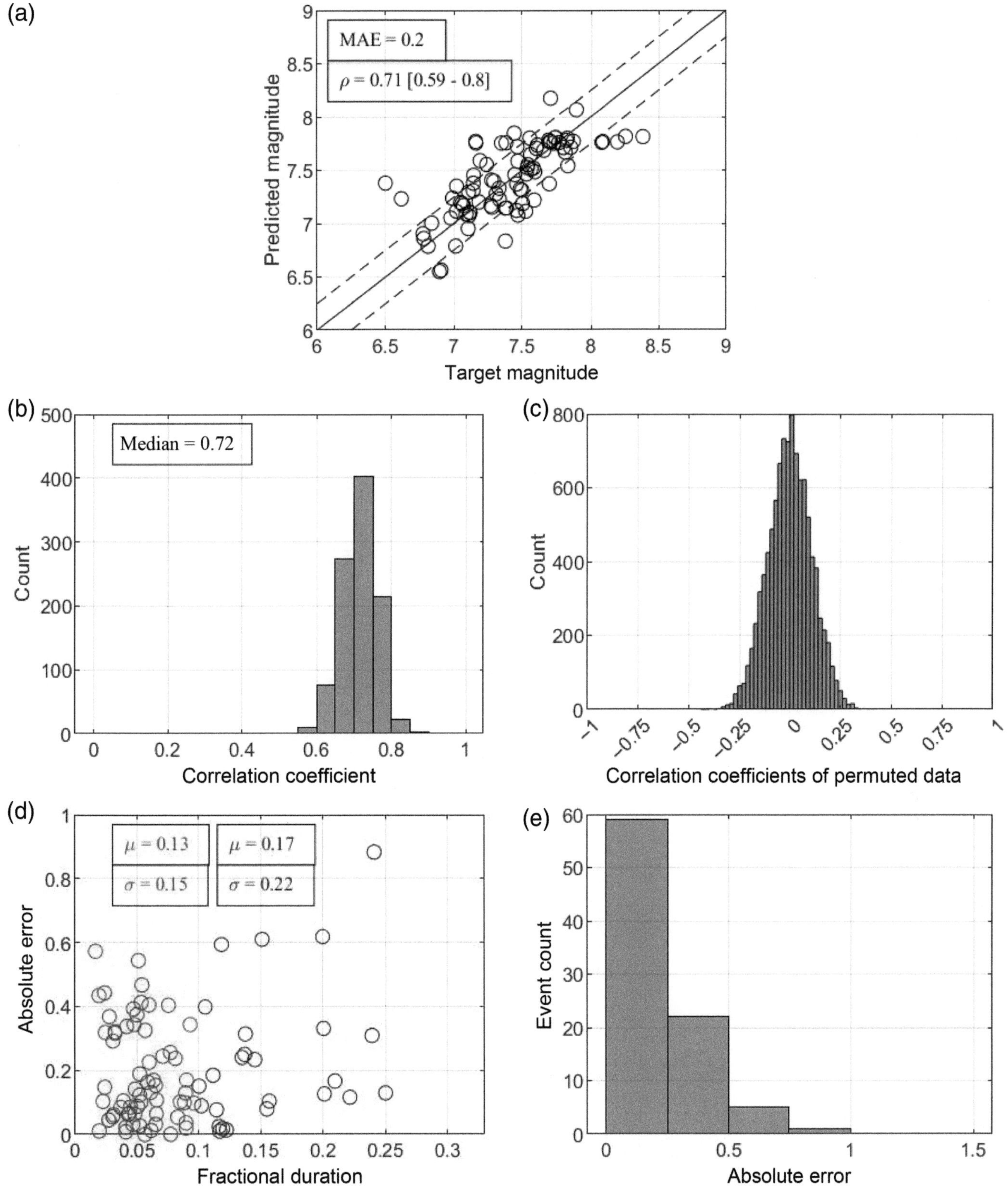

Figure 3. Assessment of the trained convolutional neural network–recurrent neural network (CNN-RNN) model. (a) Comparison between the target and predicted moment magnitudes for the random testing dataset. The ideal equality line ($y = x$) is shown by the black-solid curve, whereas ±0.25 error bounds are represented by the dashed lines; (b) bootstrap correlation coefficients for 1000 iterations; (c) correlation distribution for permuted data using 10,000 iterations; (d) fractional duration against the absolute error; and (e) histogram of the absolute error. One can see that most of the predictions fall within 0.25 error demonstrating the ability of the hybrid CNN-RNN model to learn the STF features. MAE, mean absolute error. The color version of this figure is available only in the electronic edition.

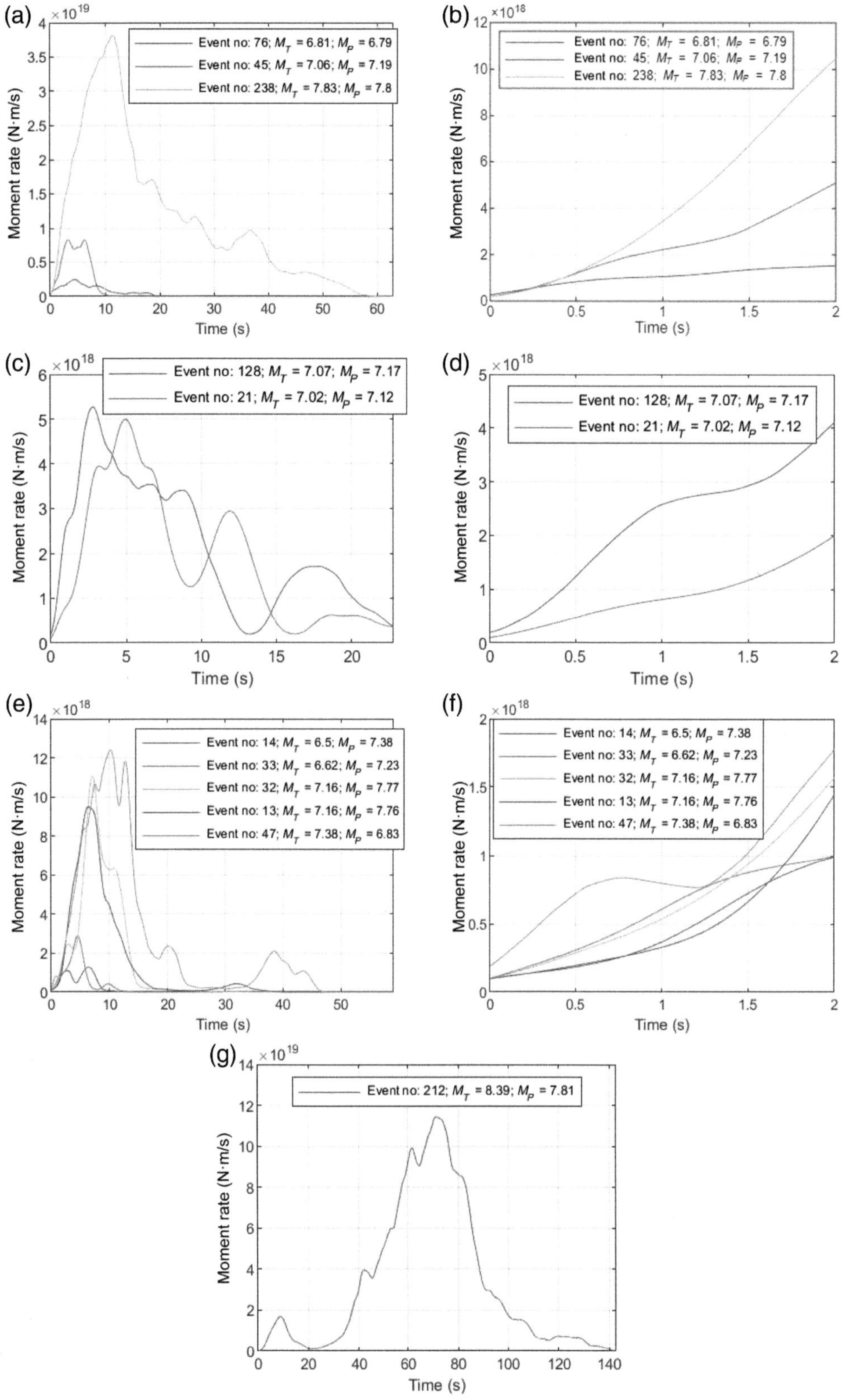

Figure 4. Assessment of the chosen hybrid CNN-RNN model using a few-selected STF samples. (a–d) STFs of the selected seismic events that exhibit strong performance. (e–g) STFs of the selected seismic events that exhibit weak performance. M_T refers to the target moment magnitude, and M_P refers to the predicted moment magnitude. Panels (b,d,f) show a zoomed-in view of the first 2 s of STFs in panels (a,c,e,g). The color version of this figure is available only in the electronic edition.

with its RNN component, is adept at learning these temporal dependencies and higher-order features directly from the sequential input.

Yet, the model's performance has a few limitations, as illustrated by the examples of events with magnitude prediction errors above 0.5 in Figure 4e–f. Particularly, as shown in Figure 4g, for an earthquake involving a more complex rupture with multiple asperities breaking sequentially, the information within the first 2 s is insufficient, with an underprediction of the moment magnitude in cases for which most of the moment release occurs during the break of later asperities. This limitation is inherent to our chosen methodology of using a very short, early time window of the STF. Despite this limitation, our study still demonstrates a statistically significant correlation between the initial 2 s STF segment and the final magnitude for the USGS dataset, at least for a significant portion of the events in this dataset.

Because of limitations discussed earlier (see the Data section), the Ye16 and SCARDEC datasets were excluded from the main analysis of the CNN-RNN model. However, for completeness, the results when these datasets are included in the training are presented in Figures S4 and S5, supporting the earlier results. Figure S4 presents the CNN-RNN model's performance on the combined USGS and Ye16 datasets. One may infer that the model performs similarly on both datasets, with correlation coefficients of 0.67 and 0.68 and MAEs of 0.21 and 0.23 for the USGS and Ye16 datasets, respectively. However, a closer examination reveals that only 50 of the 120 seismic events in the Ye16 dataset are unique (not included in the USGS dataset), and these 50 events correspond to a narrowband of magnitudes (32 events in 7–7.25), heavily influencing the apparent performance metrics of the Ye16 dataset (Fig. S4c). Given their coarse sampling rate and narrow magnitude range, including these STFs in the training of the machine learning algorithm could negatively impact generalization. This highlights the limitations of current publicly available STF datasets for comprehensive magnitude estimation and underscores the need for broader, more unified datasets for future research. Figure S5 shows the model's performance on the combined USGS, Ye16, and SCARDEC datasets, for which events with $M_w < 7$ were excluded from SCARDEC. Although the MAE decreases to 0.18, the correlation coefficient drops to 0.49. This may be attributed to the large number of events in a narrow magnitude range (7–7.5) within the SCARDEC dataset, potentially limiting the model's ability to discern subtle variations and establish stronger correlations.

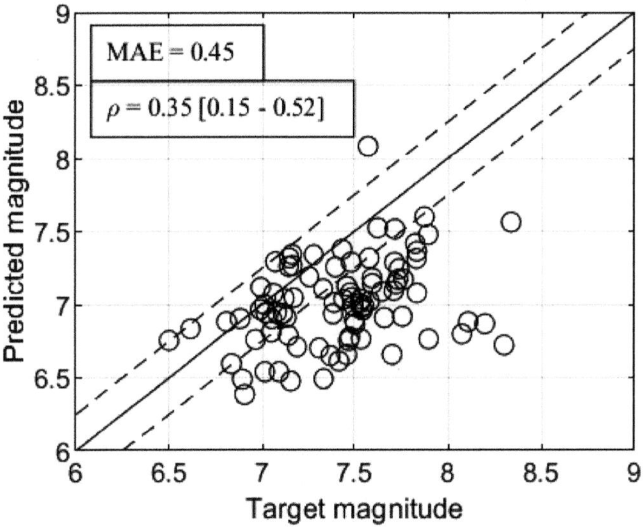

Figure 5. Assessment of machine learning model (artificial neural network model [ANN]) trained with AMA and accumulated seismic moment at 2 s as input.

Discussion

This study investigates a fundamental question in earthquake physics: can the final earthquake magnitude be predicted based on the initial rupture characteristics? Because of the large range of source durations observed in the USGS STF dataset (Fig. 2a), not all events could be assessed for strong predictability, as defined by Meier *et al.* (2021), because they require source durations exceeding 20 s for a 2 s STF observation. For the events exceeding 20 s (62 events, Fig. 3d), the CNN-RNN model exhibits strong performance, with 42 events having magnitude estimates less than 0.25 error and most predictions falling within 0.5 error (Fig. 3e). In events with durations between 6 and 20 s, 1/10–1/3 duration window, the model also performs well, with only 4 out of 25 events exceeding 0.5 error. Overall, nearly 70% (59 out of 87) of the earthquake magnitudes are estimated within 0.25 error and 93% (81 out of 87) are estimated within 0.5 error. Our findings (Fig. 3) suggest that the considered CNN-RNN model can analyze the earthquake's onset characteristics and estimate the final moment magnitude with reasonable accuracy. Strong performance is noted despite the diverse nature of recorded earthquakes.

Based on the SCARDEC STF dataset, Meier *et al.* (2021) explored the possible correlation between the final magnitude and the AMA (at 2, 5, 10, and 20 s) and reported that smaller and larger earthquakes grow similarly and can only be distinguished once the smaller earthquakes reach their peak STF. Münchmeyer *et al.* (2022) analyzed STFs from the USGS, SCARDEC, and Ye16 datasets and explored the use of multilayer neural network models in predicting the moment magnitude using five parameters of the STF at a specific time "*t*": (1) cumulative moment, (2) current moment rate, (3) average moment rate, (4) peak moment rate, and (5) current moment acceleration. The reported results indicate no definitive signs of early rupture predictability, and any such predictability exists only after the peak moment rate.

In line with these findings, our preliminary analysis (see the Data section) also revealed that simple parameters, such as the AMA (Fig. 1b) and accumulated seismic moment (Fig. 1c) at the initial stages of the STF (e.g., at 2 s), do not exhibit a clear and direct relationship with the final earthquake magnitude. Furthermore, these two parameters were given as input to an artificial neural network model (ANN) for training and predicting the final moment magnitude. Results from the optimized network are presented in Figure 5. The ANN architecture comprises four fully connected layers, each incorporating layer normalization, Swish activation, and a 25% dropout layer. A detailed description of this ANN architecture is provided in Table S2. The observed correlation coefficient of 0.35 is only comparable to that noted for the linear regression of AMA and cumulative seismic moments, as presented in Figure 1. The high MAE of 0.45 and the low correlation collectively indicate that relying solely on these basic features is insufficient for accurate magnitude prediction, necessitating more sophisticated approaches.

Although these simple characteristics of the initial stages of the STF do not show a clear relationship with the final magnitude, our results (Fig. 3) suggest that for most events in the USGS dataset, a relationship, although complex, does exist between the initial evolution of the STF and the final magnitude. The present analysis employs machine learning models, such as the CNN-RNN architecture, to analyze the STF characteristics, including their temporal evolution and higher-order derivatives. This approach differs from that of Münchmeyer *et al.* (2022), who used static STF parameters at fixed times and found limited early predictability, with

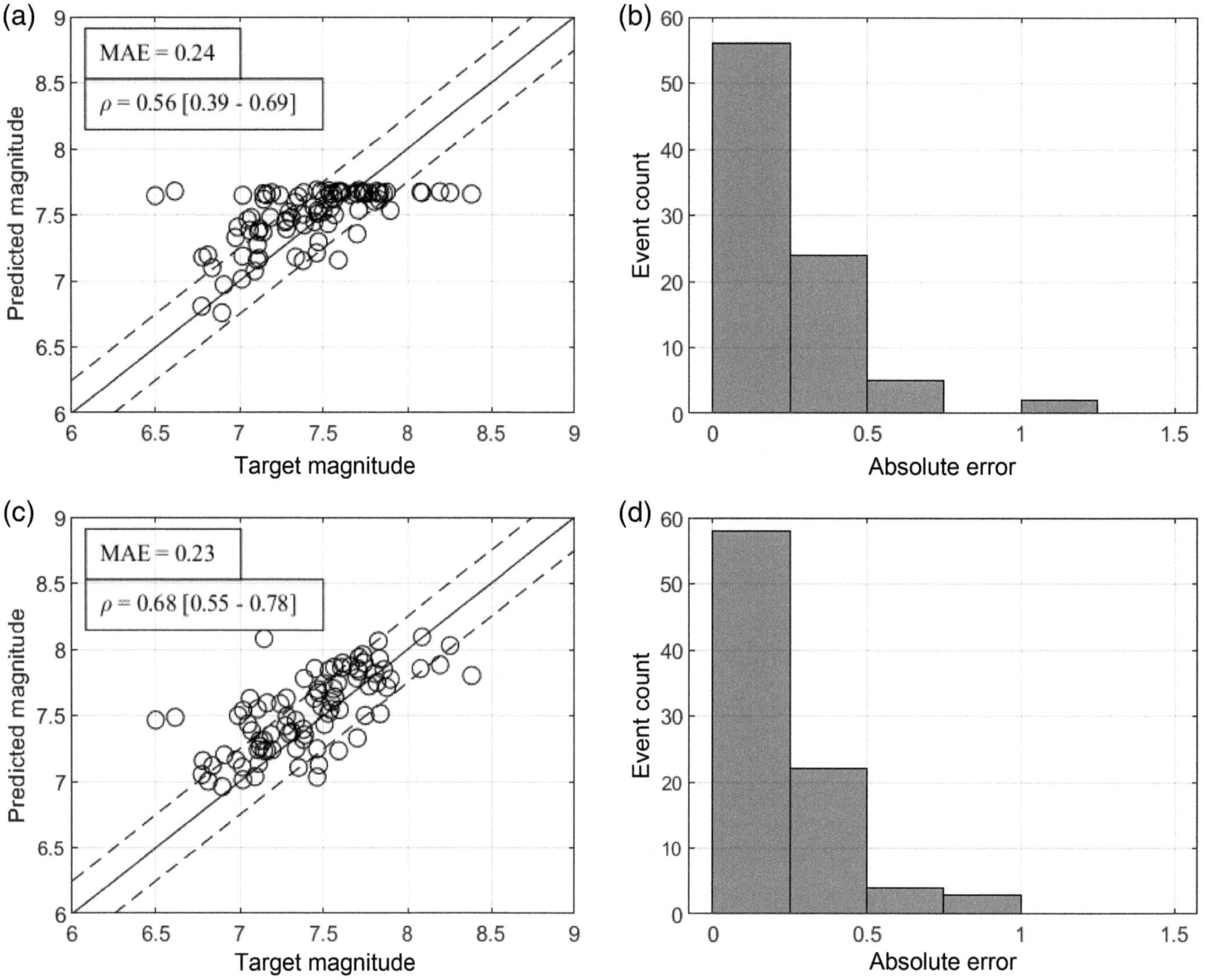

Figure 6. Optimizing STF time window duration. (a,b) Results for the initial 1 s STF window and (c,d) results for the initial 3 s STF window. The color version of this figure is available only in the electronic edition.

reliable magnitude estimation only after the peak moment rate. Specifically, the present methodology uses the temporal evolution of cumulative moment, moment rate, and moment acceleration as input features. These correspond to STF parameters 1, 2, and 5 of Münchmeyer *et al.* (2022), respectively, but are used here as continuous time series rather than static values at a specific time. By processing this richer, time-dependent information, the model learns to identify subtle features within the initial stages of an earthquake that are important for estimating its final magnitude.

To further examine the influence of the STF time-window size on model performance, Figure 6 shows the magnitude prediction of the CNN-RNN model using the initial 1 and 3 s of the STF after retraining with new input sizes. As expected, we observe a gradual decrease in MAE and a corresponding increase in correlation coefficient as the window length is extended from 1 to 3 s. Notably, the improvement in prediction between 1 (Fig. 6a) and 2 s (Fig. 3a) windows is significant, whereas the performance difference between 2 and 3 s windows (Fig. 6c) is minimal, particularly when considering the possible range of random variation in correlation values as indicated by the bootstrapping analysis (Fig. 3b). This suggests that a 2 s STF window is sufficient to capture the relevant initial characteristics for predicting the earthquake's final magnitude using the CNN-RNN model.

The findings of this study hold significant implications for the development of machine learning models. If a robust and timely relationship between early earthquake properties and final magnitude can be established, it suggests that the potential for leveraging machine learning algorithms to analyze the initial *P* wave and infer valuable insights regarding the final earthquake magnitude, before the full STF is available.

The observed correlation between the initial few seconds (~2 s) of the STF and the final moment magnitude suggests that the onset of earthquake rupture may contain fundamental information that scales with its eventual size, at least for events with $M_w \leq 7.8$ in the analyzed dataset. This is not trivial, as such events may ultimately propagate over hundreds of kilometers and last tens to a hundred seconds (Fig. 2a). The model underestimates magnitudes for the largest events ($M_w > 8$) and overestimates the smallest ones ($M_w < 6.6$), as shown in Figure 4. The results are consistent with Allen and Kanamori (2003) and Olson and Allen (2005), who showed that the predominant period of the first few seconds of *P*-wave arrivals scales with final magnitude.

These findings suggest that the rupture front may rapidly organize into a dynamic state that reflects fault conditions and energy availability, which is not well captured by static STF parameters at fixed times, but requires time-dependent information of the evolving rupture dynamics. Meier *et al.* (2021) discussed how differences in early rupture behavior may reflect nucleation processes that scale with magnitude. Melgar and Hayes (2019) suggested that although the first 1–2 s of rupture may appear similar across events, large earthquakes tend to develop a coherent and strong slip pulse for which properties scale with the final magnitude early in the rupture process. The CNN-RNN model appears to capture subtle features even within these early seconds that correlate with final magnitude, suggesting that physical differences may already be present at the onset of rupture, even if not easily observable using traditional methods. This correlation may not reflect a direct causal link, but rather a shared dependence on fault-zone properties or stress conditions that influence whether the rupture will arrest or grow. Three-dimensional numerical simulations of the earthquake cycle, for which fault behavior is explicitly modeled, can help identify the key physical factors that control early rupture evolution and its link to final magnitude.

Although this study offers encouraging results, there are limitations inherent in the USGS dataset used. Source inversion methods often involve regularization techniques, which can introduce acausality into the resulting STFs by employing techniques such as band-pass filtering, assumption of finite duration of rise time, and smoothing over subfaults (Ji, 2002; Hayes, 2017). This means that information from later times in the rupture process can influence the estimated slip at earlier times, potentially leading to spurious correlations. Although steps have been taken to mitigate this issue by carefully selecting and preprocessing the STFs (refer to the Data section for preprocessing and resampling adopted in this study for more details), it is important to recognize that these limitations may still affect the results. Future research could explore alternative data sources, such as raw seismic waveforms, to minimize the impact of acausal effects and improve the accuracy of magnitude forecasting models. Moreover, the limited magnitude range of the datasets might influence the model's generalizability. Including a larger and more diverse set of earthquakes, encompassing a broader magnitude range, could improve the model's ability to analyze the potential relationship between the earthquake rupture onset and final magnitude and predict final magnitude across various earthquake scenarios.

Conclusions

This study employed a hybrid CNN-RNN model to explore the potential relationship between earthquake onset and final moment magnitude by analyzing modeled STF from recorded earthquake (USGS dataset) data.

Although simple parameters, such as the AMA and accumulated seismic moment at the initial stages of the STF (2 s), do not exhibit a clear relationship with the final earthquake magnitude, the CNN-RNN model demonstrates an impressive performance in predicting the final magnitude. For the USGS dataset comprising of 228 field-recorded earthquakes, the model achieves high-correlation coefficients (0.71) and low-MAE values (0.21 magnitude units, for which the most magnitudes lie between 6.75 and 8.25 for the considered random testing dataset). These results showcase the model's ability to learn complex relationships within the STF data and translate them into accurate moment magnitude predictions. Although the limited range of fractional durations in the testing dataset prevents us from definitively establishing a trend between fractional duration and prediction error, the model generally achieves accurate predictions, with most errors falling within a 0.25 margin across various source durations. Strong performance (for fractional duration less than 1/10 as well as fractional duration between 1/10 and 1/3) is observed in most of the earthquakes. The results show a significantly larger gain in performance between 1 and 2 s and a minimal performance difference between 2 and 3 s. This suggests that a 2 s STF window captures a critical set of initial features within the earthquake rupture process that are useful for the model to predict the final magnitude.

Further training with a larger and more diverse dataset is necessary for improving the magnitude prediction capabilities of the CNN-RNN model. Exploring different input representations and model architectures can further improve performance.

Data and Resources

The inverted earthquake source time functions (STFs) were obtained from the publicly available databases (U.S. Geological Survey [USGS] National Earthquake Information Center [NEIC]: https://earthquake.usgs.gov/data/finitefault/, last accessed January 2025); Seismic source ChActeristics Retrieved from DEConvolvolving teleseismic body waves (SCARDEC) STFs database (http://scardec.projects.sismo.ipgp.fr/, last accessed January 2025); and with personal communication from Ye *et al.* (2016). The supplemental material contains a comprehensive flatfile summarizing the USGS events considered in this analysis. Additional details and results associated with the SCARDEC and Ye *et al.* (2016) datasets are also presented in the supplemental material.

Furthermore, the supplemental material includes the three-channel STF input data, the CNN-RNN model structure, and the associated MATLAB programs (www.mathworks.com/products/matlab, last accessed October 2025) and data necessary to fully replicate the results. The optimized weights for the trained model are archived in the Zenodo repository available at https://zenodo.org/records/17256773 (last accessed October 2025).

Declaration of Competing Interests

The authors acknowledge that there are no conflicts of interest recorded.

Acknowledgments

The authors thank Lingling Ye for sharing the source time functions (STFs) of 120 seismic events, which helped in understanding the recorded-earthquake early characteristics. This study was supported by the Israel Science Foundation (ISF) through Contract Number 1887/20.

References

Allen, R. M., and H. Kanamori (2003). The potential for earthquake early warning in southern California, *Science* **300,** no. 5620, 786–789, doi: 10.1126/science.1080912.

Allen, R. M., and D. Melgar (2019). Earthquake early warning: Advances, scientific challenges, and societal needs, *Annu. Rev. Earth Planet. Sci.* **47,** no. 1, 361–388, doi: 10.1146/annurev-earth-053018-060457.

Bonett, D. G., and T. A. Wright (2000). Sample size requirements for estimating Pearson, Kendall and Spearman correlations, *Psychometrika* **65,** no. 1, 23–28, doi: 10.1007/BF02294183.

Cho, K., B. van Merrienboer, D. Bahdanau, and Y. Bengio (2014). On the properties of neural machine translation: Encoder-decoder approaches, doi: 10.48550/arXiv.1409.1259.

Colombelli, S., A. Zollo, G. Festa, and M. Picozzi (2014). Evidence for a difference in rupture initiation between small and large earthquakes, *Nat. Commun.* **5,** no. 1, 3958, doi: 10.1038/ncomms4958.

Danré, P., J. Yin, B. P. Lipovsky, and M. A. Denolle (2019). Earthquakes within earthquakes: Patterns in rupture complexity, *Geophys. Res. Lett.* **46,** no. 13, 7352–7360, doi: 10.1029/2019GL083093.

Ellsworth, W. L., and G. C. Beroza (1995). Seismic evidence for an earthquake nucleation phase, *Science* **268,** no. 5212, 851–855, doi: 10.1126/science.268.5212.851.

Hayes, G. P. (2017). The finite, kinematic rupture properties of great-sized earthquakes since 1990, *Earth Planet. Sci. Lett.* **468,** 94–100, doi: 10.1016/j.epsl.2017.04.003.

Ide, S. (2019). Frequent observations of identical onsets of large and small earthquakes, *Nature* **573,** no. 7772, 112–116, doi: 10.1038/s41586-019-1508-5.

Ioffe, S., and C. Szegedy (2015). Batch normalization: Accelerating deep network training by reducing internal covariate shift, doi: 10.48550/arXiv.1502.03167.

Ji, C. (2002). Source description of the 1999 Hector Mine, California, earthquake, part I: Wavelet domain inversion theory and resolution analysis, *Bull. Seismol. Soc. Am.* **92,** no. 4, 1192–1207, doi: 10.1785/0120000916.

Kilb, D., and J. Gomberg (1999). The initial subevent of the 1994 Northridge, California, earthquake: Is earthquake size predictable? *J. Seismol.* **3,** no. 4, 409–420, doi: 10.1023/A:1009890329925.

Kingma, D. P., and J. Ba (2017). Adam: A method for stochastic optimization, doi: 10.48550/arXiv.1412.6980.

Meier, M., T. Heaton, and J. Clinton (2016). Evidence for universal earthquake rupture initiation behavior, *Geophys. Res. Lett.* **43,** no. 15, 7991–7996, doi: 10.1002/2016GL070081.

Meier, M.-A., J. P. Ampuero, and T. H. Heaton (2017). The hidden simplicity of subduction megathrust earthquakes, *Science* **357,** no. 6357, 1277–1281, doi: 10.1126/science.aan5643.

Meier, M.-A., J.-P. Ampuero, E. Cochran, and M. Page (2021). Apparent earthquake rupture predictability, *Geophys. J. Int.* **225,** no. 1, 657–663, doi: 10.1093/gji/ggaa610.

Melgar, D., and G. P. Hayes (2019). Characterizing large earthquakes before rupture is complete, *Sci. Adv.* **5,** no. 5, eaav2032, doi: 10.1126/sciadv.aav2032.

Minson, S. E., M.-A. Meier, A. S. Baltay, T. C. Hanks, and E. S. Cochran (2018). The limits of earthquake early warning: Timeliness of ground motion estimates, *Sci. Adv.* **4,** no. 3, eaaq0504, doi: 10.1126/sciadv.aaq0504.

Mori, J., and H. Kanamori (1996). Initial rupture of earthquakes in the 1995 Ridgecrest, California sequence, *Geophys. Res. Lett.* **23,** no. 18, 2437–2440, doi: 10.1029/96GL02491.

Münchmeyer, J., U. Leser, and F. Tilmann (2022). A probabilistic view on rupture predictability: All earthquakes evolve similarly, *Geophys. Res. Lett.* **49,** no. 13, e2022GL098344, doi: 10.1029/2022GL098344.

Olson, E. L., and R. M. Allen (2005). The deterministic nature of earthquake rupture, *Nature* **438,** no. 7065, 212–215, doi: 10.1038/nature04214.

Ramachandran, P., B. Zoph, and Q. V. Le (2017). Swish: A self-gated activation function, doi: 10.48550/arXiv.1710.05941.

Trugman, D. T., M. T. Page, S. E. Minson, and E. S. Cochran (2019). Peak ground displacement saturates exactly when expected: Implications for earthquake early warning, *J. Geophys. Res.* **124,** no. 5, 4642–4653, doi: 10.1029/2018JB017093.

Vallée, M., and V. Douet (2016). A new database of source time functions (STFs) extracted from the SCARDEC method, *Phys. Earth Planet. In.* **257,** 149–157, doi: 10.1016/j.pepi.2016.05.012.

Wang, J., Q. Ma, D. Tao, Q. Xie, and X. Ren (2022). Weak predictability of rupture growth evidenced by *P* waves: Implications for earthquake early warning, *Bull. Seismol. Soc. Am.* **112,** no. 5, 2653–2667, doi: 10.1785/0120210316.

Wang, J., Y. Yang, J. Mao, Z. Huang, C. Huang, and W. Xu (2016). CNN-RNN: A unified framework for multi-label image classification, doi: 10.48550/arXiv.1604.04573.

Ye, L., T. Lay, H. Kanamori, and L. Rivera (2016). Rupture characteristics of major and great ($M_w \geq 7.0$) megathrust earthquakes from 1990 to 2015: 1. Source parameter scaling relationships, *J. Geophys. Res.* **121,** no. 2, 826–844, doi: 10.1002/2015JB012426.

Manuscript received 25 April 2024
Published online 5 December 2025

Identifying Vehicle Signals in Continuous Seismic Data Using Unsupervised Machine-Learning Techniques

OPEN ACCESS

Chengping Chai*[1], Omar Marcillo[1], Monica Maceira[1], Ryan Kerekes[1], and Bonnie Canion[2]

Abstract

Seismic sensors deployed near roadways effectively capture ground vibrations generated by passing vehicles. Although both traditional and machine-learning algorithms have been utilized for analyzing such signals, independent validation of detected vehicle events remains limited. We applied two unsupervised machine-learning algorithms, uniform manifold approximation and projection for dimension reduction, and hierarchical density-based spatial clustering of applications with noise, to continuous seismic data collected along a road on the main campus of Oak Ridge National Laboratory. The algorithms identified seven distinct cluster labels across the entire dataset. By comparing these cluster labels with precipitation records from a nearby weather station and image-derived labels from a local camera system, we identified one cluster associated with rainfall and another with vehicle activity. Our algorithms identified a greater number of vehicle-related labels compared to the camera-derived labels because seismic data are unaffected by poor lighting conditions. The arrival times of the newly detected vehicle signals corresponded well with the road's speed limit, supporting our findings. Our algorithm outperformed the short-term average/long-term average method and k-means clustering. Our results suggest that seismic data, when analyzed with machine-learning algorithms, can complement existing vehicle monitoring systems, particularly under challenging environmental conditions.

Cite this article as Chai, C., O. Marcillo, M. Maceira, R. Kerekes, and B. Canion (2025). Identifying Vehicle Signals in Continuous Seismic Data Using Unsupervised Machine-Learning Techniques, *Seismol. Res. Lett.* **97**, 1893–1904, doi: 10.1785/0220250202.

Supplemental Material

Introduction

Continuous ground motions recorded by seismic sensors arise from a wide range of sources, including earthquakes, ocean noise, wildlife, and anthropogenic activities (e.g., Denolle and Nissen-Meyer, 2020). Seismic deployments in urban settings provide a unique opportunity to leverage seismic data for the study of anthropogenic activities. Distinct seismic signatures are produced by trains, low-flying aircrafts, and automobiles, enabling their potential use in traffic monitoring (Riahi and Gerstoft, 2015). In addition, mechanical vibrations originating from industrial facilities provide valuable seismic data that allow for the investigation of operational activities (Marcillo *et al.*, 2020; Guenaga *et al.*, 2021; Chai *et al.*, 2022, 2023). However, the diverse nature of these anthropogenic activities results in seismic signals with highly variable characteristics, complicating the detection and identification of anthropogenic seismic signals within continuous data streams. Recent advances in machine learning have significantly enhanced our ability to analyze complex seismic datasets (Arrowsmith *et al.*, 2022; Mousavi and Beroza, 2022). For example, Zhu and Beroza (2019) trained a convolutional neural network for picking signal arrival times, significantly increasing the number of detected seismic events from continuous seismic data (Liu *et al.*, 2020). Saad *et al.* (2021) developed a variational autoencoder in conjunction with a squeeze-and-excitation network to suppress background noise, resulting in more accurate seismic event source localization.

Machine-learning techniques have increasingly been applied to identify signal clusters in continuous seismic data. For example, Seydoux *et al.* (2020) integrated a deep scattering network with a Gaussian mixture model to identify nine signal clusters from a single-seismic station in Greenland near a landslide.

1. Oak Ridge National Laboratory, Oak Ridge, Tennessee, U.S.A., https://orcid.org/0000-0002-6792-6014 (CC); https://orcid.org/0000-0003-1248-2185 (MM); https://orcid.org/0000-0001-7199-811X (RK); 2. Lawrence Livermore National Laboratory, Livermore, California, U.S.A., https://orcid.org/0000-0002-5913-6362 (BC)

*Corresponding author: chaic@ornl.gov

Figure 1. A satellite image depicting the geographical locations of the seismic stations used in this study. The inset map highlights the overall study area. The color version of this figure is available only in the electronic edition.

Johnson *et al.* (2020) utilized hand-engineered features derived from seismic waveforms along with k-means clustering to delineate five signal clusters using data from a dense seismic network near the San Jacinto fault. Snover *et al.* (2020) implemented an autoencoder model in conjunction with deep embedded clustering to uncover five distinct signal groups from continuous data from a dense seismic array in Long Beach, California. Jenkins II *et al.* (2021) applied a similar deep embedded clustering technique to continuous data from the Ross Ice Shelf in Antarctica, identifying eight signal clusters. Steinmann *et al.* (2022) used wavelet transforms, deep scattering spectrum analysis, and hierarchical clustering to extract four primary clusters from data recorded in Türkiye. More recent work by Chai, Marcillo, *et al.* (2025) showcased the integration of uniform manifold approximation and projection for dimension reduction (UMAP, McInnes *et al.*, 2020) and hierarchical density-based spatial clustering of applications with noise (HDBSCAN, McInnes and Healy, 2017) to identify 11 signal clusters from continuous seismic data collected at an industrial site in Texas. Despite the successes of these studies in identifying distinct signal clusters, the validation of the resulting clusters against independent measurements has not been rigorously conducted.

To assess the effectiveness of unsupervised machine learning for signal classification, we deployed three seismic stations near a camera system at the main campus of the Oak Ridge National Laboratory (ORNL) in Oak Ridge, Tennessee, United States. Applying the methodology of Chai, Marcillo, *et al.* (2025), we employed UMAP and HDBSCAN algorithms to process the continuous seismic data acquired by these stations. The resulting signal clusters were compared against precipitation records and labels obtained from the collocated camera system to assess their correspondence with observable environmental and anthropogenic events.

Data

We analyzed continuous seismic data collected from three nodal-type seismic stations deployed along a roadway at the main campus of ORNL between 29 March 2023 and 18 April 2023 (Fig. 1). These seismic stations were deployed near a camera system, for which event labels were used to validate the results derived from the seismic data. As illustrated in Figure 2, these camera-based labels correspond well with the observed seismic waveforms. The seismic stations, designated S1, S2, and S3, were spaced approximately 15 m apart, resulting in a noticeable time delay between seismic signal arrivals across the linear array (Fig. 2). A three-

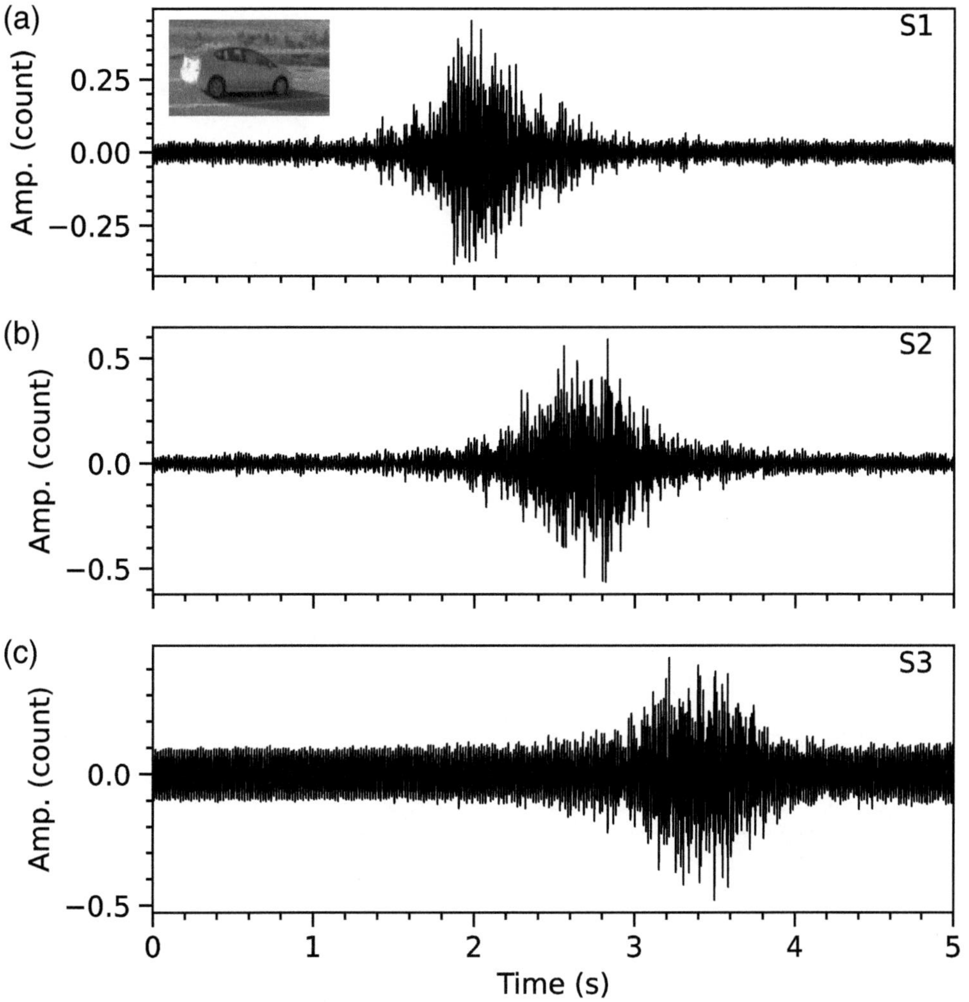

Figure 2. Example vertical-component seismograms from stations (a) S1, (b) S2, and (c) S3. The inset in panel (a) features a photograph of the vehicle associated with the seismograms recorded. The color version of this figure is available only in the electronic edition.

component GS-ONE 4.5 Hz geophone was installed at each station location with a sampling rate of 1000 Hz. The instrument response was not removed because the techniques employed do not require absolute amplitude information of ground motion. Applying the methodology of Chai, Marcillo, *et al.* (2025), we process data from each station independently to account for the significant interstation time delays of signals originating from the same source. The continuous seismic data streams were segmented into 10 s time windows without overlap. The spectra for each component were computed using the Fourier transform after applying a Hanning window. We then concatenated the spectra from three components to create input vectors for the machine-learning algorithms. Each station produced approximately 174,000 input vectors for analysis.

Methodology

Applying the methodology developed by Chai, Marcillo, *et al.* (2025), our study utilized two unsupervised machine-learning algorithms, UMAP and HDBSCAN, to analyze the input vectors derived from the continuous seismic data. The UMAP algorithm was used to reduce the dimensionality of these input vectors, whereas the HDBSCAN algorithm enabled the automatic assignment of signal labels based on the low-dimensional representation produced by UMAP. In contrast to Chai, Marcillo, *et al.* (2025), our analysis examined four different frequency bands: 1–200, 200–400, 400–600, and 600–900 Hz. UMAP was applied separately to the spectra within each frequency band, and HDBSCAN was then used to cluster the resulting 2D representations. The UMAP algorithm provides users with the flexibility to adjust various parameters, including the number of nearest neighbors considered for embedding and minimum distance allowed between points. For our analysis, the number of nearest neighbors was set to 30, a relatively small value that produced results comparable to those obtained with larger values (Fig. S1, available in the supplemental material to this article). The minimum distance between the neighbors was set to 0. Similarly, the HDBSCAN algorithm relies on key parameters such as the smallest cluster size and the smallest number of neighbors required to define a core point. HDBSCAN was configured with a minimum cluster size of 1000 and a minimum number of neighbors of 300, resulting in well-preserved major clusters and a relatively small total number of clusters (Figs. S2 and S3). Increasing the minimum cluster size reduced the overall number of clusters, whereas decreasing it yielded a greater number of clusters.

Results

The 2D UMAP representations of the input vectors revealed noticeable differences across the four frequency bands analyzed (Fig. 3). In the 1–200 Hz band, we visually identified two prominent signal groups, each exhibiting distinct internal structure. As the frequency band increased, the embeddings showed less variations (Fig. 3b–d). Specifically, the 200–400 Hz

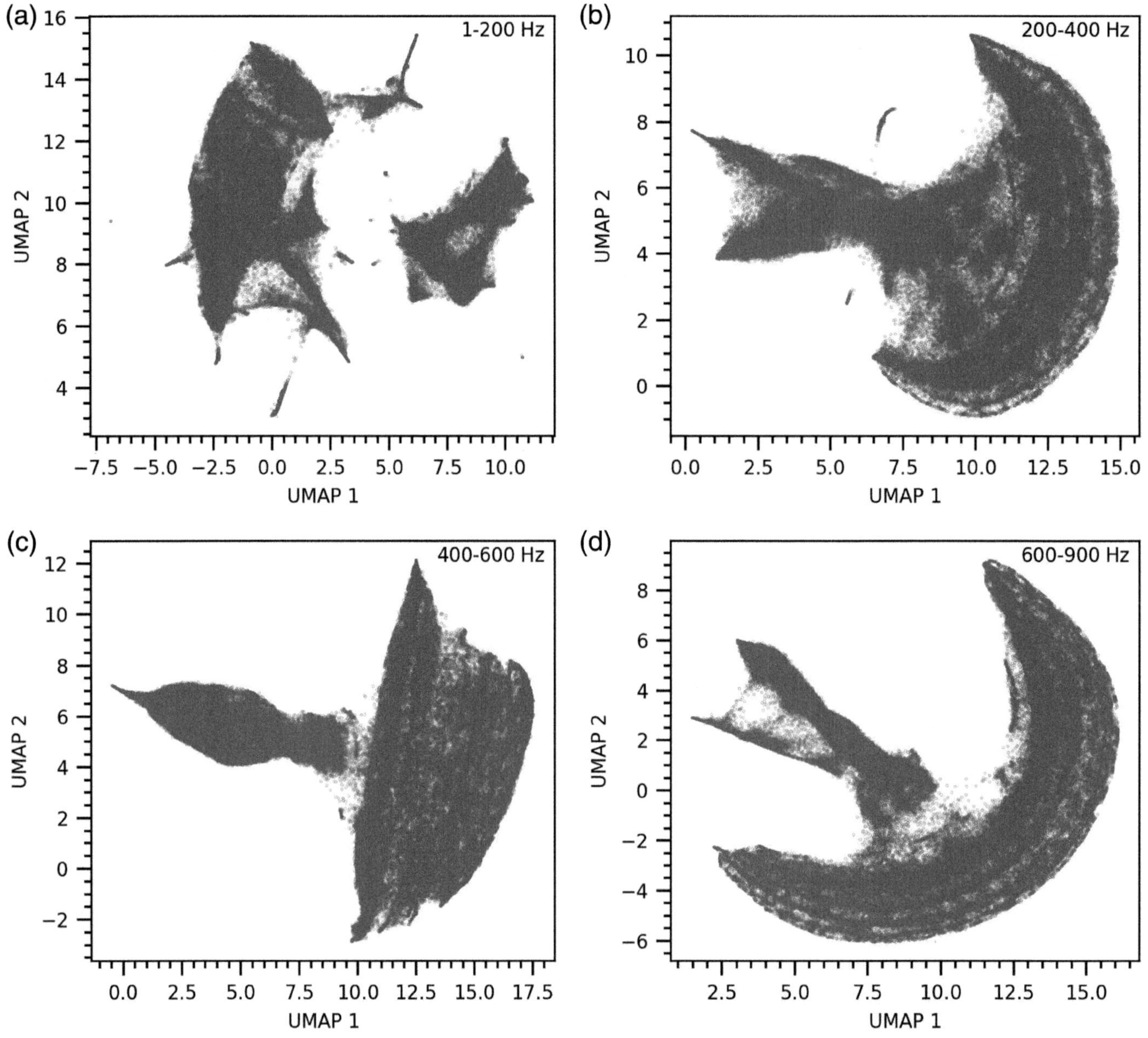

Figure 3. Two-dimensional representations of continuous seismic data generated using uniform manifold approximation and projection for dimension reduction (UMAP) for station S1, displayed across four frequency ranges: (a) 1–200, (b) 200–400, (c) 400–600, and (d) 600–900 Hz. Each dot in the figure corresponds to the power spectral density derived from a 10-s-long three-component seismic waveform.

band showed a single-dominant signal group, whereas the 400–600 and the 600–900 Hz bands each exhibited two major signal groups within their respective embeddings.

HDBSCAN algorithm identified seven distinct signal clusters (A1–A6) from data collected at station S1 (Fig. 4). Signals not assigned to any of these were grouped into a residual cluster labeled A7. The distribution of input vectors within each cluster was as follows: A1 accounted for 53.4%, A2 for 33.4%, A3 for 7.8%, A4 for 3.0%, A5 for 1.1%, A6 for 0.8%, and A7 for 0.5%. Analysis of the temporal distributions of these clusters provided insight into the likely seismic sources associated with each (Figs. 4b–g and 5). For instance, cluster A2 was predominantly active during working hours on weekdays, suggesting a strong correlation with vehicle traffic. In contrast, cluster A1 showed higher occurrence rates during nighttime and weekends, indicating that it may correspond to background noise. The reduced occurrences of cluster A1 during working hours likely reflects the increased dominance of signals from cluster A2. Because each time window is assigned a unique cluster label and the total number of time windows is fixed, a higher number of labels for one cluster naturally result in fewer labels being available for the other clusters.

To validate our clustering results and further interpret their source characteristics, we randomly selected three time windows per cluster for manual inspection (Fig. 6 and Fig. S4). As expected, seismograms and spectra within individual clusters

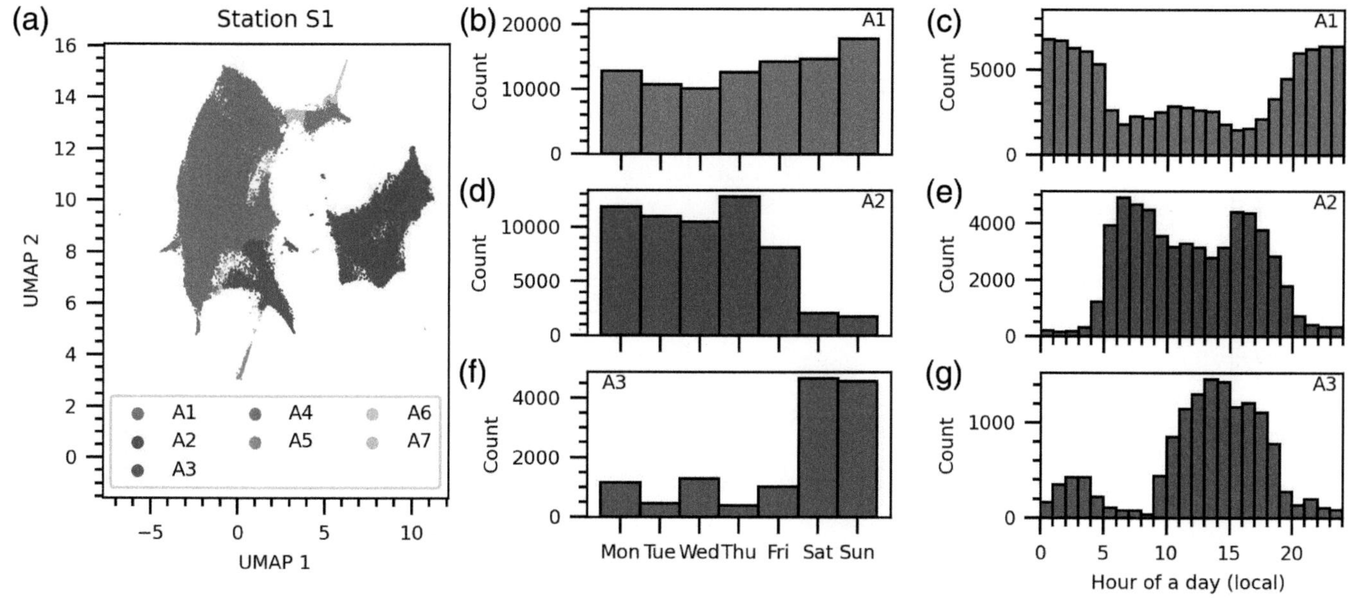

Figure 4. Signal clusters produced by hierarchical density-based spatial clustering of applications with noise (HDBSCAN) for station S1. (a) A color-coded 2D UMAP representation of the continuous seismic data, with each color denoting a different cluster. Cluster A7 contains signals that were not assigned to any cluster due to insufficient neighboring points. Panels (b,d,f) show the temporal distribution of clusters A1, A2, and A3 across each day of the week, respectively. Panels (c,e,g) present the count of signals from clusters A1, A2, and A3 for every hour of the day, respectively. The color version of this figure is available only in the electronic edition.

exhibited similar patterns, whereas those from distinct clusters displayed noticeable differences. The randomly selected seismograms from cluster A1 did not reveal any noticeable patterns (Fig. 6a), and its average spectral power was uniformly lower across the 1–200 Hz range compared to the overall dataset (Fig. 6b). In contrast, as illustrated in Figure 6c, seismograms from cluster A2 contained transient signals similar to these shown in Figure 2, and their average spectra showed higher power levels than the overall average (Fig. 6d), reinforcing the interpretation of cluster A1 as background noise and cluster A2 as vehicle-related signals. The average spectra for clusters A3 and A4 (Fig. 6f,h) exhibited higher power than the background noise (A1) but lower power than the vehicle signals (A2). We suspect that these three clusters represent slightly noisy background. Cluster A4 was characterized by very short duration, irregular impulsive signals (Fig. 6g).

Discussion

Lower dimensional representations (latent variables) of seismic data derived from other methods have demonstrated correlations with various physical features. For instance, Hu *et al.* (2024) observed that the clustering results could be reorganized based on peak frequency, frequency dominance, and temporal concentration. Similarly, Ma *et al.* (2022) reported that latent variables showed strong correlations with earthquake magnitude and corner frequency. However, in our analysis, the spectral domain was dominated by 60 Hz noise, which obscured such relationships. Consequently, our clusters (Figs. 6, 7 and Fig. S4) did not exhibit a clear correlation between latent variables and peak frequency.

To identify the sources of seismic signals, we compared the machine-learning-derived cluster labels with independent external observations. By color coding one day of continuous seismic data using these cluster labels, we discovered a strong temporal correlation between instances of cluster A4 and rainfall events. This alignment was confirmed by comparing the seismic data and cluster labels with precipitation records from a nearby weather station, suggesting that cluster A4 is likely associated with rainfall (Fig. 8). Notably, instances of cluster A2 were also detected during periods of rainfall, even when the seismograms were primarily dominated by rain-induced signals. The available precipitation records, sampled hourly, were used to estimate seismic data derived labels based on a majority vote within each hour. Among the 10 hr with precipitation rates exceeding 0.1 cm/hr, seismic data derived labels correctly identified 6 hr. Of the four misidentified hours, two were mistakenly labeled as vehicle activity (A2) due to a high prevalence of vehicle-related detections during these periods. The other two were classified as background noise (A1) because rain-related labels accounted for less than half of the detections in each hour. For dry periods (precipitation rate less than 0.1 cm/hr), the seismic data derived labels achieved an accuracy of 98.7%.

We further validated the cluster labels using image-derived labels from a collocated camera system. As illustrated in Figure 9, seismic signals in cluster A2 corresponded closely with the camera labels, which serve as an independent proxy for vehicle activity. However, camera labels were unavailable between 01:00 and 11:00 (UTC) due to poor lighting

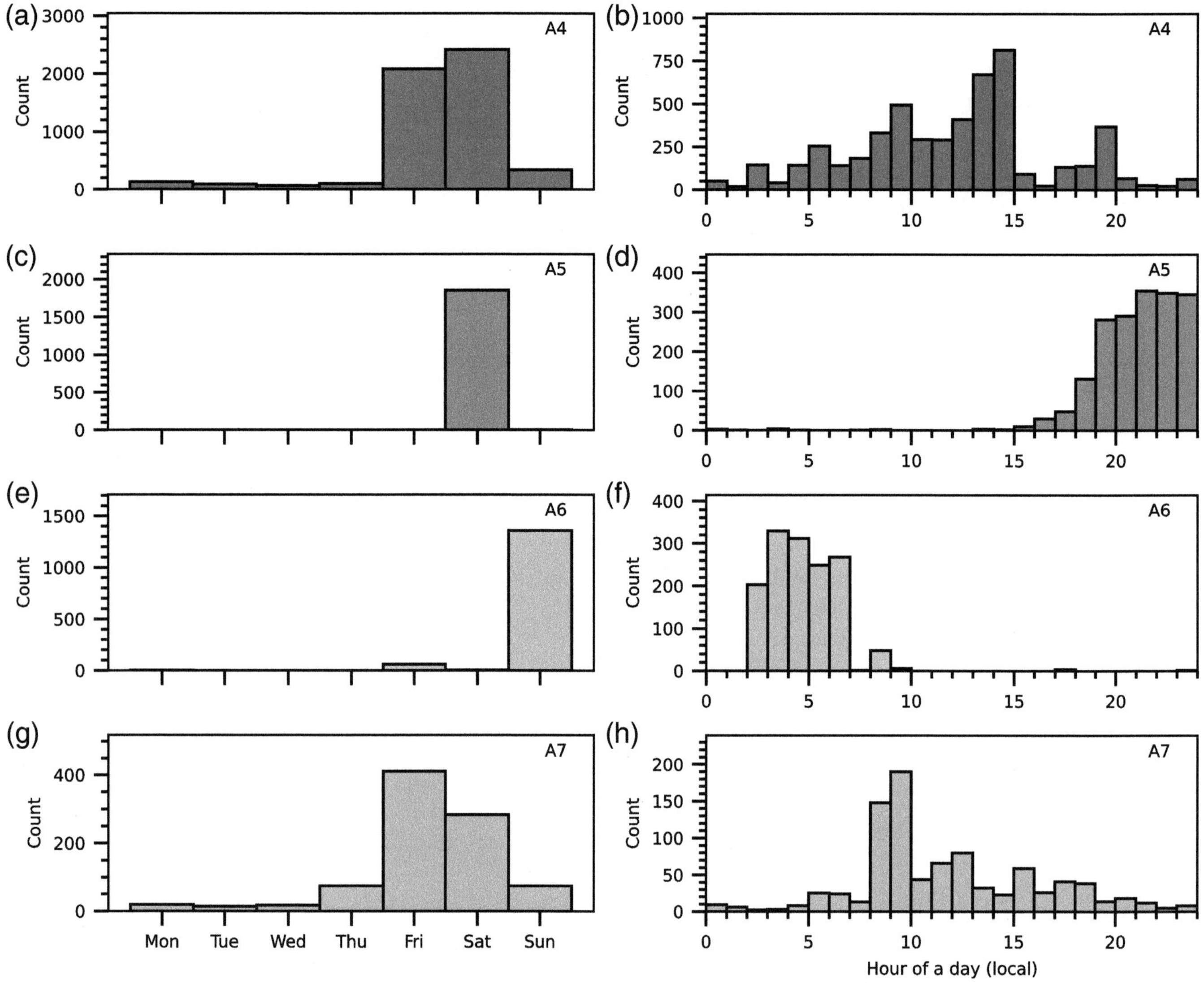

Figure 5. Temporal distribution of signal clusters A4–A7. Panels (a,c,e,g) display the daily signal counts for clusters A4, A5, A6, and A7, respectively. Panels (b,d,f,h) illustrate the hourly signal counts for these same clusters. The color version of this figure is available only in the electronic edition.

conditions. After 11:00 (UTC), we observed more instances of cluster A2 than corresponding camera labels, which we cannot validate as the camera system did not retain all video footage for postprocessing. To provide additional support for our interpretation, we selected four time windows (W1–4) that corresponded to cluster A2 and examined the waveforms from all three seismic stations (Fig. 10). Time windows W1, W2, and W4 lacked associated camera labels, whereas time window W3 included a camera label. In all cases, our analysis revealed that the recorded seismic waveforms agree with the expected arrival times based on the known speed limit of the road. These findings reinforce the conclusion that instances in cluster A2 are linked to vehicle movements.

The performance of the proposed method was compared with two alternative approaches: the short-term average/long-term average (STA/LTA) method (Allen, 1978) and k-means clustering. Because continuous camera-derived labels were not available, performance was evaluated only on time segments associated with existing camera labels. All 269 camera labels collected over one day were used for evaluation. For the STA/LTA method, the same parameters from Chai, Marcillo, *et al.* (2025) were applied. Because the STA/LTA method does not distinguish detected signals, we assume all the STA/LTA detections from our data were related to vehicle signals. The STA/LTA detections aligned reasonably well with vertical-component waveforms (Fig. S5). For k-means clustering, three-component spectra within the frequency band of 1–200 Hz served as input features. Clustering was performed using both six and two clusters. The six-cluster configuration was chosen to align with the UMAP and HDBSCAN method, treating five of the resulting six clusters as vehicle-related labels (Fig. S6). Conversely, the two-cluster configuration was used to simplify the problem, as the primary objective was distinguishing between vehicle-related labels and background noise

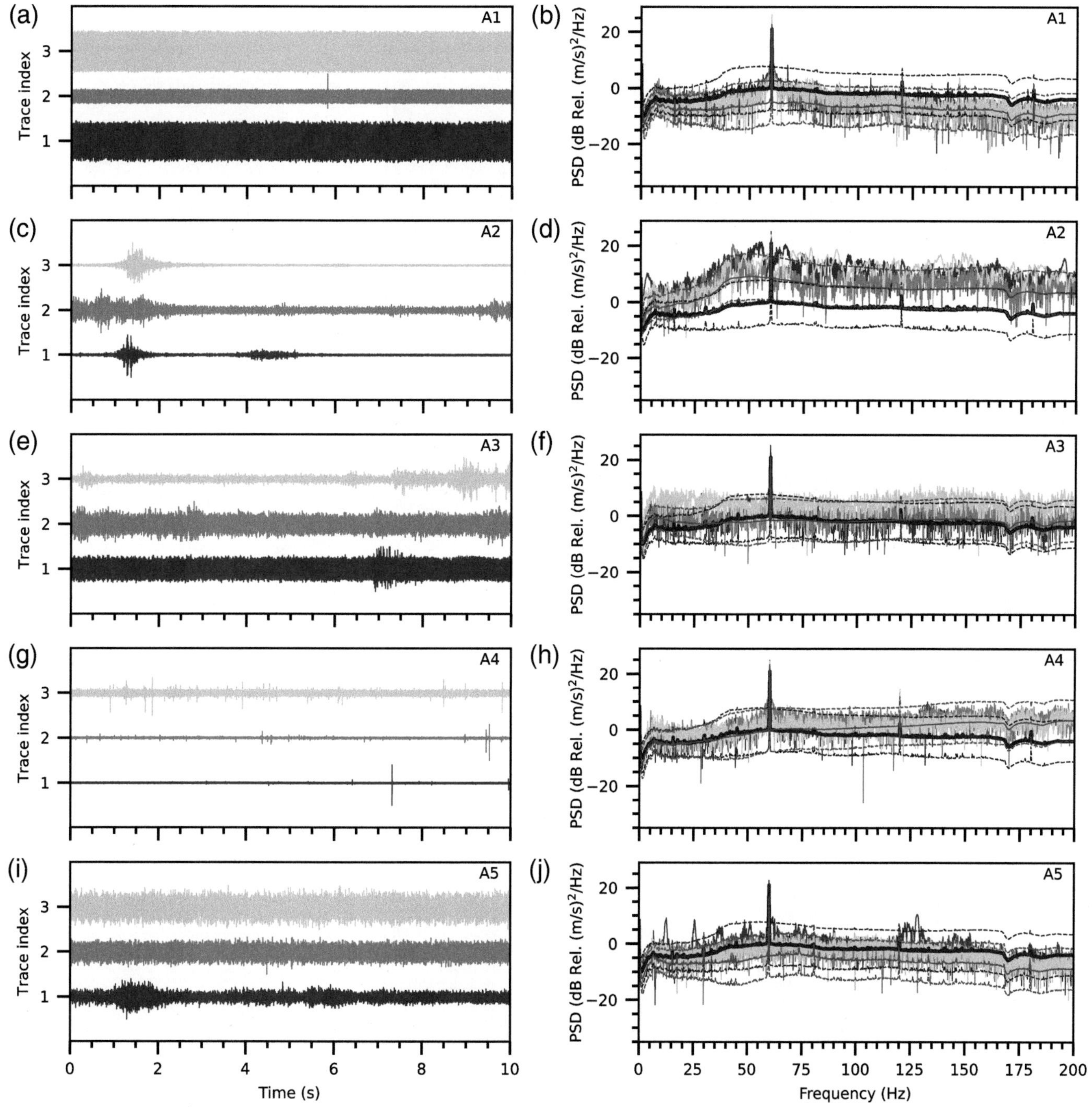

(Fig. S7). In addition, we combined the clustering results of UMAP and HDBSCAN across data from three stations to further enhance performance. The label accuracy was calculated as the ratio of correctly labeled time segments to the total number of camera labels. The resulting accuracies associated with camera-derived vehicle labels were 19.7% for k-means with two clusters, 52.4% for k-means with six clusters, 65.3% for STA/LTA, 95.5% for UMAP and HDBSCAN using data from a single station, and 97.4% for UMAP and HDBSCAN using data from three stations. Future efforts to collect continuous camera-derived labels will enable a more comprehensive performance evaluation including detailed analyses of misclassification rates.

Figure 6. (a,c,e,g,i) Randomly selected vertical-component waveform examples and (b,d,f,h,j) their corresponding spectra for clusters A1–A5 based on seismic recordings collected from station S1. Each left panel displays three waveform segments representing different time windows associated with a specific cluster. Waveform amplitudes were normalized with the maximum value. The blue curve depicts the average spectrum for the entire dataset, whereas the red curve represents the average spectrum for each individual cluster. Dashed curves show the range of one standard deviation. PSD stands for power spectral density. The color version of this figure is available only in the electronic edition.

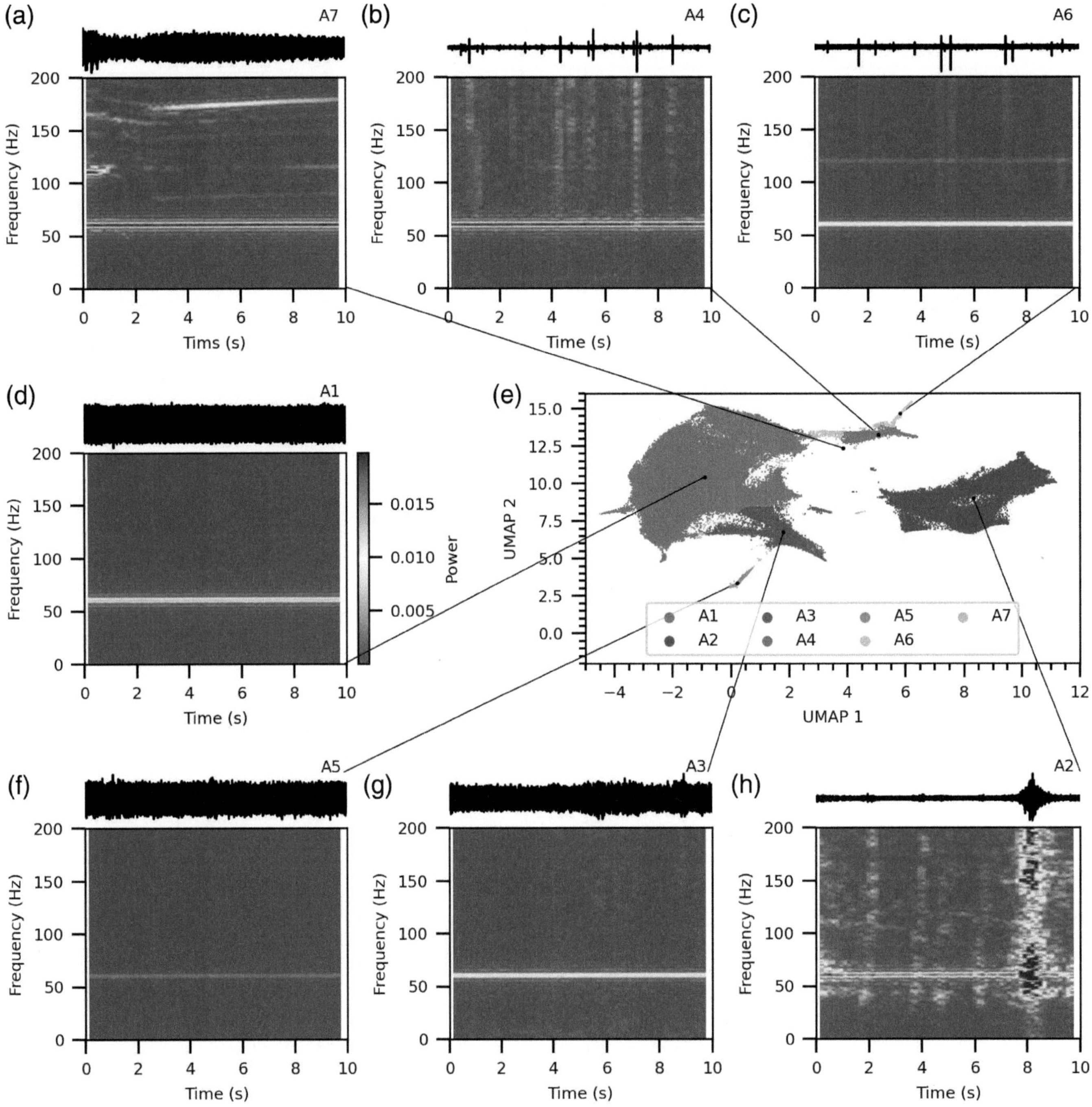

By comparing image-derived vehicle labels against the 2D representations of continuous seismic data computed across various frequency ranges, we observed that vehicle-related vectors were more distinctly separated from other vectors in the 1–200 Hz frequency band (Fig. S8). In contrast, at other frequency bands, the boundaries between vehicle-related vectors and other input vectors were less distinct, often appearing blurred or exhibiting significant overlap. While applying HDBSCAN to the 2D representations at these other frequency bands could still identify vehicle-related signals, the results were accompanied by a higher rate of misclassifications.

Figure 7. Representative vertical-component waveforms and their spectrograms for each cluster using data from station S1. Panels (a–d) and (f–h) correspond to cluster A7, A4, A6, A1, A5, A3, and A2, respectively. Panel (e) shows the signal clusters in the 2D representation with black dots indicate the location for samples used in panels (a–d) and (f–h). The waveform sample that was closest to the center of each cluster in the 2D representation was selected to represent the cluster. The color version of this figure is available only in the electronic edition.

Vehicle speed can be estimated using seismic signals recorded at multiple stations. Given the fixed distances between stations, estimating vehicle speed requires measuring the arrival-time differences of signals at these stations. However, variations in seismic signals across stations prevent cross-correlation

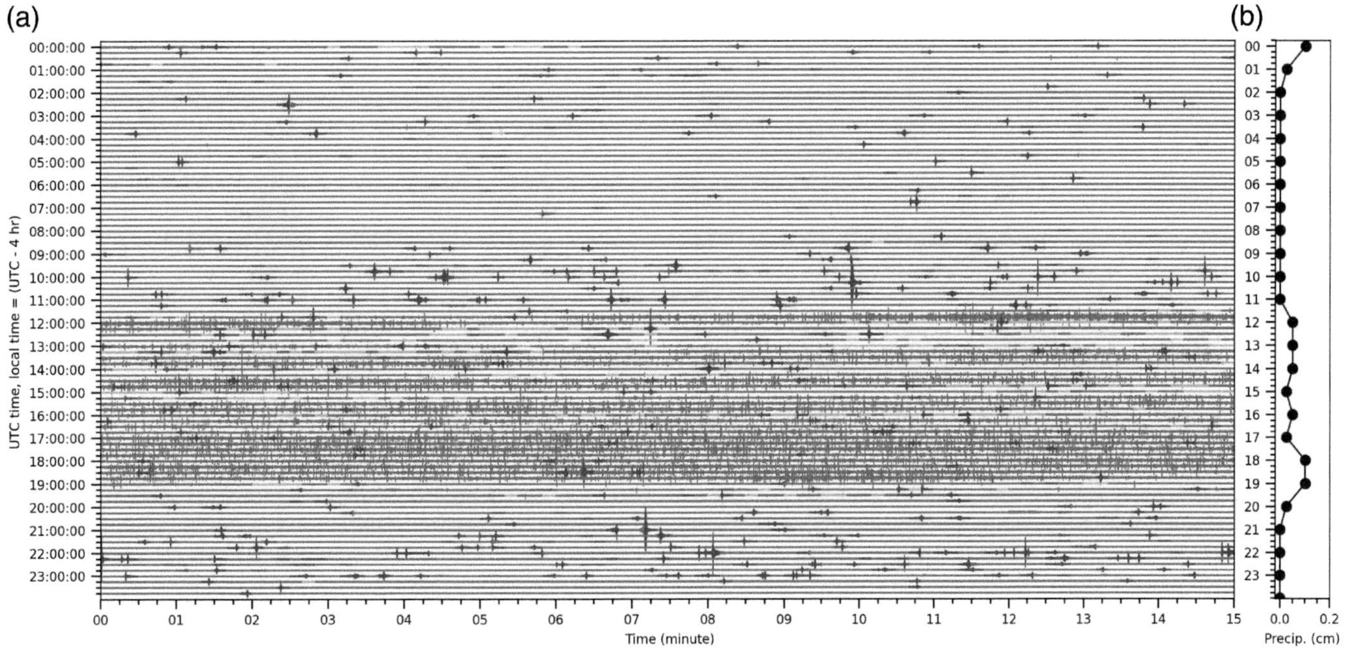

Figure 8. A comparison of seismic and precipitation data for station S1. Panel (a) presents a one-day record of continuous vertical-component seismic data, color coded according to cluster labels consistent with colors used in Figure 4a. Panel (b) displays precipitation (precip.) data from a nearby weather station. The color version of this figure is available only in the electronic edition.

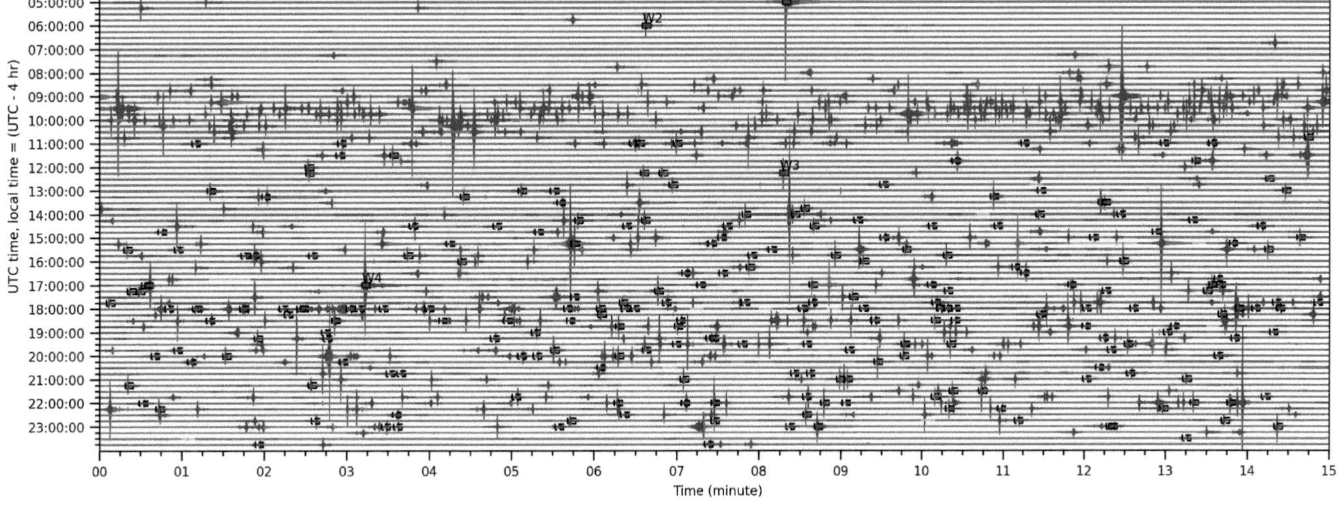

Figure 9. A comparison of one-day continuous vertical-component seismic data and camera labels for station S1. The seismic data was color coded with cluster labels consistent with colors used in Figure 4a. Black symbols represent camera labels. Blue boxes highlight the time windows selected for analysis in this figure. The color version of this figure is available only in the electronic edition.

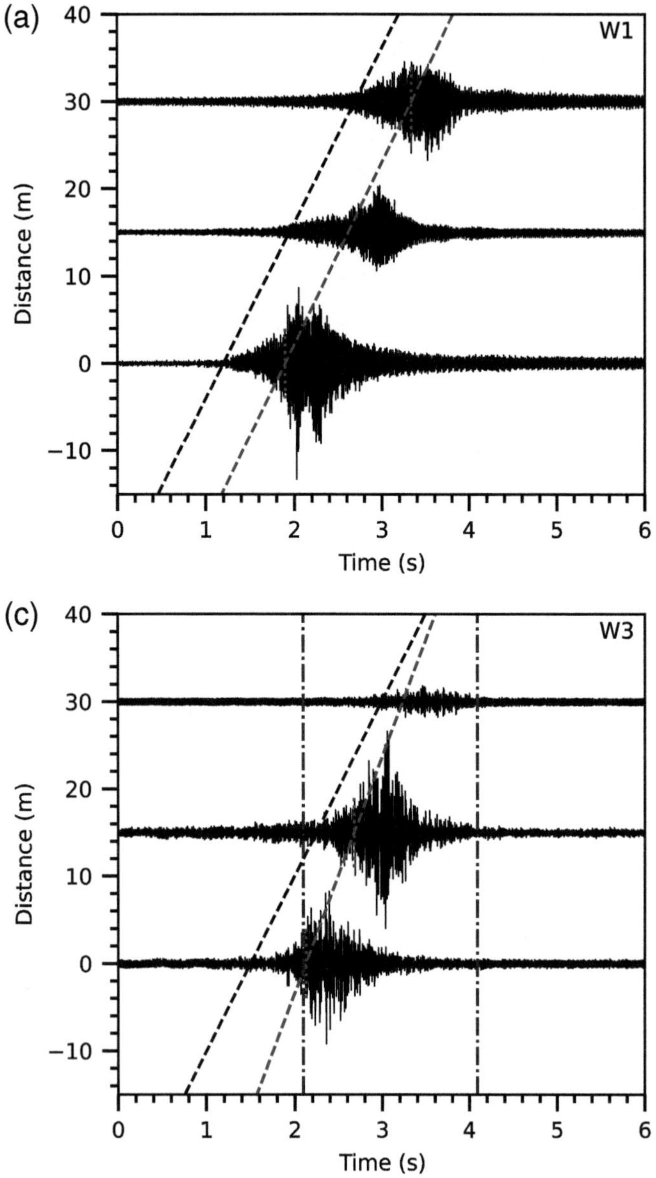

methods for determining arrival times difference reliably. To address this, we applied a deep learning model for picking signal arrival times (Chai, Rose, *et al.*, 2025) to the three-component seismograms used in Figure 10. Although the deep learning model was originally trained to analyze earthquake signals, it successfully identified signal arrival times for many waveforms automatically. The vehicle speed estimated using the deep learning model (slope of the red-dashed line in Fig. 10) matched the speed derived from manual estimation (slope of the black-dashed line in Fig. 10), showing first-order agreement. However, the deep learning model was unable to extract signal arrival times for many other vehicle-related waveforms. This limitation highlights the potential for improvement through transfer learning techniques (e.g., Chai *et al.*, 2020), which could adapt the model to better handle vehicle-related seismic signals.

Figure 10. Vertical-component seismic records from three seismic stations (S1–S3) for (a–d) four selected time windows (W1–W4). Refer to Figure 8 for the absolute times of these time windows. The blue-dashed lines indicate the corresponding camera label when available. W1, W2, and W4 lack associated camera labels. The black-dashed line shows the expected arrival time based on the vehicle speed limit for the road. The red-dotted lines show the signal arrival times measured from a deep learning model when available. The red-dashed line indicates a linear fit of the measured signal arrival times when possible. The color version of this figure is available only in the electronic edition.

Both UMAP and HDBSCAN can be leveraged to analyze new seismic data after being trained with continuous data for vehicle monitoring. Once trained, the UMAP model can project new seismic waveforms into the 2D space, providing a compact representation of the data. This 2D representation can then be passed through the pretrained HDBSCAN model to assign cluster labels, enabling the identification of vehicle-related events in the new data. Alternatively, a streamlined approach that may enhance model performance involves training a deep learning model using supervised learning techniques (e.g., Cui *et al.*, 2024). Such models can directly map seismic waveforms to labels, reducing the reliance on intermediate steps and potentially increasing prediction accuracy and efficiency.

Summary

Two unsupervised machine-learning algorithms, UMAP and HDBSCAN, were utilized to investigate continuous seismic data gathered from three stations positioned along a road at the main campus of ORNL. Using spectra of segmented seismic data as input, we generated cluster labels that revealed distinct signal patterns. At station S1, seven clusters (A1–A7) were identified, each exhibiting unique temporal distributions. Based on further analysis, we infer that cluster A1 is associated with background noise, cluster A2 is linked to vehicle activity, and cluster A4 corresponds to rainfall events. Our comparison with precipitation data from a nearby weather station confirmed that instances of cluster A4 predominantly occurred when the precipitation rate exceeded zero. Comparison with image-derived labels from a collocated camera system showed strong agreement for cluster A2, although seismic data captured more instances of vehicle activity than the camera system, likely due to limited video retention. Furthermore, the arrival times of newly detected vehicle signals in the seismic data were consistent with the local speed limits. The proposed method demonstrated superior accuracy in identifying vehicle-related signals compared to both the STA/LTA method and k-means clustering. Our results demonstrate the potential of seismic data, enhanced through unsupervised learning, to complement existing monitoring systems for vehicle detection.

Data and Resources

Waveform data used in this study are available by request only. An External Computer Access Management System (XCAMS) account and formal request must be made to gain access to waveform data through the Oak Ridge National Laboratory's (ORNL) XCAMS website (https://xcams.ornl.gov/xcams/, last accessed June 2025). For assistance on obtaining an XCAMS account, please contact the ORNL Computer Helpline at 865-241-6765 or send an email requesting assistance to helpline@ornl.gov. For further assistance accessing data, please contact Monica Maceira (maceiram@ornl.gov). The figures were prepared with Generic Mapping Tools (GMT) version 6.5.0 (Wessel *et al.*, 2019) and Matplotlib version 3.10.6 (Hunter, 2007). NumPy version 2.3.2 (Harris *et al.*, 2020), pandas version 2.3.1 (The pandas development team, 2024), and ObsPy version 1.4.2 (Beyreuther *et al.*, 2010; Megies *et al.*, 2011; Krischer *et al.*, 2015) were used to process the seismic data. Figure 1 used satellite images from Google Earth (https://www.google.com/web/, last accessed June 2025). The supplemental material to this article includes a figure (Fig. S1) showing uniform manifold approximation and projection for dimension reduction (UMAP) results obtained with varying parameter settings, a figure (Fig. S2) presenting hierarchical density-based spatial clustering of applications with noise (HDBSCAN) results with varying minimum-cluster size, a figure (Fig. S3) illustrating HDBSCAN results with varying minimum numbers of neighbors, a figure (Fig. S4) presenting examples of waveforms and corresponding spectra for clusters A6 and A7, a figure (Fig. S5) showing short-term average/long-term average (STA/LTA) detections on one-day continuous seismic data, a figure (Fig. S6) illustrating k-means clustering results with six clusters, a figure (Fig. S7) presenting k-means clustering results with two clusters, and a figure (Fig. S8) identifying vehicle labels on UMAP results computed at different frequency ranges.

Declaration of Competing Interests

The authors acknowledge that there are no conflicts of interest recorded.

Acknowledgments

The authors would like to acknowledge the U.S. Department of Energy (DOE), National Nuclear Security Administration's Office of Defense Nuclear Nonproliferation Research and Development for supporting this work. This work has been authored in part by UT-Battelle, LLC, under contract DE-AC05-00OR22725 with the U.S. DOE. The U.S. Government retains, and the publisher, by accepting the article for publication, acknowledges that the U.S. Government retains a non-exclusive, paid-up, irrevocable, worldwide license to publish or reproduce the published form of this article, or allow others to do so, for U.S. Government purposes. The views and conclusions contained in this document are those of the authors and should not be interpreted as necessarily representing the official policies, either expressed or implied, of the U.S. Government. This research used resources of the Compute and Data Environment for Science (CADES) at the Oak Ridge National Laboratory (ORNL), which is supported by the DOE Office of Science under Contract Number DE-AC05-00OR22725. DOE will provide public access to these results of federally sponsored research in accordance with the DOE Public Access Plan (http://energy.gov/downloads/doe-public-access-plan, last accessed June 2025). The authors acknowledge Erik Kabela for providing the precipitation data. The authors acknowledge helpful suggestions from Erin Cunningham. The authors thank Editor-in-Chief Allison Bent, an anonymous Associate Editor, and two anonymous reviewers for their constructive comments that significantly improve the article.

References

Allen, R. V. (1978). Automatic earthquake recognition and timing from single traces, *Bull. Seismol. Soc. Am.* **68,** no. 5, 1521–1532, doi: 10.1785/BSSA0680051521.

Arrowsmith, S. J., D. T. Trugman, J. MacCarthy, K. J. Bergen, D. Lumley, and M. B. Magnani (2022). Big data seismology, *Rev. Geophys.* **60,** no. 2, e2021RG000769, doi: 10.1029/2021RG000769.

Beyreuther, M., R. Barsch, L. Krischer, T. Megies, Y. Behr, and J. Wassermann (2010). ObsPy: A python toolbox for seismology, *Seismol. Res. Lett.* **81,** no. 3, 530–533, doi: 10.1785/gssrl.81.3.530.

Chai, C., M. Maceira, H. J. Santos-Villalobos, S. V. Venkatakrishnan, M. Schoenball, W. Zhu, G. C. Beroza, C. Thurber, and E. C. Team (2020). Using a deep neural network and transfer learning to bridge scales for seismic phase picking, *Geophys. Res. Lett.* **47,** no. 16, e2020GL088651, doi: 10.1029/2020GL088651.

Chai, C., O. Marcillo, M. Maceira, J. Park, S. Arrowsmith, J. O. Thomas, and J. Cunningham (2025). Exploring continuous seismic data at an industry facility using unsupervised machine learning, *Seism. Record* **5,** no. 1, 64–72, doi: 10.1785/0320240046.

Chai, C., O. Marcillo, M. Maceira, C. Young, and T. Karnowski (2023). Locating operational events of the cooling tower of a nuclear reactor with a very local seismic network, *Bull. Seismol. Soc. Am.* **113,** 1344–1355, doi: 10.1785/0120220216.

Chai, C., C. Ramirez, M. Maceira, and O. Marcillo (2022). Monitoring operational states of a nuclear reactor using seismoacoustic signatures and machine learning, *Seismol. Res. Lett.* **93,** no. 3, 1660–1672, doi: 10.1785/0220210294.

Chai, C., D. Rose, S. Stewart, N. Martindale, M. Adams, L. Linville, C. Stanley, A. Torres Polanco, and P. Bingham (2025). PickerXL, A large deep learning model to measure arrival times from noisy seismic signals, *Seismol. Res. Lett.* doi: 10.1785/0220240353.

Cui, X., Y. Hu, S. Ma, Z. Li, G. Liu, and H. Huang (2024). Bridging supervised and unsupervised learning to build volcano seismicity classifiers at Kilauea volcano, Hawaii, *Seismol. Res. Lett.* **95,** no. 3, 1849–1857, doi: 10.1785/0220230251.

Denolle, M. A., and T. Nissen-Meyer (2020). Quiet anthropocene, quiet Earth, *Science* **369,** no. 6509, 1299–1300, doi: 10.1126/science.abd8358.

Guenaga, D. L., C. Chai, M. Maceira, O. E. Marcillo, and A. A. Velasco (2021). Seismically detecting nuclear reactor operations using a power spectral density (PSD) misfit detector, *Bull. Seismol. Soc. Am.* **111,** no. 3, 1378–1391, doi: 10.1785/0120200267.

Harris, C. R., K. J. Millman, S. J. van der Walt, R. Gommers, P. Virtanen, D. Cournapeau, E. Wieser, J. Taylor, S. Berg, N. J. Smith, *et al.* (2020). Array programming with NumPy, *Nature* **585,** no. 7825, 357–362, doi: 10.1038/s41586-020-2649-2.

Hu, Y., Z. Li, L. Fu, and X. Liu (2024). Environment-modulated glacial seismicity near Dålk glacier in East Antarctica revealed by deep clustering, *J. Geophys. Res.* **129,** no. 4, e2023JF007593, doi: 10.1029/2023JF007593.

Hunter, J. D. (2007). Matplotlib: A 2D graphics environment, *Comput. Sci. Eng.* **9,** no. 3, 90–95, doi: 10.1109/MCSE.2007.55.

Jenkins, W. F., II, P. Gerstoft, M. J. Bianco, and P. D. Bromirski (2021). Unsupervised deep clustering of seismic data: Monitoring the ross ice shelf, Antarctica, *J. Geophys. Res.* **126,** no. 9, e2021JB021716, doi: 10.1029/2021JB021716.

Johnson, C. W., Y. Ben-Zion, H. Meng, and F. Vernon (2020). Identifying different classes of seismic noise signals using unsupervised learning, *Geophys. Res. Lett.* **47,** no. 15, e2020GL088353, doi: 10.1029/2020GL088353.

Krischer, L., T. Megies, R. Barsch, M. Beyreuther, T. Lecocq, C. Caudron, and J. Wassermann (2015). ObsPy: A bridge for seismology into the scientific Python ecosystem, *Comput. Sci. Discov.* **8,** no. 1, 014003, doi: 10.1088/1749-4699/8/1/014003.

Liu, M., M. Zhang, W. Zhu, W. L. Ellsworth, and H. Li (2020). Rapid characterization of the July 2019 Ridgecrest, California, earthquake sequence from raw seismic data using machine-learning phase picker, *Geophys. Res. Lett.* **47,** no. 4, e2019GL086189, doi: 10.1029/2019GL086189.

Ma, S., Z. Li, and W. Wang (2022). Machine learning of source spectra for large earthquakes, *Geophys. J. Int.* **231,** no. 1, 692–702, doi: 10.1093/gji/ggac215.

Marcillo, O. E., M. Maceira, C. Chai, C. Gammans, R. Hunley, and C. Young (2020). The local seismoacoustic wavefield of a research nuclear reactor and its response to reactor power level, *Seismol. Res. Lett.* **92,** no. 1, 378–387, doi: 10.1785/0220200139.

McInnes, L., and J. Healy (2017). Accelerated hierarchical density clustering, *2017 IEEE International Conf. on Data Mining Workshops (ICDMW)*, 33–42, doi: 10.1109/ICDMW.2017.12.

McInnes, L., J. Healy, and J. Melville (2020). UMAP: Uniform manifold approximation and projection for dimension reduction, available at http://arxiv.org/abs/1802.03426 (last accessed November 2025).

Megies, T., M. Beyreuther, R. Barsch, L. Krischer, and J. Wassermann (2011). ObsPy - what can it do for data centers and observatories? *Ann. Geophys.* **54,** no. 1, 47–58, doi: 10.4401/ag-4838.

Mousavi, S. M., and G. C. Beroza (2022). Deep-learning seismology, *Science* **377,** no. 6607, eabm4470, doi: 10.1126/science.abm4470.

Riahi, N., and P. Gerstoft (2015). The seismic traffic footprint: Tracking trains, aircraft, and cars seismically, *Geophys. Res. Lett.* **42,** no. 8, 2674–2681, doi: 10.1002/2015GL063558.

Saad, O. M., M. Bai, and Y. Chen (2021). Uncovering the microseismic signals from noisy data for high-fidelity 3D source-location imaging using deep learning, *Geophysics* **86,** no. 6, KS161–KS173, doi: 10.1190/geo2021-0021.1.

Seydoux, L., R. Balestriero, P. Poli, M. de Hoop, M. Campillo, and R. Baraniuk (2020). Clustering earthquake signals and background noises in continuous seismic data with unsupervised deep learning, *Nat. Commun.* **11,** no. 1, 3972, doi: 10.1038/s41467-020-17841-x.

Snover, D., C. W. Johnson, M. J. Bianco, and P. Gerstoft (2020). Deep clustering to identify sources of Urban Seismic noise in Long Beach, California, *Seismol. Res. Lett.* **92,** no. 2A, 1011–1022, doi: 10.1785/0220200164.

Steinmann, R., L. Seydoux, É. Beaucé, and M. Campillo (2022). Hierarchical exploration of continuous seismograms with unsupervised learning, *J. Geophys. Res.* **127,** no. 1, e2021JB022455, doi: 10.1029/2021JB022455.

The pandas development team (2024). pandas-dev/pandas: Pandas, *Zenodo*, doi: 10.5281/zenodo.10957263.

Wessel, P., J. F. Luis, L. Uieda, R. Scharroo, F. Wobbe, W. H. F. Smith, and D. Tian (2019). The generic mapping tools version 6, *Geochem. Geophys. Geosys.* **20,** no. 11, 5556–5564, doi: 10.1029/2019GC008515.

Zhu, W., and G. C. Beroza (2019). PhaseNet: A deep-neural-network-based seismic arrival-time picking method, *Geophys. J. Int.* **216,** no. 1, 261–273, doi: 10.1093/gji/ggy423.

Manuscript received 23 June 2025
Published online 26 November 2025

Signal Enhancement of Distributed Acoustic Sensing Data Using a Spectral Subtraction–Based Approach

Giulio Pascucci*[1], Sonja Gaviano[2], Alice Pozzoli[3], and Francesco Grigoli[1]

Abstract

Distributed acoustic sensing (DAS) is a fast-developing technology that has gained significant popularity in the seismological community, particularly for microseismic monitoring operations. Its unique capability to convert fiber-optic cables into dense seismic arrays offers numerous advantages over conventional seismic networks. This is particularly true for microseismic monitoring in extreme environments, such as deep geothermal wells, because of fiber's resistance to high temperatures. However, seismic signals acquired with DAS systems are generally characterized by higher noise levels than those acquired with standard seismometers. When working with DAS systems, traditional frequency filtering methods often fail to recover weak signals, resulting in limited noise reduction performance. In this work, we introduce a robust denoising approach that adapts a spectral subtraction–based method used in speech signal processing to improve DAS data quality. We validated our denoising workflow using both realistic synthetic data and real microseismic events recorded at the Frontier Observatory for Research in Geothermal Energy Enhanced Geothermal Systems site (Utah, United States). The results obtained with both synthetic and real DAS data demonstrate significant improvements in signal enhancement, showcasing the effectiveness of our approach even under poor signal-to-noise ratio (SNR) conditions. This method outperforms traditional frequency filtering techniques, offering a promising solution to enhance DAS signals and enabling the detection of weak seismic events characterized by low SNR.

Cite this article as Pascucci, G., S. Gaviano, A. Pozzoli, and F. Grigoli (2025). Signal Enhancement of Distributed Acoustic Sensing Data Using a Spectral Subtraction–Based Approach, *Seismol. Res. Lett.* **97**, 1905–1918, doi: 10.1785/0220250105.

Supplemental Material

Introduction

Distributed acoustic sensing (DAS) is a rapidly evolving technology able to transform fiber-optic cables into dense arrays of sensors capable of detecting seismic waves passing through the fiber, enabling continuous, high-resolution seismic monitoring over large distances (Hartog, 2017; Zhan, 2019; Fernández-Ruiz *et al.*, 2020). In recent years, DAS has become particularly useful in microseismic monitoring operations, especially in borehole settings. Typical seismological applications include onshore and offshore monitoring of natural seismicity in active tectonic (Li *et al.*, 2021; Shinohara *et al.*, 2022; Trabattoni *et al.*, 2022; Biondi *et al.*, 2025; Zhang *et al.*, 2025), volcanic (Nishimura *et al.*, 2021; Jousset *et al.*, 2022), and glacial environments (Klaasen *et al.*, 2021, 2023). Moreover, DAS offers significant advantages for monitoring induced seismicity associated with hydraulic fracturing (Karrenbach *et al.*, 2019; Zhang *et al.*, 2023; Ma *et al.*, 2024), geothermal energy exploitation (Feigl *et al.*, 2016; Lellouch *et al.*, 2020, 2021; Ajo-Franklin *et al.*, 2022; Azzola *et al.*, 2023; Lv *et al.*, 2023; Jechumtálová *et al.*, 2025), or Carbon Capture and Storage operations (Pevzner *et al.*, 2021; Bremaud *et al.*, 2023).

Optical fibers can be deployed in challenging environments, including production and injection wells, thus reducing the need for dedicated monitoring wells. The increased proximity to the reservoir significantly improves the detection capability for small-magnitude earthquakes (e.g., $M_L < 0$), enabling high-resolution microseismic monitoring. The installation in deep monitoring wells reduces the ambient noise (Rossi *et al.*, 2023), thereby enhancing the signal-to-noise ratio (SNR) and making even very weak seismic events detectable. In addition, fiber-optic cables exhibit strong resistance to high temperatures, allowing their installation in deep geothermal wells. This makes DAS systems particularly well suited for seismic data acquisition in extreme conditions. A notable example is the Frontier Observatory for Research in Geothermal Energy (FORGE) pilot

1. Department of Earth Sciences, University of Pisa, Pisa, Italy, https://orcid.org/0009-0008-3723-9003 (GP); https://orcid.org/0000-0002-2858-9756 (FG);
2. Seismix Srl, Palermo, Italy, https://orcid.org/0000-0003-3481-2923 (SG);
3. Geodynamics and Geophysical Monitoring Department (GEOM), Eni SpA, Milano, Italy
*Corresponding author: giulio.pascucci@phd.unipi.it

project in Utah (United States), which aims for safe exploitation of Enhanced Geothermal Systems (EGS; McLennan, 2022).

Moreover, fiber-optic cables deployed in borehole environments are often cemented behind casing, and the resulting mechanical coupling to the formation strongly influences the observed DAS amplitude and SNR. Cemented intervals generally provide strong microseismic signals, whereas noncemented sections tend to exhibit casing arrivals and degraded coupling. Recent work by Hart *et al.* (2025) employed fiber-optic sensing during cement placement and hydration to supervise well construction and assess coupling development.

Despite these important advantages, one main limitation of DAS systems is their lower SNR compared with conventional geophones (Lellouch *et al.*, 2020). Noise sources affecting DAS data can be of different kinds and are mainly related to the instrument (i.e., the interrogator) or to the fiber coupling (Bozzi *et al.*, 2024). The most relevant source of noise, known as common-mode noise (Lindsey *et al.*, 2020; Willis, 2022), is caused by local seismic disturbances producing vibrations near the interrogator. This noise is characterized by an infinite-velocity signal (i.e., simultaneously arriving at all channels), leading to an overprinted signal on all channel recordings simultaneously (Ellmauthaler *et al.*, 2017). Other types of noise affecting DAS measurements include high-frequency random noise (Porras *et al.*, 2024) and coherent fading noise, caused by interference patterns caused by partial loss of coherence in the laser source or backscattering effects along the fiber, producing spatially coherent amplitude variations often observed as periodic or slowly varying patterns unrelated to the seismic wavefield (Lindsey *et al.*, 2020; Willis, 2022). Another source is coupling noise, which arises from poor or inconsistent mechanical coupling between the fiber and its surrounding medium. This results in reduced SNR (Chen *et al.*, 2019) and may vary depending on whether the fiber is deployed on the surface or in a borehole. These noise sources complicate the extraction of hidden signals, reducing the overall SNR and thus limiting the detection of weak microseismic events.

Several approaches have recently been proposed to denoise DAS data. For example, Isken *et al.* (2022) introduced an adaptive frequency–wavenumber (*f-k*) filter to suppress incoherent seismic noise while amplifying the coherent wavefield. Lellouch *et al.* (2021) and Shimony and Lellouch (2024a) proposed using a combination of median and band-pass filters to enhance the SNR of the FORGE dataset. To remove the interrogator's common-mode noise across all DAS channels, Ellmauthaler *et al.* (2017) subtracted the median from all channels; Binder *et al.* (2020) applied *f-x* deconvolution and dip filtering to attenuate vertical- and horizontal-optical noise in DAS data; and Tuinstra *et al.* (2024) and Porras *et al.* (2024) applied an *f-k* filter to remove to remove the zero-wavenumber ($k = 0$) component related to this strong, coherent noise. In addition, other denoising techniques originally developed for reflection seismology have also been adapted to DAS data. For example, Qin *et al.* (2012) applied a wavelet-based method, which decomposes the seismic signal into a series of scaled and shifted versions of a selected mother wavelet to separate coherent signals from random noise. Similarly, Atterholt *et al.* (2021) adapted the curvelet transform, which considers the spatial coherence of the seismic wavefield. This makes it well suited for removing stochastic and coherent noise from DAS recordings.

With the growing popularity of deep learning (DL) techniques, several methods have also been developed to enhance the SNR of DAS data. These include supervised (Lapins *et al.*, 2023; Yang, Fomel, Wang, Chen, Chen *et al.*, 2023), unsupervised (Yang, Fomel, Wang, Chen, and Chen, 2023; Konietzny *et al.*, 2024; Saad *et al.*, 2024), and self-supervised (Van den Ende *et al.*, 2021; Xu *et al.*, 2024; Zitt *et al.*, 2025) approaches. Although some of these methods show promising results in noise reduction, they typically require large amounts of labeled data to effectively train their models. However, the limited availability of open and publicly available DAS datasets often makes these approaches impractical, especially when dealing with new data acquisitions.

In this work, we adapted a spectral subtractive algorithm traditionally used in speech enhancement for audio signals (Boll, 1979) for denoising DAS data. We first introduce the theoretical background of our denoising workflow and then evaluate its performance using both synthetic and real DAS microseismic data acquired during the April 2022 EGS stimulation campaign at the FORGE site in Utah, United States. Finally, we discuss the algorithm's performance in enhancing the SNR of a set of microseismic events characterized by different noise levels.

This framework aims to address the current limitations in DAS denoising approaches, offering a more efficient and flexible solution for improving the SNR of DAS recordings. Moreover, this method can be easily applied to multiple DAS datasets with different acquisition layouts, and it has low computational requirements, making it feasible to run on standard laptop hardware.

Oversubtraction Denoising Workflow

Let $y(n)$ denote a raw input signal (a single seismic trace of the DAS array), modeled as the sum of the signal $x(n)$ of interest and the additive noise $d(n)$:

$$y(n) = x(n) + d(n), \quad (1)$$

in which n is the discrete-time index. The raw signal $y(n)$ is first divided into overlapping frames of N samples each, tapered using a Hamming window, and transformed in the frequency domain via the fast Fourier transform (Boll, 1979; Loizou, 2013). The windowing process reduces endpoint discontinuities and is defined as (Blackman and Tukey, 1958)

$$w(n) = 0.54 - 0.46 \cos \frac{2\pi n}{N - 1} \quad 0 \leq n \leq N - 1. \quad (2)$$

In frequency domain, equation (1) then becomes:

$$Y(\omega) = X(\omega) + D(\omega), \quad (3)$$

in which $X(\omega)$ and $D(\omega)$ are the clean signal and noise spectra, respectively. Writing this in polar form:

$$Y(\omega) = |Y(\omega)|e^{j\phi_y(\omega)}, \quad (4)$$

in which $|Y(\omega)|$ is the amplitude spectrum and $\phi_y(\omega)$ is the phase spectrum of the raw signal. The noise spectrum is similarly expressed as

$$D(\omega) = |D(\omega)|e^{j\phi_d(\omega)}, \quad (5)$$

in which $|D(\omega)|$ is the noise amplitude spectrum, which is usually unknown. The noise estimation procedure is a crucial step in the denoising process, and various approaches have been proposed over the years (Ephraim and Malah, 1984; Cohen and Berdugo, 2002). In this work, we extract the noise amplitude spectrum by averaging the amplitude spectra computed for all frames sampling the portion of noise. We assume that the frames used for noise estimation do not contain any signal of interest. Substituting equations (4) and (5) into equation (3), the estimated clean signal spectrum is finally obtained as follows:

$$\tilde{X}(\omega) = [|Y(\omega)| - |\tilde{D}(\omega)|]e^{j\phi_y(\omega)}, \quad (6)$$

in which $\phi_y(\omega)$ is the raw signal's phase and $|\tilde{D}(\omega)|$ is the estimated noise amplitude spectrum. The preceding derivation of the spectral subtraction algorithm can be easily extended to the power spectrum:

$$|\tilde{X}(\omega)|^2 = |Y(\omega)|^2 - |\tilde{D}(\omega)|^2, \quad (7)$$

with $|\tilde{X}(\omega)|^2$ and $|\tilde{Y}(\omega)|^2$ as the estimates of the clean and noisy signal's power spectrum, respectively.

Finally, after subtracting the noise from the observed signal power spectra, the enhanced seismic trace is obtained by returning to the time domain by applying the inverse Fourier transform of $|\tilde{X}(\omega)|^2$ using the raw signal's phase. This process is applied iteratively to each DAS channel, and the results are combined to produce the enhanced DAS seismic recording.

A common issue that may occur when implementing equation (7) is that the enhanced signal's power spectrum ($|\tilde{X}(\omega)|^2$) becomes negative for a certain range of frequencies. To address this problem, in most conventional spectral subtractive-type algorithms, one solution is to set the negative spectral components to zero (Boll, 1979). However, this can introduce remnant noise or signal distortion in cases of inaccurate noise estimates (Berouti *et al.*, 1979). A way to overcome this problem is to prevent spectral components from going below a preset value (i.e., spectral floor) while subtracting an overestimate of the noise spectrum:

$$|\tilde{X}(\omega)|^2 = \begin{cases} |Y(\omega)|^2 - \alpha|\tilde{D}(\omega)|^2 & \text{if } |Y(\omega)|^2 > (\alpha+\beta)|\tilde{D}(\omega)|^2 \\ \beta|\tilde{D}(\omega)|^2 & \text{otherwise} \end{cases}, \quad (8)$$

in which α is the oversubtraction factor ($\alpha \geq 1$) and β is the spectral floor parameter ($0 < \beta \ll 1$). The value of β controls the amount of remaining residual noise; if it is too small, it will be highly reduced, but if it is too large, the noise will not be sufficiently attenuated. Here, α instead controls the amount of noise power spectrum subtracted from the raw signal's one in each frame, with smaller values for high-SNR frames (i.e., when signal is present) and larger ones for low-SNR frames (i.e., when noise is present):

$$\alpha = \begin{cases} 5 & \text{SNR} < 0 \text{ dB} \\ 3 - (2/20)\,\text{SNR} & \text{if } 0 \text{ dB} \leq \text{SNR} \leq 20 \text{ dB}. \\ 1 & \text{SNR} > 20 \text{ dB} \end{cases} \quad (9)$$

The SNR in the previous equation is estimated frame-by-frame for each channel of the DAS data and is calculated using the segmental SNR (SSNR), which is defined as Vondrasek and Pollak (2005):

$$\text{SSNR}_i = 10\log\left(\frac{\sum_{k=1}^{N}|Y_k(\omega)|^2}{\sum_{k=1}^{N}|\tilde{D}_k(\omega)|^2}\right). \quad (10)$$

Finally, to further enhance the algorithm's performance, an updating mechanism is applied to the noise spectrum for each frame and DAS channel. This step enables the algorithm to dynamically adapt to variations in the noise power spectrum, improving estimation accuracy under nonstationary conditions. When the SSNR (defined in equation 10) falls below a user-defined threshold, indicating that the signal is likely dominated by noise, it becomes reasonable to approximate the current noise spectrum using the observed power spectrum $|Y(\omega)|^2$. Based on this assumption, the noise estimate is updated as follows:

$$|\overline{D}(\omega)| = G|\tilde{D}(\omega)|^2 + (1-G)|Y(\omega)|^2, \quad (11)$$

in which $|\tilde{D}(\omega)|^2$ represents the previous estimate of the noise power spectrum, and $|Y(\omega)|^2$ is the current observed power spectrum. The parameter G, constrained to the range $0.1 \leq G \leq 0.9$, determines how the noise spectrum is updated during the spectral subtraction process. More specifically, G controls the balance between the old and current noise estimates; whereas higher values of G give more importance to past noise estimates, lower values give more weight to the current noisy data estimate. This update step is applied only if the SSNR defined in equation (10) falls below a user-defined threshold. Otherwise, the original noise estimate averaged over selected frames for which no signal is present remains unchanged.

A schematic representation of the full denoising workflow is shown in Figure 1, summarizing the key steps described in this section.

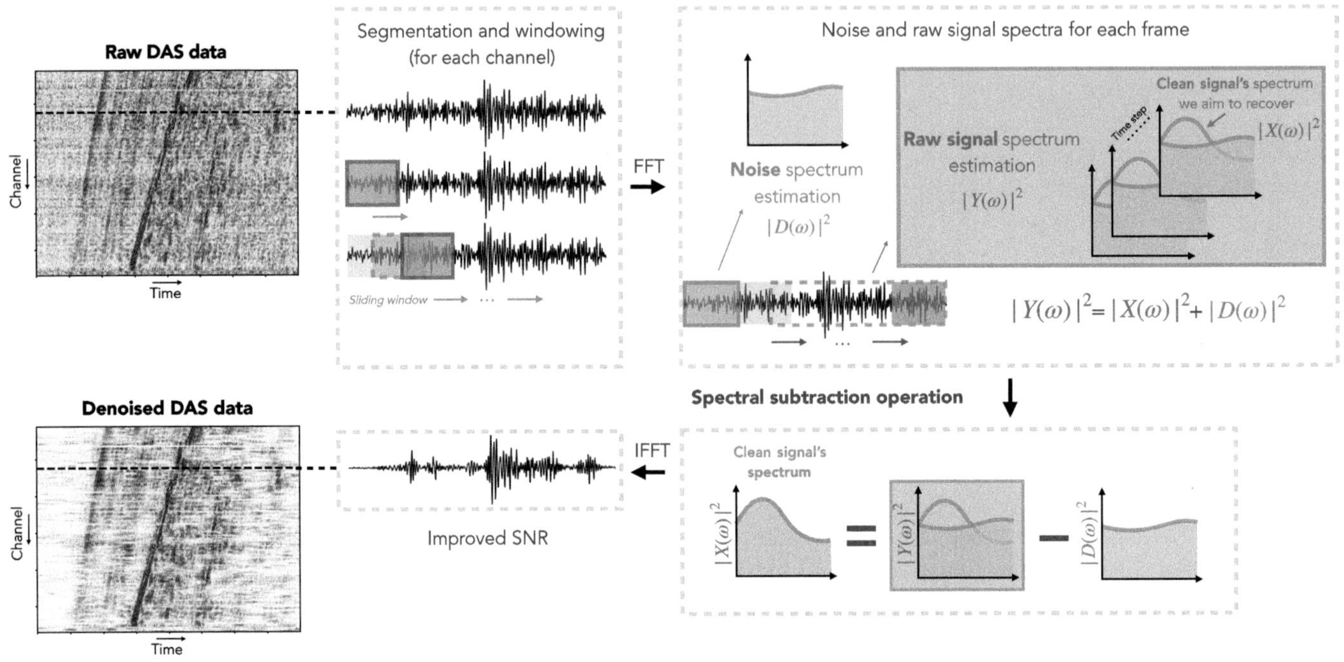

Figure 1. Simplified block diagram illustrating the workflow of spectral oversubtraction. The algorithm works channel-wise, and finally, the enhanced distributed acoustic sensing (DAS) data are displayed. FFT, fast Fourier transform; IFFT, inverse fast Fourier transform; SNR, signal-to-noise ratio. The color version of this figure is available only in the electronic edition.

Utah FORGE EGS Dataset

The FORGE site is a large-scale field laboratory located in Utah, created to advance and test new technologies for the safe and efficient development of EGS. EGS could make geothermal energy a valuable renewable resource in the long term, no longer confined to volcanic or hydrothermal regions (Vargas *et al.*, 2022). By injecting fluids at high pressure into the subsurface, EGS technology enables the creation of artificial geothermal systems that exploit the Earth's heat in a variety of environments. However, these operations are often accompanied by risks associated with induced seismicity because of changes in the local stress conditions caused by fluid injections, which can lead to the reactivation of pre-existing faults.

In these contexts, the introduction of DAS systems could allow an important step forward in the development of more efficient seismic monitoring systems. The FORGE pilot project was one of the first sites where fiber-optics sensing techniques were used for microseismic monitoring applications. In the past years, several DAS acquisition campaigns (during hydraulic stimulation operations) have been conducted at this site, including one in April 2022, from which we extracted the dataset used in this study. The seismic monitoring infrastructure consists of a surface network and two monitoring wells (78A-32 and 78B-32) spaced ~85 m apart and located ~1308 m from the injection well (16A-78-32; McLennan, 2022). The two monitoring wells are equipped with fiber-optic cables up to 989 m depth for the well 78A-32 and 1193 m depth for the well 78B-32 (Fig. 2) (Shimony and Lellouch, 2024b), which is enclosed in a metal tube and cemented in the annulus of the 5 1/2 inch casing. Using this deployment configuration, the fiber-optic cable is directly coupled to the formation, providing the optimal SNR for seismic signals propagating in the surrounding formation (Willis, 2022). Finally, DAS data were acquired with a 1 m channel spacing, a 10 m gauge length and saved with a sampling frequency of 4 kHz in 15 s segments and stored in the *.tdms* format.

At Utah FORGE, noise originates from a variety of sources and exhibits spectral, temporal, and depth variations. As discussed by Pecci *et al.* (2024), noise below 30 Hz is predominantly associated with anthropogenic activity, showing clear daily cycles and stronger amplitudes in the shallow sections of the fiber. Supporting this observation, Kalinichenko *et al.* (2025) more recently presented a model of noise decay with depth, showing that noise levels are highest at the free surface and decrease below 50–100 m. They also demonstrated that seismic noise for frequencies above 4.5 Hz is predominantly of anthropogenic origin and can penetrate to depths exceeding 200 m. In contrast, low-frequency noise (<1 Hz) appears relatively constant over time and with depth, suggesting a natural, remote origin, such as oceanic microseisms propagating laterally into the borehole as plane wavefronts. At higher frequencies (>60 Hz), noise often lacks clear temporal patterns and is interpreted as electronic or mechanical in nature, potentially originating from the interrogator unit.

Our denoising approach focuses on suppressing this depth- and frequency-dependent noise, which can vary spatially along the fiber, by exploiting the statistical characteristics of the noise

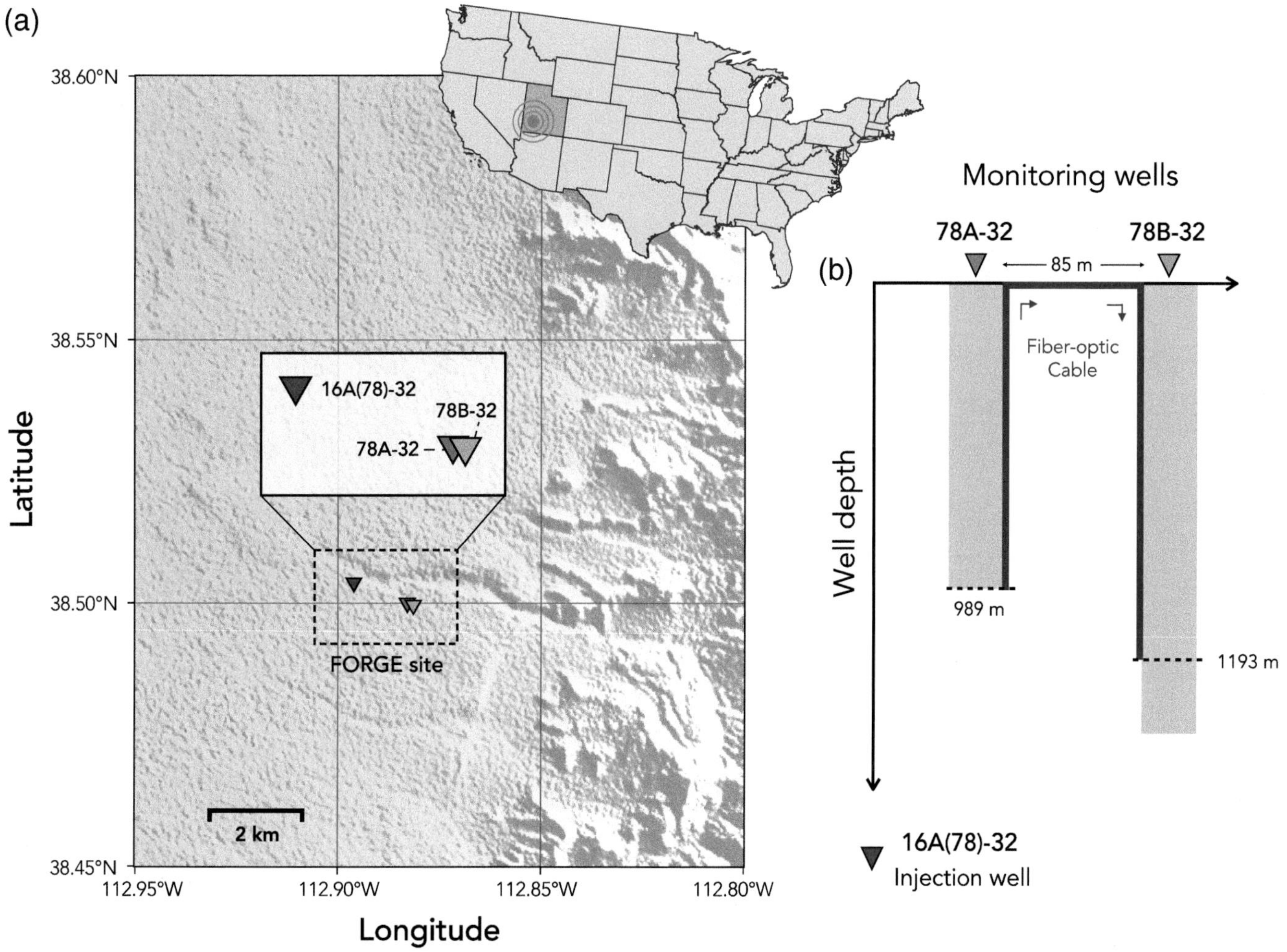

Figure 2. (a) Location map of the Frontier Observatory for Research in Geothermal Energy (FORGE) site in Utah, United States (highlighted in red in the U.S. inset map in the top right corner of the figure). Well 16A(78)-32 corresponds to the injection well, and wells 78A-32 and 78B-32 (located 1308 m from the injection well) host the fiber-optic cables of the DAS system. The data used in this study were recorded at well 78B-32. (b) Schematic illustration of the two monitoring wells (78A-32 and 78B-32) hosting the DAS system, which was used to monitor the stimulation campaign during April 2022. The color version of this figure is available only in the electronic edition.

spectrum, which differ from those of the seismic signal. This allows for improved separation between microseismic events and background noise in DAS recordings, particularly under low signal-to-noise conditions.

We first test the oversubtraction-based denoising on synthetic DAS data, simulating real noise conditions and the vertical well geometry of the FORGE EGS experiment using the spectral element software *Salvus* by Mondaic (Afanasiev *et al.*, 2018; Porras *et al.*, 2024). Next, we validate the method on 29 real microseismic events recorded at FORGE during the April 2022 stimulation, with SNR ranging from very low to high. The following sections present results from both synthetic tests and real data, highlighting three microseismic events with different SSNR levels.

Results

The results of the testing phase for the spectral oversubtraction method are presented in two steps. We first evaluate the performance of our proposed denoising workflow on synthetic data contaminated with real noise from the FORGE EGS site, allowing us to assess its effectiveness in a controlled setting. Finally, we validate our method and demonstrate its application to real DAS data recorded at FORGE, with a high, medium, and low SSNR.

Application to Synthetic DAS Data

We first generated synthetic DAS data simulating a microseismic event at the FORGE EGS site. The simulation of the synthetic event has been performed using the spectral element software *Salvus* (Afanasiev *et al.*, 2018), considering a velocity model characteristic of the FORGE site (Zhang and Pankow, 2021), with the hypocenter of the event located at a depth of 4 km and at an epicentral distance of about 8 km from the fiber. To simulate realistic conditions, we extracted real noise waveforms from the FORGE DAS dataset and added it to the waveform of the synthetic event. To represent different noise conditions, we first normalized trace-by-trace the synthetic

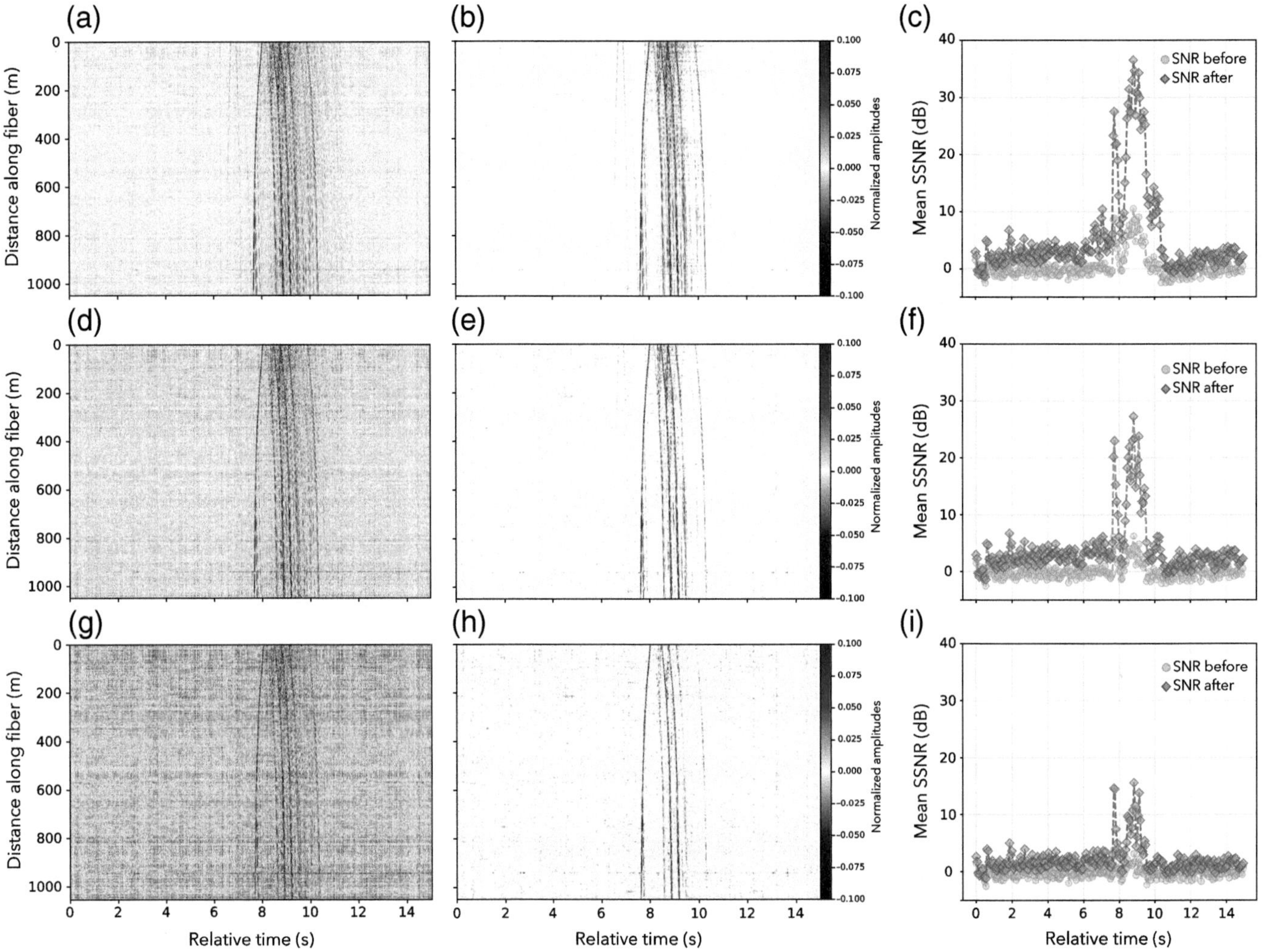

Figure 3. (a,d,g) Raw high-, medium-, and low-simulated segmental signal-to-noise ratio (SSNR) synthetic DAS data using noise extracted from FORGE Enhanced Geothermal Systems (EGS) real data. (b,e,h) Synthetic data after applying the oversubtraction denoising workflow. (c,f,i) Mean SSNR values before and after denoising, computed for all channels and each frame used for the signal segmentation phase of the workflow. The color version of this figure is available only in the electronic edition.

waveforms (with respect to the maximum absolute amplitude of each trace) and then added the real noise waveforms scaled by factors of 0.5, 1, and 2, as shown in Figure 3a,d,g. The combined dataset simulates seismic events with high-, medium-, and low-SSNR levels (i.e., mean SSNRs of 0.17, −0.11, and −0.23 dB, respectively).

In Figure 3b,e,h, the denoised synthetic data are displayed after applying the oversubtraction method discussed earlier in the previous section. The improvement in SSNR values after denoising is quite evident in Figure 3c,f,i, which illustrate the mean SSNR calculated for all channels and each frame used for signal segmentation, before and after denoising. These results clearly show the effectiveness of our denoising approach under varying noise conditions (additional details on the effects of oversubtraction on individual channels extracted at various depths from the different synthetic data are provided in Figure S1, available in the supplemental material to this article).

Application to real DAS data

We validated our denoising workflow on real DAS data from the FORGE site. More specifically, we applied it to 29 selected microseismic events with different SSNRs.

Data preprocessing. Before applying the oversubtraction denoising workflow to the real DAS data, a few preprocessing steps were applied to the raw recordings. These include (1) downsampling of the traces to increase computational efficiency; (2) demeaning each trace; (3) optionally normalizing the trace amplitudes to their respective maximum absolute values to reduce the influence of factors such as geometrical spreading, variations in receiver coupling, and nonlinear noise effects (Miah and Potter, 2017); and (4) applying a fourth-order band-pass filter (5–250 Hz). In addition, an *f*-*k* filter was applied to remove the strong common-mode noise at $k = 0$, which is characterized by signals that appear simultaneously across all channels. Importantly, in our proposed denoising workflow,

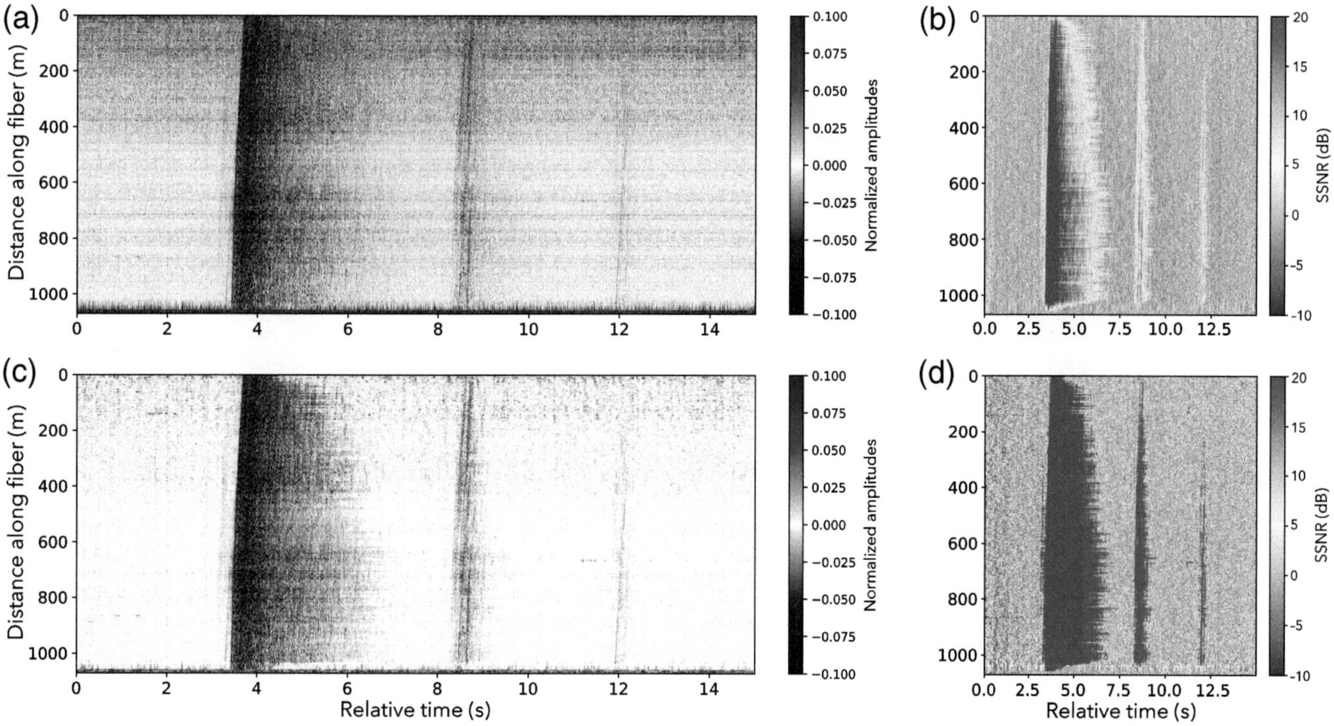

Figure 4. (a) Raw high-SSNR DAS data from FORGE (FORGE_DFIT_UTC_20220421_152924.398.tdms) after the preprocessing steps. (c) Denoised DAS data after applying the oversubtraction workflow. Panels (b,d) are the SSNR values computed for each channel of the DAS array before and after the application of the denoising framework, respectively. The color version of this figure is available only in the electronic edition.

the normalization step is not mandatory and does not affect the method's performance. To demonstrate this, we provide a comparison in Figures S2–S5, in which results with and without normalization are shown for two events of different SNRs (file names: "FORGE_DFIT_UTC_20220421_145439.398.tdms" and "FORGE_DFIT_UTC_20220421_153124.398.tdms").

First field example: High-SSNR seismic event. As a first test, we consider a high-SSNR (>30 dB) DAS recording (file name "FORGE_DFIT_UTC_20220421_152924.398.tdms"). Figure 4a shows the raw data after the preprocessing steps have been applied, and Figure 4c its denoised version after the application of the proposed oversubtraction denoising method. Furthermore, Figure 4b,d shows a clear improvement in the SSNR values when comparing raw and denoised data after using the oversubtraction, especially in correspondence of the microseismic events observed around 3.5, 8.5, and 12 s. Figure 5 shows zoomed-in sections of the seismic event between 3.2 and 4.8 s. The left and right columns show the raw and denoised data, respectively, highlighting some waveforms extracted at different depths (89, 398, and 816 m) to illustrate the denoising performance across varying depths for which differences in SNR and noise levels may occur. For this example, a value of 0.002 is used as the spectral floor parameter β using a frame size of 0.06 s. The factor G, which controls the update rate of the noise spectrum during the spectral subtraction process, is kept fixed to 0.9 for all the following examples because it showed optimal results. The noise power spectrum is estimated considering the first 30 frames (i.e., the first 0.9 s of each single channel of the DAS array), and it is updated following equation (11) as the SSNR defined in equation (10) falls below a threshold, which was determined by testing different values and using the one producing the highest SSNR as the final result. In this case, this parameter is set to 4.

Second field example: Medium-SSNR seismic event. A second test was then performed considering a DAS recording under medium SSNR (between 15 and 30 dB) condition (file name "FORGE_DFIT_UTC_20220421_155009.398.tdms"). As in the previous case, Figure 6a shows the raw data, and Figure 6c is denoised version after applying the proposed workflow. Again, the method exhibits a strong improvement in the SSNR values before (Fig. 6b) and after (Fig. 6d) denoising with the oversubtraction-based method, allowing for a better detection also of lower SSNR events, occurring around 4, 12.5, and 14 s. Figure 7 shows a close-up of the seismic event between 7.2 and 8.8 s and some extracted waveforms from the DAS array at different depths (i.e., 171, 418, and 821 m), exhibiting a clear enhancement after denoising, without affecting the signal's amplitudes or the phase. As in the previous test, a frame size of 0.06 s is used, and the noise power spectrum is estimated considering the first 30 frames (i.e., the first 0.9 s of each single channel of the DAS array). In Figure

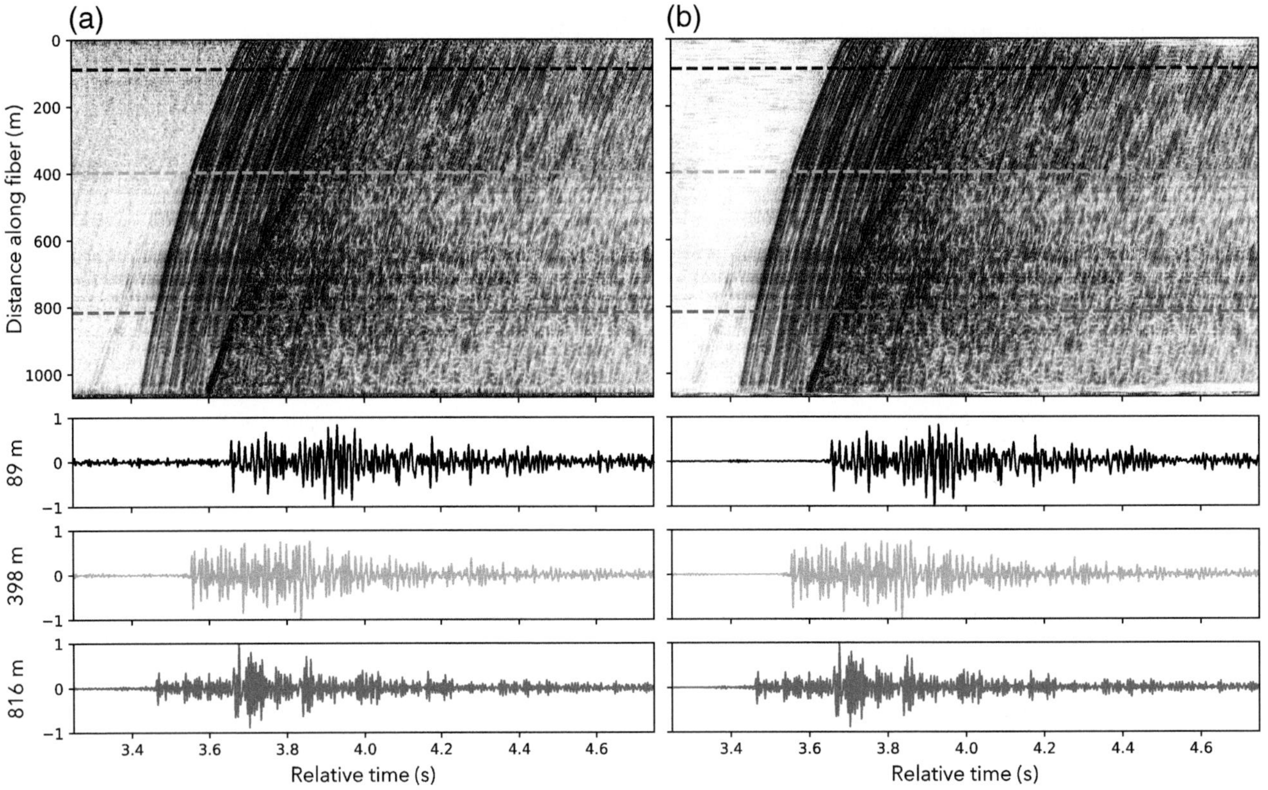

Figure 5. Zoomed-in section of the high-SSNR event around 3.4 s recorded by the DAS system, (a) before and (b) after the application of the proposed denoising framework, respectively. Three channel waveforms are extracted at different depths (89, 398, 816 m) of the DAS array and are highlighted by different colors. The color version of this figure is available only in the electronic edition.

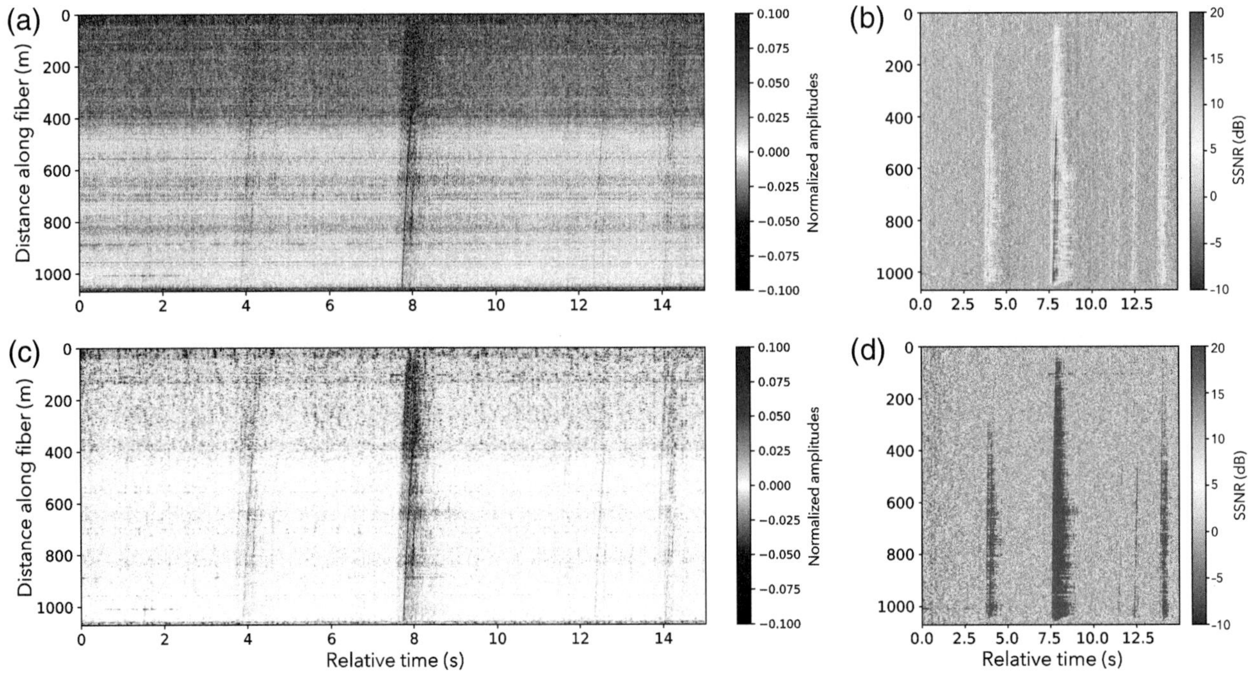

Figure 6. (a) Raw medium-SSNR DAS data from FORGE (FORGE_DFIT_UTC_20220421_155009.398.tdms) after the preprocessing steps. (c) Denoised DAS data after applying the oversubtraction workflow. Panels (b,d) are the SSNR values computed for each channel of the DAS array before and after the application of the denoising framework, respectively. The color version of this figure is available only in the electronic edition.

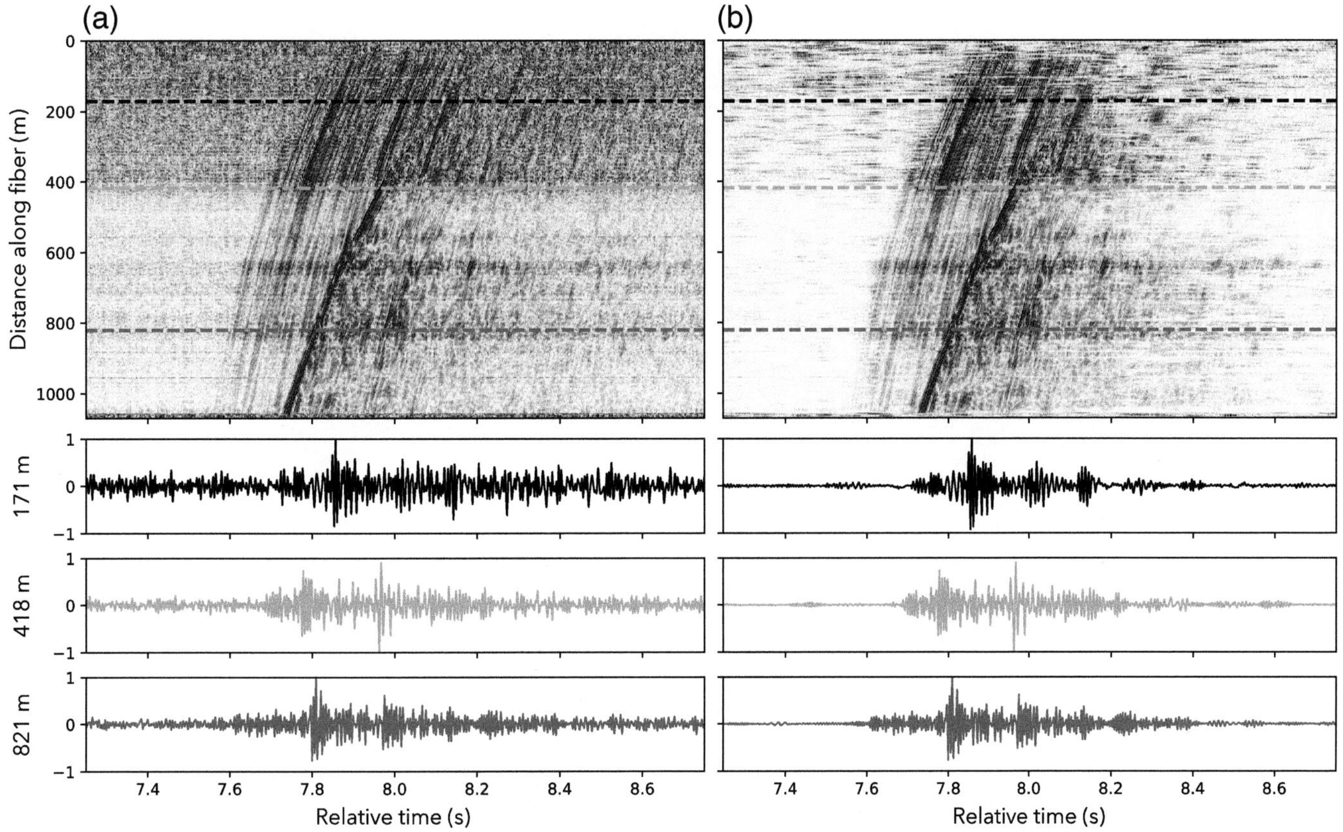

Figure 7. Zoomed-in section of the medium-SSNR event around 7.6 s recorded by the DAS system, (a) before and (b) after the application of the proposed denoising framework, respectively. Three channel waveforms are extracted at different depths (171, 418, 821 m) of the DAS array and are highlighted by different colors. The color version of this figure is available only in the electronic edition.

S6, the SSNR values computed for every channel are displayed using a different value of the spectral floor parameter β. As demonstrated, the lowest value of 0.002 as used in this example exhibits the highest SSNR values across all channels of the DAS array.

Third field example: Low-SSNR seismic event. A DAS recording under low SSNR (lower than 15 dB) conditions is then considered as a final test (file name "FORGE_DFIT_UTC_20220421_153109.398.tdms"). As shown in Figure 8a, in this case the microseismic events occurring especially around 6 and 14 s are barely visible even after the preprocessing stage described at the beginning of this section. However, a clear improvement is visible in Figure 8c after applying the proposed denoising framework. This can be better appreciated by looking at the SSNR values computed for each channel of the DAS array before (Fig. 8b) and after (Fig. 8d) applying the oversubtraction workflow. The parameters used for this test are the same as in the previous cases, demonstrating a notable improvement in SSNR after denoising and a better distinction of lower SNR events. Finally, a 1 s zoom-in around the event occurring around 3.2 s is displayed in Figure 9, along with some extracted waveforms from the DAS array at different depths (i.e., 466, 611, and 969 m). Despite the lower SSNR conditions of this selected event compared with the previous examples, in this case the oversubtraction denoiser also demonstrates a good enhancement of the selected waveforms and the overall recording in general, without affecting much of the signal's amplitudes.

Noise attenuation for the all cases are presented in Figures S7–S9. In addition, the supplemental material includes another denoising example using the proposed framework, this time applied to a weaker seismic event ("FORGE_DFIT_UTC_20220421_150754.398.tdms," Fig. S10). This event, characterized by a very low magnitude, remained undetectable even after standard preprocessing filtering procedures, which included an f-k filter to remove the $k = 0$ and a band-pass filter in the frequency range 5–250 Hz. After applying the oversubtraction denoiser, the event became much clearer and its SNR increased.

Discussion and Conclusions

This study presents a novel approach based on a spectral subtraction algorithm that has shown significant improvements in the SSNR of DAS data. The method was first tested on synthetics and then real DAS data from the FORGE EGS site, demonstrating robust performance across various SNR conditions. The algorithm effectively enhanced the SSNRs for events with different noise levels (SSNRs ranging from 10 to 40 dB). With the Utah FORGE dataset, we observed that typical values

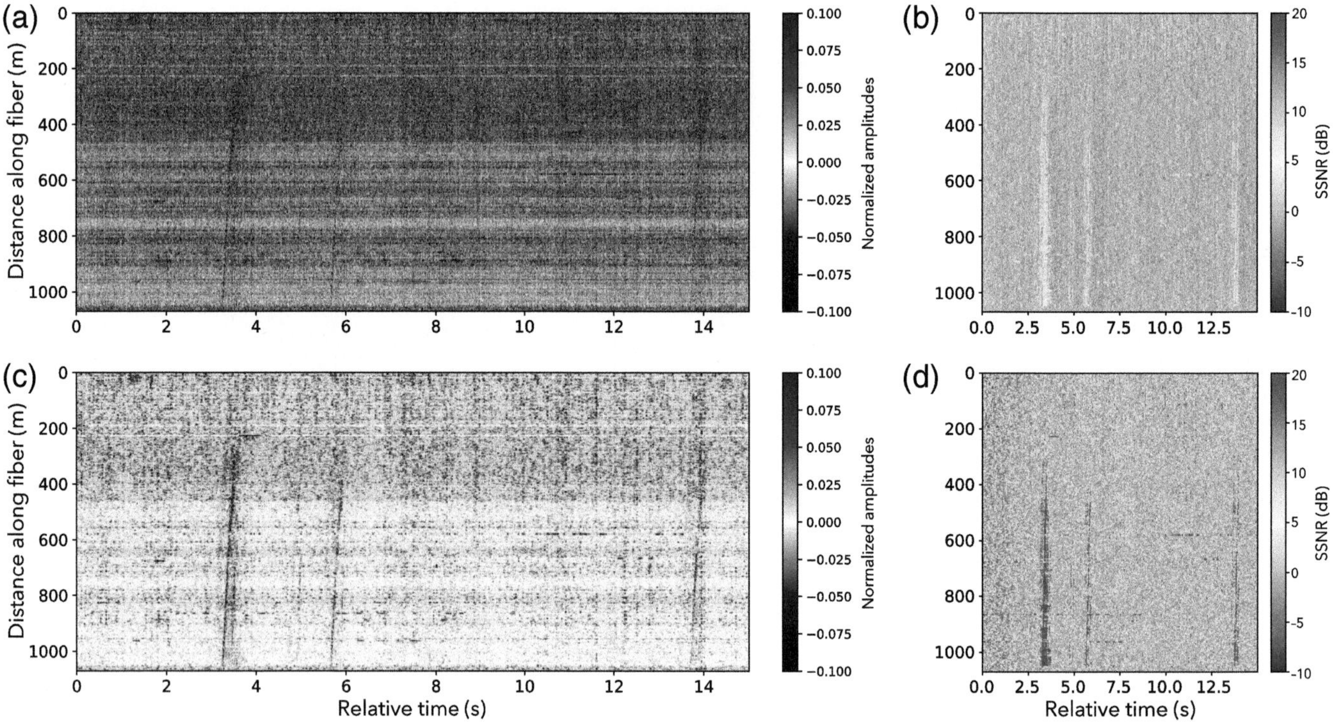

Figure 8. (a) Raw low-SSNR DAS data from FORGE (FORGE_DFIT_UTC_20220421_153109.398.tdms) after the preprocessing steps. (c) Denoised DAS data after applying the oversubtraction workflow. Panels (b,d) are the SSNR values computed for each channel of the DAS array before and after the application of the denoising framework, respectively. The color version of this figure is available only in the electronic edition.

of 0.06 s for frame size, 0.002 for the parameter β, and a G factor of 0.9 yielded optimal results under different SNR conditions, highlighting the versatility of our method in handling various noise conditions using only a few adjustable parameters. From a computational standpoint, the algorithm processed 15 s chunks of DAS recordings (i.e., 60.000 samples per trace) in ~ 1 min on a 2017 MacBook Pro (16 GB RAM, 3.1 GHz Intel Core i5). Considering a frame size of 0.06 s (i.e., 240 samples per frame), the algorithm processed a total of 499 frames per DAS channel.

Figure 10 shows the maximum SSNR values across all channels of the DAS data before and after denoising for a subset of microseismic events from the seismic catalog of Porras *et al.* (2024). Using the proposed denoising method, we successfully enhanced the SSNRs of 29 selected microseismic events, particularly those with low or very low SSNRs. The full list of these events, including their SSNR values before and after denoising, is provided in Table S1, along with their corresponding event IDs shown in Figure 10.

Compared with conventional filtering techniques (e.g., band-pass filtering, as applied, for example, in Lellouch *et al.*, 2021; Shimony and Lellouch, 2024a; Tuinstra *et al.*, 2024), and more recent machine learning (ML) or DL approaches, our spectral subtraction algorithm offers several advantages. Traditional filters cannot distinguish between signal and noise when both occupy the same frequency band, which often occurs in DAS recordings. In contrast, our algorithm targets the statistical differences between noise and signal spectra to selectively suppress noise components, even when they overlap with the signal spectrum. Similarly, multiscale transforms such as wavelet or curvelet denoising aim to suppress noise by thresholding transform coefficients. Although potentially effective, these approaches require careful parameter tuning and risk discarding low-amplitude microseismic signals, especially when the thresholds are not optimally chosen (Wang *et al.*, 2023). Our method uses instead a fixed set of interpretable parameters that control the strength of noise subtraction.

More recently, with the advances of ML and DL techniques, lots of promising results have been presented for DAS data denoising. However, these methods typically require large amounts of labeled training data, which are still a major limitation because of the lack of open-source datasets with continuous DAS data recordings. These models also often demand extensive tuning and significant computational resources (e.g., graphical processing units [GPUs]), which may not be available in many operational settings. In contrast, our spectral subtraction approach is purely signal-processing based and computationally lightweight, with no need for training or labeled data.

Moreover, we expect this method to perform well in various DAS deployment scenarios, including borehole installations with fiber-optic cables clamped outside the well's production tubing (as opposed to cemented behind casing, as in FORGE), or long seafloor cables used in offshore environments. In production wells, flow-induced noise (e.g., from turbulent flow in injection or production wells) is particularly marked when the

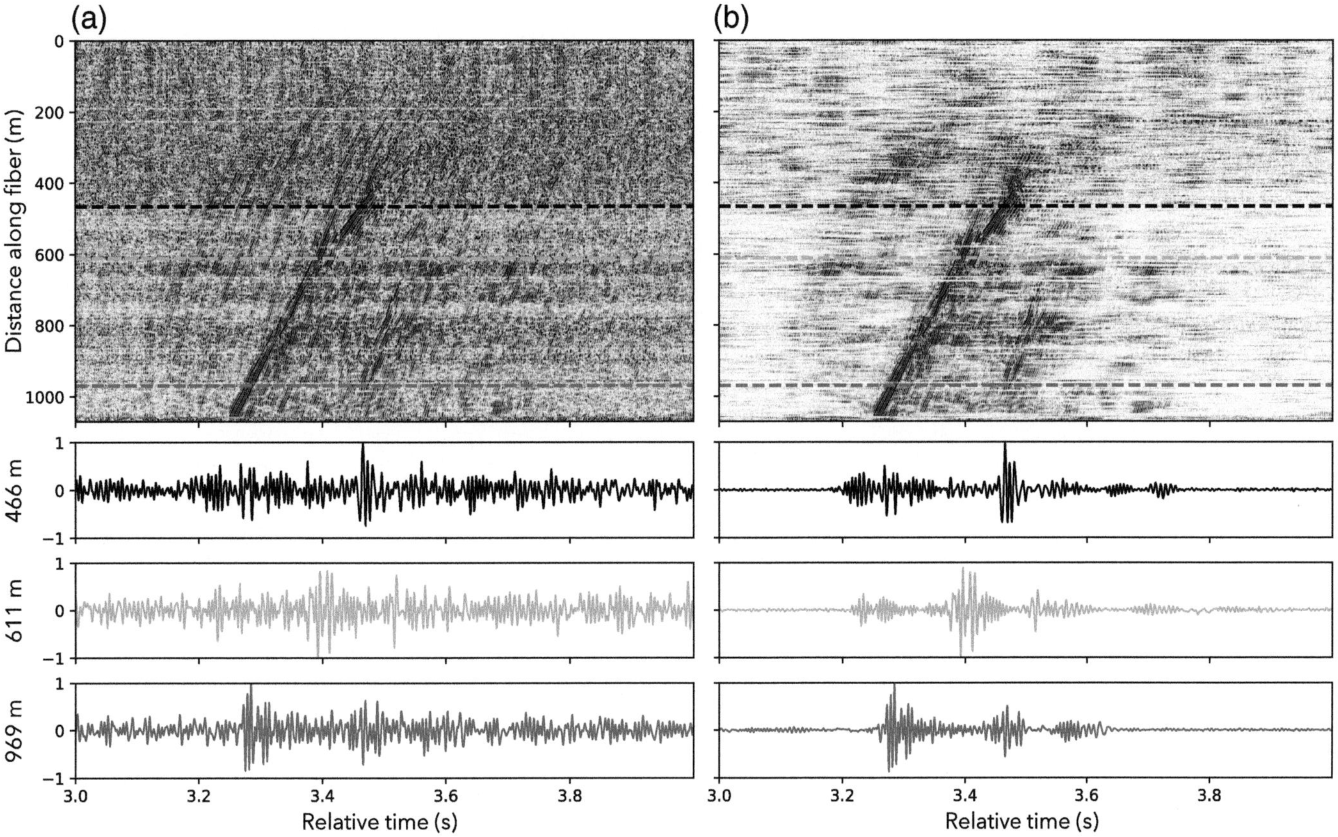

Figure 9. Zoomed-in section of the low-SSNR event around 3.2 s recorded by the DAS system, (a) before and (b) after the application of the proposed denoising framework, respectively. Three channel waveforms are extracted at different depths (466, 611, 969 m) of the DAS array and are highlighted by different colors. The color version of this figure is available only in the electronic edition.

cable is within the flow path and can mask low-amplitude signals (Zhan *et al.*, 2022, 2023). Flow noise often dominates low-frequency bands, and the use of conventional high-pass filters may suppress both the noise and valuable low-frequency signal content.

In seafloor cables, although DAS data generally benefit from higher SNR compared with surface or borehole deployments because of lower anthropogenic noise, nonoptimal seafloor coupling can locally reduce signal quality (Pelaez Quiñones *et al.*, 2023). Our method may help in this case to recover the low-amplitude signals that would otherwise remain undetected. However, because of the limited availability of open-access DAS datasets from such configurations, further testing is left for future work.

Despite its strengths, the method has some limitations. One assumption of our approach is that the noise spectrum can be estimated at the beginning of DAS recordings over frames in which no signal is present (i.e., assuming the noise is relatively stationary at the beginning of each frame). This may not hold in the presence of high-amplitude transient noise (Pecci *et al.*, 2024) or random noise spikes caused by phenomena such as laser frequency drift or laser noise (Zhirnov *et al.*, 2019), which could influence the noise spectrum estimation process and therefore reduce denoising effectiveness. Moreover, the algorithm processes each channel independently and does not currently exploit the spatial coherence across the DAS array. Consequently, it is not optimized for mitigating coherent multichannel noise (e.g., common-mode noise). Although many interrogator units include an internal reference length that can be leveraged to estimate this kind of noise and further enhance the quality of the retrieved signal (Hartog, 2017), in principle it could also be addressed more effectively by extending the proposed method to the *f*-*k* domain. Such an extension would require converting the actual trace-by-trace (1D) spectral subtraction algorithm into a 2D version using overlapping time–space patches. This could potentially eliminate the need for applying an *f*-*k* filter to remove the $k = 0$ component during the data preprocessing stage.

Finally, DAS instrumentation itself also imposes certain limitations; as previously mentioned, DAS data often contain high-amplitude transient signals or random spikes that our approach may not be able to fully remove, leaving residual noise in the output. In addition, although in the coming years we may expect improvements in DAS instrumentation and to lower the instrument's self-noise, the development of new processing techniques will continue to be essential to fully leverage the potential of DAS recordings.

In summary, we introduced a spectral subtraction algorithm for denoising DAS recordings and demonstrated its effectiveness

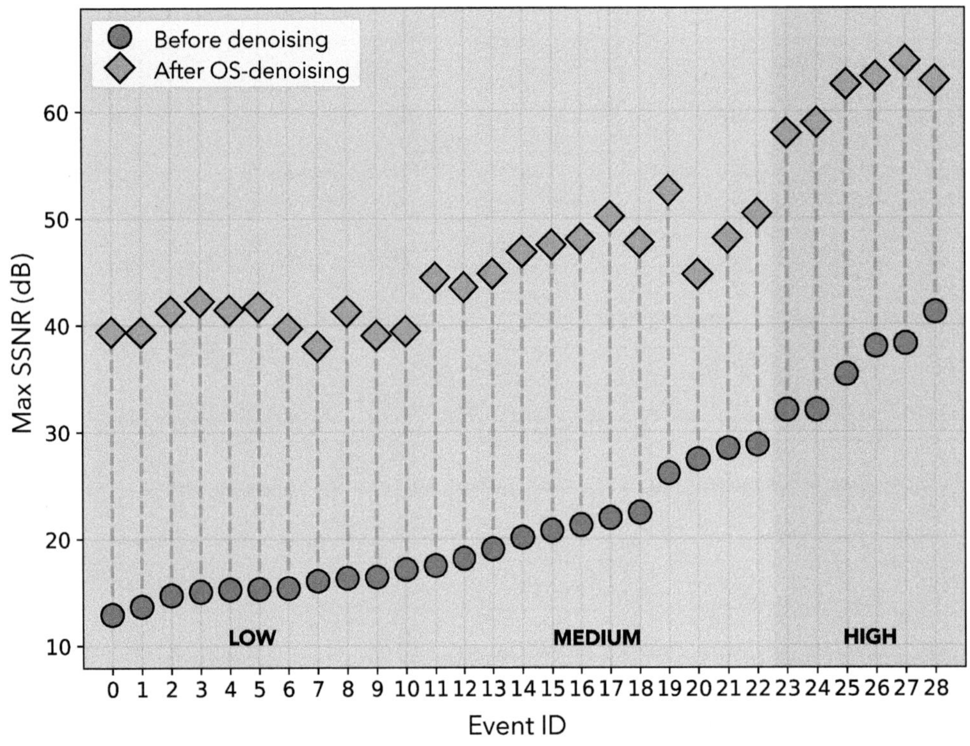

Figure 10. Improved maximum SSNR values over a selected number of microseismic events (i.e., 29) recorded at the FORGE EGS site during the stimulation occurred in April 2022, after applying the oversubtraction denoising framework. Different colors identify DAS data having different SSNR values (i.e., low, medium, and high). The color version of this figure is available only in the electronic edition.

on both synthetic and real data from the Utah FORGE EGS site. The method significantly improved the SSNRs of a selection of 29 microseismic events, particularly those under low SSNR conditions, offering several advantages over conventional filtering methods. The proposed algorithm relies on a small set of interpretable parameters, requires no labeled training data, and has a low computational cost, making it a practical and efficient plug-and-play solution for DAS data processing workflows. Although tested only on standard laptop hardware, the method could be adapted for real-time or near-real-time applications (e.g., through central processing unit– and/or GPU-based parallelization). Although this study focused on vertical-borehole DAS data for microseismic monitoring, the proposed method can be generalized and extended to other DAS use cases requiring signal enhancement. Future extensions of this work could focus on extending the algorithm into a 2D version using the *f-k* spectrum to exploit spatial coherence across channels. It would also be valuable to validate the algorithm on a broader range of DAS configurations (e.g., seafloor or horizontal cable deployments) as more datasets becomes publicly available.

Data and Resources

The Utah Frontier Observatory for Research in Geothermal Energy (FORGE) project provides complete access to fiber-optic data from the 2022 acquisition campaign, which can be downloaded from the U.S. Department of Energy (DOE) Geothermal Data Repository (doi: 10.15121/1871203). The Python code of the oversubtraction distributed acoustic sensing (DAS) denoiser, along with a Jupyter notebook tutorial demonstrating the method, is available on GitHub at https://github.com/giuliopas/DASpectralDenoiser.git (last accessed November 2025). The supplemental material contains additional figures cited in the article and a table of selected seismic events for which the denoising workflow was applied.

Declaration of Competing Interests

The authors acknowledge that there are no conflicts of interest recorded.

Acknowledgments

This work has been funded by the HORIZON EU project GEOHEAT (Grant Agreement 101147571) and the GEOTWINS project (Grant Agreement 101069750). The authors thank the reviewers for their valuable feedback and suggestions, which helped improve the quality of this work, as well as the editors for their support.

References

Afanasiev, M., C. Boehm, M. van Driel, L. Krischer, M. Rietmann, D. A. May, M. G. Knepley, and A. Fichtner (2018). Modular and flexible spectral-element waveform modelling in two and three dimensions, *Geophys. J. Int.* **216,** no. 3, 1675–1692.

Ajo-Franklin, J., V. Rodríguez Tribaldos, A. Nayak, F. Cheng, R. Mellors, B. Chi, T. Wood, M. Robertson, C. Rotermund, E. Matzel, *et al.* (2022). The imperial valley dark fiber project: Toward seismic studies using DAS and telecom infrastructure for geothermal applications, *Seismol. Res. Lett.* **93,** no. 5, 2906–2919.

Atterholt, J., Z. Zhan, Z. Shen, and Z. Li (2021). A unified wavefield-partitioning approach for distributed acoustic sensing, *Geophys. J. Int.* **228,** no. 2, 1410–1418.

Azzola, J., K. Thiemann, and E. Gaucher (2023). Integration of Distributed Acoustic Sensing (DAS) for real-time seismic monitoring of a geothermal field, *Geotherm. Energy* **11,** doi: 10.1186/s40517-023-00272-4.

Berouti, M., R. Schwartz, and J. Makhoul (1979). Enhancement of speech corrupted by acoustic noise, *ICASSP '79. IEEE International Conference on Acoustics, Speech, and Signal Processing,* Vol. 4, 208–211.

Binder, G., A. Titov, Y. Liu, J. Simmons, A. Tura, G. Byerley, and D. Monk (2020). Modeling the seismic response of individual hydraulic fracturing stages observed in a time-lapse distributed acoustic sensing vertical seismic profiling survey, *Geophysics* **85,** no. 4, T225–T235.

Biondi, E., G. Tepp, E. Yu, J. K. Saunders, V. Yartsev, M. Black, M. Watkins, A. Bhaskaran, R. Bhadha, Z. Zhan, *et al.* (2025). Real-time processing of distributed acoustic sensing data for earthquake monitoring operations, available at http://arxiv.org/abs/2505.24077 (last accessed October 2025).

Blackman, R., and J. Tukey (1958). *The Measurement of Power Spectra*, Dover Publications, New York, New York.

Boll, S. (1979). Suppression of acoustic noise in speech using spectral subtraction, *IEEE Trans. Acoust. Speech Signal Process.* **27,** no. 2, 113–120.

Bozzi, E., N. P. Agostinetti, A. Fichtner, S. Klaasen, A. Ugalde, B. Biondi, S. Yuan, T. Dahm, M. Isken, P. Paitz, *et al.* (2024). Modelling uncertainty in p-wave arrival-times retrieved from DAS data: Case-studies from 15 fibre optic cables, *Geophys. J. Int.* **239,** no. 3, 1928–1942.

Bremaud, V., E. Rebel, L. Lemaistre, and J. Vernier (2023). Capabilities of fiber optics deployed at seabed for microseismic monitoring: Northern lights case study, *The Fourth EAGE Global Energy Transition Conference and Exhibition*, Vol. 2023, 1–5.

Chen, J., J. Ning, W. Chen, X. Wang, W. Wang, and G. Zhang (2019). Distributed acoustic sensing coupling noise removal based on sparse optimization, *Interpretation* **7,** no. 2, T373–T382.

Cohen, I., and B. Berdugo (2002). Noise estimation by minima controlled recursive averaging for robust speech enhancement, *IEEE Signal Process Lett.* **9,** 12–15.

Ellmauthaler, A., M. Willis, X. Wu, and M. LeBlanc (2017). Noise sources in fiber-optic distributed acoustic sensing VSP data, *79th EAGE Conference and Exhibition 2017*, Vol. 2017, 1–5.

Ephraim, Y., and D. Malah (1984). Speech enhancement using a minimum-mean square error short-time spectral amplitude estimator, *IEEE Trans. Acoust. Speech Signal Process.* **32,** no. 6, 1109–1121.

Feigl, K., E. Reinisch, J. Patterson, S. Jreij, L. Parker, A. Nayak, X. Zeng, M. Cardiff, N. E. Lord, D. Fratta, *et al.* (2016). Porotomo natural laboratory horizontal and vertical distributed acoustic sensing data, doi: 10.15121/1778858.

Fernández-Ruiz, M. R., M. A. Soto, E. F. Williams, S. Martin-Lopez, Z. Zhan, M. Gonzalez-Herraez, and H. F. Martins (2020). Distributed acoustic sensing for seismic activity monitoring, *APL Photonics* **5,** no. 3, 030901-1–030901-16, doi: 10.1063/1.5139602.

Hart, J., B. Polat, C. Wollin, M. Lipus, F. Schölderle, T. Ledig, P. Jousset, T. Reinsch, and C. M. Krawczyk (2025). A fiber optic approach for cement placement and hydration assessment of deep geothermal boreholes, *Sci. Rep.* **15,** no. 1, 11,365.

Hartog, A. (2017). An introduction to distributed optical fibre sensors, in *Series in Fiber Optic Sensors*, A. Mendez (Editor), CRC Press, Boca Raton, Florida.

Isken, M., H. Vasyura-Bathke, T. Dahm, and S. Heimann (2022). De-noising distributed acoustic sensing data using an adaptive frequency-wavenumber filter, *Geophys. J. Int.* **231,** 944.

Jechumtálová, Z., D. Anikiev, and L. Eisner (2025). Sensitivity for monitoring array of distributed acoustic sensors (DAS) in a vertical borehole, *First Break* **43,** no. 4, 35–37.

Jousset, P., G. Currenti, B. Schwarz, A. Chalari, F. Tilmann, T. Reinsch, L. Zuccarello, E. Privitera, and C. M. Krawczyk (2022). Fibre optic distributed acoustic sensing of volcanic events, *Nat. Commun.* **13,** no. 1, 1753.

Kalinichenko, O., L. Eisner, F. Stanek, U. Bin Waheed, S. Hanafy, and Z. Jechumtálová (2025). Signal-to-noise ratio models for shallow borehole seismic monitoring, *Seismol. Res. Lett.* **96,** 3692.

Karrenbach, M., S. Cole, A. Ridge, K. Boone, D. Kahn, J. Rich, K. Silver, and D. Langton (2019). Fiber-optic distributed acoustic sensing of microseismicity, strain and temperature during hydraulic fracturing, *Geophysics* **84,** no. 1, D11–D23.

Klaasen, S., P. Paitz, N. Lindner, J. Dettmer, and A. Fichtner (2021). Distributed acoustic sensing in volcano-glacial environments—Mount meager, British Columbia, *J. Geophys. Res.* **126,** no. 11, e2021JB022358, doi: 10.1029/2021JB022358.

Klaasen, S., S. Thrastarson, Y. Çubuk Sabuncu, K. Jónsdóttir, L. Gebraad, P. Paitz, and A. Fichtner (2023). Subglacial volcano monitoring with fibre-optic sensing: Grímsvötn, Iceland, *Volcanica* **6,** no. 2, 301–311.

Konietzny, S., V. H. Lai, M. S. Miller, J. Townend, and S. Harmeling (2024). Unsupervised coherent noise removal from seismological distributed acoustic sensing data, *J. Geophys. Res.* **1,** no. 4, e2024JH000356, doi: 10.1029/2024JH000356.

Lapins, S., A. Butcher, J.-M. Kendall, T. S. Hudson, A. L. Stork, M. J. Werner, J. Gunning, and A. M. Brisbourne (2023). DAS-N2N: Machine learning distributed acoustic sensing (DAS) signal denoising without clean data, *Geophys. J. Int.* **236,** no. 2, 1026–1041.

Lellouch, A., N. J. Lindsey, W. L. Ellsworth, and B. L. Biondi (2020). Comparison between distributed acoustic sensing and geophones: Downhole microseismic monitoring of the FORGE geothermal experiment, *Seismol. Res. Lett.* **91,** no. 6, 3256–3268.

Lellouch, A., R. Schultz, N. Lindsey, B. Biondi, and W. Ellsworth (2021). Low-magnitude seismicity with a downhole distributed acoustic sensing array—Examples from the FORGE geothermal experiment, *J. Geophys. Res.* **126,** no. 1, doi: 10.1029/2020JB020462.

Li, Z., Z. Shen, Y. Yang, E. Williams, X. Wang, and Z. Zhan (2021). Rapid response to the 2019 Ridgecrest earthquake with distributed acoustic sensing, *AGU Adv.* **2,** no. 2, e2021AV000395, doi: 10.1029/2021AV000395.

Lindsey, N. J., H. Rademacher, and J. B. Ajo Franklin (2020). On the broadband instrument response of fiber-optic DAS arrays, *J. Geophys. Res.* **125,** no. 2, doi: 10.1029/2019JB018145.

Loizou, P. (2013). *Speech Enhancement: Theory and Practice*, Second Ed., Taylor & Francis, Boca Raton, Florida.

Lv, H., X. Zeng, B. Chi, G. Zhang, and C. Thurber (2023). Monitoring seismicity triggered by geothermal site shutdown with a surface DAS array at brady hot springs, *Geophys. J. Int.* **235,** no. 2, 1861–1871.

Ma, Y., J. Ajo-Franklin, A. Nayak, X. Zhu, J. Correa, and E. Kerr (2024). Distributed acoustic sensing microseismic reflection imaging for hydraulic fracture and fault lineament characterization, *Geophysics* **89,** no. 4, D183–D192.

McLennan, J. (2022). Utah FORGE: Well 16A(78)-32 stimulation data (April, 2022), doi: 10.15121/1871203.

Miah, K., and D. K. Potter (2017). A review of hybrid fiber-optic distributed simultaneous vibration and temperature sensing technology and its geophysical applications, *Sensors* **17,** no. 11, 2511.

Nishimura, T., K. Emoto, H. Nakahara, S. Miura, M. Yamamoto, S. Sugimura, A. Ishikawa, and T. Kimura (2021). Source location of volcanic earthquakes and subsurface characterization using fiber-optic cable and distributed acoustic sensing system, *Sci. Rep.* **11,** no. 1, 6319.

Pecci, D., S. Cesca, P. Niemz, K. Pankow, G. Carelli, and F. Grigoli (2024). Noise analysis of distributed acoustic sensing (DAS) data in borehole installations, *Seismol. Res. Lett.* doi: 10.1785/0220240292.

Pelaez Quiñones, J. D., A. Sladen, A. Ponte, I. Lior, J.-P. Ampuero, D. Rivet, S. Meulé, F. Bouchette, I. Pairaud, and P. Coyle (2023). High resolution seafloor thermometry for internal wave and upwelling monitoring using distributed acoustic sensing, *Sci. Rep.* **13,** no. 1, 17,459.

Pevzner, R., R. Isaenkov, S. Yavuz, A. Yurikov, K. Tertyshnikov, P. Shashkin, B. Gurevich, J. Correa, S. Glubokovskikh, T. Wood, *et al.* (2021). Seismic monitoring of a small CO_2 injection using a multi-well DAS array: Operations and initial results of Stage 3 of the CO2CRC Otway project, *Int. J. Greenhouse Gas Control* **110,** 103437, doi: 10.1016/j.ijggc.2021.103437.

Porras, J., D. Pecci, G. M. Bocchini, S. Gaviano, M. De Solda, K. Tuinstra, F. Lanza, A. Tognarelli, E. Stucchi, and F. Grigoli (2024). A semblance-based microseismic event detector for DAS data, *Geophys. J. Int.* **236,** no. 3, 1716.

Qin, Z., L. Chen, and X. Bao (2012). Wavelet denoising method for improving detection performance of distributed vibration sensor, *IEEE Photonics Technol. Lett.* **24,** no. 7, 542–544.

Rossi, C., F. Grigoli, P. Gasperini, S. Gandolfi, C. Cocorullo, T. Gukov, and P. Macini (2023). Seismic noise reduction as a function of depth recorded by a vertical array installed in a 285-m-deep borehole at a gas storage field in northern Italy, *Seismol. Res. Lett.* **94,** no. 4, 1925–1935.

Saad, O. M., M. Ravasi, and T. Alkhalifah (2024). Noise attenuation in distributed acoustic sensing data using a guided unsupervised deep learning network, *Geophysics* **89,** no. 6, V573–V587.

Shimony, E., and A. Lellouch (2024a). Microseismic event location with dual vertical DAS arrays: Insights from the FORGE 2022 stimulation, *Seismol. Res. Lett.* **95,** no. 4, 2290–2304.

Shimony, E., and A. Lellouch (2024b). Microseismic event location with dual vertical DAS arrays: Insights from the FORGE 2022 stimulation, *Seismol. Res. Lett.* **95,** no. 4, 2290–2304.

Shinohara, M., T. Yamada, T. Akuhara, K. Mochizuki, and S. Sakai (2022). Performance of seismic observation by distributed acoustic sensing technology using a seafloor cable off Sanriku, Japan, *Front. Mar. Sci.* **9,** 844506, doi: 10.3389/fmars.2022.844506.

Trabattoni, A., G. Festa, R. Longo, P. Bernard, G. Plantier, A. Zollo, and A. Strollo (2022). Microseismicity monitoring and site characterization with distributed acoustic sensing (DAS): The case of the Irpinia fault system (Southern Italy), *J. Geophys. Res.* **127,** no. 9, e2022JB024529, doi: 10.1029/2022JB024529.

Tuinstra, K., F. Grigoli, F. Lanza, A. P. Rinaldi, A. Fichtner, and S. Wiemer (2024). Locating clustered seismicity using distance geometry solvers: Applications for sparse and single-borehole DAS networks, *Geophys. J. Int.* **238,** no. 2, 661–680.

Van den Ende, M. P. A., I. Lior, J.-P. Ampuero, A. Sladen, A. Ferrari, and C. Richard (2021). A self-supervised deep learning approach for blind denoising and waveform coherence enhancement in distributed acoustic sensing data, *IEEE Trans. Neural Netw. Learn. Syst.* **34,** 3371.

Vargas, C. A., L. Caracciolo, and P. J. Ball (2022). Geothermal energy as a means to decarbonize the energy mix of megacities, *Commun. Earth Environ.* **3,** no. 1, 66.

Vondrasek, M., and P. Pollak (2005). Methods for speech SNR estimation: Evaluation tool and analysis of VAD dependency, *Radioengineering* **14,** no. 1, 6–11.

Wang, C., X. Huang, Y. Li, and K. Jensen (2023). Removing multiple types of noise of distributed acoustic sensing seismic data using attention-guided denoising convolutional neural network, *Front. Earth Sci.* **10,** doi: 10.3389/feart.2022.986470.

Willis, M. E. (2022). Distributed acoustic sensing for seismic measurements—What geophysicists and engineers need to know, Society of Exploration Geophysicists (SEG), 1–62, doi: 10.1190/1.9781560803850.

Xu, Z., B. Wu, Y. Luo, L. Yang, and Y. Chen (2024). SelfMixed: Self-supervised mixed noise attenuation for distributed acoustic sensing data, *Geophysics* **89,** no. 5, V415–V436.

Yang, L., S. Fomel, S. Wang, X. Chen, W. Chen, O. M. Saad, and Y. Chen (2023). Denoising of distributed acoustic sensing data using supervised deep learning, *Geophysics* **88,** no. 1, WA91–WA104.

Yang, L., S. Fomel, S. Wang, X. Chen, and Y. Chen (2023). Denoising distributed acoustic sensing data using unsupervised deep learning, *Geophysics* **88,** no. 4, V317–V332.

Zhan, G., Z. Liu, and W. Fei (2023). DAS VSP flow noise attenuation based on matching pursuit, **2023,** no. 1, 1–5.

Zhan, G., Y. Zhao, C. Cheng, J. Heim, W. Fei, M. Craven, S. Baker, and G. Hennenfent (2022). Noise analysis and ML denoising of DAS VSP data acquired from ESP lifted wells, *Second International Meeting for Applied Geoscience & Energy*, 597–601, doi: 10.1190/image2022-3750545.1.

Zhan, Z. (2019). Distributed acoustic sensing turns fiber-optic cables into sensitive seismic antennas, *Seismol. Res. Lett.* **91,** 1–15.

Zhang, H., and K. L. Pankow (2021). High-resolution Bayesian spatial autocorrelation (SPAC) quasi-3-D vs model of Utah FORGE site with a dense geophone array, *Geophys. J. Int.* **225,** no. 3, 1605–1615.

Zhang, J., A. Kato, A. Anil Dindar, W. Wang, S. Nakagawa, Y. Aoki, M. Shinohara, Y. Kaneda, and S. Tunç (2025). Preliminary analysis of distributed acoustic sensing (DAS) data using a submarine fiber-optic cable across the north Anatolian fault, *Seismol. Res. Lett.* doi: 10.1785/0220250049.

Zhang, Z., M. C. A. White, T. Bai, H. Qiu, and N. Nakata (2023). Characterizing microearthquakes induced by hydraulic fracturing with hybrid borehole DAS and three-component geophone data, *IEEE Trans. Geosci. Remote Sens.* **61,** 1–15.

Zhirnov, A. A., K. V. Stepanov, A. O. Chernutsky, A. K. Fedorov, E. T. Nesterov, C. Svelto, A. B. Pnev, and V. E. Karasik (2019). Influence of the laser frequency drift in phase-sensitive optical time domain reflectometry, *Opt. Spectrosc.* **127,** no. 4, 656–663.

Zitt, J., P. Paitz, A. Fichtner, F. Walter, and J. Umlauft (2025). Self-supervised coherence-based denoising of cryoseismological distributed acoustic sensing data, *J. Geophys. Res.* **2,** no. 3, doi: 10.1029/2024JH000414.

Manuscript received 24 March 2025
Published online 11 December 2025

Fiber-Optic Sensing for Earthquake Hazards Research, Monitoring, and Early Warning

OPEN ACCESS

Jeffrey J. McGuire* et al.

Abstract

The use of fiber-optic sensing systems in seismology has exploded in the past decade. Despite an ever-growing library of ground-breaking studies, questions remain about the potential of fiber-optic sensing technologies as tools for advancing if not revolutionizing earthquake-hazards-related research, monitoring, and early warning systems. A working group convened to explore these topics; we comprehensively examined the application of fiber optics in various aspects of earthquake hazards, encompassing earthquake source processes, crustal imaging, data archiving, and technological challenges. There is great potential for fiber-optic systems to advance earthquake monitoring and understanding, but to fully unlock their capabilities requires continued progress in key areas of research and development, including instrument testing and validation, increased dynamic range for applications focused on larger earthquakes, and continued improvement in subsurface and source imaging methods. A key current stumbling block results from the lack of clear data archiving requirements, and we propose an initial strategy that balances data volume requirements with preserving key data for a broad range of future studies. In addition, we demonstrate the potential for fiber-optic sensing to impact monitoring efforts by documenting the data completeness in a number of long-term experiments. Finally, we outline the features of a instrument testing facility that would enable progress toward reliable and standardized distributed acoustic sensing data. Overcoming these current obstacles would facilitate progress in fiber-optic sensing and unlock its potential application to a broad range of earthquake hazard problems.

Cite this article as McGuire, J. J., A. J. Barbour, Z. J. Spica, V. Rodríguez Tribaldos, Z. Zhan, B. P. Lipovsky, R. J. Mellors, E. Biondi, C. Yoon, M. Karrenbach, *et al.* (2025). Fiber-Optic Sensing for Earthquake Hazards Research, Monitoring, and Early Warning, *Seismol. Res. Lett.* **97**, 1919–1945, doi: 10.1785/0220250067.

Supplemental Material

Introduction

Fiber-optic sensing is revolutionizing Earth sciences by transforming fiber-optic cables into dense arrays of potentially thousands of seismic sensors measuring ground vibrations (Zhan, 2020; Lindsey and Martin, 2021; Li *et al.*, 2022). New insights into fundamental earthquake-related phenomena such as fault rupture, wavefield phenomena, and subsurface imaging are possible due to unprecedented spatial resolution and eased access to challenging sensing environments.

As fiber-optic sensing technology matures, it may have an increasingly important role in earthquake-hazards-related research and monitoring. A critical aspect of such monitoring and research is the ability to observe small-scale variations in wavefields over both long periods of time and broad areas. Distributed fiber-optic sensing technologies allow for multiscale observatories, with signals measured at evenly spaced locations along their length, and tunable spatial resolution using what's called an interrogator, which contains the laser, optical devices, and processing hardware. Using principles of interferometry, the interrogator pulses the laser and tracks backscattered light to create an array of virtual sensors measuring strain relative to a reference distance (the "gauge length"). The user is responsible for setting the temporal sampling, channel spacing, and gauge length, among other things (see also Hartog, 2017). Fiber-optic interrogators require relatively little maintenance, and fiber deployments themselves are typically reliable and durable—that is, individual fiber strands can be protected from weather and other environmental hazards via buried conduit, specialized cable jackets, and reinforced cable bundles. This implies that long-term operational expenses might be lower for fiber-optic sensing than for traditional seismic equipment.

Another benefit of using fiber optics to study earthquake sources and earth structure is that the sensitivity and dynamic

Full author list and affiliations appear at the end of this article.

*Corresponding author: jmcguire@usgs.gov

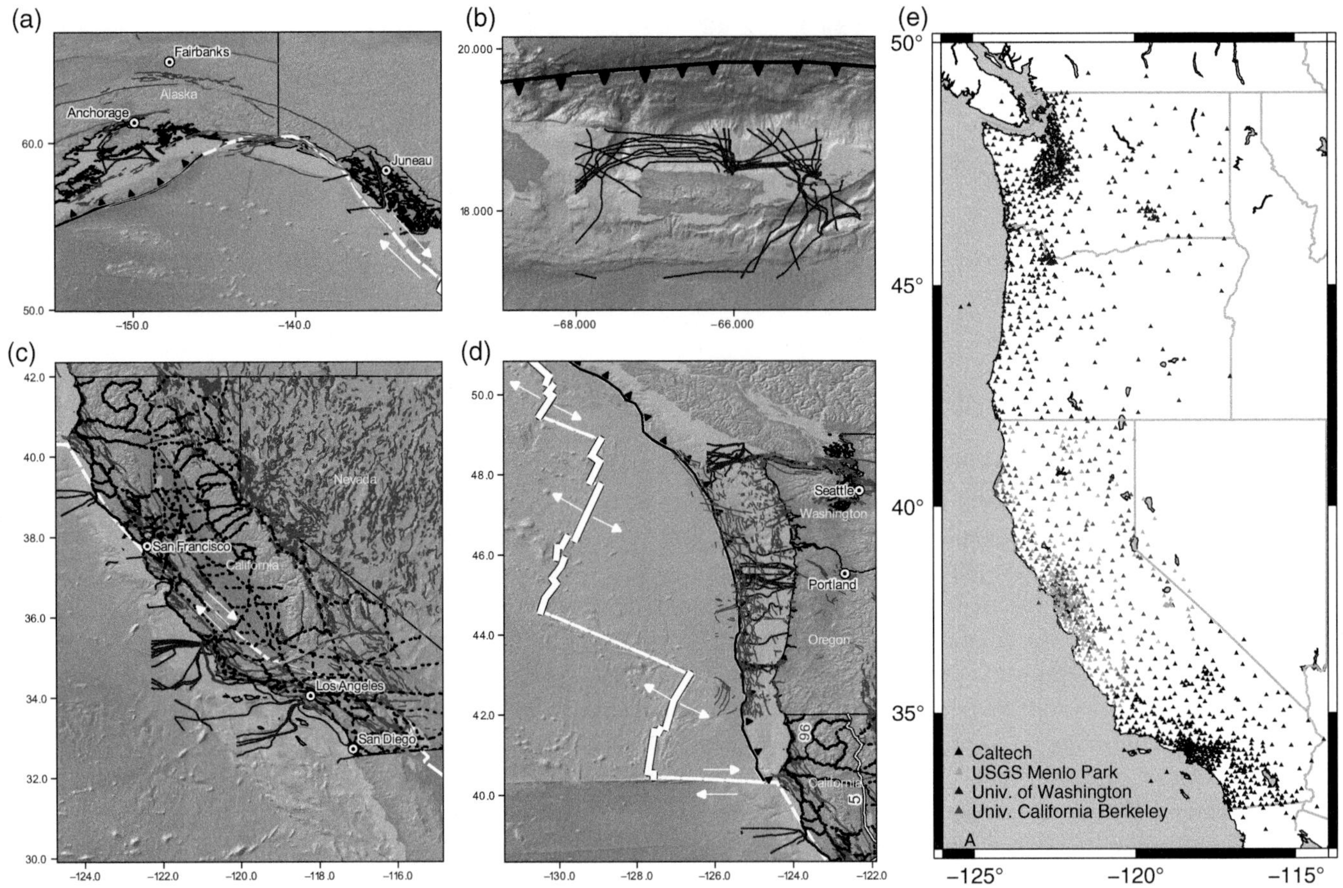

Figure 1. Maps of offshore cables (National Oceanic and Atmospheric Administration [NOAA] Office for Coastal Management, 2024) for Alaska (a), Puerto Rico (b), California (c), and Cascadia (d) regions. Cables are shown as blue lines out to variable distances between roughly 100–200 km from their landing stations. The red lines denote the U.S. Geological Survey (USGS) Quaternary faults database (USGS, 2017b). Thrust, spreading, and strike-slip tectonic plate boundaries are denoted with black lines and triangles; white thick lines and arrows; and white dashed lines and arrows, respectively. The California map denotes planned locations of fiber to be installed as part of the Middle Mile Initiative with black-dashed lines. (e) The distribution of stations for the ShakeAlert earthquake early warning (EEW) system as of July 2024 from McGuire, Ulberg, *et al.* (2025). The color version of this figure is available only in the electronic edition.

range of sensing systems can be customized. For example, fiber optics have been used in seismological applications with a broad range of signals, such as imaging the subsurface and identifying unmapped faults with ambient noise (Spica, Nishida, *et al.*, 2020; Atterholt *et al.*, 2022), measuring ground-motion amplification and attenuation (Yang *et al.*, 2022), studying the dynamics of earthquake ruptures and aftershock sequences (Li and Zhan, 2018; Li *et al.*, 2021; Li, Kim, *et al.*, 2023), and enhancing earthquake early warning (EEW) systems (Lior *et al.*, 2023; Yin *et al.*, 2023). Their applicability to offshore environments is also becoming increasingly apparent (Lindsey *et al.*, 2019; Sladen *et al.*, 2019; Williams *et al.*, 2019; Spica *et al.*, 2022; Viens *et al.*, 2022; Baillet *et al.*, 2025).

Although most experiments to date have covered relatively limited geographic areas with single fibers (~1–200 km in fiber length), the potential to expand this technology to cover wide areas using multiple data collection systems is clear from the geographic extent of existing fiber-optic coverage. For instance, in California, the state's Middle Mile Broadband Initiative (Zelezny, 2023) is installing tens of thousands of kilometers of fiber to improve internet access (Fig. 1c). This new, public resource covers the Pacific–North America plate boundary including hundreds of hazardous faults (Fig. 1). Importantly, the Middle Mile Broadband Initiative is prioritizing buried-cable installations as much as possible, which would thus enable myriad potential sites of data collection for geophysics.

Similarly, in offshore regions, submarine cables are routinely buried during installation for the portions that cross the continental shelf to avoid damage. The offshore portions of the subduction zones surrounding the United States (e.g., Alaska, Puerto Rico, and Cascadia) are covered by a large number of submarine cables installed by the telecom industry (Fig. 1). This presents an incredible opportunity for earthquake research and monitoring within the United States from regions that previously lacked continuous, real-time telemetered data. Figure 1e shows the current distribution of seismic stations within the U.S. West Coast that contribute to the

ShakeAlert EEW system (e.g., Given *et al.*, 2018; Lux *et al.*, 2024). With the exception of a handful of island stations and instruments attached to research submarine cables, the system lacks offshore data both in Cascadia and in important areas in California such as offshore Los Angeles. Because submarine cable networks expand, there is potential to fundamentally change earthquake monitoring and related studies.

Researchers are continually developing new ways to use fiber-optic sensing to measure earthquake-related phenomena such as source complexity, or changes related to fault slip such as transient deformation, temperature, and pore pressure. There are, however, outstanding issues related to data quality and other technological limitations of fiber-optic systems, and a general lack of community-adopted standards for seismology-related datasets. These challenges represent a major hurdle to broad adoption of systems, especially if they are intended to collect a substantial amount of critical data in future monitoring and research studies. Recent efforts to establish standards for distributed acoustic sensing (DAS) data (Taverna *et al.*, 2023) and metadata (Lai *et al.*, 2024), and to provide publicly accessible datasets (Weers *et al.*, 2022; Spica *et al.*, 2023; Wuestefeld *et al.*, 2024) are critical steps toward broader adoption.

Owing to the rapidly expanding set of DAS earthquake datasets and the variety of archiving approaches it can be difficult for earthquake researchers to identify appropriate datasets. To facilitate DAS data discovery for earthquake research, we have constructed a U.S. Geological Survey (USGS) web tool that connects the earthquake catalogs of the Advanced National Seismic System (ANSS), USGS fault databases, and other relevant information to specific DAS experiments with publicly available data (Sawi *et al.*, 2025).

This article represents the first major outcome from a USGS Powell Center working group (see Data and Resources) examining the use of fiber optics in earthquake hazards research and monitoring. This group is composed of an international team of experts from academia and government agencies to generate ideas and potential solutions to the complex problems surrounding these topics. In particular, this article explores the technical applications and challenges of using fiber-optic sensing technology for earthquake hazards research and monitoring. It first outlines the technologies considered by the Fiber-Optic Powell Center working group. The article then discusses how this technology can be used for imaging the structure of the Earth, and examines its potential for understanding the physics of earthquake sources and its practical use in areas like EEW systems, induced seismicity, and routine earthquake monitoring. These applications represent what the Fiber-Optic Powell Center views as three fundamental aspects of earthquake hazards.

The article further addresses the practical and logistical hurdles of implementing this technology on a larger scale. It compares the crosscutting issues of principal data quality, instrument testing, and data archiving needs for these applications, and discusses present technological limitations. This includes the need for a dedicated testing facility and the development of robust data standards and archiving strategies to manage the large volume of data generated. We also discuss the Fiber-Optic Powell Center's perceptions of the operational implications of larger-scale adoption. The article concludes with specific recommendations for creating an effective data facility to support future research.

Fiber-Optic Sensing Technology for Earthquake Seismology

The discussion in later sections hinges on a clear understanding of the fiber-optic sensing technologies considered by the Fiber-Optic Powell Center. These include any method that uses light in a fiber as the primary sensing mechanism for observing physical quantities in the earth such as strain, pressure, and temperature changes (Hartog, 2017, see Fig. 2). A critical distinction between the fiber systems considered by the Fiber-Optic Powell Center and traditional measurement systems is they can be configured to provide so called "distributed" measurements along the fiber. Distributed measurements do not predefine the location of measurements, but rather use the fiber material itself and principles of wave scattering. Linear and nonlinear scattering effects are utilized in a variety of ways: sensing devices that utilize a single light-scattering effect (e.g., Rayleigh, Raman, or Brillouin) to determine the physical observable (Fig. 2) are most common.

Advancements in fiber-optic sensing technology enabling transformative science have coincided with advances in other supporting technologies (Fig. S1, available in the supplemental material to this article). Early development of laser sources and fiber manufacturing capabilities were often driven by early adopters in the defense or telecom (telecommunications) industries. Because the commercial availability of laser and fiber technologies became increasingly common, they were typically applied to high-value sensing applications (e.g., hydraulic fracturing) where it was not economical to deploy conventional electronic sensing devices due to their unreliability or their very limited lifetime (e.g., high pressure and temperature environments). Increases in computational and data storage capabilities, cheaper high-quality optical components, and a variety of commercial fiber and cable types led to a considerable increase in fiber-optic sensing applications: for the last decade, the number of technical and scientific articles has grown exponentially (e.g., Zhan, 2020), while the technology has been propagating across technical and scientific disciplines.

The majority of the boom in fiber-optic sensing in seismology is related to the increasing popularity of DAS technology, mainly because it provides a cost-effective tool to deploy an array of dynamic strain (or strain rate) measurements in the seismic band, and in certain situations may be directly compared to data from inertial instrumentation. DAS utilizes Rayleigh-type scattering to do this (Fig. 2), wherein optical phase changes due to wave interference provide direct measures of dynamic strain. Of course, the spectrum of earthquake-related deformation is not

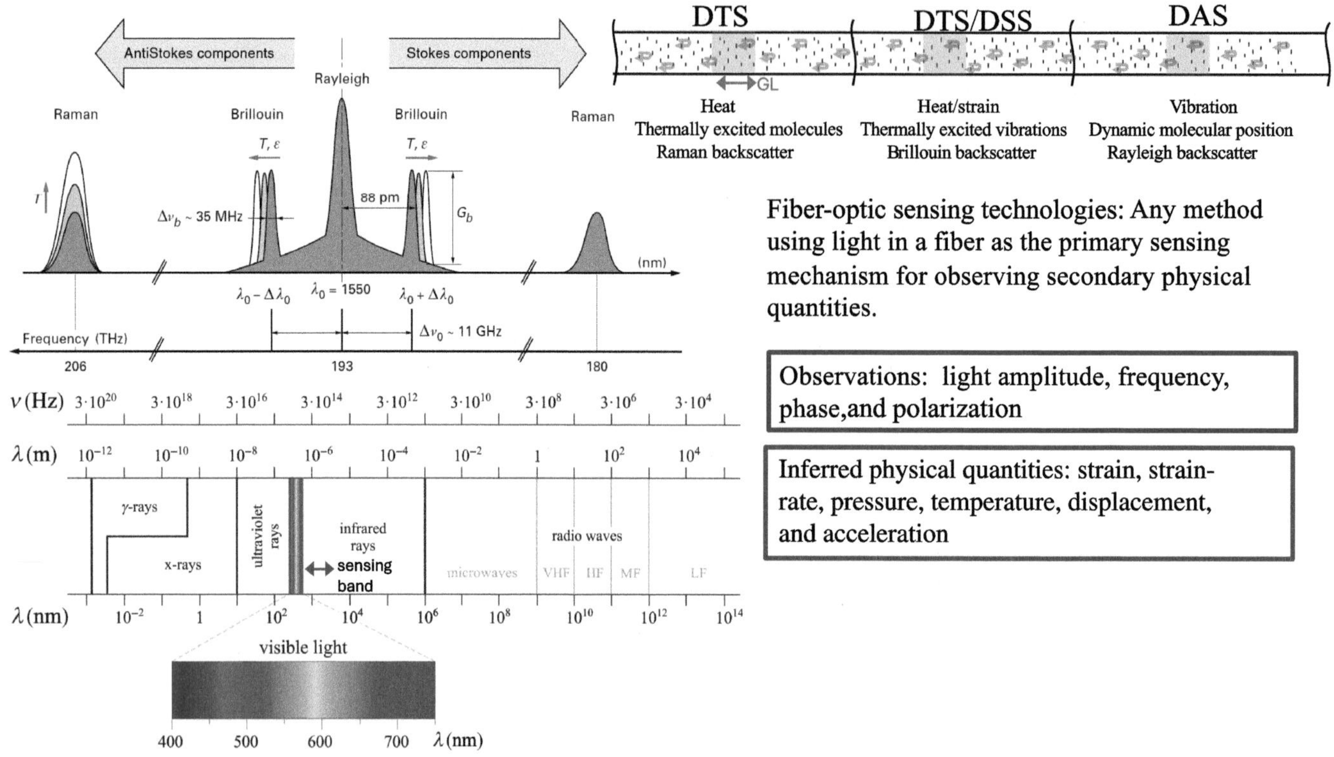

entirely dynamic, and because DAS is a relative measurement, it is not necessarily the best tool to measure (quasi)static crustal deformation; for this, there are two separate technologies, namely distributed strain sensing (DSS) and distributed temperature sensing (DTS) that utilize Brillouin and Raman scattering, respectively. DSS and DTS are typically used in more specialized applications where absolute strain or temperature measurements are needed over far-longer periods (e.g., hours to days).

Although distributed fiber-optic sensing was initially developed in the energy industry for use in relatively short fibers in boreholes and temporary experiments, the technology has rapidly matured: long-duration, semicontinuous datasets are becoming more common. Table 1 denotes some recent long-duration experiments making use of DAS for research purposes. The ability of commercially available instrumentation to take data for a year or more continuously and over ~100 km long fibers with >99% completeness is a major achievement in instrument development borne out of robust engineering and construction of the instrumentation by the industry, and the careful operational methods adopted by practitioners. This breakthrough in stability, sensitivity, and interrogation range shows that fiber-optic sensing can be a potentially cost-effective way to expand the types of seismological research and monitoring that can be done. In the following sections, we describe this in more detail, and focus on the more critical aspects of earthquake-hazards-related applications.

Applications to Earth Structure Imaging

Seismic imaging is an integral part of earthquake hazard research, from mapping and characterizing faults and fault

Figure 2. Basic principles of fiber-optic sensing. The key technologies of distributed temperature sensing (DTS), distributed strain sensing (DSS), and distributed acoustic sensing (DAS) rely on three different types of scattering mechanisms: Raman, Brillouin, and Rayleigh. They respond to different physical properties of the fiber, including heat, strain, and vibration, and they are recorded at different wavelengths relative to the transmitted signal, which is often 1550 nm (see spectrum in the top left). DAS measures phase and/or polarization at the transmitted wavelength, which are related to strain, strain rate, and temperature. DTS measures amplitude at the Raman frequency shift, which is related to temperature. DTS and DSS can use the Brillouin frequency shift measurement, which is stable and appropriate for high-sensitivity measurements and proportional to strain and temperature. Both Stokes and anti-Stokes scattering can be used depending on the interrogator design. The measurements are made on reflected light and typically averaged over a finite-gauge length (GL) denoted in the cartoon. The spectrum in the upper left is from Ferdinand (2014). The full electromagnetic spectrum is shown in the lower left. Fiber-optic sensing typically uses the range from 800 to 1700 nm wavelength in the infrared band, denoted by the red arrow. Fiber-optic interrogators measure the amplitude, frequency content, phase, and polarization of the reflected signal directly (e.g., the blue box). Those measurements are converted to estimates of physical variables along the fiber, including (e.g., the red box) strain, strain rate, pressure, temperature, displacement, acceleration, and so forth. Because of the range of physical properties that can potentially be sensed remotely, the applications of fiber-optic sensing are rapidly expanding. The color version of this figure is available only in the electronic edition.

TABLE 1
Examples of Long-Duration Distributed Acoustic Sensing (DAS) Experiments

Group	Location	Duration (mo.)	Date (yyyy/mm/dd)	Completeness	Volume (TB)	Reasons for Outages	Reference
Penn State, Mines, UAF	Utqiaġvik, Alaska	>36	2021/09/03 to present	>90% so far	>150 so far	Cable break, internet outage, cable bend, and power outage	Tourei *et al.* (2024)
Caltech	Ridgecrest, California	30	2021/08/10–2024/03/12	>95%	160	Power reboots interrogator failure	Atterholt *et al.* (2024)
Caltech	Mammoth Lk, California	24	2022/03/08–2024/03/12	>99%	97	Power reboots	Li *et al.* (2023)
USGS, Cal Poly Humboldt	Arcata, California	24	2022/12/22–2024/12/31	>99%	40	Power reboots	McGuire, Barbour, *et al.* (2025)
UNAM University of Michigan	Mexico City	15	2022/05/06–2023/07/26	~93%	124	GPS failure	Li *et al.* (2024)
UW	Mt. Rainier Ntl. Park, Washington	12	2023/08/15–2024/09/18	98%	100	Power reboots full disks	Ni *et al.* (2024)
UW	Homer, Alaska	12	2023/06/08–2024/11/06	95%	120	Power reboots	Williams *et al.* (2024)
UCB MBARI	Monterey Bay, California	>12	2022/07/21 to present	99%	>300 so far	Power outage and system updates	Romanowicz *et al.* (2023)

GPS, Global Positioning System; UCB, Univ. of California, Berkeley; UMich, University of Michigan; UNAM, Universidad Nacional Autónoma de México; USGS, U.S. Geological Survey; UW, University of Washington.

zones, to imaging basement structure and sedimentary basins. Accurate, high-resolution measurements of shear-wave velocity (V_S) in the upper few tens of meters of the subsurface underneath populated areas help constrain site amplification and improve ground-motion simulations (Denolle *et al.*, 2014). Of all applications of DAS in seismology, subsurface imaging is one of the most widespread and commonly used. DAS measurements offer new possibilities for subsurface imaging at a spatial resolution and extent previously unattainable with traditional passive seismic surveys, in a variety of environments and for a wide range of applications relevant to earthquake hazard (Fig. 3). The success of early imaging studies with DAS (Daley *et al.*, 2013; Mateeva *et al.*, 2013, 2014; Miller *et al.*, 2016) can be attributed to the fact that travel-time-based analyses, using earthquakes or the ambient seismic noise, should theoretically yield the same results for both DAS and geophone-equivalent data (Zeng *et al.*, 2017; Wang *et al.*, 2018; Nayak *et al.*, 2021), making these techniques readily applicable to DAS datasets.

Subsurface imaging with DAS in areas of high seismic hazard represents a more recent and innovative development. One of the first validations of using DAS for shallow imaging was performed by Dou *et al.* (2017) using an ambient seismic noise inversion scheme. Since then, shallow imaging with DAS has expanded to both purpose-built fibers (e.g., Lellouch *et al.*, 2019; Zeng *et al.*, 2021) and existing telecommunication infrastructure (e.g., Spica, Perton, *et al.*, 2020; Shragge *et al.*, 2021; Williams *et al.*, 2021). These studies span a variety of environments, including urban areas, remote mountains and glaciers, volcanoes, and even offshore locations (Fig. 3; see also Spica, Nishida, *et al.*, 2020). Many of the pioneering studies were essential to lay the foundations of DAS for passive seismic applications, and for example, establishing the importance of the network geometry (e.g., Daley *et al.*, 2013, 2016) or testing the effects of different types of fiber-optic cable constructions (Dou *et al.*, 2017). A few studies have also investigated near-surface imaging using active seismic sources (Costley *et al.*, 2018; Song *et al.*, 2019; Lancelle *et al.*, 2021; Vantassel *et al.*, 2022; Hong *et al.*, 2024). More recently, advances in machine learning have allowed the detection and picking of a large database of earthquake waveforms (Zhu *et al.*, 2023), which has led to the first DAS-based body-wave tomography study at the crustal scale (Biondi *et al.*, 2023).

Imaging applications relevant to USGS

Numerous factors affect the accuracy of earthquake hazard assessments, including material properties and geological structure at local and regional scales. The effect of seismic structure on earthquake ground shaking is used in USGS hazards products such as in ShakeMap (Wald *et al.*, 2022), the U.S. National Seismic Hazard Model (Petersen *et al.*, 2024), and the ShakeAlert EEW system (Lux *et al.*, 2024; McGuire, Ulberg, *et al.*, 2025) through empirical relationships. ShakeMap and the National Seismic Hazard Model use ground-motion models (GMMs) to

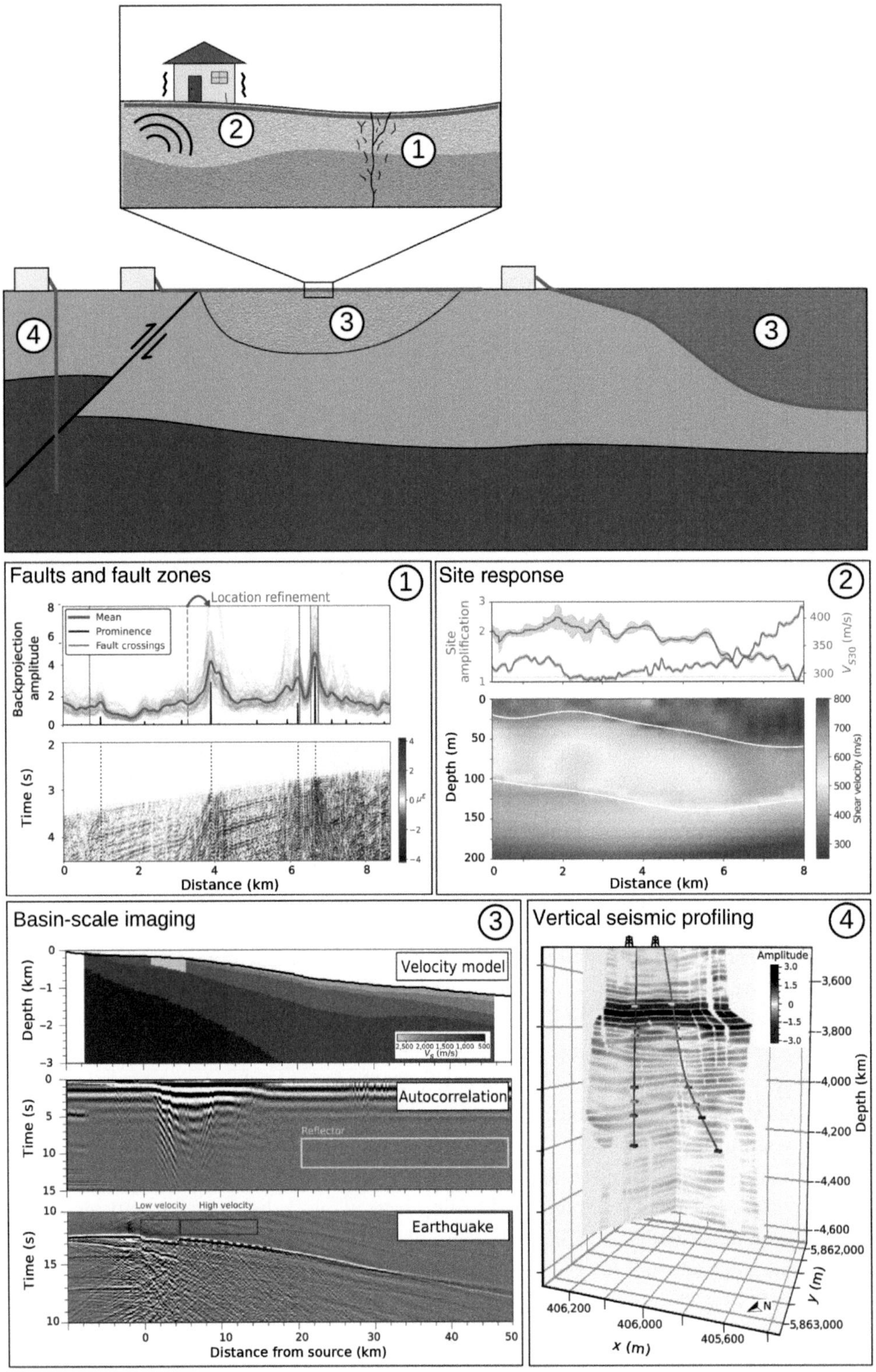

Figure 3. Schematic illustrating possible structural imaging targets with DAS and corresponding examples from onshore, offshore, and borehole fibers. Numbered callouts in schematic are: (1) fault zone mapping via backprojection of earthquake scattered waves measured by a DAS array (adapted from Atterholt *et al.*, 2022); (2) observed correlation between site amplification and a shallow structural model produced via ambient noise cross correlations of DAS channels (adapted from Yang *et al.*, 2021); (3) theoretical velocity model and retrieved auto-correlation and earthquake seismic wavefield (adapted from Spica, Nishida, *et al.*, 2020); and (4) 3D DAS vertical seismic profile (VSP) cube (adapted from Martuganova *et al.*, 2022). The color version of this figure is available only in the electronic edition.

model ground shaking for deterministic or probabilistic scenarios, respectively. The functional forms of the GMMs use the seismological partitioning of ground motion into source, path, and site effects. To model the site effects arising from different seismic structures, modern empirical GMMs use simplified parameterizations of the shallow shear-wave velocity and proxies for basin depth such as V_{S30}, the time-averaged shear-wave velocity in the top 30 m, as well as Z_1 or $Z_{2.5}$, the depths to V_S isosurfaces of 1 and 2.5 km/s, respectively. The empirical relationships between these site parameters and ground-motion amplification have been developed for broad regions, such as California or the central and eastern North America (e.g., Field, 2000; Power *et al.*, 2004; Parker *et al.*, 2016), and thus the site response models in GMMs represent the regionally averaged site effects.

Future directions in modeling earthquake ground motions are likely to include increased regionalization of the GMMs, site-response models informed by improved understanding of lateral variations in seismic velocity structure, and increased use of 3D simulations. Examples of these GMMs are available (e.g., Graves *et al.*, 2011; Abrahamson *et al.*, 2019), and advancing their use in USGS hazards products may require, among other needs, further characterization of high-resolution seismic velocity structures and their impacts on ground motions.

The imaging capabilities of DAS have the potential to support current and future USGS earthquake hazards assessments by enabling high-resolution (meter-to-kilometer scale) seismic velocity imaging, specifically at depths critical for characterizing ground-motion amplification effects. DAS can provide both dense spatial sampling over regional scales and broadband sensitivity, which enables seismic imaging at varying scales and depths. This multiresolution capability of DAS has been demonstrated in various recent studies using dark fiber, which is a fiber that exists as part of telecom infrastructure but is not actively used (e.g., for redundancy). For example, in the Imperial Valley in southern California, two days of ambient seismic noise recorded along a dark-fiber DAS array enabled the development of two different imaging products, one targeting the basin seismic structure at depths down to ~3 km with a spatial resolution of 5 km (Cheng, Ajo-Franklin, Nayak, *et al.*, 2023), and another one imaging the shallower 70 m, V_{S30}, and ground amplification with a resolution of 100 m (Cheng, Ajo-Franklin, and Rodriguez Tribaldos, 2023). The V_S model of Cheng, Ajo-Franklin, Nayak, *et al.* (2023) reveals a previously unmapped, high-velocity zone associated with hydrothermal alteration beneath the North Brawley geothermal field, as well as low-velocity anomalies associated with fault structures within the Brawley seismic zone and other previously unmapped features (Fig. 4).

In the context of improved GMMs, the Imperial Valley and other DAS imaging studies demonstrate that DAS could not only yield an increased number of V_{S30} measurements along large distances, but also has the potential to fill the "observational gap" between the very shallow and deep domains, providing additional and more accurate estimates of Z_1, $Z_{2.5}$, or Z_{sed} (depth to the sediment–basement contact) as well as information about regional velocity structure variations and basin geometry, which are important contributors to long-period motions (especially in deep basins). Higher resolution shear-wave velocity observations across broad regions can also open opportunities to investigate additional aspects of ground motion and amplification such as the relationship between seismic velocity structure and ground-motion distance attenuation (Sung *et al.*, 2023) and improved modeling of nonlinear site amplification response (Hou and Zhao, 2021). Higher resolution site response maps can also benefit systems like ShakeAlert by enabling modeling and forecasting short-wavelength variations in ground motions in areas affected by strong shaking (Parker and Baltay, 2022; Lin *et al.*, 2023; McGuire, Ulberg, *et al.*, 2025).

A sharpened view of near-surface structure and basin parameters is perhaps most important in densely populated areas, where seismic risk is generally the highest. In these areas, obtaining the necessary observational coverage using conventional sensors is challenging; however, telecom networks are abundant and widespread, which, when coupled with DAS systems, provides a new paradigm for urban imaging (e.g., Spica, Perton, *et al.*, 2020; Shragge *et al.*, 2021; Cheng, Ajo-Franklin, Nayak, *et al.*, 2023; Li *et al.*, 2023; Ji *et al.*, 2024). Moreover, except in rare cases, the location of existing fiber networks will not change, and thus dark-fiber DAS provides an unprecedented opportunity for more reliable repeated experiments for subsurface monitoring and time-dependent studies (Rodríguez Tribaldos and Ajo-Franklin, 2021; Yang and Shragge, 2023).

Improving the resolution of crustal-scale seismic velocity models is also critical to understand the contribution of deeper crustal structures to ground-motion amplification patterns (Boyd *et al.*, 2024). Recent advances in earthquake tomography approaches combining DAS with local and/or regional seismic networks have yielded *P*-wave and *S*-wave velocity models of unprecedented resolution down to depths of 15 km (Biondi *et al.*, 2023).

Beyond improving ground-motion estimations, the imaging capabilities of DAS have the potential to improve other earthquake-hazard-related products and investigations. Maps of liquefaction potential could also be improved with the addition of higher-resolution seismic velocity structure information along with ground motion and other geotechnical measurements. Recent work also suggests that the high spatial resolution of DAS may be useful in detecting and monitoring landslide processes (Ouellet *et al.*, 2024; Xie *et al.*, 2024). Dense sampling may also allow for identification and characterization of faults and fault zones that could be invisible to sparse seismic networks. Using a cable in Iceland, Jousset *et al.* (2018) observed phase delays, amplified body-wave coda, and long-period strain signals that are spatially coincident with fault zones that cross the fiber. Lindsey *et al.* (2019) observed earthquake-scattered waves with an offshore DAS array that were collocated with mapped and unmapped faults. Atterholt *et al.* (2022) developed a technique to systematically map and quantify this scattering using a fiber near the 2019 Ridgecrest earthquake sequence (Fig. 3); with modeling found that the frequency content of these scattered waves is related to the dimensionality of the fault zone, and Yang *et al.* (2022) reached a similar result using acausal and coda signals in ambient noise cross correlations. Some recent work has been directed toward using DAS for high-resolution imaging of major fault zones as well: Atterholt *et al.* (2024) used DAS to constrain the geometry of the fault damage zone of the Garlock fault and to measure the velocity contrast across the fault; and Ma *et al.* (2024) used a borehole fiber crossing the Milun thrust fault to document amplification in the fault gouge zone.

Challenges and key opportunities for future imaging research. Despite the advancements highlighted earlier, there are some significant technical challenges to providing accurate 3D tomographic velocity models of specific regions using telecom infrastructure. There is often a lack of control of the cable's precise path, type, and coupling conditions when using pre-existing fibers; this may require fit-for-purpose installations, which could be challenging in urban areas.

The linear nature of telecom grids limits imaging to 2D transects as opposed to a 3D volume. However, dense grids of fiber-optic cables in urban areas offer opportunities to move toward 2D and 3D surface-wave tomography. Simultaneous recording on multiple cables with different orientations can

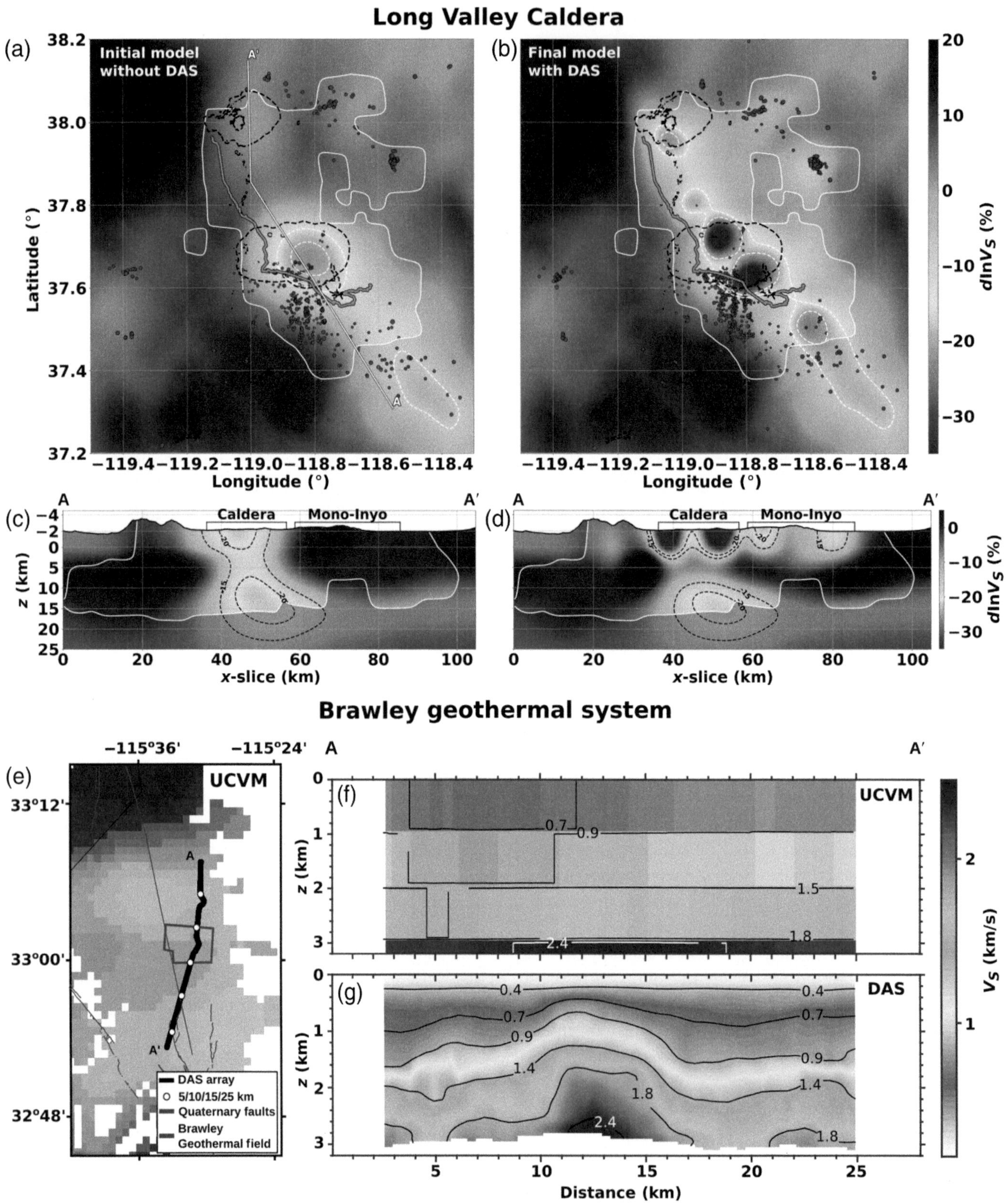

Figure 4. Comparison of tomography models with and without inclusion of DAS data for the Long Valley Caldera (a–d, modified from Biondi *et al.*, 2023) and Brawley geothermal field (e.g., modified from Cheng, Ajo-Franklin, Nayak, *et al.*, 2023) in California. (a,c) Initial shear-wave velocity anomalies from the community velocity model (Lee *et al.*, 2014); (a) a slice at 1 km depth, (c) a depth profile through the Caldera as indicated in (a). (b,d) As for (a,c), but showing velocity anomalies from DAS eikonal tomographic workflow. (e) Shear-wave velocity model at 2 km depth from the unified community velocity model (Small *et al.*, 2017). (f) Reference V_S model from the unified community velocity model along the DAS array. (g) Inverted V_S model from DAS ambient noise data. The color version of this figure is available only in the electronic edition.

yield 2D profiles that can be combined into pseudo-3D models. The combination and integration of DAS with regional networks of conventional sensors can also improve the resolution of seismic velocity models (Nayak *et al.*, 2021; Biondi *et al.*, 2023), and could enable other imaging techniques requiring multicomponent measurements such as receiver functions (Yu *et al.*, 2019) and horizontal-to-vertical spectral ratios (Spica, Perton, *et al.*, 2020). A few studies succeed at utilizing higher-mode surface waves (Dou *et al.*, 2017; Yan *et al.*, 2023) to improve shallow structural models, and this represents a key area for future work. New approaches for seamless integration of high-resolution transects with existing, lower-resolution velocity models would also help maximize the capabilities of imaging with DAS.

The directional sensitivity intrinsic to DAS arrays can complicate the interpretation of the observed seismic signals, but recent studies have demonstrated the potential for imaging using cable sections of different orientations for a variety of sources. Fang *et al.* (2023) successfully retrieved coherent Rayleigh waves originating from ocean-generated microseism based on ambient noise cross correlations using a rectangular array, and Abukrat *et al.* (2023) and Ji *et al.* (2024) demonstrate that, depending on the cable geometry, Love waves can also be retrieved from the ambient strain field and be used to image the Earth; joint inversion of Rayleigh- and Love-wave dispersion curves can significantly improve *S*-wave velocity models. Other imaging techniques that could significantly improve our understanding of the Earth's subsurface include full-waveform inversion and the use of seismic waves from teleseismic earthquakes (Fichtner, 2010; Huang *et al.*, 2015; Pan *et al.*, 2023), as well as the use of secondary phases (Atterholt and Zhan, 2024), which have been shown to significantly improve shallow Earth models in exploration geophysics (Berkhout, 2014). Great research opportunities lay ahead for fiber sensing imaging, specifically ones that aim to set new resolution standards and capabilities for tomographic studies.

Applications to Earthquake Source Physics

Another primary goal for fiber-optic applications in seismology is to enhance our comprehension of earthquake sources. By leveraging both static and dynamic strain fields, as well as signals spanning a wide range of amplitudes, we can gain valuable insights into the physics of earthquakes. This section explores current capabilities and their applications in induced seismicity, EEW, long- and short-term monitoring, and rapid response. In addition, we will discuss potential technological advancements aimed at extending the observable frequency range from the seismic band down to (quasi)static signals.

Existing capabilities

Numerous methods have been developed to analyze earthquake source parameters using DAS data, and there is now a nearly complete set of tools for initial data processing (Chen, 2023; Chambers *et al.*, 2024; Ni *et al.*, 2024). Characterizing earthquake source parameters typically begins with accurate phase picks (e.g., of direct *P* and *S* waves), and this has been nearly fully automated for DAS datasets in the PhaseNet-DAS package (Zhu *et al.*, 2023). These picks allow for the calculation of millions of event–pair differential times from a few hundred earthquakes (Biondi *et al.*, 2023), and a means to improve focal sphere coverage (Li, Zhu, *et al.*, 2023). DAS has demonstrated detection levels at least as good as the completeness of regional catalogs (Li *et al.*, 2021) (Fig. 5), indicating the potential for creating massive arrival time and ground-motion amplitude datasets. Moreover, DAS interrogator technology is continually improving, and it is now possible to acquire microearthquake data out to 100 km from the interrogator (Strumia *et al.*, 2024), and to have multiple cables interrogated simultaneously from a single interrogator.

It is well known that strainmeters are inherently sensitive to both the static and dynamic terms in the seismic wavefield (Aki and Richards, 2002; Luo *et al.*, 2021). At distances close to the fault, traditional strainmeters have the bandwidth sensitivity and dynamic range to record near- and intermediate-field terms, and stay on scale for large earthquakes (e.g., Barbour *et al.*, 2021). However, since DAS systems necessarily need to track optical phase at very high rates, it is possible for DAS waveforms to "saturate" during moderate-to-large earthquakes (e.g., Ajo-Franklin *et al.*, 2022, their fig. 8). That is, if the DAS interrogator unit (IU) loses track of optical phase, which is changing too rapidly, the relative strain is lost permanently, which will manifest in the timeseries as phase wrapping. This has nothing to do with the elastic limit of the fiber, which is on the order of 10^{-2}, but rather is largely related to acquisition settings and capabilities for phase tracking in real time (e.g., Mellors *et al.*, 2021). Recently, van den Ende *et al.* (2025) presented a comprehensive analysis of the effects of phase saturation in DAS recordings of large-magnitude earthquakes. They further proposed a postprocessing correction method to address the issue of large-amplitude wrapped phases. In our study, we adopt a simplified scaling relationship to emphasize the challenges that DAS faces in the context of EEW for large-magnitude events, which may not be applicable in all cases. Figure 6 shows anticipated thresholds for saturation for crustal earthquakes in California using typical acquisition parameters. To model the expected earthquake strain rate $\dot{\epsilon}_p$ and $\dot{\epsilon}_s$ for *P* and *S* waves, respectively, we employ the following scaling relationships (Yin *et al.*, 2023):

$$\log_{10}(\dot{\epsilon}_p) = 0.437M - 1.269\log_{10}(D) + K_p, \quad (1)$$

$$\log_{10}(\dot{\epsilon}_s) = 0.690M - 1.588\log_{10}(D) + K_s, \quad (2)$$

in which M and D indicate the earthquake magnitude and the distance from the hypocenter and the sensing point, respectively,

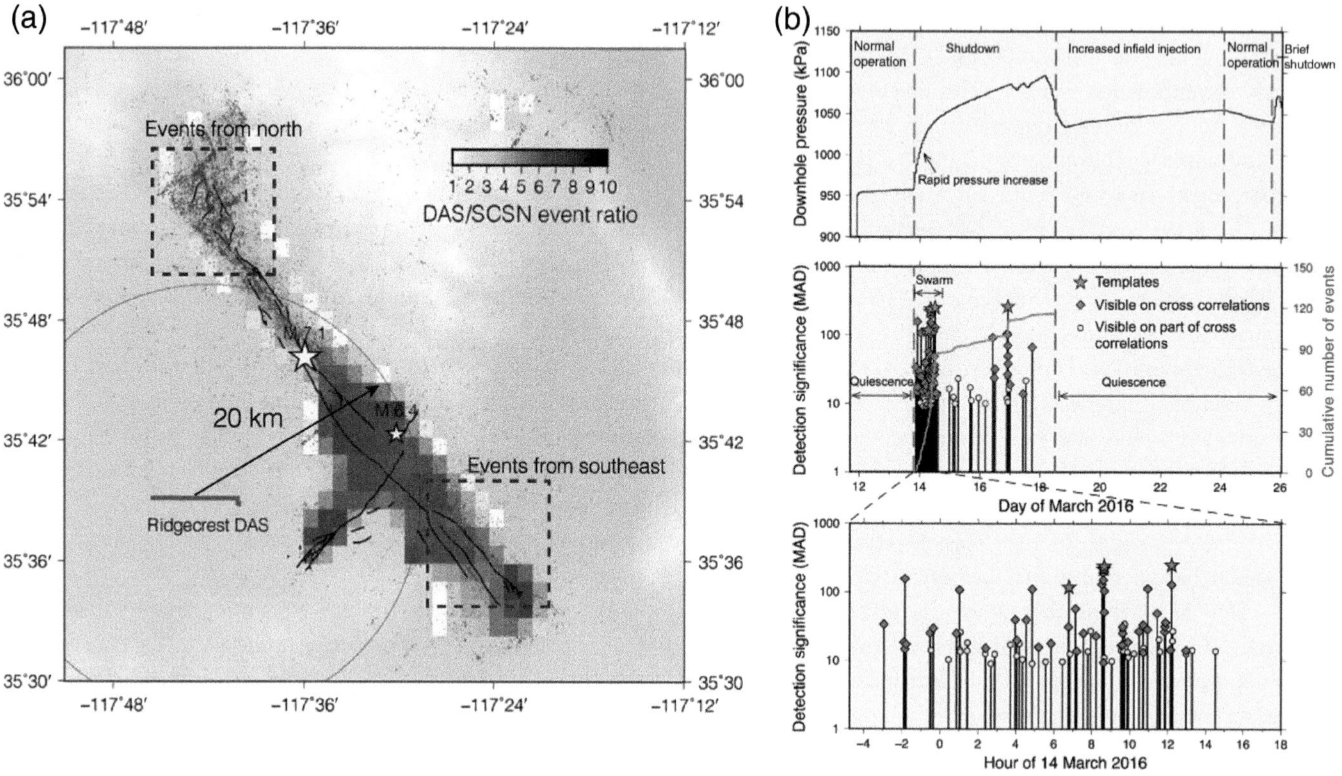

Figure 5. Improvements to event detection with DAS in (a) space, for the Ridgecrest aftershock sequence (Li *et al.*, 2021); and (b) time, for induced seismicity at the Brady geothermal field (Li and Zhan, 2018). For Ridgecrest, the ratio of detected events on DAS to the Southern California Seismic Network cataloged events ranges from equivalent to nearly a factor of 10. For Brady, the improved temporal resolution provides remarkable insight into the evolution of injection-induced seismicity, which, along with complementary downhole pressure measurements, helps constrain the physical mechanisms. The color version of this figure is available only in the electronic edition.

and the corresponding site terms are represented by K_p and K_s. These two last parameters are set to 0.3 in our computations. From the computed strain rates, we can obtain the expected phase change $d\phi$ using the following equation (Lindsey *et al.*, 2020):

$$d\phi = \frac{4\pi n G \eta}{\lambda} \frac{\dot{\epsilon}}{f_{\text{ping}}}, \tag{3}$$

in which G is gauge length, n is the fiber refractive index (e.g., 1.4682 for standard, single-mode fiber), η is the photoelastic scaling factor for longitudinal strain in isotropic material (i.e., 0.78), λ is the laser wavelength (usually, 1550.0 nm), and f_{ping} the instrument ping rate that is set by the desired instrument range (e.g., an ~100 km range corresponds to 1 kHz ping rate). If the absolute phase change exceeds 2π, the strain measurements may be compromised by unwrapping errors. This saturation phenomenon limits their use in certain seismological methods that require modelable waveforms. However, with proper acquisition parameter tuning and further advancements in interrogator technology, likely, DAS can likely reliably give complete, high-fidelity records even in the near field of large earthquakes. Understanding the utility of DAS for these methods remains an area of active research and technological development, but the community lacks testable datasets that would accelerate progress toward a solution.

With records that are not saturated, DAS provides sufficient data quality for estimating source parameters of local and regional moderate earthquakes. Magnitude estimation using DAS strains directly has been successful in both offshore and terrestrial systems from moderate-size events down to microseismicity (Yin *et al.*, 2023; Nayak *et al.*, 2024; Strumia *et al.*, 2024). DAS records can also be converted to inertial quantities and then used to determine source parameters such as duration and moment rate functions, and methods for doing this include calibrating the signal with closely located seismometers (Gök *et al.*, 2024), calculating apparent slowness across the fiber using a semblance-based slant-stack method (Lior, Sladen, Mercerat, *et al.*, 2021), or rescaling the wavefield in the frequency–wavenumber domain (Lindsey *et al.*, 2020; Lior, 2025). Alternatively, source parameters can be found using empirical Green's function methods applied to DAS records, with results closely resembling those from broadband or nodal seismometers (e.g., Chen, 2023; Lior, 2024). In addition, DAS offers the potential to record a more broadband record of ground motion than traditional seismometers, with a flat response from the spatial aliasing frequency set by the gauge length (typically kilohertz) down to frequencies of 0.008 Hz or lower (Becker *et al.*, 2020; Lindsey

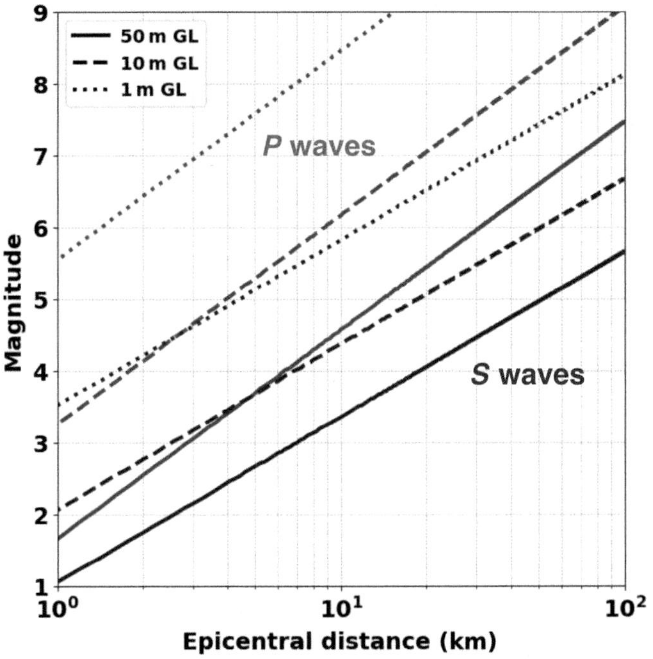

Figure 6. Conditions for optical phase wrapping as a function of epicentral distance and source magnitude, computed for different DAS gauge length (GL) values and for *P*- and *S*-wave arrivals (red and blue, respectively). The calculations are based on empirical attenuation of DAS strain-rate amplitudes (Yin *et al.*, 2023) converted to optical phase using a laser wavelength of 1550 nm, an interrogator ping rate of 1000 Hz, a fiber refractive index of 1.4682, and a photoelastic scaling factor of 0.78 (see main text). A magnitude–distance pair at a given contour is expected to generate an optical phase exceeding $\pm 2\pi$, which might lead to a phase wrapping in a DAS time series, depending on the processing capabilities of the interrogator unit; reducing the gauge length may serve to mitigate this effect, but potentially at the cost of higher noise levels. The color version of this figure is available only in the electronic edition.

et al., 2020; Paitz *et al.*, 2021). The key potential advantage of DAS for source parameter studies derives from the density of measurements, which may allow for capturing the variations over the focal sphere of key quantities like corner frequency and fall-off exponent that are expected from standard source models (Kaneko and Shearer, 2014) but challenging to resolve with widely spaced seismometers.

Induced seismicity

Induced seismicity refers to the global phenomenon of earthquakes caused by anthropogenic activities. The most common sources of induced seismicity include energy production from natural or engineered geothermal reservoirs, wastewater disposal by deep injection, hydraulic fracturing, and resource mining. Seismic hazard associated with these types of activities is often highly dynamic across regions and time, and fiber-optic sensing systems are appealing in their ability to provide high-resolution, passive monitoring of formation temperature, pressure, and strain, which are key observables needed to understand causal mechanisms. Unlike natural earthquakes, with induced seismicity, there is some level of control on the causal factors (e.g., injection), which can vary from hours to months or even years.

With geothermal energy production at both naturally occurring (conventional) reservoirs and enhanced geothermal systems, seismicity and ground deformation are expected outcomes of the continual process of fluid circulation from the reservoir to the surface, for heat and/or electricity generation, and back into the reservoir. With enhanced geothermal systems, the process of engineering tight formations to be suitable for industrial energy production requires concentrated, high-pressure injection episodes, known as “stimulations,” to create and propagate new fractures, and to hydromechanically dilate the existing fracture network. Microseismicity is commonly observed during enhanced geothermal systems simulations because of the hydraulic fracturing process itself, but also because the hydraulic conductivity of crustal rock is controlled primarily by critically stressed faults and fractures (e.g., Townend and Zoback, 2000). There is also the chance of reactivating a dormant, crustal-scale fault, like the 2019 M_w 5.5 earthquake in Pohang, South Korea (Ellsworth *et al.*, 2019). Thus, a critical aspect of understanding enhanced geothermal systems related to induced seismicity is having ultra-high-resolution monitoring of the seismic and aseismic deformation occurring before, during, and after all stages of the stimulation process (e.g., Li and Zhan, 2018; Lellouch *et al.*, 2020).

Activities related to the oil and gas industry represent the dominant sources of moderate-magnitude-induced earthquakes in the United States (Cochran *et al.*, 2024). The clearest demonstration of the benefits of using fiber-optic arrays to study the physics of induced earthquakes comes from hydraulic fracturing-related studies. Because with enhanced geothermal systems discussed earlier, hydraulic fracturing sites use stimulations to free up hydrocarbon resources. Downhole fiber-optic arrays enable high-resolution information on induced microseismicity associated with the injection process using DAS (e.g., Karrenbach *et al.*, 2019) and incorporating DSS and DTS measurements can be used not only to confirm increased flow and microseismicity associated with the stimulations, but also to measure low-frequency, quasistatic strain resulting from fracture opening (e.g., Jin and Roy, 2017). In other words, borehole fiber-optic deployments perhaps provide a general means to image the full spectrum of strain ranging from fracture initiation and growth, to slow, aseismic deformation, to seismic radiation.

Although CO_2 sequestration, as part of large-scale carbon capture and storage projects, has not seen as prolific levels of induced seismicity as, say, wastewater disposal; the potential for seismicity remains high, especially as the scales of sequestration projects increase (Ellsworth, 2013). One critical aspect of sustainable sequestration is ensuring that the CO_2 injected into the target formation remains in place, with minimal leakage. For multiple projects, DAS has helped track seismic signatures of the CO_2 injection process and map the spatial distribution of microseismicity in high resolution, revealing plume migration and possible links between plume saturation and microseismicity (Glubokovskikh *et al.*, 2021; Wang and Lawton, 2023).

Operational EEW

There are multiple EEW systems in operation across the globe (Allen and Melgar, 2019). Here, we focus on the ShakeAlert EEW system for the U.S. West Coast, which is operated by the USGS and its academic and industry partners (Given *et al.*, 2018; Kohler *et al.*, 2020). ShakeAlert's goal is to detect earthquakes within the first few seconds after they begin and provide alerts to as many users as possible before strong shaking arrives at their locations. The system relies on a dense network of traditional seismic stations throughout California, Oregon, and Washington (Fig. 1). For shallow earthquakes, ShakeAlert will often issue its first alert within four to six seconds after the earthquake origin time (Lux *et al.*, 2024). Although there is typically a zone close to the epicenter where it is not possible to provide timely warnings, ShakeAlert has already produced usable warnings before strong shaking at distances on the order of 30–50 km from the epicenter (Lux *et al.*, 2024). The underlying algorithms' performance is maximized by dense strong-motion observations close to the fault and epicenter (Chung *et al.*, 2020; Böse *et al.*, 2023) and high-speed telemetry with typical latencies of 1 s or less between the instruments in the field and network processing centers (Chung *et al.*, 2020; Stubailo *et al.*, 2020). The need for sensors close to the fault, as well as for rapid data telemetry over distances of 100s of kilometers, provides a natural argument for investigating DAS in EEW.

Quickly and reliably characterizing offshore and out-of-network earthquakes is a key challenge for any EEW system and a particular focus in subduction zones. For earthquakes located offshore with only a few stations having observed the initial *P* wave, early epicenter estimates can be mislocated by several tens of kilometers or more (Williamson *et al.*, 2023; Lux *et al.*, 2024). Offline replays of the ShakeAlert system for large Japanese earthquakes indicate that for offshore epicenters in subduction zones, the first alerts will be delayed until 12–22 s after origin time (see Table S1 and McGuire, Ulberg, *et al.*, 2025). In addition, tests using realistic Cascadia synthetic seismograms show that ShakeAlert will have difficulty providing timely warnings at high modified Mercalli intensity (MMI) levels due in part to the lack of offshore near-fault instrumentation (McGuire *et al.*, 2021; Thompson *et al.*, 2023). Essentially, the lack of offshore data wastes a crucial ~5–10 s upon the initiation of large ruptures; this is a particularly disappointing outcome, as offshore megathrust events provide some of EEW's greatest opportunities for success (McGuire *et al.*, 2021; Meier *et al.*, 2021; McGuire, Ulberg, *et al.*, 2025). The lack of offshore data is a first-order problem for ShakeAlert that can potentially be mitigated by offshore fiber-optic cables that fill this key data gap.

Deploying scientific fibers offshore is a costly proposition, but there is an abundance of fiber-optic cable deployed by the telecom industry in subduction zones like Cascadia, Alaska, and Puerto Rico (Fig. 1); and hence, there exists the possibility of utilizing those fibers for DAS-based EEW (Ide *et al.*, 2021; Lior, Sladen, Rivet, *et al.*, 2021; Farghal *et al.*, 2022; Lior *et al.*, 2023; Yin *et al.*, 2023; Gou *et al.*, 2025). However, all EEW operations will require reliable data uplinks and real-time processing, perhaps including edge computing for effective alerting systems (e.g., Ben-Zeev and Lior, 2025). Given the potential data volume of DAS systems and the unknown quality of site-specific submarine data, it could benefit from a collaborative study between academic, commercial, and governmental bodies.

Routine earthquake monitoring

Earthquake monitoring workflows, including seismic phase picking, location, and characterization, have been demonstrated to work in real time on DAS data (see previous section). DAS data are already integrated into existing real-time earthquake monitoring systems in southern California (Biondi *et al.*, 2025). DAS data can help identify smaller earthquakes missing from the existing, authoritative catalog for a region (e.g., Fig. 5), which is important for understanding seismicity rate changes. As a dense array measurement, DAS can also help improve how seismic networks discriminate local, regional, and teleseismic events (e.g., Li *et al.*, 2021) by considering signal content of the full wavefield across the array rather than with phase picks. In the near future, DAS might have the most impact on improving earthquake monitoring in sparsely instrumented regions with active faults, especially offshore, where it is expensive to deploy a limited number of ocean-bottom seismometers. In the longer term, DAS could have even more impact on earthquake monitoring if DAS data can be acquired ubiquitously with broad spatial coverage. For instance, instrumenting California's Middle Mile Broadband Initiative (Fig. 1) with enough interrogators to cover the available cables at ~100 km spacing would yield unprecedented earthquake monitoring capabilities across the full spectrum of seismic hazard and risk.

DAS, while promising, presents myriad challenges for operational earthquake monitoring. Its quality can vary greatly, and determining cable geometry and data quality thresholds is essential. Large data volumes and the need for specialized expertise can also be limiting factors. However, with careful planning and resource allocation, it may be feasible for DAS to be integrated into earthquake monitoring systems to provide valuable and perhaps unprecedented insights.

Rapid response

Typically, after a major earthquake, agencies like the USGS quickly deploy temporary, portable seismometers to record aftershocks at close distances to the fault. Collecting data provides essential information about near-fault ground motions, fault structure, earthquake source properties, and subsurface structure, but the opportunity is transient. Data are usually collected during periodic visits to each station, though real-time telemetry is also possible (e.g., Cochran *et al.*, 2020). If logistical issues are solved ahead of time, rapid response DAS data could have the same advantages described in previous sections. Cable access is the key hurdle, and agencies could establish agreements with large cable networks to enable rapid installations. A key aspect is a database of fibers that provides scientific quality data to base agreements on. Alternatively, agencies could work with commercial cable monitoring companies that are routinely recording data in seismically active areas to automatically archive subsets of those data streams based on earthquake activity.

Low-frequency strain

DAS is typically used to measure earthquake signals at frequencies above ~0.01 Hz. If DAS can reliably measure low-frequency strains, this opens up opportunities to measure aseismic faulting and deformation phenomena that occur from hours to months or longer. Such phenomena are typically observed with networks of shallow and surface creepmeters (Langbein *et al.*, 2024), complemented by satellite-based observations from continuous Global Navigation Satellite Systems stations and Interferometric Synthetic Aperture Radar (e.g., Li, Perton, *et al.*, 2023), and borehole strainmeters (e.g., Linde *et al.*, 1996). These classic technologies have varying sensitivities and noise levels, and can be affected by various nontectonic processes. With strainmeters, new, fiber-optic-based designs using Michelson interferometry show great promise for detecting small, transient, and permanent strains in the crust (e.g., Murdoch *et al.*, 2023), but these are limited to point measurements, as with prior technologies. Hence, low-frequency DAS could further complement these geodetic techniques by helping validate the source of ambiguous signals, investigate differences in dynamics along faults, and help document source propagation (e.g., Materna *et al.*, 2024) in greater detail. If low-frequency strain from fault movements can be reliably measured by dark fiber in offshore environments, DAS might enable a cost-effective complement to burgeoning seafloor geodetic techniques, especially if offshore cables cross active subduction zone faults.

To our knowledge, no study has yet observed low-frequency fault movements using DAS. However, a number of studies have reported observations of phenomena that occur over similar spatial and temporal scales, thereby suggesting that such fault zone observations may be feasible. Perhaps the most relevant analogous observation is that of Li *et al.* (2025), who describe hours-long strain transients during magmatic intrusion. In controlled injection experiments (e.g., Jin and Roy, 2017; Norbeck *et al.*, 2023), low-frequency strains have been measured reliably with downhole DAS systems (Fig. 7). More rapid, ~10 s (Currenti *et al.*, 2021, 2023) and ~100 s period signals have also been observed using DAS fundamental technical questions remain as to whether reliable low-frequency DAS strain measurements are even possible for natural deformation sources, given the strong coupling with temperature in fiber-optic systems, which is often observed to be on the order of $10^{-5}/C°$, and both the environmental controls and proximity-to-source that borehole environments can provide. Therefore, additional information is needed to distinguish between thermal and mechanical deformation effects in a DAS measurement, such as colocated DTS measurements.

With the prospect of measuring slow deformation processes, it could be worthwhile to consider building a dedicated, long-term, fault zone fiber-optic experiment to make crucial observations needed to understand earthquake sources and ruptures at close range, thermal effects, the role of aseismic processes in earthquake nucleation, the range of aseismic slip from continuous to episodic, and ultimately the conditions that promote seismic and aseismic slips. On land, a custom fiber deployment in boreholes, crossing a known fault or getting as close to the fault as possible, could reduce noise at lower frequencies and stabilize the influence of temperature; one such example is the MiDAS project in Taiwan (Ma *et al.*, 2024). Another potential target opportunity could be the San Andreas Fault Observatory at Depth (SAFOD) borehole at the creeping to locked transition zone of the San Andreas fault (Zoback *et al.*, 2011). In a short-term pilot experiment, Lellouch *et al.* (2019) successfully used earthquakes detected by DAS on a vertical fiber down to ~700 m to do shallow imaging, but the real power of these technologies would be revealed by monitoring a fiber that crosses the fault zone. The technical challenges associated with setting up a long-term fiber-optic observatory in conditions where the SAFOD borehole actually crosses the San Andreas fault are nontrivial.

Technological Challenges and Future Opportunities

As we touched on above, technological advances enabled immense progress in this field in the last decade. Though challenges remain, the Fiber-Optic Powell Center is optimistic that these can be overcome with further technological innovation.

DAS sensing systems utilize the optical Rayleigh-backscattered signal by measuring the light's amplitude, frequency, phase, and polarization (Fig. 2). All four measurement quantities are sensitive (to various degrees) to the surrounding environment, which induces strain changes on the fiber (Lu *et al.*, 2019). Some commercial sensing systems exist that only make use of light intensity changes, whereas others make use only of polarization. Most current DAS systems utilize Rayleigh-backscattered optical phase measurement and rely on coherent light amplitude, polarization, and frequency to reliably carry out optical phase measurements.

DAS sensing systems are composed of optical, photonic, and electronic components. Because those components are also used in other telecom hardware systems, they are typically

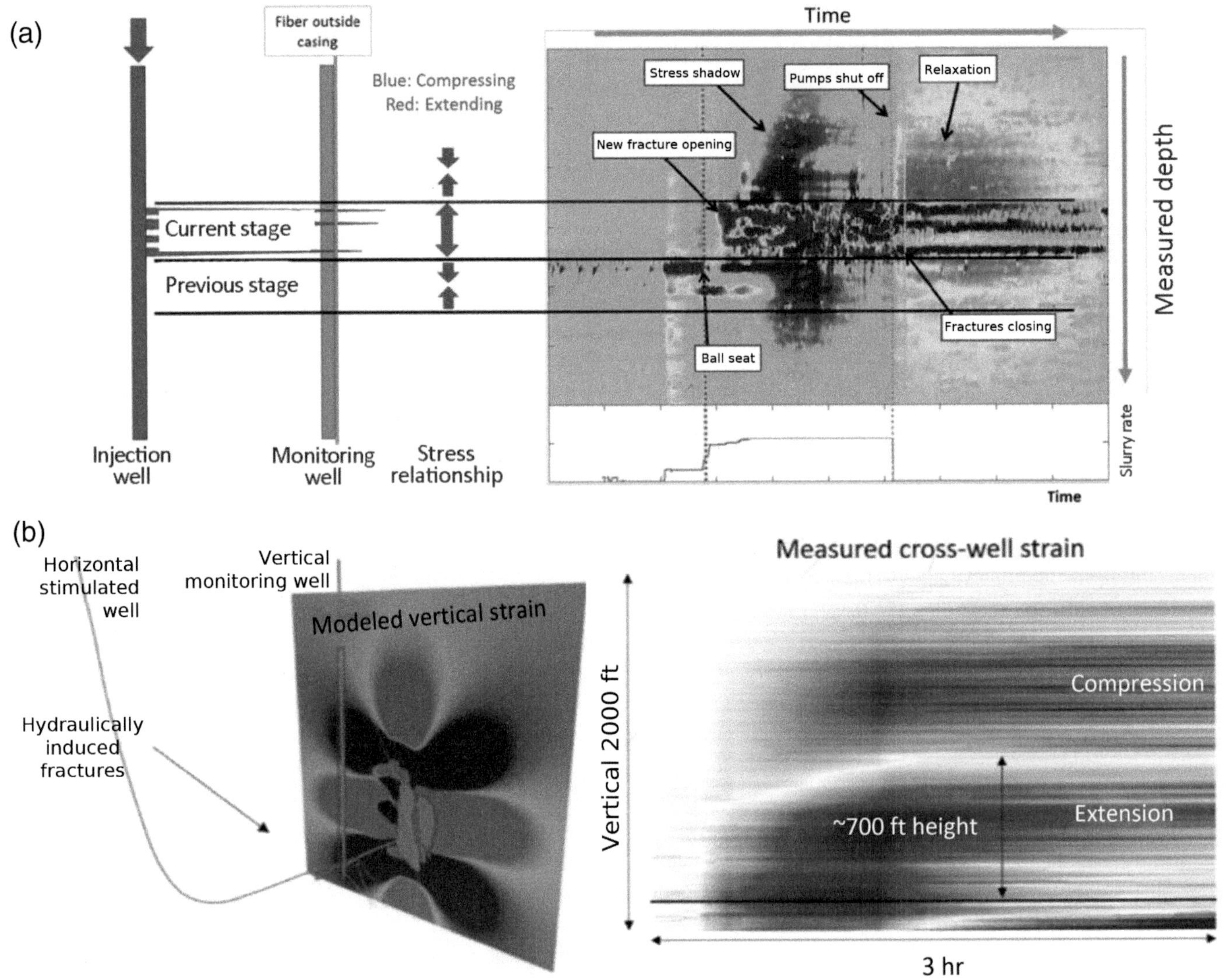

Figure 7. Low-frequency strains from high-pressure fluid injection, as measured by downhole DAS systems for (a) hydraulic fracturing (Jin and Roy, 2017) and (b) an enhanced geothermal system (modified from Norbeck *et al.*, 2023). In these examples, transient and static strains associated with reservoir stimulation are seen clearly by the DAS systems. The color version of this figure is available only in the electronic edition.

built to satisfy stringent specifications on failure rates, durability, survivability, and mechanical, thermal, and electromagnetic interference. DAS systems that use such components and are assembled while maintaining these standards exhibit considerably higher reliability. It is not unusual to see systems operating according to specifications for many years with extremely minimal hardware-induced downtime (see Table 1). Although DAS systems provide accurate and widely applicable measurements, there remain challenges that likely can be overcome by continued technology developments.

Many of the examples shown above benefit from the high sensitivity of DAS systems over a remarkably wide bandwidth. However, improving the DAS system's dynamic range could allow capturing large strain events for use in early-warning applications that need to estimate the event magnitude. Most interrogators in use today operate with a fixed gauge length, which impacts whether the setup will be more or less prone to phase wrapping, in addition to other factors (e.g., equation 3). Future implementations could output multiple simultaneous gauge length data streams while also using phase and polarization measurements in more advanced phase-tracking algorithms.

Large-scale spatial coverage (dense onshore, near-offshore, and far offshore) of the DAS system could allow adequate warning times for EEW and usability for imaging and tomographic applications. To achieve this, DAS systems would require increased sensing reach, versatile packaging, and in-system data analysis. Recent progress in the field of photonics might lead to condensed electrooptical components manufactured as dedicated integrated photonic chips or assembly boards. Not only would this save space, lower power requirements, and increase reliability, but this might also allow efficient manufacturing at scale. DAS system interrogation technology is progressing at a steady pace and is likely to take advantage of improvements of photonic and computational components that are driven by diverse commercial markets.

Minimizing latency is essential for EEW and monitoring applications. To enable efficient real-time analysis, the interrogator could directly attach to data processing chips, which would allow flexible algorithm application directly at the data source and minimize latency in deriving crucial output. Furthermore, a flexible and scalable usage paradigm for real-time, edge, and networked cloud computing could then be sustained in low-power, low-network speed, and space-constrained environments.

Although many of the above results we highlighted previously utilize already existing fiber cabling (dark, unlit fiber) as a cost-efficient way to create large sensing arrays for a variety of purposes, they often fall short in terms of optimal coverage and positioning with respect to the area under investigation. Dark fiber is more easily accessible to end users for sensing than "lit" fibers, but fiber cables are expected to progressively contain less dark fiber due to increasing network traffic volumes. Lit fibers contain live data traffic of the telecom company. The traffic is typically segmented into channels occupying discrete wavelength bands (conventional (C) and long (L) bands, etc.). Distributed fiber-optic sensing can be carried out in one of these unused wavelength band channels without impacting neighboring channels. Several DAS vendors offer passive optical hardware to safely inject and extract sensing signals onto a live/lit fiber without impacting either the network traffic or the sensing signal. Simultaneously operating network traffic and sensing will likely become the norm for submarine cable installation due to the limited number of fiber stands in those cables (Brenne *et al.*, 2024; Shi *et al.*, 2025).

Where dedicated fit-for-purpose fiber installations are possible, they have in the past provided great improvement to noise floor, sensitivity, coupling, repeatability, and area of illumination. In addition to the geometrical layout, specialty fiber cables and engineered fiber cores can be deployed to enhance strain-sensing characteristics and noise floor. Thus, for high-value applications, such as a fault zone observatory, a dedicated purpose-designed fiber installation could be considered when deployment plans are drawn up.

As the examples provided earlier show, there is tremendous insight into the natural earth system when complementary and concurrent measurements are made. Although current DAS systems often measure just one modality—dynamic strain—it is possible to incorporate other modalities, such as absolute strain (e.g., DSS) or temperature (e.g., DTS), into the same system. In other words, it may be possible to obtain all measurements with a single interrogator connected to a single fiber or fiber bundle, which would dramatically lower operational costs and might lead to novel large-scale applications in earthquake hazards research.

Testing Facility

Significant effort has been invested to quantify the performance and response of DAS interrogators. The current state-of-the-art standards for quantifying the performance of DAS interrogators are the SEAFOM specifications (SEAFOM, 2024). These specifications provide a number of procedures for measurement of performance parameters, including dynamic range, frequency response, fidelity, self-noise, spatial resolution, crosstalk, loss budget, and sensor reflection effect tests. All these tests are important for the applications discussed in the present study. There are several ways that the SEAFOM specifications could be augmented to be more useful within the scope of earthquake hazards applications. The three main issues we address are frequency bandwidth, instrumental transfer function phase, and the use of well-characterized testing facilities.

Earthquake studies most often involve seismic frequencies from 0.01 to 100 Hz. However, in tests with variable frequency, the SEAFOM specifications generally limit the lowest frequency to some percentage of the Nyquist frequency, for example, 1% of Nyquist for the dynamic range test (see SEAFOM, 2024, their section 4.2) and 2% of Nyquist for the frequency response test (see SEAFOM, 2024, their section 4.3). For a typical Nyquist frequency of 20 Hz, this would limit low frequencies to 0.2 Hz (5 s periods and shorter), which is not low enough for teleseismic earthquake studies. Modifying the SEAFOM specifications to include frequencies as low as 0.01%-of-Nyquist would likely be adequate for most teleseismic earthquake studies, while including frequencies as low as 0.001% would allow the same 20 Hz sampled DAS interrogator to be tested at the 54 min period of Earth's gravest normal mode. Testing at these low frequencies may also be beneficial to other fields of study outside the earthquake sciences, such as in physical oceanography (e.g., Williams *et al.*, 2023).

Modern DAS interrogators exploit a wide range of optical, electrical, and digital schemes to deliver geophysically relevant strain or strain-rate data streams (Hartog, 2017). As is true of any physical system, certain components (e.g., lenses, delay lines, dispersive optical elements, resistor–capacitor circuits, and digital filters) may result in an instrumental transfer function with a frequency-dependent phase shift. Such phase shifts may asymptotically act as spatial or temporal differentiators or integrators, implying that an interrogator may have variable response characteristics below a given component's characteristic frequency. This behavior is not captured in the present SEAFOM specification because the SEAFOM frequency response test explicitly excludes quantification of the transfer function phase response (see SEAFOM, 2024, their section 7.2). Future research could seek to quantify this response.

Facilities with well-understood seismic noise characteristics, such as the USGS Albuquerque Seismic Laboratory, help systematically quantify the performance of seismic instrumentation. In testing a particular seismometer, the Albuquerque Seismic

Laboratory routinely uses three of the same seismometers in close spatial proximity to quantify the self-noise of the instrument (Sleeman *et al.*, 2006); this eliminates pervasive noise sources such as microseism. Quiet facilities are beneficial because they may have the ability to minimize 50/60 Hz noise by running equipment entirely on DC power. They may also have the ability to maintain thermal stability and thereby minimize thermal impacts on optical (i.e., laser) and inertial components. The SEAFOM specification does not exclude measurements made in noisy laboratory environments. Therefore, it may be beneficial to establish a dedicated testing facility for this purpose. An added benefit obtained from this proposed testing facility might be a set of interrogator standards relevant to sensing earthquakes; these could help new DAS users decide how to invest in the system that best meets their sensing needs, while also providing benchmarks as the interrogator technologies improve over time.

Data Standards and Archiving Strategies

The Fiber-Optic Powell Center identified three grand challenges related to managing the immense data volumes created by distributed sensing experiments, specifically ones related to archiving, metadata, and hardware and storage; we discuss each challenge in detail subsequently.

Challenge 1: Archiving

Long-term data archiving of DAS remains a primary challenge due to the large data volumes (100s of TB for a single dataset) (Ni *et al.*, 2024). Even with modern data storage technology, the cost and effort needed to store these volumes, either in dedicated hardware or in a cloud environment, are substantial. The ongoing increase in the number of DAS experiments, as well as potential new uses such as regional earthquake monitoring and EEW, which would require continuous monitoring over possibly hundreds or thousands of kilometers of fiber, suggests that data archiving needs could feasibly reach 1000 TB/yr. Table 2, which lists a few existing DAS datasets, illustrates the problem, which is unprecedented in this field and lacks clear guidelines to follow. The popularity of DAS data is rapidly growing, and two existing archives, such as PubDAS (Spica *et al.*, 2023; Wuestefeld *et al.*, 2024) and the Department of Energy geothermal data repository (GDR; see Data and Resources) are already serving hundreds of users and supporting total downloads of over 140 TBs (e.g., Fig. 8). Internationally, at least one large DAS experiment is archived and available in near-real time (Rivet *et al.*, 2025), demonstrating the feasibility of this approach for high-value datasets.

In contrast, most seismic data collected for research or monitoring purposes using funding from the National Science Foundation or the USGS is archived in its entirety at a trusted digital repository (TDR). For websites, please see Data and Resources. For USGS-sponsored data, TDRs are approved by a review process to ensure the long-term fiscal stability and

TABLE 2
Example Distributed Acoustic Sensing (DAS) Datasets

Organization	Name	Location	Type	Volume (TB)	Duration (dy)	IUs	Gauge (m)	Channel Spacing (m)	Range (km)	Samp. (Hz)	Data Rate (GB/dy)	Reference
NTNU	DAS4Whale	Svalbard, Norway	Dark fiber	308	44	1	8	4	120	645	7000	Bouffaut *et al.* (2022)
University of Wisconsin	PoroTomo	Nevada	Custom	81	15	1	10	2	8.4	1000	5400	Wang *et al.* (2018)
University of Washington	RAPID	Offshore Oregon	Dark fiber	26	5	3	30	2	160	200	1733	Shi *et al.* (2025)
LBL	Imperial Valley	California	Dark fiber	240	440	1	10	4	28	500	545	Ajo-Franklin *et al.* (2022)
PSU	FORSEE	Pennsylvania	Custom	46	270	1	10	2	5	500	170	Zhu *et al.* (2021)
USGS	Arcata	California	Dark fiber	28	244	1	8	2	15	250	115	McGuire, Barbour, *et al.* (2025)
Caltech	Ridgecrest	California	Dark fiber	122	1095	1	50	10	100	100	111	Atterholt *et al.* (2024)
Caltech	Mammoth	California	Dark fiber	152	730	2	20	10	50	100	104	Biondi *et al.* (2023)
Caltech	Pasadena	California	Dark fiber	22	365	1	16	10	10	100	60	Wang *et al.* (2020)

IU, interrogator unit; LBL, Lawrence Berkeley Lab; USGS, U.S. Geological Survey; NTNU, Norwegian University of Science and Technology; PSU, Pennsylvania State University.

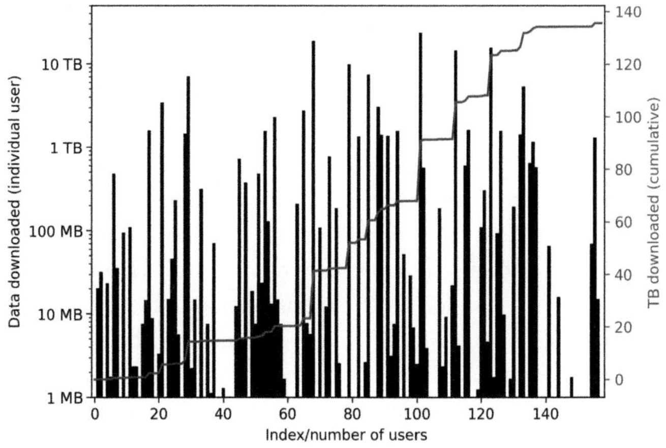

Figure 8. History of data downloads by user since the PubDAS archive began in 2023 at the University of Michigan (Spica *et al.*, 2023). The repository contains 9 different DAS datasets, including 32 subsets from the Global DAS Month initiative (Wuestefeld *et al.*, 2024) and about 110 TB of DAS data. The white spaces represent users who have connected to the database but have not downloaded data yet. The color version of this figure is available only in the electronic edition.

proper conventions for data management, access, and security of the archived data. For traditional seismic data, this has been feasible given the rapid improvement in storage capabilities, as the entire seismic data archive at EarthScope (over >50 yr of data) is currently about 1 petabyte. The archiving requirements are typically part of the data management plan that is part of all federal grants. One example is the USGS ANSS data policy for traditional seismic data, which requires the archiving of all monitoring data and derived data products in a TDR (see Data and Resources). If an archiving policy with similarly complete requirements were to apply directly to DAS data, the storage and data-serving requirements for large-scale, multi-fiber applications could be financially intractable.

USGS-sponsored data collection must adhere to data archiving specifications as both a Federal Record and as defined for specific data management plans. These rules constitute a Records Designation and are specific to particular data types and experiment types; they mandate duration and disposition of the data and associated metadata. In this section, we further describe the scale of the archiving and distribution problems, explore possible solutions, and suggest a path forward.

Challenge 2: Metadata

A secondary challenge for DAS is that a widely accepted metadata standard does not yet exist. Interrogator units (IUs) generally output their internal settings in headers attached to the raw data, but these headers may not, by default, contain critical information related to the experiment itself. However, community standardization efforts are well underway. Initial metadata standards have been developed to provide such information for the benefit of scientific reproducibility, most notably by the DAS-Research Coordination Network (RCN, Lai *et al.*, 2024) and ProDML (https://www.energistics.org/prodml-data-standards, last accessed June 2025). Currently, an updated version of the DAS-RCN metadata framework of Lai *et al.* (2024) is being proposed by the International Federation of Digital Seismograph Networks (FDSN) as the metadata format for describing DAS datasets (https://docs.fdsn.org/projects/das-metadata/en/draft/, last accessed June 2025). Thus, for this work, we use the DAS-RCN framework of Lai *et al.* (2024) with the expectation that it evolves into the global metadata standard in the near future, and that metadata volumes will be very small with respect to the raw data volumes.

There are a few key categories that DAS metadata should include to cover seismological experiments (Taverna *et al.*, 2023; Lai *et al.*, 2024):

1. Overview: a description of the experiment (geographical location, times, etc.), the institutions and people involved, and funding agencies;
2. Cable and fiber: details related to the fiber-optic cable(s) that were monitored and the sensing environment; and
3. Interrogator: details related to the IU, including manufacturer, model, and so forth; and
4. Acquisition: details related to IU settings (sampling rates, gauge length, etc.), pre- and post-processing, and so forth; and
5. Channels: locations of sensing segments along the fiber and other details pertinent to the experiment.

Challenge 3: Hardware and storage

Solutions to the issue of long-term data storage will likely involve balancing cost, accessibility, and reliability. Some common options include:

1. Portable hard drives, which are affordable and easy to access, but limited in capacity and susceptible to physical damage;
2. local equipment racks, which are scalable using hard disks or RAID systems, but can be complex to manage and may not offer remote access;
3. computational facility storage, which may be ideal for cloud computing integration, but access may be restricted due to competing demands within the facility's budget and storage limitations; and,
4. commercial cloud storage, which offers scalability, remote access, and potentially high reliability, but costs may increase significantly with data volume and frequent access.

The GDR utilizes commercial cloud storage to standardize and store DAS data primarily related to energy-related experiments (Weers *et al.*, 2022); the GDR archive already contains about 275 TB of DAS data from just a few experiments and is rapidly expanding (Taverna *et al.*, 2023). For scale, this is equivalent to more than a quarter of all seismic data archived by EarthScope (see Data and Resources), but from datasets collected over a far smaller fraction of time.

Assuming there are constraints on resources and storage capabilities, archived DAS data volumes will likely need to be significantly reduced relative to the raw data volumes (or streams). This reduction in size includes extended long-term storage (>10 yr). Multiple possibilities exist to achieve these reductions. One option is data reduction involving expunging subsets of data, either by downsampling, windowing (either in time or space), or lossy compression. Lossy compression can achieve significant reductions in volume (factors of 5–100) but introduces data errors and waveform distortion that may have adverse impacts on future research; the exact type of error depends on the compression scheme and data characteristics. The overall archiving strategy may need to include both data reduction and a variety of storage types. Therefore, it could be beneficial to consider trade-offs between different types of storage and their costs, the associated risk of data loss, and the level of accessibility.

Data processing needs remain an important consideration as well because this will place additional constraints on storage, access, internal standardization, and downloads. For example, some types of analysis require the capability to extract selected data windows from a large dataset based on spatial or temporal ranges (e.g., ambient noise imaging), while others may need to scan through entire datasets (e.g., template matching). Burdensome download costs might be alleviated by conducting data processing online using cloud-based computing resources (Ni *et al.*, 2024), although this approach adds an extra layer of complexity to the design and implementation of a DAS TDR.

Proposed archiving strategy and records designations

The Fiber-Optic Powell Center proposes the following archiving strategy be considered. These are based on different classes of data collection and the distinctions in archiving requirements inherent in the definition of USGS official Records, namely the distinctions between "Permanent" versus "Temporary" Records (see Data and Resources). In the purview of the Fiber-Optic Powell Center, an effective strategy distinguishes large-scale monitoring applications compared to targeted research experiments because they can differ dramatically in scale, goals, and potential usage in the future. Some datasets will span years and 100s of kilometers of cable range, while others may last only a few days or be in a borehole, for instance. Experimental applications may have dramatically different temporal sampling rates compared to monitoring applications. Some may yield perplexing results that might be better understood in the future.

A key aspect of the proposed strategy for monitoring applications involves permanently archiving predefined temporal subsets around earthquakes in a reference catalog (e.g., the ANSS Comprehensive Earthquake Catalog, U.S. Geological Survey [USGS], 2017a). Although monitoring networks record and process data continuously, a wide variety of research efforts rely on the permanent archiving of a subset of this data that contains the records from earthquakes. A similar strategy adopted by the Center for Engineering Strong-Motion Data has been effective in serving the most valuable subset of large continuous datasets to a key user community. However, the point of departure for DAS experiments and the Center for Engineering Strong-Motion Data examples is their broader and more diverse applicability; hence, we have divided the proposed DAS archiving requirements into three broad categories:

1. Test or testing facility datasets,
2. targeted experiments, and
3. continuous, long-term monitoring networks.

For each category, we distinguish the needs for both Temporary and Permanent Records, and the duration of Temporary Record storage. The overall goal of this scheme is to optimize the balance between cost-effective DAS data collection and the preservation of key subsets for future research efforts by the broader community.

A key feature of these definitions is having built-in flexibility. For instance, the minimum earthquake source magnitude for permanent archiving in some networks may be substantially higher than in others due to differences in seismicity rates. For example, in Alaska, many magnitude >4 earthquakes happen every week, but in Oregon, those events happen only once every few years. For datasets produced from testing facilities or in situ testing experiments, it is desirable to archive all of the data permanently. Because these datasets tend to be relatively small, they do not require extensive resources. They also provide sanity checks and the ability to verify properties of deployed systems. For datasets from targeted experiments, we encourage a flexible definition where the experiment lead could propose and negotiate permanent storage of an entire dataset at a TDR, even if it is anticipated to be larger than the nominal size limits, funding capabilities notwithstanding. Finally, the options for cold (high latency) storage are rapidly evolving at data centers and may allow for longer retention times for temporary archives. In any case, it would be beneficial for these recommendations to be revisited every few years by the community, both as new archiving options become available and as the associated costs change.

Testing facility or calibration datasets

Calibration tests or datasets from formal testing facilities are the most straightforward to provide recommendations about, as they are expected to be some of the smallest datasets due to relatively short cables and possibly intermittent operation. These tests are also extremely valuable to preserve in their entirety because they can be used to investigate the source of abnormal behavior of similar systems in field deployments. Relatively few laboratory datasets exist currently, and because it is expensive to set up and conduct these tests, the costs of archiving the data represent a relatively small part of the overall cost. Thus, the recommendation is fairly straightforward that all these datasets should be treated like Permanent Records and all continuous data archived at a TDR. Providing extensive metadata is critical to interpretation and reproducibility, and if possible, all ancillary data relevant to a given test should also be included.

Targeted experiments

These are temporary deployments for Principal Investigator (PI)-driven experiments with a set of predefined scientific goals, and we expect that they will range greatly in their scale. This class includes, for example, aftershock deployments, active source experiments, injection monitoring experiments, and other short-term data collection efforts. The data archiving details should be determined on an experiment-by-experiment basis using the data management plan agreed on by the funders, but, in general, we expect that many of these experiments will be small enough to allow permanent archiving at a TDR, particularly those below a predefined data volume limit. Experiments larger than this data volume threshold could follow an archiving strategy similar to that described subsequently. The minimum level of permanent archiving could match the requirements of the nearest permanent ANSS regional seismic network. Experiments will vary widely in their goals, staffing, and geologic environment, and there are no specific products that should be required to be archived.

Temporary Records:

1. Continuous data will be stored with the PI, and data that has not been archived at a TDR are destroyed after 5 yr unless it is part of an ongoing experiment.

Permanent Records:

1. For local earthquakes, ten minutes before and after every catalog earthquake with $M \geq M_{\mathrm{thresh}}$ within R_{thresh} of any point along the cable being monitored. The magnitude threshold, M_{thresh}, would likely be ~4 and the distance threshold R_{thresh} would likely be ~100 km, but these could be unique for each network to allow higher cutoffs in very active locations. Similarly, for local earthquakes with $M_{\mathrm{min}} \leq M < M_{\mathrm{thresh}}$, save 2 min before and after the origin time. M_{min} is likely to be ~2, but this magnitude range could be set to match the practice of the nearest regional network.
2. For every catalog earthquake with $M > 6$ within 100 km of any point on the cable, save 10 days before and no fewer than 30 days after to allow for studies related to aftershocks and rupture kinematics, enhanced catalog development, EEW algorithm development, and so forth.
3. The full continuous data during key time periods during the experiment is to be archived, such as during fluid injection episodes in induced seismicity experiments, or early aftershocks, or during active source experiments.
4. Longer durations of continuous data below data volume limit are allowed if funding is available and it is consistent with the data management plan.
5. Additional options that could be added:
   i. No derived products are required for these experiments.
   ii. The dataset is required to be archived with a compression ratio of JPEG or better.

Continuous long-term data streams. Continuous DAS monitoring networks, both permanent (e.g., within seismic networks) and semipermanent (e.g., induced seismicity target regions), will likely cover up to hundreds of kilometer of cable and operate continuously for years at a time at the same temporal sampling as with network seismometers, which would yield massive data volumes. Individual networks could conceivably exceed 1000 TB/yr. Of the three categories considered by the Fiber-Optic Powell Center, this is the most difficult to project future needs for. The recommendations that follow will need to be reviewed and adjusted over time based on feedback from a wide range of stakeholders.

In large earthquake sequences, seismic networks may be overwhelmed with cataloging small earthquakes in real time. Thus, a key feature for DAS in network monitoring is having a rolling buffer of the full continuous dataset that can be accessed for multiple weeks/months to allow flexibility in characterizing active sequences.

The subsetting of these datasets for Permanent Records would be based on an official earthquake catalog and the exact criteria could be modifiable by specific networks to match their regions' activity levels without overwhelming the archive. The high spatial density of DAS data is not generally required for routine seismological studies and hence the permanent archiving of a small number of regularly spaced channels with high data quality will greatly improve long-term data usage without the burden of the full dataset. For the parameter ranges discussed subsequently, it is likely that less than 10% of the total dataset would be archived as Permanent Records based on recent experience.

Furthermore, it is important to consider how DAS-derived products are to be handled. ANSS routinely produces well-defined products from raw seismic data, such as the arrival times of specific seismic waves and the peak ground shaking at stations for a given earthquake. If similar products are derived from DAS datasets, the associated increase in storage is not likely to be burdensome. Furthermore, systems are already in place to store and distribute these types of derived products, and those products are widely used by the scientific and engineering communities; the Fiber-Optic Powell Center recommends similar products be calculated from the DAS data and archived similarly.

Below are recommendations for handling datasets with a Temporary Records distinction. All temporary records are to be archived in a lossless format unless otherwise specified.

Each separate cable/dataset would be required to have an approximately one-month rolling buffer of the full continuous dataset that would not be required to be made public. For data outside this rolling buffer, the following options would then be required:

Option 1: The data are destroyed immediately, similar to triggered strong-motion data.

Option 2: The data are destroyed after a longer temporary archive of ~1 yr but with a low-speed access device (local or cloud).

Option 3: A lossy compressed version of the data (e.g., JPEG, ZFP) would be archived on site for a longer temporary period of ~2 yr (Lindstrom, 2014; Issah and Martin, 2024).

Option 4: A progressive scheme based on reducing channel density with time. For example, After 1 month, delete half the channels. After 6 months, reduce to 25%, after 1 yr, it will be reduced to 10% of original, and so forth. After 5 yr, delete completely except for the permanent requirements below.

Subsequent are the recommendations for datasets having a Permanent Records distinction, which are required to be made public:

1. For local earthquakes, ten minutes before and after every catalog earthquake with $M \geq M_{thresh}$ within R_{thresh} of any point along the cable being monitored. The magnitude threshold, M_{thresh}, would likely be ~4 and the distance threshold R_{thresh} would likely be ~100 km, but these could be unique for each network to allow higher cutoffs in very active locations. Similarly, for local earthquakes with $M_{min} \leq M < M_{thresh}$, save 2 min before and after the origin time. M_{min} is likely to be ~2, but this magnitude range could be set by each network.
2. For every catalog earthquake with $M > 6$ within 100 km of any point on the cable, save 10 days before and no fewer than 30 days after to allow for studies related to aftershocks and rupture kinematics, enhanced catalog development, EEW algorithm development, and so forth.
3. For any EEW alert that is not associated with an ANSS earthquake save the same time windows as (1) above.
4. Continuous data for a small subset of channels giving reliable data; the subsetting criteria could be based on even spacing (e.g., every 10 km), or sections of channels, but the overall spatial coverage should be comparable to the average interstation distance in the densest part of a typical monitoring network.
5. For derived, event-based products such as phase picks and peak strain-rate values, save values for all good channels for all earthquakes with $M \geq M_{min}$. As in (1), M_{min} is likely to be 2, but this magnitude range could be set by each network.

Making these data publicly available with minimal lead time would increase their utilization in a variety of research projects beyond the initial monitoring. Any specific requirements would need to be defined beforehand; ANSS time requirements might be a useful guide.

Recommendations for an effective DAS data facility. Permanently archived DAS data are recommended to be stored at a TDR similar to other USGS-funded seismic data. Although there are many possibilities for such a data center, decisions will need to be made in terms of optimizing trade-offs between costs, accessibility, and ease of use of permanent records for research purposes. There could be multiple data centers designed to handle different aspects of these trade-offs, but the Fiber-Optic Powell Center discussed the key features of a single TDR that would enable the most efficient use of DAS data by researchers. In the purview of the Fiber-Optic Powell Center, the following represents top priorities in a DAS TDR: Metadata that is easily and quickly searchable; adherence to generally accepted standards (e.g., findable, accessible, interoperable, and reusable, Wilkinson *et al.*, 2016); an automated quality assessment system to evaluate datasets in aggregate; the ability to download subsets of data (spatially or temporally); capabilities for online/cloud processing, notably without downloading to the user's machine; and secure access and storage. The utility of DAS for earthquake hazards research will be accelerated if an appropriate TDR can be identified soon.

Compared to a standard data repository, a DAS-optimized TDR should allow users to download large amounts of raw data quickly, similar to how GDR operates (Weers *et al.*, 2022). For instance, the 81 TB PoroTomo dataset (Wang *et al.*, 2018) is frequently downloaded from the GDR, and we expect future targeted experiments will be in a similar size range (tens of terabytes). Similarly, it is likely that users will want to download entire continuous datasets from, say, induced seismicity experiments to study triggering mechanisms, fault-zone observatories, or aftershock datasets to study microseismicity and the temporal evolution of crustal properties (see Introduction and Fiber-Optic Sensing Technology for Earthquake Seismology sections).

Conclusion

Fiber-optic sensing technologies have now been used in nearly every aspect of earthquake-hazards-related research and monitoring. Considering both the breadth of applications covered by prior work, and the observational and operational needs of hazards related applications, serves to clarify the immense potential these technologies have for driving a revolution in sensing capabilities and physical understanding of the earthquake source, earth structure, and wavefield. To make lasting inroads, however, the community must move beyond seminal, PI-driven research, toward building consensus on metadata standards and data archiving strategies, building the infrastructure for preserving and accessing immense volumes of data, establishing a test facility, and working to eliminate any remaining doubt that the future of fiber optics in seismology indeed shines brightly.

Data and Resources

There were no new data collected as part of this article. There were no new analysis codes developed as part of this article. The U.S. Geological Survey (USGS) Powell Center working groups are described at https://www.usgs.gov/centers/john-wesley-powell-center-for-analysis-and-synthesis (last accessed September 2025). The Department of Energy geothermal data repository (GDR) data were available at https://gdr.openei.org/ (last accessed June 2025). Example repositories of seismic data collected for research or monitoring purposes were available at https://earthscope.org, https://www.marine-geo.org/, https://scedc.caltech.edu, https://ncedc.org, or https://www.sciencebase.gov (last accessed June 2025). The USGS Advanced National Seismic System (ANSS) data policy for traditional seismic data was available at https://www.usgs.gov/media/files/anss-data-and-products-policy (last accessed June 2025). All seismic data archived by EarthScope were available at https://ds.iris.edu/data/distribution (last accessed June 2025). The definition of USGS official Records, namely the distinctions between 'Permanent' versus 'Temporary' Records were available at https://www.usgs.gov/survey-manual (last accessed June 2025). The supplemental material contains one figure that describes the evolution of fiber optic sensing capabilities. It contains one table that demonstrates the delayed EEW alert times for offshore earthquakes.

Declaration of Competing Interests

The authors acknowledge that there are no conflicts of interest recorded.

Acknowledgments

This working group was principally supported by the U.S. Geological Survey (USGS) John Wesley Powell Center for Analysis and Synthesis (https://www.sciencebase.gov/catalog/item/6328d47ad34e71c6d67b7942, last accessed June 2025), and received supplemental funds from the National Science Foundation Division of Earth Sciences. The authors thank Jill Baron for guidance in organizing a productive working group. The authors thank Demi Bingham, Asha Varma, and Asena Tongamoa for help with workshop organizing. The authors thank Nate Lindsey for numerous contributions to the working group and the content of this article. The authors thank the Powell Center for supporting the postdoctoral positions of Q. Shi and J. Atterholt. The authors thank the various participants and guest speakers during the course of this project, including Sean Ahdi, Josh Callahan, Sireesh Dadi, Stas Glubokovskikh, Dara Goldberg, Alex Hatem, Mike Hines, Evan Hirakawa, Kathleen Hodgkinson, Kishor Jaiswal, Ge Jin, Valey Kamalov, Yuanyuan Ma, Mikael Mazur, Marla Meehl, Josh Nelson, Cody Rotermund, Justin Rubinstein, Amir Salaree, Kenichi Soga, Connie Stewart, Nicole Taverna, Aleksei Titov, William Wilcock, Ethan Williams, William Yeck, Ellen Yu, and Mark Zumberge. L. V. was supported by the ground-based nuclear detonation detection and low-yield nuclear monitoring programs funded by the National Nuclear Security Administration, Defense Nuclear Nonproliferation Research and Development; this article has been coauthored by L. V. with number LA-UR-25-20865 by Triad National Security, LLC, under contract with the U.S. Department of Energy (Number 89233218CNA000001). The authors thank Sumant Jha for help with figures. The authors thank Rob Skoumal, Voon Hui Lai, and two anonymous reviewers for comments that strengthened this article.

Any use of trade, firm or product names is for descriptive purposes only and does not imply endorsement by the U.S. Government.

References

Abrahamson, N. A., N. M. Kuehn, M. Walling, and N. Landwehr (2019). Probabilistic seismic hazard analysis in California using nonergodic ground-motion models, *Bull. Seismol. Soc. Am.* **109,** no. 4, 1235–1249.

Abukrat, Y., P. Sinitsyn, M. Reshef, and A. Lellouch (2023). Directional sources and distributed acoustic sensing deployments for nearsurface characterization, *Geophysics* **88,** no. 6, WC121–WC131.

Ajo-Franklin, J., V. Rodríguez Tribaldos, A. Nayak, F. Cheng, R. Mellors, B. Chi, T. Wood, M. Robertson, C. Rotermund, E. Matzel, *et al.* (2022). The Imperial Valley dark fiber project: Toward seismic studies using DAS and telecom infrastructure for geothermal applications, *Bull. Seismol. Soc. Am.* **93,** no. 5, 2906–2919.

Aki, K., and P. Richards (2002). *Quantitative Seismology*, University Science Book.

Allen, R. M., and D. Melgar (2019). Earthquake early warning: Advances, scientific challenges, and societal needs, *Annu. Rev. Earth Planet. Sci.* **47,** no. 1, 361–388.

Atterholt, J., and Z. Zhan (2024). Fine-scale southern California Moho structure uncovered with distributed acoustic sensing, *Sci. Adv.* **10,** no. 48, eadr3327, doi: 10.1126/sciadv.adr3327.

Atterholt, J., Z. Zhan, Z. Shen, and Z. Li (2022). A unified wavefield-partitioning approach for distributed acoustic sensing, *Geophys. J. Int.* **228,** no. 2, 1410–1418.

Atterholt, J., Z. Zhan, Y. Yang, and W. Zhu (2024). Imaging the Garlock fault zone with a fiber: A limited damage zone and hidden bimaterial contrast, *J. Geophys. Res.* **129,** no. 7, e2024JB028900, doi: 10.1029/2024JB028900.

Baillet, M., D. Rivet, A. Trabattoni, J. Chèze, F. Peix, D. Ambrois, M. van den Ende, C. Vernet, R. Sánchez-Olavarria, and S. E. Barrientos (2025). Automatic earthquake catalogs from a permanent DAS offshore network, doi: 10.22541/essoar.174326522.29064769/v4.

Barbour, A. J., J. O. Langbein, and N. S. Farghal (2021). Earthquake magnitudes from dynamic strain, *Bull. Seismol. Soc. Am.* **111,** no. 3, 1325–1346.

Becker, M. W., T. I. Coleman, and C. Ciervo (2020). Distributed acoustic sensing as a distributed hydraulic sensor in fractured bedrock, *Water Resour. Res.* **56,** no. 9, e2020WR028140, doi: 10.1029/2020WR028140.

Ben-Zeev, S., and I. Lior (2025). Earthquake location with distributed acoustic sensing subarray beamforming with implications for earthquake early warning, *Seismol. Res. Lett.* **96,** no. 4, 2453–2462.

Berkhout, A. (2014). An outlook on the future of seismic imaging, Part I: Forward and reverse modelling, *Geophys. Prospect.* **62,** no. 5, 911–930.

Biondi, E., G. Tepp, E. Yu, J. K. Saunders, V. Yartsev, M. Black, M. Watkins, A. Bhaskaran, R. Bhadha, Z. Zhan, *et al.* (2025). Real-time processing of distributed acoustic sensing data for earthquake monitoring operations, doi: 10.48550/arXiv.2505.24077.

Biondi, E., W. Zhu, J. Li, E. F. Williams, and Z. Zhan (2023). An upper-crust lid over the Long Valley magma chamber, *Sci. Adv.* **9,** no. 42, eadi9878, doi: 10.1126/sciadv.adi9878.

Böse, M., J. Andrews, R. Hartog, and C. Felizardo (2023). Performance and next-generation development of the finite-fault rupture detector (FinDer) within the United States West Coast ShakeAlert warning system, *Bull. Seismol. Soc. Am.* **113,** no. 2, 648–663.

Bouffaut, L., K. Taweesintananon, H. J. Kriesell, R. A. Rorstadbotnen, J. R. Potter, M. Landro, S. E. Johansen, J. K. Brenne, A. Haukanes, O. Schjelderup, *et al.* (2022). Eavesdropping at the speed of light: Distributed acoustic sensing of baleen whales in the Arctic, *Front. Mar. Sci.* **9,** 901,348.

Boyd, O. S., D. Churchwell, M. P. Moschetti, E. M. Thompson, M. C. Chapman, O. Ilhan, T. L. Pratt, S. K. Ahdi, and S. Rezaeian (2024). Sediment thickness map of united states atlantic and gulf coastal plain strata, and their influence on earthquake ground motions, *Earthq. Spectra* **40,** no. 1, 89–112.

Brenne, J. K., A. Sladen, P. Pecci, J. P. Morten, J. Pelaez, J. Jacobsen, A. Calsat, P. Plantady, J.-P. Ampuero, D. Rivet, *et al.* (2024). NonIntrusive DAS coexisting in telecom networks, *Optical Fiber Communication Conference*, Optica Publishing Group, M4E-3 pp.

Chambers, D., G. Jin, A. Tourei, A. H. S. Issah, A. Lellouch, E. Martin, D. Zhu, A. Girard, S. Yuan, T. Cullison, *et al.* (2024). Dascore: A python library for distributed fiber optic sensing, *Seismica* **3,** no. 2, 10-26443.

Chen, X. (2023). Source parameter analysis using distributed acoustic sensing-An example with the porotomo array, *Geophys. J. Int.* **233,** no. 3, 2208–2214.

Cheng, F., J. B. Ajo-Franklin, A. Nayak, V. R. Tribaldos, R. Mellors, P. Dobson, and I. V. D. F. Team (2023). Using dark fiber and distributed acoustic sensing to characterize a geothermal system in the imperial valley, southern California, *J. Geophys. Res.* **128,** no. 3, e2022JB025240, doi: 10.1029/2022JB025240.

Cheng, F., J. B. Ajo-Franklin, and V. Rodriguez Tribaldos (2023). High-resolution near-surface imaging at the basin scale using dark fiber and distributed acoustic sensing: Toward site effect estimation in urban environments, *J. Geophys. Res.* **128,** no. 9, e2023JB026957, doi: 10.1029/2023JB026957.

Chung, A. I., M.-A. Meier, J. Andrews, M. Böse, B. W. Crowell, J. J. McGuire, and D. E. Smith (2020). Shakealert earthquake early warning system performance during the 2019 ridgecrest earthquake sequence, *Bull. Seismol. Soc. Am.* **110,** no. 4, 1904–1923.

Cochran, E. S., J. L. Rubinstein, A. J. Barbour, and J. O. Kaven (2024). Induced seismicity strategic vision, *Circular 1509*, U.S. Geological Survey, Reston, Virginia.

Cochran, E. S., E. Wolin, D. E. McNamara, A. Yong, D. Wilson, M. Alvarez, N. van der Elst, A. McClain, and J. Steidl (2020). The U.S. Geological Survey's rapid seismic array deployment for the 2019 Ridgecrest earthquake sequence, *Seismol. Res. Lett.* **91,** no. 4, 1952–1960.

Costley, R. D., G. Galan-Comas, C. K. Kirkendall, J. E. Simms, K. K. Hathaway, M. W. Parker, S. A. Ketcham, E. W. Smith, W. R. Folks, T. W. Milburn, *et al.* (2018). Spectral analysis of surface waves with simultaneous fiber optic distributed acoustic sensing and vertical geophones, *J. Environ. Eng. Geophys.* **23,** no. 2, 183–195.

Currenti, G., M. Allegra, F. Cannavo, P. Jousset, M. Prestifilippo, R. Napoli, M. Sciotto, G. Di Grazia, E. Privitera, S. Palazzo, *et al.* (2023). Distributed dynamic strain sensing of very long period and long period events on telecom fiber-optic cables at Vulcano, Italy, *Sci. Rep.* **13,** no. 1, 4641.

Currenti, G., P. Jousset, R. Napoli, C. Krawczyk, and M. Weber (2021). On the comparison of strain measurements from fibre optics with a dense seismometer array at Etna volcano (Italy), *Solid Earth* **12,** no. 4, 993–1003.

Daley, T., D. Miller, K. Dodds, P. Cook, and B. Freifeld (2016). Field testing of modular borehole monitoring with simultaneous distributed acoustic sensing and geophone vertical seismic profiles at Citronelle, Alabama, *Geophys. Prospect.* **64,** no. 5, 1318–1334.

Daley, T. M., B. M. Freifeld, J. Ajo-Franklin, S. Dou, R. Pevzner, V. Shulakova, S. Kashikar, D. E. Miller, J. Goetz, J. Henninges, *et al.* (2013). Field testing of fiber-optic distributed acoustic sensing (DAS) for subsurface seismic monitoring, *Lead. Edge* **32,** no. 6, 699–706.

Denolle, M., E. Dunham, G. Prieto, and G. Beroza (2014). Strong ground motion prediction using virtual earthquakes, *Science* **343,** no. 6169, 399–403.

Dou, S., N. Lindsey, A. M. Wagner, T. M. Daley, B. Freifeld, M. Robertson, J. Peterson, C. Ulrich, E. R. Martin, and J. B. Ajo-Franklin (2017). Distributed acoustic sensing for seismic monitoring of the near surface: A traffic-noise interferometry case study, *Sci. Rep.* **7,** no. 1, 11,620.

Ellsworth, W. L. (2013). Injection-induced earthquakes, *Science* **341,** no. 6142, 1,225,942.

Ellsworth, W. L., D. Giardini, J. Townend, S. Ge, and T. Shimamoto (2019). Triggering of the Pohang, Korea, earthquake (M_w 5.5) by enhanced geothermal system stimulation, *Seismol. Res. Lett.* **90,** no. 5, 1844–1858.

Fang, J., Y. Yang, Z. Shen, E. Biondi, X. Wang, E. F. Williams, M. W. Becker, D. Eslamian, and Z. Zhan (2023). Directional sensitivity of DAS and its effect on Rayleigh-wave tomography: A case study in Oxnard, California, *Bull. Seismol. Soc. Am.* **94,** no. 2A, 887–897.

Farghal, N. S., J. K. Saunders, and G. A. Parker (2022). The potential of using fiber optic distributed acoustic sensing (DAS) in earthquake early warning applications, *Bull. Seismol. Soc. Am.* **112,** 1416–1435.

Ferdinand, P. (2014). The evolution of optical fiber sensors technologies during the 35 last years and their applications in structure health monitoring, *EWSHM–7th European Workshop on Structural Health Monitoring*, Nantes, France.

Fichtner, A. (2010). *Full Seismic Waveform Modelling and Inversion*, Springer Science and Business Media.

Field, E. H. (2000). A modified ground-motion attenuation relationship for southern California that accounts for detailed site classification and a basin-depth effect, *Bull. Seismol. Soc. Am.* **90,** no. 6B, S209–S221.

Given, D., R. M. Allen, A. S. Baltay, P. Bodin, E. S. Cochran, K. Creager, R. M. de Groot, L. S. Gee, E. Hauksson, T. H. Heaton, *et al.* (2018). Revised technical implementation plan for the ShakeAlert system—An earthquake early warning system for the west coast of the United States, *U.S. Geol. Surv. Open-File Rept. 2018-1155.*

Glubokovskikh, S., R. Pevzner, E. Sidenko, K. Tertyshnikov, B. Gurevich, S. Shatalin, A. Slunyaev, and E. Pelinovsky (2021). Downhole distributed acoustic sensing provides insights into the structure of short-period ocean-generated seismic wavefield, *J. Geophys. Res.* **126,** no. 12, e2020JB021463, doi: 10.1029/2020JB021463.

Gök, R., W. R. Walter, J. Barno, C. Downie, R. J. Mellors, K. Mayeda, J. Roman-Nieves, D. Templeton, and J. Ajo-Franklin (2024). Reliable earthquake source parameters using distributed acoustic sensing data derived from coda envelopes, *Seismol. Res. Lett.* **95,** no. 4, 2208–2220.

Gou, Y., R. M. Allen, W. Zhu, T. Taira, and L.-W. Chen (2025). Leveraging submarine DAS arrays for offshore earthquake early warning: A case study in Monterey Bay, California, *Seismol. Res. Lett.* **115,** 516–532.

Graves, R., T. H. Jordan, S. Callaghan, E. Deelman, E. Field, G. Juve, C. Kesselman, P. Maechling, G. Mehta, K. Milner, *et al.* (2011). CyberShake: A physics-based seismic hazard model for southern California, *Pure Appl. Geophys.* **168,** 367–381.

Hartog, A. H. (2017). *An Introduction to Distributed Optical Fibre Sensors*, CRC Press.

Hong, H., F. Yin, Y. Lei, Y. Li, and B. Wang (2024). 3d near-surface p-wave velocity structure imaging with distributed acoustic sensing and electric hammer source, *Earthq. Res. Adv.* **4,** no. 3, 100,274.

Hou, R., and J. X. Zhao (2021). A simulation-based nonlinear site amplification model for ground-motion prediction equations in Japan, *Earthq. Eng. Eng. Vib.* **20,** no. 4, 843–862.

Huang, H.-H., F.-C. Lin, B. Schmandt, J. Farrell, R. B. Smith, and V. C. Tsai (2015). The Yellowstone magmatic system from the mantle plume to the upper crust, *Science* **348,** no. 6236, 773–776.

Ide, S., E. Araki, and H. Matsumoto (2021). Very broadband strain-rate measurements along a submarine fiber-optic cable off Cape Muroto, Nankai subduction zone, Japan, *Earth Planets Space* **73,** no. 1, 1–10.

Issah, A. H. S., and E. R. Martin (2024). Impact of Lossy compression errors on passive seismic data analyses, *Seismol. Res. Lett.* **95,** 1675–1686.

Ji, Q., B. Luo, and B. Biondi (2024). Exploiting the potential of urban DAS grids: Ambient-noise subsurface imaging using joint Rayleigh and Love waves, *Seismol. Res. Lett.* **95,** no. 3, 1794–1811.

Jin, G., and B. Roy (2017). Hydraulic-fracture geometry characterization using low-frequency das signal, *Lead. Edge* **36,** 975–980.

Jousset, P., T. Reinsch, T. Ryberg, H. Blanck, A. Clarke, R. Aghayev, G. P. Hersir, J. Henninges, M. Weber, and C. M. Krawczyk (2018). Dynamic strain determination using fibre-optic cables allows imaging of seismological and structural features, *Nat. Commun.* **9,** no. 1, 2509.

Kaneko, Y., and P. M. Shearer (2014). Seismic source spectra and estimated stress drop derived from cohesive-zone models of circular subshear rupture, *Geophys. J. Int.* **197,** no. 2, 1002–1015.

Karrenbach, M., S. Cole, A. Ridge, K. Boone, D. Kahn, J. Rich, K. Silver, and D. Langton (2019). Fiber-optic distributed acoustic sensing of microseismicity, strain and temperature during hydraulic fracturing, *Geophysics* **84,** no. 1, D11–D23.

Kohler, M. D., D. E. Smith, J. Andrews, A. I. Chung, R. Hartog, I. Henson, D. D. Given, R. de Groot, and S. Guiwits (2020). Earthquake early warning ShakeAlert 2.0: Public rollout, *Seismol. Res. Lett.* **91,** no. 3, 1763–1775.

Lai, V. H., K. M. Hodgkinson, R. W. Porritt, and R. Mellors (2024). Toward a metadata standard for distributed acoustic sensing (DAS) data collection, *Seismol. Res. Lett.* **95,** no. 3, 1986–1999.

Lancelle, C. E., J. A. Baldwin, N. Lord, D. Fratta, A. Chalari, and H. F. Wang (2021). Using distributed acoustic sensing (DAS) for multichannel analysis of surface waves (MASW), in *Distributed Acoustic Sensing in Geophysics: Methods and Applications*, 213–228.

Langbein, J., R. G. Bilham, H. A. Snyder, and T. Ericksen (2024). Summary of Creepmeter Data from 1980 to 2020—Measurements Spanning the Hayward, Calaveras, and San Andreas faults in Northern and Central California, *U.S. Geol. Surv. Open File Rept. 2024-1011.*

Lee, E.-J., P. Chen, T. H. Jordan, P. B. Maechling, M. A. Denolle, and G. C. Beroza (2014). Full-3-d tomography for crustal structure in southern california based on the scattering-integral and the adjoint-wavefield methods, *J. Geophys. Res.* **119,** no. 8, 6421–6451.

Lellouch, A., N. J. Lindsey, W. L. Ellsworth, and B. L. Biondi (2020). Comparison between distributed acoustic sensing and geophones: Downhole microseismic monitoring of the forge geothermal experiment, *Bull. Seismol. Soc. Am.* **91,** no. 6, 3256–3268.

Lellouch, A., S. Yuan, Z. Spica, B. Biondi, and W. L. Ellsworth (2019). Seismic velocity estimation using passive downhole distributed acoustic sensing records: Examples from the San Andreas fault observatory at depth, *J. Geophys. Res.* **124,** no. 7, 6931–6948.

Li, J., E. Biondi, E. R. Heimisson, S. Puel, Q. Zhai, S. Zhang, V. Hjörleifsdottir, X. Wei, E. Bird, A. Klesh, *et al.* (2025). Minute-scale dynamics of recurrent dike intrusions in Iceland with fiber-optic geodesy, *Science* **388,** no. 6752, 1189–1193.

Li, J., T. Kim, N. Lapusta, E. Biondi, and Z. Zhan (2023). The break of earthquake asperities imaged by distributed acoustic sensing, *Nature* **620,** no. 7975, 800–806.

Li, J., W. Zhu, E. Biondi, and Z. Zhan (2023). Earthquake focal mechanisms with distributed acoustic sensing, *Nat. Commun.* **14,** no. 1, 4181.

Li, Y., M. Karrenbach, and J. Ajo-Franklin (2022). *Distributed Acoustic Sensing in Geophysics: Methods and Applications*, Vol. 268, John Wiley and Sons.

Li, Y., M. Perton, L. Ermert, F. J. Sánchez-Sesma, L. I. E. Maya, and Z. J. Spica (2024). Monitoring spatiotemporal seismic velocity changes using seismic interferometry and distributed acoustic sensing in Mexico City, *J. Geophys. Res.* **130,** doi: 10.1029/2024JB030697.

Li, Y., M. Perton, B. Gaite, S. Ruiz-Barajas, and Z. J. Spica (2023). Near-surface characterization using distributed acoustic sensing in an urban area: Granada, Spain, *Geophys. J. Int.* **235,** no. 2, 1849–1860.

Li, Z., and Z. Zhan (2018). Pushing the limit of earthquake detection with distributed acoustic sensing and template matching: A case study at the Brady geothermal field, *Geophys. J. Int.* **215,** no. 3, 1583–1593.

Li, Z., Z. Shen, Y. Yang, E. Williams, X. Wang, and Z. Zhan (2021). Rapid response to the 2019 Ridgecrest earthquake with distributed acoustic sensing, *AGU Adv.* **2,** no. 2, e2021AV000395, doi: 10.1029/2021AV000395.

Lin, R., G. A. Parker, J. J. McGuire, and A. S. Baltay (2023). Applications of nonergodic site response models to shakealert case studies in the Los Angeles area, *Bull. Seismol. Soc. Am.* **113,** no. 3, 1324–1343.

Linde, A. T., M. T. Gladwin, M. J. Johnston, R. L. Gwyther, and R. G. Bilham (1996). A slow earthquake sequence on the San Andreas fault, *Nature* **383,** no. 6595, 65–68.

Lindsey, N. J., and E. R. Martin (2021). Fiber-optic seismology, *Annu. Rev. Earth Planet. Sci.* **49,** 309–336.

Lindsey, N. J., T. C. Dawe, and J. B. Ajo-Franklin (2019). Illuminating seafloor faults and ocean dynamics with dark fiber distributed acoustic sensing, *Science* **366,** no. 6469, 1103–1107.

Lindsey, N. J., H. Rademacher, and J. B. Ajo-Franklin (2020). On the broadband instrument response of fiber-optic DAS arrays, *J. Geophys. Res.* **125,** no. 2, e2019JB018145, doi: 10.1029/2019JB018145.

Lindstrom, P. (2014). Fixed-rate compressed floating-point arrays, *IEEE Trans. Vis. Comp. Graphic* **20,** 2674–2683.

Lior, I. (2024). Accurate magnitude and stress drop using the spectral ratios method applied to distributed acoustic sensing, *Geophys. Res. Lett.* **51,** no. 1, e2023GL105153, doi: 10.1029/2023GL105153.

Lior, I. (2025). Earthquake source parameter estimation using distributed acoustic sensing and frequency wavenumber scaling, *Bull. Seismol. Soc. Am.* **115,** no. 3, 1267–1278.

Lior, I., D. Rivet, J.-P. Ampuero, A. Sladen, S. Barrientos, R. Sánchez-Olavarria, G. A. Villarroel Opazo, and J. A. Bustamante Prado (2023). Magnitude estimation and ground motion prediction to harness fiber optic distributed acoustic sensing for earthquake early warning, *Sci. Rep.* **13,** no. 1, 424.

Lior, I., A. Sladen, D. Mercerat, J.-P. Ampuero, D. Rivet, and S. Sambolian (2021). Strain to ground motion conversion of distributed acoustic sensing data for earthquake magnitude and stress drop determination, *Solid Earth* **12,** no. 6, 1421–1442.

Lior, I., A. Sladen, D. Rivet, J.-P. Ampuero, Y. Hello, C. Becerril, H. F. Martins, P. Lamare, C. Jestin, S. Tsagkli, and M. Christos (2021). On the detection capabilities of underwater distributed acoustic sensing, *J. Geophys. Res.* **126,** no. 3, e2020JB020925, doi: 10.1029/2020JB020925.

Lu, P., N. Lalam, M. Badar, B. Liu, B. T. Chorpening, M. P. Buric, and P. R. Ohodnicki (2019). Distributed optical fiber sensing: Review and perspective, *Appl. Phys. Rev.* **6,** 041,302.

Luo, B., G. Jin, and F. Stanek (2021). Near-field strain in distributed acoustic sensing-based microseismic observation, *Geophysics* **86,** no. 5, P49–P60.

Lux, A. I., D. Smith, M. Böse, J. J. McGuire, J. K. Saunders, M. Huynh, I. Stubailo, J. Andrews, G. Lotto, B. Crowell, *et al.* (2024). Status and performance of the ShakeAlert earthquake early warning system: 2019-2023, *Bull. Seismol. Soc. Am.* doi: 10.1785/0120230259.

Ma, K.-F., S. von Specht, L.-W. Kuo, H.-H. Huang, C.-R. Lin, C.-J. Lin, C.-S. Ku, E.-S. Wu, C.-Y. Wang, W.-Y. Chang, and P. Jousset (2024). Broad-band strain amplification in an asymmetric fault zone observed from borehole optical fiber and core, *Commun. Earth Environ.* **5,** no. 1, 402.

Martuganova, E., M. Stiller, B. Norden, J. Henninges, and C. M. Krawczyk (2022). 3D deep geothermal reservoir imaging with wireline distributed acoustic sensing in two boreholes, *Solid Earth* **13,** no. 8, 1291–1307.

Mateeva, A., J. Lopez, J. Mestayer, P. Wills, B. Cox, D. Kiyashchenko, Z. Yang, W. Berlang, R. Detomo, and S. Grandi (2013). Distributed acoustic sensing for reservoir monitoring with VSP, *Lead. Edge* **32,** no. 10, 1278–1283.

Mateeva, A., J. Lopez, H. Potters, J. Mestayer, B. Cox, D. Kiyashchenko, P. Wills, S. Grandi, K. Hornman, B. Kuvshinov, W. Berlang, Z. Yang, and R. Detomo (2014). Distributed acoustic sensing for reservoir monitoring with vertical seismic profiling, *Geophys. Prospect.* **62,** no. 4, 679–692.

Materna, K., R. Bürgmann, D. Lindsay, R. Bilham, T. Herring, B. Crowell, and W. Szeliga (2024). Shallow slow slip events in the imperial valley with along-strike propagation, *Geophys. Res. Lett.* **51,** no. 12, e2023GL108089, doi: 10.1029/2023GL108089.

McGuire, J. J., A. J. Barbour, C. Stewart, V. Yartsev, M. Karrenbach, M. Hemphill-Haley, R. C. McPherson, K. Stockdale, C. Yoon, and T. Sawi (2025). The GorDAS distributed acoustic sensing experiment above the cascadia locked zone and subducted Gorda slab, *Seismol. Res. Lett.* **96,** 2489–2503.

McGuire, J. J., D. E. Smith, A. D. Frankel, E. A. Wirth, S. K. McBride, and R. M. de Groot (2021). Expected warning times from the ShakeAlert earthquake early warning system for earthquakes in the Pacific Northwest, *U.S. Geol. Surv. Rept. 2021-1026*, Reston, Virginia, Version 1.0: March 10, 2021; Version 1.1: 24 March 2021.

McGuire, J. J., C. W. Ulberg, A. I. Lux, M. Böse, J. R. Andrews, D. E. Smith, B. W. Crowell, J. R. Murray, I. Henson, R. Hartog, *et al.* (2025). ShakeAlert version 3: Expected performance in large earthquakes, *Bull. Seismol. Soc. Am.* **115,** 533–561.

Meier, M.-A., J.-P. Ampuero, E. Cochran, and M. Page (2021). Apparent earthquake rupture predictability, *Geophys. J. Int.* **225,** no. 1, 657–663.

Mellors, R. J., R. Abbott, D. Steedman, D. Podrasky, and A. Pitarka (2021). Modeling subsurface explosions recorded on a distributed fiber optic sensor, *J. Geophys. Res.* **126,** no. 12, e2021JB022690, doi: 10.1029/2021JB022690.

Miller, D., T. Daley, D. White, B. Freifeld, M. Robertson, J. Cocker, and M. Craven (2016). Simultaneous acquisition of distributed acoustic sensing VSP with multi-mode and single-mode fibre-optic cables and 3C-geophones at the Aquistore CO_2 storage site, *CSEG Recorder* **41,** no. 6, 28–33.

Murdoch, L. C., S. DeWolf, L. N. Germanovich, S. Moysey, A. Hanna, S. Roudini, and R. Moak (2023). Using the shallow strain tensor to characterize deep geologic reservoirs, *Water Resour. Res.* **59,** no. 2, e2022WR032920, doi: 10.1029/2022WR032920.

Nayak, A., J. Ajo-Franklin, and I. V. D. F. Team (2021). Measurement of surface-wave phase-velocity dispersion on mixed inertial seismometer-distributed acoustic sensing seismic noise cross-correlations, *Bull. Seismol. Soc. Am.* **111,** no. 6, 3432–3450.

Nayak, A., J. Correa, and J. Ajo-Franklin (2024). Seismic magnitude estimation using low-frequency strain amplitudes recorded by das arrays at far-field distances, *Bull. Seismol. Soc. Am.* **114,** no. 4, 1818–1838.

Ni, Y., M. A. Denolle, R. Fatland, N. Alterman, B. P. Lipovsky, and F. Knuth (2024). An object storage for distributed acoustic sensing, *Seismol. Res. Lett.* **95,** no. 1, 499–511.

National Oceanic and Atmospheric Administration (NOAA) Office for Coastal Management (2024). Submarine cables, available at https://www.fisheries.noaa.gov/inport/item/66190 (last accessed October 2024).

Norbeck, J., T. Latimer, C. Gradl, S. Agarwal, S. Dadi, E. Eddy, S. Fercho, C. Lang, E. McConville, A. Titov, *et al.* (2023). A review of drilling, completion, and stimulation of a horizontal geothermal well system in North-Central Nevada, *Proc. of the 48th Workshop on Geothermal Reservoir Engineering Stanford University*, Stanford, California, 6–8 February 2023, Number SGP-TR-224, pp. 6–8.

Ouellet, S. M., J. Dettmer, M. J. Lato, S. Cole, D. J. Hutchinson, M. Karrenbach, B. Dashwood, J. E. Chambers, and R. Crickmore (2024). Previously hidden landslide processes revealed using distributed acoustic sensing with nanostrain-rate sensitivity, *Nat. Commun.* **15,** no. 1, 6239.

Paitz, P., P. Edme, D. Gräff, F. Walter, J. Doetsch, A. Chalari, C. Schmelzbach, and A. Fichtner (2021). Empirical investigations of the instrument response for distributed acoustic sensing (DAS) across 17 octaves, *Bull. Seismol. Soc. Am.* **111,** no. 1, 1–10.

Pan, W., L. Qu, K. A. Innanen, J. Dettmer, M. Macquet, D. Lawton, and Y. Wang (2023). Imaging near-surface s-wave velocity and attenuation models by full-waveform inversion with distributed acoustic sensing-recorded surface waves, *Geophysics* **88,** no. 1, R65–R78.

Parker, G. A., and A. S. Baltay (2022). Empirical map-based nonergodic models of site response in the greater Los Angeles area, *Bull. Seismol. Soc. Am.* **112,** no. 3, 1607–1629.

Parker, G. A., J. A. Harmon, G. M. Atkinson, R. B. Darragh, W. J. Silva, and Y. M. Hashash (2016). Towards the development of community consensus on site amplification in Central and Eastern North America, *Tech. Rept. U.S. Geol. Surv.*, available at https://earthquake.usgs.gov/cfusion/external_grants/reports/G16AP00005.pdf (last accessed November 2024).

Petersen, M. D., A. M. Shumway, P. M. Powers, E. H. Field, M. P. Moschetti, K. S. Jaiswal, K. R. Milner, S. Rezaeian, A. D. Frankel, A. L. Llenos, *et al.* (2024). The 2023 U.S. 50-state national seismic hazard model: Overview and implications, *Earthq. Spectra* **40,** no. 1, 5–88.

Power, M., R. Borcherdt, and J. Stewart (2004). Site amplification factors from empirical studies, *Report Prepared for the Pacific Earthquake Engineering Research Center by NGA Working Group*, 5 pp.

Rivet, D., M. Baillet, A. Trabattoni, M. Van Den Ende, J. Cheze, C. Maron, R. Sánchez, and S. Barrientos (2025). Three marine fibre-optic cables offshore central Chile [Data set], doi: 10.15778/RESIF.F1.

Rodríguez Tribaldos, V., and J. B. Ajo-Franklin (2021). Aquifer monitoring using ambient seismic noise recorded with distributed acoustic sensing (DAS) deployed on dark fiber, *J. Geophys. Res.* **126,** no. 4, e2020JB021004, doi: 10.1029/2020JB021004.

Romanowicz, B., R. Allen, K. Brekke, L. Chen, Y. Gou, I. Henson, J. Marty, D. Neuhauser, B. Pardini, T. Taira, *et al.* (2023). SeaFOAM: A year-long DAS deployment in Monterey bay, California, *Seismol. Res. Lett.* **94,** no. 5, 2348–2359.

Sawi, T., P. Puri, S. Haefner, J. McGuire, A. J. Barbour, C. Yoon, V. R. Tribaldos, Z. Spica, and J. Blair (2025). Fiber optic seismology interactive map, available at https://www.usgs.gov/tools/fiber-optic-seismology-experiment-interactive-map (last accessed October 2025).

SEAFOM (2024). DAS parameter definitions and tests, *Measuring Sensor Performance Document SEAFOM MSP-02 V2.0*, available at https://seafom.com/published-documents/ (last accessed October 2025).

Shi, Q., E. F. Williams, B. P. Lipovsky, M. A. Denolle, W. S. Wilcock, D. S. Kelley, and K. Schoedl (2025). Multiplexed distributed acoustic sensing offshore central Oregon, *Seismol. Res. Lett.* **96,** no. 2A, 784–800.

Shragge, J., J. Yang, N. Issa, M. Roelens, M. Dentith, and S. Schediwy (2021). Low-frequency ambient distributed acoustic sensing (DAS): Case study from Perth, Australia, *Geophys. J. Int.* **226,** no. 1, 564–581.

Sladen, A., D. Rivet, J. P. Ampuero, L. De Barros, Y. Hello, G. Calbris, and P. Lamare (2019). Distributed sensing of earthquakes and ocean-solid Earth interactions on seafloor telecom cables, *Nat. Commun.* **10,** no. 1, 5777.

Sleeman, R., A. van Wettum, and J. Trampert (2006). Three-channel correlation analysis: A new technique to measure instrumental noise of digitizers and seismic sensors, *Bull. Seismol. Soc. Am.* **96,** no. 1, 258–271.

Small, P., D. Gill, P. J. Maechling, R. Taborda, S. Callaghan, T. H. Jordan, K. B. Olsen, G. P. Ely, and C. Goulet (2017). The SCEC unified community velocity model software framework, *Seismol. Res. Lett.* **88,** no. 6, 1539–1552.

Song, Z., X. Zeng, C. H. Thurber, H. F. Wang, and D. Fratta (2019). Imaging shallow structure with active-source surface wave signal recorded by distributed acoustic sensing arrays, *Earthq. Sci.* **31,** no. 4, 208–214.

Spica, Z. J., J. Ajo-Franklin, G. C. Beroza, B. Biondi, F. Cheng, B. Gaite, B. Luo, E. Martin, J. Shen, C. Thurber, *et al.* (2023). PubDAS: A PUBlic distributed acoustic sensing datasets repository for geosciences, *Bull. Seismol. Soc. Am.* **94,** no. 2A, 983–998.

Spica, Z. J., J. C. Castellanos, L. Viens, K. Nishida, T. Akuhara, M. Shinohara, and T. Yamada (2022). Subsurface imaging with ocean-bottom distributed acoustic sensing and water phases reverberations, *Geophys. Res. Lett.* **49,** e2021GL095287, doi: 10.1029/2021GL095287.

Spica, Z. J., K. Nishida, T. Akuhara, F. Pétrélis, M. Shinohara, and T. Yamada (2020). Marine sediment characterized by ocean-bottom fiber-optic seismology, *Geophys. Res. Lett.* **47,** no. 16, e2020GL088360, doi: 10.1029/2020GL088360.

Spica, Z. J., M. Perton, E. R. Martin, G. C. Beroza, and B. Biondi (2020). Urban seismic site characterization by fiber-optic seismology, *J. Geophys. Res.* **125,** no. 3, e2019JB018656, doi: 10.1029/2019JB018656.

Strumia, C., A. Trabattoni, M. Supino, M. Baillet, D. Rivet, and G. Festa (2024). Sensing optical fibers for earthquake source characterization using raw DAS records, *J. Geophys. Res.* **129,** no. 1, e2023JB027860, doi: 10.1029/2023JB027860.

Stubailo, I., M. Alvarez, G. Biasi, R. Bhadha, and E. Hauksson (2020). Latency of waveform data delivery from the southern California seismic network during the 2019 Ridgecrest earthquake sequence and its effect on ShakeAlert, *Seismol. Res. Lett.* **92,** no. 1, 170–186.

Sung, C.-H., N. Abrahamson, and M. Lacour (2023). Methodology for including path effects due to 3d velocity structure in nonergodic ground-motion models, *Bull. Seismol. Soc. Am.* **113,** no. 5, 2144–2163.

Taverna, N., J. Weers, S. Porse, A. Anderson, Z. Frone, and E. Holt (2023). An update on the geothermal data repository's data standards and pipelines: Geospatial data and distributed acoustic sensing data, *Technical Report*, National Renewable Energy Laboratory (NREL), Golden, Colorado.

Thompson, M., J. Renate Hartog, and E. A. Wirth (2023). A population-based performance evaluation of the ShakeAlert earthquake early warning system for M 9 megathrust earthquakes in the Pacific Northwest, U.S.A, *Bull. Seismol. Soc. Am.* **114,** no. 2, 1103–1123.

Tourei, A., X. Ji, G. Rocha dos Santos, R. Czarny, S. Rybakov, Z. Wang, M. Hallissey, E. R. Martin, M. Xiao, T. Zhu, *et al.* (2024). Mapping permafrost variability and degradation using seismic surface waves, electrical resistivity, and temperature sensing: A case study in Arctic Alaska, *J. Geophys. Res.* **129,** no. 3, e2023JF007352, doi: 10.1029/2023JF007352.

Townend, J., and M. D. Zoback (2000). How faulting keeps the crust strong, *Geology* **28,** no. 5, 399–402.

U.S. Geological Survey (USGS) (2017a). Advanced National Seismic System (ANSS) comprehensive catalog of earthquake events and products: Various, doi: 10.5066/F7MS3QZH.

USGS (2017b). Quaternary fault and fold database for the United States, available at https://www.usgs.gov/natural-hazards/earthquake hazards/faults (last accessed July 2025).

van den Ende, M., A. Trabattoni, M. Baillet, and D. Rivet (2025). An analysis of the dynamic range of distributed acoustic sensing for earthquake early warning, *Seismica* **4,** no. 1.

Vantassel, J. P., B. R. Cox, P. G. Hubbard, and M. Yust (2022). Extracting high-resolution, multi-mode surface wave dispersion data from distributed acoustic sensing measurements using the multichannel analysis of surface waves, *J. Appl. Geophys.* **205,** 104,776.

Viens, L., L. F. Bonilla, Z. J. Spica, K. Nishida, T. Yamada, and M. Shinohara (2022). Nonlinear earthquake response of marine sediments with distributed acoustic sensing, *Geophys. Res. Lett.* **49,** no. 21, e2022GL100122, doi: 10.1029/2022GL100122.

Wald, D. J., C. B. Worden, E. M. Thompson, and M. Hearne (2022). ShakeMap operations, policies, and procedures, *Earthq. Spectra* **38,** no. 1, 756–777.

Wang, H. F., X. Zeng, D. E. Miller, D. Fratta, K. L. Feigl, C. H. Thurber, and R. J. Mellors (2018). Ground motion response to an ml 4.3 earthquake using co-located distributed acoustic sensing and seismometer arrays, *Geophys. J. Int.* **213,** no. 3, 2020–2036.

Wang, X., E. F. Williams, M. Karrenbach, M. G. Herráez, H. F. Martins, and Z. Zhan (2020). Rose Parade seismology: Signatures of floats and bands on optical fiber, *Seismol. Res. Lett.* **91,** no. 4, 2395–2398.

Wang, Y., and D. C. Lawton (2023). Time-lapse impedance variations using DAS VSP data during CO2 injection at the CMC Newell County Facility, Alberta, Canada, *Third International Meeting for Applied Geoscience & Energy*, Society of Exploration Geophysicists and American Association of Petroleum Geologists, 1750–1754.

Weers, J., A. Anderson, and N. Taverna (2022). The geothermal data repository: Ten years of supporting the geothermal industry with open access to geothermal data, *Technical Report*, National Renewable Energy Laboratory (NREL), Golden, Colorado.

Wilkinson, M. D., M. Dumontier, I. J. Aalbersberg, G. Appleton, M. Axton, A. Baak, N. Blomberg, J.-W. Boiten, L. B. da Silva Santos, P. E. Bourne, *et al.* (2016). The FAIR guiding principles for scientific data management and stewardship, *Sci. Data* **3,** no. 1, 1–9.

Williams, E. F., M. Denolle, S. Abadi, K. Aderhold, P. Bodin, V. Gaete-Elgueta, E. M. Golos, B. P. Lipovsky, Y. Ni, Q. Shi, *et al.* (2024). Cook Inlet DAS (CIDAS) BADGER experiments: Studying structure, seismicity, ocean waves, and acoustics offshore southern Alaska with hybrid networks integrating distributed acoustic sensing and seismometers, *Fall AGU Meeting*.

Williams, E. F., M. R. Fernández-Ruiz, R. Magalhaes, R. Vanthillo, Z. Zhan, M. González-Herráez, and H. F. Martins (2019). Distributed sensing of microseisms and teleseisms with submarine dark fibers, *Nat. Commun.* **10,** no. 1, 1–11.

Williams, E. F., M. R. Fernández-Ruiz, R. Magalhaes, R. Vanthillo, Z. Zhan, M. Gonzalez-Herraez, and H. F. Martins (2021). Schölte wave inversion and passive source imaging with ocean-bottom DAS, *Lead. Edge* **40,** no. 8, 576–583.

Williams, E. F., A. Ugalde, H. F. Martins, C. E. Becerril, J. Callies, M. Claret, M. R. Fernandez-Ruiz, M. Gonzalez-Herraez, S. Martin-Lopez, J. L. Pelegri, *et al.* (2023). Fiber-optic observations of internal waves and tides, *J. Geophys. Res.* **128,** no. 9, e2023JC019980, doi: 10.1029/2023JC019980.

Williamson, A., A. Lux, and R. Allen (2023). Improving out of network earthquake locations using prior seismicity for use in earthquake early warning, *Bull. Seismol. Soc. Am.* **113,** no. 2, 664–675.

Wuestefeld, A., Z. J. Spica, K. Aderhold, H.-H. Huang, K.-F. Ma, V. H. Lai, M. Miller, L. Urmantseva, D. Zapf, and D. C. Bowden (2024). The global DAS month of February 2023, *Seismol. Res. Lett.* **95,** no. 3, 1569–1577.

Xie, T., C.-C. Zhang, B. Shi, Z. Chen, and Y. Zhang (2024). Integrating distributed acoustic sensing and computer vision for real-time seismic location of landslides and rockfalls along linear infrastructure, *Landslides* **21,** 1941–1959.

Yan, Y., X. Chen, J. Li, J. Guan, C. Xi, and H. Liu (2023). Inversion of multimodal dispersion curves from distributed acoustic sensing measurements for subsurface imaging: A field case of Garner Valley, California, *J. Appl. Geophys.* **214,** 105,070.

Yang, J., and J. Shragge (2023). Long-term ambient seismic interferometry for constraining seasonal subsurface velocity variations in urban settings: A distributed acoustic sensing (DAS) case study, *Geophys. J. Int.* **234,** no. 3, 1973–1984.

Yang, L., X. Liu, and G. C. Beroza (2021). Revisiting evidence for widespread seismicity in the upper mantle under Los Angeles, *Sci. Adv.* **7,** no. 4, eabf2862, doi: 10.1126/sciadv.abf2862.

Yang, Y., J. W. Atterholt, Z. Shen, J. B. Muir, E. F. Williams, and Z. Zhan (2022). Sub-kilometer correlation between near-surface structure and ground motion measured with distributed acoustic sensing, *Geophys. Res. Lett.* **49,** e2021GL096503, doi: 10.1029/2021GL096503.

Yin, J., W. Zhu, J. Li, E. Biondi, Y. Miao, Z. J. Spica, L. Viens, M. Shinohara, S. Ide, K. Mochizuki, *et al.* (2023). Earthquake magnitude with DAS: A transferable data-based scaling relation, *Geophys. Res. Lett.* **50,** no. 10, e2023GL103045, doi: 10.1029/2023GL103045.

Yu, C., Z. Zhan, N. J. Lindsey, J. B. Ajo-Franklin, and M. Robertson (2019). The potential of DAS in teleseismic studies: Insights from the Goldstone experiment, *Geophys. Res. Lett.* **46,** no. 3, 1320–1328.

Zelezny, S. (2023). Broadband or bust: California's plan to close the digital divide, *Univ. Pac. Law Rev.* **54,** 206.

Zeng, X., C. Lancelle, C. Thurber, D. Fratta, H. Wang, N. Lord, A. Chalari, and A. Clarke (2017). Properties of noise cross-correlation functions obtained from a distributed acoustic sensing array at Garner Valley, California, *Bull. Seismol. Soc. Am.* **107,** no. 2, 603–610.

Zeng, X., C. H. Thurber, H. F. Wang, D. Fratta, and K. L. Feigl (2021). High-resolution shallow structure at Brady hot springs using ambient noise tomography (ANT) on a trenched distributed acoustic sensing (DAS) array, in *Distributed Acoustic Sensing in Geophysics: Methods and Applications*, 101–110.

Zhan, Z. (2020). Distributed acoustic sensing turns fiber-optic cables into sensitive seismic antennas, *Seismol. Res. Lett.* **91,** no. 1, 1–15.

Zhu, T., J. Shen, and E. R. Martin (2021). Sensing earth and environment dynamics by telecommunication fiber-optic sensors: An urban experiment in Pennsylvania, USA, *Solid Earth* **12,** no. 1, 219–235.

Zhu, W., E. Biondi, J. Li, J. Yin, Z. E. Ross, and Z. Zhan (2023). Seismic arrival-time picking on distributed acoustic sensing data using semi-supervised learning, *Nat. Commun.* **14,** no. 1, 8192.

Zoback, M., S. Hickman, W. Ellsworth, and , and The SAFOD Science Team (2011). Scientific drilling into the San Andreas fault zone; an overview of SAFOD's first five years, *Sci. Drill.* **11,** 14–28.

Authors and Affiliations

Jeffrey J. McGuire: U.S. Geological Survey, Earthquake Science Center, Moffett Field, California, U.S.A., https://orcid.org/0000-0001-9235-2166; **Andrew J. Barbour:** U.S. Geological Survey, Earthquake Science Center, Vancouver, Washington, U.S.A., https://orcid.org/0000-0002-6890-2452; **Zack J. Spica:** Department of Earth and Environmental Sciences, University of Michigan, Ann Arbor, Michigan, U.S.A., https://orcid.org/0000-0002-9259-1973; **Verónica Rodríguez Tribaldos:** GFZ Potsdam, Potsdam, Germany Earth and Environmental Sciences Area, Lawrence Berkeley National Laboratory, Berkeley, California, U.S.A., https://orcid.org/0000-0002-1325-0434; **Zhongwen Zhan:** Seismological Laboratory, California Institute of Technology, Pasadena, California, U.S.A., https://orcid.org/0000-0002-5586-2607; **Bradley P. Lipovsky:** Department of Earth and Space Sciences, University of Washington, Seattle, Washington, U.S.A.; **Robert J. Mellors:** Institute of Geophysics and Planetary Physics, Scripps Institution of Oceanography, UC San Diego, La Jolla, California, U.S.A.; **Ettore Biondi:** Seismological Laboratory, California Institute of Technology, Pasadena, California, U.S.A., https://orcid.org/0000-0002-3305-0982; **Clara Yoon:** U.S. Geological Survey, Earthquake Science Center, Pasadena, California, U.S.A., https://orcid.org/0000-0003-4521-3889; **Martin Karrenbach:** Seismics Unusual LLC, Brea, California, U.S.A., https://orcid.org/0000-0003-2190-8598; **Adam T. Ringler:** Albuquerque Seismological Laboratory, U.S. Geological Survey, Albuquerque, New Mexico, U.S.A., https://orcid.org/0000-0002-9839-4188; **James Atterholt:** U.S. Geological Survey, Geologic Hazards Science Center, Golden, Colorado, U.S.A., https://orcid.org/0000-0003-1603-5518; **Avinash Nayak:** Earth and Environmental Sciences Area, Lawrence Berkeley National Laboratory, Berkeley, California, U.S.A., https://orcid.org/0000-0001-7913-7189; **Theresa Sawi:** U.S. Geological Survey, Earthquake Science Center, Moffett Field, California, U.S.A., https://orcid.org/0000-0001-5938-6743; **Loïc Viens:** Los Alamos National Laboratory, Los Alamos, New Mexico, U.S.A., https://orcid.org/0000-0002-7975-7799; **Eileen R. Martin:** Colorado School of Mines, Golden, Colorado, U.S.A., https://orcid.org/0000-0002-3420-4971; **Allen L. Husker:** Seismological Laboratory, California Institute of Technology, Pasadena, California, U.S.A., https://orcid.org/0000-0003-1139-0502; **Paul Bodin:** Department of Earth and Space Sciences, University of Washington, Seattle, Washington, U.S.A.; **Morgan P. Moschetti:** U.S. Geological Survey, Geologic Hazards Science Center, Golden, Colorado, U.S.A., https://orcid.org/0000-0001-7261-0295; **Qibin Shi:** Department of Earth and Space Sciences, University of Washington, Seattle, Washington, U.S.A., https://orcid.org/0000-0002-4211-9187; **Nathaniel C. Miller:** U.S. Geological Survey, Coastal and Marine Science Center, Woods Hole, Massachusetts, U.S.A., https://orcid.org/0000-0003-3271-2929; and **Prisha Puri:** University of Missouri, M.U. Institute for Data Science and Informatics, Columbia, Missouri, U.S.A., https://orcid.org/0009-0006-0700-8832

Manuscript received 24 February 2025
Published online 7 November 2025

Near-Surface High-Frequency Spectral Decay Kappa (κ) Model of *S* Waves in Western-Central Sichuan, China

Pengfei Dang*[1], Jie Cui[2], Bingyan Zhao[1], and Qifang Liu[3]

Abstract

The Longmenshan fault zone in the western-central region of Sichuan is one of the active earthquake areas in China and is characterized by frequent earthquakes. We used 4260 seismic components of 165 earthquakes with magnitudes ranging from 3.5 to 6.0 recorded by 168 stations in western-central Sichuan, China, to estimate the high-frequency decay parameter kappa (κ) of the horizontal and vertical components in this region. The estimated horizontal kappa values are almost twice those of the vertical kappa values, and the difference in the kappa values between the two horizontal components is not significant. In addition, we investigated the influence of earthquake size and site classification on the κ_0 value. The results revealed that the κ_0 value gradually increased as the soil layer changed from rock to soft, and the κ_0 value strongly depended on the near-surface site conditions. When the site type was the same, the κ_0 value increased with magnitude, indicating that the κ_0 value is influenced by both site and source effects. The relationships between the kappa values and the local magnitude were defined as $\kappa = 0.00403\ M_L + 0.01748$ for the horizontal component and $\kappa = 0.00496\ M_L + 0.00369$ for the vertical component. The single-station κ_0 value also indicated that there was not much difference in the κ_0 values between the two horizontal components, which were significantly greater than the κ_0 value of the vertical component. Finally, the relationships for the horizontal and vertical components between κ_0 and V_{S30} were defined as $\kappa_0 = (0.1032 \pm 0.0989)-0.0118 \ln(V_{S30})$ and $\kappa_0 = (0.1491 \pm 0.1043)-0.0222 \ln(V_{S30})$, respectively, which indicates that the relationship is weak without considering the influence of magnitude. The estimated kappa values for western-central Sichuan, China, may provide a fundamental basis for the study of seismic attenuation and fine simulation of ground-motion fields in this region.

Cite this article as Dang, P., J. Cui, B. Zhao, and Q. Liu (2025). Near-Surface High-Frequency Spectral Decay Kappa (κ) Model of *S* Waves in Western-Central Sichuan, China, *Seismol. Res. Lett.* **97**, 1946–1964, doi: 10.1785/0220250225.

Supplemental Material

Introduction

The Longmenshan fault zone, located in the central region of Sichuan, China, has been in a relatively active stage since the Wenchuan earthquake with a magnitude of 7.9 in 2008. Several small- and large-sized earthquakes with magnitudes of 1.0–7.0 have occurred in the region (Yang *et al.*, 2005), including the M_w 6.6 Lushan earthquake in 2013 (Bai *et al.*, 2016; Zhang, Li, *et al.*, 2024; Liu *et al.*, 2025) and the M_s 7.0 Jiuzhaigou earthquake in 2017 (Wu *et al.*, 2023), which indicates that the Longmenshan fault zone has been in a relatively active state. The Longmenshan fault zone and Xianshuihe fault zone in central Sichuan are large and important earthquake fault zones on the eastern edge of the Qinghai-Tibet plateau. They are among the areas with the strongest inland deformation in the world, with the steepest global terrain elevation, the most frequent earthquakes, and the most severe geological disasters (Zhang, Li, *et al.*, 2024). The Longmenshan fault zone is the most important earthquake-prone area in China and is characterized mainly by thrust ground motion (Li *et al.*, 2006; Hubbard and Shaw, 2009), whereas the Xianshuihe fault zone has experienced 17 earthquakes with magnitudes greater than 6.0 since 1975 (Zhang, Ma *et al.*, 2024), which are characterized mainly by strike-slip ground motion (Wen *et al.*, 1989; Klinger, 2010; Zielke *et al.*, 2015). The northeast section of the Longmenshan fault zone is adjacent to the Minshan uplift on the west side. The western boundary of the Minshan uplift is the Minjiang fault, the eastern boundary is the Huya fault,

1. School of Civil and Environmental Engineering and Geography Science, Ningbo University, Ningbo, China, https://orcid.org/0000-0001-6780-6453 (PD); 2. School of Civil Engineering and Transportation, Guangzhou University, Guangzhou, China; 3. School of Civil Engineering, Suzhou University of Science and Technology, Suzhou, China.

*Corresponding author: iempengfeid@qq.com

and the southern and northern boundaries are the Longmenshan structural belt and the East Kunlun fault, respectively. It is a south–north-trending neotectonic uplift that differs significantly from the landforms on the east and west sides (Hu *et al.*, 2024). Its formation mechanism is closely related to the movement mode of the east–west boundary fault since the neotectonic period of the fault (Ma, 1989). Taking the Minshan uplift as the boundary, the Longmenshan fault zone can be divided into the northeast section and the southwest section (Chen *et al.*, 2007). The northeast section is characterized by the exposed Jiaoziding basement complex and the development of the Tangwangzhai syncline (Li *et al.*, 2020), with weaker Quaternary activity (Chen *et al.*, 2008).

When the frequency exceeds a specific frequency, the Fourier amplitude spectrum (FAS) of the S wave rapidly decreases at high frequencies (Aki, 1967; Brune, 1970). The spectral attenuation feature can be represented by two types of filters: the kappa filter, which is defined as $\exp(-\pi f \kappa)$ (Anderson and Hough, 1984), and the $f_{\max}$ filter, which is defined as $[1 + (f/f_{\max})^8]^{-1/2}$ (Hanks, 1982). In the field of seismology, kappa filters are commonly used to describe the attenuation characteristics of the FAS at high frequencies (Boore, 2003), and some studies suggest that it is possible to better estimate the ground motion at a certain site by incorporating high-frequency decay characteristics into regional attenuation functions (Cotton *et al.*, 2006; Laurendeau *et al.*, 2013; Neighbors *et al.*, 2015). One common method for calculating the high-frequency attenuation of S-wave FAS is to observe the exponential decay of the kappa factor (Anderson and Hough, 1984). Parameter kappa is one of the critical input parameters for stochastic ground-motion simulation (Dang *et al.*, 2022, 2023; Luo and Peng, 2024; Mao *et al.*, 2024; Shi and Zhang, 2024; Dang, Cui, and Liu, 2025; Yu *et al.*, 2025). In recent years, several studies have investigated the distance, earthquake size, fault type, site condition, and focal depth dependency of kappa based on earthquake recordings from various regions worldwide (Papageorgiou and Aki, 1983; Parolai and Bindi, 2004; Askan *et al.*, 2014; Fu and Li, 2017; Kumar *et al.*, 2020; Sertcelik *et al.*, 2022). The spectral decay parameter, kappa, is well known to be related to distance; however, there are different opinions on whether the spectral decay parameter κ is fundamentally a source effect (Kumar *et al.*, 2020), a site effect (Anderson and Hough, 1984), or a combination of source and site effects (Tsai and Chen, 2000; Campbell, 2009). Because the kappa values calculated at stations with different distances from the sources include path attenuation, eliminating these effects to determine the physical parameters that describe local site attenuation is necessary. Moreover, the estimation of the spectral decay parameter kappa is closely related to the geological materials of the site; thus, the kappa (κ_0) value at a distance of 0 km is defined and used extensively. A common application of kappa in site effects is to adjust the site amplifications calculated via the quarter-wavelength technique (Boore and Joyner, 1997). Another use of kappa in evaluating local site conditions is to investigate the potential correlations between site parameters, V_{S30} (the average shear-wave velocity of the soil layer within a range of 30 m from the surface), and kappa (Drouet *et al.*, 2010; Edwards *et al.*, 2011; Van Houtte *et al.*, 2011). In addition, single-station κ_0 values are generally applied to correct the acceleration spectrum of site effects before the source effect is studied (Margaris and Hatzidimitriou, 2002; Oth *et al.*, 2010; Lancieri *et al.*, 2012). Recently, kappa has also been used in ground-motion prediction equation (GMPE) calibration for different regions with different site conditions (Cotton *et al.*, 2006; Douglas *et al.*, 2006; Houtte *et al.*, 2014). Interestingly, different authors have estimated kappa values with alternative methods, which may result in incompatible values (Askan *et al.*, 2014) because kappa estimation is sensitive to several factors, such as the selected dataset, approach, near-surface geology, source mechanism, and focal depth. To address this issue, extensive research has been conducted on the variability of kappa calculations, and several remedial measures have been taken to achieve more stable and uniform results (Ktenidou *et al.*, 2013).

In this study, we collected a strong ground motion dataset from western-central Sichuan, China, with different source characteristics, site classes, and epicentral distances. The study area has experienced many major earthquakes that caused major structural and economic losses, notably during the 2008 M_w 7.9 Wenchuan earthquake (Han *et al.*, 2016; Zhu *et al.*, 2020). The reason for choosing western-central Sichuan, China, is that the seismic activity in this area has generated a large dataset, and because of the active faults near densely populated areas, this region is associated with significant earthquake hazards and risks. However, there has not yet been a systematic investigation of the kappa parameter via the ground-motion recordings in western-central Sichuan, China.

The basic objective of this study was to measure kappa empirically and calculate zero-distance κ_0 values in western-central Sichuan, China, within the framework for which it is used in ground-motion simulations and GMPE adjustments. In this case, based on the scheme given by Askan *et al.* (2014), we established a kappa model related to distance and site classification. In this study, we investigated the magnitude dependence of the estimated kappa values as well; thus, we fitted a single-station kappa and its relationship with the site parameter V_{S30} and then compared it with the regional models. Finally, we explored the empirical relationship among kappa, magnitude and site parameter V_{S30} and compared it with models from other regions. The kappa values in this study were manually calculated according to the S-wave portion of the horizontal and vertical kappa components for each recording. The robust regression was used to fit the relationship between the horizontal and vertical kappa values and the distance.

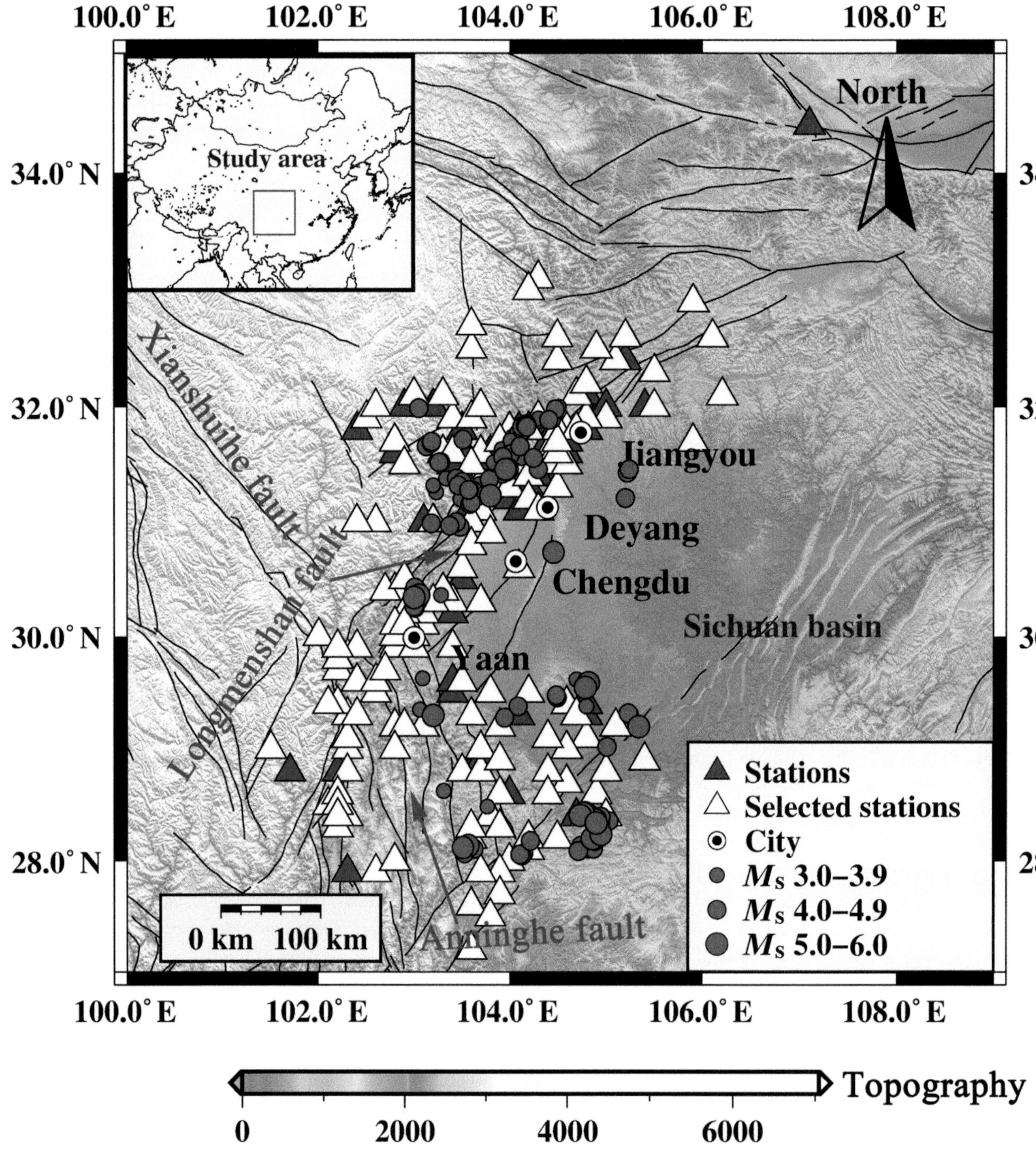

Figure 1. Distibutions of selected earthquake events (red circles, scaled by surface-wave magnitude) and strong-motion stations (white triangles) used in this analysis. The inset map in the upper left corner shows the location of the study area on the map of China. The red triangles represent the stations not used in this study. The color version of this figure is available only in the electronic edition.

Dataset

In this study, 4260 three-component (e.g., east–west [EW]; north–south [NS]; up–down [UD]) recordings from 165 earthquake events with magnitudes ranging from 3.5 to 6.0, which triggered a total of 168 strong-motion stations in western-central Sichuan, China, from 2007 to 2022 were collected (Fig. 1). In this dataset, there are 55 earthquake events with a magnitude range of 3.5–3.9, represented by small circles; 86 earthquake events with a magnitude range of 4.0–4.9, represented by medium circles; and 24 earthquake events with a magnitude range of 5.0–6.0, represented by large circles. Earthquake records with magnitudes less than 3.5 were not included because the corner frequencies of these small seismic events are relatively high, which may affect the estimation of

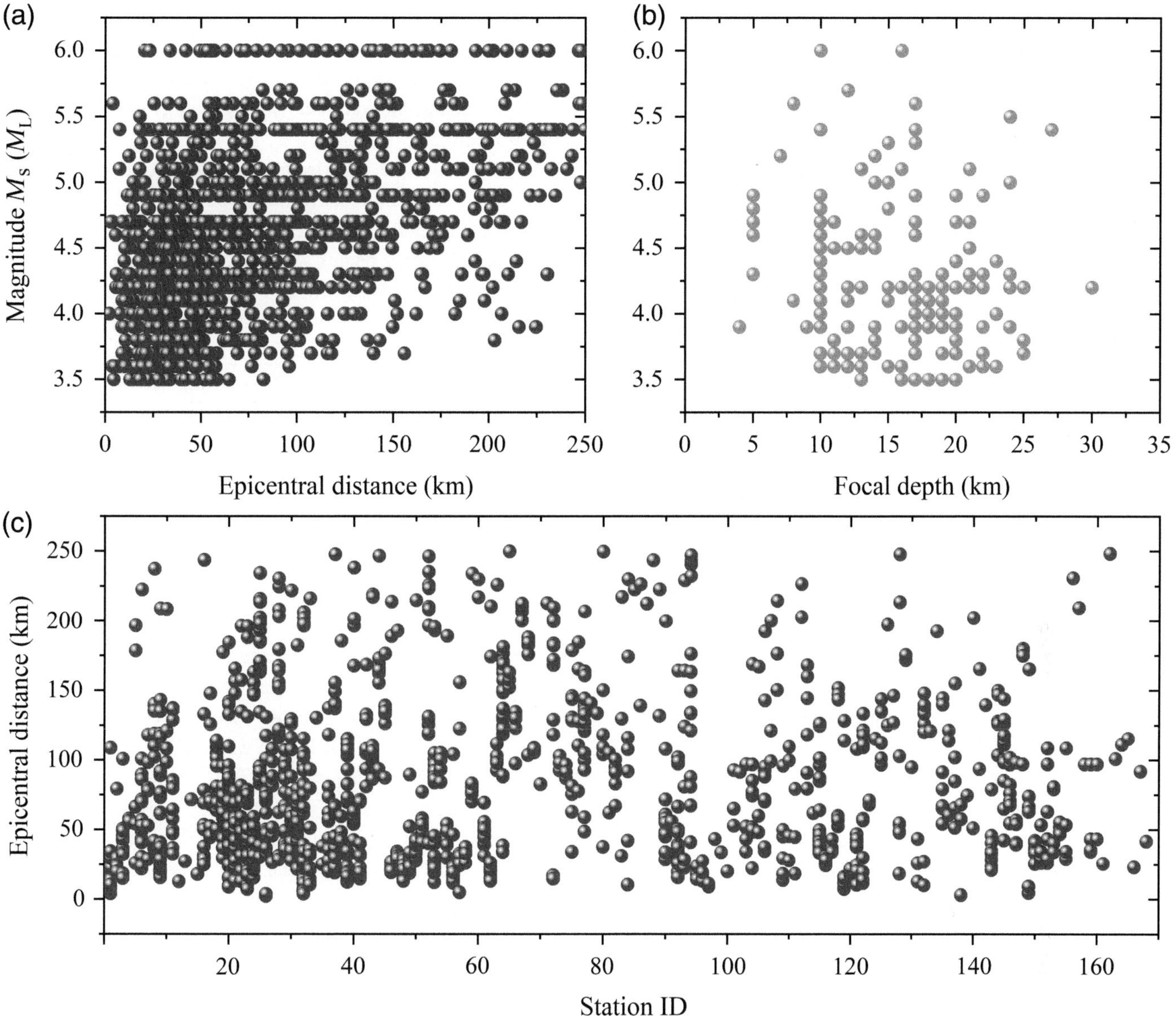

kappa values. In addition, earthquakes with magnitudes greater than 6.0 were not used because large events may cause nonlinear behavior at local sites, resulting in deviations in the kappa value (Askan *et al.*, 2014). All the records released by the China Strong-Motion Network Centre have a sampling time interval of 0.005 s. The magnitude of these earthquake events given by the header files of the raw data includes the local magnitude (M_L) and surface-wave magnitude (M_s); we used an empirical relationship between the two magnitudes to convert the surface-wave magnitude to the local magnitude, which is defined as $M_s = 1.13\ M_L - 1.08$ (Wang, Wang, *et al.*, 2010). The relationships between magnitude and epicentral distance, magnitude and source depth, and the range of epicentral distance recorded by each strong-motion station are shown in Figure 2, which indicates that the depth distribution of the seismic source is within the range of 4–30 km and that the epicentral distance is within the range of 2–250 km. The earthquake ID, time of occurrence (local time), magnitude, latitude, and longitude of the epicenter, and source depth of the 165 earthquake events selected in this study are summarized in Table S1, available in the supplemental material to this article.

Figure 2. Dataset selected for this analysis. (a) Magnitude and epicentral distance distributions of selected earthquake events, (b) magnitude and focal depth distributions of selected earthquake events, and (c) epicentral distance ranges of the earthquake recordings at each strong-motion station. The color version of this figure is available only in the electronic edition.

The raw acceleration time history of each component was first processed, and a baseline correction was used. Then, a Butterworth filter with a filtering range of 0.1–60 Hz was applied to all the selected acceleration records. Because the signal-to-noise ratio (SNR) for small earthquakes at low frequencies is poor, the spectral ratio at frequencies lower than 0.5 Hz is not reliable, and the spectral ratio value amplitude always falls within the low-frequency range because of the increased noise for small earthquake events. Under these circumstances, the S wave was then extracted. The onset of the S wave was determined according to the abruptly increasing point in the Husid plot (Husid, 1967), and the ending time of the S wave was set to this point, at which time the cumulative root mean square function begins to decrease over time (Hassani and Atkinson, 2015). The event (event ID: 0111226004652) recorded at the station (station ID: 051MXN) was selected to illustrate the extraction step of the S wave (Fig. S1). The maximum S-wave window length was set to 15 s to avoid the influence of coda waves (Moya *et al.*, 2000; Drouet and Chevrot, 2008). The Hanning window function was performed at the beginning and end of the extracted S waves to eliminate truncation errors, and the length of the Hanning window was 10% of the S-wave length (Dang *et al.*, 2024; Dang, Cui, Yang, and Song, 2025). In addition, the noise window of each waveform was selected from the pre-event portion, with the noise window length being the same as the corresponding S-wave length. In this study, we removed seismic records with SNR values less than 3. Notably, as long as the energy portion of the S waves is extracted, the window length used has little impact on the estimation of kappa (Tsai and Chen, 2000; Douglas *et al.*, 2010; Neighbors *et al.*, 2015). After preliminary screening according to the above principles, 4260 well-recorded three-component acceleration waveforms from 165 small- and medium-sized events recorded at 168 strong-motion stations were selected. The related detailed information of the selected strong-motion stations, such as the station name, coordinates, V_{S30}, and site class, is summarized in Table S2.

Askan *et al.* (2014) estimated kappa values with smoothed and unsmooth FAS and reported that the smoothing step was necessary for stable kappa values. Therefore, both the S wave and noise wave were transformed to the frequency domain via the fast Fourier transform algorithm. To avoid sudden changes in the FAS, the FAS curves were smoothed between 0.25 and 50 Hz via the windowing function (Konno and Ohmachi, 1998):

$$W(f,f_c) = \left[\frac{\sin(\log(f/f_c)^b)}{\log(f/f_c)^b}\right]^4, \quad (1)$$

in which f_c, f, and b denote the central frequency, frequency, and filtering parameters, respectively; in this study, the filtering parameter b was set to 20. In this case, the smoothed horizontal FAS and vertical FAS values were obtained.

Kappa Determination

Kappa is defined as the fall-off attenuation of the FAS in the high-frequency range above 1 Hz (Anderson and Hough, 1984; Castro *et al.*, 1990). To estimate the high-frequency attenuation parameter kappa, the method proposed by Anderson and Hough (1984) was used; in this case, the high-frequency spectral attenuation is defined as follows:

$$A(f) = A_0 \exp(-\pi f \kappa), f > f_e, \quad (2)$$

in which the amplitude A_0 depends on the source and path properties, and the frequency f_e indicates the frequency over which the FAS are approximated with a linear decay on a log-linear space, and the frequency f_e is generally greater than the corner frequency.

In this study, the high-frequency attenuation kappa value was estimated by measuring the slope k of the S-wave FAS in a log-linear scale at high frequencies. The frequencies where the amplitude decay begins and ends are referred to as f_e and f_x, respectively, because the linear portion in the log-linear scale is visually determined. The width of the ($\Delta f = f_x - f_e$) windows should be greater than 10 to ensure the accuracy of the kappa estimation (Ktenidou *et al.*, 2013), and the wide range of ($f_x - f_e$) windows allows for estimation of the bias due to high-frequency local amplifications (Douglas *et al.*, 2010). Thus, herein, the slope of the linear portion was obtained by fitting a line to the FAS curve via the least-squares approach (Fig. S1).

Site effects may significantly affect the estimation of kappa values. Parolai and Bindi (2004) reported that if the fundamental resonance frequency of a site is less than the frequency f_e, kappa estimation will be reliable and unbiased. To isolate high-frequency site effects from source effects, the kappa value is estimated at frequencies greater than the corner frequency of the earthquake event. It is also essential to avoid including resonance peaks because of site effects in the linear portion, and the parameter f_e value was set to 1.5 times the fundamental resonance frequency of the site (Palmer and Atkinson, 2020). The horizontal-to-vertical (H/V) spectral ratio method of Lermo and Chávez-García (1993) can be used to approximately determine the fundamental resonance frequency of a site. In this study, we plotted the H/V spectral ratio curves of 168 selected strong-motion stations and thus obtained the fundamental resonance frequencies of class C and class D sites and unknown sites (Fig. S2). In this case, 90% of the acceleration recordings had a fundamental resonance frequency of less than 8 Hz for the class C site, less than 6 Hz for the class D sites, and less than 10 Hz for the unknown sites (Fig. 3). Therefore, the high-pass cutoff frequencies f_e for class C, class D, and unknown sites were determined to be 12 Hz (= 8 × 1.5 Hz), 9 Hz (= 6 × 1.5 Hz), and 15 Hz (= 10 × 1.5 Hz), respectively. In addition, the low-pass cutoff frequency f_x was manually determined based on the FAS of the S wave and was basically in the range of 35–50 Hz.

After the values of parameters f_e and f_x are determined, the high-frequency attenuation kappa (κ) of the acceleration spectrum can be calculated via the following equation:

$$\kappa = -k/\pi, \quad (3)$$

in which k is the slope of the S-wave FAS in linear–log space and can be calculated by $k = \Delta \ln A/\Delta f$ (Douglas *et al.*, 2010). In this case, the high-frequency attenuation kappa (κ) from

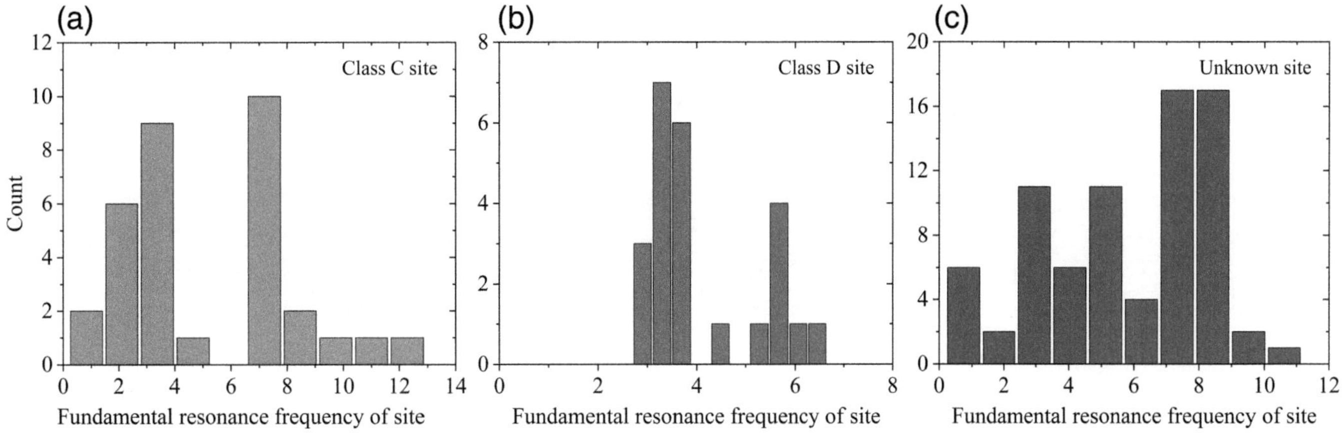

Figure 3. Fundamental resonance frequencies of the (a) class C site, (b) class D site, and (c) unknown site. The color version of this figure is available only in the electronic edition.

each component for all 165 selected earthquake events recorded at 168 strong-motion stations in the western-central Sichuan region, China, was estimated. The estimated kappa (κ) values of different earthquake records recorded at the same station are different because of the influence of the path effect on the kappa values. For this purpose, we used the following equation to estimate the zero-distance κ_0 value related to the site (Anderson and Hough, 1984):

$$\kappa = \kappa_0 + m \times R, \tag{4}$$

in which κ (s), κ_0 (s), m (s/km), and R (km) denote the kappa value calculated from each earthquake record, the zero-distance kappa value, the fitting coefficient, and the epicentral distance, respectively. Research has shown that the zero-distance κ_0 value is site-dependent and can provide information on near-surface attenuation within a few kilometers, where coefficient m is considered a proxy for regional attenuation and is related to the study area. The zero-distance $\kappa_0$value is unique between each station and depends on the geological conditions near the strong-motion station. This study investigated the local site dependence of kappa parameters at different sites and analyzed the impact of earthquake magnitude on kappa estimation under different geographical conditions.

Results and Discussion

The high-frequency attenuation factor κ is an important parameter in seismology and earthquake engineering. It is widely used in determining source parameters, studying regional medium attenuation characteristics, earthquake GMPEs, simulating earthquake ground motion, compiling earthquake ground-motion parameter zoning maps, and analyzing ground-motion characteristics. In addition, the V_S–kappa corrections significantly influence the seismic hazard assessments (Biro and Renault, 2013). As a new step, it was tried to develop a generalized methodology by deriving parameterized relationships from preprocessed evaluation. On the one hand, this enables the application of V_S–kappa corrections to specific GMPEs (Cotton *et al.*, 2006). On the other hand, it can also provide a constraint for the damping parameter $D_{\min}$ (Xu *et al.*, 2020; Pozo *et al.*, 2023). To study the high-frequency attenuation characteristics of different components of ground motion, we calculated the high-frequency decay parameters of the EW, NS, and UD three-component ground motion separately, as shown in Figure 4. Figure 4 shows that the difference between the estimated kappa values of the EW and NS components is small, whereas the two horizontal kappa values are significantly larger than the UD component, which indicates that the observed slow decay of the vertical component can be attributed to its heightened sensitivity to variations in near-surface shear-wave velocity (Motazedian, 2006). Notably, the difference between event-related kappa values in the horizontal and vertical components indicates that zero-distance $\kappa_0$exhibits site-specific dependence on attenuation effects in shallow subsurface layers. The results are consistent with the conclusions drawn by Askan *et al.* (2014) based on the 522-component ground-motion data of 142 small- and medium-sized earthquakes with magnitudes ranging from 3.0 to 6.0 in northwest Türkiye. These findings also confirm that site conditions are an important factor affecting kappa estimation. In this scheme, the site where the station is located was divided into three categories according to the National Earthquake Hazards Reduction Program (NEHRP) standard in the United States. Among them, 37 stations had V_{S30} values ranging from 360 to 760 cm/s, 29 stations had V_{S30} values between 180 and 360 cm/s, and 102 stations did not have V_{S30} values (Table S2). It should be noted that the V_{S30} values of some stations in Table S2 were derived from drilling data, whereas the V_{S30} values of some stations were obtained from the Pacific Earthquake Engineering Research Center (PEER) database. The V_{S30} of the remaining stations was calculated via the empirical relationship equation provided by Wang, Xie, *et al.* (2010) for the western-central Sichuan region. In the seismic design code provided by the China Ministry of

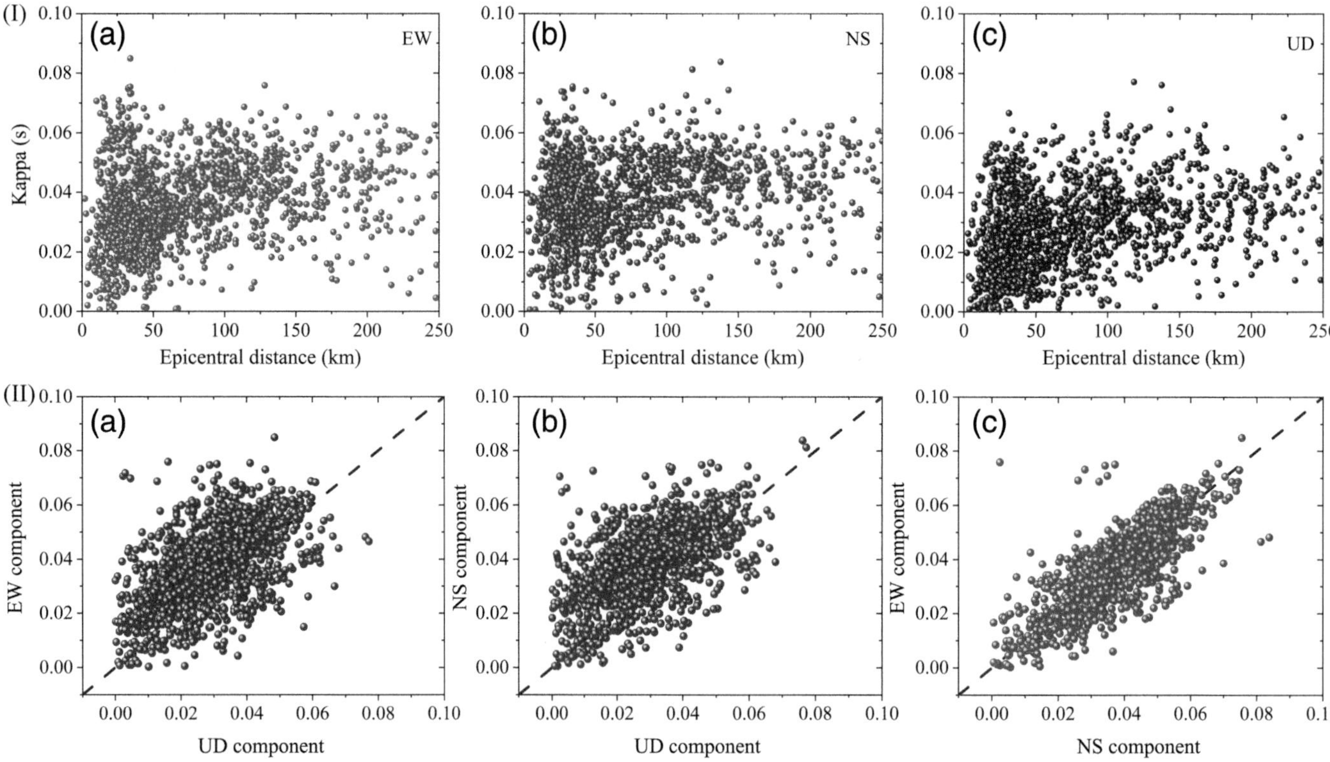

Figure 4. Top panels (I): (a–c) distribution of the high-frequency attenuation parameter kappa values with the epicentral distance. Bottom panels (II): (a) comparison of the kappa values obtained from the east–west (EW) and up–down (UD) components, (b) comparison of the kappa values obtained from the north–south (NS) and UD components, and (c) comparison of the kappa values obtained from the EW and NS components. The dashed line in each subplot represents the case in which the variables represented by the *x*- and *y*-axis are equal. The color version of this figure is available only in the electronic edition.

Construction, the site conditions are determined by the equivalent shear-wave velocity (V_{Se}) and the depth to the rock (H_{top}). In this scheme, it is assumed that the shear-wave velocity is a constant value of 500 m/s below the measured depth. Based on this assumption, the V_{S30} value for each station is computed as $V_{S30} = 30/[(H_{top}/V_{Se}) + (30 - H_{top})/500]$ (Wang, Xie, *et al.*, 2010).

Effect of site class on kappa values

To analyze the factors influencing the spectral decay parameters in detail, we investigated two factors: site conditions and earthquake magnitude. First, we used the Shapiro–Wilk test to check whether the data followed a normal distribution, as shown in Figure S3. In addition, the test results are shown in Table S3. The results show that the kappa values estimated for class C, class D, and unknown sites generally follow a normal distribution. In this case, we derived the relationship between kappa and distance for class C, class D, and unknown sites using the robust regression method. To avoid the trend of nonuniform patterns between residuals and estimation values, we performed the Huber–White sandwich estimator in robust regression analysis to estimate the robust standard deviation. The standard deviations and standard errors of robust regression and Huber–White sandwich estimator are shown in Tables S4 and S5. The results indicate that at a confidence level of $\alpha = 0.05$, the zero-distance κ_0 values estimated in this study are significant and reliable. The results revealed that the kappa models for the EW, NS, and UD components of class C sites were as follows: $\kappa = 9.58135 \times 10^{-5}R + (0.03037 \pm 0.00129)$, $\kappa = 8.81436 \times 10^{-5}R + (0.03243 \pm 0.00116)$, and $\kappa = 1.25328 \times 10^{-4}R + (0.01485 \pm 0.00106)$ (Fig. 5I). The kappa models for the EW, NS, and UD components of class D sites were defined as $\kappa = 8.93839 \times 10^{-5}R + (0.03334 \pm 0.00132)$, $\kappa = 7.30205 \times 10^{-5}R + (0.03537 \pm 0.00129)$, and $\kappa = 8.63401 \times 10^{-5}R + (0.02203 \pm 0.00155)$, respectively (Fig. 5II). The kappa models for estimating the EW, NS, and UD components of unknown sites are $\kappa = 3.10713 \times 10^{-5}R + (0.03283 \pm 0.00081)$, $\kappa = 3.64886 \times 10^{-5}R + (0.03351 \pm 0.00080)$, and $\kappa = 5.78011 \times 10^{-5}R + (0.02476 \pm 0.00074)$, respectively (Fig. 5III). The results show that the κ_0 values of the two components estimated for class C sites are 0.03037 and 0.03243, and the κ_0 values estimated for class D sites are 0.03334 and 0.03537, both of which are greater than the corresponding κ_0 values for class C sites. This finding indicates that the high-frequency attenuation of seismic components in soft soil sites is faster. In addition, we also found that the estimated κ_0 values of the horizontal component for both class C and class D sites are almost twice those of their vertical component κ_0 values, indicating that the high-frequency attenuation of the vertical component is slow. This may be due to the greater sensitivity of the horizontal component to changes in shear-wave velocity in near-surface sedimentary layers (Motazedian, 2006). For the vertical component, the κ_0 values estimated for the class C and class D sites are 0.01485 and 0.02203, respectively. The same conclusion has also been reached for unknown sites. This fully demonstrates that the estimation of κ_0 is closely related to the near-surface site conditions. This finding is consistent with the conclusion of Kumar *et al.* (2020) on the κ_0 in the Himalayan seismic zone of the Indian plate.

Effects of earthquake size and site class on kappa values

To investigate the influence of magnitude and site conditions on the kappa values, we further classified the data into three categories based on magnitude ranges of 3.5–3.9, 4.0–4.9, and 5.0–6.0. Each category was further divided into three groups based on C, D, and unknown site types. In this study, we also conducted Shapiro–Wilk tests on each dataset. The results are shown in Figures S4–S6. The results indicate that, except for a few groups, the data of most groups generally follow a normal distribution. The kappa models for the EW, NS, and UD components of class C sites estimated from earthquake with magnitudes of 3.5–3.9 are $\kappa = 1.82262 \times 10^{-4}R + (0.02135 \pm 0.00288)$, $\kappa = 1.75805 \times 10^{-4}R + (0.02409 \pm 0.00227)$, and $\kappa = 2.12526 \times 10^{-4}R + (0.00933 \pm 0.00179)$, respectively (Fig. 6I). The kappa models for the EW, NS, and UD components of class D sites are $\kappa = 1.09982 \times 10^{-4}R + (0.03134 \pm 0.0032)$, $\kappa = 9.21592 \times 10^{-5}R + (0.0331 \pm 0.00286)$, and $\kappa = 6.1084 \times 10^{-5}R + (0.02194 \pm 0.00379)$, respectively (Fig. 6II), whereas the kappa models for the EW, NS, and UD components of unknown sites are $\kappa = 1.37261 \times 10^{-5}R + (0.0328 \pm 0.00174)$, $\kappa = 4.68621 \times 10^{-5}R + (0.03356 \pm 0.00158)$, and $\kappa = 7.29061 \times 10^{-5}R + (0.02208 \pm 0.00145)$, respectively (Fig. 6III). This indicates that the κ_0 values of the two horizontal components estimated from records with small magnitudes of 3.5–3.9 are also greater than the corresponding κ_0 values of the vertical components under different site conditions. Similarly, the κ_0 values of class C sites are smaller than those of class D sites. The kappa models for the EW, NS, and UD components of class C sites estimated from earthquake recordings with magnitude of 4.0–4.9 are $\kappa = 1.06281 \times 10^{-4}R + (0.03192 \pm 0.00166)$, $\kappa = 1.05279 \times 10^{-4}R + (0.03308 \pm 0.00149)$, and $\kappa = 1.25867 \times 10^{-4}R + (0.01537 \pm 0.00149)$, respectively (Fig. 7I). The kappa models for the EW, NS, and UD components of class D sites are as follows: $\kappa = 8.29143 \times 10^{-5}R + (0.03335 \pm 0.00213)$, $\kappa = 5.87316 \times 10^{-5}R + (0.03608 \pm 0.00216)$, and $\kappa = 8.1989 \times 10^{-5}R + (0.02187 \pm 0.00244)$, respectively (Fig. 7II). The kappa models for the EW, NS, and UD components of unknown sites are $\kappa = 3.70966 \times 10^{-5}R + (0.03161 \pm 0.00114)$, $\kappa = 4.41361 \times 10^{-5}R + (0.03251 \pm 0.00115)$, and $\kappa = 5.25383 \times 10^{-5}R + (0.02607 \pm 0.00109)$, respectively (Fig. 7III). In addition, the kappa models for the EW, ND, and UD components of class C sites estimated from earthquake records with magnitudes of 5.0–6.0 are $\kappa = 4.70624 \times 10^{-5}R + (0.03501 \pm 0.00316)$, $\kappa = 3.09511 \times 10^{-5}R + (0.03855 \pm 0.00322)$, and $\kappa = 9.13225 \times 10^{-5}R + (0.01903 \pm 0.00294)$, respectively (Fig. 8I). The kappa models for the EW, NS, and UD components of class D sites are $\kappa = 5.10548 \times 10^{-5}R + (0.04104 \pm 0.00282)$, $\kappa = 3.77169 \times 10^{-5}R + (0.04284 \pm 0.0028)$, and $\kappa = 4.03856 \times 10^{-5}R + (0.0316 \pm 0.00342)$, respectively (Fig. 8II). The kappa models for the EW, NS, and UD components of unknown sites are $\kappa = 1.59312 \times 10^{-6}R + (0.03806 \pm 0.00184)$, $\kappa = 2.1883 \times 10^{-5}R + (0.03548 \pm 0.00186)$, and $\kappa = 4.96827 \times 10^{-5}R + (0.02551 \pm 0.00163)$, respectively (Fig. 8III). The estimation results of κ_0 based on magnitude and site conditions are shown in Table 1, which indicates that site conditions have a significant effect on the calculation of κ_0, with softer sites yielding higher κ_0 values. For the same site type, the smaller the magnitude of the earthquake event is, the smaller the calculated κ_0 value. This study demonstrates that both earthquake magnitude and site conditions significantly influence the estimation of κ_0. Our findings are consistent with previous research results, such as Gariel and Campillo (1989), Purvance and Anderson (2003), Wen and Chen (2012), Perron *et al.* (2017), Tsurugi *et al.* (2020), Biro *et al.* (2022), Altindal and Askan (2022), and Biro (2024). These researchers consistently observed that kappa values increase with magnitude and identified both site and source effects as contributing factors to kappa variability. In this study, we also compared the effects of different site types and earthquake magnitudes on the fitting coefficient m, as shown in Table 1. The results indicate that at class C sites, the m values estimated from earthquake records with magnitudes of 3.5–4.9 are significantly lower than those estimated from earthquakes with magnitudes of 5.0–6.0, and there is no significant difference in the m values estimated from the three components. However, without considering the magnitude factor, there is not much difference in the m values of the two horizontal components estimated under different site conditions.

To verify the relationship between kappa and magnitude, we used an empirical relationship between the surface-wave magnitude and local magnitude to convert the surface-wave magnitude into a local magnitude. In addition, we directly combined the kappa values of the two horizontal components into a dataset, defined as the horizontal kappa value. Therefore, the relationships between the kappa values of the horizontal and vertical components and the local magnitude can be defined as follows (Fig. 9a,b):

$$\kappa = 0.00403M_L + (0.01748 \pm 0.00202), \tag{5}$$

$$\kappa = 0.00496M_L + (0.00369 \pm 0.00278). \tag{6}$$

Figure 9c compares the relationship between kappa and local magnitude fitted in this study with those in other studies. The

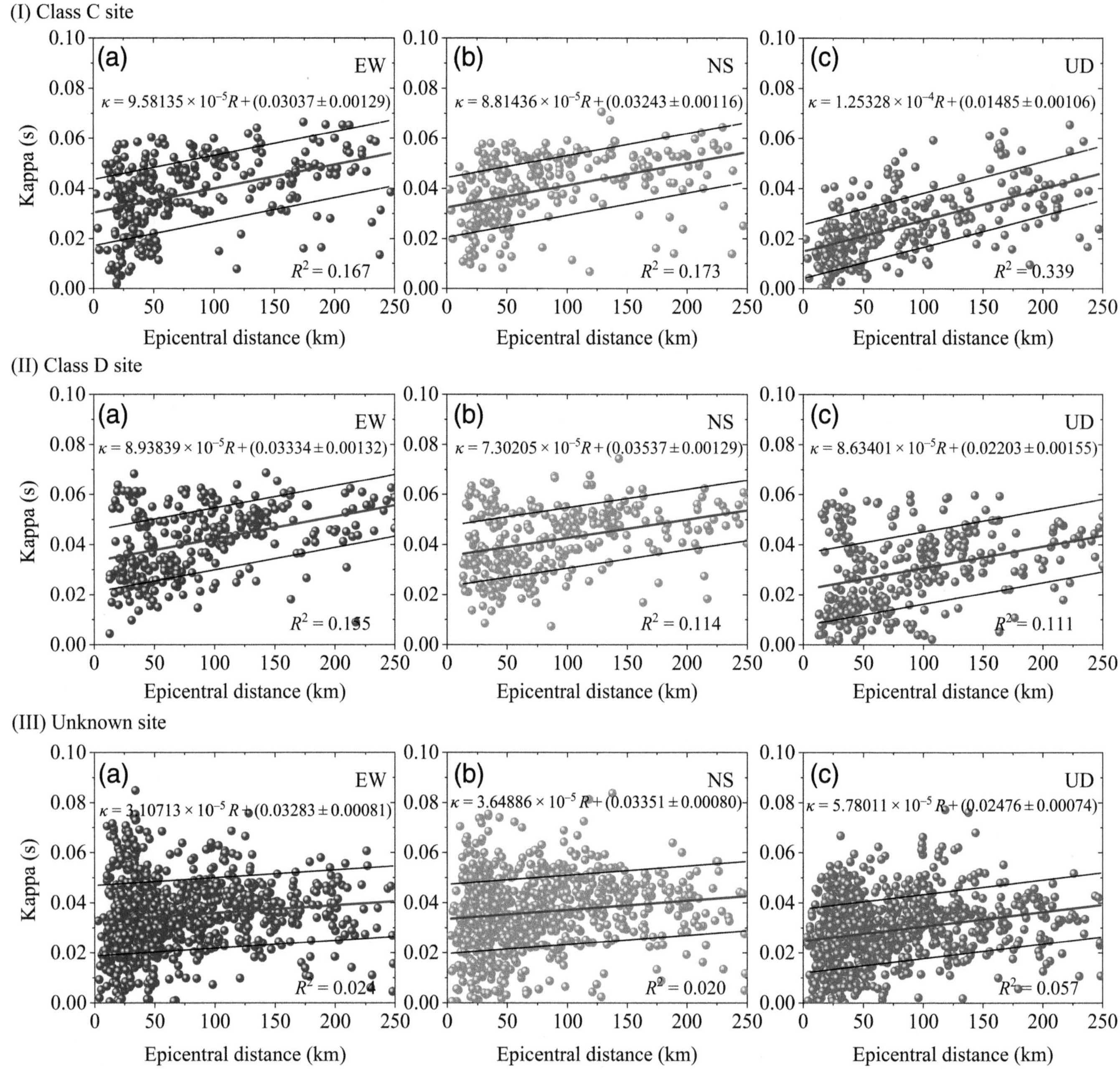

Figure 5. (I) Variations in high-frequency attenuation kappa values obtained from the (a) EW, (b) NS, and (c) UD components of all earthquakes with the epicentral distance for class C sites. (II) Variations in the high-frequency attenuation kappa values obtained from the (a) EW, (b) NS, and (c) UD components with the epicentral distance for class D sites. (III) Variations in the high-frequency attenuation kappa values obtained from the (a) EW, (b) NS, and (c) UD components with the epicentral distance at unknown sites. The color version of this figure is available only in the electronic edition.

results show that Sertcelik *et al.* (2022) estimated a larger kappa value than the results in this study did, which may be due to differences in the near-surface site characteristics of the two study regions. The relationship between kappa and M_L in the Marmara region by Sertcelik *et al.* (2022) is $\kappa = 0.0118M_L + 0.013$, this region is influenced by the right-lateral strike-slip caused by the North Anatolian fault zone and the north–south extensional regime in western Anatolia. Because of the collision of the India Asia plate, the tectonic environment in the western-central Sichuan region is complex, and seismic activity is very active. This study area includes both the relatively stable geological environment of the Sichuan basin and the active geological environment of the Songpan Garze Orogen region (Fu *et al.*, 2019). On the other hand, the conversion between magnitudes (M_L and M_s, M_L, and M_D, in which M_D is a duration magnitude) may be a reason for the differences. The difference in the relationship between magnitude and kappa also indicates that the kappa values have strong regional characteristics.

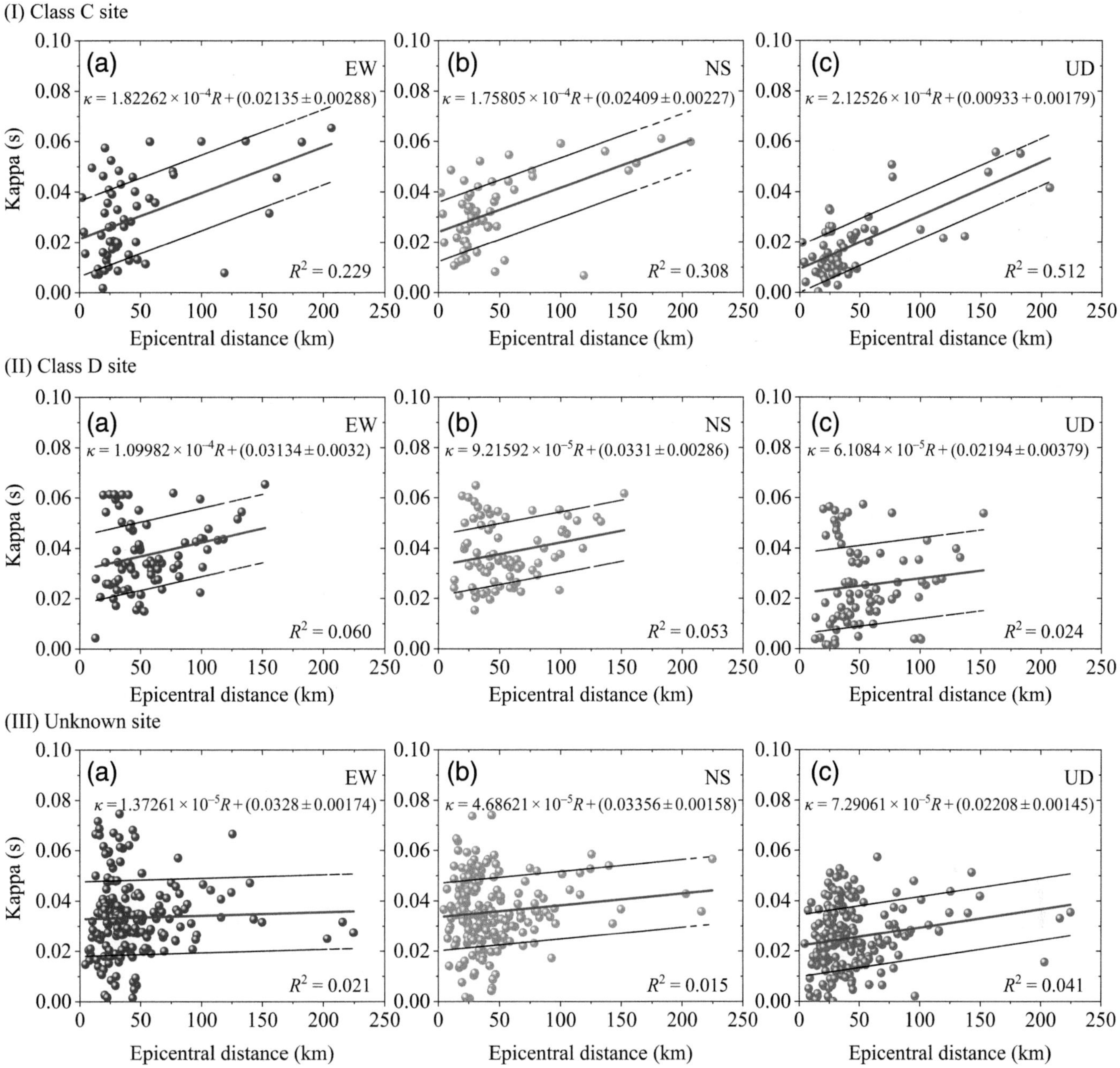

Figure 6. (I) Variations in high-frequency attenuation kappa values obtained from the (a) EW, (b) NS, and (c) UD components of earthquakes ($3.5 \le M < 4.0$) with the epicentral distance for class C sites. (II) Variation in the high-frequency attenuation kappa values obtained from the (a) EW, (b) NS, and (c) UD components with the epicentral distance for class D sites. (III) Variations in the high-frequency attenuation kappa values obtained from the (a) EW, (b) NS, and (c) UD components with the epicentral distance for unknown sites. The color version of this figure is available only in the electronic edition.

Zero-distance κ_0 estimation for a single station

Because the κ_0 value of a single station is an important input parameter for the stochastic finite-fault model, exploring the correlation between κ_0 and V_{S30} and its application in site classification is crucial. Therefore, this study also determined the κ_0 values for each strong-motion station. Among the 168 strong-motion stations, only 60 strong ground motions have earthquake recordings greater than 10. We fitted the κ_0 values of the selected 60 stations via equation (4), as shown in Table S2. Some stations, such as stations 51HSS, 51HSD, 53YSZ, 51NXT, 51SMW, and 51LZT, have a record count greater than 5, and stations 51KDT and 51AXY have a record count less than 5. Interestingly, we derived negative κ_0 values, which indicate a positive trend in amplitude with increasing frequency, which is meaningless and may be due to inaccurate estimation (Palmer and Atkinson, 2020). The symbol "–" in columns 3–5 of the Table S2 indicates that due to limited recordings, the κ_0 values have not been consistently obtained, and the κ_0 value of the UD component of station 51HSS is negative and we assume

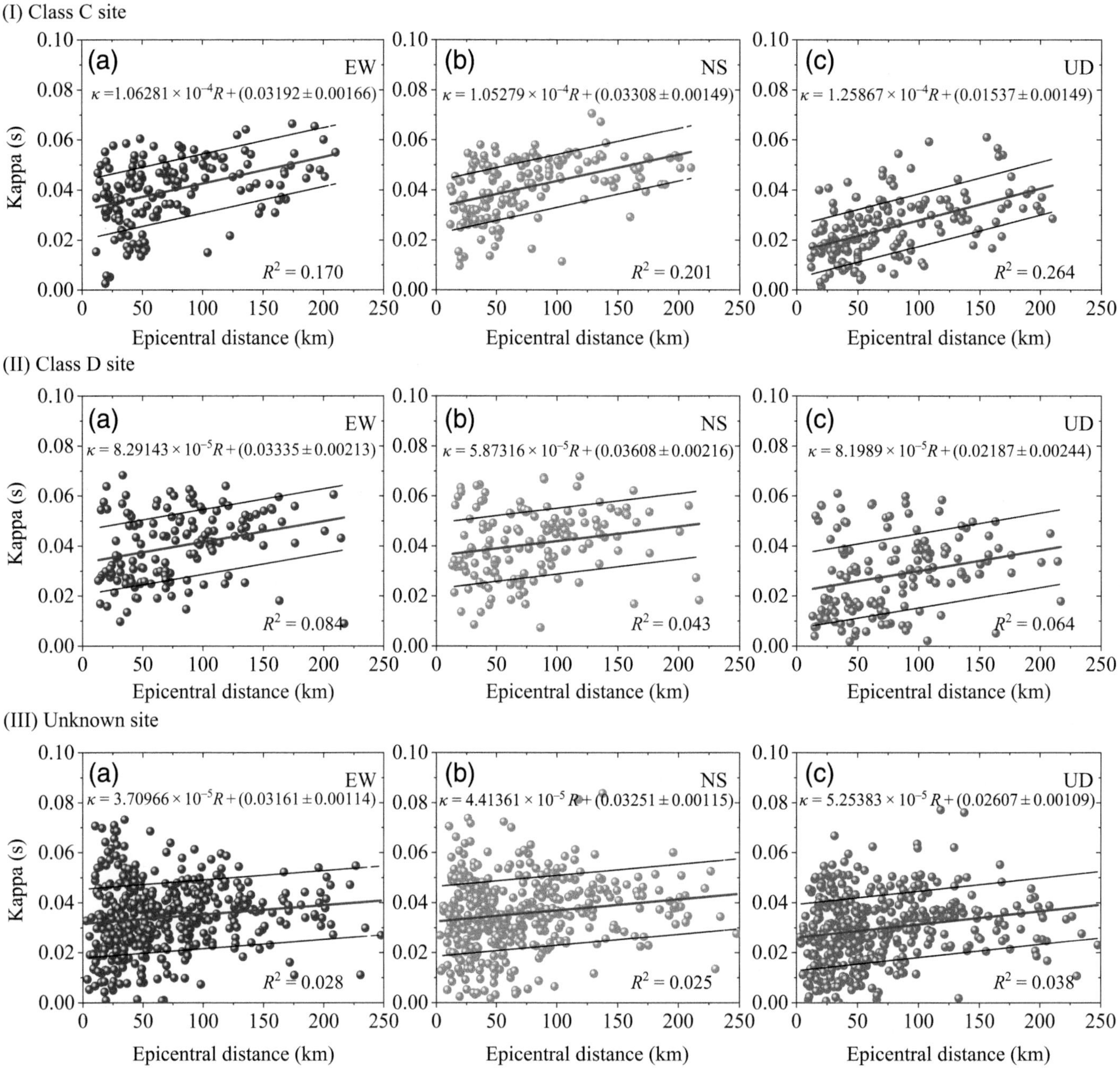

Figure 7. (I) Variations in high-frequency attenuation kappa values obtained from the (a) EW, (b) NS, and (c) UD components of earthquakes ($4.0 \le M < 5.0$) with the epicentral distance for class C sites. (II) Variation in the high-frequency attenuation kappa values obtained from the (a) EW, (b) NS, and (c) UD components with the epicentral distance for class D sites. (III) Variations in the high-frequency attenuation kappa values obtained from the (a) EW, (b) NS, and (c) UD components with the epicentral distance at unknown sites. The color version of this figure is available only in the electronic edition.

that negative kappa should be interpreted as κ_0 value close to zero, which may be due to the small difference in the epicentral distance corresponding to the earthquake records recorded by the station. Notably, the κ_0 values of stations with fewer records may be unstable. In some cases, Pozo *et al.* (2023) pointed out that either due to the dispersion of values or due to the few remaining values after filtering, we may obtain negative m. Therefore, in this study, we selected several typical stations with many records (>9) and present the fitting results in Figure 10. The kappa model of station 51BCB in the UD component fitted by the least-squares method is $\kappa = -1.0624 \times 10^{-6} R + 0.02611$, and the fitting coefficient m value is negative. Based on the mainshock sequences of the 2008 Wenchuan earthquake in China, Sun *et al.* (2013) estimated the kappa model for the UD component of ground motion in the study area as $\kappa = -2.0813 \times 10^{-7} R + 0.01261$, where R is the epicentral distance. When R is changed to the fault distance, the estimated kappa model of the UD component is $\kappa = 5.6086 \times 10^{-5} R + 0.00855$. However, the robust

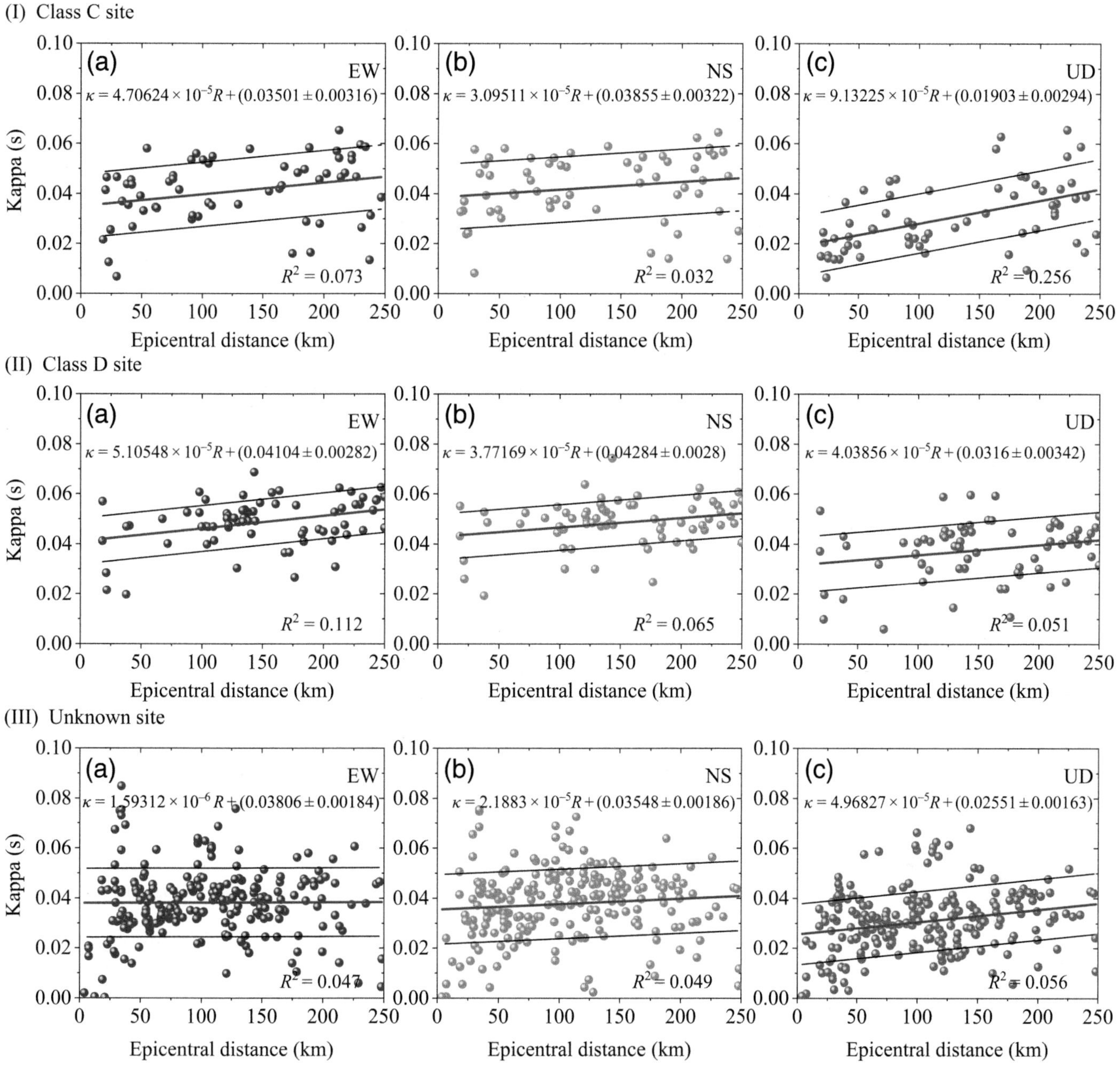

Figure 8. (I) Variations in high–frequency attenuation kappa values obtained from the (a) EW, (b) NS, and (c) UD components of earthquakes ($5.0 \le M \le 6.0$) with the epicentral distance for class C sites. (II) Variations in the high-frequency attenuation kappa values obtained from the (a) EW, (b) NS, and (c) UD components with the epicentral distance for class D sites. (III) Variations in the high-frequency attenuation kappa values obtained from the (a) EW, (b) NS, and (c) UD components with the epicentral distance at unknown sites. The color version of this figure is available only in the electronic edition.

regression method is used to refit the results of station 51BCB, and the kappa model in the UD component is $\kappa = 2.91046 \times 10^{-6}R + (0.02643 \pm 0.00175)$. In addition, based on a recording of an **M** 4.7 earthquake recorded by station FIAM at 68.8 km of hypocentral distance, Castro *et al.* (2022) obtained significantly different kappa values using different $\Delta f = f_x - f_e$ ranges. The kappa value was 0.0123 s for $\Delta f = 8$–20 Hz, 0.0374 s for $\Delta f = 10$–30 Hz, and 0.0713 s for $\Delta f = 16$–30 Hz. Therefore, the negative m value may be attributed to the use of the epicentral distance, an inappropriate fitting method, or different $f_x - f_e$ ranges. The κ_0 value of a single station also indicates that there was not much difference in the κ_0 values between the two horizontal components, which were significantly greater than the κ_0 value of the vertical component.

The high-frequency attenuation parameter κ_0 value at a distance of 0 km is related to the local site conditions where the station is located. Previous conclusions have shown that the κ_0 value gradually increases as the site conditions change from

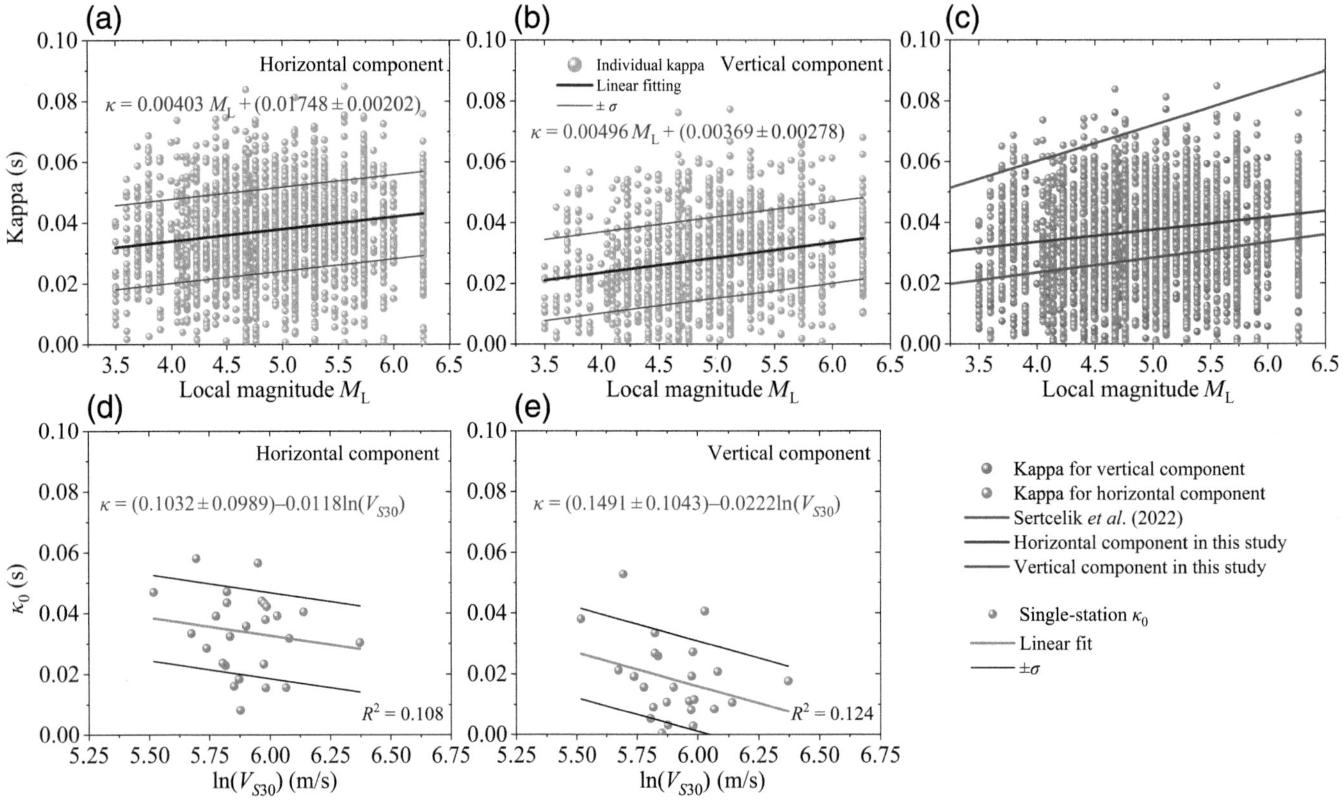

Figure 9. Variation in the high-frequency attenuation parameter kappa value with the local magnitude M_L for the (a) horizontal component and (b) vertical component. The blue and red solid lines represent the linear-fit model and $\pm\sigma$ range, respectively. (c) Comparison with the relationship between kappa and local magnitude (M_L) given by other studies. Relationship between the zero-distance kappa value (κ_0) obtained from strong-motion stations and the S-wave velocity V_{S30} for the (d) horizontal component and (e) vertical component. The color version of this figure is available only in the electronic edition.

TABLE 1

Comparison of the κ_0 (s) Values and Fitting Coefficient $m(\times 10^{-5}$ s/km) Values for Different Site Conditions and Magnitude Ranges

Site Conditions and Magnitude Bins			κ_0-EW	κ_0-NS	κ_0-UD	m-EW	m-NS	m-UD
Site class dependence (all magnitudes)	Class C site		0.03037	0.03243	0.01485	9.58135	8.81436	0.125328
	Class D site		0.03334	0.03537	0.02203	8.93839	7.30205	8.63401
	Unknown site		0.03283	0.03351	0.02476	3.10713	3.64886	5.78011
Different site conditions and magnitude ranges	Class C site	M_s 3.5–4.0	0.02135	0.02409	0.00933	0.182262	0.175805	0.212526
		M_s 4.0–5.0	0.03192	0.03308	0.01537	0.106281	0.105279	0.125867
		M_s 5.0–6.0	0.03501	0.03855	0.01903	4.70624	3.09511	9.13225
	Class D site	M_s 3.5–4.0	0.03134	0.03310	0.02194	0.109982	9.21592	6.1084
		M_s 4.0–5.0	0.03335	0.03608	0.02187	8.29143	5.87316	8.1989
		M_s 5.0–6.0	0.04104	0.04284	0.03160	5.10548	3.77169	4.03856
	Unknown site	M_s 3.5–4.0	0.03280	0.03356	0.02208	1.37261	4.68621	7.29061
		M_s 4.0–5.0	0.03161	0.03251	0.02607	3.70966	4.41361	5.25383
		M_s 5.0–6.0	0.03806	0.03548	0.02551	15.9312	2.1883	4.96827

EW, east–west; NS, north–south; UD, up–down.

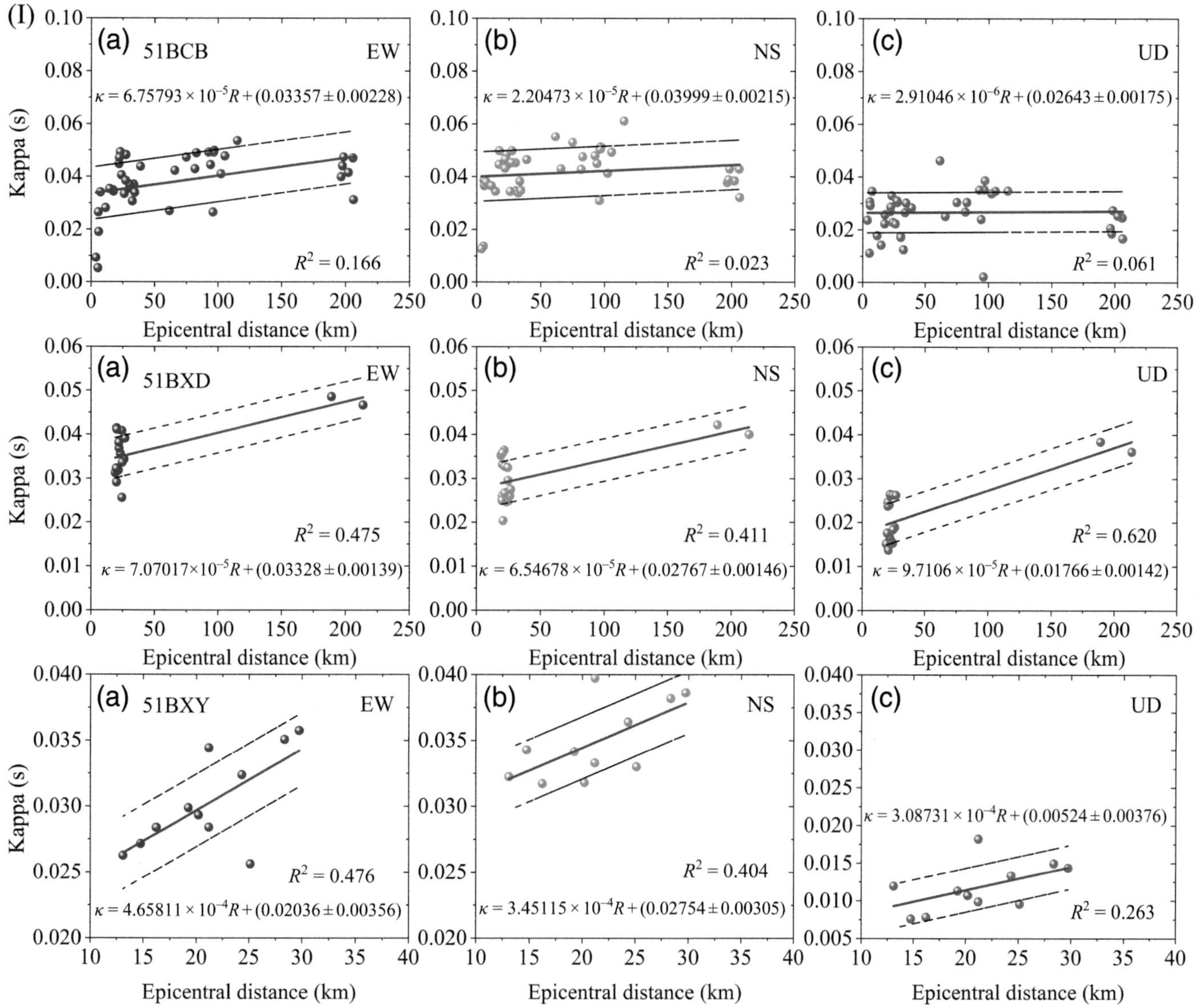

Figure 10. (I,II) High-frequency attenuation kappa models of six selected strong-motion stations calculated from the (a) EW, (b) NS, and (c) UD components. The color version of this figure is available only in the electronic edition. *(Continued)*

rock to soft soil (Askan *et al.*, 2014; Neighbors *et al.*, 2015). In this scheme, we investigated the potential relationship between the κ_0 values and V_{S30} for 60 selected stations, as shown in Figure 9d,e, indicating that the relationships between κ_0 and $\ln(V_{S30})$ for the horizontal and vertical components are as follows:

$$\kappa_0 = (0.1032 \pm 0.0989) - 0.0118 \ln(V_{S30}), \tag{7}$$

$$\kappa_0 = (0.1491 \pm 0.1043) - 0.0222 \ln(V_{S30}). \tag{8}$$

In this case, the κ_0 value of a single station is calculated by taking the arithmetic mean of the $\kappa_0$values in two horizontal components. Equations (7) and (8) indicate that the relationship between κ_0 and V_{S30} is weak without considering the influence of magnitude. In this study, the V_{S30} values for the stations were obtained from three primary sources: drilling data, the PEER database, and an empirical relationship. To enhance the reliability of our fitting results, we selected 26 stations with a record count greater than 9 and confirmed V_{S30} values. Among them, the V_{S30} values of 16 stations were calculated from drilling data, the V_{S30} values of 2 stations were determined via empirical relationship, and the V_{S30} values of 8 stations were sourced from the PEER database. To validate the derived relationship between κ_0 and V_{S30}, we conducted statistical analysis of the station's V_{S30} data from both drilling data and the PEER database (Fig. S7). The resulting relationships for 16 stations in both horizontal and vertical components are $\kappa_0 = (0.1612 \pm 0.1405) - 0.022 \ln(V_{S30})$ and $\kappa_0 = (0.2535 \pm 0.1779) - 0.0402 \ln(V_{S30})$.

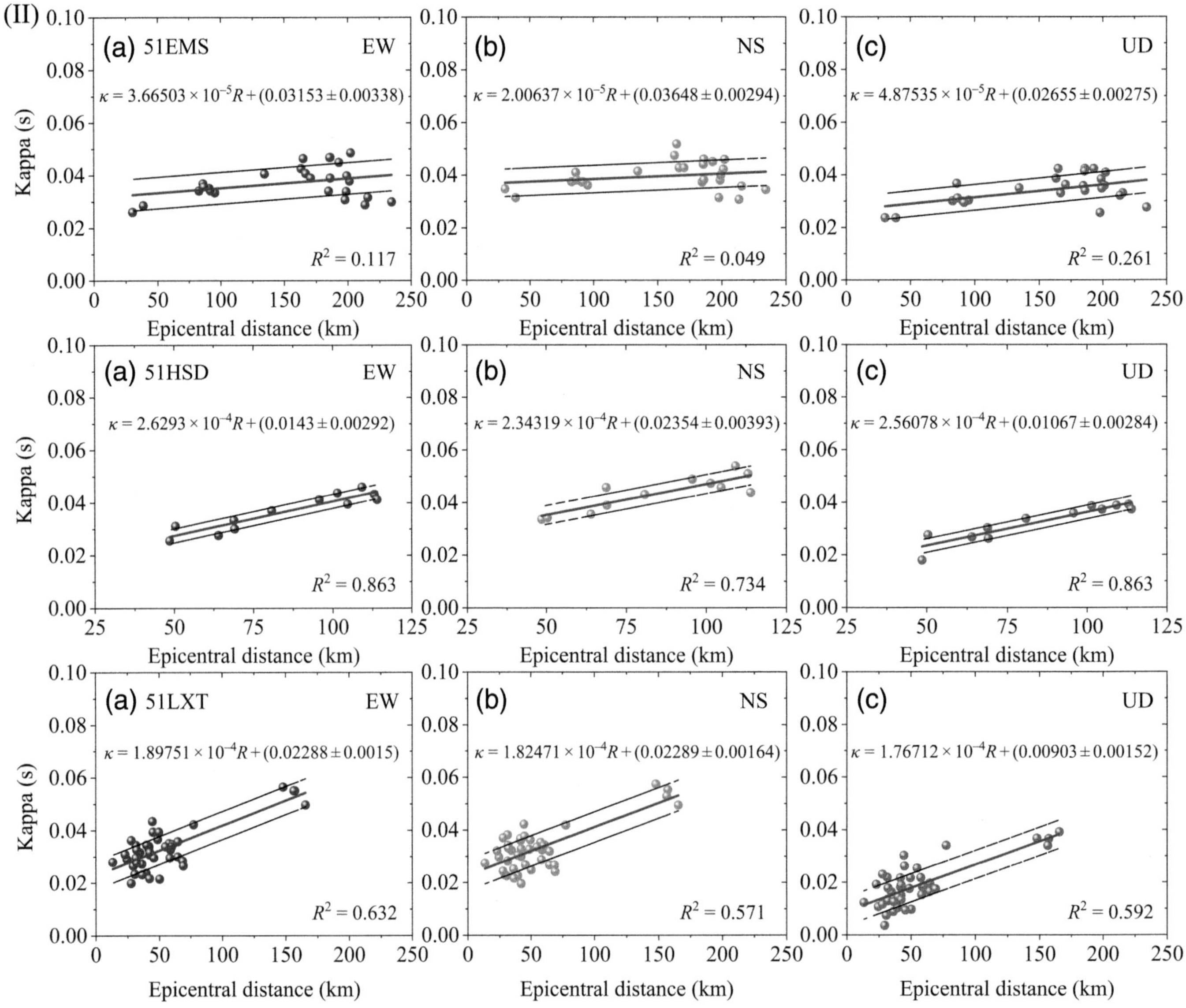

Figure 10. Continued

The relationship between κ_0 and V_{S30} for eight stations in both horizontal and vertical components are $\kappa_0 = (0.11834 \pm 0.09542) - 0.01352 \ln(V_{S30})$ and $\kappa_0 = (0.0326 \pm 0.1147) - 0.00234 \ln(V_{S30})$. Regional statistical analyses reveal a consistent trend where κ_0 values gradually decrease with increasing V_{S30}. However, significant regional variations in these relationships were observed, suggesting that the near-surface soil layer at each station's location exerts a measurable influence on the derived $\kappa_0 - V_{S30}$ correlation.

In the probabilistic seismic hazard analysis, high-frequency attenuation parameters serve as critical validation metrics for seismic attenuation relationships. Statistical analysis of κ parameters based on existing earthquake records is particularly important. Empirical studies demonstrate that a 0.012 s increase in κ_0 can reduce the relative error between simulated and observed peak ground acceleration values by ~40% (Fu and Li, 2017) and a 10 ms reduction in κ_0 increase the amplitude of the response spectra within the 0.1–0.2 s period range by 0.2g (Tanircan and Dikmen, 2018; Tao *et al.*, 2025). Normally, lower kappa values always result in a higher level of ground motion, and higher kappa values correspond to a lower level of ground motion (Mittal *et al.*, 2021). The study in the Effects of earthquake size and site class on kappa values section indicates that the kappa values are correlated with both site and magnitude. However, we did not establish an ideal relation model between κ_0 and the site parameter V_{S30} within different magnitude ranges because the number of stations with V_{S30} values in different magnitude ranges is very limited, and the resulting relationship equation may be unreliable. This exploration requires further research to collect strong-motion records for analysis.

Conclusion

In our scheme, we investigated the kappa values estimated from 4260 three-component recordings recorded by 168 selected strong-motion stations from 165 earthquake events with magnitudes ranging from 3.5 to 6.0 in western-central Sichuan, China. The influences of earthquake size, site class and epicentral distance on kappa values were analyzed for the EW, NS, and UD components. These regional kappa models for both horizontal and vertical components are presented for future use in stochastic finite-fault models and GMPE adjustments (Askan *et al.*, 2014; Houtte *et al.*, 2014). In addition, the single-station kappa values were fitted to investigate the potential correlations between κ_0 and V_{S30}. However, we did not establish an ideal relation model between κ_0 and the site parameter V_{S30} within different magnitude ranges because the number of stations with V_{S30} values in different magnitude ranges is very limited. This exploration requires further research to collect strong-motion records for analysis. Finally, the relationship between the kappa value and local magnitude was fitted, and the relationship between the zero-distance κ_0 and V_{S30} was also obtained. The conclusions of this study are consistent with those of research studies from other regions worldwide. The main conclusions of this study are as follows:

1. The estimated spectral decay parameter kappa (κ) of the three-component ground motion shows that the difference between the kappa values of the EW and NS components is small, whereas the two horizontal kappa values are significantly larger than those of the UD component, which indicates that the vertical component of the lower crust ground motion decays slowly.
2. The zero-distance κ_0 values estimated for class D sites are 0.03334 and 0.03537, both of which are greater than the corresponding κ_0 values for class C sites, 0.03037 and 0.03243. This finding indicates that the high-frequency attenuation of seismic components in soft soil sites is faster. In addition, the estimated κ_0 values of the horizontal component for both the class C and class D sites are almost twice those of their vertical component κ_0 values, indicating that the high-frequency attenuation of the vertical component is slow. This may be due to the greater sensitivity of the horizontal component to changes in shear-wave velocity in near-surface sedimentary layers. For the vertical component, the κ_0 values estimated for the class C and class D sites are 0.01485 and 0.02203, respectively. The same conclusion has also been reached for unknown sites. This fully demonstrates that the estimation of κ_0 is closely related to the near-surface site conditions.
3. The estimation results of the zero-distance κ_0 based on magnitude and site conditions indicate that site conditions have a significant effect on the calculation of κ_0, with softer sites yielding higher κ_0 values. For the same site type, the smaller the magnitude of the earthquake event is, the smaller the calculated κ_0 value. This finding indicates that both magnitude and site conditions have a significant effect on the κ_0 estimation. However, there is no significant difference in the fitting coefficient m estimated from the three components. In addition, without considering the magnitude factor, there is not much difference in the m values of the two horizontal components estimated under different site conditions.
4. The zero-distance κ_0 value of a single station also indicates that there was not much difference in κ_0 values between the two horizontal components, which were significantly greater than the κ_0 value of the vertical component. The relationship between κ_0 and V_{S30} is weak without considering the influence of magnitude. In addition, the relationship between kappa and local magnitude indicates that Sertcelik *et al.* (2022) estimated a larger kappa value than the results of this study indicate, which may be due to differences in kappa values caused by near-surface site characteristics. This also indicates that kappa values have strong regional characteristics.

Data and Resources

The acceleration waveforms used in this study are provided by the Institute of Engineering Mechanics, China Earthquake Administration, upon reasonable request (csmnc@iem.ac.cn). Figure 1 was made using Generic Mapping Tools (GMT; Wessel *et al.*, 2013) version 5.4.4 (https://gmt-china.org/#download, last accessed February 2020). The remaining figures were made using the Origin software version OriginPro 2024b, which can be downloaded from https://www.originlab.com/demodownload.aspx (last accessed December 2024). The MATLAB-based code used for data processing and kappa estimation was written by Pengfei Dang, and the data used in this study can be obtained upon resonable request, and the MATLAB software can be downlaoded from https://www.mathworks.com/products/matlab (last accessed May 2024). The supplemental material consists of five tables and seven figures.

Declaration of Competing Interests

The authors acknowledge that there are no conflicts of interest recorded.

Acknowledgments

The authors are thankful to the China Strong Ground Motion Networks Center for providing the strong ground motion data selected in this study and the American Journal Experts for providing the linguistic assistance during the preparation of the original and revised article. Moreover, the authors are also thankful to anonymous reviewers and the editors for their meticulous editing and critical comments that improved the article. The research was undertaken with the National Key Research and Development Program of China (Grant Number 2022YFC3003601), National Natural Science Foundation of China (Grant Numbers 42204050 and 52378523), and Exploration Project of Zhejiang Natural Science Foundation (Grant Number ZX2024000700).

References

Aki, K (1967). Scaling law of seismic spectrum, *J. Geophys. Res.* **72,** 1217–1231.

Altindal, A., and A. Askan (2022). Predictive kappa (k) models for Turkey: Regional effects and uncertainty analysis, *Earthq. Spectra* **38,** no. 4, 2479–2499.

Anderson, J. G., and S. E. Hough (1984). A model for the shape of the Fourier amplitude spectrum of acceleration at high frequencies, *Bull. Seismol. Soc. Am.* **74,** 1969–1993.

Askan, A., F. N. Sisman, and O. Pekcan (2014). A regional near-surface high frequency spectral attenuation (kappa) model for northwestern Turkey, *Soil Dynam. Earthq. Eng.* **65,** 113–125.

Bai, Y. Z., X. W. Xu, T. M. Li, and B. G. Zhou (2016). Spectrum characteristics of strong ground motion during the Lushan earthquake and correlation analysis of the resulting disaster, *China Earthq. Eng. J.* **38,** no. 4, 570–580 (in Chinese).

Biro, Y. (2024). Magnitude dependency of spectral decay parameter (kappa) in EAF related events, *18th World Conf. on Earthquake Engineering*, Milan, Italy, 30 June–5 July 2024.

Biro, Y., and P. Renault (2013). A parameterized relation for Vs-Kappa corrections to adjust the global ground motion prediction equations to Swiss NPP sites, *22nd Conf. on Structural Mechanics in Reactor Technology*, San Francisco, California, 18–23 August 2013.

Biro, Y., B. Siyahi, and B. Akbas (2022). Spectral decay parameter (k) analysis for a single fault source and an automatic selection procedure for spectral flattening frequency (f_x), *Soil Dynam. Earthq. Eng.* **153,** 107,122.

Boore, D. M. (2003). Simulation of ground motion using the stochastic method, *Pure Appl. Geophys.* **160,** no. 3, 635–676.

Boore, D. M., and W. B. Joyner (1997). Site amplifications for generic rock sites, *Bull. Seismol. Soc. Am.* **87,** 327–341.

Brune, J. N. (1970). Tectonic stress and the spectra of seismic shear waves from earthquakes, *J. Geophys. Res.* **75,** 4997–5009.

Campbell, K. W. (2009). Estimates of shear-wave Q and κ_0 for unconsolidated and semiconsolidated sediments in eastern North America, *Bull. Seismol. Soc. Am.* **99,** no. 4, 2365–2392.

Castro, R. R., J. G. Anderson, and S. K. Singh (1990). Site response, attenuation, and source spectra of S-waves along the Guerrero, Mexico, subduction zone, *Bull. Seismol. Soc. Am.* **80,** 1481–1503.

Castro, R. R., L. Colavitti, C. A. Vidales-Basurto, F. Pacor, S. Sgobba, and G. Lanzano (2022). Near-source attenuation and spatial variability of the spectral decay parameter kappa in central Italy, *Seismol. Res. Lett.* **93,** no. 4, 2299–2310.

Chen, G. G., F. J. Ji, R. J. Zhou, J. Xu, B. G. Zhou, X. G. Li, and Y. Q. Ye (2007). Primary research of activity segmentation of Longmenshan fault zone since late-Quaternary, *Seismol. Geol.* **29,** no. 3, 657–673 (in Chinese).

Chen, L. C., J. Chen, J. F. Liu, F. Li, X. P. Yang, and Y. K. Ran (2008). Investigation of late Quaternary activity along the northern range-front fault, Longmenshan, *Seismol. Geol.* **30,** no. 3, 710–722 (in Chinese).

Cotton, F., F. Scherbaum, J. J. Bommer, and H. Bungum (2006). Criteria for selecting and adjusting ground-motion models for specific target regions: Application to Central Europe and rock sites, *J. Seismol.* **10,** 137–156.

Dang, P. F., J. Cui, and Q. F. Liu (2025). Research progress on input parameter models for stochastic finite fault ground motion simulation, *China Earthq. Eng. J.* doi: 10.20000/j.1000-0844.20250311002 (in Chinese).

Dang, P. F., J. Cui, M. J. Ma, and Y. D. Li (2023). Simulation of the 2022 M_w 6.6 Luding, China, earthquake by a stochastic finite-fault model with a nonstationary phase, *Soil Dynam. Earthq. Eng.* **172,** 108,035.

Dang, P. F., J. Cui, H. F. Yang, and J. Song (2024). Regional spectral characteristics, quality factor and site responses in western-central Sichuan, China (I): Application of parametric generalized inversion technique, *Soil Dynam. Earthq. Eng.* **176,** 108,303.

Dang, P. F., J. Cui, H. F. Yang, and J. Song (2025). Estimation of source characteristics, site effects and path attenuation in Sichuan basin, China, using a non-parametric generalized inversion technique, *Geophys. J. Int.* **240,** no. 2, 1028–1047.

Dang, P. F., C. Wang, W. H. Qi, and Y. D. Li (2022). An updated stochastic finite fault modeling: Application to the M_w 6.0 earthquake in Jiashi, China, *Soil Dynam. Earthq. Eng.* **162,** 107,450.

Douglas, J., H. Bungum, and F. Scherbaum (2006). Ground motion prediction equations for southern Spain and southern Norway obtained using the composite model perspective, *J. Earthq. Eng.* **10,** 33–72.

Douglas, J., P. Gehl, L. F. Bonilla, and C. Gelis (2010). A κ model for mainland Frace, *Pure Appl. Geophys.* **167,** 1303–1315.

Drouet, S., and S. Chevrot (2008). Simultaneous inversion of source spectra, attenuation parameters, and site responses: Application to the data of French Accelerometric Network, *Bull. Seismol. Soc. Am.* **98,** 198–219.

Drouet, S., F. Cotton, and P. Guéguen (2010). *Vs*30, κ, regional attenuation and M_w from small magnitude events accelerograms, *Geophys. J. Int.* **182,** 880–898.

Edwards, B., D. Faeh, and D. Giardini (2011). Attenuation of seismic shear-wave energy in Switzerland, *Geophys. J. Int.* **185,** 967–984.

Fu, L., and X. J. Li (2017). The kappa (κ_0) model of the Longmenshan region and its application to estimation of strong ground-motion by the Wenchuan Ms8.0 earthquake, *Chin. J. Geophys.* **60,** no. 8, 2935–2947 (in Chinese).

Fu, L., X. J. Li, F. Wang, and S. Chen (2019). A study of site response and regional attenuation in the Longmen Shan region, eastern Tibetan plateau, SW China, from seismic recordings using the generalized inversion method, *J. Asian Earth Sci.* **181,** 103,887.

Gariel, J. -C., and M. Campillo (1989). The influence of the source on the high-frequency behavior of the near-field acceleration spectrum: A numerical study, *Geophys. Res. Lett.* **16,** no. 4, 279–282.

Han, B., L. Zdravkovic, S. Kontoe, and D. M. G. Taborda (2016). Numerical investigation of the responses of the Yele rockfill dam during the 2008 Wenchuan earthquake, *Soil Dynam. Earthq. Eng.* **88,** 124–142.

Hanks, T. C. (1982). f_{max}, *Bull. Seismol. Soc. Am.* **72,** 1867–1879.

Hassani, B., and G. M. Atkinson (2015). Referenced empirical ground-motion model for eastern north America, *Seismol. Res. Lett.* **86,** 477–491.

Houtte, C. V., O. J. Ktenidou, T. Larkin, and C. Holden (2014). Hard-site calculations for κ_0 (kappa) Calculations for Christchurch, New Zealand, and comparison with local ground-motion prediction models, *Bull. Seismol. Soc. Am.* **104,** no. 4, 1899–1913.

Hu, N., F. Long, Y. Wang, and L. X. Xu (2024). The spatial and temporal characteristics of present-day seismicity in northeastern Longmenshan fault zone, *Seismol. Geol.* **46,** no. 4, 856–875 (in Chinese).

Hubbard, J., and J. H. Shaw (2009). Uplift of the Longmen Shan and Tibetan plateau, and the 2008 Wenchuan (M = 7.9) earthquake, *Nature* **458,** no. 7235, 194–197.

Husid, P. (1967). *Gravity Effects on the Earthquake Response of Yielding Structures*, California Institute of Technology, California.

Klinger, Y. (2010). Relation between continental strike-slip earthquake segmentation and thickness of the crust, *J. Geophys. Res.* **115,** no. B7, doi: 10.1029/2009JB006550.

Konno, K., and T. Ohmachi (1998). Ground-motion characteristics estimated from spectral ratio between horizontal and vertical components of microtremor, *Bull. Seismol. Soc. Am.* **88,** 228–241.

Ktenidou, O. J., C. Gelis, and L. F. Bonilla (2013). A study on the variability of kappa (κ) in a borehole: Implications of the computation process, *Bull. Seismol. Soc. Am.* **103,** 1048–1068.

Kumar, V., S. Chopra, P. Choudhury, and D. Kumar (2020). Estimation of near surface attenuation parameter kappa (κ) in northwest and northeast Himalaya region, *Soil Dynam. Earthq. Eng.* **136,** 106,237.

Lancieri, M., R. Madariaga, and F. Bonilla (2012). Spectral scaling of the aftershocks of the Tocopilla 2007 earthquake in northern Chile, *Geophys. J. Int.* **189,** no. 1, 469–480.

Laurendeau, A., F. Cotton, O. J. Ktenidou, L. F. Bonilla, and F. Hollender (2013). Rock and stiff-soil site amplification: Dependency on Vs30 and kappa (κ_0), *Bull. Seismol. Soc. Am.* **103,** no. 6, 3131–3148.

Lermo, J., and F. J. Chávez-García (1993). Site effect evaluation using spectral ratios with only one station, *Bull. Seismol. Soc. Am.* **83,** 1574–1594.

Li, C. L., H. B. Li, H. Wang, L. Zhang, Z. M. Sun, J. J. Zhang, K. Yun, and J. J. Zhang (2020). Rock characteristics and internal structures of the Beichuan fault zone at Nanba outcrop in the northeastern segment of the 2008 Wenchuan seismogenic fault, *Acta Petrol. Sinica* **36,** no. 10, 3192–3208 (in Chinese).

Li, Y., R. J. Zhou, A. L. Densmore, and M. A. Ellis (2006). Geomorphic evidence for the late Cenozoic strike-slipping and thrusting in Longmen Mountain at the eastern margin of the Tibetan plateau, *Quat. Sci.* **26,** no. 1, 40–51 (in Chinese).

Liu, P., C. Liu, X. Z. Chen, H. Wang, C. G. Wei, Y. R. Fan, F. Chen, and Y. X. Wu (2025). Directionality of Newmark displacement during the Lushan M_w 6.8 earthquake in 2013, *China Earthq. Eng. J.* **47,** no. 2, 437–447 (in Chinese).

Luo, C. R., and Y. B. Peng (2024). Stochastic simulation of earthquake ground motions based on improved finite-fault model, *Soil Dynam. Earthq. Eng.* **176,** 108,336.

Ma, X. Y. (1989). *Lithospherical Dynamics Atlas of China*, China Cartographic Publishing House, Beijing, 1–16 (in Chinese).

Mao, L., Y. C. Shi, Y. X. Lu, and K. Liu (2024). Three-component ground motion simulation for the 2023 Ms 6.2 earthquake in Jishishan, Gansu, based on the stochastic finite-fault method, *China Earthq. Eng. J.* **46,** no. 4, 778–790 (in Chinese).

Margaris, B. N., and P. M. Hatzidimitriou (2002). Source spectral scaling and stress release estimates using strong-motion records in Greece, *Bull. Seismol. Soc. Am.* **92,** 2926–2941.

Mittal, H., B. Sharma, M. Sandhu, and D. Kumar (2021). Spatial distribution of high-frequency spectral decay factor kappa (κ) for Delhi, India, *Acta Geophys.* **69,** 2113–2127.

Motazedian, D. (2006). Region-specific key seismic parameters for earthquakes in northern Iran, *Bull. Seismol. Soc. Am.* **96,** 1383–1395.

Moya, A., J. Aguirre, and K. Irikura (2000). Inversion of source parameters and site effects from strong ground motion records using genetic algorithms, *Bull. Seismol. Soc. Am.* **90,** 977–992.

Neighbors, C., E. J. Liao, E. S. Cochran, G. J. Funning, A. I. Chung, J. F. Lawrence, C. Christensen, M. Miller, A. Belmonte, and H. H. A. Sepulveda (2015). Investigation of the high-frequency attenuation parameter, κ (kappa), from aftershocks of the 2010 M_w 8.8 Maule, Chile earthquake, *Geophys. J. Int.* **200,** 200–215.

Oth, A., D. Bindi, S. Parolai, and D. Di Giacomo (2010). Earthquake scaling characteristics and the scale-(in)dependence of seismic energy-to-moment ratio: Insights from KiK-net data in Japan, *Geophys. Res. Lett.* **37,** L19304, doi: 10.1029/2010GL044572.

Palmer, S. M., and G. M. Atkinson (2020). The high-frequency decay slope of spectra (kappa) for M ≥ 3.5 earthquakes on rock sites in eastern and western Canada, *Bull. Seismol. Soc. Am.* **110,** no. 2, 471–488.

Papageorgiou, A. S., and K. Aki (1983). A specific barrier model for the quantitative description of inhomogeneous faulting and prediction of strong ground motion. I. Description of the model, *Bull. Seismol. Soc. Am.* **73,** no. 3, 693–722.

Parolai, S., and D. Bindi (2004). Influence of soil-layer properties on κ evaluation, *Bull. Seismol. Soc. Am.* **94,** 349–356.

Perron, V., F. Hollender, P. Y. Bard, C. Gelis, C. Guyonnet-Benaize, B. Hernandez, and O. J. Ktenidou (2017) Robustness of kappa (k) measurement in low-to-moderate seismicity area: Insight from a site-specific study in Provence, France, *Bull. Seismol. Soc. Am.* **107,** no. 5, 256–275.

Pozo, I., G. Montalva, and M. Miller (2023). Assessment of kappa values in the Chilean subduction zone for interface and in-slab events, *Seismol. Res. Lett.* **94,** no. 1, 385–398.

Purvance, M. D., and J. G. Anderson (2003). A comprehensive study of the observed spectral decay in strong-motion accelerations recorded in Guerrero, Mexico, *Bull. Seismol. Soc. Am.* **93,** 600–611.

Sertcelik, F., D. Akcay, H. Livaoglu, and S. Gerdan (2022). The spectral decay parameter kappa in Marmara region, Turkey, *Arabian J. Geosci.* **15,** 271.

Shi, H. B., and Y. S. Zhang (2024). Strong ground motion simulation of the Qinghai M 6.9 earthquake on January 8, 2022, *China Earthq. Eng. J.* **46,** no. 3, 680–691 (in Chinese).

Sun, X. D., X. X. Tao, S. S. Duan, and C. Q. Liu (2013). Kappa (κ) derived from accelerograms recorded in the 2008 Wenchuan mainshock, Sichuan, China, *J. Asian Earth Sci.* **73,** 306–316.

Tanircan, G., and S. U. Dikmen (2018). Variation of high frequency spectral attenuation (kappa) in vertical arrays, *Soil Dynam. Earthq. Eng.* **113,** 406–414.

Tao, Z. R., M. C. H. Zhang, Y. M. Zhao, J. Hao, and P. Xiao (2025). Research progress on the high-frequency decay parameter kappa (κ) of Fourier amplitude spectrum of acceleration, *World Earthq. Eng.* **41,** no. 2, 42–52 (in Chinese).

Tsai, C. C. P., and K. C. Chen (2000). A model for the high-cut process of strong-motion accelerations in terms of distance, magnitude, and site condition: an example from the SMART 1 array, Lotung, Taiwan, *Bull. Seismol. Soc. Am.* **90,** 1535–1542.

Tsurugi, M., R. Tanaka, T. Kagawa, and K. Irikura (2020). High-frequency spectral decay characteristics of seismic records of inland crustal earthquakes in Japan: Evaluation of the f_{max} and κ models, *Bull. Seismol. Soc. Am.* **110,** 452–470.

Van Houtte, C., S. Drouet, and F. Cotton (2011). Analysis of the origins of κ (Kappa) to computed hard rock to rock adjustment factors for GMPEs, *Bull. Seismol. Soc. Am.* **101,** 2926–2941.

Wang, D., L. L. Xie, N. A. Abrahamson, and S. Y. Li (2010). Comparison of strong ground motion from the Wenchuan, China, earthquake of 12 May, 2008 with the next generation attenuation (NGA) ground-motion models, *Bull. Seismol. Soc. Am.* **100,** no. 5B, 2381–2395.

Wang, S. Y., J. Wang, Y. X. Yu, Q. Wu, A. J. Gao, and M. T. Gao (2010). The empirical relation between M_L and Ms based on bulletin of seismological observations of Chinese stations, *Earthq. Res. China* **26,** 14–22 (in Chinese).

Wen, J., and X. Chen (2012). Variations in fmax along the ruptured fault during the M_w 7.9 Wenchuan earthquake of 12 May 2008, *Bull. Seismol. Soc. Am.* **102,** no. 3, 991–998.

Wen, X. Z., C. R. Allen, Z. L. Luo, H. Qian, H. W. Zhou, and W. S. Huang (1989). Segmentation, geometric features, and their seismotectonic implications for the Holocene Xianshuihe fault zone, *Acta Seismol. Sinica* **11,** no. 4, 362–372 (in Chinese).

Wessel, P., W. H. F. Smith, R. Scharroo, J. Luis, and F. Wobbe (2013). Generic mapping tools: Improved version released, *Eos Trans. AGU* **94,** no. 45, 409.

Wu, M., X. D. Yang, and J. Liu (2023). Discussion on the correlation between the water- level anomaly of the Shiquan well and the Jiuzhaigou M 7.0 earthquake, *China Earthq. Eng. J.* **45,** no. 2, 441–446 (in Chinese).

Xu, B., E. M. Rathje, Y. Hashash, J. Stewart, K. Campbell, and W. J. Silva (2020). κ_0 for soil sites: Observations form KiK-net sites and their use in constraining small-strain damping profiles for site response analysis, *Earthq. Spectra* **36,** no. 1, 111–137.

Yang, Z. X., F. Waldhauser, Y. T. Chen, and P. G. Richard (2005). Double-difference relocation of earthquakes in central-western China, 1992-1999, *J. Seismol.* **9,** no. 2, 241–264.

Yu, R. F., Q. L. Yang, J. R. Xu, Y. S. Song, H. Zhou, and Y. X. Yu (2025). Maximum credible ground motion evaluation based on broadband stochastic finite-fault method: A case study for Baihetan dam in China, *Soil Dynam. Earthq. Eng.* **190,** 109,168.

Zhang, L., H. B. Li, H. Wang, Q. Wu, S. H. Yang, Z. M. Sun, J. L. Si, C. Marie-Luce, Y. Cao, Y. Zheng, *et al.* (2024). Deformation mechanism of large earthquake fault zone in the Tibetan plateau, *Acta Geosci. Sinica* **45,** no. 6, 854–870 (in Chinese).

Zhang, S. X., X. M. Ma, X. X. Yin, H. C. Ju, Z. D. Wang, and W. Q. Wan (2024b). Relocation of the 2022 Ms 6.1 and 2013 Ms 7.0 earthquake sequences in Lushan, Sichuan Province, and their tectonic relationship, *China Earthq. Eng. J.* **46,** no. 5, 1223–1233 (in Chinese).

Zhu, L., X. J. Pei, S. H. Cui, S. Y. Wang, X. C. Zhang, and Y. F. Liang (2020). On the initiation mechanism of the Daguangbao landslide triggered by the 2008 Wenchuan (Ms 7.9) earthquake, *Soil Dynam. Earthq. Eng.* **137,** 106,272.

Zielke, O., Y. Klinger, and J. R. Arrowsmith (2015). Fault slip and earthquake recurrence along strike-slip faults-contributions of high-resolution geomorphic data, *Tectonophysics* **638,** 43–62.

Manuscript received 7 July 2025
Published online 5 November 2025

Wavenumber Limitation of Medium in the Finite-Difference Modeling of Seismic-Wave Propagation: A Proof of Concept

Jozef Kristek[1,2], Jaroslav Valovcan[1], Peter Moczo[*1,2], Miriam Kristekova[1,2], Rune Mittet[3,4], and Martin Galis[1,2]

Abstract

When developing a finite-difference (FD) scheme, one of the key aspects that must be addressed is the spatial discretization of material parameters and the implementation of material interfaces. Mittet (2017) and Moczo *et al.* (2022) recently suggested a novel approach based on the wavenumber limitation of the medium. They demonstrated that, due to spatial discretization, a model of the medium must be wavenumber-limited by a wavenumber k_m smaller than the Nyquist wavenumber. Mittet (2021a) and Valovcan *et al.* (2024) proved that the wavefield (numerically simulated or exact) in a k_m-limited medium can only be accurate up to $k_m/2$. Here, we numerically demonstrate a perfect subcell resolution (capability to sense the position of interface within a grid cell) of FD modeling based on the wavenumber-limited medium using a finite spatial low-pass filter. The finding that it is possible to use a finite-length filter for wavenumber limitation of the medium is of key importance for the next development of the concept in terms of computational efficiency. We demonstrate an unprecedented accuracy for a canonical model—a material interface between two homogeneous half-spaces. The time–frequency envelope and phase misfits between the FD solution and the exact analytical solution are surprisingly small and are the same for any position of the interface within a grid spacing. We show that the misfits for the reflected and transmitted waves are solely due to grid dispersion. We compare the accuracy of the FD solution for the wavenumber-limited medium with that for the harmonically averaged modulus (Moczo *et al.*, 2002). The FD modeling based on the wavenumber-limited medium is considerably more accurate. The proof of concept of the wavenumber limitation of the medium should be followed by development of a practical way of wavenumber limitation using finite spatial filters in 2D and 3D elastic problems.

Cite this article as Kristek, J., J. Valovcan, P. Moczo, M. Kristekova, R. Mittet, and M. Galis (2025). Wavenumber Limitation of Medium in the Finite-Difference Modeling of Seismic-Wave Propagation: A Proof of Concept, *Seismol. Res. Lett.* **97**, 1965–1975, doi: 10.1785/0220250256.

Introduction

Discretization (sampling) of a continuous signal causes its spectrum to become periodic, introducing potential aliasing, unlike the original continuous spectrum, which is typically nonperiodic and unbounded. This is true for time signals and for functions of spatial coordinates.

The equation of motion and constitutive law include material parameters (e.g., density and elastic moduli) depending on spatial coordinates, and wavefield variables (e.g., particle velocity and stress) that are functions of both spatial coordinates and time.

The finite-difference (FD) method applies relatively simple discretization in space to the material parameters and discretization in space and time to wavefield variables. Therefore, consequences of discretization must be analyzed in the time, space, frequency, and wavenumber domains.

FD schemes for modeling seismic-wave propagation have been developed approximately since the mid-60s of the twentieth century. At that time, the finite-element method dominated. It was just the relatively simple notion of discretization in time and space that motivated seismologists to apply the FD approach to seismic-wave propagation.

The development of the FD schemes has usually been based on necessary analysis of consistency, stability, and subsequently

1. Faculty of Mathematics, Physics and Informatics, Comenius University Bratislava, Bratislava, Slovakia, https://orcid.org/0000-0002-2332-541X (JK); https://orcid.org/0000-0001-5276-9311 (PM); https://orcid.org/0000-0001-9017-5952 (MK); https://orcid.org/0000-0002-5375-7061 (MG); 2. Earth Science Institute, Slovak Academy of Sciences, Bratislava, Slovakia; 3. Allton AS, Stavanger, Norway; 4. RMGS OMS, Trondheim, Norway

*Corresponding author: moczo@fmph.uniba.sk

grid dispersion as a consequence of discretization in time and space. The analysis usually assumed a harmonic plane wave in a homogeneous medium and was performed in the time–space domain. We refer to Moczo *et al.* (2014), Jiang and Zhang (2021), Liu (2022), Koene *et al.* (2022), Zhou *et al.* (2022, 2024), and Chen *et al.* (2024) for a basic overview of the FD method.

Considerably less obvious was how to properly represent material heterogeneity, mainly the internal interface, in the spatial grid. What has been missing was the appropriate account for consequences of the spatial discretization of the medium and wavefield in the wavenumber domain. We refer to Mittet (2017), Mittet (2021a,b), Moczo *et al.* (2022), and Valovcan *et al.* (2023, 2024) for the recent overview of the problem of accuracy of implementation of the material interface and for fundamental insight into accuracy through the wavenumber domain analysis. We do not repeat here the numerous references to relevant contributions present in the articles mentioned. However, we want to especially acknowledge Mora (1986), Holberg (1987), Igel *et al.* (1995), and Fichtner (2011) who pointed out the important aspect of the wavenumber-domain view in replacing spatial derivatives by the wavenumber-limited discrete operators.

In this article, we focus on the possibility to use a finite-length filter in the spatial domain for wavenumber limitation of a heterogeneous medium (bandlimitation of the wavenumber spectrum of a material parameter). For examining accuracy and subcell resolution of an FD solution based on the wavenumber-limited representation of a heterogeneous medium, we use a stringent canonical model of a sharp heterogeneity—a material interface between two homogeneous half-spaces. We compare the FD solution with the exact solution.

Because we are addressing the FD method, we will use the term "grid spacing," here denoted as h, for the sampling step in the spatial domain and "time step" for the sampling step in the time domain. We will briefly cover the well-known aspects and recent surprising findings related to the spatial discretization of the medium and the wavefield.

Introducing Considerations on Wavefields in a Homogeneous Medium

Assume a spatial grid with a grid spacing h. If a function is discretized (sampled) with a grid spacing h, its Fourier wavenumber spectrum is periodic with period

$$2\,\frac{\pi}{h} =: 2k_N(h). \tag{1}$$

The relation defines the Nyquist wavenumber k_N: if the sampling with h should not cause aliasing, the range of the wavenumber spectrum must be limited by

$$k_{\max} \le \frac{\pi}{h} \equiv k_N(h). \tag{2}$$

In other words, a discrete spatial grid with grid spacing h cannot support wavenumbers larger than $k_N(h)$. (Note that here we fix, for a while, the grid spacing h, not k_{max}.)

Assume a source of a wavefield with spectrum limited by ω_{max} and a homogeneous medium with wavespeed c. These two parameters determine the maximum wavenumber k_{max} and the corresponding minimum wavelength λ_{min} of the wavefield:

$$k_{\max} = \frac{\omega_{\max}}{c}, \quad \lambda_{\min} = \frac{2\pi}{k_{\max}}. \tag{3}$$

In other words, in the homogeneous medium, the exact wavefield is wavenumber limited if the source is frequency limited. Assume now a spatial grid with grid spacing h. Relations (2) and (3) imply that the minimum number of grid spacings per λ_{min} must be at least 2:

$$N_{\lambda\min} := \frac{\lambda_{\min}}{h} = 2\frac{k_N}{k_{\max}} \ge 2. \tag{4}$$

In FD modeling, this criterion is applied to the minimum wavelength, that is in the spatial domain. The criterion usually does not pose a concern in the time domain because the stability of a scheme imposes considerably more severe restriction to values of the time step (discretization in time).

All this has been well known since the beginning of the development of FD schemes. We included this explicit brief explanation just because it is the first step of consideration. The second step may be found to be quite surprising by many.

Phenomenon of Wavefield Accuracy Limit in a Wavenumber-Limited Heterogeneous Medium

We say that a function of spatial coordinates (e.g., a material parameter or wavefield variable) is wavenumber limited if its wavenumber Fourier spectrum is nonzero only up to some finite wavenumber. Otherwise, we say that the function is not wavenumber limited. For example, contrary to the homogeneous medium, a material parameter in the heterogeneous medium might not be wavenumber limited.

Importantly, no matter whether the medium is wavenumber limited or not, the exact wavefield in any heterogeneous medium is not wavenumber limited (see Valovcan *et al.*, 2024).

The spatial grid discretizes (samples) a material parameter as a function of spatial coordinates. The spatial discretization does not remove a potential wavenumber content above the Nyquist wavenumber $k_N(h)$. So, obviously, assuming a grid spacing h, if the wavenumber spectrum of a material parameter is effectively nonzero above $k_N(h)$, the medium must be wavenumber limited by $k_N(h)$ prior to the spatial discretization.

The question is what happens with a wavefield (in principle not wavenumber limited) in the k_N-limited medium. Mittet (2017) was the first to address this fundamental question and obtained preliminary indications for the answer in his investigation of the interface error. Later, Mittet (2021a) reported that if the discrete grid model of a medium coincides with the true medium up to some wavenumber, the simulated wavefield is accurate only up to half of this wavenumber. Valovcan *et al.* (2024) analyzed the question in relation to both the exact and numerically simulated wavefields.

Here, we briefly outline the exemplary 1D test case presented by Valovcan *et al.* (2024). Consider a model of a thin homogeneous layer between two identical homogeneous half-spaces. We apply a wavenumber bandlimitation to the model with three different values of the limiting wavenumber k_m: $k_m = 2\pi/\lambda_m = \{2\pi, 4\pi, 10\pi\}\mathrm{m}^{-1}$. (Note that, due to the structure of the governing equations, the wavenumber limitation must be applied to compliance and density.) Thus, there are four models: the exact model and the three wavenumber-limited models. The wavefield in each model is due to a plane-wave incident in the lower half-space and propagating upward to the thin layer and the upper half-space. Let f_m be the frequencies of the wavefield corresponding to k_m.

For each model we used the matrix (i.e., exact) method. We approximated the wavenumber-limited models by the stack of thin layers and checked that further reduction of the layer thickness does not change the result in the considered frequency range. We calculated the wave transmitted from the lower half-space through the thin layer into the upper half-space and the wave reflected at the thin layer back to the lower half-space.

The transmitted wave in each wavenumber-limited model is the same as the transmitted wave in the exact model in the entire frequency range, that is, in the entire corresponding range of wavenumbers.

Results for the reflected waves may be considered surprising. Systematically, the reflected wave in each wavenumber-limited model exists and is the same as the reflected wave in the exact model only up to frequency $f_m/2$, that is, only up to wavenumber $k_m/2$.

For the model of two half-spaces, the result is the same except that the reflected wave exists also beyond $f_m/2$ or $k_m/2$. Beyond this limit, the reflected wave is, however, very different from the exact wave in the exact model.

We emphasize that we speak about exact wavefields, not wavefields obtained by a numerical method.

Consequence of Wavefield Accuracy Limit for the FD Modeling

The phenomenon of wavefield accuracy limit in a wavenumber-limited medium has a serious consequence for the FD modeling. If we want the wavefield to be accurate up to wavenumber k_{max}, we must limit the model of the medium by wavenumber $k_m = 2k_{max}$. What does it mean for the choice of grid spacing? If grid spacing h is needed for fulfilling condition $k_{max} \le k_N(h)$, then it is obvious that twice the smaller grid spacing $h/2$ is needed for fulfilling condition $k_{max} \le 2k_N(h) = k_N(h/2)$.

Practically taken: no matter which FD scheme we use, if we want the wavefield to be accurate up to wavenumber $k_{max} = 2\pi/\lambda_{min}$, we must

1. choose such grid spacing h that $h \le \lambda_{min}/4$,
2. wavenumber limit the medium by $2k_{max}$, and
3. discretize (sample) the wavenumber-limited medium using the grid spacing h.

It seems to us that it is not easy to intuitively understand this relation between the wavenumber limitation of the medium and wavenumber limitation of the wavefield. Valovcan *et al.* (2024) provided an explanation based on the application of the Lippmann–Schwinger equation in the Born approximation of the first order for scattered wavefields.

How to Wavenumber Limit the Medium?

If we know that, given a spatial grid, the medium must be correspondingly wavenumber limited, let us look at the wavenumber limitation itself.

An ideal filter for the k_m limitation of the material parameter $M(z)$ for a scheme without grid dispersion would be

$$\tilde{F}(k) = \begin{cases} 1; & 0 \le k \le k_m \\ 0; & k_m < k \end{cases}, \tag{5}$$

in which k_m would be equal to a corner wavenumber k_{cor} and a cutoff wavenumber k_{cut},

$$k_m = k_{cor} = k_{cut}, \tag{6}$$

as illustrated in Figure 1a.

The problem is that the ideal filter is not applicable because the corresponding wavenumber-limited medium would have an infinite spatial extent with nonnegligible variations of the value of the material parameter over relatively large spatial extent. What "relatively" means may depend on the model heterogeneity, size of the computational region, the source, and extent of an FD stencil.

Therefore, we must use a filter with $k_{cor} < k_{cut}$. The value of k_{cor} must be larger than or equal to k_m, and k_{cut} must be smaller than or equal to k_N. The best possibility would be $k_{cor} = k_m = 2k_{max}$, that is, k_{cor} would correspond to $h = \lambda_{min}/4$. The filter is illustrated in Figure 1b.

The choice of k_{cut} has several aspects to be considered. Depending on the FD scheme, more than four grid spacings per λ_{min} might be required due to grid dispersion. The minimum wavespeed in the wavenumber-limited medium may be smaller than c_{min} due to oscillatory character of the wavenumber-limited medium. Because of these two aspects, k_{cut} should be sufficiently larger than $k_{cor} = k_m$. Therefore, instead of the grid spacing $h = \lambda_{min}/4$ we should use a grid spacing

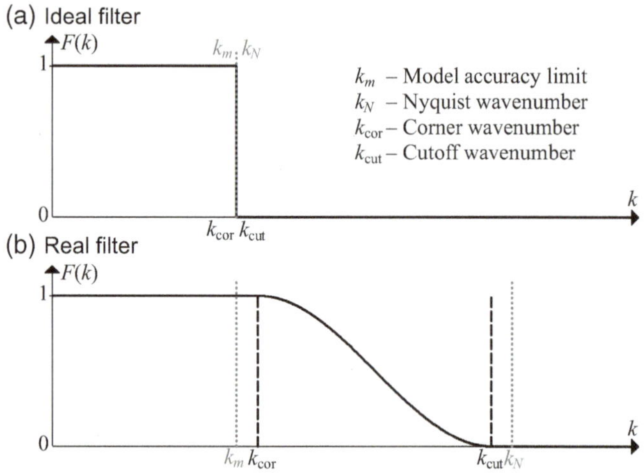

Figure 1. (a) An ideal wavenumber filter for k_m limitation of a material parameter. (b) Real filter.

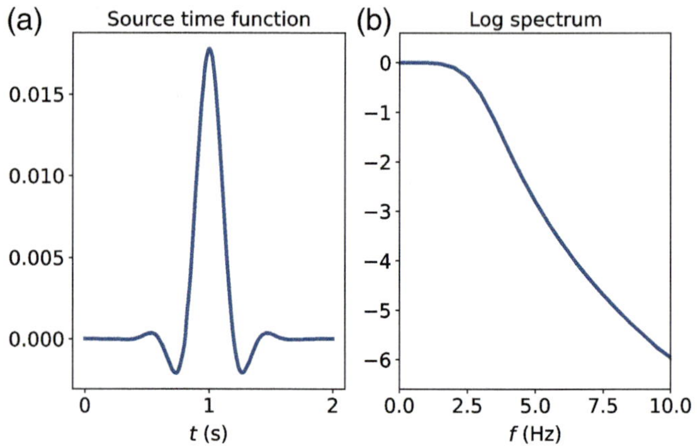

Figure 2. (a) Source time function and its (b) amplitude Fourier spectrum.

$$h_{cut} = \frac{k_{cor}}{k_{cut}} h = \frac{k_{cor}}{k_{cut}} \frac{1}{4} \frac{c_{min}}{f_{max}}. \quad (7)$$

Obviously, the values of k_{cut} and k_{cor} determine the spatial extent of the nonnegligible variations of the wavenumber-limited medium.

As already mentioned, in practice, that is in numerical simulations, the spatial extent is limited by the material heterogeneity, the finite grid, the free surface, and possibly also by the source. The corresponding limitations for the spatial extent of the wavenumber-limited medium could potentially cause values of k_{cut} larger than those required by the grid dispersion of the FD scheme. Therefore, it is necessary to make an approximation as a compromise in the presence of several factors affecting accuracy of the modeling. The compromise mainly relates to the wavenumber filter.

Denoting a material parameter by P and filter by F, we recall the relation

$$\mathcal{F}^{-1}_{k\to z}\{\tilde{F}(k)\ \tilde{P}(k)\} = F(z) * P(z). \quad (8)$$

We see that in practice it might be reasonable to (1) design a filter in the wavenumber domain, (2) transform it to the spatial domain with sampling considerably finer than the grid spacing, (3) restrict its spatial extent using a suitable window, (4) check the spatially restricted filter in the wavenumber domain, and, if acceptable, (5) apply the filter in the spatial domain through the convolution with the material parameter, and (6) downsample the material parameter.

Numerical Test: Accuracy of a Reflected Wave

Configuration

Consider a 1D problem for a model of two homogeneous half-spaces. The wavespeeds in the lower and upper half-spaces are 300 and 100 m/s, respectively. A constant density of 2500 kg/m^3 is assumed. A plane wave is generated 600 m beneath the interface. The source time function is obtained by application of the Butterworth filter to the Fourier spectrum of the Dirac impulse and a subsequent application of the Blackman window in the time domain. The source time function and its amplitude Fourier spectrum are shown in Figure 2. The spectral amplitude falls by three orders approximately at the frequency of 5 Hz. Therefore, we will consider this frequency as a reasonable maximum frequency of the wavefield. The corresponding minimum wavelength is $\lambda_{min} = 100$ m/s/5 Hz $= 20$ m, and the corresponding maximum wavenumber is $k_{max} = 2\pi/\lambda_{min} = \pi/10$ m^{-1}.

The plane wave propagates upward in the lower half-space and reaches the interface. A transmitted wave propagates upward in the upper half-space, and a reflected wave propagates downward in the lower half-space. As explained in the exemplary 1D test presented by Valovcan *et al.* (2024), we should be primarily interested in the reflected wave. We "record" the reflected wave at the position where the plane wave was generated.

For the considered medium-wavefield configuration, we compare three independent solutions for the reflected wave:

- ES is an exact analytical solution.
- FDA is an FD method (staggered-grid, velocity–stress, fourth order in space, second order in time) with arithmetically averaged compliance, that is, harmonically averaged elastic modulus (Moczo *et al.*, 2002, 2014). We use 10 grid spacings per λ_{min}. (This choice is "cautious," ensuring sufficiently small grid-dispersion error without conflicting with the goal of the test.) This means grid spacing $h = 2$ m. Consequently, $k_N = \pi/2$ m^{-1}.
- FDWL is an FD method (staggered-grid, velocity–stress, fourth order in space, second order in time) with a wavenumber-limited medium. If we want to have the wavefield

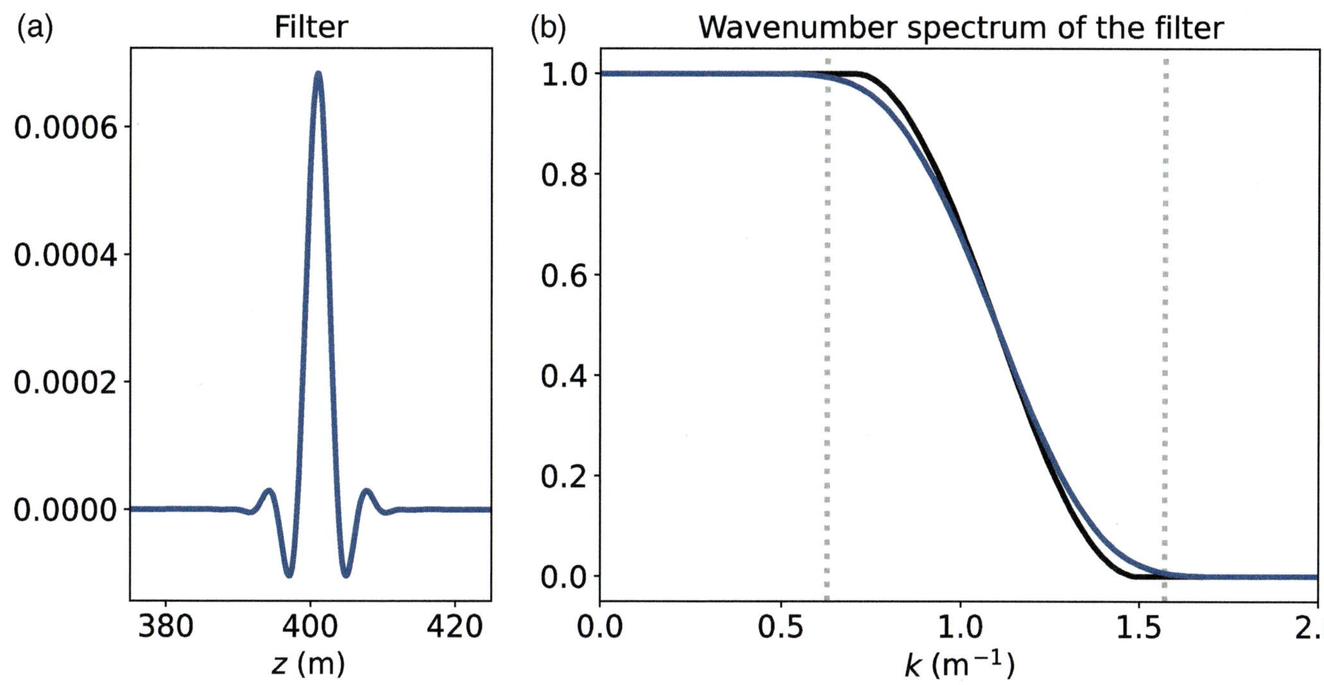

Figure 3. (a) Final spatial filter used for the wavenumber limitation of the medium. (b) Solid black—originally designed filter (as in Fig. 1b), which has an infinite spatial extent. Solid blue—the final (truncated) filter corresponding to the spatial filter in panel (a). The left-vertical dotted bar corresponds to the wavenumber accuracy limit k_m. The right-vertical dotted bar corresponds to the Nyquist wavenumber k_N.

sufficiently accurate up to wavenumber $k_{\max} = \pi/10\ \mathrm{m}^{-1}$, we must limit the medium by $k_m = 2k_{\max} = \pi/5\ \mathrm{m}^{-1}$.

Wavenumber limitation using a spatial filter

For the wavenumber limitation of the medium, we first designed a filter in the wavenumber domain:

$$\tilde{F}(k) = \begin{cases} 1 & k \in [0, k_{\mathrm{cor}}] \\ \frac{1}{2}\left[1 + \cos\left(\pi \frac{k - k_{\mathrm{cor}}}{k_{\mathrm{cut}} - k_{\mathrm{cor}}}\right)\right] & k \in [k_{\mathrm{cor}}, k_{\mathrm{cut}}] . \\ 0 & k \geq k_{\mathrm{cut}} \end{cases} \tag{9}$$

Values of k_{cor} (which must be larger than k_m) and k_{cut} (which must be smaller than k_N) used for the numerical test were, 0.7 and 1.5 m^{-1}, respectively.

The corresponding filter in the spatial domain was obtained by the inverse Fourier transform. Because it has an infinite spatial extent, it must be truncated. We truncated it using the Blackman window

$$W_B = \begin{cases} 0.42 - 0.50\cos\left(\pi \frac{z - z_c + w}{w}\right) + 0.08\cos\left(2\pi \frac{z - z_c + w}{w}\right); |z - z_c| \leq w \\ 0; |z - z_c| > w \end{cases} . \tag{10}$$

The filter is truncated at its zero values at half-width w from its center at z_c. Expertly, we chose $w \approx 12.5h$. The final filter in the spatial and wavenumber domain is shown in Figure 3. As can be seen in Figure 3b, the truncation in the spatial domain slightly modifies the filter in the wavenumber domain. Still, however, for $k < k_m$ it is $\tilde{F}(k) \approx 1$, and for $k > k_{\mathrm{cut}}$ it is $\tilde{F}(k) \approx 0$.

The wavenumber limitation itself is performed by a convolution of the spatial filter with the original compliance.

FDA and FDWL solutions

Assuming the fixed position of the source, each ES, FDA, and FDWL solution corresponds to a specific position of the true interface in a spatial FD grid. This is because both FDA and FDWL approaches make it possible to consider an arbitrary position of the interface within a grid spacing (in 1D this means anywhere within one grid cell).

In the FDA approach, we account for a position of the interface within a grid spacing by evaluating effective grid modulus at grid position (here, e.g., $I + 1/2$) as an integral harmonic average between grid points I and $I + 1$ (Moczo *et al.*, 2002, 2014)

$$M^H_{I+1/2} \equiv \left[\frac{1}{h}\int_{z_I}^{z_{I+1}} \frac{1}{M(z)} \mathrm{d}z\right]^{-1} . \tag{11}$$

The harmonic averaging of the modulus is equivalent to arithmetic averaging of the compliance. Moczo *et al.* (2002, 2014) demonstrated a very good level of accuracy and very good subcell resolution of this representation of the material interface.

In the FDWL approach, we apply wavenumber limitation to compliance. Then, we calculate the corresponding modulus. Although we did not apply the limitation to the modulus itself, we call it the wavenumber-limited modulus. Then we simply position, say $M^{\mathrm{WL}}_{I+1/2}$, in the grid points. In Figure 4, we show

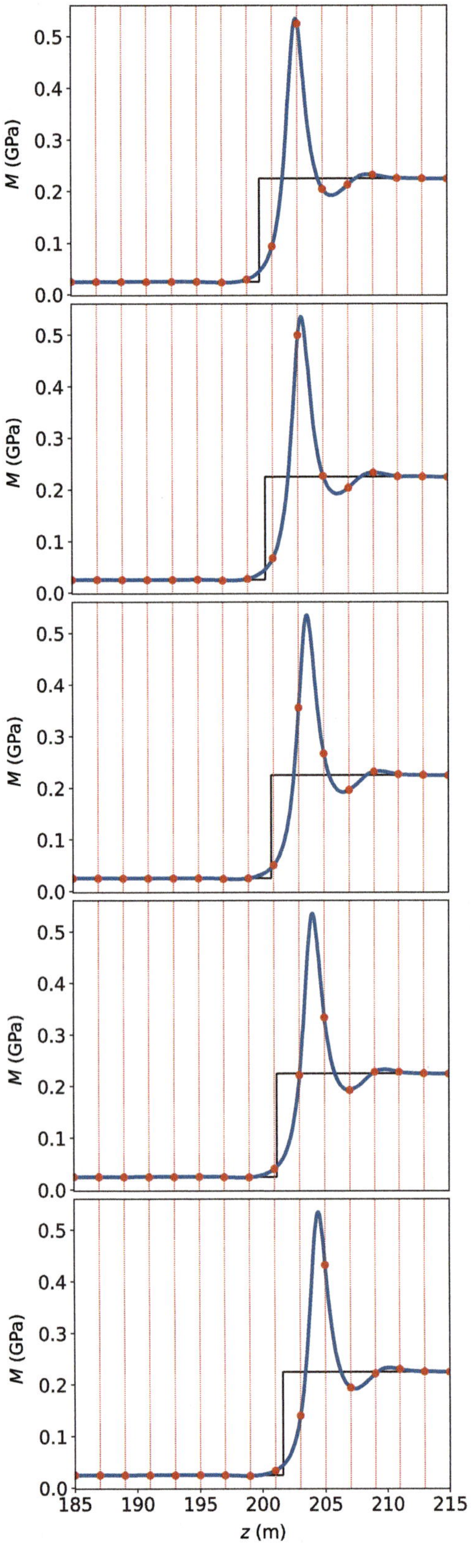

Figure 4. Five positions of the material interface in the spatial grid used for finite-difference (FD) simulations. The true modulus $M(z)$ is shown in solid black. Red-dotted lines represent grid lines (in 1D representing grid positions of stress). Solid-blue line represents the wavenumber limited modulus $M^{\mathrm{WL}}(z)$, and red dots represent values of $M^{\mathrm{WL}}_{I+1/2}$ entering the FD scheme for the FDWL simulation.

five different positions of the interface within a grid spacing. In each of the five panels, the red-dotted lines represent grid lines (in 1D representing grid points—positions of stress and thus also modulus in the staggered grid). The true modulus $M(z)$ is shown in solid black, and the wavenumber-limited modulus $M^{\mathrm{WL}}(z)$ is shown in solid blue. Red dots represent values of $M^{\mathrm{WL}}(z)$ sampled by the spatial grid, that is, $M^{\mathrm{WL}}_{I+1/2}$ values. Note that just these sampled values represent the wavenumber-limited medium in the FD scheme.

We can clearly see that each position of the true interface in the grid (shown in solid black) is represented in the wavenumber-limited medium by differently positioned samples (red dots) of $M^{\mathrm{WL}}(z)$. Note that only in two positions of the interface is $M^{\mathrm{WL}}(z)$ sampled close to its peak value.

Comparison of FDA and FDWL with the exact solution

We removed the incident wave from the total wavefield in the lower half-space to obtain the reflected wave. We compare reflected waves in the three solutions, that is, exact, FDA, and FDWL, in Figure 5 using time–frequency envelope misfit (TFEM) and time–frequency phase misfit (TFPM) according to Kristekova *et al.* (2009). The figure consists of five panels. Each panel compares three solutions for one of the five positions of the material interface in the grid shown in Figure 4. The position is indicated in the left column. The left of the comparing panels shows TFEM and TFPM between the FDA and the exact solutions. The right panel shows TFEM and TFPM between the FDWL and the exact solutions. Signal of the reflected wave is also shown for all three solutions. The values of the single-valued envelope misfit (EM) and phase misfit (PM) evaluated over the entire time and frequency ranges are also shown.

There are two most striking features of the comparison: (a) TFEM and TFPM between the FDWL and exact solutions do not change with the position of the interface in the grid, and the maximum EM and PM are as low as 0.08% and 0.07%, respectively; (b) TFEM and TFPM between the FDA and exact solution vary, but they are all smaller than or equal to 0.38% and 0.09%, respectively. This is why we cannot recognize FD seismograms from the exact seismograms and see only one (red) color of the seismogram. In other words, both FD solutions are excellent and with subcell resolution, but FDWL is simply better because its accuracy does not change with the position of the interface in the grid.

The accuracy of the FDWL solution for any position of the interface in the grid can be demonstrated also in Figure 6. Again, we compare FDA versus the exact solution and FDWL versus the exact solution. Here, we show only time envelope misfit, however, for 13 positions within a grid spacing. All misfits between the FDA and the exact solution are shown in the left frame. We can see that misfits for different positions of the interface differ from each other. At the same time, they are all very small—the absolute values are less than 0.5%. The

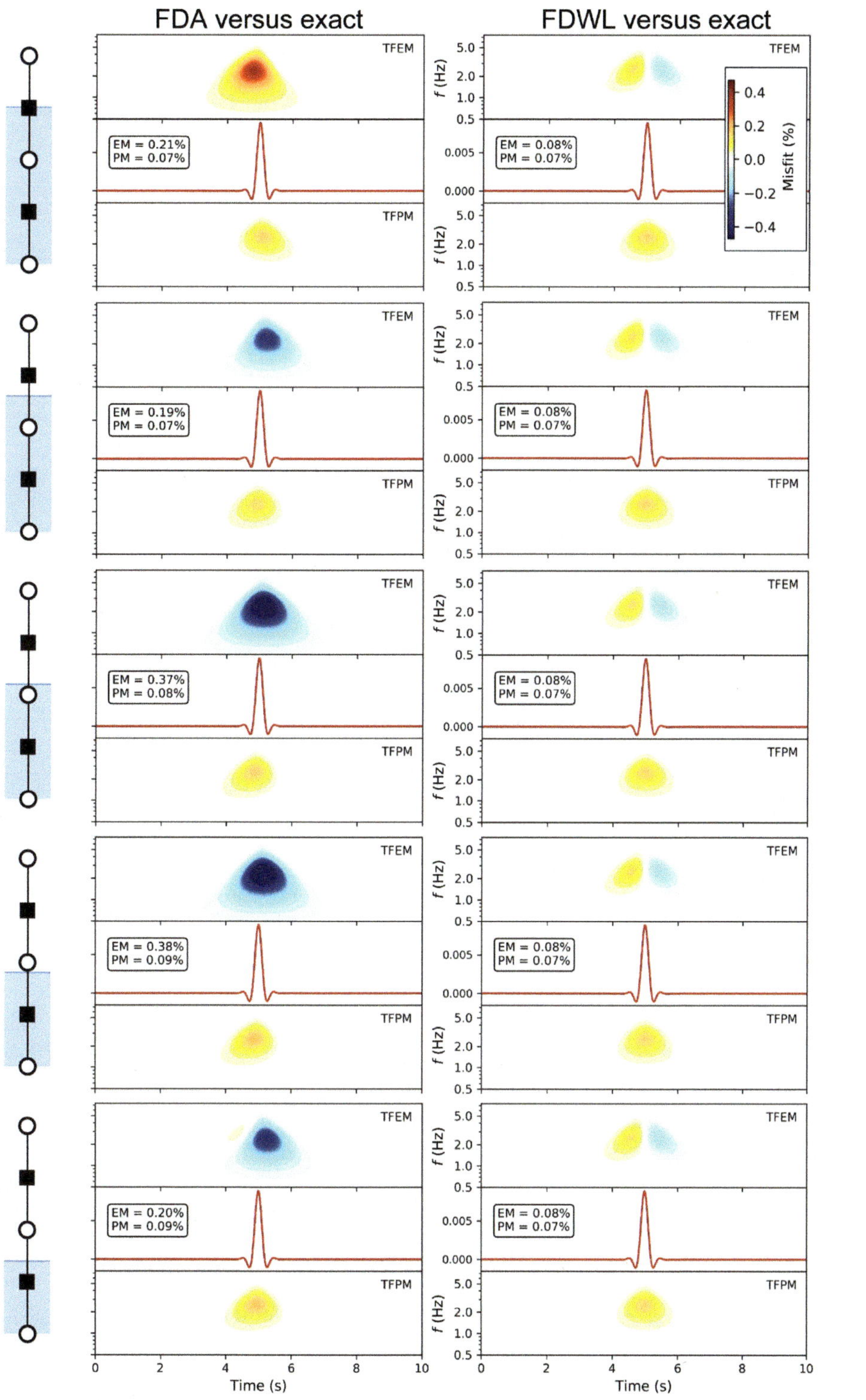

Figure 5. Comparison of the FDA (FD with arithmetically averaged compliance—corresponding to the harmonically averaged modulus) and FDWL (FD with wavenumber-limited compliance) solutions with the exact analytical solution using time–frequency envelope misfit (TFEM) and time–frequency phase misfit (TFPM) for the wave reflected from the interface between two half-spaces. The left column shows positions of the material interface in the FD spatially staggered grid. Circles represent grid positions of the stress; black squares represent grid positions of the particle velocity. Signals of the reflected waves are also shown. The exact solution is in solid red, the FD solutions in solid black (not seen due to very good agreement between signals). Single-valued envelope misfit (EM) and phase misfit (PM) evaluated over the entire time and frequency ranges are also shown.

comparison between FDWL and the exact solution confirms what we could see already in Figure 5—the misfit is the same for all positions of the interface in the grid.

In Figure 6, we also show the misfits between the FD solutions and the exact solution for the direct wave. By the direct wave, we mean the wave propagating in the homogeneous medium with material properties of the lower half-space, and propagating the same time as is the time between the radiation of the wave and recording the reflected wave at the receiver. (The same time in the same medium is important to have the same cumulative effect of the grid dispersion.) We can see that the misfit for the direct wave is the same as the misfit for the reflected waves (plural because we consider reflected waves simulated using FDWL for 13 positions of the interface in the grid). This means that there is no interface error in the FDWL solutions and the misfit quantifies nothing else than the grid-dispersion error! The absence of the interface error in all FDWL solutions is a very significant result. The meaning of this result is nothing less than the proof of concept of the wavenumber-limited representation of the material heterogeneity!

Numerical Test: Accuracy Across the Entire Model

In the first numerical test, we looked at the accuracy of the reflected wave at a distance from the interface, which is considerably larger than the extent of the spatial filter used for the wavenumber limitation.

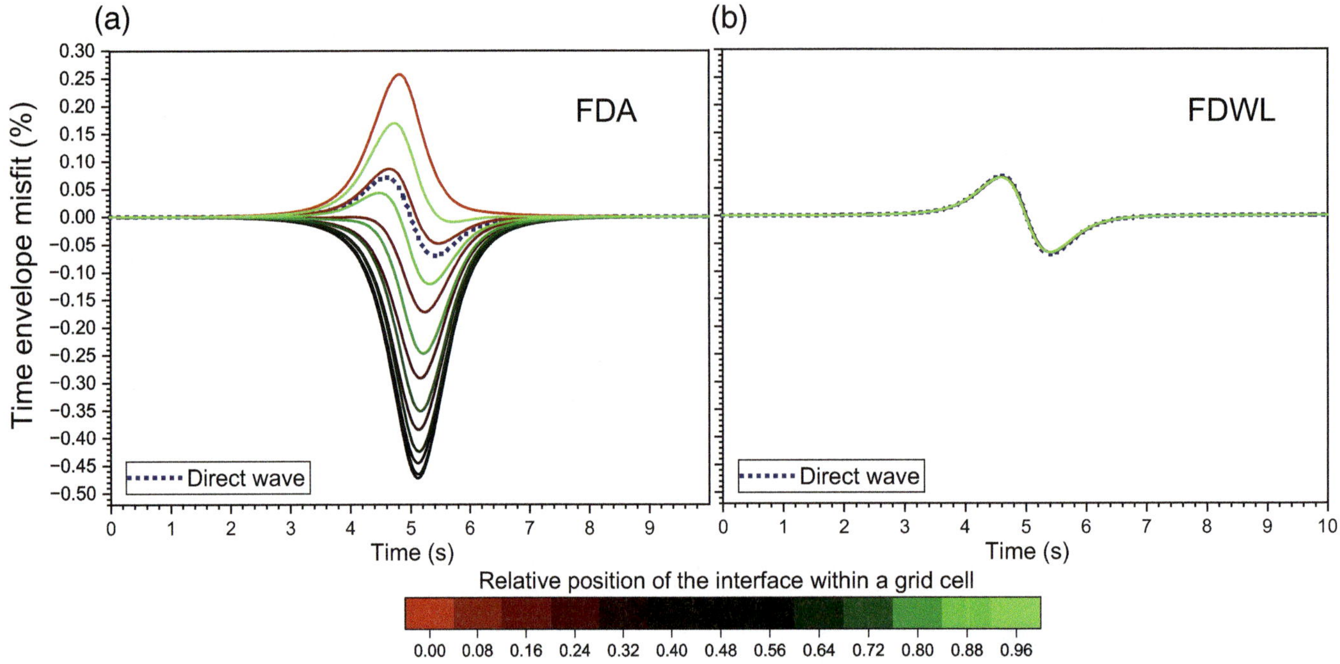

Figure 6. Comparison of (a) FDA (FD with harmonically averaged modulus) and (b) FDWL (FD with wavenumber-limited medium) solutions with the exact analytical solution using time envelope misfit for the wave reflected from the interface between two half-spaces (solid lines with color corresponding to the position of the interface in the grid) and for the direct wave (blue-dotted line). Thirteen positions of the material interface within a grid spacing are considered.

Here, we will look at the accuracy of the wavefield across the entire model. Therefore, we will include also the transmitted wave in the upper half-space.

Configuration and methods of computation

The wavefield-medium configuration is the same as that in the first numerical test. We applied the same three methods to compute the total wavefield. In the upper half-space we obviously obtained the transmitted wave, whereas in the lower half-space we removed the incident wave from the total wavefield to obtain the reflected wave.

Comparison of FDA and FDWL with the exact solution

We compare the three solutions, exact, FDA, and FDWL, using single-valued EM and PM according to Kristekova *et al.* (2009). Figure 7 shows EM and PM between the FD and exact solutions. FDA indicates the EM and PM between FDA and ES. FDWL indicates the EM and PM between FDWL and ES. Both EM and PM are shown as functions of the absolute position of receiver with respect to the interface and the relative position of the interface within a grid spacing. Position 0 m of the receiver (on the vertical axis) corresponds to the top of the grid cell within which we position the interface. Relative position 0.0 of the interface (on the horizontal axis) means the interface at the grid position of the particle velocity (see the top panel in Fig. 5). Relative position 1.0 means the interface just one grid spacing lower—again at the grid position of the particle velocity. For example, point [0.4, 200] means that the receiver is at $z = 200$ m and the interface is at $z = 0.4\ h = 0.8$ m, which means that the receiver is 199.2 m below the interface.

We can easily see several striking features. The two most important at first sight are the principal difference between FDA and FDWL, and the small values of both EM and PM for both FD solutions.

The largest values of PM are restricted to a thin effective layer around the interface in both FD solutions. In the FDA solution, they are smaller than 0.5%, and the thickness of the effective layer is determined by the spatial extent of the FD stencil. In the FDWL solution, they are smaller than 2%, and the thickness of the layer is determined by both the spatial extents of the FD stencil and the filter. Outside the effective layers, PM for both FD solutions is very small.

The largest values of EM are restricted to a thin layer around the interface in the FDWL solution, for which they are smaller than 0.75%. As in the case of PM, the thickness of the layer is determined by both the spatial extents of the FD stencil and the filter. Outside the layer, the extremely small values of EM are caused solely by the grid dispersion (recall Fig. 6). It is very clear that we do not see any dependence of EM or PM on the relative position of the interface within a grid spacing. We should not hesitate to speak about the perfect subcell resolution of the FDWL solution.

In the case of FDA, the largest value of EM is about 0.4% in the lower half-space with higher wavespeed and about 0.15 % in the upper half-space. The largest values are not restricted only to the vicinity of the interface. The amplitude of EM changes only

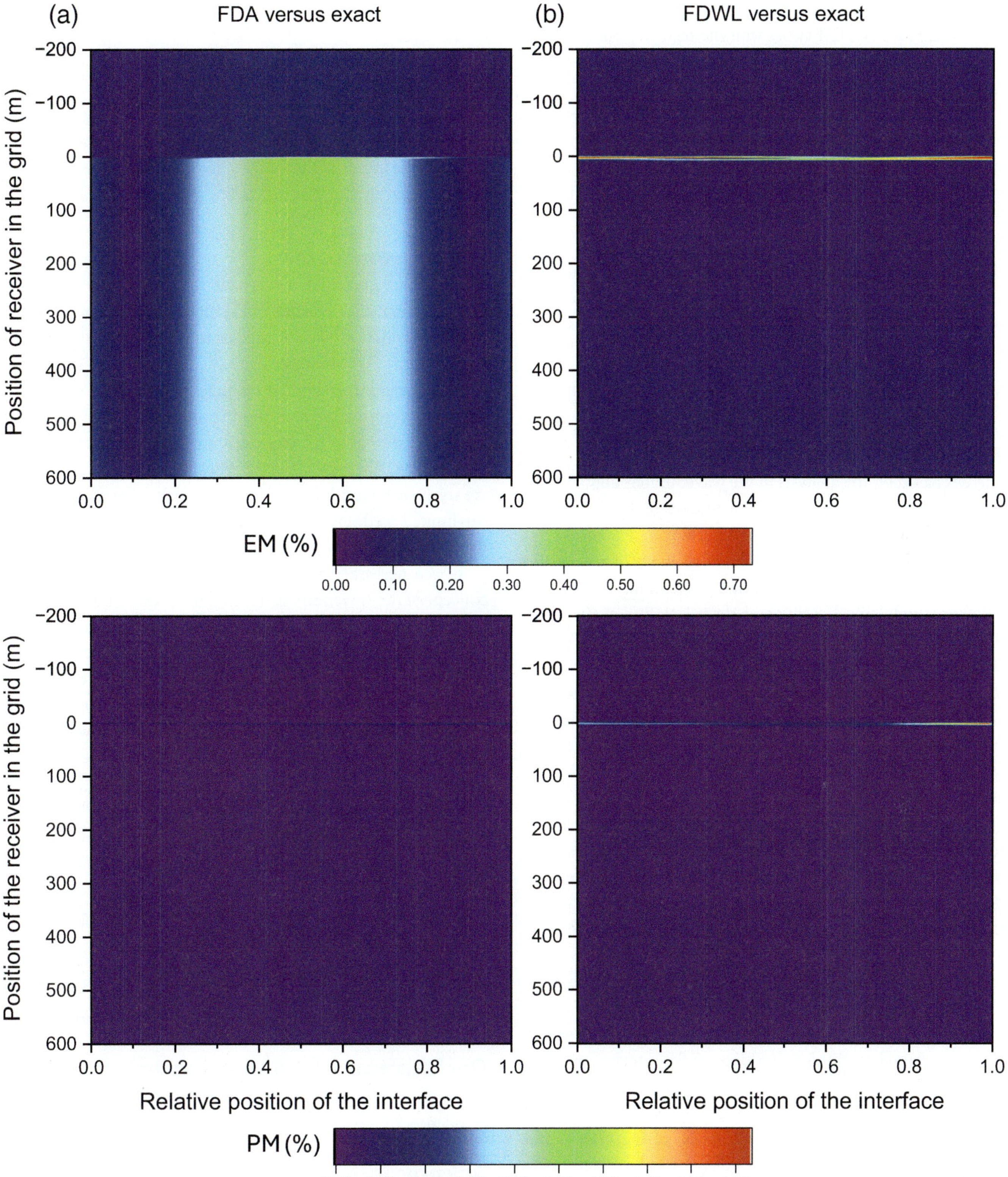

Figure 7. Comparison of (a) FDA and (b) FDWL versus the exact solution for the model of two homogeneous half-spaces. The differences between FD and the exact solutions are quantified by single-valued time-frequency envelope misfit (EM) and single-valued time-frequency phase misfit (PM). The misfit values are overall very small. The principal difference between the FDA and FDWL solutions is that the accuracy of the FDWL solution does not depend on the relative position of the interface within a grid spacing—we may speak of the perfect subcell resolution of the FDWL solution. The misfits of the FDWL solution in the half-spaces are only due to grid dispersion—not affected by the interface error.

slightly with the distance from the interface due to grid dispersion. However, EM varies with the relative position of the interface within a grid spacing. Recall that this variation does not exist in FDWL solution.

EM of both the transmitted and reflected waves in FDA is related to the spatial extent of the fourth-order operator. We checked this by evaluating also EM and PM for the FDA wavefield obtained using a second-order FD scheme. EM and PM are smaller in the second-order solution. This is related to the fact that the harmonic averaging of modulus (Moczo *et al.*, 2002) is applied over one grid spacing and thus is more suitable for the second-order scheme (using an operator with a shorter stencil). Obviously, such an approach requires finer spatial sampling.

Conclusions

This study is a necessary logical continuation, literally a proof of concept, of our current investigations on the accuracy of FD schemes based on the analysis in the wavenumber domain. We have performed a detailed numerical analysis of the accuracy of the implementation of a material interface in FD modeling, following the recently identified limit of accuracy of a wavefield in a wavenumber-limited model of the medium.

For methodological clarity and clean isolation of the effect of wavenumber limitation of the medium, we investigated the accuracy of the reflected and the transmitted waves in a 1D problem of two homogeneous half-spaces. We calculated the wavefield using three methods: exact analytical method, FD scheme (FDA) for arithmetically averaged compliance (i.e., harmonically averaged modulus) and FD scheme (FDWL) for wavenumber-limited medium.

We used a finite-extent spatial filter to wavenumber limit the medium. We evaluated the TFEMs and TFPMs between the FDA and the exact solution as well as the misfits between the FDWL and the exact solution in the entire computational domain. The results of the analysis may be formulated as follows.

1. The time–frequency misfits between the FD and the exact analytical solutions are very small.
2. Both FDA and FDWL have the subcell resolution capability —they can sense different positions of the interface within a grid spacing.
3. However, there is a principal difference between FDA and FDWL. Whereas the subcell resolution of the FDA is not perfect (the misfit between the FDA and the exact solution varies a little bit with position of the interface within a grid spacing), the misfit between the FDWL and the exact solution is the same and very small for any position of the interface within a grid spacing. The misfits in FDWL for the reflected and transmitted waves are solely caused by the grid dispersion of the FD scheme. In other words: FDWL exhibits a perfect subcell resolution, and the demonstrated nature and level of accuracy may be considered proof of concept of the wavenumber limitation of the medium.
4. The largest values of the EM are restricted to a thin layer around the interface in the FDWL solution, for which they are smaller than 0.75%. The thickness of the layer is determined by the spatial extents of the FD stencil and the filter. The most important is the fact that in FDWL, the error at, and very near, the interface does not propagate into half-spaces.

The main conclusion

We have numerically demonstrated accuracy of the implementation of a material interface in FD modeling based on the wavenumber limitation of the medium. We used a finite-extent spatial filter to wavenumber limit the medium. The FD scheme for the wavenumber-limited medium has a perfect subcell resolution: the misfit between the FD and exact solutions is very small and the same for any position of the interface within a grid spacing. The misfits for the reflected and transmitted waves are solely due to grid dispersion. FD modeling for the wavenumber-limited medium is considerably more accurate than that for the harmonically averaged modulus.

It was necessary to provide a detailed numerical proof of concept of the wavenumber-limited medium in the fundamental methodological model—a material interface between the two homogeneous half-spaces. The next step will be to develop finite-extent spatial filtering to wavenumber limit the medium in 2D and 3D. We assume that development of a practical "recipe" will be a challenging task. If successfully developed, we assume that the spatial filtering in 2D and 3D will be applicable also in other most important numerical-modeling methods—spectral-element method (e.g., Komatitsch and Vilotte, 1998; Lyu *et al.*, 2020), discontinuous Galerkin method (e.g., Käser and Dumbser, 2006; Wolf *et al.*, 2020), and the recent and promising distributional FD method (e.g., Masson, 2023; Lyu *et al.*, 2024)—inside an element in which material parameters are functions of spatial coordinates.

Data and Resources

There are no new data or resources to report for this article.

Declaration of Competing Interests

The authors acknowledge that there are no conflicts of interest recoded.

Acknowledgments

The authors thank reviewers Wei Zhang and Chao Lyu for their reviews, which helped them to improve the article. This work was supported by the Slovak Research and Development Agency under the Contract Number APVV-24-0311 (Project SANEFF).

References

Chen, H., K. Chen, L. Wang, H. Zhou, H. Zhang, and W. Sun (2024). An efficient immersed free surface boundary method for 3-D scalar seismic waves finite-difference modeling in presence of topography, *IEEE Trans. Geosci. Remote Sens.* **62,** 1–12.

Fichtner, A. (2011). *Full Seismic Waveform Modelling and Inversion*, Springer, Heidelberg, Germany.

Holberg, O. (1987). Computational aspects of the choice of operator and sampling interval for numerical differentiation in large-scale simulation of wave phenomena, *Geophys. Prospect.* **37,** no. 6, 629–655.

Igel, H., P. Mora, and B. Riollet (1995). Anisotropic wave propagation through finite-difference grids, *Geophysics* **60,** no. 4, 1203–1216.

Jiang, L., and W. Zhang (2021). TTI equivalent medium parametrization method for the seismic waveform modelling of heterogeneous media with coarse grids, *Geophys. J. Int.* **227,** 2016–2043.

Käser, M., and M. Dumbser (2006). An arbitrary high-order discontinuous Galerkin method for elastic waves on unstructured meshes – I. The two-dimensional isotropic case with external source terms, *Geophys. J. Int.* **166,** 855–877.

Koene, E. F. M., J. Wittsten, and J. O. A. Robertsson (2022). Finite-difference modelling of 2-D wave propagation in the vicinity of dipping interfaces: A comparison of anti-aliasing and equivalent medium approaches, *Geophys. J. Int.* **229,** 70–96.

Komatitsch, D., and J.-P. Vilotte (1998). The spectral element method: An efficient tool to simulate the seismic response of 2D and 3D geological structures, *Bull. Seismol. Soc. Am.* **88,** 368–392.

Kristekova, M., J. Kristek, and P. Moczo (2009). Time-frequency misfit and goodness-of-fit criteria for quantitative comparison of time signals, *Geophys. J. Int.* **178,** 813–825.

Liu, Y. (2022). Removing the stability limit of the time-space domain explicit finite-difference schemes for acoustic modeling with stability condition-based spatial operators, *Geophysics* **87,** no. 3, T205–T223.

Lyu, C., Y. Capdeville, and L. Zhao (2020). Efficiency of the spectral element method with very high polynomial degree to solve the elastic wave equation, *Geophysics* **85,** no. 2, T33–T43.

Lyu, C., Y. Masson, B. Romanowicz, and L. Zhao (2024). Introduction to the distributional finite difference method for 3D seismic wave propagation and comparison with the spectral element method, *J. Geophys. Res.* **129,** no. 4, e2023JB027576, doi: 10.1029/2023JB027576.

Masson, Y. (2023). Distributional finite-difference modelling of seismic waves, *Geophys. J. Int.* **233,** 264–296.

Mittet, R. (2017). On the internal interfaces in finite-difference schemes, *Geophysics* **82,** no. 4, T159–T182.

Mittet, R. (2021a). On the pseudospectral method and spectral accuracy, *Geophysics* **86,** no. 3, T127–T142.

Mittet, R. (2021b). Small-scale medium variations with high-order finite-difference and pseudospectral schemes, *Geophysics* **86,** no. 5, T387–T399.

Moczo, P., J. Kristek, and M. Galis (2014). *The Finite-Difference Modelling of Earthquake Motions: Waves and Ruptures*, Cambridge University Press, Cambridge, United Kingdom.

Moczo, P., J. Kristek, M. Kristekova, J. Valovcan, M. Galis, and D. Gregor (2022). Material interface in the finite-difference modeling: A fundamental view, *Bull. Seismol. Soc. Am.* **113,** no. 1, 281–296.

Moczo, P., J. Kristek, V. Vavryčuk, R. J. Archuleta, and L. Halada (2002). 3D heterogeneous staggered-grid finite-difference modeling of seismic motion with volume harmonic and arithmetic averaging of elastic moduli and densities, *Bull. Seismol. Soc. Am.* **92,** no. 8, 3042–3066.

Mora, P. (1986). Elastic finite differences with convolutional operators, *Stanford Explor. Proj. Rep.* **48,** 277–289.

Valovcan, J., P. Moczo, J. Kristek, M. Galis, and M. Kristekova (2023). Can higher-order finite-difference operators be applied across a material interface? *Bull. Seismol. Soc. Am.* **113,** no. 5, 1924–1937.

Valovcan, J., P. Moczo, J. Kristek, M. Galis, and M. Kristekova (2024). How accurate numerical simulation of seismic waves in a heterogeneous medium can be? *Bull. Seismol. Soc. Am.* **114,** no. 5, 2287–2309.

Wolf, S., A.-A. Gabriel, M. Bader (2020). Optimisation and local time stepping of an ADER-DG scheme for fully anisotropic wave propagation in complex geometries, in *Computational Science – ICCS 2020*, V. V. Krzhizhanovskaya, *et al.* (Editors), Lecture Notes in Computer Science, Vol. 12,139, Springer, Cham, Switzerland.

Zhou, H., Y. Liu, and J. Wang (2022). Elastic wave modeling with high-order temporal and spatial accuracies by a selectively modified and linearly optimized staggered-grid finite-difference scheme, *IEEE Trans. Geosci. Remote Sens.* **60,** 1–22.

Zhou, H., L. Zhang, and Y. Zhang (2024). Simulation of scalar wave propagation with high-order temporal and spatial accuracy by a new multi-axial staggered-grid finite-difference scheme, *Bull. Seismol. Soc. Am.* **115,** no. 1, 1–21.

Manuscript received 4 August 2025
Published online 9 December 2025

Insights into ShakeAlert Earthquake Early Warning Alert Delivery by the MyShake Platform from Rapid Post-Event Analyses

OPEN ACCESS

Savvas Marcou*[1], Stephen Thompson[1], Angela I. Lux[1], Amy L. Williamson[1], Suresh Raman[1], Julien Marty[1], and Richard M. Allen[1]

Abstract

The U.S. Geological Survey's ShakeAlert earthquake early warning (EEW) system provides EEW alerts to the U.S. West Coast. ShakeAlert EEW alerts are distributed by alert delivery partners, such as the MyShake smartphone app, supported by earthquake warning in California and CalOES. MyShake has been delivering alerts since 2019 and currently serves over 2 million active EEW users. As alerts reach an ever-increasing number of users, there is a growing need to rapidly assess system performance and provide answers to commonly asked questions by EEW recipients about their EEW experience. MyShake harvests detailed alert delivery data from EEW recipients, including alert delivery latencies. We first present a retrospective analysis of MyShake delivery latencies across a large number of events. Latency is not a single number, but rather a distribution. We find the median of the 20th and 50th percentile delivery latencies across the events was 2.03 and 2.90 s, respectively. We find latencies have remained constant even with an increasing number of users while confirming they need to be considered for realistic warning time calculations. We leverage delivery latency data to develop a near-real-time, fully automated workflow that can produce data-driven warning time estimates for MyShake users. We develop user-friendly graphical products to present our results, including a joint map of median warning time contours and shaking distribution, and discuss how useful insights can be created for the general public and expert users alike. Our products can be rapidly disseminated via social media to satisfy the public's desire for information. Our results can also complement other efforts to assess ShakeAlert alerting performance, such as the Did-You-Feel-It supplemental EEW questionnaire. In addition, our workflow produces technical diagnostics that enable rapid detection of failures along the ShakeAlert–MyShake alerting pipeline.

Cite this article as Marcou, S., S. Thompson, A. I. Lux, A. L. Williamson, S. Raman, J. Marty, and R. M. Allen (2025). Insights into ShakeAlert Earthquake Early Warning Alert Delivery by the MyShake Platform from Rapid Post-Event Analyses, *Seismol. Res. Lett.* **XX**, 1976–1989, doi: 10.1785/0220250037.

Supplemental Material

Introduction

Earthquake early warning (EEW) aims to identify regions about to experience strong earthquake ground motion and alert them before strong ground motion arrives (Allen and Melgar, 2019). EEW systems (EEWSs) are proliferating globally at a fast pace (Allen and Stogaitis, 2022). Although a large body of scientific literature focuses on improving the efficacy of the systems that detect and characterize earthquakes in real time, detailed consideration of how alerts are delivered is lacking. The ability of an EEWS to deliver alerts quickly and efficiently, and provide users with adequate information to enable situational awareness, is also key to its success. Because EEWS expands, it becomes essential to rapidly assess end-to-end performance (from earthquake detection to alert delivery) in the immediate aftermath of an alert, in terms of the timeliness of alert arrival with respect to shaking and the success of the system in warning those who feel shaking. This is especially important as not all users who feel shaking will always get an alert, and some alerts will always arrive after shaking (Minson *et al.*, 2022). At the same time, social science research indicates that rapid alert delivery prompts the public to seek more information (e.g., Goltz *et al.*, 2024), highlighting the need for information to be made rapidly available to users. Rapid and effective communication helps avoid speculation, builds trust,

1. Berkeley Seismological Laboratory, University of California, Berkeley, Berkeley, California, U.S.A., https://orcid.org/0000-0003-3961-773X (SM); https://orcid.org/0000-0002-3767-6018 (AIL); https://orcid.org/0000-0003-1481-725X (ALW); https://orcid.org/0000-0003-4293-9772 (RMA)

*Corresponding author: savvas.marcou@berkeley.edu

and establishes an authoritative narrative (Seeger, 2006; Haynes *et al.*, 2008; McBride *et al.*, 2019).

In the United States, the U.S. Geological Survey (USGS) runs the ShakeAlert system, which has been sending out public alerts to U.S. West Coast users since October 2019 (Given *et al.*, 2018). The USGS is responsible for coordinating the operation of the real-time earthquake detection and characterization portion of the system. As a means of offering public information, the USGS publishes information about the performance of ShakeAlert via the event pages on the USGS Comprehensive Catalog (ComCat; U.S. Geological Survey [USGS] Earthquake Hazards Program, 2017). Recent efforts to establish post-alert information for ShakeAlert users include the development of post-alert messaging, aimed at helping users make sense of their experience of EEW (McBride *et al.*, 2020), as well as attempts to collect more information about users' experience of EEW using post-event surveys (Goltz *et al.*, 2023, 2024). However, the vast majority of users will get alerts via one of the ShakeAlert delivery partners, who are responsible for disseminating the alerts issued by ShakeAlert, and thus form an essential part of users' experience of EEW. One of these delivery partners is the MyShake smartphone app.

MyShake is a free app available for both Android and iOS smartphone devices that was initially developed to provide a global smartphone-based EEW system (Kong *et al.*, 2016). It has been downloaded over 4 million times globally. With the support of the state of California Governor's Office for Emergency Services (CalOES), MyShake has evolved into an official delivery platform for ShakeAlert EEW messages (Strauss *et al.*, 2020), delivering alerts since 2019. As of the end of 2024, MyShake has sent over 4 million alerts. User feedback from user emails and app reviews on the Google Play and Apple App stores indicates there are several common questions posed by MyShake users after an alert:

- Was I located within the alert area?
- I felt shaking. Why did I not get an alert?
- I did not feel shaking, but I got an alert?
- I got an alert, but it came after the shaking. Why?

These questions clearly indicate there is an appetite among users for more information about their experience. Uniquely, MyShake routinely harvests user data that can be used to assess user experience of EEW (Patel and Allen, 2022). However, there is potential for these data to be used more broadly in assessing the performance of ShakeAlert end-to-end, from alert generation to alert delivery, beyond its use in interpreting user experience.

EEW system performance is often judged in terms of the warning time available to users. Warning time is typically defined as the time a user has between the moment they have received an EEW message and the moment strong ground motion of a given level of interest (commonly termed the target threshold in the EEW literature) arrives at their location. It is thus the difference between the time it takes for strong ground motion to propagate from the earthquake source to the user's location, and the total time it takes for the end-to-end EEW pipeline to detect, characterize, publish, and deliver an alert. All components of the EEW pipeline take up a finite amount of time and thus take away from the available warning time. However, in the EEW literature, especially for studies evaluating the performance of individual algorithms (e.g., Allen *et al.*, 2009; Böse *et al.*, 2018; Minson *et al.*, 2020), warning time is often calculated without accounting for delivery delays, instead assuming that users get alerts instantaneously (i.e., as soon as they are issued). This yields an upper bound for warning time estimates because they are the maximum expected times; any delivery delays take away from available warning time. This assumption is often made due to the large variability of latencies across individual delivery mechanisms. Although alert delivery delays should not play a major role for machine-to-machine systems, where alerts are directly received from the issuing alert servers, recent work (e.g., Patel and Allen, 2022; McBride *et al.*, 2023) has shown that delivery latency becomes an issue for mass, personalized alert delivery to individual members of the general public. In these cases, alert delivery providers need to process an alert message from an EEW system and distribute it to the intended recipients, introducing non-negligible delays. As such, a realistic representation of the warning time experienced by the vast amount of EEW end-users must account for delivery latencies (Wald, 2020).

In this work, we present a methodology that leverages MyShake user data to assess the warning time performance of the ShakeAlert–MyShake alerting pipeline while at the same time producing insights that can address common user information needs. We first assess the utility of MyShake alert delivery latency data and present macroscopic properties of this unique dataset. We then put forth a fully automated, near-real-time approach for producing a consistent technical analysis of alerting performance following any individual earthquake that activates the ShakeAlert system and results in public alerts being sent by MyShake. We use alert delivery data collected from users to produce rapid data-driven estimates of the warning time distribution. We present user-friendly visualizations that aid in understanding user experience and gaining rapid insights into alerting performance, as well as directly addressing commonly asked questions posed by MyShake users. We also demonstrate how our workflow can isolate individual elements of the EEW pipeline to detect potential issues.

ShakeAlert

The USGS has been operating the ShakeAlert EEWS in collaboration with academic institutions and state agencies since 2012. ShakeAlert has been delivering public alerts in California since October 2019, in Oregon since March 2021, and in Washington since May 2021 (McBride *et al.*, 2022). ShakeAlert alert issuance

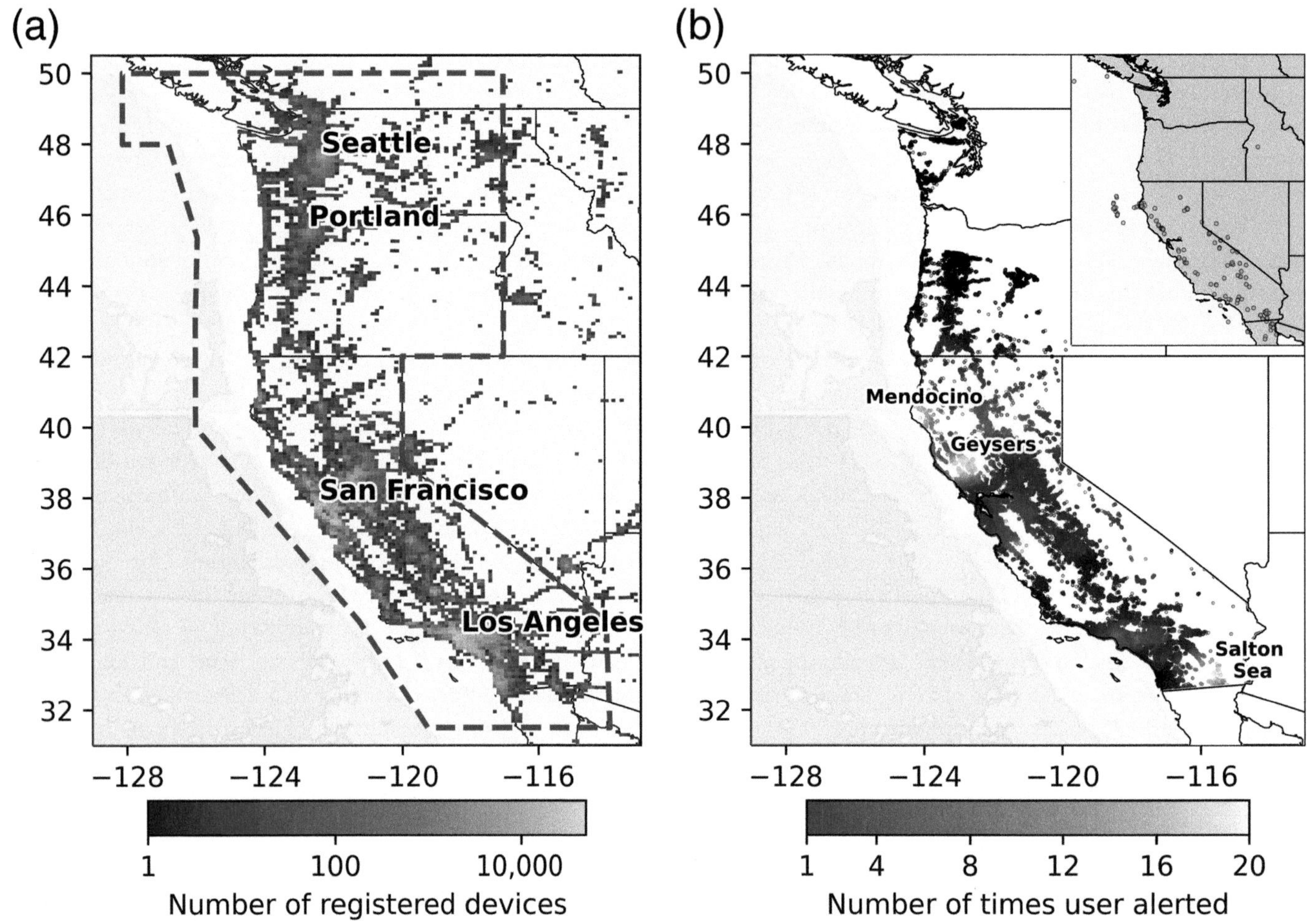

Figure 1. MyShake users and alerting history. (a) Distribution of MyShake users on the U.S. West Coast, as of July 2024. Users are grouped in 10 × 10 km cells. The red outline shows the ShakeAlert reporting region (Given *et al.*, 2018; Kohler *et al.*, 2020). (b) Number of times locations were alerted by MyShake between the start of public alerting on 19 October 2019, and 31 December 2024. The dots are sampled in space according to absolute population counts. The inset shows the locations of ShakeAlert estimated epicenters, plotted as orange dots, for all events considered. We plot the location associated with the alert update with the maximum modified Mercalli intensity (MMI) 3 contour radius. The color version of this figure is available only in the electronic edition.

is distributed across three layers (Kohler *et al.*, 2020): the data, production, and alert layers (see Fig. S1, available in the supplemental material to this article, for a schematic view). The data layer ingests ground-motion data from a real-time dense seismic network across the three states. The production layer comprises three EEW algorithms that rapidly detect earthquakes and issue source parameter estimates. Their source estimates are averaged by the solution aggregator (SA), and then passed to the ground-motion module (eqinfo2GM, Thakoor *et al.*, 2019), which then uses the aggregated source estimate to forecast the areas expected to experience ground shaking at modified Mercalli intensity (MMI) 2 through 9. This ground-shaking forecast is issued as contour and grid products. The contour product defines the area expected to feel shaking of a given intensity as an eight-sided polygon. The grid product defines the expected shaking on a 20 km spatial grid. Finally, the alert layer is responsible for publishing a ShakeAlert EEW alert, including the source estimate and ground-motion forecast, if the estimated magnitude exceeds M 3.5. This alert is broadcast to users by various licensed operators (LtOs, see Data and Resources for a list of LtOs) who use a variety of alerting thresholds (Given *et al.*, 2018; Chung *et al.*, 2020). For public alerting, an alert is issued for earthquakes with ShakeAlert magnitude estimates M 4.5 and greater, to any region within the ShakeAlert reporting region (Fig. 1) that is expected to experience MMI 3 (weak) shaking or stronger.

ShakeAlert mass public alerts are delivered via the Federal Emergency Management Agency's (FEMA) wireless emergency alerts (WEA) system as well as via smartphone-based platforms, such as the MyShake app (available for Android and iOS devices) and the Android earthquake alerts system (available on Android phones) (Chung *et al.*, 2020; Kohler *et al.*, 2020). Recent work has aimed to evaluate the delivery latency of various delivery platforms used in the ShakeAlert EEW pipeline. Using controlled testing, McBride *et al.* (2023) evaluated latencies for the WEA system, which alerts users within the MMI 4+ region when the ShakeAlert estimated magnitude exceeds M 5.0. For the version they tested, they found WEA added a median delivery delay of 8–10 s. Meanwhile, Patel and Allen (2022) examined delivery receipt data from smartphone devices that MyShake alerted during five events and found median delivery latencies of 3–5 s. It is thus clear that warning time assessments that ignore delivery latency will inevitably end up overestimating warning time.

MyShake App: Alerting Strategy and Previous Alert Delivery Performance Analyses

MyShake has been delivering public alerts in California since October 2019, in Oregon since March 2021, and in Washington since January 2022. About 2 million of MyShake's active users are now located across the three states served by ShakeAlert (Fig. 1a). MyShake uses the ShakeAlert contour product to alert users expected to feel MMI 3 (weak) or stronger shaking, for all earthquakes with a ShakeAlert estimated magnitude of $M \geq 4.5$. Each user is alerted only once for every distinct earthquake. MyShake alerts take over a user's screen and are accompanied by an alert tone followed by the audible message "Earthquake. Drop, Cover, Hold on. Shaking Expected" (Patel and Allen, 2022). As of 16 December 2024, MyShake sent 4.2 million alerts for 147 cataloged earthquakes. Following the M 6.4 Tofino earthquake offshore British Columbia in July 2024, when users in Washington were alerted for the first time, MyShake has now alerted users across all three states served by ShakeAlert. Current data show that at least one alert has been delivered via MyShake to all populated locations within California (Fig. 1b). Regions with high background seismicity levels, like the Mendocino area, as well as swarm-producing areas, like the Geysers and Salton Sea areas, have been alerted over 15 times.

MyShake alerts users based on their location. MyShake uses either dynamically reported locations by device location services, or a static location reported by users upon registration (termed HomeBase). MyShake stores an alerting cache of user locations using 10 × 10 km military grid reference system (MGRS) cells for all three states offering ShakeAlert EEW. MyShake servers continuously watch all six ShakeAlert alert servers for new alert updates. Once a new event message is received, the server computes all MGRS cells that intersect with the MMI 3 polygon. It then pushes a list of all users found within these cells to message distribution services, which are tasked with delivering alert messages to smartphones as quickly as possible. On receipt of further ShakeAlert updates, the server checks whether they update an event in progress (if locations and origin times are within 100 km and 16 s, respectively), or are a new event. Because MyShake receives information from multiple alert servers, this filtering procedure ensures that redundant alert information is filtered out and the latest information is being used. For any incoming message deemed to be an update to an existing event, it computes which cells lie within the new MMI 3 polygon and have not been alerted yet, and then forwards user lists to distribution. To keep processing latencies low, MyShake assigns groups of users to parallel processing threads, which process incoming ShakeAlert updates in parallel, independently of each other (Patel and Allen, 2022). Each MyShake thread will always check for the latest update received across the six ShakeAlert servers whenever it becomes free to do so (i.e., finishes processing a previously received update). As such, MyShake does not issue alerts for every single individual update received from ShakeAlert. For the benefit of the reader, we provide a schematic overview of how MyShake interacts with ShakeAlert in Figure S1.

Patel and Allen (2022) produced the first assessment of alert delivery latency performance using data routinely harvested by MyShake. The MyShake server requests an alert delivery receipt from all alerted devices. These receipts contain performance data on alerting performance and are received by MyShake servers within the first 15 min of an alert being issued. More specifically, receipts record the times at which different processing steps are completed during the MyShake alerting workflow. Patel and Allen (2022) presented the alert acknowledgment time metric, which is the time between the receipt of ShakeAlert message by MyShake and the moment an individual user's device displayed the alert, and thus represents the total MyShake delivery latency. They used this metric to calculate warning times to the S-wave arrival for a small dataset from five representative events in California in 2020, for which MyShake delivered a total of just over 120,000 alerts. However, MyShake has since delivered millions of alerts, and as such, a more comprehensive evaluation of latency data and how it can be used to analyze warning time performance in the aftermath of EEW alerts is due.

Analysis of MyShake Alert Delivery Latency

The first step in developing a workflow for calculating and visualizing the warning times MyShake users experience is to assess the latency data MyShake harvests. MyShake harvests receipts from user devices that contain the time at which a MyShake phone received an alert message, as well as the time a ShakeAlert message was received. The difference between the two timestamps gives the added delivery delay MyShake adds for delivering alerts to its users. This term was introduced by Patel and Allen (2022) as the alert acknowledgement time, but in this work, we refer to it as MyShake delivery latency (t_{delivery}), for simplicity. Currently, MyShake harvests these latency measurements from user devices via two distinct avenues. One is based on rapid message receipts (MRs), which are immediately available from a small subset of alerted devices, and were used by Patel and Allen (2022) in their analysis. A more complete collection of latency measurements is available from analytics (AN) services provided by message distribution services 3–5 days after an event. The MR dataset is a subset of the AN dataset. We macroscopically analyze both datasets to reaffirm the importance of including latency in warning time calculations, although detailed spatiotemporal analysis is beyond the scope of this article. For the purposes of calculating warning time consistently, in near-real time, including latency, we also verify if there is agreement between MR-based rapid results and the more complete AN-based results.

In Figure 2, we show the 20th, 50th, and 80th percentiles of alert delivery latency calculated from the MR and AN methods for 33 events processed by MyShake between September 2022 and December 2024, for which MyShake sent 10,000 or more alerts. We select this period for analysis because it represents the time after which alert delivery was parallelized. It is important to consider the percentiles of the latency distribution for any given event, rather than a single number, because MyShake delivery latency has a long-tailed distribution, as previously shown by Patel and Allen (2022). As we will demonstrate in Figure 3, the long-tailed latency distribution in turn causes the warning time distribution to have a waterfall-like appearance.

We observe from Figure 2 that 50th percentile delivery latency has remained largely constant, even as the number of users has increased. The August 2024 **M** 5.2 Lamont earthquake, for which MyShake sent 517,354 alerts, stands as a clear outlier with delivery latencies around 20 s. This was caused by some of the parallel alerting runs used by MyShake (see the MyShake App: Alerting Strategy and Previous Alert Delivery Performance Analyses section) experiencing a connection timeout issue to one of MyShake's message distribution partners. For earthquakes for which MyShake sent out similar numbers of alerts, such as the August 2024 **M** 4.4 Highland Park event (381,255 alerts), the September 2024 **M** 4.7 Malibu event (425,217 alerts), or the December 2024 **M** 7.0 Cape Mendocino event (468,247 alerts), median MyShake latencies generally remained around 5 s. We also note that there are differences between earthquakes. These are driven by highly event-specific factors that are beyond the scope of this article.

Over all the earthquakes considered here, using the complete AN dataset, the medians of the 20th, 50th, and 80th percentiles were 2.03, 2.90, and 4.64 s, respectively. In other words, one can typically expect that 20% of users sent a MyShake alert will receive it 2.03 s or less after MyShake receives a ShakeAlert message, whereas 50% of users will receive it 2.90 s or earlier, following receipt of a ShakeAlert message. Meanwhile, 20% of users can expect to receive an alert more than 4.64 s after MyShake receives a relevant ShakeAlert message. If we want to emphasize performance in events where a large number of alerts is sent, we can calculate the same metrics, but weight the results by the number of alerts sent. This yields values of 2.87, 4.14, and 5.66 s, respectively (4.91, 6.18, and 7.72 s with the anomalous Lamont event included). These observations hint that events with larger numbers of alerts sent, seem to have slightly larger median delivery latencies. We confirm this by considering the unweighted median of the 50th percentile latency for 23 events with 10,000–100,000 alerts sent (2.59 s) versus that for 9 events with over 100,000 alerts sent, excluding the Lamont event (3.67 s). Figure 2 also shows that the relative ratio of the 80th percentile to the median is consistently larger than the ratio of the median to the 20th percentile. This indicates that MyShake delivery latency forms a long-tailed (right-skewed) distribution, confirming the observations of Patel and Allen (2022). It also suggests that alert delivery latency must be accounted for, especially for events where large numbers of users have to be alerted.

Comparing latency estimates from rapid MRs and complete AN in Figure 2 shows that our MR-based rapid results are equivalent to the more complete AN dataset for 20th and 50th latency percentiles, and that reliable warning time estimates that incorporate delivery latencies can be obtained in a rapid manner. Rapid MR results tend to overestimate the tail of the latency distribution (80th percentiles), perhaps due to a greater sensitivity of the tail to spuriously large individual latencies resulting from the small size of the MR dataset (around 5 times smaller than the AN dataset). This means that rapidly estimated warning times (i.e., using MRs) are rather conservative. Regardless of this result, any calculation of warning times, including MyShake delivery latency, whether using MR or AN-based latency, should yield consistent results.

Methodology for Creating User Insights from EEW Performance Data

Using the latency data analyzed in the previous section, we can put forth a workflow for assessing the performance of the ShakeAlert–MyShake EEW pipeline. Our workflow aims to estimate warning time provided to users in a near-real-time, automated manner, as well as isolate potential sources of delays in alert delivery. Issues can originate from any of the ShakeAlert layers (impacting alert issuance times), from the MyShake side (affecting alert delivery time), or a combination of the two.

Data

We compile data from three sources:

- Alert delivery receipts automatically returned to the MyShake servers by MyShake devices receiving an EEW message (Patel and Allen, 2022). These provide latency (t_{delivery}) measurements, and can be MRs or ANs (see the Analysis of MyShake Alert Delivery Latency section), depending on the time at which the analysis is run.
- ShakeAlert alert message contents from the six ShakeAlert alert layer servers.
- Authoritative event information (origin information, ShakeMap) from regional networks contributing to the Advanced National Seismic System (ANSS) and stored in the USGS ComCat.

Calculating and visualizing warning times

We estimate the warning time t_{warn} for the ith user, as the time the user has before the arrival of the first S wave at their location, using the equation

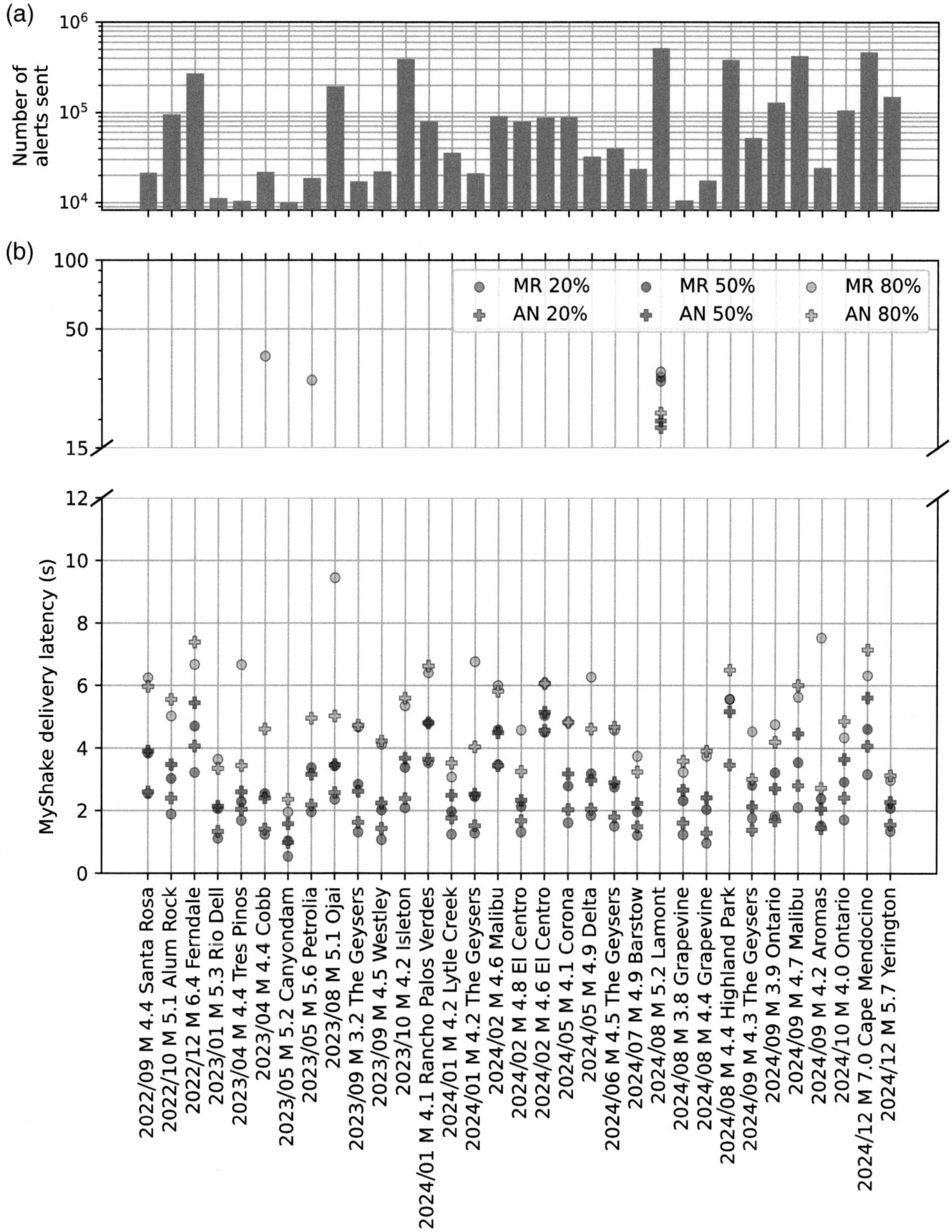

Figure 2. Comparison of rapidly determined MyShake latency estimates using delivery receipts, against latency estimates compiled using receipts returned by the message distribution services, and the number of alerts sent. (a) Number of alerts sent by MyShake per event. (b) Calculated latency percentiles. The circles indicate results calculated using the rapid message receipts (MR), and crosses show results using the more voluminous analytics (AN) dataset, which takes days to arrive. We plot the 20th (green), 50th (purple), and 80th (orange) percentiles of the latency distributions from both datasets. We consider here all events since late 2022 for which MyShake sent 10,000 or more alerts and for which both rapid receipt-based and complete analytics-based measures of latency were available. The color version of this figure is available only in the electronic edition.

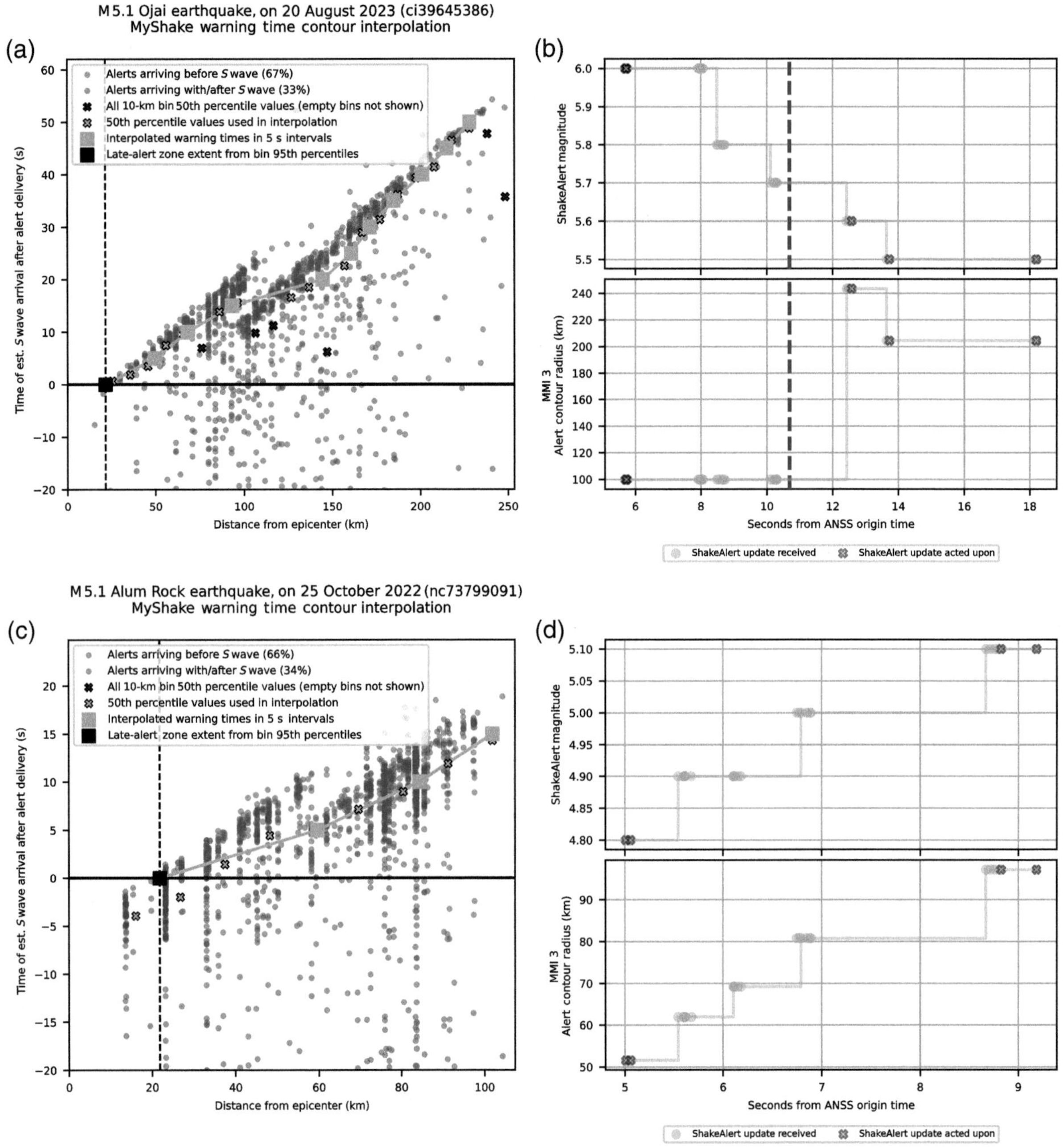

Figure 3. Graphical illustration of the MyShake warning time interpolation workflow. We show results for the **M** 5.1 Ojai earthquake on 20 August 2023, and the **M** 5.1 Alum Rock earthquake on 25 October 2022. (a) Warning time interpolation scatter plot for the Ojai earthquake. The dots represent receipts from individual devices, and plot the time of estimated *S*-wave arrival time (based on a constant *S*-wave moveout velocity $V_S = 3.5$ km/s) after the alert arrival reported by the device, against epicentral distance. The crosses show the median warning time in equally spaced epicentral distance bins. The gold crosses represent points used for interpolating warning time against epicentral distance, and blue crosses are points discarded (because they do not fit our imposed increasing trend with distance). The gold line represents the interpolated warning time as a function of epicentral distance, in 5 s bins. The line is anchored to the interpolated distance of zero warning time inferred from bin 95th percentiles. The zero warning time distance is marked by a black square crossed by a dashed line. The gold squares represent points extracted at regular intervals from the interpolated gold line for the purpose of plotting warning time contours (see Fig. 1). (b) ShakeAlert alert update evolution. The top panel shows the magnitude estimate evolution as received by the MyShake backend from the six ShakeAlert alert layer servers, while the bottom panel shows the evolution of the MMI 3 contour radius. Updates that MyShake acted upon (i.e., issued alerts) are highlighted as crosses. The red line indicates the end of the alert pause (5 s from the first alert). (c) As in (a), but for the Alum Rock earthquake. (d) As in (b), but for the Alum Rock earthquake. Note the different horizontal and vertical axis extents between panels (a) and (c), and (b) and (d). ANSS, Advanced National Seismic System. The color version of this figure is available only in the electronic edition.

$$t_{\text{warn}} = \frac{R_{\text{hyp}}}{V_S} - t_{\text{alert}} - t_{\text{delivery}}, \quad (1)$$

in which R_{hyp} is the distance from the event hypocenter (from ComCat) to the user's location, V_S is a constant *S*-wave velocity of 3.5 km/s, t_{alert} is the time after the ANSS origin time at which a ShakeAlert message is received by MyShake, and t_{delivery} is the MyShake delivery latency (the time taken by MyShake to deliver a received ShakeAlert message pertaining to the user's location, as previously defined). t_{delivery} is computed from information contained in MyShake alert delivery receipts, following Patel and Allen (2022). MyShake delivery latencies form a long-tailed distribution (Patel and Allen, 2022) and as such, calculating warning times using these latency data produces a distribution of warning times against hypocentral distance (Fig. 3) with a waterfall-like appearance.

We assume that the earliest possible arrival of strong motion at user locations is given by the arrival of the initial *S* wave from the hypocenter, propagating at a velocity of 3.5 km/s. This moveout tracks the first exceedance of MMI 3–4 shaking (Minson *et al.*, 2020; Cochran *et al.*, 2022). For most earthquakes, using *S*-wave moveout as a proxy for the arrival of strong shaking provides conservative (i.e., shorter) warning time estimates compared to using higher MMI levels to mark the arrival of strong shaking. However, for some very large-magnitude earthquakes, it is likely that MMI 3–4 shaking will be exceeded during the *P* wave (Minson *et al.*, 2019; Wald, 2020), making warning times shorter than assumed here. Given this assumption of a constant *S*-wave velocity, the warning time to the initial *S* wave is simply an increasing function of distance from the earthquake epicenter, controlled by alert issuance times and median delivery latency.

We observe this readily from a scatterplot of warning time against epicentral distance in Figure 3a for users alerted in the August 2023 **M** 5.1 Ojai earthquake. There are two populations of linearly increasing warning time, which we can readily associate with the ShakeAlert alert updates. The first line corresponds to the initial **M** 6.0 alert that was issued at 5 s from origin time that had its MMI 3 contour restricted to 100 km by the ShakeAlert alert pause feature (Lux *et al.*, 2024), as seen in Figure 3b. This feature was introduced in 2023 and limits all contours to 100 km in the first 5 s following an initial $M \geq 5.0$ estimate to prevent overalerting due to magnitude overestimation. The second line corresponds to the later **M** 5.6 update issued at 12.7 s from origin time, with an unrestricted MMI 3 contour radius of 245 km (note that the alert pause did not release the contours at 5 s from the first alert; see further discussion in the Results and Discussion section). This was the last update that triggered delivery of MyShake alerts for this event. The last two updates that MyShake acted upon estimated a lower magnitude of **M** 5.5 and involved no significant change in the epicenter estimate (see Fig. S3a). They thus did not cause any expansion of the alert area, and no further users were alerted.

A similar trend of expanding alert areas is observed for the **M** 5.1 Alum Rock in October 2022 in the South Bay area. The initial alert, with a magnitude estimate of *M* 4.8, alerted users out to 50 km. ShakeAlert issued further updates at *M* 4.9 and 5.0 within 2 s of this initial update (see Fig. 3), but MyShake did not act on these as its processing threads were busy processing the initial alert. MyShake issued its final alerts to the maximum MMI 3 alert area extent of around 100 km on receipt of ShakeAlert's final and peak magnitude estimate of *M* 5.1, received 8.7 s from origin time, 3.7 s after the initial alert. The scattered "waterfall" of points below the prominent lines of warning time represents the long tail of the warning time distribution. These are devices that received the alerts later than the majority of devices at the same location, due to a device-specific delay in the delivery pipeline. Metrics collected from the MyShake production system indicate that devices that receive alerts over cellular networks (rather than through a Wi-Fi connection) tend to experience greater delivery latencies.

We produce an estimate of median warning time against distance as described in Figure 3. We first calculate the median warning time in successive distance bins. Then, we interpolate through these medians, including only medians that fit an increasing trend with distance. The interpolated trend with distance is then subsampled at regular warning time intervals to obtain median warning time contours. These are plotted over the shaking distribution obtained from ShakeMap, shown in Figure 4. We make the choice to only use median values with an increasing trend with distance in order to make the summary maps easier for people to understand. As seen from the examples in Figure 3a, warning times may actually decrease with distance. This happens mainly due to the timing of later updates, or because of the ShakeAlert "alert pause" feature. It can also happen if a distance bin with very few points includes data points with a very large latency, severely skewing the median warning time in that bin. Our method ignores points that do not fit an increasing trend to mitigate spurious bins with little data, but still manages to capture any at-large decrease due to the timing of updates (see shallowing of the interpolated trend in Fig. 3a in response to the later update in the Ojai event), ensuring that its median warning time estimate is not skewed by minor anomalies in the data. We also calculate the radius of the "late-alert zone," that is the area in which alerts arrive after the *S* wave (i.e., were late). We calculate this from the 95th, rather than the 50th, percentile of warning time, so as to ensure this zone strictly encloses people who are very unlikely to have been alerted in time. Using the 50th percentile would have meant that 50% of users within the late-alert zone would have experienced a positive warning time.

Our workflow also produces a suite of plots for diagnosing the performance of different parts of the alerting pipeline, including histograms of MyShake alert delivery latency and plots depicting the temporal evolution of source parameters and MMI 3 contours published by ShakeAlert, following

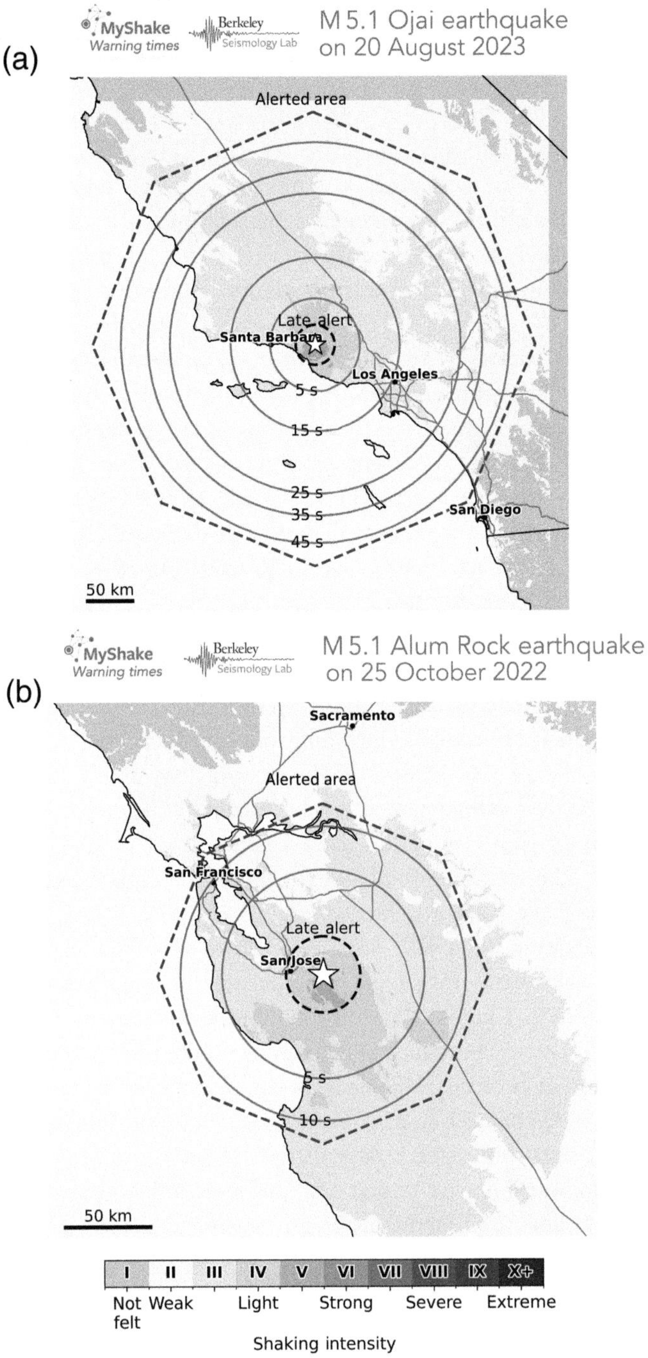

Figure 4. Median warning time contour maps for (a) the 20 August 2023 **M** 5.1 Ojai earthquake, and (b) the 25 October 2022 **M** 5.1 Alum Rock earthquake. The turquoise contours show median warning time to the initial *S* wave, as calculated from interpolation of user data. The extent of the largest MMI 3 contour is shown as a green-dashed eight-sided polygon. The black-dashed circle shows the estimated radius of the late-alert zone, using 95th percentiles of warning time. Warning time contours are plotted atop the MMI shaking intensity grid from the U.S. Geological Survey (USGS) ShakeMap product, queried automatically from the USGS Comprehensive Catalog (ComCat). The color version of this figure is available only in the electronic edition.

Patel and Allen (2022) (see Fig. S3 for examples from the Ojai and Alum Rock earthquakes). We run our workflow in near-real-time, starting 15 min after the first report of a MyShake alert. This allows for the collection of a satisfactory number of alert delivery receipts and for the initial ComCat event parameters to be consolidated. We rerun our analysis automatically at set time intervals following an earthquake, with the last analysis run at 3 days after the origin time. This ensures we incorporate the most complete MyShake latency dataset possible (using AN latency measurements), as well as the latest and most accurate ComCat event parameters (e.g., origin, magnitude) and data products (ShakeMap). These products are updated because more information becomes available, and regional network operators perform manual review and revision of the initial automatic versions of event data products.

Results and Discussion

Using warning time visualizations to interpret alerting performance

We illustrate the outputs of our workflow using two example events: the **M** 5.1 Ojai earthquake in southern California on 20 August 2023, for which MyShake sent 194,168 alerts, and the October 2022 **M** 5.1 Alum Rock (South San Francisco Bay area) earthquake, for which MyShake sent 95,272 alerts. We choose these moderate-magnitude events because they occurred close to densely populated areas in northern and southern California, prompting delivery of alerts to a large number of users who were also likely to have felt at least weak shaking. They also involved a significant temporal evolution in the ShakeAlert source parameters (Fig. 3b,d), providing a good case study for how alerting performance is affected by evolving EEW source estimates. We present workflow outputs produced using the rapid MR latency dataset to highlight how insights can be rapidly gained. Later reruns of the analysis, using the complete AN dataset, produce results with less scatter owing to the larger amount of data, but remain fully consistent with the results presented in this article.

The central output of our automated workflow is a median warning time map, designed using user-friendly principles. We show the map for our two example events in Figure 4. The map displays contours of median warning time to the first *S* wave (produced via interpolation), plotted atop the shaking distribution calculated by the USGS ShakeMap software. The octagon shows the maximum extent of alerting. We also plot the "late alert zone," or area in which alerts were delivered after the estimated arrival of the *S* wave, as a black dashed line labeled "Late Alert." We sought to create a map that is accessible to the nontechnical, nonexpert user. We plot the largest cities within the map area, as well as main highways, to help users locate themselves. We use a color scale for shaking intensity that is in line with the hazard communication recommendations of Schneider *et al.* (2023), and is also used by popular news outlets like the Los Angeles Times and the New York Times in recent coverage of large earthquake events (e.g., Robles *et al.*, 2023; Winton *et al.*,

2023). In the MMI shaking legend, we simplify the description of shaking levels compared to the standard ShakeMap scale published by the USGS. We omit peak ground velocity and acceleration conversions to MMI shaking that might confuse nonexperts, and instead provide textual descriptions of shaking experience for every second step on the MMI scale.

Plotting warning time contours spatially atop a shaking distribution is sometimes done in the EEW literature (see Wald, 2020, for an example), but it is not currently done in the context of the publicly available analyses of ShakeAlert performance on the ComCat event pages (see Data and Resources for the links to the ShakeAlert event pages for the Ojai and Alum Rock events). Plotting warning time and shaking distribution on the same graphic serves to unify the two main elements that will define an experience of an earthquake for a user with access to EEW: the amount of shaking they experienced and how much warning time they got before shaking arrived at their location. These are also recurring themes in frequently asked questions by MyShake users, such as why they did or did not receive an alert, or figuring out why they got alerted after they felt shaking (see Introduction).

Our analysis and user-friendly visualizations (Figs. 4 and 5) readily serve to answer these frequently asked questions and quickly build up a picture of user experience in a particular event. For instance, using our map, one can readily see that in the Ojai event, very few people who experienced intensity 5 (moderate) or greater shaking should have expected an alert to reach them before shaking. By plotting the extent of alerting, our map also immediately shows that people in San Diego, some of whom may have felt shaking, did not receive an alert. The alert was issued beyond the extent of felt MMI 3 shaking, owing to the ShakeAlert magnitude overestimate (**M** 6.0). Conversely, the map for the Alum Rock event conveys the fact that those who feel shaking will not always get an alert. More specifically, it shows how some locations that experience shaking of intensity that matches or exceeds the alert threshold may not be issued an alert. In this case, even though ShakeAlert accurately estimated the magnitude, the region of felt MMI 3 shaking extended beyond the alerted region to the southeast, owing to southeast-directed rupture directivity causing elevated ground shaking in this direction (Hirakawa *et al.*, 2023).

For the technical user (e.g., EEW seismologists interested in alert issuance and delivery, and members of the MyShake team), the map, viewed together with the plots shown in Figures 3 and 5, serves to make sense of the amount of warning time experienced on average by users in an event. For instance, in the **M** 5.1 Ojai earthquake, the step decrease in warning times at 100–150 km seen in Figure 3, can be readily tied to the increased distance between the 15 and 25 s median warning time contour, compared to the distance between the 5 and 15 s contour. Users who received 5–15 s of warning were covered by the initial alert, whereas users receiving larger amounts of warning were only alerted due to the later **M** 5.6 update, issued around 7 seconds after the first. The mode of individual user warning times for the Ojai event is found in the 10–20 s interval (see Fig. 5b). This interval can be approximated by the 15-s median warning time contour intersecting the outskirts of the heavily populated Los Angeles urban area in the map in Figure 4a (also see Fig. S2).

A similar interpretation can be made for the Alum Rock event by jointly looking at Figures 1b, 3b, and 5c,d. Users within 50 km from the epicenter were covered by the initial **M** 4.8 alert (Fig. 3d). A rather significant portion of users (34%, Fig. 5d) received late alerts, and from the late-alert zone plotted on the map in Figure 1b, we can tie most of these users to the major population center in San Jose (see also detailed distribution in Fig. S2). As the alert area expanded to cover the East Bay and the city of San Francisco with the peak and final update (see Fig. S3d), a much larger number of users was alerted. This is seen by the large number of points we can associate with the second linear trend in Figure 5c, as well as the large peak between 5 and 10 s in Figure 5d. The median warning time contour of 10 s in Figure 4b encloses parts of San Francisco and the East Bay and provides another view into the same observations discussed earlier.

Given the user-friendly design principles we use, discussed earlier, our map is optimized for sharing over social media, where it is likely to be seen by a large number of information-seeking users. It can also be used for briefings to local government officials, using simple, descriptive arguments like the ones we provide for the example Ojai and Alum Rock events. The map can complement public messages sent according to the post-alert messaging protocol for ShakeAlert developed by McBride *et al.* (2020). Figure 5 is a reduced version of Figure 3 without the details of warning time interpolation. It is meant for public dissemination, as a representation of warning times driven by real-world data contributed by users, featuring also a simple histogram of warning times (see Fig. 5b,d). By sharing these simple analyses with the public over the course of many events, we hope to get across simple but key points about the realities of EEW and earthquake shaking that are key for greater public understanding and reducing misconceptions: the existence of a late-alert zone, increasing warning times and decreasing shaking intensity with increasing distance from the epicenter, and the fact that warning time is a distribution, rather than a single number.

Our workflow was developed in early 2023 and has been used by the MyShake platform operationally ever since to derive rapid insights about alerting performance. We exemplify the type of insight that can be gained from its graphical outputs through the examples of the Alum Rock and Ojai earthquakes. Currently, we disseminate results for events for which alerts were sent to a large area via X (formerly Twitter), through the MyShake account (see Data and Resources for an example). An internal website is maintained with a complete archive of analyses for all past events. Future planned improvements include developing a public-facing resource much like

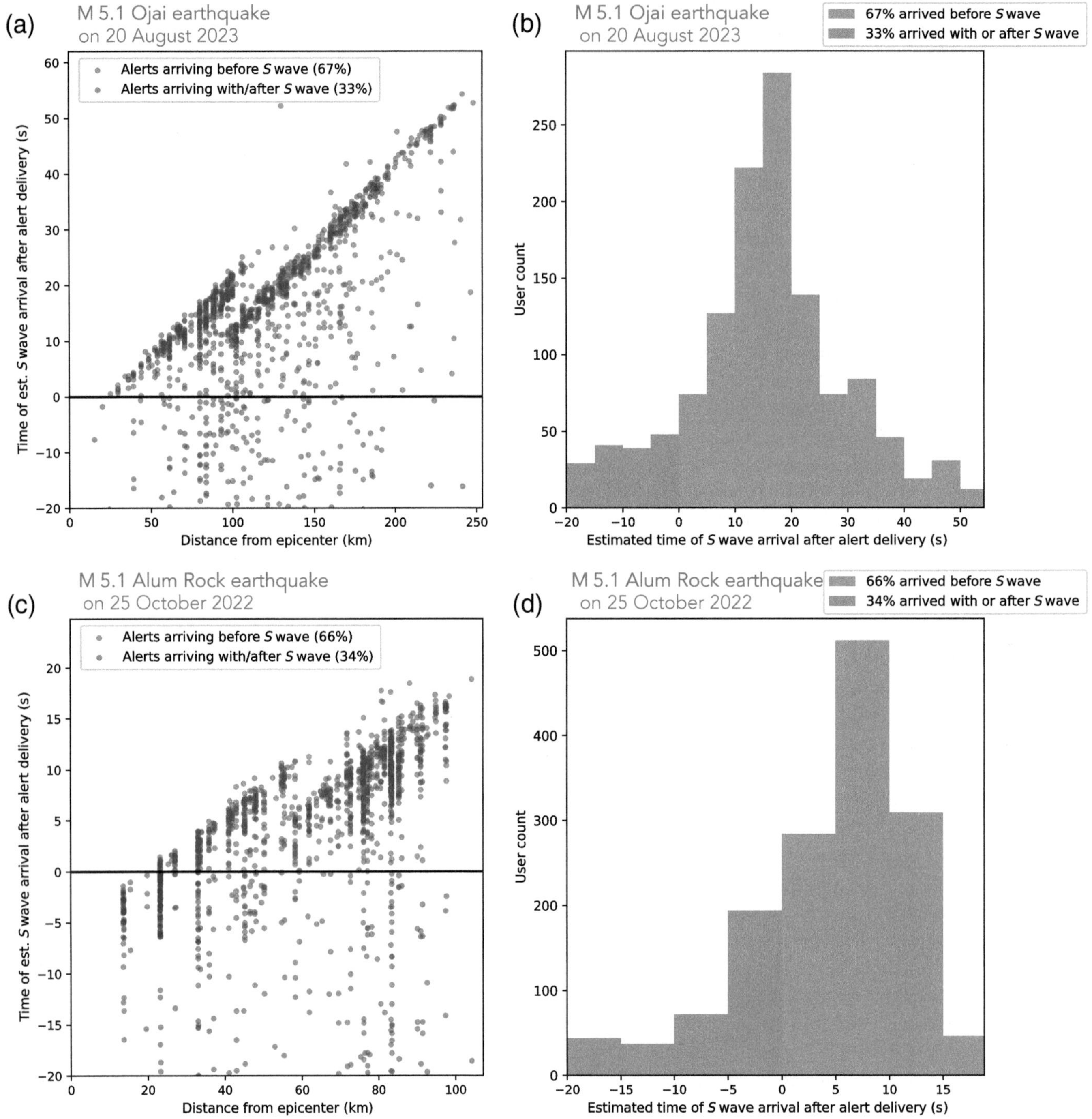

the ShakeAlert tab on the ComCat event pages, where members of the general public who use MyShake, as well as technical stakeholders, will be able to access the outputs of our rapid analysis. However, we have also used this workflow retrospectively for all events for which there have been MyShake public alerts, producing an archive of MyShake warning time performance over time. Such an archive of self-consistent analyses of alerting performance could facilitate detailed future study of the variation of warning times in space and the effectiveness of MyShake's MMI 3 alerting threshold, which is beyond the scope of the study being presented here.

Figure 5. Visualizations of MyShake warning time distributions for public dissemination. (a) Warning time to the *S* wave plotted against epicentral distance for the Ojai earthquake. (b) Histogram of *S*-wave warning time for the Ojai earthquake. Note that user counts are derived from the number of receipts received. (c) As (a), but for the Alum Rock earthquake. (d) As (b), but for the Alum Rock earthquake. Note the different scaling used on the vertical and the horizontal axes for the two events. The color version of this figure is available only in the electronic edition.

Comparisons with other routine ShakeAlert warning time performance assessments

Our workflow produces results that can be readily compared with the data collected from EEW message recipients using the USGS Did-You-Feel-It (DYFI) EEW supplemental questionnaire, which collects information about users' experience of EEW across all delivery platforms (Goltz *et al.*, 2023, 2024). We find that in the Ojai earthquake, 68% of MyShake users received an alert before or with the *S*-wave arrival; Goltz *et al.* (2024) find that 66% of DYFI-EEW respondents received an alert before or during shaking. The Goltz *et al.* (2024) DYFI questionnaire dataset and analysis are not MyShake-specific, but rather incorporate the responses of users who received alerts from WEA or any of the independent smartphone-based alert delivery mechanisms (e.g., MyShake or the Android earthquake alerts system). The DYFI questionnaire and associated analyses also do not distinguish between alert delivery platforms in deriving their warning time estimates; the number of recipients receiving alerts from each platform is thus unknown. At a basic level, it suggests that the MyShake user experience, as derived from quantitative data, is in line with general trends in user experience across all platforms. This consistency of results from our analysis and the DYFI questionnaire is encouraging. It indicates that results derived using fully automatic device-to-server data (like this study) broadly match what people actually report their experience to be. It therefore opens up the possibility for running comparisons of automated estimates of warning time and the size of the late-alert zone (like ours) with those from surveys of users, with a view to validating assumptions used in estimating warning time. It also hints at the potential of integrated data collection for further analysis if MyShake and other LtOs delivering alerts prompt their users to respond to the DYFI questionnaire. Harvesting such information, along with continued evaluation of the effectiveness of the graphical products developed here via user feedback (e.g., following Rochford *et al.*, 2018), could massively improve the understanding of overarching trends in user experience of EEW.

Technical diagnostics

Finally, our workflow also provides technical diagnostics of alert delivery performance in the minutes after an event. A complete view of the alerting pipeline, split into the alerting (ShakeAlert-controlled) and delivery (MyShake-controlled) components, allows for rapidly pinpointing potential problematic areas of the system and determining sources of alert delivery delays. For example, we were able to detect a bug with the implementation of the recently added "alert pause" feature (Lux *et al.*, 2024) in the ShakeAlert alert layer. The alert pause restricts all MMI contours for updates issued within the first 5 s following an initial alert update to 100 km, to reduce overalerting if the magnitude is initially overestimated. At the 5 s mark, the system is supposed to release a repeat of the most recent update with unrestricted contours. In early 2023, we noticed that alert layer updates did not reflect the expected behavior (see Fig. S4 for an example using the **M** 5.6 Petrolia earthquake on 21 May 2023); immediate reporting to the USGS resulted in this previously unidentified bug being fixed.

Conclusion

We propose a method for assessing the performance of the ShakeAlert–MyShake EEW alerting pipeline, in terms of the warning time available to users, using latency data routinely harvested by MyShake. We first retrospectively analyze MyShake delivery latencies over time. We use real-world data from two distinct datasets (one rapid dataset available minutes after an event, MR, and another more complete dataset, AN, available within a few days). We find that the two datasets give equivalent results, and thus verify the suitability of rapid results for alerting performance assessments. Over all events for which MyShake sent 10,000 or more alerts from September 2022 to December 2024, we find the median of the 20th and 50th percentile delivery latencies across the events was 2.03 and 2.90 s, respectively. We find that alert delivery latency is significant for calculating the warning time available to users, but show it has remained constant even as the number of MyShake users has increased. We then propose a method for combining real-world alert delivery latency data together with ShakeAlert outputs in the immediate aftermath of an event to develop warning time assessments. We present a series of newly developed graphical products meant for public dissemination. We discuss how these products can provide immediate insight into user experience and alerting performance, both in terms of warning time and the success of alerting those who felt shaking. These graphics can be shared via social media and other means to aid with rapid post-alert communication with the public and address commonly asked questions by EEW recipients. We show that results from this workflow can be readily integrated with other current efforts, such as the DYFI supplemental questionnaire, to assess ShakeAlert alert quality. It also produces valuable, rapid insights into technical system performance, for both the alert issuance (ShakeAlert) and the alert delivery (MyShake) side. Future work should focus on evaluating the success of these products in communicating their key points through direct engagement with the general MyShake user base via user surveys and targeted focus groups. These outcomes could feed directly into refining the graphical products presented here.

Data and Resources

MyShake data reported in this article are correct as of 10 January 2025. MyShake latency data used in the analysis presented in Figure 2 are made available as a csv file in a Zenodo repository: doi: 10.5281/zenodo.17096468. Detailed outputs from the ShakeAlert alert layer that are used here are openly available only to ShakeAlert licensed operators (LtOs). They can be requested from the U.S. Geological Survey (USGS) on a case-by-case basis. Event data were compiled by querying the Advanced National Seismic System (ANSS) Comprehensive Earthquake Catalog (ComCat, U.S. Geological Survey Earthquake Hazards Program, 2017) accessed at https://earthquake.usgs.gov/data/comcat/ (last accessed May 2025), using the Python package libcomcat (Hearne and Schovanec, 2022). Figures were compiled using the matplotlib (Hunter, 2007) and CartoPy (Met Office, 2015) packages in Python. The results of the MyShake event analysis workflow are posted to the MyShake account on X (https://x.com/MyShakeApp/, last accessed November 2025). An example post for the 12 September 2024 **M** 4.7 Malibu earthquake can be found at https://x.com/MyShakeApp/status/1834339815724286435 (last accessed November 2025). The list of ShakeAlert LtOs can be found at https://www.shakealert.org/system-information/license-to-operate-lto-technical-partners/ (last accessed November 2025). The publicly available analyses of ShakeAlert performance discussed in the text are available at https://earthquake.usgs.gov/earthquakes/eventpage/ci39645386/shake-alert (Ojai earthquake) and https://earthquake.usgs.gov/earthquakes/eventpage/nc73799091/shake-alert (Alum Rock earthquake). Both websites were last accessed in November 2025. The supplemental material includes four supplemental figures.

Declaration of Competing Interests

The authors acknowledge that there are no conflicts of interest recorded.

Acknowledgments

The authors would like to thank David J. Wald of the U.S. Geological Survey (USGS) for providing an updated ShakeMap for the Ojai earthquake. The authors are grateful for the contributions and support from current and former MyShake team and Berkeley Seismology Laboratory members for their assistance and feedback on this work: Steven Allen, Aya Ibayashi, Akie Mejia, Mark Ballew, Ivan Henson, and Sarina Patel. This work was funded by the California Governor's Office of Emergency Services (Cal OES), Agreement Number A221010272.

References

Allen, R. M., and D. Melgar (2019). Earthquake early warning: Advances, scientific challenges, and societal needs, *Annu. Rev. Earth Planet. Sci.* **47,** no. 1, 361–388.

Allen, R. M., and M. Stogaitis (2022). Global growth of earthquake early warning, *Science* **375,** no. 6582, 717–718.

Allen, R. M., H. Brown, M. Hellweg, O. Khainovski, P. Lombard, and D. Neuhauser (2009). Real-time earthquake detection and hazard assessment by ElarmS across California, *Geophys. Res. Lett.* **36,** no. 5, L00B08, doi: 10.1029/2008GL036766.

Böse, M., D. E. Smith, C. Felizardo, M.-A. Meier, T. H. Heaton, and J. F. Clinton (2018). FinDer v.2: Improved real-time ground-motion predictions for M2–M9 with seismic finite-source characterization, *Geophys. J. Int.* **212,** no. 1, 725–742.

Chung, A. I., M. Meier, J. Andrews, M. Böse, B. W. Crowell, J. J. McGuire, and D. E. Smith (2020). ShakeAlert earthquake early warning system performance during the 2019 Ridgecrest earthquake sequence, *Bull. Seismol. Soc. Am.* **110,** no. 4, 1904–1923.

Cochran, E. S., J. K. Saunders, S. E. Minson, J. Bunn, A. Baltay, D. Kilb, C. O'Rourke, M. Hoshiba, and Y. Kodera (2022). Alert optimization of the PLUM earthquake early warning algorithm for the western United States, *Bull. Seismol. Soc. Am.* **112,** no. 2, 803–819.

Given, D. D., R. M. Allen, A. S. Baltay, P. Bodin, E. S. Cochran, K. Creager, R. M. de Groot, L. S. Gee, E. Hauksson, T. H. Heaton, *et al.* (2018). Revised technical implementation plan for the ShakeAlert system—An earthquake early warning system for the West Coast of the United States, *U.S. Geol. Surv. 2018-1155 Ser.: Open-File Rept. IP-098251*, Reston, Virginia, Code Number: 2018-1155.

Goltz, J. D., D. J. Wald, S. K. McBride, R. DeGroot, J. K. Breeden, and A. Bostrom (2023). Development of a companion questionnaire for "Did You Feel It?": Assessing response in earthquakes where an earthquake early warning may have been received, *Earthq. Spectra* **39,** no. 1, 434–453.

Goltz, J. D., D. J. Wald, S. K. McBride, E. Reddy, V. Quitoriano, and J. K. Saunders (2024). The Ojai California earthquake of 20 August 2023: Earthquake early warning performance and alert recipient response in the M_w 5.1 event, *Seismol. Res. Lett.* **95,** 2745–2760.

Haynes, K., J. Barclay, and N. Pidgeon (2008). The issue of trust and its influence on risk communication during a volcanic crisis, *Bull. Volcanol.* **70,** no. 5, 605–621.

Hearne, M., and H. E. Schovanec (2022). USGS LibComCat, doi: 10.5066/P91WN1UQ.

Hirakawa, E., G. A. Parker, A. Baltay, and T. Hanks (2023). Rupture directivity of the 25 October 2022 M_w 5.1 Alum Rock earthquake, *The Seism. Rec.* **3,** no. 2, 144–155.

Hunter, J. D. (2007). Matplotlib: A 2D graphics environment, *Comput. Sci. Eng.* **9,** no. 3, 90–95.

Kohler, M. D., D. E. Smith, J. Andrews, A. I. Chung, R. Hartog, I. Henson, D. D. Given, R. de Groot, and S. Guiwits (2020). Earthquake early warning ShakeAlert 2.0: Public rollout, *Seismol. Res. Lett.* **91,** no. 3, 1763–1775.

Kong, Q., R. M. Allen, L. Schreier, and Y.-W. Kwon (2016). MyShake: A smartphone seismic network for earthquake early warning and beyond, *Sci. Adv.* **2,** no. 2, e1501055.

Lux, A. I., D. Smith, M. Böse, J. J. McGuire, J. K. Saunders, M. Huynh, I. Stubailo, J. Andrews, G. Lotto, B. Crowell, *et al.* (2024). Status and performance of the ShakeAlert earthquake early warning system: 2019–2023, *Bull. Seismol. Soc. Am.* **114,** 3041–3062.

McBride, S. K., A. Bostrom, J. Sutton, R. M. de Groot, A. S. Baltay, B. Terbush, P. Bodin, M. Dixon, E. Holland, R. Arba, *et al.* (2020). Developing post-alert messaging for ShakeAlert, the earthquake early warning system for the West Coast of the United States of America, *Int. J. Disaster Risk Reduct.* **50,** 101,713.

McBride, S. K., A. L. Llenos, M. T. Page, and N. van der Elst (2019). EarthquakeAdvisory: Exploring discourse between government officials, news media, and social media during the 2016 Bombay Beach Swarm, *Seismol. Res. Lett.* **91,** no. 1, 438–451.

McBride, S. K., H. Smith, M. Morgoch, D. Sumy, M. Jenkins, L. Peek, A. Bostrom, D. Baldwin, E. Reddy, R. de Groot, *et al.* (2022). Evidence-based guidelines for protective actions and earthquake early warning systems, *Geophysics* **87,** no. 1, WA77–WA102.

McBride, S. K., D. F. Sumy, A. L. Llenos, G. A. Parker, J. McGuire, J. K. Saunders, M.-A. Meier, P. Schuback, D. Given, and R. de Groot (2023). Latency and geofence testing of wireless emergency alerts intended for the ShakeAlert® earthquake early warning system for the West Coast of the United States of America, *Saf. Sci.* **157,** 105,898.

Met Office (2015). Cartopy: a cartographic python library with a Matplotlib interface, available at http://scitools.org.uk/cartopy (last accessed January 2025).

Minson, S. E., A. S. Baltay, E. S. Cochran, T. C. Hanks, M. T. Page, S. K. McBride, K. R. Milner, and M.-A. Meier (2019). The limits of earthquake early warning accuracy and best alerting strategy, *Sci. Rep.* **9,** no. 1, 2478.

Minson, S. E., E. S. Cochran, J. K. Saunders, S. K. McBride, S. Wu, A. S. Baltay, and K. R. Milner (2022). What to expect when you are expecting earthquake early warning, *Geophys. J. Int.* **231,** no. 2, 1386–1403.

Minson, S. E., J. K. Saunders, J. J. Bunn, E. S. Cochran, A. S. Baltay, D. L. Kilb, M. Hoshiba, and Y. Kodera (2020). Real-time performance of the PLUM earthquake early warning method during the 2019 M 6.4 and 7.1 Ridgecrest, California, earthquakes, *Bull. Seismol. Soc. Am.* **110,** no. 4, 1887–1903.

Patel, S. C., and R. M. Allen (2022). The MyShake App: User experience of early warning delivery and earthquake shaking, *Seismol. Res. Lett.* **93,** no. 6, 3324–3336.

Robles, P., A. Chang, J. Holder, L. Leatherby, S. Reinhard, and A. Wu (2023). Mapping the damage from the earthquake in Turkey and Syria, *The New York Times*, available at https://www.nytimes.com/interactive/2023/02/06/world/turkey-earthquake-damage.html (last accessed January 2025).

Rochford, K., J. A. Strauss, Q. Kong, and R. M. Allen (2018). MyShake: Using human-centered design methods to promote engagement in a smartphone-based global seismic network, *Front. Earth Sci.* **6,** 237.

Schneider, M., F. Cotton, and P.-J. Schweizer (2023). Criteria-based visualization design for hazard maps, *Nat. Hazards Earth Syst. Sci.* **23,** no. 7, 2505–2521.

Seeger, M. W. (2006). Best practices in crisis communication: An expert panel process, *J. Appl. Commun. Res.* **34,** no. 3, 232–244.

Strauss, J. A., Q. Kong, S. Pothan, S. Thompson, R. F. Mejia, S. Allen, S. Patel, and R. M. Allen (2020). MyShake citizen seismologists help launch dual-use seismic network in California, *Front. Commun.* **5,** 32.

Thakoor, K., J. Andrews, E. Hauksson, and T. Heaton (2019). From earthquake source parameters to ground-motion warnings near you: The ShakeAlert earthquake information to ground-motion (eqInfo2GM) Method, *Seismol. Res. Lett.* **90,** no. 3, 1243–1257.

U.S. Geological Survey (USGS) Earthquake Hazards Program (2017). Advanced National Seismic System (ANSS) comprehensive catalog of earthquake events and products, doi: 10.5066/F7MS3QZH.

Wald, D. J. (2020). Practical limitations of earthquake early warning, *Earthq. Spectra* **36,** no. 3, 1412–1447.

Winton, R., R.-G. Lin II, C. Stone, and S. Rust (2023). *Magnitude 5.1 Earthquake Strikes Ojai Area, Rattling Nerves as Hilary Pounds Southland*, Los Angeles Times, California, available at https://www.latimes.com/california/story/2023-08-20/5-0-magnitude-earthquake-strikes-ojai-area (last accessed January 2025).

Manuscript received 29 January 2025
Published online 5 December 2025

Searching for Seismic Precursors—The Barry Landslide Hazard

OPEN ACCESS

Gabrielle K. Davy*[1], Michael E. West[2], Ezgi Karasözen[2], and John J. Lyons[3]

Abstract

The Barry Landslide, located in Barry Arm of Prince William Sound, Alaska, poses a major hazard due to its steep, unstable slopes, and the potential for a massive landslide-generated tsunami. With an estimated volume of 500–700 million cubic meters, the Barry Landslide could trigger highly destructive waves. In this study, we focus on seismic signals from the Barry Landslide, which are critical for providing timely tsunami warnings. Since the summer of 2020, the region has been instrumented to monitor the landslide, but the seismic record is complicated by the presence of nearby glaciers and frequent regional earthquakes. Among these signals, we analyze a specific class of short-duration, high-frequency seismic events that exhibit strong seasonal variability, increasing in rate from late summer to midwinter before ceasing abruptly in late winter or early spring. Our analysis suggests that the source of these signals is likely near or beneath Cascade Glacier, adjacent to the landslide, rather than within the landslide mass itself. We apply detection algorithms to construct a time history for this signal type, which we then compare with environmental factors like precipitation, temperature, and slope displacement data from ground-based radar and remote sensing. Correlations indicate that these seismic events may be driven by seasonal hydrological changes, particularly the freeze-up of subglacial water pathways. Although these events are not directly linked to landslide motion, they serve as indirect markers of subsurface hydrological conditions that influence slope stability. Our findings highlight the complex interplay between glaciers, groundwater, and landslide dynamics, emphasizing the need for multiparameter monitoring to assess evolving geohazards in the region.

Cite this article as Davy, G. K., M. E. West, E. Karasözen, and J. J. Lyons (2025). Searching for Seismic Precursors—The Barry Landslide Hazard, *Seismol. Res. Lett.* **97**, 1990–2001, doi: 10.1785/0220250205.

Supplemental Material

Introduction

Landslides are among the most destructive natural hazards, and their impacts can be magnified when they generate tsunamis. Tsunamigenic landslides, which displace large volumes of rock or ice into water, can produce waves that travel rapidly, posing risk to life and infrastructure. For example, in 1958, an earthquake triggered a rockslide into Lituya Bay, Alaska, producing a wave that reached 530 m in height and traveled at up to 210 km per hour, killing two people (Miller, 1960).

Two of the largest landslide-generated tsunamis in modern history occurred in the past decade. In 2015, the Taan Fjord slide in Alaska displaced about 55 million cubic meters of debris, and generated a wave that ran 193 m up the opposite slope (Gualtieri and Ekström, 2018; Higman *et al.*, 2018). In 2017, a landslide on the southwest coast of Greenland displaced 45 million cubic meters of debris into the fjord, producing a tsunami that reached the village of Nuugaatsiaq 20 km away. This wave killed four people, injured nine, and washed away 11 buildings (Gauthier *et al.*, 2018).

As the climate warms, melting permafrost and receding glaciers compromise the stability of slopes. Steep slopes that were once buttressed by glaciers no longer have this support. New potentially hazardous landslides are continually being discovered, and failures of such slopes have increased (Coe *et al.*, 2018; Schaefer *et al.*, 2023).

The Barry Landslide, located in Prince William Sound, Alaska, is arguably the type-example of this hazard in the United States (Dai *et al.*, 2020) (Fig. 1a). The potentially unstable slope, located on the western side of the fjord, has an approximate width of 2.7 km and rises about 1.5 km from the fjord to the headscarp. It has exhibited slow movement over recent decades and is situated in a seismically active region. The slope is heavily faulted (Schaefer *et al.*, 2023) (Fig. 1b), and if it were to collapse as a single unit, the volume of the

1. Department of Geosciences, University of Alaska Fairbanks, Fairbanks, Alaska, U.S.A., https://orcid.org/0009-0003-7230-2382 (GKD); 2. Alaska Earthquake Center, Geophysical Institute, University of Alaska Fairbanks, Fairbanks, Alaska, U.S.A., https://orcid.org/0000-0003-1140-1427 (EK); 3. U.S. Geological Survey, Alaska Volcano Observatory, Anchorage, Alaska, U.S.A.

*Corresponding author: gdavy@alaska.edu

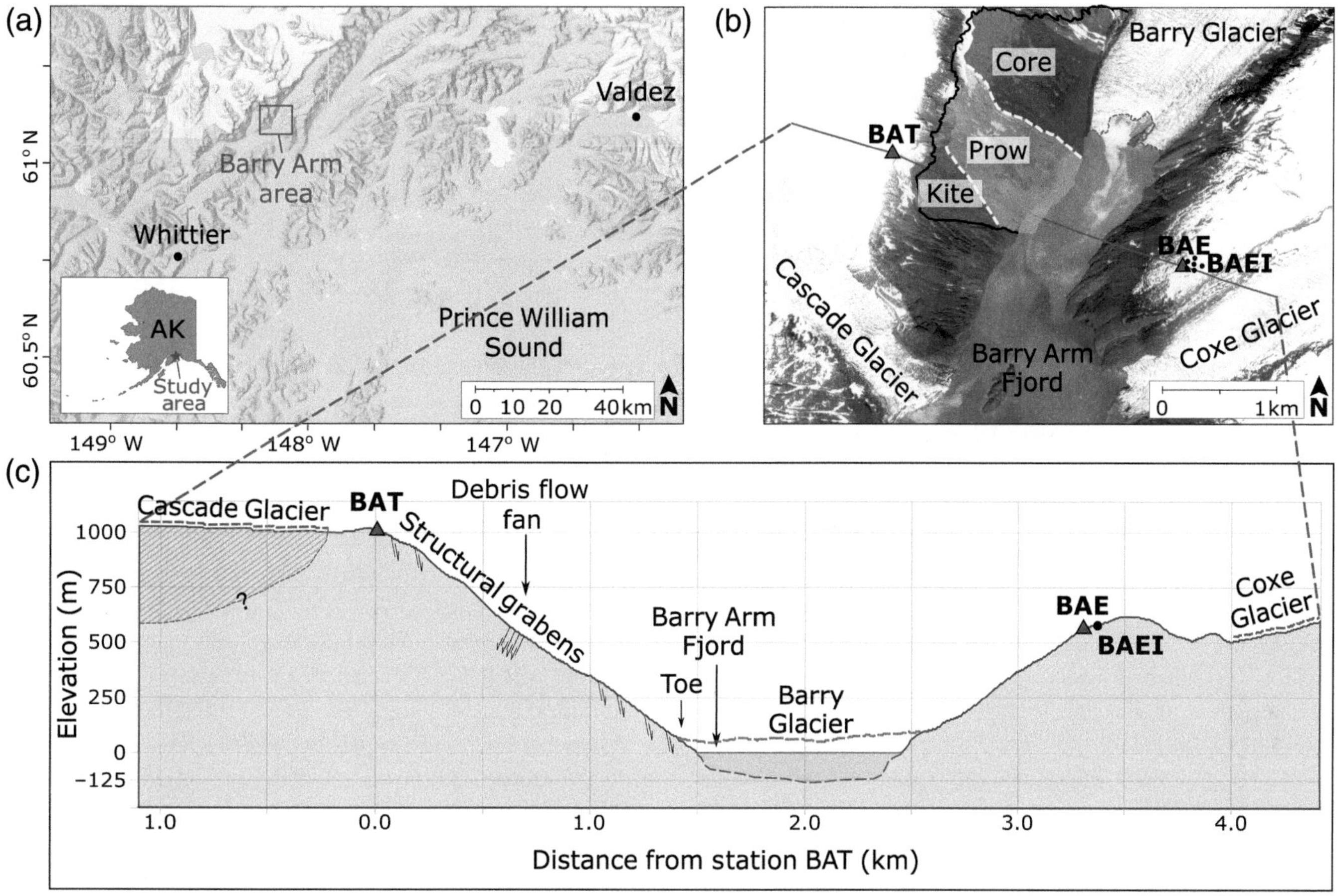

Figure 1. (a) Location of the Barry Arm area in relation to Prince William Sound and nearby communities, as well as location in relation to Alaska. (b) Barry Arm fjord detail showing the location of the Cascade, Coxe, and Barry Glaciers, as well as seismic stations BAT and BAE, and infrasound BAEI, and where the cross section is taken. The colored sections of the slope indicate the Kite (blue), Prow (yellow), and Core (red)—these locations are where the slope is most active. (c) Barry Arm fjord cross-section diagram (1:1 scale) illustrating glacier features, fjord depth (slope profile derived from Google Earth; Google, n.d.), station locations, and structural features modified from Schaefer *et al.* (2023) Boundary for Cascade Glacier is inferred. The color version of this figure is available only in the electronic edition.

slide is estimated to be 500–700 million cubic meters (Dai *et al.*, 2020). Simulations of its tsunami potential demonstrate that towns including Whittier, Valdez, and Cordova would be impacted (Barnhart *et al.*, 2021) (Fig. 1a).

Since 2020, the Barry Arm region has been well instrumented, providing a unique opportunity to study the hazard (Fig. 1c). Geophysical records are affected, however, by the presence of nearby glaciers, which generate a wide variety of seismic signals (Neave and Savage, 1970; Wolf and Davies, 1986; Qamar, 1988; Bartholomaus *et al.*, 2012; Walter *et al.*, 2012), complicating efforts to isolate signals originating in the landslide slope.

Several landslides have produced precursory signals that were identified after slope failures, including the Nuugaatsiaq landslide (Poli, 2017), the Askja caldera landslide (Schöpa *et al.*, 2018), and the Irazu volcano landslide (Chávez *et al.*, 2023). Long-period automated waveform monitoring has played a role in the detection and characterization of such slides after they have occurred (Ekström and Stark, 2013; Karasözen and West, 2024). However, these approaches have not provided advance warning. Monitoring landslide precursors is challenging because there are no geophysical signals that are known to manifest consistently across different slides. If such precursory events were consistently detectable, they could enable targeted monitoring and provide timely warnings, potentially allowing for evacuations before a landslide occurs. One example of advanced recognition comes from Iliamna volcano, where slides are driven primarily by glacial activity rather than catastrophic rock failure (Huggel *et al.*, 2007; Toney *et al.*, 2021). Understanding and establishing consistent patterns across various types of landslides would greatly enhance our predictive capabilities and improve hazard mitigation.

In this study, we focus on seismic signals observed at Barry Landslide, collected from seismic stations positioned on top of, and across from, the slide. We identified a variety of seismic event types, such as frequent rockfalls, snow avalanches, and unique short, high-frequency events that we term short-impulsive or SI events. These short impulses show temporal variability, suggesting they could be linked to other activities on the slope with the potential to inform early warnings.

Although Barry Landslide is not a unique hazard in the region, the confluence of instrumentation and research efforts makes it an ideal location for researching rock failures in the coastal alpine environment. This study examines a three-year data set, analyzing the spatial and temporal distribution of one specific type of promising seismic signal (SI events) and its connection to environmental drivers and slope movement, providing insights that may be applied to similar hazards elsewhere.

Data

We use a combination of seismic, weather, infrasound, and radar data. Each data set provides a different perspective on the slope's behavior and environmental conditions.

Seismic data are collected from real-time monitoring stations positioned around Barry Arm. The Barry Arm East (AK.BAE) station, located across the fjord from the slide, was installed in 2020 by the Alaska Earthquake Center. Barry Arm Top (AK.BAT), positioned on the slide itself, was installed in 2021, replacing an early site that was lost in an avalanche (BAW). Both stations use broadband seismic sensors with sampling rates of 100 Hz and have strong motion sensors as well (Alaska Earthquake Center, University of Alaska Fairbanks, 1987).

Weather stations that record temperature, humidity, and precipitation are collocated near the seismic stations. These are maintained by the Alaska Division of Geological and Geophysical Surveys (see Data and Resources).

An infrasound array (AV.BAEI), positioned near the BAE seismic station, records acoustic signals. Operated by the Alaska Volcano Observatory, this six-element array has a sampling rate of 100 Hz and is telemetered in near-real time (Alaska Volcano Observatory, U.S. Geological Survey, 1988). This array is particularly valuable for determining the direction, or back azimuth, to events and for distinguishing between subsurface seismic events and surface disturbances like avalanches and landslides (Lyons *et al.*, 2024).

A ground-based radar located across the fjord from the landslide monitors surface movements across the Barry Arm slope. The radar system, operated by the U.S. Geological Survey, provides continuous seasonal monitoring of slope deformation, capturing millimeter-level changes. This information complements the seismic and infrasound data by providing a direct measurement of physical changes in the landscape (Schaefer *et al.*, 2023).

Common event types

Barry Arm is a seismically active region, where the seismic records are often busy with signals from earthquakes, glacier activity, and other sources. Differentiating slope-related signals from other sources presents considerable challenges. To address this, we conducted a manual examination of the seismic record over more than a year, reviewing seismic waveforms and daily spectrograms to develop an understanding of what constitutes baseline activity (Text S1, available in the supplemental material to this article). By comparing waveforms across multiple stations —BAT (and its predecessor BAW), BAE, and KNK (a regional station 35 km to the north)—we can isolate tectonic earthquakes. Regional tectonic earthquakes are easily identified because they move across stations with a consistent waveform shape and amplitude (Fig. 2a).

In addition, glaciers generate prominent seismic signals. Glacier events are due primarily to calving and are extremely frequent. The signals are distinct due to their emergent nature, with a dominance of around 1–2 Hz energy. These glacier events are usually observed on both local seismic stations (BAT and BAE) and the BAEI infrasound (Fig. 2b), with their calculated back azimuth pointing to the glacier terminus.

During daily monitoring reviews, we routinely observed the extended rumbles characteristic of rockfalls (see Text S1 for details). They can have a low, rolling onset or a sharp, impulsive start. Either way, their duration typically extends from 20 s to several minutes, with a tapering coda and a wide range of amplitudes. Rockfalls are often clear in the infrasound record and have back azimuths consistent with the landslide (Fig. 2c).

We frequently observed a fourth type of event at station BAT, characterized by a very short duration (1–4 s) and a high signal-to-noise ratio. We refer to these as short-impulsive, or SI, events. Unlike calving signals and earthquakes, SI events observed at BAT are not seen across the fjord at BAE on either seismic or infrasound sensors, suggesting they occur near BAT and are likely not surficial events (Fig. 2d). Some SI events exhibit *P*- and *S*-wave arrivals (Fig. 3), further distinguishing them from surficial events. Their impulsive nature suggests they likely originate from small brittle-failure fractures. On rare occasions, events with a similar signal are observed on BAE. These events are not observed at BAT and are presumably coming from the rocks or glaciers on the east (at station BAE) side of the fjord. Because these are away from the landslide, we do not consider them here.

Although the origins of calving signals, rockfalls, and earthquakes are well understood, the SI events are enigmatic. The suggestion that they are fracture events not occurring at the surface caught our attention. If these events are tied to progressive failure inside the mountain slope, they hold the potential to act as precursory signals. For this reason, we undertook an effort to catalog these BAT-specific SI events, estimate their location, and map their occurrence through time.

Methods and Results

Time history of SI events

To identify patterns and correlations in SI events, we build a time history of these signals. We construct a training data set by manually identifying SI events throughout one day, 19 September 2023, during a period of known movement on the slide.

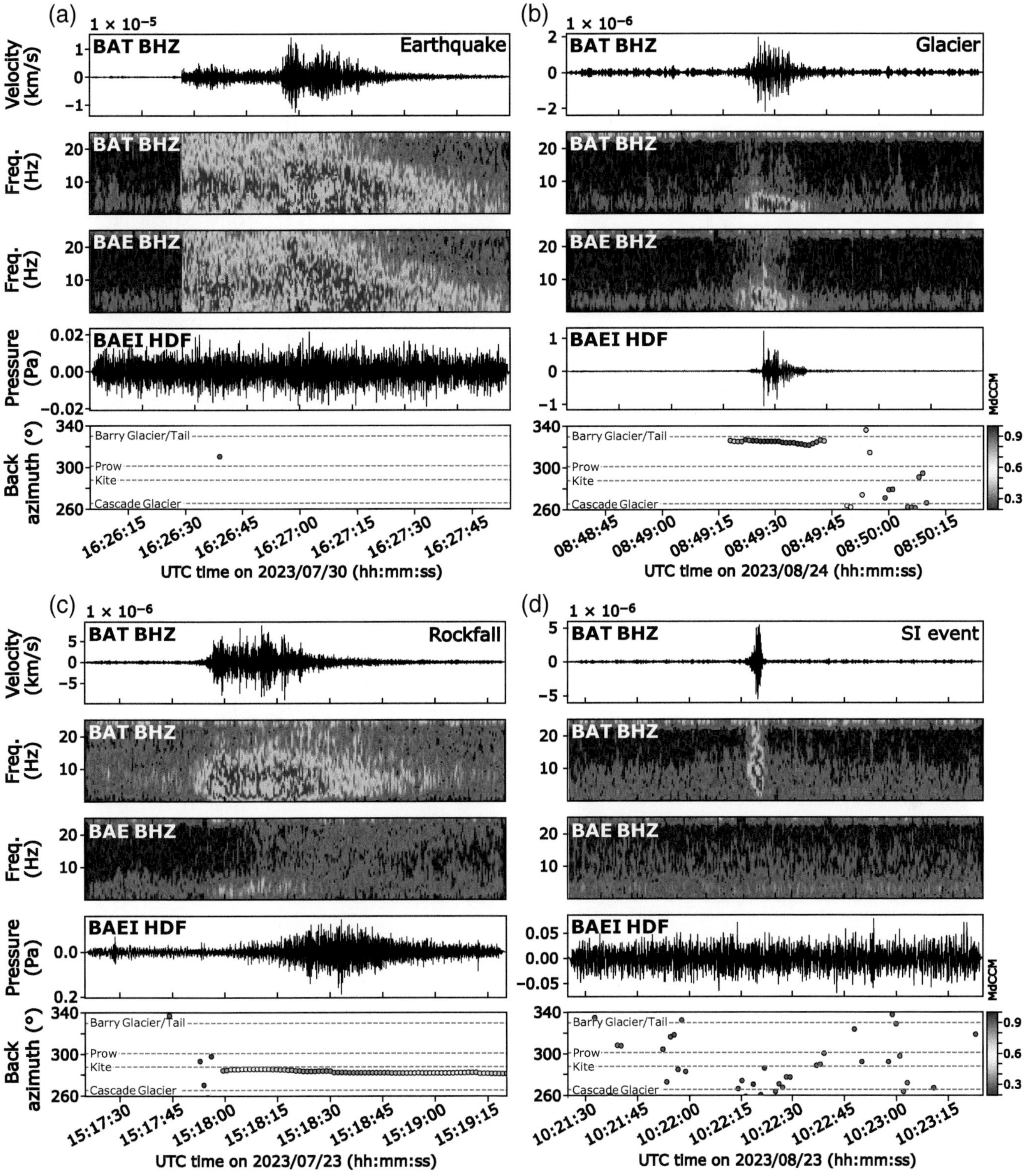

We employ the antelope-based detection tool *dbdetect*, which utilizes a short-term average to long-term average (STA/LTA) algorithm (Allen, 1982). We adjust the parameters to capture the training SI events while minimizing the detection of other types of events (see Text S2). We apply a high-pass filter at 5 Hz to emphasize the high-frequency characteristics of SI events. Because local earthquakes are difficult to completely filter

Figure 2. Seismogram, spectrogram, and infrasound (top to bottom) of an (a) earthquake, (b) glacier event, (c) rockfall, and (d) short-impulsive (SI) event. Note that SI events do not appear on infrasound, nor station BAE, whereas rockfall and glacier events are present on infrasound and both seismic stations, and earthquakes are visible on both seismic stations (see Fig. 1 for station locations). The color version of this figure is available only in the electronic edition.

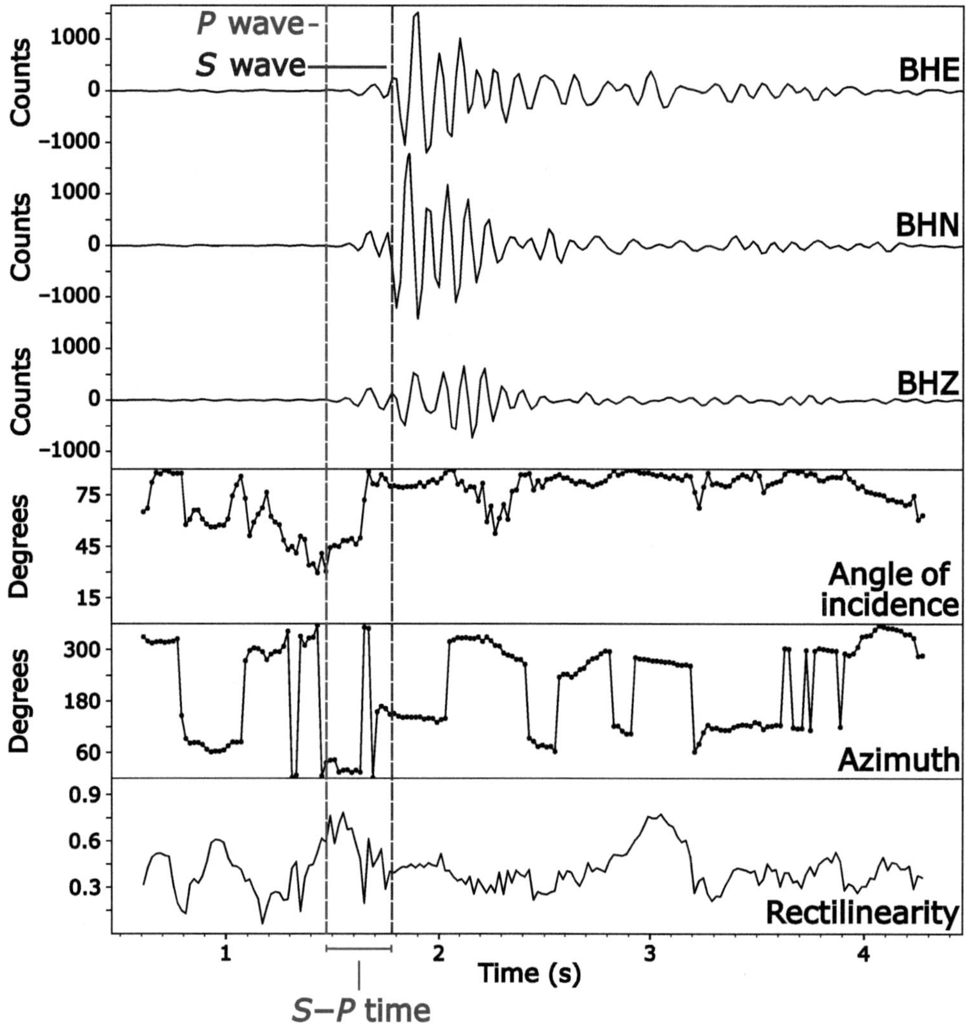

Figure 3. Particle motion and polarization analysis of an SI event on station BAT. The seismogram is high-pass filtered at 5 Hz. *P*-wave (green) and *S*-wave (blue) picks are made manually. The color version of this figure is available only in the electronic edition.

out, we exclude events with durations longer than 4 s, effectively removing earthquakes and calving events that tripped the detector (Text S3). We reprocessed this training day repeatedly to determine the best parameter set, ultimately recovering 35 out of 39 SI events while limiting false positives to just six non-SI detections (see Text S2 for parameter details).

We then apply our detection algorithm to three years of data, yielding a total of 32,877 SI events. We note that this period includes significant data gaps during the winter and spring months when heavy snow load inhibits real-time data transmission (Fig. 4).

SI events and environmental drivers

We observe a strong annual cycle in SI events. We investigate the potential correlations to weather by examining rainfall and temperature records (Fig. 4). Weather metrics in this region are highly cyclic as well, though offset in time from the SI events. From late

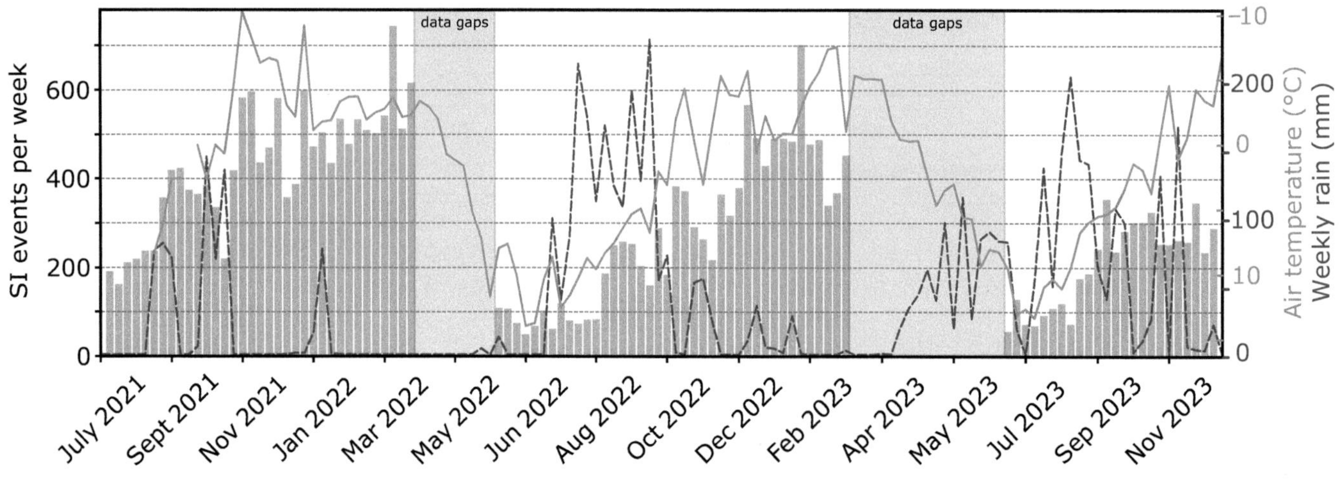

Figure 4. Histogram of SI events overlain with air temperature (orange) and weekly rainfall (purple) from July 2021 to December 2023. Note the data gaps in seismic stations from April to May 2022 and March to June 2023. The color version of this figure is available only in the electronic edition.

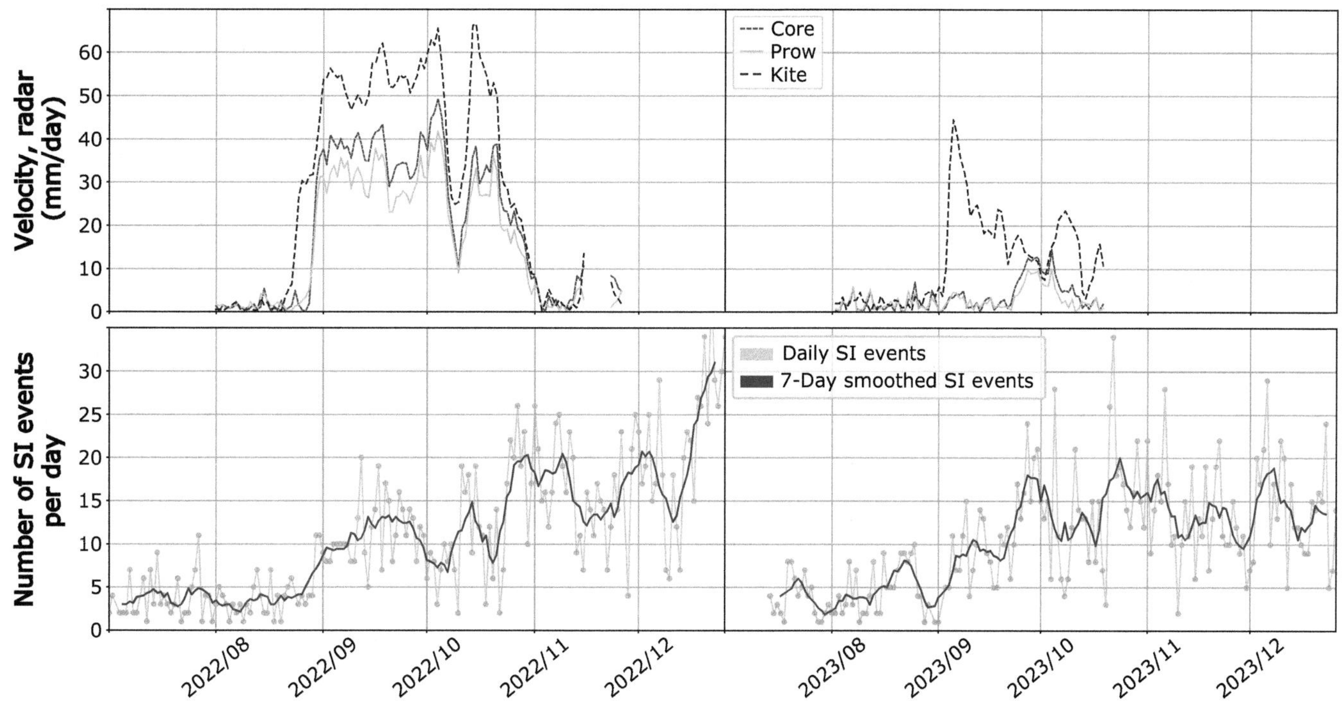

September to mid-January, the rate of SI events increases gradually. Toward late winter (February–March), these events cease, decreasing much more rapidly than they emerged in the fall.

Rainfall increases in the early summer and peaks by early fall, ceasing as winter sets in. We note increases in SI events at around the same time rainfall peaks in the late summer and fall. Air temperature steadily increases from early winter to midsummer, and steadily decreases from midsummer to early winter. The air temperature shows a rough inverse correlation to the rate of SI events.

SI events and landslide movement

A ground-based radar system that tracks millimeter-scale displacement on the slope is located across from the Barry Landslide (Schaefer *et al.*, 2023). We compare slope displacement with SI events to determine whether there is any correlation. Correlation between SI events and displacement would suggest that SI signals are the product of landslide movement.

There are three main kinematic sections of the Barry slope–Kite, Prow, and Core (Fig. 1b). The radar results show that the landslide moved slowly in 2022 and 2023 (Fig. 5). In 2022, widespread movement began on 21 August 2022, and slowed to no movement in November. The rate of movement ranged from 30 mm to more than 65 mm per day, for a cumulative displacement of around 7 m. The displacement in 2023 was slower and shorter in duration, beginning at the end of August, and ending in late October, with a cumulative displacement of just over one meter (Karasözen *et al.*, 2023; Schaefer *et al.*, 2023). There were no large movements observed in the radar outside of these time periods.

Figure 5. Radar data of the movement of the Barry Landslide slope (top) versus number of SI events per day (bottom) for 2022 (left) and 2023 (right). SI events include the entire range of azimuths but are filtered by rectilinearity of a value of 0.5 or greater. [Radar data are preliminary and may change with updated processing, but overall patterns are expected to remain constant.] The color version of this figure is available only in the electronic edition.

We observed a notable rise in the rate of SI event detections concurrent with movement, particularly during the initial periods when the Kite accelerates. However, the rate of SI events continued to increase even after the slope activity stops.

Polarization analysis

SI events are only observed on a single station, complicating efforts to derive a location. Without the ability to use typical network-based location methods, we infer location using a combination of particle motions and the time difference between *P*- and *S*-phase arrivals.

Polarization analysis allows us to determine the angle of incidence, azimuth, and rectilinearity of *P*-wave phase arrivals (Montalbetti and Kanasewich, 1970; Ereditato and Luongo, 1994). The angle of incidence is a measure of how steeply the signal arrives at the station, whereas the azimuth indicates the horizontal direction of travel. Rectilinearity—the degree to which particle motion aligns with the direction of propagation—is valuable because it tells us when the azimuth and angle of incidence parameters are trustworthy. All parameters can be derived from the covariance matrix of the three ground-motion components (Montalbetti and Kanasewich, 1970).

We calculate polarization using the method of Flinn (1965) as implemented in ObsPy (Beyreuther *et al.*, 2010).

We use particle motion to estimate the polarization of the P wave and the back azimuth to the seismic source. Polarization is computed from a short segment of waveform centered on the detection time, specifically from one second before to four seconds after our pick (Fig. 3). Although we tested more elaborate approaches for selecting azimuth and angle of incidence, we found that using the single sample closest to the detection time gave the most reliable results.

Polar plots of these results help visualize the azimuth and angle of incidence of the SI events. These parameters only have meaning when the rectilinearity is high. To ensure we are only using reliable estimates of direction, we use polarization results with rectilinearity greater than or equal to 0.5 (Text S4). Out of the 32,877 detections, 11,685 meet this criterion. We observe that a large portion of events have azimuths between 10° and 60° (measured clockwise from north), and angles of incidence of 30°–70° (measured with respect to vertical) (Fig. 6; Text S5).

This suggests that these signals come from the southwest (relative to station BAT) and travel upward at a steep angle. These angles of incidence are relatively steep for seismic events that are occurring at close distances. This could indicate that they are coming from deep under the station. We note, however, that near-surface structures can significantly influence this angle, so we treat that interpretation with caution.

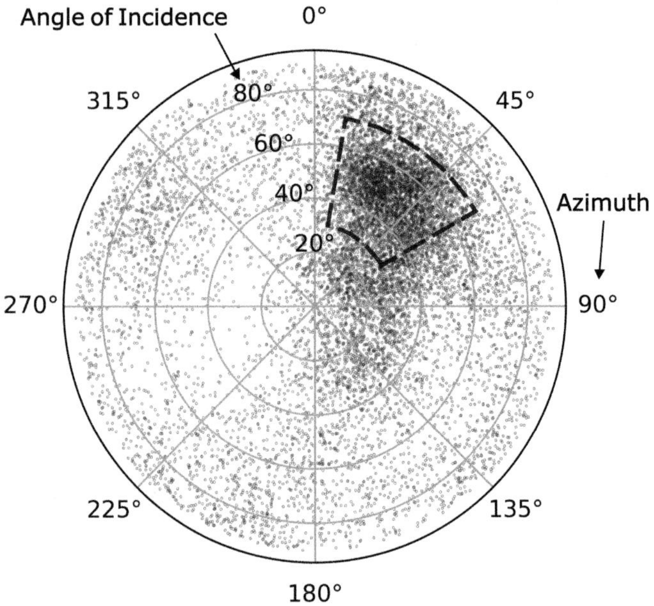

Figure 6. Polar plot of all SI events with a rectilinearity value greater than or equal to 0.5. Note the red-dashed outline on the plot—this area is the cluster of events that we further analyze and calculate source locations for. The color version of this figure is available only in the electronic edition.

Repeating events

Many of the SI events are similar in appearance. The waveform similarity suggests they are coming from one or a small number of source areas. To assess this, we analyze the catalog for families of similar, or repeating, events. We use the REDPy package to categorize our data set into families of repeating seismic events, after significantly tuning for our data type (Text S6) (Hotovec-Ellis, 2025). We again limit this analysis to events with azimuths of 10°–60° (back azimuths of 190°–240°) and angles of incidence of 30°–70°.

We observe a particular waveform (family 1) that recurs annually over the full three-year study (Fig. 7a). In addition, we observe several smaller families that are limited to specific seasons, alongside larger families that appear more frequently in late 2022 and 2023 but are absent in 2021 (families 0/2, 3, and 5). We also note that family 2 is closely related to family 0. There are fewer events in family 1 in 2023 compared to previous years, which is consistent with the overall reduction in detected events (Fig. S1).

Source location

We use S–P times and back azimuths to estimate the source location for each of these families. Stacked waveforms from each family allow us to extract more reliable P and S arrivals. We calculate the distance to the source by assuming apparent velocities of $V_P = 3$–5 km/s and $V_S = 1.8$–3.0 km/s. We acknowledge that these values are assumptions only. However, the wide range brackets are feasible velocities for shallow fractured bedrock. We estimate the range of source distances as

$$\text{Distance} = \frac{(S - P) \cdot V_P \cdot V_S}{V_P - V_S}. \quad (1)$$

Assuming that each family originates from a single location and that the scatter of azimuths in the 10°–60° range represents measurement error, then we can derive a single back azimuth for each event along with an uncertainty (Table 1). Combining these observations, we infer a source region one to two kilometers southwest of station BAT in the direction of Cascade Glacier (Fig. 7b). We do not attempt to backproject the angle of incidence of these signals. Given the extreme topography, highly fractured rock, and complex near surface rock and ice environment, we have no velocity model. However, bending incoming ~5–10 Hz seismic energy to a steep angle of incidence would require substantial velocity contrast in the top few hundred meters. This seems unlikely given that the mountain is essentially a single outcrop of fractured metamorphic rock (Dai *et al.*, 2020).

Discussion

The families of similar waveforms demonstrate persistent seismic sources. Their repeated occurrence indicates a regularly triggered phenomenon. Although the back azimuth and S–P

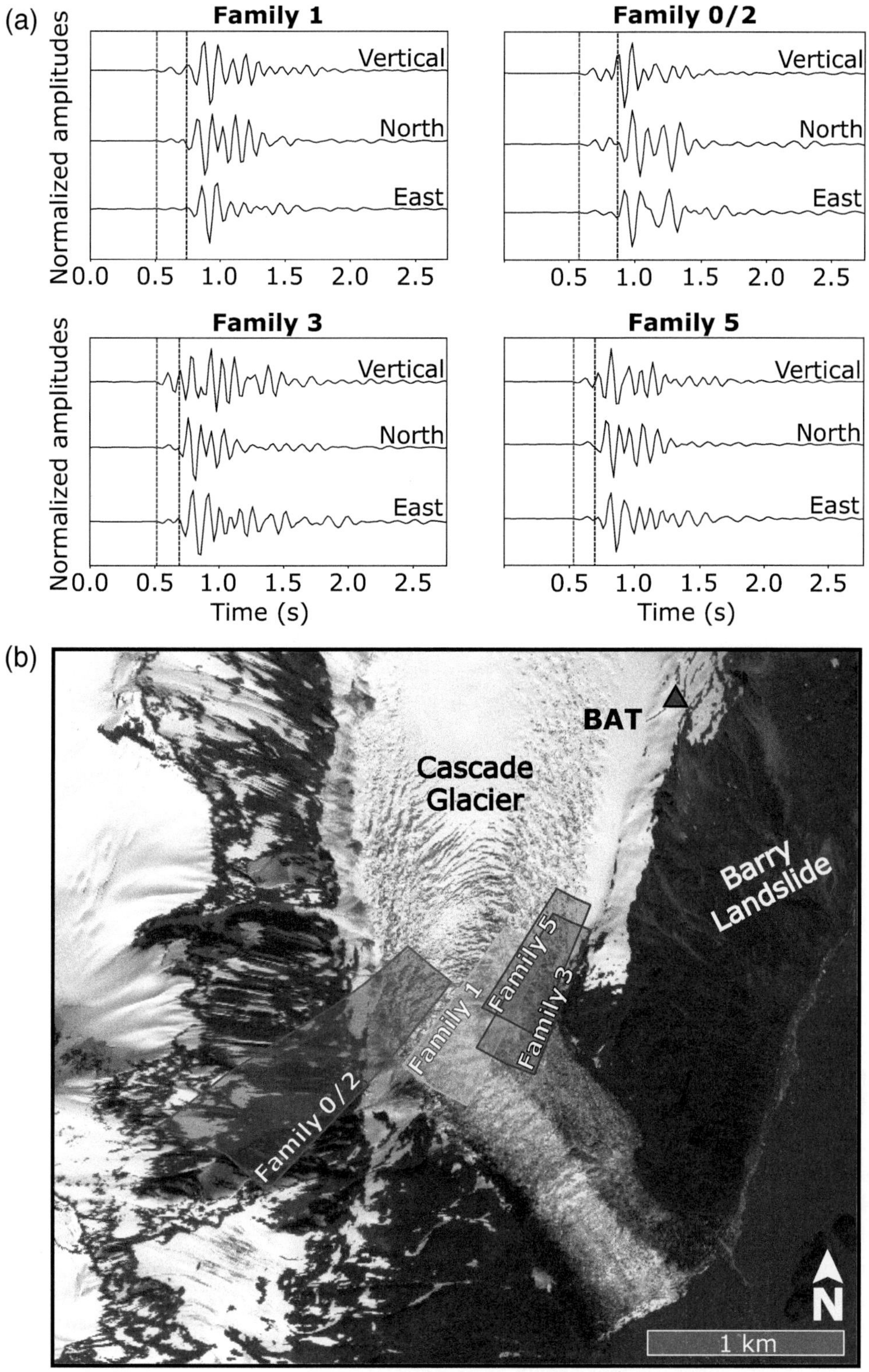

Figure 7. Stacked family waveforms and source location of the families in Barry Arm. Each waveform represents 30 stacked waveforms from (a) family 1, (b) family 0/2, (c) family 3, and (d) family 5 distributed evenly through time. (e) The approximate source location of each family. Imagery plotted using Google Earth (Google, n.d.). The color version of this figure is available only in the electronic edition.

time provide a rough location, the angle of incidence may suggest something about depth. The width and topography of the valley suggest that the Cascade Glacier is no more than a few hundred meters thick. The steep angles of *P*-wave incidence argue against a source near the surface of the glacier, though crevassing and other cracking events are known to produce waveforms with similar characteristics (West *et al.*, 2010). Deeper sources would be at or below the base of the glacier. Candidate explanations include basal events at the rock–ice interface and fracturing in the rock beneath the glacier.

The time history of these events provide additional clues. Together with location and the observation that these sources tend to be repetitive, we examine the possibilities that they are tied to slope movement, that they track the glacier's dynamics, or reflect weather-driven influences (Fig. 8). The time history of SI events is strongly seasonal—as are most other observables including rainfall, temperature, and slope movement. Though we find that many of these covary on a similar annual cycle, their relative timing is insightful.

The close correlation between SI events and the initial onset of movement in the Kite block in fall 2022 and 2023 is tantalizing. However, we note the SI events were strong in 2021 even though no significant motion occurred on the landslide. Moreover, SI events continue and even increase well into the winter, long after slope displacement has ceased. This suggests to us that SI events are not a direct reflection of

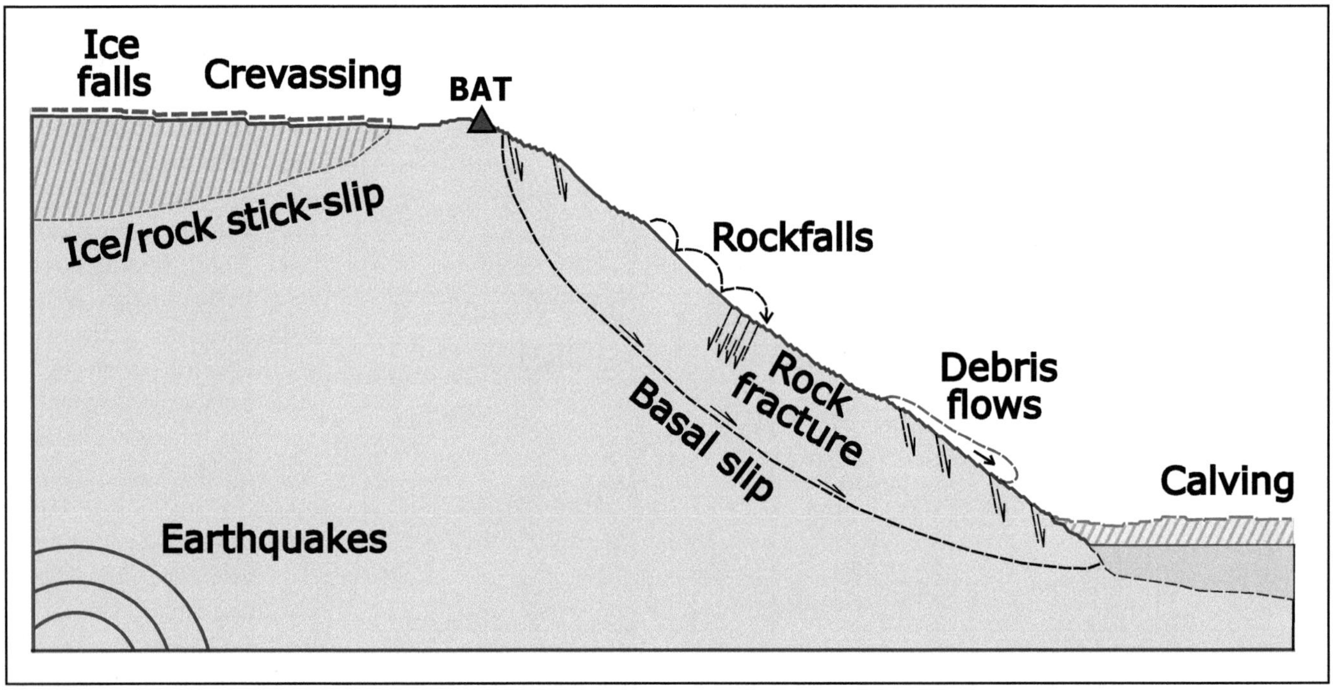

Figure 8. Diagram cross section of the Cascade Glacier and Barry Arm west slope depicting possible sources of seismic events. Slope profile derived from Google Earth (Google, n.d.). The color version of this figure is available only in the electronic edition.

slope movement but perhaps related to an environmental influence that itself could be a trigger for slope activity.

Velocity data generated using auto-RIFT and provided by the National Aeronautics and Space Administration MEaSUREs ITS_LIVE project (Gardner *et al.*, 2018, 2022), of Cascade Glacier indicate continual, consistent motion of 400–600 m per year with slight increases around May and June, and slight decreases between November and January (Fig. S2). If SI events reflect fracturing of the glacier because it navigates the complex fjord topography, we would expect some correlation between their rate and the speed of the glacier. However, the seasonal velocity fluctuations do not align at all with the rate of SI events. For this reason, it is difficult to reconcile the occurrence of SI events with phenomena that result from glacier flow, such as crevassing or basal stick slip.

Water, both from rain and melt, can lubricate the base of the glacier, promoting sliding. This happens when influxes of surface water impinge on the basal surface, raising pore pressure and, conceptually, floating the glacier (Cuffey and Paterson, 2010). Melt water peaks in midsummer, as a function of temperature. But SI events begin in late summer and increase through the fall and into winter, long after sources of subglacial melt have vanished. Any model that connects rainfall with SI events would need to explain months of delay between these two.

A fourth possibility is tied to the spring waters that are well observed across the face of the landslide. These waters are believed to originate beneath the glacier and driven eastward through the fractured rock, emerging as springs on the surface of the slide (Wolken *et al.*, 2024). A recent paper by Langet and Silverberg (2023) describes similar signals—which they refer to as low-frequency slope quakes—arising in a landslide-prone area in Norway, with a pattern that also correlates with seasonal moisture and freezing. Their events share characteristics with our SI events, including short-duration (<4 s) frequency content predominantly below 25 Hz, and a seasonal trend, with increased activity from October to February and quieter periods from June to September. They attribute this to water in rock fractures freezing and thawing as temperatures oscillate between 0° and 4°C. Although we do not have temperature records from the base of Cascade Glacier, it is reasonable that our SI events result from similar mechanisms, with water in fractures or

TABLE 1
Waveform Families and Their Calculated Source Locations from Station BAT

Family	*S–P* Time (s)	Distance (km)	Average Back Azimuth ± STD
0/2	0.3	1.4–2.3	223° ± 9°
1	0.23	1.0–1.7	213° ± 10°
3	0.2	0.9–1.5	205° ± 10°
5	0.18	0.8–1.4	208° ± 10°

S–P times calculated from manually picked *P*- and *S*-wave times from stacked family waveforms—described in the Repeating events section. Distance calculated using equation (1). Back azimuth calculation described in the Source location section. STD, standard deviation.

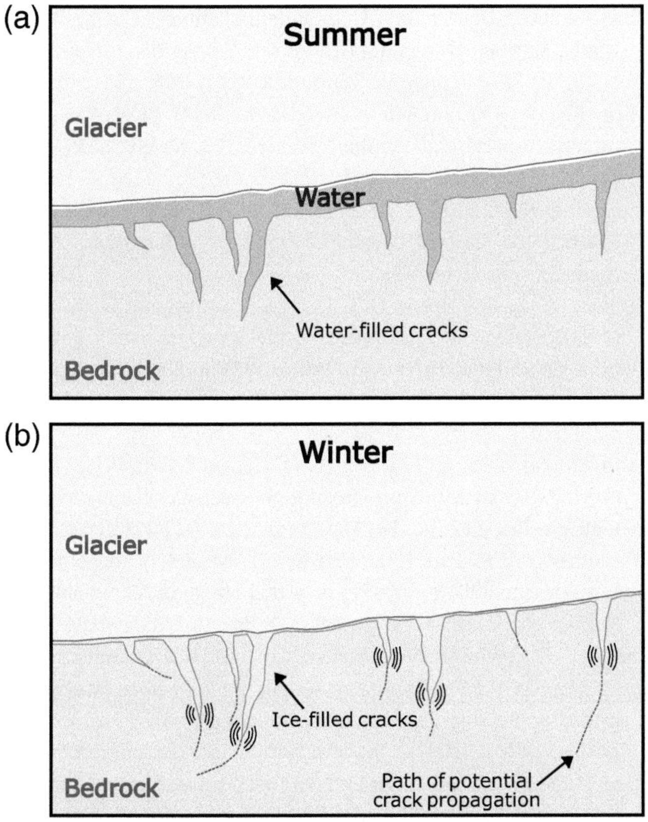

Figure 9. Seasonal "freeze-up" cycle of subglacial (a) summer and (b) winter pathways. The color version of this figure is available only in the electronic edition.

microcracks freezing and thawing seasonally, generating the observed seismic signals.

We find the most plausible source of these events to be in the rock under, or near, Cascade Glacier. We postulate that these events represent small fractures driven by a combination of hydrostatic pressure or annual freezing (Fig. 9). The locations agree with the back azimuths and are consistent with arrival angles observed at station BAT. The impulsive high-frequency waveforms are what one would expect from tiny brittle failure events. Their seasonal pattern, which does not align with rainfall or warm temperatures, appears more in line with the annual freeze up cycle. Because the heat flux of summer waters from the surface of the glacier begin to shut down (Fig. 9a), the base of the glacier returns to colder subfreezing temperatures. Flow from the glacier into the surrounding rock tapers off, also shutting down the influx of warmer surface waters. Because these waters stagnate in the cold rock, they expand, cracking the rock around them (Fig. 9b). Because individual pathways expand incrementally, these tiny fractures occur repeatedly in nearly the same place. Each fracture has the same basic orientation leading to highly similar seismic records. Eventually, the flow paths freeze up, bringing these small fracture events to a stop (St. Lawrence and Qamar, 1979; Métaxian *et al.*, 2003; Armstrong and Anderson, 2020). Our data suggest this happens in the February timeframe (Fig. 4). When the melt waters return in early summer, warm water returns to the base of the glacier, subglacial pathways open up, and underground springs pick up in volume. Because the water is melting, these processes are largely aseismic. Late in the summer season, the freeze up cycle begins again.

We acknowledge this is not the only possible explanation. A similar process might also occur in the basal regions of the glacier itself. That is, pathways in the lower parts of the glacier freeze up in the fall creating a similar fracturing process. The only difference is that they might occur in the lower glacier ice and not the surrounding rock. Though we cannot distinguish between these, we note that both are explained by the annual water cycle and freezing process. In that sense, both explanations for SI seismic events reflect the gradual shutdown of the hydraulic system that feeds the Barry Landslide from behind, tracking a similar phenomenon.

Conclusions

Seismic waveforms, source locations, and minimal or absent infrasound support the idea that SI events are not a direct consequence of surficial processes on the Barry Landslide. Their highly repetitive nature suggests they originate from fixed locations and recur annually. These annual cycles do not correlate directly with environmental variables such as temperature or precipitation though they may still be drivers via more complex interactions.

These events generally intensify during the same annual time frame as the two well-constrained periods of slope movement identified by radar data. However, they also occur in at least one year without observed slope movement and continue to increase in rate long after landslide movement ceases. Estimated seismic source locations indicate that these events may originate behind the landslide, likely at some depth within or beneath Cascade Glacier. If accurate, these locations further complicate a direct connection between SI events and landslide creep.

Our understanding of the deep interior of Cascade Glacier and the underlying rock is limited, yet this region is the most likely source of these events. They may originate from deep within the glacier itself or in the fractured rock beneath it. Regardless, the subglacial environment experiences significant seasonal changes, with warm meltwater infiltrating in spring and early summer before gradually tapering off later in the year. It is likely that SI events are linked to this seasonal process, potentially reflecting the progressive freeze-up in the latter half of the year as the heat flux of water from the surface declines.

If true, these events could serve as markers that do have relevance to the landslide and its associated hazard. It is possible they track the hydraulic system behind the landslide, giving them some value for hazard monitoring. For instance, if these events failed to appear in early fall or emerged significantly later than usual, it could signal prolonged hydraulic activity behind the landslide, potentially suggesting elevated landslide risk. Although this interpretation involves a fair amount of speculation, it highlights the diverse geophysical signals within the landslide environment, each offering unique insights into slope stability—whether or not they are directly linked to movement.

Data and Resources

All data used in this article came from published sources listed in the references. Seismic and infrasound waveform data are available through Incorporated Research Institutions for Seismology (IRIS) Data Management Center and the Alaska Earthquake Center. Radar data are provided by the U.S. Geological Survey Landslide Program. Weather data are available through the Alaska Division of Geological and Geophysical Surveys (https://dggs.alaska.gov/weatherstations/). Glacial velocity data are generated using auto-RIFT (Gardner *et al.*, 2018) and is provided by the NASA MEaSUREs ITS_LIVE project (Gardner *et al.*, 2022) (ITS_LIVE, last accessed January 2025). Imagery from Maxar Technologies, Landsat/Copernicus, retrieved from https://earth.google.com. The authors use Antelope Seismic Software for some processing. ObsPy is available through: https://www.obspy.org. REDPy is available through: Hotovec-Ellis (2025). All websites were last accessed in November 2025. The supplemental material includes Text S1 describing our daily review of spectrograms, Text S2, which details tuning *dbdetect* for waveform analysis, Text S3 explaining how longer duration events are removed from our catalog, Text S4 depicting how we determined our rectilinearity filter, Text S5 detailing our selection of the location in which we run analysis on SI events, and Text S6 describing the parameters chosen for REDPy; Figures S1–S5, which depict family timelines of optimized parameters of REDPy, the velocity of the Cascade Glacier over a three-year period, a sample short-impulsive (SI) event overlain by the short-term average (STA)/long-term average (LTA) function, polar plots of all SI events filtered by rectilinearity, and cluster analysis of SI events and their different waveforms; and Table S1 describing optimized parameters for detecting SI events using an STA/LTA algorithm.

Declaration of Competing Interests

The authors acknowledge that there are no conflicts of interest recorded.

Acknowledgments

This work was supported by U.S. Geological Survey Cooperative Agreement G23AC00441. The authors thank Alicia Hotovec-Ellis for assistance and troubleshooting with the use of REDPy, as well as for her constructive comments on the article. The authors also thank an anonymous reviewer, whose comments further improved the quality and clarity of the article.

Any use of trade, firm, or product names is for descriptive purposes only and does not imply endorsement by the U.S. Government.

References

Alaska Earthquake Center, University of Alaska Fairbanks (1987). Alaska Geophysical Network [Data set], *International Federation of Digital Seismograph Networks*, doi: 10.7914/SN/AK.

Alaska Volcano Observatory, U.S. Geological Survey (USGS) (1988). Alaska Volcano Observatory [Data set], *International Federation of Digital Seismograph Networks*, doi: 10.7914/SN/AV.

Allen, R. (1982). Automatic phase pickers: Their present use and future prospects, *Bull. Seismol. Soc. Am.* **72,** no. 6B, S225–S242, doi: 10.1785/BSSA07206B0225.

Armstrong, W. H., and R. S. Anderson (2020). Ice-marginal lake hydrology and the seasonal dynamical evolution of Kennicott Glacier, Alaska, *J. Glaciol.* **66,** no. 259, 699–713, doi: 10.1017/jog.2020.41.

Barnhart, K. R., R. P. Jones, D. L. George, J. A. Coe, and D. M. Staley (2021). Preliminary assessment of the wave generating potential from landslides at Barry Arm, Prince William Sound, Alaska, *U.S. Geol. Surv. Open-File Rept. 2021-1071*, 28 pp., doi: 10.3133/ofr20211071.

Bartholomaus, T. C., C. F. Larsen, S. O'Neel, and M. E. West (2012). Calving seismicity from Iceberg–Sea surface interactions, *J. Geophys. Res.* **117,** no. F4, F04029, doi: 10.1029/2012JF002513.

Beyreuther, M., R. Barsch, L. Krischer, T. Megies, Y. Behr, and J. Wassermann (2010). ObsPy: A python toolbox for seismology, *Seismol. Res. Lett.* **81,** no. 3, 530–533, doi: 10.1785/gssrl.81.3.530.

Chávez, E., S. Y. Schwartz, J. F. Pacheco, C. Muller, N. J. Finnegan, and B. M. Higman (2023). Precursory seismic signals before catastrophic landslides in Costa Rica: From slow to fast slip, *AGU Fall Meeting*, Abstract (T31H-0287), available at https://agu.confex.com/agu/fm23/meetingapp.cgi/Paper/1391193 (last accessed November 2025).

Coe, J. A., E. K. Bessette-Kirton, and M. Geertsema (2018). Increasing rock-avalanche size and mobility in Glacier Bay National Park and Preserve, Alaska detected from 1984 to 2016 Landsat imagery, *Landslides* **15,** no. 3, 393–407, doi: 10.1007/s10346-017-0879-7.

Cuffey, K. M., and W. S. B. Paterson (2010). *The Physics of Glaciers*, Elsevier, Massachusetts, 175–222.

Dai, C., B. Higman, P. J. Lynett, M. Jacquemart, I. M. Howat, A. K. Liljedahl, A. Dufresne, J. T. Freymueller, M. Geertsema, M. W. Jones, *et al.* (2020). Detection and assessment of a large and potentially tsunamigenic Periglacial Landslide in Barry arm, Alaska, *Geophys. Res. Lett.* **47,** no. 22, e2020GL089800, doi: 10.1029/2020GL089800.

Ekström, G., and C. P. Stark (2013). Simple scaling of catastrophic landslide dynamics, *Science* **339,** no. 6126, 1416–1419, doi: 10.1126/science.1232887.

Ereditato, D., and G. Luongo (1994). Volcanic tremor wave field during quiescent and eruptive activity at Mt. Etna (Sicily), *J. Volcanol. Geoth. Res.* **61,** nos. 3/4, 239–251, doi: 10.1016/0377-0273(94)90006-X.

Flinn, E. A. (1965). Signal analysis using rectilinearity and direction of particle motion, *Proc. IEEE* **53,** no. 12, 1874–1876, doi: 10.1109/PROC.1965.4462.

Gardner, A. S., M. Fahnestock, and T. Scambos (2022). MEaSUREs ITS_LIVE landsat image-pair glacier and ice sheet surface velocities, *NSIDC-0775, Version 1* [Data Set], NASA National Snow and Ice Data Center Distributed Active Archive Center, Boulder, Colorado USA doi: 10.5067/IMR9D3PEI28U.

Gardner, A. S., G. Moholdt, T. Scambos, M. Fahnstock, S. Ligtenberg, M. BroekeVan Den, and J. Nilsson (2018). Increased west Antarctic and unchanged east Antarctic ice discharge over the last 7 years, *Cryosphere* **12,** no. 2, 521–547, doi: 10.5194/tc-12-521-2018.

Gauthier, D., S. A. Anderson, H. M. Fritz, and T. Giachetti (2018). Karrat Fjord (Greenland) tsunamigenic landslide of 17 June

2017: Initial 3D observations, *Landslides* **15,** no. 2, 327–332, doi: 10.1007/s10346-017-0926-4.

Google (n.d.). Barry Arm area, Prince William Sound, Alaska [Satellite imagery], *Google Earth*, available at https://earth.google.com/ (last accessed May 2024).

Gualtieri, L., and G. Ekström (2018). Broad-band seismic analysis and modeling of the 2015 Taan Fjord, Alaska Landslide using instaseis, *Geophys. J. Int.* **213,** no. 3, 1912–1923, doi: 10.1093/gji/ggy086.

Higman, B., D. H. Shugar, C. P. Stark, G. Ekström, M. N. Koppes, P. Lynett, A. Dufresne, P. J. Haeussler, M. Geertsema, S. Gulick, *et al.* (2018). The 2015 landslide and tsunami in Taan Fiord, Alaska, *Sci. Rep.* **8,** no. 1, 12,993, doi: 10.1038/s41598-018-30475-w.

Hotovec-Ellis, A. J. (2025). REDPy – Repeating earthquake detector in Python (Version 1.2.0), *U.S. Geol. Surv. Software Release*, doi: 10.5066/P1FRCP22.

Huggel, C., J. Caplan-Auerbach, C. F. Waythomas, and R. L. Wessels (2007). Monitoring and modeling ice-rock avalanches from ice-capped volcanoes: A case study of frequent large avalanches on Iliamna volcano, Alaska, *J. Volcanol. Geoth. Res.* **168,** nos. 1/4, 114–136, doi: 10.1016/j.jvolgeores.2007.08.009.

Karasözen, E., G. Davy, M. E. West, B. D. Collins, M. Einbund, J. J. Lyons, C. Miles, D. M. Staley, L. Toney, and G. J. Wolken (2023). Can a diverse array of monitoring techniques reveal insights into precursor activity in the Barry Arm Landslide, Alaska? *AGU Fall Meeting*, Abstract (NH11E-0672), available at https://agu.confex.com/agu/fm23/meetingapp.cgi/Paper/1410786 (last accessed November 2025).

Karasözen, E., and M. E. West (2024). Toward the rapid seismic assessment of landslides in Coastal Alaska, *Seism. Rec.* **4,** no. 1, 43–51, doi: 10.1785/0320230044.

Langet, N., and F. M. J. Silverberg (2023). Automated classification of seismic signals recorded on the Åknes rock slope, Western Norway, using a convolutional neural network, *Earth Surf. Dynam.* **11,** no. 1, 89–115, doi: 10.5194/esurf-11-89-2023.

Lyons, J. J., D. Fee, W. A. Thelen, A. M. Iezzi, and A. G. Wech (2024). Infrasound for volcano monitoring, in *Recommended Capabilities and Instrumentation for Volcano Monitoring in the United States*, Flinders A. F., J. B. Lowenstern, M. L. Coombs, and M. P. Poland (Editors), U.S. Geological Survey Scientific Investigations Report 2024-5062-C, 11 p., doi: 10.3133/sir20245062C.

Métaxian, J.-P., S. Araujo, M. Mora, and P. Lesage (2003). Seismicity related to the glacier of Cotopaxi volcano, Ecuador, *Geophys. Res. Lett.* **30,** no. 9, 1–4, doi: 10.1029/2002GL016773.

Miller, D. J. (1960). The Alaska earthquake of July 10, 1958: Giant wave in Lituya Bay, *Bull. Seismol. Soc. Am.* **50,** no. 2, 253–66, doi: 10.1785/BSSA0500020253.

Montalbetti, J. F., and E. R. Kanasewich (1970). Enhancement of teleseismic body phases with a polarization filter, *Geophys. J. Int.* **21,** no. 2, 119–129, doi: 10.1111/j.1365-246X.1970.tb01771.x.

Neave, K. G., and J. C. Savage (1970). Icequakes on the Athabasca glacier, *J. Geophys. Res.* **75,** no. 8, 1351–1362, doi: 10.1029/JB075i008p01351.

Poli, P. (2017). Creep and slip: Seismic precursors to the Nuugaatsiaq landslide (Greenland), *Geophys. Res. Lett.* **44,** no. 17, 8832–8836, doi: 10.1002/2017GL075039.

Qamar, A. (1988). Calving Icebergs: A source of low-frequency seismic signals from Columbia Glacier, Alaska, *J. Geophys. Res.* **93,** no. B6, 6615–6623, doi: 10.1029/JB093iB06p06615.

Schaefer, L. N., J. A. Coe, K. Wikstrom-Jones, B. D. Collins, D. M. Staley, M. E. West, E. Karasozen, C. Miles, G. J. Wolken, R. P. Daanen, *et al.* (2023). Kinematic evolution of a large paraglacial landslide in the Barry Arm Fjord of Alaska, *J. Geophys. Res.* **128,** no. 11, e2023JF007119, doi: 10.1029/2023JF007119.

Schöpa, A., W-A. Chao, B. P. Lipovsky, N. Hovius, R. S. White, R. G. Green, and J. M. Turowski (2018). Dynamics of the Askja Caldera July 2014 Landslide, Iceland, from seismic signal analysis: Precursor, motion and aftermath, *Earth Surf. Dynam.* **6,** no. 2, 467–485, doi: 10.5194/esurf-6-467-2018.

St. Lawrence, W., and A. Qamar (1979). Hydraulic transients: A seismic source in volcanoes and glaciers, *Science* **203,** no. 4381, 654–656, doi: 10.1126/science.203.4381.654.

Toney, L., D. Fee, K. E. Allstadt, M. M. Haney, and R. S. Matoza (2021). Reconstructing the dynamics of the highly similar May 2016 and June 2019 Iliamna volcano (Alaska) ice–rock avalanches from seismoacoustic data, *Earth Surf. Dynam.* **9,** no. 2, 271–293, doi: 10.5194/esurf-9-271-2021.

Walter, F., J. M. Amundson, S. O'Neel, M. Truffer, M. Fahnestock, and H. A. Fricker (2012). Analysis of low-frequency seismic signals generated during a multiple-iceberg calving event at Jakobshavn Isbræ, Greenland, *J. Geophys. Res.* **117,** no. F1, F01036, doi: 10.1029/2011JF002132.

West, M. E., C. F. Larsen, M. Truffer, S. O'Neel, and L. LeBlanc (2010). Glacier microseismicity, *Geol. Soc. Am.* **38,** no. 4, 319–322, doi: 10.1130/G30606.1.

Wolf, L. W., and J. N. Davies (1986). Glacier-generated earthquakes from Prince William Sound, Alaska, *Bull. Seismol. Soc. Am.* **76,** no. 2, 367–379, doi: 10.1785/BSSA0760020367.

Wolken, G. J., B. D. Collins, and D. Medrzycka (2024). Understanding the influence of glaciers on the Barry Arm Landslide, Prince William Sound, Alaska, *AGU Fall Meeting*, Abstract EP53G-03, available at https://agu.confex.com/agu/agu24/meetingapp.cgi/Paper/1633561 (last accessed November 2025).

Manuscript received 24 June 2025
Published online 19 November 2025

An Improved Method for Inverting the Spatiotemporal Stress Field Using Focal Mechanism Data and Its Application in Sichuan–Yunnan Region, China

OPEN ACCESS

Xiangyun Guo[1] and Zhenyue Li[*1,2]

Abstract

This study introduces a novel iterative method for regional stress field inversion using focal mechanism data. By integrating key techniques from homogeneous stress inversion, the method enhances the accuracy of stress estimation. Seismic events are first clustered based on their spatial distribution to define distinct stress partitions. Fault planes are then identified using a fault instability criterion, and the conventional assumption of uniform shear stress across all planes is relaxed. Stress continuity between adjacent partitions is also enforced to produce a smooth stress field. The method is applied to both synthetic data and earthquake data from the seismically active Sichuan–Yunnan region of China. Results show that although the principal stress orientations are consistent with those obtained from conventional approaches, the proposed method yields more reliable stress shape ratios that better align with the regional tectonic setting.

Cite this article as Guo, X., and Z. Li (2025). An Improved Method for Inverting the Spatiotemporal Stress Field Using Focal Mechanism Data and Its Application in Sichuan–Yunnan Region, China, *Seismol. Res. Lett.* **97**, 2002–2015, doi: 10.1785/0220250101.

Introduction

Crustal stress serves as the fundamental driving force behind plate tectonics. Accurate determination of regional stress states is crucial for reconstructing tectonic evolution processes, interpreting tectonic phenomena, and understanding earthquake nucleation and rupture mechanism (Sibson, 1982; Angelier, 1984; Zoback, 1992). Earthquakes are caused by instantaneous fault displacements driven by tectonic stress, making the orientation of seismogenic faults and their slip directions (i.e., focal mechanisms) valuable carriers of stress information (Wallace, 1951; Michael, 1984, 1987; Hardebeck and Michael, 2006; Martínez-Garzón *et al.*, 2016). Because most earthquakes occur in the mid-to-lower crust, focal mechanism analysis has become not only essential but also frequently the only available approach for studying stress conditions at these depths. At present, many scholars have constructed a variety of methods for inverting homogeneous (e.g., Gephart and Forsyth, 1984; Michael, 1987; Vavryčuk, 2014; Beaucé *et al.*, 2022) and spatiotemporal (e.g., Hardebeck and Michael, 2006; Martínez-Garzón *et al.*, 2016) stress fields based on focal mechanisms (Cheng *et al.*, 2023; Kuang *et al.*, 2023). The primary distinctions among homogeneous stress inversion methods lie in the optimization algorithms employed, whether the assumption of equal shear stress on the fault planes is adopted, and the criteria for selecting the fault plane from the two nodal planes of the focal mechanism. In addition to these differences, spatiotemporal methods also differ in terms of stress partitioning strategies and whether they smooth the stress between adjacent partitions. The specific differences among these methods are detailed in Table 1. The optimal combination of techniques in current homogeneous stress inversion includes linearized solving, selecting the fault plane from the two nodal planes of the focal mechanism based on fault instability, and accounting for variations in shear stress magnitudes across different faults. This approach is precisely what Beaucé *et al.* (2022) proposed. Their method is an extension of the iterative inversion framework developed by Vavryčuk (2014). At each iteration step, the current stress is applied to all faults, and the resulting shear stress magnitudes are assigned to the respective faults to construct the equations for stress inversion. Through synthetic tests, they demonstrated that this approach significantly improves the accuracy of stress inversion.

Because of the increased complexity of spatiotemporal stress inversion compared to homogeneous methods, the development of spatiotemporal stress field inversion techniques has not kept pace with advancements in homogeneous approaches. A representative approach for inverting spatiotemporal data is the

1. Institute of Geophysics, China Earthquake Administration, Beijing, China, https://orcid.org/0009-0009-1931-154X (ZL); 2. Now at Institute of Disaster Prevention, Langfang, China

*Corresponding author: li_zhenyue@foxmail.com

TABLE 1
Comparison of Different Stress Field Inversion Methods

Methods	Dimension	Partitioning Method	Algorithm	Whether the Shear Stresses of the Faults Are Equal	Method of Selecting the Fault Plane	Whether the Stress Field Is Smooth or Not
Gephart and Forsyth (1984)	0	\	Grid Search	No	Slip misfit	\
Michael (1987)	0	\	Linear	Yes	Randomly	\
Vavryčuk (2014)	0	\	Linear iteration	Yes	Instability	\
Beaucé *et al.* (2022)	0	\	Linear iteration	No	Instability	\
Hardebeck and Michael (2006)	≥0	Grid	Linear	Yes	Randomly	Yes
Martínez-Garzón *et al.* (2016)	≥0	Cluster	Linear iteration	Yes	Instability	Yes
This article	≥0	Cluster	Linear iteration	No	Instability	Yes

"\" indicates that partitioning or smoothing is not applicable to the stress inversion.

damped stress field inversion method developed by Hardebeck and Michael (2006). This method divides the data into different temporal or spatial grids and inverts the stress within each grid using the approach of Michael (1984), while applying smoothing constraints between adjacent temporal or spatial grids to ensure smooth stress variations. These constraints help mitigate artificial stress anomalies caused by inappropriate data partitioning or insufficient data within individual grids. There are three aspects of this method that can be improved: (1) because of the uneven spatial distribution of earthquakes, the use of regular grid partitioning may result in significant disparities in the number of seismic events across different regions. Regions with fewer data are less likely to yield reliable results. (2) The method of Hardebeck and Michael (2006) randomly selects the fault plane from the two nodal planes of each focal mechanism to perform stress inversion. (3) The method assumes equal shear stress magnitudes on all faults. These three factors can reduce the accuracy of the derived stress field.

Martínez-Garzón *et al.* (2016) proposed a method aimed at addressing the first two limitations. For the first, they employed a clustering approach to partition regions based on the spatial distribution of earthquakes. This ensures that regions with dense seismic activity are divided into smaller partitions, whereas sparsely populated regions are assigned larger partitions, thus guaranteeing sufficient data within each partition to constrain the stress tensor. For the second point, after partitioning, they used the iterative method of Vavryčuk (2014) to invert the stress within each partition separately. After obtaining the stress results for each partition, they decide whether to apply damped least squares to refine the result based on the extent of the stress differences between the partitions. If significant stress differences were observed between partitions, damped least-squares inversion was performed on the fault planes selected from the iterative inversion of each partition.

In this article, we focus on the three aspects of improvement and propose a new inversion strategy. For the first point, following the approach of Martínez-Garzón *et al.* (2016), we adopt a spatial clustering method for focal mechanisms to establish partitions. For the second and third points, we integrate the methods of Beaucé *et al.* (2022) and Hardebeck and Michael (2006) to develop an iterative damped least-squares approach. In the following sections, after presenting the theoretical framework of the proposed method, we apply it to invert the stress field in the Sichuan–Yunnan region of China using both synthetic and real focal mechanism data. By comparing the results with those derived from other approaches, we demonstrate the effectiveness and reliability of our method.

Method

Stress partitioning

In conventional 2D stress field inversion, focal mechanism data are typically partitioned into different regions using regular grids (Hardebeck and Michael, 2006). However, due to the spatial clustering of earthquakes, this approach has a significant drawback: some grids may contain insufficient data to reliably determine the stress field. Although the damped stress inversion method can constrain the stress in adjacent grids through smoothing, it still fails to yield credible stress field results when neighboring grids also lack sufficient data. To address the spatial clustering of earthquakes, some studies (e.g., Martínez-Garzón *et al.*, 2016; Nouri *et al.*, 2023) have adopted the K-means clustering method to spatially group earthquakes, treating each cluster as a separate stress partition. This approach has the advantage of creating smaller partitions in areas with dense seismic activity and larger partitions in areas with sparse activity, thereby ensuring that each partition contains an adequate amount of data. In this study, we also adopted the spatial clustering method for partitioning earthquakes.

Applying smoothing constraints between adjacent irregular partitions requires a nuanced approach. Martínez-Garzón *et al.* (2016) proposed a method where, after K-means clustering, the study area is first divided into regular grids. The centroid of each cluster is then assigned to the nearest grid point, and smoothing constraints are applied to partitions corresponding to directly adjacent grid points. However, this approach of determining neighbors by dividing the study area into regular grids is indirect. In our method, we define neighboring partitions as those for which centroids are within a specified distance (e.g., 2°) from the centroid of the target partition. In addition, if the angle between the connecting lines of these neighbors and the target partition is too small (e.g., <60°), the neighbor with the farther centroid distance is discarded.

Stress inversion

Assuming that we have already identified the fault planes from the two nodal planes of each focal mechanism, we first construct the inversion equations following the damped stress field inversion method of Hardebeck and Michael (2006), as shown in the following equation:

$$\phi(\boldsymbol{m}_{\text{all}}) = \|\boldsymbol{d}_{\text{all}} - \mathbf{G}_{\text{all}}\boldsymbol{m}_{\text{all}}\|_2^2 + \alpha^2\|\mathbf{L}\boldsymbol{m}_{\text{all}}\|_2^2. \quad (1)$$

The first part of equation (1) represents the data-fitting residual, whereas the second part imposes constraints on the model. The parameter α is the damping coefficient, which balances the weights of these two parts in the objective function. The matrix $\mathbf{L}$ is the flattening matrix, which enhances the smoothness of the stress field between adjacent partitions. The forms of these parameters are as follows:

$$\mathbf{G}_{\text{all}} = \text{diag}(\mathbf{G}_1 \quad \mathbf{G}_2 \quad \cdots \quad \mathbf{G}_k \quad \mathbf{G}_{k+1} \quad \cdots \quad \mathbf{G}_r), \quad (2)$$

$$\boldsymbol{m}_{\text{all}} = [\boldsymbol{m}_1 \quad \boldsymbol{m}_2 \quad \ldots \quad \boldsymbol{m}_k \quad \boldsymbol{m}_{k+1} \quad \ldots \quad \boldsymbol{m}_r]^T, \quad (3)$$

$$\boldsymbol{d}_{\text{all}} = [\boldsymbol{d}_1 \quad \boldsymbol{d}_2 \quad \cdots \quad \boldsymbol{d}_k \quad \boldsymbol{d}_{k+1} \quad \cdots \quad \boldsymbol{d}_r]^T, \quad (4)$$

$$\mathbf{L} = \begin{bmatrix} \mathbf{I} & -\mathbf{I} & \ldots & 0 & 0 & \ldots \\ \mathbf{I} & 0 & \ldots & -\mathbf{I} & 0 & \ldots \\ 0 & \mathbf{I} & \ldots & 0 & -\mathbf{I} & \ldots \\ & & \ldots & & & \ldots \\ 0 & 0 & \ldots & \mathbf{I} & -\mathbf{I} & \ldots \\ & & \ldots & & & \ldots \end{bmatrix}. \quad (5)$$

In equations (2)–(4), the subscript "all" refers to all partitions, whereas "k" indicates the index of a partition, with a total of r partitions. In equation (5), the number of rows in matrix $\mathbf{L}$ corresponds to the total number of neighboring partitions, and $\mathbf{I}$ is a 5×5 identity matrix (because under the assumption of a deviatoric stress tensor, the stress tensor for a single region has five independent components). For a given partition, $\boldsymbol{m}$ and $\boldsymbol{d}$ are linearly related:

$$\boldsymbol{d} = \mathbf{G}\boldsymbol{m}. \quad (6)$$

In the formula,

$$\mathbf{G} = \begin{bmatrix} n_{i1}(n_{i2}^2 + 2n_{i3}^2) & n_{i2}(1 - 2n_{i1}^2) & n_{i3}(1 - 2n_{i1}^2) & n_{i1}(-n_{i2}^2 + n_{i3}^2) & -2n_{i1}n_{i2}n_{i3} \\ n_{i2}(-n_{i1}^2 + n_{i3}^2) & n_{i1}(1 - 2n_{i2}^2) & -2n_{i1}n_{i2}n_{i3} & n_{i2}(n_{i1}^2 + 2n_{i3}^2) & n_{i3}(1 - 2n_{i2}^2) \\ n_{i3}(-2n_{i1}^2 - n_{i2}^2) & -2n_{i1}n_{i2}n_{i3} & n_{i1}(1 - 2n_{i3}^2) & n_{i3}(-n_{i1}^2 - 2n_{i2}^2) & n_{i2}(1 - 2n_{i3}^2) \end{bmatrix}, \quad (7)$$

$$\boldsymbol{m} = [\sigma_{11} \quad \sigma_{12} \quad \sigma_{13} \quad \sigma_{22} \quad \sigma_{23}]^T, \quad (8)$$

$$\boldsymbol{d} = \tau_i[s_{i1} \quad s_{i2} \quad s_{i3}]^T. \quad (9)$$

In equation (7), n represents the fault normal vector, in which the first subscript denotes the fault index, and the second subscript indicates the component of the normal vector. In equation (8), $\boldsymbol{\sigma}$ is the stress tensor. In equation (9), s represents the slip direction of the fault, with the subscripts having the same meaning as those for the fault normal vector, and $\boldsymbol{\tau}$ is the shear stress vector on the fault. Equations (6)–(9) describe the inversion of the stress tensor (deviatoric stress) for a single region. However, because the expression for $\boldsymbol{d}$ in equation (9) includes the magnitude of the shear stress on the fault, the stress cannot be directly inverted using equation (6). To solve this problem, Michael (1984) proposed an approach by assuming that the magnitudes of the shear stress on all faults are equal (set to 1), and then solving for a deviatoric stress tensor that best satisfies this assumption. The spatiotemporal stress field inversion method of Hardebeck and Michael (2006) also constructs equation (1) based on this assumption. However, because the magnitudes of the shear stress on different faults vary, the stress derived under this assumption deviates to some extent from the true stress. In our new method, following the approach of Beaucé *et al.* (2022), we use the stress tensor obtained from the previous iteration to calculate the magnitudes of the shear stress on each fault and assign them to equation (9). By minimizing equation (1) with respect to $\boldsymbol{m}_{\text{all}}$, the stress for each partition is obtained as follows:

$$(\mathbf{G}_{\text{all}}^T\mathbf{G}_{\text{all}} + \alpha^2\mathbf{L}^T\mathbf{L})\boldsymbol{m}_{\text{all}} = \mathbf{G}_{\text{all}}^T\boldsymbol{d}_{\text{all}}. \quad (10)$$

In equation (10), the size of the matrix depends on the amount of focal mechanism data. If the dataset is small, the spatial distribution of stress can be directly obtained by solving the equation. If the dataset is large, the conjugate gradient method can be employed for solving. In addition, it is important that because the shear stress on each fault is only relative in magnitude, the absolute values of the stress tensor obtained for each region are not physically meaningful. Instead, we can only determine the orientations of the three principal stress axes and the shape ratio between the three principal stresses:

$$R = \frac{\sigma_1 - \sigma_2}{\sigma_1 - \sigma_3}. \quad (11)$$

In equation (11), σ_1, σ_2, and σ_3 are the magnitudes of the maximum, intermediate, and minimum principal stresses, respectively. From a physical perspective, the stress parameter R determines the shape of the stress ellipsoid and normal stress surface (Lund and Townend, 2007).

Integrated stress inversion workflow

The use of equation (10) to solve the stress field requires identifying the fault plane from the two nodal planes of each focal mechanism. However, which of the nodal planes corresponds to the actual fault plane remains an unknown. Hardebeck and Michael (2006) adopted the approach of Michael (1984) by randomly selecting the fault plane from each focal mechanism and then solving for the stress field. Clearly, because the equations incorporate auxiliary fault planes, the resulting stress field may deviate from the true stress field. In the context of homogeneous stress inversion problems, Vavryčuk (2014) proposed an iterative inversion strategy to simultaneously determine the fault plane and the stress tensor. At each iteration step, the instability of the two nodal planes of each focal mechanism is calculated based on the stress tensor from the previous step, and the nodal plane with higher instability is selected as the more likely fault plane. Because this method relies on the assumption of equal shear stress magnitudes on all faults, Beaucé *et al.* (2022) mitigated the impact of this assumption on the inversion results by updating the shear stress magnitudes on all faults at each iteration step. Clearly, this approach to handling fault planes and shear stress magnitudes can be integrated into spatiotemporal stress field inversion. The specific computational workflow is as follows.

1. Specify an appropriate number of partitions and use the K-means clustering method to divide the focal mechanism data into the specified categories.
2. Determine the smoothing relationships for stresses between different partitions.
3. Randomly select one nodal plane from the two nodal planes of each focal mechanism in each partition, assume equal shear stress magnitudes on all faults, test different damping coefficient values, calculate the stress field using equation (10) for each case, plot the L-curve, and determine the appropriate value for the damping coefficient.
4. Fix the damping coefficient, randomly select one nodal plane from the two nodal planes of each focal mechanism in each partition, assume equal shear stress magnitudes on all faults, and compute the initial stress solution using equation (10).
5. Based on the initial stress of each partition, select the nodal plane with higher instability from the two nodal planes of the focal mechanisms within the corresponding partition and calculate the shear stress magnitudes on all faults to assign to equation (9).
6. Update equation (10) and solve the updated stress field.
7. Repeat steps (5) and (6) until the stress results converge.

We employ the Monte Carlo approach (Aster *et al.* 2018) to assess the uncertainty in the stress results. Specifically, we randomly perturb all focal mechanisms by a certain degree (e.g., Gaussian-distributed noise with a mean of 0° and a standard deviation of 10°) and then perform stress inversion steps (4–7) on the noisy focal mechanisms. This process of adding noise and performing inversion is repeated independently for a certain number of times. Finally, the distribution of these stress results is used to quantify the uncertainty.

Applications in Sichuan–Yunnan Region

Focal mechanisms data

The focal mechanism data used in this study are sourced from the research of Sheng *et al.* (2022), comprising a total of 1302 events recorded from January 1970 to July 2019. Figure 1a shows the spatial distribution of these focal mechanisms, revealing a clustered pattern of earthquakes, which makes the data suitable for spatial partitioning using clustering methods. Figure 1b,c displays the distribution of earthquake depths and magnitudes respectively, indicating that the depths are primarily concentrated between 0 and 20 km, whereas the magnitudes mainly range from 3 to 6. Figure 1d presents the density distribution of focal mechanism types on the triangle diagram (Frohlich, 1992), showing that the focal mechanisms in the study region are predominantly strike-slip and uncertain types.

Spatial partitioning and damping coefficient

The data within the study area are divided into 20 clusters according to the epicenter locations of the earthquakes using the K-means clustering method. Each cluster serves as a spatial partition, as shown in Figure 2. The purpose of dividing the space into several regions is not only to be able to invert the data within each partition separately. More importantly, while inverting the data within each partition, smooth constraints are added to the stresses of the adjacent partitions. This additional constraint is in line with the nature of the gradual change of the stress field in the real situation and can also, to some extent, eliminate the spurious stress abrupt changes caused by inappropriate partitioning or too little data within the region. In the figure, the centroids connected by red lines indicate the smoothing of stresses between the corresponding partitions. We define partitions as neighbors if the distance between their centroids is less than 2°. For each target partition, we connect its centroid to those of its neighbors. If the angle between two connecting lines is less than 60°, the neighbor with the larger centroid distance is excluded. Figure 3 shows the trade-off curve for different damping coefficients, for which the horizontal axis represents the model length (measured by the L2 norm of the model) and the vertical axis represents the standard deviation of the data-fitting residuals. The red triangle marks our optimal damping choice, which is 1.5.

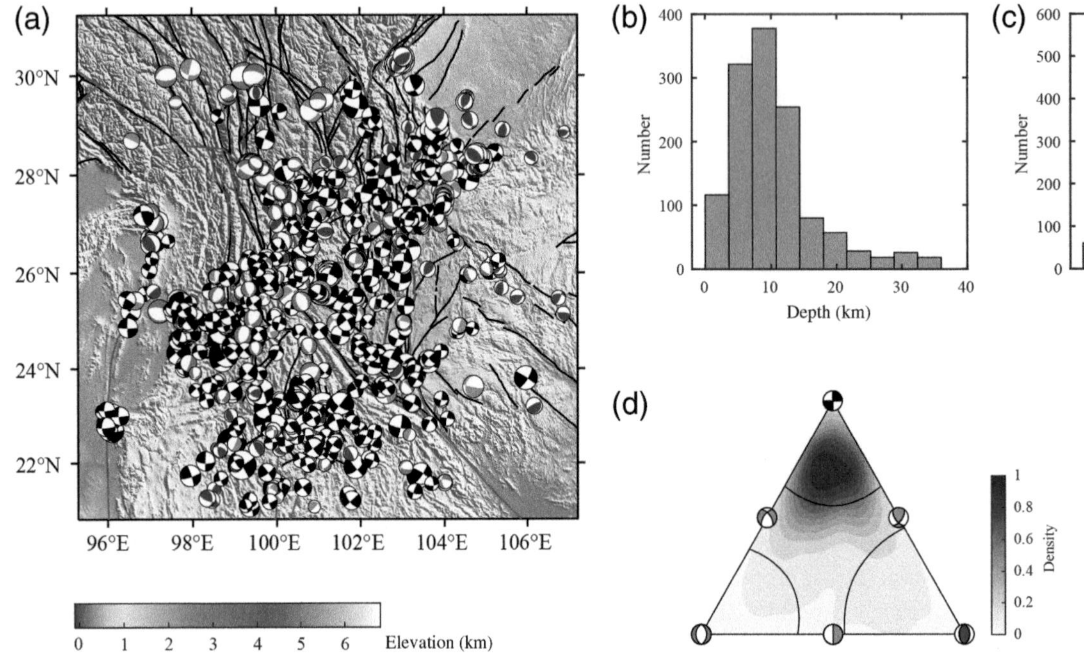

Figure 1. Distribution of focal mechanisms in the (a) Sichuan–Yunnan region, (b) statistics of earthquake depth, (c) magnitude, and (d) density distribution of focal mechanism type. In panel (a), the size of the focal mechanism plot is proportional to the magnitude of the earthquakes. The red, blue, black, and green focal mechanism plots represent the focal mechanism types of thrust, normal, strike-slip, and uncertain types, respectively. The black curves are the active faults (Deng *et al.*, 2003), and the magenta curves are the block boundaries. In panel (d), the black arc in the figure represents the classification standard of Frohlich (1992). The color version of this figure is available only in the electronic edition.

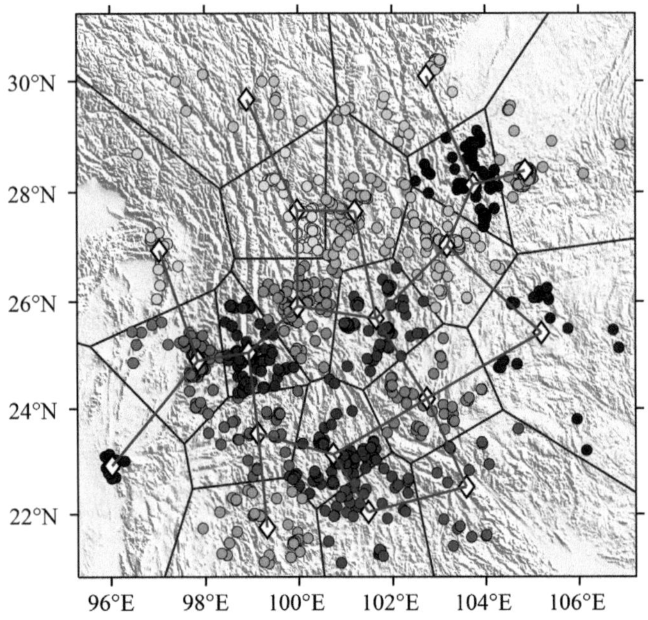

Figure 2. Spatial partitioning of stresses (blue Voronoi polygons) and smoothing relations of stresses between neighboring partitions (red line segments). The points of the same color in the figure belong to the same spatial partition, the diamonds are the corresponding mass centers, and the two mass centers connected by the red lines indicate the smoothing of the stresses of these two regions. The color version of this figure is available only in the electronic edition.

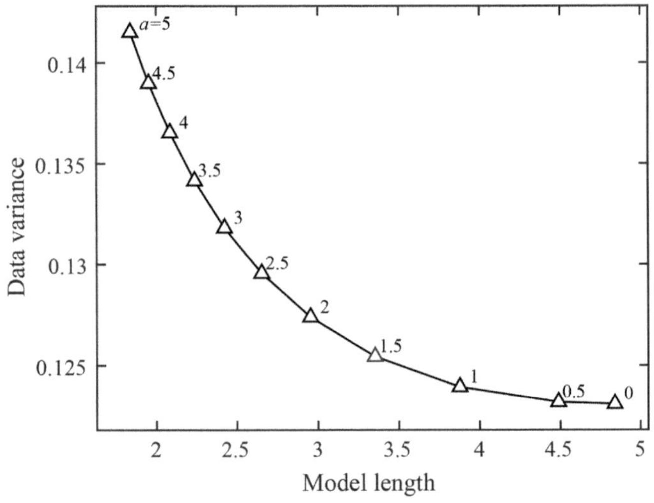

Figure 3. Dependence between data misfit and model length, calculated from a discrete set of damping parameters (damping values are indicated beside each triangle symbol). The selected damping parameter is shown with a red triangle symbol. The color version of this figure is available only in the electronic edition.

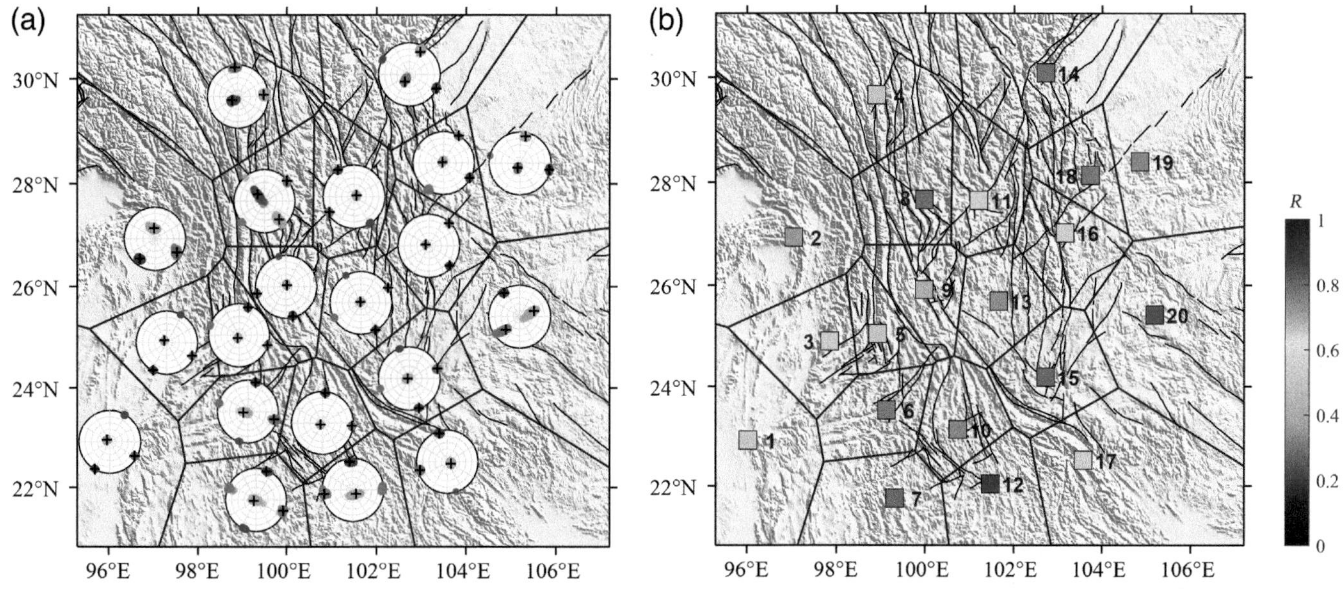

Figure 4. (a) Optimal stress directions and their uncertainties, and (b) the distribution of optimal R values. In panel (a), the red, green, and blue points represent the uncertainty ranges of the σ_1, σ_2, and σ_3 axes, respectively, and the black crosses indicate the optimal stress axes. The blue numbers in panel (b) indicate the partition number. The color version of this figure is available only in the electronic edition.

Results of stress field

Figures 4 and 5 show the results of the stress field inversion. Figure 4a shows the optimal stress orientations and their uncertainties obtained by repeating the stress inversion 500 times with random noise of 10° amplitude added to the focal mechanisms. It can be observed that stress orientations exhibit very small uncertainties across all partitions. Figure 4b shows the spatial distribution of the optimal stress ratio (R value), with the partition numbers labeled on the map. Figure 5 displays the optimal solutions of the R values for each partition along with their uncertainty ranges, showing that the R values in each region have a maximum uncertainty of ±0.2. Figure 6 depicts the orientations of the maximum horizontal principal stress (SH_{max}; Lund and Townend, 2007) and their uncertainties, which also show very small uncertainties. As shown in Figures 4a and 6, the stress field within the study area is predominantly strike slip, although localized regions exhibit normal or thrust faulting regimes. In strike-slip stress regimes, the azimuth of SH_{max} corresponds to the orientation of the σ_1 axis (Li *et al.*, 2025). When viewed along the southeast direction, the orientation of the σ_1 axes extends in an arc from the north-northwest–south-southeast direction to both sides, with dip angles close to horizontal. The σ_2 axes have a nearly vertical dip angle, whereas the σ_3 axes are oriented perpendicular to the σ_1 axes with a dip angle close to horizontal. Such stress distribution in the study area is attributed to the ongoing collision of the Indian plate with the Eurasian plate, which has resulted in uplift of the Tibetan plateau and lateral extrusion of material. The distribution characteristics of the principal stress axes are consistent with the results of previous studies (e.g., Cui *et al.*, 2006; Zhao *et al.*, 2013; Tian *et al.*, 2019), which serves as evidence of the validity of the methodology used in this article.

Regarding the stress ratio, the study area generally exhibits high R values, averaging around 0.7. However, six regions—numbered 1, 3, 4, 5, 8, and 9—display slightly lower R value anomalies, averaging around 0.5. In terms of deviatoric stress, when $R > 0.5$, $\sigma_2 < 0$, indicating that the σ_2 axis is under tensile stress, and the magnitude of this tensile stress is smaller than that of σ_3. The high R values obtained from the inversion suggest that the study area is subjected to strong compressive forces, resulting in a tensile stress state in all directions within the plane perpendicular to the compression axis. This observation is consistent with the dynamic background of the region. The six areas with lower R values are spatially connected, and the data amounts in regions 3, 5, 8, and 9 are

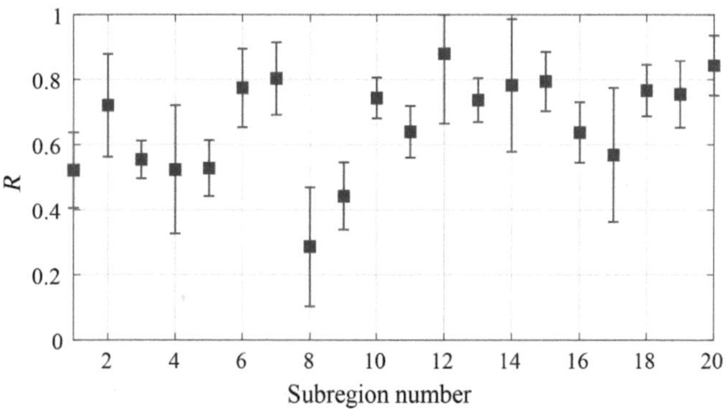

Figure 5. Optimal R values and uncertainty ranges for each region. The color version of this figure is available only in the electronic edition.

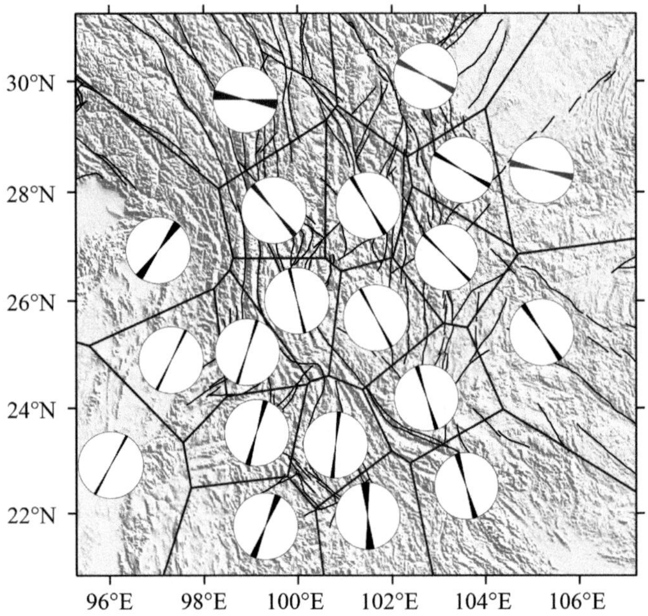

Figure 6. Orientations of SH_{max} and their uncertainty ranges for each region. In the figure, the direction of the sector indicates the orientation of SH_{max}, the central angle of the sector represents the uncertainty range, and the fill color denotes the stress type. Blue: normal, red: thrust, and black: strike slip. The color version of this figure is available only in the electronic edition.

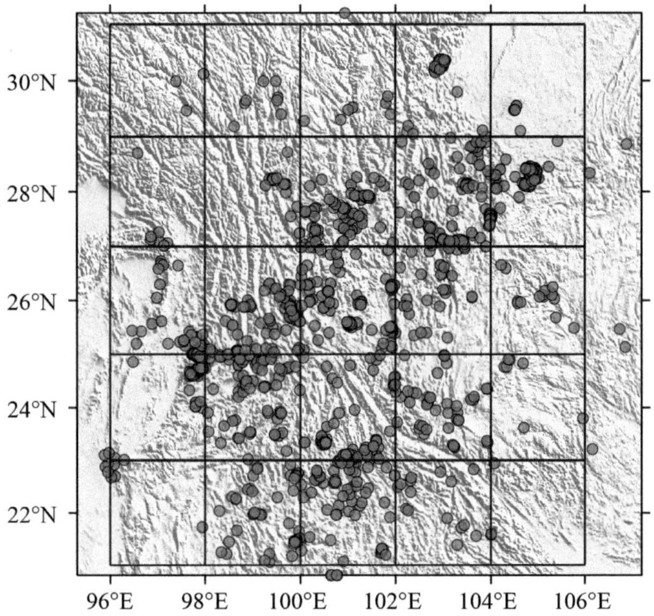

Figure 7. Stress partition based on a regular grid in methods 1 and 3. The color version of this figure is available only in the electronic edition.

sufficiently large, indicating that the low R value anomalies are likely to be real phenomena.

Comparison with results of other methods

This section compares the results of our method with those obtained from three other methods to highlight the advantages of our approach. The three methods are as follows: method 1: the damped stress field inversion method of Hardebeck and Michael (2006), using regular grid partitioning (Figs. 7 and 8); method 2: The same partitioning and stress smoothing strategy as our method (Fig. 9a), but retaining the stress inversion approach of Hardebeck and Michael (2006); method 3: regular grid partitioning (Fig. 9b) combined with our proposed algorithm for stress inversion. For methods 1 and 2, the uncertainties of the results are derived by performing 500 times stress inversion with random fault-plane selections, for which the optimal solution corresponds to the one with the smallest data residual among the 500 results. For methods 1 and 3, the stress smoothing strategy involves smoothing stress between directly adjacent grids (excluding diagonally adjacent grids), and only grids containing more than 10 focal mechanisms are inverted. Based on the trade-off curves of data residuals versus model length, the optimal damping coefficient for all three methods is determined to be 1.5.

Figure 7 shows the stress partitioning based on regular grids with a size of 2° × 2°. The results obtained using method 1 are shown in Figures 8 and 10a. Figure 8a shows the optimal stress orientations and their uncertainties. Figure 8b shows the spatial distribution of the optimal stress R values superimposed on the topographic map. Figure 10a shows the uncertainty ranges of the R values for each partition. Comparing Figures 4 and 5 with Figures 8 and 10a, the spatial variations in stress orientations obtained by our method and method 1 are consistent. However, there are significant differences in the distribution of the R values, although both methods exhibit small uncertainties in the R values. The most notable difference is that the R values obtained by method 1 fluctuate around 0.5 across different partitions, with a slightly increasing trend from northwest to southeast, and the overall mean R value is smaller than that obtained by our method.

In addition to differences in the computational approach, our method and method 1 also differ in their stress partitioning strategies. To assess the contribution of stress partitioning to the differences in R values, we conducted stress inversion using method 2. The results indicate that the stress orientations within each partition are consistent with those in Figure 4a, but the R values (Figs. 9a, 10b) exhibit significant differences compared to both our method and method 1. The R values obtained by method 2 fluctuate around 0.5, similar to those from method 1, but the amplitude of these fluctuations is considerably larger. Previous studies (e.g., Vavryčuk, 2014; Martínez-Garzón *et al.*, 2016) have shown that the instability criterion can more accurately identify the fault plane from focal mechanisms, thereby enhancing the accuracy of R value. Furthermore, accounting for variations in shear stress magnitudes across different fault planes also contributes to

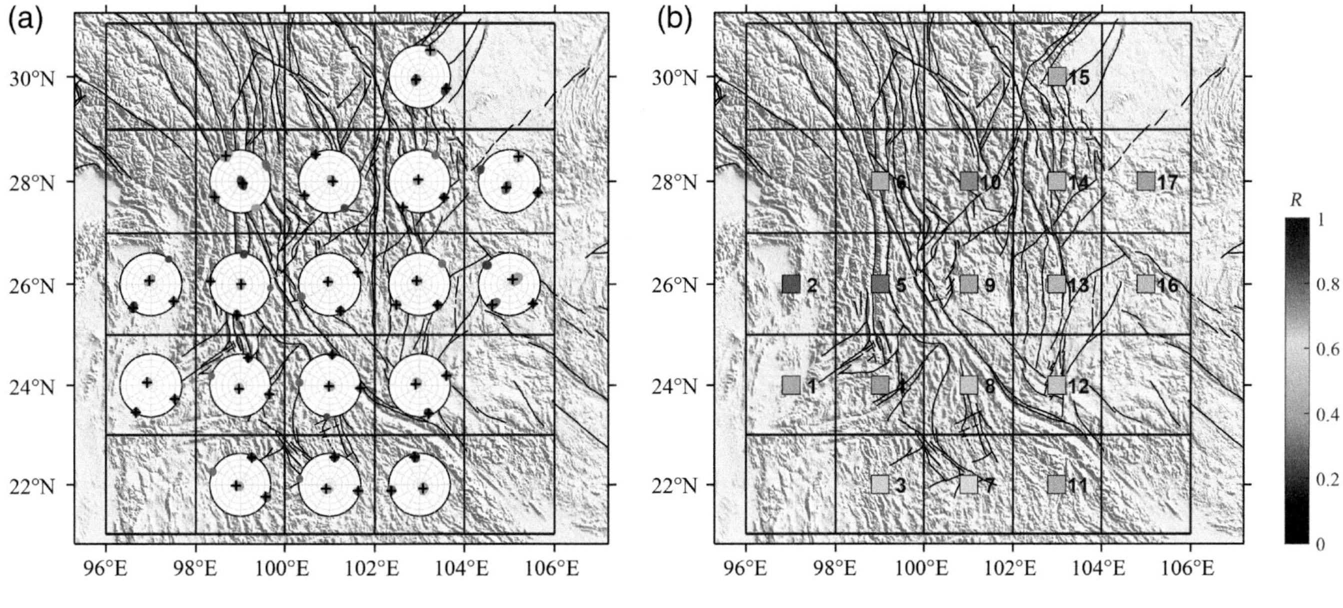

Figure 8. (a) Optimal stress direction and its uncertainty, and (b) the optimal R values obtained by method 1. The color version of this figure is available only in the electronic edition.

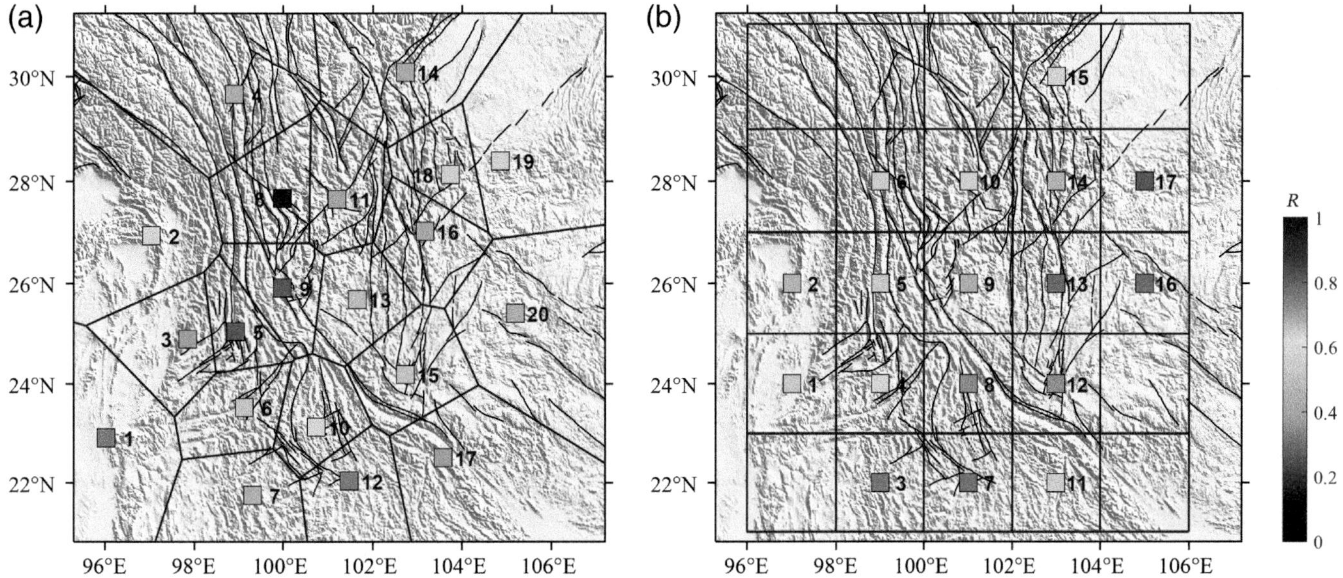

Figure 9. Distribution of the optimal R values obtained by methods (a) 2 and (b) 3. The color version of this figure is available only in the electronic edition.

constructing more reliable R value (Beaucé *et al.*, 2022). Therefore, it is expected that the R values obtained by our method differ significantly from those of methods 1 and 2. The stress orientations obtained using method 3 are consistent with those from other methods, and the R values (Figs. 9b, 10c) exhibit a high degree of agreement with the results from our method. This similarity stems from the fact that the algorithms used to compute the stress field are identical. Notably, the R values from method 3 display smoother distribution. This smoothing effect occurs because the regular grid partitioning does not account for the clustering characteristics of earthquakes. When data from different stress regimes are grouped into the same grid, it inherently smooths the stress field. Combined with the smoothing effect of the damping coefficient, this results in a stress field that has undergone double smoothing, effectively suppressing weaker R value anomalies. This further underscores the suitability of the partitioning method advocated in this study.

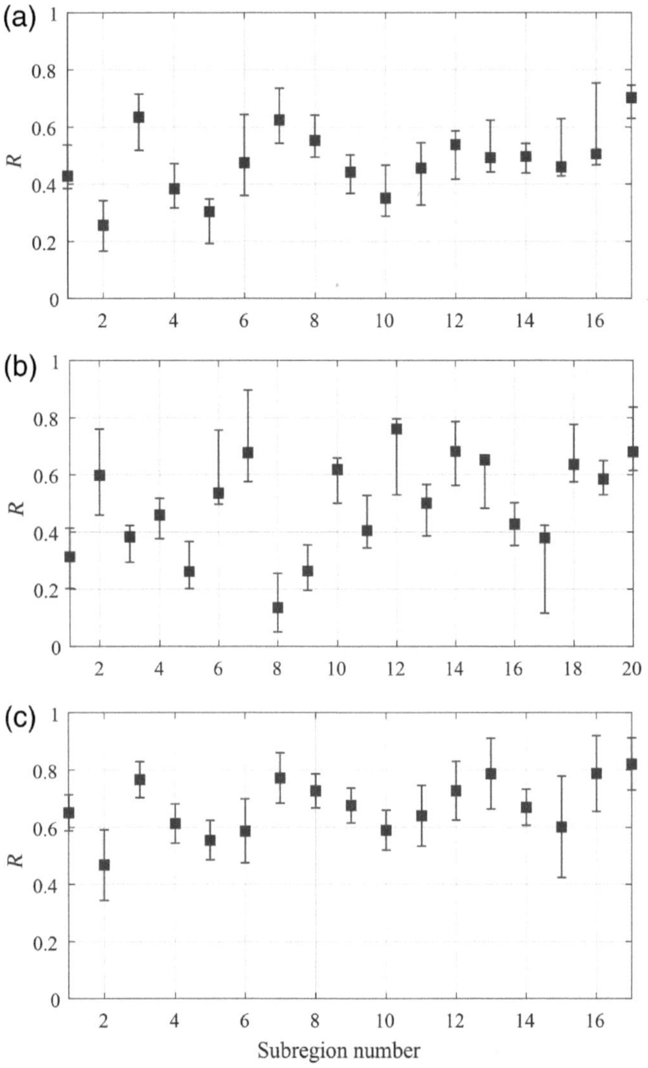

Figure 10. Optimal R values and their uncertainty ranges for each partition obtained by methods (a) 1, (b) 2, and (c) 3. The color version of this figure is available only in the electronic edition.

Synthetic tests

We also designed synthetic tests to more rigorously demonstrate that the proposed method can yield more accurate stress results than other approaches. Specifically, we used the stress partitioning and stress results derived from real data in the Sichuan–Yunnan region (Fig. 4) as a forward model, assuming homogeneous stress within each partition. Based on this model, we calculated the instability (Vavryčuk, 2014) and slip deviation (the angular difference between the theoretical and observed slip directions) of both nodal planes for each focal mechanism in each partition. A nodal plane was identified as the simulated fault if its instability coefficient exceeded 0.8 and its slip deviation was less than 30°. This is a relatively stringent criterion, ensuring that the faults belong to the same stress regime. If both nodal planes met these criteria, the one with the higher instability was selected, if neither met the criteria, the corresponding focal mechanism was discarded. The discarded mechanisms may indicate inappropriate stress partitioning, events unrelated to the regional background stress field, or substantial misfits in the focal mechanism inversion. The remaining focal mechanisms were retained as synthetic data under the assumed stress field, and the slip deviations were used to simulate observational noise. Table A1 shows the number of focal mechanisms in each subregion of the Sichuan–Yunnan region for both the original data and the synthetic tests. This synthetic model of stress and data distribution was then used to evaluate the accuracy of different stress inversion methods.

The synthetic test results indicate that, despite using different datasets, the stress fields obtained with the proposed method and the conventional inversion approach closely resemble those derived from the real data. Both methods produce comparable spatial variations in stress orientations; however, substantial differences emerge in the inferred stress shape ratio. Notably, only the proposed method accurately reproduces the spatial distribution of the shape ratio, clearly demonstrating its superiority. Details of the synthetic test results are provided in the Appendix.

Discussion

This study adopts the same stress parameters smoothing strategy between adjacent regions as that proposed by Hardebeck and Michael (2006). The stress tensor within each partition is represented by five parameters (as defined in equation 8), and smoothing is applied directly to these parameters to ensure a gradual transition across neighboring regions. These parameters implicitly encode both the orientations and shape ratio of the principal stresses. As a result, the inversion process simultaneously smooths both aspects. When adjacent partitions exhibit similarity in one aspect (e.g., orientation) but large differences in the other (e.g., shape ratio), the smoothing primarily acts on the component with greater contrast. If both aspects differ significantly, the smoothing is distributed across both.

Apparent stress discontinuities between adjacent partitions —such as the interchange of principal stress axes—may result from suboptimal partitioning or data limitations, such as a small number of focal mechanisms or high similarity among them, which limit the ability to reliably constrain the stress tensor. In such cases, a broad spectrum of stress solutions may fit the data equally well, and the one with the lowest misfit may be erroneous, showing significant deviation from the surrounding stress field. The application of a smoothing constraint can help suppress such spurious anomalies. If the stress discontinuity is genuine and the partition contains sufficient focal mechanism data, the stress will be well constrained, and the smoothing constraint will not override it, as doing so would substantially increase the data misfit. Conversely, if the discontinuity is genuine but the focal mechanism data are sparse, the limited data may not penalize smoothing-induced deviations strongly enough, and the true stress variation may be artificially smoothed out. However, even in the absence of smoothing, stress anomalies inferred from only a few data points lack robustness and should be interpreted with caution.

Conclusions

This study proposes an improved method for inverting the spatiotemporal stress field and we use data from the Sichuan–Yunnan region to illustrate the principles and workflow of spatial stress field inversion, which represents the most common application in stress analysis. The methods for other dimensions differ only in how data are partitioned spatially and temporally. The damped stress field inversion method proposed by Hardebeck and Michael (2006) offers an effective approach for inverting spatiotemporal stress fields. However, this method is based on the homogeneous stress inversion approach of Michael (1987) to invert stress within each partition. Recent studies (Vavryčuk, 2014; Martínez-Garzón *et al.*, 2016; Beaucé *et al.*, 2022) have shown that the practice of randomly selecting the fault plane from the two nodal planes of each focal mechanism in the Michael (1987) method, as well as the assumption of equal shear stress magnitudes on all fault planes, can reduce the accuracy of stress inversion. As a result, new homogeneous stress inversion methods have been developed to address these shortcomings. Nevertheless, these two improvements have not yet been extended to spatiotemporal stress inversion. The main contribution of this study is to propose a strategy that incorporates these two improvements from homogeneous methods into the damped stress field inversion method, thereby improving the accuracy of spatiotemporal stress field inversion results.

Our new method discards the strategy of using regular grids for stress spatial partitioning, as employed by Hardebeck and Michael (2006), and instead adopts a spatial clustering approach for partitioning focal mechanisms. This approach adjusts the size of each partition according to the clustering characteristics of earthquake spatial distribution, ensuring that each partition contains sufficient data to produce reliable results. We also propose a method for smoothing stress between adjacent partitions under this partitioning strategy. Using focal mechanism data from the Sichuan–Yunnan region, we provide a detailed explanation of our inversion method and compare the results obtained from different partitioning strategies and computational approaches. The results demonstrate that the computational approach has a significantly greater impact on the stress field results than the partitioning scheme. In the context of homogeneous stress inversion, the two improvements primarily enhance the accuracy of stress R value. As expected, the stress orientations derived from our proposed method are largely consistent with those obtained using traditional methods, whereas the R values exhibit notable differences.

The R values obtained for the Sichuan–Yunnan region using our method are relatively high, with a mean value of approximately 0.7, whereas the traditional methods produce a mean R value of around 0.5. The continuous subduction and compression of the Indian plate against the Eurasian plate drive the ongoing uplift of the Tibetan Plateau and the southeastward material flow through the Sichuan–Yunnan region (England and Houseman, 1986; Zhang *et al.*, 2004; Royden *et al.*, 2008). As a result, the stress background in this area is expected to be dominated by uniaxial compression, which corresponds to higher R values. This indirectly confirms the ability of our new method to provide more accurate stress R values. This study compares the results obtained from two partitioning methods and shows that the spatial clustering approach for focal mechanisms identifies a slightly lower R value anomaly band compared to the regional average. In contrast, the traditional regular grid partitioning method groups focal mechanisms from different stress regimes into the same grid, which inherently smoothes the spatial stress field. Combined with the smoothing effect of the inversion algorithm itself, the resulting double-smoothed stress field inevitably weakens the characteristics of stress anomalies to some extent. Based on these findings, we recommend the spatial clustering approach for partitioning focal mechanisms.

Data and Resources

The focal mechanism dataset for the Sichuan–Yunnan region is from Sheng *et al.* (2022). The MATLAB program (version 2021a, https://www.mathworks.com/products/matlab.html) for spatiotemporal stress field inversion developed in this study is publicly available on GitHub (https://github.com/li-zhenyue/spatiotemporal-stress-inversion) for interested readers to download and use. Both websites were last accessed in October 2025.

Declaration of Competing Interests

The authors acknowledge that there are no conflicts of interest recorded.

Acknowledgments

This work is supported by the National Natural Science Foundation of China (42474090) and Free Exploration Research Grants. The authors would like to thank the two anonymous reviewers for their valuable feedback and insightful suggestions, which significantly improved this work.

References

Angelier, J. (1984). Tectonic analysis of fault slip data sets, *J. Geophys. Res.* **89,** no. B7, 5835–5848, doi: 10.1029/JB089iB07p05835.

Aster, R. C., B. Borchers, and C. H. Thurber (2018). *Parameter Estimation and Inverse Problems*, Third Ed., Elsevier, Amsterdam, The Netherlands.

Beaucé, E., R. D. Van Der Hilst, and M. Campillo (2022). An iterative linear method with variable shear stress magnitudes for estimating the stress tensor from earthquake focal mechanism data: Method and examples, *Bull. Seismol. Soc. Am.* **112,** no. 3, 1224–1239, doi: 10.1785/0120210319.

Cheng, Y., R. M. Allen, and T. Taira (2023). A new focal mechanism calculation algorithm (refoc) using inter-event relative radiation patterns: Application to the earthquakes in the Parkfield area, *J. Geophys. Res.* **128,** no. 3, e2022JB025006, doi: 10.1029/2022JB025006.

Cui, X., F. Xie, and H. Zhang (2006). Recent tectonic stress field zoning in Sichuan-Yunnan region and its dynamic interest, *Acta Seismol. Sin.* **19,** no. 5, 485–496, doi: 10.1007/s11589-006-0501-x.

Deng, Q., P. Zhang, Y. Ran, X. Yang, W. Min, and Q. Chu (2003). Basic characteristics of active tectonics of China, *Sci. China Earth Sci.* **46,** no. 4, 356–372, doi: 10.1360/03yd9032.

England, P., and G. Houseman (1986). Finite strain calculations of continental deformation: 2. Comparison with the India-Asia Collision Zone, *J. Geophys. Res.* **91,** no. B3, 3664–3676, doi: 10.1029/JB091iB03p03664.

Frohlich, C. (1992). Triangle diagrams: Ternary graphs to display similarity and diversity of earthquake focal mechanisms, *Phys. Earth Planet. In.* **75,** nos. 1/3, 193–198, doi: 10.1016/0031-9201(92)90130-N.

Gephart, J. W., and D. W. Forsyth (1984). An improved method for determining the regional stress tensor using earthquake focal mechanism data: Application to the San Fernando earthquake sequence, *J. Geophys. Res.* **89,** no. B11, 9305–9320, doi: 10.1029/JB089iB11p09305.

Hardebeck, J. L., and A. J. Michael (2006). Damped regional-scale stress inversions: Methodology and examples for southern California and the Coalinga aftershock sequence, *J. Geophys. Res.* **111,** no. B11, doi: 10.1029/2005JB004144.

Kuang, W., C. Yuan, J. Zhang, and W. Zhang (2023). Relative focal mechanism inversion and its application to Ridgecrest sequence, *Seismol. Res. Lett.* **94,** no. 1 305–317, doi: 10.1785/0220210370.

Li, Z., Y. Wan, R. Liu, and X. Guo (2025). Can the azimuth of the horizontal principal stress indicate the azimuth of the three-dimensional principal stress? *Pure Appl. Geophys.* **182,** 2039–2053, doi: 10.1007/s00024-025-03704-3.

Lund, B., and J. Townend (2007). Calculating horizontal stress orientations with full or partial knowledge of the tectonic stress tensor, *Geophys. J. Int.* **170,** no. 3, 1328–1335, doi: 10.1111/j.1365-246X.2007.03468.x.

Martínez-Garzón, P., Y. Ben-Zion, N. Abolfathian, G. Kwiatek, and M. Bohnhoff (2016). A refined methodology for stress inversions of earthquake focal mechanisms, *J. Geophys. Res.* **121,** no. 12, 8666–8687, doi: 10.1002/2016JB013493.

Michael, A. J. (1984). Determination of stress from slip data: Faults and folds, *J. Geophys. Res.* **89,** no. B13, 11,517–11,526, doi: 10.1029/JB089iB13p11517.

Michael, A. J. (1987). Use of focal mechanisms to determine stress: A control study, *J. Geophys. Res.* **92,** no. B1, 357–368, doi: 10.1029/JB092iB01p00357.

Nouri, A., B. Rahimi, V. Vavryčuk, and F. Ghaemi (2023). Spatially varying crustal stress along the Zagros seismic belt inferred from earthquake focal mechanisms, *Tectonophysics* **846,** 229653, doi: 10.1016/j.tecto.2022.229653.

Royden, L. H., B. C. Burchfiel, and R. D. Van Der Hilst (2008). The geological evolution of the Tibetan Plateau, *Science* **321,** no. 5892, 1054–1058, doi: 10.1126/science.1155371.

Sheng, S., X. Hu, X. Wang, Y. Wan, H. Li, Z. Li, X. Tian, X. Wang, and S. Zhang (2022). Study on the crustal stress field of Yunnan and its adjacent areas, *Chin. J. Geophys.* **65,** no. 9, 3252–3267, doi: 10.6038/cjg2022P0383.

Sibson, R. H. (1982). Fault zone models, heat flow, and the depth distribution of earthquakes in the continental crust of the United States, *Bull. Seismol. Soc. Am.* **72,** no. 1, 151–163.

Tian, J., Y. Luo, and L. Zhao (2019). Regional stress field in Yunnan revealed by the focal mechanisms of moderate and small earthquakes, *Earth Planet. Phys.* **3,** no. 3, 243–252, doi: 10.26464/epp2019024.

Vavryčuk, V. (2014). Iterative joint inversion for stress and fault orientations from focal mechanisms, *Geophys. J. Int.* **199,** no. 1, 69–77, doi: 10.1093/gji/ggu224.

Wallace, R. E. (1951). Geometry of shearing stress and relation to faulting, *J. Geol.* **59,** no. 2, 118–130, doi: 10.1086/625831.

Zhang, P., Z. Shen, M. Wang, W. Gan, R. Bürgmann, P. Molnar, Q. Wang, Z. Niu, J. Sun, J. Wu, *et al.* (2004). Continuous deformation of the Tibetan Plateau from global positioning system data, *Geology* **32,** no. 9, 809–812, doi: 10.1130/G20554.1.

Zhao, L., Y. Luo, T. Liu, and Y. Luo (2013). Earthquake focal mechanisms in Yunnan and their inference on the regional stress field, *Bull. Seismol. Soc. Am.* **103,** no. 4, 2498–2507, doi: 10.1785/0120120309.

Zoback, M. L. (1992). First- and second-order patterns of stress in the lithosphere: The World Stress Map Project, *J. Geophys. Res.* **97,** no. B8, 11,703–11,728, doi: 10.1029/92JB00132.

Appendix

We conducted synthetic experiments to evaluate the effectiveness of the improved stress inversion method proposed in this study. Details of the stress model and the generation of focal mechanism data for the synthetic tests are described in the Synthetic tests section. The spatial distribution of the synthetic focal mechanisms across the subregions is shown in Figure A1a, and the number of focal mechanisms in each subregion is given in Table A1.

We first compare the stress inversion results obtained by the method proposed in this study with those derived from the Hardebeck and Michael (2006) approach. To isolate the differences between the two algorithms, both methods employed the same actual zoning scheme and stress smoothing strategy (as shown in Fig. 2). Figure A2 shows the stress orientations and R values from our method, Figure A4a presents the uncertainty ranges of R values in each subregion. Figures A3 and A4b display the corresponding results from the Hardebeck and Michael (2006) method.

Comparing the true stress model with the results from both methods reveals that the spatial distribution of stress orientations is consistent with the true stress field, and uncertainties within each subregion are relatively small. However, significant differences arise in the recovered stress shape ratios: our method better reproduces the spatial variation of R values, whereas the Hardebeck and Michael (2006) method tends to underestimate them overall, despite both methods reporting similarly low uncertainty ranges for R in each subregion.

In addition, we performed stress inversion using the Hardebeck and Michael (2006) method with a regular grid partitioning scheme (referred to as the classical method), with the

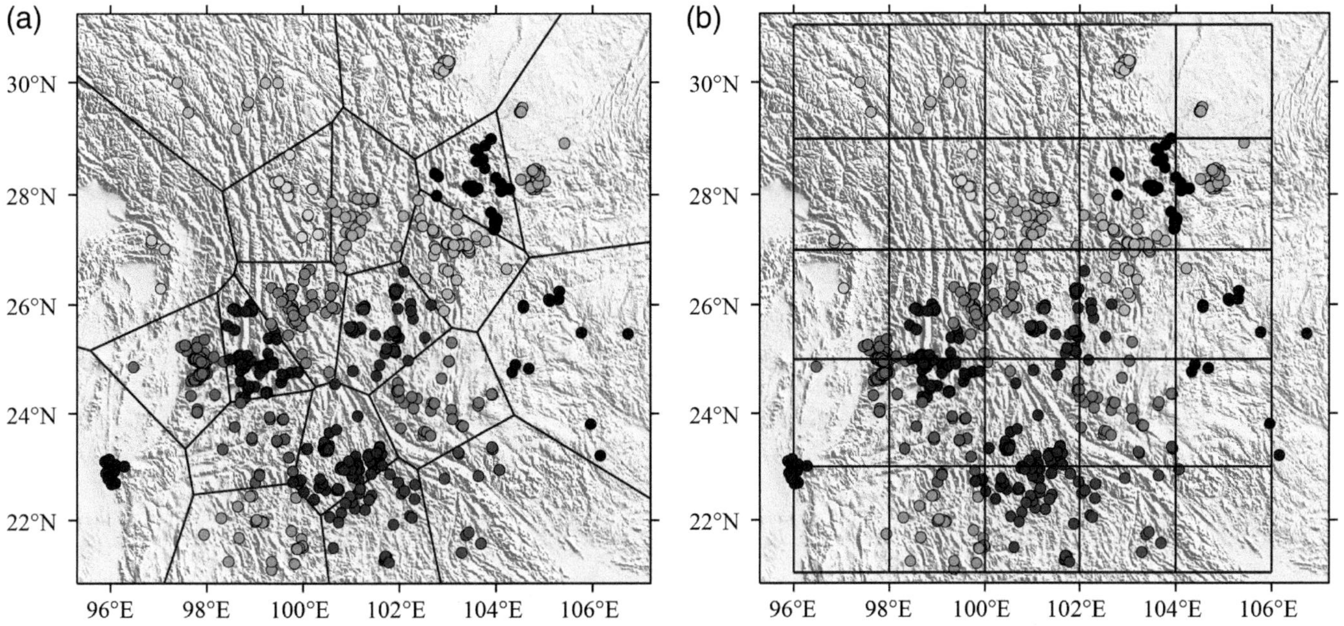

Figure A1. Stress partitioning of focal mechanism data for the (a) synthetic test and (b) regular grid partitioning. Different colors of scatter points represent earthquake events, with points of the same color belonging to the same stress regime. The color version of this figure is available only in the electronic edition.

partitioning and inversion results shown in Figures A1b, A4, and A5c. It can be seen that the stress orientations obtained by the classical method are consistent with those from the previous two methods, whereas the stress shape ratios are similar to those in Figure A3. This is expected, as both results are derived using the same inversion algorithm. The *R* value distribution from the classical method appears smoother, which is attributed to the use of regular grid partitioning that groups data from different stress regimes into the same grid cells, thereby enhancing the spatial smoothing of the stress field.

These synthetic test comparisons provide strong validation for the effectiveness of our method. By refining the strategy for selecting the fault plane from the two nodal planes and incorporating differences in shear stress across faults, the proposed approach achieves more accurate stress estimations compared to the other two methods.

TABLE A1
Focal Mechanism Counts in Each Subregion of the Sichuan–Yunnan Region for the Original Data and the Synthetic Tests

Partition Number	Number of Original Events	Number of Synthetic Events	Partition Number	Number of Original Events	Number of Synthetic Events
1	10	10	11	87	52
2	14	4	12	38	29
3	264	169	13	76	56
4	12	7	14	46	30
5	102	69	15	45	33
6	28	17	16	92	73
7	38	24	17	17	11
8	39	14	18	83	48
9	89	53	19	82	35
10	114	83	20	21	13

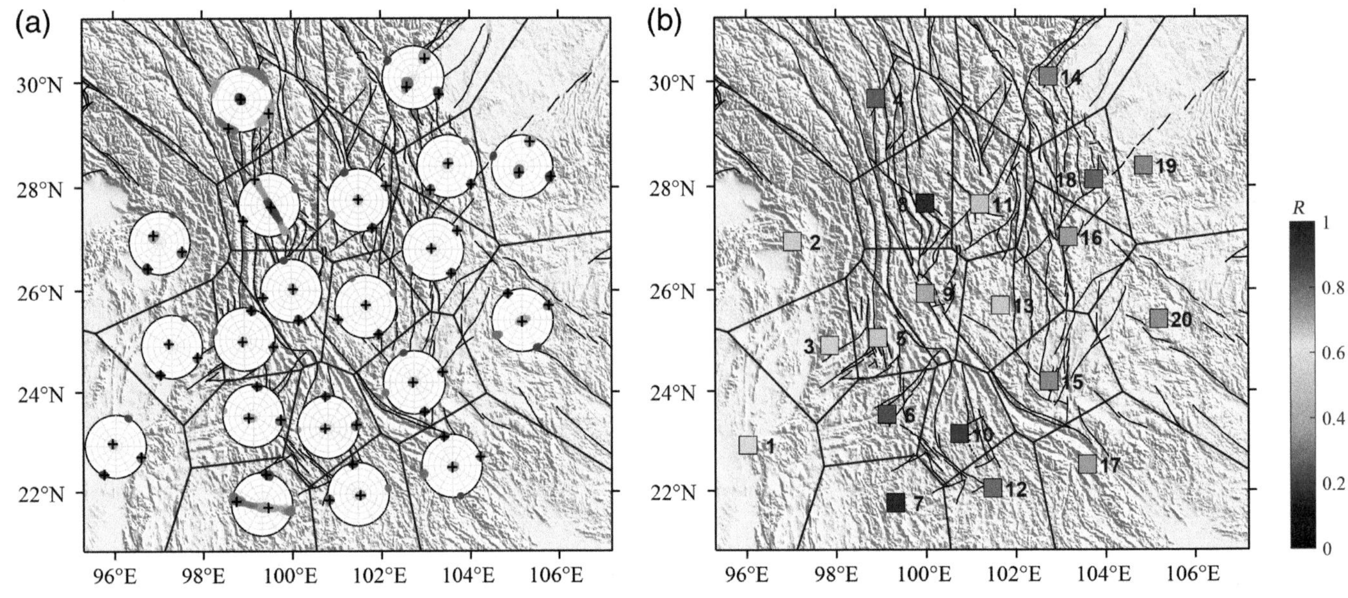

Figure A2. (a) Stress orientations and (b) *R* values obtained using the method proposed in this study. The interpretation of each panel corresponds to that in Figure 4. The color version of this figure is available only in the electronic edition.

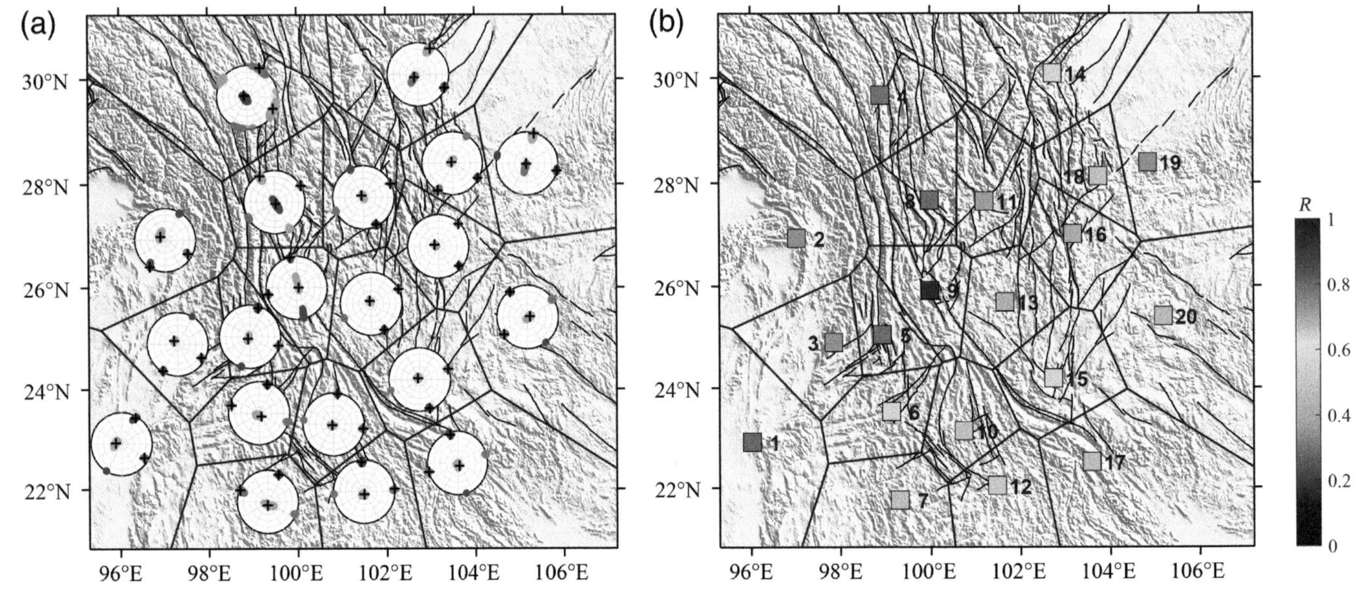

Figure A3. (a) Stress orientations and (b) *R* values inverted using the method of Hardebeck and Michael (2006) with the correct data partitioning. The interpretation of each panel corresponds to that in Figure 4. The color version of this figure is available only in the electronic edition.

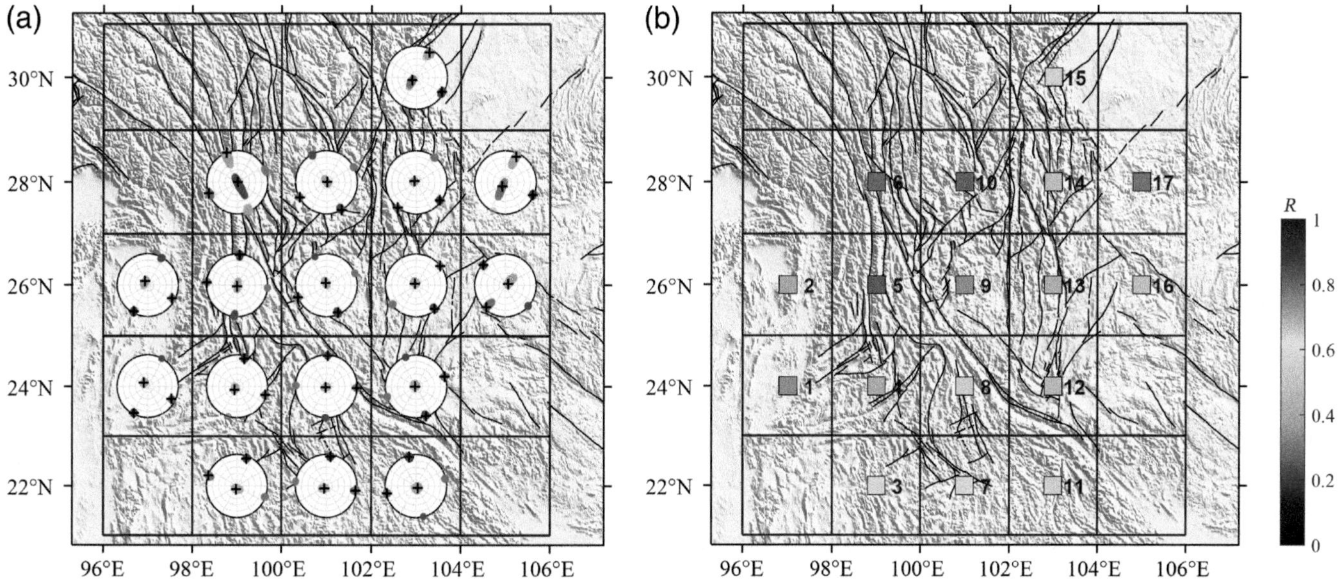

Figure A4. (a) Stress orientations and (b) R values obtained from stress inversion using the method of Hardebeck and Michael (2006) under a grid-based partitioning scheme. The interpretation of each panel corresponds to that in Figure 8. The color version of this figure is available only in the electronic edition.

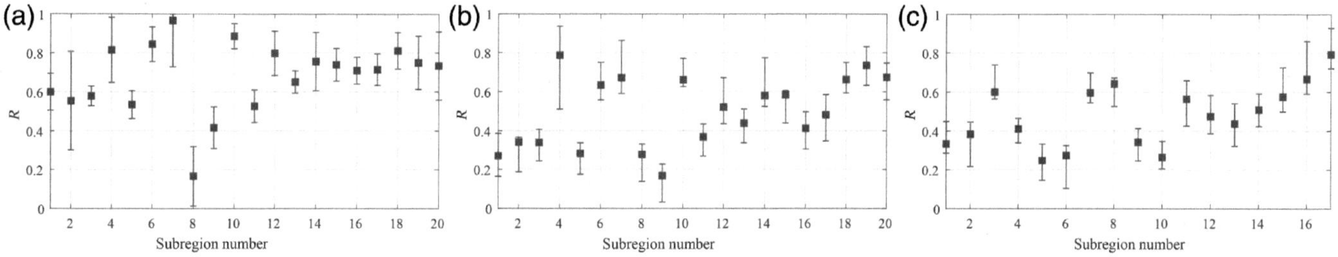

Figure A5. Optimal R values and their uncertainty ranges for each subregion obtained using different methods. (a) The method proposed in this study, (b) the method of Hardebeck and Michael (2006) with the correct data partitioning, and (c) the method of Hardebeck and Michael (2006) with grid-based partitioning. The color version of this figure is available only in the electronic edition.

Manuscript received 19 March 2025
Published online 24 October 2025

Lower Crustal Density: Method and Uncertainty Quantification

OPEN ACCESS

Yitan Wang*[1], Raymond M. Russo[1], and Yuanhang Lin[2]

Abstract

Lower crustal density (ρ_1) plays a fundamental role in understanding lithospheric structure, tectonic evolution, and gravity modeling, yet it remains difficult to constrain directly. This study introduces a new method to estimate ρ_1 and its uncertainty ($\delta\rho_1$) using P_s/P amplitude ratios derived from receiver functions and Zoeppritz equations, which account for seismic impedance contrasts at the Moho. The method requires a parameter set including compressional and shear-wave velocities of the lower crust and upper mantle (α_1,β_1,α_2,β_2), upper mantle density (ρ_2), ray parameter (p), and P_s/P ratio. We constructed a parameter inclusion model to explore a full range of theoretical values and used velocity pairs extracted from CRUST1.0, LITHO1.0, and Shen and Ritzwoller (2016). Monte Carlo simulations incorporating sharp and gradational Moho structures, with and without added noise, were used to test the method under relative realistic conditions. We calculated and density contrast ($\Delta\rho/\rho$) and evaluated their relationships with model parameters using Pearson correlation coefficients. Shear-wave velocities have the strongest impact on and $\delta\rho_1$, whereas shows the weakest correlation. The mean is ~10%. Comparison with CRUST1.0 shows similar density values but low correlation, reflecting fundamental methodological differences. In addition, uncertainty estimates using from Shen and Ritzwoller (2016) confirm that has limited influence on and $\Delta\rho/\rho$, supporting the reliability of our method. Compared with the approach of Aki and Richards (2002) and Julià (2007), our approach yields more stable, broadly applicable results, enabling in situ ρ_1 estimation for regional and global applications using widely available receiver function data.

Cite this article as Wang, Y., R. M. Russo, and Y. Lin (2025). Lower Crustal Density: Method and Uncertainty Quantification, *Seismol. Res. Lett.* **97**, 2016–2035, doi: 10.1785/0220250233.

Supplemental Material

Introduction

Understanding the lower crustal density (ρ_1) is essential for advancing our knowledge of Earth's internal structure, dynamic processes, gravity, and terrestrial evolution (e.g., Woollard, 1959; Kamber, 2015; Artemieva and Shulgin, 2019; Pappa *et al.*, 2019). The lower crust forms the base of the continental crust, typically extending from ~20 to 40 km depth, and is critical to understanding lithospheric composition and strength (e.g., Woollard, 1959; White, 1993; Rudnick and Fountain, 1995; Tassara *et al.*, 2006; Schmandt *et al.*, 2015). Because it is rarely exposed at the surface, much of our understanding comes from indirect geophysical observations and limited xenolith data.

Previous studies have extensively explored the composition and structure of the lower crust using seismic velocities, xenolith samples, and gravity modeling. Global compilations suggest that the lower crust is typically mafic, with seismic velocities ($V_P \sim 6.8$ to 7.4 km/s, $V_S \sim 3.6$ to 4.2 km/s) and densities ranging from ~2.9 to 3.2 $\mathrm{g/cm^3}$, although substantial regional variability exists (e.g., Holbrook *et al.*, 1992; Christensen and Mooney, 1995; Hacker *et al.*, 2015; Faccenna and Becker, 2020; Kalmár and Balázs, 2025). Xenolith studies provide direct sampling of deep crustal rocks but are limited in spatial coverage and may not represent broad crustal averages. The crust–mantle transition, or Moho, may appear as either a sharp discontinuity or a gradational zone, depending on tectonic history (Jarchow and Thompson, 1989). Although traditional seismic studies focus on arrival times to map this boundary, these methods offer limited sensitivity to gradual transitions or direct density constraints. Receiver function studies have traditionally focused on arrival times to constrain Moho depth and velocity contrasts (e.g., Ammon *et al.*, 1990; Zhu and Kanamori, 2000), with fewer efforts aimed at using amplitude information. Amplitude ratios such as P_s/P have been discussed in the context of Moho sharpness or shear velocity contrasts (e.g., Kumar *et al.*, 2005; Julià

1. Department of Geological Sciences, University of Florida, Gainesville, Florida, U.S.A., https://orcid.org/0000-0003-2804-6337 (YW); https://orcid.org/0000-0003-1960-0084 (RMR); 2. Department of Computer and Information Science and Engineering, University of Florida, Gainesville, Florida, U.S.A., https://orcid.org/0000-0002-8570-1898 (YL)

*Corresponding author: ytwang.geophysics@gmail.com

et al., 2000), but their potential for directly constraining ρ_1 remains underused. Crustal structure models such as CRUST1.0 (Laske *et al.*, 2013) incorporate seismic constraints and a priori assumptions to provide global estimates of velocity and density. However, these models are designed for broad regional applications and are not directly sensitive to impedance contrasts or wavefield behavior. Other methods, such as gravity inversion and ambient noise tomography, offer additional insights but often suffer from trade-offs between resolution and uncertainty, particularly in distinguishing compositional versus thermal effects (e.g., Cammarano and Romanowicz, 2007; Afonso *et al.*, 2008). These limitations highlight the need for a method that can constrain ρ_1 using widely available seismic observations. Our study builds on existing receiver function (RF) theory and amplitude sensitivity analysis to develop such a method, aiming to improve density estimates in tectonically diverse regions.

The primary goal of this study is to introduce and evaluate a forward-modeling method to estimate ρ_1 from direct P and converted P_s amplitudes using Zoeppritz equations (Aki and Richards, 2002). We determine ρ_1 and its uncertainty of propagation ($\delta\rho_1$) by analyzing conversions at the Mohorovičić (Moho; Mohorovičić, 1910) discontinuity. In practice, P and P_s amplitudes should be taken from observed RFs; in this study, we use P_s/P ratio as input to establish the theoretical foundation that relates amplitude behavior to subsurface density variations. Although this study focuses on establishing the theoretical framework, the long-term objective is to apply the method to real-RF data to estimate ρ_1 in situ and ultimately construct regional or global maps of ρ_1.

We construct a parameter inclusion model (PIM) that systematically samples a broad space of seismic parameters, including lower crustal and upper mantle velocities (α_1,α_2,$\beta_1\beta_2$), upper mantle density (ρ_2), ray parameter (p), and the P_s/P ratio, at fixed intervals. It has no constraints or uncertainty, making it theoretical and free from biases introduced by specific methodologies or constraints. Velocity pairs extracted from CRUST1.0 (Laske *et al.*, 2013), LITHO1.0 (Pasyanos *et al.*, 2014), and Shen and Ritzwoller (2016; SR) are treated as realistic subsets within the broader PIM space to assess the method's sensitivity, uncertainty, and robustness. As the velocity models do not uniquely prescribe values for p, ρ_2, and P_s/P, these parameters were treated as independent variables and assigned values within defined ranges that were applied uniformly across the PIM and all model subsets.

To examine structural realism, we generated Monte Carlo (Metropolis and Ulam, 1949) ensembles of sharp and gradational Moho scenarios, with and without additive noise ($\sigma = 0.08$) applied to the P_s/P ratio. The gradational Moho thickness was maintained at 15 km throughout to preserve meaningful velocity contrasts at the top, middle, and base of the transition zone. Although the parameters were randomly selected, their ranges matched those used in the PIM models. These simulations assess how structure and noise affect density estimates while maintaining the same parameter bounds as the PIM.

We compute the mean and standard deviation of ρ_1 and estimate $\delta\rho_1$ using propagation of uncertainty (Ku, 1966). We analyze parameter–density relationships using Pearson correlation coefficients (PCCs). We further evaluated the variability of the estimates using both the uncertainties of propagation and their percentage relative to the mean density, as well as the coefficient of variation (CV; standard deviation divided by mean) to test robustness under realistic conditions. Finally, we compared the density contrast ($\Delta\rho/\rho$) derived from our method with those from Aki and Richards (2002) and Julià (2007) to assess its performance relative to existing approaches.

We examined the reliability of our amplitude-based ρ_1 method by comparing our results with CRUST1.0 densities (which rely on empirical $V_P - \rho$ relations) using mean absolute error (MAE), root mean squared error (rmse), and z-scores (incorporating our uncertainties); we also report PCC to characterize linear consistency.

To evaluate the influence of input parameter uncertainty on ρ_1 estimates, we incorporated lower crustal shear-wave velocity uncertainty ($\delta\beta_1$) from the SR model. This allowed us to determine how realistic variations in affect the resulting density estimates and their sensitivities. By comparing density uncertainties and sensitivities derived using with those from our method, we aim to assess the practical robustness and applicability of the approach under real-world conditions in future work.

Method and Models

In this study, we developed a new method to estimate ρ_1 using the Zoeppritz equations (Aki and Richards, 2002). Our method requires seven key input parameters: lower crustal and upper mantle V_P, V_S, upper mantle density, ray parameter, and the P_s/P ratio. We used predefined velocity models. We did not use P_s/P ratios extracted from real RF data because this study focuses on the development and theoretical evaluation of the method. We systematically varied the ray parameter ρ_2 and P_s/P ratios. Details of the parameter setup are provided in the following sections.

To evaluate the method under realistic conditions, we applied three established velocity models: CRUST1.0, LITHO1.0, and SR. These models provide global coverage and allow comparison with existing estimates, including direct comparisons with ρ_1 and ρ_2 in CRUST1.0 and uncertainty evaluation using SR. Because the method depends exclusively on defined parameter sets, geographic locations, and Moho depth were not specified (i.e., identical input combinations yield the same ρ_1). A detailed description of the velocity models is provided in the Models with real velocity pairs section.

We applied the PIM, which integrates diverse parameter combinations to build a comprehensive framework for estimating ρ_1 from seismic data. To approximate realistic Earth structures, we also tested sharp and gradational Moho transitions, introduced random parameter variability, and added noise to assess method stability. The detailed setups are described in the Self-designed model—the PIM section.

Together these comparisons help determine whether the method can produce reliable density estimates with relatively low uncertainties and whether it can be confidently applied to a variety of crustal structures.

Method

Lower crustal density calculation. We developed a method to calculate ρ_1 and its $\delta\rho_1$. The mathematical details are provided in the supplemental material (mathematical derivations), available to this article. Because the method is based on *P*-to-*S* conversions, specifically the P_s/P amplitude ratios, we refer to it as the "amplitude-based method" (AB method). As shown in Figure 1, the required parameters include $\alpha_1,\beta_1,\alpha_2,\beta_2,p,\rho_2$, and P_s/P, with incident and transmitted angles (i_1,j_1,i_2,j_2) determined from the velocities and ray parameter using Snell's law.

The original equations are based on eqn 5.40 from Aki and Richards (2002) and are presented in the following equation:

$$\acute{P}\acute{P} = 2\rho_2 \frac{\cos(i_2)}{\alpha_2} F\alpha_2/(\alpha_1 D),$$
$$\acute{P}\acute{S} = -2\rho_2 \frac{\cos(i_2)}{\alpha_2} Gp\alpha_2/(\beta_1 D). \quad (1)$$

Therefore, set the $\frac{\acute{P}\acute{S}}{\acute{P}\acute{P}}$ as *R*, which represents the P_s/P ratio:

$$R = -\frac{Gp\alpha_1}{\beta_1 F}, \quad (2)$$

$$D = EF + GHp^2, \quad (3)$$

in which the terms *F*, *G*, *D*, and related expressions are defined in the supplemental material (mathematical derivations section 1).

In practice, the direct *P* and P_s amplitudes can be extracted from RFs. In this study, we directly provide *R* as input. Set $\chi = R\frac{\beta_1}{p\alpha_1}$, and substitude *G* and *F* with equation (2):

$$\chi = R\frac{\beta_1}{p\alpha_1} = -\frac{G}{F} = -\frac{\rho_2 M + \rho_1 N}{\rho_2 P + \rho_1 Q}, \quad (4)$$

in which

$$M = p\alpha_1(1 - 2\beta_2^2 p^2) - 2p\beta_2 \cos(i_1)\cos(j_2),$$
$$N = 2p\beta_1^2 \cos(i_1)\frac{\cos(j_2)}{\beta_2} - p\alpha_1(1 - 2\beta_1^2 p^2),$$
$$P = \cos(j_1)(1 - 2\beta_2^2 p^2) + 2\beta_2 p^2 \beta_1 \cos(j_2),$$
$$Q = 2\beta_1^2 p^2 \cos(j_1) + \beta_1(1 - 2\beta_1^2 p^2)\frac{\cos(j_2)}{\beta_2}. \quad (5)$$

Thus, ρ_1 is

$$\rho_1 = -\frac{\rho_2(M + \chi P)}{N + \chi Q}. \quad (6)$$

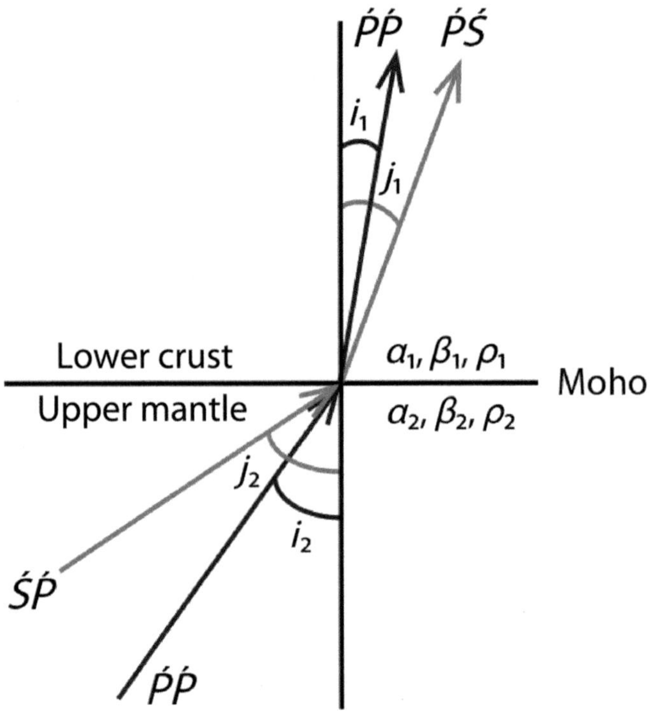

Figure 1. *P-to-S* wave conversion at the Moho. The compressional waves (*P* waves) are shown in blue, and the shear waves (*S* waves) are shown in red. Parameters in the lower crust are denoted with "1," and parameters in the upper mantle are denoted with "2." The angles associated with compressional waves are labeled as "i," and those associated with shear waves are labeled as "j." The color version of this figure is available only in the electronic edition.

Because χ is determined by the input parameters, equation (7) can be used to calculate ρ_1. A comprehensive derivation is presented in the supplemental material (mathematical derivations section 2).

Determining the range for reliable density estimates

Lower crustal constraints

For each ρ_1, we restricted its value to a reasonable range, with a lower bound ϵ and an upper bound set by ρ_2. Therefore, because $\rho_1 < \rho_2$, by applying to equation (7), we have

$$\chi < -\frac{M + N}{P + Q}. \quad (7)$$

This constraint on χ ensures that we obtain a meaningful ρ_1. Applying the lower bound ϵ to equation (7), we obtained

$$\frac{M + \chi P}{N + \chi Q} < -\frac{\epsilon}{\rho_2}. \quad (8)$$

Based on the range adopted for α_1, β_1, α_2, β_2, *p*, *R*, and ρ_2, the lowest calculated ρ_1 is 2.602 g/cm^3, occurring when $\alpha_1 = 6.2$ km/s, $\beta_1 = 3.8$ km/s, $\alpha_2 = 6.9$ km/s, $\beta_2 = 4.1$ km/s, $p = 0.05$ s/km, $R = 0.07$, and $\rho_2 = 3.35$ g/cm^3. In this study, we set the lower bound $\epsilon = 2.6\ \mathrm{g/cm^3}$. This indicates that the lowest ρ_1 falls within the reasonable range we set at the beginning. In practice, equation (7) will be used to obtain a reasonable ρ_1.

Incident angle constraints

To minimize scattering and improve the reliability of the P_s/P ratio, we restricted the P-wave incident angles to near-vertical values. In RF practice, large incident angles often introduce strong noise and complexity, lowering the usable signal-to-noise ratio (SNR). Following Ryberg and Weber (2000), we therefore adopt the commonly used range [23°, 37°], which is considered reasonable for real data and yields acceptable SNR levels. In some cases, applying an even narrower selection can further reduce noise in the input data (e.g., Kind *et al.*, 1995; Ryberg and Weber, 2000); this narrower window represents an optional more stringent filter for higher quality subsets.

Using Snell's low, $p = \sin i_2/\alpha_2$, we convert these angle ranges into constraints on the ray parameter. For typical upper mantle velocities ($\alpha_2 = 6.9 - 8.5$ km/s), the [23°, 37°] window corresponds to $\in$[0.045,0.087]s/km. To maintain consistency across models, we adopt a working range of $\in$[0.04,0.07] s/km, which keeps the incident angles within or close to the accepted observational range. The mathematical details are provided in the supplemental material (mathematical derivations section 2).

Propagation of uncertainty. We applied eqn 2.11 from Ku (1966) to calculate the propagation uncertainty of ρ_1. This method evaluates how uncertainties in the variables affect the overall uncertainty in the results, revealing the impact of parameter uncertainties on the estimates (Ku, 1966). According to eqn (7), the uncertainty in ρ_1, denoted as $\delta\rho_1$ is calculated as follows:

$$\delta\rho_1 = \sqrt{\sum_{x=\alpha_1}^{\chi}\left(\frac{\partial\rho_1}{\partial x}\delta x\right)^2}, \tag{9}$$

in which x can be variables α_1,β_1,α_2,β_2, and p. To determine $\delta\rho_1$ using equation (10), we must calculate the partial derivative of all the variables included in equation (7). The partial derivative of ρ_1, ρ_2, and χ with respect to each variable are provided in the supplemental material (mathematical derivations section 3 and 4).

To evaluate the effect of step size (δx), we tested a range of values (e.g., 0.1, 0.01, 0.001, and 0.0001) and observed that $\delta\rho_1$ decreased with smaller δx. For example, $\delta x = 0.1$ resulted in $\delta\rho_1 \approx 0.35$, and $\delta x = 0.01$,0.001, and 0.0001 yielded $\delta\rho_1$ values of ~0.035, ~0.0035, and ~0.00035, respectively. Although the relationship was not strictly proportional, the results exhibited a consistent scaling trend. Based on these tests, we selected $\delta x = 0.01$ as a balanced and practical interval that mitigates overestimation from larger steps while maintaining numerical stability and computational efficiency across all variables in equation (9).

Correlation analysis of variables to ρ_1 and $\delta\rho_1$. We used the PCC to measure the linear correlation between parameter sets (i.e., α_1,β_1,α_2,β_2,p,ρ_2,P_s/P), and ρ_1, as well as $\delta\rho_1$ (Benesty *et al.*, 2009). The PCC measures normalized covariance, ranging from −1 to 1, with values near 1 indicating strong positive correlation and values near −1 indicating strong negative correlation (Benesty *et al.*, 2009).

We analyzed the PCC between parameter sets ρ_1 uncertainty across all four models (i.e., CRUST1.0, LITHO1.0, SR, and PIM). In addition, we examined the PCC between ρ_1 and $\delta\rho_1$ to assess the correlation between density and its uncertainty. It provides insight into the ρ_1 variation, expressed as $\delta\rho_1/\rho_1$.

Analysis of lower crustal density variability

Density variation analysis

The main factors influencing variations across the Moho are the velocity and density discontinuities. We aimed to analyze density contrasts, denoted as $\Delta\rho/\rho$, to evaluate the reliability of ρ_1 estimates. The primary factor is the difference in density across the Moho (i.e., $\Delta\rho = \rho_2 - \rho_1$). We used the mean values of α, β, and ρ above and below the Moho, defining sensitivities as $\Delta\alpha/\alpha$, $\Delta\beta/\beta$, and $\Delta\rho/\rho$. We calculated these velocity and density contrasts based on all four models.

We also calculated the PCC between velocity contrasts (i.e., $\Delta\alpha/\alpha$ and $\Delta\beta/\beta$) and $\Delta\rho/\rho$ to demonstrate the correlation between them. Similarly, we calculated the PCC between $\Delta\rho/\rho$ and seven key parameters to illustrate the correlations between them. Analyzing these variations shows how parameter affects density calculation.

$\Delta\rho/\rho$ comparison

According to Aki and Richards (2002), their eqn 5.46 provides an approximation for calculating $\acute{P}\grave{P}$ and $\acute{P}\grave{S}$ We followed the two-step process of Julià (2007) to calculate $\Delta\rho$ using the same parameter sets as in the AR and AB methods. The ρ_2 values from these sets were then used to convert $\Delta\rho$ into ρ, allowing direct calculation of $\Delta\rho/\rho$ for comparison. The mathematical derivations are provided in the supplemental material (mathematical derivations section 5.1, 5.2).

For clarity, we refer to results from the AR method as AR results and those from Julià (2007) as Julià results. For consistency across methods, we constrained the outputs by requiring $\rho_1 < \rho_2$ and $\Delta\rho/\rho > 0$, matching the conditions used in the AB method. Although our method yields exact ρ_1 estimates, both the AR and the Julià methods provided $\Delta\rho/\rho$. Therefore, we also express our results in terms of $\Delta\rho/\rho$ to place all three methods in equal footing.

We compared the three different $\Delta\rho/\rho$ values using the methods outlined in the Density variation analysis section. For the Julià results, we used β_0 derived from various parameter combinations as outlined by Julià (2007). The differences between these values will reveal the correlation between $\Delta\rho/\rho$, and $\Delta\beta/\beta$ and $\Delta\alpha/\alpha$. A lower $\Delta\rho/\rho$ indicates more reliable results.

ρ_1 comparison between CRUST1.0 and AB method. To evaluate the consistency between our amplitude-based ρ_1 estimates and the empirical densities from the CRUST1.0 model, we compiled all available combinations of lower crustal and upper mantle seismic velocities and their associated densities (ρ_1, ρ_2) from CRUST1.0, resulting in a total of 1214 unique structural configurations. Each configuration represents a distinct set of velocity and density parameters, allowing for a direct comparison with our density estimates. To make the comparison, we used the CRUST1.0 V_P, V_S, and ρ_2 values as fixed inputs to our AB method. Because CRUST1.0 does not provide ray parameters or P_s/P ratios, we varied them within the ranges established in the Introduction of models section to complete the parameter sets. Using these parameter sets, we calculated ρ_1 with our method and then compared the results directly with the ρ_1 values reported in CRUST1.0 under the same velocity and density conditions.

Although both approaches aim to estimate ρ_1, they rely on fundamentally different methodologies. CRUST1.0 densities are empirically assigned from $V_P - \rho$ relationships (Christensen and Mooney, 1995), but our method derives ρ_1 from amplitudes ratios governed by Zoeppritz equations, which are sensitive to impedance contrasts and incidence angles under controlled wavefield conditions. As a result, the two datasets are expected to be comparable in magnitude but may differ in how they respond to variations in crustal structure.

To quantify the difference between our method and CRUST1.0, we computed the MAE and rmse between the two sets of ρ_1. The formulas are given by

$$\mathrm{MAE} = \frac{1}{n}\sum_{i=1}^{n} |\rho_i^a - \rho_i^c|, \mathrm{rmse} = \sqrt{\frac{1}{n}\sum_{i=1}^{n}(\rho_i^a - \rho_i^c)^2}, \tag{10}$$

in which ρ_i^a and ρ_i^c are the amplitude-based and CRUST1.0-derived ρ_1 for the *i*th parameter set, and n is the total number of valid comparisons. MAE captures the average difference, and rmse emphasizes larger discrepancies, providing complementary measures of model agreement: whereas MAE indicates typical deviations, rmse gives greater weight to outliers.

To assess the difference relative to the uncertainty in our estimates, we also computed z-scores (Zill, 2020) using

$$z_i = \frac{|\rho_i^a - \rho_i^c|}{\delta\rho_i}, \tag{11}$$

in which $\delta\rho_i$ is the propagation uncertainty calculated using equation (9) based on the same parameter sets, with full derivations provided in the supplement (mathematical derivations sections 3 and 4). The z-score measures the difference between the two models relative to the AB uncertainty (Zill, 2020). Values ≤ 1 indicate agreement within uncertainty, 1–2 reflect moderate deviations, and >2 suggest discrepancies beyond expected bounds. PCC were also calculated to assess linear consistency between the two sets of ρ_1 estimates.

Analysis of $\delta\rho_1$ using Shen and Ritzwoller $\delta\beta_1$. The uncertainty of propagation analysis (details in the Propagation of uncertainty section and supplemental material mathematical derivations sections 3 and 4) shows that β_1 is the most influential parameter for both ρ_1 and $\delta\rho_1$ (e.g., Brocher, 2005). To evaluate how shear-wave velocity uncertainty ($\delta\beta_1$) affects density estimates, we used the Shen and Ritzwoller (2016) model, which provides velocity pairs across the western United States based on Bayesian Monte Carlo inversions. We incorporated the $\delta\beta_1$ values to the velocity pair and obtained a total of 2220 distinct velocity-$\delta\beta_1$ combinations. The analysis will help assess the reliability of the method when applied to real velocity pairs. SR only provides $\delta\beta_1$ for the western United States, which does not cover all possible $\delta\beta_1$ in the entire parameter set.

We varied the available velocity pairs (i.e., α_1, α_2, and β_2) with each β_1 that has an available $\delta\beta_1$. For each velocity pair, we varied β_1 from $\beta_1 - \delta\beta_1$ to $\beta_1 + \delta\beta_1$, ensuring that $\beta_1 + \delta\beta_1 < \beta_2$, with corresponding parameter ranges for ρ_2 (3.30–3.37 g/cm^3), and P_s/P (0.01–0.25). If $\beta_1 + \delta\beta_1 \geq \beta_2$, the upper limit was set to β_2. β_1 was sampled in 0.01 km/s steps, and the result for each velocity set was averaged to determine the ρ_1 and $\delta\rho_1$. We varied the ray parameter from 0.04 to 0.07 s/km in 0.01 s/km increments, consistent with values typically used for *P-to-S* conversions. The parameter sets were applied in equations (7) and (9) to calculate ρ_1 and $\delta\rho_1$, allowing us to assess how $\delta\beta_1$ influences the resulting density uncertainty under realistic conditions.

To quantify relationships, we computed PCC between $\delta\beta_1$ and $\delta\rho_1$ and between β_1 and $\Delta\rho$ or $\Delta\rho/\rho$. These analyses assess how velocity uncertainty propagates into density uncertainty and highlight links between shear velocity and density contrasts. Because SR only provides $\delta\beta_1$ in continental regions of the western United States, no equivalent oceanic analysis was conducted.

Introduction of models

As outlined earlier, this study estimates using the seven parameters, including velocities from CRUST1.0, LITHO1.0, and SR models. Because real RFs are not used, the ray parameter, P_s/P ratio, and ρ_2 were assigned predefined ranges. To explore a broader parameter space, we applied the PIM. For both sharp and gradational Moho models, parameter sets were generated using a Monte Carlo approach to simulate natural variability. Synthetic noise was introduced to assess the stability and reliability of the AB method under realistic conditions.

In velocity models, each longitude and latitude point is associated with specific values for lower crustal and upper mantle velocities and ρ_2. However, when geographic coordinates and Moho depth are excluded, the number of unique combinations of these parameters across the entire model is limited. For this study, we considered only the unique combinations of input parameters rather than the full spatial grids because our method depends exclusively on a defined set of seven parameters.

Therefore, geographic location and Moho depth do not influence the estimates, and identical parameter sets yield the same ρ_1. Similarly, the PIM, sharp Moho, and gradational Moho tests were designed to sample parameter combinations directly, isolating the effects of seismic parameters without reference to specific depths or locations.

Models with real velocity pairs. We tested three different velocity models in this study: CRUST1.0, LITHO1.0, and SR. The three velocity models are derived from real data, meaning they represent actual geological structures and include the noise inherent in real-world observations (LITHO1.0, SR) or variations in models obtained from different studies and types of seismic data (CRUST1.0). CRUST1.0 and LITHO1.0 are global models with uniform resolution, containing the most possible parameter sets under real conditions and allowing us to test whether the method is applicable to global-scale studies of ρ_1. SR only provides velocity pairs for the western United States, with longitude ranging from −124.75° to −100° and latitude from 28.25° to 49°.

The three velocity models (CRUST1.0, LITHO1.0, and SR) are constrained by different datasets or methodologies. CRUST1.0 provides V_P, V_S, and ρ from global seismic data, with V_S and ρ scaled from V_P (Nafe and Drake, 1957; Christensen and Mooney, 1995; Brocher, 2005). LITHO1.0 is mainly an upper mantle V_S model, in which the crustal V_S adopted from CRUST1.0 was adjusted (and V_P and ρ rescaled) to fit surface-wave dispersion data (Pasyanos *et al.*, 2014). SR constrained V_S in the lower crust and upper mantle using surface-wave dispersion from ambient noise and earthquake data. Therefore, a direct comparison of ρ_1 estimates derived from different models is somewhat challenging because of their distinct constraints and methodologies. Instead, we focus on analyzing ρ_1 within each individual velocity model rather than comparing results across models.

CRUST1.0 provides ρ_1 and ρ_2 for direct comparison with our estimates, and SR supplies $\delta\beta_1$ used to assess their impact on ρ_1 and AB method stability under realistic conditions. Applying velocity pairs extracted from these velocity models provides insight into how real velocity pairs, along with their associated noise, influence ρ_1 estimates using this method.

As previously described, we used real velocity pairs from the models to analyze ρ_1 and $\delta\rho_1$ under real conditions, including noise. The velocity ranges of the extracted velocity pairs from each model are listed in Table S1. Because p, ρ_2, and P_s/P are not uniquely constrained by these velocity models, we set them independently over shared ranges: $p = 0.04 - 0.07$ s/km, $\rho_2 = 3.30 - 3.37$ g/cm^3, and $0 < P_s/P \leq 0.25$ (Wang *et al.*, 2024), applied consistently across PIM and all model subsets. Ratios >0.25 were excluded to remain consistent with theoretical predictions of maximum P_s amplitudes given the modeled Moho velocity contrasts (e.g., McCamy *et al.*, 1962). Using Snell's law, $= \frac{\sin\theta}{V}$, in which θ is the incident or transmitted angle of the incoming compressional wave, we determined i and j using the ray parameters and velocities.

For each velocity pair, we rounded the values to one decimal place. Under this criterion, if the four velocities are not all identical to a previously recorded set, the combination is considered a new velocity pair. Based on this, we obtained 120 from CRUST1.0, 515 from LITHO1.0, and 147 velocity pairs from SR, across both the lower crust and upper mantle. The following values, derived from the CRUST1.0 model, serve as an example input parameter set: $\alpha_1 = 6.8$ km/s, $\beta_1 = 3.9$ km/s, $\alpha_2 = 8.2$ km/s, $\beta_2 = 4.5$ km/s, $p = 0.04$ s/km, $P_s/P = 0.16$, and $\rho_2 = 3.35$ g/cm^3. For convenience, we refer to the models using real velocity pairs by the names of their respective velocity datasets, that is, CRUST1.0, LITHO1.0, and SR, even though only the available velocity pairs from these models are applied.

Self-designed model—the PIM. We applied the PIM, which systematically incorporates a wide range of possible parameter combinations, effectively covering most scenarios likely to be encountered in real-world observations. PIM is built by varying α_1,α_2, β_1, β_2, p, ρ_2, and the P_s/P ratio at fixed intervals, generating a broad set of theoretical ρ_1 estimates. Unlike the other three models, which are based on real-world parameters and include velocity uncertainties, PIM does not account for parameter uncertainties and instead provides evenly spaced values within defined ranges. This approach creates a comprehensive reference framework, serving as a practical "dictionary" of ρ_1 estimates that is used both to explore the possible range of density values and to provide parameter sets for method comparisons (i.e., AR, Julià, and AB).

For each parameter in our PIM, we predefined a given range (as listed in Table S1), with an interval of 0.01 for all variables. An example set of input parameters from the PIM is: $\alpha_1 = 6.8$ km/s, $\beta_1 = 3.7$ km/s, $\alpha_2 = 8.2$ km/s, $\beta_2 = 4.2$ km/s, $p = 0.05$ s/km, $P_s/P = 0.12$, and $\rho_2 = 3.35$ g/cm^3. We calculated the ρ_1 and uncertainty for each parameter set, covering a broad range of scenarios. For all the velocity models, we averaged ρ_1 and uncertainty across different values of p,P_s/P, and ρ_2 to obtain an average density and uncertainty for each velocity pair. We also calculated the mean density and uncertainty for each model.

Sharp Moho model. In addition to the real velocity models and the PIM model, we tested a set of randomly generated velocity models to evaluate the impact of the sharp Moho structure on the ρ_1 estimated from the AB method. To better reflect natural variability, we used a Monte Carlo approach to randomly generate lower crustal, upper mantle velocities, and ρ_2 within the same ranges defined in the PIM model. Ray parameters were sampled over the range [0.04, 0.07] s/km, and P_s/P amplitude ratios were varied from 0.01 to 0.25, both with a step size of 0.01. To capture compositional variation, we constrained V_P/V_S ratios to 1.70–1.87 in the noise-free models, with lower values (1.70–1.77) representing felsic compositions and higher values (1.77–1.87) indicating more mafic materials (Wang *et al.*, 2024). In total, we generated 10,000 random parameter sets representing sharp Moho models.

To account for observational uncertainty and natural variability in P_s/P ratios, we applied Monte Carlo perturbations to the P_s/P values. Previous studies show that P_s/P typically varies from ~0.05 to 0.15 because of factors such as Moho structure and SNR (e.g., Kind *et al.*, 1995; Rychert and Shearer, 2009). Based on this, we used a standard deviation of 0.08 to represent moderate observational uncertainty (Li *et al.*, 2019). This value provides a realistic estimate of noise while avoiding systematic bias in the correlation between synthetic and observed P_s/P ratios. When synthetic noise is introduced, the resulting V_P/V_S ratios broaden to 1.52–1.97, spanning the full range of physically plausible values for crustal and mantle lithologies. This demonstrates that the framework is capable of reproducing both typical lower crustal values and the wider range observed in natural data. For each Monte Carlo realization, random noise was drawn from a normal distribution $N(0, 0.08)$ and added to the original P_s/P values. A total of 10,000 parameter sets were generated for the sharp Moho model with noise included.

For both the Monte Carlo sharp Moho models with and without noise, we calculated the mean and standard deviation of the results and performed propagation of uncertainty. Moreover, we computed the CV (Kendall, 1948), defined as the ratio of standard deviation to the mean. This metric is used to evaluate the relative variability of the density estimates and to assess the stability of the results under random parameter combinations (Kendall, 1948).

Gradational Moho model. In addition to the two-layer model representing a sharp Moho, we explored scenarios with a gradational Moho structure, which is commonly observed in real Earth settings. The gradational models were constructed by assuming that the transition from lower crust to upper mantle occurs over a 15 km thickness (e.g., Wang *et al.*, 2024). The 15-layer representation provides a reasonable gradient while preserving realistic velocity contrasts across depth. For each model, *P*- and *S*-wave velocities were randomly sampled using the Monte Carlo method within the same parameter ranges used for the sharp Moho case and PIM model. These values were then sorted in ascending order to define 15 layers representing an increasing velocity gradient across the Moho. The V_P/V_S ratio for each layer was constrained to fall within a realistic range of 1.70–1.87 (e.g., Wang *et al.*, 2024). In addition, ρ_2 and ray parameters were randomly generated within defined bounds using the same Monte Carlo framework.

The 15-layer transition zone results in varying α_1 and β_1 at different depths, leading to different parameter sets for estimating ρ_1. To evaluate how depth within the gradational Moho affects ρ_1, we selected three representative depths characterized by distinct lower crustal velocities: the shallowest layer, the median layer, and the layer just above the upper mantle. For simplicity, we refer to these as the top layer, midpoint layer, and base layer, respectively.

The velocities ρ_2, ray parameter, and P_s/P ratio ranges follow those in the PIM model, with ray parameter and P_s/P sampled at 0.01 intervals. The upper mantle velocities and density were held fixed within each model and shared across the three selected depths. Using the Monte Carlo method, we generated 10,000 velocity structures for each depth.

Similar to the sharp Moho model, we applied the Monte Carlo method to add synthetic noise to the P_s/P ratios in the gradational Moho models to represent more realistic observational conditions. A standard deviation of 0.08 was used to generate the noise, consistent with the sharp Moho case, and the resulting noises were added to the P_s/P ratios. The same parameter ranges and constraints were applied to both the noise-free and noisy gradational Moho models. The P_s/P ratio extends from 1.50 to 1.96, and 10,000 velocity structures with noise were generated for each of the three depths.

We note that in this study, amplitudes were not modeled with explicit frequency-dependent transmission effects, which are expected for a gradational interface. In real applications, such effects should be considered when extracting the P_s/P ratio. However, the AB method itself only requires the P_s/P ratio as input, regardless of how it is obtained. For this reason, we sampled the ratio within the range 0.01–0.25, providing a practical way to evaluate the robustness of the AB method under gradational structure while still representing the variability associated with frequency-dependent effect.

For each case, we calculated the mean and standard deviation of ρ_1, performed propagation of uncertainty, and CV to evaluate their behavior and relationship.

Lower Crustal Density Estimates

Lower crustal density and uncertainty

Using the method derived in the Method section, we calculated ρ_1 based on different parameter sets from the four models. According to Table 1, the mean ρ_1 varies slightly among models but remains within a narrow and geophysically reasonable range of 2.946–3.012 g/cm^3. The result of the PIM is 2.992 g/cm^3, representing the theoretical estimate derived from the full range of possible parameter values. Importantly, the close agreement of the mean ρ_1 values across independent velocity models indicates that the method is not strongly model dependent, which supports its robustness when applied to real velocity pairs. The SR model, which only covers the contiguous U.S. continental structure, yields the highest mean among the four models, consistent with the expectation of relatively dense continental lower crust.

Propagation of uncertainty. We calculated the propagation of ρ_1 uncertainty using equation (9). Table 1 presents

TABLE 1
Density Analysis Including Mean Density, Mean Propagation of Uncertainty, Mean Standard Deviation, and the Mean Ratio of Uncertainty to Density

Velocity Model	ρ_1 (g/cm³)	$\delta\rho_1$ (g/cm³)	σ (g/cm³)	$\delta\rho_1/\rho_1$
CRUST1.0	2.960	0.079	0.065	0.105
SR	3.012	0.065	0.057	0.097
LITHO1.0	2.946	0.105	0.061	0.122
PIM	2.992	0.081	0.094	0.096

PIM, parameter inclusion model. SR, Shen and Ritzwoller (2016).

the average results for $\delta\rho_1$, the standard deviation (σ), and the mean of $\delta\rho_1/\rho_1$.

As a result, the $\delta\rho_1$ and σ across all models are relatively small, indicating the consistency of the density estimates and the robustness of the method (Table 1). The last column presents the relative uncertainty of ρ_1, with $\delta\rho_1/\rho_1$ around 10%, demonstrating the reliability of the results. The PIM shows an uncertainty of 9.6%, representing the $\delta\rho_1/\rho_1$ without constraints or methodological biases, further supporting the robustness of the estimates. For the other three models, which incorporate different constraints, the $\delta\rho_1/\rho_1$ values are 10.5%, 9.7%, and 12.2% for CRUST1.0, LITH1.0, and SR, respectively.

Correlation analysis

The PCC results are presented in Table 2. We analyzed the correlation between all the parameters and both ρ_1 and $\delta\rho_1$. Because the PIM covers the most extensive set of parameters without constraints, it reflects correlations with minimal bias and provides a relatively complete representation of the PCC landscape. The analysis shows that α_1, β_2, the ray parameter, and ρ_2 are negatively correlated with ρ_1, whereas only α_1, β_1, and α_2 are negatively correlated with $\delta\rho_1$.

In the PIM, β_1 and β_2 across the Moho are most strongly correlated with both ρ_1 and $\delta\rho_1$, whereas α_1 and α_2 show the weakest (Fig. 2, Figs. S1–S3, Table 2). Specifically, the PCC between α_2 and ρ_1 is 0.020 and between α_2 and $\delta\rho_1$ is −0.033, indicating that upper mantle V_P has little impact on the calculation and uncertainty of ρ_1. In addition, the ray parameter shows a strong negative correlation with and a modest positive correlation with $\delta\rho_1$. Here, ρ_2 has a small PCC, indicating a weak correlation with ρ_1. It shows that in real practice, ρ_2 has little effect on both ρ_1 and $\delta\rho_1$. Notably, the correlation between P_s/P and $\delta\rho_1$ is significant. This suggests that a higher P_s/P ratio increases $\delta\rho_1$.

Similar results are depicted in Figure 2 and Figure S2, which provides more detailed insights into the distribution of different parameters. In the figures, the lighter the circle color, the lower the parameter value. The results show a negative correlation between ρ_1 and $\delta\rho_1$ (i.e., the negative slopes in the figure).

For β_1, in the PIM result, a lower value leads to higher ρ_1 and $\delta\rho_1$ (Fig. 2b, Table 2). For β_2, a lower value primarily leads

TABLE 2
Pearson Correlation Coefficient Between Lower Crustal Density or Its Propagation of Uncertainty and Key Parameters Analyzed in the Study, Based on Four Different Velocity Models

	Parameters						
Velocity Model	α_1	β_1	α_2	β_2	p	ρ_2	P_s/P
CRUST1.0							
ρ_1	0.054	0.062	−0.247	−0.263	−0.424	0.010	−0.225
$\delta\rho_1$	−0.428	−0.415	0.594	0.615	0.257	0.025	0.581
SR							
ρ_1	−0.047	−0.034	−0.122	−0.133	−0.373	0.010	−0.100
$\delta\rho_1$	−0.187	−0.223	0.233	0.274	0.294	0.022	0.347
LITHO1.0							
ρ_1	0.042	0.043	−0.114	−0.121	−0.487	0.007	−0.344
$\delta\rho_1$	−0.485	−0.495	0.431	0.450	0.263	0.017	0.588
PIM							
ρ_1	−0.034	0.126	0.020	−0.251	−0.281	−0.036	0.047
$\delta\rho_1$	−0.069	−0.406	−0.033	0.313	0.131	0.045	0.470

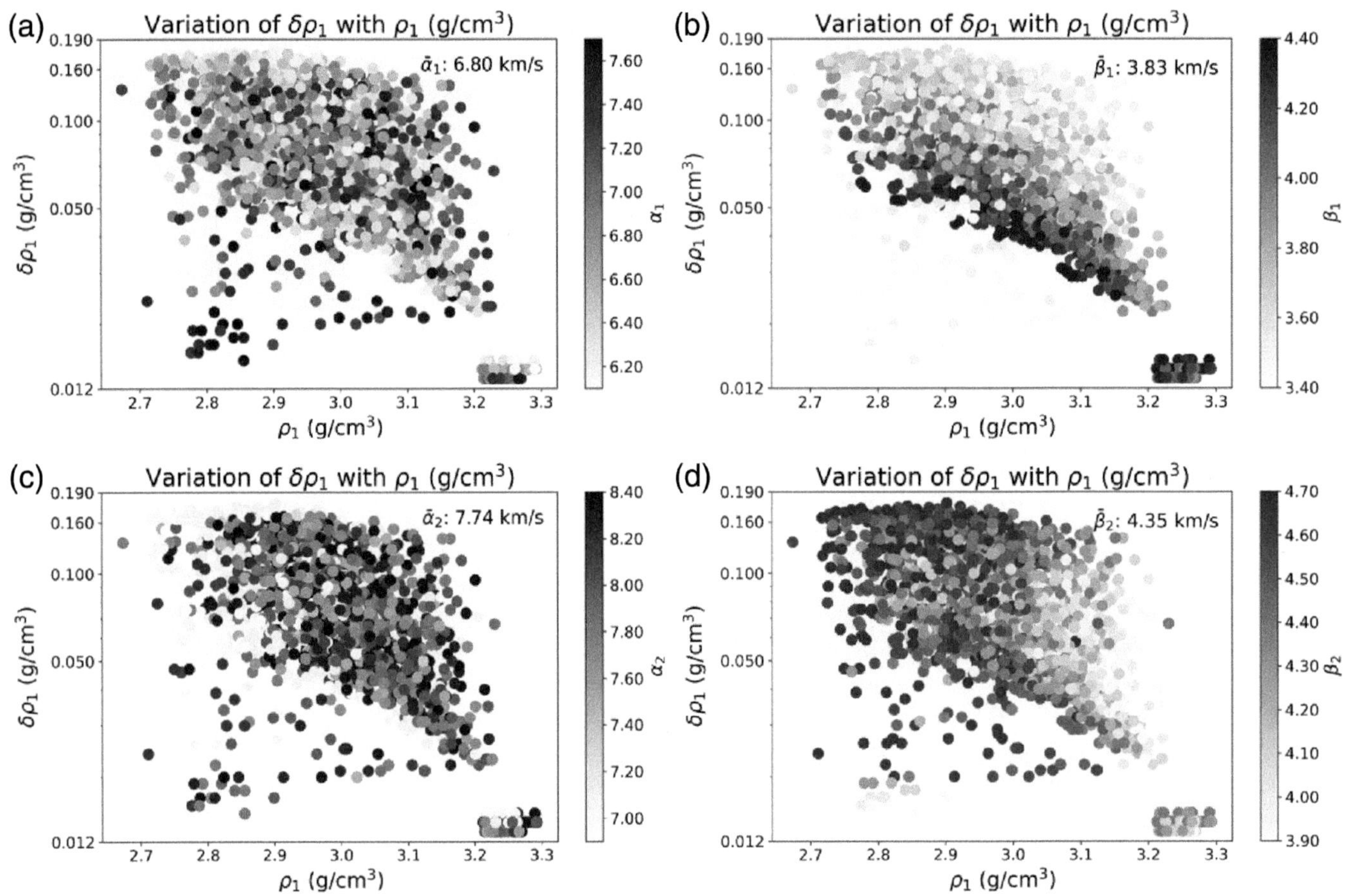

Figure 2. Correlation between ρ_1 and $\delta\rho_1$ from the parameter inclusion model (PIM). The lighter the color, the lower the parameter. (a) Lower crustal V_P, (b) lower crustal V_S, (c) upper mantle V_P, and (d) upper mantle V_S. The color version of this figure is available only in the electronic edition.

to higher ρ_1, whereas a low β_2 can also lead to lower $\delta\rho_1$ (Fig. 2d, Table 2). However, the compressional velocities are more evenly distributed (Fig. 2a,c). Both Figure 2b,d and the analysis suggest that the relationship between shear waves, ρ_1, and $\delta\rho_1$ is more consistent compared to other parameters.

The other three velocity models exhibit PCC values between the parameters and ρ_1 and $\delta\rho_1$ (Fig. S1, Table 2) using real velocity pairs. The uneven distribution of parameter sets across the range, along with the differing constraints and methodologies applied in each model, introducing additional variabilities. However, this variability does not appear to significantly impact the reliability of the estimates.

In the SR model, the β_1 show negative correlations with $\delta\rho_1$ (Fig. S1b (B), Table 2), and the upper mantle velocities are negatively correlated with ρ_1 (Fig. S1b (D), Table 2). Among the parameters, β_2 and the ray parameter have the strongest influence on ρ_1, whereas ρ_2 has the smallest impact on both ρ_1 and $\delta\rho_1$. In the CRUST1.0 model, upper mantle velocities have a relatively strong influence on both ρ_1 and $\delta\rho_1$ (Fig. S1a, Table 2). Similarly, the ray parameter remains the most influential factor for ρ_1, whereas ρ_2 has the smallest impact on both ρ_1 and $\delta\rho_1$ (Table 2). Lower crustal velocities are negatively correlated with $\delta\rho_1$, whereas upper mantle velocities are positively correlated with $\delta\rho_1$ and negatively correlated with ρ_1 (Fig. S1a, Table 2). In addition, P_s/P shows a positive correlation with $\delta\rho_1$ (Table 2, Fig. S2). Despite differences in constraints, the LITHO1.0 model exhibits similar parameter correlations with ρ_1 and $\delta\rho_1$ (Table 2), emphasizing the overall trends observed in the other models.

Furthermore, we analyzed the correlation between ρ_1 and $\delta\rho_1$ to assess the sensitivity of ρ_1. The results are presented in Table S2. It shows that for all four models, ρ_1 and $\delta\rho_1$ are negatively correlated, with PCC values ranging from −0.310 to −0.390, as also illustrated in Figure 2 and Figure S1. This demonstrates a universal trend that ρ_1 derived from our method has a similar influence on $\delta\rho_1$, regardless of the velocity pairs used. A high ρ_1 tends to result in a relatively low $\delta\rho_1$. The PCC results indicate that real velocity pairs, despite differences in noise and constraints, do not significantly affect the correlations between the estimates and their uncertainties, supporting the reliability of the method in practical applications.

These correlation results indicate that parameters are the primary contributors to variations in density estimates and their uncertainties. In practice, it means that constraining β_1 and β_2 is critical for minimizing uncertainty in ρ_1, whereas

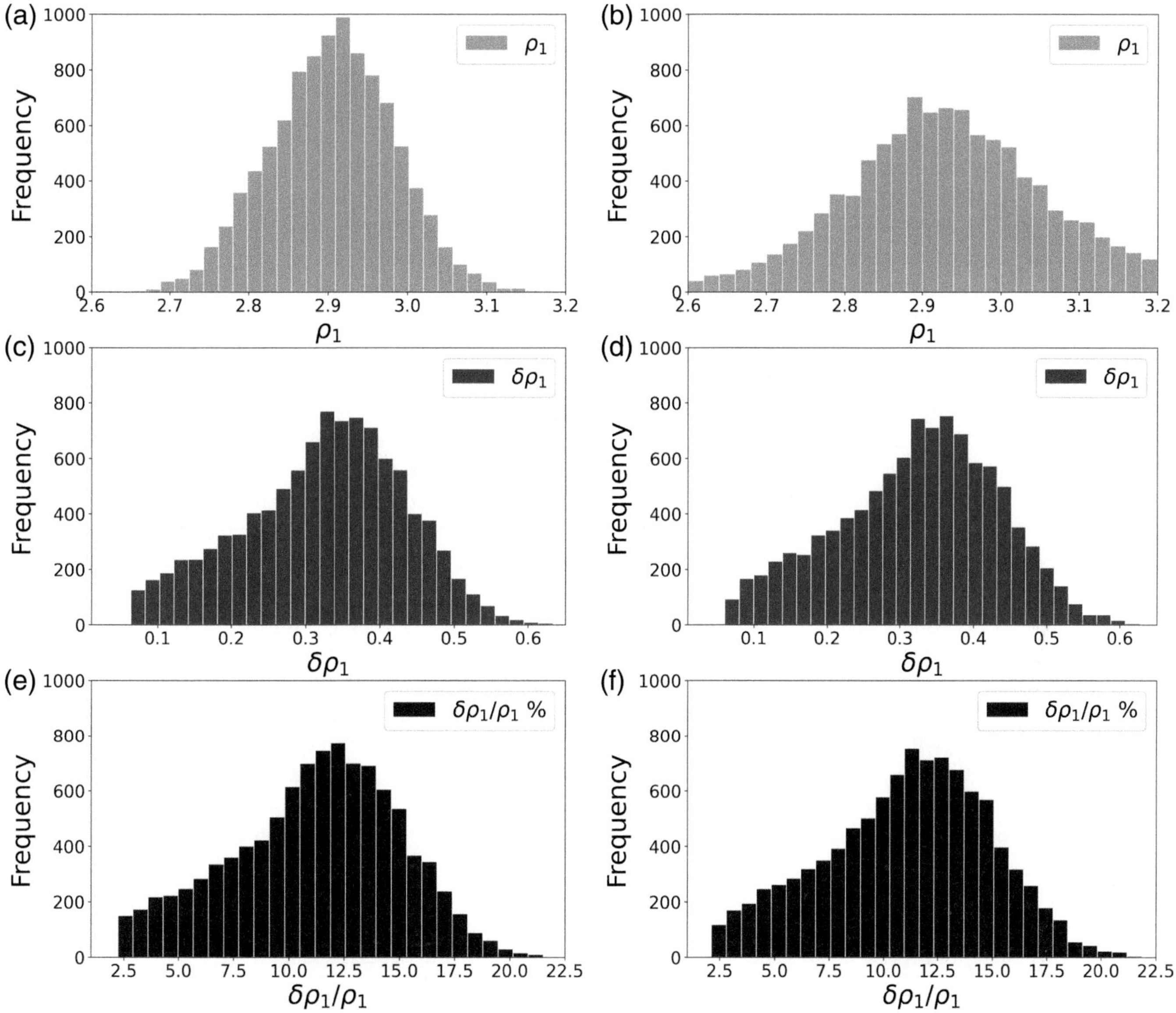

uncertainties in ρ_2 or α_2 have relatively minor influence. The positive correlation between P_s/P and $\delta\rho_1$ further implies that measurements with higher P_s/P ratios may be associated with greater uncertainty, which should be considered when selecting and weighting data. Overall, the correlation analysis highlights the key parameters that require tighter constraints in real applications of the method.

Figure 3. Distributions of ρ_1, $\delta\rho_1$, and $\delta\rho_1/\rho_1$ for the sharp Moho model with and without synthetic noise. (a,c,e) Without noise and (b,d,f) with noise. (a,b) ρ_1, (c,d) $\delta\rho_1$, and (e,f) $\delta\rho_1/\rho_1$. The color version of this figure is available only in the electronic edition.

Monte Carlo models

Sharp Moho. The mean of ρ_1 in the noise-free sharp Moho model is 2.91 ± 0.08 g/cm^3, consistent with the typical density of global lower crust (e.g., Christensen and Mooney, 1995). The distribution of ρ_1 values is shown in Figure 3a, in which the highest frequency occurs near 2.91 g/cm^3, aligning with the calculated mean (Table S3). The distribution is approximately normal, as expected from the central limit theorem (Rice, 2007), because is derived from a combination of several normally or uniformly distributed input parameters, which together tend to produce a normal distribution. The mean of the propagated uncertainty in ρ_1 is 0.32 ± 0.11 g/cm^3 (Table S3). The distribution of the propagated uncertainties is shown in Figure 3c, in which the highest frequency occurs around 0.35 g/cm^3 and follows a normal distribution as well.

We also computed the relative uncertainty, that is, $\delta\rho_1/\rho_1$. The mean of this ratio is 0.112 ± 0.038, as shown in Figure 3e and Table S3, which exhibits a near-normal distribution. This relative uncertainty is consistent with results from the other four models and is slightly higher than the value from the PIM. This is expected, as the PIM uses systematically varied parameters, whereas the current model uses random combinations, leading to higher variability in the resulting ρ_1. The normal distribution of $\delta\rho_1/\rho_1$ follows the central limit theorem and supports the reliability of the estimates (Fig. 3e).

The CV is 0.027 (Table S3), indicating that varies by only 2.7% relative to its mean, reflecting low variability. The small CV suggests that estimates from the noise-free sharp Moho model are highly consistent and robust, even with randomly sampled input parameters.

When noise is included in the analysis, the mean and standard deviation of ρ_1 increase to $2.93 \pm 0.12/\mathrm{cm}^3$ (Table S3). Both the average density and its spread become larger because of the introduction of noise, contributing to greater variability in the results. The propagation of uncertainty is similar in both noisy and noise-free cases because it depends on unchanged partial derivatives and input uncertainties (Table S3, Fig. 3). The presence of noise in the output affects the observed spread in ρ_1 but not the analytically propagated uncertainty derived from input distributions.

$\delta\rho_1/\rho_1$ is also very similar between the two cases (Table S3). The value in the noisy model is slightly smaller, likely because the higher mean density reduces the ratio, even if the absolute uncertainty increases. This subtle difference highlights the stabilizing effect of normalization in relative metrics.

The CV increases from 0.027 in the noise-free model to 0.041 in the noisy model, reflecting a rise in relative variability (Table S3). However, this value remains low, indicating that even under random parameter combinations and added noise, the ρ_1 estimates for the sharp Moho model are still robust and reliable.

Gradational Moho. The gradational Moho model introduces additional complexity because of the continuous velocity and density gradient across the Moho transition. Table S4 and Figure 4 and Figure S3 present the results for the three depth levels within the 15-km-thick transition zone. The mean ρ_1 values are very close across the top, midpoint, and bottom layers, indicating that the average density is not strongly depth dependent within the gradient. However, the standard deviation of ρ_1 increases with depth, reflecting greater variability in density estimates at deeper levels.

In contrast, both $\delta\rho_1$ and its standard deviation decrease with increasing depth (Table S4). The trend suggests that $\delta\rho_1$ becomes smaller toward the base of the transition zone, likely because the velocity contrast between adjacent layers becomes smaller, resulting in more gradual amplitude variations and reduced sensitivity to input parameter changes, which improves the stability of the estimates. Consequently, the relative uncertainty and its standard deviation also decrease with depth, consistent with the decreasing $\delta\rho_1$. The observed decrease in and with depth highlights that deeper layers within the gradational Moho structure provide relatively reliable and robust estimates of ρ_1. On the other hand, the CV increases with depth, with values of 0.027, 0.031, and 0.049 for the top, midpoint, and bottom layers, respectively (Table S4). This increase occurs because decreases, but the standard deviation of grows at deeper depths, leading to a higher CV. Despite this upward trend, the CV values remain low, indicating that the relative variability of is still limited, and the results are statistically stable. It suggests that considering the vertical gradient is important when interpreting *P-to-S* converted amplitudes in regions with a gradational Moho.

The distribution of in the top and midpoint layers follows a near-normal distribution, indicating relatively consistent estimates across randomly generated parameter sets (Fig. 4). In contrast, the base layer exhibits a bimodal distribution, with the highest frequency centered around $2.75\ \mathrm{g/cm}^3$ and a secondary peak near $3.05\ \mathrm{g/cm}^3$ (Fig. 4g). This bimodal pattern may result from the combined effects of more complex parameter interactions at greater depths, for which lower crustal properties increasingly resemble those of the upper mantle, affecting amplitude behavior and density estimates. The peak around $2.75\ \mathrm{g/cm}^3$ likely corresponds to parameter combinations for which the density remains more representative of lower crustal properties, whereas the peak near $3.05\ \mathrm{g/cm}^3$ reflects combinations approaching upper mantle characteristics. Because the base layer is located at the lower end of the 15 km gradational Moho, it captures influences from both crustal and mantle structures. The bimodal distribution arises from this transitional setting, for which random parameter combinations produce densities that tend to group around either crust-like or mantle-like values. The relatively high standard deviation in this layer may also reflect this increased complexity. We believe this is due to weaker *P-to-S* conversions in the gradational Moho model. At greater depths, lower crustal velocities become closer to upper mantle values, making the transition smoother. As a result, the amplitude response flattens, and different combinations can produce similar low amplitudes. This nonuniqueness can result in a bimodal or multimodal distribution in the estimated values, especially when multiple theoretical models (e.g., from Monte Carlo sampling) are considered. This suggests that the depth within the gradational Moho affects the properties of: the deeper the layer, the greater the influence from the upper mantle on the estimated density.

On the other hand, the distributions of and across all depths are consistent with the statistical trends shown in Table S4 and Figure 4. The peak frequency in the base layer is the lowest among the three depths, indicating a narrower spread and reduced variability in the uncertainty estimates. This supports the interpretation that result robustness improves with depth because smaller impedance contrasts and weaker *P-to-S* conversions make the amplitude response less sensitive to parameter changes, leading to more stable estimates and uncertainties.

When noise is included, the overall trends in ρ_1, $\delta\rho_1$, $\delta\rho_1/\rho_1$, and CV remain consistent with the noise-free results (Table S4 and Fig. S3). However, the mean values and standard deviations of all these quantities are higher than in the noise-free

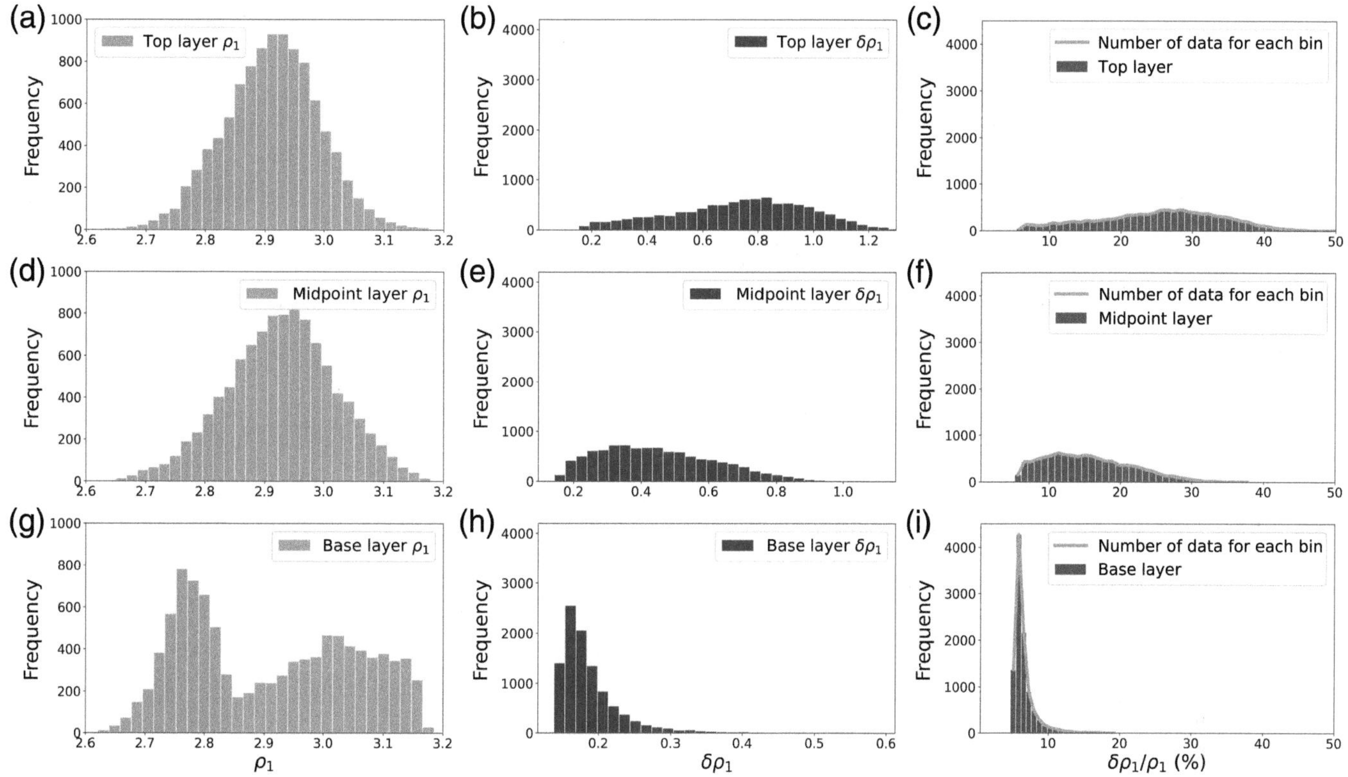

Figure 4. Distributions of ρ_1, $\delta\rho_1$, and $\delta\rho_1/\rho_1$ for the top, midpoint, and base layers of the gradational Moho model without noise. Panels (a,d,g) show the distributions of ρ_1, panels (b,e,h) show the corresponding propagated uncertainties $\delta\rho_1$, and panels (c,f,i) present the relative uncertainties $\delta\rho_1/\rho_1$. Each column corresponds to a specific depth layer: (a–c) top, (d–f) midpoint, and (g–i) base. The color version of this figure is available only in the electronic edition.

case. This indicates that the added noise increases the randomness and variability in the results, as expected. In Figure S3, the distributions of ρ_1 in the top and midpoint layers still follow a normal distribution, suggesting that these depths are relatively stable under the influence of noise. However, for the base layer, ρ_1 appears to follow a more normal distribution compared with the bimodal shape seen in the noise-free case. This suggests that the addition of noise smooths out the parameter sensitivity contrast at greater depths, reducing the effects of the discrete parameter groupings that caused the bimodal distribution. As a result, the noise introduces variability that partially obscures the distinct responses associated with specific parameter combinations, leading to a more uniform distribution. This behavior suggests that noise can homogenize the model's response, particularly at greater depths for which upper mantle properties influence the estimates. Even so, the deeper layers still exhibit relatively stable and values, indicating that the base of the gradational Moho remains a stable region for estimating ρ_1, even in the presence of noise.

In summary, for the gradational Moho model, $\delta\rho_1$ decreases with depth, suggesting that estimates become more reliable closer to the Moho discontinuity, for which the impedance contrast is smoothest. The bimodality of in the base layer reflects the increasing influence of upper mantle properties, suggesting that the midpoint and top layers are less affected by the upper mantle. As a result, the midpoint layer, which shows relatively low uncertainties and minimal upper mantle influence, becomes a reasonable choice for estimating ρ_1. However, if minimizing uncertainty is the primary goal, the base layer, despite its bimodality, offers the lowest uncertainty. The addition of noise increases uncertainties at all depths and partially obscures the distinct responses associated with specific parameter combinations. However, the presence of noise does not alter the overall trends observed in the gradational Moho model.

ρ_{lc} between CRUST1.0 and AB method

We compared ρ_1 between CRUST1.0 and the AB method. CRUST1.0 yields 2.96 ± 0.065 g/cm^3, whereas the AB method gives 2.98 ± 0.070 g/cm^3, both consistent with global lower crustal averages (e.g., Holbrook *et al.*, 1992; Christensen and Mooney, 1995; Hacker *et al.*, 2015), supporting the reliability of the amplitude-based approach. This agreement suggests that the AB method can effectively reproduce large-scale ρ_1. The MAE and rmse between the two results are 0.070 and 0.086, respectively, both of which are small, indicating that the estimates are numerically similar when based on the same parameter sets.

We also calculated the z-scores to evaluate the differences between the two results, as shown in Figure 5. Most points cluster

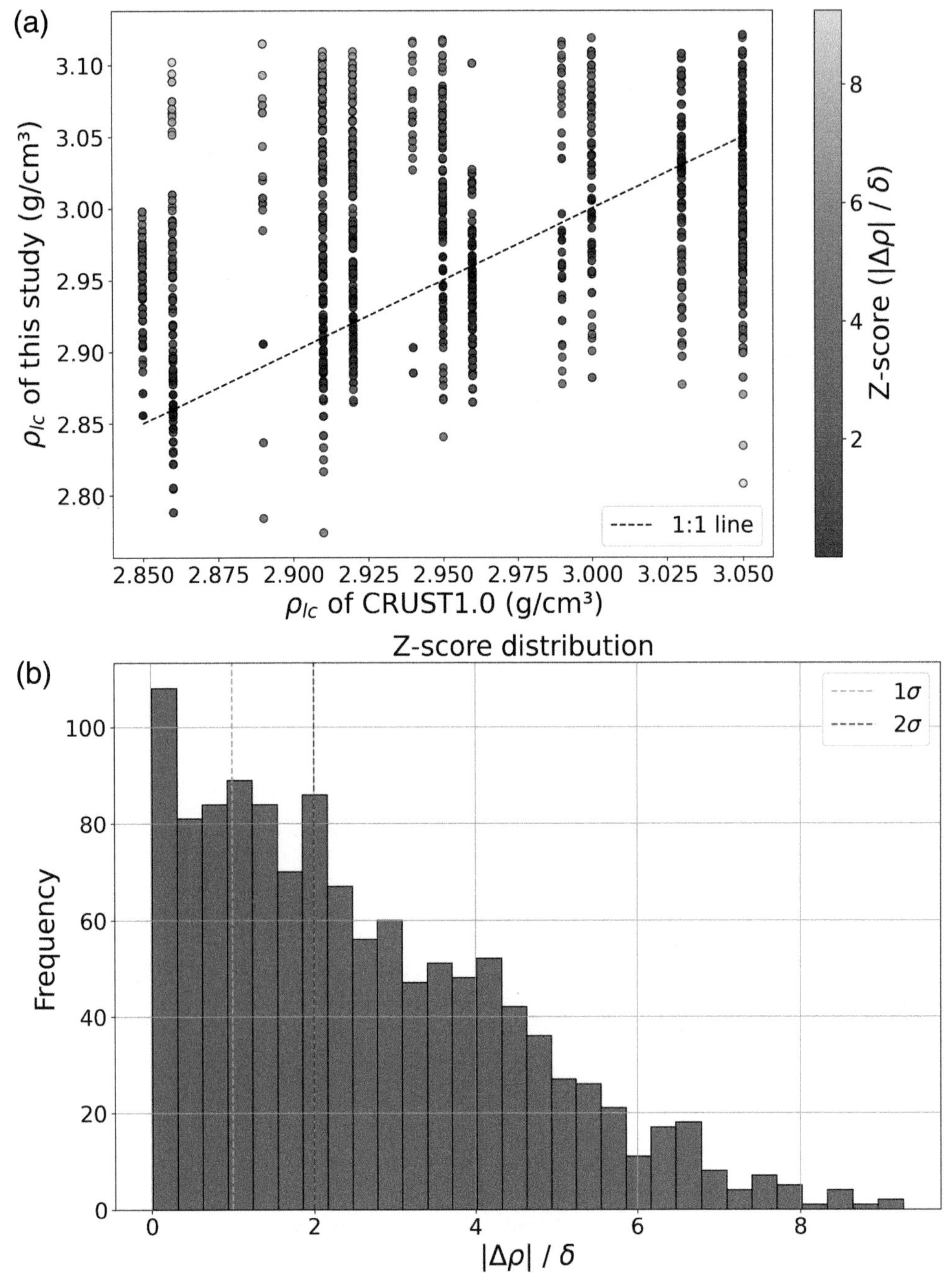

Figure 5. (a) Comparison of from AB method versus CRUST1.0, colored by the Z-score ($|\Delta\rho|/\delta$). The dashed line represents the 1:1 reference line. (b) Histogram of Z-scores quantifying the difference between AB method and CRUST1.0, normalized by the propagated uncertainty. Vertical-dashed lines indicate the 1σ (orange) and 2σ (red) thresholds. The color version of this figure is available only in the electronic edition.

around the 1:1 line and appear dark in color, indicating low z-scores. Points that deviate substantially from the 1:1 line correspond to relatively high z-scores and are shown in more yellow colors. This pattern suggests that the two estimates are generally consistent, and the low Z-scores indicate that the differences fall within the expected uncertainty bounds based on the propagation of uncertainties. Overall, the close agreement between the results supports the reliability of the method. For Figure 5b, more z-scores fall below 2, even with a large number below 1, indicating a large fraction of ρ_1 differ from CRUST1.0 by $<1\sigma$. Even where differences exist, ~53% of the results fall within 2σ, suggesting that the estimates from this study are relatively consistent with CRUST1.0.

The PCC between the two results is 0.002, close to zero, indicating weak linear correlation. It is expected given the fundamentally different methodologies used in CRUST1.0 and the AB approach. As a result, the two estimates do not vary linearly with one another across parameter space. However, the lack of linear correlation does not undermine the robustness of our results. Instead, it highlights the distinct physical basis of each approach. Despite these differences, the similarity in mean values, small MAE and rmse, and low z-scores demonstrate that both approaches converge on comparable magnitudes of ρ_1. Moreover, the differences between individual estimates are generally small and show little systematic dependence on parameter values. The lack of parameter-linked bias indicates that the AB method produces stable estimates across a wide range of conditions, supporting its overall reliability.

Parameter Variations and Uncertainty Response

Density variation analysis

We calculated the $\Delta\alpha/\alpha$, $\Delta\beta/\beta$, and $\Delta\rho/\rho$ across Moho and PCC between $\Delta\alpha/\alpha$ and $\Delta\rho/\rho$, as well as $\Delta\beta/\beta$ and $\Delta\rho/\rho$, using all four models. The results are shown in Figure 6 and Tables S5 and S6. The mean values of $\Delta\rho/\rho$ over $\Delta\alpha/\alpha$ and $\Delta\rho/\rho$ over $\Delta\beta/\beta$ are presented in Table S5. These ratios indicate how uncertainties in the measurement of *P*- ($\Delta\alpha/\alpha$) and *S*-wave ($\Delta\beta/\beta$) velocities propagate to uncertainties in the density contrast ($\Delta\rho/\rho$) (i.e., $\frac{\Delta\rho/\rho}{\Delta\alpha/\alpha}, \frac{\Delta\rho/\rho}{\Delta\beta/\beta}$). A higher ratio implies that variations in compressional or shear-wave velocities have a strong influence on the density contrast, potentially because of changes in composition, porosity, or fluid content (e.g., Gardner *et al.*, 1974; Rabbel *et al.*, 2013; Anovitz and Cole, 2015; Malvoisin *et al.*, 2015). Conversely, a lower ratio indicates that the density remains relatively stable, suggesting a more uniform material (e.g., Rabbel *et al.*, 2013; Lücke, 2014).

Theoretically, according to the PIM, the ratio of $\Delta\rho/\rho$ to $\Delta\beta/\beta$ is very close to 1, indicating that shear-wave variations strongly govern density behavior (Table S5). Similarly, for the CRUST1.0 and SR models, $\Delta\beta/\beta$ is also close to 1, whereas LITHO1.0 shows the lowest ratio. In contrast, $\Delta\alpha/\alpha$ deviates more from 1, indicating weaker influence of compressional velocities. The variation in these ratios across different models reflects the impact of model constraints and the extent of model coverage in shaping parameter–density relationships.

The PCC correlation between $\Delta\alpha/\alpha$ and $\Delta\rho/\rho$ is generally weaker than that between $\Delta\beta/\beta$ and $\Delta\rho/\rho$ across all models, indicating a consistent universal trend (as shown in Table S6). In the theoretical results using PIM, $\Delta\alpha/\alpha$ is negatively correlated with $\Delta\rho/\rho$, but in the other three models with real velocity pairs, the correlation becomes relatively positive. On the other hand, $\Delta\beta/\beta$ is positively correlated with $\Delta\rho/\rho$ across all models. The larger PCC value between $\Delta\beta/\beta$ and $\Delta\rho/\rho$ compared with $\Delta\alpha/\alpha$ and $\Delta\rho/\rho$ suggests a stronger correlation between shear-wave velocity and $\Delta\rho/\rho$ across the Moho. Similarly, although the values vary, all three constrained models show a stronger correlation between shear-wave velocity and $\Delta\rho/\rho$ across the Moho than between compressional-wave velocity and $\Delta\rho/\rho$. This supports the idea that shear-wave variations have a greater influence on $\Delta\rho/\rho$ across the Moho, regardless of the constraints in the base models (Table S6), and that the use of real velocity pairs further strengthens the correlation between shear-wave velocity and $\Delta\rho/\rho$ across Moho.

Figure 6 and Figures S4 and S5 illustrate the relationship between $\Delta\alpha/\alpha$, $\Delta\beta/\beta$, and $\Delta\rho/\rho$. The PIM results present a comprehensive view of the relationship between $\Delta\alpha/\alpha$, $\Delta\beta/\beta$, and $\Delta\rho/\rho$ (Fig. 6), whereas the other constrained models illustrate these relationships using real velocity pairs (Fig. S4). In the figures (left column), the correlation between $\Delta\alpha/\alpha$ and $\Delta\rho/\rho$ appears to be inconsistent because the results (dots) are relatively evenly distributed, indicating that $\Delta\alpha/\alpha$ contributes less to $\Delta\rho/\rho$. The parameters (colors), on the other hand, also reflect the influence of $\Delta\alpha/\alpha$ to $\Delta\rho/\rho$. The point colors are evenly distributed, supporting this observation. In Figure 6a, the color of the data points gradually becomes lighter as $\Delta\alpha/\alpha$ increases, indicating a correlation between $\Delta\alpha/\alpha$ and α_1. However, for $\Delta\rho/\rho$, the data points remain evenly distributed, further supporting the idea that $\Delta\alpha/\alpha$ contributes less to $\Delta\rho/\rho$ across the Moho. The consistency of these patterns across all four models highlights the reliability of the method in practical applications.

Figure 6 and Figures S4 and S5 (right column) show the relationship between $\Delta\beta/\beta$ and $\Delta\rho/\rho$. There is a noticeable region in the middle of the figure with fewer available data points across all models and parameters (Fig 6, Figs. S4 and S5 right column). This suggests a universal limitation. The orange line in Figure 6b, for instance, represents the curve of $\Delta\rho/\rho$ as a function of $\Delta\beta/\beta$, denoted as $\Delta\rho/\rho = f(\Delta\beta/\beta)$. The mathematical details of this function are provided in the supplemental material mathematical derivations section 6. The figure shows that less data are available along this line, indicating that in practice, parameter sets located in this region may yield less reliable results.

The parameter sets that align with the curve $\Delta\rho/\rho = f(\Delta\beta/\beta)$ represent critical transitions for which small changes in $\Delta\beta/\beta$ can lead to significant changes in $\Delta\rho/\rho$. The transitions might be associated with phase changes in the material, variations in fluid content, or other significant geological processes. This could also suggest that these parameter sets represent less common or extreme material properties or conditions that result in much higher densities outside the reasonable range. Further study is needed to better understand the limitations of these parameter sets and the reason behind the scarcity of available data in these regions.

Figure 7 (bottom figure of each subfigure) provides details about the PCC values between $\Delta\alpha/\alpha$ and $\Delta\beta/\beta$ to $\Delta\rho/\rho$ through the Moho using the PIM. As α_1 and β_2 increase, the PCC values gradually increase (Fig. 7a,d, blue lines), whereas with an increase β_1, the PCC values decrease (Fig. 7b, blue line). The variation in PCC values with increasing α_2 is relatively subtle, supporting the idea that α_2 has a minimal impact on ρ_1. This trend is not always consistent across the other three models using real velocity pairs (as shown in Fig. S6), suggesting that unevenly distributed velocity pairs and different constraints and methodologies can lead to inconsistencies in $\Delta\rho/\rho$ and introduce extra uncertainty into the calculations.

In Table S7, we calculated the PCC between $\Delta\rho/\rho$ and the parameters of interest using the full range of available parameter sets. For theoretical results using PIM, the results show that α_2 has the least correlation with $\Delta\rho/\rho$, whereas β_2 and the ray parameter have the greatest impact. ρ_1 and α_2 are negatively correlated with $\Delta\rho/\rho$, whereas the other parameters are positively correlated. When examining the results from the three models with real velocity pairs, the ray parameter is consistently positively correlated with $\Delta\rho/\rho$ and exhibits the strongest correlation among all variables. In addition, β_2 consistently has the strongest correlation with $\Delta\rho/\rho$ compared with other velocity parameters. This indicates a global trend regardless of the different constraints and development methods of the velocity pairs. In the two global velocity models,

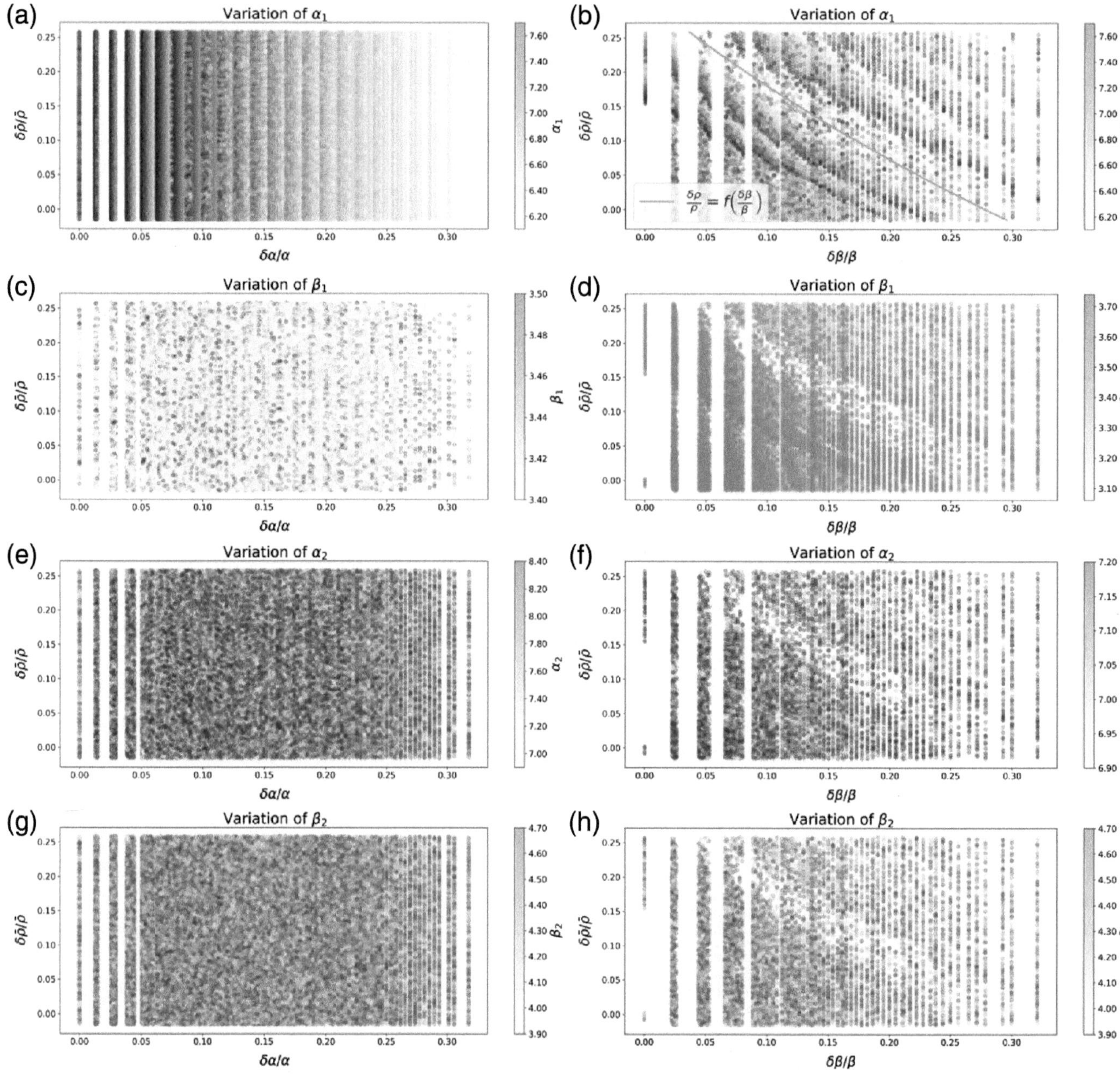

Figure 6. Correlation between compressional wave sensitivity or shear-wave sensitivity and density sensitivity across the Moho. The model used is the PIM. (a,c,e,g) Compressional wave sensitivity versus density sensitivity. (b,d,f,h) Shear-wave sensitivity versus density sensitivity. The lighter the color, the lower the parameter value. (a,b) α_1, (c,d) β_1, (e,f) α_2, and (g,h) β_2. The color version of this figure is available only in the electronic edition.

whereas the lower crustal velocities are negatively correlated, the remaining parameters are positively correlated. For the SR model, which represents continental structures, all parameters are positively correlated with $\Delta\rho/\rho$. These findings suggest that the ray parameter, which exhibits the highest PCC among all parameters, plays a substantial role in influencing $\Delta\rho/\rho$ in both the theoretical model and those using real velocity pairs.

Although incident angle is not shown explicitly, it is implicitly constrained by the ray parameter and velocity bounds, limiting i_2 to ~23° to 37°, a range consistent with near-vertical incidence in RF practice. Within this range, i_2 dependence is minor compared with velocity and density effects (e.g., Kind *et al.*, 1995; Ligorría and Ammon, 1999; Ryberg and Weber, 2000), allowing the analysis to focus on parameter-driven variability under realistic angular conditions.

Density variation comparison between the PIM, Aki and Richards, and Julià (2007) approaches

In addition to the AB method, alternative approaches to evaluate $\Delta\rho/\rho$ were presented by Aki and Richards (2002) and Julià (2007). We compared our results with those from AR approximation and Julià's method using the PIM for consistency. According to the Analysis of lower crustal density variability section, supplemental material (mathematical derivatives 5.1)

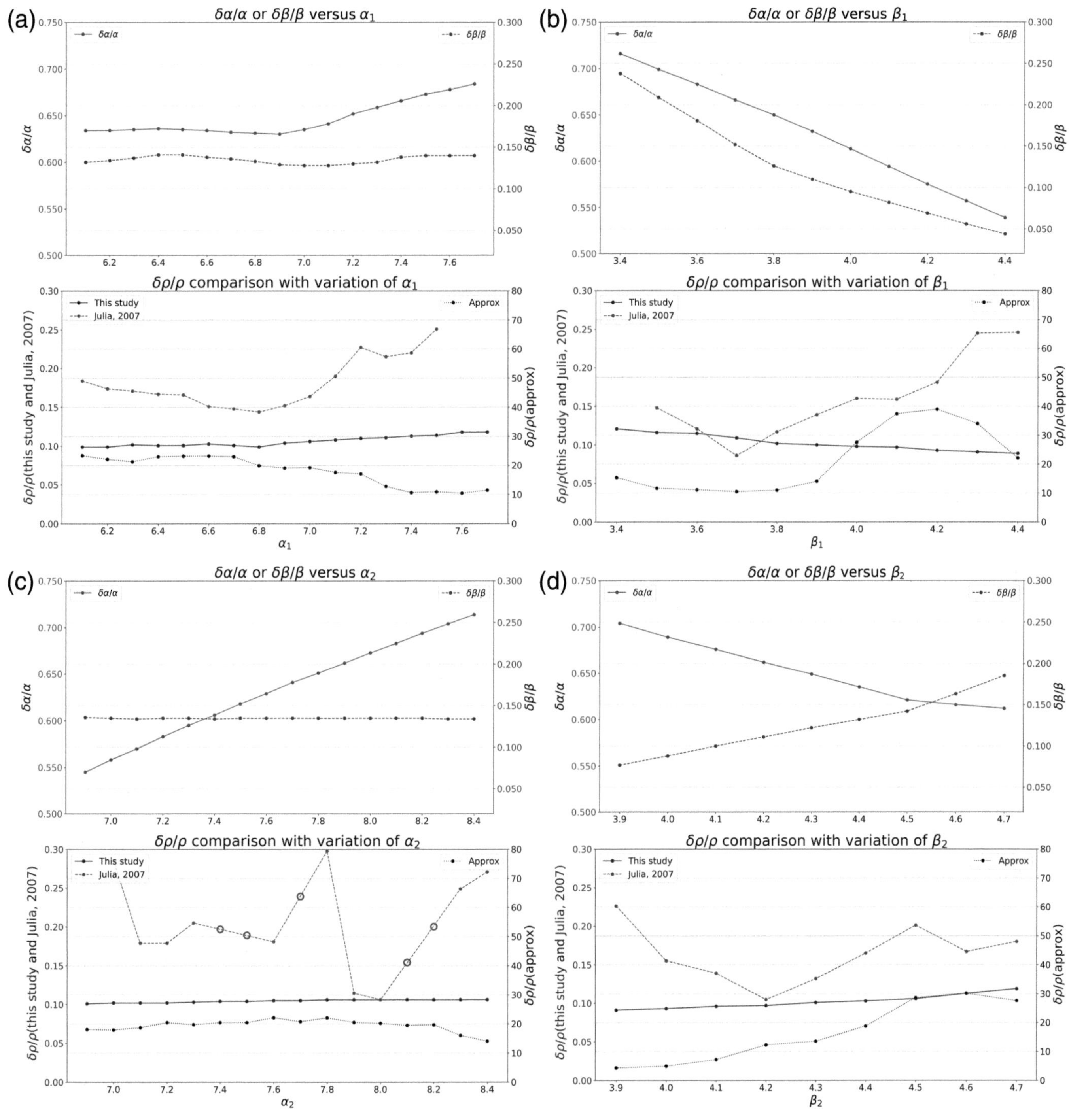

Figure 7. Pearson correlation coefficient (PCC) values from the PIM showing correlations between $\delta\alpha/\alpha$, $\delta\beta/\beta$, $\delta\rho/\rho$, and the key parameters of interest, based on each data point, e.g., $\alpha_1 = 2.6$. The top panel in each subfigure shows PCC values between $\delta\alpha/\alpha$ (left y axis), $\delta\beta/\beta$ (right y axis), and different parameters. The bottom panel shows PCC values between $\delta\rho/\rho$ and the same parameters. The left y axis represents values from Julià (2007) and this study, while the right y axis represents values from the AR method. Red circles indicate missing data in Julià (2007) results. Panels (a)–(g) represent the comparisons between $\delta\alpha/\alpha$, $\delta\beta/\beta$, or $\delta\rho/\rho$ and different parameters: (a) α_1, (b) β_1, (c) α_2, (d) β_2, (e) P_s/P ratio, (f) ray parameter, and (g) ρ_2. The color version of this figure is available only in the electronic edition. *(Continued)*

and equation (10), we calculated the $\Delta\rho/\rho$ using all three methods. The ratios between the results are listed in Table 3, Figure 7, and Figure S6. These ratios show that the $\Delta\rho/\rho$ across the Moho varies significantly among the methods.

The result from the AB method has the smallest value, but AR's method produces the largest. Julià's method produces values that fall between those obtained from the other two methods. The acceptable range for $\Delta\rho/\rho$, based on the density ranges

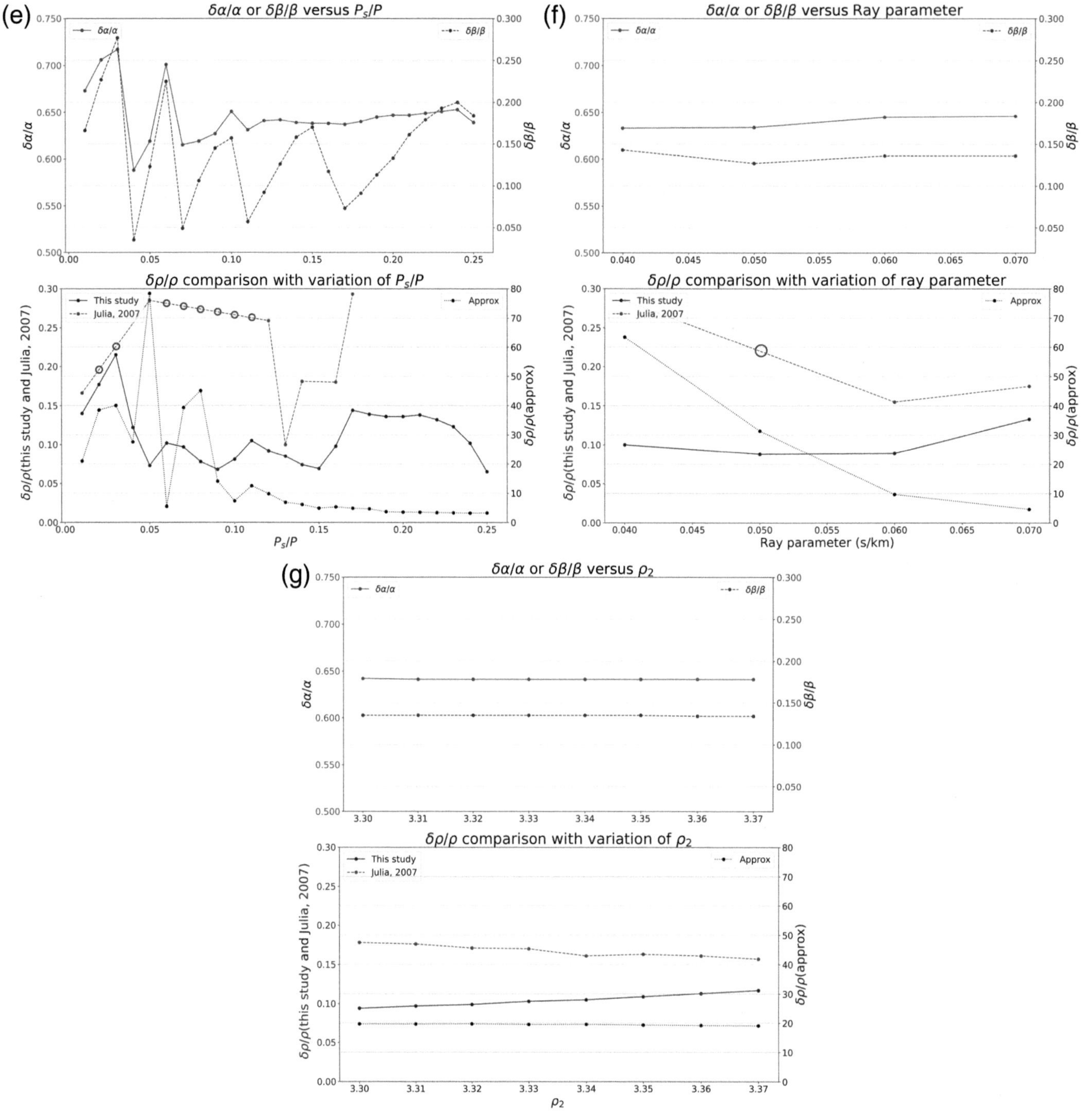

Figure 7. Continued

used in this study, is (0.0, 0.267], indicating that the methods by AR approximation cannot be applied to obtain reasonable ρ_1.

The details of the $\Delta\rho/\rho$ from the AB, AR, and Julià methods are presented in Figure 7 and Figure S6. The $\Delta\rho/\rho$ from the AB method shows consistent variation with parameter changes, except for the P_s/P ratio (Fig. 7). For instance, in this study, $\Delta\rho/\rho$ increases with ρ_2, whereas the AR and Julià methods show a slight decrease (Fig. 7g). Figure 7f shows that ray parameter affects $\Delta\rho/\rho$ differently: higher values reduce sensitivity in AR but increase it in the Julià method. For ρ_2, its influence on $\Delta\rho/\rho$ is minor, so fluctuations are barely noticeable (Fig. 7g). For other parameters, neither the AR nor the Julià method exhibits a clear pattern of variation, suggesting that the impact of parameters on these methods is unpredictable.

TABLE 3
$\delta\rho/\rho$ Ratios Based on the Method from This Study, AR Approximation, and Julià's Method Across the Four Velocity Models

	Approximate Velocity			
	CRUST1.0	**SR**	**LITHO1.0**	**PIM**
Aki and Richards (2002) method	25.60	26.09	25.44	26.09
Julià (2007) method	0.192	0.187	0.196	0.183
Amplitude-based method	0.106	0.097	0.122	0.103

The parameter inclusion model (PIM) was used for the calculations.

Figure 7 (red circles) also reveals that Julià does not consistently yield estimates for all parameter sets. For example, in Figure 7f, no results are available for a ray parameter of $p = 0.05$ s/km, and in Figure 7e, no data exist when the P_s/P ratio exceeds 0.16. No ρ_1 were obtained from the CRUST1.0 model using Julià's method (Fig. S6a). Litho1.0 provided more estimates (Fig. S6b), whereas the SR model yielded fewer results because it only includes continental data (Fig, S6c). These limitations highlight that the Julià method does not produce valid estimates for certain parameter settings. In contrast, the amplitude-based approach provides results across a broader range of tested parameters.

Correlation between $\delta\rho_1$ and $\delta\beta_1$

It is important to understand how $\delta\beta_1$ affects $\delta\rho_1$, as previous studies have shown that β_1 has one of the strongest impacts on $\delta\rho_1$ (e.g., Shen and Ritzwoller, 2016; Table 2). The SR model provides the β_1 and its uncertainty in the western contiguous United States, making it the only velocity model among the four that includes $\delta\beta_1$. Therefore, we used the β_1 values with associated uncertainty to calculate the corresponding propagation uncertainty $\delta\rho_1$. We also calculated $\Delta\rho/\rho$ and $\Delta\beta/\beta$ and analyzed these uncertainties in relation to β_1.

We applied equation (2) from Shen and Ritzwoller (2016) to calculate the $\delta\rho_1$ based on the $\delta\beta_1$ from the SR dataset. The mean ρ_1 from SR is 2.85 ± 0.11 g/cm^3, whereas the mean ρ_1 from this study is 3.01 ± 0.10 g/cm^3. The average ρ_1 obtained using this method is ~0.16 g/cm^3 higher than SR; however, the standard deviation remains of the same order of magnitude. The mean $\delta\beta_1$ from SR is 0.12 km/s, with the corresponding $\delta\rho_1$ calculated as 3.04×10^{-3} g/cm^3 and the mean $\Delta\rho/\rho$ as 0.07 ± 0.05. This suggests that $\delta\beta_1$ has a minimal effect on $\delta\rho_1$, but its influence on $\Delta\rho/\rho$ is relatively large. The mean $\delta\rho_1$ obtained using this method is 0.065 g/cm^3, whereas the mean $\Delta\rho/\rho$ based on the same SR velocity pair is 0.10 ± 0.06, which remains within the same order of magnitude as the SR results.

It is important that the calculation methods differ (e.g., eqn (2) in Shen and Ritzwoller, 2016 vs. equation 6 in this study), leading to differences in the mean and standard deviation results. However, the similarity in the order of magnitude of $\Delta\rho/\rho$ between the two results supports the reliability this method when applied to real-world velocity pairs with real uncertainties.

We compared the PCC values obtained using the AB method with those derived from the method outlined by Shen and Ritzwoller (2016). Comparing the PCC values of β_1 and $\delta\rho_1$, result from this study reports ~ −0.233, which is smaller than ~0.984 from SR (Table S8). This suggests that the β_1 data with uncertainty from real observations show stronger correlation to $\delta\rho_1$ from SR than this study. Similarly, the PCC between β_1 and $\delta\rho/\rho$ is 0.192 in SR, >0.008 in this study. In addition, the PCC between $\delta\beta_1$ and $\delta\rho_1$ is −0.201 in SR compared with 0.019 in this study. The PCC between β_1 and $\delta\rho_1$ in this study is smaller than that obtained using the SR method, further supporting this observation.

The correlation between β_1 and $\delta\rho_1$ in this study is positive, but the others are negative. Here, $\delta\beta_1$ shows a weak correlation with $\Delta\rho/\rho$, suggesting it has little influence on $\Delta\rho/\rho$. Furthermore, the low-PCC value between and confirms that uncertainty in has minimal impact on the uncertainty of (Table S8).

Conclusion

We developed a new method to calculate ρ_1, $\delta\rho_1$, and $\Delta\rho/\rho$ across the Moho. In addition, we analyzed the correlations between parameters $[\alpha_1,\beta_1,\alpha_2,\beta_2,p,\rho_2,P_s/P]$ and ρ_1, $\delta\rho_1$, and $\Delta\rho/\rho$.

The mean ρ_1 across all four models falls within a reasonable range of 2.946–3.012 g/cm^3, demonstrating the method's reliability. The PIM result is 2.992 g/cm^3, representing the theoretical estimate derived from the broad range of possible parameter values. The consistency of results across different models further validates the robustness of the approach.

The estimates obtained from the Monte Carlo sharp and gradational Moho models are consistent with the PIM results, supporting the reliability and robustness of the AB method. The addition of synthetic noise increases uncertainty but still yields results consistent with the noise-free models. Among the three depth layers in the gradational Moho structure, the base layer exhibits the lowest uncertainty, though it is influenced by upper mantle properties. In contrast, the top and midpoint layers are not affected by the upper mantle, with the midpoint layer showing moderate uncertainty.

The differences in constraints and the development of velocity models affect the correlation between ρ_1 (or its sensitivity) and various parameters. However, some global trends remain consistent across models. The average $\delta\rho_1/\rho_1$ is ~10% indicates the reasonable accuracy of the ρ_1 calculation. The method has been validated as reasonable through uncertainty.

Whereas α_2 is less correlated with both ρ_1 and $\delta\rho_1$ than the other parameters, the shear-wave velocities have the strongest correlation with ρ_1. The ray parameter also has a strong negative correlation on density calculation, and β_1 shows the strongest negative correlation with $\delta\rho_1$.

The comparison of between CRUST1.0 and the AB method reveals general similarities in the estimates, but the low correlation between them highlights their differing emphases and development approaches. Comparisons of $\Delta\rho/\rho$ among this method, AR approximation, and Julià's method indicate that the AB method yields more consistent results, but the AR and Julià methods either show limited reliability or do not produce results for certain parameter sets. In addition, the similar $\Delta\rho/\rho$ obtained from the same model (i.e., velocity pairs extracted from SR) between the real $\delta\beta_1$ from SR and AB method further supports the reliability of the estimates derived in this study for practical applications.

Further experiments are needed to test the method's uncertainty in different regions, such as oceanic areas, to evaluate how reliably ρ_1 can be determined using this approach. Applying the method to real receiver functions will be the next step to demonstrate its performance on observational data. In the framework of a follow-up study, such validation on real measurements will be essential for the method to be considered fully valid, acceptable, and broadly applicable. The scarcity of data on the relationship between shear-wave sensitivity and $\Delta\rho/\rho$ (Fig. 6) emphasizes the limitations of the velocity sets in determining ρ_1 using the method from this study. This may indicate transitional or extreme density regions, which requires further study.pt

Data and Resources

The velocity models used in this study, CRUST1.0, LITHO1.0, and Shen and Ritzwoller (2016), are publicly available. The CRUST1.0 model (Laske *et al.*, 2013) was downloaded from https://igppweb.ucsd.edu/~gabi/crust1.html, the LITHO1.0 model (Pasyanos *et al.*, 2014) from https://ds.iris.edu/ds/products/emc-litho10, and the Shen and Ritzwoller (2016) model from https://ds.iris.edu/ds/products/emc-us2016. All scripts used for data processing and visualization were written in Python and are available from the corresponding author upon reasonable request. All websites were last accessed in December 2024. The supplemental material for this article includes mathematical derivations, Tables S1–S8, and Figures S1–S6.

Declaration of Competing Interests

The authors acknowledge that there are no conflicts of interest recorded.

Acknowledgments

The authors appreciate Gabi Laske from Scripps Institution of Oceanography, University of California San Diego, for her thoughtful review and valuable feedback on the article. The authors also appreciate the efforts of Yuxin Huang from Colgate University, and Yang Zhao from Shanghai University of Finance and Economics for reviewing the mathematical derivatives.

References

Afonso, J. C., M. Fernandez, G. Ranalli, W. L. Griffin, and J. A. D. Connolly (2008). Integrated geophysical-petrological modeling of the lithosphere and sublithospheric upper mantle: Methodology and applications, *Geochem. Geophys. Geosys.* **9,** no. 5, doi: 10.1029/2007GC001834.

Aki, K., and P. G. Richards (2002). Quantitative Seismology, Second Ed., University Science Books, Mill Valley, California.

Ammon, C. J., G. E. Randall, and G. Zandt (1990). On the nonuniqueness of receiver function inversions, *J. Geophys. Res.* **95,** no. B10, 15,303–15,318, doi: 10.1029/JB095iB10p15303.

Anovitz, L. M., and D. R. Cole (2015). Characterization and analysis of porosity and pore structures, *Rev. Mineral. Geochem.* **80,** no. 1, 61–164, doi: 10.2138/rmg.2015.80.04.

Artemieva, I. M., and A. Shulgin (2019). Making and altering the crust: A global perspective on crustal structure and evolution, *Earth Planet. Sci. Lett.* **512,** 8–16, doi: 10.1016/j.epsl.2019.01.033.

Benesty, J., J. Chen, Y. Huang, and I. Cohen (2009). Pearson correlation coefficient, in *Noise Reduction in Speech Processing*, Chap. 5, Springer Topics in Signal Processing, Vol. 2, 1–4, Springer, Berlin, Heidelberg, doi: 10.1007/978-3-642-00296-0_5.

Brocher, T. M. (2005). Empirical relations between elastic wavespeeds and density in the Earth's crust, *Bull. Seismol. Soc. Am.* **95,** no. 6, 2081–2092, doi: 10.1785/0120050077.

Cammarano, F., and B. Romanowicz (2007). Insights into the nature of the transition zone from physically constrained inversion of long-period seismic data, *Proc. Natl. Acad. Sci.* **104,** no. 22, 9139–9144, doi: 10.1073/pnas.0608075104.

Christensen, N. I., and W. D. Mooney (1995). Seismic velocity structure and composition of the continental crust: A global view, *J. Geophys. Res.* **100,** no. B6, 9761–9788, doi: 10.1029/95JB00259.

Faccenna, C., and T. W. Becker (2020). Topographic expressions of mantle dynamics in the Mediterranean, *Earth Sci. Rev.* **209,** 103327, doi: 10.1016/j.earscirev.2020.103327.

Gardner, G. H. F., L. W. Gardner, and A. Gregory (1974). Formation velocity and density—The diagnostic basics for stratigraphic traps, *Geophysics* **39,** no. 6, 770–780, doi: 10.1190/1.1440465.

Hacker, B. R., P. B. Kelemen, and M. D. Behn (2015). Continental lower crust, *Annu. Rev. Earth Planet. Sci.* **43,** no. 1, 167–205, doi: 10.1146/annurev-earth-050212-124117.

Holbrook, W. S., W. D. Mooney, and N. I. Christensen (1992). The seismic velocity structure of the deep continental crust, in *Continental Lower Crust*, D. M. Fountain, R. Arculus, and R.W. Kay (Editors), Elsevier, Amsterdam, The Netherlands, 1–43.

Jarchow, C. M., and G. A. Thompson (1989). The nature of the Mohorovicic discontinuity, *Annu. Rev. Earth Planet. Sci.* **17,** 475.

Julià, J. (2007). Constraining velocity and density contrasts across the crust—mantle boundary with receiver function amplitudes, *Geophys. J. Int.* **171,** no. 1, 286–301, doi: 10.1111/j.1365-2966.2007.03502.x.

Julià, J., C. J. Ammon, R. B. Herrmann, and A. M. Correig (2000). Joint inversion of receiver function and surface wave dispersion observations, *Geophys. J. Int.* **143,** no. 1, 99–112, doi: 10.1046/j.1365-246x.2000.00217.x.

Kalmár, D., and A. Balázs (2025). Upper and lower crustal deformation and residual topography in a continental back-arc: Inferences from the Pannonian-Transylvanian Basins, *Tectonophysics* **894,** 230572, doi: 10.1016/j.tecto.2024.230572.

Kamber, B. S. (2015). The evolving nature of terrestrial crust from the Hadean, through the Archaean, into the Proterozoic, *Precambrian Res.* **258,** 48–82, doi: 10.1016/j.precamres.2014.12.007.
Kendall, M. G. (1948). *The Advanced Theory of Statistics*, Vol. 1, Charles Griffin and Co., London, United Kingdom.
Kind, R., G. L. Kosarev, and N. V. Petersen (1995). Receiver functions at the stations of the German Regional Seismic Network (GRSN), *Geophys. J. Int.* **121,** no. 1, 191–202, doi: 10.1111/j.1365-246X.1995.tb03520.x.
Ku, H. H. (1966). Notes on the use of propagation of error formulas, *J. Res. Natl. Bureau Stand.* **70C,** no. 4, 263–273.
Kumar, P., X. Yuan, R. Kind, and G. Kosarev (2005). The lithosphere-asthenosphere boundary in the Tien Shan-Karakoram region from S receiver functions: Evidence for continental subduction, *Geophys. Res. Lett.* **32,** no. 7, doi: 10.1029/2004GL022291.
Laske, G., G. Masters, Z. Ma, and M. Pasyanos (2013). Update on CRUST1.0—A 1-degree global model of Earth's crust, *Geophys. Res. Abs.* **15,** no. 15, 2658.
Li, J., X. Song, P. Wang, and L. Zhu (2019). A generalized H-κ method with harmonic corrections on Ps and its crustal multiples in receiver functions, *J. Geophys. Res.* **124,** no. 4, 3782–3801, doi: 10.1029/2018JB016356.
Ligorría, J. P., and C. J. Ammon (1999). Iterative deconvolution and receiver-function estimation, *Bull. Seismol. Soc. Am.* **89,** no. 5, 1395–1400, doi: 10.1785/BSSA0890051395.
Lücke, O. H. (2014). Moho structure of Central America based on three-dimensional lithospheric density modelling of satellite-derived gravity data, *Int. J. Earth Sci.* **103,** 1733–1745, doi: 10.1007/s00531-012-0787-y.
Malvoisin, B., Y. Y. Podladchikov, and J. C. Vrijmoed (2015). Coupling changes in densities and porosity to fluid pressure variations in reactive porous fluid flow: Local thermodynamic equilibrium, *Geochem. Geophys. Geosys.* **16,** no. 12, 4362–4387, doi: 10.1002/2015GC006019.
McCamy, K., R. P. Meyer, and T. J. Smith (1962). Generally applicable solutions of Zoeppritz' amplitude equations, *Bull. Seismol. Soc. Am.* **52,** no. 4, 923–955, doi: 10.1785/BSSA0520040923.
Metropolis, N., and S. Ulam (1949). The Monte Carlo method, *J. Am. Stat. Assoc.* **44,** no. 247, 335–341, doi: 10.1080/01621459.1949.10483310.
Mohorovičić, A. (1910). Potres od 8/X 1909.(Das Beben vom 8. X. 1909), *Jahrbuch des meteorologischen Observatoriums in Zagreb (Agram) für das Jahr*, 1909, 1 pp. (in German).
Nafe, J. E., and C. L. Drake (1957). Variation with depth in shallow and deep water marine sediments of porosity, density and the velocities of compressional and shear waves, *Geophysics* **22,** no. 3, 523–552, doi: 10.1190/1.1438386.
Pappa, F., J. Ebbing, and F. Ferraccioli (2019). Moho depths of Antarctica: Comparison of seismic, gravity, and isostatic results, *Geochem. Geophys. Geosys.* **20,** no. 3, 1629–1645, doi: 10.1029/2018GC008111.
Pasyanos, M. E., T. G. Masters, G. Laske, and Z. Ma (2014). LITHO1.0: An updated crust and lithospheric model of the Earth, *J. Geophys. Res.* **119,** no. 3, 2153–2173, doi: 10.1002/2013JB010626.
Rabbel, W., M. Kaban, and M. Tesauro (2013). Contrasts of seismic velocity, density and strength across the Moho, *Tectonophysics* **609,** 437–455, doi: 10.1016/j.tecto.2013.06.020.
Rice, J. A. (2007). *Mathematical Statistics and Data Analysis*, Vol. 371, Thomson/Brooks/Cole, Belmont, California.
Rudnick, R. L., and D. M. Fountain (1995). Nature and composition of the continental crust: A lower crustal perspective, *Rev. Geophys.* **33,** no. 3, 267–309, doi: 10.1029/95RG01302.
Ryberg, T., and M. Weber (2000). Receiver function arrays: A reflection seismic approach, *Geophys. J. Int.* **141,** no. 1, 1–11, doi: 10.1046/j.1365-246X.2000.00077.x.
Rychert, C. A., and P. M. Shearer (2009). A global view of the lithosphere-asthenosphere boundary, *Science* **324,** no. 5926, 495–498, doi: 10.1126/science.1169754.
Schmandt, B., F. C. Lin, and K. E. Karlstrom (2015). Distinct crustal isostasy trends east and west of the Rocky Mountain Front, *Geophys. Res. Lett.* **42,** no. 23, 10–290, doi: 10.1002/2015GL066593.
Shen, W., and M. H. Ritzwoller (2016). Crustal and uppermost mantle structure beneath the United States, *J. Geophys. Res.* **121,** no. 6, 4306–4342, doi: 10.1002/2016JB012887.
Tassara, A., H. J. Götze, S. Schmidt, and R. Hackney (2006). Three-dimensional density model of the Nazca plate and the Andean continental margin, *J. Geophys. Res.* **111,** no. B9, doi: 10.1029/2005JB003976.
Wang, Y., R. M. Russo, and Y. Lin (2024). Use of decision tree ensembles for crustal structure imaging from receiver functions, *Geophys. J. Int.* **238,** no. 3, 1429–1450.
White, R. S. (1993). Melt production rates in mantle plumes, *Phil. Trans. Roy. Soc. Lond. A* **342,** no. 1663, 137–153, doi: 10.1098/rsta.1993.0010.
Woollard, G. P. (1959). Crustal structure from gravity and seismic measurements, *J. Geophys. Res.* **64,** no. 10, 1521–1544, doi: 10.1029/JZ064i010p01521.
Zhu, L., and H. Kanamori (2000). Moho depth variation in southern California from teleseismic receiver functions, *J. Geophys. Res.* **105,** no. B2, 2969–2980, doi: 10.1029/1999JB900322.
Zill, D. G. (2020). *Advanced Engineering Mathematics*, Jones & Bartlett Learning, Burlington, Massachusetts.

Manuscript received 10 July 2025
Published online 7 November 2025

Basin Geometry and Crustal Structure in and Around the Jianghan Basin of Central China: Implications for Geothermal Prospecting

Rong Huang*[1,2], Penglong Wei[1,3], Lei Liu[4,5], Fengxu Wang[1], Shaoqian Hu[1], Kaifeng Zhao[1,2], and Yinhe Luo[1,2]

Abstract

Basin geometry and underneath crustal structures are important for unraveling deep geothermal resources. Here, we used teleseismic waveform data from 58 broadband seismic stations in and around the Jianghan basin in central China to determine the geometry of the basin and the crustal structure using nonlinear waveform inversion and modified H–κ receiver function stacking methods. The results reveal two prominent basin subsidence centers (>5 km deep), coinciding with Moho uplifts (~5 km), indicative of isostatic compensation and possible upwelling of the mantle. The crustal anisotropy obtained exhibits a divergent pattern from these centers and aligns with the regional north-northeast–south-southwest extension direction. The two subsidence centers also coincide with high-crustal ratios V_P/V_S and high-surface heat flow, suggesting that the thin crust beneath the basin and mantle upwelling contribute to the geothermal reservoir in the region.

Cite this article as Huang, R., P. Wei, L. Liu, F. Wang, S. Hu, K. Zhao, and Y. Luo (2025). Basin Geometry and Crustal Structure in and Around the Jianghan Basin of Central China: Implications for Geothermal Prospecting, *Seismol. Res. Lett.* **97**, 2036–2049, doi: 10.1785/0220250133.

Supplemental Material

Introduction

The continental lithosphere of the Chinese mainland is composed of several terranes that collided at different times and are sutured together along a series of nearly east–west-trending sutures (Huang *et al.*, 1977; Qiu *et al.*, 2006; Zhang *et al.*, 2013). However, the current surface topography as well as crustal and lithospheric thicknesses of China exhibit a distinct east–west difference separated by a nearly north–south gravity lineament (NSGL). The crustal thickness in the eastern part is generally less than 40 km and the lithosphere thickness ranges from 80 to 100 km, whereas the western part has a thicker crust (>40 km) and lithosphere (150–200 km; Zhu *et al.*, 2012; Li *et al.*, 2015; Stern *et al.*, 2018). The NSGL roughly coincides with the western edge of the stagnant Pacific subducted plate in the mantle transition zone (Huang and Zhao, 2006). It is considered to be the transition zone from the Yanshan tectonic domain and the Himalayan tectonic domain in the Chinese mainland (Yang *et al.*, 2005). The Jianghan basin is located in the middle section of NSGL (Fig. 1). To its west, the crustal deformation is mostly compressional as manifested by the thrusting and nappe tectonics of the Dabashan orogenic belt onto the southern Sichuan basin (Li *et al.*, 2011; Dong *et al.*, 2013). To its east, the deformation is extensional as manifested by the development of the Jianghan rift basin (Dong *et al.*, 2007; He *et al.*, 2011).

The Jianghan basin, developed on the Yanshanian fold basement in eastern China, is located on the northern edge of the South China block and adjacent to the NSGL (Fig. 1). As a typical inland rift basin, it has undergone three stages of evolution: (1) the foreland basin stage (Middle Triassic to Late Jurassic), dominated by compression from the Qinling-Dabie thrust nappe and formation of a checkerboard fault system; (2) the fault basin stage (Cretaceous to Tertiary), transition to extensional tectonics, with faults reactivated as normal faults and accompanied by basin rotation and intense magmatic activity; and (3) the depression basin stage (since the Tertiary), with reduced fault control, cessation of magmatism, and widespread Quaternary sedimentation (Dai, 1996; Liu *et al.*, 2000; Wang, Mei, *et al.*, 2018). By modeling the geothermal history of hydrocarbon-bearing basins based on borehole data in the southern Jianghan basin, the basin was in a stable low heat flow state (50–55 mW/m^2) before the Indosinian Period (240 Ma), bounded by the Qianbei-Tianmen River fault (Fig. 1), with the

1. Hubei Subsurface Multi-scale Imaging Lab (SMIL), School of Geophysics and Geomatics, China University of Geosciences, Wuhan, China, https://orcid.org/0000-0001-5377-9060 (RH); https://orcid.org/0009-0006-6870-3951 (PW); https://orcid.org/0000-0001-5250-4153 (SH); 2. State Key Laboratory of Geological Processes and Mineral Resources, China University of Geosciences, Wuhan, China; 3. CCTEG Xi'an Research Institute (Group) Co., Ltd, Xi'an, China; 4. Geophysical Exploration Brigade of Hubei Geological Bureau, Wuhan, China; 5. Hubei Key Laboratory of Resource and Eco- Environment Geology, Hubei Geological Bureau, Wuhan, China

*Corresponding author: huangrong@cug.edu.cn

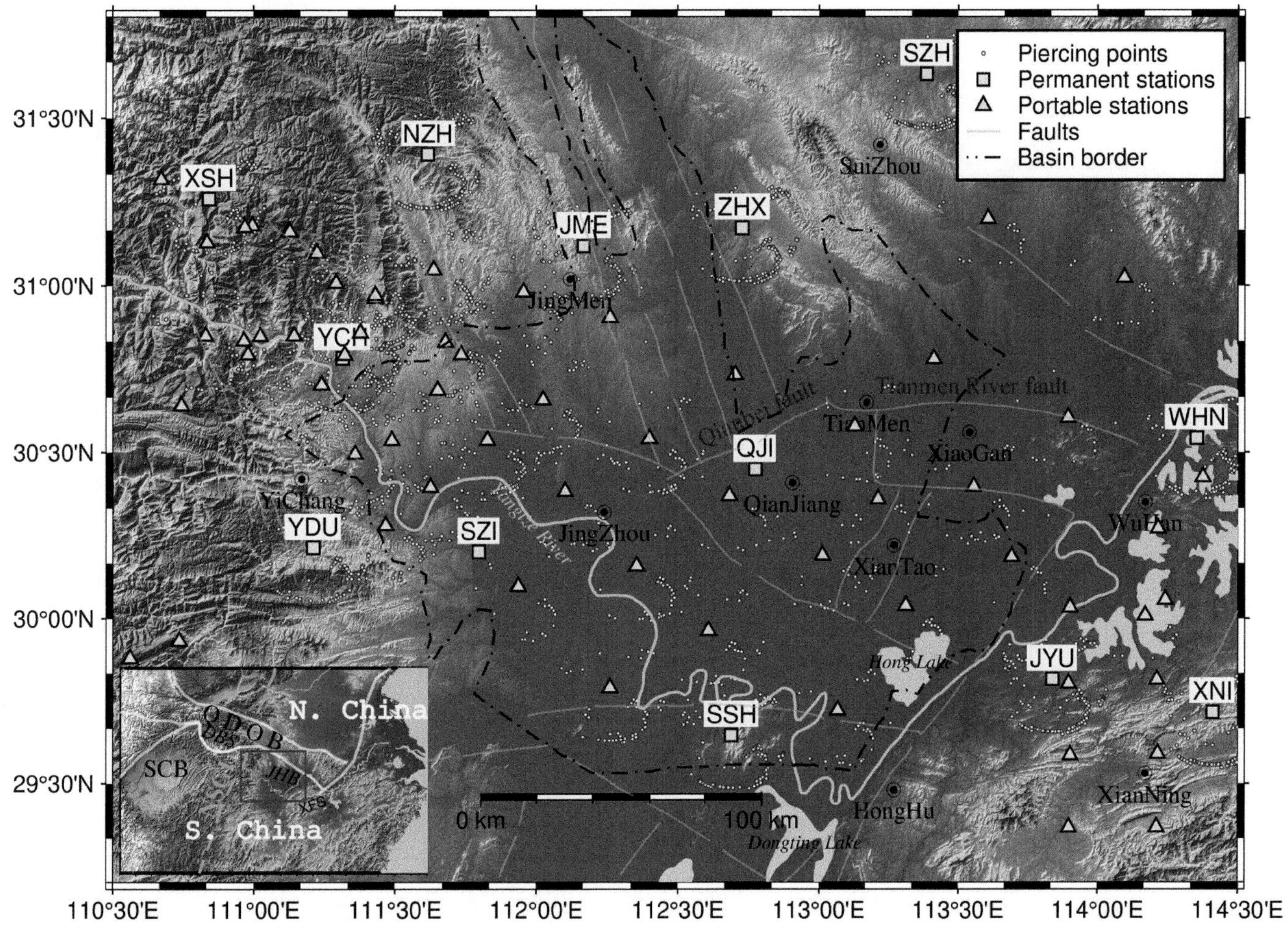

Figure 1. Topography of the sediment thicknesses of the Jianghan basin and its surrounding area, showing the distribution of piercing points of Moho (gray dots), permanent (black squares), and portable seismic stations (black triangles). The inset map in the lower left shows the study area (the red square) within the Chinese mainland, with abbreviations for various geologic units. DBS, Dabashan Mt.; JHB, Jianghan basin; JME, Jing Men; NSGL, north–south gravity lineament; QDOB, Qinling-Dabie Orogenic Belt; QJI, Qian Jiang; SCB, Sichuan basin; SZH, Sui Zhou; WHN, Wu Han; XFS, Xuefengshan Mt.; XNI, Xian Ning; YCH, Yi Chang. Station codes (e.g., JME, JYU, NZH, QJI, SSH, SZH, SZI, WHN, XNI, XSH, YCH, YDU, ZHX) represent the names of individual broadband seismic stations. The color version of this figure is available only in the electronic edition.

northern part of the basin reaching a peak during the Middle Yanshan Period (155 Ma; ~72 mW/m^2), and the southern part peaking during the Late Yanshan Period (40 Ma; ~76 mW/m^2); after the Late Himalayan Period, the heat flow rapidly declined, and the basin began to cool, forming a geothermal pattern of high in the north and low in the south, and strong in the east and weak in the west (Li *et al.*, 2010). The basin contains thick evaporites, brine resources rich in potassium, lithium, and iodine (Yu *et al.*, 2022), and hundreds of meters of organic-rich shale (Paleogene), with geological conditions for shale gas extraction (Guo *et al.*, 2012), and rich in geothermal resources as characterized by stratified geothermal reservoirs and conductive heating (Li *et al.*, 2016).

Since the start of seismic exploration in the Jianghan basin in 1958, a series of discoveries have been garnered, particularly in the basin tectonics. Extensive research has found that basement and crustal structures influence the formation and evolution of the basin. However, previous studies have primarily been based on drilling and 2D active-source seismic exploration and lacked 3D high-resolution seismic data and studies. To date, research on the deep structure of the Jianghan basin has mainly stemmed from seismic wide-angle reflection (Zhang *et al.*, 2009), lithospheric mantle tomography (Ouyang *et al.*, 2014) and anisotropy (Zhang *et al.*, 2011), ambient noise tomography (Zhou *et al.*, 2012; Luo *et al.*, 2013; Gao and Chen, 2017; Wei *et al.*, 2022), and other comprehensive geological and geophysical studies (Jiang *et al.*, 2007). These studies show that the upper crust of the Jianghan basin exhibits low velocities from 5 to 10 km depths, a positive radial anisotropy (Ouyang *et al.*, 2015), whereas the upper mantle displays high-velocity characteristics (Wang, Huang, and Liu, 2018). In addition, a distinct lateral heterogeneous high-velocity anomaly band is present in the basin and was speculated to be the result of a magmatic intrusion in the lower crust (Gao and Chen, 2017), which controlled the eastward migration of the basin's subsidence center (Wang, Mei, *et al.*,

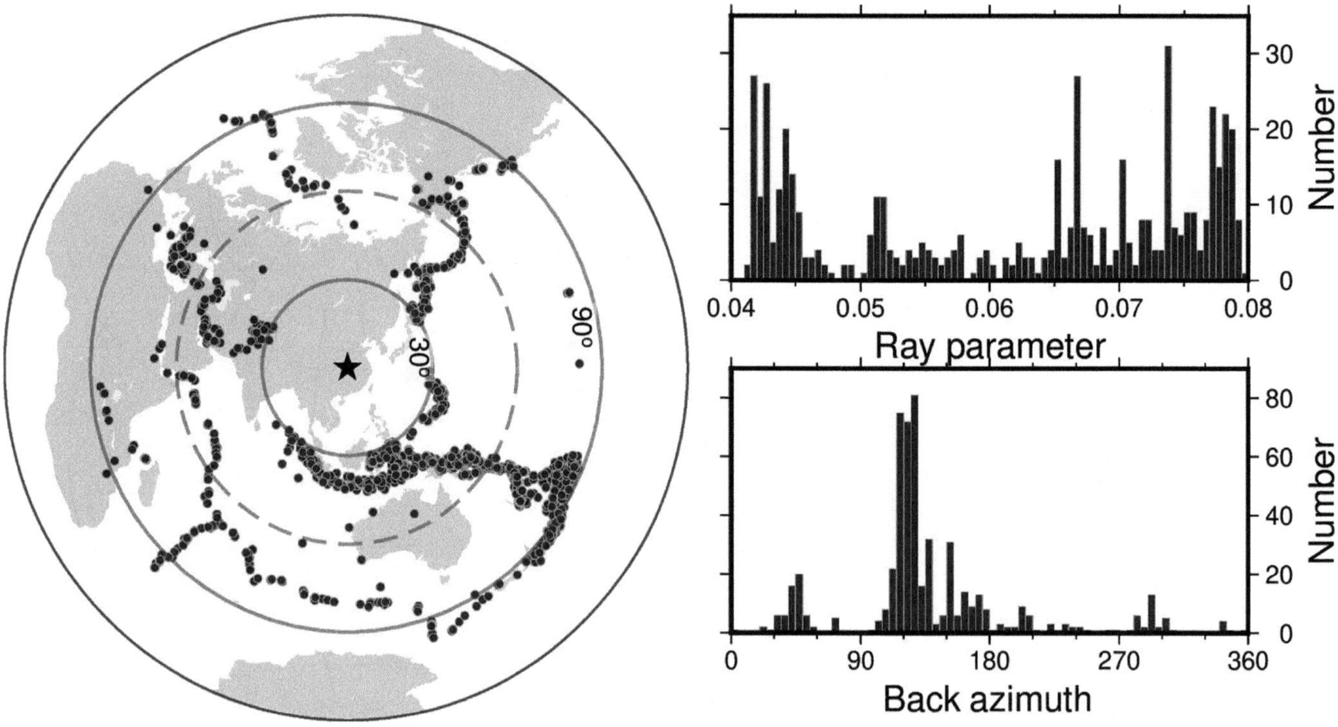

Figure 2. Seismic events used in the study and the distributions of back azimuths and ray parameters. The black dots represent the epicenters of the teleseismic events used in this study. The black star marks the location of the Jianghan Basin study area.

2018). Nevertheless, a detailed investigation of 3D high-resolution basement and crustal structures in the Jianghan basin is needed (Wu *et al.*, 2018, 2020).

In this study, we used 58 broadband seismic stations in and around the Jianghan basin and the teleseismic *P*-wave receiver functions methods to conduct a high-resolution analysis of the basin and underlying crust structures. The combined characteristics of the Jianghan basin and crustal structures are important to exploring deep geothermal and hydrocarbon resources. Li *et al.* (2010) suggested that the coupling between sediment thickness and Moho geometry may directly influence the thermal maturation of hydrocarbon source rocks. This study aims to fill our knowledge gaps in the study area by (1) obtaining the geometries of the top of the basement and the Moho and crustal anisotropy through waveform inversion and H-κ stacking of receiver functions; (2) correlating the basin geometry and crustal thickness with surface heat flow data; and (3) exploring the dynamic link among crustal thinning, magmatic underplating, and geothermal resource distribution, in the framework of the tectonic evolution of the South China block under the influence of the Western Pacific subduction and India-Eurasia collision.

Data and Methods

Data used in this study were collected from 46 portable stations and 12 permanent stations of the CEArray China National Seismic Network (Zheng *et al.*, 2010) deployed in and around the Jianghan basin (Fig. 1). The portable stations operated in three phases, for which phase 1 of 19 stations from June 2017 to June 2018, phase 2 of 14 stations from July 2018 to December 2019, and phase 3 of 13 stations from June 2022 to June 2023. Permanent station data spanned from January 2017 to December 2019. The station spacing of ~20 km provides a lateral resolution of ~10 km for deep crustal structures based on the piecing point distribution of teleseismic *P*-wave at the Moho (Fig. 1). However, because the H-κ method incorporates crustal multiples for which piercing points are three to four times farther from the station than those of *Ps* alone, its lateral resolution for this region is accordingly 30–40 km.

Teleseismic *P*-wave receiver function calculation

We first converted the raw continuous waveform data recorded by broadband three-component seismometers in the miniSEED format into the Seismic Analysis Code format. Based on the catalog from Incorporated Research Institutions for Seismology, we selected 569 teleseismic events of magnitudes larger than 5 and epicentral distances between 30° and 90° (Fig. 2) and then extracted their *P*-wave waveform from 10 s before to 100 s after the theoretical *P*-wave arrival time and high signal-to-noise ratios (SNRs). After removing the mean and linear trend, and rotating the two horizontal components to the radial and transverse directions, we filtered the waveforms with a band-pass filter of 0.05–2 Hz. Finally, we calculated radial and transverse receiver functions using a time-domain iterative deconvolution (Ligorria and Ammon, 1999) with 100 iterating times and a Gaussian parameter of 3. This Gaussian parameter corresponds to a low-pass filter cutoff frequency of ~1.5 Hz. By checking the

TABLE 1
Model Parameter Search Space (Minimum, Step, Maximum) Used in the NNA Inversion

Layer	H (km)	V_S^t (km/s)	V_S^b (km/s)	V_P/V_S	Q_P	Q_S
Case 1	[0.5: 0.2: 7.0]	[0.2: 0.1: 3.0]	[1.0: 0.2: 3.0]	[2.0: 0.1: 4.0]	400	200
Case 2	[0.5: 0.2: 5.0]	[0.2: 0.1: 2.0]	[1.0: 0.2: 3.0]	[2.0: 0.1: 4.0]	400	200
	[0.5: 0.2: 5.0]	[1.0: 0.1: 3.0]	[2.0: 0.2: 3.0]	[2.0: 0.1: 4.0]	400	200
Basement	Half-space	3.43	3.43	1.75	1200	600

NNA, nearest neighborhood algorithm.

similarity of receiver functions from adjacent azimuths, we ultimately obtained 2280 high-quality receiver functions.

Waveform inversion of basin receiver functions

We adopted the nearest neighborhood algorithm (NNA) to invert basin station receiver function waveforms for basin velocity structures. The algorithm uses a velocity model of multiple sedimentary layers on top of the basement crust. The model assumes a linear *S*-wave velocity (V_S) variation and constant V_P/V_S ratio in each layer. It uses the Thomson–Haskell propagation matrix algorithm (Haskell, 1964) to calculate the theoretical receiver functions of different models and searches for the best model for which predicted receiver functions match the observed receiver functions. The basement *S*-wave velocity was fixed to 3.43 km/s based on borehole measurements and regional seismic profiling in the Jianghan basin, which indicate that the crystalline basement consists of Mesozoic granites with $V_S = 3.4$–3.5 km/s (Wu *et al.*, 2018; Wang, Mei, *et al.*, 2018).

For NNA search, it is critical to select proper model parameters. Each layer of the model is determined by layer thickness (H), *S*-wave velocity (V_S^t) at the top, *S*-wave velocity (V_S^b) at the bottom, V_P/V_S ratio, and Q values. In most circumstances, the sedimentary layer was considered as a single layer (case 1). However, the waveform fits for some stations with one sedimentary layer was not good. For these stations, two sedimentary layers were used (case 2). The search ranges of other model parameters are listed in Table 1. Receiver functions of basin stations are usually complex due to reverberations in the low-velocity basin. We manually selected receiver functions with high quality and eliminated those stations with a limited number of receiver functions. Ultimately, we obtained basin velocity models of 21 stations in the Jianghan basin. The results are listed in Table S1, available in the supplemental material to this article. Figure 3 shows an example. Uncertainties of the best model parameters were estimated using the best 100 models in the NNA search space. The standard deviation of basin thickness ranges from 0.2 km for stations with high-quality receiver functions (SNR > 8) to 0.5 km for stations with lower SNR (<5).

H-κ stacking of basin-station receiver functions

Teleseismic *P* waves, when propagating through the Moho or the sediment-basement discontinuity beneath a seismic station, generate *P*-to-*S* converted waves (*Ps*). The *P* and *Ps* waves reflect repeatedly in the low-velocity crust and sedimentary layers to generate a distinct high-amplitude reverberation following the primary phase (Fig. 4). The basin reverberation often masks the Moho *Ps* phase and renders the traditional H-κ stacking method (Zhu and Kanamori, 2000) ineffective to determine the crustal thickness and V_P/V_S ratio.

For basin stations, the largest phase in the receiver functions is the *P*-to-*S* converted wave at the top of the basement (*Pbs*), followed by the Moho converted phase *PmS* and its multiples (*PPms* and *PSms*). Amplitudes of the basin multiples (*PPbs* and *PSbs*) are usually lower than the *Pbs*'s amplitude because of the high attenuation in the basin. To suppress the influence of basin reverberation on the Moho *Ps*, Yu *et al.* (2015) designed a filter in the form:

$$F(\omega) = 1 + r_0 e^{-i\omega\Delta t},$$

in the frequency domain, in which r_0 is the reflection coefficient at the sediment-basement interface and Δt is the two-way travel time in the basin. The reflection coefficient r_0 is estimated as the amplitude ratio of the first trough (A_{trough}) and peak (A_{peak}) in the receiver functions, whereas Δt is measured by their time separation.

After removing the basin reverberation using the filter, receiver functions of a basin station were stacked using a modified H-κ stacking method (Yu *et al.*, 2015):

$$S(H,\kappa) = \omega_1 r(t_1 + \delta t) + \omega_2 r(t_2 + \Delta t - \delta t) + \omega_3 r(t_3 + \Delta t),$$

in which δt is the time delay of *Pbs*. ω_i are weighting factors for *PmS*, *PPmS*, and *PSmS* that satisfy $\sum_{i=1}^{3} \omega_i = 1$. In this study, we set them to be 0.5, 0.4, and 0.1, respectively. We searched crystalline crust thickness from 20 to 70 km and the crustal V_P/V_S ratio from 1.6 to 2.0 (Fig. 5). We obtained the best-estimated crystalline crust thickness and V_P/V_S ratio of 22 basin stations (Table S2).

H-κ-c stacking of receiver functions

When the Moho discontinuity is not flat and/or the crust is anisotropic, the *Pms* arrival time will vary with ray's back-azimuth θ. In case of a tilted Moho, the arrival time varies in a term of $\cos\theta$. For crustal azimuthal anisotropy, the variation

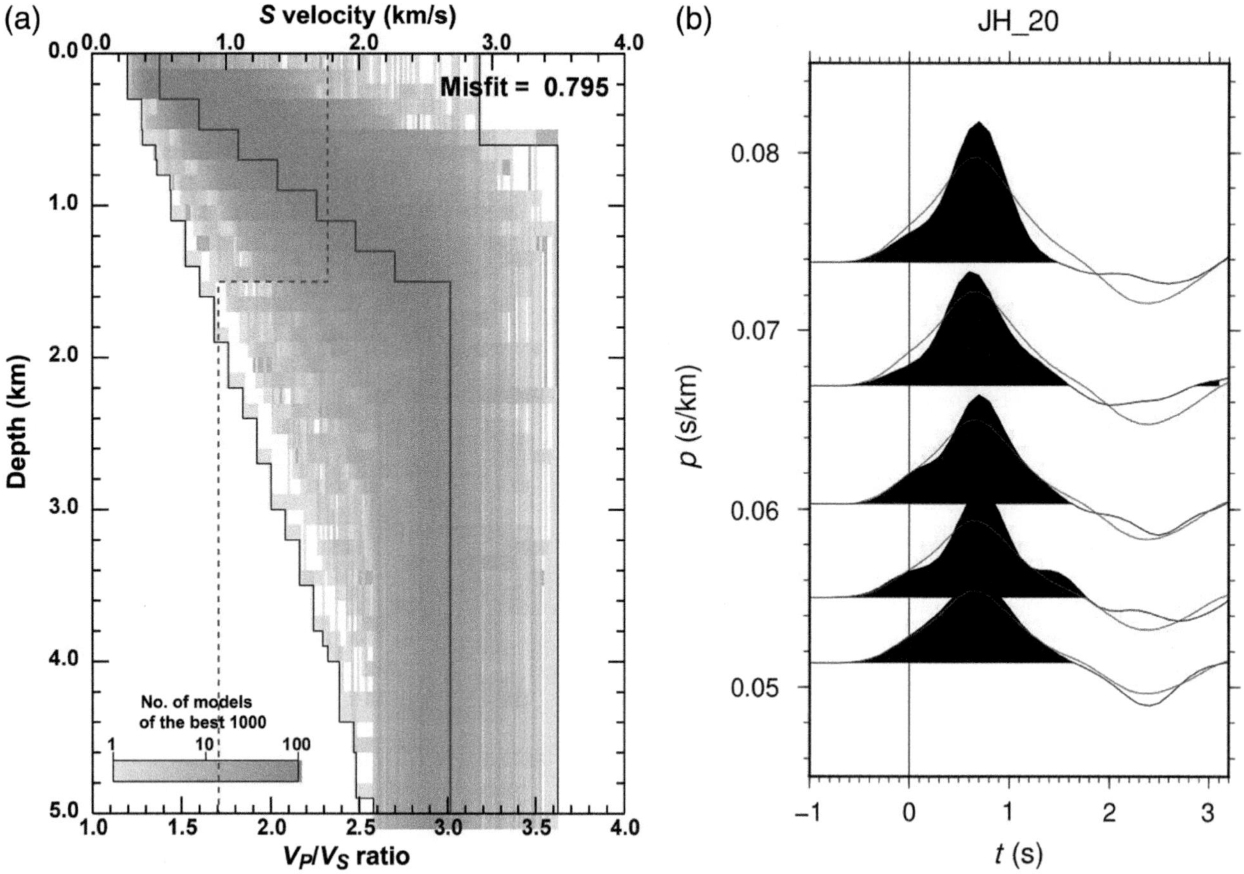

Figure 3. Results of the nearest neighborhood algorithm (NNA) at the station JH_20 located in the basin area. The colored area in panel (a) shows the best 1000 V_S models among the entire searched model space (the gray-shaded area), and the red lines are the best V_S model (solid) and V_P/V_S ratios (dotted). Panel (b) displays the waveform fits between observations (black) and best-model-predicted receiver functions (red). The color version of this figure is available only in the electronic edition.

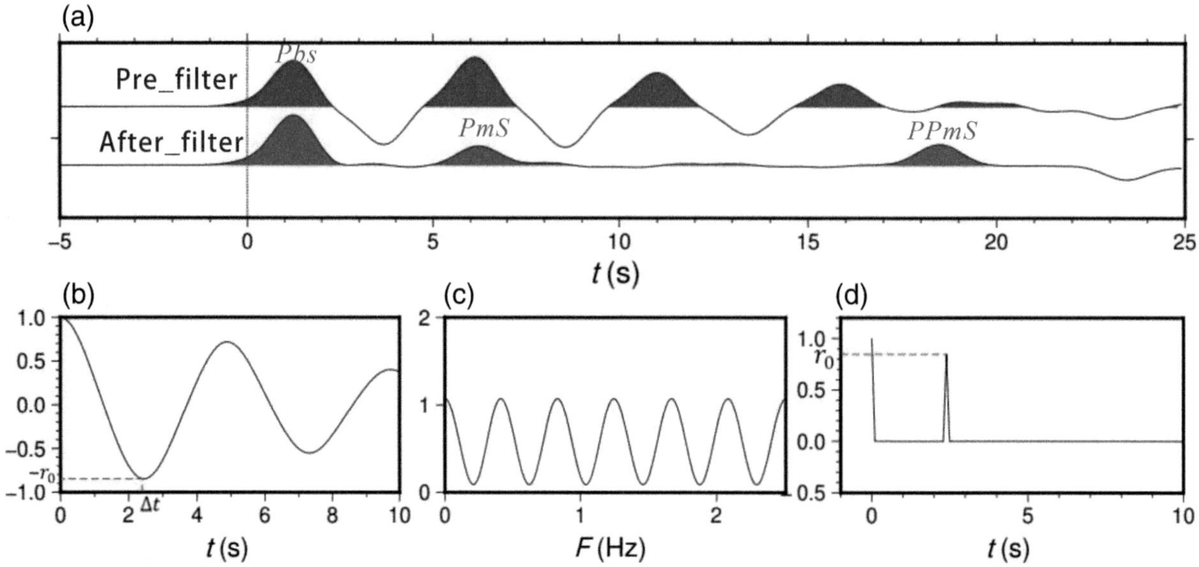

Figure 4. (a) Comparison of receiver functions before and after the basin-reverberation filtering. The dotted lines indicate the zero-time reference. (b) Autocorrelation of a receiver function, showing the two-way travel-time (Δt) and intensity of the basement reflection (r_0) for constructing the filter in the frequency domain (c). (d) The corresponding filter in the time domain. The color version of this figure is available only in the electronic edition.

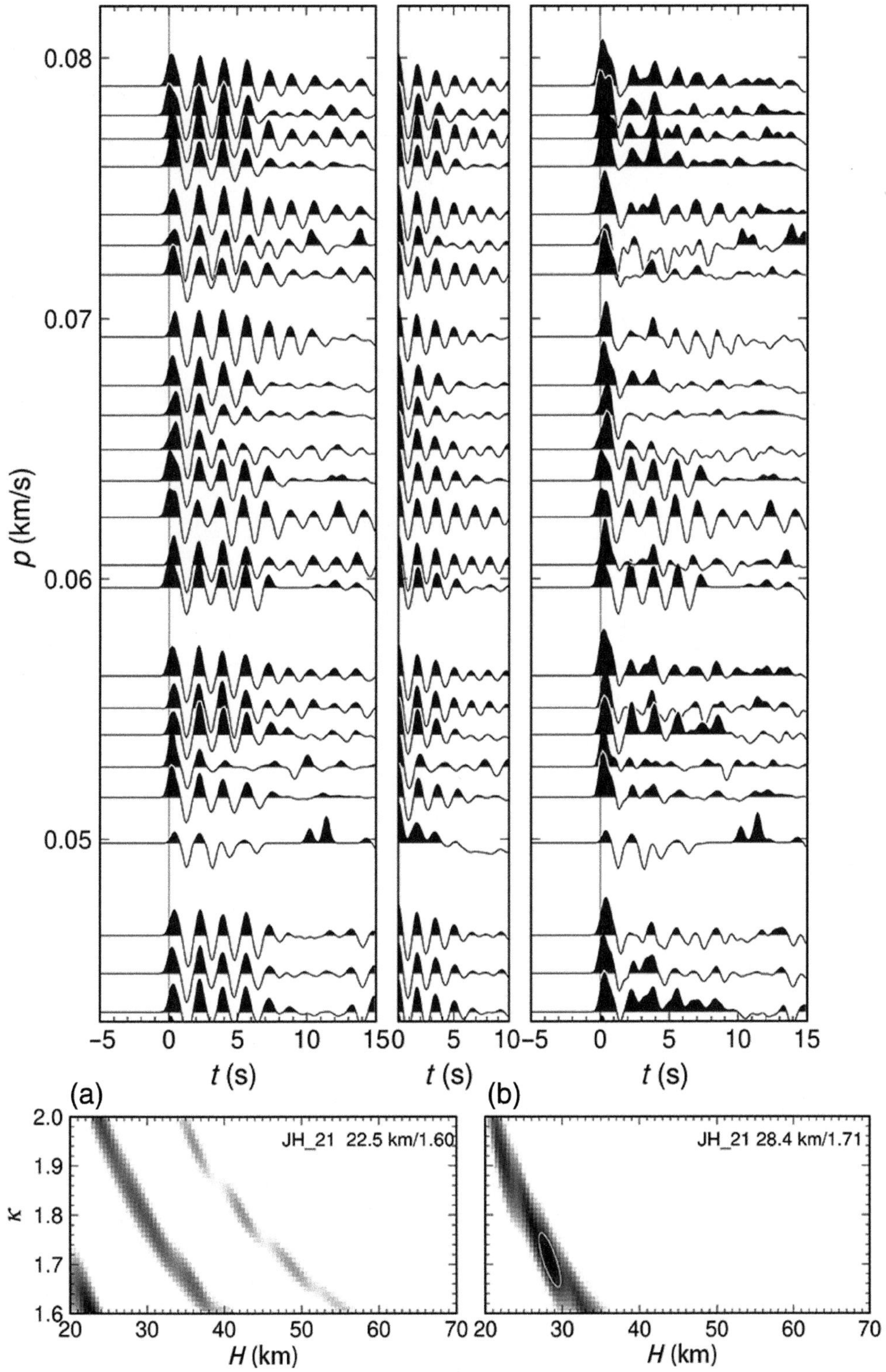

Figure 5. Comparison of results from the (a) traditional H-κ and (b) basin-corrected H-κ-b stacking methods at station JH_21. The blue shading represents the stacking energy, with darker shades indicating higher confidence. The white dashed oval outline highlights the region of maximum stacking energy, which corresponds to the best-estimated crustal thickness (H) and V_P/V_S ratio (κ). The color version of this figure is available only in the electronic edition.

follows $\cos 2\theta$. In general, the arrival time as a function of the back azimuth can be expressed as (Li *et al.*, 2019)

$$f(\theta) = A_0 + A_1 \cos(\theta - \theta_1) + A_2 \cos 2(\theta - \theta_2),$$

in which A_0 represents the reference arrival time of *Ps*. A_1 and θ_1 are the time delay and dipping direction of the Moho, respectively. A_2 is the time delay caused by the crustal azimuthal anisotropy, and θ_2 is the fast-wave direction of the crustal anisotropy.

We applied the harmonic analysis to all stations for which receiver function back-azimuthal gap was less than 90°. All the receiver functions were corrected to a reference ray parameter p = 0.06 km/s and then stacked in a 5° back-azimuth bin. We used the traditional H-κ stacking technique to determine the *Ps* reference arrival time. Other model parameters were determined from the best-harmonic fitting of the Moho *Ps* amplitudes. In the end, the Moho dipping angles as well as crustal azimuthal anisotropy direction and magnitude beneath 19 stations were obtained (Table S3). Figure 6 shows two examples.

We corrected receiver functions for the arrival time delays to the *Pms* phase and its multiples due to the dipping Moho and crustal azimuthal anisotropy. We then applied the H-κ-c stacking method to the corrected receiver functions to determine crustal thickness and V_P/V_S ratio beneath stations in the surrounding mountainous areas. The stacking weights were set to 0.5, 0.4, and 0.1. Figure 7 shows a comparison of results before and

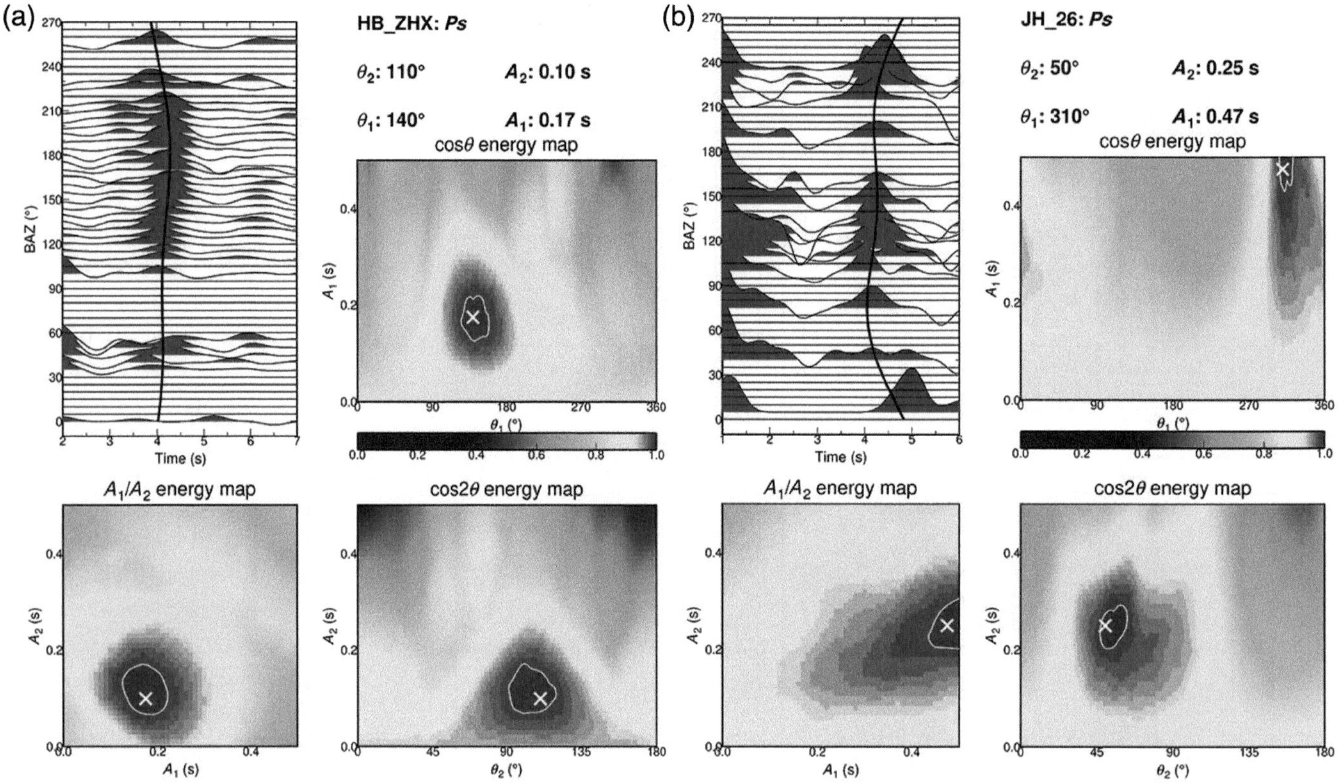

Figure 6. Results of the harmonic fitting analysis for stations (a) HB_ZHX and (b) JH_26. Each panel shows the grid-search energy diagrams for $\cos\theta$, A_1/A_2, and $\cos 2\theta$, respectively. The best-harmonic fitting curves and best-fit parameters are shown at the top. The bolded black lines in the top panel of each example show the best harmonic fitting curve for the *Pms* arrival time. The red shading in the lower panels represents the grid-search energy for the corresponding parameters. The white "X" marks the location of the best-fitting parameter values (A_1/θ_1 for Moho tilt and A_2/θ_2 for anisotropy). The color version of this figure is available only in the electronic edition.

after the correction. We obtained crustal thicknesses and V_P/V_S ratio beneath a total of 26 stations (Table S2), we also calculated the differences in the average crustal thickness H and the average crustal velocity ratio, showing a maximum 3-km variation in crustal thickness and 0.1 variation in V_P/V_S ratio.

Results and Discussion

Sediment thickness, crustal thickness, and azimuthal anisotropy

Here, we obtained sediment thickness variation in the Jianghan basin (Fig. 8). The sediment thickness changes from 1.3 to 6.1 km, with an average of 3.3 km. Overall, the sediments in the southern edge, central region, and parts of the northwest are relatively thick (>5 km), whereas the northern, northeastern, and some eastern areas are relatively thin (<2 km). There are two significant subsidence centers: one in the southwestern part of the Jingmen city, with a radius of ~20 km and maximum thickness >5.5 km, and another one between Qianjiang and Xiantao with a radius of 15 km and maximum thickness >5 km.

The crustal thicknesses beneath stations in the basin were obtained by summing the crystalline crust thickness from H-κ-b stacking and sediment thickness from the NNA inversion beneath each station (Table S2), whereas the crustal thicknesses beneath the stations in the surrounding mountainous areas were directly obtained from the H-κ-c stacking of the receiver functions. The results show that the Moho depth varies from 26.1 to 40.8 km, with an average of 33.2 km, in the Jianghan basin and its southern area. In other surrounding areas, the Qinling-Dabie orogenic belt in the north has an overall depth of ~35 km, and the area west to the NSGL has a Moho depth exceeding 40 km.

From the harmonic analysis of *Pms* delay times, the time delays A_1 and A_2 reveal the magnitudes of Moho tilt and crustal anisotropy, whereas the corresponding angles θ_1 and θ_2 are the directions of Moho tilt and fast wave in crustal anisotropy, respectively.

The results show coherent variations of Moho tilt direction and the fast-wave direction in the basin area (Figs. 8, 9). The fast-wave directions radiate outward from the first basin subsidence center for which the crustal anisotropy magnitude exceeds 0.5 s.

The fast-wave directions of crustal anisotropy exhibit a divergent pattern and align with the regional north-northeast–south-southwest deformation direction from Global Positioning System measurements (Wang *et al.*, 2001). This suggests that crustal anisotropy is primarily controlled by crustal stretching and fault reactivation (Liu *et al.*, 2015) under the current

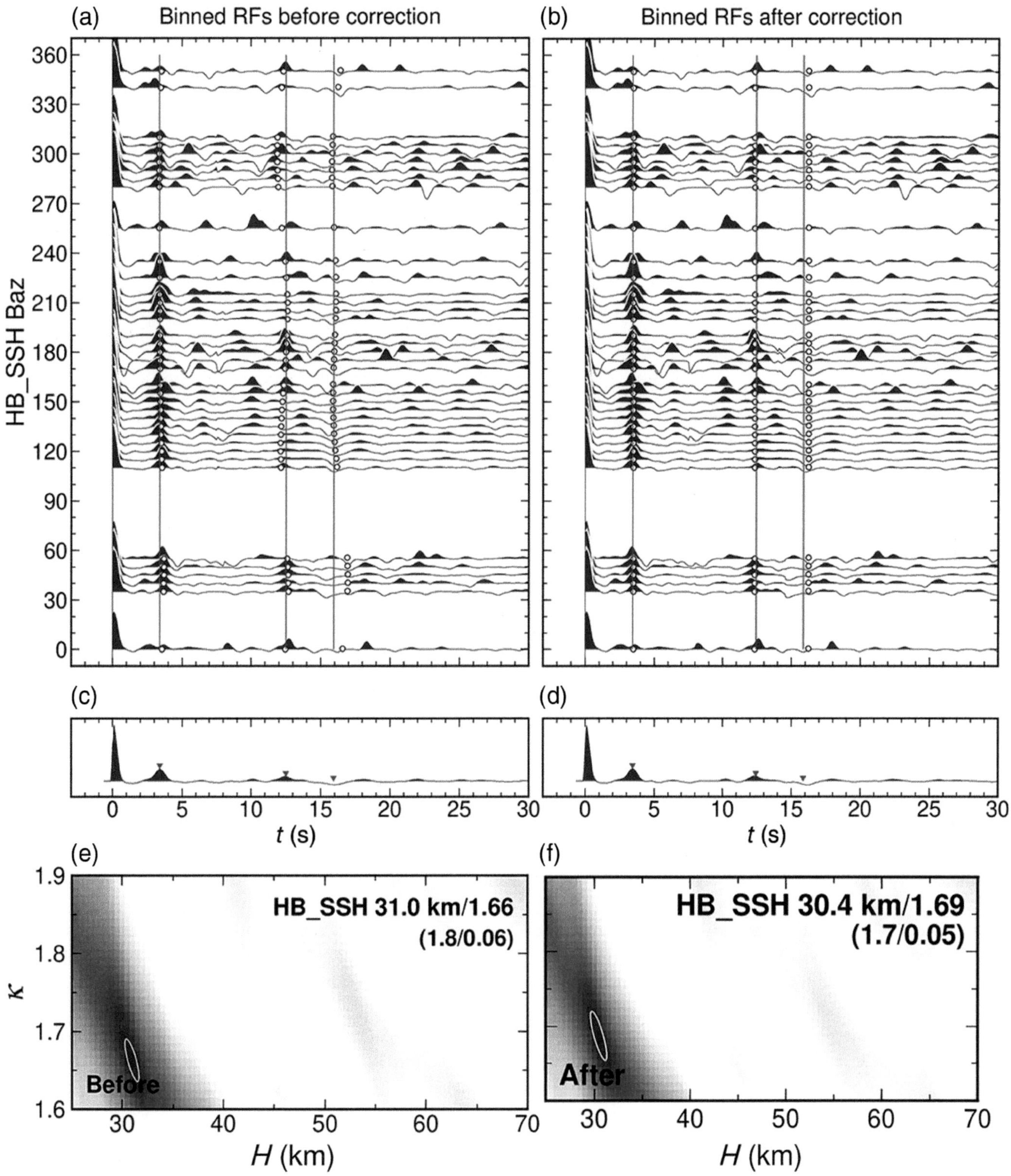

Figure 7. Comparison of results from (a,c,e) H-κ and (b,d,f) H-κ-c stacking method at the station HB_SSH located in the mountainous area. The blue shading represents the stacking energy. The red vertical lines mark the theoretical arrival times for the *Pms* phase and its multiples. The white dots are the observed receiver function (RF) amplitudes at the predicted times. The red triangles are the predicted RF amplitudes from the best-fitting model. The white dashed oval outlines highlight the region of maximum stacking energy corresponding to the best-estimated H and κ. The color version of this figure is available only in the electronic edition.

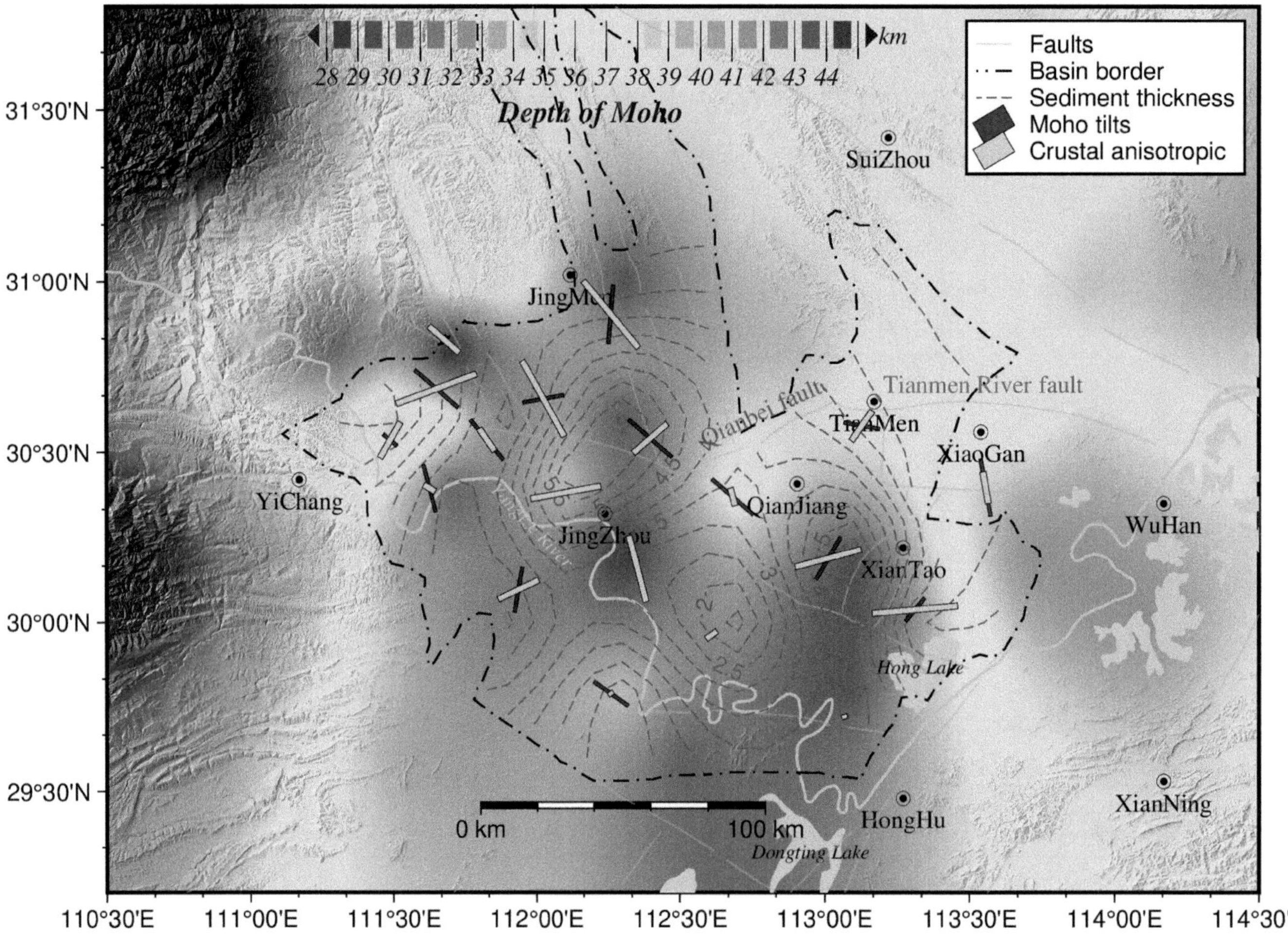

Figure 8. Moho depth and tilt, crustal anisotropy, and sediment thickness beneath the Jianghan basin and its surrounding area, as well as the contour of the Moho tilts and crustal anisotropy. The color version of this figure is available only in the electronic edition.

extensional regime. The divergent crustal anisotropy patterns could arise from a vertical material flow beneath the subsidence centers and is consistent with high V_P/V_S ratios (>1.80) in these areas, which likely reflect partial melt (Christensen, 1996) or hydrated mineral assemblages. In contrast, the eastern region shows less regularity and weaker average crustal anisotropy, with a subtle radiating pattern centered around the second subsidence center. This reflects a stronger crustal anisotropy in the northern part and weaker in the southern part. Overall, there is a trend of outward radiation. It also reflects an upward bulging of the Moho within the region, which indicates a concentrated upwelling of mantle material in the area (Zhang *et al.*, 2009, 2023).

Crustal thinning and its implications

The Jianghan basin was developed on a crustal basement that has undergone a series of tectonic deformations. The crustal thickness and the average V_P/V_S ratio reflect the structural morphology and the compositional components of the crustal material. A strong negative correlation exists between the sediment thickness and Moho depth, consistent with isostatic compensation models (Watts, 2001). Independent gravity anomaly data further confirm this anticorrelation, showing Bouguer gravity lows (<−50 mGal) over the subsidence centers. In the study region, the Moho depth in the area west of the NSGL is over 40 km. Zhang *et al.* (2009) used a 300-km-long seismic profile to show that the Moho depth in this region was approximately 42 km, and they suggested that the NSGL is a primary crustal thinning zone in China, where the crust thins from 40 to 50 km in the west to about 30 km in the eastern Jianghan basin. Our results accurately depict the morphology of this north–south thinning zone.

In this study, the average Moho depth within the Jianghan basin was found to be 33 km. Wei *et al.* (2022) conducted a study on lithospheric deformation in the East Qinling-Dabie orogenic belt using ambient noise tomography. Four velocity profiles crossing the Jianghan basin show Moho depths of approximately 30–35 km (Wei *et al.*, 2022), which are consistent with our findings. Previous studies have indicated the presence of a secondary "V" or "Y" shaped crustal thinning zone in southeastern China, east of the primary thinning zone (Huang *et al.*, 2015; Han *et al.*, 2023). The Jianghan basin is

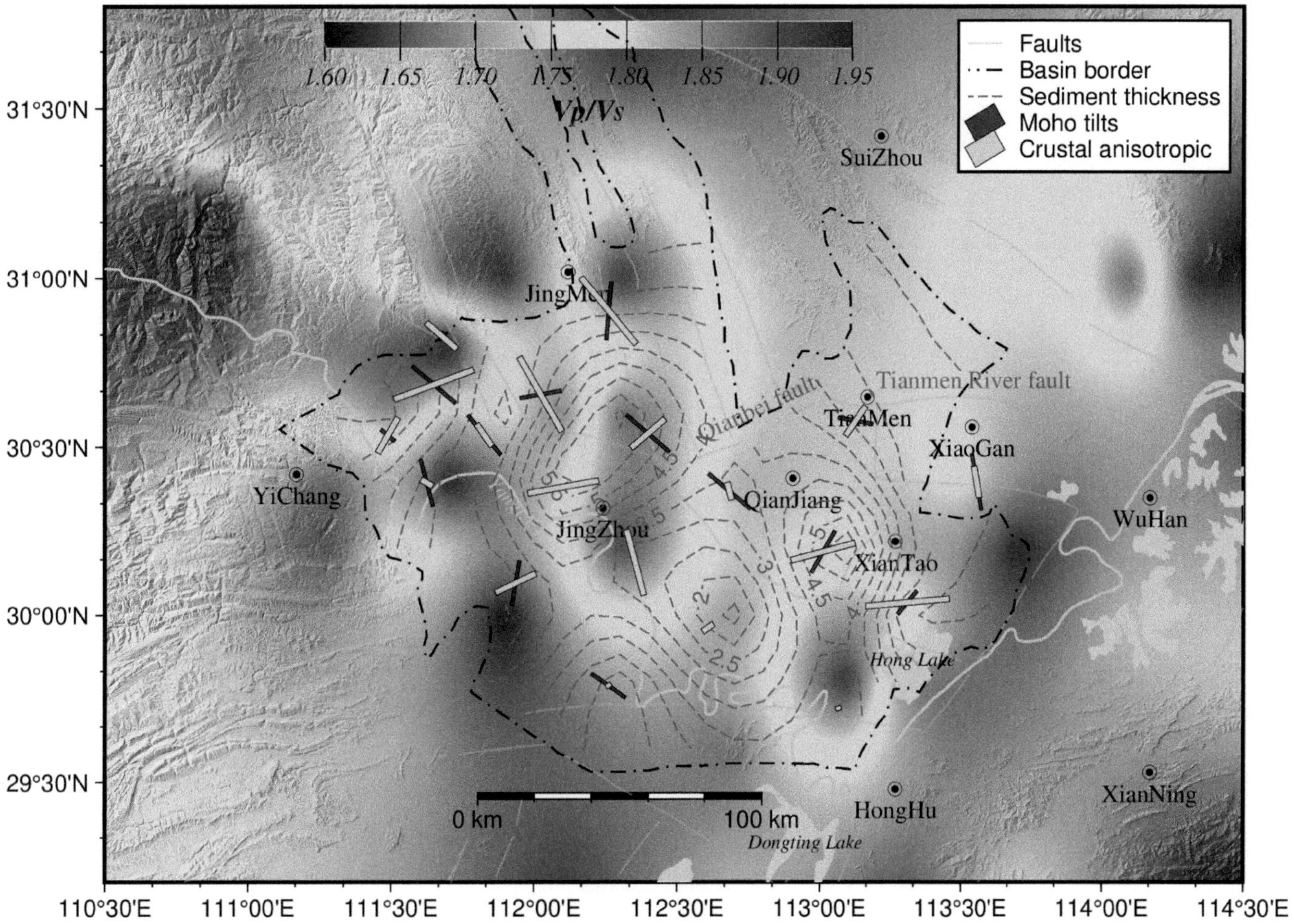

located in the left branch terminus of this secondary thinning zone. Our results reveal that the thinning zone extends northward to 31.5° N, and notably, another branch extends westward into the mountainous region of western Hubei at approximately 100 km. The low V_P/V_S ratios (<1.7) in the western branch of the thinning zone suggest a felsic-dominated crust, likely composed of Mesozoic granites as evidenced by stratigraphic data (Wu *et al.*, 2018), which is associated with the absence of mountain roots in orogenic belts. Two possible mechanisms could explain the observation: (1) delamination of dense mafic lower crust into the mantle, supported by mantle xenoliths with eclogitic signatures (Gao *et al.*, 1995; Huang *et al.*, 2014; Wang *et al.*, 2014; Gao and Chen, 2017); and (2) magmatic underplating and intrusion of basaltic melts in the crust, which is consistent with high V_P/V_S ratios (>1.8) in the basin center. The coexistence of both processes is possible, with delamination dominating in the west and underplating in the east.

Geothermal prospecting

Seismic anisotropy is widely recognized to exist in the crust and upper mantle, primarily arising from the preferred orientation of rock fractures, fluid inclusions, and the lattice orientation of minerals such as olivine (Long and Becker, 2010). The overall crustal anisotropy within the Jianghan basin is relatively weak. Combined with its thinner crust and higher V_P/V_S ratio compared with the surrounding area, it suggests that the Jianghan basin tectonics is primarily extensional (Mu *et al.*, 2023). Our results indicate that the crustal anisotropy and Moho tilt within the Jianghan basin are characterized by an outward divergence from the two subsidence centers in the basin. The Moho morphology in these two regions exhibits an upward bulge, further validating the model of outward divergence for both crustal anisotropy and Moho tilt.

Figure 9. Crustal V_P/V_S ratios, sediment thicknesses, Moho tilts, and crustal anisotropy beneath the Jianghan basin and its surrounding area. The color version of this figure is available only in the electronic edition.

To further understand the geothermal resources in the Jianghan basin, we analyzed the distribution of heat flows based on previous research (Jiang *et al.*, 2019). The results indicate that the distribution of the heat flow in the Jianghan basin is closely related to regional geological structure. High heat flow often corresponds to tectonic activity zones associated with uplift, faulting, and rapid subsidence processes. In the subsidence center areas, the Moho is relatively shallow,

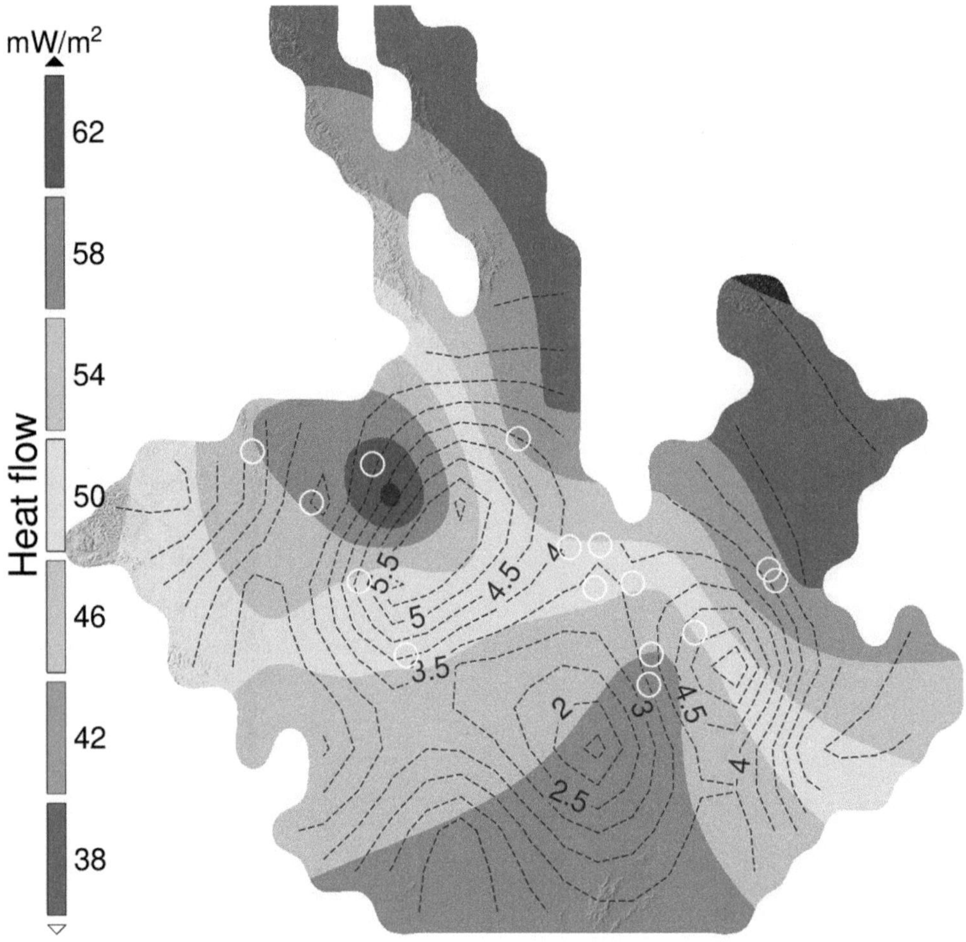

Figure 10. Heat flows in milliwatts per square meter of the Jianghan basin, modified from Jiang *et al.* (2019). The white circles are 19 measurement points. The black-dashed contours are sediment thicknesses in this study. The color version of this figure is available only in the electronic edition.

approximately by 28 km, which increases the geotherm gradient. The outward divergence of crustal anisotropy and Moho tilt, along with a high V_P/V_S ratio, suggests high deep geothermal energy in these regions. The areas also have a thick sedimentary layer, with thicknesses from 5 to 6 km, which act as an insulating cover to reduce heat dissipation. Other areas with thin sedimentary cover of less than 3 km in thickness would allow heat to dissipate more easily (He *et al.*, 2022).

Geothermal heat flow peaks near the subsidence centers (Fig. 10) show a moderate positive correlation with sediment thickness, suggesting that thick sediments act as thermal insulators. However, the highest heat flow values (>65 mW/m^2) occur in areas with thin sediments (<3 km) but high basement heat production, indicating that both sediment insulation and radiogenic heat contribute to the thermal regime. Future studies should integrate thermochronology data to disentangle these effects.

The integration of high-resolution crustal structure and geothermal data reveals that the Jianghan basin's subsidence centers act as dual heat convergence zones, where crustal thinning, mantle upwelling, and sediment insulation jointly regulate the geothermal regime (Fig. 11). This model not only advances our understanding of intracontinental rift dynamics but also provides a template for geothermal exploration in similar basins worldwide. However, the lack of mantle anisotropy data restricts deeper dynamic interpretations. Future studies should integrate magnetotelluric imaging and thermochronology to resolve finer-scale thermal processes and validate the proposed heat conduction model.

Conclusions

In this study, we employed a total of 58 three-component broadband seismic stations in and around the Jianghan basin, and adopted the teleseismic *P*-wave receiver function methods to obtain a high-resolution basin and crustal structures. The results are as follows.

1. **Basin-Moho coupling:** two basin subsidence centers (>5 km sediment thickness) spatially correlate with Moho uplifts (~5 km), reflecting isostatic compensation and mantle upwelling. This anticorrelation is consistent with gravity anomalies and supports a flexural response to Mesozoic–Cenozoic extension.
2. **Crustal anisotropy dynamics:** divergent fast-axis orientations around the subsidence centers, with delay times >0.5 s, align with the regional north-northeast–south-southwest extensional deformation direction. We attribute this pattern to crustal stretching and vertical mantle flow, facilitated by lower crustal delamination in the west and magmatic underplating in the east.
3. **Geothermal implications:** the subsidence centers act as dual heat convergence zones, where thick sediments insulate upward heat flux, whereas shallow Moho and high V_P/V_S ratios (>1.76) enhance conductive heat transfer. This mechanism explains the observed geothermal anomalies (~65 mW/m^2) and provides a template for targeting deep geothermal reservoirs in similar rift basins.

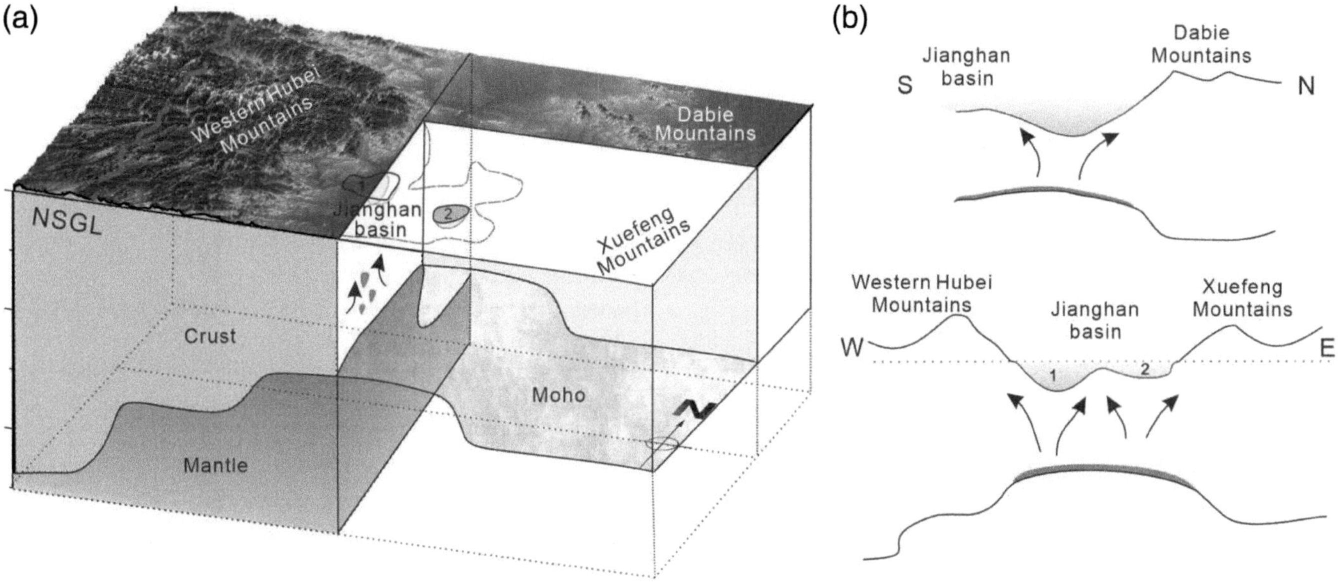

Figure 11. (a) A 3D diagram showing the crustal structure, sediment thickness variation, and an upward conduction of geothermal energy in the Jianghan basin, as well as (b) the north–south and east–west trans-sections through the two subsidence centers, where regions 1 and 2 correspond to the two centers. In the 3D diagram (a), the black arrows represent the upward conduction of geothermal energy. The orange layer represents the sedimentary basin. The red, upward-bulging line represents the Moho discontinuity. The red shading in the mantle signifies areas of mantle upwelling. In the cross-sections (b), the orange shading represents the thick sedimentary fill in the two subsidence centers, and the red line and shading again represent the shallow Moho and mantle upwelling beneath these centers. The color version of this figure is available only in the electronic edition.

Data and Resources

Waveform data of permanent stations for this study were obtained from Data Management Centre of China National Seismic Network at Institute of Geophysics, China Earthquake Administration (SEISDMC, doi: 10.7914/SN/CB). Earthquake locations and magnitudes are from the earthquake catalogs of China Earthquake Networks Center (CENC) and Incorporated Research Institutions for Seismology (IRIS) at http://irsc.ut.ac.ir/. We used the Seismic Analysis Code (SAC) available from the IRIS Data Management Center (DMC) for seismic waveform analysis. Figures are plotted via Generic Mapping Tools (GMT) v. 6 (Wessel *et al.*, 2019). The supplemental material includes Tables S1–S3 cited in the article. Waveform data of temporary stations and results for this article are available upon request to the corresponding author at huangrong@cug.edu.cn.

Declaration of Competing Interests

The authors acknowledge that there are no conflicts of interest recorded.

Acknowledgments

The authors thank Editor-in-Chief Allison Bent and two anonymous reviewers for their in-depth reviews and valuable comments. This work was supported by the National Key Research and Development Program of China (Grant Number 2024YFF0807300), Natural Science Foundation of Hubei Province of China (Grant Numbers 2024AFD379 and 2023AFD211), and the Research Fund Program of Hubei Key Laboratory of Resources and Eco-Environment Geology (Grant Number HBREGKFJJ-202406).

References

Christensen, N. I. (1996). Poisson's ratio and crustal seismology, *J. Geophys. Res.* **101,** no. B2, 3139–3156.

Dai, S. (1996). Discussion on the regional structural features of Jianghan Basin since the indosinian movement, *J. Geomech.* **2,** no. 4, 80–84 (in Chinese with English abstract).

Dong, S., R. Gao, and A. Yin (2013). What drove continued continent-continent convergence after ocean closure? Insights from high-resolution seismic-reflection profiling across the Daba Shan in central China, *Geology* **41,** no. 6, 671–674.

Dong, S., Y. Zhang, and C. Long (2007). Jurassic tectonic revolution in China and new interpretation of the Yanshan Movement, *Acta Geol. Sin.* **81,** no. 11, 1449–1461 (in Chinese with English abstract).

Gao, J., and Y. Chen (2017). Ambient noise tomography of northern part of South China, *Prog. Geophys.* **32,** no. 4, 1423–1431 (in Chinese with English abstract).

Gao, S., Z. Zhao, T. Luo, and B. Zhang (1995). Petrological model, chemical composition and possible genesis of the crust along Yichuan-Yichang global geoscience transect(ggt) in east Qinling, *Acta Petrol. Sin.* **11,** no. 2, 213–226 (in Chinese with English abstract).

Guo, X., T. Guo, Z. Wei, H. Zhang, R. Liu, Z. Liu, and W. Wang (2012). Thoughts on shale gas exploration in southern China, *Eng. Sci.* **14,** no. 6, 101–105 (in Chinese with English abstract).

Han, R., D. Yang, Q. Li, R. Huang, H. Zhang, J. Li, H. Chen, Z. Ye, and W. Fu (2023). Receiver function imaging of dense seismic array and deep dynamic mechanism beneath the eastern South China, *Sci. China Earth Sci.* **66,** 1289–1308.

Haskell, N. (1964). Radiation pattern of surface waves from point sources in a multi-layered medium, *Bull. Seismol. Soc. Am.* **54,** no. 1, 377–393.

He, K., R. Huang, and Y. Xu (2022). Crustal structures beneath the Northern Jiangsu Basin and its surrounding areas: Implications for geothermal prospecting, *J. Geophys. Eng.* **19,** no. 3, 316–325.

He, Z., X. Wang, S. Li, Y. Wo, and Y. Zhou (2011). Yanshan Movement and its influence on petroleum preservation in middle-upper Yangtze region, *Petroleum Geol. Exp.* **33,** no. 1, 1–11 (in Chinese with English abstract).

Huang, J., and D. Zhao (2006). High-resolution mantle tomography of China and surrounding regions, *J. Geophys. Res.* **111,** no. B9, doi: 10.1029/2005JB004066.

Huang, R., Y. Xu, L. Zhu, and K. He (2015). Detailed moho geometry beneath southeastern china and its implications on thinning of continental crust, *J. Asian Earth Sci.* **112,** 42–48.

Huang, R., L. Zhu, and Y. Xu (2014). Crustal structure of Hubei Province of China from teleseismic receiver functions: Evidence for lower crust delamination, *Tectonophysics* **636,** 286–292.

Huang, T. K., C. Jen, C. Jiang, C. Chang, and Z. Xu (1977). An outline of the tectonic characteristics of China, *Acta Geol. Sin.* **2,** 117–135 (in Chinese with English abstract).

Jiang, G., S. Hu, and Y. Shi (2019). Terrestrial heat flow of continental China: Updated dataset and tectonic implications, *Tectonophysics* **753,** 36–48.

Jiang, W., T. Hao, Y. Xu, Z. Liu, D. Zhu, and G. Tu (2007). Comprehensive geological and geophysical study in middle southern region of China, *Chin. J. Geophys.* **50,** no. 1, 171–183 (in Chinese with English abstract).

Li, J., X. Song, and P. Wang (2019). A generalized h- method with harmonic corrections on Ps and its crustal multiples in receiver functions, *J. Geophys. Res.* **24,** no. 4, 3782–3801.

Li, Q., R. Gao, H. Wang, J. Zhang, P. Li, Z. Lu, Y. Guan, and H. Hou (2011). Lithospsheric structure of northeastern Sichuan-Dabashan basin-range system and top-deep deformation coupling, *Acta Petrol. Sin.* **27,** no. 3, 612–620 (in Chinese with English abstract).

Li, W., J. Ye, Y. Liao, and L. Wang (2016). The preliminary research on the geothermal resource evaluation of jianghan plain, *Resources Environ. Eng.* **30,** no. 6, 882–894 (in Chinese with English abstract).

Li, X., P. Zhu, and T. Kusky (2015). Has the Yangtze craton lost its root? A comparison between the north China and Yangtze cratons, *Tectonophysics* **655,** 1–14.

Li, Z., P. Zhao, Z. Sun, Y. Yuan, and Y. Zhao (2010). A study on maturity evolution of lower silurian marine hydrocarbon source rocks and thermal history in the southern Jianghan basin, *Chin. J. Geophys.* **53,** no. 12, 2918–2928 (in Chinese with English abstract).

Ligorria, J. P., and C. J. Ammon (1999). Iterative deconvolution and receiver-function estimation, *Bull. Seismol. Soc. Am.* **89,** 1395–1400.

Liu, H., H. Liang, X. Li, J. Yin, D. Zhu, and L. Liu (2000). The coupling mechanisms of mesozoic–cenozoic rift basins and extensional mountain system in eastern China, *Earth Sci. Front.* **4,** 173–182 (in Chinese with English abstract).

Liu, S., W. Li, K. Wang, T. Qian, and C. Jiang (2015) Late Mesozoic development of the southern Qinling-Dabieshan foreland fold-thrust belt, Central China, and its role in continent-continent collision, *Tectonophysics* **644,** 220–234.

Long, M., and T. Becker (2010). Mantle dynamics and seismic anisotropy, *Earth Planet. Sci. Lett.* **297,** 341–354.

Luo, Y., Y. Xu, and Y. Yang (2013). Crustal radial anisotropy beneath the Dabie orogenic belt from ambient noise tomography, *Geophys. J. Int.* **195,** no. 2, 1149–1164.

Mu, Q., R. Huang, and J. Yan (2023). Constraining the crustal structure of the southern segment of the north-south gravity lineament by the receiver function h-k-c method, *Earth Sci. Front.* **30,** no. 5, 369–383 (in Chinese with English abstract).

Ouyang, L., H. Li, and Q. Lu (2015). Crustal shear wave velocity structure and radial anisotropy beneath the Middle-Lower Yangtze River metallogenic belt and surrounding areas from seismic ambient noise tomography, *Chin. J. Geophys.* **58,** no. 12, 4388–4402 (in Chinese with English abstract).

Ouyang, L., H. Li, Q. Lü, Y. Yang, X. Li, G. Jiang, G. Zhang, D. Shi, D. Zheng, S. Sun, *et al.* (2014). Crustal and uppermost mantle velocity structure and its relationship with the formation of ore districts in the Middle-Lower Yangtze River region, *Earth Planet. Sci. Lett.* **408,** 378–389.

Qiu, R., T. Li, J. Deng, S. Zhou, Q. Xiao, T. Ye, and S. Geng (2006). Petrological structure, types and inhomogeneity of the lithosphere beneath continental China, *Geol. China* **33,** no. 4, 842–851 (in Chinese with English abstract).

Stern, R. J., S. Li, and G. R. Keller (2018). Continental crust of China: A brief guide for the perplexed, *Earth Sci. Rev.* **179,** 72–94.

Wang, C., E. Sandvol, and L. Zhu (2014). Lateral variation of crustal structure in the Ordos block and surrounding regions, North China, and its tectonic implications, *Earth Planet. Sci. Lett.* **387,** 198–211.

Wang, D., L. Mei, Y. Liu, L. Wu, C. Min, and J. Luo (2018). Mesozoic-cenozoic episodic subsidence and migration of Jianghan basin in extensional composite basin-mountain system, *Earth Sci.* **43,** no. 11, 4180–4192 (in Chinese with English abstract).

Wang, Q., J. Huang, and Z. Liu (2018). Pn velocity and anisotropy of uppermost mantle beneath East China and adjacent regions, *Chin. J. Geophys.* **61,** no. 7, 2750–2759 (in Chinese with English abstract).

Wang, Q., P. Zhang, and J. T. Freymuller (2001). Present-day crustal deformation in China constrained by global positioning system measurements, *Science* **294,** 574–577.

Watts, A. B. (2001). *Isostasy and Flexure of the Lithosphere*, Vol. 139, Cambridge University Press, Cambridge, 365 pp.

Wei, Y., S. Zhang, M. Li, T. Wu, Y. Hua, Y. Zhang, and J. Cai (2022). Regional lithospheric deformation beneath the East Qinling-Dabie orogenic belt based on ambient noise tomography, *Geophys. J. Int.* **228,** no. 2, 1294–1312.

Wessel, P., J. F. Luis, L. Uieda, R. Scharroo, F. Wobbe, W. H. F. Smith, and D. Tian (2019). The generic mapping tools version 6, *Geochem. Geophys. Geosys.* **20,** no. 11, 5556–5564, doi: 10.1029/2019GC008515.

Wu, L., L. Mei, Y. Liu, D. A. Paton, J. Luo, L. Yu, D. Wang, C. Min, M. Li, L. Guo, *et al.* (2018). The stratigraphic and structural record of the Cretaceous Jianghan Basin, central China: Implications for initial rifting processes and geodynamics, *Cretaceous Res.* **90,** 21–39.

Wu, L., L. Mei, D. A. Paton, Y. Liu, C. Shen, and Z. Liu (2020). Basement structures have crucial influence on rift development: Insights from the Jianghan Basin, Central China, *Tectonophysics* **39,** no. 2, e2019TC005671, doi: 10.1029/2019TC005671.

Yang, B., W. Liu, and X. Wang (2005). Geophysical characteristics of Daxinganling gravitational gradient zone in the East China and its geodynamic mechanism, *Chin. J. Geophys.* **48,** no. 1, 86–97 (in Chinese with English abstract).

Yu, X., C. Liu, and C. Wang (2022). Genesis of lithium brine deposits in the Jianghan basin and progress in resource exploration: A review, *Earth Sci. Front.* **29,** no. 1, 107–123 (in Chinese with English abstract).

Yu, Y., J. Song, and K. Liu (2015). Determining crustal structure beneath seismic stations overlying a low-velocity sedimentary layer using receiver functions, *J. Geophys. Res.* **120,** no. 5, 3208–3218.

Zhang, G., A. Guo, and Y. Wang (2013). Tectonics of south China continent and its implications, *Sci. China Earth Sci.* **56,** 1804–1828 (in Chinese with English abstract).

Zhang, H., Q. Lü, and X. E. A. Wang (2023). Seismically imaged lithospheric delamination and its controls on the Mesozoic Magmatic Province in South China, *Nat. Commun.* **14,** 2718.

Zhang, L., Y. Yao, W. Liao, J. Li, Q. Wang, and D. Wang (2011). Research on the upper mantle seismic anisotropy beneath Hubei and its geodynamic implication, *Chin. J. Geophys.* **54,** no. 1, 35–43 (in Chinese with English abstract).

Zhang, Z., Z. Bai, and W. Mooney (2009). Crustal structure across the Three Gorges area of the Yangtze platform, central China, from seismic refraction/wide-angle reflection data, *Tectonophysics* **475,** nos. 3/4, 423–437.

Zheng, X., Z. Yao, J. Liang, and J. Zheng (2010). The role played and opportunities provided by IGP DMC of China National Seismic Network in Wenchuan earthquake disaster relief and researches, *Bull. Seismol. Soc. Am.* **100,** no. 5B, 2866–2872.

Zhou, L., J. Xie, W. Shen, Y. Zheng, Y. Yang, H. Shi, and M. H. Ritzwoller (2012). The structure of the crust and uppermost mantle beneath SouthChina from ambient noise and earthquake tomography, *Geophys. J. Int.* **189,** no. 3, 1565–1583.

Zhu, L., and H. Kanamori (2000). Moho depth variation in southern California from teleseismic receiver functions, *J. Geophys. Res.* **105,** no. B2, 2969–2980.

Zhu, R., Y. Xu, and G. Zhu (2012). Destruction of the North China craton, *Sci. China Earth Sci.* **55,** 1565–1587.

Manuscript received 30 April 2025
Published online 27 October 2025

Long-Period Ground Motions from Dynamic Rupture Simulations of Large Earthquakes on the Creeping Hayward–Calaveras–Rodgers Creek Fault System

Ruth A. Harris*[1], Michael Barall[1], Grace A. Parker[1], and Evan T. Hirakawa[1]

Abstract

The Hayward, Calaveras, and Rodgers Creek faults in the San Francisco Bay region of California have a high probability of producing a large earthquake in the next decades. Although these faults creep, the creep is insufficient to keep up with their relatively rapid slip rates on their deepest sections, so they have been storing tectonic strain since their last large earthquakes, with the Hayward's and Rodgers Creek's more than 150 yr ago. We do not know what the next large Hayward–Calaveras–Rodgers Creek earthquakes will look like or how strongly they will shake the San Francisco Bay region. Harris *et al.* (2021) used the 3D dynamic (spontaneous) rupture method to simulate large earthquakes on these creeping faults. In this article, we examine the resulting simulated long-period (T > 1 s) ground shaking from 0 to 50 km distance, for earthquakes nucleating on the Hayward fault and earthquakes nucleating on the Rodgers Creek fault. We compare these simulated long-period ground motions with the Boore *et al.* (2014) well-established empirically based ground-motion model suitable for the slowest material velocity in our 3D velocity structure. We find that the simulated long-period ground motions from the creeping-fault earthquake scenarios produce a reasonable agreement with the empirical expectations if frictional cohesion is included only where it is appropriate.

Cite this article as Harris, R. A., M. Barall, G. A. Parker, and E. T. Hirakawa (2025). Long-Period Ground Motions from Dynamic Rupture Simulations of Large Earthquakes on the Creeping Hayward–Calaveras–Rodgers Creek Fault System, *Seismol. Res. Lett.* **97**, 2050–2063, doi: 10.1785/0220250194.

Supplemental Material

Introduction

The Hayward fault and its connected companions—the Rodgers Creek and Calaveras faults (Ponce *et al.*, 2004; Watt *et al.*, 2016; Fig. 1)—have a high probability of producing a large (magnitude 6.7 or greater) earthquake in the San Francisco Bay area (Aagaard *et al.*, 2016). The faults also creep, slipping aseismically (e.g., Radbruch and Lennert, 1966; Burgmann *et al.*, 2000; Lienkaemper *et al.*, 2012; Harris *et al.*, 2021). The interplay between the interseismic fault creep and large coseismic rupture has been contemplated and debated for decades; however, we do know that all three faults produced large earthquakes in the past (e.g., Budding *et al.*, 1991; Yu and Segall, 1996; Hecker *et al.*, 2005; Boatwright and Bundock, 2008; Lienkaemper *et al.*, 2010; Hirakawa *et al.*, 2023). This information informs us that large earthquakes are likely to occur again. What we do not yet know are the details of the next large earthquake ruptures or their associated ground-shaking intensities, and therefore we do not know the specifics of how the highly populated San Francisco Bay area will be affected.

To remedy this situation of uncertainty in future earthquake-generated ground-shaking characteristics, computational simulations of large scenario earthquakes on the Hayward fault have been conducted over the years. Larsen *et al.* (1997) and Aagaard *et al.* (2010) used kinematic rupture simulations, whereby the earthquake source, including the fault rupture extent, was prescribed, then the ground shaking was simulated based on this assumed earthquake source. In more recent work, Rodgers *et al.* (2020) used the kinematic rupture method with an assumed earthquake source and a sophisticated modeling method to produce simulations of 0–10 Hz ground motions.

In this study, rather than using the aforementioned kinematic rupture approach, which uses a predetermined earthquake source, we instead use results from the dynamic (spontaneous) rupture approach. The dynamic rupture method has been used to simulate real or scenario earthquakes in other tectonic regions, and it has also been used for simulating large earthquakes on the

1. USGS Earthquake Science Center, Moffett Field, California, U.S.A., https://orcid.org/0000-0002-9247-0768 (RAH); https://orcid.org/0000-0001-7724-8563 (MB); https://orcid.org/0000-0002-9445-2571 (GAP); https://orcid.org/0000-0002-5720-0850 (ETH)

*Corresponding author: harris@usgs.gov

The congruence in dynamic rupture simulations between a physically self-consistent earthquake source and the resulting ground motions has been explored from a range of perspectives over the years. These include studies implementing dynamic rupture simulations to discover which earthquake models best match a specific earthquake's ground motions (e.g., Peyrat and Olsen, 2004; Gallovič *et al.*, 2019; Tinti *et al.*, 2021), and studies that examined how well scenario earthquake sources, for either a specific fault rupture or a generic fault setting, match the set of ground-motion data encapsulated by a ground-motion model (GMM) (e.g., Guatteri *et al.*, 2003; Olsen *et al.*, 2009; Withers *et al.*, 2018). In this article, we use detailed 3D simulations of large scenario earthquakes on the creeping Hayward, Calaveras, and Rodgers Creek faults, and examine how similar the resulting long-period ($T > 1$ s) ground motions are to the empirical expectations from a GMM.

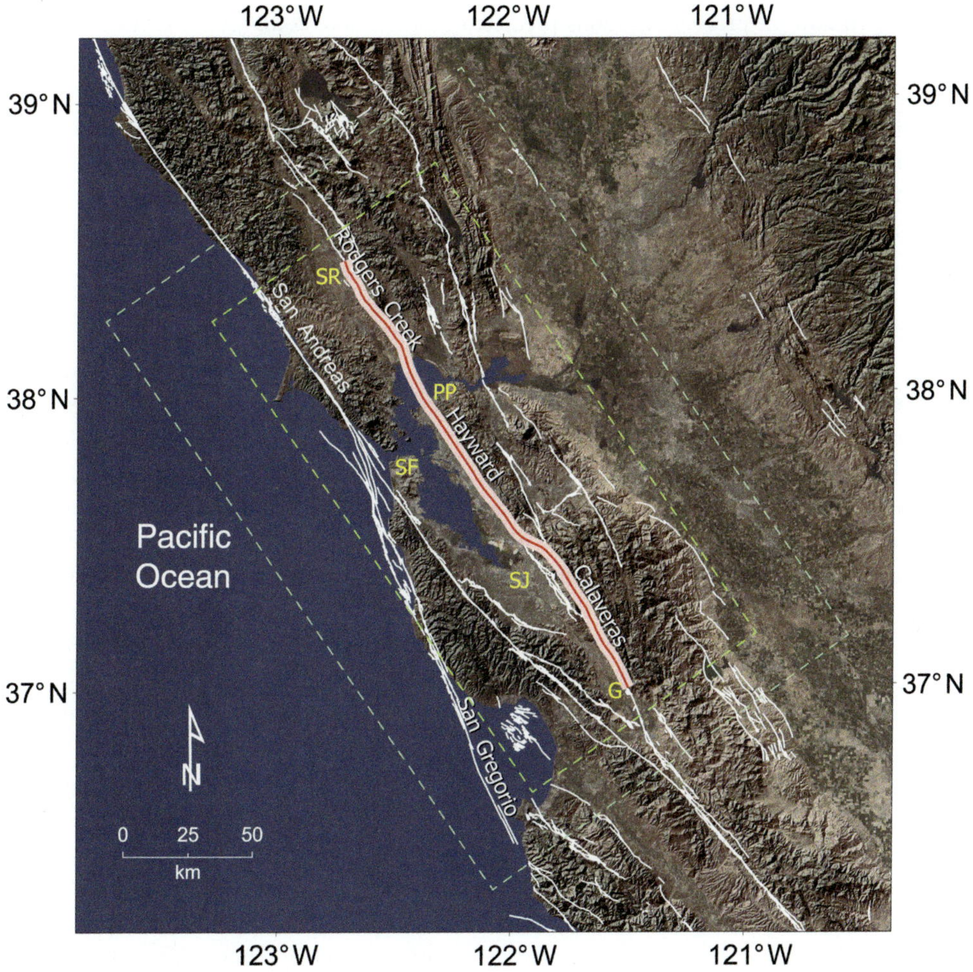

Figure 1. Map view of the fault setting for our dynamic earthquake rupture and ground-motion simulations. The red curve shows the trace of the 196 km long 3D fault surface we use; it is the same as the main fault surface in Harris *et al.* (2021) and a 3D view of this fault surface is shown in Figure 2a. It encompasses the southern part of the Rodgers Creek fault, starting in Santa Rosa (SR), continues southeast through Point Pinole (PP), and all of the Hayward fault, and ends near Gilroy (G) on the Calaveras fault. SF is San Francisco, SJ is San Jose. The outer green-dashed box shows the approximate outside boundaries of our 3D finite-element mesh at Earth's surface. The inner green-dashed box shows the approximate outer boundaries of where our ground-motion stations are located on Earth's surface. These stations are at 250 m spacing within 2.5 km of the fault trace, and at 500 m spacing from 2.5 to 50 km from the fault trace, except beyond the two ends of the fault trace, where the stations stop at 10 km along strike distance. The faults (white lines) are from the U.S. Geological Survey (USGS) and California Geological Survey (CGS) Quaternary fault and fold database (U.S. Geological Survey [USGS] and California Geological Survey [CGS], 2024).

Method—Part I: Dynamic Rupture Simulations

Harris *et al.* (2021) used the 3D dynamic rupture finite-element code, FaultMod (Barall, 2024) to simulate large earthquakes nucleating on the Hayward and Rodgers Creek faults (Fig. 1). The FaultMod code has been tested extensively using the entire suite of exercises provided by the Southern California Earthquake Center-U.S. Geological Survey dynamic rupture code verification group (Harris *et al.*, 2018; see Data and Resources). For the present study, we investigate the ground motions produced by a subset of the suite of dynamic rupture simulations presented in Harris *et al.* (2021). This subset focuses on the cases where the simulated earthquakes nucleate on either the Hayward fault or the Rodgers Creek fault. Because geodetic and other observations reveal that the Hayward, Rodgers Creek, Hayward, Calaveras, and Rodgers Creek faults in the San Francisco Bay area (Harris *et al.*, 2021). The dynamic rupture method is advantageous in that the earthquake source itself is not predetermined, but instead it is a result of the interactions among the assumed stress, friction, rock properties, and fault geometry, starting when the earthquake nucleates and continuing throughout the time-dependent evolution of the earthquake rupture. This means that dynamic rupture simulations are physically self-consistent. For an in-depth explanation of how dynamic rupture simulations work, see Ramos *et al.* (2022).

and Calaveras faults creep, and it is not yet known how the presence of fault creep affects ground motions for creeping-fault earthquakes larger than magnitude 6.5–6.6 (Harris and Abrahamson, 2014; Harris, 2017), this article only examines ground motions from the simulations in Harris *et al.* (2021) where this creep was taken into consideration. Harris *et al.* (2021) accounted for the fault creep by examining two possibilities: the first where the initial shear stresses for the dynamic rupture simulations were assigned to be lower, where the faults interseismically slip at 1 mm/yr or faster, the second where the cutoff was 3 mm/yr. In this article, we concentrate on the ground motions produced by the Harris *et al.* (2021) creeping-fault cases, which assumed that the dynamic rupture simulations' initial shear stresses are lower where the Hayward, Rodgers Creek, and Calaveras fault surfaces interseismically creep at 3 mm/yr or faster. These fault-surface creep regions, where the initial shear stresses were assumed to be lower, are shown in Figures 2f, 3, and 4. For all the simulations, the assumptions about the 3D velocity structure, fault friction, and 3D fault geometry are summarized in Text S1 and Table S1, available in the supplemental material to this article, detailed in Harris *et al.* (2021) and depicted here in Figure 2.

Harris *et al.* (2021) used slip-weakening friction (Andrews, 1976),

$$\tau_{\text{friction}}(t) = C_0 + \mu(d)\sigma_n(t), \tag{1}$$

in which $\tau_{\text{friction}}(t)$ is the time-dependent shear stress while the fault is sliding, C_0 is frictional cohesion, d is the accumulated amount of fault slip, $\mu(d)$ is the slip-dependent coefficient of friction, and $\sigma_n(t)$ is the time-dependent normal stress. The value of $\mu(d)$ decreases linearly from a higher "static" value to a lower "dynamic" value as the slip d increases from 0 to a critical value d_c, and remains constant thereafter. This study's rock-unit-dependent friction values are the same as in Harris *et al.* (2021), as shown in Figure 2. The present study's choices of C_0 values are also the same as those used in Harris *et al.* (2021), with C_0 either set to zero or linearly tapered from 2 MPa at the Earth's surface down to 0 at 3-km depth, here called "with 3-km cohesion."

Because of computational constraints, the minimum shear-wave velocity (rock property value) in the Harris *et al.* (2021) dynamic rupture models was truncated at 1950 m/s. Also, due to computational constraints, the elements in the Harris *et al.* (2021) finite-element mesh are 250 m hexahedra near the faults, and change to 500 m hexahedra starting at about 2.5 km from the faults. This element sizing means that the simulations can resolve periods of 1 s and longer near the propagating rupture front, and periods of 2 s and longer elsewhere, so these longer periods are where we focus our attention in this article.

Method—Part II: GMM

We compare the ground motions produced by our elastic 3D dynamic earthquake rupture simulations with the ground motions predicted by the Boore *et al.* (2014) GMM, hereafter called "BSSA14." The BSSA14 GMM is described in detail in the Appendix. Every GMM has a defined range of parameters where it is designed to operate best. Among these parameters are the earthquake magnitude, distance from the fault rupture, and time-averaged shear-wave velocity in the upper 30 m (V_{S30}). The BSSA14 GMM has a proposed range of applicability of 150–1500 m/s for V_{S30}, with the upper limit being a higher V_{S30} value than some other GMM's encompass, a reason for our choosing this GMM. In our simulations, due to computational limitations, we had to truncate the San Francisco Bay area 3D velocity structure's slowest shear-wave velocity at 1950 m/s, so we still use the Boore *et al.* (2014) formulas, but we set V_{S30} equal to 1950 m/s. In the BSSA14 GMM, site response does not scale with V_{S30} for values greater than 760–1000 m/s in the period range considered here. In other words, the site response in BSSA14 is constant between 760–1000 and 1500 m/s. We assume this constant scaling behavior extrapolates beyond 1500 m/s to 1950 m/s, and use the BSSA14 GMM with $V_{S30} = 1950$ m/s as the input.

Results

We present a 1 Hz low-pass-filtered version of the ground motions produced by Harris *et al.* (2021) dynamic rupture models of large scenario earthquakes nucleating on the creeping Hayward fault and large scenario earthquakes nucleating on the creeping Rodgers Creek fault. The filtering was done for this article because the higher frequencies in the ground motions were not well resolved by the Harris *et al.* (2021) simulations, which had to use relatively large element sizes in the finite-element mesh, and were primarily an investigation into the earthquake sources. Instead, it is just the lower frequency aspects of the Harris *et al.* (2021) ground motions that are dependable. The magnitudes of the scenarios we examine range from **M** 6.94 to 7.29, depending on the total length of the rupture and whether or not frictional cohesion is included. For these dynamic rupture scenarios, we use the subset of Harris *et al.* (2021) cases that did take the fault creep into account by assuming that the shear stress at the beginning of the simulations was lower on the fault surfaces in the locations where the faults interseismically creep at 3 mm/yr or faster. We next compare the (1 Hz low-pass filtered) ground motions generated by these four scenario earthquakes nucleating on the Hayward fault or on the Rodgers Creek fault, with the BSSA14 GMM.

We plot an intensity measure of horizontal ground motion, 5% damped pseudospectral acceleration (PSA), for each Earth surface location in our finite-element model out to 50 km R_{JB} distance from the ruptured fault surface. R_{JB} is the distance from a given point on the Earth's surface to the closest point on the surface projection of the fault surface that slipped. We note that for ruptures reaching the along-strike ends of the fault surface, we just go out to 10 km beyond the fault ends,

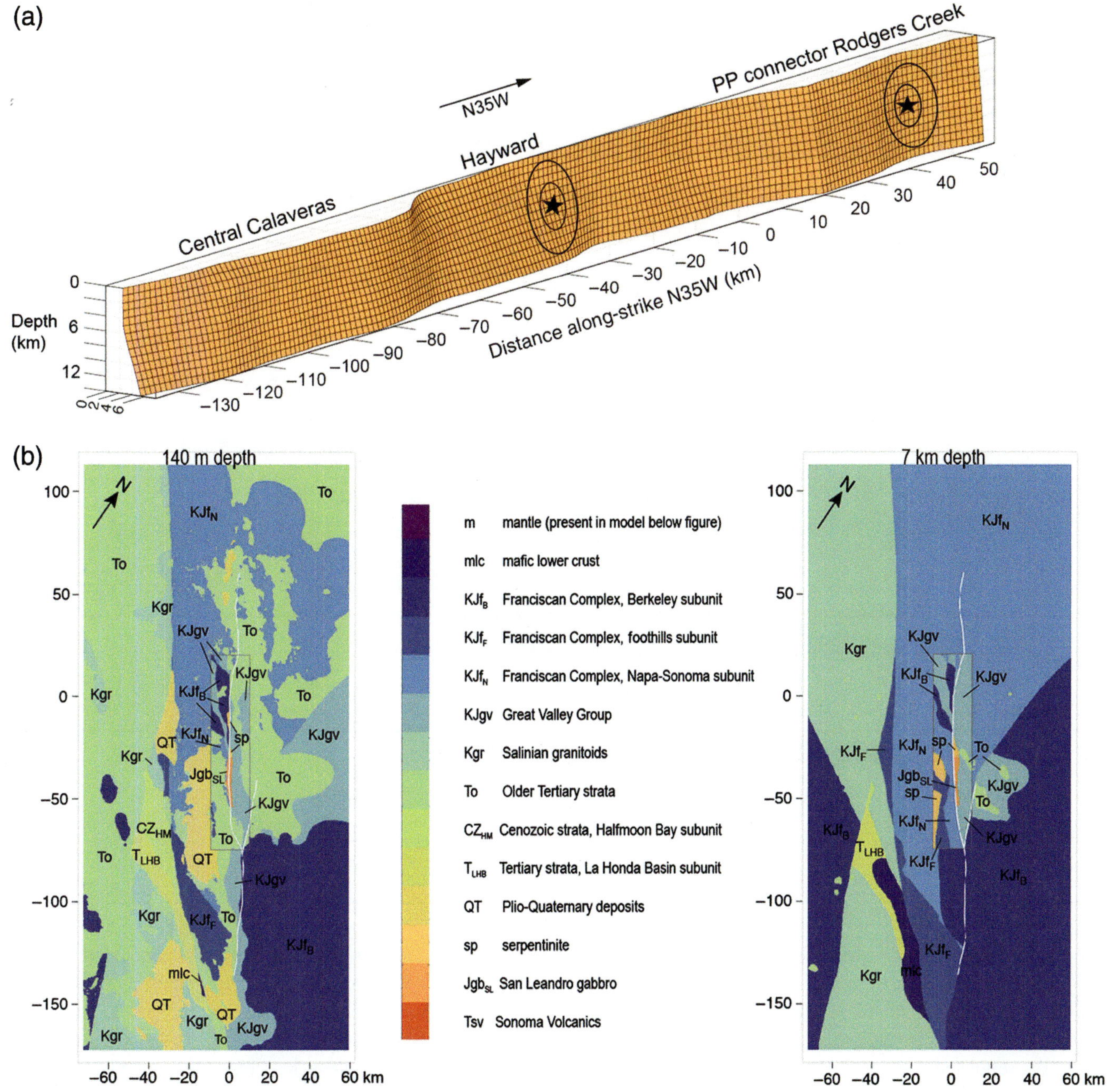

Figure 2. Ingredients used in our 3D finite-element dynamic rupture simulations. Panels (b)–(f) are modified from figures in Harris *et al.* (2021). Please also see Text S1 and Table S1. (a) The fault surface, depicted with 1-km mesh elements for better viewing (the actual elements are 250 m). The circles show where the rupture nucleates on the Hayward fault, 40 km southeast of Point Pinole (PP), or on the Rodgers Creek fault, 40 km northwest of Point Pinole. (b) Horizontal map view of the rock units in the 3D geologic model at two depths. The 3D geologic model is constructed from the Hayward geologic model (Graymer *et al.*, 2005; Phelps *et al.*, 2008) and the Big Bay geologic model (Jachens *et al.*, 2006). The rock units are used to determine the rock properties. (c) Rock units touching the east face and the west face, respectively, of the fault surface. (d) The corresponding shear-wave velocity in our 3D velocity model, using the rock units along with the Brocher (2008) empirical relations. (e) The dynamic coefficient of friction on the fault surface, based on the rock units' friction. Slip-weakening friction, shown in the plot to the right, is assumed. (f) The interseismic slip-rate pattern on the fault surface. Where the interseismic slip rate is 3 mm/yr or faster, the initial shear stress in the dynamic rupture simulations is assumed to be lower. *(Continued)*

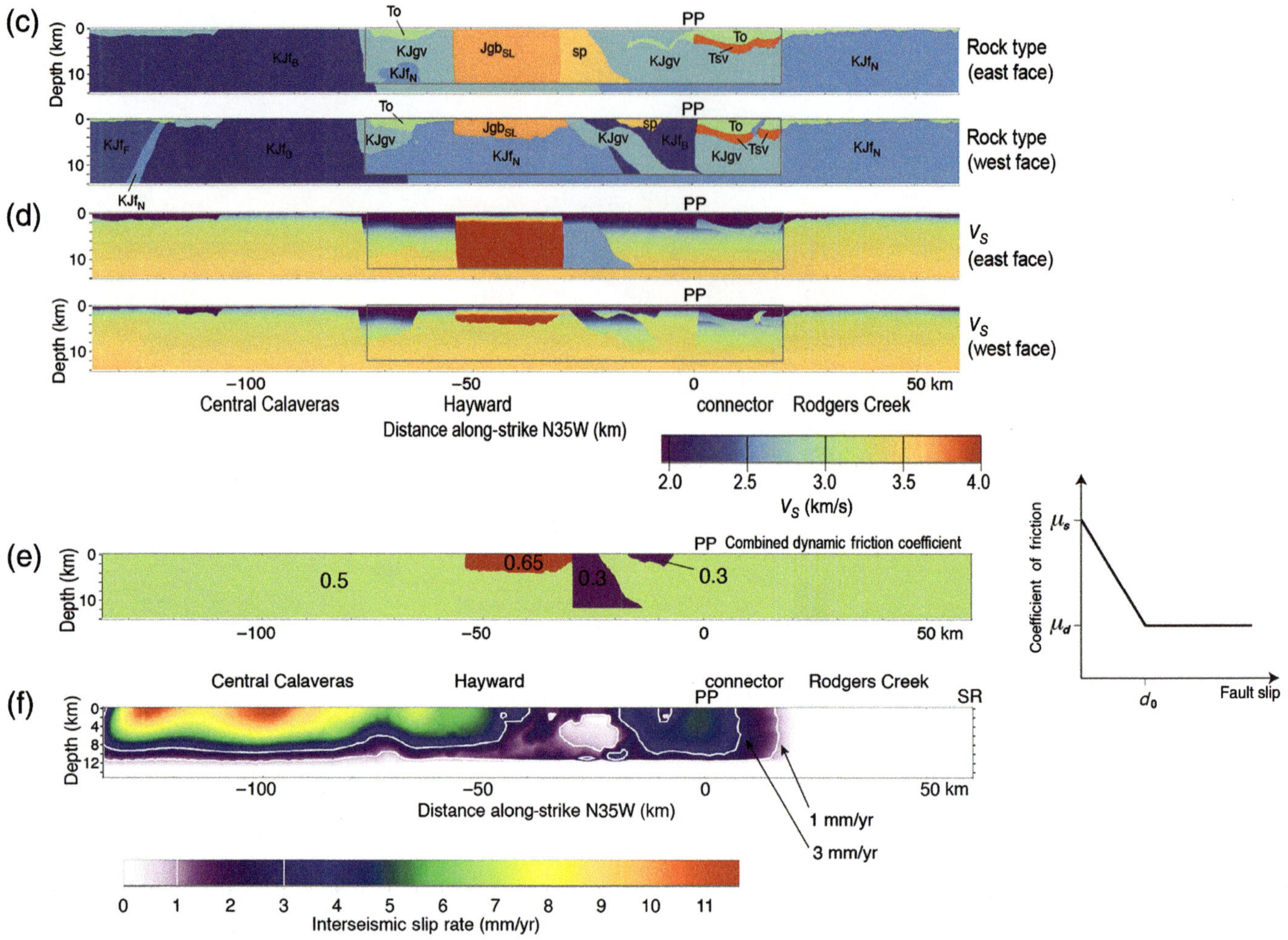

Figure 2. Continued

due to our finite-element mesh's boundary constraints. For both intensity measures, we use the RotD50 horizontal component of the motion (Boore, 2010). Please see the Appendix for the details of how RotD50 and PSA are calculated. Figure 3 shows the simulated and the GMM's ground-motion intensity as a function of distance for the scenario of a large earthquake nucleating on the Rodgers Creek fault. The figure shows two simulations, one without frictional cohesion and one with frictional cohesion. Figure 4 compares the simulated and the GMM's ground-motion intensity for the scenario of a large earthquake nucleating on the Hayward fault, one case without frictional cohesion, and one case with frictional cohesion.

Discussion

We have examined the ground motions produced by 3D dynamic rupture simulations of large earthquakes nucleating on the Rodgers Creek and Hayward faults. We show that some of the models produce simulated ground motions (PSA) which, on average, are similar to those predicted by an empirically based GMM out to 50 km distance from the ruptured fault surface. This is our result, even though Harris *et al.* (2021) did not intentionally tune the dynamic rupture parameters to lead to intensities consistent with GMMs; rather, the simulations were originally conducted to better understand what large earthquakes may look like on creeping faults, under typically assumed friction and stress conditions, known fault geometry, and 3D seismic velocity structure.

For the rupture nucleating on the Rodgers Creek fault (Fig. 3), the initial shear stress on the Rodgers Creek fault is at a higher level, making it closer to failure, so including cohesion in the upper few kilometers of the fault surface reduces the ground motions by tempering the rupture's interactions with Earth's free surface. The result is that for the Rodgers Creek nucleation site, the rupture produces median ground motions more in agreement with the Boore *et al.* (2014) GMM if cohesion is included in the friction equation (right side of Fig. 3c–f).

In contrast, the median of the ground motions produced by the simulated rupture nucleating on the Hayward fault is lower than the GMM if cohesion is included (right side of Fig. 4c–f). This might be occurring because the Hayward fault already has

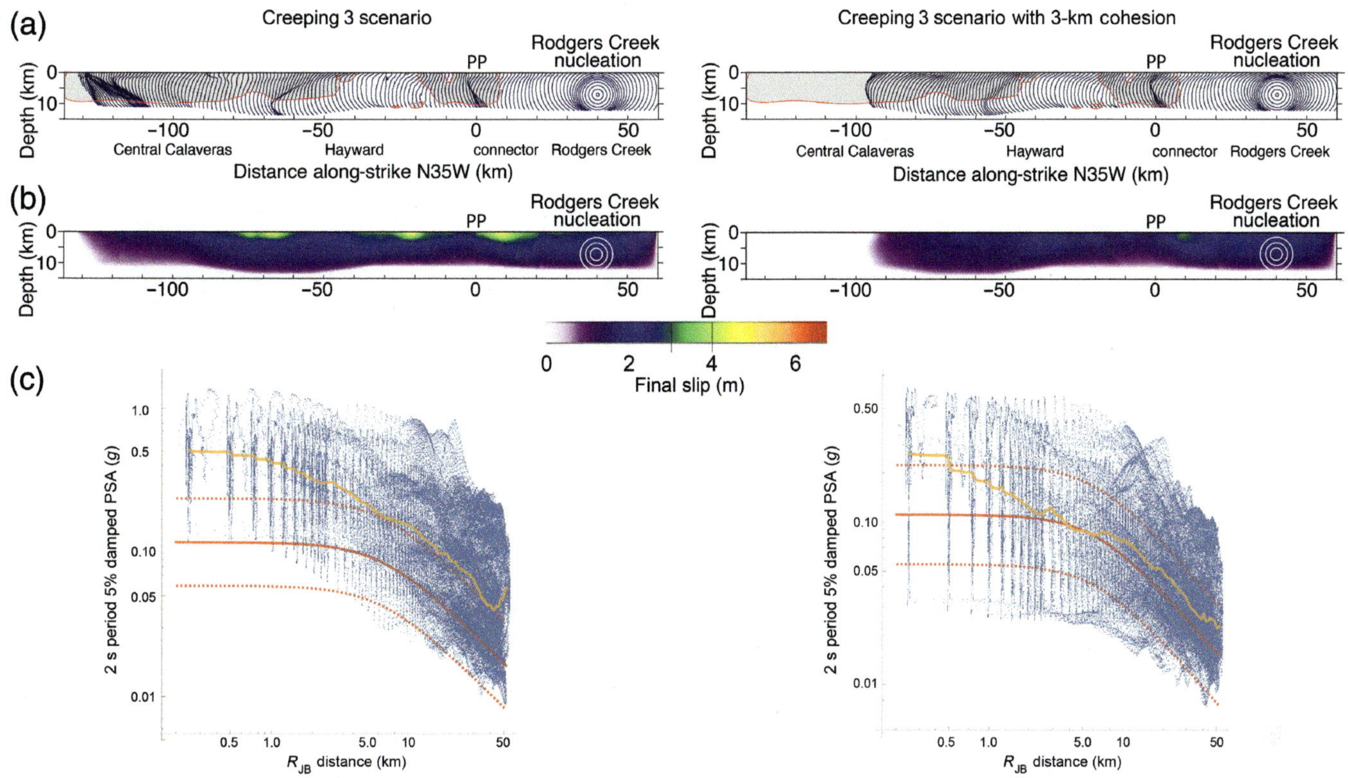

Figure 3. Earthquake rupture was nucleated on the Rodgers Creek fault 40 km northwest of Point Pinole (PP), and spontaneously propagated along the fault. (Left column) Simulation with no cohesion. The earthquake's moment magnitude is 7.29 (Right column) Simulation with cohesion. The earthquake's moment magnitude is 7.19. (a) The progress of the rupture front on the fault surface is shown by the rupture front contours at 1 s intervals. Shading indicates where the interseismic fault creep is faster than 3 mm/yr, so lower initial shear stress at the beginning of the dynamic rupture simulation was assumed (from Harris *et al.*, 2021, their figs. 9a and 11a). (b) Final slip on the fault surface after the rupture has stopped (from Harris *et al.*, 2021, their figs. 9b and 11b). (c–f) Simulated ground motions at the Earth's-surface stations in the finite-element model versus the ground motions predicted by the Boore *et al.* (2014) ground-motion model (GMM). The depicted ground motions are pseudospectral acceleration (PSA) at 2, 3, 5, and 7.5 s periods. The three GMM curves in each plot show the median value (solid red) and plus and minus one standard deviation (both red dashed), respectively. Each blue dot in each plot represents one point on the Earth's surface in the simulation; the horizontal axis indicates the point's distance from the portion of the fault that ruptured, and the vertical axis indicates the value of PSA at that point. The jagged orange curve shows the median of these data. This curve is created by first computing a moving median with a window size of 1601 points, and then smoothing it using a moving average filter with a window size of 801 points. All the ground motions are RotD50 (see the Appendix). The simulations are low-pass filtered at 1 Hz before calculating PSA. Note that the vertical scales are not all the same in these ground-motion plots. (*Continued*)

a significant portion of its total rupture area at a lower initial shear stress due to the creeping regions (denoted by the shading in Fig. 4a), even without the contribution of cohesion. For the Hayward nucleation case, if we include the shallow cohesion too, we are in effect doubling the resistance to fault rupture, and thereby, reducing the simulated ground motion more than expected. Therefore, the median ground motions generated by rupture nucleating on the Hayward fault match the GMM prediction better if there is no cohesion in the friction equation.

These results remind us that not only do we need to better understand the rupture behavior and ground motions hazard of creeping faults, but that the nucleation sites for earthquakes in general can affect not only rupture propagation and extent, but also ground motions. This is the situation here for our creeping-fault rupture simulations, as well as for others' locked-fault rupture simulations (e.g., Oglesby and Mai, 2012).

Caveats for our results are that, for computational efficiency, the slowest shear-wave velocities in the Harris *et al.* (2021) 3D rock (velocity) model are 1950 m/s, which is faster than the slowest shear-wave velocities in the 3D San Francisco Bay area velocity model (Hirakawa and Aagaard, 2022). Including these slower velocities might affect the ground-motion results. Similarly, implementing smaller elements in the finite-element mesh, which would allow for higher frequencies to be resolved, might lead to different conclusions

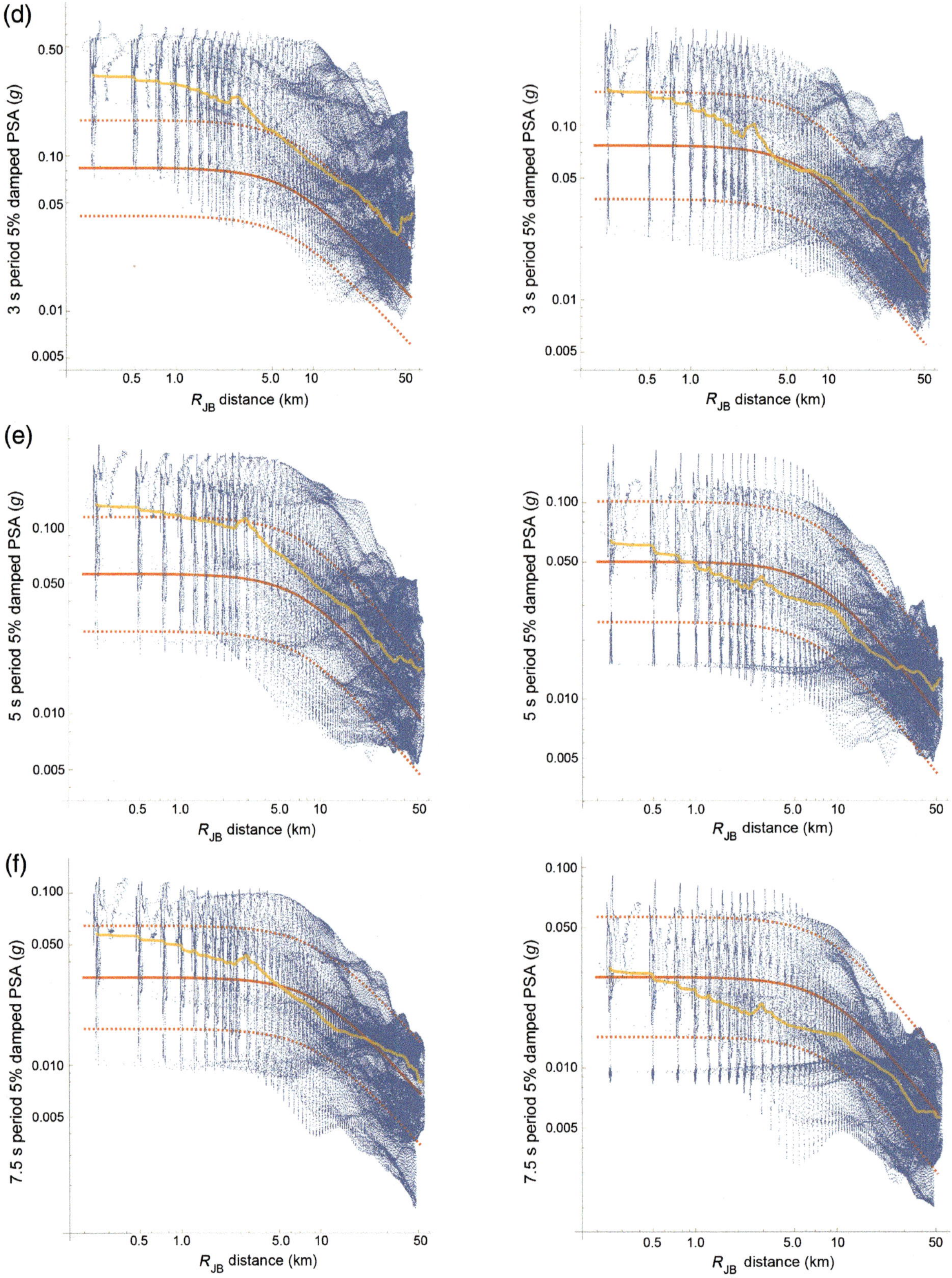

Figure 3. Continued

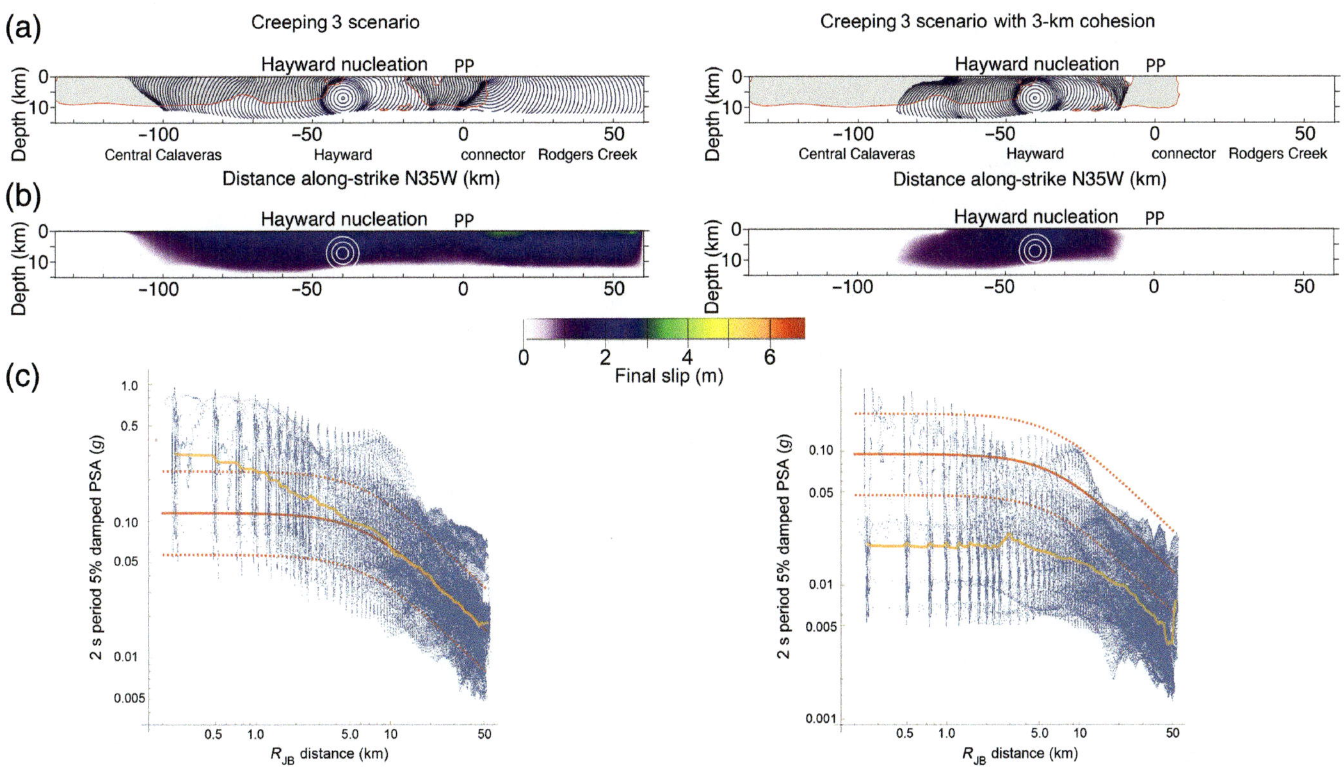

Figure 4. Similar to Figure 3, except that the rupture was nucleated on the Hayward fault 40-km southeast of Point Pinole (PP). (Left column) Simulation with no cohesion. The earthquake's moment magnitude is 7.24. (Right column) Simulation with cohesion. The earthquake's moment magnitude is 6.94. (a) The progress of the rupture front on the fault surface is shown by the rupture front contours at 1 s intervals. Shading indicates where the interseismic fault creep is faster than 3 mm/yr, so lower initial shear stress at the beginning of the dynamic rupture simulation was assumed (from Harris *et al.*, 2021, their figs. 9a and 11a). (b) Final slip on the fault surface after the rupture has stopped (from Harris *et al.*, 2021, their figs. 9b and 11b). (c–f) Simulated ground motions at the Earth's-surface stations in the finite-element model versus the ground motions predicted by the Boore *et al.* (2014) GMM. The depicted ground motions are PSA at 2, 3, 5, and 7.5 s periods. The three GMM curves in each plot show the median value (solid red), and plus and minus one standard deviation (both red dashed), respectively. Each blue dot in each plot represents one point on the Earth's surface in the simulation; the horizontal axis indicates the point's distance from the portion of the fault that ruptured, and the vertical axis indicates the value of PSA at that point. The jagged orange curve shows the median of these data. This curve is created by first computing a moving median with a window size of 1601 points, and then smoothing it using a moving average filter with a window size of 801 points. All the ground motions are RotD50 (see the Appendix). The simulations are low-pass filtered at 1 Hz before calculating PSA. Note that the vertical scales are not all the same in these ground-motion plots. *(Continued)*

when comparing the simulations with the GMM at a higher frequency range. Higher frequency dynamic rupture simulations could allow for a test of the idea that magnitude 6.7 and larger creeping-fault earthquakes and locked-fault earthquakes may produce similar peak ground velocity and peak ground acceleration, as was evidenced in the empirical study by Harris and Abrahamson (2014) for smaller earthquakes. Earth's surface topography in this region might also make a difference, especially at higher frequencies. We note that Harris *et al.* (2021) did not include anelastic attenuation in the finite-element model's rock properties; instead, all wave propagation was elastic. They also did not include a proxy for inelastic yielding, such as the method of nonlinear radiation damping (Barall and Harris, 2023), but it appears that the long-period ($T > 1$ s) ground motions are already sufficiently close to the GMM, if elastic rock response is implemented along with reasonable assumptions about where to apply frictional cohesion. Anelastic attenuation might affect the results, especially at farther distances from the faults, but we do not expect it to appreciably affect the long-period ground motions within the 50 km distance examined here.

Conclusions

The dynamic earthquake rupture method was used by Harris *et al.* (2021) to simulate large scenario earthquakes on the creeping Hayward, Calaveras, and Rodgers Creek faults in the San Francisco Bay area. The method produces earthquake sources physically self-consistent with detailed assumptions about these faults' 3D geometry, initial stress conditions based on the fault slip-rate pattern, rock properties from the region's 3D geologic model, and fault friction based on the rock types. We examined the long-period ($T > 1$ s) ground shaking produced by these

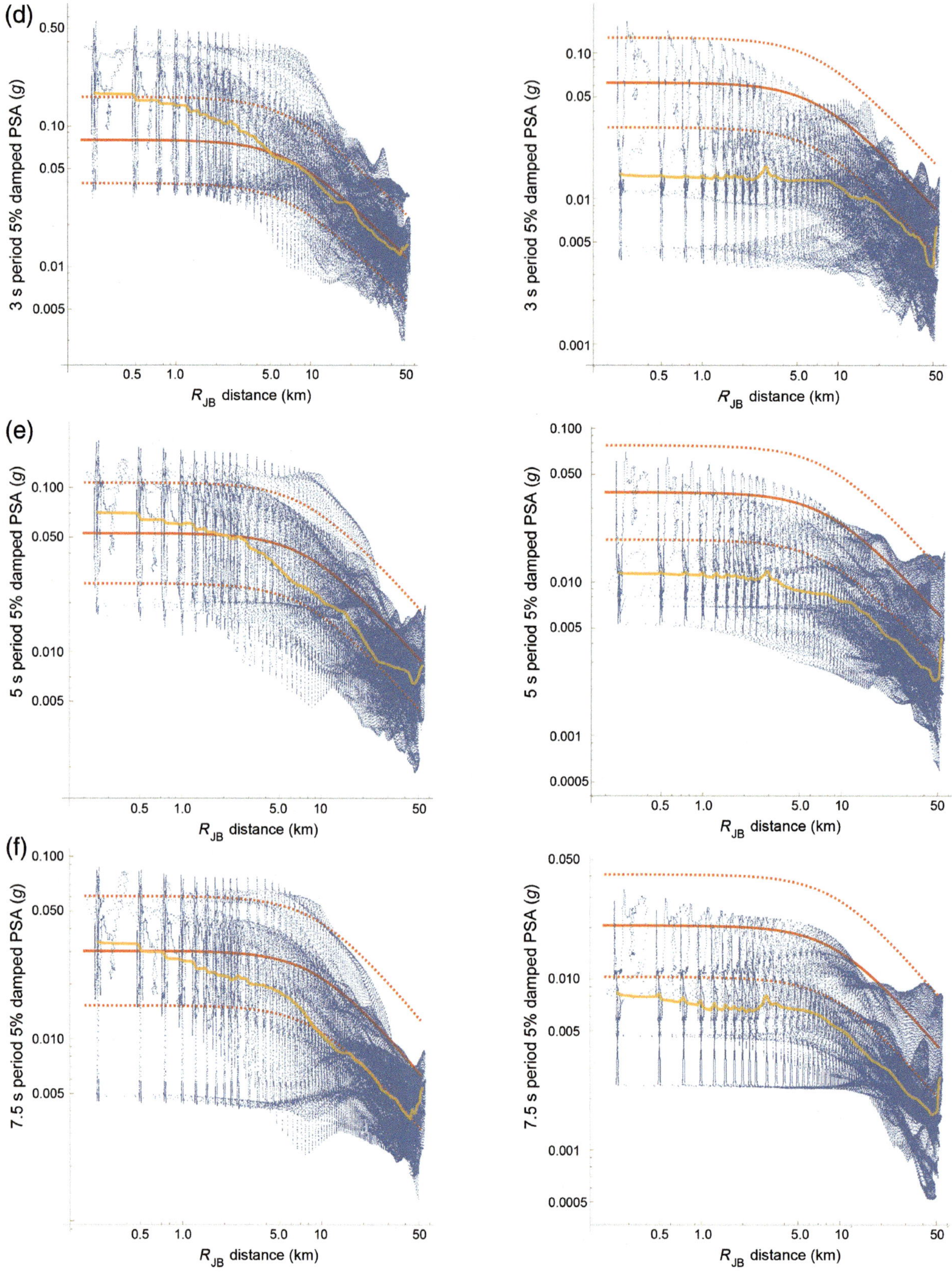

Figure 4. Continued

large scenario earthquakes and compared them with an empirically based GMM. From 0 to 50 km distance from the fault ruptures, the medians of the simulated ground motions appear to be in the range of the Boore *et al.* (2014) GMM, if frictional cohesion is only included where appropriate. Our work's findings suggest that viable long-period ground-motion estimates may be produced using dynamic rupture simulations of large earthquakes on creeping faults.

Data and Resources

The numerical simulation results in this article were performed using the FaultMod finite-element code (Barall, 2024). The input files for the dynamic rupture simulations are available at doi: 10.5061/dryad.d7wm37q0n. The Boore *et al.* (2014) (BSSA14) ground-motion model (GMM) was calculated using OpenSHA (https://opensha.org, last accessed June 2025). Some more information about the Statewide (formerly Southern) California Earthquake Center (SCEC) dynamic rupture code verification group is available at https://strike.scec.org/cvws (last accessed September 2025). This article's supplemental material includes detailed information about the assumed dynamic rupture parameters and also explains which Harris *et al.* (2021) dynamic rupture simulations were used to produce the ground motions presented in this article.

Declaration of Competing Interests

The authors acknowledge that there are no conflicts of interest recorded.

Acknowledgments

Thank you to Luke Blair for creating the San Francisco Bay area fault map in Figure 1 and Phil Dawson for the depiction of the fault surface in Figure 2a. Thank you to Rob Graves, Kyle Withers, and Annemarie Baltay Sundstrom for thoughtful U.S. Geological Survey (USGS) internal reviews and suggestions. *SRL* journal reviewers Kim Olsen and an anonymous reviewer provided valuable suggestions which the authors used to improve the article.

Any use of trade, firm, or product names is for descriptive purposes only and does not imply endorsement by the U.S. Government.

References

Aagaard, B. T., J. L. Blair, J. Boatwright, S. H. Garcia, R. A. Harris, A. J. Michael, D. P. Schwartz, and J. S. DiLeo (2016). Earthquake outlook for the San Francisco Bay region 2014–2043 (ver. 1.1, August 2016), *U.S. Geol. Surv. Fact Sheet 2016-3020*, doi: 10.3133/fs20163020.

Aagaard, B. T., R. W. Graves, A. Rodgers, T. M. Brocher, R. W. Simpson, D. Dreger, N. A. Petersson, S. C. Larsen, S. Ma, and R. C. Jachens (2010). Ground-motion modelling of Hayward fault scenario earthquakes, Part II: Simulation of long-period and broadband ground motions, *Bull. Seismol. Soc. Am.* **100,** no. 6, 2945–2977, doi: 10.1785/0120090379.

Andrews, D. J. (1976). Rupture propagation with finite stress in antiplane strain, *J. Geophys. Res.* **81,** no. 20, 3575–3582, doi: 10.1029/JB081i020p03575.

Barall, M. (2024). FaultMod - Finite-element earthquake fault model, *U.S. Geol. Surv. Software Release*, doi: 10.5066/P14MGULF.

Barall, M., and R. A. Harris (2023). Nonlinear radiation damping: A new method for dissipating energy in dynamic earthquake rupture simulations, *The Seismic Record* **3,** no. 2, 69–76, doi: 10.1785/0320230001.

Boatwright, J., and H. Bundock (2008). Modified Mercalli intensity maps for the 1868 Hayward earthquake plotted in ShakeMap format, *U.S. Geol. Surv. Open-File Rept. 2008-1121*, available at https://pubs.usgs.gov/of/2008/1121 (last accessed September 2025).

Boore, D. M. (2010). Orientation-independent, nongeometric-mean measures of seismic intensity from two horizontal components of motion, *Bull. Seismol. Soc. Am.* **100,** no. 4, 1830–1835, doi: 10.1785/0120090400.

Boore, D. M., J. P. Stewart, E. Seyhan, and G. M. Atkinson (2014). NGA-West 2 equations for predicting PGA, PGV, and 5%-damped PSA for shallow crustal earthquakes, *Earthq. Spectra* **30,** no. 3, 1057–1085, doi: 10.1193/070113EQS184M.

Bozorgnia, Y., N. A. Abrahamson, L. Al Atik, T. D. Ancheta, G. M. Atkinson, J. W. Baker, A. Baltay, D. M. Boore, K. W. Campbell, B. S.-J. Chiou, *et al.* (2014). NGA-West2 research project, *Earthq. Spectra* **30,** no. 3, 973–987, doi: 10.1193/072113EQS209M.

Brocher, T. M. (2008). Compressional and shear-wave velocity versus depth relations for common rock types in northern California, *Bull. Seismol. Soc. Am.* **98,** no. 2, 950–968, doi: 10.1785/0120060403.

Budding, K. E., D. P. Schwartz, and D. H. Oppenheimer (1991). Slip rate, earthquake recurrence, and seismogenic potential of the Rodgers Creek fault zone, northern California: Initial results, *Geophys. Res. Lett.* **18,** no. 3, 447–450, doi: 10.1029/91GL00465.

Burgmann, R., D. Schmidt, R. M. Nadeau, M. d'Alessio, E. Fielding, D. Manaker, T. V. McEvilly, and M. H. Murray (2000). Earthquake potential along the northern Hayward fault, *Science* **289,** no. 5482, 1178–1182, doi: 10.1126/science.289.5482.1178.

Gallovič, F., Ľ. Valentová, J.-P. Ampuero, and A.-A. Gabriel (2019). Bayesian dynamic finite-fault inversion: 2. Application to the 2016 M_w 6.2 Amatrice, Italy, earthquake, *J. Geophys. Res.* **124,** 6970–6988, doi: 10.1029/2019JB017512.

Graymer, R. W., D. A. Ponce, R. C. Jachens, R. W. Simpson, G. A. Phelps, and C. M. Wentworth (2005). Three-dimensional geologic map of the Hayward fault, northern California: Correlation of rock units with variations in seismicity, creep rate, and fault dip, *Geology* **33,** 521–524, doi: 10.1130/G21435.1.

Guatteri, M., P. M. Mai, G. C. Beroza, and J. Boatwright (2003). Strong ground-motion prediction from stochastic-dynamic source models, *Bull. Seismol. Soc. Am.* **93,** no. 1, 301–313, doi: 10.1785/0120020006.

Harris, R. A. (2017). Large earthquakes and creeping faults, *Rev. Geophys.* **55,** 169–198, doi: 10.1002/2016RG000539.

Harris, R. A., and N. A. Abrahamson (2014). Strong ground motions generated by earthquakes on creeping faults, *Geophys. Res. Lett.* **41,** 3870–3875, doi: 10.1002/2014GL060228.

Harris, R. A., M. Barall, B. Aagaard, S. Ma, D. Roten, K. Olsen, B. Duan, D. Liu, B. Luo, K. Bai, *et al.* (2018). A suite of exercises for verifying dynamic earthquake rupture codes, *Seismol. Res. Lett.* **89,** no. 3, 1146–1162, doi: 10.1785/0220170222.

Harris, R. A., M. Barall, D. A. Lockner, D. E. Moore, D. A. Ponce, R. W. Graymer, G. Funning, C. A. Morrow, C. Kyriakopoulos, and D. Eberhart-Phillips (2021). A geology and geodesy based model of dynamic earthquake rupture on the Rodgers Creek-Hayward-Calaveras fault system, California, *J. Geophys. Res.* **126,** e2020JB020577, doi: 10.1029/2020JB020577.

Hecker, S., D. Pantosti, D. P. Schwartz, J. C. Hamilton, L. M. Reidy, and T. J. Powers (2005). The most recent large earthquake on the Rodgers Creek fault, San Francisco Bay area, *Bull. Seismol. Soc. Am.* **95,** no. 3, 844–860, doi: 10.1785/0120040134.

Hirakawa, E., and B. Aagaard (2022). Evaluation and updates for the USGS San Francisco Bay region 3D seismic velocity model in the east and north bay portions, *Bull. Seismol. Soc. Am.* **112,** no. 4, 2070–2096, doi: 10.1785/0120210256.

Hirakawa, E., G. A. Parker, A. Baltay, and T. Hanks (2023). Rupture directivity of the 25 October 2022 M_w 5.1 Alum Rock earthquake, *Seism. Rec.* **3,** no. 2, 144–155, doi: 10.1785/0320230013.

Jachens, R. C., R. W. Simpson, R. W. Graymer, C. M. Wentworth, and T. M. Brocher (2006). Three-dimensional geologic map of northern California: A foundation for earthquake simulations and other predictive modeling, *AGU Fall Meeting Abstracts*, Vol. 2006, S51B-1265.

Kalkan, E. (2019). Spectral acceleration, velocity and displacement spectra, *MATLAB Central File Exchange*, available at https://www.mathworks.com/matlabcentral/fileexchange/57906-spectral-acceleration-velocity-and-displacement-spectra (last accessed November 2023).

Larsen, S., M. Antolik, D. Dreger, C. Stidham, C. Schultz, A. Lomax, and B. Romanowicz (1997). 3-D models of seismic wave propagation: Simulating scenario earthquakes along the Hayward fault, *Seismol. Res. Lett.* **68,** 328.

Lienkaemper, J. J., F. S. McFarland, R. W. Simpson, R. G. Bilham, D. A. Ponce, J. J. Boatwright, and S. J. Caskey (2012). Long-term creep rates on the Hayward fault: Evidence for controls on the size and frequency of large earthquakes, *Bull. Seismol. Soc. Am.* **102,** no. 1, 31–41, doi: 10.1785/0120110033.

Lienkaemper, J. J., P. L. Williams, and T. P. Guilderson (2010). Evidence for a twelfth large earthquake on the southern Hayward fault in the past 1900 years, *Bull. Seismol. Soc. Am.* **100,** no. 5A, 2024–2034, doi: 10.1785/0120090129.

Oglesby, D. D., and P. M. Mai (2012). Fault geometry, rupture dynamics and ground motion from potential earthquakes on the North Anatolian fault under the Sea of Marmara, *Geophys. J. Int.* **188,** 1071–1087, doi: 10.1111/j.1365-246X.2011.05289.x.

Olsen, K. B., S. M. Day, L. A. Dalguer, J. Mayhew, Y. Cui, J. Zhu, V. M. Cruz-Atienza, D. Roten, P. Maechling, T. H. Jordan, *et al.* (2009). ShakeOut-D: Ground motion estimates using an ensemble of large earthquakes on the southern San Andreas fault with spontaneous rupture propagation, *Geophys. Res. Lett.* **36,** L04303, doi: 10.1029/2008GL036832.

Peyrat, S., and K. B. Olsen (2004). Nonlinear dynamic rupture inversion of the 2000 western Tottori, Japan, earthquake, *Geophys. Res. Lett.* **31,** L05604, doi: 10.1029/2003GL019058.

Phelps, G. A., R. W. Graymer, R. C. Jachens, D. A. Ponce, R. W. Simpson, and C. M. Wentworth (2008). Three-dimensional geologic map of the Hayward fault zone, San Francisco Bay region, California, *U.S. Geol. Surv. Scientific Investig. Map 3045*, doi: 10.3133/sim3045.

Ponce, D. A., R. W. Simpson, R. W. Graymer, and R. C. Jachens (2004). Gravity, magnetic, and high-precision relocated seismicity profiles suggest a connection between the Hayward and Calaveras faults, northern California, *Geochem. Geophys. Geosys.* **5,** Q07004, doi: 10.1029/2003GC000684.

Power, M., B. Chiou, N. Abrahamson, Y. Bozorgnia, T. Shantz, and C. Roblee (2008). An overview of the NGA project, *Earthq. Spectra* **24,** no. 1, 3–21, doi: 10.1193/1.2894833.

Radbruch, D. H., and B. J. Lennert (1966). Damage to culvert under Memorial Stadium, University of California, Berkeley, caused by slippage in the Hayward fault zone, *Bull. Seismol. Soc. Am.* **56,** no. 2, 295–304.

Ramos, M. D., P. Thakur, Y. Huang, R. A. Harris, and K. J. Ryan (2022). Working with dynamic earthquake rupture models: A practical guide, *Seismol. Res. Lett.* **93,** no. 4, 2096–2110, doi: 10.1785/0220220022.

Rodgers, A. J., A. Pitarka, R. Pankajakshan, B. Sjögreen, and N. A. Petersson (2020). Regional-scale 3D ground-motion simulations of M_w 7 earthquakes on the Hayward fault, northern California resolving frequencies 0–10 Hz and including site-response corrections, *Bull. Seismol. Soc. Am.* **110,** no. 6, 2862–2881, doi: 10.1785/0120200147.

Tinti, E., E. Casarotti, T. Ulrich, T. Taufiqurrahman, D. Li, and A.-A. Gabriel (2021). Constraining families of dynamic models using geological, geodetic and strong ground motion data: The M_w 6.5, October 30th, 2016, Norcia earthquake, Italy, *Earth Planet. Sci. Lett.* **576,** 117,237, doi: 10.1016/j.epsl.2021.117237.

U.S. Geological Survey (USGS) and California Geological Survey (CGS) (2024). Quaternary fault and fold database for the United States, available at https://www.usgs.gov/programs/earthquake-hazards/faults (last accessed August 2024).

Wang, L.-J. (1996). Processing of near-field earthquake accelerograms, *California Institute of Technology Rept. EERL 96-04*, available at https://authors.library.caltech.edu/records/e0wfb-mfb25 (last accessed November 2023).

Watt, J., D. Ponce, T. Parsons, and P. Hart (2016). Missing link between the Hayward and Rodgers Creek faults, *Sci. Adv.* **2,** no. 10, e1601441, doi: 10.1126/sciadv.1601441.

Withers, K. B., K. B. Olsen, S. M. Day, and Z. Shi (2018). Ground motion and intraevent variability from 3D deterministic broadband (0–7.5 Hz) simulations along a nonplanar strike-slip fault, *Bull. Seismol. Soc. Am.* **109,** no. 1, 229–250, doi: 10.1785/0120180006.

Yu, E., and P. Segall (1996). Slip in the 1868 Hayward earthquake from the analysis of historical triangulation data, *J. Geophys. Res.* **101,** 16101–16118, doi: 10.1029/96JB00806.

Appendix

Part 1: Calculating pseudo-spectral acceleration

Definition of PSA. Pseudo-spectral acceleration, or PSA, is frequently used as a measure of ground-motion intensity during an earthquake, at a single point on the Earth's surface. PSA is defined by two parameters: an oscillator period T measured in seconds, and a damping factor ξ, which is dimensionless. Commonly, T has values in the range of 0.01–10.0 s, and ξ is often taken to be 5% or 0.05. The PSA itself has units of g, the gravitational acceleration (e.g., Power *et al.*, 2008).

A very simple model of a structure is a vertical column that sits upon and is fastened to a rigid base, and supports a mass M at the top. The base is attached firmly to the ground (Fig. A1).

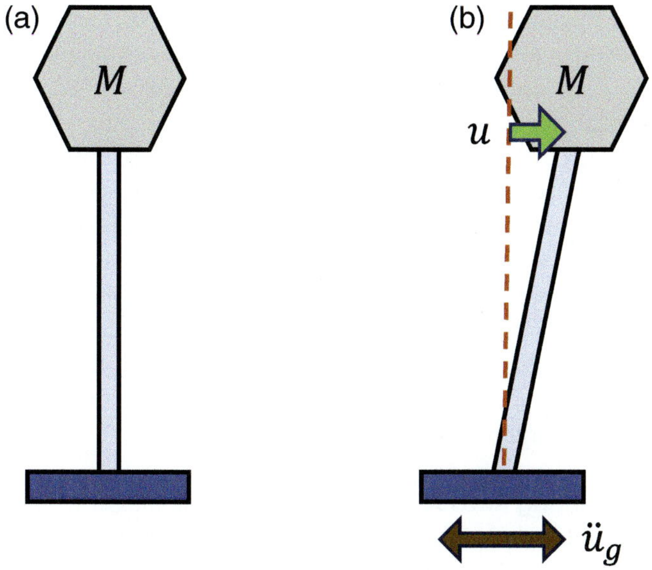

Figure A1. (a) A very simple model of a structure. A vertical column supports a mass M attached at the top. The bottom of the column is attached to a rigid base, which is anchored to the ground. (b) When earthquake ground motion shakes the structure, it oscillates like an inverted pendulum. The time-varying horizontal ground acceleration $\ddot{u}_g$ moves the base from side to side. The time-varying horizontal displacement of the mass relative to the base is called u.

When the ground shakes, the structure is assumed to vibrate like a damped oscillator in response. Usually, only horizontal ground motions are considered, in which case the mass oscillates back and forth and side to side horizontally.

For a single degree of freedom (SDOF), the equation of motion of the damped oscillator is

$$\ddot{u} + 2\xi\omega\dot{u} + \omega^2 u = -\ddot{u}_g, \quad \text{(A1)}$$

in which u is the displacement of the mass relative to the base, $\omega = 2\pi/T$ is the undamped oscillator frequency in radians per second, and $\ddot{u}_g$ is the ground acceleration. By convention, T is the natural period of the undamped oscillator, that is, the period in the case $\xi = 0$.

The PSA is then defined to be

$$\text{PSA} = \omega^2 \max|u(t)|, \quad \text{(A2)}$$

in which the maximum is taken over all times t of interest.

The PSA is a measure of the peak lateral force, neglecting damping forces, that the column must be able to sustain during the earthquake to avoid failure. To see this, note that the total acceleration of the mass is $\ddot{u} + \ddot{u}_g$. Setting $\xi = 0$ in equation (A1) and rearranging terms, this acceleration is equal to $-\omega^2 u$, and so the force is $-M\omega^2 u$, and the maximum force is M * PSA. Another way of saying this is that $M\omega^2 u$ is the amount of static force (i.e., slowly applied force) that must be applied to the top of the column to produce the deflection u of the top of the column relative to the base. So, M * PSA is the amount of static force that must be applied to the top of the column to produce the maximum deflection.

Algorithm for calculating SDOF PSA

We now describe an algorithm for computing PSA for a single degree of freedom. Suppose we are given a sequence of times, $t_0,t_1,\ldots t_N$. Suppose that the ground acceleration is constant within each time interval. We write

$$\ddot{u}_g(t) = a_i \quad \text{for } t_{i-1} < t < t_i. \quad \text{(A3)}$$

Then the following algorithm (Algorithm A1), written in pseudo-code, computes the analytically exact value of $\omega^2 u(t_i)$ for each time t_i (Wang, 1996; Kalkan 2019).

ALGORITHM A1

```
INPUT
    t[i] = Sequence of times tᵢ, for 0 ≤ i ≤ N, in seconds.
    a[i] = Ground accelerations aᵢ in the intervals
tᵢ₋₁ < t < tᵢ.
    period = Undamped oscillator period T, in seconds.
    xi = Damping factor.
    g = Acceleration of gravity, in the same units as aᵢ.
OUTPUT
    wwu[i] = Value of ω²u(tᵢ), in units of g.
    wwud[i] = Value of ω²u̇(tᵢ), in units of g/s.
ALGORITHM
    # Initialize oscillator to be at rest at initial time
    wwu[0] ← 0
    wwud[0] ← 0
    # Process each time interval
    for i = 1, …, N
begin
     # Calculate some intermediate values
```

(Continued next page.)

ALGORITHM A1 (continued)

```
    r ← 1.0/g

    dt ← t[i] - t[i-1]

    w ← 2.0*PI/period

    z ← sqrt(1.0 - xi * xi)

    c ← cos(dt*w*z)

    s ← sin(dt*w*z)

    f ← exp(-dt*w*xi)

    # Calculate the propagator matrix

    mae11 ← f*(c + (s*xi)/z)

    mae12 ← (f*s)/(w*z)

    mae21 ← -((f*s*w)/z)

    mae22 ← f*(c - (s*xi)/z)

    mab1 ← r*(-1.0 + c*f + (f*s*xi)/z)

    mab2 ← -((f*r*s*w)/z)

    # Recurrence relation

    wwu[i] ← mae11*wwu[i-1] + mae12*wwud[i-1] +
mab1*a[i]

    wwud[i] ← mae21*wwu[i-1] + mae22*wwud[i-1] +
mab2*a[i]

end
```

The ground accelerations a_i and the gravitational acceleration g must be given in the same units. If the ground accelerations are given in m/s^2, then g should be 9.8. If the ground accelerations are given in cm/s^2, then g should be 980.

For the single degree of freedom, we can then calculate the PSA as

$$\mathrm{PSA} = \max_{0 \le i \le N} |\omega^2 u(t_i)|. \tag{A4}$$

To obtain useful results, the time intervals $t_i - t_{i-1}$ should be small relative to the oscillator period T. Although the algorithm produces mathematically correct results regardless of the size of the time intervals, the resulting PSA may not be useful unless the ground motions are sampled many times within each oscillator period.

In practice, it is usually desired to calculate the response of several oscillators with the same period and damping factor, instead of just one. This is needed, for example, to calculate the response for two orthogonal directions of horizontal ground motion, or for the response at different points on the Earth's surface. The algorithm is easily modified to accommodate multiple oscillators by including a recurrence relation for each oscillator, each with its own ground acceleration.

In our dynamic rupture simulations, we sample the results at intervals of 0.1 s, so the times t_i are spaced 0.1 s apart. These intervals are larger than the timestep used in the simulation. For example, if the timestep is 0.01 s, then we sample the simulation results once in every 10 timesteps. This has the effect of filtering out high-frequency noise. For each time t_i, the finite-element code provides a particle velocity v_i. Then, we apply the above algorithm, taking $a_i = (v_i - v_{i-1})/(t_i - t_{i-1})$.

Calculating RotD50 PSA. At each point on the Earth's surface, horizontal ground motion has two degrees of freedom, which we denote as x and y. The two components of horizontal ground accelerations in each time interval are a_{xi} and a_{yi}. Using the above algorithm, it is possible to compute two components of oscillator motion at each time, which we denote $\omega^2 u_x(t_i)$ and $\omega^2 u_y(t_i)$.

The RotD50 algorithm is a way to combine the two components of oscillator motion into a single PSA value (Boore, 2010). To do this, we consider the oscillator motion in many azimuths, not just the x and y directions. For an azimuth angle θ, the oscillator motion in the θ direction is

$$\omega^2 u_\theta(t_i) = (\cos\theta)\omega^2 u_x(t_i) + (\sin\theta)\omega^2 u_y(t_i). \tag{A5}$$

We now choose a set of K equally spaced azimuth angles, spanning π radians, by defining $\theta(k) = k\pi/K$ for $k = 0,1,\ldots,K-1$. The reason we only need to span π radians, instead of 2π radians, is that adding π to θ just reverses the sign of u_θ, which has no effect on the PSA. Now, for each k, we can compute a PSA in the $\theta(k)$ azimuth:

$$\mathrm{PSA}_k = \max_{0 \le i \le N} |\omega^2 u_{\theta(k)}(t_i)| \quad \text{for } k = 0,1,\ldots,K-1. \tag{A6}$$

The RotD50 PSA is defined to be the median of the set $\{\mathrm{PSA}_0, \mathrm{PSA}_1, \ldots, \mathrm{PSA}_{K-1}\}$.

In our calculations, we take $K = 101$ so that the median is well defined.

The number 50 appearing in RotD50 refers to the 50th percentile, which is the median. The notation generalizes to other percentiles. For example, RotD75 refers to the 75th percentile of the set $\{\mathrm{PSA}_0, \mathrm{PSA}_1, \ldots, \mathrm{PSA}_{K-1}\}$, whereas RotD100 refers to the 100th percentile which is the maximum.

Part 2: Boore *et al.* (2014) ground-motion model

The Boore *et al.* (2014) (BSSA14) ground-motion model (GMM) was developed as part of the Next Generation Attenuation-West2 project (Bozorgnia *et al.*, 2014) to estimate the median and standard deviation of ground-motion shaking intensities for shallow earthquakes in active tectonic regions. The model has a generalized form of equation (A7), where an intensity measure ($\ln Y$, e.g., PSA for a given oscillator period) is the sum of a median model with components representative of the earthquake source (F_E), seismic wave propagation path (F_P), and local site conditions (F_S), plus an error term quantified using the number of standard deviations away from the median, ε_n times a standard deviation model σ:

$$\ln Y = F_E(\mathbf{M},\text{mech}) + F_P(R_{\text{JB}},\mathbf{M},\text{region}) + F_S(V_{S30},R_{\text{JB}},\mathbf{M},\text{region},z_1) + \varepsilon_n \sigma(\mathbf{M},R_{\text{JB}},V_{S30}). \quad \text{(A7)}$$

Model input parameters include moment magnitude ($\mathbf{M}$), fault rupture mechanism (mech), the closest distance to the surface projection of the fault plane (the Joyner–Boore distance, R_{JB}), geographic region, the time-averaged shear-wave velocity in the upper 30 m (V_{S30}), and the depth to the 1 km/s shear-wave velocity horizon (z_1).

The earthquake source scaling (F_E) is parameterized as equation (A8), in which U, SS, NS, and RS are dummy variables taking on the value of 0 or 1 depending on if the earthquake rupture mechanism is unspecified, strike slip, normal, or reverse, respectively,

$$F_E = \begin{cases} e_0 U + e_1 SS + e_2 NS + e_3 RS + e_4(\mathbf{M}-\mathbf{M}_h) + e_5(\mathbf{M}-\mathbf{M}_h)^2 & \mathbf{M} \le \mathbf{M}_h \\ e_0 U + e_1 SS + e_2 NS + e_3 RS + e_6(\mathbf{M}-\mathbf{M}_h) & \mathbf{M} > \mathbf{M}_\mathbf{h} \end{cases}. \quad \text{(A8)}$$

The path term (F_P; equation A9) depends on a modified Joyner–Boore distance, R (equation A10), which enforces near-source saturation of the ground motion at distance h. The F_P term includes a magnitude-dependent geometrical spreading slope that controls the distance fall-off with the natural logarithm of R, and an anelastic attenuation term that scales with R and has variations that depend on region via the Δc_3 modifier to the c_3 coefficient.

$$F_P = [c_1 + c_2(\mathbf{M}-\mathbf{M}_{\text{ref}})]\ln(R/R_{\text{ref}}) + (c_3 + \Delta c_3)(R - R_{\text{ref}}), \quad \text{(A9)}$$

$$R = \sqrt{R_{\text{JB}}^2 + h^2}. \quad \text{(A10)}$$

The site term F_S (equation A11) includes linear (F_{lin}), nonlinear (F_{nl}), and sediment depth ($F_{\delta z_1}$) terms. The linear term controls how the site amplification scales with V_{S30} (equation A12). The nonlinear term (equations A13 and A14) captures nonlinear soil damping for soft soils (low V_{S30}) at short periods and large shaking intensities. The shaking intensity is characterized as an estimate of peak ground acceleration (PGA) for a $V_{S30} = 760$ m/s at the site of interest, PGA_r, in units of g. Finally, the ground-motion scales with the sediment depth parameterized using z_1. Because V_{S30} and z_1 are correlated, $F_{\delta z_1}$ is conditioned on the differential depth (δz_1) between the z_1 value at the site of interest and the average z_1 given the V_{S30} at the site of interest, $\mu_{z_1}(V_{S30})$ (equations A16 and 17). The $\mu_{z_1}(V_{S30})$ given in equation (A17) is calibrated for California, but BSSA14 also has a $\mu_{z_1}(V_{S30})$ model calibrated for use in Japan:

$$F_S = F_{\text{lin}} + F_{\text{nl}} + F_{\delta z_1}, \quad \text{(A11)}$$

$$F_{\text{lin}} = \begin{cases} c\ln\left(\frac{V_{S30}}{V_{\text{ref}}}\right) & V_{S30} \le V_c \\ c\ln\left(\frac{V_c}{V_{\text{ref}}}\right) & V_{S30} > V_c \end{cases}, \quad \text{(A12)}$$

$$F_{\text{nl}} = f_1 + f_2 \ln\left(\frac{\text{PGA}_r + f_3}{f_3}\right), \quad \text{(A13)}$$

$$f_2 = f_4[\exp\{f_5(\min(V_{S30},760) - 360)\} - \exp\{f_5(760 - 360)\}], \quad \text{(A14)}$$

$$F_{\delta z_1} = \begin{cases} 0 & T < 0.65 \\ f_6 \delta z_1 & T \ge 0.65 \text{ and } \delta z_1 \le f_7/f_6 \\ f_7 & T \ge 0.65 \text{ and } \delta z_1 > f_7/f_6 \end{cases}, \quad \text{(A15)}$$

$$\delta z_1 = z_1 - \mu_{z_1}(V_{S30}), \quad \text{(A16)}$$

$$\ln(\delta z_1) = \frac{-7.15}{4}\ln\left(\frac{V_{S30}^4 + 570.94^4}{1360^4 + 570.94^4}\right) - \ln(1000). \quad \text{(A17)}$$

Coefficients of the model in equations (A8)–(A17) (e_0–e_5, $\mathbf{M}_h$, $\mathbf{M}_{\text{ref}}$, R_{ref}, c_1–c_3, Δc_3, h, c, V_c, V_{ref}, and f_1–f_5) are available as the supplemental material to the original BSSA14 publication.

Manuscript received 14 June 2025
Published online 21 November 2025

RMS and Hierarchical Agglomerative Clustering to Build Template Event Catalogs of Tectonic Tremors

Gerardo Mendo-Pérez[1], Hiromichi Nagao[*1,2], and Yoshikazu Terada[3]

Abstract

Since their discovery in 2002, the detection of slow earthquakes and their precise locations in subduction zones have become important topics of interest in seismology. These earthquakes can potentially be linked to the generation of large megathrust earthquakes. Traditionally, tectonic tremors and low-frequency earthquakes (LFE) are identified using two different methods: envelope cross-correlation method and template matching, respectively. In particular, the template matching method identifies seismic events by means of quantifying the similarity between observations and master signals known as templates. Although powerful, it relies heavily on the template event catalog used. This method has not been used to detect tremor signals due to their stochastic nature and relatively low signal-to-noise ratio values. However, under the assumption that the tremor waveforms may be composed of several LFE, we may build tremor waveform catalogs. To address these points, recent research has been focusing on improving template matching. In this regard, we present the You Only Search Once (YOSO) method, which creates template catalogs based on automatic detection and classification of waveforms associated with seismic slow earthquakes. The YOSO method comprises three stages: identification of events using a root mean square (RMS)-based detector, estimation of the duration of each detected event by calculating the RMS amplitude decay curves, and their classification using a hierarchical clustering scheme. We applied the YOSO method to synthetic seismograms and observed seismograms from Hi-net broadband stations located in central Shikoku, Japan. YOSO retrieved tremor-related waveforms with durations ranging from 100 to 400 s in the 2–8 Hz frequency band. By determining first-order hypocenters and comparing them with existing catalogs, we confirmed that the waveforms correspond to tremor waveforms. This method provides a new scheme for template-based detection without the dependence on existent template catalogs.

Cite this article as Mendo-Pérez, G., H. Nagao, and Y. Terada (2025). RMS and Hierarchical Agglomerative Clustering to Build Template Event Catalogs of Tectonic Tremors, *Seismol. Res. Lett.* **97**, 2064–2081, doi: 10.1785/0220240392.

Supplemental Material

Introduction

Slow earthquakes are a type of fault-slip phenomenon that occur at longer characteristic times than regular earthquakes (Ide *et al.*, 2007, 2008; Obara, 2020; Nishikawa *et al.*, 2023). Most slow earthquakes have been reported in the subduction zones of Japan (Obara, 2002; Shelly *et al.*, 2007; Obara *et al.*, 2010; Beroza and Ide, 2011; Obara and Kato, 2016; Nakano *et al.*, 2018, 2019; Mizuno and Ide, 2019; Takemura, Matsuzawa, *et al.*, 2019; Takemura, Noda, *et al.*, 2019; Toh *et al.*, 2020; Uchida *et al.*, 2020; Aiken and Obara, 2021; Tamaribuchi *et al.*, 2022; Kaneko *et al.*, 2023; Ohta *et al.*, 2023), Cascadia (Rogers and Dragert, 2003; Wech and Creager, 2008; Aguiar *et al.*, 2009; Kao *et al.*, 2009; Ghosh *et al.*, 2015; Bartlow, 2020; Wech, 2021), Mexico (Frank *et al.*, 2013,2014; Plata-Martinez *et al.*, 2021), New Zealand (Chamberlain *et al.*, 2014; Todd and Schwartz, 2016; Todd *et al.*, 2018), and Taiwan (Tang *et al.*, 2010; Sun *et al.*, 2015; Aguiar *et al.*, 2017; Peng *et al.*, 2019). Although these are classified as seismic (very low-frequency earthquakes [VLFE], low-frequency earthquakes [LFE], and tectonic tremors) and geodetic (short- and long-term slow slip events), both are aligned to fault-slip process in subduction systems, and their relation is still a topic of research (Ide and Beroza, 2023). In addition, the potential link between slow and fast earthquakes and the many unsolved mysteries related to source physical processes are also of interest in current research.

1. Earthquake Research Institute, The University of Tokyo, Tokyo, Japan, https://orcid.org/0000-0002-5239-4377 (GM-P); https://orcid.org/0000-0003-4314-5093 (HN); 2. Graduate School of Information Science and Technology, The University of Tokyo, Tokyo, Japan; 3. Graduate School of Engineering Science, The University of Osaka, Osaka, Japan, https://orcid.org/0000-0002-4509-1108 (YT)

*Corresponding author: nagaoh@eri.u-tokyo.ac.jp

The task of detecting seismic slow earthquakes is challenging. Both LFE and tremor are observed in the 1–10 Hz frequency band (Obara, 2002), and the frequency band of VLFE is between 0.02 and 0.05 Hz (Ide *et al.*, 2007; Ito *et al.*, 2007). In addition, the amplitudes of LFE and tremor are less than 1 mm/s in surface stations of Shikoku, Japan (Ide, 2008), and sometimes these events may have the same amplitude level as the background noise. Another issue is that some deep LFE and tectonic tremor waveforms may present no clear *P*- and *S*-wave onsets in the Shikoku area (Obara, 2002), and their waveforms are similar to those of noise.

Several detection techniques have been developed to systematically identify and extract tremor signals in seismic data. One of the most commonly used methods to detect tremor activity is the envelope cross-correlation method, which estimates the correlation between the root mean square (RMS) envelopes from different stations to obtain the distribution of the arrival times of tremors (Obara, 2002).

Another method that has proven useful for detecting seismic slow earthquake waveforms is the template matching (or matched filter) algorithm (Gibbons and Ringdal, 2006; Shelly *et al.*, 2007). This method computes the correlation coefficient between a seismic trace and a master signal (template) to search for waveforms similar to the template within the trace. Detections are declared when the correlation coefficient surpasses a user-defined threshold value. Shelly *et al.* (2007) applied this technique to detect LFE waveforms in the seismic traces of Hi-net stations in Shikoku, Japan. With this implementation, they demonstrated that tectonic tremors can be considered as a swarm of LFE.

The performance of the template matching algorithm depends on the waveform used to perform the search. Because many earthquake event catalogs are available, a template matching algorithm can be applied relatively easily. A strong disadvantage of template matching is the lack of generalization of this method, that is, it cannot identify events that are not similar to template signals. For this reason, there has been active research toward the improvement of template matching, focusing on the development of methods to create template catalogs using machine learning. Mu *et al.* (2018) applied convolutional neural networks (CNNs) to identify earthquake signals for template matching algorithms. Senobari *et al.* (2024) estimate the autocorrelation between signals enabling to apply template matching algorithm without the need of templates. Although these methods improve the performance of template matching, some issues arise when mapping traces with low signal-to-noise ratio (SNR). In addition, current methodologies that improve template matching performance for detecting slow earthquakes signals are still in research (Senobari *et al.*, 2024).

In the context of seismic slow earthquake detection, it may also be plausible to apply template matching using tremor waveform templates. As mentioned earlier, Shelly *et al.* (2007) demonstrated that LFE may be considered as the "building blocks" of tremor. The origin of the LFE associated with tremor is presumably due to shear slip in the interface between plates in the subduction zones (Ide *et al.*, 2007; Shelly *et al.*, 2007; Kato and Nakagawa, 2020). Therefore, in this study, we present a method for creating catalogs of template signals of tectonic tremors with nonfixed time lengths that can be used along with template matching. We called this method You Only Search Once (YOSO), and it consists of three steps: (1) we detect the events in band-pass-filtered seismic traces between 1 and 10 Hz using an RMS amplitude detector, (2) the algorithm estimates the duration of each event by calculating the slopes of the RMS amplitude decay curves, and (3) we use hierarchical clustering (Murtagh and Contreras, 2011) to separate the detections into different event families. We used the maximum amplitude of the detections, the duration of the detections, and the correlation coefficient between detections as metrics to cluster them. In addition, we calculate uniform manifold approximation and projection (UMAP) graphs (McInnes *et al.*, 2020) to visually distinguish cluster distributions in low-dimensional spaces.

We applied the YOSO method to seismic records from the Hi-net station in central Shikoku, Japan, and compare our generated catalogs with existent catalogs. Our results show that the proposed framework might be useful for creating template catalogs of both LFE and tremor. In addition, we show that tremor sequences may be identified by template-based methods.

Methods

The YOSO method attempts to build template catalogs of waveforms associated with tectonic tremors without prior identification in recordings from inland seismometers. The method comprises three stages: event detection, estimation of the duration of each detection, and event classification (Fig. 1a).

In the detection stage, the algorithm calculates the RMS in moving windows throughout the seismic trace to obtain the signal envelope (Fig. 1b). The RMS method is a common procedure in seismology: it is implemented in the frequency-scanning method for earthquake detection (Sit *et al.*, 2012; Katakami *et al.*, 2017) and used for the identification of microseismicity in volcanic environments (Castañeda-Bastida, 2018). We calculate RMS using time windows of 1.0 s with 50% overlap. Subsequently, we use a peak detection algorithm (Duarte and Watanabe, 2021) to identify the peaks above the threshold. In this step, we retrieve all the signals associated with RMS peaks that surpass a predefined amplitude threshold. The threshold is set as twice the median absolute deviation (MAD) value of the RMS envelope, and the peaks are identified within time windows of 2.5 s to avoid close detection duplicates due to neighbor peaks.

Once the algorithm detects events, it estimates the duration of each detection by calculating RMS amplitude decay curves (or RMS curves). These curves keep track of the change in RMS in different time windows. We define a set of window sizes that

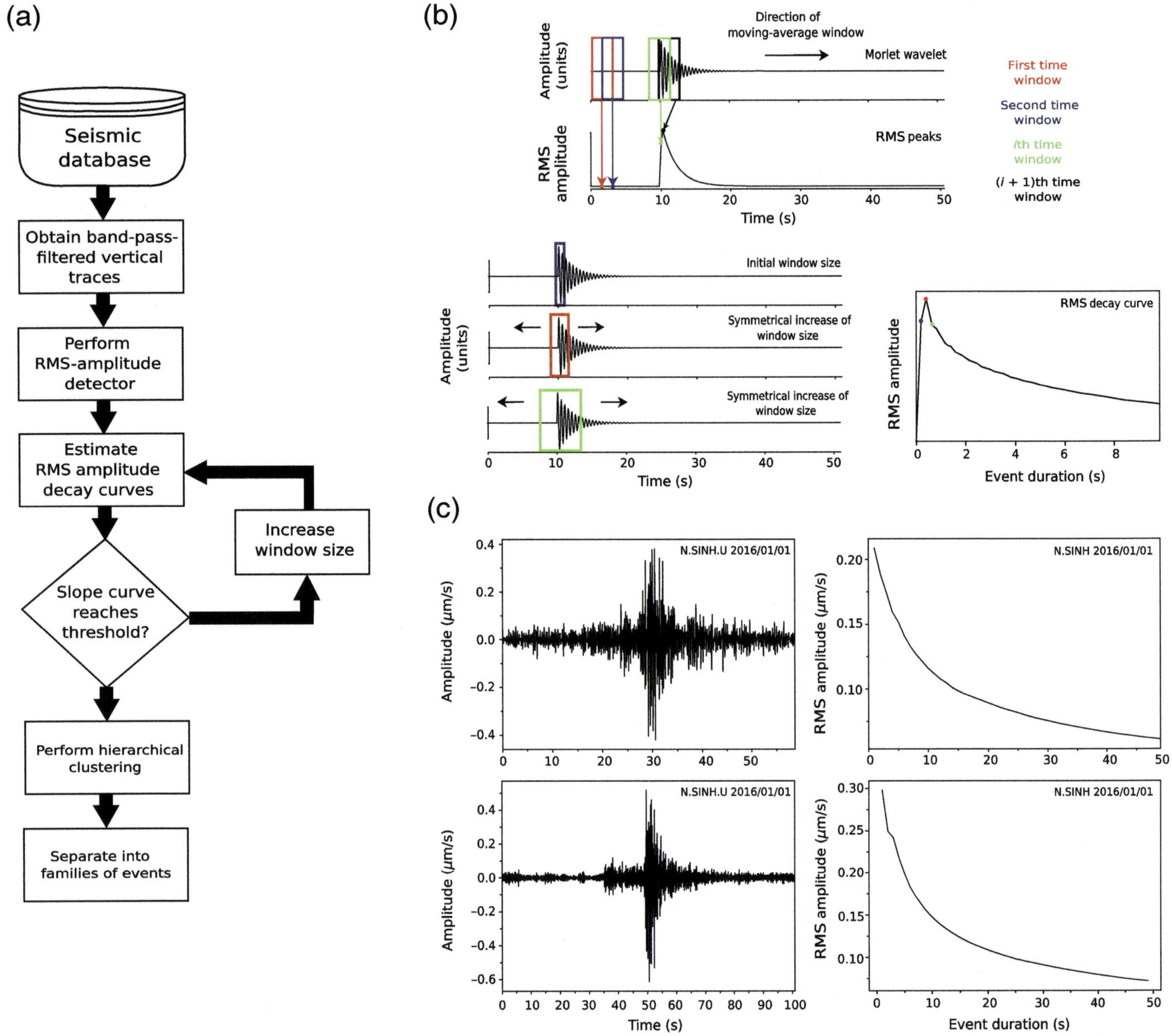

Figure 1. (a) Flowchart of the You Only Search Once (YOSO) method. (b) Scheme of the YOSO procedure applied on a dummy waveform. First, we run a detector that keeps track of the changes in the root mean square (RMS) amplitude of the filtered trace. Each color in the trace corresponds to different time windows, and the RMS peaks are plotted in the same colors as their corresponding window. Next, we determine the duration of each event by estimating the RMS amplitude decay. Each color corresponds to a different time-window length, and the colors are associated with the color point on the right side of the figure. The black arrows indicate the direction of increase in windows. (c) Examples of RMS decay curves associated with two observed events.

range from 10 to 500 s to create the RMS curves. The center of all windows is the time position of the maximum RMS amplitude, previously obtained in the detection stage. To create the curves, we iteratively calculate the RMS of each detection by retrieving portions of the event with the same size as each element of the window set (Fig. 1c).

The algorithm estimates the duration of each event by estimating the slope of the RMS curves. Assuming that each envelope peak is associated with a seismic event, the signal energy decreases proportionally with an increase in the searched time window until the amplitude values approach the mean amplitude of the trace. Hence, the energy must follow a decay proportional to the decay of the RMS of the form $A_{\mathrm{RMS}}(t) = A_{\max(\mathrm{RMS})}\exp(-bt)$ in the absence of any other signal or high-amplitude noise near the detection. If the slope of the curve is close to zero, the RMS is no longer associated with the signal. For this reason, the duration corresponds to the point where the slope of RMS decay curve is below a threshold value.

The threshold of the RMS curve slope ranges from 10^{-16} to 10^{-9}, allowing the retrieval of long-duration signals (~500 s) to shorter duration signals (up to 10 s), respectively. We found by trial and error that the slope threshold of 10^{-15} retrieves signals between 50 and 400 s (see Fig. S1, available in the supplemental material to this article).

In the third stage, the algorithm separates the detections into families of events. The RMS maps the amplitude changes of the seismic trace, and the peaks correspond to signals unrelated to the trace mean values. Thus, the algorithm retrieves events without knowledge of their origin. LFE and tremors have amplitude values above the mean amplitude of the trace. However, local and regional earthquakes, anthropogenic activity, landslides, and ocean–ocean interaction may be present in the detections. For this reason, in the clustering stage we attempt to separate the events into different groups by means of a common metric between these.

YOSO method classifies events by applying hierarchical agglomerative clustering (Benvegna *et al.*, 2011, 2013; Mullner, 2011; Murtagh and Contreras, 2011; Steinke *et al.*, 2023; Yates *et al.*, 2023). To perform clustering, we set measures to quantify the relationship between events: amplitude ratio, duration ratio, and correlation coefficient.

Consider two detections obtained in previous stages, E_i and E_j. The amplitude ratio (AR) is defined as

$$\mathrm{AR}_{ij} = \frac{\min(\max(\mathrm{RMS}(E_i)), \max(\mathrm{RMS}(E_j)))}{\max(\max(\mathrm{RMS}(E_i)), \max(\mathrm{RMS}(E_j)))}, \quad (1)$$

in which $\max(\mathrm{RMS}(E_i))$ is the maximum RMS peak value of E_i, and $\max(\mathrm{RMS}(E_j))$ is the maximum RMS peak value of E_j. The form of equation (1) is set to constrain the AR values in the interval [0,1]. Similarly, we define the event duration ratio (DR) as

$$\mathrm{DR}_{ij} = \frac{\min(T_i, T_j)}{\max(T_i, T_j)}, \quad (2)$$

in which T_i is the duration of E_i, and T_j is the duration of E_j. Because E_i and E_j have different lengths, the denominator in equation (2) corresponds to the event with the longest duration between E_i and E_j to constrain the DR range within [0,1]. Finally, the cross-correlation coefficient is defined as (Gibbons and Ringdal, 2006)

$$\mathrm{CC} = \max(\mathrm{CC}) = \max\left(\frac{\sum_{i=1}^{N_s} E_i E_{j-k}}{\sqrt{\sum_{i=1}^{M} E_i E_i}\sqrt{\sum_{i=1}^{N} E_j E_j}}\right), \quad (3)$$

in which M and N are the lengths of E_i and E_j, N_s is the number of samples of the event with the shortest length between E_i and E_j, and k is the time lag between E_i and E_j. In equation (3), E_j has shorter duration than E_i, but the order can be interchangeable and depends on the duration of each event.

The correlation coefficient measures the similarity between two signals, whereas the dissimilarity score measures the difference between two data sets (Benvegna *et al.*, 2011, 2013; Yates *et al.*, 2023). The dissimilarity scores are distance estimations between values of a chosen measure (AR, DR, and CC) in a spatial dimension. Thus, we use the results obtained from equations (1)–(3) to estimate dissimilarity scores matrices. We use the correlation distance (Székely *et al.*, 2007):

$$c = 1 - \frac{(\mathbf{x} - \bar{\mathbf{x}}) \cdot (\mathbf{y} - \bar{\mathbf{y}})}{\|(\mathbf{x} - \bar{\mathbf{x}})\|_2 \|(\mathbf{y} - \bar{\mathbf{y}})\|_2}, \quad (4)$$

as the dissimilarity score, in which $\mathbf{x}$ and $\mathbf{y}$ are two different vectors obtained from the measure matrix, $\bar{\mathbf{x}}$ and $\bar{\mathbf{y}}$ indicate the mean of $\mathbf{x}$ and $\mathbf{y}$, respectively, and $\mathbf{x} \cdot \mathbf{y}$ is the dot product between $\mathbf{x}$ and $\mathbf{y}$. The dissimilarity score matrix is decomposed into several row vectors to estimate the distance value from a matrix of observations. The distance is zero if $\mathbf{x}$ and $\mathbf{y}$ are independent, and the second term of equation (4) is somehow similar to Pearson's correlation coefficient formula (Székely *et al.*, 2007).

Using the dissimilarity score matrices, the algorithm separates the detections into different families of events using hierarchical clustering, which is an unsupervised machine learning algorithm used in classification problems. In hierarchical clustering, each data set element is considered as a cluster or singleton node. These elements are then agglomerated into clusters of more elements, merging them into families of elements based on statistical distance metrics that measure the proximity between one event/cluster and another until a single cluster is reached (Bar-Joseph *et al.*, 2001; Mullner, 2011; Murtagh and Contreras, 2011; Yates *et al.*, 2023). The hyperparameter that controls the separation between events is the clustering threshold.

Common methods for hierarchical clustering include the following: single linkage, ward linkage, average linkage, and complete linkage (Mullner, 2011; Murtagh and Contreras, 2011). The differences among these methods lie in the choice of the interconnecting distance between the elements within the cluster and the distance between the two elements of different clusters. Single linkage considers the minimum distance between two dissimilarity values between clusters, complete linkage considers the maximum interconnecting dissimilarity, average linkage considers the mean interconnecting values, and ward linkage considers the interconnecting distance between two centroids (Mullner, 2011). The association is based on pairwise distance matrices between data set elements. Statistical metrics such as Euclidean, cosine, and correlation distances are used to build distance matrices (Mullner, 2011). We regard the dissimilarity score matrix as the distance matrix. After trial and error, we determine that by setting the clustering threshold at the 30th percentile of the dissimilarity score values, we obtain clearer cluster structures when using this value.

In addition, we applied the UMAP method (McInnes *et al.*, 2020), a dimensionality reduction technique that generates "fuzzy" topological structures in lower dimensions, facilitating a visual representation of the cluster distribution. We need to define two parameters to generate UMAP graphs: the number of nearest-neighbors N_{nn} and the minimum distance between

TABLE 1

Parameters Used in the You Only Search Once (YOSO) Method for Retrieving Template Events from Seismic Traces Recorded from 1 January 2016

Hyperparameter	Value
RMS window size	1.0 s
RMS window overlap	50%
RMS threshold	2 * MAD (envelope)
RMS slope threshold	10^{-15}
Clustering threshold	30th percentile of correlation distance

MAD, median absolute deviation; RMS, root mean square.

data points d_{min}. N_{nn} balances the global and local representations of the data set in lower dimensions. A small N_{nn} value implies a local structure, whereas higher values depict the general distribution of the data. d_{min} determines the distance between data points in the lower dimensions (McInnes *et al.*, 2020). A small d_{min} results in more data points being associated with each feature in the lower dimensions. We set N_{nn} to 5 and d_{min} to 0.5 because we obtain more balance between local and global topological structure of score data.

We applied the YOSO method using synthetic data to evaluate the performance of the RMS detector and the ability of YOSO to estimate durations tracking the RMS decay. Synthetic data were generated using the Brownian Walk model (Ide, 2008). Subsequently, we applied the YOSO procedure to the continuous seismic traces recorded by the Hi-net stations N.SINH, N.IKWH, and N.SJOH and F-net broadband station N.OKWF, which operates in Shikoku (Fig. 2) (Okada *et al.*, 2004; Obara *et al.*, 2005). We present the results obtained using the vertical seismic traces due to the presence of the *P* wave, which aids in identifying local/regional earthquake sources. However, YOSO method is not restricted to only using the vertical channel, and it is also applied to the rest of the channels to retrieve the templates (see Fig. S6).

After we identified the events using the YOSO method, we applied the amplitude source model (Battaglia and Aki, 2003) to obtain the epicenter distribution of the detections. We obtained the detections from eight Hi-net stations (N.SINH, N.SADH, N.IKWH, N.MTYH, N.KYDH, N.MKIH, N.AYKH, and N.MNOH) (Fig. 2). The obtained distribution is an approximate estimation because of the high uncertainty of the model to locate point sources. This model assumes that the signal amplitude follows an exponential decay of amplitude, which is mainly controlled by geometrical spreading. We assume the sources are distributed in a grid with latitude and longitude increments of 0.01° that cover the entire Shikoku area at a fixed depth of 30 km (Fig. 2). As misfit function, we use the mean square error function (MSE). In an attempt to improve the results and following the original procedure from Battaglia and Aki (2003), we apply gradient descent algorithm (Tarantola, 2005) to the initial solutions of the grid search. We set the central frequency to 4.5 Hz and *S*-wave propagation velocity to 3.5 km/s. We associated the detections across stations by estimating the theoretical arrival times of *S*-wave propagation through a homogeneous medium. Seismic events associated with only two stations were excluded. The solutions were obtained using a path-averaged intrinsic quality factor for *S*-waves (Q) value of 336. This value has been reported in previous research works related to depth-dependence attenuation (Yabe *et al.*, 2014; Yabe and Ide, 2014) for crustal layers at depths below 50 km.

Results

We tested the performance of the detection and duration estimation stages of the YOSO method by applying it to synthetic data. For this purpose, we used synthetic tremor signals obtained by the Brownian Walk model (Ide, 2008). Following Ide (2008), we used an *S*-wave velocity of 4000 m/s, rigidity modulus μ of 40 GPa, characteristic damping α of 0.02 1/s, diffusion coefficient σ of 400 $m/s^{1/2}$, and radius of the circular fault of 40 km as parameters. These values produce synthetic tremors with a constant moment rate of 5×10^{12} $N \cdot m/s$, which agrees with the moment rate estimated from observed data (Ide, 2008).

The results obtained using synthetic data are shown in Figure 3. The upper panel in Figure 3a shows the synthetic seismogram filtered in the frequency range of 2–8 Hz, and the lower panel in Figure 3a shows the RMS peaks calculated from the synthetic seismogram. Each dot corresponds to the time position of each detection. These detections were obtained using the double of the mean of the RMS peaks as a threshold. This threshold value was set after several tests with the YOSO method using different threshold values and aims to retrieve low-SNR signals. Figure 3b shows all the RMS curves associated with detections in Figure 3a. The RMS curve slope threshold was set to 10^{-7} to determine the duration. We observe that most of the RMS curves harshly decrease near 100 s. In contrast, the decrease of RMS amplitudes is slower for the curves associated with high-RMS amplitudes. The detections are highlighted in red in Figure 3c. All detections are constrained in between durations of 10 and 120 s, and most of these have a duration of around 40 s. (Fig. 3d). This distribution may shift to detections with higher duration when relaxing the RMS curve threshold (see Fig. S1).

We applied the YOSO method to the 24-hr vertical seismic trace of the Hi-net stations in eastern Shikoku (Fig. 2) from 1 January 2016. From here, we focus on the results obtained from the Hi-net station N.SINH, and the results from the rest of the stations are displayed in Figures S3–S8. Figure 4 displays the results obtained by applying the YOSO method. We identified 169 events using YOSO for durations between 10 and 490 s. The hyperparameters used to obtain the detections are listed in Table 1. At this stage, local and regional earthquakes, slow earthquakes, and noise may be obtained after running the

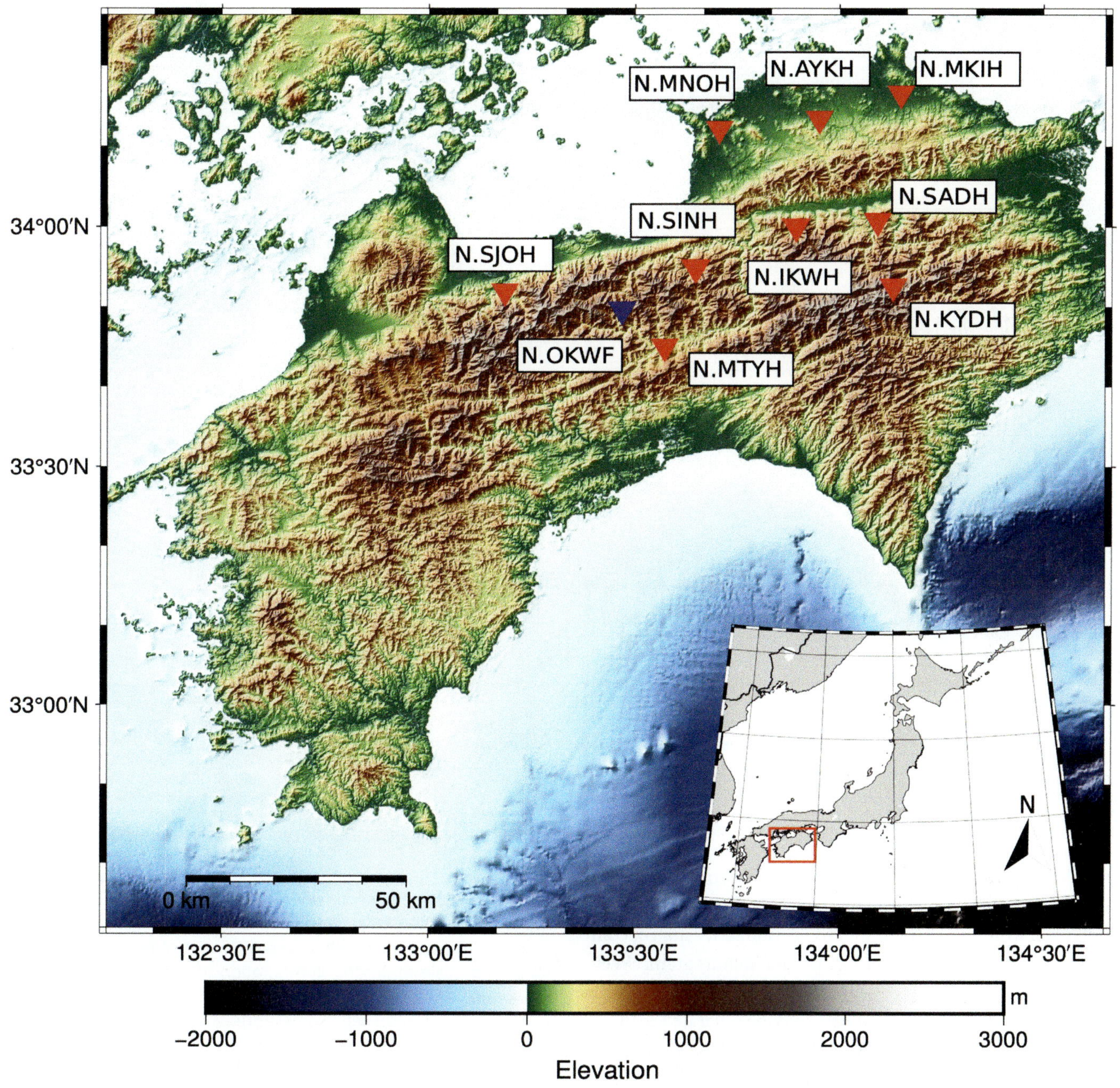

Figure 2. Map of Shikoku area. The inset shows the relative position of Shikoku to Japan. The red inverted triangles point to the locations of Hi-net stations, and the blue inverted triangle shows the position of the F-net broadband stations.

RMS detector. The detection rate depends on the amplitude and the RMS window size. Therefore, in the RMS decay curves (Fig. 4c), we used a semilogarithmic scale to better observe their behavior. We used trial time window sizes between 10 and 500 s, but the curves were truncated to half the duration (up to 250 s). Most of the curves exhibit smooth decay, with amplitudes ranging between 0.01 and 0.1 μm/s. An increase of the size of the RMS window and the RMS detector threshold reduces the probability of obtaining noise. However, this also increases the probability of missing small events. The estimated duration of each detection depends entirely on the slope threshold (see Figs. S1 and S2). Conversely, the amplitude may not follow a decrease when the duration increases for some RMS slopes, resulting in errors in the duration estimation.

At this point, identifying the type of event retrieved using this method is challenging. Consequently, we classified the signals using hierarchical clustering. Figure 5 illustrates the distribution of event families after applying hierarchical clustering for detection. We used average linkage on the dissimilarity score matrix using AR as the clustering metric. The dendrogram shows that the observations have been separated into six clusters with correlation distances below 0.2 (Fig. 5a).

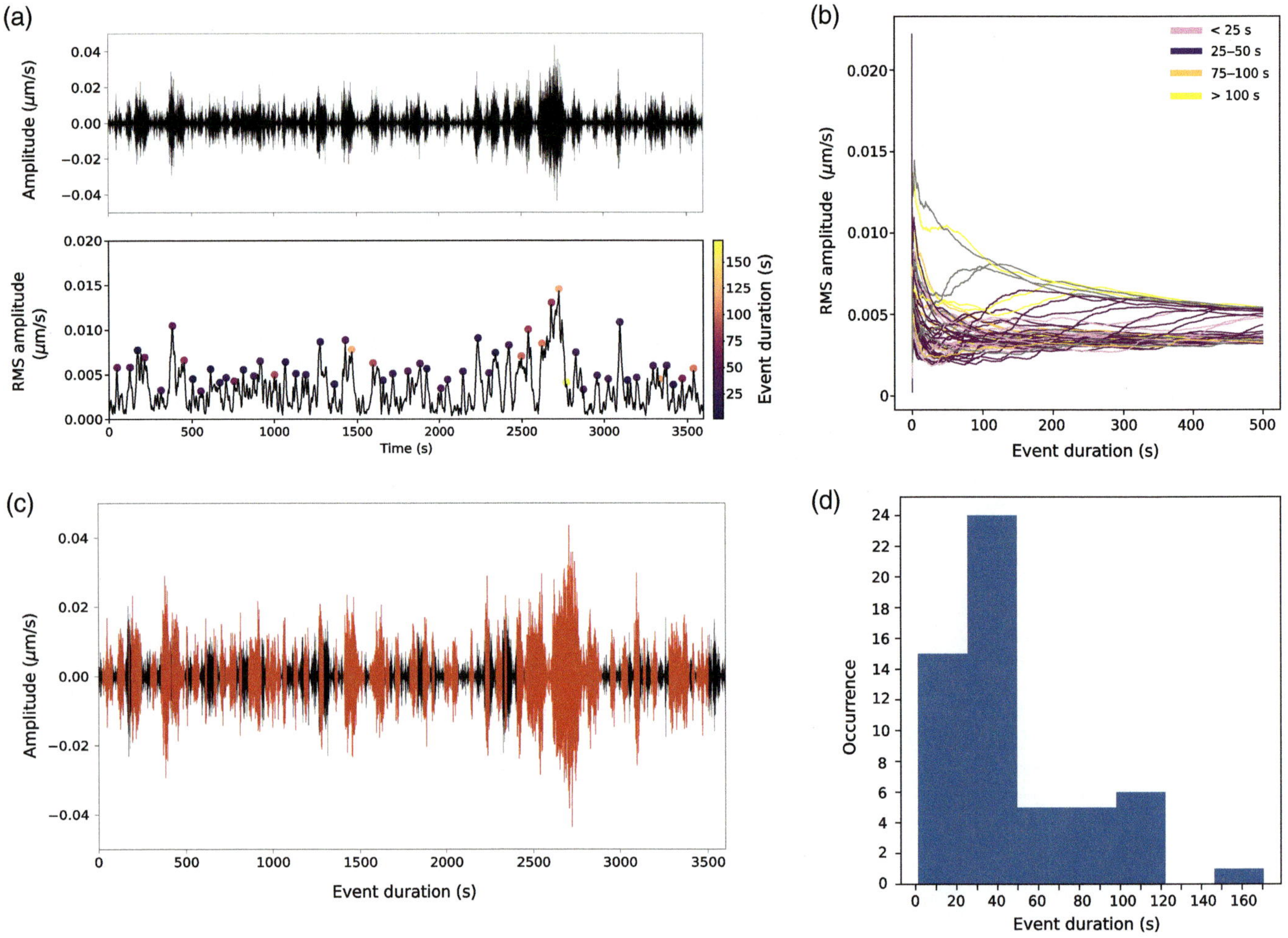

Figure 3. (a) Upper panel: Synthetic seismogram created using the Brownian Walk model for slow earthquakes (Ide, 2008). Lower panel: RMS peaks calculated from the synthetic seismogram. Each dot is associated with a detected event obtained by YOSO. The color scale represents the duration of each event. (b) RMS decay curves calculated from the detections obtained in Figure 1a. Each color represents a duration range. (c) Detections (red signals) retrieved from the synthetic seismograms for which duration is estimated by the RMS amplitude decay curves shown in Figure 1b. (d) Histogram of the retrieved events from the synthetic seismogram.

The dissimilarity matrix values (Fig. 5b) were sorted according to the leaves in the dendrogram shown in Figure 5a. Hence, each pixel from top to bottom of the dissimilarity matrix coincides with the value presented in the dendrogram. Well-defined patterns of low dissimilarity were observed within the matrix, indicating that the data may be separated into signals of varying amplitudes (Fig. 5b). One of these clusters has an element with a dissimilarity score of 0.2, corresponding to the event with the highest amplitude within the trace. A total of 5–6 clusters were obtained per station. The mean duration of all events is ~150 s, and most events were within the range of 100–200 s. The distribution differs slightly at the N.OKWF station, where more events within the 200–300 s range were recovered. This may reflect a higher uncertainty in the duration estimation for the waveforms at this station. The N.OKWF station belongs to the broadband F-net network, meaning that this station is installed on the surface and is more susceptible to recording background and anthropogenic noise than the rest of the stations (see Figs. S2–S5).

The corresponding UMAP plots of the data set are depicted in Figure 5c,d. Each UMAP is associated with the number of each cluster and amplitude distribution, respectively. We observe well-defined data clusters in the UMAP plot associated with low dissimilarity scores (<0.2) and coincides with the number of clusters shown in Figure 5a. Although some points with high dissimilarity scores were also present within certain clusters, this UMAP structure suggests our data set can be clustered using an amplitude-based metric. This can be observed in Figure 5d where we have the same cluster distribution but with the amplitude values.

Figure 6 displays the boxplots associated with the amplitude and duration values per cluster, and some examples of the waveforms associated with two clusters. We observe a clear separation of events with amplitudes in the range of 0.1–1 μm/s. This

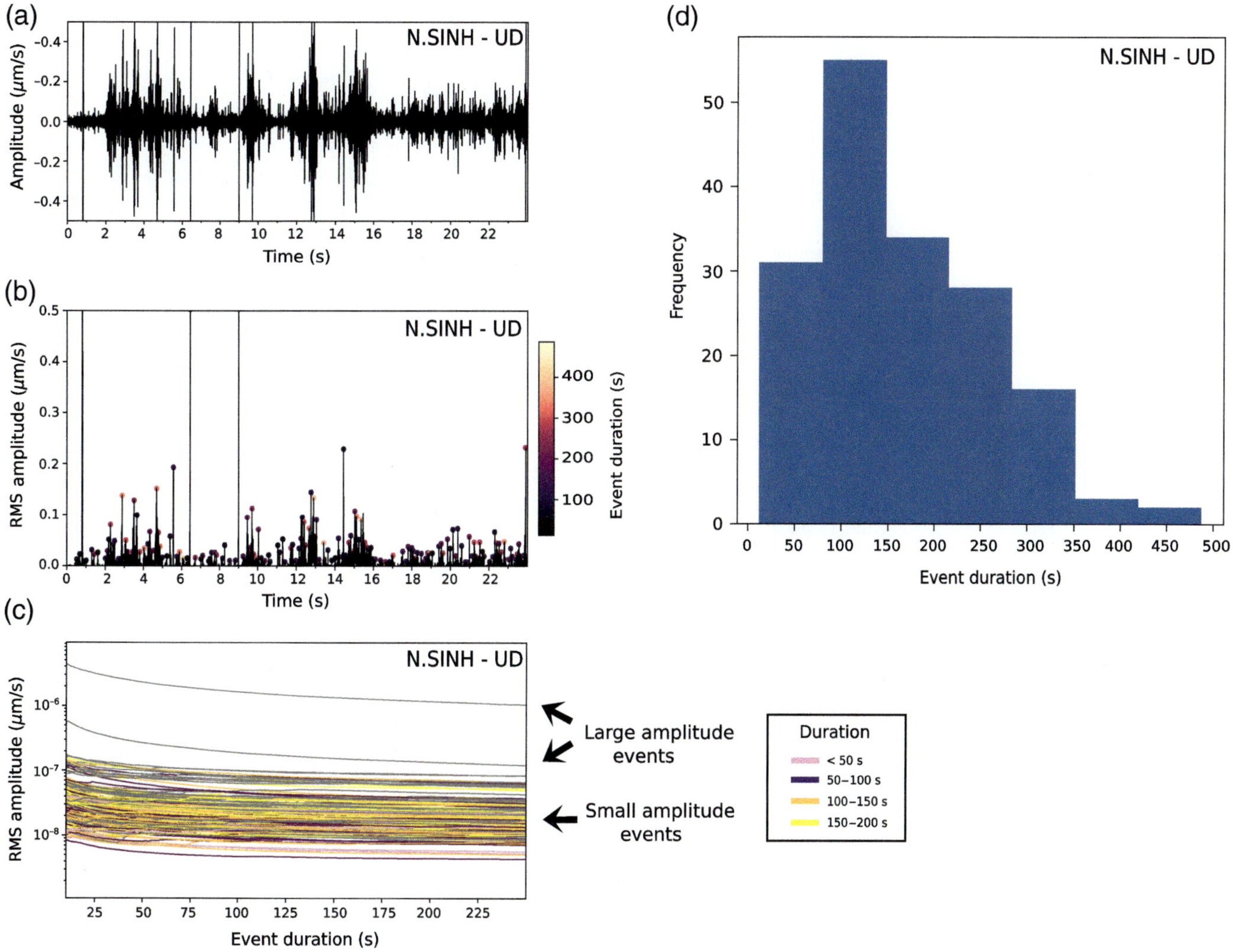

Figure 4. (a) 24-hr-long-filtered (2–8 Hz) vertical seismic record of N.SINH station from 1 January 2016. (b) RMS peaks associated with the trace. The dots represent detections, and the color scale is associated with its duration. The RMS envelope was obtained using windows of 1.0 s with a 50% overlap; the RMS detector threshold was set at twice the mean absolute deviation value of the envelope. (c) RMS decay curves associated with the detections of the N.SINH station. The horizontal axis represents the half-duration of each trial duration. The RMS decay curves threshold was set to 10^{-15}. (d) Histogram of detections obtained using the YOSO method, with each bin representing time-window increments between 40 and 60 s. The gray color in (b,c) indicates events with durations outside the duration range.

range may broaden to 0.001–10 μm/s depending on the observation point (see Figs. S2–S4). We observe that the total duration of the waveforms lies between 100 and 400 s, but some outliers may appear with durations outside this range (Fig. 6b). At this point, we suggest that most of the tremor-related waveforms lie between clusters C2 and C5 for amplitude-based classification. C1 and C5 are related to events with the highest and lowest amplitudes that may be related to local and regional earthquakes and noise, respectively.

We also applied the YOSO method using the CC and DR values, and the results are shown in Figure 7. The dissimilarity scores associated with CC range between 0.6 and 1.0, with an average of 0.48 and a standard deviation of 0.35. These results reveal a predominance of high dissimilarity scores, indicating significant waveform shape variations and complicating the clustering process. The UMAP plot does not show an evident distinction between observations (Fig. 7c, upper panel). Conversely, the distribution of scores associated with the DR exhibits well-defined patterns. The mean correlation distance was ~0.014, with a standard deviation of 0.08. The UMAP plots reveal a distribution of six clusters (Fig. 7c,d). And, similar to the AR, these also can be separated in using duration ranges. For duration-based clustering, the tremor waveforms may lie in clusters C3–C5. In contrast, the UMAP plots of CC values show a scattered distribution of events with no clear distinction of CC families (Fig. 7c, lower panel). We must emphasize that the YOSO method is not applied to the vertical channel only. We have also applied the YOSO method to both horizontal channels (see Fig. S6), obtaining the same clustering distribution as the vertical trace.

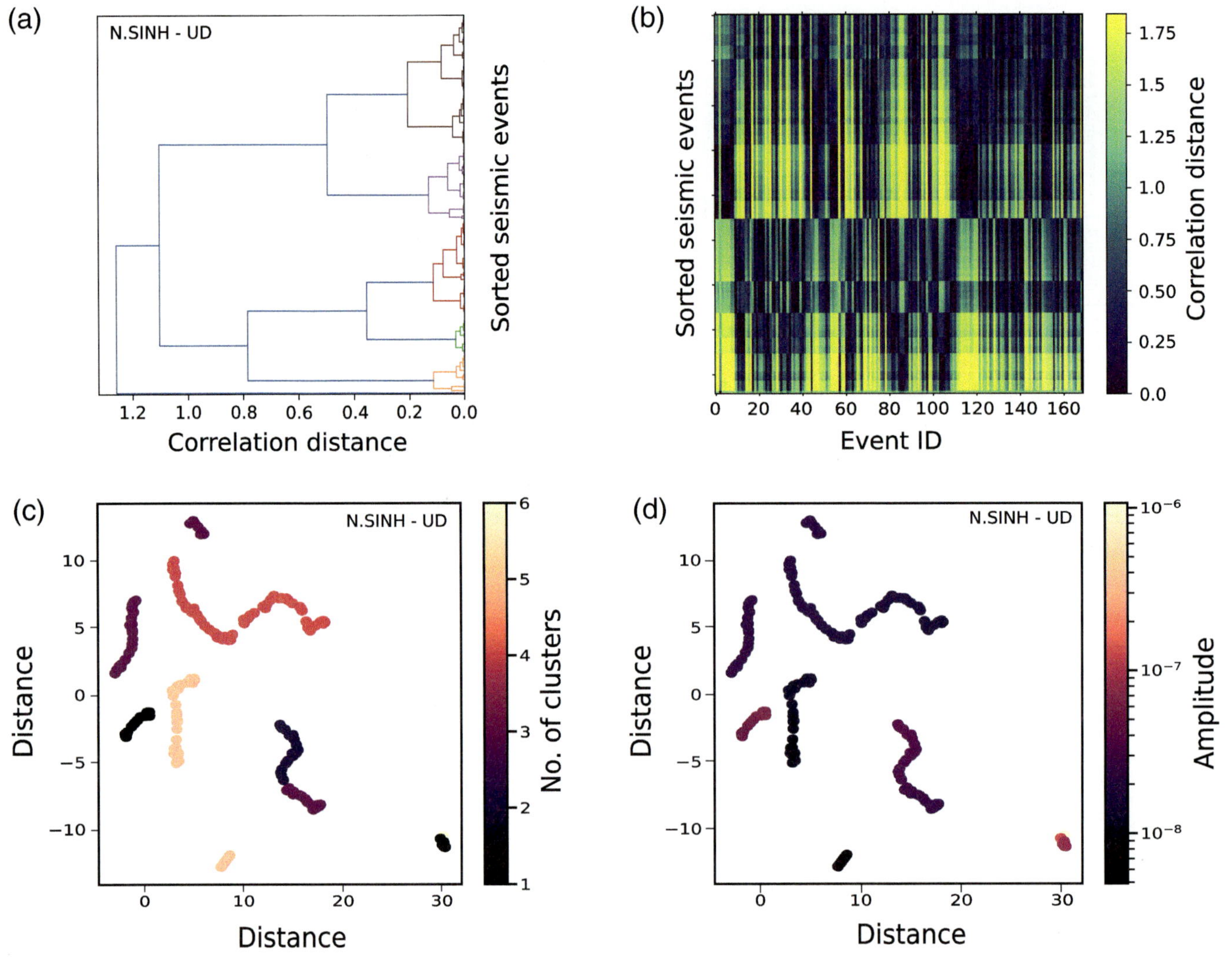

Figure 5. (a) Dendrogram, (b) sorted dissimilarity matrix, (c) uniform manifold approximation and projection (UMAP) plot associated with the detections, and (d) the same as (c) but showing the RMS amplitude values of the detections instead of the number of clusters. The observations were obtained from 1 January 2016 vertical trace of the station N.SINH.

Thus far, we have qualitatively evaluated the separation of the detections into clusters, but this approach alone is insufficient to determine the optimal separation of data set elements into clusters. Therefore, we evaluated the clustering performance using metrics that assess the distance between elements within each cluster relative to the separation between clusters. These metrics are the Silhouette score (Rousseeuw, 1987), the Davis–Bouldin score (Davies and Bouldin, 1979), and the Calinski–Harabasz score (Calinski and Harabasz, 1972).

The choice of these scores is based on the absence of ground-truth detections to validate the clustering results. We provide a brief description of each score as follows: considering two clusters, C_i and C_j, the Silhouette score (S) (Rousseeuw, 1987; Pedregosa *et al.*, 2011) is defined as

$$S = \frac{\bar{b} - \bar{a}}{\max(\bar{a},\bar{b})}, \tag{5}$$

in which $\bar{a}$ is the mean distance between the elements of cluster C_i, and $\bar{b}$ is the mean distance of the elements of C_i to the elements of the nearest cluster C_j. The score, normalized to the maximum distance between $\bar{a}$ and $\bar{b}$, ranges from −1 to 1. The data set can be separated into well-defined clusters if the S value approaches to 1. Because S approaches zero, the data set may be composed of overlapping clusters, resulting in no clear cluster distribution.

The Davies–Bouldin score (DB) (Davies and Bouldin, 1979; Pedregosa *et al.*, 2011),

$$DB = \frac{1}{k}\sum_{i=1}^{k} \max_{i \neq j} R_{ij}, \tag{6}$$

$$R_{ij} = \frac{s_i + s_j}{d_{ij}}, \tag{7}$$

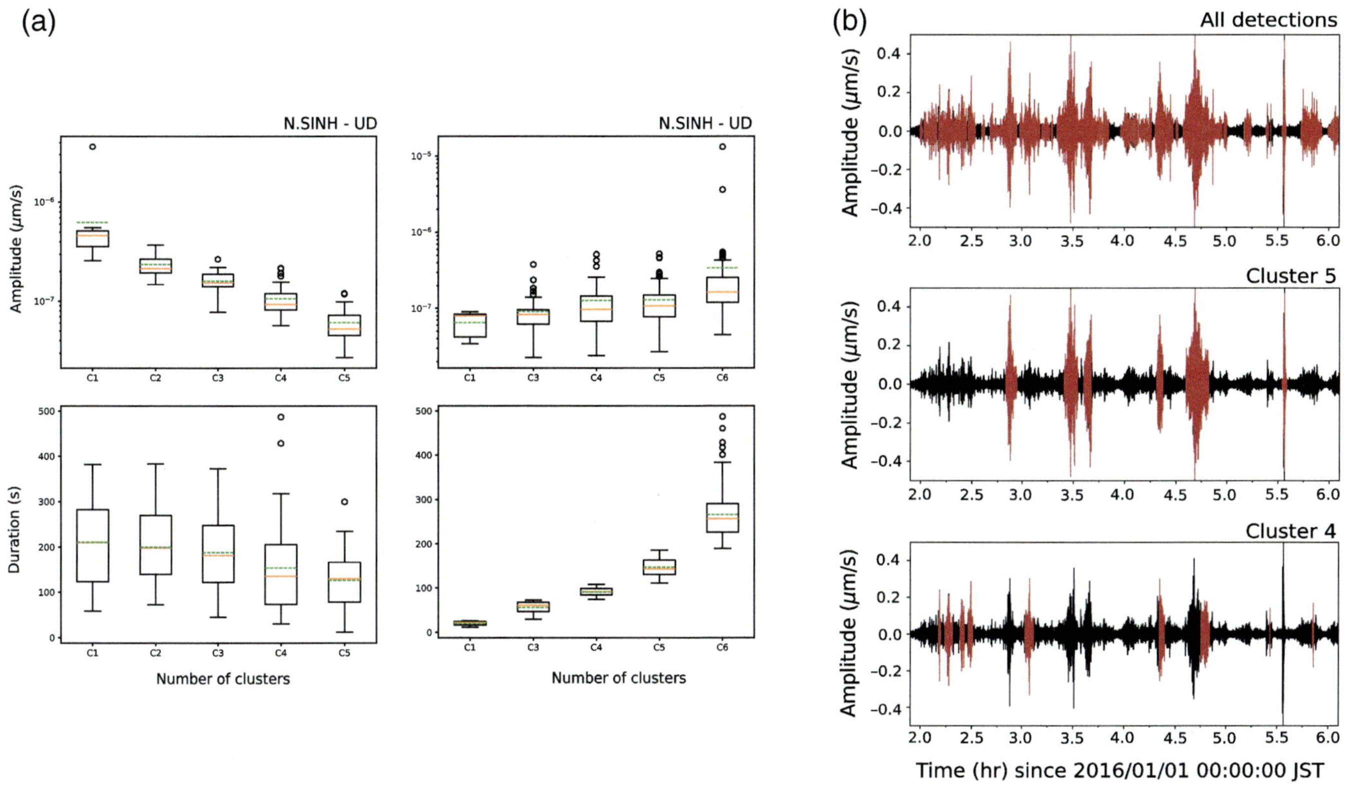

Figure 6. (a) Boxplots associated with the clusters obtained from the vertical trace of station N.SINH from 1 January 2016. The left column corresponds to the clusters using the amplitude ratio (AR) value, and the right column corresponds to the clusters obtained from duration ratio (DR) value. (b) Detections obtained from the vertical trace of station N.SINH from 1 January 2016 02:00:00–06:00:00 JST. The waveforms highlighted in red indicate detection. All detections are shown in the upper panel, and the detections associated with clusters 4 and 5 are shown in the middle and lower panels, respectively.

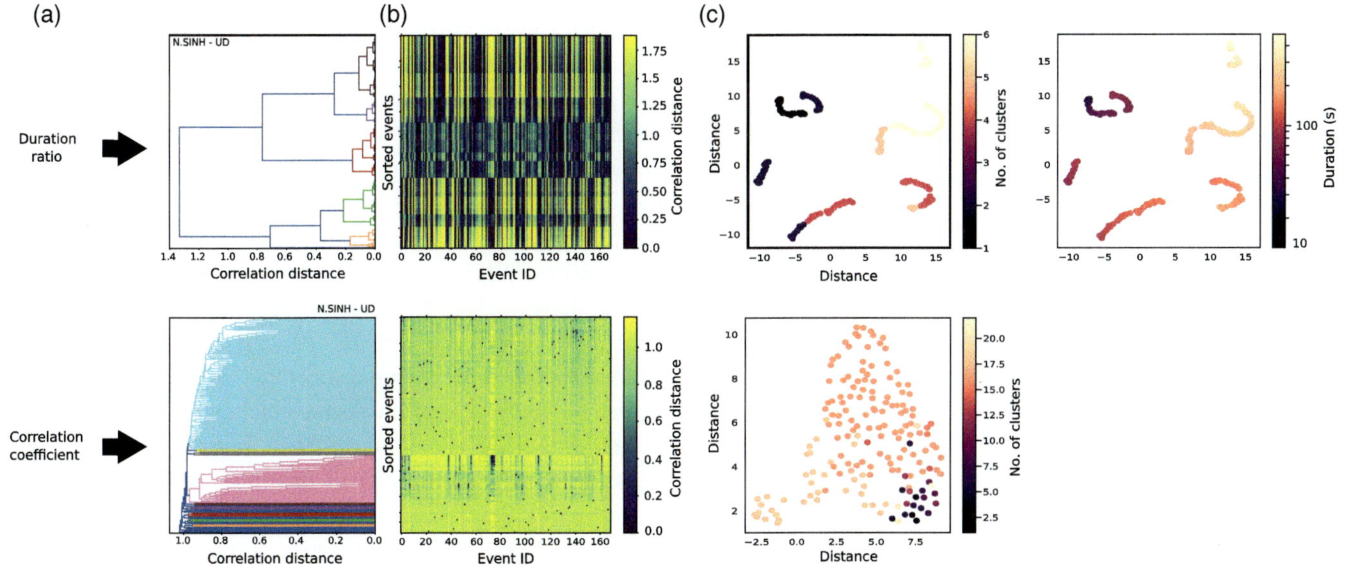

Figure 7. (a) Dendrogram, (b) sorted heat map associated with the dissimilarity matrix, and (c) UMAP plots using DR (upper row) and correlation coefficient (CC) (lower row) at station N.SINH obtained from 1 January 2016 trace.

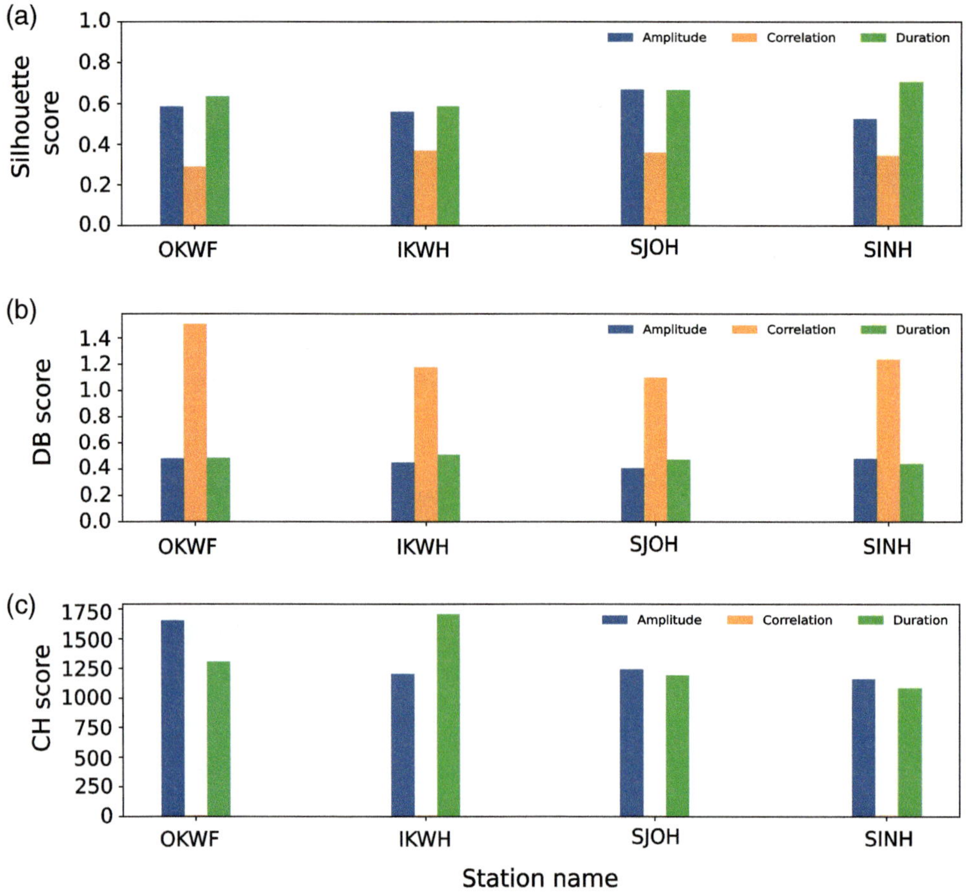

Figure 8. (a) Silhouette, (b) Davies–Bouldin, and (c) Calinski–Harabasz scores of the clusters associated with detections from stations N.SINH, N.OKWH, N.IKWH, and N.SJOH recorded on 1 January 2016. These scores were calculated using AR (blue), CC (orange), and DR (green) values.

in which R_{ij} is defined as the similarity between two clusters, and k is the number of clusters. R_{ij} is dependent on the average distance s_i from elements within C_i to the cluster centroid and the distance d_{ij} between C_i and C_j. We estimate the Euclidean distance to measure the distance between clusters. Note that this distance is different from the one used to separate the detections in the clustering scheme. The lower the DB score the better the data set separation into clusters. Finally, the Calinski–Harabasz score (CH) (Calinski and Harabasz, 1972; Pedregosa *et al.*, 2011) is defined as

$$\mathrm{CH} = \frac{tr(B_k)}{tr(W_k)} \times \frac{n_E - k}{k - 1}, \tag{8}$$

$$B_k = \sum_{i=1}^{k} n_i (c_i - c_E)(c_i - c_E)^T, \tag{9}$$

$$W_k = \sum_{i=1}^{k} \sum_{x \in C_i} (c_i - c_E)(c_i - c_E)^T, \tag{10}$$

in which B_k and W_k represent the between- and within-cluster dispersion matrices, respectively. Here, c_i denotes the centroid of cluster C_i, and C_E is the centroid of data set E. This score, also known as the variance ratio criterion (Calinski and Harabasz, 1972; Pedregosa *et al.*, 2011), is used to evaluate the dispersion of elements within clusters and that in the overall cluster distribution. High CH scores indicate effective clustering.

Figure 8 shows the S, DB, and CH scores estimated from the clustering distribution of the YOSO method using the records from Hi-net stations N.SINH, N.SJOH, N.IKWH, and the F-net station N.OKWH. Using AR, the S, DB, and CH range from 0.52–0.66, 0.40–0.47, and 1160–1652, respectively. Using DR, the scores range from 0.58–0.70, 0.44–0.50, and 1085–1706, respectively. And using CC, the scores were 0.28–0.34, 1.09–1.50, and 7.12–8.45, respectively. A visual inspection of Figure 8 and the reported S, CH, and DB ranges indicate that both AR and DR are more effective metrics for clustering events than the CC, yielding comparatively favorable results.

The epicenter distribution for our detections using the YOSO method is shown in Figure 9a. All these epicenters belong to events recorded on 1 January 2016. For comparison, we plotted the cluster centroids of tremor obtained by the National Research Institute for Earth Science and Disaster Prevention (NIED) using the method proposed by Obara *et al.* (2010) (Fig. 9a, blue points), epicenter distribution obtained by Mizuno and Ide (2019) (Fig. 9a, red points), and the event distribution from Ohta *et al.* (2023) (Fig. 9a, green points). We used the results obtained from eight stations from eastern Shikoku (Fig. 9a, black inverted triangles). The epicentral estimation obtained from the YOSO detections is more widespread in comparison to the other two catalogs. We estimate the location difference of our catalog by measuring the distance between each coincident event in both catalogs. We assume the Mizuno and Ide (2019) catalog as the ground truth; hence, this location difference measures the uncertainty of the obtained locations. The differences range

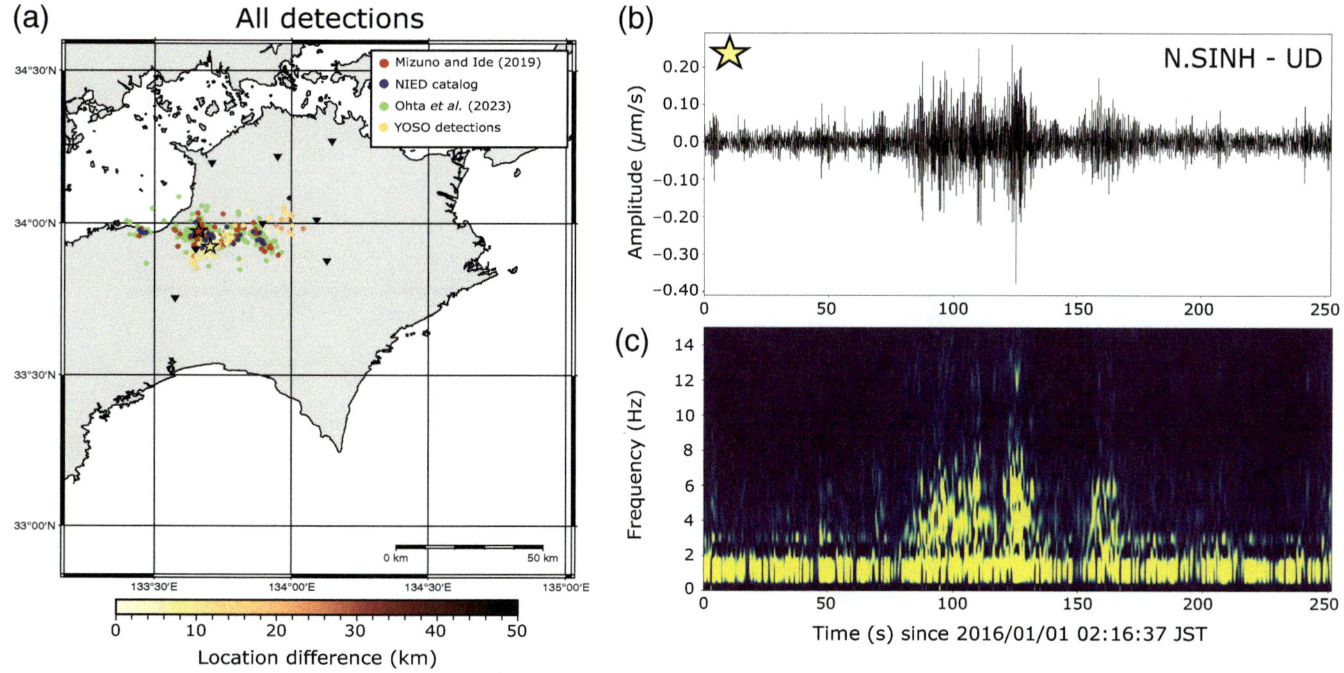

Figure 9. (a) Distribution of epicenters associated with the detections obtained by the YOSO method (brown points). For comparison, we also show the tremor cluster centroid catalog obtained by National Research Institute for Earth Science and Disaster Prevention (NIED) using the method proposed by Obara *et al.* (2010) (blue dots), the catalog obtained from Mizuno and Ide (2019) (red dots), and the catalog from Ohta *et al.* (2023) (green dots). The color scale represents the location difference of each point in comparison to Mizuno and Ide (2019) detections. All epicenters were calculated assuming a fixed depth of 35 km. (b,c) Example of detected tremor waveform and its associated spectrogram. The yellow star in (a) points to its spatial position. The location from Mizuno and Ide (2019) catalog for the same event is pointed out by the red star.

between epicenters lies within 0.75–50 km, reflecting the high uncertainty of this location method. However, most of the detections have a location difference between 5.3 and 13.22 km. In addition, the high uncertainty does not mean that we are not retrieving the same events. In Figure 9b,c, we show an example of a tremor waveform identified by the YOSO method. This event occurred on 1 January at 02:16:37 JST (Fig. 9a, brown and green stars). Its frequency content ranges from 1 to 10 Hz and is more present around 80–175 s, for which the amplitude is higher. The location of this event is ~6 km apart from the location obtained by Mizuno and Ide (2019), and 3 km from the closest centroids of the NIED catalog. The events with higher uncertainty (above 20 km) are the ones that are farther to the epicenter distribution. Even if the events obtained from YOSO do not exactly coincide, the distribution is closer to the distribution of other catalogs. We must highlight that our locations are not as accurate as other catalogs due to the simplicity of the location method. In addition, the number of stations and parameters used to obtain the locations is different for each method. Other epicenter estimations were performed using other Q values lower than 1000, without any change in the epicenter distribution (see Fig. S16).

The obtained tremor waveforms from the YOSO method are used as templates in the template matching method. Here, we applied the template matching method as follows: (1) both template and traces are down sampled from 100 to 20 Hz, (2) the algorithm computes the correlation coefficients (CC) between each one of the templates and the traces of all components, (3) we sum the absolute value CC of all channels, and (4) we sum again obtained CC values from all stations. This procedure is almost the same as the one described by Shelly *et al.* (2006). However, we apply a different threshold value due to the use of absolute values of CC. Instead of using the median absolute deviation, we set the threshold as the mean of the summed CC. In the supplemental material, we show some results obtained from template matching using only one of the horizontal channels (Figs. S12 and S13) and all three channels of N.SINH station (Figs. S14 and S15).

Figure 10 shows two examples of the application of template matching using seismic data from 1 to 5 January 2016. As templates, we used the two tremor waveforms retrieved from cluster number 5 identified in Hi-net station N.SINH. For comparison, we also show the seismic traces from N.SINH, N.IKWH, and N.SADH stations. In both examples, we observe an increase in the summed CC values that coincides with the positions where there is an amplitude increase in the trace. In addition, we observe that the peaks associated with the summed CC functions coincide. Note that the summed CC values from Figure 10a are noisier than the CC value from Figure 10b. This coincides with the fact that EV00 duration is shorter than EV08.

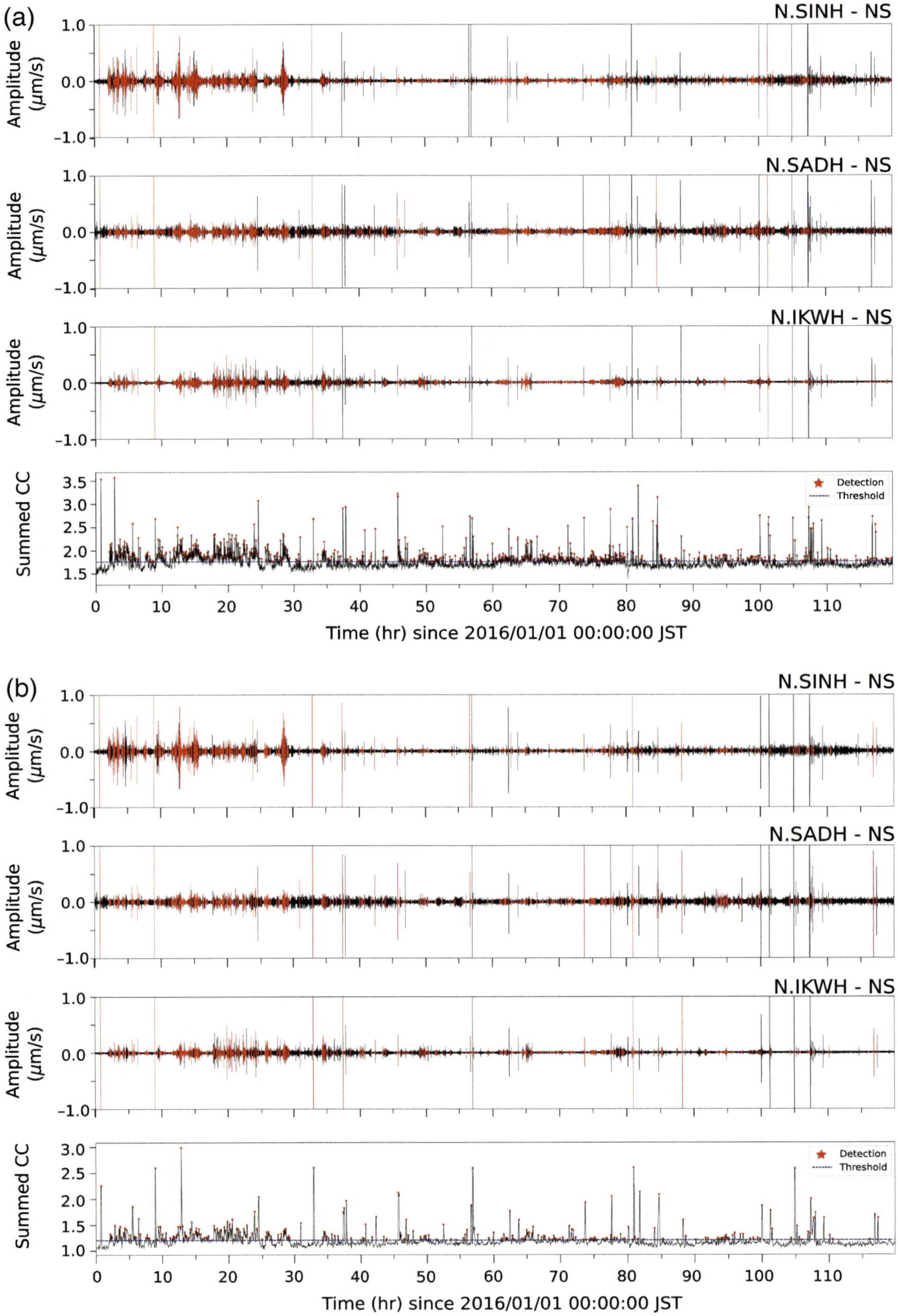

Figure 10. Example of results from template matching from 1 to 5 January using two templates: (a) EV00 and (b) EV08 with lengths of ~170 and 440 s, respectively. Both templates belong to cluster number 5 from Hi-net station N.SINH. The CC values shown in the last panel of each figure correspond to the sum of all CC obtained from all components of the used Hi-net stations. The red dots point out the detections, and the blue line indicates the threshold value.

The template matching analysis was extended to two weeks, from 1 to 14 January 2016. The number of templates used was increased to 13, using 50% overlap between time windows, and using the mean of the summed CC values as the detection threshold. The detections from all templates are compared to each other to select only coherent detections. We keep the detections that were obtained by at least 10 templates. The results obtained are compared with the catalogs from Mizuno and Ide (2019) and Ohta *et al.* (2023) to assess the performance of the YOSO method and the template matching. We will refer to Mizuno and Ide (2019) and Ohta *et al.* (2023) catalogs as MI and OT catalogs, respectively. In this period, MI catalog has 357 events, and OT catalog has 812 events. Using template matching, we detected 837–11,459 events. This range accounts for the total number of events detected per template. We remove false detections by comparing similar detections across all templates. We remove 33%–93% of false detections from the rest of the templates. In addition, all events with amplitude values above 1 μm/s are also discarded. Hence, our catalog comprises 758 tremor detections in eastern Shikoku during this period. Assuming that either MI or OT catalogs are ground truth, we compared the time of each event of the MI and OT catalogs with the events of our catalog to assess the method performance. The parameters to build MI, OT, and our catalog are different. In account to this variability of the parameters and the uncertainty in the event times between catalogs, we set a time window of tolerance of 1200 s and distance up to 50 km to between events of different catalogs to compare them. Under these assumptions, the template matching has a detection precision between 70% and 80%. However, this is not conclusive information. If we compare the events of both MI and OT catalogs, we will observe that the times of the events also do not coincide. In contrast, the epicentral distribution of both catalogs coincides. Our catalog has different distribution than MI and OT catalogs (Fig. 9). However, this issue is related to the uncertainty in the source location rather than a false detection problem.

Discussion

Detecting deep tectonic tremors using records from inland seismometers has been a challenge for researchers because of their relatively low-amplitude waveforms compared with those of other seismic events. In the Nankai region, tremors usually appear as continuous waveforms with durations between 20 and 200 s. The identification of deep tremor in seismic traces across Hi-net station is purely based in the envelope estimation, which is a common feature in different stations, and it keeps direct relation to the seismic moment rate (Ide *et al.*, 2008). Tremors have also been demonstrated to occur as swarms for LFE earthquakes (Shelly *et al.*, 2007). The waveform amplitudes were below 1 mm/s, the dominant frequencies between 2 and 8 Hz (Obara, 2002; Shelly *et al.*, 2007; Ide *et al.*, 2008), and the scaled energy (Kanamori and Rivera, 2006) is $\sim 10^{-10}$ (Ide, 2008; Ide *et al.*, 2008).

Focusing on the latter quantity, the scaled energy is defined as the radiated energy normalized by the scalar moment magnitude (Kanamori and Rivera, 2006). The radiated energy for slow earthquakes is $\sim 0.23 \times 10^{18}$ times the square envelope amplitude (Ide *et al.*, 2008), and the scalar moment magnitude M_0 of each detection depends on the dimensions of the rupture zone. One valid approach for estimating the scalar moment magnitude is to consider the unbounded and bounded slip zones $M_0 = k_b T$ and $M_0 = k_u T^3$, in which K_b and K_u are the coefficients for the bounded and unbounded slip regions, respectively. The K_b and K_u coefficients depend on the stress drop, slip region dimensions, and seismic wave propagation speed (Gomberg *et al.*, 2016). Based on the previously mentioned information, we estimated the scaled energy of the detections obtained using the YOSO method. We observed that most of the retrieved waveforms with amplitudes below 0.1 μm/s had scaled energy values within the range 10^{-11}–10^{-9}. Although there is a difference of one order of magnitude with respect to previous observations, we can infer that the detections are associated with tremor waveforms.

In addition, we estimated the coherence between the clusters obtained from YOSO from different stations (see Figs. S8 and S9). Most of the coherence values falls in the 0.1–0.5 range, being more common the coherence value between 0.2 and 0.4. Although this coherence value seems low, these results match with other coherence estimation values obtained from array observations to locate deep low-frequency tremor in the Kii peninsula (Sagae *et al.*, 2021), confirming that the tremor waveforms are present in our detections. A potential limitation of the coherence analysis is that common earthquakes may present high coherence values in the same frequency band as LFE and tremor. This coherence analysis is performed outside the current framework, and future work is aimed to integrate coherence estimations to further improve tremor accuracy.

The amplitude source model (Battaglia and Aki, 2003) yielded a more widespread epicenter distribution than other catalogs. In addition, the depth estimates are poorly resolved.

We highlight that the YOSO method detects seismic events using RMS and performs preclassification using hierarchical clustering to create template catalogs. We emphasize that the YOSO method does not perform event location or phase associations. More accurate and reliable hypocenter estimations can be obtained using other methods (Obara, 2002; Maeda and Obara, 2009; Obara *et al.*, 2010; Mizuno and Ide, 2019), which leverages the seismic energy decay instead of the amplitude, and the travel-time difference between similar envelopes across seismic stations. Further studies consider the addition of hypocenter estimation using ML-based methods that will result in more reliable estimations than the amplitude source model.

An important feature of the YOSO method is the search on each channel independently, and the consideration of the vertical channel may be controversial. It is a fact that LFE and tremor are more visible in horizontal channels due to their relation to their source mechanism. However, the reason behind the selection of the vertical channel is to address seismic signals associated with earthquakes where *P*-wave arrivals are clearer than in the horizontal channels. The latter does not mean that we do not apply and/or use the rest of the channels. In fact, the YOSO method is applied on the three channels, and these are needed for the estimation of the seismic energy and template matching. In Figure S6, we observe that the detections distribution and the cluster structure do not dramatically change between channels.

So far, we have shown that we can apply template matching to detect tremor waveforms in seismic data (Fig. 10). However, several templates may be needed to fully map tremor sequences. Assuming that the tremor is composed of several LFE, the tremor waveform is dependent on the LFE waveforms. Thus, any change of LFE waveforms will produce waveforms that differ from the recovered tremor templates. Downsampling the tremor templates enhances the coherency of the tremor waveforms, thus increasing the CC values. This approach may help reduce the number of required templates. Further work will focus on this issue.

Although the YOSO framework is useful for template matching, this method has several limitations. First, the YOSO method is highly sensitive to the parameters used. In particular, the RMS decay curve slope threshold is the most critical. The slope threshold is a constant that determines the duration of short- and long-duration events. A slope threshold of 10^{-7} will retrieve signals with shorter durations (between 10 and 20 s), which are more coincident with LFE durations. However, large earthquakes could be trimmed, resulting in false detections. The choice of this parameter depends on the type of the target signal, and the most suitable value is found by trial and error. A second limitation is the hierarchical clustering scheme used. In this study, we selected straightforward metrics to perform clustering successfully. In general, the hierarchical scheme provided satisfactory results. However, for some stations, the elements within the clusters are inconsistent, and classification errors may arise. Further analysis is needed to explore other hierarchical clustering schemes.

Another limitation is related to the identification of the source of families of the events. In a homogeneous medium without any kind of source, we have a perfect separation of events with different sources. Of course, the presence of external factors, noise of different sources, and medium heterogeneity make challenging the task of classification. Therefore, we need to validate clustering results from several observation points. For this reason, in this work we attempt to validate our results by estimating approximate epicentral distribution and similar scaled energies. Although we have shown some results that prove that some clusters are related to tremor waveforms, we recall that the YOSO method does not perform event location and phase association. Further improvement is aimed to add location information for clustering.

Finally, the YOSO method is based on the RMS envelopes, which is a time-domain feature needed for validating and locating tremor sources. From the time lag envelopes, we obtain the source location, and the envelope correlation serves as a weight factor to validate tremor-related envelopes (Ide *et al.*, 2008; Maeda and Obara, 2009; Mizuno and Ide, 2019; Obara, 2020). Further work is aimed at improving this method to better constrain the nature of the families of detections by adding this information, which is crucial for tremor identification.

Conclusions

In this work, we present the YOSO method to create template catalogs of tremor waveforms from seismic data. This method is based on the estimation of the RMS to determine the time position and duration of each event, and the classification of the detections using hierarchical clustering into families of events. This method was applied to physics-based synthetic data (Ide, 2008) and observations from Hi-net stations in eastern Shikoku, Japan. We classified the detections obtained from the RMS detector using amplitude, duration, and correlation metrics. Among the three metrics, the amplitude ratio provided the best classification. The scaled energy of the detections lies between 10^{-11} and 10^{-9}, which is not significantly different from the typical values reported in previous studies. We have applied the YOSO method and template matching to locate tremor from 1 to 14 January 2016, identifying a total of 758 events. The relative location of these detections coincides with previous catalogs. The YOSO method proves useful, alongside template matching, as an algorithm for supplying template waveforms and gives rapid assessment of tremor activity. The limitations of this method are related to its high sensitivity to input parameters. This method provides a new scheme for seismic event detection without the dependence on template catalogs, producing reliable results. Future work will aim to improve this method by extending it to identify earthquake signals from different sources with the aim of combining the YOSO method and template matching to create an autonomous methodology with the potential to generate reliable and accurate detections.

Data and Resources

The seismic data and the site amplification factors were obtained from the National Research Institute for Earth Science and Disaster Prevention (NIED) Hi-net website (https://www.hinet.bosai.go.jp/, last accessed August 2025). Data analysis and plotting were performed using Matplotlib (Hunter, 2007), ObsPy (Beyreuther *et al.*, 2010), SciPy (Virtanen *et al.*, 2020), and PyGMT (Tian *et al.*, 2024). The uniform manifold approximation and projection (UMAP) method was downloaded from https://umap-learn.readthedocs.io/en/latest/ (last accessed August 2025) and implemented using the following examples from the same source. The YOSO source code and some examples can be found in https://github.com/GerardoMendo/YOSO (last accessed

October 2025). The supplemental material includes the calculations obtained with You Only Search Once (YOSO) method associated with stations N.OWKF, N.SJOH, and N.IKWH, coherence values from Hi-net stations and template matching examples using station N.SINH. We show the root mean square (RMS) peaks, RMS decay curves, UMAP plots, dendrograms, and sorted heat maps for amplitude ratio, duration ratio, and correlation coefficients.

Declaration of Competing Interests

The authors acknowledge that there are no conflicts of interest recorded.

Acknowledgments

This study was supported by the MEXT Project for Seismology Toward Research Innovation with Data of Earthquakes (STAR-E) Number JPJ010217. The key ideas in this study were derived from the activities of the MEXT Volcano Practical Human Resource Development Support Program Japan, the MEXT The Third Earthquake and Volcano Hazards Observation and Research Program (Earthquake and Volcano Hazard Reduction Research), JST NEXUS, Japan Number JPMJNX25C5, the JSPS KAKENHI Grant-in-Aid for Scientific Research (A) Number 23H00466, Fund for the Promotion of Joint International Research (International Collaborative Research) Number 23KK0181, Grant-in-Aid for Challenging Research (Pioneering) Number 25K21806, and Earthquake Research Institute, University of Tokyo Joint Research ERI JURP 2025-A-03, 2024-B-01, and 2025-B-01. The authors thank Naoshi Hirata, Kazushige Obara, Keisuke Yano, Masaaki Imaizumi, Tomoki Tokuda, and Shinya Katoh for their valuable feedback on this work. Finally, the authors thank the three anonymous reviewers for reviewing and giving their comments. The authors believe that their feedback will improve the quality of this document.

References

Aguiar, A. C., K. Chao, and G. C. Beroza (2017). Tectonic tremor and LFEs on a reverse fault in Taiwan, *Geophys. Res. Lett.* doi: 10.1002/2016GL072148.

Aguiar, A. C., T. I. Melbourne, and C. W. Scrivner (2009). Moment release rate of Cascadia tremor constrained by GPS, *J. Geophys. Res.* doi: 10.1029/2008JB005909.

Aiken, C., and K. Obara (2021). Data-driven clustering reveals more than 900 small magnitude slow earthquakes and their characteristics, *Geophys. Res. Lett.* doi: 10.1029/2020GL091764.

Bar-Joseph, Z., D. K. Gifford, and T. S. Jaakkola (2001). Fast optimal leaf ordering for hierarchical clustering, *Bioinformatics* doi: 10.1093/bioinformatics/17.suppl_1.S22.

Bartlow, N. M. (2020). A long-term view of episodic tremor and slip in Cascadia, *Geophys. Res Lett.* doi: 10.1029/2019GL085303.

Battaglia, J., and K. Aki (2003). Location of seismic events and eruptive fissures on the Piton de la Fournaise volcano using seismic amplitudes, *J. Geophys. Res.* doi: 10.1029/2002JB002193.

Benvegna, F., A. D'Alessandro, G. Lo Bosco, D. Luzio, L. Pinello, and D. Tegolo (2011). A new dissimilarity measure for clustering seismic signals, in *Image Analysis and Processing—ICIAP 2011*, G. Maino and G. L. Foresti (Editors), doi: 10.1007/978-3-642-24088-1.

Benvegna, F., G. Lo Bosco, and D. Tegolo (2013). Dissimilarity measures for the identification of earthquake focal mechanisms, in *Image Analysis and Processing—ICIAP 2013*, A. Petrosino (Editor), doi: 10.1007/978-3-642-41184-7.

Beroza, G. C., and S. Ide (2011). Slow earthquakes and nonvolcanic tremor, *Annu. Rev. Earth Planet. Sci.* **39,** 271–296, doi: 10.1146/annurev-earth-040809-152531.

Beyreuther, M., R. Barsch, L. Krischer, T. Megies, Y. Behr, and J. Wassermann (2010). ObsPy: A Python toolbox for seismology, *Seismol. Res. Lett.* **81,** 530–533, doi: 10.1785/gssrl.81.3.530.

Calinski, T., and J. Harabasz (1972). A dendrite method for cluster analysis, *Commun. Stat.* doi: 10.1080/03610927408827101.

Castañeda-Bastida, E. (2018). Análisis y caracterización espectral de la microsismicidad y la actividad eruptiva del Volcán de Fuego de Colima, *Master Thesis*, Universidad Nacional Autónoma de México, Repositorio de tesis TESIUNAM, available at https://ru.dgb.unam.mx/bitstream/20.500.14330/TES01000772012/3/0772012.pdf (last accessed October 2024) (in Spanish).

Chamberlain, C. J., D. R. Shelly, J. Townend, and T. A. Stern (2014). Low-frequency earthquakes reveal punctuated slow slip on the deep extent of the Alpine fault, New Zealand, *Geochem. Geophys. Geosys.* **15,** 2984–2999, doi: 10.1002/2014GC005436.

Davies, D. L., and D. W. Bouldin (1979). A cluster separation measure, *IEEE Trans. Pattern Anal. Mach. Intell.* doi: 10.1109/TPAMI.1979.4766909.

Duarte, M., and R. N. Watanabe (2021). Notes in scientific computing for biomechanics and motor control, *Zenodo* doi: 10.5281/zenodo.4599319.

Frank, W. B., N. M. Shapiro, A. L. Husker, V. Kostoglodov, A. Romanenko, and M. Campillo (2014). Using systematically characterized low-frequency earthquakes as a fault probe in Guerrero, Mexico, *J. Geophys. Res.* doi: 10.1002/2014JB011457.

Frank, W. B., N. M. Shapiro, V. Kostoglodov, A. L. Husker, M. Campillo, J. S. Payero, and G. A. Prieto (2013). Low-frequency earthquakes in the Mexican Sweet Spot, *Geophys. Res. Lett.* **40,** 2661–2666, doi: 10.1002/grl.50561.

Ghosh, A., E. Huesca-Pérez, E. Brodsky, and Y. Ito (2015). Very low frequency earthquakes in Cascadia migrate with tremor, *Geophys. Res. Lett.* doi: 10.1002/2015GL063286.

Gibbons, S. J., and F. Ringdal (2006). The detection of low magnitude seismic events using array-based waveform correlation, *Geophys. J. Int.* **165,** no. 1, 149–166, doi: 10.1111/j.1365-246X.2006.02865.x.

Gomberg, J., A. Wech, K. Creager, K. Obara, and D. Agnew (2016). Reconsidering earthquake scaling, *Geophys. Res. Lett.* doi: 10.1002/2016GL069967.

Hunter, J. D. (2007). Matplotlib: A 2D graphics environment, *Comput. Sci. Eng.* doi: 10.1109/MCSE.2007.55.

Ide, S. (2008). A Brownian walk model for slow earthquakes, *Geophys. Res. Lett.* doi: 10.1029/2008GL034821.

Ide, S., and G. C. Beroza (2023). Slow earthquake scaling reconsidered as a boundary between distinct modes of rupture propagation, *Proc. Natl. Acad. Sci. Unit. States Am.* doi: 10.1073/pnas.2222102120.

Ide, S., G. C. Beroza, D. R. Shelly, and T. Uchide (2007). A scaling law for slow earthquakes, *Nature* doi: 10.1038/nature05780.

Ide, S., K. Imanishi, Y. Yoshida, G. C. Beroza, and D. R. Shelly (2008). Bridging the gap between seismically and geodetically detected slow earthquakes, *Geophys. Res. Lett.* **35,** no. 10, doi: 10.1029/2008GL034014.

Ito, Y., K. Obara, K. Shiomi, S. Sekine, and H. Hirose (2007). Slow earthquakes coincident with episodic tremors and slow slip events, *Science* doi: 10.1126/science.1134454.

Kaneko, R., H. Nagao, S. Ito, H. Tsuruoka, and K. Obara (2023). Detection of deep low-frequency tremors from continuous paper records at a station in southwest Japan about 50 years ago based on convolutional neural network, *J. Geophys. Res.* doi: 10.1029/2022JB024842.

Kao, H., S. J. Shao, H. Dragert, and G. Rogers. (2009). Northern Cascadia episodic tremor and slip: A decade of tremor observations from 1997 to 2007, *J. Geophys. Res.* doi: 10.1029/2008JB006046.

Kanamori, R., and L. Rivera (2006). Energy Partitioning During an Earthquake, in *Earthquakes: Radiated Energy and the Physics of Faulting*, R. Abercrombie, A. McGarr, G. Di Toro, and H. Kanamori (Editors), doi: 10.1029/GM170.

Katakami, S., Y. Yamashita, H. Yakiwara, H. Shimizu, Y. Ito, and K. Ohta (2017). Tidal response in shallow tectonic tremors, *Geophys. Res. Lett.* doi: 10.1002/2017GL074060.

Kato, A., and S. Nakagawa (2020). Detection of deep low-frequency earthquakes in the Nankai subduction zone over 11 years using a matched filter technique, *Earth Planets Space* doi: 10.1186/s40623-020-01257-4.

Maeda, T., and K. Obara (2009). Spatiotemporal distribution of seismic energy radiation from low-frequency tremor in western Shikoku, Japan, *J. Geophys. Res.* doi: 10.1029/2008JB006043.

McInnes, L., J. Healy, and J. Melville (2020). UMAP: Uniform manifold approximation and projection for dimension reduction, doi: 10.48550/arXiv.1802.03426.

Mizuno, N., and S. Ide (2019). Development of a modified envelope correlation method based on maximum-likelihood method and application to detecting and locating deep tectonic tremors in western Japan, *Earth Planets Space* **71,** 40.

Mu, D., P. Cicotti, Y. Cui, E. Lee, F. J. Langer, J. Qiu, H. J. Lee, and C. Morrin (2018). Deep learning for seismic template recognition, *Proc. of the Practice and Experience on Advanced Research Computing: Seamless Creativity*, doi: 10.1145/3219104.3219133.

Mullner, D. (2011). Modern hierarchical, agglomerative clustering algorithms, doi: 10.48550/arXiv.1109.2378.

Murtagh, F., and P. Contreras (2011). Algorithms for hierarchical clustering: An overview, *WIRES Data Min. Knowl.* doi: 10.1002/widm.53.

Nakano, M., T. Hori, E. Araki, S. Kodaira, and S. Ide (2018). Shallow very-low-frequency earthquakes accompany slow slip events in the Nankai subduction zone, *Nat. Commun.* doi: 10.1038/s41467-018-03431-5.

Nakano, M., S. Yabe, H. Sugioka, M. Shinohara, and S. Ide (2019). Event size distribution of shallow tectonic tremor in the Nankai trough, *Geophys. Res. Lett.* doi: 10.1029/2019GL083029.

Nishikawa, T., S. Ide, and T. Nishimura (2023). A review on slow earthquakes in Japan trench, *Progr. Earth Planet. Sci.* doi: 10.1186/s40645-022-00528-w.

Obara, K. (2002). Nonvolcanic deep tremor associated with subduction in Southwest Japan, *Science* doi: 10.1126/science.1070378.

Obara, K. (2020). Characteristic activities of slow earthquakes in Japan, *Proc. Jpn. Acad. B* doi: 10.2183/pjab.96.022.

Obara, K., and A. Kato (2016). Connecting slow earthquakes to huge earthquakes, *Science* **353,** 253–257.

Obara, K., K. Kasahara, S. Hori, and Y. Okada (2005). A densely distributed high-sensitivity seismograph network in Japan: Hi-net by National Research Institute for Earth Science and Disaster Prevention, *Rev. Sci. Ins.* doi: 10.1063/1.1854197.

Obara, K., S. Tanaka, T. Maeda, and T. Matsuzawa (2010). Depth-dependent activity of non-volcanic tremor in southwest Japan, *Geophys. Res. Lett.* doi: 10.1029/2010GL043679.

Ohta, K., K. Shiomi, and T. Matsuzawa (2023). Complex interaction, striations, and periodicity of deep tremor surrounding a tremor gap in the Central Nankai subduction zone, Japan, *J. Geophys. Res.* doi: 10.1029/2022JB025373.

Okada, Y., K. Kasahara, S. Hori, K. Obara, S. Sekiguchi, H. Fujiwara, and A. Yamamoto (2004). Recent progress of seismic observation networks in Japan -Hi-net, F-net, K-NET and Kik-net, *Earth Planets Space* doi: 10.1186/BF03353076.

Pedregosa, F., G. Varoquaux, A. Gramfort, V. Michel, B. Thirion, O. Grisel, M. Blondel, P. Prettenhofer, R. Weiss, V. Dubourg, *et al.* (2011). Scikit-learn: Machine learning in Python, *J. Machine Learn. Res.* available at http://jmlr.org/papers/v12/pedregosa11a.html (last accessed August 2025).

Peng, W., K. H. Chen, and S. Toda (2019). Evaluating the association between tectonic tremors and earthquakes in Taiwan from 7 years catalogs, *J. Geophys. Res.* doi: 10.1029/2018JB017258.

Plata-Martinez, R., S. Ide, M. Shinohara, E. S. Garcia, N. Mizuno, L. A. Dominguez, T. Taira, Y. Yamashita, A. Toh, T. Yamada, *et al.* (2021). Shallow slow earthquakes to decipher future catastrophic earthquakes in the Guerrero seismic gap, *Nat. Commun.* doi: 10.1038/s41467-021-24210-9.

Rogers, G., and H. Dragert (2003). Episodic tremor and slip on the Cascadia subduction zone: The chatter of silent slip, *Science* doi: 10.1126/science.1084783.

Rousseeuw, P. J. (1987). Silhouettes: A graphical aid to the interpretation and validation of cluster analysis, *J. Comput. Appl. Math.* **20,** 53–65, doi: 10.1016/0377-0427(87)90125-7.

Sagae, K., H. Nakahara, T. Nishimura, and K. Imanashi. (2021). High resolution location of deep low-frequency tremors beneath Kii Peninsula, Nankai subduction zone, Japan, using data from a dense seismic array, *Geophys. J. Int.* doi: 10.1093/gji/ggab004.

Senobari, N. S., P. M. Shearer, G. J. Funning, Z. Zimmerman, Y. Zhu, P. Brisk, and E. Keogh (2024). The matrix profile in seismology: Template matching of everything with everything, *J. Geophys. Res.* doi: 10.1029/2023JB027122.

Shelly, D. R., G. C. Beroza, and S. Ide (2007). Non-volcanic tremor and low-frequency earthquake swarms, *Nature* doi: 10.1038/nature05666.

Shelly, D. R., G. C. Beroza, S. Ide, and S Nakamula (2006). Low-frequency earthquakes in Shikoku, Japan, and their relationship to episodic tremor and slip, *Nature* doi: 10.1038/nature04931.

Sit, S., M. Brudzinski, and H. Kao (2012). Detecting tectonic tremor through frequency scanning at a single station: Application to the Cascadia margin, *Earth Planet. Sci. Lett.* doi: 10.1016/j.epsl.2012.08.002.

Steinke, B., A. D. Jolly, R. Carniel, D. E. Dempsey, and S. J. Cronin (2023). Identification of seismo-volcanic regimes at Whakaari/White Island (New Zealand) via systematic tuning of an unsupervised classifier, *J. Geophys. Res.* doi: 10.1029/2022JB026221.

Sun, W. F., Z. Peng, C. H. Lin, and K. Chao (2015). Detecting deep tectonic tremor in Taiwan with a dense array, *Bull. Seismol. Soc. Am.* doi: 10.1785/0120140258.

Székely, G. J., M. L. Rizzo, and N. K. Bakirov (2007). Measuring and testing dependence by correlation of distances, *Ann. Stat.* doi: 10.1214/009053607000000505.

Takemura, S., T. Matsuzawa, A. Noda, T. Tonegawa, Y. Asano, T. Kimura, and K. Shiomi (2019). Structural characteristics of the Nankai trough shallow plate boundary inferred from shallow very low frequency earthquakes, *Geophys. Res. Lett.* doi: 10.1029/2019GL082448.

Takemura, S., A. Noda, T. Kubota, Y. Asano, T. Matsuzawa, and K. Shiomi (2019). Migrations and clusters of shallow very low frequency earthquakes in the regions surrounding shear stress accumulation peaks along the Nankai trough, *Geophys. Res. Lett.* doi: 10.1029/2019GL084666.

Tamaribuchi, K., M. Ogiso, and A. Noda (2022). Spatiotemporal distribution of shallow tremors along the Nankai trough, southwest Japan, as determined from waveform amplitudes and cross-correlations, *J. Geophys. Res.* doi: 10.1029/2022JB024403.

Tang, C. C., Z. Peng, K. Chao, C. C. Chen, and C. H. Lin (2010). Detecting low-frequency earthquakes within non-volcanic tremor in southern Taiwan triggered by the 2005 M_w 8.6 Nias earthquake, *Geophy. Res. Lett.* doi: 10.1029/2010GL043918.

Tarantola, A. (2005). *Inverse Problem Theory and Methods for Model Parameter Estimation*, Society for Industrial and Applied Mathematics.

Tian, D., L. Uieda, W. J. Leong, Y. Fröhlich, W. Schlitzer, M. Grund, M. Jones, L. Toney, J. Yao, Y. Magen, *et al.* (2024). PyGMT: A Python interface for the Generic Mapping Tools (v0.12.0), *Zenodo* doi: 10.5281/zenodo.3781524.

Todd, E. K., and S. Y. Schwartz (2016). Tectonic tremor along the northern Hikurangi Margin, New Zealand, between 2010 and 2015, *J. Geophys. Res.* doi: 10.1002/2016JB013480.

Todd, E. K., S. Y. Schwartz, K. Mochizuki, L. M. Wallace, A. F. Sheehan, S. C. Webb, C. A. Williams, J. Nakai, J. Yarce, B. Fry, *et al.* (2018). Earthquakes and tremor linked to seamount subduction during shallow slow slip at the Hikurangi Margin, New Zealand, *J. Geophys. Res.* **123,** 6769–6783.

Toh, A., W. J. Chen, N. Takeuchi, D. S. Dreger, W. C. Chi, and S. Ide (2020). Influence of a subducted oceanic ridge on the distribution of shallow VLFEs in the Nankai trough as revealed by moment tensor inversion and cluster analysis, *Geophys. Res. Lett.* doi: 10.1029/2020GL087244.

Uchida, N., R. Takagi, Y. Asano, and K. Obara (2020). Migration of shallow and deep slow earthquakes toward the locked segment of the Nankai megathrust, *Earth Planet. Sci. Lett.* doi: 10.1016/j.epsl.2019.115986.

Virtanen, P., R. Gommers, T. E. Oliphant, M. Haberland, T. Reddy, D. Cournapeau, E. Burovski, P. Peterson, W. Weckesser, J. Bright, *et al.* (2020). SciPy 1.0: Fundamental algorithms for scientific computing in Python, *Nat. Meth.* 261–272.

Wech, A. G. (2021). Cataloging tectonic tremor energy radiation in the Cascadia subduction zone, *J. Geophys. Res.* doi: 10.1029/2021JB022523.

Wech, A. G., and K. C. Creager (2008). Automated detection and location of Cascadia tremor, *Geophys. Res. Lett.* doi: 10.1029/2008GL035458.

Yabe, S., and S. Ide (2014). Spatial distribution of seismic energy rate of tectonic tremors in subduction zones, *J. Geophys. Res.* doi: 10.1002/2014JB011383.

Yabe, S., A. S. Baltay, S. Ide, and G. C. Beroza (2014). Seismic-wave attenuation determined from tectonic tremor in multiple subduction zones, *Bull. Seismol. Soc. Am.* **104,** no. 4, 2043–2059, doi: 10.1785/0120140032.

Yates, A., C. Caudron, P. Lesage, A. Mordret, T. Lecocq, and J. Soubestre (2023). Assessing similarity in continuous seismic cross-correlation functions using hierarchical clustering: Application to Ruapehu and Piton de la Fournaise volcanoes, *Geophys. J. Int.* doi: 10.1093/gji/ggac469.

Manuscript received 4 October 2024
Published online 14 November 2025

The Intensity Gap: A Global Analysis of Who Responds to the Crowdsourced "Did You Feel It?" System

Elijah Knodel*[1], David J. Wald[2], Vincent Quitoriano[2], and Sabine Loos[1]

Abstract

The U.S. Geological Survey's (USGS) "Did You Feel It?" (DYFI) system is an internet tool that collects shaking intensity observations through crowdsourcing. It produces maps and provides supplementary data to ShakeMap, which offers near-real-time maps of ground motion resulting from significant earthquakes around the globe. Barriers such as technology and language make DYFI an unequally accessible tool, however, leading to a less comprehensive view of an earthquake's impact in certain regions. Here, we analyze users' global interaction with DYFI to evaluate its accessibility. We employ web analytics to quantify how users access DYFI, and perform inference modeling to predict each country's response rate to DYFI. The panel dataset built for this inference model combines physical earthquake parameters from the USGS with socioeconomic data from the World Bank and the Central Intelligence Agency for 151 countries from 2009 to 2020. Our web analytics show that users predominantly access DYFI through mobile devices and are often referred through social media. In addition, results from the inference model reveal that socioeconomic parameters, including primary language spoken and broadband internet subscriptions, alongside physical earthquake parameters such as average shaking intensity, have a significant effect on a country's response rate to DYFI. As a result of this analysis, we establish a country priority index for improved DYFI awareness and accessibility. This index considers regions of the world lacking seismic station coverage that face barriers to DYFI access, such as language, technology, and other factors. Consequently, the USGS has made evaluating DYFI's performance on mobile devices a priority and has begun incorporating and monitoring the use of additional languages within the DYFI system. Furthermore, our analyses suggest specific nations with low response rates could benefit from targeted outreach in conjunction with partner agencies in each country.

Cite this article as Knodel, E., D. J. Wald, V. Quitoriano, and S. Loos (2026). The Intensity Gap: A Global Analysis of Who Responds to the Crowdsourced "Did You Feel It?" System, *Seismol. Res. Lett.* **XX**, 2082–2106, doi: 10.1785/0220250168.

Introduction

The U.S. Geological Survey (USGS) has been operating "Did You Feel It?" (DYFI) since 1999 in California, since 2000 for the rest of the United States, and since 2004 globally (Quitoriano and Wald, 2020). To date, DYFI has received more than eight million responses, covering large portions of the globe. Analogous systems around the world are typically implemented at the national level–for example, Italy's Hai Sentito Il Terremoto (Sbarra *et al.*, 2010; Tosi *et al.*, 2015) and various adaptations of the USGS DYFI software in countries such as Canada, New Zealand, and others. For a full list of analogous national systems, please see Goded *et al.* (2017). The European-Mediterranean Seismological Center (EMSC) provides the only other widely used global community-science method for collecting earthquake felt reports (Bossu *et al.*, 2016). Yet, the EMSC Felt Reports system is based on users' selection of picture-based intensities, not formal macroseismic intensity values, which would require the collection of users' detailed observations for validation and reproducibility.

DYFI has led to a number of benefits for the general populace exposed to earthquakes, emergency responders, and the scientific community. DYFI benefits exposed populations—where often tens of thousands of DYFI contributors have a direct ability to engage with a federal agency and contribute to citizen science efforts (Goltz *et al.*, 2020). This ability to engage can offer

1. Department of Civil and Environmental Engineering, University of Michigan, Ann Arbor, Michigan, U.S.A., https://orcid.org/0009-0007-2571-2118 (EK); https://orcid.org/0000-0001-7190-3432 (SL); 2. Geologic Hazards Science Center, U.S. Geological Survey, Golden, Colorado, U.S.A., https://orcid.org/0000-0002-1454-4514 (DJW); https://orcid.org/0000-0003-4157-1101 (VQ)

*Corresponding author: knodel@umich.edu

educational value where citizens are familiarized with concepts such as intensity, and thus, an increased understanding of their risk (Celsi *et al.*, 2005). Scientifically, DYFI has been shown to be an accurate measure of ground motion when a large number of DYFI responses are recorded (Atkinson and Wald, 2007). Thus, the output of DYFI is directly used as shaking constraints for USGS products such as the ShakeMap (Wald *et al.*, 2022), an important input for loss estimates provided by the Prompt Assessment of Global Earthquakes for Response (PAGER; Quitoriano and Wald, 2020). PAGER and ShakeMap, in turn, inform stakeholders such as humanitarian specialists and emergency managers responding to an earthquake and serving exposed populations (Thompson *et al.*, 2019;Wald, 2023; Loos *et al.*, 2024).

One key to capturing a more accurate estimate of shaking is the quantity and spatial coverage of DYFI responses (Atkinson and Wald, 2007). This is especially the case in regions where fewer seismic stations exist, such as the Central and Eastern United States (CEUS) or many countries in the developing world. Take, for example, the Haiti 2010 earthquake—an event that led to the deaths of over 200,000 people and over $8 billion U.S. losses, exceeding the nation's gross domestic product (Calais *et al.*, 2010). At the time of the earthquake, no seismic stations existed —the only on-the-ground measurements of shaking were those provided by DYFI (Eberhard *et al.*, 2010). A more accurate estimate of shaking could have aided situational awareness and better focused response. Countries, such as Haiti, that do not have an analogous DYFI system and lack seismic stations to constrain shaking estimates, stand to benefit from increased contributions to the USGS DYFI system. The goal of this study is to understand how access to DYFI can be increased in countries that would benefit from its results.

We build upon several studies that have evaluated the factors that influence DYFI contribution. Mak and Schorlemmer (2016) performed a thorough regression analysis to estimate DYFI responses per ZIP code in the United States, while accounting for multiple factors simultaneously. This analysis was done for all earthquakes (n = 614) greater than M_w 4 in the United States (comparing results for California and the CEUS) between 2000 and 2014. The study is rigorous and finds that DYFI responses depend on both earthquake and socioeconomic status parameters. Hough and Martin (2021b) also performed an analysis of who responds to DYFI, specifically assessing response rates (or the number of DYFI responses normalized by population) per ZIP code in California and per district in India. Compared to Mak and Schorlemmer (2016), the analysis presented by Hough and Martin (2021b) is valuable in that it is a cross-cultural comparison between India and the United States (e.g., California), and it has a greater focus on the influence of socioeconomic factors, such as household income, on DYFI engagement. The Hough and Martin (2021b) study evaluates a few widely felt earthquakes (n = 6) and analyzes the individual relationship between response rates, shaking intensity, and socioeconomic variables. Aspects of the correlation analysis in Hough and Martin (2021b) were critiqued in Wald (2021), which Hough and Martin refined in a reply (Hough and Martin, 2021a) and Hough's follow-on study (Hough, 2021). Specifically, Hough's follow-on study expanded upon their earlier work by collectively analyzing additional earthquakes (n = 21) in California and using a spatial approach, finding that economically advantaged ZIP codes were correlated with high DYFI response rates (Hough, 2021). Our study aims to build upon the strengths and concepts of these foundational analyses, including the regression analysis presented in Mak and Schorlemmer (2016) and the detailed focus on socioeconomic factors contributing to DYFI engagement presented in Hough and Martin (2021b) and Hough (2021). Here, we extend the statistical analysis to the global level and investigate between-country differences in DYFI response rates for all recorded major earthquakes from 2009 to 2020 (n = 1758).

Given that DYFI responses have been collected for over two decades around the globe (Quitoriano and Wald, 2020), an opportunity exists to conduct a global empirical analysis of the factors that contribute to DYFI response rates for all earthquakes and countries around the world to understand current limitations and potentially improve access to DYFI in places where it matters the most. Specifically, we answer the following research questions (Q).

Q1. How do earthquake-affected populations interact with DYFI?
Q2. What are the factors that influence the number of responses to DYFI globally?
Q3. Which countries would benefit from increased DYFI accessibility?

To address these questions, we draw on multiple data sources and methods. We begin with a web traffic analysis, which informs a subsequent regression analysis using statistical inference techniques. This regression is applied to panel data that links DYFI responses with earthquake and population variables over a 12-yr period (2009–2020), during which consistent DYFI data are available for 151 countries. By leveraging statistical inference methods, we are able to identify significant relationships between factors and DYFI responses. We also primarily focus on population variables that may explain differences in DYFI responses, such as internet access. Using the results of these analyses, we identify the countries that would benefit from increased access to DYFI through a composite priority index. Already, as a result of this analysis, the USGS is increasing access in identified countries through language translation and improved sharing.

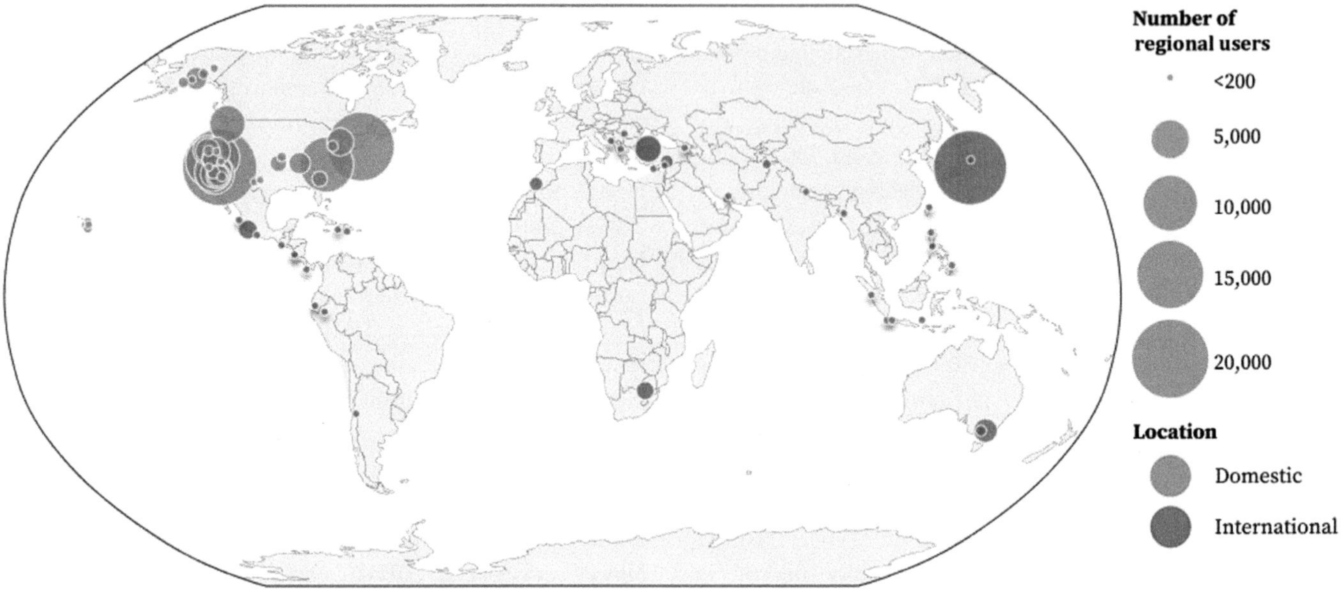

Figure 1. Web traffic data were analyzed for 80 earthquakes. Locations and number of regional users for earthquakes from 2019 to 2023 used in web traffic analysis. The color version of this figure is available only in the electronic edition.

Question 1: How do Earthquake-Affected Populations Interact with DYFI?

We conduct a web traffic analysis to understand how contributors in the earthquake-affected region access and interact with DYFI. Web traffic data describe how people interact with websites, and its value for directly estimating the area where an earthquake is felt, has been studied in-depth by the EMSC through the method called "flash-sourcing" (Bossu *et al.*, 2008, 2011, 2014). Here, we instead leverage web traffic data to gain insight into how people complete the crowdsourced DYFI questionnaire, including information about their device and the path they took to reach the form. Using these insights, we can define tangible ways to increase access to DYFI.

Question 1: Web traffic analysis

To contribute to DYFI, individuals must complete a Felt Report questionnaire, which includes a series of questions such as "Was it difficult to stand and/or walk?" and, for indoor situations, "Did objects rattle, topple over, or fall off shelves?" Responses to these questions are translated into a community decimal intensity (CDI), which takes values between 1 (not felt) and 9+ (violent shaking). CDI is calibrated to be on the same scale as the metric used for ShakeMap, modified Mercalli intensity (MMI), allowing intensity estimates from DYFI to be incorporated into USGS intensity maps (Dengler and Dewey, 1998; U.S. Geological Survey, 2025).

For our analysis of interaction with the DYFI Felt Report page, we use data recorded within a week of the earthquake because interaction with DYFI is minimal beyond this period. We source web traffic data from Google Analytics, as detailed in the Data and Resources.

Our analysis covers earthquake events from 2019 to 2023, with a large majority of events (96%) occurring after 2020. The dataset begins in 2019 because Google Analytics data in prior years tends to be rounded or overly aggregated. Many events in 2019 and 2020 also had this data quality issue, which resulted in there being only three events included prior to 2021. We used the USGS Earthquake Catalog to select events, filtering for high-impact events, identified by their PAGER alert level, and high-exposure events, indicated by the number of DYFI responses (Earle *et al.*, 2009). We include all events with a yellow or higher PAGER alert level from 2019 to 2023, given that they had at least 100 DYFI responses. The remaining events in our sample are those with the greatest number of responses to DYFI, with the intention of having an equal number of events in the United States (domestic) and outside the United States (international) to facilitate comparison. Although users can contribute to DYFI for either a specific earthquake through that earthquake's event page or a general unknown event, we only examine web traffic for users who filled out a Felt Report through an earthquake's event page because web traffic cannot be analyzed for unknown events.

The resulting sample has 80 earthquakes, 40 domestic and 40 international. International events span 6 continents and 26 countries, and domestic events span 13 states, with magnitudes across the entire sample ranging between M_w 3.6 and 7.8, as shown in Figure 1. All sampled events are included in Table A1.

Several Google Analytics metrics measure engagement with a webpage, including *users*, or the number of unique devices that interact with a given webpage; *sessions*, or the number of distinct, time-separated visits to a webpage; and *pageviews*, or the number of times a webpage is viewed (Google Analytics, 2024). A single *user* could have multiple *sessions* in which they visit the Felt Report page, and within each *session*, they could have multiple Felt Report *pageviews*. Here, because we are interested in the characteristics of unique users of the Felt Report page, we analyze *users*. Although likely uncommon, we were unable to account for occurrences in which the same person visited a DYFI Felt Report page using multiple devices.

To only consider data for users who are most likely to be affected by the earthquake, we define *regional users* as the *users* within the region where the earthquake occurred. Location information is available for web users who grant location access to Google Analytics, for which the user's IP address typically reveals their nearest city, region (state), and country. We did not have access to individual IP addresses. We filtered *users* to only include those *regional users* that are located in the states (if in the United States) or in the countries (if outside the United States) that experienced some level of shaking as reflected by that earthquake's ShakeMap. If an earthquake had shaking in multiple states or countries, *users* from each state or country with shaking would be considered *regional users*. For the 80 events, 44% of *users* could not be determined to be *regional users* and were excluded from analysis. For international earthquakes in which large, highly populated countries were impacted (such as China and India), *users* in regions without shaking (as indicated by ShakeMap) that had more *users* than regions with shaking were not counted as *regional users*. In this analysis, we are unable to account for the unlikely scenario in which a person uses a virtual private network (VPN) to alter their device's perceived location to near an earthquake event. In addition, people who disable Google Analytics tracking permissions are not included in this analysis, resulting in available web traffic data for a total of 38% of DYFI responses in our sample, as dictated by Table A1. However, trends among available user data should be consistent with the full population, given that the number of users per event is still large.

To understand how DYFI is accessed both physically and digitally, we analyzed *regional users* of the Felt Report page using two main Google Analytics dimensions: *device category* and *referral source*. We also examined browser language data, but found it to be largely influenced by the location of the earthquake. *The device category* gives the type of device (mobile device, desktop, or tablet) used to access the Felt Report. *Referral source* specifies the domain of the webpage the user was on before entering the USGS Earthquake domain and viewing the Felt Report (Google Analytics, 2024). These chosen dimensions can be directly influenced by the USGS through their development and publicizing of the Felt Report page.

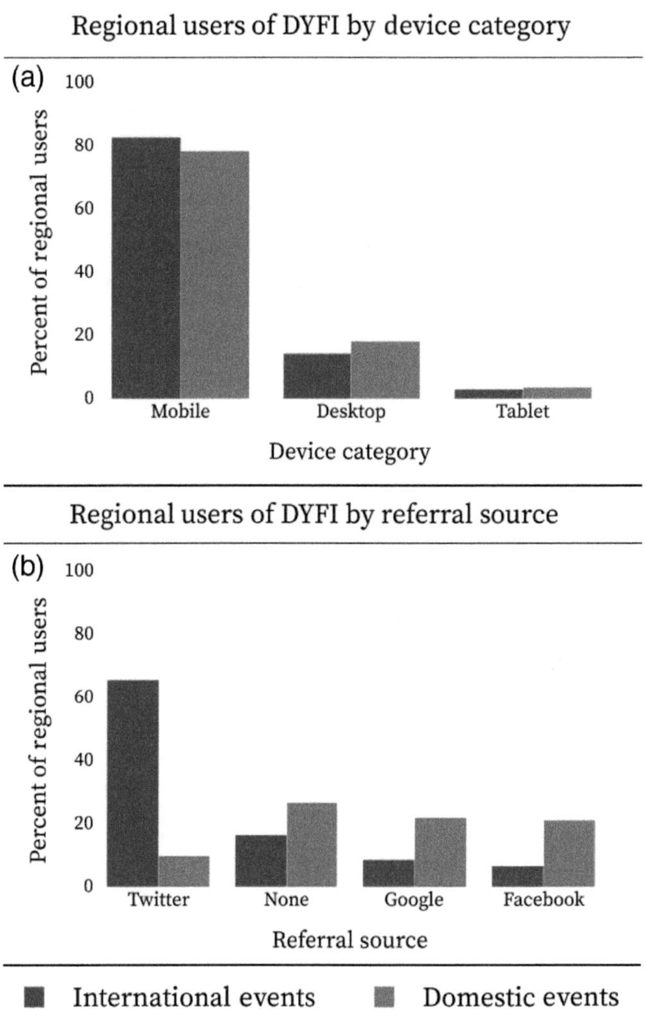

Figure 2. Earthquake-affected populations (regional users) physically and digitally access "Did You Feel It?" (DYFI) through different means. Bar charts show the number of regional users that access an event's Felt Report page by (a) device category and (b) referral source aggregated across 40 domestic events (orange) and 40 international events (teal). Only the four most common referral sources are shown (b). The 2021 M_w 5.9 Chiba, Japan, accounts for 63% of all international regional users. The color version of this figure is available only in the electronic edition.

Question 1: Results and discussion

Across all 80 events, we find that a large majority of *regional users* access the DYFI Felt Report via mobile device, as shown in Figure 2a. This includes 83% of international and 78% of domestic users. The second-most-used device is on desktop computers, and the third-most is via tablet. There is a negligible difference in device access between the international and domestic events.

Overall, users are referred to the Felt Report from numerous referral sources, including Twitter, Google, and Facebook, as shown in Figure 2b. The "None" referral source indicates that Google Analytics tracked no referral before the USGS Earthquake domain, which can occur if a user is directly linked to the Felt Report page from a separate application, such as an email or messaging app. Therefore, although the "None" source cannot be specifically tracked, it is likely a proxy for external messages, such as the USGS Earthquake Notification

Figure 3. Social media can significantly increase DYFI interaction. Social media interactions surrounding "Did You Feel It?" and the 2021 M_w 5.9 Chiba, Japan, earthquake. Arrows point from the original tweet to responses to that tweet. The color version of this figure is available only in the electronic edition.

Service. For domestic events, *regional users* are somewhat evenly distributed across these referral sources. However, for international events, a large percentage (66%) of users were referred from Twitter.

The considerable number of Twitter referrals for international events is largely due to tremendous user interaction following the 2021 M_w 5.9 Chiba, Japan, earthquake. Shortly after the earthquake, a local Japanese resident posted a tweet, encouraging others in Japan to fill out the USGS DYFI Felt Report (Fig. 3). This tweet gained thousands of retweets, with some Twitter users commenting how they were using translators to fill out the form. Altogether, the tweet was largely responsible for the 17,429 *regional users* who interacted with the Chiba earthquake's Felt Report page, the second most *regional users* of all 80 events. This great citizen science response highlights the power of social media to rapidly spread information and increase engagement. Although the Chiba earthquake tweet was an exceptional case, Twitter remains the most common referral source for international events overall.

Question 2: What Factors Influence DYFI Responses?

Although the web analysis provides insight into user-specific interaction behavior, it is only available for select years and countries, and lacks detail on the characteristics that motivate global DYFI response. To determine the factors that influence global DYFI responses, we leverage statistical inference methods using a panel dataset that links country-year DYFI responses with earthquake and population variables for 151 countries over 12 yr (2009–2020). Regressing on data in its panel (longitudinal) form accounts for changes in the response variable over time as well as differences between individuals (countries). This is preferable to summarizing temporal data for each country and using a generalized linear model because it preserves time-dependent information and has a greater number of observations.

Question 2: Panel data

A panel dataset describes subjects over time. Here, we construct a country-year panel dataset by aggregating all variables annually (t), ensuring that most seismically active countries experience at least one earthquake event with DYFI responses, and aligning with the national level (c) at which most population variables are reported.

Because ShakeMap is generated at a higher magnitude threshold of M_w 5.4 outside of the United States, compared

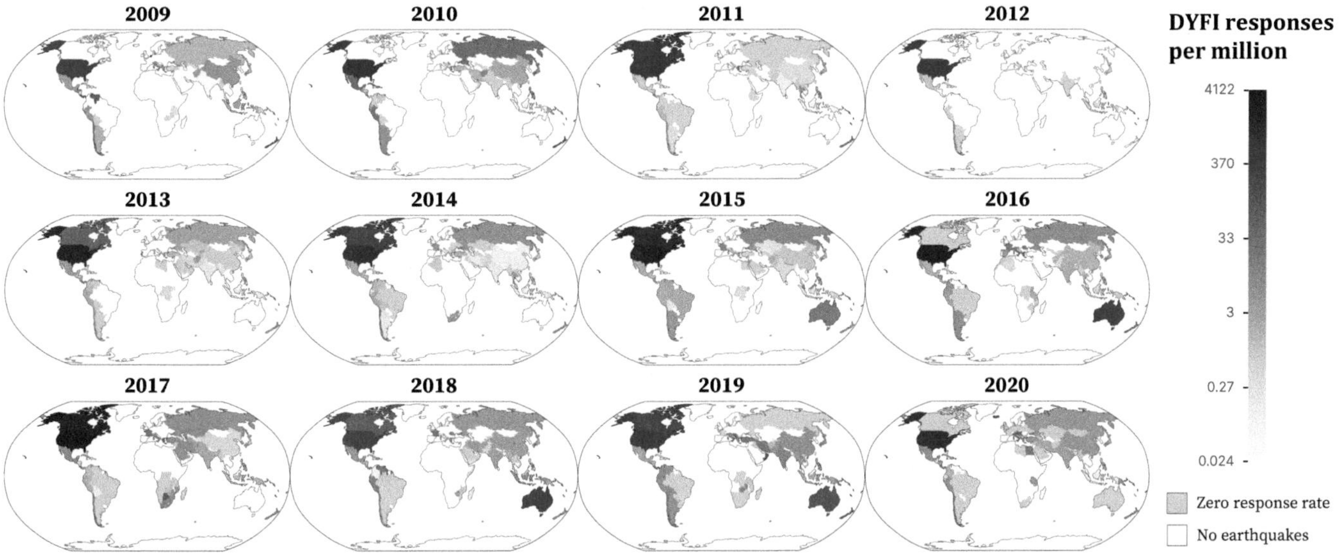

Figure 4. DYFI response rates over time. Grid of maps visualize response rate to DYFI for each year in the dataset (2009–2020). Response rates are transformed on a log scale and presented as DYFI responses per million people exposed to shaking. Countries are colored gray if they experienced earthquakes but had zero responses to DYFI for the year. The color version of this figure is available only in the electronic edition.

to the domestic threshold of M_w 3.5, we only include events of M_w 5.4 and greater. DYFI responses that occurred outside of a country's boundaries and in areas with zero population or a population less than the number of responses were also removed. Countries without any earthquake data and countries without data reported by the World Bank were removed from the analysis. The final panel dataset spans 151 countries between the years of 2009 and 2020. The dataset begins in 2009, one of the first years in which DYFI saw sustained and widespread global participation, with representation from 57 countries.

In our analysis, the dependent variable is DYFI response rate y per country per year (y_{ct}). Similar to Mak and Schorlemmer (2016) and Hough (2021), our explanatory variables (X_{ct}) are a combination of earthquake variables, largely from the USGS, and population variables, largely from the World Bank or the Central Intelligence Agency (CIA; see Data and Resources). Although we aimed to include similar variables as both studies, it was not always possible due to data availability. However, the regression analysis accounts for unobserved heterogeneity due to unexplained variables.

Overall, we evaluate a total of 52 explanatory variables, 36 from the USGS, 15 from the World Bank, and 1 from the CIA. Table A2 provides a full list of variables and their descriptions. Figure 4 visualizes country DYFI response rates (y) over time, and Figure 5 visualizes a subset of the explanatory variables in the dataset. Those identified as most influential for DYFI response rates are explained in further detail subsequently.

DYFI response rate (y_{ct}). DYFI response rate is the dependent variable in our analysis, normalizing the number of DYFI responses by the exposed population (defined as *TotalDYFIResponseRate* in Table A2). As done in other studies (Hough, 2021; Hough and Martin, 2021b), we use response rate rather than including population exposure as an explanatory variable to mitigate against the complex relationship between DYFI responses and population (Mak and Schorlemmer, 2016; Boatwright and Phillips, 2017).

The number of DYFI responses is the number of people who completed the questionnaire on the Felt Report page, introduced in the previous section for question 1. The Felt Report requires location information for CDI assignments, making location and date information available for each response. Felt Report responses were available on a 10 km grid, including the number of responses and the estimated exposed population per grid cell. Gridded population data are time-specific and originally sourced from Oak Ridge National Laboratory's (ORNL) LandScan (see Data and Resources; Quitoriano and Wald, 2020).

To aggregate the timestamped, grid-level Felt Report data to the country-year level, we grouped the grids by country and year and, within each country-year pair, summed the number of DYFI responses and separately summed the approximate population exposed to shaking (defined as *TotalDYFIResponses* and *TotalGriddedPopulation* in Table A2. The DYFI response rate y_{ct} used for analysis is the ratio of total responses to total population:

$$y_{ct} = \frac{\text{Total DYFI responses per country per year}}{\text{Total exposed population per country per year}}. \tag{1}$$

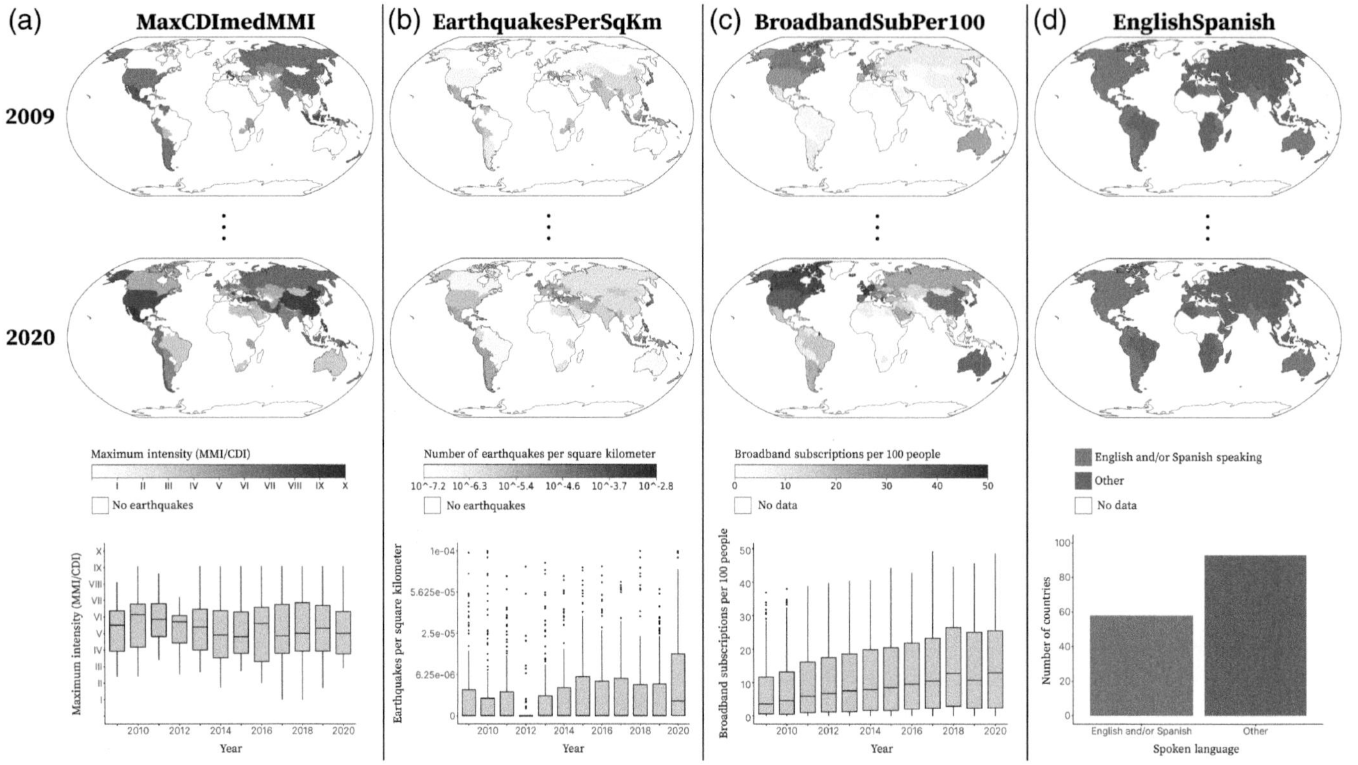

Figure 5. Explanatory variables over time. Grid of maps and charts visualize a subset of explanatory variables over time. Each column visualizes a different variable in the dataset: (a) *MaxCDImedMMI*, (b) *EarthquakesPerSqKm* (on a log scale), (c) *BroadbandSubPer100*, and (d) *EnglishSpanish*. These are the independent variables in the final statistical inference model. The first two rows show the spatial distribution of each variable for the first (2009) and last (2020) years of the compiled dataset. Intermediate years are not shown. The bottom row shows the temporal or categorical distribution of each variable. Each box in the box plot describes the variable's distribution across all 151 countries in a given year. Box plots for *EarthquakesPerSqKm* and *BroadbandSubPer100* have upper limits of 1×10^{-4} and 50, respectively, for visualization purposes. Missing values are not visualized. A bar chart is used for *EnglishSpanish*, because it is constant over time. The color version of this figure is available only in the electronic edition.

Earthquake variables (X_{ct}). We expect more DYFI responses in countries with frequent or large earthquakes. Therefore, we use multiple earthquake variables to capture a country's seismic hazard, which come from the USGS ShakeMap Atlas (see Data and Resources).

To represent intensity over the country, we calculate the maximum intensity across all earthquakes in that country and year ($MaxCDImedMMI_{ct}$). At the grid level, prior to aggregation, this metric uses the CDI value if there were DYFI responses in that grid; otherwise, it uses the grid's median MMI value from ShakeMap. We calculated and tested alternative summary statistics to the maximum per country-year pair, such as the minimum, average, and several quantiles, which are described in Table A2.

For seismically active countries, several earthquakes often occur in the same year. To account for earthquake frequency and the physical size of a country, we calculate earthquake density $EarthquakesPerSqKm_{ct}$ as the ratio of the number of earthquakes per year to a country's land area. Some earthquake variables exhibit a data anomaly in 2012 due to potential data acquisition issues. Because this anomaly was captured by both explanatory and dependent variables, we kept the year 2012 in the dataset.

Other seismic hazard variables tested describe characteristics such as magnitude and the number of grid cells exposed to shaking. These can be found in Table A2.

Population variables (X_{ct}). As noted in other studies of DYFI, response rate is also related to characteristics of the responding population (Mak and Schorlemmer, 2016; Hough and Martin, 2021b). To describe population variables for all countries, we used data from the World Bank and the CIA World Factbook (see Data and Resources). Our initial selection of population variables was informed by the socioeconomic status variables used by Mak and Schorlemmer (2016) and Hough and Martin (2021b), the results of the web analysis, and our own intuition regarding factors that could potentially influence DYFI response rate. Given the global scale of our analysis, population variable inclusion was constrained by which variables were available for all countries.

Similar to Mak and Schorlemmer (2016), we include primary spoken language. Felt Report is a language-dependent form that

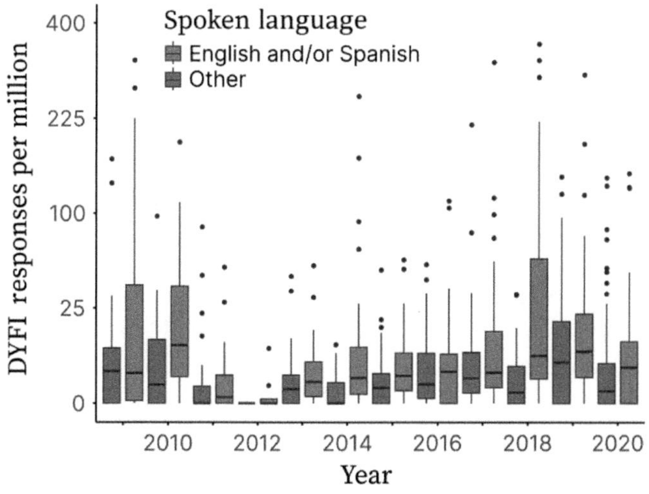

Figure 6. English- and Spanish-speaking countries tend to have higher DYFI response rates. Temporal box plots of response rate by country spoken language. For illustrative purposes, response rates are capped at 400 responses per million people exposed to shaking, and missing values are excluded from the visualization. The color version of this figure is available only in the electronic edition.

only supported English and Spanish at the time of this research, thus we created a binary indicator of a country's primary spoken language, $EnglishSpanish_c$. For $EnglishSpanish_c$ to be true, a country must have English or Spanish as an official language, or at least 25% of its residents must speak English or Spanish as their first language. Language data were sourced from the CIA World Factbook (see Data and Resources), which has data that are static in time, so $EnglishSpanish_c$ is constant across all years in the dataset. We used the most recent language estimates relative to the time of data sourcing (2023), with the year of estimate varying by country. The relationship between $EnglishSpanish_c$ and y_{ct} is visualized in Figure 6. For each year, response rates in English- and Spanish-speaking countries tend to be higher than those in non-English- and non-Spanish-speaking countries.

Similar to previous studies, we include education indicators, such as the proportion of the population enrolled in tertiary education ($TertiarySchoolPct_{ct}$) and government expenditure on education ($GovExpenditureEdu_{ct}$), and wealth indicators, such as gross domestic product per capita ($GDPcap_{ct}$). These variables were sourced from the World Bank (see Data and Resources).

Because DYFI is only available online and most users access DYFI via mobile devices, as found in the web analysis, we incorporate variables related to mobile phones and internet access. These variables include of cell phone subscriptions per 100 people ($CellSubPer100_{ct}$) and broadband (high-speed internet) subscriptions per 100 people ($BroadbandSubPer100_{ct}$). These variables were also sourced from the World Bank (see Data and Resources).

The subset of explanatory variables included in our selected model is visualized in Figure 5. All other initial population variables are included in Table A2.

Question 2: Regression analysis

Here, we leverage panel regression methods, a class of statistical regression that allows for the evaluation of explanatory variable effects on the dependent variable while accounting for unobserved covariates through the spatial and temporal heterogeneity of the panel dataset (Angrist and Pischke, 2008). Because the dependent variable, DYFI response rate (y_{ct}), is censored and only takes values between 0 and 1, we model DYFI response rates using a Tobit regression Colonescu, (2016) with mixed effects:

$$y^*_{ct} = \beta_{0c} + \sum_i^k \beta_i x_{ict} + \mu_c + \delta_t + \varepsilon_{ct}, \tag{2}$$

in which y^*_{ct} is a latent variable for the response rate, $\beta_0 c$ is the fitted intercept varying for each country c, x_{ict} is an earthquake or population variable i for country c and year t, β_i is the fitted coefficient for each variable, μ_c is the unobserved country-dependent error term, δ_t is the unobserved time-dependent error term, and ε_{ct} is a general error term. The mixed effects allow separate random intercepts and slopes to be estimated per country.

The observed response rate is derived from

$$y_{ct} = \begin{cases} y^{*2}_{ct} & \text{if } y^*_{ct} > 0 \\ 0 & \text{if } y^*_{ct} \le 0 \end{cases}. \tag{3}$$

Equation (3) ensures predicted values are greater than 0. We square the latent variable as we actually model the square root of DYFI response rate to reduce its skew and maintain zero values.

All continuous explanatory variables were standardized to facilitate comparison between variables and ensure variables with large variances do not dominate the model's fit. Because the maximum-observed response rate is 0.005, we do not impose an upper limit on y^*_{ct}. We use the plm package in R to fit the Tobit model to our panel data using maximum-likelihood estimation (see Data and Resources).

It is worth noting that this dataset becomes unbalanced when it is modeled, meaning each country does not have an equal number of observations. Observations are excluded from the model fit if they have a missing value for any of the model variables, and many country-year pairs are without an earthquake occurrence, causing those observations to lack a value for y_{ct} (among additional variables). Of the 1812 observations in the dataset, 1058 have a y_{ct} value that is missing.

Although a substantial part of the dataset has missing data, it does not appear to impact model results. Alternative models, which are detailed in Table A3, filled missing values in y_{ct} and arrived at very similar results based on the significance and direction of the coefficients in each model.

To evaluate the impact of each explanatory variable on DYFI response rate, we estimate their marginal effects, which give the predicted change in the response variable based on a one-unit increase of the explanatory variable. In an ordinary least-squares fit, the marginal effects are represented by the coefficients alone, but additional calculations are required to get these values in a Tobit regression. The marginal effect for the intercept E_0 is

$$E_0 = \hat{\beta}_0 \Phi\left(\frac{\hat{\beta}_0}{v}\right) + v\phi\left(\frac{\hat{\beta}_0}{v}\right), \quad (4)$$

in which $\hat{\beta}_0$ is the fitted intercept, v is the standard deviation of the model's error term (ε), Φ is the standard normal cumulative density function, and ϕ is the standard normal probability density function (Croissant and Millo, 2018). In general, $\hat{\beta}_i$ is the fitted estimate for the ith variable.

Marginal effects (E_i) for each explanatory variable x_i were calculated using

$$E_i = \frac{e_i}{\sigma_{x_i}}, \quad (5)$$

in which σ_{x_i} is the standard deviation of x_i and

$$e_i = \hat{\beta}_{0i} \Phi\left(\frac{\hat{\beta}_{0i}}{v}\right) + v\phi\left(\frac{\hat{\beta}_{0i}}{v}\right) - E_0, \quad (6)$$

$$\hat{\beta}_{0i} = \hat{\beta}_0 + \hat{\beta}_i. \quad (7)$$

Because we model the square root of the DYFI response rate, E_i is a marginal effect in relation to $\sqrt{y}$. To obtain an untransformed marginal effect, we use the relationship $y = (\sqrt{y})^2$ and differentiate with respect to x_i. This yields an instantaneous slope that varies with y, thus we plug in the average response rate $\bar{y}$ to arrive at our final marginal effects $\frac{\partial y}{\partial x_i}$, which have units of responses per exposed population:

$$\frac{\partial y}{\partial x_i} = 2 \times \sqrt{\bar{y}} \times E_i, \quad (8)$$

in which

$$E_i = \frac{\partial \sqrt{y}}{\partial x_i}. \quad (9)$$

For variable selection, we first removed explanatory variables relating to seismic stations because these variables describe another source of shaking intensity data, rather than earthquake or population characteristics. We also removed all variables that quantified the population exposed to shaking because this information is already present in y_{ct}. To determine the yearly summary statistic variables to consider in our model selection, we performed an exploratory data analysis that led us to keep all "maximum" variables ($MaxCDImedMMI_{ct}$, $MaxMagnitude_{ct}$, etc.) because they had the strongest correlation with DYFI response rate. This initial variable thinning reduced our pool of 52 explanatory variables to 19. We used forward selection to choose from the remaining pool, iteratively adding variables to the model based on their contribution to model fit, as evaluated by minimizing the Akaike information criterion (AIC; Akaike, 1974). In this pool, we also included several variable transformations (logarithmic, square root, etc.) and interaction terms. If an interaction term between two explanatory variables is significant, this means that the relationship between an explanatory variable and the response variable is different based on the value of the other explanatory variable. We carried out the forward selection process both manually and pseudo-randomly, adding variables to the model in no particular order, which led us to select a final model with four explanatory variables and one interaction term. All model fits were recorded, compared, and evaluated for interpretability to arrive at the final model:

$$\begin{aligned} y^*_{ct} = {} & \beta_{0c} + \beta_1 MaxCDImedMMI_{ct} \\ & + \beta_2 EarthquakesPerSqKm_{ct} + \beta_3 EnglishSpanish_c \\ & + \beta_4 BroadbandSubPer100_{ct} + \beta_5 EnglishSpanish_c \\ & * BroadbandSubPer100_{ct} + \mu_c + \delta_t + \varepsilon_{ct}, \end{aligned} \quad (10)$$

in which the final response rate can be calculated using equation (3). Uncertainty in the coefficient estimates β_i were estimated via 100 bootstrapped samples.

Notable measures not included in this model are the country's $MaxMagnitude_{ct}$ (maximum-magnitude earthquake), $TertiarySchoolPct_{ct}$, and $GDPcap_{ct}$. Unlike Mak and Schorlemmer (2016), who found magnitude to be a significant explanatory variable, $MaxMagnitude_{ct}$ did not have a strong relationship with response rate in our global analysis. This may be related to the fact that magnitude does not describe what is experienced at the Earth's surface as well as intensity does. Although $TertiarySchoolPct_{ct}$ had a substantial positive relationship with response rate, we excluded it from the model because 700 out of the 1812 country-year pairs lacked data for $TertiarySchoolPct_{ct}$, which would have significantly reduced the number of observations available for modeling. $GDPcap_{ct}$ also had a strong relationship with response rate, but it had a high correlation with $BroadbandSubPer100_{ct}$ as well, introducing multicollinearity issues if both measures were included in a model (Alin, 2010). Models with $BroadbandSubPer100_{ct}$ resulted in better fits to the data than models with $GDPcap_{ct}$, justifying its inclusion.

The interaction term between $EnglishSpanish_c$ and $BroadbandSubPer100_{ct}$ was included because it yielded a model with the lowest AIC.

TABLE 1
Coefficient Estimates and Variable Marginal Effects for the Fitted Model

Fitted Coefficient	x_i	Nontechnical Name for x_i	Estimate (β_i)	Marginal Unit	Marginal Effect in DYFI Responses per Million People Exposed to Shaking*
$\hat{\beta}_0$	(Intercept)		0.0001968		
$\hat{\beta}_1$	*MaxCDImedMMI*	Shaking intensity	0.0028222†	1 MMI	8.62
$\hat{\beta}_2$	*EarthquakesPerSqKm*	Earthquake density	0.0012222†	1 earthquake per **1000** km^2 per year	3.84
$\hat{\beta}_3$	*EnglishSpanish*	Spoken language	0.0029576†	Speaking a DYFI-supported language	16.6 **greater** than countries speaking other languages
$\hat{\beta}_4$	*BroadbandSubPer100*	Broadband subscriptions	0.0014210‡	1 broadband subscription per 100 people	0.59 in countries that speak a **language** that is **not supported** by DYFI
$\hat{\beta}_5$	*EnglishSpanish* * *BroadbandSubPer100*	Spoken language, broadband interaction	0.0012540	1 broadband subscription per 100 people	1.10 in countries that speak a **language** that is **supported** by DYFI (0.51 greater)

Coefficient estimates are based on standardized variables, thus they have comparable scales. The "Marginal Unit" specifies the (unstandardized) variable increase required for the estimated effect on the number of "Did You Feel It?" (DYFI) responses, which is given in the "Marginal Effect" column to its right. Marginal effect values were calculated using equations (4)–(8).

*Marginal effect calculations assume an initial DYFI response rate of 0.00001981 (19.81 responses per million people exposed to shaking), which is the average global response rate.

†$p < 0.001$.

‡$p < 0.01$.

To ensure that this selection of explanatory variables yields consistent results under different choices of response variables, transformations, and handling of missing values, we fit several other models as a robustness check. Table A3 gives the results for these models. In addition, diagnostic plots for the final model are available in Figures A1 and A2.

Question 2: Results and discussion

From our fitted model, the earthquake and population variables most significant in explaining DYFI response rate are shaking intensity ($MaxCDImedMMI_{ct}$), spoken language ($EnglishSpanish_c$), broadband subscriptions ($BroadbandSubPer100_{ct}$), and earthquake density ($EarthquakesPerSqKm_{ct}$), as shown in Table 1 and visualized in Figure 7. All of these variables have a positive relationship (positive coefficient and marginal effect) with response rate, meaning increases in each contribute to greater DYFI response rates.

Spoken language is the largest contributing factor overall. Countries with a population that speaks a language compatible with the Felt Report have higher response rates (16.6 responses per million people higher) on average. This effect is shown in Figure 7 by the greater intercepts associated with the lines for English- and Spanish-speaking countries, compared to countries that speak other languages. Language comprehension is a fundamental prerequisite for responding to DYFI, creating a barrier for populations that do not speak English or Spanish.

Regardless of a country's spoken language, increased broadband subscriptions have a significant relationship with responses to DYFI. Marginal effect calculations show that an additional broadband subscription per 100 people corresponds to a higher rate of DYFI responses (0.59 responses per million people exposed) in countries that do not speak a language compatible with DYFI. In countries where a DYFI-compatible language is spoken, greater broadband internet access per capita further amplifies this increased response rate. Our model has a positive interaction term between spoken language and broadband subscriptions, meaning that an additional broadband subscription per 100 people coincides with an even greater DYFI response rate (1.10 responses per million people) in English- and Spanish-speaking countries. The compounding effect of broadband subscriptions and spoken language on DYFI response rate is illustrated by the differing slopes in Figure 7a. This effect is also likely influenced by the language barrier. Although greater internet accessibility generally leads to higher DYFI engagement, countries with strong digital infrastructure and a larger proportion of English or Spanish speakers are better positioned to have high response rates, as more people are able to easily engage with the platform.

These results for spoken language and broadband subscriptions provide statistical evidence that strengthens the claims made by Hough and Martin (2021b) and Hough (2021) on a broader, global scale.

Earthquake variables, as expected, have a significant effect on DYFI response rate. Shaking intensity has a strong relationship with response rate (Fig. 7b), with an increase in

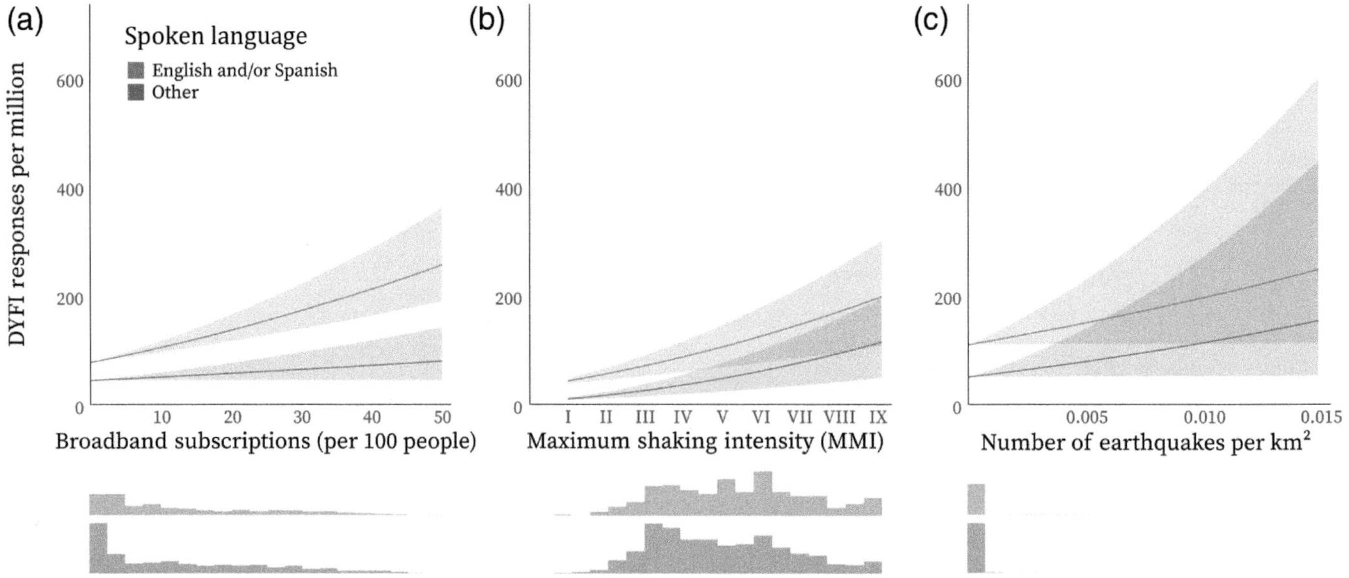

Figure 7. Individual variable impacts on DYFI response rate. Line plots with confidence bounds visualize the modeled relationship between quantitative explanatory variables and DYFI response rate, by country's spoken language, while holding all other variables constant (at their mean value). Quantitative explanatory variables plotted are (a) broadband subscriptions, (b) shaking intensity, and (c) earthquake density. Based on 100 bootstrapped samples, the lines correspond to the median coefficients, and the bounds reflect a 95% confidence interval derived from the same bootstrapping process. Response rate values were calculated using equations (3)–(7). Below the plots are histograms of explanatory variables by country spoken language, including data from all years (2009–2020). The color version of this figure is available only in the electronic edition.

maximum-shaking intensity of 1 corresponding to an average increase in DYFI responses of 8.62 responses per million people. This relationship may be explained by stronger surface shaking causing greater societal impact, which in turn motivates people to share their experiences and learn more about the event. This positive relationship between intensity and DYFI responses is consistent with Mak and Schorlemmer (2016) and Hough and Martin (2021b).

Earthquake density and DYFI response rate also have a strong relationship. Holding all other factors constant, a country that experiences an additional earthquake per 1000 km^2 per year is expected to see an increase of 3.84 DYFI responses per million people. One possible interpretation of this relationship is that populations in seismically active countries are likely more familiar with earthquakes and related resources, such as DYFI.

In Figure 7c, the confidence bounds for the marginal effects of earthquake density on DYFI response rate are wider than those for broadband subscriptions and shaking intensity. Earthquake density values are typically very low, but a few seismically active, small-area countries have high values, causing greater uncertainty in estimates for the impact of high earthquake density on response rate.

Question 3: Where Can DYFI Responses Be Increased?

Based on the results from the statistical inference model, we develop a priority index to identify countries where improved DYFI access is likely to lead to increased engagement. With this priority index, we build upon the significant variables identified from question 2, and also include an additional variable to account for the relative importance of increased access to DYFI, given other sources of ground-motion data in a country. For example, in a country such as Japan that has a dense network of seismic stations, an additional DYFI response is valuable for earthquake perception, but is not as influential on the final estimate of shaking distribution in the ShakeMap as compared to a country that has a sparse set of stations. Our index assigns equal weight to each country's relative position across all variables to generate a composite metric for country prioritization.

Question 3: Data

For the priority index, we build upon the dataset from question 2 to identify where DYFI access can be increased in the future. Our goal is to characterize each country by the variables identified as important for DYFI access in question 2 and include additional information on seismic stations. Here, we include six variables: *TotalDYFIResponseRate*, *EnglishSpanish*, *BroadbandSubPer100*, *MaxCDImedMMI*, *TotalGriddedPopulation*, and *StationsPerCapita*. Each of these variables was collapsed to remove the time dimension, as described subsequently.

For *EnglishSpanish* and *BroadbandSubPer100*, we select the countries' most recent values (from 2020). For *MaxCDImedMMI*, we use the countries' largest recorded shaking intensity between 2009 and 2020. Because we are

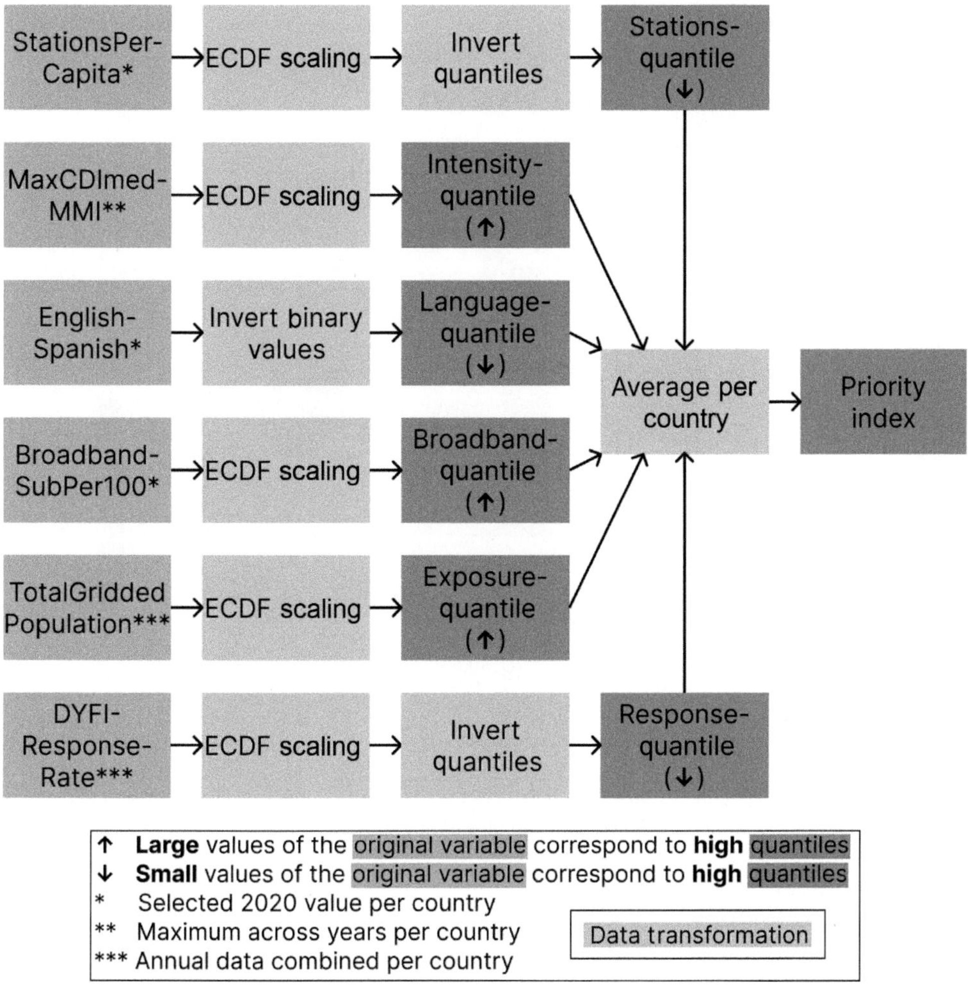

Figure 8. Calculating the country priority index. The diagram flows left to right, starting with input variables, transforming them into country quantiles, and averaging quantiles to create the priority index. Empirical cumulative distribution function (ECDF) scaling involves constructing an ECDF to assign country quantiles for each variable. For further details on the priority index calculation, see Figure A3. The color version of this figure is available only in the electronic edition.

identifying countries where DYFI responses could be improved, we also use the DYFI response rate variable (*TotalDYFIResponseRate*) as an input factor in the priority index, which we recalculate over 2009–2020. We use *TotalGriddedPopulation*—which represents the total population exposure to shaking each year—as our measure of earthquake density and exposure, summing its annual values from 2009 to 2020. This approach is used instead of *EarthquakesPerSqKm* because *TotalGriddedPopulation* reflects the number of people potentially able to respond to DYFI, a dimension that *EarthquakesPerSqKm* does not capture.

In addition to the variables we found in the model, we add the ratio of ShakeMap-input seismic stations and a country's population *StationsPerCapita*. Here, we use seismic station location data from the International Federation of Digital Seismograph Networks (FDSN), selecting data from 2020 (see Data and Resources).

Question 3: Priority index

We create a composite priority index that averages the relative standing of countries across each variable to identify countries that are most likely to benefit from improved DYFI accessibility. This is similar to creating a composite index score for a country (OECD and JRC, 2008).

Figure 8 outlines the calculation of the priority index, with greater detail available in Figure A3. For the quantitative variables, we create empirical cumulative distribution functions (ECDFs) to assign quantiles to each country, giving them a value ranging from 0 to 1 for each variable. The *EnglishSpanish* variable remains binary, with non-English- and non-Spanish-speaking countries being assigned as 1.

We use results from the inference model to determine a variable's direction of influence on the priority ranking, as specified by the vertical arrows in the quantile boxes in Figure 8. For example, although limited high-speed internet subscriptions hinder DYFI interaction, broadband infrastructure is nearly impossible to modify. Larger values of *BroadbandSubPer100* indicate that a country's population is better equipped to access the DYFI Felt Report, suggesting a high potential for increased engagement. For variables in which smaller values represent higher priority, such as *StationsPerCapita*, quantiles are inverted (e.g., 0.01 becomes 0.99).

After computing variable quantiles for each country, they are averaged with equal weights to form the composite priority index. This index ranges from 0 to 1, with higher values representing greater priority for improved DYFI accessibility.

Question 3: Results and discussion

The priority index highlights that non-English-speaking Asian and Central European countries would most benefit from having improved for improved DYFI access, as shown in Figure 9 and Table 2. The top 10 ranked countries have a historical

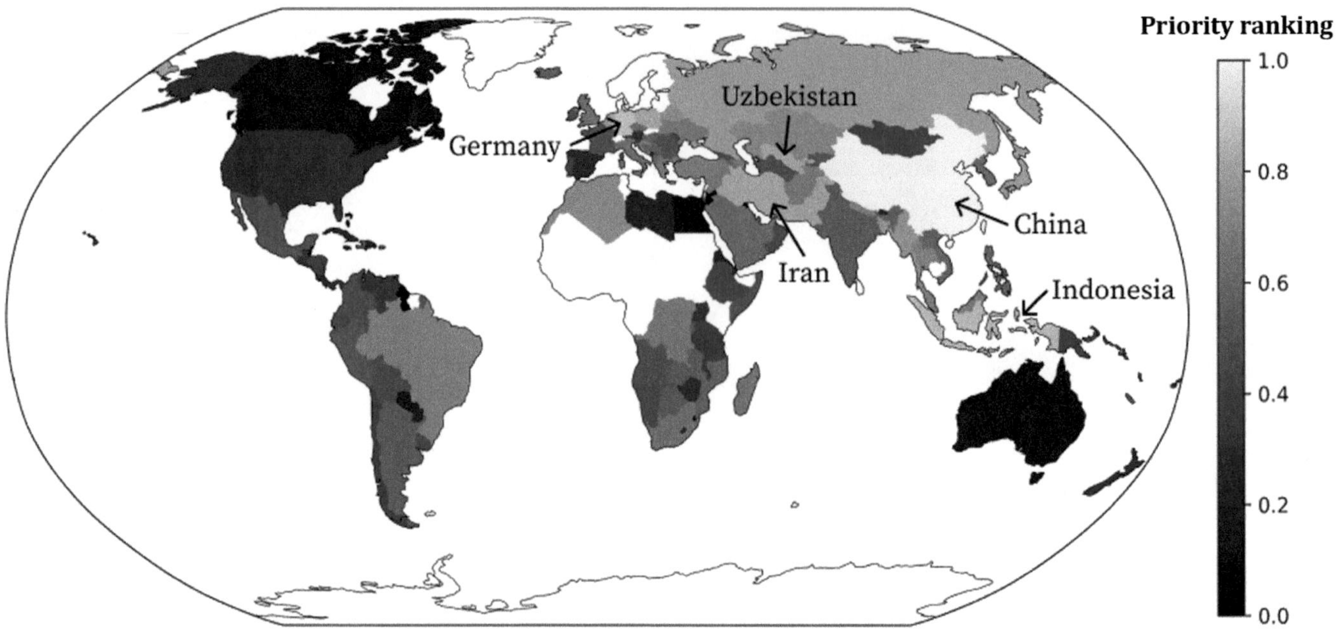

Figure 9. Mapped results of the composite priority index. Countries with the highest priority for improved DYFI accessibility are labeled. White-colored countries had no recorded earthquakes from 2009 to 2020. The color version of this figure is available only in the electronic edition.

DYFI response rate below the global median and seismic station coverage that places each of them in the bottom 20% globally. Although they are unified in these aspects, they differ in their seismic and technological contexts.

Indonesia and several countries in the Middle East and South Asia (Iran, Iraq, and Pakistan) have high-priority indices due to intense earthquake hazards. These countries are very seismically active, with large populations exposed to earthquakes, yet they have few or no seismic stations in the FDSN. In addition, their limited high-speed internet coverage compared to other high-priority countries makes it harder for them to engage with DYFI.

Central European countries, such as Germany, Poland, and the Netherlands, also have high-priority indices, though they face lower earthquake hazards. High-intensity earthquakes are less common, resulting in lower population exposure and a reduced need for a seismic station network. However, these countries have high broadband internet coverage, giving them greater potential to engage with DYFI when an earthquake does occur.

Countries with high DYFI response rates and populations that speak a DYFI-compatible language, such as Costa Rica,

TABLE 2
Variable Quantile Breakdown for the Composite Priority Index

Country	Priority	Stations	Intensity	Language	Broadband	Exposure	DYFI Response Rate
China	**0.92**	0.96	1.00	1.00	0.85	0.98	0.73
Germany	**0.85**	0.83	0.62	1.00	0.96	0.67	1.00
Indonesia	**0.83**	0.97	1.00	1.00	0.28	0.99	0.76
Uzbekistan	**0.81**	1.00	0.52	1.00	0.51	0.83	0.99
Iran	**0.81**	1.00	0.89	1.00	0.47	0.93	0.56
Poland	**0.81**	1.00	0.54	1.00	0.68	0.62	1.00
Iraq	**0.81**	1.00	0.81	1.00	0.53	0.90	0.60
Netherlands	**0.80**	1.00	0.59	1.00	0.97	0.48	0.77
Pakistan	**0.80**	1.00	0.83	1.00	0.17	0.95	0.85
Russia	**0.79**	0.88	0.79	1.00	0.72	0.75	0.60

The top 10 countries for improved "Did You Feel It?" (DYFI) accessibility are listed in descending order.

Venezuela, and New Zealand, tend to have low-priority indices. Similarly, many African countries, with their low seismic hazard, have low-priority indices, or no priority index was calculated due to a lack of recorded earthquakes in the dataset.

Built on variables with a statistically significant relationship to DYFI response rate, the composite priority index offers an immediate application of the model results. Countries with the highest priority are those where efforts to increase interaction with DYFI are most likely to result in substantial increases in response rate. These efforts can meaningfully expand public and scientific understanding of seismic activity in countries that need it most, all without the need for costly seismic infrastructure.

Conclusion

In this first comprehensive global analysis of DYFI, we found that a large majority of DYFI respondents access the Felt Report page via mobile device, with social media being a primary driver for engagement. In addition, we observed that socioeconomic factors, such as high-speed internet infrastructure and primary spoken languages, along with the intensity and frequency of earthquakes, significantly influence DYFI response rates globally. Our findings add to those of previous studies (Mak and Schorlemmer, 2016; Hough, 2021; Hough and Martin, 2021b) by presenting a thorough statistical analysis of 1758 earthquakes around the world. Overall, the results of this study suggest that with improved DYFI accessibility, non-English-speaking Asian and Central European countries are most likely to see large increases in DYFI interaction.

Moving forward, efforts to improve the accessibility of DYFI can take many forms. For example, technological approaches could include building a social media presence to raise awareness of DYFI among populations exposed to shaking, as well as optimizing the questionnaire for a smoother user experience on mobile devices. Language, specifically, has been an integral factor contributing to DYFI engagement, and as a result, the USGS has already begun supporting languages beyond English and Spanish, including Chinese and German. To further enhance language accessibility, more languages could be incorporated—such as Indonesian or Persian—based on those spoken in priority countries, or reliance on language could be reduced through visual aids. When adapting DYFI to be more accessible in various parts of the world, it could be beneficial to tailor the questionnaire to the local population, considering the geographical, cultural, and structural differences that may influence their experience with the earthquake. Furthermore, collaborating with partner agencies in countries with high-priority indices is not only encouraged but also required when relevant in-country partners exist, to ensure that the questionnaire is accessible and understandable to their residents.

This study aims to develop the first global analysis of DYFI accessibility to support future engagement efforts by the USGS. As with any global analysis, trade-offs exist between leveraging consistent, globally available data sources and more accurate country-specific sources. For example, the developed panel dataset leverages The World Bank and the CIA World Factbook, which provide consistent socioeconomic variables as opposed to country-level census data, which have differences in collection methodologies and frequencies between countries. Because of this, some variables may be underestimated, like spoken language, as the CIA World Factbook only provides information for first languages spoken by country, regardless of the percentage of the population that may speak English or Spanish. Therefore, some effects may be underestimated, though the results of this study are useful for initial decision-making with which to engage. Continued engagement will, of course, depend on more detailed information on each country's socioeconomic makeup.

Considering data limitations, the results do capture overall trends in DYFI access among countries.

In this study, we found that interaction with DYFI—a key input into USGS rapid loss estimates used to inform humanitarian response—is influenced not only by earthquake characteristics, but also by access to resources and language comprehension. Thus, disadvantaged populations that do not speak a DYFI-compatible language are unfavorably positioned to provide on-the-ground measurements that calibrate shaking estimates influencing emergency response. For emergency managers to better serve earthquake-affected populations, it is crucial to reduce the barriers that prevent people from documenting their experiences. It is also critical to acknowledge the existence of these barriers, particularly when considering potentially marginalized populations whose impacts from the earthquake may have been underestimated. With the global reach of the USGS earthquake products, earthquake-affected populations and scientific communities around the world stand to benefit from increased spatial coverage of DYFI, making it essential that its barriers to access are reduced in the areas that need it most.

Data and Resources

Google Analytics user data were acquired through the Digital Analytics Program and the Technology Transformation Services at the U.S. General Services Administration (U.S. General Services Administration, 2024). This aggregated user data is available from the authors upon request. All "Did You Feel It?" (DYFI) data for this analysis are publicly available at http://earthquake.usgs.gov/dyfi. The U.S. Geological Survey (USGS) Comprehensive Catalog (ComCat) has a webpage interface, application programming interface (API), and associated command-line tool (libcomcat) for retrieving earthquake event information, including DYFI data. Raw, anonymized DYFI data are available upon request from the USGS. Earthquake data were sourced from the USGS ShakeMap Atlas (Marano *et al.*, 2024). Data for population exposed to shaking comes from Oak Ridge National Laboratory (ORNL) LandScan (Sims *et al.*, 2023). Socioeconomic data were collected from the World Bank, (2023), and language data were scraped using Python from the Central Intelligence Agency (CIA) World Factbook (Central Intelligence Agency, 2023). Seismic station location data were gathered from the International Federation of Digital Seismograph Networks (FDSN; International Federation of Digital Seismograph Networks, 2023) and the station list for ShakeMap (U.S. Geological Survey, 2011). Statistical analyses were conducted in R using the plm package (Croissant *et al.*, 2024).

Declaration of Competing Interests

The authors acknowledge that there are no conflicts of interest recorded.

Acknowledgments

This research was conducted under the financial support of the University of Michigan and the U.S. Geological Survey (USGS). The authors thank *Seismological Research Letters* reviewers and Max Schneider for their feedback that helped them improve this work. Conceptualization: S. L., E. K., D. W.; methodology: E. K., S. L.; data collection: V. Q., E. K.; formal analysis: E. K., S. L.; writing—original draft: E. K.; visualization: E. K.; writing—review and editing: S. L., V. Q., D. W., E. K.; funding acquisition: S. L., D. W.; project administration: S. L.

References

Akaike, H. (1974). A new look at the statistical model identification, *IEEE Trans. Autom. Control* **19,** no. 6, 716–723.

Alin, A. (2010). Multicollinearity, *Wiley Interdiscip. Rev. Comput. Stat.* **2,** no. 3, 370–374.

Angrist, J. D., and J.-S. Pischke (2008). Mostly harmless econometrics: An empiricist's companion, in *Mostly Harmless Econometrics*, Princeton University Press, Princeton, New Jersey.

Atkinson, G. M., and D. J. Wald (2007). "Did You Feel It?" Intensity data: A surprisingly good measure of earthquake ground motion, *Seismol. Res. Lett.* **78,** no. 3, 362–368.

Boatwright, J., and E. Phillips (2017). Exploiting the demographics of "Did You Feel It?" responses to estimate the felt area of moderate earthquakes in California, *Seismol. Res. Lett.* **88,** no. 2A, 335–341.

Bossu, R., S. Gilles, G. Mazet-Roux, F. Roussel, L. Frobert, and L. Kamb (2011). Flash sourcing, or rapid detection and characterization of earthquake effects through website traffic analysis, *Ann. Geophys.* **54,** no. 6, doi: 10.4401/ag-5265.

Bossu, R., M. Landès, F. Roussel, R. Steed, G. Mazet-Roux, S. S. Martin, and S. Hough (2016). Thumbnail-based questionnaires for the rapid and efficient collection of macroseismic data from global earthquakes, *Seismol. Res. Lett.* **88,** no. 1, 72–81.

Bossu, R., S. Lefebvre, Y. Cansi, and G. Mazet-Roux (2014). Characterization of the 2011 Mineral, Virginia, earthquake effects and epicenter from website traffic analysis, *Seismol. Res. Lett.* **85,** no. 1, 91–97.

Bossu, R., G. Mazet-Roux, V. Douet, S. Rives, S. Marin, and M. Aupetit (2008). Internet users as seismic sensors for improved earthquake response, *EOS Trans. AGU* **89,** no. 25, 225–226.

Calais, E., A. Freed, G. Mattioli, F. Amelung, S. Jónsson, P. Jansma, S.-H. Hong, T. Dixon, C. Prépetit, and R. Momplaisir (2010). Transpressional rupture of an unmapped fault during the 2010 Haiti earthquake, *Nature Geosci.* **3,** no. 11, 794–799.

Celsi, R., M. Wolfinbarger, and D. Wald (2005). The effects of earthquake measurement concepts and magnitude anchoring on individuals' perceptions of earthquake risk, *Earthq. Spectra* **21,** no. 4, 987–1008.

Central Intelligence Agency (2023). Languages - the world factbook, available at https://www.cia.gov/the-world-factbook/field/languages/ (last accessed January 2023).

Colonescu, C. (2016). *Principles of Econometrics with R.*

Croissant, Y., and G. Millo (2018). *Panel Data Econometrics with R*, John Wiley & Sons, Hoboken, New Jersey.

Croissant, Y., G. Millo, and K. Tappe (2024). Linear models for panel data, available at https://github.com/ycroissant/plm (last accessed January 2025).

Dengler, L. A., and J. W. Dewey (1998). An intensity survey of households affected by the Northridge, California, earthquake of 17 January, 1994, *Bull. Seismol. Soc. Am.* **88,** 441–462.

Earle, P. S., D. J. Wald, K. S. Jaiswal, T. I. Allen, M. G. Hearne, K. D. Marano, A. J. Hotovec, and J. Fee (2009). Prompt assessment of global earthquakes for response (PAGER): A system for rapidly determining the impact of earthquakes worldwide, *U.S. Geol. Surv. Numbered Series 2009-1131.*

Eberhard, M., S. Baldridge, J. Marshall, W. Mooney, and G. Rix (2010). The mw 7.0 Haiti earthquake of January 12, 2010: USGS/EERI advance reconnaissance team report, *U.S. Geol. Surv. Open-File Rept. 2010-1048.*

Goded, T., N. Horspool, M. Gerstenberger, S. Canessa, and A. Lewis (2017). Macroseismic intensity assessment method for online questionnaires in New Zealand, *Proc. of the 16th World Conference on Earthquake Engineering*, Santiago de Chile, Chile, Paper 1109, 12 pp.

Goltz, J. D., H. Park, V. Quitoriano, and D. J. Wald (2020). Human behavioral response in the 2019 Ridgecrest, California, earthquakes: Assessing immediate actions based on data from "Did You Feel It?", *Bull. Seismol. Soc. Am.* **110,** no. 4, 1589–1602.

Google Analytics (2024). Ga4 dimensions & metrics explorer (last accessed August 2024).

Hough, S. E. (2021). Contributed reports of widely felt earthquakes in California, United States: If They Felt it, Did They Report it? *Front. Earth Sci.* **9,** doi: 10.3389/feart.2021.770445.

Hough, S. E., and S. S. Martin (2021a). Reply to "comment on 'which earthquake accounts matter?' by Susan E. Hough and Stacey S. Martin" by David J. Wald, *Seismol. Res. Lett.* **93,** no. 1, 506–511.

Hough, S. E., and S. S. Martin (2021b). Which earthquake accounts matter? *Seismol. Res. Lett.* **92,** no. 2A, 1069–1084.

International Federation of Digital Seismograph Networks (2023). About the FDSN, available at https://www.fdsn.org/about/ (last accessed January 2023).

Loos, S., M. Karr, M. Macías, E. Knodel, D. Wald, K. Ludwig, L. Peek, and P. Lee (2024). Publicly available yet not fully accessible: Strategies for equitably sharing post-earthquake loss information., *Proceedings from the 18th World Conference on Earthquake Engineering. 18th World Conference on Earthquake Engineering*, Milan, Italy.

Mak, S., and D. Schorlemmer (2016). What makes people respond to "Did You Feel It"? *Seismol. Res. Lett.* **87,** no. 1, 119–131.

Marano, K. D., M. Hearne, K. S. Jaiswal, E. M. Thompson, C. B. Worden, and D. J. Wald (2024). Shakemap atlas 4.0 and Atlascat: An archive of the recent and the historical earthquake

Shakemaps, and impacts for global hazard analyses and loss model calibration, *Seismol. Res. Lett.* **95,** no. 2A, 879–899.
OECD and JRC (2008). *Handbook on Constructing Composite Indicators: Methodology and User Guide*, OECD Publishing, Paris, France.
Quitoriano, V., and D. J. Wald (2020). USGS "Did You Feel It?—Science and lessons from 20 years of citizen science-based microseismology, *Front. Earth Sci.* **8,** doi: 10.3389/feart.2020.00120.
Sbarra, P., P. Tosi, and V. De Rubeis (2010). Web-based macroseismic survey in Italy: Method validation and results, *Nat. Hazards* **54,** no. 2, 563–581.
Sims, K., A. Reith, E. Bright, J. Kaufman, J. Pyle, J. Epting, J. Gonzales, D. Adams, E. Powell, M. Urban, *et al.* (2023). Landscan global 2022 Data set, available at https://landscan.ornl.gov/ (last accessed August 2023).
Thompson, E. M., S. K. McBride, G. P. Hayes, K. E. Allstadt, L. A. Wald, D. J. Wald, K. L. Knudsen, C. B. Worden, K. D. Marano, R. W. Jibson, *et al.* (2019). USGS near-real-time products—and their use—for the 2018 Anchorage earthquake, *Seismol. Res. Lett.* **91,** no. 1, 94–113.
Tosi, P., P. Sbarra, V. De Rubeis, and C. Ferrari (2015). Macroseismic intensity assessment method for web questionnaires, *Seismol. Res. Lett.* **86,** no. 3, 985–990.
U.S. General Services Administration (2024). Digital analytics program (DAP) guide, available at https://digital.gov/guides/dap (last accessed January 2024).
U.S. Geological Survey (2011). Shakemap station data for the 2011 Tohoku, Japan earthquake, available at https://earthquake.usgs.gov/earthquakes/eventpage/official20110311054624120_30/shakemap/stations (last accessed July 2025).
U.S. Geological Survey (2025). DYFI scientific background, available at https://earthquake.usgs.gov/data/dyfi/background.php (last accessed April 2025).
Wald, D. J. (2021). Comment on "which earthquake accounts matter?" by S. E. Hough and S. S. Martin, *Seismol. Res. Lett.* **93,** no. 1, 500–505, doi: 10.1785/0220210072.
Wald, D. J. (2023). Alerting the globe of consequential earthquakes, *Perspect. Earth Space Sci.* **4,** no. 1, e2022CN000200, doi: 10.1029/2022CN000200.
Wald, D. J., C. B. Worden, E. M. Thompson, and M. Hearne (2022). ShakeMap operations, policies, and procedures, *Earthq. Spectra* **38,** no. 1, 756–777.
World Bank (2023). World bank open data, available at https://data.worldbank.org/ (last accessed January 2023).

Appendix

Appendix includes tables describing sampled events used in the web analysis (Table A1), variables in the global panel dataset (Table A2), and results from alternative statistical models (Table A3). It also contains model diagnostic plots (Figs. A1 and A2) and a more detailed diagram of the priority metric calculation (Fig. A3).

TABLE A1
All Sampled Events Included in the Web Analysis

Event Name	Event ID	DYFI Responses	Total Users	Regional Users	Year
M_w 7.1—Ridgecrest, California	ci38457511	24,382	23,721	18,581	2019
M_w 3.6—Bliss Corner, Massachusetts	us7000cc4d	19,612	16,284	15,148	2020
M_w 5.1—Sparta, North Carolina	se60324281	66,710	44,083	9,662	2020
M_w 5.9—Chiba, Japan	us6000fsl6	5,679	21,703	17,429	2021
M_w 6.0—Antelope Valley, California	nc73584926	25,976	8,459	6,174	2021
M_w 4.3—Carson, California	ci39812319	10,294	5,672	4,996	2021
M_w 6.2—Petrolia, California	nc73666231	4,401	3,639	1,978	2021
M_w 5.9—Mount Buller, Australia	us7000fd9v	5,839	2,126	1,846	2021
M_w 4.0—Williamsville, Missouri	nm60363582	5,442	3,791	1,533	2021
M_w 5.9—Port Alsworth, Alaska	us6000geb1	1,886	735	391	2021
M_w 4.3—Gypsum, Kansas	us6000gaga	811	576	318	2021
M_w 5.3—Calipatria, California	ci39919392	1,173	490	313	2021
M_w 6.2—Naalehu, Hawaii	hv72748782	3,485	717	282	2021
M_w 4.9—Harding-Birch Lakes, Alaska	ak021bt4ffvw	1,085	421	232	2021
M_w 5.2—Kukuihaele, Hawaii	hv72565662	1,335	261	149	2021

Data are ordered by year and number of regional users. Totals across all events are given in the final row. DYFI, "Did You Feel It?"
(Continued next page.)

TABLE A1 (continued)
All Sampled Events Included in the Web Analysis

Event Name	Event ID	DYFI Responses	Total Users	Regional Users	Year
M_w 4.7—San Simeon, California	nc73644630	619	251	129	2021
M_w 7.0—Acapulco, Mexico	us7000f93v	654	510	113	2021
M_w 5.7—Chile–Argentina border region	us7000fr0v	450	96	75	2021
M_w 6.2—Falam, Myanmar	us7000fx45	333	130	73	2021
M_w 5.7—Talisay, Philippines	us7000fen1	211	82	70	2021
M_w 6.7—Hukay, Philippines	us6000eyfk	317	116	60	2021
M_w 7.2—Nippes, Haiti	us6000f65h	362	436	52	2021
M_w 6.4—Bandar Abbas, Iran	us7000fu12	207	152	50	2021
M_w 7.5—Barranca, Peru	us7000fxq2	274	263	23	2021
M_w 6.2—Yilan, Taiwan	us6000fx56	113	160	21	2021
M_w 6.7—Burica, Panama	us6000exs5	225	106	17	2021
M_w 6.3—Masachapa, Nicaragua	us7000fskw	110	97	16	2021
M_w 5.6—Corral del Risco, Mexico	us7000eik4	110	47	15	2021
M_w 5.1—Alum Rock, California	nc73799091	24,216	22,163	8,098	2022
M_w 6.4—Ferndale, California	nc73821036	5,950	6,287	2,864	2022
M_w 6.1—Duzce, Türkiye	us7000irp8	1,686	4,045	2,355	2022
M_w 4.0—Palomar Observatory, California	ci39928087	5,793	2,393	1,955	2022
M_w 7.6—Aguililla, Mexico	us7000i9bw	1,171	2,344	1,172	2022
M_w 4.5—Medford, Oklahoma	ok2022cedc	4,766	1,879	933	2022
M_w 4.1—Bay Point, California	nc73740051	5,796	1,736	861	2022
M_w 3.9—Stillmore, Georgia	se60400186	2,352	1,754	762	2022
M_w 4.0—Santa Paula, California	ci40194736	2,096	660	526	2022
M_w 4.7—Hōlualoa, Hawaii	hv73019747	1,600	1,017	490	2022
M_w 5.2—Cantwell, Alaska	ak0221pb6nv5	1,362	514	350	2022
M_w 4.7—Wailua, Hawaii	hv72889347	847	211	148	2022
M_w 4.8—Deep Springs, California	nc73674211	526	353	139	2022
M_w 6.0—Bandar-e Lengeh, Iran	us6000hz8x	488	315	136	2022
M_w 4.5—Waimea, Hawaii	hv72956917	754	166	113	2022
M_w 5.2—Range Hill, Texas	tx2022yplg	2,405	237	95	2022
M_w 6.2—Nueva Concepción, Guatemala	us7000gl8w	431	215	95	2022
M_w 7.3—Namie, Japan	us6000h519	452	299	73	2022
M_w 6.6—Pólis, Cyprus	us7000gaqu	486	247	70	2022
M_w 4.7—Tyonek, Alaska	ak0228vb1a7q	1,400	186	64	2022
M_w 5.7—Ljubinje, Bosnia and Herzegovina	us6000hfqj	464	188	60	2022
M_w 6.6—Labuan, Indonesia	us7000gbu4	140	97	45	2022

Data are ordered by year and number of regional users. Totals across all events are given in the final row. DYFI, "Did You Feel It?"
(Continued next page.)

TABLE A1 (continued)
All Sampled Events Included in the Web Analysis

Event Name	Event ID	DYFI Responses	Total Users	Regional Users	Year
M_w 6.1—Bukittinggi, Indonesia	us6000gzyg	212	112	31	2022
M_w 5.3—Metsavan, Armenia	us7000gkl5	117	40	26	2022
M_w 5.5—Flórina, Greece	us7000gaex	154	93	23	2022
M_w 5.6—Sukabumi, Indonesia	us7000ir9t	161	60	23	2022
M_w 7.0—Dolores, Philippines	us6000i5rd	664	332	15	2022
M_w 6.6—Masachapa, Nicaragua	us6000hf75	159	63	13	2022
M_w 5.1—Ojai, California	ci39645386	14,126	7,510	4,693	2023
M_w 4.3—Port Townsend, Washington	uw61965081	10,892	6,323	4,253	2023
M_w 5.5—Lake Almanor, California	nc73886731	7,025	3,419	2,539	2023
M_w 4.2—Malibu Beach, California	ci40161279	11,376	6,234	2,429	2023
M_w 3.8—West Seneca, New York	us6000jlqv	5,920	4,556	2,389	2023
M_w 4.5—Eagle River, Alaska	ak0238gji26s	2,191	2,097	1,597	2023
M_w 4.2—Palomar Observatory, California	ci39508378	7,603	2,176	1,392	2023
M_w 4.2—Isleton, California	nc73948665	7,895	1,724	1,254	2023
M_w 4.9—Gauteng, South Africa	us7000k7q8	1,377	1,193	1,048	2023
M_w 6.8—Al Haouz, Morocco	us7000kufc	1,294	1,365	607	2023
M_w 7.8—Türkiye earthquake sequence	us6000jllz	2,035	2,125	583	2023
M_w 3.8—Mickleham, Australia	us7000k4me	1,588	409	389	2023
M_w 3.6—Madison, Ohio	us7000krer	1,403	611	385	2023
M_w 5.4—Rio Dell, California	nc73827571	976	747	351	2023
M_w 6.5—Jurm, Afghanistan	us7000jln7	1,084	445	286	2023
M_w 5.6—Lelesti, Romania	us6000jnqz	646	262	201	2023
M_w 5.2—Canyondam, California	nc73887046	1,350	250	160	2023
M_w 5.2—Coalson Draw, Texas	tx2023vxae	1,241	314	133	2023
M_w 5.0—Matanzas, Dominican Republic	us6000jkqk	629	169	128	2023
M_w 5.7—Dailekh, Nepal	us7000l8p5	372	147	97	2023
M_w 7.1—Gili Air, Indonesia	us7000krjx	628	213	72	2023
M_w 6.3—Uzunbag, Türkiye	us6000jqcn	546	479	67	2023
M_w 7.6—Mindanao, Philippines	us7000lff4	351	366	59	2023
M_w 6.8—Balao, Ecuador	us7000jl3s	194	162	38	2023
Total		331,485	226,426	126,431	

Data are ordered by year and number of regional users. Totals across all events are given in the final row. DYFI, "Did You Feel It?"

TABLE A2
Variable Descriptions and Sources for the Global Inference Model

Variable	Category	Description	Source
CountryName	Identifier	Name of the country	
CountryCode	Identifier	Country's ISO 3166-1 alpha-3 code	ISO
CountryNumber	Identifier	World Bank Official Boundaries country code	World Bank
EnglishSpanish_CIA	Population	Binary variable indicating if the country has an official or major language of English or Spanish, or if English or Spanish is the first language for more than 25% of the population. This variable is assigned a 1 if true, 0 otherwise	CIA World Factbook
Year	Time	Year corresponding to the data	
Population_WB	Population	The population of a country during a given year, including all residents regardless of legal status or citizenship	World Bank
LandAreaSqKm_WB	Population	The country's total area in square kilometers	World Bank
UrbanPopPct_WB	Population	Percentage of a country's population living in urban areas (the same as 100 —RuralPopPct_WB)	World Bank
RuralPopPct_WB	Population	Percentage of a country's population living in rural areas (the same as 100 —UrbanPopPct_WB)	World Bank
InternetPct_WB	Population	Percentage of a country's population that has used the internet in the last three months, using any sort of device	World Bank
CellSubPer100_WB	Population	Number of subscriptions to a public mobile telephone service per 100 people in a country	World Bank
ElectAccessPct_WB	Population	The percentage of a country's population that has access to electricity	World Bank
ElectAccessUrbanPct_WB	Population	The percentage of a country's population living in urban areas that has access to electricity	World Bank
ElectAccessRuralPct_WB	Population	The percentage of a country's population living in rural areas that has access to electricity	World Bank
BroadbandSubPer100_WB	Population	Number of fixed subscriptions to high-speed access to the public Internet per 100 people in a country	World Bank
GDPcap_WB	Population	Gross domestic product (GDP) per capita based on purchasing power parity (PPP) in constant 2017 international dollars	World Bank
JournalArtNo_WB	Population	Number of scientific and engineering articles published per country per year	World Bank
PrimarySchoolPct_WB	Population	Percentage of total individuals enrolled in primary education of the population of the age group eligible for primary education	World Bank
TertiarySchoolPct_WB	Population	Percentage of total individuals enrolled in tertiary education of the population of the age group eligible for tertiary education	World Bank
GovExpenditureEdu_WB	Population	Total government expenditure on education expressed as a percentage of the country's GDP	World Bank
NumStations_USGS	Stations	Number of ShakeMap stations within the country's boundaries	FDSN
StationsPerSqKm_USGS	Stations	Number of ShakeMap stations divided by the total land area of the country (NumStations_USGS/LandAreaSqKm_WB)	FDSN, World Bank

The Category column defines the type of variable as one of the following: identifier, time, population, stations, earthquake, exposure, or responses. Data sources for these variables are the World Bank, Central Intelligence Agency (CIA), International Federation of Digital Seismograph Networks (FDSN), U.S. Geological Survey (USGS), and LandScan (see Data and Resources). DYFI, "Did You Feel It?"
(Continued next page.)

TABLE A2 (continued)
Variable Descriptions and Sources for the Global Inference Model

Variable	Category	Description	Source
StationsPerCapita_USGS	Stations	Number of ShakeMap stations divided by the country's population (NumStations_USGS/Population_WB)	FDSN, World Bank
CDImedMMI_USGS (Mean, Sd, Min, Q1, Median, Q3, Max)	Earthquake	CDI (Community Decimal Intensity) is a metric resulting from DYFI and is an aggregate of the weighted sums of the various indices of the DYFI questionnaires. The metric, medMMI, is the median modified Mercalli Intensity (MMI) of the grid cell, which is a shaking intensity measure that results from ShakeMap. CDI and MMI are on the same scale. So, CDImedMMI is equal to the CDI value when there are DYFI responses, otherwise it is equal to the medMMI value. These summary statistics describe the shaking intensity of all grids that experienced shaking	USGS
Magnitude_USGS (Mean, Sd, Min, Q1, Median, Q3, Max)	Earthquake	Summary statistics of the magnitude of earthquakes (event-based rather than grid based)	USGS
GriddedPopulation_USGS (Mean, Sd, Min, Q1, Median, Q3, Max)	Exposure	Summary statistics of the estimated population per grid that experienced shaking	USGS, LandScan
GridsNo_USGS (Mean, Sd, Min, Q1, Median, Q3, Max)	Exposure	Summary statistics of the number of grid cells associated with each earthquake	USGS
DYFIResponsesNo_USGS (Mean, Sd, Min, Q1, Median, Q3, Max)	Responses	Summary statistics of the number of DYFI responses in each grid that experienced shaking	USGS
DYFIResponseRate_USGS (Mean, Sd, Min, Q1, Median, Q3, Max)	Responses	Summary statistics of the DYFI response rate per grid that experienced shaking. The response rates are the number of responses divided by the approximate population within the grid. If there were responses in a grid with a population of 0, no response rate for that grid is calculated	USGS, LandScan
GridResponseRate_USGS (Mean, Sd, Min, Q1, Median, Q3, Max)	Responses	Summary statistics of the grid response rate for each earthquake. The grid response rate is the number of grid cells with at least one DYFI response divided by the number of grid cells exposed to shaking for that earthquake	USGS
NumEarthquakes_USGS	Earthquake	Number of earthquakes that led to USGS ShakeMap and/or DYFI responses	USGS
EarthquakesPerSqKm_USGS	Earthquake	Number of earthquakes divided by the total land area of the country (NumEarthquakes_USGS/LandAreaSqKm_USGS)	USGS, World Bank
TotalGriddedPopulation_USGS	Exposure	Total (approximate) population exposed to shaking due to earthquakes over the year. Population within the same grid can be counted multiple times if that grid experienced multiple earthquakes	USGS, LandScan
AvgGriddedPopulationPerQuake_USGS	Exposure	Average population exposed to shaking per earthquake (TotalGriddedPopulation_USGS/NumEarthquakes_USGS)	USGS, LandScan
TotalGrids_USGS	Exposure	Total number of grid cells exposed to shaking across all earthquakes. Grids can be counted multiple times if they experienced multiple earthquakes	USGS
NumEarthquakesWithResponses_USGS	Responses	Count of the number of earthquakes that led to at least one DYFI response	USGS
EarthquakeResponseRate_USGS	Responses	Proportion of earthquakes with at least one DYFI response (NumEarthquakesWithResponses_USGS/NumEarthquakes_USGS)	USGS
TotalDYFIResponses_USGS	Responses	Total number of DYFI responses across all earthquakes	USGS
TotalDYFIResponseRate_USGS (y_{ct})	Responses	Total number of DYFI responses divided by the total population exposed to shaking (TotalDYFIResponses_USGS/TotalGriddedPopulation_USGS)	USGS, LandScan
DYFIResponsesPerQuake_USGS	Responses	Total number of DYFI responses divided by the number of earthquakes (TotalDYFIResponses_USGS/NumEarthquakes_USGS)	USGS

The Category column defines the type of variable as one of the following: identifier, time, population, stations, earthquake, exposure, or responses. Data sources for these variables are the World Bank, Central Intelligence Agency (CIA), International Federation of Digital Seismograph Networks (FDSN), U.S. Geological Survey (USGS), and LandScan (see Data and Resources). DYFI, "Did You Feel It?"
(Continued next page.)

TABLE A2 (continued)
Variable Descriptions and Sources for the Global Inference Model

Variable	Category	Description	Source
TotalGridsWithResponses_USGS	Responses	Total number of grid cells with at least one DYFI response across all earthquakes	USGS
TotalGridResponseRate_USGS	Responses	Number of grid cells with at least one DYFI response divided by the total number of grid cells (TotalGridsWithResponses_USGS/TotalGrids_USGS)	USGS

The Category column defines the type of variable as one of the following: identifier, time, population, stations, earthquake, exposure, or responses. Data sources for these variables are the World Bank, Central Intelligence Agency (CIA), International Federation of Digital Seismograph Networks (FDSN), U.S. Geological Survey (USGS), and LandScan (see Data and Resources). DYFI, "Did You Feel It?"

TABLE A3
Alternative Models

Model	Estimate	Response Variable	Observations
Chosen model	MaxCDImedMMI: 0.0028222*	sqrt(TotalDYFIResponseRate)	Total: 705
	EarthquakesPerSqKm: 0.0012222*		Left censored: 202
	EnglishSpanish: 0.0029576*		Uncensored: 503
	BroadbandSubPer100: 0.001421†		
	EnglishSpanish‡ BroadbandSubPer100: 0.001254		
Alternate response variable 1	MaxCDImedMMI: 0.085098*	sqrt(TotalGridResponseRate)	Total: 705
	EarthquakesPerSqKm: 0.038722*		Left censored: 202
	EnglishSpanish: 0.092905*		Uncensored: 503
	BroadbandSubPer100: 0.064442*		
	EnglishSpanish‡ BroadbandSubPer100: −0.013019		
Alternate response variable 2	MaxCDImedMMI: 0.18705*	sqrt(MaxDYFIResponseRate)	Total: 705
	EarthquakesPerSqKm: 0.01177		Left censored: 202
	EnglishSpanish: 0.11156†		Uncensored: 503
	BroadbandSubPer100: 0.031		
	EnglishSpanish‡ BroadbandSubPer100: 0.10336‡		
Alternate response variable 3	MaxCDImedMMI: 0.108156*	sqrt(MaxGridResponseRate)	Total: 705
	EarthquakesPerSqKm: 0.069687*		Left censored: 202
	EnglishSpanish: 0.084631†		Uncensored: 503
	BroadbandSubPer100: 0.086638*		
	EnglishSpanish‡ BroadbandSubPer100: −0.022803		

Bold variables indicate that the missing values for that variable are filled with zero. Underlined variables indicate that the missing values for that variable are filled with 0.0000001 (for applying a log transformation).
*$p < 0.001$.
†$p < 0.01$.
‡$p < 0.05$.
(Continued next page.)

TABLE A3 (continued)
Alternative Models

Model	Estimate	Response Variable	Observations
Untransformed response variable	MaxCDImedMMI: 1.007×10^{-4}*	TotalDYFIRepsonseRate	Total: 705
	EarthquakesPerSqKm: 4.326×10^{-5}†		Left censored: 202
	EnglishSpanish: 1.080×10^{-4}†		Uncensored: 503
	BroadbandSubPer100: 2.92×10^{-5}		
	EnglishSpanish‡ BroadbandSubPer100: 9.640×10^{-5}†		
Missing values filled with 0	**MaxCDImedMMI**: 0.0074988*	sqrt(**TotalDYFIResponseRate**)	Total: 1683
	EarthquakesPerSqKm: 0.0020336*		Left censored: 1180
	EnglishSpanish: 0.0025756†		Uncensored: 503
	BroadbandSubPer100: 0.0011937‡		
	EnglishSpanish‡ BroadbandSubPer100: 0.0009085		
Log model	**MaxCDImedMMI**: 60.9305*	log(TotalDYFIResponseRate)	Total: 1683
	EarthquakesPerSqKm: 9.4740*		Left censored: NA
	EnglishSpanish: 5.9427†		Uncensored: NA
	BroadbandSubPer100: 2.5003		
	EnglishSpanish‡ BroadbandSubPer100: −3.1631		

Bold variables indicate that the missing values for that variable are filled with zero. Underlined variables indicate that the missing values for that variable are filled with 0.0000001 (for applying a log transformation).
*$p < 0.001$.
†$p < 0.01$.
‡$p < 0.05$.

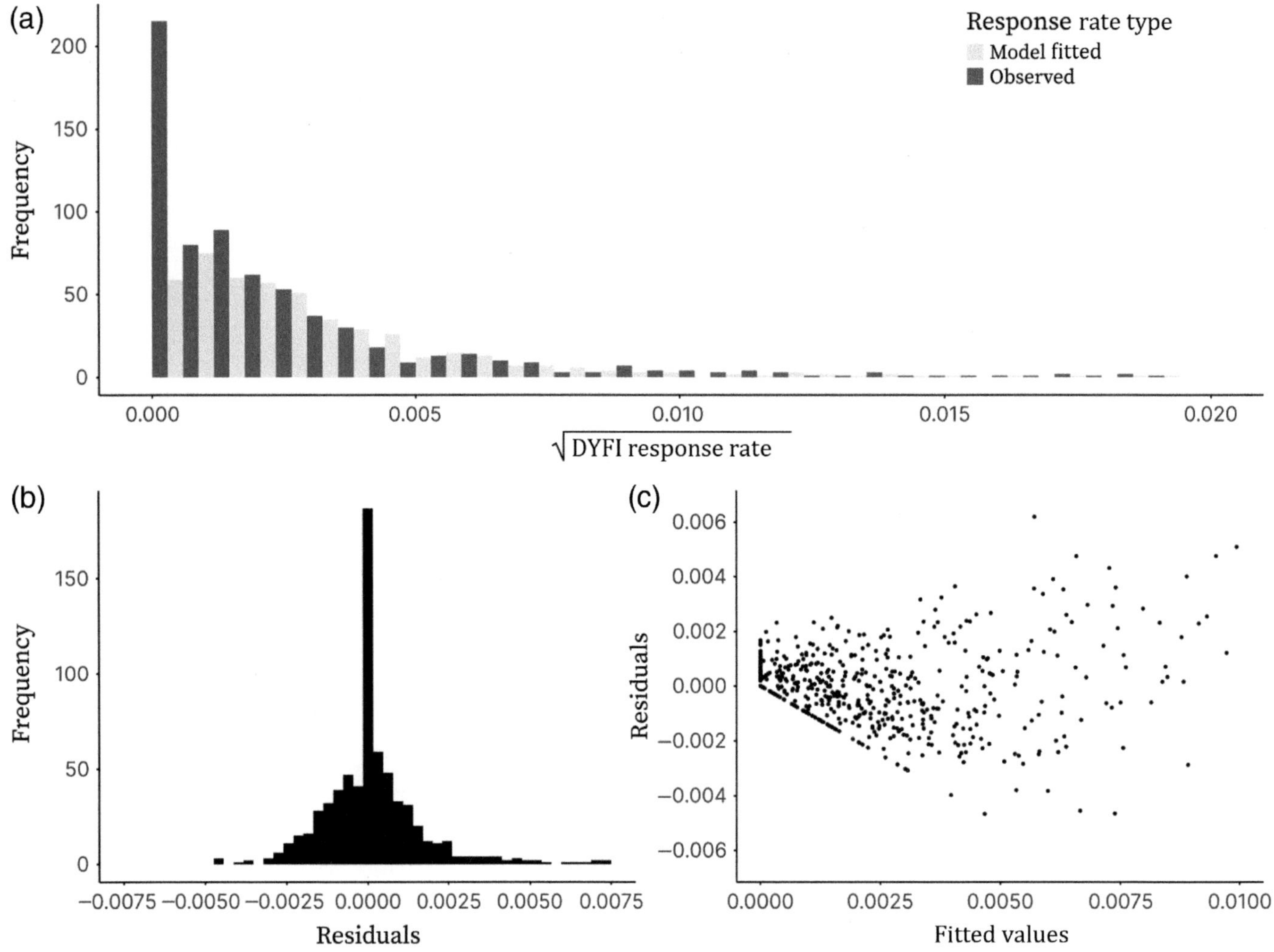

Figure A1. Detailed view of model diagnostic plots. Each plot focuses on an *x* value range that captures the densest portion of the data. For the full plots, see Figure A2. (a) The side-by-side histogram compares the fitted and observed y^*_{ct} values. (b) The distribution of residuals is given in the single histogram. (c) The scatterplot compares the fitted values to their residuals.

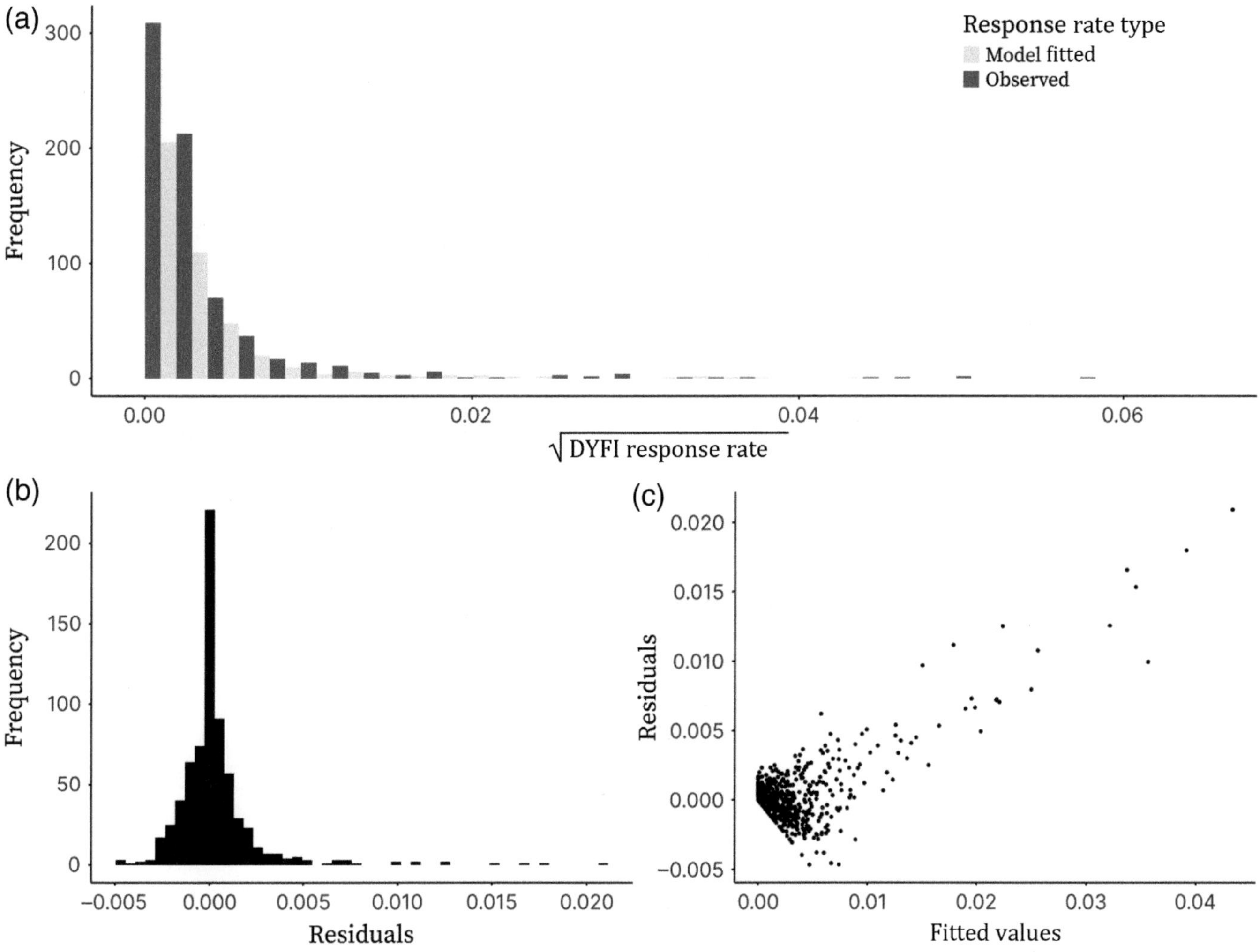

Figure A2. Complete view of model diagnostic plots. Same as Figure A1 but zoomed out.

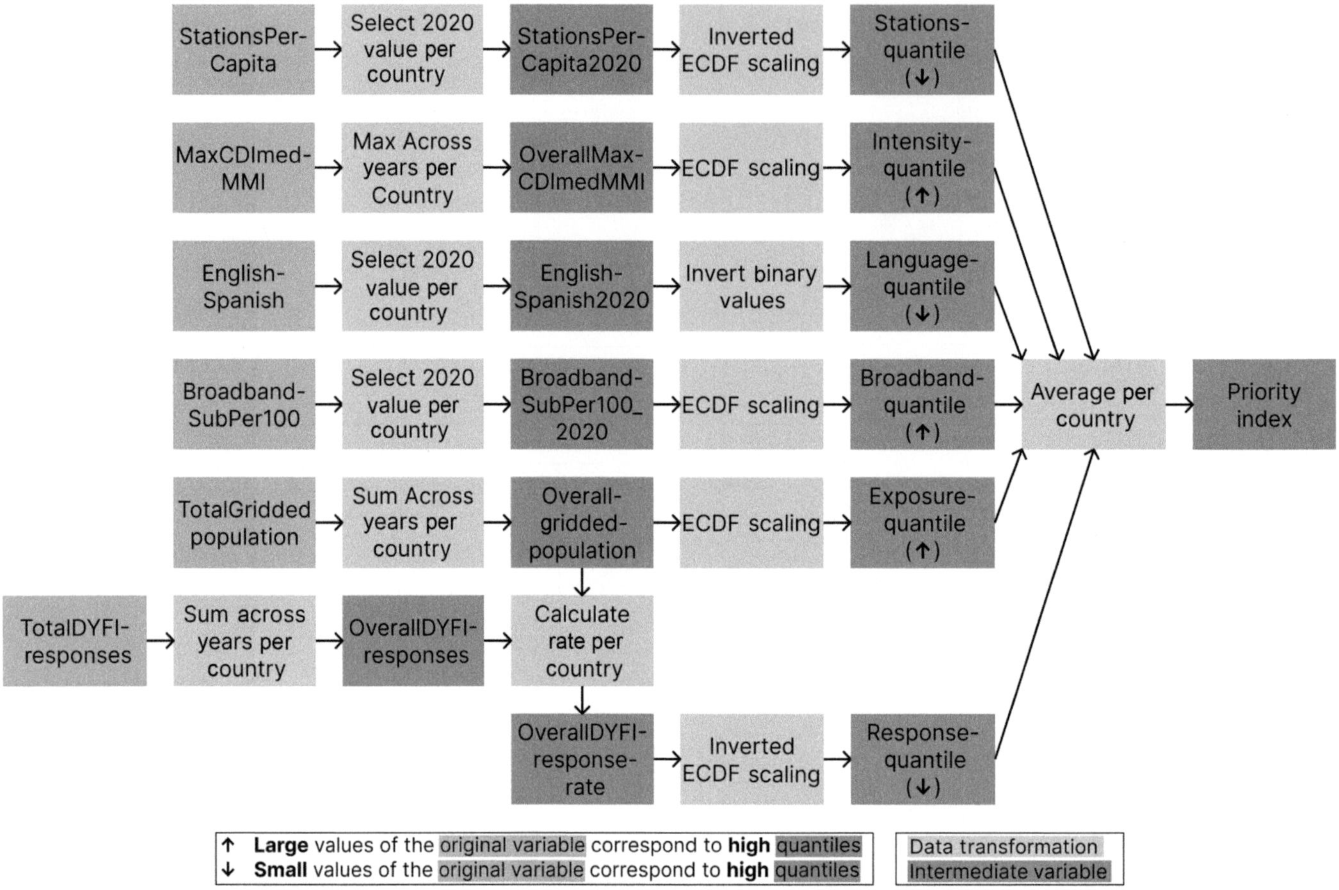

Figure A3. Detailed diagram showing the calculation of the country priority index. Same as Figure 8 but expanded to show all steps taken. The color version of this figure is available only in the electronic edition.

Manuscript received 18 May 2025
Published online 3 November 2025

Environmental Effects on Broadband Seismic Noise: A Year-Long Assessment from Maitri Station, Dronning Maud Land, East Antarctica

Satish Saha[†1], Rahul Biswas[*†1], and Prakash Kumar[1]

Abstract

We present a detailed year-long characterization of seismic noise at the Maitri station (MAIT) in East Antarctica, based on continuous three-component waveform data from 2023. Using probabilistic power spectral density and probability density function analysis, we assess spectral behavior across vertical (HHZ) and horizontal (HHN, HHE) components over a broad period range (0.1–100 s). The vertical component records the lowest noise in the microseism (1–20 s) and long-period (> 20 s) bands, consistent with reduced tilt sensitivity and robust bedrock installation, whereas at short periods (< 1 s) levels are comparable to or slightly higher than the horizontals. Seasonal and month-wise analyses reveal clear environmental modulation: microseism noise intensifies during December–June, with amplitudes increasing by up to ~15 dB, consistent with reduced sea-ice extent and enhanced Southern Ocean wave activity, whereas long-period fluctuations correlate with temperature-induced strain and wind variations. Short-period noise remains at low levels, with only seasonal elevations linked to summer field activity, highlighting the lack of persistent anthropogenic noise. Across all components and frequencies, power spectral density levels remain bounded by global new high and low noise models, demonstrating the station's high-fidelity performance. These results position MAIT as a benchmark site for polar seismic studies and inform strategies for future broadband deployments in extreme environments.

Cite this article as Saha, S., R. Biswas, and P. Kumar (2025). Environmental Effects on Broadband Seismic Noise: A Year-Long Assessment from Maitri Station, Dronning Maud Land, East Antarctica, *Seismol. Res. Lett.* **97**, 2107–2115, doi: 10.1785/0220250219.

Supplemental Material

Introduction

Characterizing seismic noise is fundamental for evaluating the performance of broadband seismic stations because it constrains their sensitivity to low-amplitude ground motion and underpins the reliability of local to global seismic analyses. Beyond earthquake detection, seismic noise studies provide valuable insights into Earth system processes, including atmosphere–ocean interactions, cryospheric variability, and other environmental dynamics (Bensen *et al.*, 2007; Ardhuin *et al.*, 2011). Seismic noise is commonly categorized by period bands, each associated with distinct source mechanisms. In the short-period range (0.1–1 s), noise in populated areas primarily arises from anthropogenic activity such as transport and industrial operations. In contrast, at remote polar stations such as MAIT, anthropogenic contributions are substantially reduced, though not entirely absent, as activities at scientific bases during field seasons can contribute to short-period noise. Instead, noise in this band is generally dominated by instrument self-noise, wind-induced vault vibrations, and thermal strain from diurnal temperature fluctuations (Ringler and Hutt, 2010; Anthony *et al.*, 2015; Doody *et al.*, 2018; Johnson *et al.*, 2019; Frankinet *et al.*, 2020).

The microseism band (1–20 s) is dominated by oceanic sources. Within this band, secondary microseisms (1–10 s), generated by the nonlinear interaction of opposing wave systems, are particularly sensitive to storm activity over the Southern Ocean and typically reach peak amplitudes during austral winter in open-ocean regions. In contrast, at Antarctic coastal stations such as MAIT, their amplitudes are suppressed in winter due to seasonal sea-ice extent, which damps wave–coast interactions and limits microseism generation (Stutzmann *et al.*, 2000; Grob *et al.*, 2011; Wolin *et al.*, 2015). Primary microseisms (10–20 s), produced by direct wave–coast interactions, are likewise diminished during winter when sea ice reduces coastal coupling. At

1. National Geophysical Research Institute, CSIR, Hyderabad, India, https://orcid.org/0000-0003-4438-8695 (SS); https://orcid.org/0000-0001-8177-526X (RB)

*Corresponding author: rbiswas92.ngri@csir.res.in

†These authors contributed equally to this work.

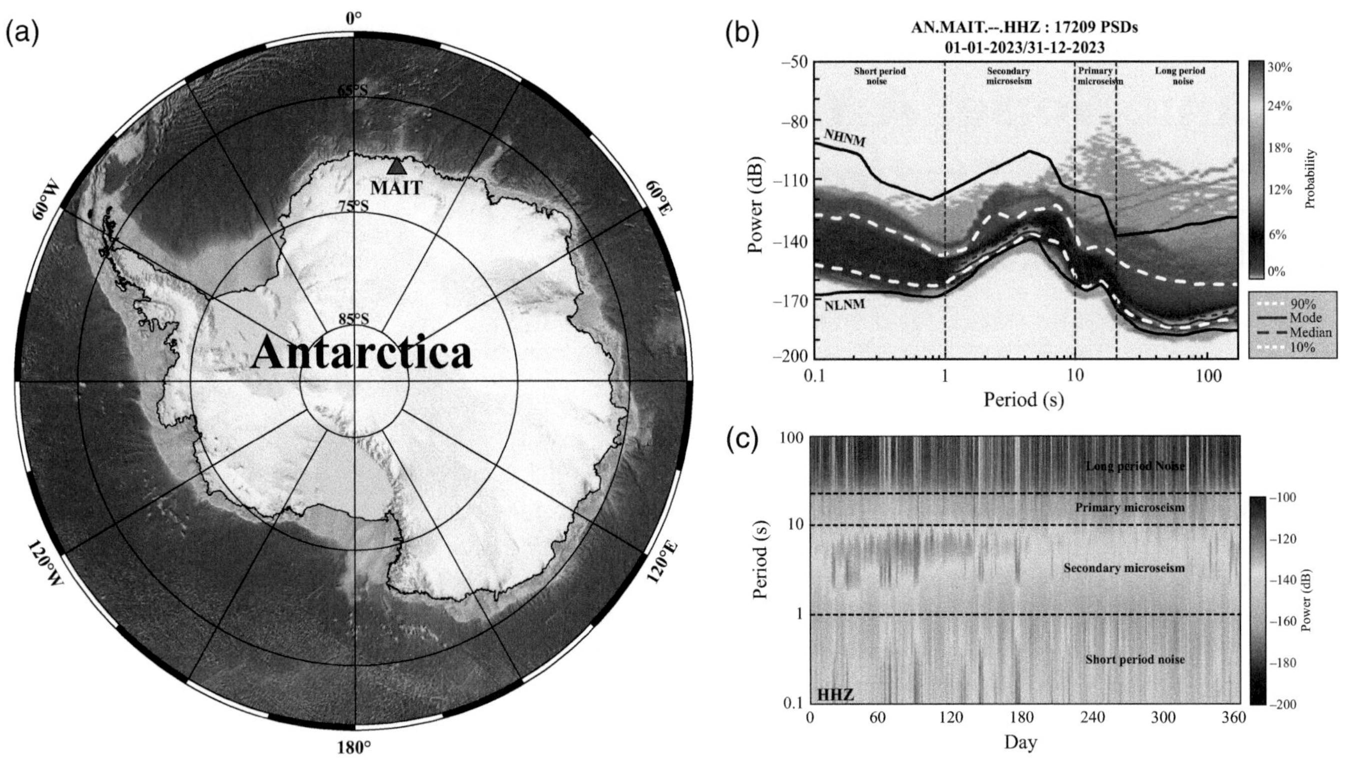

Figure 1. Location and seismic noise characteristics of the Maitri station (MAIT) broadband station in East Antarctica. (a) Map showing the position of MAIT (70°45′52″ S, 11°44′03″ E) within the Antarctic continent. (b) Probabilistic power spectral density (PPSD) distribution for the vertical (HHZ) component during 2023, computed from 17,209 hourly windows. Color scale denotes probability density, and global new low noise model (NLNM) and new high noise model (NHNM) curves are shown for reference. (c) Time–period spectrogram of the HHZ component highlighting seasonal variations across short-period, microseism, and long-period bands. The color version of this figure is available only in the electronic edition.

longer periods (20–100 s), seismic noise reflects tilt, atmospheric pressure variability, and thermal gradients, with enhanced amplitudes observed in horizontal components due to their greater tilt sensitivity (Beauduin *et al.*, 1996; McNamara and Buland, 2004; Zürn *et al.*, 2007, 2022).

Given its geographic isolation, stable bedrock setting, and minimal anthropogenic influence, the MAIT station, operated under the Indian Antarctic Program and situated in the Schirmacher Oasis of central Dronning Maud Land, offers a uniquely favorable site for long-term seismological monitoring. Although prior studies have reported preliminary noise characteristics at MAIT (Saha and Srinagesh, 2021), they did not provide seasonally resolved analyses using probabilistic power spectral density–probability density function (PPSD–PDF) methods. To address this gap, we present a comprehensive assessment of seismic noise at MAIT based on the most recent complete calendar year of continuous high-quality recordings (2023). This data set provides a robust benchmark for evaluating seasonal and diurnal variability under current Antarctic conditions. Employing the PPSD–PDF method of McNamara and Buland (2004), we examine spectral characteristics across short-period, microseism, and long-period bands. The analysis further incorporates seasonal and diurnal variability, enabling a refined interpretation of environmental influences and a systematic evaluation of the station's performance under extreme polar conditions.

Study Area and Station Description

The MAIT station is located in the Schirmacher Oasis, a coastal ice-free region of central Dronning Maud Land, East Antarctica, at 70°45′52″ S, 11°44′03″ E. Situated approximately 100 km inland from the continental margin at an elevation of ~50 m above sea level (Fig. 1), the station is strategically deployed on exposed Precambrian bedrock. MAIT was deployed on 26 January 1998 and upgraded to broadband operation in January 2001. It operates in a tectonically stable and low-noise environment, characterized by limited anthropogenic influence and minimal seasonal snow cover, providing favorable conditions for continuous seismic monitoring under polar conditions.

The station is equipped with a Güralp CMG-3T broadband seismometer, featuring a flat velocity response from 0.0083 to 50 Hz and a sensitivity of 2000 V/m/s. The sensor is installed in a custom-designed, thermally insulated vault mechanically coupled to bedrock to minimize tilt and thermal effects. The vault is located about 0.5 km from the main Maitri base, further reducing anthropogenic noise (Ministry of Earth Sciences [MoES], 1998). At this distance, wind-building interactions are unlikely to dominate the seismic spectra, although localized anthropogenic contributions during summer field campaigns may still be detectable in the short-period band. A RefTek 130-01/3 digitizer with 24-bit resolution is used for data acquisition, housed in a thermally regulated enclosure ~15 m from the sensor and connected via a subterranean conduit. Timing is maintained using a Global Positioning System module, and the system is powered by a 12 V battery array engineered for subzero environments.

MAIT continuously records three-component seismic waveforms at 100 Hz sampling rate, with data archived in miniSEED format and retrieved periodically for analysis. The design and operational stability of the installation ensure low site noise and high data fidelity. A summary of instrumentation and configuration details is provided in Table 1. As shown in Figure 1, the station recorded 17,209 valid power spectral density (PSD) windows in 2023, underscoring its excellent operational continuity and suitability for long-term geophysical studies in Antarctica.

TABLE 1
Specifications of the Seismometer and Data Acquisition System Installed at the MAIT Seismic Station, East Antarctica

Serial Number	Parameter	Details
Seismometer specifications (Güralp CMG-3T)		
1	Model	Güralp CMG-3T
2	Type	Triaxial, orthogonal
3	Feedback mechanism	Force balance with capacitive displacement transducer
4	Frequency band	0.0083 (120 s)–50 Hz
5	Sensitivity	2000 V/m/s
6	Dynamic range	>140 dB at the rate of 5 Hz
7	Self noise	Below NLNM from 100 s to 10 Hz
8	Calibration	Coil resistance: 1000 Ω; Sensitivity: 10 m/s^2/A
9	Power consumption	~1.1 W
10	Operating temperature	−20°C to + 60°C
Data acquisition system specifications (RefTek 130-01/3)		
1	Model	RefTek 130-01/3
2	Type	24-bit A/D converter
3	Input channels	3
4	Sampling rate	100 samples per second
5	Dynamic range	>132 dB at the rate of 100 samples per second
6	Internal storage	Compact flash card (capacity varies)
7	External storage	Optional via PCMCIA (up to 32 GB)
8	Data format	miniSEED
9	Power consumption	~1.2 W
10	Operating temperature	−30°C to + 70°C

MAIT, Maitri station; NLNM, new low noise model; PCMCIA, Personal Computer Memory Card International Association.

Data and Methods

We analyzed continuous broadband seismic data recorded at the MAIT station in East Antarctica from January to December 2023. The data set includes vertical (HHZ), north–south (HHN), and east–west (HHE) components of ground motion, sampled at 100 Hz and archived in miniSEED format. Instrument response corrections were applied to retrieve absolute ground velocity, and spectral amplitudes are reported in decibels (dB).

Seismic noise characteristics were quantified using the PPSD–PDF framework of McNamara and Buland (2004). Hour-long, 50%-overlapping time windows were used to ensure adequate temporal resolution. Spectral processing was performed with the open-source PQLX software, enabling robust statistical characterization of noise across the 0.1–100 s period range. For each component, PDFs were computed to extract the mode, median, and 10th and 90th percentile bounds. These spectra were evaluated against the global new low noise model (NLNM) and new high noise model (NHNM) benchmarks (Peterson, 1993). The resulting PPSD distributions reveal distinct peaks associated with secondary and primary microseisms and stable background trends across the short- and long-period bands.

To assess the azimuthal dependence of ambient seismic noise, a directionality analysis was conducted following the conceptual framework of Bensen *et al.* (2008), adapted here for single-station polarization evaluation. Continuous three-component data were segmented into 10 min windows with 2 min overlaps and band-pass filtered in one-third-octave frequency bands centered between 0.1 and 100 s. For each window, the covariance matrix of the horizontal components (HHN and HHE) was computed to derive the dominant polarization azimuth and its corresponding strength, retaining only windows with polarization strength ≥6 dB. The resulting azimuths were grouped into 10° bins to generate rose diagrams depicting the directional distribution of horizontal motion at each period. These were compared with meteorological data to investigate environmental influences on horizontal noise variability.

Results and Discussion

Component-wise noise characteristics

PPSD estimates for the three-component broadband installation at MAIT over 2023 reveal consistent low-noise performance across HHZ, HHN, and HHE channels (Fig. 2). All components remain bounded by the NLNM and NHNM curves. HHZ exhibits the lowest PSD levels at long periods, consistent with its reduced sensitivity to tilt, whereas at short periods its PSD is comparable to, or slightly higher than, that of the horizontal components. The vertical channel shows

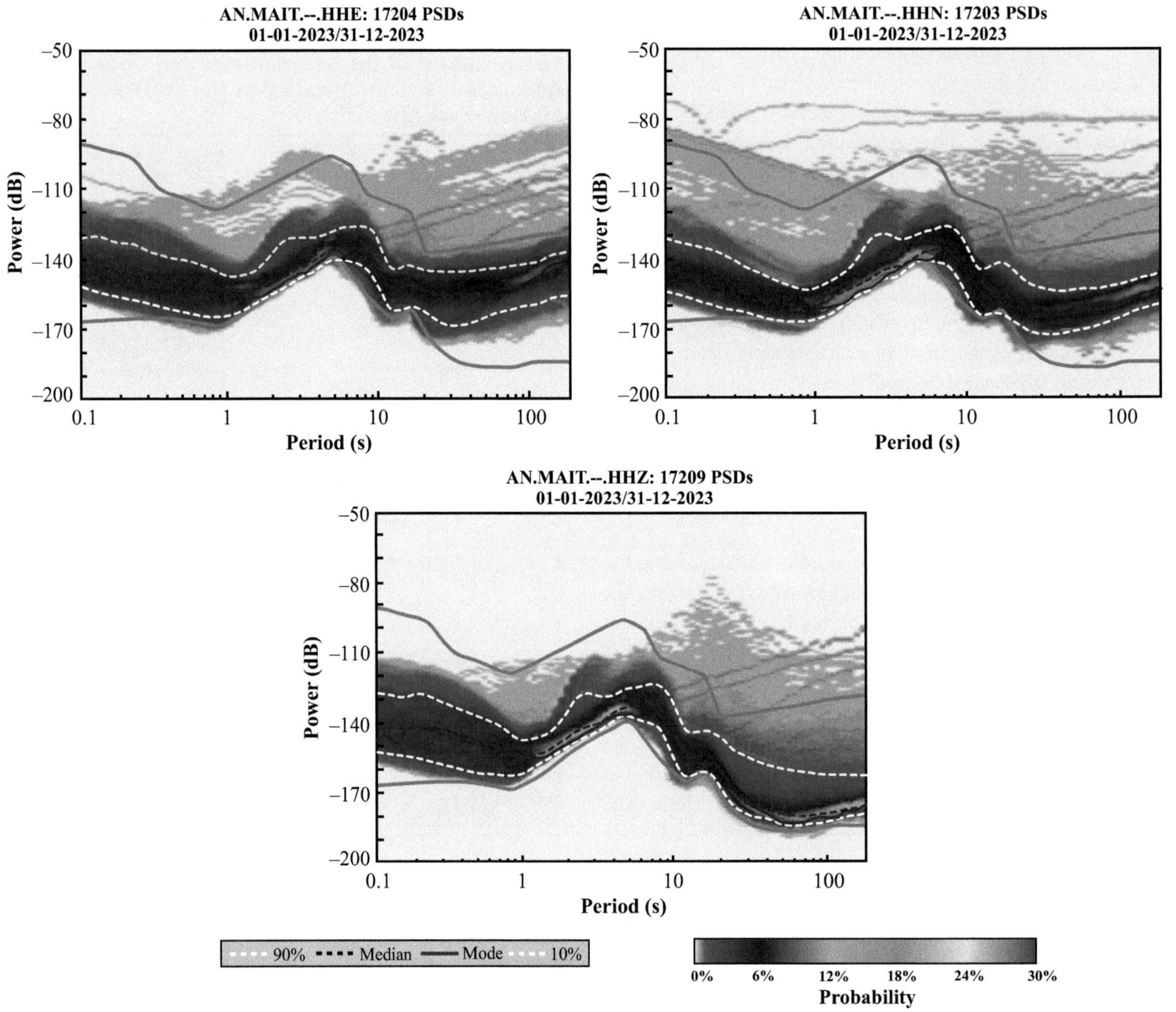

Figure 2. PPSD distributions for the vertical (HHZ), north–south (HHN), and east–west (HHE) components recorded at MAIT during 2023. Each panel shows over 17,000 hourly power spectral density (PSD) windows spanning the full year, color coded by probability density (0%–30%) with the NHNM and NLNM bounds overlaid. Summary statistics include the mode (black-solid line), median (black dashed), and the 10th and 90th percentiles (white dashed), highlighting the station's low-noise performance and spectral stability across all components and periods (0.1–100 s). The color version of this figure is available only in the electronic edition.

particularly low noise in the secondary microseism band, suggesting effective mechanical coupling of the vault to bedrock and reduced sensitivity to thermal tilt effects (Ringler and Hutt, 2010; Grob *et al.*, 2011; Anthony *et al.*, 2015; Doody *et al.*, 2018). The horizontal components display elevated long-period PSD levels, consistent with tilt-induced noise from wind loading and thermal expansion effects. HHN and HHE are broadly similar, although HHN exhibits slightly lower noise at long periods compared to HHE, indicating symmetric environmental forcing, possibly influenced by prevailing katabatic winds. Despite these variations, all channels demonstrate performance well within global reference bounds, confirming the low-noise performance and operational integrity of the station. A supplementary comparison with other Antarctic stations (Fig. S1, available in the supplemental material to this article) further illustrates that MAIT exhibits comparable or lower PSD levels, thereby reinforcing its reliability in the regional network.

Seasonal noise variation

Seismic PSD levels at MAIT exhibit pronounced seasonal modulation across all three components. In the short-period band, noise is elevated across HHE, HHN, and HHZ from December to June (Fig. 3), primarily due to anthropogenic activity

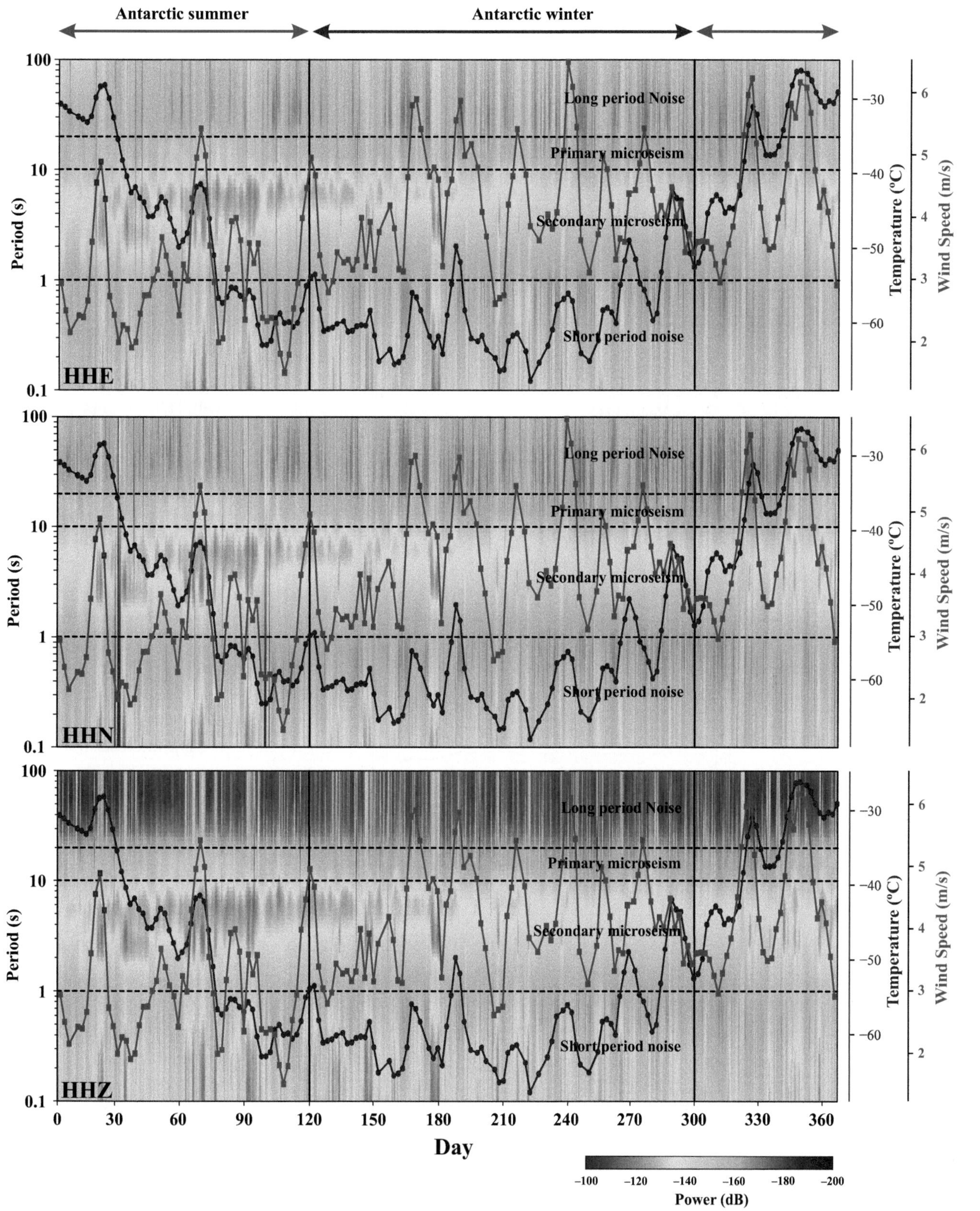

Figure 3. Daily spectrograms of PPSD for the HHE, HHN, and HHZ components at MAIT during 2023. Each panel spans the full period range (0.1–100 s) and displays daily variations in seismic spectral power (dB). Shading indicates relative energy levels, with warmer colors representing higher spectral power. Overlaid curves show smoothed surface air temperature (blue) and wind speed (red). The austral summer (November–April) and winter (May–October) periods are annotated above. The color version of this figure is available only in the electronic edition.

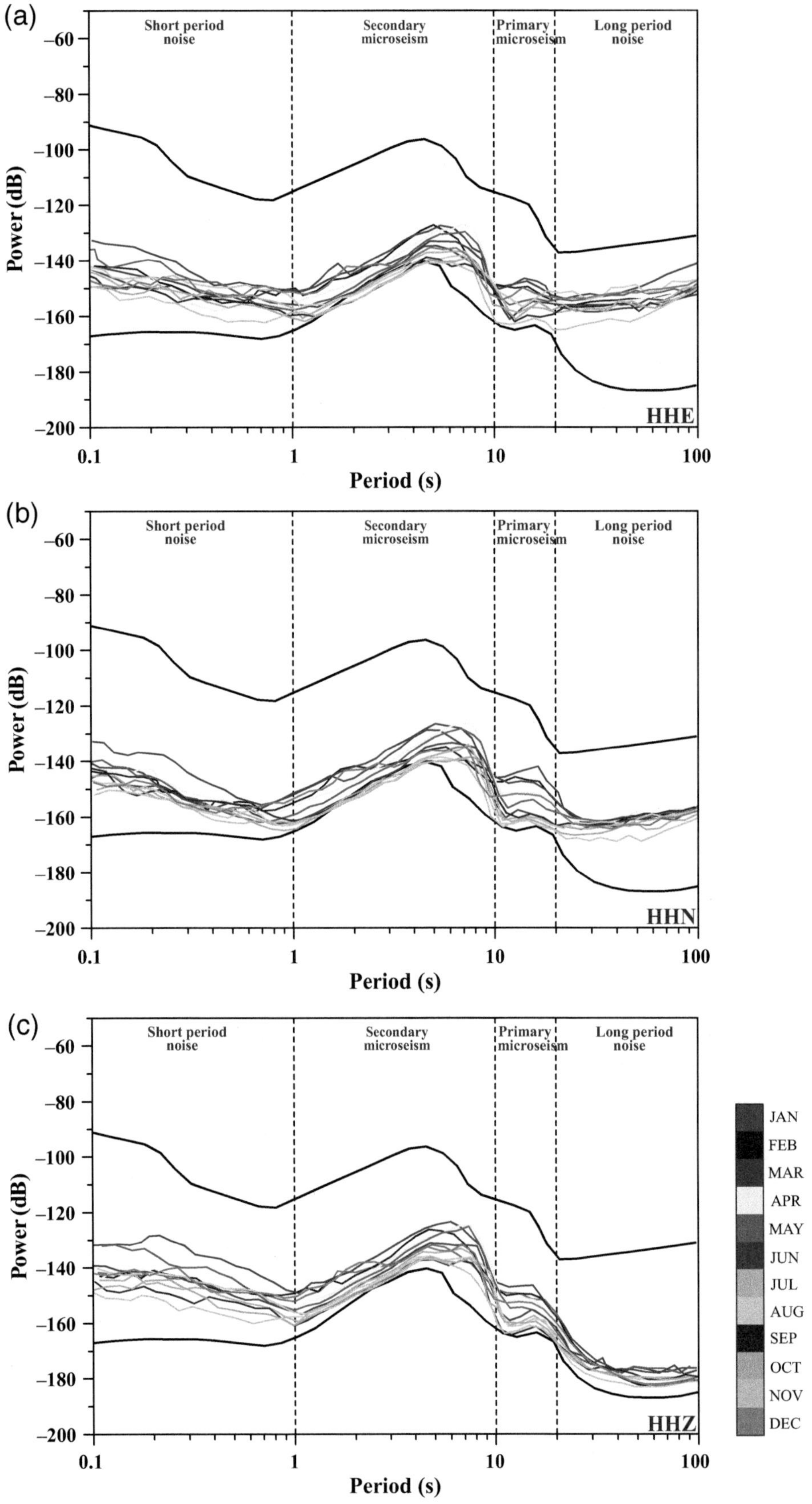

Figure 4. Monthly median PSD curves for the (a) east–west (HHE), (b) north–south (HHN), and (c) vertical (HHZ) components at MAIT during 2023. The color version of this figure is available only in the electronic edition.

associated with summer scientific campaigns and logistical operations. Correlation analysis shows only weak association with wind and moderate association with temperature (Figs. S2, S3), indicating that meteorological effects play a secondary role compared to anthropogenic contributions. Monthly PSDs indicate variations of ~10 dB, ranging from −145 dB in winter to −135 dB in summer (Fig. 4). PSD levels are comparable across all three components, with HHZ in some cases slightly higher than the horizontals, suggesting that both vertical and horizontal sensors capture wind-induced and near-surface environmental effects, though the horizontals are generally more tilt-sensitive (Beauduin *et al.*, 1996; Stutzmann *et al.*, 2000; Grob *et al.*, 2011; Anthony *et al.*, 2015; Johnson *et al.*, 2019; Frankinet *et al.*, 2020; Chaput *et al.*, 2023).

The microseism band shows the most pronounced seasonal variability, with PSD levels peaking from December to June (Fig. 3). HHZ exhibits an ~15 dB increase from winter minima (~−155 dB) to summer maxima (~−140 dB), consistently showing the strongest response across components (Fig. 5). These summer peaks align with reduced sea-ice extent and enhanced coastal wave activity, which promote effective Rayleigh-wave generation and coastal coupling (Grob *et al.*, 2011; Anthony *et al.*, 2015; Turner *et al.*, 2020). The broader duration of elevated noise in HHN and HHE, extending beyond the sharp summer maximum observed in HHZ, is further supported by wind

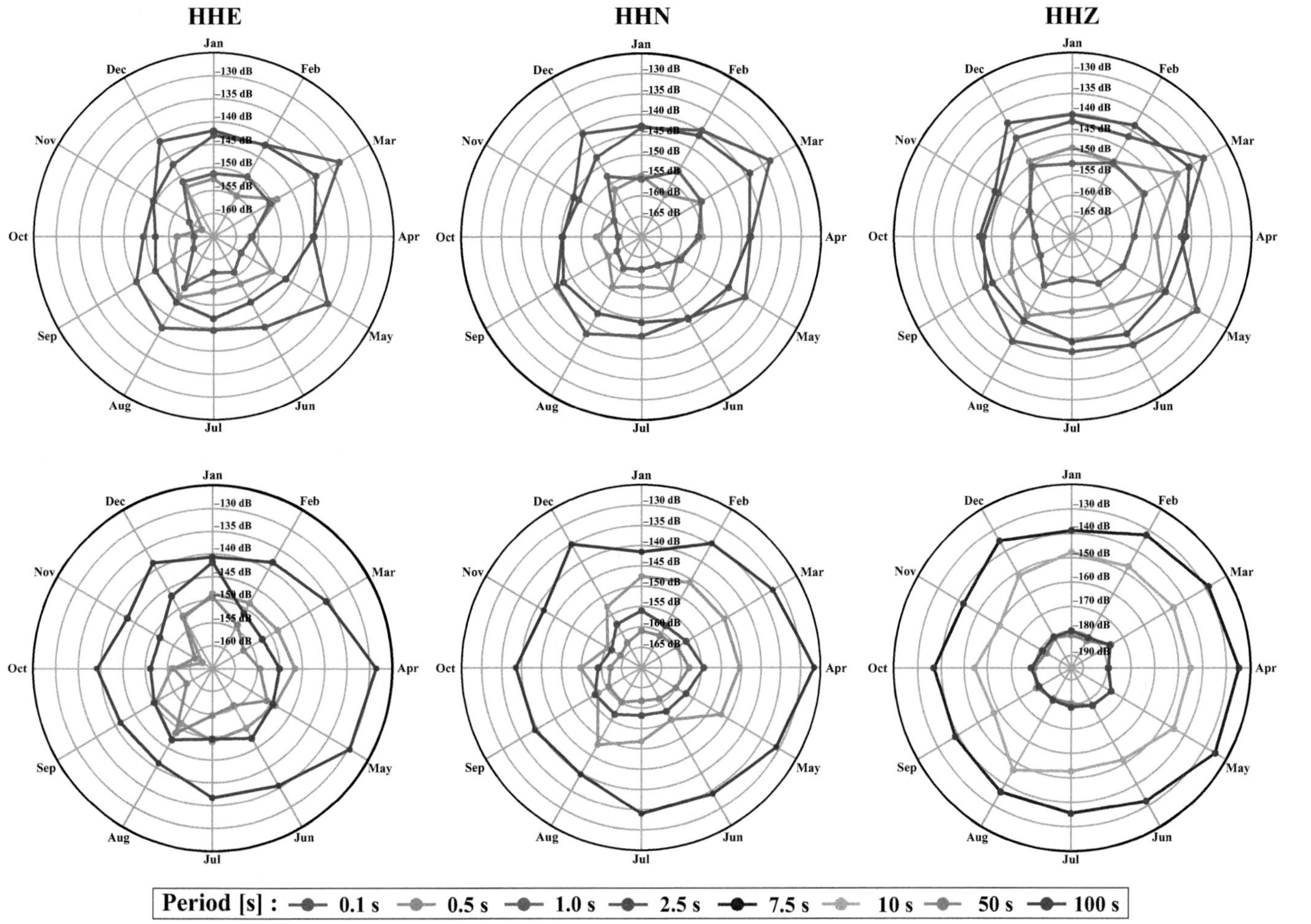

directionality analysis (Figs. S4, S5), suggesting enhanced susceptibility of the horizontal components to local wind forcing and directional sensitivity to ocean wave fields. At short periods (0.1–1 s), strong azimuthal clustering toward the east–southeast indicates coupling with dominant surface wind regimes, whereas at intermediate microseismic periods (2.5–10 s), azimuths exhibit weaker coherence, reflecting a combined influence of wind activity and oceanic swell. Toward longer periods (>20 s), broader eastward orientations emerge, consistent with Southern Ocean swell propagation. These patterns collectively highlight that wind forcing modulates short-period horizontal noise, whereas oceanic processes dominate the longer-period bands. Despite these seasonal variations, correlation with local meteorological parameters remains negligible (Figs. S2, S3), confirming that Southern Ocean wave climate and sea-ice extent primarily governs the variability of these bands. The timing and persistence of elevated noise may vary interannually with Antarctic sea-ice extent, which controls the efficiency of coastal wave coupling and Rayleigh-wave generation. Comparable behavior has been reported in Alaska, where wind- and river-driven signals exhibit weak correlation with seismic noise despite pronounced seasonal trends (Smith and Tape, 2019).

Figure 5. Monthly median PSD values for the HHE, HHN, and HHZ components at MAIT across selected periods (0.1, 0.5, 1.0, 2.5, 7.5, 10, 50, and 100 s) for the year 2023. The color version of this figure is available only in the electronic edition.

At long periods, horizontal components remain consistently noisier than the vertical component throughout the year (Fig. 3). Monthly PSDs show noise amplitudes in the horizontals that are 10–15 dB higher (∼−145 to −150 dB) compared to HHZ (∼−160 dB), reflecting their greater tilt sensitivity and susceptibility to thermally induced ground deformation and barometric pressure variations (Beauduin *et al.*, 1996; Webb, 2002; Ringler and Hutt, 2010). HHZ remains consistently quiet across this band, underscoring its high fidelity in capturing long-period signals.

Additional PSD distributions, including intermediate variability and band-specific transitions, are provided in the supplemental material (Figs. S6–S8). Collectively, these observations demonstrate that MAIT records local atmospheric forcing at short and long periods and remote oceanic forcing in the microseism band, highlighting its value for monitoring cryosphere–atmosphere interactions.

Interpretation and context

The noise characteristics recorded at MAIT underscore its suitability as a high-quality broadband seismic station in East Antarctica. The quiet short-period background in winter provides optimal conditions for detecting weak teleseismic phases and facilitates advanced analyses such as receiver functions and ambient noise interferometry. Seasonal modulation in the microseism band reflects strong environmental forcing, with austral summer enhancements highlighting MAIT's sensitivity to cryosphere–ocean–atmosphere interactions. This sensitivity underscores MAIT's role as a passive environmental observatory for monitoring sea-ice retreat and Southern Ocean wave activity. The extended persistence of elevated noise in the horizontal components further points to contributions from wind-induced tilt and directional wave interactions.

At long periods, the vertical component remains remarkably stable, reaffirming its reliability for surface-wave and normal-mode investigations. The coherence of seasonal and month-wise variability across bands and components suggests that seismic noise at MAIT is primarily governed by natural surface processes. These findings validate the station's mechanical and environmental stability and highlight its dual role as both a low-noise seismic observatory and a monitor of atmosphere–cryosphere interactions in Antarctica. Importantly, this study advances beyond the preliminary assessment of Saha and Srinagesh (2021) by presenting the first seasonally and diurnally resolved PPSD–PDF analysis at MAIT. This refined approach establishes a robust benchmark for 2023, quantifies band-specific noise variability, and directly links microseism amplitudes to sea-ice extent and Southern Ocean wave climate, thereby complementing earlier long-term but less temporally resolved work. With PSD levels consistently within the NLNM–NHNM bounds, MAIT is well positioned for both global seismic monitoring and regional investigations of polar environmental processes.

Conclusions

This study provides a comprehensive spectral characterization of seismic noise at the MAIT broadband station in East Antarctica, emphasizing its suitability for low-noise broadband operation in polar environments. The vertical component consistently maintains low-PSD levels across all period bands, reflecting superior mechanical isolation and minimal environmental coupling. In contrast, the horizontal components are more susceptible to wind-induced tilt and thermal effects, especially in the short- and long-period ranges. Variations are most pronounced within the microseism band, for which amplitudes reach ~15 dB and track closely with environmental drivers such as sea-ice retreat, ocean wave activity, and surface meteorology. These observations confirm that MAIT not only meets global standards for seismic station performance but also functions effectively as a passive observatory of atmosphere–cryosphere interactions. Consistently, low-PSD levels within the NLNM–NHNM bounds highlight MAIT's capability for long-term seismic and environmental research in Antarctica.

Data and Resources

Broadband seismic waveform data from the MAIT station are available upon reasonable request to Director, Council of Scientific and Industrial Research-National Geophysical Research Institute (CSIR-NGRI). Surface air temperature and wind speed data used in this study were obtained from the JASE2007 station archive hosted by the Antarctic Meteorological Research and Data Center (AMRDC) at the University of Wisconsin–Madison, accessible at https://amrdcdata.ssec.wisc.edu/ (last accessed September 2025). All processed power spectral density (PSD) products and analysis scripts are available from the corresponding author upon request. The supplemental material for this article includes Figures S1–S8, which illustrate comparative PSD analyses, environmental correlations, noise directionality, and monthly probabilistic PSD (PPSD) distributions for Maitri Station, Dronning Maud Land, East Antarctica.

Declaration of Competing Interests

The authors acknowledge that there are no conflicts of interest recorded.

Acknowledgments

The authors gratefully acknowledge the National Centre for Polar and Ocean Research (NCPOR), Ministry of Earth Sciences, Government of India, for managing the seismic data acquisition at Maitri station under the Indian Antarctic Programme. The authors thank the India Meteorological Department (IMD) and the logistical teams stationed at Maitri for maintaining the continuous operation of the broadband seismic station under challenging polar conditions. The authors also appreciate the support from Council of Scientific and Industrial Research-National Geophysical Research Institute (CSIR-NGRI), Hyderabad, for providing the computational and research infrastructure necessary for this study. This research did not receive any specific grant from funding agencies in the public, commercial, or not-for-profit sectors.

References

Anthony, R. E., R. C. Aster, D. Wiens, A. Nyblade, S. Anandakrishnan, A. Huerta, J. P. Winberry, T. Wilson, and C. Rowe (2015). The seismic noise environment of Antarctica, *Seismol. Res. Lett.* **86,** 89–100.

Ardhuin, F., E. Stutzmann, M. Schimmel, and A. Mangeney (2011). Ocean wave sources of seismic noise, *J. Geophys. Res.* **116,** doi: 10.1029/2011JC006952.

Beauduin, R., P. Lognonné, J. Montagner, S. Cacho, J. Karczewski, and M. Morand (1996). The effects of the atmospheric pressure changes on seismic signals or how to improve the quality of a station, *Bull. Seismol. Soc. Am.* **86,** 1760–1769.

Bensen, G., M. Ritzwoller, M. Barmin, A. L. Levshin, F. Lin, M. Moschetti, N. Shapiro, and Y. Yang (2007). Processing seismic ambient noise data to obtain reliable broad-band surface wave dispersion measurements, *Geophys. J. Int.* **169,** 1239–1260.

Bensen, G., M. Ritzwoller, and N. M. Shapiro (2008). Broadband ambient noise surface wave tomography across the United States, *J. Geophys. Res.* **113,** doi: 10.1029/2007JB005248.

Chaput, J., R. Aster, M. Karplus, N. Nakata, P. Gerstoft, P. Bromirski, A. Nyblade, R. Stephen, and D. Wiens (2023). Near-surface seismic anisotropy in Antarctic glacial snow and ice revealed by high-frequency ambient noise, *J. Glaciol.* **69,** 773–789.

Doody, C., A. T. Ringler, R. E. Anthony, D. C. Wilson, A. A. Holland, C. R. Hutt, and L. D. Sandoval (2018). Effects of thermal variability on broadband seismometers: Controlled experiments, observations, and implications, *Bull. Seismol. Soc. Am.* **108,** 493–502.

Frankinet, B., T. Lecocq, and T. Camelbeeck (2020). Wind-induced seismic noise at the Princess Elisabeth Antarctica Station, *The Cryosphere Discussions* **2020,** 1–16.

Grob, M., A. Maggi, and E. Stutzmann (2011). Observations of the seasonality of the Antarctic microseismic signal, and its association to sea ice variability, *Geophys. Res. Lett.* **38,** doi: 10.1029/2011GL047525.

Johnson, C. W., F. Vernon, N. Nakata, and Y. Ben-Zion (2019). Atmospheric processes modulating noise in Fairfield nodal 5 Hz geophones, *Seismol. Res. Lett.* **90,** 1612–1618.

McNamara, D. E., and R. P. Buland (2004). Ambient noise levels in the continental United States, *Bull. Seismol. Soc. Am.* **94,** 1517–1527.

Ministry of Earth Sciences (MoES) (1998). Site noise survey and installation details of the Maitri broadband seismic station, Antarctica, *Technical Report Government of India*, available at https://incois.gov.in/essdp/ViewMetadata?fileid=0d1acca2-9ab9-424e-a5d5-b675e5959c96 expedition Science and Support Data Portal (ESSDP) (last accessed September 2025).

Peterson, J. R. (1993). Observations and modeling of seismic background noise, *Technical Rept. U.S. Geol. Surv. 93-322*, doi: 10.3133/ofr93322.

Ringler, A., and C. Hutt (2010). Self-noise models of seismic instruments, *Seismol. Res. Lett.* **81,** 972–983.

Saha, S., and D. Srinagesh (2021). Seismic noise characteristics of Maitri broadband seismic station in Antarctica: Using power spectral density estimation, *IOSR J. Appl. Geol. Geophys. (IOSR-JAGG)* **9,** 01–11.

Smith, K., and C. Tape (2019). Seismic noise in central Alaska and influences from rivers, wind, and sedimentary basins, *J. Geophys. Res.* **124,** 11,678–11,704.

Stutzmann, E., G. Roult, and L. Astiz (2000). GEOSCOPE station noise levels, *Bull. Seismol. Soc. Am.* **90,** 690–701.

Turner, R. J., M. Gal, M. A. Hemer, and A. M. Reading (2020). Impacts of the cryosphere and atmosphere on observed microseisms generated in the Southern Ocean, *J. Geophys. Res.* **125,** e2019JF005354, doi: 10.1029/2019JF005354.

Webb, S. C. (2002). Seismic noise on land and on the sea floor, in *International Geophysics*, W. H. K. Lee, H. Kanamori, P. C. Jennings, and C. Kisslinger (Editors), Vol. 81, Academic Press, New York, New York, 305–318.

Wolin, E., S. van der Lee, T. A. Bollmann, D. A. Wiens, J. Revenaugh, F. A. Darbyshire, A. W. Frederiksen, S. Stein, and M. E. Wysession (2015). Seasonal and diurnal variations in long-period noise at SPREE stations: The influence of soil characteristics on shallow stations' performance, *Bull. Seismol. Soc. Am.* **105,** 2433–2452.

Zürn, W., J. Exß, H. Steffen, C. Kroner, T. Jahr, and M. Westerhaus (2007). On reduction of long-period horizontal seismic noise using local barometric pressure, *Geophys. J. Int.* **171,** 780–796.

Zürn, W., T. Forbriger, R. Widmer-Schnidrig, P. Duffner, and A. T. Ringler (2022). Modelling tilt noise caused by atmospheric processes at long periods for several horizontal seismometers at BFO—A reprise, *Geophys. J.Int.* **228,** 927–943.

Manuscript received 3 July 2025
Published online 14 November 2025

Lithosphere Tectonic Regionalization of China and Surrounding Regions from Unsupervised Learning Analysis of Surface-Wave Dispersion Data

Jiao Yang[1], Han Zhang*[2], Sidao Ni[2], Zefeng Li[1,3], and Xuewei Bao[4]

Abstract

Tectonic regionalization characterizes the primary variation of Earth's lithosphere and is critical for the quantitative investigation of geodynamic evolution. Although classification of lithospheric blocks based on crustal rock types has been successful, tectonic regionalization with information on deep crustal and mantle structures could provide an alternative perspective due to the addition of mantle structure information. Rayleigh-wave phase velocity dispersion data quantify crustal and upper mantle structures and are thus suitable for deep tectonic regionalization. Here, we used a variational autoencoder (VAE), an unsupervised machine learning method, to classify Rayleigh-wave dispersion maps at 8–120 s in China and its surrounding regions. VAE can compress high-dimensional and nonlinear data to a minimal set of latent variables, which allows a quantitative tectonic regionalization. We found that two latent variables are sufficient to represent the general variations of the dispersion maps. The two latent variables are spatially correlated with topography and the effective elastic thickness of the lithosphere. By generating dispersion curves using even samples from the latent space, we can categorize the continental lithosphere in and around China into four distinct types visually, potentially reflecting different lithospheric activities (e.g., magmatic activities) and composition states related to the physical properties of the lithosphere. We also find that dispersion curves with large reconstruction loss are indicative of regions with relatively poor data resolution. The information extracted from dispersion curves enables us to better understand the integral lithospheric structure from shallow to deep.

Cite this article as Yang, J., H. Zhang, S. Ni, Z. Li, and X. Bao (2025). Lithosphere Tectonic Regionalization of China and Surrounding Regions from Unsupervised Learning Analysis of Surface-Wave Dispersion Data, *Seismol. Res. Lett.* **97**, 2116–2127, doi: 10.1785/0220240374.

Supplemental Material

Introduction

As a traditional framework for dividing the lithosphere into blocks, plate tectonics provides insights into understanding the lithosphere's evolution. The classic plate tectonics theory divides the lithosphere into stable plates and deforming boundary zones between them (e.g., Hasterok *et al.*, 2022). Generally, the intraplate region is relatively stable and has fewer geological activities, whereas areas adjacent to plate boundaries are characterized by more frequent tectonic activities and complex geological phenomena (e.g., Chapman and Solomon, 1976; Gordon and Stein, 1992). Since East Asia is situated at the junction of the Philippine plate, Eurasian plate, and Indian plate (Hasterok *et al.*, 2022), mainland China and its surroundings within East Asia include active tectonic movements, making the area an important window to study the evolution of the Earth's lithosphere (Lv *et al.*, 2011; Zhao *et al.*, 2011). Using numerous data from this densely instrumented region (e.g., Bao *et al.*, 2015; Shen *et al.*, 2016; Han *et al.*, 2022; Li *et al.*, 2022), there is a desire to seek a new way to divide the region and provide additional information on its evolution.

Seismic velocity models, which indicate the 3D structure within the lithosphere, provide a basis to classify the lithosphere. High-resolution tomography reveals the structural features of the Earth's interior, like boundaries of cratons or distribution of partial melts (e.g., Wang *et al.*, 2017;Debayle *et al.*, 2020), and serves as a crucial reference for the intricate

1. Laboratory of Seismology and Physics of Earth's Interior, School of Earth and Space Sciences, University of Science and Technology of China, Hefei, China, https://orcid.org/0000-0003-4405-8872 (ZL); 2. State Key Laboratory of Precision Geodesy, Innovation Academy for Precision Measurement Science and Technology, Chinese Academy of Sciences, Wuhan, China, https://orcid.org/0000-0003-0362-433X (HZ); 3. Mengcheng National Geophysical Observatory, University of Science and Technology of China, Mengcheng, China; 4. Key Laboratory of Geoscience Big Data and Deep Resource of Zhejiang Province, School of Earth Sciences, Zhejiang University, Hangzhou, China, https://orcid.org/0000-0001-8836-405X (XB)

*Corresponding author: hanzhang@apm.ac.cn

lithospheric structures. However, discrepancies between these models, which are less relevant to the lithosphere's features, can sometimes be apparent and potentially reflect different sensitivity of data to the structure, coupling relationships of inversion parameters, or the uncertainty of the initial model in the inversion process (Zhang *et al.*, 2022). Therefore, choosing tomographic models may lead to discrepancies when classifying the lithosphere. In contrast to *S*-wave velocity models derived from traditional two-step inversion process (e.g., Yao *et al.*, 2006, 2008; Yang *et al.*, 2008), dispersion curves established with phase velocity values extracted at a specific geographic coordinate from phase velocity maps at different periods are generally more consistent, possibly due to the uniformity of the data, fewer inversion parameters, and avoiding the choice of damping and smoothing parameters when inverting for V_S (Zhang *et al.*, 2023). Besides, surface-wave dispersion curves also reflect the lithosphere's elastic parameter characteristics, allowing quantitative lithosphere classification. Therefore, we expect classification of lithospheric structure using dispersion maps to be relatively reliable.

Representing high-dimensional dispersion data with several independent key features enables objective regionalization. However, conventional techniques, such as the principal component analysis (PCA), which occasionally necessitate retention of over 10 principal components to capture >80% of the data variance, become inefficient when processing complex nonlinear data (e.g., Hashemi, 2013; Okada *et al.*, 2017). The commonly adopted B-spline parameterization well addresses the nonlinear variation of phase velocities at different periods, but it is not clear whether those coefficients are correlated or not (Chen *et al.*, 2006). Nevertheless, newly developed machine learning techniques have proven effective in extracting primary features from high-dimensional and nonlinear geophysical data (e.g., Johnson *et al.*, 2020; Jenkins *et al.*, 2021; Li, 2022; Steinmann *et al.*, 2021; Ma *et al.*, 2022; Zhou *et al.*, 2024).

A novel unsupervised approach VAE can extract crucial information from data without prior knowledge or assumptions (Kingma and Welling, 2014). To comprehensively classify the lithosphere using dispersion curves, a method that reflects these holistic trends is more appropriate. VAE can effectively capture hidden features that reflect variations in overall dispersion curves through neural networks while reconstructing the original curves using these features, thereby preserving essential information about dispersion curves (e.g., Li, 2022; Ma *et al.*, 2022; Zhang *et al.*, 2024). This method has been applied in the extraction of global lithospheric features using dispersion curves, which can indicate the lithosphere's physical properties (Zhang *et al.*, 2024). By examining these hidden features and corresponding dispersion curves, we can accurately classify lithospheric structures.

In this study, we applied the VAE method to uncover hidden lithospheric structure information using Rayleigh-wave phase velocity dispersion maps in China and its surroundings. The input dispersion curves contain more short-period data, with a period range of 8–120 s, than previous global applications, with a period range of 25–250 s, therefore allowing regionalization with shallower structure information. We categorized the lithospheric structure within the designated area by analyzing the extracted features and synthetic dispersion curves corresponding to the reduced number of features.

Regional Dispersion Curves Classified by VAE

This study utilized the Rayleigh-wave phase velocity dispersion curves, which are established with phase velocity values extracted at a specific geographic coordinate from phase velocity maps at different periods by Bao *et al.* (2015) and Li *et al.* (2022) as the intermediate input in the inversion of the *S*-wave velocity model from two-point (source–receiver) phase velocity dispersion curves. It is noteworthy that the dispersion curves here are from dispersion maps in the inversion process of *S*-wave velocity, which are different from the two-point dispersion used in the direct inversion of Rayleigh-wave dispersion (Fang *et al.*, 2015). These curves used in the study were derived from seismic data collected from the networks in and surrounding the Chinese mainland, like the Chinese Regional Seismic Network, temporary seismic stations in the Tibetan plateau, and permanent global seismic stations situated within or around the study area. The data were obtained from a combination of ambient noise tomography (8–50 s) and surface-wave tomography using earthquakes (20–120 s). The seismic stations covered nearly the whole study area, which promises comprehensive ray coverage and reliable Rayleigh-wave phase velocities within the period range from 8 to 120 s. We chose this dataset because it covers a larger area and a wider period range among the models we found. We aim to see the structural variation within the lithosphere, so we chose a wider period range dataset. Considering the phase velocity sensitivity kernel relative to the average 1D shear-wave profile over the study area (Li *et al.*, 2022) (Fig. S1, available in the supplemental material to this article), the longest period is sensitive to V_S down to around 200 km depth, which is deep enough for the lithosphere structure. The shortest period provides more detailed shallow information. Compared to other datasets, dispersion curves derived by Bao *et al.* (2015) and Li *et al.* (2022) offer a denser sampling, with 30 points within the specified period range, and allow the capture of finer structural variations in the lithosphere. To include dispersion curves with less uncertainty, we specifically selected curves within regions having large station densities according to Li *et al.* (2022). Despite the implemented quality control to enhance the reliability of the results, we observed anomalies in some dispersion curves in which phase velocities at 50 and 60 s were significantly higher than those at 80 s. The finding contradicts global phase velocities at larger scales (Ekström, 2011), and these particular data are situated at the peripheries of the inversion area. This could be attributed to an increasing uncertainty

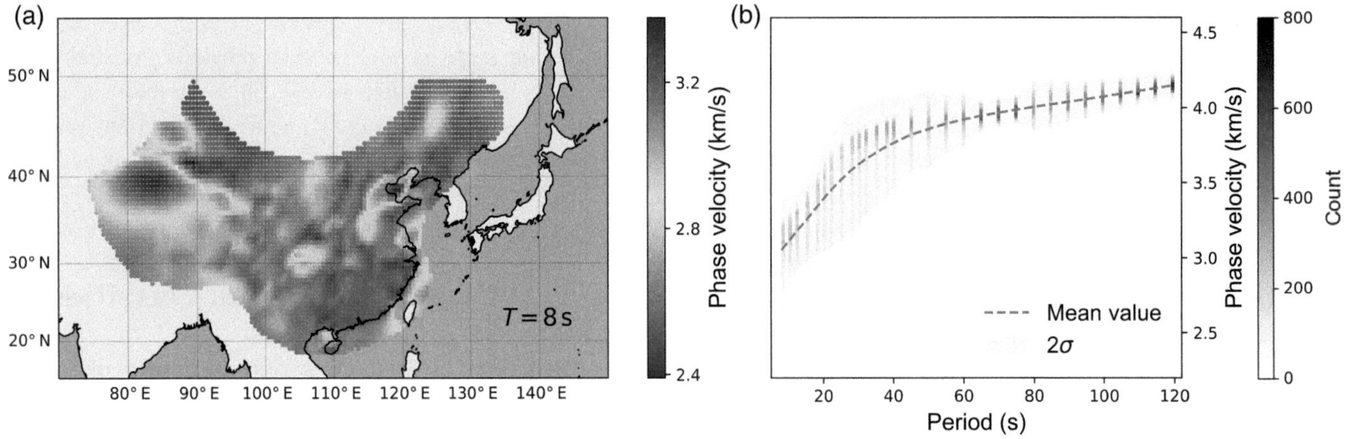

Figure 1. Rayleigh-wave phase velocity map after removing discrepant data: (a) spatial distribution of Rayleigh-wave phase velocities at the period of 8 s in the study area, the background colors represent the Rayleigh-wave phase velocities; (b) a 2D histogram of phase velocity dispersion curves at periods ranging from 8 to 120 s used in the study area, the background colors correspond to the distribution of Rayleigh-wave phase velocities within each period. The dashed line represents the arithmetic mean of all phase velocity dispersion curves. The gray shaded area represents the area within the data's two standard deviation range. The color version of this figure is available only in the electronic edition.

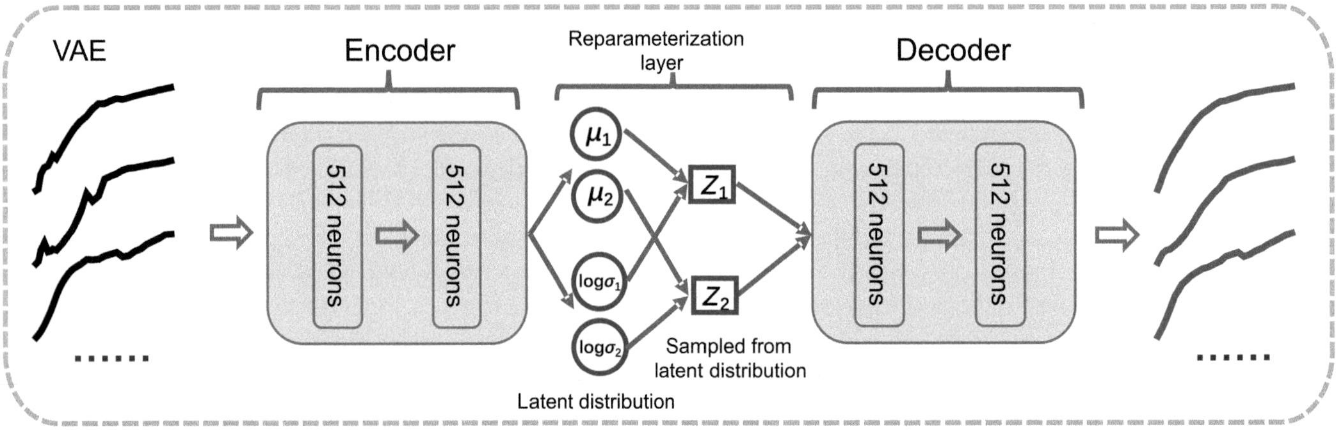

Figure 2. Variational autoencoder (VAE) network structure. It consists of an encoder and a decoder containing two fully connected layers with 512 neurons in each. The bottleneck (reparameterization layer) consists of two latent variables constrained to follow the normal distributions. The color version of this figure is available only in the electronic edition.

at boundaries during the inversion process (e.g., Shen *et al.*, 2016). Thus, we excluded the anomalous dispersion curves to enhance data reliability and achieve more stable classification results. After the preprocessing steps, we retained 4342 dispersion curves on a spatial grid of 0.5° × 0.5° (Fig. 1).

VAE was utilized to extract features from dispersion curves. Its network architecture includes an encoder, a decoder, and a reparameterization layer (Kingma and Welling, 2014). Specifically, the encoder reduces high-dimensional input into low-dimensional intermediate variables (i.e., the mean value and standard deviation of a Gaussian distribution), and the reparameterization layer generates latent variables (i.e., the extracted z values) following a Gaussian distribution based on these mean values and standard deviations. The latent variable is the key feature used to reconstruct the input. The decoder then reconstructs the input data using these latent variables (Fig. 2). We built the architecture following Li (2022), where both the encoder and decoder consist of two fully connected layers with 512 neurons in each layer (Fig. 2). Given the unknown influence of the feature's number on dispersion curves, we must test and confirm the appropriate number of latent variables to represent the data's features. Therefore, we determined the optimal number of latent variables by comparing reconstruction loss for latent dimensions in a range of one to five. To optimize network parameters and achieve an optimal model, we define the following loss function (Kingma and Welling, 2014):

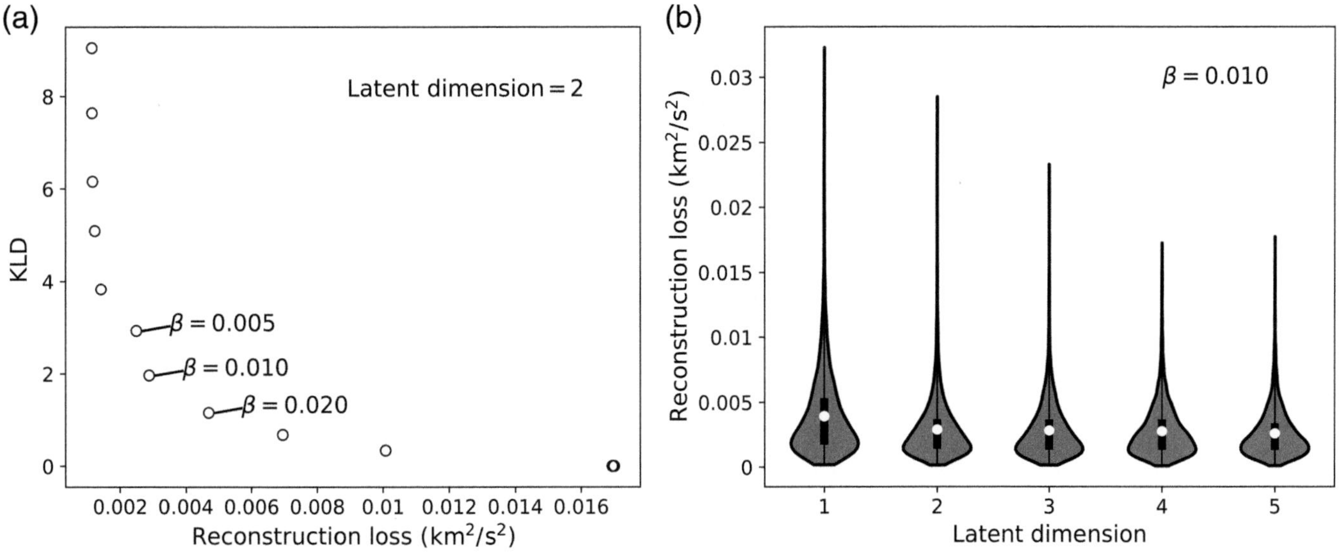

Figure 3. Parameter tests on various β values and latent dimensions. (a) The effect of different β values. The variations of reconstruction loss and Kullback–Leibler divergence (KLD) as β values change (latent dimension = 2); (b) the reconstruction loss changes when setting different latent dimensions ($\beta = 0.01$). The violin plot for each latent dimension represents the reconstruction loss distribution of different latent dimensions. The central white dots and the black rectangle's upper and lower boundaries represent the mean, upper quartile, and lower quartile of the reconstruction loss distribution, respectively. The color version of this figure is available only in the electronic edition.

$$\text{Loss} = \sum_{i}^{M}\sum_{j}^{N_P}\frac{(C_i^{\text{in}}(T_j) - C_i^{\text{out}}(T_j,z,\beta))^2}{N_P * M} + \beta \times \frac{1}{2} \times \sum_{i}^{M}\sum_{k}^{N_Z}(-\log\sigma_{ik}^2 - 1 + \sigma_{ik}^2 + \mu_{ik}^2). \quad (1)$$

The index i represents the ith dispersion curve sample in the entire dataset. The index j indicates the jth period sample point in the dispersion curve, and the index k denotes the kth latent variable extracted from one dispersion curve. M indicates the total number of dispersion curves. N_P represents the number of period sampling points in a dispersion curve. N_Z represents the number of latent dimensions (Fig. 3b). T_j refers to the jth period. $C_i^{\text{in}}(T_j)$ and $C_i^{\text{out}}(T_j,z,\beta)$ are the phase velocity of the ith dispersion curve (input) at period T_j and the corresponding output phase velocity at the same period T_j. σ_{ik} and μ_{ik} are the standard deviation and mean values of the kth z value (e.g., Z_1, Z_2 in Fig. 2) extracted from the ith dispersion curve. β is used to balance the two parts in the loss function. Specifically, the first term calculates the similarity between the input and output using the mean square error (MSE) over a period range. It is referred to as the reconstruction loss. The second term, namely KLD (Kullback–Leibler divergence), assesses the disparity between the latent variable distribution and the standard normal distribution. The weight of KLD within the loss function is represented by β, which is used to balance reconstruction loss and KLD during optimization (Higgins *et al.*, 2017). As we assume the Gaussian distribution of the latent variables for computational simplicity, we use β to constrain the value of KLD and ensure a Gaussian distribution of the latent variables. However, the optimal value of β varies across datasets influenced by multiple factors, and the appropriate β value for the dispersion curves used in this study remains unclear. We use the dataset as the model input because we intend to use these dispersion curves as the proxy to classify the lithosphere in the study area. Consequently, we introduced a 4342×30 matrix of dispersion curves into the model as an input and tested the impact of different β values. By plotting reconstruction loss and KLD derived from the model on the x-axis and y-axis, respectively, we chose a β value of 0.01 near the turning point, which achieves a relative balance between the two values above (Fig. 3a).

We randomly assigned 80% of the dispersion curves as the training dataset for the neural network, whereas the remaining 20% was used for validation to acquire a model. After extensive testing, we determined that an optimal learning rate of 1×10^{-3} and a batch size of 32 resulted in convergence after 200 epochs. We used the rectified linear unit as the activation function in this study. Throughout the network training process, we utilized the Adam optimizer (Kingma and Ba, 2015) to update the network parameters.

Two normally distributed latent variables adequately represent the overall variation of the dispersion curves (Fig. 3b, Table 1). Although it was speculated that a higher latent space dimension offers a better fit to the data, our tests using these 4342 dispersion curves on various latent dimensions show unexpected results. With only one latent variable, the reconstruction loss has a mean value of approximately 0.00393 km^2/s^2, and the upper and lower quartile values are up to approximately 0.00531 km^2/s^2 and 0.00172 km^2/s^2. Adding one more latent

TABLE 1
Mean, Lower, and Upper Quartiles of the Reconstruction Loss (Latent Dimension from 1 to 5)

Latent Dimension	Mean Misfit (km^2/s^2)	Upper Quartile (km^2/s^2)	Lower Quartile (km^2/s^2)
1	0.00393	0.00531	0.00172
2	0.00288	0.00370	0.00137
3	0.00281	0.00367	0.00131
4	0.00276	0.00368	0.00132
5	0.00259	0.00338	0.00129

variable drops the mean reconstruction loss to approximately 0.00288 km^2/s^2, with the upper and lower quartile reconstruction losses of 0.00370 km^2/s^2 and 0.00137 km^2/s^2. When we set three latent variables in the hidden layer, the mean reconstruction loss reduces to approximately 0.00281 km^2/s^2, and the upper and lower quartile of reconstruction loss reduces to 0.00367 km^2/s^2 and 0.00131 km^2/s^2. In the case of four latent variables, instead of producing a better fitting to the input data, the reconstructed dispersion curves show a mean reconstruction loss of approximately 0.00276 km^2/s^2 with the upper and lower quartile reconstruction loss values of 0.00368 km^2/s^2 and 0.00132 km^2/s^2, whereas the mean reconstruction loss with five latent variables reduces to 0.00259 km^2/s^2. We hypothesize that the slightly higher quartile values with four latent variables are led by a trade-off between β and the latent dimension. Using four latent variables necessitates a smaller β value to increase the relative weight of reconstruction loss in equation (1) and to drive it to lower values (see Fig. S2). Therefore, the reconstruction loss levels suggest that two latent variables are sufficient to capture the main features of dispersion curves after tests.

The two latent variables primarily impact changes in dispersion curves' slopes at short to medium periods and those at long periods. We input virtual latent variables at every 0.5 interval from −2.5 to 2.5 into the decoder to generate a set of dispersion curves and to visualize their variations with latent variables (Fig. 4a). An increase in the Z_1 results in a decline in the slopes of dispersion curves at short to medium periods (~40 s), which means that the velocity transition within the depth range weakens. Similarly, an increase in the second latent variable primarily leads to an increase in the slope contrast between medium (~80 s) and long periods.

Variation of dispersion curves with latent variables provides a quantificational basis for the lithosphere's classification related to its velocities and elastic properties. By reconstructing these dispersion curves' variations related to the latent variables, we can expose the overall changes in the shapes of the dispersion curves. The trends allow us to categorize the dispersion curves into four distinct types within the study area (Fig. 4). We divided the dispersion curves visually and set the thresholds of the four subregions as follows: R1 ($Z_1 : 1\text{–}2.5$, $Z_2 : -2.5 \text{ to } 1$); R2 ($Z_1 : 1\text{–}2.5$, $Z_2 : 1\text{–}2.5$); R3 ($Z_1 : -2.5 \text{ to } 1$, $Z_2 : -2.5 \text{ to } 1$); and R4 ($Z_1 : -2.5 \text{ to } 1$, $Z_2 : 1\text{–}2.5$).

We distinguish the four regions according to the shapes of the dispersion curves visually. The phase velocities of dispersion curves generated when $Z_1 < 1$ increase faster with period than those generated when $Z_1 > 1$ at short periods. The phase velocities of dispersion curves generated when $Z_2 > 1$ increase faster with period than those generated when $Z_2 < 1$ at long period ends. Although the group velocity reflects the slopes of phase velocity, the systematic errors of group velocity measurement and inversion are large (Shapiro and Singh, 1999), which can make it difficult to identify the curve's variation. The division is not fully objective, but we classified the area with the thresholds to divide it into subregions (Fig. 4c). The area with Z_1 smaller than 1 tends to have a thinner crust, whereas the area with Z_1 larger than 1 tends to have a thicker crust. The curves with Z_2 larger than 1 might have lower velocities at the lithospheric mantle depth.

The R3 and R4 regions, collectively accounting for approximately 84% of our study area, are two major dispersion curve types. These regions predominantly correspond to areas beyond the Tibetan plateau. The R4 region correlates more strongly with active tectonic units, such as the Yunnan–Guizhou plateau and the Cathaysian block. In contrast, the R3 region aligns more closely with stable blocks such as the western North China craton and Sichuan basin. The remaining two types, constituting approximately 16% of the area, are primarily associated with the Tibetan plateau area. The R2 region is approximately situated in the Songpan terrane, western Sichuan plateau, and Tanggula Mountains area, whereas the R1 region mainly encompasses locations in the Kunlun Mountains, northern Tibetan plateau, and the Himalayas. Because of gradual changes in curve shapes between different dispersion curve types, transitional colors are used to show the continuous changes close to the thresholds.

Compared to conventional surface-wave inversion methods, the VAE approach reconstructs dispersion curves that fit the general trends of curve shapes and promise the reflection of observed velocity variations with fewer variables. This approach bypasses specific physical processes and simplifies calculations. The correlation coefficient between the two latent variables is approximately 0.0082, suggesting that they likely reflect different features in the dispersion curves. Given that surface waves are particularly sensitive to *S*-wave velocity variations, *S*-wave velocities can be obtained using dispersion curves for traditional surface-wave inversion. Although these *S*-wave velocities provide insights into structural characteristics within the Earth's interior at various depths, they may exhibit relatively high correlation coefficients between horizontal distribution maps at neighboring depths due to vertical

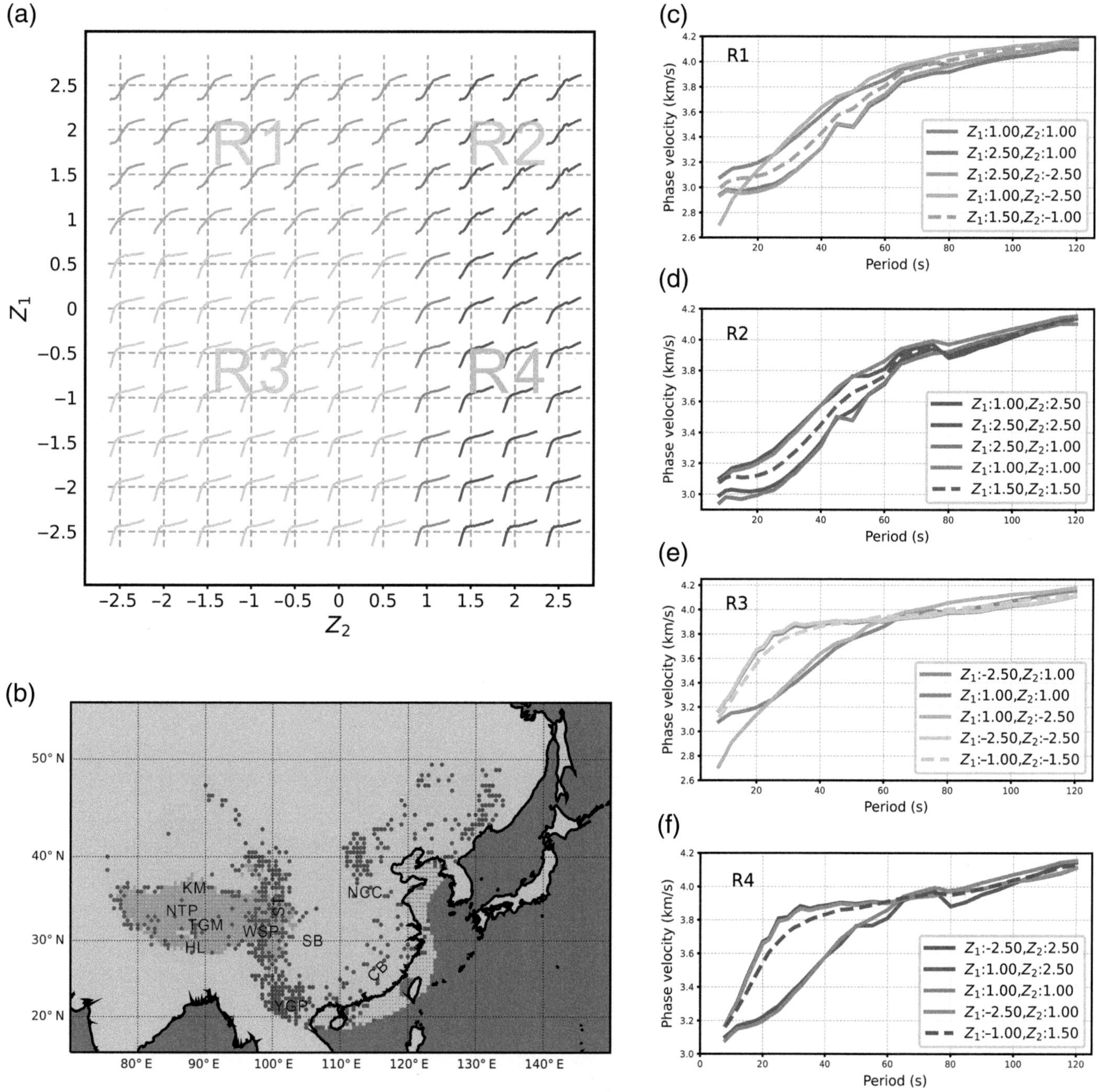

Figure 4. The classification diagram in the study area. (a) Dispersion curves generated by the VAE model for the subregions of the study area. The curves' colors correspond to four regions in (b); (b) geographical distributions of the different dispersion curves. Gradient colors represent transitions between different types. The abbreviations represent different geological units: CB, Cathaysian block; HL, the Himalayas; KM, Kulun Mountain; NCC, North China craton; NTP, North Tibetan plateau; SB, Sichuan basin; ST, Songpan terrane; TGM, Tanggula Mountain; WSP, western Sichuan plateau; and YGP, Yunnan–Guizhou plateau; (c) dispersion curve shape variations in R1; (d) dispersion curve shape variations in R2; (e) dispersion curve shape variations in R3; (f) dispersion curve shape variations in R4. The curve ($Z_1 = 1, Z_2 = 1$) is the same in all figures and can be used for relative comparison. The color version of this figure is available only in the electronic edition.

smoothing (Zhang and Ritzwoller, 2024). These interdependent parameters may contain redundant information, hindering the effective description of overall lithospheric characteristics using a limited number of parameters. Besides, when we compare the dispersion curves generated by the VAE model and synthetic dispersion curves forward modeled from the 85-layer 3D V_S model inverted from the surface-wave dispersion data (Li *et al.*, 2022), it shows similar levels of reconstruction loss (Fig. 5), promising the extraction of the curve shapes by VAE. The mean value and standard deviation of reconstruction loss are 0.0029 km^2/s^2 and 0.0022 km^2/s^2 with VAE-generated dispersion curves, whereas those values are 0.00065 km^2/s^2 and 0.00080 km^2/s^2 with physics-based dispersion curves.

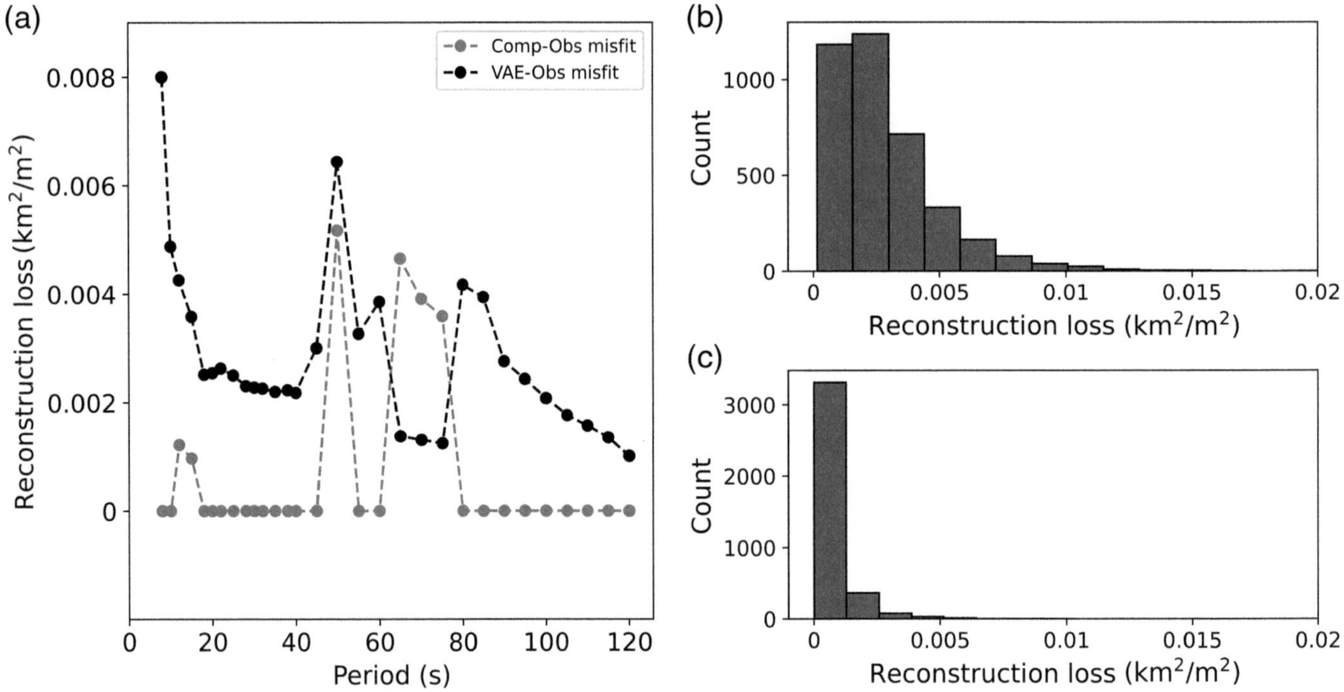

Figure 5. Comparisons between dispersion curves generated by different methods and observations in the whole region: (a) mean reconstruction loss variation within the study area for synthetic dispersion curves calculated using the *S*-wave velocity model derived from Li *et al.* (2022) and VAE-generated dispersion curves in the period range of 8–120 s; (b) the mean reconstruction loss over the periods at all spatial grid point for VAE-generated dispersion curves compared with observed dispersion curves; (c) the reconstruction loss distribution of synthetic dispersion curves calculated using physics-based forward modeling from the 3D V_S model compared with observed dispersion curves. The color version of this figure is available only in the electronic edition.

Even in the R1 group with the worst fit among the four types (Fig. S3), the mean reconstruction loss is around 0.00323 km^2/s^2. The VAE-generated dispersion curves reflect the general variation of curve shapes and ignore some minor features; therefore, they have a relatively larger reconstruction loss. However, the general variations concentrate the classification on the main features with relatively smooth generated curves. Compared with the reconstructed dispersion curves by VAE using one latent variable (see supplemental material), the dispersion curves derived by the inverse transformation of PCA using the first component have a larger mean reconstruction loss (0.0044 km^2/s^2). The reconstruction loss levels are similar when using two principal components, which have a mean reconstruction loss of 0.0021 km^2/s^2 and upper and lower quantiles of 0.0030 km^2/s^2 and 0.00075 km^2/s^2, compared to VAE using two latent variables. The VAE might show better results when it is applied to more complex nonlinear data. In addition, we classify the region using the thresholds of −0.3, 0, and 0.3 for the first principal component. The classification according to the first principal components can reliably classify the Tibetan plateau from the remaining region but contains small inlaid areas, which are difficult to interpret (Figs. S4 and S5).

Implications for Tectonics in China and Its Surroundings

The spatial patterns of the two latent variables closely align with surface tectonic features. The values of the first latent variable (Fig. 6a) generally decrease from west to east. Areas adjacent to mountain ranges and high plateaus, such as the Tianshan Mountains and the Tibetan plateau, predominantly display high values of this latent variable. Conversely, regions near the North China Plain and the northeast China Plain are predominantly characterized by low values. The distribution of the second latent variable (Fig. 6b) typically exhibits a clear discontinuity between high and low values. Areas near certain high plateaus, such as the Yunnan–Guizhou plateau, and hilly regions like the Shandong Peninsula, predominantly manifest high values of this latent variable. Conversely, regions adjacent to sedimentary basins, such as the Tarim basin or coastal sedimentary basins, are predominantly associated with low values.

The results of the VAE model indicate that classification through analyzing the dispersion curves correlates with geological structures. The R1 and R3 types can be distinguished from the R2 and R4 types, respectively, based on the second latent variable's values, with the main difference lying in the dispersion curves' shapes at medium (~80 s) to long periods. Curve variations with the second latent variable suggest that R1 and R3 types correspond to lower values of this variable, indicating generally higher velocities at longer periods (mean phase velocity of 4.08 km/s over 80 s), primarily sensitive to the

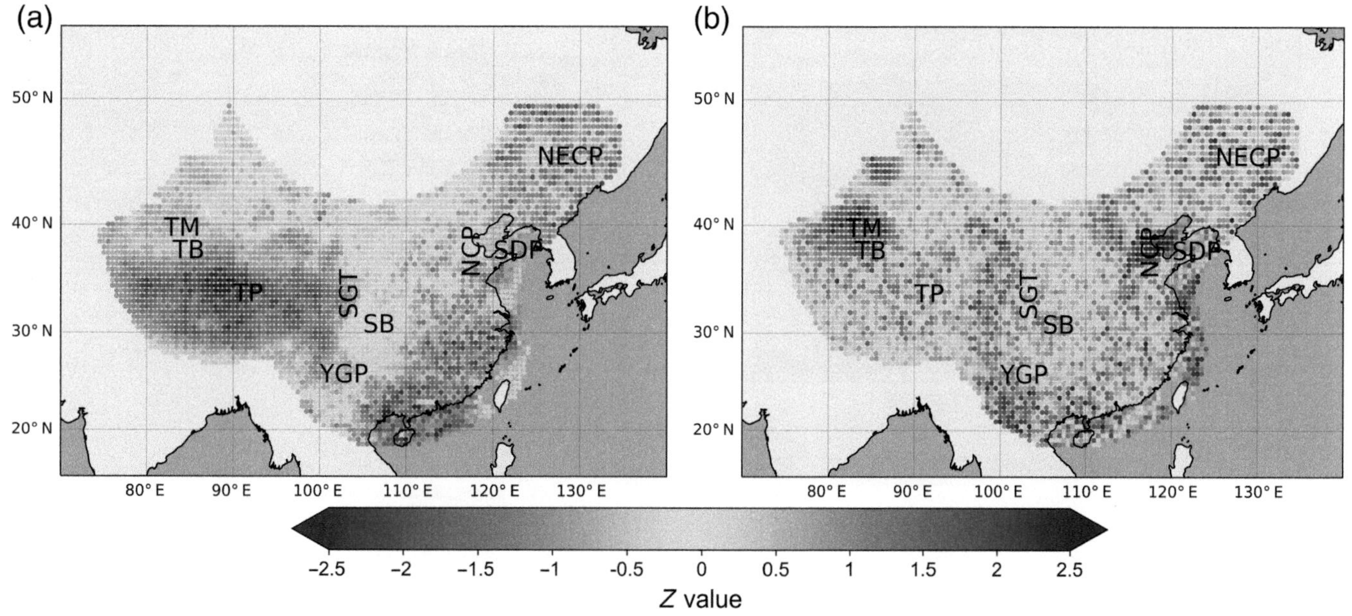

Figure 6. Spatial distributions of two latent variables: (a) Z_1 and (b) Z_2 plotted with the same color scale. The abbreviations in the figures represent different geological units: NCP, North China Plain; NECP, northeastern China Plain; SB, Sichuan basin; SGT, Songpan-Ganzi terrane; SP, Shandong Peninsula; TB, Tarim basin; TM, Tianshan Mountain; TP, Tibetan plateau; and YGP, Yunnan-Guizhou plateau. The color version of this figure is available only in the electronic edition.

lithospheric mantle. Our inferred depths are not exact due to a broad range of depth sensitivity for phase velocity at each period (Fig. S1). On the other hand, R2 and R4 types, which show generally lower velocities at longer periods (mean phase velocity of 4.02 km/s over 80 s) primarily sensitive to the mantle (Fig. 4), exhibit higher values of the second latent variable. The distinction between R1, R2 types and R3, R4 types primarily lies in velocity changes of short to medium periods within the crust. Notably, due to its thicker crust in the Tibetan plateau area, short-period phase velocity increases more slowly with period compared with those in other regions. Consequently, the Tibetan plateau related to R1 and R2 types can be differentiated from other areas, which correspond to R3 and R4 (Fig. 4). Outside the Tibetan plateau, type R3 exhibits relatively higher average velocities at longer periods (mean phase velocity of 4.08 km/s over 80 s), primarily sensitive to the lithospheric mantle, which suggests probably a higher shear modulus. This may correspond to areas with fewer magmatic activities, like stable cratons (e.g., Sichuan basin, Ordos block, Yangtze craton, and Tarim basin). Although R3 takes up 74% within the whole region, 94% of areas in the cratons (Hasterok *et al.*, 2022) belong to the R3 type, which indicates a concentration of craton lithosphere in the region. Conversely, type R4 indicates a lower average velocity at longer periods (mean phase velocity of 4.03 km/s over 80 s) in the lithospheric mantle with stronger lithospheric activity. Its relatively lower phase velocities may be attributed to the magma formed by upwelling hot materials (e.g., Chen *et al.*, 2023) or modification of the lithospheric mantle (Wang *et al.*, 2017). In the Tibetan plateau region, although the phase velocity variations in the shallow part of this region are different from those in the other regions, the general lithospheric mantle's velocity difference between R1 and R2 (0.066 km/s) is similar to that between R3 and R4 (0.053 km/s). Type R2 has a relatively lower average velocity (with a mean value of 4.01 km/s over 80 s) in the lithospheric mantle compared with type R1 (with a mean value of 4.08 km/s over 80 s), which may be induced by the hot material upwelling in the mantle. This process may affect both the crust and the mantle (Chen *et al.*, 2017; Li *et al.*, 2019).

The misfits between the dispersion curves generated by VAE and the input dispersion curves at each grid point reflect the extent of deviations between the VAE model and observation, which potentially indicates regions with poor data resolution (Fig. 7). At each period, we compute the L2 norm of misfit at each grid point relative to the sum of L2 norm misfits within the study area as the relative misfit:

$$\text{Relative misfit}_{i,j} = \frac{||C_i^{\text{in}}(T_j) - C_i^{\text{out}}(T_j)||}{\sum_i^{M=4342}(||C_i^{\text{in}}(T_j) - C_i^{\text{out}}(T_j)||)}, \quad (2)$$

as a metric to quantify disparities between the observed and generated dispersion curves. The $(||C_i^{\text{in}}(T_j) - C_i^{\text{out}}(T_j)||)$ is the L2 norm misfit value, i represents ith dispersion curve sample in the entire dataset, in and out represent the input and output phase velocities, and T_j represents the jth period within the 30-period samples. The observed dispersion curves exhibit apparent disparities compared with the curves generated by the VAE model. Here, we calculated the 90th percentile of the reconstruction loss within the study area over the entire period

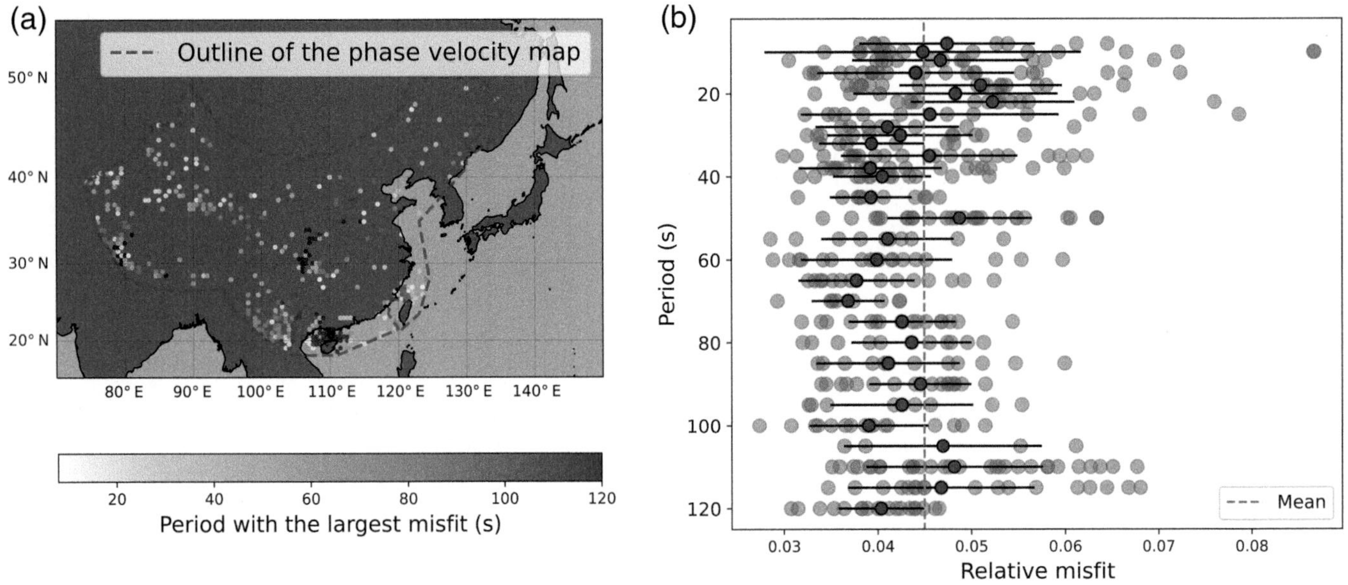

Figure 7. Distribution of relative misfits at different periods. (a) The positions of the curves where the reconstruction loss is greater than the 90th percentile. The colors, ranging from white to dark brown, represent increasing periods with the maximum misfit in a curve. The red-dashed line is the boundary of the study area. (b) The distribution of the maximum relative misfits. The gray dashed line represents the mean of all relative misfit values. The light brown solid circles at each period show the maximum relative misfit among the 30 sampled points in a dispersion curve, and locations corresponding to these curves are shown in (a). The dark brown solid circle at each period represents the mean relative misfit within each period. The error bar represents one standard deviation of relative misfits within each period. The color version of this figure is available only in the electronic edition.

range and used it as the threshold (0.0056 km^2/s^2, Fig. 3b). Afterward, we picked all the dispersion curves with reconstruction loss larger than the threshold and their corresponding relative misfits calculated by equation (2). We selected the largest relative misfit in every dispersion curve and its corresponding periods, and plotted the spatial distribution of the picked periods on the map (Fig. 7a). In addition, we plotted the picked period with its corresponding relative misfit in Figure 7b. The dark brown solid points in Figure 7b describe the mean values of all the light-colored circles within the same period, and the solid lines represent one standard deviation of the light-colored circles within the same period. The gray-dashed line represents the overall mean relative misfit value of light-colored circles. The means of these relative misfit values corresponding to different periods (light-colored circles in Fig. 7b) surpass the overall mean over all periods (the gray-dashed line in Fig. 7b) at period range from 8 to 30 s, and from 105 to 120 s. Locations with large relative misfit values at periods shorter than 30 s are sparsely distributed (Fig. 7a). Whereas checkerboard tests show velocity anomalies greater than 1° × 1° can be reliably recovered (Li *et al.*, 2022), these scattered points corresponding to large relative misfits with periods shorter than 30 s show no clustering and therefore, likely reflect random deviations rather than real velocity anomalies. In contrast, areas with large relative misfits at periods longer than 105 s are clustered at the boundary of the study area, and are likely caused by poor resolution due to reduced station density (generally lower than 5 in 2° × 2° grid; Fig. S6). In addition, we plotted the density map of all the relative misfits corresponding to dispersion curves with reconstruction loss exceeding the 90th percentile to show their distribution at different periods (Fig. S7).

Based on the extracted features, we have identified that one latent variable exhibits a strong correlation with topography, whereas the other is most likely to be correlated with the lithosphere's effective elastic thickness (Lu *et al.*, 2020; Fig. 8). We additionally compared the spatial variation of latent variables with crustal thickness and lithospheric thickness (Fig. S8). The topography dataset is the ETOPO1.0 model derived from direct remote sensing observations, with a spatial resolution of 1 arcmin, and we downsampled the topography data to 0.5° × 0.5°. The crustal thickness is from inversion of Rayleigh-wave dispersion curves by Li *et al.* (2022); the spatial resolution of the model is 1° × 1°. The lithospheric thickness is from LITHO1.0, which originates from inversion of high-resolution surface-wave dispersion maps, with a spatial resolution of 1° × 1° (Pasyanos *et al.*, 2014). The effective elastic thickness describes the thickness of an equivalent elastic plate that results in the same deformation as observed, and it was inverted from the topography and gravitational anomaly data by Lu *et al.* (2020), with a spatial resolution of 2° × 2°. The two latent variables significantly influence the variations of dispersion curves at the lithospheric scale. The correlation analysis reveals that these latent variables are associated with different physical quantities. Specifically, the correlation coefficient between

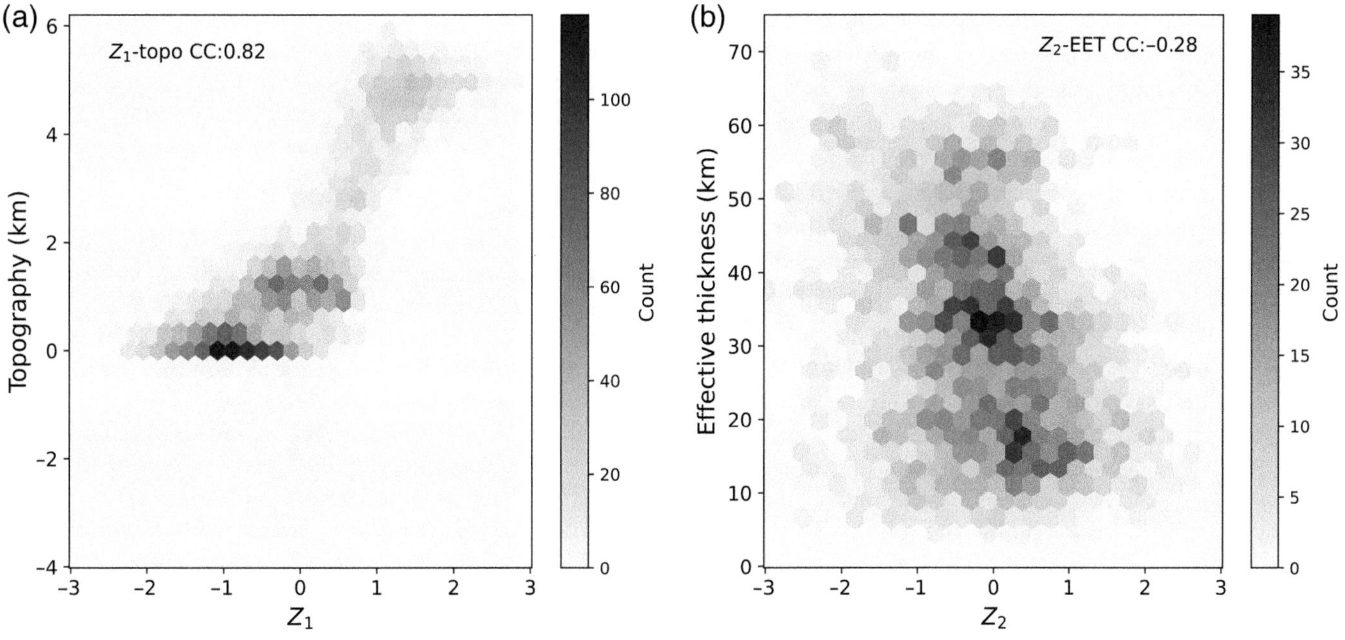

Figure 8. Correlations between latent variables and two specific physical parameters: (a) the correlation between the first latent variable and topography. The color scale corresponds to the number of points at different locations; (b) the correlation between the second latent variable and effective elastic thickness. The color scale corresponds to the number of points at different locations. The color version of this figure is available only in the electronic edition.

the first latent variable and topography is around 0.82, and that between the second latent variable and effective elastic thickness is approximately −0.28. We prefer physical parameters with a larger correlation coefficient. Although the correlation coefficient between the first latent variable and the crustal thickness from the Li *et al.* (2022) model is larger (CC = 0.88), we choose topography because it is a directly observed parameter. However, the correlation between the second latent variable and effective elastic thickness is not as significant as the association between the first latent variable and the topography, potentially due to other complex factors at play. This finding suggests that classification based on latent variables extracted from dispersion curves may provide insights into the dynamic processes, which in turn reflect on changes in topography and effective elastic thickness related to lithospheric strength.

Inverting a V_S model using fundamental-mode surface-wave dispersion only gives nonunique results. We think such nonuniqueness might be a consequence of overparameterized V_S models. Because of the overparameterization, building a V_S model from the dispersion data requires prior assumptions on subsurface structures, regularizations, or independent constraints.

However, choosing prior information may be subjective and lead to biased V_S models. In contrast, our VAE model offers a more objective input data compression, enabling more robust classifications. We find that two free variables are sufficient to fit the data and therefore suggest that most V_S models are indeed overparameterized. Therefore, to build more robust multilayer seismic models, we will need to add more observations with independent sensitivity. Our machine learning approach can easily extend to joint inversion with other seismic, geophysical, geochemical, and so forth data. Because the encoder–decoder network does not require specific physical modeling, other datasets can be easily added by appending them after the dispersion curves. The weights of individual datasets in the loss function need to be adjusted to balance their contributions. The interpretation of lithosphere structures here is incomplete because we only use one seismic dataset. But, regarding the information in the dispersion data, the extracted latent variables should be a good proxy.

Alternatively, we can parameterize models using fewer variables to speed up the inversions and reduce the uncertainties. Recently, Tsai *et al.* (2023) proposed a geological parametrization to better evaluate acceptable models without introducing an excessive number of parameters. Adopting a priori knowledge helps decrease dependence on ad hoc factors such as regularization and smoothing. In the future, it is possible to combine our approach and their geological parametrization to build a data-driven tomography model.

Conclusion

Using the VAE method, we observe that two latent variables adequately capture the primary variations in the 8–120 s Rayleigh-wave dispersion curve data in mainland China and its surrounding regions. The variations in dispersion curves exhibited in the latent space enable us to classify the lithosphere around China into four categories, especially with diverse lithosphere activities in or outside the Tibetan plateau regions. In addition to the four categories primarily delineated by the dominant trend of the dispersion curve, unusually large reconstruction losses are observed between the measured and reconstructed curves at some locations. The large reconstruction losses in these regions may be attributed to relatively poor model resolution associated with sparse station distribution when inverting phase velocity travel times. The correlation analysis reveals that the two latent variables are associated with topography (correlation coefficient = 0.82) and an effective elastic thickness model (correlation coefficient = −0.28) separately, suggesting that these two factors likely play a predominant role in shaping the dispersion maps compared to other physical parameters we considered.

Data and Resources

Phase velocity maps, 3D V_S model and the synthetic dispersion curves forward modeled from the 3D V_S model were provided by Mengkui Li (Li *et al.*, 2022). Topography in this study is from ETOPO1.0 available at https://ngdc.noaa.gov/mgg/global/relief/ETOPO1/tiled/ (last accessed December 2023). Lithospheric thickness in this study is from LITHO1.0 available at ~https://igppweb.ucsd.edu/~gabi/litho1.0.html (last accessed January 2025). Dispersion curve and sensitivity kernel computational software disba is available at https://pypi.org/project/disba/ (last accessed December 2023). The supplemental material contains eight figures, including sensitivity kernel of phase velocity at representative periods, reconstruction losses with four latent variables and those belonging to four types (R1–R4), principal component analysis (PCA) analysis with one principal component, station density map, and correlation analysis with four physical parameters.

Declaration of Competing Interests

The authors acknowledge that there are no conflicts of interest recorded.

Acknowledgments

The authors are grateful to the editor and two anonymous reviewers for their constructive comments and suggestions. This study is supported by the National Natural Science Foundation of China (Grant Numbers 42488301, 42030311, 42304071, and 42374055). Zefeng Li is supported by Anhui Provincial Key R&D Program (Number 2022m07020002). The authors thank Chun-Feng Li and Zhezhe Lu for providing their effective elastic thickness model. The authors thank Mengkui Li for providing synthetic dispersion curves using *S*-wave models, station information, and constructive comments.

References

Bao, X., X. Song, and J. Li (2015). High-resolution lithospheric structure beneath mainland china from ambient noise and earthquake surface-wave tomography, *Earth Planet. Sci. Lett.* **417,** 132–141, doi: 10.1016/j.epsl.2015.02.024.

Chapman, M. E., and S. C. Solomon (1976). North American-Eurasian plate boundary in northeast Asia, *J. Geophys. Res.* **81,** no. 5, 921–930, doi: 10.1029/JB081i005p00921.

Chen, K., Y. Lin, W. Shen, X. Xu, W. Wang, and S. Liu (2023). The origin of the Tengchong volcano: A review of geophysical and geochemical studies, *Rev. Geophys. Planet. Phys.* **54,** no. 2, 216–230.

Chen, M., F. Niu, J. Tromp, A. Lenardic, C.-T. A. Lee, W. Cao, and J. Ribeiro (2017). Lithospheric foundering and underthrusting imaged beneath Tibet, *Nat. Commun.* **8,** no. 1, 15659, doi: 10.1038/ncomms15659.

Chen, Q., N. Huang, S. Riemenschneider, and Y. Xu. (2006). A B-spline approach for empirical mode decompositions, *Adv. Comput. Math.* **24,** no. 1, 171–195, doi: 10.1007/s10444-004-7614-3.

Debayle, E., T. Bodin, S. Durand, and Y. Richard (2020). Seismic evidence for partial melt below tectonic plates, *Nature* **586,** no. 7830, 555–559, doi: 10.1038/s41586-020-2809-4.

Ekström, G. (2011). A global model of love and Rayleigh surface wave dispersion and anisotropy, 25–250 s, *Geophys. Res. Lett.* **187,** no. 3, 1668–1686, doi: 10.1111/j.1365-246X.2011.05225.x.

Fang, H., H. Yao, H. Zhang, Y. C. Huang, and R. D. van der Hilst. (2015). Direct inversion of surface wave dispersion for three-dimensional shallow crustal structure based on ray tracing: Methodology and application, *Geophys. J. Int.* **201,** no. 3, 1251–1263, doi: 10.1093/gji/ggv080.

Gordon, R. G., and S. Stein (1992). Global tectonics and space geodesy, *Science* **256,** no. 5055, 333–342, doi: 10.1126/science.256.5055.333.

Han, S., H. Zhang, H. Xin, W. Shen, and H. Yao (2022). USTClitho2.0: Updated unified seismic tomography models for Continental China lithosphere from joint inversion of body-wave arrival times and surface-wave dispersion data, *Seismol. Res. Lett.* **93,** no. 1, 201–215, doi: 10.1785/0220210122.

Hashemi, S. (2013). Seismicity characterization of Iran: A multivariate statistical approach, *Math. Geosci.* **45,** 705–723.

Hasterok, D., J. A. Halpin, A. S. Collins, M. Hand, C. Kreemer, M. G. Gard, and S. Clorie (2022). New maps of global geological provinces and tectonic plates, *Earth Sci. Rev.* **231,** 104,069, doi: 10.1016/j.earscirev.2022.104069.

Higgins, I., I. Matthey, A. Pal, C. Burgess, X. Glorot, M. Botvinick, S. Mohamed, and A. Lerchner (2017). beta-VAE: Learning basic visual concepts with a constrained variational framework, *International Conf. on Learning Representations (ICLR)*, available at https://openreview.net/forum?id=Sy2fzU9gl (last accessed January 2024).

Jenkins, W. F., II, P. Gerstoft, M. J. Bianco, and P. D. Bromirski (2021). Unsupervised deep clustering of seismic data: Monitoring the ross ice shelf, Antarctica, *J. Geophys. Res.* **126,** no. 9, doi: 10.1002/essoar.10505894.3.

Johnson, C. W., Y. Ben-Zion, H. Meng, and F. Vernon (2020). Identifying different classes of seismic noise signals using unsupervised learning, *Geophys. Res. Lett.* 47, no. 15, doi: 10.1029/2020GL088353.

Kingma, D. P., and J. Ba (2015). Adam: A method for stochastic optimization, *International Conf. on Learning Representations (ICLR)*, available at https://arxiv.org/abs/1412.6980v5 (last accessed January 2024).

Kingma, D. P., and M. Welling (2014). Auto-encoding variational Bayes, *Proc. International Conf. on Learning Representations (ICLR)*, Vol. 19, 121, doi: 10.48550/arXiv.1312.6114.

Li, M., X. Song, J. Li, and X. Bao (2022). Crust and upper mantle structure of East Asia from ambient noise and earthquake surface wave tomography, *Earthq. Sci.* **35,** no. 2, 71–92, doi: 10.1016/j.eqs.2022.05.004.

Li, Z. (2022). A generic model of global earthquake rupture characteristics revealed by machine learning, *Geophys. Res. Lett.* **49,** no. 8, e2021GL096464, doi: 10.1029/2021GL096464.

Li, Z., B. Guo, Q. Liu, J. Chen, S. Li, and S. Qi (2019). P-wave structure of upper mantle beneath the Northeastern Tibetan plateau from multi-scale seismic tomography, *Chin. J. Geophys.* **62,** no. 4, 1244–1255, doi: 10.6038/cjg2019J0392.

Lu, Z., C. Li, S. Zhu, and P. Audet (2020). Effective elastic thickness over the Chinese mainland and surroundings estimated from a joint inversion of bouguer admittance and coherence, *Phys. Earth Planet. In.* **301,** 106,456, doi: 10.1016/j.pepi.2020.106456.

Lv, X., Z. Shao, P. Hao, D. Chen, and Z. Fu (2011). Preliminary comparison of seismicity between eastern Asia western Asia and eastern Mediterranean region, *Earthquake* **31,** no. 3, 77–91.

Ma, S., Z. Li, and W. Wang (2022). Machine learning of source spectra for large earthquakes, *Geophys. J. Int.* **231,** no. 1, 692–702, doi: 10.1093/gji/ggac215.

Okada, A., M. Toriumi, and Y. Kaneda. (2017). Feature extraction of global seismicity by principal component analysis, *2017 International Conference on Control, Artificial Intelligence, Robotics and Optimization (ICCAIRO)*, 278–282, doi: 10.1109/ICCAIRO.2017.71.

Pasyanos, M. E., T. G. Masters, G. Laske, and Z. Ma (2014). LITHO1.0: An updated crust and lithospheric model of the earth, *J. Geophys. Res.* **119,** no. 3, 2153–2173, doi: 10.1002/2013JB010626.

Shapiro, N. M., and S. K. Singh (1999). A systematic error in estimating surface-wave group-velocity dispersion curves and a procedure for its correction, *Bull. Seismol. Soc. Am.* **89,** 1138–1142, doi: 10.1785/BSSA0890041138.

Shen, W., M. H. Ritzwoller, D. Kang, Y. Kim, F. Lin, J. Ning, W. Wang, Y. Zheng, and L. Zhou (2016). A seismic reference model for the crust and uppermost mantle beneath China from surface wave dispersion, *Geophys. J. Int.* **206,** no. 2, 954–979, doi: 10.1093/gji/ggw175.

Steinmann, R., L. Seydoux, É. Beaucé, and M. Campillo (2021). Hierarchical exploration of continuous seismograms with unsupervised learning, *J. Geophys. Res.* **127,** no. 1, doi: 10.1029/2021JB022455.

Tsai, V. C., C. Huber, and C. A. Dalton (2023). Towards the geological parametrization of seismic tomography, *Geophys. J. Int.* **234,** no. 2, 1447–1462, doi: 10.1093/gji/ggad140.

Wang, X., Y. Li, Z. Ding, L. Zhu, C. Wang, X. Bao, and Y. Wu (2017). Three-dimensional lithospheric S wave velocity model of the NE Tibetan plateau and Western North China Craton, *J. Geophys. Res.* **122,** no. 8, 6703–6720, doi: 10.1002/2017JB014203.

Yang, Y., A. Li, and M. H. Ritzwoller (2008). Crustal and uppermost mantle structure in southern Africa revealed from ambient noise and teleseismic tomography, *Geophys. J. Int.* **174,** no. 1, 235–248, doi: 10.1111/j.1365-246X.2008.03779.x.

Yao, H., C. Beghein, and R. D. van der Hilst (2008). Surface wave array tomography in SE Tibet from ambient seismic noise and two-station analysis–II. Crustal and upper-mantle structure, *Geophys. J. Int.* **173,** no. 1, 205–219, doi: 10.1111/j.1365-246X.2007.03696.x.

Yao, H., R. D. van der Hilst, and M. V. de Hoop (2006). Surface-wave array tomography in SE Tibet from ambient seismic noise and two-station analysis–I. Phase velocity maps, *Geophys. J. Int.* **166,** no. 2, 732–744, doi: 10.1111/j.1365-246X.2006.03028.x.

Zhang, H., S. Ni, L. Liu, and B. Schmandt (2024). Two effective degrees of freedom can represent the dominant features of global Rayleigh wave dispersion maps, *Geophys. Res. Lett.* **51,** no. 12, e2024GL108449, doi: 10.1029/2024GL108449.

Zhang, S., and M. H. Ritzwoller (2024). Applying machine learning to characterize and extrapolate the relationship between seismic structure and surface heat flow, *Geophys. J. Int.* **238,** no. 3, 1201–1222, doi: 10.1093/gji/ggae218.

Zhang, X., X. Song, and J. Li (2022). A comparative study of seismic tomography models of the Chinese continental lithosphere, *Earthq. Sci.* **35,** no. 3, 161–185, doi: 10.1016/j.eqs.2022.05.005.

Zhang, X., X. Song, and F. Wang (2023). A comparative study of seismic tomography models of southwest China, *Earthq. Sci.* **36,** no. 1, 15–39, doi: 10.1016/j.eqs.2023.02.006.

Zhao, D., S. Yu, and E. Ohtani (2011). East Asia: Seismotectonics, magmatism and mantle dynamics, *J. Asian Earth Sci.* **40,** no. 3, 689–709, doi: 10.1016/j.jseaes.2010.11.013.

Zhou, Z., P. Gerstoft, and K. Olsen (2024). Graph-learning approach to combine multiresolution seismic velocity models, *Geophys. J. Int.* **238,** no. 3, 1353–1365, doi: 10.1093/gji/ggae212.

Manuscript received 18 September 2024
Published online 18 November 2025

Bedrock Offset Across the Wasatch Fault in Salt Lake City, Utah, from Teleseismic Converted Phases and Its Geologic Implications

HyeJeong Kim*[1,2], James C. Pechmann[1], Fan-Chi Lin[1], Adam P. McKean[3], and Christian L. Hardwick[3]

Abstract

In 2018, 32 three-component geophones were deployed in a linear array with ~90 m average station spacing across the active East Bench fault (EBF) in Salt Lake City, Utah. This west-dipping normal fault is a relatively young section of the Wasatch fault zone which cuts through the northeastern Salt Lake basin (SLB), west of and mostly parallel to the older Foothill fault section at the base of the Wasatch Range. Here, we investigate the variation of bedrock depth across the fault by examining the first peak of teleseismic receiver functions (RFs) along the linear array. The arrival time of this initial phase at stations in the SLB is particularly sensitive to the depth of a velocity discontinuity, referred to as R2, between semi-consolidated sediment and bedrock, which is consolidated sedimentary rock in most of the SLB. We observe that the first peak times are very similar on either side of the EBF but shift abruptly by ~0.7 s across the fault. Based on two recent 1D velocity models, one for each side of the fault, this time shift indicates a vertical R2 offset of 810 ± 290 m across the EBF. This offset likely reflects the accumulated slip on the fault since the fault's activation. Combining this offset with a current slip rate of 1.2 ± 0.2 mm/yr, based on paleoseismic studies of the Wasatch fault, and a range of models for how this slip rate may have changed over time, our best estimate for the age of the EBF is 0.7–1.4 Ma. From the R2 offset and the distance between stations over which it is observed, we calculate that the EBF has a minimum average dip of 81° ± 3° in the top 1100 m.

Cite this article as Kim, H.J., J. C. Pechmann, F.-C. Lin, A. P. McKean, and C. L. Hardwick (2025). Bedrock Offset Across the Wasatch Fault in Salt Lake City, Utah, from Teleseismic Converted Phases and Its Geologic Implications, *Seismol. Res. Lett.* **97**, 2128–2137, doi: 10.1785/0220250236.

Supplemental Material

Introduction

The Wasatch fault zone (WFZ) is a west-dipping normal fault zone on the western edge of the Wasatch Range, which forms the boundary between physiographic provinces of the Basin and Range to the west and the Middle Rocky Mountains and Colorado plateau to the east (Fig. 1a). The WFZ has been active since 12 ± 2 Ma (Ehlers *et al.*, 2003) to ~18 Ma (Parry and Bruhn, 1987), which is the middle Miocene. This fault is the largest source of the elevated earthquake hazard across the Wasatch Front region of north-central Utah (Petersen *et al.*, 2014, 2024; Wong *et al.*, 2016). Understanding the fault geometry and slip rate of each fault segment is critically important for constructing earthquake rupture scenarios and estimating earthquake recurrence intervals (Wong *et al.*, 2016; Petersen *et al.*, 2014, 2024). Although paleoseismic trenching provides direct evidence of fault parameters near the surface (e.g., DuRoss *et al.*, 2016), obtaining constraints on fault displacement and geometry at depths beyond several meters remains challenging. In addition, there are practical difficulties with conducting paleoseismic trenching in an urban area.

The East Bench fault (EBF) in the northeastern Salt Lake basin (SLB) is part of the Salt Lake City segment of the WFZ (Fig. 1a). The EBF lies west of and runs roughly parallel to the Foothill fault (FF), which is an older range-bounding fault along the northern Salt Lake segment. The EBF "stepped out" to the west from the FF relatively recently in the history of the WFZ and has now replaced the FF as the primary active trace of the WFZ in the northeastern SLB (Marsell, 1969; Scott

1. Department of Geology and Geophysics, University of Utah, Salt Lake City, Utah, U.S.A., https://orcid.org/0000-0002-8271-4319 (HJK); https://orcid.org/0000-0002-6726-9640 (JCP); https://orcid.org/0000-0003-0394-6830 (F-CL); 2. Now at Université Côte d'Azur, Observatoire de la Côte d'Azur, CNRS, IRD, Géoazur, Valbonne, France; 3. Utah Geological Survey, Salt Lake City, Utah, U.S.A., https://orcid.org/0000-0002-0207-4340 (CLH)

*Corresponding author: hkim.geo@gmail.com; hyejeong.kim@utah.edu

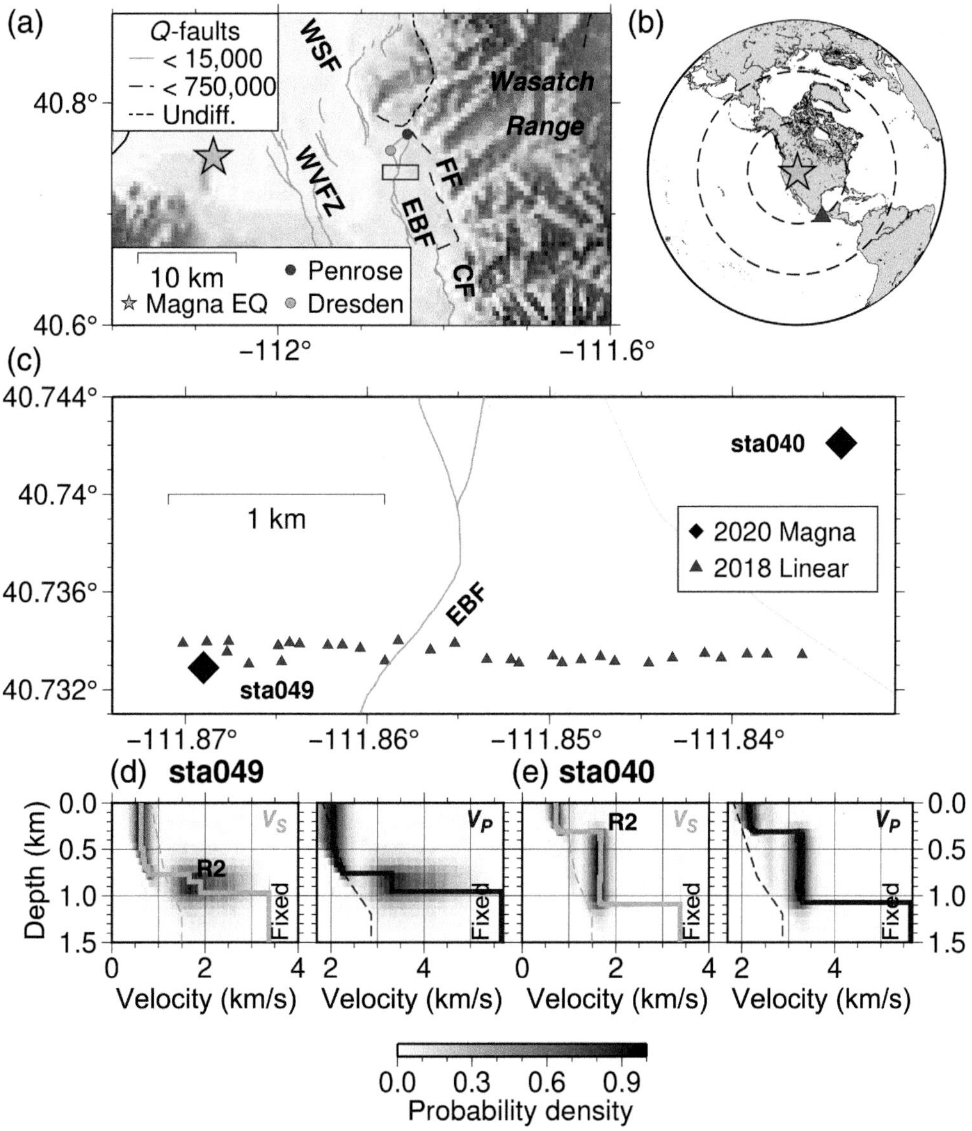

Figure 1. An overview of the data used in this study. (a) The tectonic setting of the study area (red box). The yellow star marks the epicenter of the 18 March 2020 M_w 5.7 Magna earthquake. The red and blue circles mark the locations of the Penrose Drive (DuRoss *et al.*, 2014) and Dresden Place (Garr, 1986) trenching sites, respectively. The major Quaternary faults ("Q-faults"; U.S. Geological Survey and Utah Geological Survey, 2023) are shown in different line types and colors according to their age of most recent movement, as indicated in the key; their names are abbreviated as follows: CF, Cottonwood fault; EBF, East Bench fault; FF, Foothill fault; WSF, Warm Springs fault; WVFZ, West Valley fault zone. (b) The locations of the teleseismic event used for the receiver function (RF) analysis (red triangle) and the Magna earthquake (yellow star). The dashed circles mark 30° and 60° epicentral distances from the location of the array. (c) Map of the area of the red box in (a) showing the distribution of stations used for the RF analysis as red triangles and the surface trace of the EBF. The two dark blue diamonds mark the locations of stations that provided the velocity models for migration, determined by Kim *et al.* (2025; Fig. S2) from joint inversion of RFs and Rayleigh-wave data. McKean's (2020) geologic map of this area shows colluvium and alluvial fan deposits on the western side of the EBF, with alluvial fan deposits plus lacustrine silt and clay from Lake Bonneville on the eastern side. (d) The velocity model beneath station sta049, used to represent the hanging wall, and (e) the velocity model beneath station sta040, used to represent the footwall, in the RF migration. The thin dashed lines are the V_P and V_S velocity models simplified from the WFCVM (Magistrale *et al.*, 2008). Stations sta040 and sta049 were deployed in 2020 by Allam (2020). The color version of this figure is available only in the electronic edition.

and Shroba, 1985; Machette *et al.*, 1992; Personius and Scott, 1992). The FF offsets pre-Lake Bonneville deposits (Early–Middle Pleistocene) along its northern extent, but no evidence for Holocene ruptures on this fault has been reported (McKean, 2020; Anderson *et al.*, 2024). In contrast, a paleoseismic investigation on the northern end of the EBF found that five Holocene surface-faulting earthquakes had occurred at this site and determined a latest Pleistocene and Holocene vertical slip rate of 0.5–0.9 mm/yr (DuRoss *et al.*, 2014; DuRoss and Hylland, 2015). The exact timing of the slip transfer from the FF to the EBF is unknown, and it may not yet be complete. Both faults are included as seismic sources in the 2023 National Seismic Hazard Model (Hatem *et al.*, 2022).

Ambient noise surface-wave studies have demonstrated the possibility of imaging fault zone structures using dense arrays (Wang *et al.*, 2021; Biondi *et al.*, 2024). In the SLB, Gkogkas *et al.* (2021) inverted Rayleigh-wave phase velocity measurements between 0.4 and 1.1 s period from a dense linear array across the EBF (Fig. 1c). They found an asymmetric low-velocity anomaly near the surface trace of EBF that they interpreted as a fault damage zone. Although surface-wave dispersion measurements do not have the resolution to resolve sharp vertical velocity changes, their results indicate a sedimentary layer that is ~300 m thick east of the EBF and gradually thickens toward the west. On the west side of the EBF, the top of the bedrock is deeper than the resolution depth (<400 m) of their study, based on the results of Kim *et al.* (2025) (e.g., Fig. 1d).

In comparison to surface-wave measurements, *P*-to-*S* converted phases (i.e., the *Ps* phase) from teleseismic earthquakes are more sensitive to vertical velocity discontinuities and have been employed to improve constraints on the structure of sedimentary basins (e.g., Agostinetti *et al.*, 2018; Berg *et al.*, 2021; Agrawal *et al.*, 2022). These teleseismic converted phases are analyzed using the receiver function (RF) method. An RF is the radial component record of a teleseismic *P*-wave arrival from which the vertical component record has been deconvolved to remove the source time function and obtain the near-receiver seismic response (Langston, 1979). Where there is a low-velocity sediment layer at the surface, the *P*- and *S*-wave ray paths are refracted to nearly vertical. Hence, the first significant peak in the RF is usually the *Ps* phase generated at the base of the layer, which arrives later than the first peak in the vertical component (i.e., the *P* wave).

In our recent study of the entire SLB, stations located on the sedimentary basin fill showed significant time delays in RF peaks (Kim *et al.*, 2025). We jointly inverted the RF initial peak waveform, the Rayleigh wave ellipticity (Rayleigh wave H/V; Zeng *et al.*, 2022), and the Rayleigh-wave phase velocity at each station to obtain a set of station-specific 1D shear-wave velocity (V_S) profiles in the SLB. These inverted velocity models confirm that the first peak in the RFs mostly corresponds to the *Ps* phase generated at a strong impedance contrast within the SLB referred to as R2. We note that in some areas with multiple near-surface impedance contrasts, the RF maximum peak can be the *PpPs* phase, a multiple that crosses a seismic discontinuity as a *P* wave, reflects off the surface, and then converts to an upgoing *S* wave at the discontinuity (Zhu and Kanamori, 2000; Kim *et al.*, 2025).

R2 is the strongest of three prominent seismic reflectors within the SLB that Hill *et al.* (1990) identified on seismic reflection data, sonic logs, and density logs from the northern Salt Lake Valley and named R1, R2, and R3 in order of increasing depth. Following Arnow and Mattick (1968) and Mattick (1970), Hill *et al.* (1990) interpreted these reflectors to be the boundaries separating the following four generalized geologic units: unconsolidated Quaternary sediments, semi-consolidated Tertiary sediments, Tertiary sedimentary and volcanic bedrock, and older basement rocks. All the units above R3, the top of the basement rocks, were deposited in the SLB as it formed due to downward movement along the Wasatch fault (Mattick, 1970; Hill *et al.*, 1990). Kim *et al.*'s (2025) model reveals >1 km of lacustrine and alluvial deposits above R2 within an intra-basin graben between the west-dipping EBF to the east and the east-dipping antithetic West Valley fault zone (WVFZ) to the west (Fig. 1a; DuRoss and Hylland, 2015; Zeng *et al.*, 2022). Note that R2, the boundary between semi-consolidated Tertiary sediments and the underlying Tertiary sedimentary and volcanic bedrock, is a lithification horizon. Because the degree to which sediments are lithified depends on both their age and depth of burial, and the rate of subsidence varies across the SLB, R2 is not necessarily the same age everywhere. We are not aware of any precise dates for the R2 horizon anywhere in the SLB. However, volcanic tuffs and ashes from western Salt Lake Valley exposures of the Salt Lake Formation, which may be correlative with the younger rocks between R2 and R3 in the SLB, range in age from 4.4 ± 1.0 Ma to 6.6 Ma (Clark *et al.*, 2020). The oldest rocks between R2 and R3 in the SLB would be those formed from sediments deposited shortly after the WFZ became active at 12 ± 2 Ma to 18 Ma (Ehlers *et al.*, 2003; Parry and Bruhn, 1987).

Although Hill *et al.*'s (1990) four-layer basin model was developed for the SLB, this basic model appears to apply to other extensional basins in the Wasatch Front region based on limited sonic log and seismic reflection data (Magistrale *et al.*, 2008; Pechmann *et al.*, 2010; Stephenson *et al.*, 2012). Sonic logs from the region show that R2 is clearly the largest of the three velocity discontinuities of Hill *et al.* (1990) and is the only one that is easily identifiable on these logs without lithologic information. The sharp *P*-wave velocity increase at R2 takes place over a vertical distance of 20–100 m, depending on the location and how the bounds of the velocity increase are defined (Hill *et al.*, 1990; Pechmann *et al.*, 2010). These observations, in combination with the modeling of Kim *et al.* (2025), give us confidence that the *Ps* phase that we identify in our receiver functions is generated at the R2 discontinuity.

In this study, we analyze RFs of the dense linear array across the EBF (Fig. 1c) to investigate with high lateral resolution the variation of bedrock depth (i.e., R2) across the fault. Because we do not have surface-wave measurements along the linear array that are sensitive to structure below 400 m depth to facilitate V_S model inversions, we migrate the time-domain RFs into the depth domain (Dueker and Sheehan, 1997) using existing velocity models. We use two 1D velocity models from our recent study (Kim *et al.*, 2025), one velocity model on each side of the EBF, to account for shallow velocity differences between the footwall and hanging wall (Fig. 1d,e). We show that our approach resolves sharp sediment thickness changes across the EBF, which enables us to determine a minimum near-surface dip on this fault and the amount of vertical fault displacement accumulated since its activation. Furthermore, this displacement, combined with estimates of the current slip rate on the Salt Lake City segment and some assumptions about the transfer of slip from the FF to the EBF, allows us to evaluate the timing of the initiation of slip on the EBF. This EBF age estimate adds to our knowledge of how the Wasatch fault has changed and evolved with time.

Data and Methods

RF analysis along the linear array

For the RF analysis, we utilized three-component 5-Hz geophones that were deployed for approximately a month starting in early February of 2018 (Lin and Kim, 2018). The east–west linear array consisted of 32 stations distributed along a 2.9 km section of 1700 South Street that crosses the EBF (Fig. 1c). We found two candidate RF events in the U.S. Geological Survey Preliminary Determination of Epicenters (PDE) catalog that occurred during the time of operation of the array and also met our other criteria, namely an epicentral distance between 25° and 90° and a magnitude ≥ 6.0. To compute an RF, we deconvolved the vertical component from the radial component of a teleseismic *P*-wave record using the extended time multi-taper correlation method (Shibutani *et al.*, 2008). For the deconvolution, we used time windows relative to the theoretical *P*-wave arrival time of −35 to +102.5 s for the signal and −135 to −35 s for the pre-signal noise. The RFs were Gaussian low-pass filtered ($e^{-\omega^2/4a^2}$) with $\boldsymbol{a} = 3.5$, which corresponds to a corner frequency of ~0.81 Hz. We imposed two criteria for quality assurance. First, the signal-to-noise ratios (SNRs) for both the radial- and vertical-component waveforms should be larger than $\sqrt{2.5}$. Here, we define the noise and signal windows as the time between −80 and −10 s and −10 and 60 s relative to the expected *P*-wave arrival time, respectively. The SNR was measured by taking the root mean square ratio between the signal and noise windows, after removing the instrument response and band-pass filtering between 0.1 and 1.0 Hz. The second criterion is that the RFs should have an SNR greater than 1.0 to discard RFs affected by deconvolution instabilities.

Of the two teleseismic events, only the 16 February 2018 M_w 7.2 southern Mexico earthquake provided RFs that passed the SNR criteria (Fig. 1b). All the RFs from this teleseism have an SNR > 1.30, except for one with SNR = 1.18, and 77% are above 1.50. The majority (~75%) of the radial- and vertical-component SNRs are above 2.7 and 4.3, respectively (Fig. S1, available in the supplemental material to this article). This teleseismic event has a back azimuth of ~150°, which is roughly parallel to the strike of the southern EBF (Fig. 1a). Hence, the radial RFs should be minimally affected by scattered seismic energy from the fault zone.

We measured the time delay of the first peak of the RF by measuring the time of the RF's maximum amplitude within the time interval −1 to +2 s (Fig. 2, Fig. S1b). Because there is no other positive peak that precedes the first peak, we interpret this peak as the *P*-to-*s* converted phase from the R2 discontinuity. Benefiting from the dense station spacing of ~90 m (Fig. 1c), and the fact that an RF is only sensitive to structure right beneath the station (especially in slow shallow velocity areas), the 2018 linear array can resolve R2 depth changes with high horizontal spatial resolution.

Migration of RFs to depth

We migrated the time-domain RFs into the depth domain (Gurrola *et al.*, 1994; Dueker and Sheehan, 1997) by employing velocity models from the seismic data inversions by Kim *et al.* (2025) (Fig. 1d,e, Fig. S2). The migration assumes that each point in the time-domain RF corresponds to a *Ps* phase converted at some depth. We used two 1D velocity models to migrate the RFs, one for stations on the west (hanging-wall) side of the fault (Fig. 1d) and the other for stations on the east (footwall) side (Fig. 1e). We used only the part of each velocity model that is above the R2 interface ($V_S < 1.5$ km/s) and inserted an underlying half-space. We note that the elevations of the migrated RF first peaks do not change significantly when using different cutoff frequencies for the Gaussian low-pass filter (Fig. 3c). Hence, the possibility that the first RF peaks consist of mixed *Ps* and *PpPs* phases instead of *Ps* only can be disregarded (e.g., Cunningham and Lekic, 2019). Next, we calculate the difference between the average elevations of the maximum first peak amplitudes, which we interpret as R2, on each side of the fault to obtain the R2 displacement. Here, we use sea level as the reference elevation because the surface elevation along the array decreases westward.

The accuracy of the migration results depends on the accuracy of the 1D velocity models. To estimate the uncertainty in the R2 displacement, we also migrated the RFs using the ensembles of 1D velocity models that come from the Bayesian inversions of Kim *et al.* (2025; Fig. 1d,e). We converted the posterior distributions of the two velocity models into two distributions of average R2 elevations, one for the hanging wall (Fig. S3a) and one for the footwall (Fig. S3b). Then, we randomly selected a mean R2 elevation from each distribution and calculated the difference. Repeating the last step 20,000 times, we obtained a distribution of R2 displacements (Fig. S3c) from which we computed the standard deviation (Table 1, Fig. 2d).

To further investigate the sensitivity of the calculated R2 displacement to the velocity models, we also migrated the RFs using two other velocity models. The first model is a simplified version of the Wasatch Front Community Velocity model (WFCVM; Magistrale *et al.*, 2008), consisting of the velocity gradients used in this model between the R1 and R2 discontinuities and constant velocities below 1200 m (dashed lines in Fig. 1d,e). The WFCVM between R1 and R2 was constructed from sonic log data and an empirical relation between *P*- and *S*-wave velocities (V_P and V_S, respectively). The second model is a hybrid velocity model consisting of the ambient noise tomography model of Gkogkas *et al.* (2021) from 0 to 400 m depth and the simplified WFCVM below this depth.

Results

RF first peak time variation across the EBF

Observed RF peak delay times increase sharply by ~0.7 s from east to west across the EBF (Fig. 2a,b). The increase occurs over a short distance (≤157 m) between stations on opposite sides of the fault, as seen in the map view (Fig. 2a) and in the time-domain RFs (Fig. 2b). The sharp lateral change in RF peak delay times demonstrates that the RFs provide outstanding lateral resolution of the R2 elevation variations. This result is consistent with previous RF studies, which have demonstrated that RFs have the capability to resolve lateral discontinuity

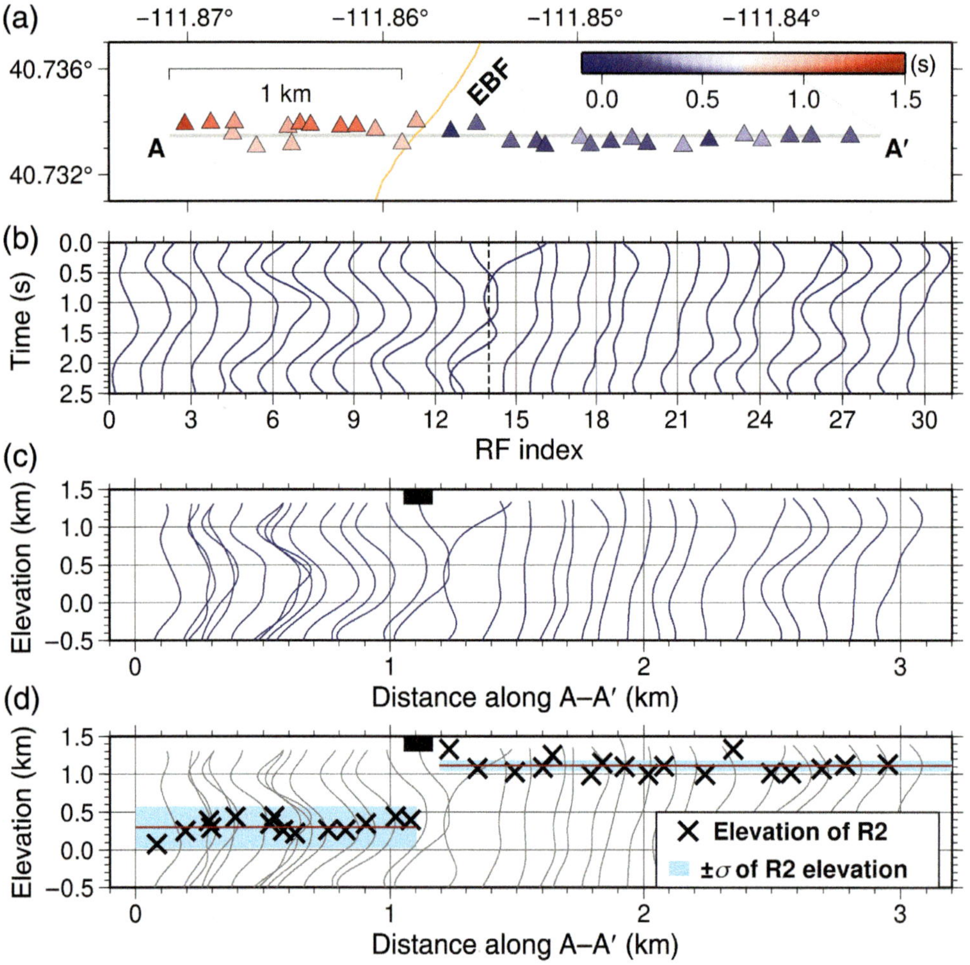

Figure 2. Observed RFs for the stations in the linear part of the array in Figure 1c. (a) Map view of the stations and the surface trace of the EBF. The colors show RF peak delay times as indicated by the color map in the upper right. (b) The time domain RFs, aligned in order from west to east along the A–A′ profile in (a). The vertical dashed line marks the surface trace location of the EBF relative to the station indices. (c) RFs migrated to depth using the velocity models for the footwall and hanging wall indicated by the thick solid lines in Figure 1d,e, respectively. The RFs are plotted at the projections of their corresponding station locations onto the A–A′ profile in (a). Elevations are relative to sea level. The solid black box on this profile and the one below it marks the location of the EBF surface trace. (d) Depth-migrated RFs, with the elevations of the RF peaks marked by black crosses at the projections of the station locations on the cross-section. The red thin lines show the average elevations of the crosses, which we interpret as R2 elevations, in the hanging wall (left; west) and the footwall (right; east) of the EBF. The light blue shading marks the $\pm 1\sigma$ range of the mean R2 elevations.

variations smaller than the Fresnel zone half-width, particularly at shallow depths (e.g., Lekić and Fischer, 2017). For reference, the Fresnel zone half-width for P-to-s RFs with an ~1 Hz cut-off frequency ($\boldsymbol{a}$ = 3.5) at ~1.0 km depth, based on the velocity structure in Figure 1d, is approximately 1.7 km. For this velocity structure and the teleseism that we used to compute our RFs, the horizontal offset of a Ps ray path between a 1.0 km deep R2 discontinuity and the ground surface is ~56 m. This short offset distance, in combination with the ~150° back azimuth of the teleseism, suggests that the piercing points of P-to-s converted phases recorded by stations closest to the fault are on the same side of the fault as the station.

R2 depths across the EBF

Similar to the shift of RF time delays across the fault, the migrated RFs show a clear R2 elevation change across the fault (Fig. 2c). The average R2 elevations on the hanging wall and footwall (red lines in Fig. 2d), rounded to the nearest 10 m with one standard deviation error bars, are 300 ± 280 m and 1110 ± 70 m, respectively. These elevations differ by 810 ± 290 m (Table 1). The small variations in R2 depths on both sides of the fault (Figs. 2d and 3c) are probably at least partially due to small-scale velocity variations that are not accounted for by our two reference velocity models (Fig. 1d,e).

Using different velocity models for the migration results in different R2 elevations (Fig. 3a,b). Migration with the simplified WFCVM results in a much deeper R2 (Fig. 3a) on both sides of the fault and a larger R2 offset of 1420 m. The deeper R2s are due to the lower V_P/V_S ratios in the WFCVM compared to our preferred reference models (Kim *et al.*, 2025). The R2 displacement from the migration with Gkogkas *et al.*'s (2021) model is 719 m (Fig. 3b), which falls within the uncertainty range of our preferred estimate. However, Gkogkas *et al.*'s (2021) model produces more variability in the R2 elevation on the hanging-wall side than the other models. For example, a ~500 m deepening of the R2 elevation is observed around X = 0.7 km when using the Gkogkas *et al.* (2021) model (Fig. 3b), whereas this deepening is less prominent when using the other velocity models (Fig. 3). This difference reflects the small-scale lateral velocity variations present in the 2D velocity model of Gkogkas *et al.* (2021), which are not present in the other velocity models (Fig. 1d,e).

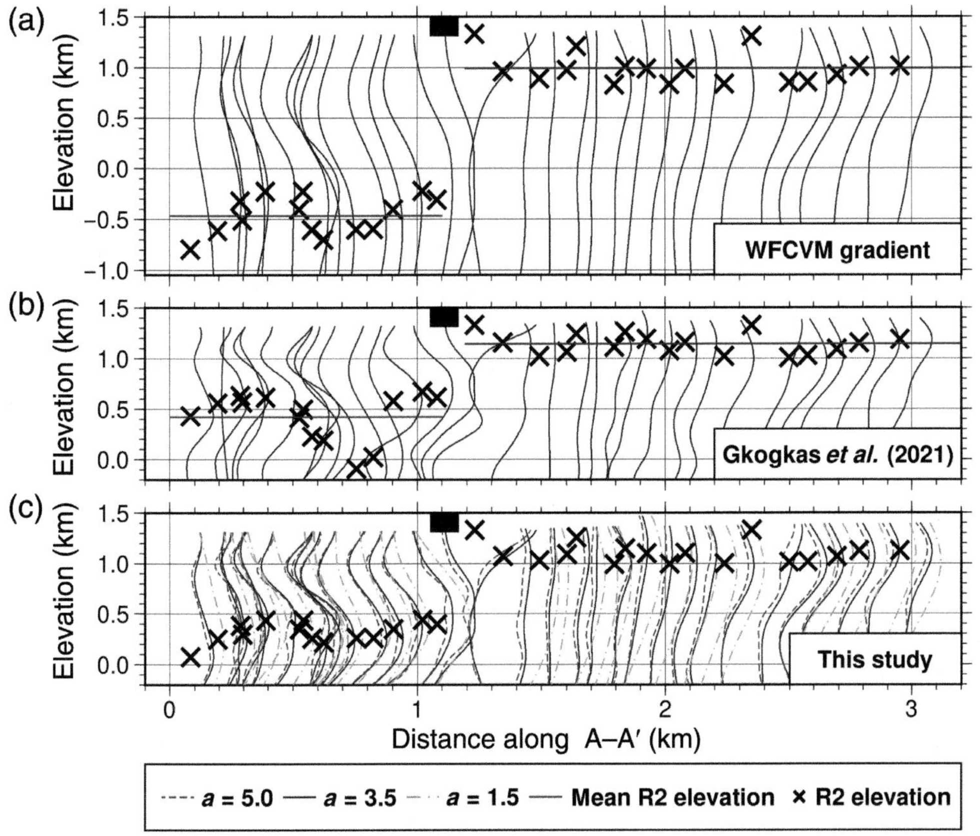

Figure 3. Depth migrated RFs using different velocity models: (a) the modified WFCVM (dashed lines in Figs. 1d,e; Magistrale *et al.*, 2008); (b) Gkogkas *et al.*'s (2021) velocity model, extended below its maximum depth of 400 m from the surface by combining with the modified WFCVM; and (c) the models in Figures 1d,e. The black crosses are the R2 elevations determined from the RFs. The thin red solid lines show the average elevations of the crosses in the hanging wall (left; west) and the footwall (right; east) of the EBF. In (c), the different line types denote RFs constructed using different values of the Gaussian low-pass filter ($e^{-\omega^2/4a^2}$) parameter ***a***. The red dashed, blue solid, and green dashed–dotted lines denote ***a*** values of 5.0, 3.5, and 1.5, respectively, which correspond to cut-off frequencies of approximately 1.3, 0.81, and 0.35 Hz. The black crosses are the R2 elevations determined using RFs filtered with parameter ***a*** = 3.5, as in Figure 2d. The solid black boxes at ~1.1 km along the A–A′ profiles in (a), (b), and (c) mark the location of the EBF surface trace. The color version of this figure is available only in the electronic edition.

Discussion

We utilize our estimated R2 displacement to constrain two basic parameters for the EBF: the near-surface dip angle and the length of time that the fault has been active.

Dip angle of the EBF

The measured R2 displacement, in combination with the horizontal distance separating the R2 depth measurements on the two sides of the fault, provides a lower limit to the dip angle of the fault plane. In the plane of the cross-section of Figure 2d, the vertical R2 displacement occurs over a maximum horizontal distance of 151 m, which is the distance between the two closest stations on the opposite sides of the EBF measured along the A–A′ profile (Figs. 2a and 4b). From this maximum distance, and our preferred R2 depth offset of 810 m with a 1σ uncertainty of 290 m, we determine a minimum apparent dip angle of 79° with a range of 74°–82°. Correcting this apparent dip on the cross-section to the true fault dip, which is the dip normal to the local EBF strike of 40° (Fig. 2a), the near-surface dip on the EBF is >81° ± 3°.

TABLE 1
Measurements of R2 Elevations and Vertical Displacement (m)

R2 Measurement	Mean Using Maximum Probability Models from Figure 1d,e	Standard Deviation (from Fig. S3)
Footwall (east side) elevation	1112	73
Hanging-wall (west side) elevation	298	275
Elevation difference across the fault	813	288

Note. The mean R2 elevations are from depth-migrated RFs using the maximum probability velocity models in Figure 1d,e. These models are constructed by selecting the maximum probability velocity at each depth in 15 m increments from an ensemble of models from the Bayesian inversion (see Kim *et al.*, 2025). The standard deviations are from the mean R2 elevation distributions in Figure S3.

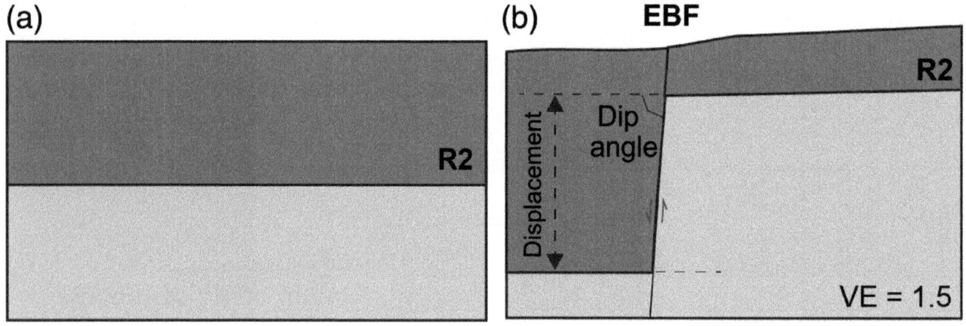

Figure 4. Schematic cartoon showing how we interpret the difference of R2 elevations observed in this study, with a vertical exaggeration (VE) of ~1.5:1. (a) The approximately flat R2 surface before movement on the fault. (b) The displaced R2 surface resulting from normal slip on the East Bench fault (EBF). The vertical R2 offset labeled "displacement" is the displacement of 810 ± 290 m that we measured in this study. The ground surface shown mimics the actual present-day topography. The color version of this figure is available only in the electronic edition.

This steep near-surface dip is typical of young normal fault scarps in unconsolidated materials (McCalpin, 1996). We note that this number is consistent with the 85° ± 5° dip observed at shallow depths (<5 m) in two trenches at the northern end of the EBF (DuRoss *et al.*, 2014; red circle, Fig. 1a). It is also consistent with dips of ~86° and 74° that Liberty *et al.* (2021) interpreted for the top ~300 m of the EBF from seismic reflection profiles crossing this fault at 700 South and 800 South Streets, respectively, after corrections for true dip. The dips of DuRoss *et al.* (2014) and Liberty *et al.* (2021), and our minimum dip of 81°(±3°), are all steeper than the dip of ~70° measured in a bedrock exposure of the Warm Springs fault, the next fault section to the north of the EBF in the Salt Lake City segment of the WFZ (Fig. 1a; Bruhn *et al.*, 1992; McKean and Anderson, 2024). All these near-surface dip angles contrast with the much shallower dip angle of 30°–35° at ~9–12 km depth on the Warm Springs fault, which several studies have inferred from the moment tensor solutions and aftershock distribution for the 2020 M_w 5.7 Magna earthquake (Pang *et al.*, 2020; Kleber *et al.*, 2021; Pechmann *et al.*, 2023). These studies interpreted a listric geometry for the Warm Springs fault, which may extend southward to the EBF.

Activation age of the EBF

We estimated how long the EBF has been slipping to create the observed R2 displacement, using a range of assumptions for how the slip rate may have varied with time. This calculation assumes that before slip began on the EBF, the R2 surface was flat and continuous across the future location of this fault (Fig. 2a). We consider this assumption to be plausible, based on the relatively flat R2 elevations observed on both sides of the fault (Fig. 2d) and the interpretation of R2 as a sedimentary horizon separating semi-consolidated Tertiary sediments from underlying consolidated Tertiary sedimentary rocks.

Text S1 and Table S1 summarize slip-rate estimates for the EBF, which come from two paleoseismic trenching sites (Fig. 1a): the Penrose Drive site (DuRoss *et al.*, 2014; DuRoss and Hylland, 2015) and the Dresden Place site (Garr, 1986; Machette *et al.*, 1992). The Dresden Place slip rates are poorly constrained minimum rates of 0.31 and 0.32 mm/yr for two different late Quaternary time periods. The Holocene Penrose Drive slip rate of 0.5–0.9 mm/yr (DuRoss *et al.*, 2014) is less than DuRoss and Hylland's (2015) preferred slip rate for the whole Salt Lake City segment, which is a middle to late Holocene rate of 1.0–1.4 mm/yr. This difference may be at least partially because the Penrose Drive site is only 0.67 km from the northern end of the EBF, within an en echelon fault stepover and possible displacement transfer zone between the EBF and the Warm Springs fault to the north.

The slip rate on the EBF may have varied with time because the transfer of slip to this fault section from the older FF along the range front may have been gradual and is not necessarily complete. Hence, we assume two simple end-member models for the slip-rate history on the EBF to determine a plausible range of ages for the initiation of slip on this fault. For both models, we assume that the current EBF slip rate is DuRoss and Hylland (2015) preferred average slip rate for the Salt Lake City segment as a whole, which is 1.2 ± 0.2 mm/yr (1σ uncertainty). We propagate errors considering that our R2 displacement measurement and the assumed slip rate are independent of each other (Lee and Forthofer, 2006). Our first model is a step function model in which the transfer of slip from the FF to the EBF fault occurs instantaneously. In this model, the time interval since slip began on the EBF is simply $810 \pm 290\ \text{m}/(1.2 \pm 0.2 \times 10^{-3}\ \text{m/yr}) = 0.7 \pm 0.3$ Ma. Although this model is unrealistic, it provides a minimum age for the EBF. In our second model, we assume that the slip rate on the EBF increases linearly from the time that slip begins until the present. In this case, the average slip rate on the fault during the time that it is active is half of the current slip rate, and the estimated EBF age is 1.4 ± 0.5 Ma. We consider it unlikely that the slip transfer from the FF to the EBF occurred as gradually as in the linear model. However, this model provides a reasonable upper limit to the age of the EBF. Note that even though the current slip rate that we are assuming for the EBF is an average rate over the last 7.7 ka (DuRoss and Hylland, 2015), this time period is only ~1% of the minimum age of the fault and is therefore negligible. Our estimated age range for the EBF fault of 0.7 ± 0.3 to 1.4 ± 0.5 Ma is compatible with the qualitative assessment of Personius and Scott (1992) that "The height of these larger [40–50 m] scarps along the EBF suggests surface faulting along the EBF during much of the middle and late Quaternary." Importantly, our estimated maximum age for the EBF is younger than the likely age of the R2 discontinuity, which is in Tertiary basin fill sediments and therefore older than 2.6 Ma.

Future applications of RFs for fault studies

Detection of the sharp displacement of the R2 discontinuity using RFs from the linear array data opens up the possibility for future studies of fault geometry, slip rate, and age using dense seismic arrays. For example, observations of the variations in R2 offsets along the EBF would provide some important clues into how the slip transfer from the FF to the EBF developed over time. Temporary geophone deployments could also be used to obtain detailed maps of R2 depths throughout the SLB and other sedimentary basins in the Wasatch Front region, which would improve analyses of ground shaking hazards. In this region, due to a high degree of urbanization, it is easier, less invasive, and more cost-effective to determine R2 depths with the RF method than with drilling or active seismic source methods. Finally, RFs from temporary geophone deployments across faults in the Wasatch Front region and elsewhere could potentially yield information on fault dips, displacements, slip rates, and/or duration of faulting. The success of such studies would depend on the existence of detectable impedance contrasts that can be correlated across the fault and/or dated, plus the availability of any other necessary information, such as, in the case of our study, a slip rate.

Careful consideration is required while utilizing RFs to investigate faults and sedimentary basin structures. First, it should be ensured that the interpreted peaks are robust. The possibility of the first large peak being the *PpPs* phase instead of the *Ps* phase is discussed in Kim *et al.* (2025). In this study, we ensured the lack of frequency dependence in the RF peak delay times and the lack of a smaller peak preceding the peak that we are interpreting. Second, a reliable velocity model must be chosen to transform the RFs from the time domain to the depth domain. In this study, we used recent velocity models developed from in situ seismic observations (Gkogkas *et al.*, 2021; Kim *et al.*, 2025). Conversely, to some extent, we can use RFs to evaluate the accuracy of the velocity model. The difference in R2 elevation between our velocity models for the two sides of the EBF, ~600 m, accounting for a station elevation difference of ~100 m (Fig. 1d,e), is within the uncertainty range of the R2 displacement from the RF migration (Table 1), showing that the RFs and the velocity models are reasonably consistent.

Summary

In this study, we used *Ps* converted phases in teleseismic RFs, combined with local velocity models, to image an 810 m vertical bedrock offset caused by movement on the EBF. Because the *Ps* phase is generated at the relatively shallow boundary between the bedrock and the overlying low V_S semi-consolidated sediments, the phase conversion points are almost directly beneath the station locations, which provides good lateral resolution. The RFs show that the 810 ± 290 m vertical offset across the fault occurs over a maximum distance of 157 m, the distance between the two closest stations to the surface trace on the footwall and hanging wall. From this information, we calculate a minimum near-surface fault dip of 81° ± 3°. In addition, from the bedrock offset, assuming a current slip rate of 1.2 ± 0.2 mm/yr from paleoseismic studies and a range of scenarios for the slip-rate transfer from the FF to the EBF, our best estimate for when the transfer began is 0.7–1.4 Ma. We envision more applications of the RF method to map fault-related displacements in the urbanized SLB and elsewhere in the region.

Data and Resources

The 2018 linear array data can be found at doi: 10.7914/SN/9H_2018 (Lin and Kim, 2018) and can be obtained from the EarthScope Consortium's Seismological Facility for the Advancement of Geoscience Data Management Center (SAGE DMC; https://ds.iris.edu/ds/nodes/dmc, last accessed December 2025). The velocity models used in the migration can be found in the supplemental material and the Zenodo Repository at doi: 10.5281/zenodo.14010756 (Kim, 2024) and doi: 10.5281/zenodo.17787625 (Kim, 2025). The supplemental material for this article includes Figures S1–S3, Text S1, and Table S1.

Declaration of Competing Interests

The authors acknowledge that there are no conflicts of interest recorded.

Acknowledgments

This study was supported by the U.S. Geological Survey Earthquake Hazards Program, Award Number G23AP00021. H. Kim and F.-C. Lin also acknowledge support from the National Science Foundation project EAR 1753362. Utah Geological Survey staff members Greg McDonald, Stephanie Carney, and Stefan Kirby improved this article through their reviews. Comments from an anonymous reviewer and Christopher B. DuRoss helped improve the article. The authors appreciate the work of the student volunteers who helped install the nodes and are thankful to the residents of the Salt Lake Valley area who agreed to host a seismometer for research.

References

Agostinetti, N. P., F. Martini, and J. Mongan (2018). Sedimentary basin investigation using receiver function: An East African rift case study, *Geophys. J. Int.* **215,** no. 3, 2105–2113, doi: 10.1093/gji/ggy405.

Agrawal, S., C. M. Eakin, and J. O'Donnell (2022). Characterizing the cover across South Australia: A simple passive-seismic method for estimating sedimentary thickness, *Geophys. J. Int.* **231,** no. 3, 1850–1864, doi: 10.1093/gji/ggac294.

Allam, A. (2020). Response to the Mar 18, 2020 M 5.7 Magna, UT Earthquake [Data set], *International Federation of Digital Seismograph Networks*, doi: 10.7914/SN/2A_2020.

Anderson, Z. W., A. P. McKean, and A. W. Yonkee (2024). Interim geologic map of the Fort Douglas quadrangle, Salt Lake, Davis, and Morgan Counties, Utah, *Utah Geol. Surv. Open-File Rept. 767*, 32 pp., 2 plates, scale 1:24,000, doi: 10.34191/OFR-767.

Arnow, T., and R. E. Mattick (1968). Thickness of valley fill in the Jordan Valley east of the Great Salt Lake, Utah, *U.S. Geol. Surv. Profess. Pap. 600-B*, B79–B82, available at https://pubs.usgs.gov/pp/0600b/report.pdf (last accessed December 2025).

Berg, E. M., F.-C. Lin, V. Schulte-Pelkum, A. Allam, H. Qiu, and K. Gkogkas (2021). Shallow crustal shear velocity and *Vp*/*Vs* across southern California: Joint inversion of short-period Rayleigh wave ellipticity, phase velocity, and teleseismic receiver functions, *Geophys. Res. Lett.* **48,** e2021GL092626, doi: 10.1029/2021GL092626.

Biondi, E., J. Castellanos, and R. Clayton (2024). Imaging urban hidden faults with ambient noise recorded by dense seismic arrays, *Seismol. Res. Lett.* **95,** 2280–2289, doi: 10.1785/0220230408.

Bruhn, R. L., P. R. Gibler, W. Houghton, and W. T. Parry (1992). Structure of the Salt Lake segment, Wasatch normal fault zone: Implications for rupture propagation during normal faulting, in *Assessment of Regional Earthquake Hazards and Risk Along the Wasatch Front, Utah, U.S. Geol. Surv. Prof. Pap., 1500*, P. L. Gori and W. W. Hays (Editors), U.S. Government Printing Office, Washington, D. C., H1–H25.

Clark, D. L., C. G. Oviatt, and D. A. Dinter (2020). Geologic map of the Tooele 30′ × 60′ quadrangle, Tooele, Salt Lake, and Davis Counties, Utah, *Utah Geol. Surv. Map 284DM*, 48 pp., 2 appendices, 4 plates, scale 1:62,500, doi: 10.34191/M-284DM.

Cunningham, E., and V. Lekic (2019). Constraining crustal structure in the presence of sediment: A multiple converted wave approach, *Geophys. J. Int.* **219,** no. 1, 313–327, doi: 10.1093/gji/ggz298.

Dueker, K. G., and A. F. Sheehan (1997). Mantle discontinuity structure from midpoint stacks of converted P to S waves across the Yellowstone hotspot track, *J. Geophys. Res.* **102,** no. B4, 8313–8327, doi: 10.1029/96JB03857.

DuRoss, C. B., and M. D. Hylland (2015). Synchronous ruptures along a Major Graben-Forming fault system: Wasatch and West Valley fault zones, Utah, *Bull. Seismol. Soc. Am.* **105,** no. 1, 14–37, doi: 10.1785/0120140064.

DuRoss, C. B., M. D. Hylland, G. N. McDonald, A. J. Crone, S. F. Personius, R. D. Gold, and S. A. Mahan (2014). Holocene and latest Pleistocene paleoseismology of the Salt Lake City segment of the Wasatch fault zone, Utah, at the Penrose Drive trench site, in *Evaluating Surface Faulting Chronologies of Graben-Bounding Faults in Salt Lake Valley, Utah--New Paleoseismic Data from the Salt Lake City Segment of the Wasatch Fault Zone and the West Valley Fault Zone--Paleoseismology of Utah*, C. B. DuRoss and M. D. Hylland (Editors), Vol. 24, Utah Geological Survey Special Study 149, 1–39, 6 appendices, 1 plate, CD.

DuRoss, C. B., S. F. Personius, A. J. Crone, S. S. Olig, M. D. Hylland, W. R. Lund, and D. P. Schwartz (2016). Fault segmentation: New concepts from the Wasatch fault zone, Utah, USA, *J. Geophys. Res. Solid Earth* **121,** 1131–1157, doi: 10.1002/2015JB012519.

Ehlers, T. A., S. D. Willett, P. A. Armstrong, and D. S. Chapman (2003). Exhumation of the central Wasatch Mountains, Utah: 2. Thermokinematic model of exhumation, erosion, and thermochronometer interpretation, *J. Geophys. Res.* **108,** no. B3, doi: 10.1029/2001JB001723.

Garr, J. D. (1986). Findings of fault investigation at the Dresden Apartment Development, 550 South 900 East, Salt Lake City, Utah, *Technical Rept. Delta Job No. 1729A*, Delta Geotechnical Consultants, available at https://geodata.geology.utah.gov/pages/download.php?direct=1&noattach=true&ref=477&ext=pdf&k= (last accessed December 2025).

Gkogkas, K., F.-C. Lin, A. A. Allam, and Y. Wang (2021). Shallow damage zone structure of the Wasatch fault in Salt Lake City from ambient-noise double beamforming with a temporary linear array, *Seismol. Res. Lett.* **92,** no. 4, 2453–2463, doi: 10.1785/0220200404.

Gurrola, H., J. B. Minster, and T. Owens (1994). The use of velocity spectrum for stacking receiver functions and imaging upper mantle discontinuities, *Geophys. J. Int.* **117,** 427–440.

Hatem, A. E., C. M. Collett, R. W. Briggs, R. D. Gold, S. J. Angster, P. M. Powers, E. H. Field, M. Anderson, J. Y. Ben-Horin, T. Dawson, *et al.* (2022). Earthquake geology inputs for the U.S. National Seismic Hazard Model (NSHM) 2023 (western US) (ver. 2.0, February 2022), *U.S. Geol. Surv. data release*, doi: 10.5066/P9AU713N.

Hill, J., H. Benz, M. Murphy, and G. T. Schuster (1990). Propagation and resonance of SH waves in the Salt Lake Valley, Utah, *Bull. Seismol. Soc. Am.* **80,** 23–42.

Kim, H. J. (2024). Velocity models from "Seismic Imaging of the Salt Lake Basin Using Joint Inversion of Receiver Functions and Rayleigh Wave Data", *Zenodo*, doi: 10.5281/zenodo.14010756.

Kim, H. J. (2025). Velocity model used for migration in "Bedrock Offset Across the Wasatch Fault in Salt Lake City, Utah, from Teleseismic Converted Phases and Its Geologic Implications", *Zenodo*, doi: 10.5281/zenodo.17787625.

Kim, H. J., F.-C. Lin, J. C. Pechmann, C. L. Hardwick, and A. P. McKean (2025). Seismic imaging of the Salt Lake basin using joint inversion of receiver functions and Rayleigh wave data, *J. Geophys. Res. Solid Earth* **130,** e2024JB030927, doi: 10.1029/2024JB030927.

Kleber, E., A. P. McKean, A. I. Hiscock, M. D. Hylland, C. L. Hardwick, G. N. McDonald, Z. W. Anderson, S. D. Bowman, G. C. Willis, and B. A. Erickson (2021). Geologic setting, ground effects, and proposed structural model for the 18 March 2020 M_w 5.7 Magna, Utah, earthquake, *Seismol. Res. Lett.* **92,** 710–724, doi: 10.1785/0220200331.

Langston, C. A. (1979). Structure under Mount Rainier, Washington, inferred from teleseismic body waves, *J. Geophys. Res.* **84,** no. B9, 4749–4762, doi: 10.1029/JB084iB09p04749.

Lee, E. S., and R. N. Forthofer (2006). Strategies for variance estimation, in *Strategies for Variance Estimation*, Second Ed., SAGE Publications, Inc., 23–39, doi: 10.4135/9781412983341.n4.

Lekić, V., and K. M. Fischer (2017). Interpreting spatially stacked *Sp* receiver functions. *Geophys. J. Int.* **210,** no. 2, 874–886, doi: 10.1093/gji/ggx206.

Liberty, L. M., J. St. Clair, and A. P. McKean (2021). A broad, distributed active fault zone lies beneath Salt Lake City, Utah, *Seism. Rec.* **1,** no. 1, 35–45, doi: 10.1785/0320210009.

Lin, F.-C., and H. J. Kim (2018). Salt lake linear nodal array 2018, *International Federation of Digital Seismograph Networks*, doi: 10.7914/SN/9H_2018.

Machette, M. N., S. F. Personius, and A. R. Nelson (1992). Paleoseismology of the Wasatch fault zone: A summary of recent investigations, interpretations, and conclusions, in *Assessment of Regional Earthquake Hazards and Risk Along the Wasatch Front, Utah, U.S. Geol. Surv. Profess. Pap. 1500-A-J*, P. L. Gori and W. W. Hays (Editors), A1–A71.

Magistrale, H., K. B. Olsen, and J. C. Pechmann (2008). Construction and verification of a Wasatch front community velocity model, *U.S. Geol. Surv. Technical Rept. no. HQGR.060012*, Reston, Virginia, 14 pp.

Marsell, R. E. (1969). The Wasatch fault zone in north central Utah, in *Guidebook of Northern Utah*, M. L. Jensen (Editor), Utah Geological and Mineralogical Survey Bulletin, Vol. 82, 125–139, doi: 10.34191/B-82.

Mattick, R. E. (1970). Thickness of unconsolidated to semiconsolidated sediments in Jordan Valley, Utah, *U.S. Geol. Surv. Profess. Pap. 700-C*, C119–C124, available at https://pubs.usgs.gov/pp/0700c/report.pdf.

McCalpin, J. P. (1996). Paleoseismology in extensional tectonic environments, in *Paleoseismology*, J. P. McCalpin (Editor), Academic Press, San Diego, California, 588 pp.

McKean, A. P. (2020). Geologic map of the Sugar House quadrangle, Salt Lake County, Utah, *Utah Geol. Surv. Map 285DM*, 27 pp., 2 plates, scale 1:24,000, doi: 10.34191/M-285DM.

McKean, A. P., and Z. W. Anderson (2024). Interim geologic map of the Salt Lake City North quadrangle, Salt Lake and Davis Counties, Utah, *Utah Geol. Surv. Open-File Rept. 768DM*, 38 pp., 2 plates, scale 1:24,000, doi: 10.34191/OFR-768DM.

Pang, G., K. D. Koper, M. Mesimeri, K. L. Pankow, B. Baker, J. Farrell, J. Holt, J. M. Hale, P. Roberson, R. Burlacu, *et al.* (2020). Seismic analysis of the 2020 Magna, Utah, earthquake sequence: Evidence for a Listric Wasatch fault, *Geophys. Res. Lett.* **47,** e2020GL089798, doi: 10.1029/2020GL089798.

Parry, W. T., and R. L. Bruhn (1987). Fluid inclusion evidence for minimum 11 km vertical offset on the Wasatch fault, Utah, *Geology* **15,** 67–70.

Pechmann, J. C., K. J. Jensen, and H. Magistrale (2010). Constraints on the near surface seismic velocity structure of the Wasatch front region, Utah, from Sonic log analyses. Abstracts of the annual meeting. *Seismol. Res. Lett.* **81,** no. 2, 284–388, doi: 10.1785/gssrl.81.2.284.

Pechmann, J. C., I. G. Wong, C. B. DuRoss, M. D. Hylland, A. J. Crone, S. F. Personius, A. P. McKean, W. J. Arabasz, D. P. Schwartz, S. S. Olig, *et al.* (2023). A logic tree for the subsurface geometry of the Salt Lake City segment of the Wasatch fault in light of the 2020 Magna, Utah, earthquake, *Proceedings Volume, Basin and Range Earthquake Summit, 17–20 October 2022*, A. I. Hiscock, E. Williams, E. J. Kleber, and S. D. Bowman (Editors), Utah Geological Survey Miscellaneous Publication 177 (electronic poster), Salt Lake City, Utah.

Personius, S. F., and W. E. Scott (1992). Surficial geologic map of the Salt Lake City segment and parts of adjacent segments of the Wasatch fault zone, Davis, Salt Lake, and Utah Counties, Utah (1992), *U.S. Geol. Surv. Misc. Invest. Series Map I-2106*, scale 1:50,000, doi: 10.3133/i2106.

Petersen, M. D., M. P. Moschetti, P. M. Powers, C. S. Mueller, K. M. Haller, A. D. Frankel, Y. Zeng, S. Rezaeian, S. C. Harmsen, O. S. Boyd, *et al.* (2014). Documentation for the 2014 update of the United States national seismic hazard maps, *U.S. Geol. Surv. Open-File Rept. 2014-1091*, 243 pp., doi: 10.3133/ofr20141091.

Petersen, M. D., A. M. Shumway, P. M. Powers, E. H. Field, M. P. Moschetti, K. S. Jaiswal, K. R. Milner, S. Rezaeian, A. D. Frankel, A. L. Llenos, *et al.* (2024). The 2023 US 50-state National Seismic Hazard Model: Overview and implications, *Earthq. Spectra* **40,** no. 1, 5–88, doi: 10.1177/87552930231215428.

Scott, W. E., and R. R. Shroba (1985). Surficial geologic map of an area along the Wasatch fault zone in the Salt Lake Valley, Utah, *U.S. Geol. Surv. Open-File Rept. 85-448*, 18 pp., doi: 10.3133/ofr85448.

Shibutani, T., T. Ueno, and K. Hirahara (2008). Improvement in the extended-time multitaper receiver function estimation technique, *Bull. Seismol. Soc. Am.* **98,** no. 2, 812–816, doi: 10.1785/0120070226.

Stephenson, W. J., J. K. Odum, R. A. Williams, J. H. McBride, and I. Tomlinson (2012). Characterization of intrabasin faulting and deformation for earthquake hazards in southern Utah Valley, Utah, from high-resolution seismic imaging, *Bull. Seismol. Soc. Am.* **102,** no. 2, 524–540, doi: 10.1785/0120110053.

U.S. Geological Survey and Utah Geological Survey (2023). Quaternary fault and fold database for the United States, available at https://www.usgs.gov/natural-hazards/earthquake-hazards/faults (last accessed May 2023).

Wang, X., Z. Zhan, M. Zhong, P. Persaud, and R. W. Clayton (2021). Urban basin structure imaging based on dense arrays and Bayesian array-based coherent receiver functions, *J. Geophys. Res.* **126,** e2021JB022279, doi: 10.1029/2021JB022279.

Wong, I. G., W. R. Lund, C. DuRoss, P. Thomas, W. Arabasz, A. J. Crone, M. D. Hylland, N. Luco, S. S. Olig, J. C. Pechmann, *et al.* (2016). *Earthquake Probabilities for the Wasatch Front Region in Utah, Idaho, and Wyoming*, Miscellaneous Publication 16-3 Utah Geological Survey, Utah Department of Natural Resources.

Zeng, Q., F.-C. Lin, and A. A. Allam (2022). 3D shear wave velocity model of Salt Lake Valley via Rayleigh wave ellipticity across a temporary geophone array, *Seism. Rec.* **2,** no. 2, 127–136, doi: 10.1785/0320220016.

Zhu, L., and H. Kanamori (2000). Moho depth variation in southern California from teleseismic receiver functions, *J. Geophys. Res.* **105,** no. B2, 2969–2980, doi: 10.1029/1999JB900322.

Manuscript received 14 July 2025
Published online 15 December 2025

PyGRT: An Efficient and Integrated Python Package for Computing Synthetic Seismograms in a Layered Half-Space Model

Dengda Zhu[1,2], Jian Wang*[2,3], Jinlai Hao[2,3], Shi Yao[1,2], Ya Xu[1,2], Tao Xu[1,2], and Zhenxing Yao[3]

Abstract

Synthetic seismograms play a crucial role in understanding Earth's internal structure and focal mechanisms. Although established methods remain fundamental, advancements in computational tools and optimizations are crucial for improving stability, efficiency, and accessibility in modern seismic modeling. Here, we introduce PyGRT, an open-source Python package designed to calculate synthetic seismograms for a point source in a layered half-space model. Built on the generalized reflection-transmission matrix method and the discrete wavenumber method, PyGRT integrates the peak-trough averaging method and Filon's integration method to handle diverse source–receiver distributions. To optimize performance, PyGRT uses C for its core computational tasks, accelerated with OpenMP for parallel processing, whereas Python provides a user-friendly interface. This dual-language approach combines efficiency with ease of use, offering a flexible and extensible framework for seismic modeling. The modular design includes both low-level C and high-level Python interfaces, enabling high-performance computing, easy customization, and streamlined data processing. PyGRT outperforms traditional tools in stability for high-frequency calculations, computational speed, and accessibility. It serves as a practical and versatile resource, providing both researchers and beginners with a robust tool for seismic-wave simulation and theoretical exploration.

Cite this article as Zhu, D., J. Wang, J. Hao, S. Yao, Y. Xu, T. Xu, and Z. Yao (2025). PyGRT: An Efficient and Integrated Python Package for Computing Synthetic Seismograms in a Layered Half-Space Model, *Seismol. Res. Lett.* **97**, 2138–2153, doi: 10.1785/0220250057.

Introduction

Recent advances in computational techniques have made it possible to model synthetic seismograms in complex 3D media (Tromp *et al.*, 2008; Bozdağ *et al.*, 2016; Burdick and Lekić, 2017), whereas 1D models remain essential in many studies. The reason is that, first, Earth's structure can be approximated as a 1D layered sphere (Dziewonski and Anderson, 1981; Kennett and Engdahl, 1991; Kennett *et al.*, 1995), which offers computational efficiency and adequate modeling accuracy in wide range of applications, and second, 1D models provide an essential stepping stone in the calibration and validation of more complex models. Currently, researchers are increasingly focused on developing more stable and user-friendly programs to meet the growing demands of seismic studies (Beyreuther *et al.*, 2010; Cabieces *et al.*, 2022; Xu *et al.*, 2025).

Under near-field conditions, it is common to simplify the model to a horizontally layered half-space in a Cartesian coordinate system. Historically, open-source software packages used to calculate full-waveform synthetic seismograms for a point source in a such model have relied on two main methods: the Thomson–Haskell matrix propagation method (Thomson, 1950; Haskell, 1953) and the discrete wavenumber method (DWM; Bouchon, 1981). Notable examples of these packages include FK (Zhu and Rivera, 2002), QSEIS (Wang, 1999), and CPS330 (Herrmann, 2013), the latter of which provides a wide range of tools for both seismology education and research (see Data and Resources). FK simplifies its usage by employing PERL (practical extraction and report language) scripts to generate the necessary input files for running the program. QSEIS addresses numerical instability at high frequencies by orthogonalizing matrices during the matrix propagation. CPS330

1. Key Laboratory of Deep Petroleum Intelligent Exploration and Development, Institute of Geology and Geophysics, Chinese Academy of Sciences, Beijing, China, https://orcid.org/0009-0004-7933-3357 (DZ); https://orcid.org/0000-0002-7649-1737 (YX); 2. University of Chinese Academy of Sciences, Beijing, China, https://orcid.org/0000-0002-9623-9221 (JH); 3. Key Laboratory of Planetary Science and Frontier Technology, Institute of Geology and Geophysics, Chinese Academy of Sciences, Beijing, China, https://orcid.org/0000-0002-4029-1266 (ZY)

*Corresponding author: jianwang@mail.iggcas.ac.cn

stands out as a comprehensive toolkit, offering programs for seismic data processing, waveform simulation, focal mechanism inversion, and velocity inversion. It also includes methods for computing synthetic seismograms, such as modal summation, generalized ray theory, and so forth, which are beyond the scope of this article. All software packages aforementioned were written in FORTRAN77— a programming language widely used in scientific computing in the past. These programs have made significant contributions to seismological research, providing robust performance and compatibility with legacy systems, and remain valuable resources for both researchers and educators in seismology. However, with the increasing demands for user-friendly interfaces, seamless integration with modern scientific computing tools, and support for advanced computational techniques, there is a growing need for more accessible and flexible solutions.

Here, we present PyGRT, an open-source Python software package designed to efficiently compute synthetic seismograms for a point source in a layered half-space model. PyGRT seamlessly blends the high-performance computing power of C with the user-friendly flexibility and extensibility of Python, making it a highly advantageous tool in the modern computing ecosystem. To tackle the numerical instability that arises at high frequencies, unlike QSEIS, PyGRT uses the generalized reflection-transmission (R/T) matrix method (GRTM), originally developed by Kennett and Kerry (1979), and later refined by Yao and Harkrider (1983), to compute the kernel function. This is followed by the application of the DWM (Bouchon, 1981) to evaluate the wavenumber integral. To address the slow convergence of integrals when the source and receiver are at close or same depths, PyGRT employs the peak-trough averaging method (PTAM; Zhang *et al.*, 2003), which efficiently computes the convergence value without requiring an increase in the integration upper limit. For large epicentral distances, PyGRT enhances computational speed by replacing traditional trapezoidal integration with Filon's integration method (FIM; Filon, 1930; Apsel and Luco, 1983; Frazer and Gettrust, 1984; Ji and Yao, 1995), allowing for larger integration steps and significantly improving efficiency. By integrating these advanced techniques, PyGRT offers a faster and more versatile solution for calculating synthetic seismograms across a wide range of source–receiver distributions. The code has been meticulously redeveloped based on the principles outlined in the relevant research papers, ensuring both accuracy and performance. This makes PyGRT a powerful and educational tool for researchers and beginners in seismology.

In the following sections, we will first outline the main computational methods used in PyGRT, including GRTM, DWM, PTAM, and FIM. Then, we will walk through how PyGRT is programmed and structured, and compare the results produced by different methods and programs. Finally, we will evaluate PyGRT's performance in terms of numerical stability, computational efficiency, and its extensibility.

Method

By applying the integral transform, the wave equation will be solved in the frequency domain. In cylindrical coordinates, the Helmholtz potential function is introduced, transforming the problem of solving the vector wave equation into one of solving the scalar wave equation corresponding to the potential function. The fundamental solution of each scalar wave equation can be expressed as

$$I_m(\omega) = \int_0^{+\infty} F(k,\omega) J_m(kr) k dk, \quad m = 0,1,2, \tag{1}$$

in which ω is the angular frequency, k is the wavenumber, and r is the epicentral distance, $J_m(kr)$ is the mth-order Bessel function, the kernel function $F(k,\omega)$ is the response of the medium, and each Green's function spectra will be a linear combination of formulas similar to formula (1). In PyGRT, we use GRTM to calculate the kernel function, DWM to calculate the integral of formula (1), PTAM and FIM to adjust and optimize the integral in special cases, and finally, inverse fast Fourier transform (IFFT) to obtain the time series of Green's function.

GRTM

Consider a horizontally layered half-space model, for which each layer has its own thickness and elastic properties. In cylindrical coordinates, the stress and displacement can be expressed using vector surface harmonics (Ben-Menahem and Jit Singh, 1968), with the expansion coefficients linked to Helmholtz potential functions through matrices. By enforcing the continuity of stress and displacement at each layer boundary, the potential functions for *P–SV* wave coupling between layers can be connected using 2 × 2 matrices (whereas *SH* waves use scalars), including both reflected and transmitted upgoing and downgoing wavefields. The generalized R/T coefficients for multiple layers can then be computed recursively. As a result, when the receiver is positioned at the free surface, the displacement integrands can be expressed as

$$\mathbf{Q}(\omega,k) = (\mathbf{M}_U + \mathbf{M}_D\tilde{\mathbf{R}})(\mathbf{I} - \mathbf{R}_D^{RS}\tilde{\mathbf{R}})^{-1}\mathbf{T}_U^{RS}(\mathbf{I} - \mathbf{R}_D^{SL}\mathbf{R}_U^{FS})^{-1}(\mathbf{R}_D^{SL}\mathbf{\Sigma}_D - \mathbf{\Sigma}_U), \tag{2}$$

in which $\tilde{\mathbf{R}}$ is the reflection coefficient matrix on the free surface, $(\mathbf{M}_U + \mathbf{M}_D\tilde{\mathbf{R}})$ is the receiver function matrix, $\mathbf{\Sigma}$ is the source coefficient vector. The superscripts of the R/T coefficients indicate the layer range described by these coefficients, in which F, R, and S represent the free surface, the plane of the receiver, and the plane of the source, respectively. The subscripts U and D denote the upgoing and downgoing wavefields, respectively. Formula (2) computes the result of *P–SV* waves coupled together, with $\mathbf{Q}$ being a 2 × 1 vector, and *SH* waves have a similar formula in scalar form. With the availability of borehole seismometers in recent years, researchers need to calculate the synthetic seismograms of the buried receivers. For such problems, formulas similar to (2) can be applied for a solution. For further details, refer to Kennett and Kerry (1979) and Yao and Harkrider (1983).

DWM

Bouchon (1981) proposed a method in which auxiliary sources are periodically placed along concentric circles centered on the real source in space. This allows the integral in formula (1) to be transformed into a summation over discrete wavenumbers, expressed as

$$I_m(\omega) = \Delta k \sum_{n=1}^{\infty} F(k_n,\omega) J_m(k_n r) k_n, \tag{3}$$

in which $\Delta k = 2\pi/L$, $k_n = n\Delta k$, the characteristic length L represents the radius of the minimum concentric circle. In practice, we always compute signals within a finite time window T. To ensure that the signals received within this time window T are solely generated by the real source—meaning that signals from the nearest auxiliary source have not yet reached the receiver—Bouchon (1981) proposed that the characteristic length must satisfy:

$$\begin{cases} \sqrt{(L-r)^2 + z^2} > \alpha T \\ r < L/2 \end{cases}, \tag{4}$$

in which r is the epicentral distance, z is the source depth, α is the maximum P-wave velocity in the model.

To avoid the impact of singularities in the kernel function $F(k,\omega)$ on calculations and the aliasing effects caused by discretization, Bouchon (1981) proposed adding a small imaginary component $-i\,\omega_I$ to the angular frequency, effectively turning it into a complex number. This shifts all singularities of the kernel function $F(k,\omega)$ away from the real axis in the complex plane, making the integral along the real axis feasible. The addition of an imaginary frequency is equivalent to introducing a decay factor $e^{-\omega_I t}$ in the time domain. Therefore, after performing an inverse Fourier transform to convert the frequency-domain results back to the time domain, the time-domain solution must be multiplied by an inverse decay factor $e^{+\omega_I t}$ to correct for the influence of the imaginary frequency. For a detailed discussion on the effects of time window length and imaginary frequency, refer to Bouchon (1981).

In addition to explicitly setting an upper limit for the discrete wavenumber summation, PyGRT allows users to predefine a convergence precision e to control the summation process (Yao and Harkrider, 1983). The summation is considered convergent, and the k-loop terminates, when the following condition is met:

$$\frac{|F(k_j,\omega) J_m(k_j r) k_j|}{|\sum_{n=1}^{j} F(k_n,\omega) J_m(k_n r) k_n|} < e,\ m = 0,1,2. \tag{5}$$

Because this condition must be satisfied for every order of the Bessel function, the k-loop will not terminate prematurely near the zeros of the Bessel function.

PTAM

The integral in formula (1) is an improper integral with an upper limit of infinity. Therefore, when performing the discrete method based on formula (3), we need to apply a truncation. In other words, the process of computing the improper integral in formula (1) can be broken down into solving a definite integral and evaluating a limit, as expressed in the following two steps:

$$P_m(k,\omega) = \int_0^k F(s,\omega) J_m(sr) s ds, \quad m = 0,1,2, \tag{6}$$

$$I_m(\omega) = \lim_{k\to\infty} P_m(k,\omega). \tag{7}$$

The definite integral in formula (6) can be solved using DWM by formula (3). Therefore, we often choose a large upper limit for the integral to ensure the result converges (the limit defined in formula 7 exists). When the source and receiver depths are significantly different, the integral converges quickly, and using a large upper limit to estimate the convergent value is effective (Fig. 1). However, when the source and receiver depths are close or even the same, the integral converges very slowly. To maintain computational accuracy, we often need to use an extremely large upper limit, which significantly reduces computational efficiency (Fig. 2).

To address this challenge, based on the principle of repeated averaging, Zhang *et al.* (2003) proposed PTAM, a computationally efficient method for estimating the convergence value of integrals. This method is not only mathematically robust but also straightforward to implement. Figure 2c illustrates the fundamental effectiveness of PTAM. When the wavenumber exceeds the critical wavenumber, a certain number of peaks and troughs can be continuously extracted from $P_m(k,\omega)$ (red pluses in Fig. 2c), forming a series $M_0(n)$ that oscillates near the convergence value. We define the ith order reduced series $M_i(n)$ as follows:

$$M_i(n) = \frac{1}{2}[M_{i-1}(n+1) + M_{i-1}(n)], i = 1,2,3..., \tag{8}$$

as $n \to +\infty$, $M_i(n)$, and $M_0(n)$ share the same limit, and higher-order reduced series converge more rapidly (Zhang *et al.*, 2003). In practical applications, for an oscillating series of N points, up to $N-1$ orders of reduced series can be obtained recursively. Therefore, the final convergence value estimated by PTAM is taken as $M_{N-1}(0)$. For further details on the empirical selection of the critical wavenumber in PTAM, the method for extracting peaks and troughs, proof of validity, and additional numerical examples, refer to Zhang *et al.* (2003).

FIM

From GRTM, it is evident that the kernel function $F(k,\omega)$ in formula (1) depends solely on the medium's physical properties

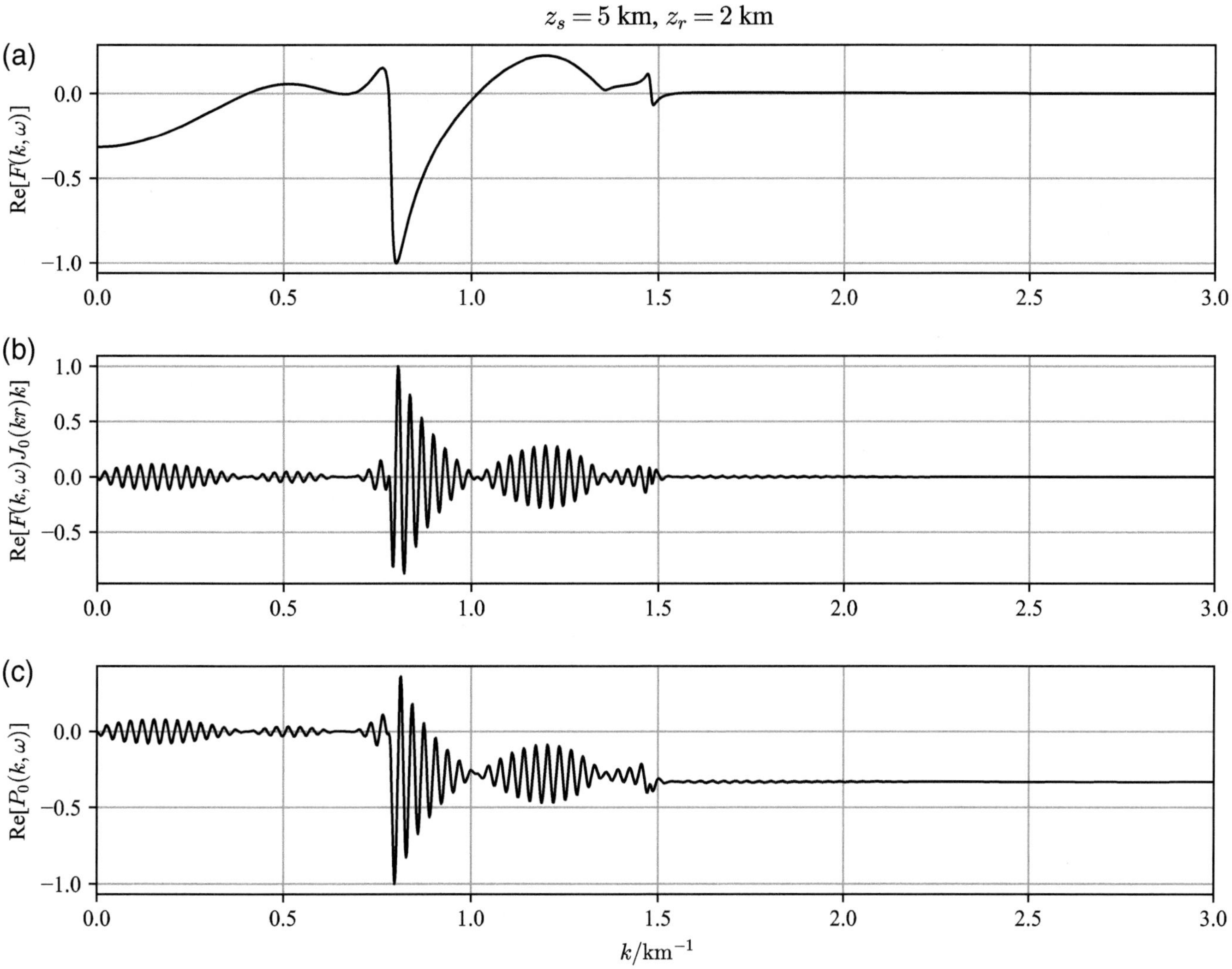

Figure 1. Real parts of (a) the kernel function $F(k,\omega)$, (b) the integrand $F(k,\omega)J_m(kr)k(m = 0)$, and (c) the integral $P_m(k,\omega)$ versus wavenumber k at a frequency $f = 1$ Hz. Half-space model (Table 1) is used. The source depth $z_s = 5$ km. The receiver depth $z_r = 2$ km. The epicentral distance $r = 200$ km. All traces here are normalized by the maximum absolute value.

and the depths of the source and receiver, but not on the epicentral distance. As shown in Figure 3, when the epicentral distance is small, the behavior of the integrand is primarily governed by the kernel function $F(k,\omega)$. However, when the epicentral distance is large, the behavior of the integrand is dominated by the Bessel function. Moreover, as the epicentral distance increases, the integrand oscillates more rapidly, requiring smaller integration steps Δk in DWM, which significantly reduces computational efficiency.

To improve computational efficiency for far-field scenarios, the semi-analytical FIM was proposed (Filon, 1930; Apsel and Luco, 1983; Frazer and Gettrust, 1984; Ji and Yao, 1995). The core idea of FIM is to divide the integration range into multiple intervals. When the argument of the Bessel function is large, the kernel function and the Bessel function within each interval can be approximated using interpolation polynomials and asymptotic expressions, respectively. This allows for an analytical solution within each interval. The final result is then the sum of the analytical solutions from all intervals. Because the integration intervals are only influenced by how well the interpolation polynomial fits the kernel function—and not by the Bessel function—and because the kernel function's behavior is independent of the epicentral distance, FIM does not suffer from the integration intervals limitations of DWM. This enables the use of relatively larger integration steps, thereby enhancing computational efficiency for large epicentral distances. Currently, PyGRT employs FIM based on two-point linear interpolation (Ji and Yao, 1995), with the specific formulas detailed in the corresponding article.

Code Implementation

The PyGRT codebase is divided into two components: Python and C (Fig. 4). PyGRT is packaged as several Python modules, and users can effortlessly compile the C library and install the

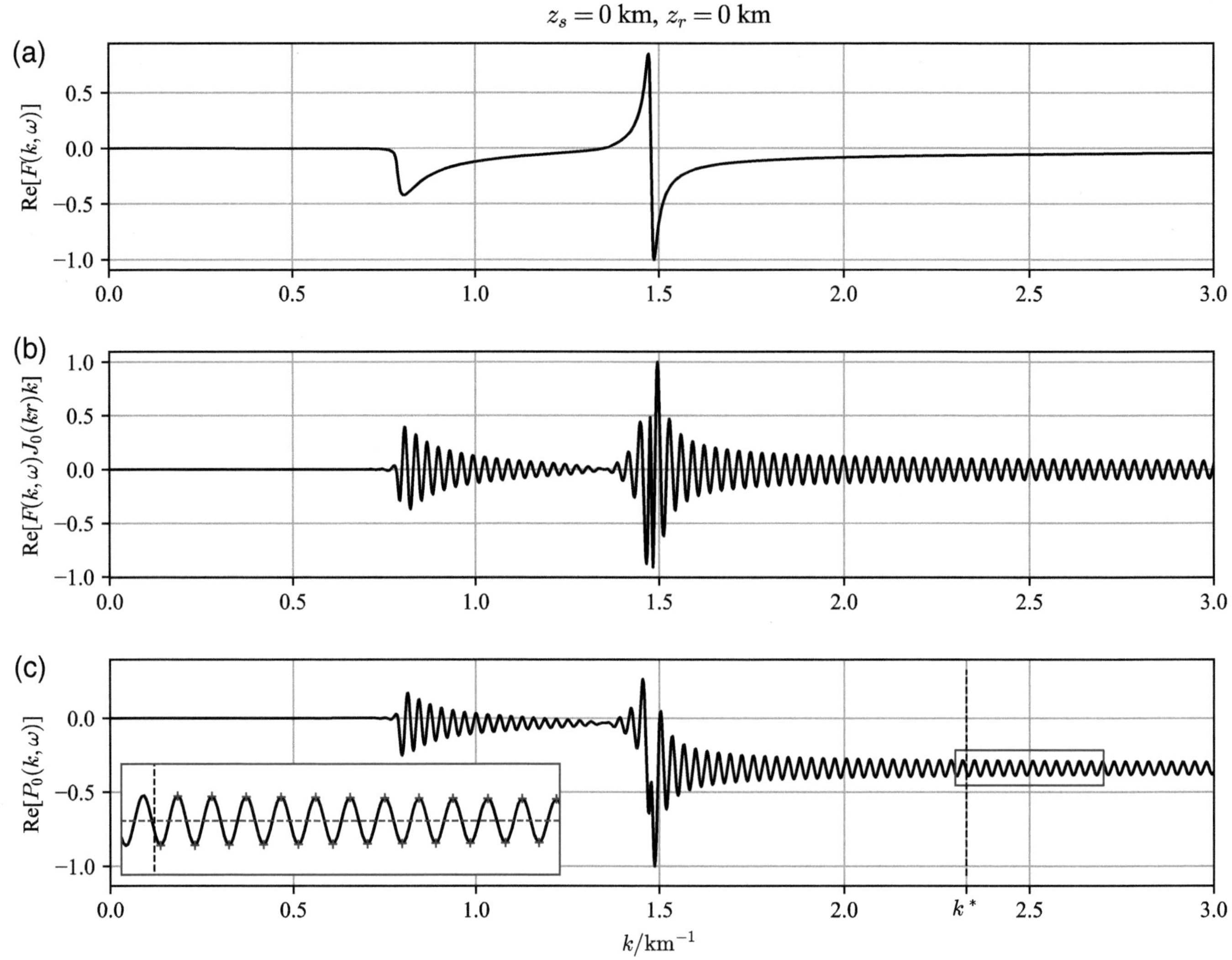

entire package with a simple "pip" command. The Python layer includes wrappers and type conversions for the C library interfaces, making it easy for users to harness the power of Python while taking advantage of the speed and efficiency of C for complex computations.

Figure 2. Similar to Figure 1, but $z_s = z_r = 0$ km. In panel (c), k^* is the critical wavenumber, beyond which the integral $P_m(k,\omega)$ becomes an oscillatory curve with a monotonically and smoothly decaying envelope, the red pluses are the picked peaks and troughs, and the red-dashed line denotes the estimated convergency value by applying the peak-trough averaging method (PTAM). The color version of this figure is available only in the electronic edition.

The core computational tasks in PyGRT are implemented in C and organized into modular components, with each module stored in its own source file. For example, the R/T matrix is handled in "layer.c," matrix propagation in "propagate.c," PTAM in "ptam.c," and FIM in "fim.c." The dynamic library file, "libgrt.so," can be compiled using the "make" command. To streamline function interfaces, model-related variables are stored in structures within the C code. Once the Green's function spectra are computed, the results are stored in memory, and the corresponding memory addresses are returned to Python.

Because calculations for different frequencies are independent, PyGRT leverages OpenMP for parallel processing at the C level. This allows wavenumber integrations for different frequencies to be computed simultaneously across multiple threads, significantly boosting performance. Importantly, PyGRT's C code is written entirely in C, without relying on Python bindings, Cython (a hybrid of Python and C), or CPython (the standard Python interpreter). This design ensures that advanced users can directly integrate PyGRT's dynamic library, "libgrt.so," into their own scientific codes written in C, FORTRAN, or other languages, without any additional dependencies. In addition, PyGRT's C code includes multiple main functions, which are automatically compiled into executable files during installation. This provides users with the flexibility to run PyGRT via traditional command-line arguments, catering to a variety of use cases.

The Python code in PyGRT is designed with an object-oriented approach, featuring classes such as the Green's function class (pygrn.py) and the model class (pymod.py), all of which

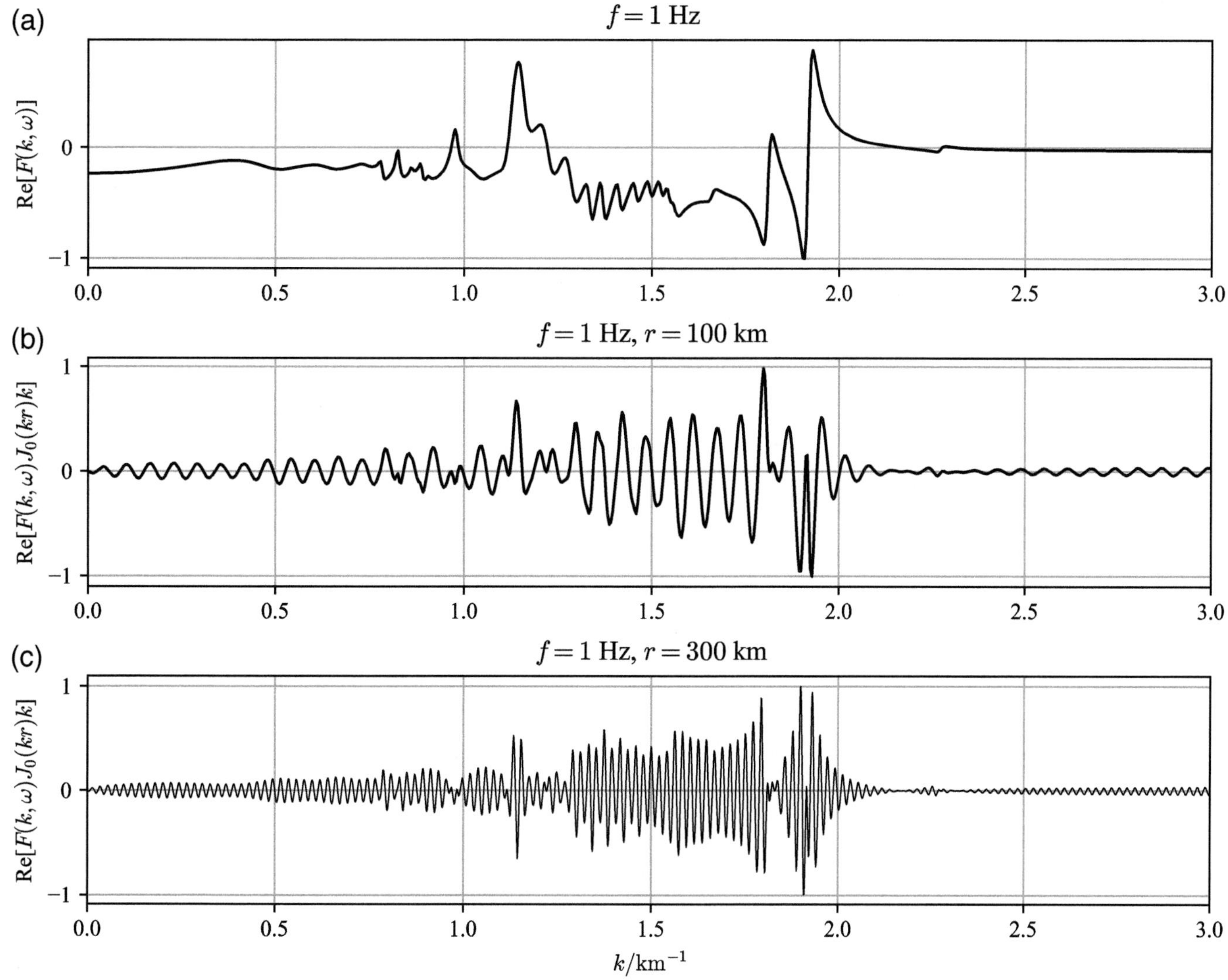

Figure 3. Real parts of (a) the kernel function $F(k,\omega)$ and (b,c) the integrand $F(k,\omega)J_m(kr)k(m = 0)$ at a frequency $f = 1$ Hz. Eight-layer model (Table 2) is used. The source depth $z_s = 2$ km. The receiver depth $z_r = 0$ km. The epicentral distance (b) $r = 100$ km and (c) $r = 300$ km, respectively. All traces are normalized by the maximum absolute value.

utilize NumPy arrays for efficient numerical operations. To bridge Python with high-performance C code, the built-in "ctypes" library is used to import external C libraries, with function interfaces (c_interfaces.py) and C structures (c_structures.py) defined to enable seamless computation in Python. For user convenience, PyGRT comes preloaded with commonly used source time functions (signals.py), such as rectangular, parabolic, and trapezoidal waveforms, as well as utility functions for signal processing (utils.py), including operations such as convolution, integration, differentiation, and saving data to Seismic Analysis Code files (Goldstein *et al.*, 2003). Users can simply import the Python package and call the provided functions to generate synthetic seismograms for various seismic sources, making the tool both powerful and accessible.

Examples

A software package producing correct results is the baseline requirement. Here, we will provide examples to demonstrate the reliability and accuracy of the synthetic seismograms generated by PyGRT, as well as the effectiveness of the PTAM and FIM modules. All results were computed on an Intel(R) Core(TM) Ultra 7 155H processor.

Example 1: Green's function

The first example features the three-component Green's functions within an eight-layer model (Table 2), which was designed to simulate near-field seismic recordings from the Milrow nuclear test (Burdick *et al.*, 1984). We compared PyGRT's results with CPS330, including explosion source, single force source (vertical and horizontal), and dislocation source (45° dip slip, 90° dip slip, and strike slip; Fig. 5). The results show remarkable agreement across all phases of multiple reflections and transmissions, whether in low- or high-frequency ranges.

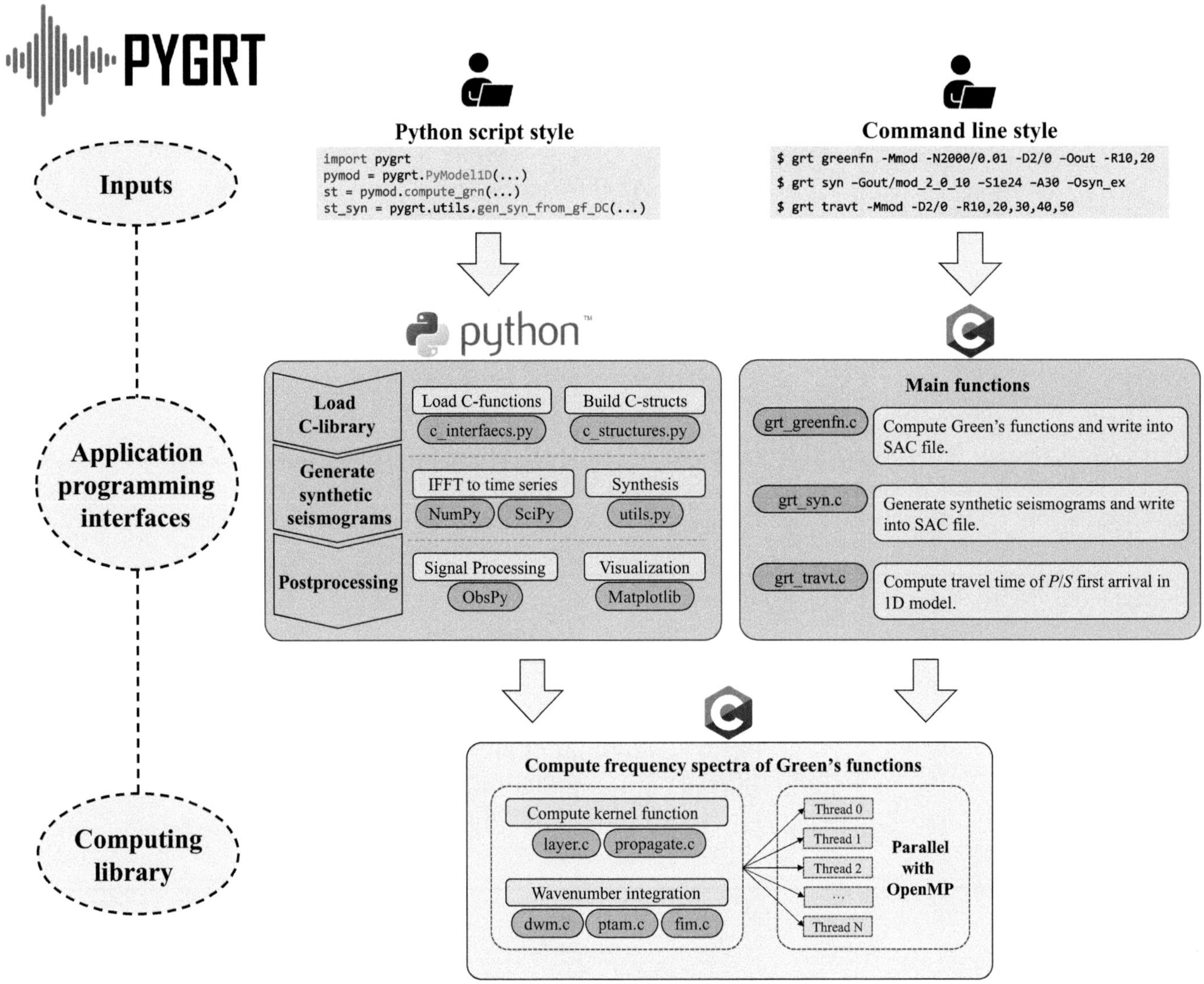

It is worth noting that two programs used identical DWM parameters (e.g., wavenumber integration limits and intervals). However, PyGRT's use of OpenMP-based multithreaded parallel computing allows it to process multiple frequencies simultaneously, giving it a significant edge in computational efficiency. For instance, with 22 threads, PyGRT completed the calculations in about 1/16 the time of CPS330. Although computational performance can also depend on program design and compiler optimizations for different languages (C and FORTRAN), from a user's perspective, PyGRT offers a highly efficient tool without compromising accuracy. Its results align closely with those from traditional codes, further confirming PyGRT's reliability.

Example 2: Lamb's problem

The second example focuses on solving Lamb's problem (Lamb, 1904). Lamb's problem originally deals with calculating the surface displacement response caused by a vertical force applied to the surface of a half-space. Lamb provided an exact integral solution to this problem. In the early twentieth century, when computers were not yet available, researchers had to rely on advanced mathematical techniques to study Lamb's problem and extend it to different types of sources and varying depths for both the source and receiver. With the rise of modern computing, we can now use numerical methods to solve such problems. However, the source and receiver are at the same depth in Lamb's problem; numerical integration becomes inefficient—convergence slows dramatically, results grow unstable, and programs such as CPS330 and FK struggle to handle it. This is where the PTAM, introduced aforementioned, becomes indispensable.

Figure 4. Code structure diagram of PyGRT, illustrating the integration of Python and C for computing synthetic seismograms. The diagram showcases the dual-language architecture, for which Python provides a user-friendly interface, and C handles high-performance computations. This combination leverages the flexibility of Python for data processing and visualization, while utilizing the speed of C for core calculations, optimized with OpenMP for parallel processing. See the Code Implementation section for more information. IFFT, inverse fast Fourier transform; and SAC, Seismic Analysis Code. The color version of this figure is available only in the electronic edition.

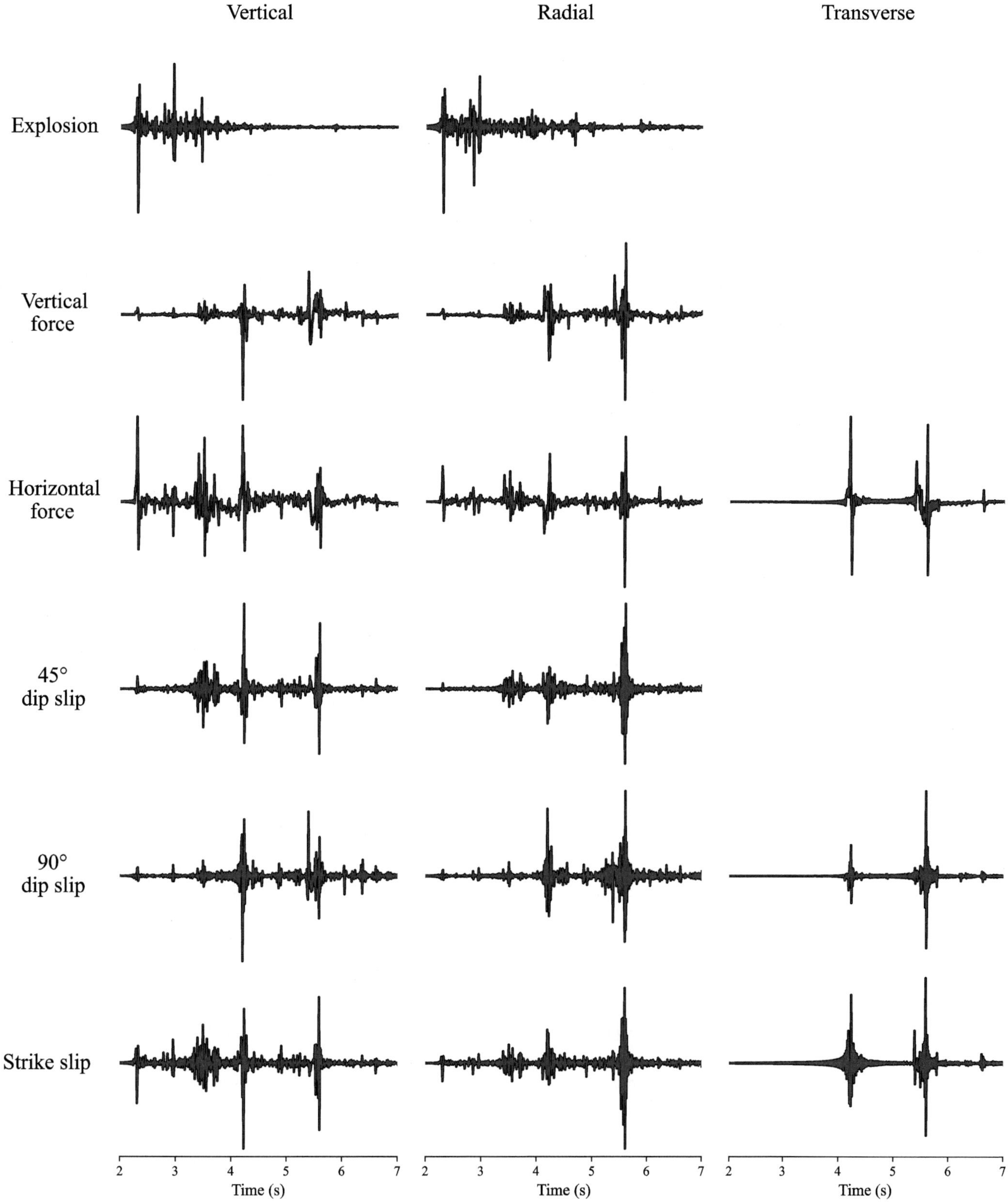

In this example, we compare the numerical results from PyGRT with those derived from earlier mathematical analyses. Figures 6 and 7 show the comparisons for a vertical force (Pekeris, 1955) and a horizontal force (Chao, 1960) on the surface of a half-space model (Table 1), respectively. The results demonstrate strong agreement between PyGRT's numerical

Figure 5. Comparison of the three-component (vertical, radial, and transverse) Green's functions of CPS330 (thick-black line) and PyGRT (thin-red line) for the eight-layer model (Table 2). The source depth $z_s = 2$ km. The receiver depth $z_r = 0$ km. The epicentral distance $r = 10$ km. The sampling frequency is 100 Hz. The color version of this figure is available only in the electronic edition.

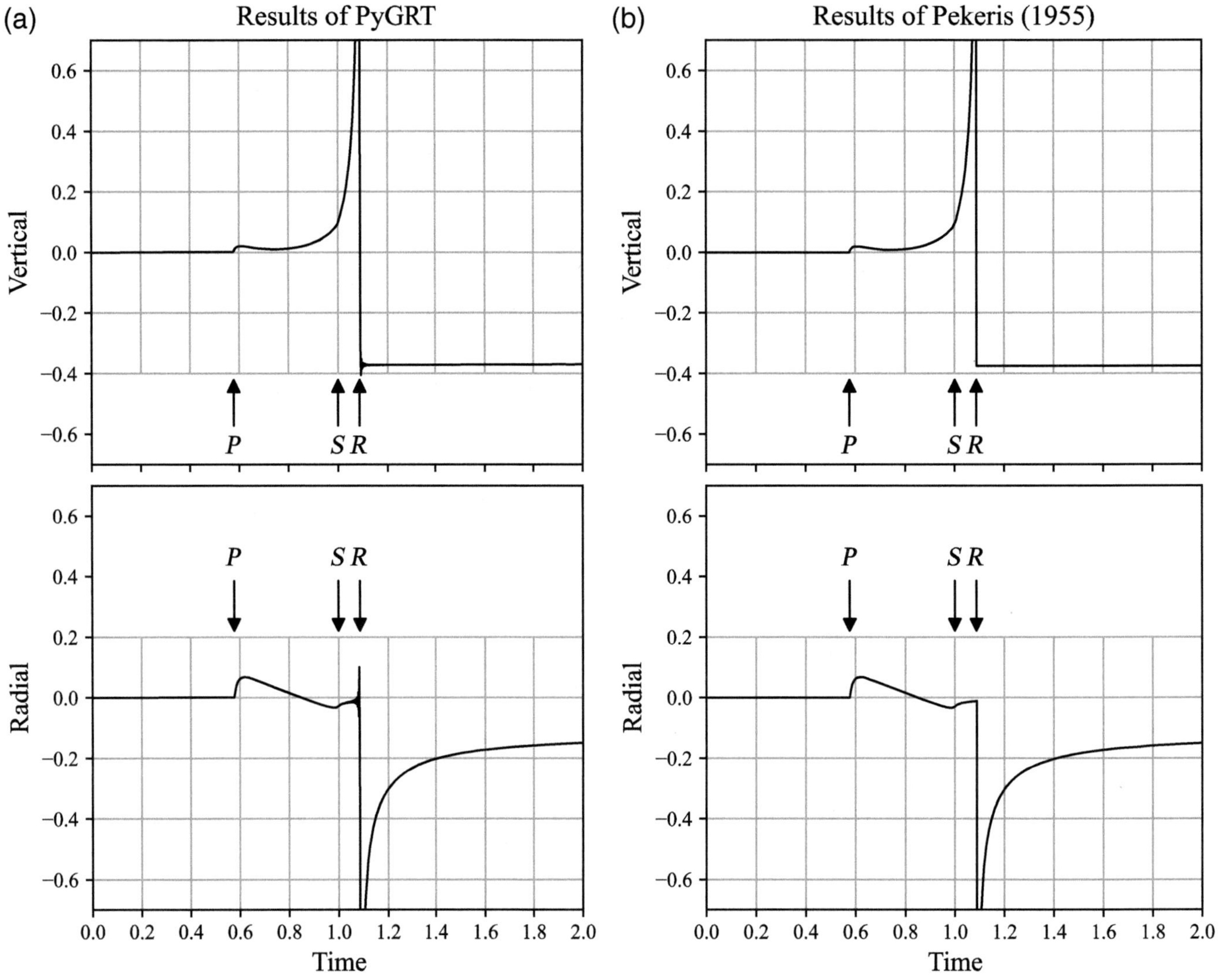

Figure 6. Comparison of the surface vertical and radial displacements of (a) PyGRT and (b) Pekeris (1955), resulting from a vertical force on the surface of the half-space model (Table 1). The displacements are scaled by $\pi\mu r$, and the time is scaled by β/r. "*P*," "*S*," and "*R*" indicate the arrival time of *P* wave, *S* wave, and the Rayleigh wave. All traces are convolved with the step function.

results and the earlier analytical solutions, confirming PyGRT's accuracy. However, numerical results exhibit oscillations at sharp transitions, such as the arrival times of major seismic phases. This is a well-known phenomenon called the Gibbs effect (Gibbs, 1899), which occurs when reconstructing sharp time-domain signals from their frequency spectra. Increasing the number of sampling points can reduce the oscillation range but will not eliminate it. Switching the source function from a step function to a ramp function can help mitigate this issue.

Example 3: Far-field seismogram

In the third example, FIM is used to calculate synthetic seismograms in an eight-layer model (Table 2) for large epicentral distances. At such distances, the integration oscillates more rapidly. This requires using smaller integration steps, which slows down calculations. However, the FIM takes advantage of a key feature: the behavior of its kernel function depends only on the properties of the model and not on the epicentral distances. This allows the FIM to use larger integration steps, significantly improving computational efficiency. Figure 8 compares the results of synthetic seismograms calculated using the DWM and FIM for large epicentral distances, generated with the PyGRT software package. The results show that the FIM produces consistent seismograms even with integration steps four times larger than those used by the DWM, while reducing computation time to just one-fourth of the DWM's. One minor difference is that the FIM produces slightly smaller amplitudes compared to the DWM. This is because the FIM implementation in PyGRT uses a zero-order approximation for the Bessel function and ignores near-field effects. However, as the epicentral distance increases, this difference becomes negligible (Ji and Yao, 1995).

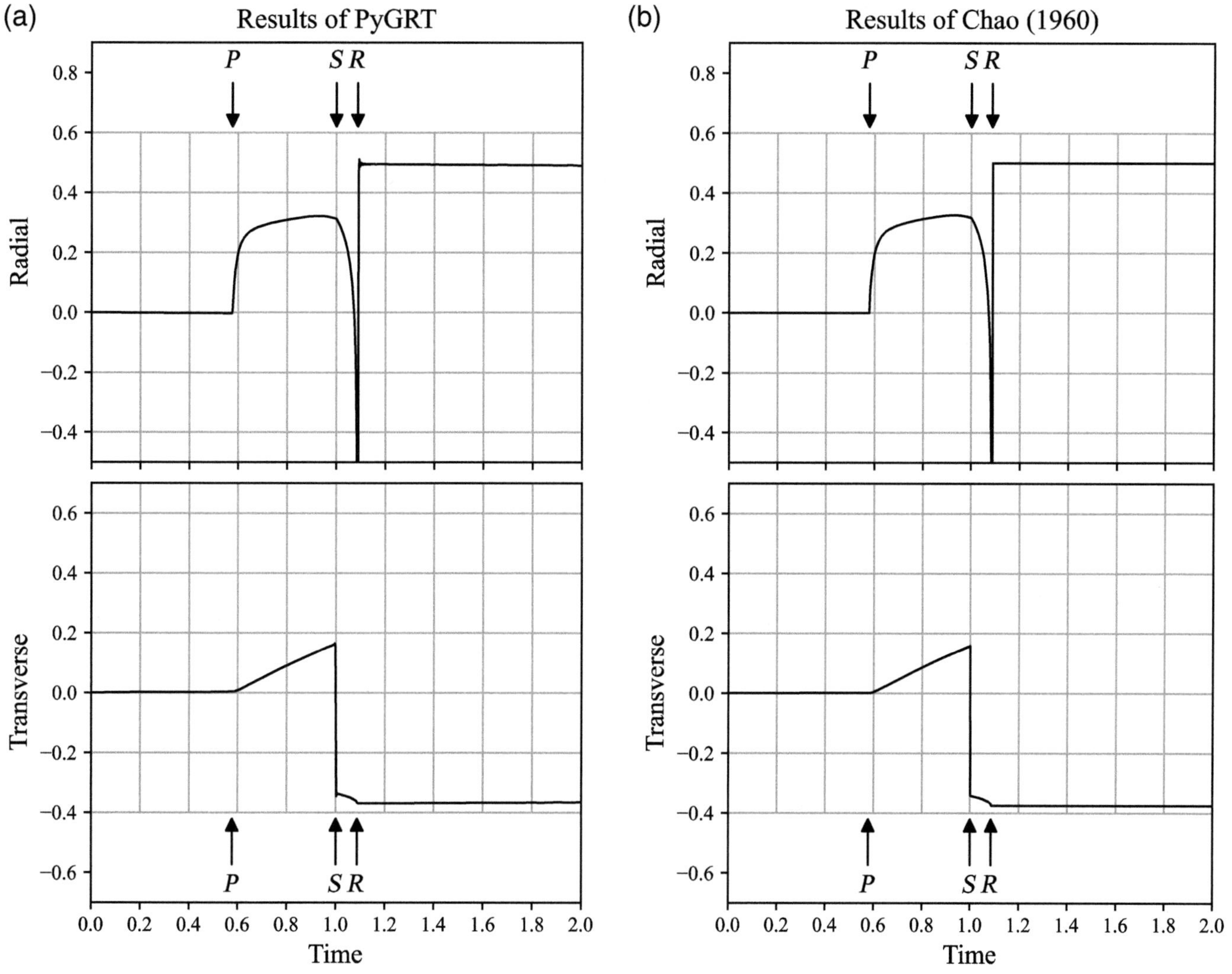

Figure 7. Comparison of the surface radial and transverse displacements of (a) PyGRT and (b) Chao (1960), resulting from a horizontal force on the surface of the half-space model (Table 1). The displacements are scaled by $\pi\mu r$, and the time is scaled by β/r. "*P*," "*S*," and "*R*" indicate the arrival time of the *P* wave, the *S* wave, and the Rayleigh wave. All traces are convolved with the step function.

Example 4: Comparison with observed waveform

In the fourth example, we compare the synthetic seismograms computed by PyGRT with actual observed waveforms. In Figure 9, the instrument responses in observed waveforms were removed to obtain the displacement records. Synthetic displacement seismograms were generated by computing synthetic Green's functions based on a flattened preliminary reference Earth model (Dziewonski and Anderson, 1981) and combining them with the moment tensor solution provided by the Global Centroid Moment Tensor project (Ekström *et al.*, 2012). The comparison shows a good fit for the first *P*-wave waveforms, demonstrating the correctness and practical value of PyGRT's computations. In fact, this comparison process is a key step in focal mechanism inversion, such as in the classic "Cut and Paste" method (Zhao and Helmberger, 1994). Therefore, from a practical standpoint, PyGRT can be correctly integrated into workflows for focal mechanism inversion and also other areas of seismology.

Discussion

In practice, researchers place greater emphasis on the numerical stability, computational efficiency, and extensibility of software packages. Throughout the development of PyGRT, we have consistently adhered to these guiding principles. The following discussion elaborates on these aspects.

Numerical stability

In PyGRT's computational framework, the matrix propagation in GRTM is the most demanding in terms of numerical stability. The method for computing synthetic seismograms in layered media using matrix propagation dates back to Thomson (1950)

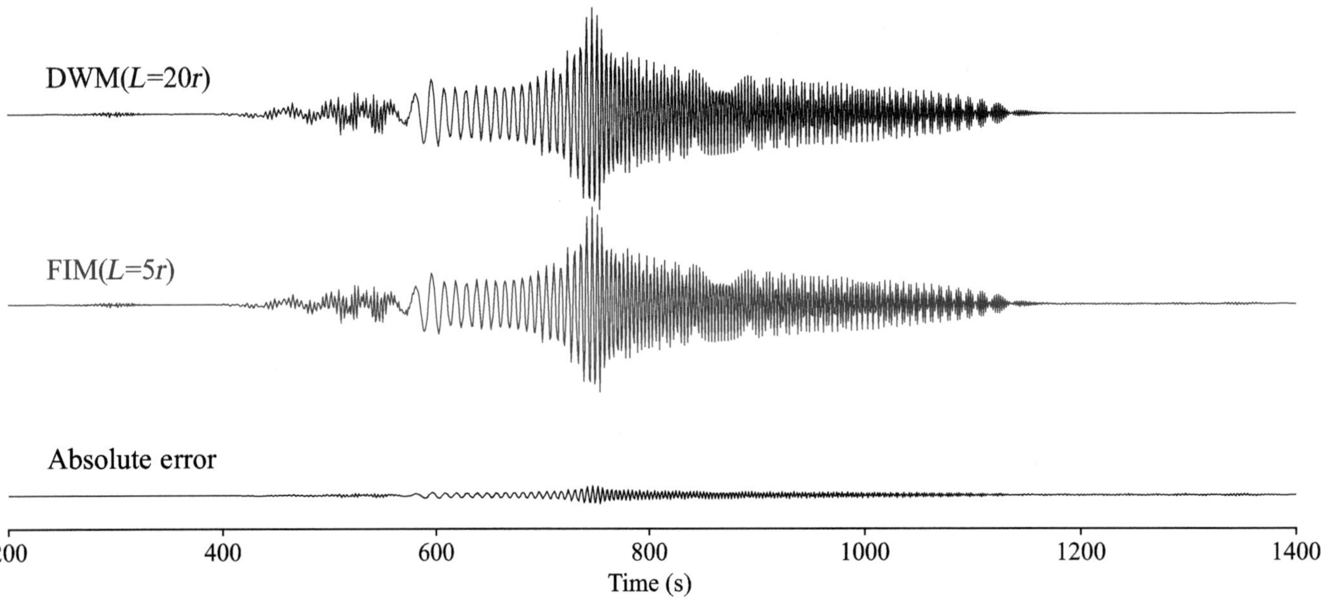

Figure 8. Comparison of the vertical displacements of the discrete wavenumber method (DWM) and Filon's integration method (FIM) for the eight-layer model (Table 2). An explosion at a depth of 2 km is used, recorded on the surface at an epicentral distance of 1800 km. The sampling frequency is 1 Hz. The last curve indicates the absolute error of FIM relative to DWM. All traces are convolved with the step function. The color version of this figure is available only in the electronic edition.

and was later refined and expanded by Haskell (1953), forming what is now known as the Thomson–Haskell propagator. However, researchers later discovered that this approach introduces exponentially growing terms during propagation, leading to numerical instability, especially at high frequencies. To resolve this issue, Kennett and Kerry (1979) developed the GRTM, which avoids these growing exponential terms and ensures stable high-frequency calculations (Chin *et al.*, 1984). PyGRT adopts a slightly modified version of the GRTM formulation compared to Yao and Harkrider (1983). To further improve numerical stability, we have reorganized the equations, factoring out higher-order terms of the wavenumber, which prevents large numbers from swallowing small numbers when the wavenumber is large.

Simulating site effects requires calculating high-frequency seismic waves. To improve numerical stability, Wang (1999) introduced an orthogonalization step into the Thomson–Haskell propagator method. This approach was tested by modeling the pronounced site effects observed during multiple aftershocks of the 1993 Latur earthquake in India (Baumbach *et al.*, 1994). For comparison, we applied the same test case to PyGRT. We used the simple model from Baumbach *et al.* (1994; Table 3), for which a 5 m low-velocity soil layer sits atop a 300 m basalt layer, potentially causing local amplification. PyGRT implements the Futterman (1962) attenuation model to handle the quality factor Q in each layer, critical for high-fidelity site-effect simulations. The source is a 45° dip-slip dislocation point source, positioned in a granite half-space at a depth of 3 km (Wang, 1999). It is worth noting that although Wang (1999) capped the highest calculated frequency at 50 Hz in the original example, PyGRT pushes this limit to 100 Hz to further test its capabilities.

Figure 10a shows the synthetic seismograms of the Killari model computed using PyGRT. To better illustrate the effect

TABLE 1
Layer Parameters of Half-Space Model

Thickness (km)	*P*-Wave Velocity (km/s)	*S*-Wave Velocity (km/s)	Density (g/cm^3)
∞	8.00	4.62	3.30

TABLE 2
Layer Parameters of Eight-Layer Model

Thickness (km)	*P*-Wave Velocity (km/s)	*S*-Wave Velocity (km/s)	Density (g/cm^3)
0.2	3.4	1.7	2.3
0.6	3.7	1.9	2.4
0.5	4.2	2.1	2.4
0.5	4.6	2.3	2.5
0.7	4.9	2.8	2.6
0.5	5.1	2.9	2.7
6.0	5.9	3.3	2.7
28.0	6.9	4.0	2.8
∞	8.2	4.7	3.2

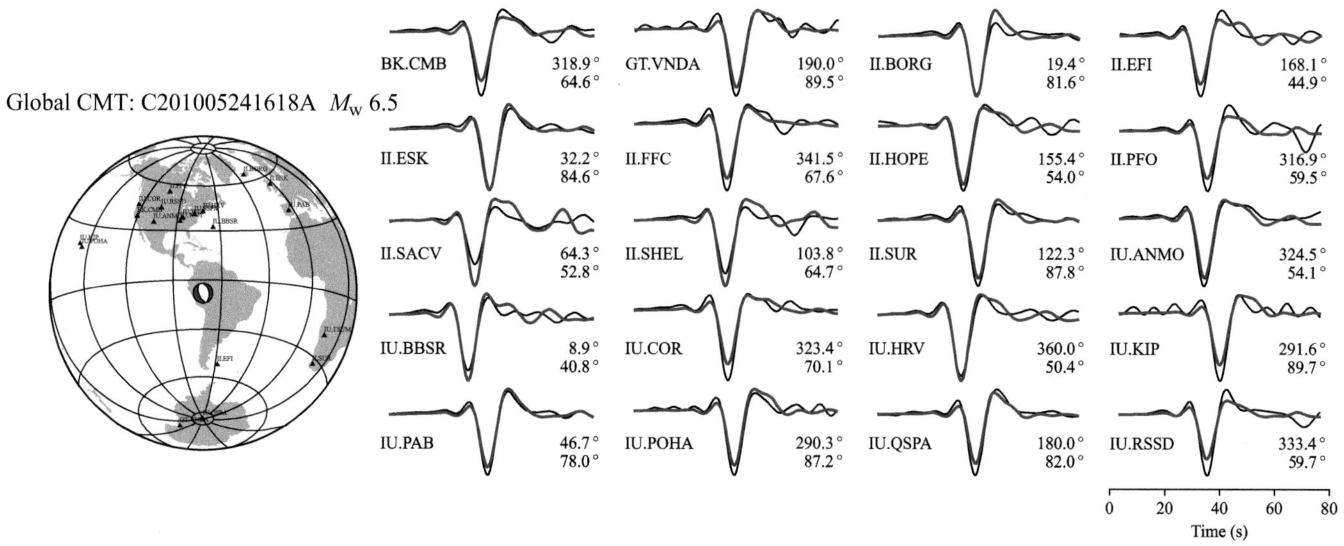

Figure 9. Comparison of 20 Z-component teleseismic recordings for the 24 May 2010 M_W 6.5 Brazil earthquake. The focal mechanism of the earthquake (beachball) and the locations of 20 stations (black triangles) are plotted on the left side. In each panel, the red and black lines denote the synthetic and observed displacement, respectively. The text and values under the waveforms denote the station name, azimuth, and epicentral distance in degrees. Global CMT, Global Centroid Moment Tensor. The color version of this figure is available only in the electronic edition.

of the sandy soil layer, we also ran a simulation with a modified version of the model, for which the 5 m soil layer was replaced by the underlying basalt. The comparison reveals that although the vertical component remains largely unchanged, the presence of the soil layer significantly amplifies ground motion in the two horizontal components. In addition, a near-monochromatic resonance appears in the *S*-wave coda. Figure 10b presents the corresponding frequency spectra, for which this resonance effect is even more pronounced. Both horizontal components exhibit distinct spectral peaks at regular frequency intervals, which can be explained using a simple theoretical analysis. Because of the large velocity contrast between the soil and basalt layers, the shear wave can be approximated as a vertically incident wave upon reaching the soil layer. In this case, the phase delay caused by a single reflection is given by

$$\Delta\phi = 2\pi \frac{2h}{\beta/f} - \pi, \tag{9}$$

in which h is the soil layer thickness, β/f is the wavelength, $-\pi$ denotes the phase shift of half-wavelength caused by the reflection at the soil-basalt interface. When the phase delay satisfies $\Delta\phi = 2n\pi$, the wavefield undergoes constructive interference, leading to an increase in amplitude, and the resonance frequency is given by

$$f_n = (2n+1)\frac{\beta}{4h}, \; n = 0,1,2,..., \tag{10}$$

in which $\beta = 200$ m/s, $h = 5$ m for the soil layer. As a result, it can be easily calculated that vibration amplification occurs at intervals of 20 Hz, starting from 10 Hz. This explains the spectral characteristics observed in Figure 10b.

However, Figure 10b also reveals a broad spectral peak around 60 Hz in the vertical component, which is not easily discernible in Figure 10a. In addition, due to the limited frequency range, this phenomenon was not observed in the example results of Wang (1999). This peak can be explained using the same analytical approach as before, with the only modification being the substitution of β with the *P*-wave velocity of the soil layer, $\alpha = 1200$ m/s, into equation (10), which yields a calculated peak at 60 Hz.

TABLE 3
Layer Parameters of the Killari Area Model (Baumbach *et al.*, 1994)

Thickness (km)	*P*-Wave Velocity (km/s)	*S*-Wave Velocity (km/s)	Density (g/cm³)	Q_P	Q_S
0.005	1.2	0.2	1.3	80	20
0.3	4.5	2.6	2.5	500	220
∞	6.0	3.5	2.7	800	270

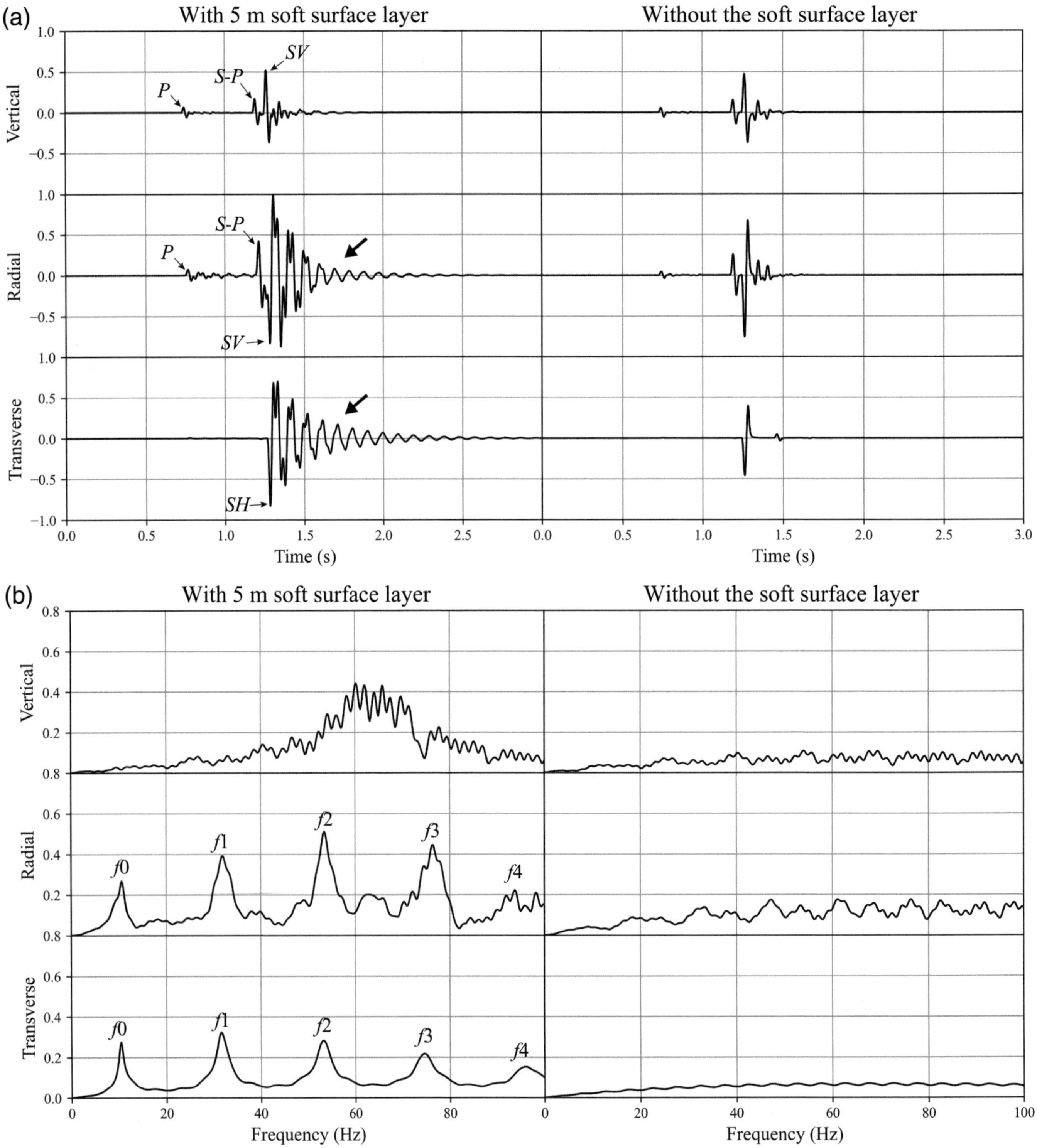

Figure 10. (a) Three-component synthetic seismograms (left) for the Killari model (Table 3), compared with the reference seismograms (right) computed for the simplified model without the soil layer. A 45° dip-slip source at a depth of 3 km is used, recorded at an epicentral distance of 3 km and an azimuth of 45°. All traces are convolved with a wavelet, which is proportional to $1/\tau \cdot \sin^3(\pi t/\tau)$, for $0 \le t \le \tau$, else 0, with $\tau = 50$ ms. The sampling frequency is 200 Hz. All traces are computed by PyGRT and scaled by the maximum absolute value of the radial component. (b) The amplitude spectra of the corresponding synthetic seismograms, but for an impulse source ($\tau \to 0$).

While using PyGRT to simulate site effects, we even tested increasing the maximum frequency to 5 kHz and still obtained stable and accurate results. Although such high frequencies are not necessary in this case, this test demonstrates PyGRT's robustness in handling high-frequency wave simulations.

Computational efficiency

In synthetic seismogram calculations, tasks of different frequencies can be processed independently, making parallel

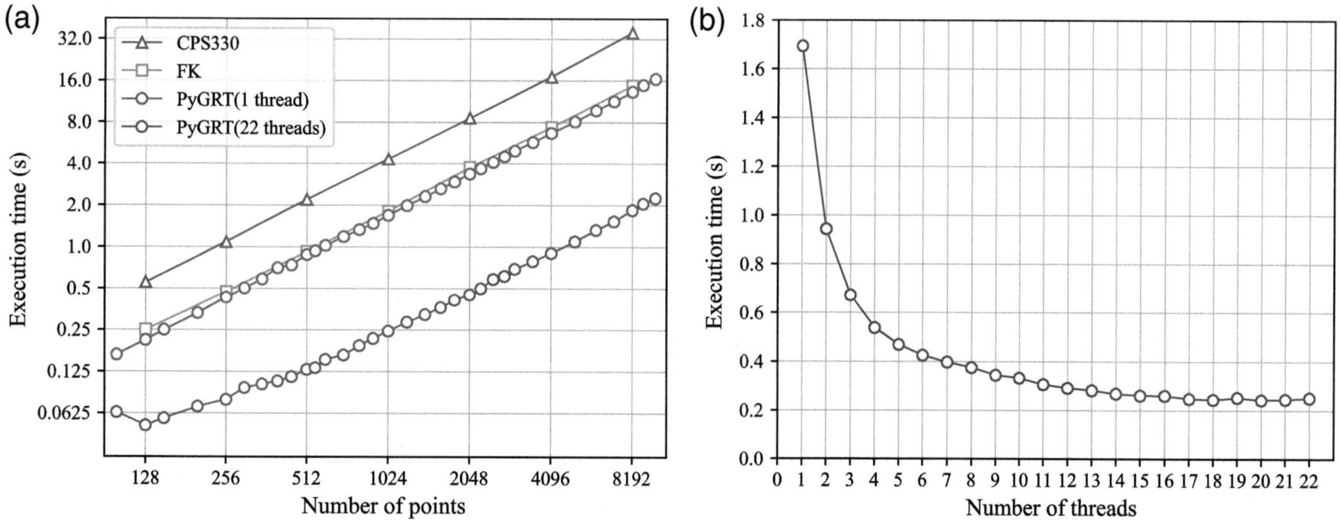

Figure 11. (a) Execution time of CPS330, FK, and PyGRT (with 1 thread and 22 threads) computing the Green's functions of a dislocation source with various numbers of points. (b) Execution time of PyGRT with various numbers of threads when the number of points is 1024. Here, the eight-layer model is used. A dislocation source at a depth of 2 km is used, recorded on the surface at an epicentral distance of 10 km. The sampling frequency is 100 Hz. Each point is the average execution time of five repeated runs. The color version of this figure is available only in the electronic edition.

computation straightforward. PyGRT takes advantage of this using OpenMP directives to parallelize frequency loops, enabling multithreading for improved efficiency. However, higher frequencies require more extensive wavenumber integration, increasing computational workload. If tasks were assigned to threads statically, some threads would finish early and sit idle, leading to inefficiencies. To prevent this, PyGRT employs OpenMP's "schedule" directive with a "guided" strategy, dynamically balancing the workload across threads. This ensures that computational resources are used efficiently, minimizing idle time and maximizing performance.

Figure 11a compares the execution times of three software packages—CPS330, FK, and PyGRT—for calculating Green's functions of a dislocation source with different time series lengths. All other parameters remain the same as in Figure 5 to ensure consistency. To ensure a fair comparison, all three programs use the same DWM parameters, such as the wavenumber integration limits and intervals, so that the number of kernel function evaluations remains the same. To better assess PyGRT's efficiency, we also included a single-threaded version in the comparison. The results show that single-threaded PyGRT runs slightly faster than FK, likely due to differences in programming implementation and compiler optimizations for C and FORTRAN. CPS330, on the other hand, runs more slowly, possibly due to redundant computations required for broader package compatibility or frequent read and write operations involving its custom file formats. The advantage of PyGRT's multithreading is particularly striking. When running on 22 threads—the maximum supported by the Intel(R) Core(TM) Ultra 7 155H processor—it achieves speeds 8 times faster than single-threaded PyGRT and FK, and 20 times faster than CPS330. A key limitation of CPS330 and FK is that they can only process series lengths that are powers of two. This is because they rely on the traditional fast Fourier transform (FFT) algorithm, which requires such lengths for efficient computation. In contrast, PyGRT has no such restriction because it utilizes SciPy (in Python) and FFTW (in C) (see Data and Resources) to perform FFT calculations. These libraries incorporate various modern FFT algorithms that can efficiently handle arbitrary series lengths. This flexibility allows researchers to choose time window lengths and sampling rates more freely when computing synthetic seismograms, offering greater adaptability in seismic studies.

Figure 11b illustrates how PyGRT's computation time varies with the number of threads. The results show that increasing the thread count significantly reduces computation time, improving efficiency in a manner that closely follows an inverse relationship with the number of threads. The benefits of multithreading will become more pronounced when processing larger datasets or computing higher frequency values.

Extensibility

Ensuring a software package is highly extensible makes it easier to maintain and extend with new features. PyGRT is built with both C and Python, each designed with extensibility in mind. The core computations are handled in C using a modular approach. Key data structures, such as model parameters and complex frequency-domain series, are encapsulated in structs, making function interfaces clearer and simplifying data exchange between the C library and Python. To improve maintainability and readability, different computational modules are organized into separate source and header files. For example, PyGRT currently supports three methods for wavenumber integration—DWM, PTAM, and FIM. Each method has its own dedicated source and header file, along with static helper functions that operate independently to avoid cross-interference. Users can easily switch between methods by adjusting a single parameter. This modular structure not only helps developers maintain and extend the software systematically but also makes it easier for advanced users to understand the underlying calculations by reading the source code.

Python's ease of use and flexibility have made it the language of choice for scientific computing. Today, most computational programs are either written in Python or use it as an interface—and PyGRT is no exception. What sets PyGRT apart is its ability to leverage the speed of C libraries while maintaining the versatility of Python. Instead of writing computed frequency spectra to disk, PyGRT keeps them in memory, enabling seamless integration with Python's robust scientific computing ecosystem, including NumPy and SciPy, for tasks such as IFFT, filtering, convolution, integration, and differentiation. The processed time series are structured using the Stream and Trace class of the seismological data processing library ObsPy (Beyreuther *et al.*, 2010; see Data and Resources), making it easier to analyze, visualize, and store seismic data in multiple formats.

Leveraging PyGRT's extensibility, we plan to integrate the Self-Adaptive FIM (SAFIM; Chen and Zhang, 2001) for wavenumber integration. Unlike conventional approaches that rely on fixed steps, SAFIM dynamically adjusts the integration interval based on the behavior of the kernel function, improving efficiency and accuracy. In addition, we will enhance PyGRT's capabilities by enabling output of stress and rotation components and optimizing synthetic seismogram computations at varying depths within the same layer (Yao and Zheng, 1984). Because kernel calculations for different frequencies and wavenumbers are independent, implementing graphic processing unit parallel computing in PyGRT is also a viable direction for future development.

Conclusion

We present PyGRT, an open-source Python package for efficiently computing synthetic seismograms for a point source in a layered half-space model. PyGRT combines the computational efficiency of C, optimized with OpenMP for parallel processing, with the flexibility and user friendliness of Python. This dual-language architecture enables seamless integration into modern computational workflows, making PyGRT a versatile tool for seismic modeling.

By integrating PTAM and FIM, PyGRT effectively handles diverse source–receiver distributions, including challenging scenarios such as close or same source–receiver depths and large epicentral distances. Extensive tests confirm PyGRT's accuracy and outstanding stability at high frequencies.

PyGRT's modular design ensures future extensibility, allowing for the integration of new features and methodologies. Its performance, validated against traditional programs, demonstrates significant improvements in computational efficiency without compromising accuracy. PyGRT bridges the gap between high-performance computing and user accessibility, offering a practical and efficient solution for synthetic seismogram computation in both research and educational contexts.

Data and Resources

PyGRT is available at https://github.com/Dengda98/PyGRT. QSEIS is available at https://github.com/pyrocko/fomosto-qseis. FK can be obtained at https://www.eas.slu.edu/People/LZhu/home.html. CPS330 can be obtained at https://www.eas.slu.edu/eqc/ComputerPrograms Seismology. ObsPy is available at https://github.com/obspy/obspy. SciPy can be obtained at https://scipy.org. NumPy can be obtained at https://numpy.org. FFTW can be obtained at https://www.fftw.org. The observed waveform data used in this study are available from the Incorporated Research Institutions for Seismology (IRIS). All websites were last accessed in November 2025.

Declaration of Competing Interests

The authors acknowledge that there are no conflicts of interest recorded.

Acknowledgments

The authors thank Editor-in-Chief Allison Bent and two anonymous reviewers for their constructive comments. The authors appreciate the technical support from the Supercomputing Laboratory, Institute of Geology and Geophysics, Chinese Academy of Sciences (IGGCAS). This study was funded by the Strategic Priority Research Program of the Chinese Academy of Sciences (XDA0430204), the CAS Project for Young Scientists in Basic Research (YSBR-082), and the Deep Earth National Science and Technology Major Project (2024ZD1002905).

References

Apsel, R. J., and J. E. Luco (1983). On the Green's functions for a layered half-space. Part II, *Bull. Seismol. Soc. Am.* **73,** no. 4, 931–951, doi: 10.1785/BSSA0730040931.

Baumbach, M., H. Grosser, H. Schmidt, A. Paulat, A. Rietbrock, C. R. Rao, P. S. Raju, D. Sarkar, and I. Mohan (1994). Study of foreshocks and aftershocks of the intraplate Latur earthquake of September 30, 1993, India, in Latur earthquake, *Geol. Soc. India Mem.* 33–63.

Ben-Menahem, A., and S. Jit Singh (1968). Multipolar elastic fields in a layered half space, *Bull. Seismol. Soc. Am.* **58,** no. 5, 1519–1572, doi: 10.1785/BSSA0580051519.

Beyreuther, M., R. Barsch, L. Krischer, T. Megies, Y. Behr, and J. Wassermann (2010). ObsPy: A Python toolbox for seismology, *Seismol. Res. Lett.* **81,** no. 3, 530–533, doi: 10.1785/gssrl.81.3.530.

Bouchon, M. (1981). A simple method to calculate Green's functions for elastic layered media, *Bull. Seismol. Soc. Am.* **71,** no. 4, 959–971, doi: 10.1785/BSSA0710040959.

Bozdağ, E., D. Peter, M. Lefebvre, D. Komatitsch, J. Tromp, J. Hill, N. Podhorszki, and D. Pugmire (2016). Global adjoint tomography:

First-generation model, *Geophys. J. Int.* **207,** no. 3, 1739–1766, doi: 10.1093/gji/ggw356.

Burdick, L. J., T. Wallace, and T. Lay (1984). Modeling near-field and teleseismic observations from the Amchitka Test Site, *J. Geophys. Res.* **89,** no. B6, 4373–4388, doi: 10.1029/JB089iB06p04373.

Burdick, S., and V. Lekić (2017). Velocity variations and uncertainty from transdimensional P-wave tomography of North America, *Geophys. J. Int.* **209,** no. 2, 1337–1351, doi: 10.1093/gji/ggx091.

Cabieces, R., A. Olivar-Castaño, T. C. Junqueira, J. Relinque, L. Fernandez-Prieto, J. Vackár, B. Rösler, J. Barco, A. Pazos, and L. García-Martínez (2022). Integrated Seismic Program (ISP): A new Python GUI-based software for earthquake seismology and seismic signal processing, *Seismol. Res. Lett.* **93,** no. 3, 1895–1908, doi: 10.1785/0220210205.

Chao, C.-C. (1960). Dynamical response of an elastic half-space to tangential surface loadings, *J. Appl. Mech.* **27,** no. 3, 559–567, doi: 10.1115/1.3644041.

Chen, X., and H. Zhang (2001). An efficient method for computing Green's functions for a layered half-space at large epicentral distances, *Bull. Seismol. Soc. Am.* **91,** no. 4, 858–869, doi: 10.1785/0120000113.

Chin, R. C. Y., G. W. Hedstrom, and L. Thigpen (1984). Matrix methods in synthetic seismograms, *Geophys. J. Int.* **77,** no. 2, 483–502, doi: 10.1111/j.1365-246X.1984.tb01944.x.

Dziewonski, A. M., and D. L. Anderson (1981). Preliminary reference Earth model, *Phys. Earth Planet. In.* **25,** no. 4, 297–356, doi: 10.1016/0031-9201(81)90046-7.

Ekström, G., M. Nettles, and A. M. Dziewoński (2012). The global CMT project 2004–2010: Centroid-moment tensors for 13,017 earthquakes, *Phys. Earth Planet. In.* **200–201,** 1–9, doi: 10.1016/j.pepi.2012.04.002.

Filon, L. N. G. (1930). III.—On a quadrature formula for trigonometric integrals, *Proc. Roy. Soc. Edinb.* **49,** 38–47, doi: 10.1017/S0370164600026262.

Frazer, L. N., and J. F. Gettrust (1984). On a generalization of Filon's method and the computation of the oscillatory integrals of seismology, *Geophys. J. Int.* **76,** no. 2, 461–481, doi: 10.1111/j.1365-246X.1984.tb05056.x.

Futterman, W. I. (1962). Dispersive body waves, *J. Geophys. Res.* **67,** no. 13, 5279–5291, doi: 10.1029/JZ067i013p05279.

Gibbs, J. W. (1899). Fourier's series, *Nature* **59,** no. 1539, 606–606, doi: 10.1038/059606a0.

Goldstein, P., D. Dodge, M. Firpo, and L. Minner (2003). SAC2000: Signal processing and analysis tools for seismologists and engineers, in *International Geophysics*, W. H. K. Lee, H. Kanamori, P. C. Jennings, and C. Kisslinger (Editors), Academic Press, International Handbook of Earthquake and Engineering Seismology, Part B, London, United Kingdom, 1613–1614, doi: 10.1016/S0074-6142(03)80284-X.

Haskell, N. A. (1953). The dispersion of surface waves on multilayered media, *Bull. Seismol. Soc. Am.* **43,** no. 1, 17–34, doi: 10.1029/SP030p0086.

Herrmann, R. B. (2013). Computer programs in seismology: An evolving tool for instruction and research, *Seismol. Res. Lett.* **84,** no. 6, 1081–1088, doi: 10.1785/0220110096.

Ji, C., and Z. Yao (1995). The study of the method for broadband regional synthetic seismogram (in Chinese with English abstract), *Acta Geophys. Sin.* **38,** no. 4, 460–468.

Kennett, B. L. N., and E. R. Engdahl (1991). Traveltimes for global earthquake location and phase identification, *Geophys. J. Int.* **105,** no. 2, 429–465, doi: 10.1111/j.1365-246X.1991.tb06724.x.

Kennett, B. L. N., E. R. Engdahl, and R. Buland (1995). Constraints on seismic velocities in the Earth from traveltimes, *Geophys. J. Int.* **122,** no. 1, 108–124, doi: 10.1111/j.1365-246X.1995.tb03540.x.

Kennett, B. L. N., and N. J. Kerry (1979). Seismic waves in a stratified half space, *Geophys. J. Int.* **57,** no. 3, 557–583, doi: 10.1111/j.1365-246X.1979.tb06779.x.

Lamb, H. (1904). I. On the propagation of tremors over the surface of an elastic solid, *Phil. Trans. Roy. Soc. Lond.* **203,** nos. 359/371, 1–42, doi: 10.1098/rsta.1904.0013.

Pekeris, C. L. (1955). The seismic surface pulse, *Proc. Natl. Acad. Sci.* **41,** no. 7, 469–480, doi: 10.1073/pnas.41.7.469.

Thomson, W. T. (1950). Transmission of elastic waves through a stratified solid medium, *J. Appl. Phys.* **21,** no. 2, 89–93, doi: 10.1063/1.1699629.

Tromp, J., D. Komatitsch, and Q. Liu (2008). Spectral-element and adjoint methods in seismology, *Commun. Comput. Phys.* **3,** no. 1, 1–32.

Wang, R. (1999). A simple orthonormalization method for stable and efficient computation of Green's functions, *Bull. Seismol. Soc. Am.* **89,** no. 3, 733–741, doi: 10.1785/BSSA0890030733.

Xu, M., S. Hao, J. Chen, B. Zhang, and P. Tong (2025). SurfATT: High-performance package for adjoint-state surface-wave travel-time tomography, *Seismol. Res. Lett.* doi: 10.1785/0220240206.

Yao, Z., and D. G. Harkrider (1983). A generalized reflection-transmission coefficient matrix and discrete wavenumber method for synthetic seismograms, *Bull. Seismol. Soc. Am.* **73,** no. 6A, 1685–1699, doi: 10.1785/BSSA07306A1685.

Yao, Z., and T. Zheng (1984). A generalized reflection-transmission coefficient matrix and discrete wavenumber method for synthetic seismograms (II)—For multiple sources at different depths, *Acta Geophys. Sin.* **27,** no. 4, 338–348.

Zhang, H., X. Chen, and S. Chang (2003). An efficient numerical method for computing synthetic seismograms for a layered half-space with sources and receivers at close or same depths, *Pure Appl. Geophys.* **160,** 467–486.

Zhao, L.-S., and D. V. Helmberger (1994). Source estimation from broadband regional seismograms, *Bull. Seismol. Soc. Am.* **84,** no. 1, 91–104.

Zhu, L., and L. A. Rivera (2002). A note on the dynamic and static displacements from a point source in multilayered media: A note on the dynamic and static displacements from a point source, *Geophys. J. Int.* **148,** no. 3, 619–627, doi: 10.1046/j.1365-246X.2002.01610.x.

Manuscript received 18 February 2025
Published online 12 December 2025

Ground-Motion Models at Your Fingertips: Easy, Rapid, and Flexible Analysis with eGSIM

Riccardo Zaccarelli*[1], Graeme Weatherill[1], Dino Bindi[1], and Fabrice Cotton[1,2]

Abstract

eGSIM is an OpenQuake-based Python library and web application for analysis and interpretation of ground motions (observed and/or simulated) and ground-motion models (GMMs). Developed in the frameworks of the European Facilities for Earthquake Hazard and Risk and the European Plate Observing System (EPOS), the eGSIM webservice can be used in many applications, from data visualization through its graphical user interface in the user's browser, to programmatic access to its application programming interface in the user's code. Its core functionalities are based on two types of GMMs comparisons: "Model-to-Model," in which the expected ground motions and aleatory variabilities are compared for a range of user-configurable scenarios, and "Model-to-Data," in which the GMMs can be compared against databases of ground motion observations. We showcase eGSIM's main features and highlight many of the potential applications, before illustrating its use in an exploratory analysis comparing ground motions from observations and physics-based simulations. These examples demonstrate not only the ease with which eGSIM can perform common analysis of GMMs for hazard and risk modelling, but also its versatility for application to other customized exploratory analyses and for integration in state-of-the-art high-performance-computing workflows.

Cite this article as Zaccarelli, R., G. Weatherill, D. Bindi, and F. Cotton (2026). Ground-Motion Models at Your Fingertips: Easy, Rapid, and Flexible Analysis with eGSIM, *Seismol. Res. Lett.* **97**, 2154–2166, doi: 10.1785/0220250228.

Introduction

One of the most critical components of earthquake hazard and risk analysis is the ground-motion model (GMM), which predicts the expected ground shaking at a location from a given scenario along with its aleatory variability. Hundreds of GMMs have been published in the scientific literature, and while the application of rigorous selection criteria (Cotton *et al.*, 2006; Bommer *et al.*, 2010) will rapidly narrow this down to a smaller set of candidate models for any given application, the likely users such as engineers, seismologists, hazard and risk modelers, and so forth, are often still confronted with a choice of high-quality GMMs to consider for use in their applications. Regardless of whether a user is aiming to identify a single GMM for use as a backbone model in a logic tree (or simply for exploration) or multiple models to describe the epistemic uncertainty in their analysis, the selection of suitable GMMs will require them to address several key questions: (1) how do the models compare with one other in terms of scaling with source, path, and site properties? (2) Do the models capture well the median and variability of observed (or even simulated) earthquake ground motions in a region and, if not, are systematic biases present with respect to the source, path, and site effects? For researchers, it has often been a common practice to create their own code to either implement the GMMs based on the descriptions in the publications or download from several popular online repositories and develop their own applications for such analysis. This process, however, can be time-consuming and potentially prone to error and inconsistency, because minor mistakes, misinterpretations, and divergent methods for calculating the GMM inputs can impact the resulting analysis. As a result, what should be a relatively routine and standard analysis can quickly become costly, and the results are sometimes difficult to reproduce. Recognizing the need to make exploration of GMMs and comparison of GMMs against ground-motion data an easy, robust, and reproducible process, we present eGSIM (pronounced ee-jee-sim),

1. GFZ Helmholtz Centre for Geosciences, Potsdam, Germany, https://orcid.org/0000-0001-9133-1750 (RZ); https://orcid.org/0000-0001-9347-2282 (GW); https://orcid.org/0000-0002-8619-2220 (DB); https://orcid.org/0000-0002-9242-3996 (FC); 2. Institute of Geosciences, University of Potsdam, Potsdam, Germany

*Corresponding author: riccardo.zaccarelli@gfz.de

an online tool for ground shaking intensity models (GSIM, used synonymously with GMM in this article).

eGSIM (Zaccarelli and Weatherill, 2020) is a Python library and free-to-use web application (hereafter also referred to as web platform or web service) built upon OpenQuake (Pagani *et al.*, 2014), a widely used, open-source software for Probabilistic Seismic Hazard Assessment (PSHA) developed by the Global Earthquake Model (GEM). Using OpenQuake's Hazard Library as a dependency (owing to OpenQuake's ongoing development, eGSIM aims to keep in alignment with recent versions of the software but does not always adopt the latest version after each release owing to the cost of maintaining compatibility), eGSIM makes available to its users hundreds of GMMs, as well as various tools for undertaking calculations of source to site geometry. eGSIM also benefits from OpenQuake's well-established testing and quality assurance process for the implementation of hundreds of GMMs collected from the scientific literature; therefore, ensuring total consistency between the GMMs used for comparison against strong-motion records and those used within the OpenQuake PSHA calculation engine itself.

eGSIM's primary objective is to assist its users, which comprise engineering seismologists, seismic hazard/risk modelers, and many others, with the process of understanding and identifying GMMs for application in seismic hazard analysis, addressing three main questions: how do different GMMs compare against each other (referred here as model-to-model comparison), how do GMMs compare against strong-motion data, for example, recorded for a particular region, or synthetically generated (model-to-data comparison), and how can modelers be assisted in the nontrivial process of converting synthetic or observed strong-motion data and metadata from heterogeneous sources (e.g., webservices, local files) and formats (e.g., XML, miniSEED) into a so-called flatfile, a parametric tabular file of ground-motion data and associated metadata that are widely used in the strong-motion community but lack the necessary standardization to be used seamlessly without guidance.

A second, but no less important, objective of eGSIM is to provide straightforward and seamless interaction with its core scientific library. Sticking closely to the FAIR principles for research software (findable, accessible, interoperable, and reusable; see Barker *et al.*, 2022), eGSIM implements a Python web application, which in turn makes it not only installable as a Python package but also deployable as a web service. Set up and online since 2019, the eGSIM webservice allows users to compute and retrieve data via two distinct and easy-to-use interfaces:

- a graphical user interface (GUI) accessible in the user's browser at Data and Resources, conceived mostly for simple operations such as becoming familiar with eGSIM, computing and downloading results, visualizing interactively, and downloading results plots, uploading user-defined flatfiles, and performing visual inspection of the data before usage.
- an application programming interface (API) accessible from a user's custom code. This is best suited for scientists and developers aiming to retrieve data from eGSIM programmatically, for example, to perform their own further analysis, produce custom plots, as a task within a sequential processing, or even in a script to be routinely run as a scheduled job. The web API is a set of uniform resource locators (URLs), that is, internet addresses that specify where a resource (such as a web page, image, or, in our case, eGSIM computed data) can be found. The benefits of performing web requests to the API in the user's code, compared with installing eGSIM and calling its functions directly, mean that there is no need to use the Python programming language and its environments, no external libraries to download, and no potential installation burden.

In this article, we present the key features of eGSIM and provide some example illustrations of the sorts of workflows that it can facilitate, from the most basic exploration of GMMs to more advanced and customized analysis. The GUI is freely accessible at the website in Data and Resources, whereas the source code of eGSIM is available at Data and Resources under The GNU Affero General Public License, version 3. To illustrate the API usage, a set of Jupyter Notebooks is available from an additional public GitHub repository (see Data and Resources), which are intended to remain always up-to-date with any changes in the API. Notebooks implementing the workflows described in this article are contained within this set. All notebooks and a general API documentation page are also accessible from the GUI. eGSIM is one of the key services that form part of the European Facility for Earthquake Hazard and Risk (see Data and Resources), one of the three pillars of the Seismology Thematic Core Service of the European Plate Observation System (EPOS Seismology) (see Data and Resources).

eGSIM: Features, Usage, and Workflows

eGSIM is designed to address two core types of analysis: comparison of GMMs with one another for various scenario configurations ("Model-to-Model" analysis) and comparison of GMMs against ground-motion data ("Model-to-Data" analysis). Performing eGSIM analysis always requires as input a list of GMM names (from the list of OpenQuake GMM class names available) and intensity measure types (IMTs) such as peak ground acceleration (PGA), peak ground velocity (PGV), spectral acceleration, SA(T) (with T being the spectral acceleration period, in s). In a typical scenario, users want to select models from specific publications, whereby the models can be filtered and selected by author and year from the full list of those available, or by geographic location using the GMMs proposed for use in specific regions. One common case, for example, may be to select GMMs used in existing seismic

TABLE 1
Main Uniform Resource Locators (URLs) of the eGSIM Application Programming Interface (API) (Mid 2025)

Resource	API URL	Returned Data Format
Available GMMs	https://egsim.gfz.de/api/query/models?name=<text>, https://egsim.gfz.de/api/query/models?lat=<number>&lon=<number> (last accessed December 2025)	JSON
Model-to-model comparison	https://egsim.gfz.de/api/query/predictions (last accessed December 2025)	HDF, CSV
Model-to-data comparison	https://egsim.gfz.de/api/query/residuals (last accessed December 2025)	HDF, CSV

The resource providing the available ground-motion models (GMMs) is intended to help users discover the OpenQuake model information that can be given as input for model-to-data and model-to-model comparisons.

hazard models for a region, as described in the corresponding scientific literature (e.g., Woessner *et al.*, 2015; Danciu *et al.*, 2021). At the time of writing, the seismic hazard models used to suggest GMMs for comparison are taken from recent European projects; however, other regionalization from elsewhere in the world may be added in the future because the software has been designed to handle this seamlessly. An exhaustive list of all available GMMs and relative information (name and docstring, the IMTs they are defined for, required ground-motion properties) is available in the eGSIM GUI or via a specific API URL (first row in Table 1) that can be built with a custom <text> for the name parameter (e.g., a GMM publication year or author name) or geographic location (latitude [lat] and longitude [lon] parameters). The URL can be used in custom code or typed directly in the browser address bar to nicely display all information in the browser window (tested with Firefox and Chrome).

Model-to-model comparison

Model-to-model comparison is intended to be primarily an exploratory tool in which users can rapidly configure a scenario (select GMMs and intensity measures for a given rupture and site configuration) and then compute the median ground motions and the standard deviations of the GMMs (for reference, see the National Seismic Hazard Mapping Project GMMs software. More details are available in Data and Resources). The rupture and site configurations offer the user the chance to choose not only the earthquake magnitude(s) and source-to-site distance(s) for the comparisons, but also to provide further information to configure the earthquake rupture (e.g., strike, dip, rake, aspect ratio, and scaling relation) and the site (e.g., 30 s averaged shear-wave velocity over the first 30 m of the crust, V_{S30}, depth to the V_S 1.0 km/s layer, $Z_{1.0}$, etc.). This information is needed because eGSIM will use other functions from OpenQuake's hazard library to generate a corresponding 3D earthquake rupture plane and position the sites at locations with the required distances from the rupture (and/or the hypocenter if one or more of the selected GMMs use point-source distance metrics). The use of a synthetic rupture plane allows for internal consistency between GMMs that use different source-to-site distance metrics, rather than assuming equivalence or empirical conversion between the metrics. This can be especially important if comparing GMMs in the near-source region. The input parameters for the selected GMMs are returned with the results of the comparisons when downloading the data through the GUI or using the programmatic API. This can allow the users to make further comparisons between predictor variables, or to plot results with respect to different predictors, if they wish.

In Figure 1, we illustrate in a few screenshots a typical model-to-model comparison performed through the GUI, which affords the user the possibility to compare GMMs for scenarios easily and without any specific coding knowledge. GMMs can be compared with respect to distance, magnitude, and/or spectral period, all represented in the GUI in the form of interactive (zoom, pan) and customizable (appearance and visibility) trellis plots that can be downloaded in several common image formats suitable for online or journal publication (PNG, PDF, and SVG). This can be useful in a variety of contexts, including teaching students about the fundamentals of GMMs in seismic hazard and risk analysis, all the way through to selection and comparison of GMMs for application in PSHA projects. Yet although the GUI is intuitive and fast, the types of comparisons available are limited to the most common encountered in practice. More sophisticated analysis is still possible with eGSIM; however, if one exploits the programmatic API. The "Model-to-Model" notebook included within the eGSIM-client library illustrates how to use the API to access, download, and visualize the GMM data in a custom manner. It also provides illustrations of different types of analysis that are possible using a relatively small amount of Python code and commonly used libraries. This includes a demonstration of how to compare the site amplification scaling of a set of models, and how to generate a Sammon's projection similar to those presented in Scherbaum *et al.* (2010) and exploited more heavily in the NGA-East (Next Generation Attenuation Relationships for Central and Eastern North America) (Goulet *et al.*, 2021).

Model-to-data comparison

For model-to-data comparison, ground-motion data, be it observed or even simulated, must also be provided to compare it with the predictions from the selected GMMs. Ground-motion data are commonly stored in a tabular data file (i.e., a flatfile), with records arranged in rows and their fields in

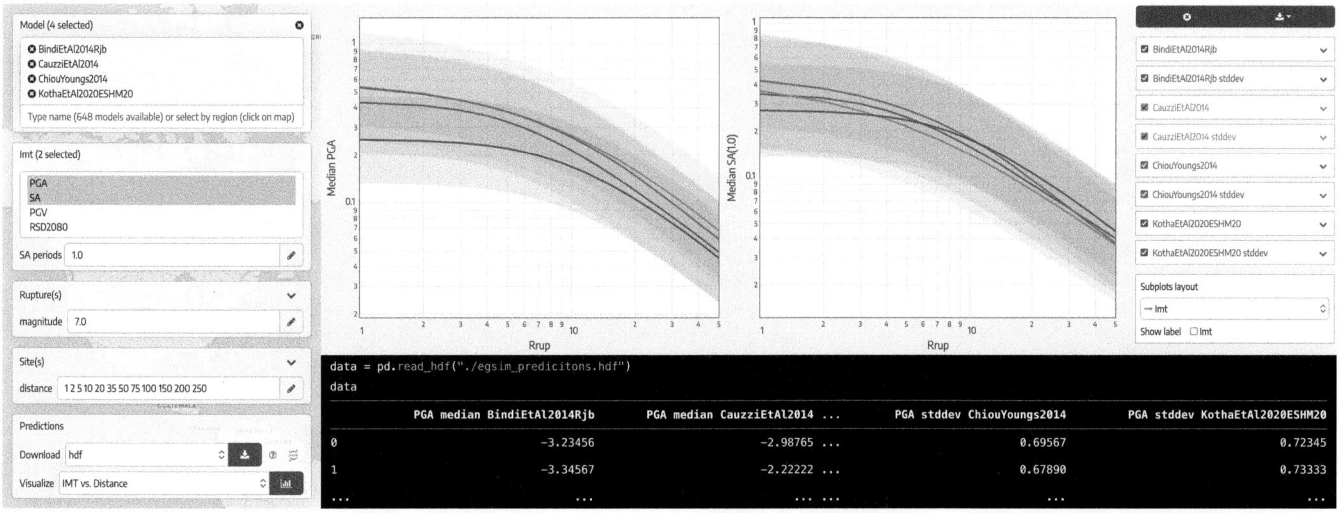

Figure 1. Graphical user interface (GUI) components of the model-to-model comparison in the user browser: the scenario configuration panel (left) and the produced interactive, customizable, and downloadable plots (upper right, in which the shaded areas indicate the standard deviation around the median). Plots data can also be downloaded as a tabular structure (HDF or CSV format) and opened in custom code, for example, as a pandas DataFrame in Python (lower right panel showing a Jupyter notebook snapshot. In custom code, the same data can be retrieved directly via the application programming interface (API), eliminating the need to download and reopen the file. IMT, intensity measure type; PGA, peak ground acceleration; PGV, peak ground velocity; and SA, spectral acceleration. The color version of this figure is available only in the electronic edition.

columns. In eGSIM, each field must include the ground-motions intensity measures and the corresponding metadata (e.g., magnitude, style-of-faulting, rupture properties, source-to-site distances, and site properties), as required by the selected models to compute their predictions. The data for the comparisons can be uploaded either as a user-defined file or selected from one of several hosted directly by the platform (indicated by a simple string of text denoting the chosen flatfile). As of 2025, eGSIM features three predefined flatfiles ("esm2018," "kiknet2024", and "knet2024"), that is, the Engineering Strong-motion flatfile (ESM, Lanzano *et al.*, 2019) along with two separate flatifles for the Japanese KIK-net (Kiban–Kyoshin network) and K-NET (Kyoshin network) databases recently compiled by Loviknes *et al.* (2025). Additional flatfiles may be added in the future because the software has been designed to handle this seamlessly. No check or conversion between horizontal intensity measure components is made (e.g., as recorded geometric mean, RotD50, etc.), so users are required to compile their flatfile(s) using horizontal-component definitions appropriate to the selection of GMMs.

The compilation of a user-defined flatfile is a nontrivial procedure because it requires the processing of observed or synthetic time histories, the collection and harmonization of metadata, and finally export into a table with eGSIM-compatible field names and consistent data types. As such, even the conversion from existing flatfiles can be tricky due to the lack of standardization, that is, different naming abbreviations or incompatible computation procedures, or missing or incomplete fields for critical metadata needed for GMM comparison. To partially facilitate this task, users can get insight through the GUI (see Data and Resources) on how their flatfile should be compiled and which fields should be provided according to their selection of GMMs. Once compiled, users can then upload their flatfile to the platform temporarily for local use (i.e., not for public dissemination) through the API or GUI, and optionally use the latter (see Data and Resources) to conduct exploratory analysis of the composition of the flatfile with respect to the different fields found within (see Figure 2).

In any tool involving a flatfile, whether it's a flatfile visualization or model-to-data analysis, eGSIM offers the possibility to select records to a smaller subset via a query string composed of common comparison and logical operators (>, <, >=, <=, ==, !=, &, |, ~) applied on the flatfile fields (e.g., "(mag > 6) & (rrup <= 100)"). This can be helpful to select only the parts of the data for which the user is interested for their comparisons, without needing to select the flatfiles offline and/or upload different flatfiles for each subset. It can also reduce the time needed for the platform to execute certain analytical operations, and as such, it is recommended for predefined flatfiles, which are usually relatively big in size (careful precautions have been implemented on top of Python libraries checks to prevent the injection of potentially harmful code via query expressions).

Model-to-data analysis, when comparing existing GMMs against observed data, primarily focuses on distributions of residuals such that

$$\ln Y_{ES} = \mu_{ES}(m_E, R_{ES}, \theta_{ES}) + \delta_{ES}, \quad (1)$$

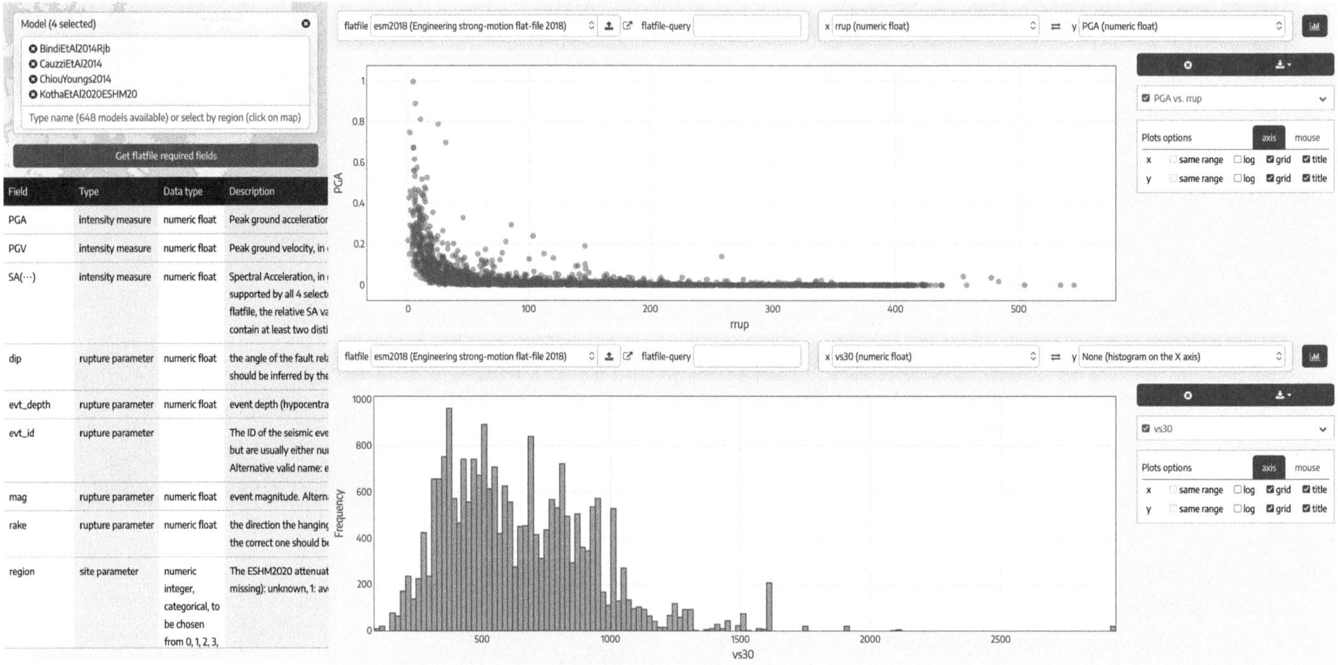

in which Y_{ES} is the ground motion at site S reported for event E, $\mu_{ES}(m_E,R_{ES},S_S,\theta_{ES})$ is the median ground motion predicted by the GMM for an earthquake of magnitude m at a distance R from site S. θ_{ES} is the set of additional source and site parameters required by the GMM and δ_{ES} is the total residual, which is a Gaussian-distributed variable $N = (0,\sigma)$. eGSIM determines this term for the selected GMMs and observations, but goes further to deconstruct this into its random-effects terms: δB_E and δW_{ES}, the between-event and within-event variability respectively:

$$\ln Y_{ES} = \mu_{ES}(m_E,R_{ES},\theta_{ES}) + \delta B_E + \delta W_{ES}. \quad (2)$$

The random-effects residuals are described by Gaussian distributions: $\delta B_E = N(0,\tau)$ and $\delta W_{Es} = N(0,\phi)$.

Determination of the random-effects residuals has been a critical step in the derivation of GMMs for several decades, and indeed, eGSIM determines δB_E using the maximum-likelihood formulation presented by Abrahamson and Youngs (1992). Making these random-effects residuals available and easy to determine provides a more detailed and critical insight into the differences between the model and the data. By default, the random-effects residuals are returned normalized by the between-event and within-event standard deviations of the required GMM. This is helpful to provide a first-order estimate of the overall fit of the models to data based on the differences in mean and variance compared with a standard normal distribution (0, 1). If the user wishes to apply different tools to extract further crossed and/or nested random effects using the widely established linear-mixed-effects regression library *lme4* in R (Bates *et al.*, 2015), or even explore Bayesian analyses using tools such as PyMC (Abril-Pla *et al.*, 2023) or STAN (see

Figure 2. GUI components of the flatfile compilation guidance and visualization tools in the user browser: panel indicating the user-selected choice of ground-motion models (GMMs) (top left), the automatically generated table indicating the required attributes given the GMM selection (bottom left), the flatfile upload and visualization page with two exploratory analysis plots that can be shown with it (right). The color version of this figure is available only in the electronic edition.

Data and Resources), then eGSIM can still be used to extract the non-normalized total residuals (δ_{ES}) and the predictor variables upon which the more complex analyses are based. Programmatic use of the service via the API opens the possibility to use eGSIM for the GMMs and data comparison, and combine it with other tools for more advanced analysis.

Users may also be interested in applying common scoring metrics to rank the relative fit of selected models to the data, including log-likelihood analysis (Scherbaum *et al.*, 2009), Euclidean distance-based ranking (Kale and Akkar, 2014), or simply descriptive statistics of the relative fits to the data. eGSIM can return these aggregation metrics instead of per-record residuals.

As with the model-to-model comparison tools, the GUI allows for rapid implementation of many common exploratory analysis without the need for the user to create their own code or software implementation of the GMMs, offering various interactive and customizable plotting functionalities including histograms of the residuals as well as scatter plots showing trends (using least squares) with respect to different predictor variables found in the flatfile. Users requiring more comprehensive statistical analysis are strongly recommended to download the data in their code or use the API directly. This too

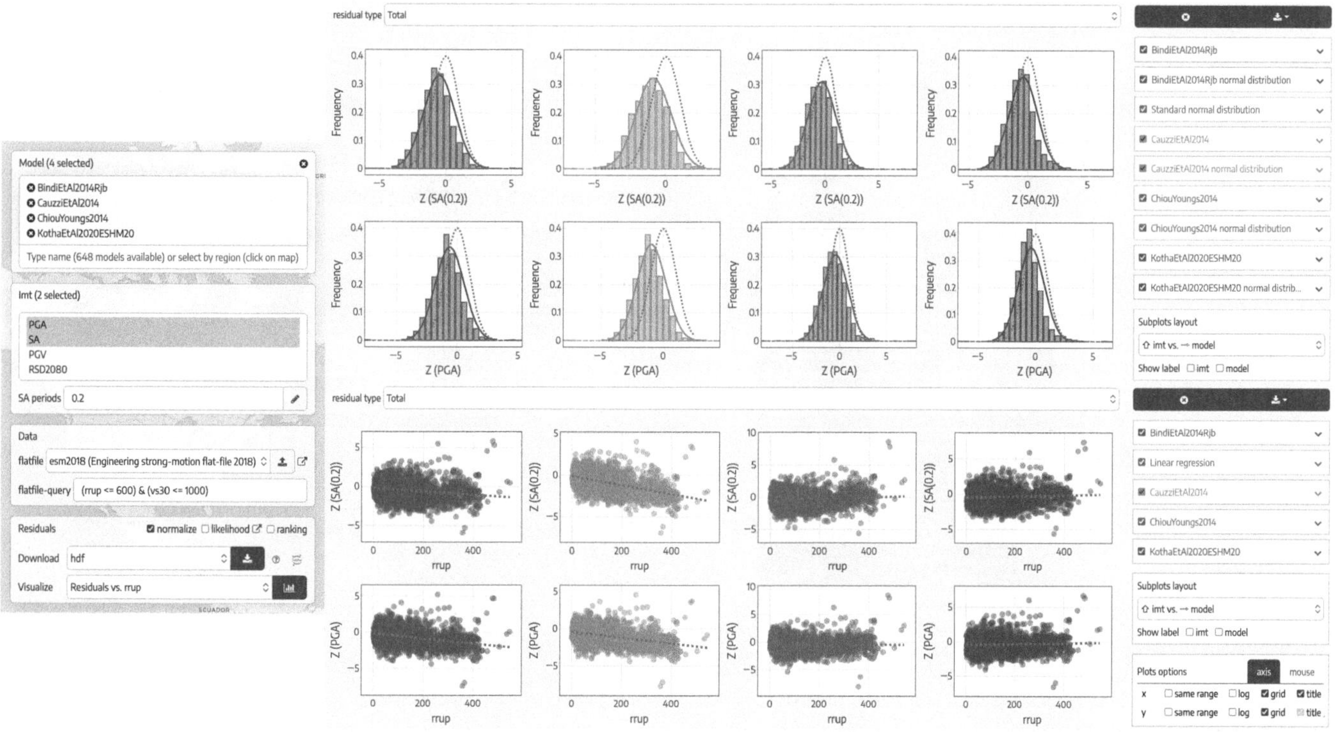

allows for more complex insights into the differences between models and data to be identified and explored in just a matter of minutes (see Fig. 3). With the programmatic API option, however, not only can users retrieve the results of the comparisons to visualize with their own preferred tools, but a wide array of novel use cases also emerges. One such example is the possibility to retrieve the random-effects residuals for databases of ground motions automatically and even rapidly following a large earthquake (provided that the flatfile is created automatically), and this can be integrated alongside other web services for data access and processing.

Figure 3. GUI components of the model-to-data comparison in the user browser: configuration panel with choice of GMM, IMT, flatfile, and analysis type (left), total distribution of the ground-motion residuals (top right), and distribution of the random-effects residuals with respect to the predictor variable (bottom right). As for the model-to-model case (see Fig. 1), all plots are interactive, customizable, and can be downloaded as an image, whereas plot data can also be downloaded as a tabular structure (HDF or CSV format) and opened in custom code (or retrieved directly in custom code via the API, eliminating the need to download and reopen the file). The color version of this figure is available only in the electronic edition.

A final example usage will be illustrated in the next section, and that is how to use eGSIM to compare databases of physics-based simulations against databases of observed ground-motion data. Although eGSIM was initially conceived as a means of exploring the fit of GMMs to observed strong-motion data, it is, in fact, agnostic as to the origin of the data that is an input into it, and consequently, any analysis with eGSIM can also include ground motions taken from broadband velocity records as well as ground motions from simulations. This can make it a useful tool in the process of testing and validating physics-based simulations against observations, either for single events or for large databases comprising multiple events (e.g., Leeet *al.*, 2022). Indeed, Rezaeian *et al.* (2023) outline the key steps needed to validate a simulation platform for use in GMM development or PSHA, many of which relate to assessing trends in the mixed-effects residuals with respect to source, path, and site parameters. These steps can be easily implemented using eGSIM, meaning that eGSIM can be used as part of a general testing platform for simulations. In the next section, we will illustrate this workflow in a simple application of eGSIM in which we compare databases of observed ground motion in Europe against physics-based simulations.

Comparing simulations and observations

To illustrate the type of analysis that eGSIM can perform rapidly, we will use its API to compare the between- and within-event residuals from two data sets: a flatfile of European strong ground motion observations adapted from the ESM flatfile (Lanzano *et al.*, 2019), and a flatfile of ground-motion intensities from a set of physics-based earthquake simulations for predominantly (though not exclusively) European earthquakes (BB-SPEEDset flatfile v.2.3, Paolucci *et al.*, 2021). For more information about the flatfiles, refer to Data and Resources. The physics-based simulations in the BB-SPEEDset are generated using the spectral elements in elastodynamics with the discontinuous Galerkin (SPEED) code for low-frequency deterministic simulation, which is combined with high-

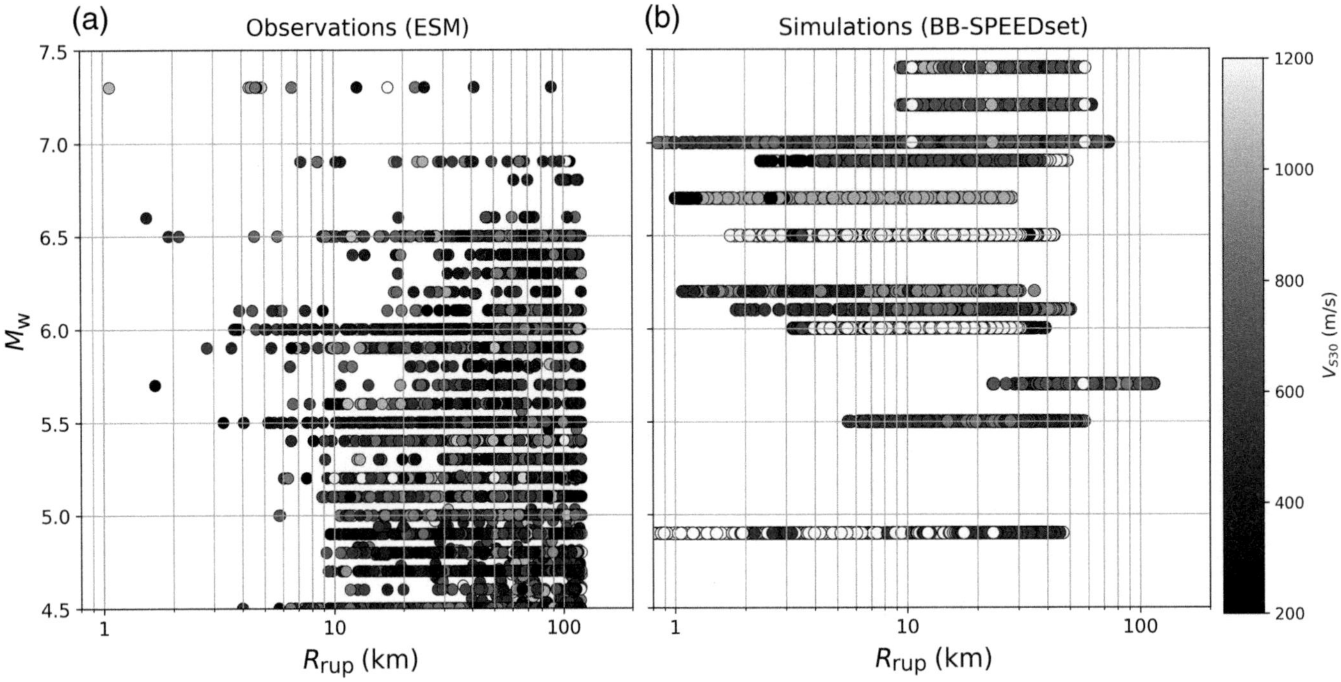

Figure 4. Distribution of the data set of observed ground motions from European strong motion (ESM) (a) and simulated ground motions from BB-SPEEDset (b) with respect to magnitude, distance, and V_{S30}. The color version of this figure is available only in the electronic edition.

frequency ground motion conditioned on the low-frequency motion using an artificial neural network technique (AN2BB) (Paolucci *et al.*, 2018). The receiver locations for most of the earthquakes in the BB-SPEEDset are limited to distances less than 100 km from the rupture. We therefore limit the comparison from both data sets to earthquakes with moment magnitude $M_w > 4.5$, distance to rupture (R_{rup}) ≤ 120 km and with hypocentral depth less than 35 km (query string "(rrup <= 120.0) & (mag > = 4.5) & (evt_-depth <= 35.0)"). The respective compositions of the two data sets are shown in Figure 4. A Jupyter notebook containing the entire workflow shown here can be found in the egsim-client repository (see Data and Resources).

The eGSIM API is used to retrieve the normalized residuals with respect to four GMMs (selected based on their demonstrated applicability to European earthquakes): Bindi *et al.* (2014), Cauzzi *et al.* (2015), Chiou and Youngs (2014), and Kotha *et al.* (2020) adapted for use in the 2020 European seismic hazard model (Weatherill *et al.*, 2020; Danciu *et al.*, 2021). The distribution of between-event residuals, δB_E with respect to magnitude, and within-event residuals δW_{ES} with respect to rupture distance, are shown in Figures 5 and 6, respectively, for four intensity measures (PGV, PGA, and response pseudospectral acceleration at periods of 0.2 and 2.0 s, SA(0.2) and SA(2.0)).

The distribution of δB_E shows that with the exception of the ESHM20 GMM, which is calibrated to much of the observed data set and thus displays no significant trend, for most intensity measures and GMMs, there is a weak positive trend with magnitude, with more positive residuals observed at larger magnitudes. In the simulation data, however, there is a significant positive trend with most of the simulated earthquakes producing positive residual terms across the magnitude range, with significantly higher positive residuals for earthquakes with $M_w \geq 6.5$.

For the within-event residuals, δW_{ES}, the distributions for the observed ground motions appear to show slightly higher values in the very near field for many GMMs (again, except ESHM20, which is generally well centered), whereas for the simulated ground motions δW_{ES} also tends toward moderately positive values in the near field. Only one simulated event considers receiver distances longer than R_{rup} 60 km (a simulation of the 2019 Sea of Marmara earthquake, M_w 5.7), so trends in δW_{ES} for longer distances reflect the particularities of this earthquake.

Despite attempting a fair comparison between the two data sets by limiting the analysis to comparable magnitude and distance ranges, systematic differences are present between the observed and simulated data. BB-SPEEDset contains simulations from 37 events, which comprise a mixture of simulations of past events and of hypothetical scenarios, the latter often representing a single scenario earthquake with several alternative parameterizations. However, within both data sets, there are four common events for which we have both observed and simulated ground motions: 1980 M_w 6.9 Irpinia, 2009 M_w 6.3 L'Aquila, 2012 M_w 6.1 Emilia-Romagna first shock, and 2016 6.4 M_w Central Italy second shock. Three of the four

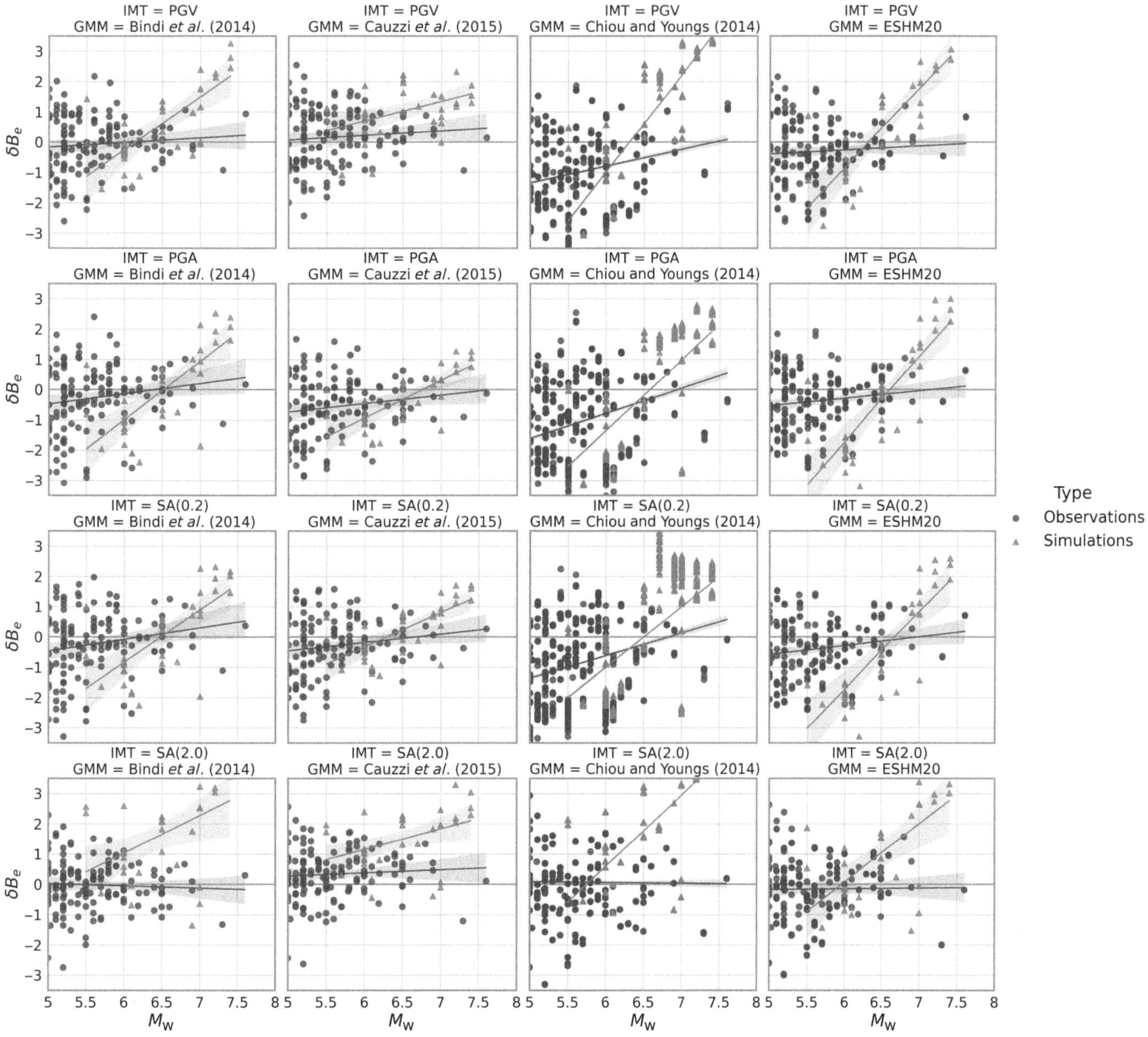

Figure 5. Distribution of between-event residuals δB_E with respect to magnitude for each selected GMM (columns) and ground-motion intensity measure (rows). The color version of this figure is available only in the electronic edition.

earthquakes are normal-faulting events (Irpinia, L'Aquila, and Central Italy), whereas the Emilia-Romagna earthquake occurred on a reverse fault. The distribution of observed recording stations and simulated receiver positions with respect to the rupture plane is shown for each event in Figure 7.

Limiting our analysis to just the Kotha *et al.* (2020) ESHM20 GMM, we first consider the variation in δB_E with period (plus PGA and PGV) for each event (Fig. 8), and then we show the trend in δW_{ES} with distance for each event and intensity measure (Fig. 9). This provides more insight that allows us to understand the differences between observed and simulated GMMs and posit some potential explanations.

For the L'Aquila, Central Italy, and Emilia-Romagna events, the configuration of receivers in the simulations is such that the density is increased above the rupture plane in the up-dip position, whereas for the Irpinia simulation, the receivers are more distributed (see Fig. 7). It is notable then that the between-event residuals for the first three events show a pronounced and sudden upward trend with period for $T \geq 1$ s, in which the simulated ground motions are based on the deterministic simulation rather than the artificial neural network (ANN). This likely reflects strong hanging wall or near-fault effects that are overrepresented in the BB-SPEEDset owing to the high density of receivers in the regions most strongly affected by near-fault amplification. For the Irpinia event, a similar relative trend in δB_E with period is seen in both the observed and simulated motions, albeit the simulated motion is systematically higher. A second influencing factor is the differences in

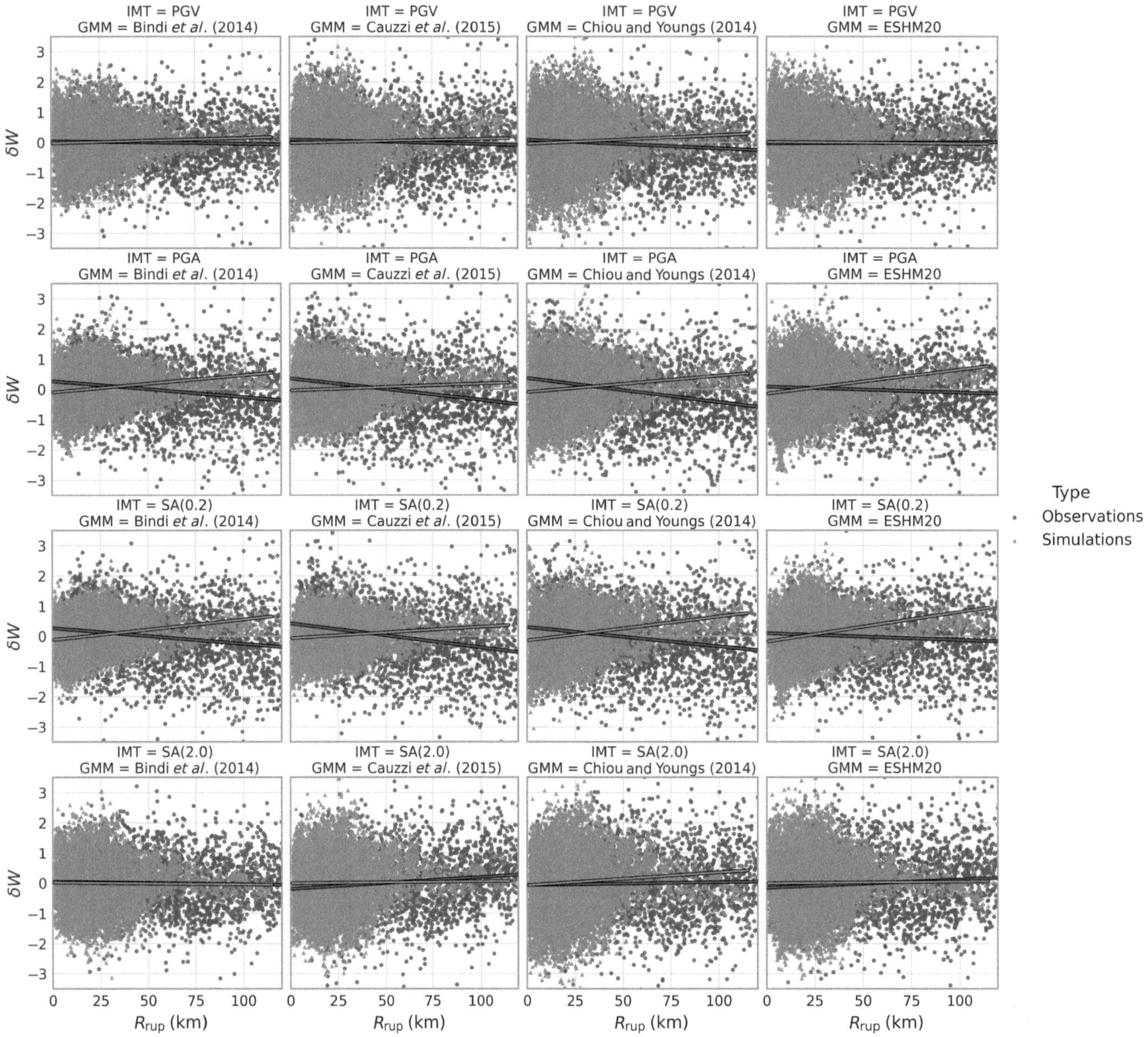

Figure 6. Distribution of within-event residuals δW_{ES} with respect to magnitude for each selected GMM (columns) and ground-motion intensity measure (rows). The color version of this figure is available only in the electronic edition.

assumed site condition for the simulations compared with the range of V_{S30} values seen for the observed records (as shown in Fig. 4). Arguably the closest agreement in δB_E for shorter periods occurs for the Emilia-Romagna earthquake, in which the assumed soil velocity of V_{S30} 300 m/s in the simulations comes into close agreement with the range of observed V_{S30}. For Central Italy and L'Aquila, the simulations tend to assume either a rock or very hard-rock condition with $V_{S30} > 900$ m/s (except for receivers in the basin close to L'Aquila in which $V_{S30} \approx 405$ m/s), whereas the observed stations have a range of values tending toward stiffer soils, this resulting in higher short-period ground motion. The systematic differences between the assumed rock-site conditions of the simulations and the predominantly soil and stiff soil conditions for most of the observation sites introduce a bias toward lower ground motions at higher frequencies in the simulations, which, in the mixed-effects residuals, propagates into the between-event term.

Comparison of δW_{ES} for each event reveals a less clear picture. Strong negative trends in δW_{ES} with distance are present in the simulations for the PGV and SA(2.0) residuals of the Emilia-Romagna and Irpinia events (see Fig. 9). These then appear less pronounced for PGA and SA(0.2) in which the high-frequency part of the simulations from the ANN is more dominant. Such trends are less obvious for the L'Aquila and Central Italy earthquake simulations, which appear generally

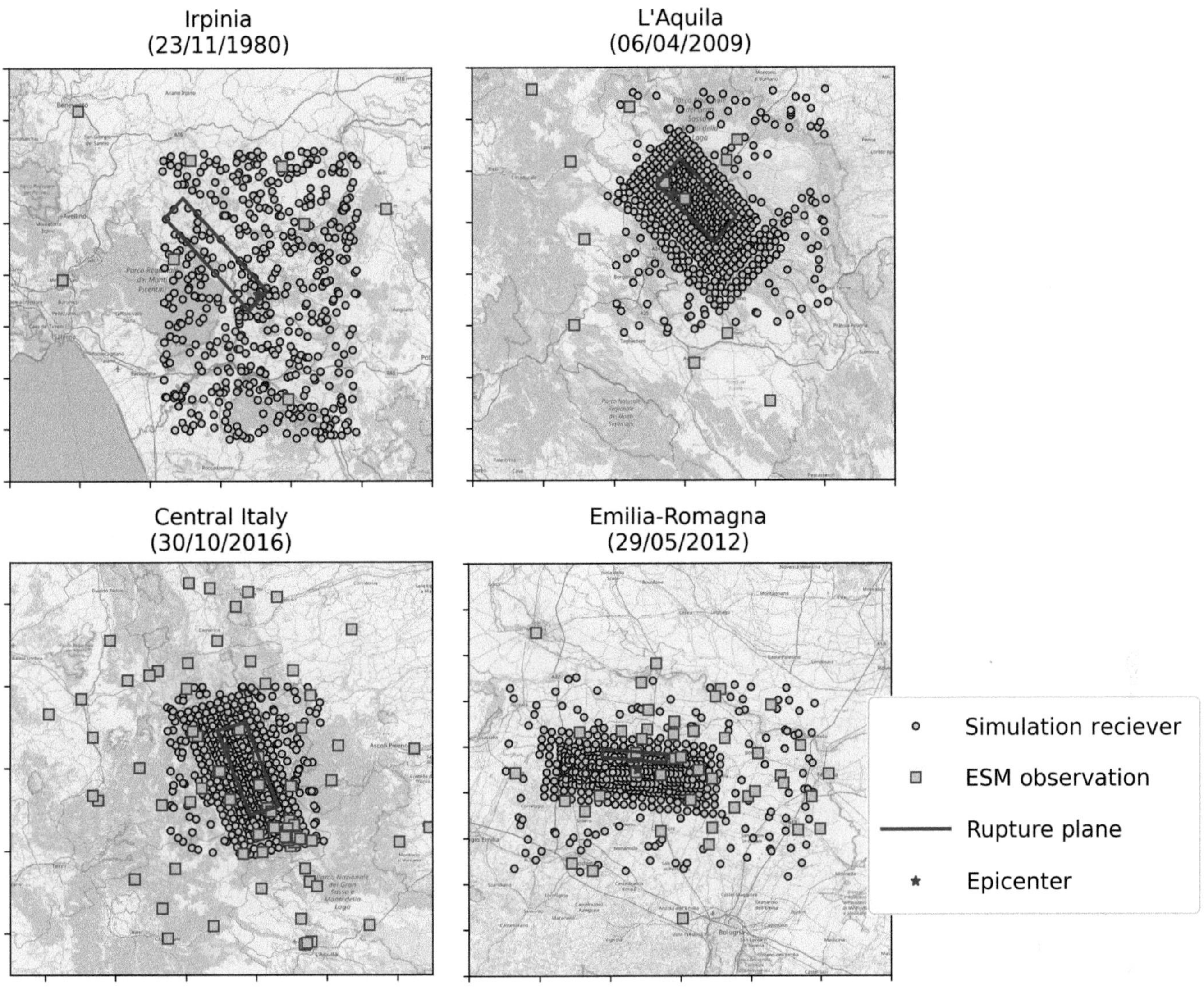

Figure 7. Configurations of the simulation receiver and observed recording stations with respect to the rupture planes of the four selected earthquakes for comparison (surface projections shown as red polygons). The color version of this figure is available only in the electronic edition.

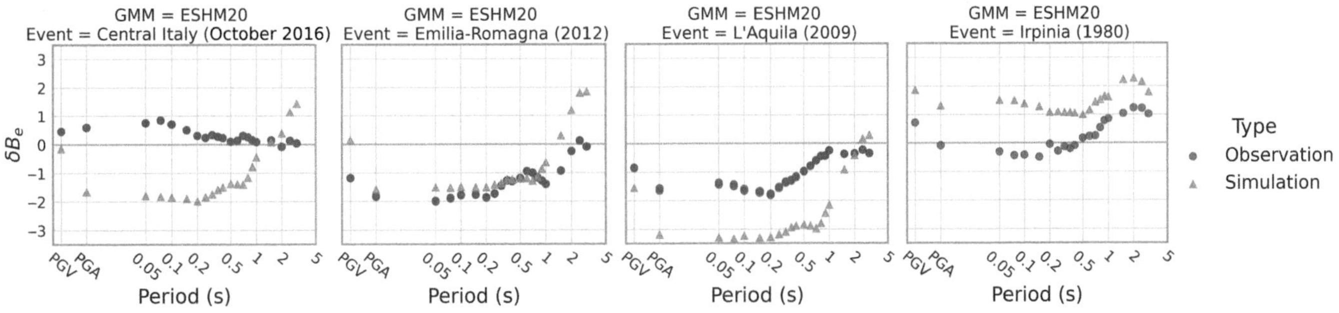

Figure 8. Variation in δB_E with intensity measure/period for each of the four earthquakes, with respect to the Kotha *et al.* (2020) ESHM20 GMM. The color version of this figure is available only in the electronic edition.

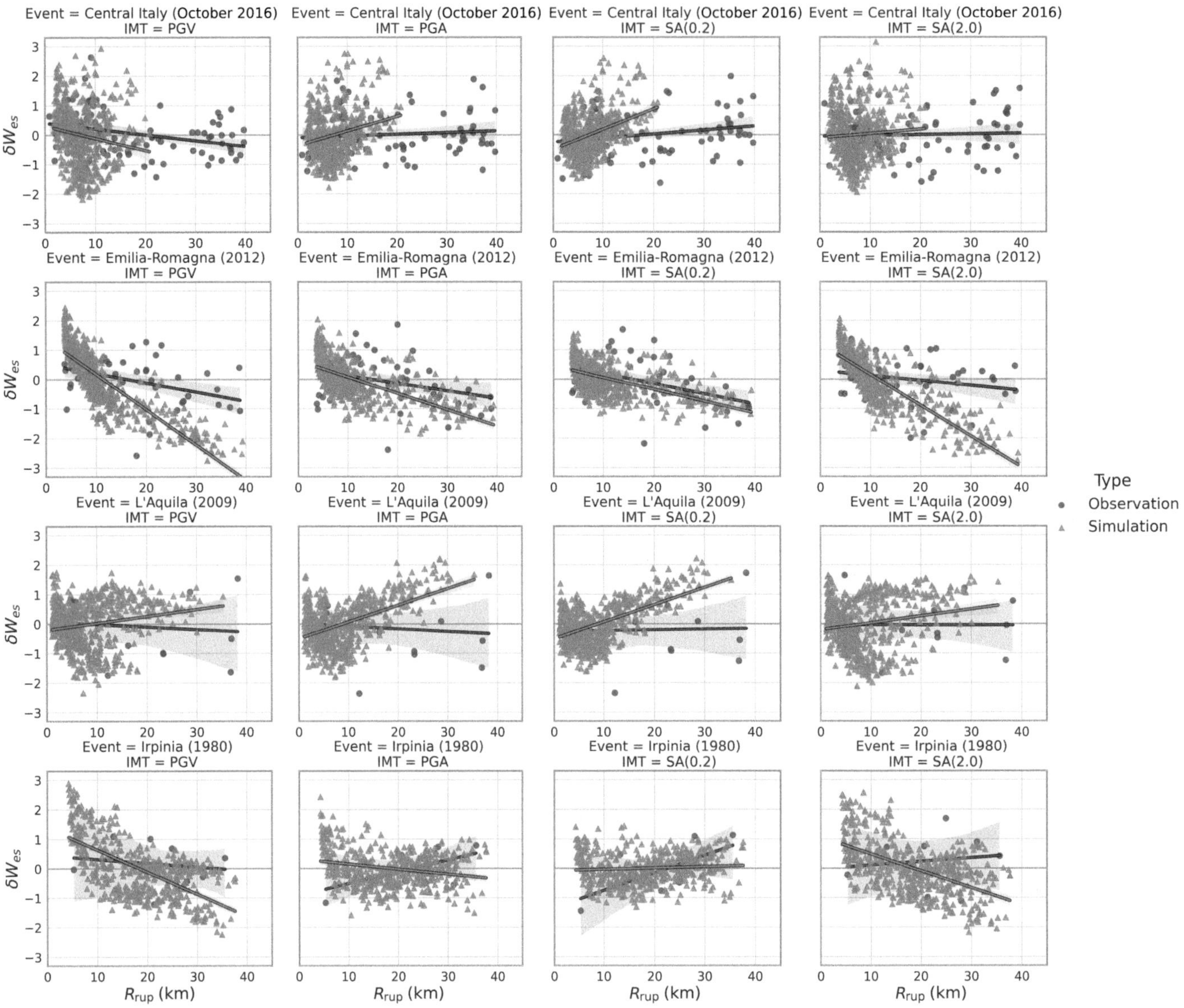

Figure 9. Variation in δW_{ES} with intensity measure (columns) for each of the four earthquakes (rows), with respect to the Kotha *et al.* (2020) ESHM20 GMM. The color version of this figure is available only in the electronic edition.

better centered in the very near-fault region ($R_{\text{rup}} \leq 15$ km), with less pronounced change with distance.

The comparison shown here aims to illustrate the types of analysis to which eGSIM can be easily applied. In this case, we can largely conclude that differences between simulations and observations in terms of the residual trends emerging from the data sets can be predominantly attributed to the receiver configuration. In a testing and validation framework, this could be partly remedied by comparing only the ground motions simulated at the observation sites, whereas the BB-SPEED simulations here were clearly configured to focus on understanding the near-fault phenomena that are ill-represented in the observed ground motions.

Conclusions

In this article, we illustrated with a few examples what the eGSIM platform can do, and how users can integrate it into their own workflows thanks to its dual interfaces (GUI and API). In the API examples, we have shown how, with a few lines of code, analysis of any sort of flatfile, whether it's observed or simulated ground motion, or even a hybrid of the two if required, can be done efficiently, even more so as users become familiar with its customizable features. In the same way, it is possible to perform models' comparison for hypothetical earthquake scenarios, inspect all available models in detail, or—from within the GUI—get insights into the complex operation of flatfile compilation or inspect visually any flatfile before usage. The API performances are on the order of a few seconds for the types of standard residual computations exemplified in this article and in the Jupyter notebooks. These results, though always to be considered with a margin of variability due to external factors (first and foremost, potential internet connection bottlenecks when using web services), show promising potential for the integration of eGSIM in complex high-performance computing workflows.

With eGSIM we aim to provide long-term sustainable software that can be scalable and cope with new emerging use case scenarios. Over the last decade, the rapid increase in the number of available seismological data, typically through webservices and standard protocols (e.g., the The International Federation of Digital Seismograph Networks) fostered the adoption of new algorithms capable of understanding patterns and relationships in big data (machine and deep learning) and new technologies such as remote cloud storage, data lakes, digital twin technology. Software code has evolved from being deployable mainly locally on the developer computer (typically, through simple Notebooks or scripts) to quickly produce material for scientific publications, to community-driven, continuously integrated, and tested software that can also be safely deployed in many operating systems and environments, and even interoperate with external software tools and data formats to form a complex chain of operations. For instance, routine data center jobs or, more recently, high-performance computing workflows, require a much higher level of effort and maintenance. In this framework, eGSIM satisfies a wide range of use cases. When tasks are executed in parallel, in which CPU usage can become a bottleneck, the eGSIM web API enables remote execution, thereby reducing local memory consumption. Conversely, in sequential workflows (typically in high-performance computing), in which execution time can be the critical bottleneck, eGSIM can be installed and used as a Python package. This approach bypasses the web API and, while requiring a steeper learning curve to directly call core functions, allows local execution on the CPU with greater control over optimization. In any case, eGSIM assures that its input and output data are well documented and as much as possible standardized to facilitate the integration into any user workflows.

Our vision is to use eGSIM as a cornerstone component of a testing and validation framework to automatically retrieve ground-motion data to test and validate numerical simulations. The challenges in building this sort of ecosystem are several: plugging together different pieces of software, integrating different, nonstandardized data formats into our input/output chain, dealing with potential lack of metadata, which is required because the data itself in GMM comparisons and tuning potential performance bottlenecks. However, we have shown how eGSIM already addresses many of these issues and has been implemented to flexibly accommodate many others to come, being applicable to IT developers, scientific researchers, and practitioners spanning a wide level of expertise.

Data and Resources

eGSIM (version 3.0) is implemented in Python (https://www.python.org) using the following libraries: OpenQuake (https://www.globalquakemodel.org/product/openquake-engine), Pandas (https://pandas.pydata.org), PyTables (https://www.pytables.org/), and, for its web-related functionalities (web application programming interface [API] and web application backend), the libraries Django (https://www.djangoproject.com) and Plotly (https://plotly.com/python/). The web graphical user interface (GUI) (web application frontend) has been implemented using HTML, CSS, the CSS library Bootstrap (https://getbootstrap.com/docs/5.0/getting-started/introduction/), JavaScript, the JavaScript framework VueJs (https://vuejs.org), and the JavaScript libraries Plotly (https://plotly.com/javascript/) for plot display and Leaflet (https://leafletjs.com/) for maps display. eGSIM source code is hosted on GitHub (https://github.com) at the address https://github.com/rizac/eGSIM, as well as the repository eGSIM-client (https://github.com/rizac/egsim-client) containing several Jupyter notebooks (https://jupyter.org/) that exemplify the eGSIM API usage in Python. All notebooks' examples require the Python library Requests (https://requests.readthedocs.io/en/latest/) to seamlessly send HTTP requests in Python. The eGSIM webservice is hosted on a Linux-based server of the Helmholtz Centre for Geosciences, GFZ (https://www.gfz.de/), and has been deployed using Nginx (https://nginx.org/) as the primary HTTP server and Gunicorn (https://gunicorn.org/) as the Python WSGI application server. In this article, the authors used the BB-SPEEDset flatfile (https://speed.mox.polimi.it/bb-speedset/) and the European Strong-Motion (ESM) 2018 flatfile (https://esm-db.eu/#/products/flat_file). The authors also mentioned the National Seismic Hazard Mapping Project (NSHMP) ground-motion models software (https://earthquake.usgs.gov/ws/nshmp/gmm), the Stan package (https://github.com/stan-dev/stan), and the International Federation of Digital Seismograph Networks (https://www.fdsn.org/about/). A graphical user interface (GUI) accessible in the user's browser at https://egsim.gfz.de. All the websites were last accessed in June 2025.

Declaration of Competing Interests

The authors acknowledge that there are no conflicts of interest recorded.

Acknowledgments

The development of eGSIM has been made possible with support and funding from the European Facility for Earthquake Hazard and Risk (EFEHR), a pillar of the Seismology Thematic Core Service European Plate Observation System (EPOS), and the Horizon Europe project DT Geo "A Digital Twin for Geophysical Extremes" (Grant Number 101058129). The authors thank both the EFEHR Executive Committee and its broader community for their continued support, engagement with, and promotion of eGSIM. OpenQuake is provided by the Global Earthquake Model. The authors would like to thank Chiara Smerzi and Roberto Paolucci for making the BB-SPEED simulations available, and two anonymous reviewers for their constructive comments and valuable suggestions.

References

Abrahamson, N. A., and R. R. Youngs (1992). A stable algorithm for regression analysis using the random effects model, *Bull. Seismol. Soc. Am.* **82,** no. 1, 505–510.

Abril-Pla, O., V. Andreani, C. Carroll, L. Dong, C. J. Fonnesbeck, M. Kochurov, R. Kumar, J. Lao, C. C. Luhmann, O. A. Martin, *et al.* (2023). PyMC: A modern and comprehensive probabilistic programming framework in Python, *PeerJ Comput. Sci.* **9,** no. e1516, doi: 10.7717/peerj-cs.1516.

Barker, M., N. P. Chue Hong, D. S. Katz, A.-L. Lamprecht, C. Martinez Ortiz, F. Psomopoulos, J. Harrow, L. J. Castro, M. Gruenpeter, P. A. Martinez, *et al.* (2022). Introducing the FAIR principles for research software, *Sci. Data* **9,** no. 1, 622.

Bates, D., M. Mächler, B. Bolker, and S. Walker (2015). Fitting linear mixed-effects models using lme4, *J. Stat. Software* **67,** no. 1, 1–48, doi: 10.18637/jss.v067.i01.

Bindi, D., M. Massa, L. Luzi, G. Ameri, F. Pacor, R. Puglia, and P. Augliera (2014). Pan-European ground-motion prediction equations for the average horizontal component of PGA, PGV, and 5%-damped PSA at spectral periods up to 3.0 s using the RESORCE dataset, *Bull. Earthq. Eng.* **12,** no. 1, 391–430, doi: 10.1007/s10518-013-9525-5.

Bommer, J. J., J. Douglas, F. Scherbaum, F. Cotton, H. Bungum, and D. Fäh (2010). On the selection of ground-motion prediction equations for seismic hazard analysis, *Seismol. Res. Lett.* **81,** no. 5, 783–793, doi: 10.1785/gssrl.81.5.7831.

Cauzzi, C., E. Faccioli, M. Vanini, and A. Bianchini (2015). Updated predictive equations for broadband (0.01–10 s) horizontal response spectra and peak ground motions, based on a global dataset of digital acceleration records, *Bull. Earthq. Eng.* **13,** no. 6, 1587–1612, doi: 10.1007/s10518-014-9685-y.

Chiou, B. S.-J., and R. R. Youngs (2014). Update of the Chiou and Youngs NGA model for the average horizontal component of peak ground motion and response spectra, *Earthq. Spectra* **30,** no. 3, 1117–1153.

Cotton, F., F. Scherbaum, J. J. Bommer, and H. Bungum (2006). Criteria for selecting and adjusting ground-motion models for specific target regions: Application to Central Europe and rock sites, *J. Seismol.* **10,** no. 2, 137–156, doi: 10.1007/s10950-005-9006-7.

Danciu, L., S. Nandan, C. Reyes, R. Basili, G. Weatherill, C. Beauval, A. Rovida, S. Vilanova, K. Sesetyan, P. Y. Bard, *et al.* (2021). The 2020 update of the European Seismic Hazard Models—ESHM20: Model overview, *EFEHR Technical Rept. 001 v1.0.0*, doi: 10.12686/a15.

Goulet, C. A., Y. Bozorgnia, N. Kuehn, L. Al Atik, R. R. Youngs, R. W. Graves, and G. M. Atkinson (2021). NGA-East ground-motion characterization model part I: Summary of products and model development, *Earthq. Spectra* **37,** no. 1_suppl, 1231–1282, doi: 10.1177/87552930211018723.

Kale, Ö., and S. Akkar (2014). A new procedure for selecting and ranking ground-motion prediction equations (GMPEs): The Euclidean distance-based ranking (EDR) method, *Bull. Seismol. Soc. Am.* **103,** no. 2A, 1069–1084, doi: 10.1785/0120120134.

Kotha, S. R., G. Weatherill, D. Bindi, and F. Cotton (2020). A regionally-adaptable ground-motion model for shallow crustal earthquakes in Europe, *Bull. Earthq. Eng.* **18,** no. 9, 4091–4125, doi: 10.1007/s10518-020-00869-1.

Lanzano, G., S. Sgobba, L. Luzi, R. Puglia, F. Pacor, C. Felicetta, M. D'Amico, F. Cotton, and D. Bindi (2019). The pan-European Engineering Strong Motion (ESM) flatfile: Compilation criteria and data statistics, *Bull. Earthq. Eng.* **17,** no. 2, 561–582, doi: 10.1007/s10518-018-0480-z.

Lee, R. L., B. A. Bradley, P. J. Stafford, R. W. Graves, and A. Rodriguez-Marek (2022). Hybrid broadband ground-motion simulation validation of small magnitude active shallow crustal earthquakes in New Zealand, *Earthq. Spectra* **38,** no. 4, 2548–2579, doi: 10.1177/87552930221109297.

Loviknes, K., S. von Specht, H. Lilienkamp, A. Händel, and F. Cotton (2025). KiK-NET and K-NET flatfile with automatically processed ground motions, *GFZ Data Services*, doi: 10.5880/GFZ.LKUT.2025.001.

Pagani, M., D. Monelli, G. Weatherill, L. Danciu, H. Crowley, V. Silva, P. Henshaw, L. Butler, M. Nastasi, L. Panzeri, *et al.* (2014). OpenQuake engine: An open hazard (and risk) software for the global earthquake model, *Seismol. Res. Lett.* **85,** no. 3, 692–702, doi: 10.1785/0220130087.

Paolucci, R., F. Gatti, M. Infantino, C. Smerzini, A. G. Özcebe, and M. Stupazzini (2018). Broadband ground motions from 3D physics-based numerical simulations using artificial neural networks, *Bull. Seismol. Soc. Am.* **108,** no. 3A, 1272–1286.

Paolucci, R., C. Smerzini, and M. Vanini (2021). BB-SPEEDset: A validated dataset of broadband near-source earthquake ground motions from 3D physics-based numerical simulations, *Bull. Seismol. Soc. Am.* **111,** no. 5, 2527–2545, doi: 10.1785/0120210089.

Rezaeian, S., J. P. Stewart, N. Luco, and C. A. Goulet (2023). Findings from a decade of ground motion simulation validation research and a path forward, *Earthq. Spectra* **40,** no. 1, 346–378, doi: 10.1177/87552930231212475.

Scherbaum, F., E. Delavaud, and C. Riggelsen (2009). Model selection in seismic hazard analysis: An information-theoretic perspective, *Bull. Seismol. Soc. Am.* **99,** no. 6, 3234–3247, doi: 10.1785/0120080347.

Scherbaum, F., N. M. Kuehn, M. Ohrnberger, and A. Koehler (2010). Exploring the proximity of ground-motion models using high-dimensional visualization techniques, *Earthq. Spectra* **26,** no. 4, 1117–1138, doi: 10.1193/1.3478697.

Weatherill, G., S. R. Kotha, and F. Cotton (2020). A regionally-adaptable "scaled backbone" ground motion logic tree for shallow seismicity in Europe: Application to the 2020 European seismic hazard model, *Bull. Earthq. Eng.* **18,** no. 11, 5087–5117, doi: 10.1007/s10518-020-00899-9.

Woessner, J., D. Laurentiu, D. Giardini, H. Crowley, F. Cotton, G. Grünthal, G. Valensise, R. Arvidsson, R. Basili, M. B. Demircioglu, *et al.* (2015). The 2013 European seismic hazard model: Key components and results, *Bull. Earthq. Eng.* **13,** no. 12, 3553–3596, doi: 10.1007/s10518-015-9795-1.

Zaccarelli, R., and G. Weatherill (2020). eGSIM—A python library and web application to select and test ground motion models, *GFZ Data Services*, doi: 10.5880/GFZ.2.6.2023.007.

Manuscript received 8 July 2025
Published online 26 January 2026

Present to Past Reflection? Notes on the 1114/5 C.E. Earthquake Sequence After the February 2023 Türkiye Doublet

Motti Zohar*[1] and Jefferson Williams[1]

Abstract

This study examines the seismic sequence of 1114/5 C.E. which occurred in southern Türkiye through the lens of the well-documented February 2023 Türkiye doublet. By drawing parallels between the two, the analysis compares the spatial distribution of damage, temporal clustering, and tectonic context to better constrain the poorly understood twelfth-century scenario. A systematic re-evaluation of the historical sources was conducted with attention to their inherent uncertainties. Using kernel density estimation (KDE) on interpreted intensity data points, we identified two persistent hotspots of destruction near Kahramanmaraş–Elbistan and near Antakya in both the 1114/5 and 2023 sequences, suggesting a recurring pattern of seismic energy release along distinct fault segments. The examination of the spread and severity of the damage indicated that at least one of the 1114/5 earthquakes likely exceeded magnitude 7, comparable to the 2023 doublet. Paleoseismological evidence further supports a dual-fault rupture scenario in 1114/5, analogous to stress-triggered ruptures observed in 2023. This reverse-historic approach using recent seismicity to constrain pre-instrumental earthquakes provides a useful pathway for reconstructing ancient seismic sequences and underscores the capability of the East Anatolian fault zone to generate large earthquakes.

Cite this article as Zohar, M., and J. Williams (2025). Present to Past Reflection? Notes on the 1114/5 C.E. Earthquake Sequence After the February 2023 Türkiye Doublet, *Seismol. Res. Lett.* **97**, 2167–2178, doi: 10.1785/0220250252.

Supplemental Material

Introduction

Earthquakes may occur as a single abrupt event or a sequence of occurrences, occasionally followed by a noticeable strain (Gomez *et al.*, 2007). When a sequence of successive earthquakes occurs, the strongest event—the mainshock—may be preceded by mild foreshocks and/or followed by weaker aftershocks. A sequence lacking one clearly dominant earthquake is referred to as a swarm, whereas a succession of several mainshock–aftershock sequences is referred to as a seismic storm (Kisslinger, 1996; Utsu, 2002). Doublets are pairs of successive strong earthquakes that occur due to a power-law recurrence mechanism (Kagan and Jackson, 1999). In such cases, one earthquake can trigger a second large event at distances of several kilometers, potentially involving different tectonic segments (Nissen *et al.*, 2016; Ye *et al.*, 2016). It does not mean, however, that two successive earthquakes with similar magnitudes are necessarily a doublet scenario; they can also reflect foreshock–main or main–aftershock scenarios because there is no upper limit for an aftershock size, although generally the size of the largest aftershock is close to one magnitude degree smaller than the mainshock (e.g., Chen and Wang, 2012).

The period during which earthquakes have been quantitatively monitored is less than 150 yr since the deployment of the first seismographs (Dewey and Byerly, 1969). Because seismic cycles may exceed this instrumental timeframe, pre-instrumental earthquakes provide critical insight for examining long-term regional seismicity (e.g., Guidoboni and Ferrari, 1989; Toppozada *et al.*, 2002; Grünthal *et al.*, 2009; Sharman *et al.*, 2013; Rockwell, 2016; Zohar, 2020). However, the characterization of pre-instrumental earthquakes is occasionally constrained by limited source material (Stucchi *et al.*, 2004; Woessner and Wiemer, 2005), requiring scrutiny and critical evaluation (e.g., Karcz, 2004; Ambraseys, 2005). Given the relatively short instrumental period, historical earthquake accounts are frequently used to infer patterns of present and future seismic activity. The rationale behind this is that seismic activity appears to be cyclic. Thus, earthquake patterns tend to repeat themselves in terms of location, size, the spread

1. School of Environmental Sciences, University of Haifa, Haifa, Israel, https://orcid.org/0000-0002-6567-7296 (MZ); https://orcid.org/0000-0002-2737-2635 (JW)

*Corresponding author: motti.zohar@univ.haifa.ac.il

of the damage, and triggered environmental effects (e.g., McGuire, 2008; Uchida and Bürgmann, 2019). The goal of this article, however, is to work the other way around. That is, instead of examining past scenarios to reflect upon future activity, we constrain a historical earthquake(s) scenario using present-day, well-recorded seismic activity. As a test case, two earthquake sequences were selected: the February 2023 Türkiye doublet (Chen *et al.*, 2023; Petersen *et al.*, 2023) and the 1114/5 C.E. sequence, which is believed to have occurred in the same geographic region as the 2023 doublet (Meghraoui *et al.*, 2025) as well as be its predecessor (Stucchi *et al.*, 2024). Like other historical earthquake scenarios, the interpretation of the 1114/5 C.E. sequence includes several unresolved enigmas to be addressed. First are the apparent discrepancies among historical sources, leading to significant interpretation disagreements between modern twenty-first-century catalogs (e.g., Guidoboni and Comastri, 2005; Sbeinati *et al.*, 2005; Ambraseys, 2009). Second is the chronology of the earthquake sequence, specifically, whether it is composed of two or three large events. Third is the uncertainty regarding the extent and severity of the reported damage, making it difficult to attribute individual damage reports to specific events within the sequence. Finally, the source parameters, such as the epicenters and magnitude estimates, remain elusive (Nalbant *et al.*, 2002).

Following the 2023 Türkiye sequence, our research question is whether and to what degree its characteristics resemble those of the twelfth-century C.E. historical sequence. The underlying hypothesis is that, if a meaningful similarity can be established, the 2023 sequence may be used to help constrain and better characterize the 1114/5 sequence, thereby providing new insights into the historical earthquakes.

2023 Türkiye Sequence

On 6 February 2023, at 01:17:32 (UTC), a devastating earthquake (namely the Pazarcık event, M_w 7.8) hit south-central Türkiye. The earthquake with an epicenter at 37.288° N, 37.043° E and a focal depth of 8.6 km (Disaster and Emergency Management Authority [AFAD], see Data and Resources), occurred on the Pazarcık fault along the East Anatolian fault zone (EAFZ, see Arpat and Şaroğlu, 1972), about 32 km west of Gaziantep. Hancilar *et al.* (2023) suggested a strike-slip movement with a length of 290 km, whereas Zabci *et al.* (2023) and Karabulut *et al.* (2023) suggested a northeast–southwest rupture length of 350 km with coseismic slip of up to 8 m on the Pazarcık fault. Over the next eight hours, the main event was followed by several dozen additional earthquakes (M > 4), including a magnitude M_w 6.7 earthquake at 01:28:16, which struck less than 15 km from the epicenter. Then, at 10:24:47 (UTC), another destructive earthquake (namely the Elbistan event, M_w 7.5) with an epicenter at 38.089° N, 37.239° E and focal depth of 7 km (AFAD, see Data and Resources) occurred on the Cardak fault along the Sürgü–Misis fault zone (SMFZ, see Kaymakci *et al.*, 2010), some 20 km south of Elbistan. Cetin *et al.* (2023) suggested a 160 km rupture length with observed surface displacements ranging from 2 to 8 m, whereas Meghraoui *et al.* (2025) suggested east–west trending of 150 km with coseismic slip of 4.1 m on the Kirikhan segment. On 20 February 2023, another strong event occurred (M_w 6.4) with an epicenter along a southern splay of the Amanos fault, close to the Türkiye–Syria border near the city of Antakya (Hatay) (Karabulut *et al.*, 2023) (Fig. 1a). The two largest events (M 7.8 and 7.5) caused widespread alarm in southern Türkiye and northern Syria (see intensities and isoseismal maps in Fig. 1b,c), resulting in massive damage with fatalities and injuries exceeding 50,000 and 100,000, respectively (Dal Zilio and Ampuero, 2023). Nearly 20,000 buildings collapsed, and more than 350,000 were reported to be damaged. The cities that were damaged most are Kahramanmaras, Adiyaman, Hatay, Osmaniye, Gaziantep, Malatya, Adana, Diyarbakir, Elazig, and Kilis (Ozkula *et al.*, 2023).

The two mainshocks were classified as a doublet occurrence for initiating on two separate faults, with the first M 7.8 earthquake triggering the second M 7.5 earthquake (Jia *et al.*, 2023; Melgar *et al.*, 2023; Toda *et al.*, 2023; Toda and Stein, 2024). The depth of the aftershocks varies from a few kilometers up to more than 40 km, but the majority (more than 90%) are less than 15 km. The aftershocks associated with the two strands continued to occur frequently during the following months. Figure 2 presents the temporal distribution of earthquakes (M ≥ 3.5) for more than two years after the mainshocks occurred and during the first three months (between 6 February 2023 and 5 May 2023). It demonstrates continuous activity of aftershocks along the SMFZ (the events elongated horizontally approximately at latitude 38° N) and EAFZ (between latitudes ~36° to 37° N) rupture zones, reinforcing a bifurcated seismicity on the two different strands. The number of aftershocks decays in time in accordance with the power law of Gutenberg and Richter (1944), suggesting the existence of secondary aftershock activity (Raykova *et al.*, 2024), which supports the suggestion of the two mainshocks forming a doublet.

1114/5 C.E. Sequence

Revisiting the historical sources

In 1114 C.E., or possibly in both 1114 and 1115 C.E., two to three major earthquakes hit southern Türkiye, followed by a few months of aftershocks. The first earthquake occurred on 10 August 1114. Fulcher of Chartres (1058–1127 C.E.), living in Jerusalem at the time and considered a reliable source (Krey, 2012, p. 30), briefly mentioned it: "Later, on the Feast of St. Lawrence, there was an earthquake" (Chartres, 1969, p. 210). A more embellished version appears in the *Estoire de Jerusalem et d'Antioche*, a vernacular Old French chronicle that draws heavily from Fulcher along with other sources. It echoes Fulcher's timeline, stating that "[...] at the Feast of Saint Lawrence, an earthquake affected us," but then dramatically

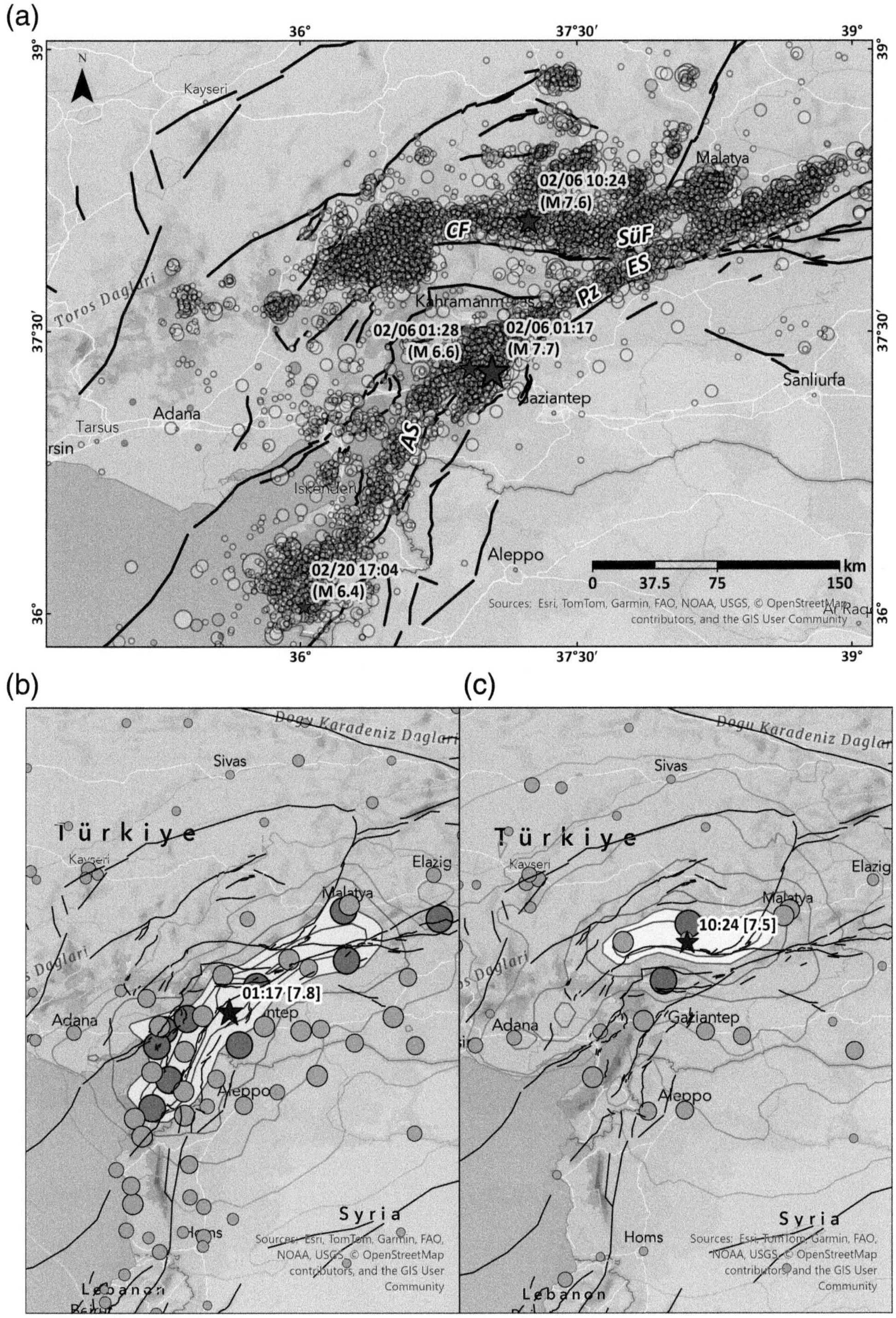

Figure 1. (a) The earthquakes (M ≥ 3) in Türkiye between 6 February 2023 and 10 June 2025. The four large earthquakes (M > 6) are noted in red stars along with the magnitude. Also portrayed are the East Anatolian fault zone (EAFZ, Arpat and Şaroğlu, 1972) segments of Amanos fault (AS); Erkenek (ES); Pazarcık (Pz); Pütürge (PS), and the Sürgü-Misis fault zone (SMFZ, Kaymakci *et al.*, 2010) segments of Çardak (CF); Göksun bend (Gb); Savrun (SaS); and Sürgü (SüF) (Emre *et al.*, 2018). Source of the events: Disaster and Emergency Management Authority (AFAD) (see Data and Resources). (b) Intensity data points (IDPs) and isoseismals for the M 7.8 Pazarcık earthquake (for source website, see Data and Resources). (c) IDPs and isoseismals for the M 7.5 Elbistan earthquake (for source website, see Data and Resources). The area delineated by isoseismals ≥7 is shown in yellow for both (b) and (c). The color version of this figure is available only in the electronic edition.

expands the account: "all the coastal cities and castles collapsed, and the people died" (Estoire-Jerus, 1895, p. 645). The chronicle continues with descriptions of destruction in Maras and Trihalet, although these are details that likely conflate Fulcher's later reference to a "greater quake," which presumably refers to an earthquake that struck on 29 November 1114. Ambraseys (2009, p. 282) accepts this broader narrative cautiously, suggesting that while the extent of coastal destruction is probably exaggerated, the 10 August shock was "probably felt in Antioch," with a possible offshore epicenter in the Bay of Iskenderun. He attributes supporting evidence to Fulcher, Walter the Chancellor, Robert of Torigni (Robert of Torigni, 1889), and the *Estoire*. On closer inspection, the passage that Ambraseys attributes to Fulcher actually originates from the *Secunda pars historiae Iherosolimitane*, an anonymous and loosely structured continuation of Fulcher's chronicle, which is sometimes attributed to Lisiard of Tours. Though it includes material beyond Fulcher's endpoint, Guidoboni and Comastri (2005, p. 70) describe it as "a kind of epitome" of his original work, blending summary, repetition, and additions. Additional description appears in *Secunda pars* stating: "In April or in May and the following [months?], a horrible earthquake struck. Some parts of the city of Mamistria were overturned, and many towns in the region of Antioch were affected —some partially destroyed, others completely—along with loss of life." This version

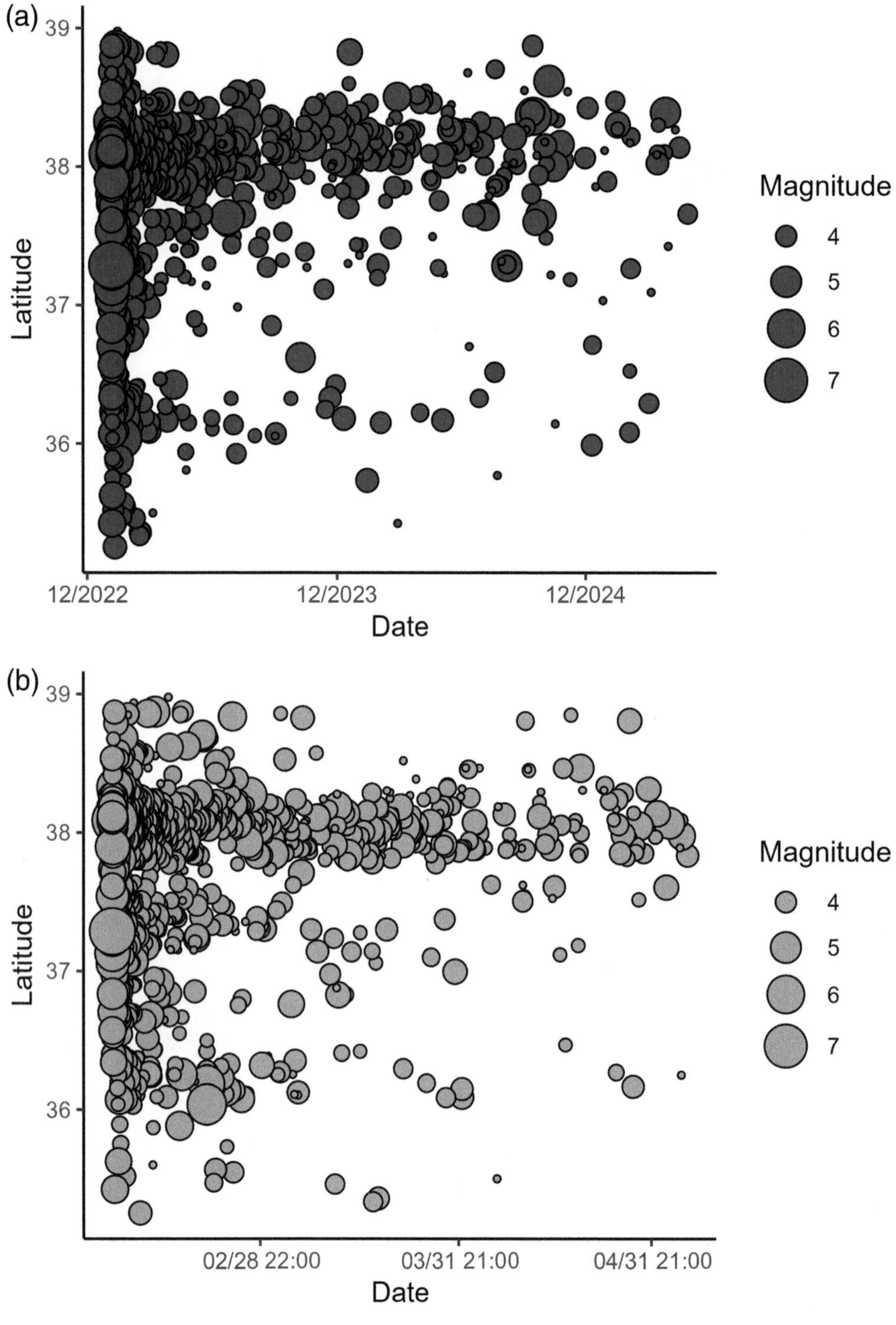

Figure 2. (a) Spatiotemporal distribution of the earthquake occurrences (M ≥ 3.5) between 5 February 2023 and 12 June 2025. (b) The same distribution portrayed in (a) but focused on the first three months (between 6 February 2023 and 5 May 2023). Note the distribution along latitude ~38° N and ~36°–37° N denoting the activity along the northern and southern strands of the Sürgü–Misis fault zone (SMFZ) and East Anatolian fault zone (EAFZ), respectively (source: the Türkiye AFAD catalog, see Data and Resources). The color version of this figure is available only in the electronic edition.

August reference. Importantly, unlike *Secunda pars*, Fulcher himself does not state that the 10 August 1114, C.E. earthquake was felt in Antioch, nor does he mention coastal destruction like *Estoire*. Regarding the other sources cited by Ambraseys, Walter the Chancellor does not refer to an earthquake occurring in the spring, summer, or on 10 August 1114. Robert of Torigni, by contrast, briefly mentions an undated earthquake in 1114 that appears consistent with the 29 November event and may also reflect elements of the 13 November earthquake. Robert subsequently seems to describe the same 29 November earthquake as recurring, or more likely being rereported, in 1115. Thus, although an earthquake near the EAFZ may have occurred and been felt as farther south as Jerusalem (more than 600 km away), the most plausible interpretation is that Fulcher was describing localized shaking in Jerusalem or the broader region of Palestine. Subsequent derivative accounts appear to have embellished the event and introduced chronological confusion.

The second earthquake struck on the night of 13 November, though sources differ on whether it occurred in 1114 or 1115 C.E. Among modern catalogs, the date and region are agreed upon among Guidoboni and Comastri (2005) and Ambraseys (2009), but they disagree about the size of the event. The former argues that this was the biggest event in the sequence, whereas the latter

conflates multiple seismic events, including possibly the 13 and 29 November earthquakes, into a vague and imprecise time frame that lacks the chronological clarity of Fulcher's 10

suggests the third earthquake was the largest of the two. Contemporaneous sources Fulcher of Chartres and Walter the Chancellor report that it destroyed part of the city of

Mamistra (Misis) (Walter the Chancellor, 1999, p. 82 and Chartres, 1969, p. 210). During that event, Abbot Anselm of Gembloux (twelfth century C.E.)—a contemporaneous source writing from Belgium possibly echoing reports from returning Crusaders—described how, in the suburbs of Antioch, the ground opened (possibly due to fissures or landslides), houses collapsed, people were killed, and several towers along with nearby structures were destroyed (Anselm in Bethmann, Abbot Anselm, 1844, pp. 375–376, in Latin). However, it seems he misdated the damage in Antioch as local, and a contemporaneous source, Walter the Chancellor, indicates that Antioch was heavily damaged in the earthquake on 29 November rather than in the earthquake on 13 November. Writing more than 200 yr later, Andrea Dandolo added that Cilicia and Mamistra and the surrounding area were especially affected, with aftershocks causing people to fear being swallowed by the earth (Dandolo and Pastorello, 1938–1958, p. 230).

The third reported earthquake occurred a day before the Feast of Saint Andrew on the night of 29 November. This event is documented by over two dozen sources. Some of the most important sources are Walter the Chancellor, Matthew of Edessa, Ibn al-Jawzi, Michael the Syrian, Chronicon Ad Annum 1234, Kemal ad-Din, the Chronicle of Sembat, and Bar Hebraeus (Walter the Chancellor, 1999, pp. 81–87; Matthew of Edessa, 1993, pp. 216–217; Ibn al-Jawzi in Ambraseys, 2009, p. 290; Michael the Syrian, 1899–1910, p. 200; Chronicon ad annum 1234, 1916–1937, v. 2, pp. 58, 60; Kemal ad-Din, Ibn al-ʿAdīm, 1884, p. 607; the Sparapet Sembat, 1869, p. 614; and Bar Hebraeus, 1932, p. 247). This event left a strong historical imprint and appears to have been the largest of the 1114/1115 C.E. earthquake. Contemporaneous sources, Walter the Chancellor and Matthew of Edessa, wrote long, detailed accounts of the earthquake from opposite ends of the fault rupture. Walter was in Antioch when the earthquake struck. He wrote about an "immense and terrible earthquake in Antioch and its region," noting how the townspeople frantically attempted to flee their collapsing structures. By morning, he observed the extensive destruction, stating, "… the vast scale of the wretched disaster was clear beneath the ruin both of men and of other things." (Walter the Chancellor, 1999, p. 81). Reports came in that Marash had been "entirely destroyed with its lord and bishop … the clergy and all the people," and Mamistra also experienced significant damage (Walter the Chancellor, 1999, p. 82). In addition, destruction was feared in al-Atharib and "other Antiochene borders." Walter described aftershocks —"each day, the earthquake threatened for hopeless hours." Walter also noted that many people in Antioch slept outside, which also suggests continuing aftershocks (Walter the Chancellor, 1999, p. 83). In addition, Walter referred to the danger of "threatening" earthquakes persisting for five months, indicating a prolonged period of aftershocks (Walter the Chancellor, 1999, p. 84). Of the sources mentioned earlier, only Walter dated the earthquake to 29 November 1115 C.E. The other sources dated it to 29 November 1114 C.E. For this, and the reasons stated subsequently, Walter likely provided an incorrect year.

According to Walter, after the earthquake, Roger of Salerno, the ruler of the Principality of Antioch, repaired earthquake-damaged fortifications in his realm (Walter the Chancellor, 1999, p. 84). Roger's intelligence agents later returned from their reconnaissance missions, reporting that there was public rejoicing within the Seljuk Empire over the widespread ruin and destruction in Syria. They also relayed that the "Sultan" had assembled an army with the aim of conquering Roger's domain and other parts of Syria, assuming that the earthquake had significantly weakened regional defenses (Walter the Chancellor, 1999, pp. 86–87). Then Walter discusses events leading up to the Battle of Tell Danith (also known as the Battle of Sarmin). Bursuq ibn Bursuq launched an invasion and was met by a broad military alliance: Lulu, the de facto ruler of Aleppo; Tughtegin of Damascus; Il-Ghazi of Mardin; and Crusader forces from the four principal states —Edessa, Antioch, Tripoli, and Jerusalem. Following a period of inconclusive engagements, Roger launched a surprise attack and decisively defeated Bursuq ibn Bursuq's forces at the Battle of Tell Danith on 15 September 1115. This well-dated battle seems to preclude a 1115 C.E. date for the 29 November earthquake, as Roger's post-earthquake repairs took place before this battle and in preparation for expected military activity, not after. Because Walter tells us that the 13 November earthquake struck before the 29 November earthquake, this would suggest that the 13 November earthquake also struck in 1114 C.E. Thus, it appears that the 13 and 29 November earthquakes occurred within 16 days of each other in 1114.

Matthew of Edessa also composed a first-hand account of the 29 November earthquake, likely written from a monastery near Kaysun. He recorded occurrences of landslides, rockfalls, loud noises, seismic concussions, and the cries of those trapped beneath the rubble. (Matthew of Edessa, 1993, p. 216). Matthew also noted ongoing aftershocks (Matthew of Edessa, 1993, pp. 216–217). Reports emerged from other locations, indicating that Samosata, Hisn-Mansur, and Raban were destroyed along with Kaysun (Matthew of Edessa, 1993, p. 217). In a probable exaggeration, Matthew claimed there were no survivors in Marash and reported 40,000 fatalities (Matthew of Edessa, 1993, p. 217). Mamistra was reported to be similarly affected (Matthew of Edessa, 1993, p. 217). Many towns and districts, particularly in the territory of the Crusader States, were said to be destroyed (Matthew of Edessa, 1993, p. 217). Matthew further described damage and loss of life at the Basilian Monastery in the Black Mountains near Marash, and perhaps at the Mashchgavor (Mashkur) Monastery (Matthew of Edessa, 1993, p. 217). Following the earthquake, Matthew wrote that snow covered the land (Matthew of Edessa, 1993, p. 217).

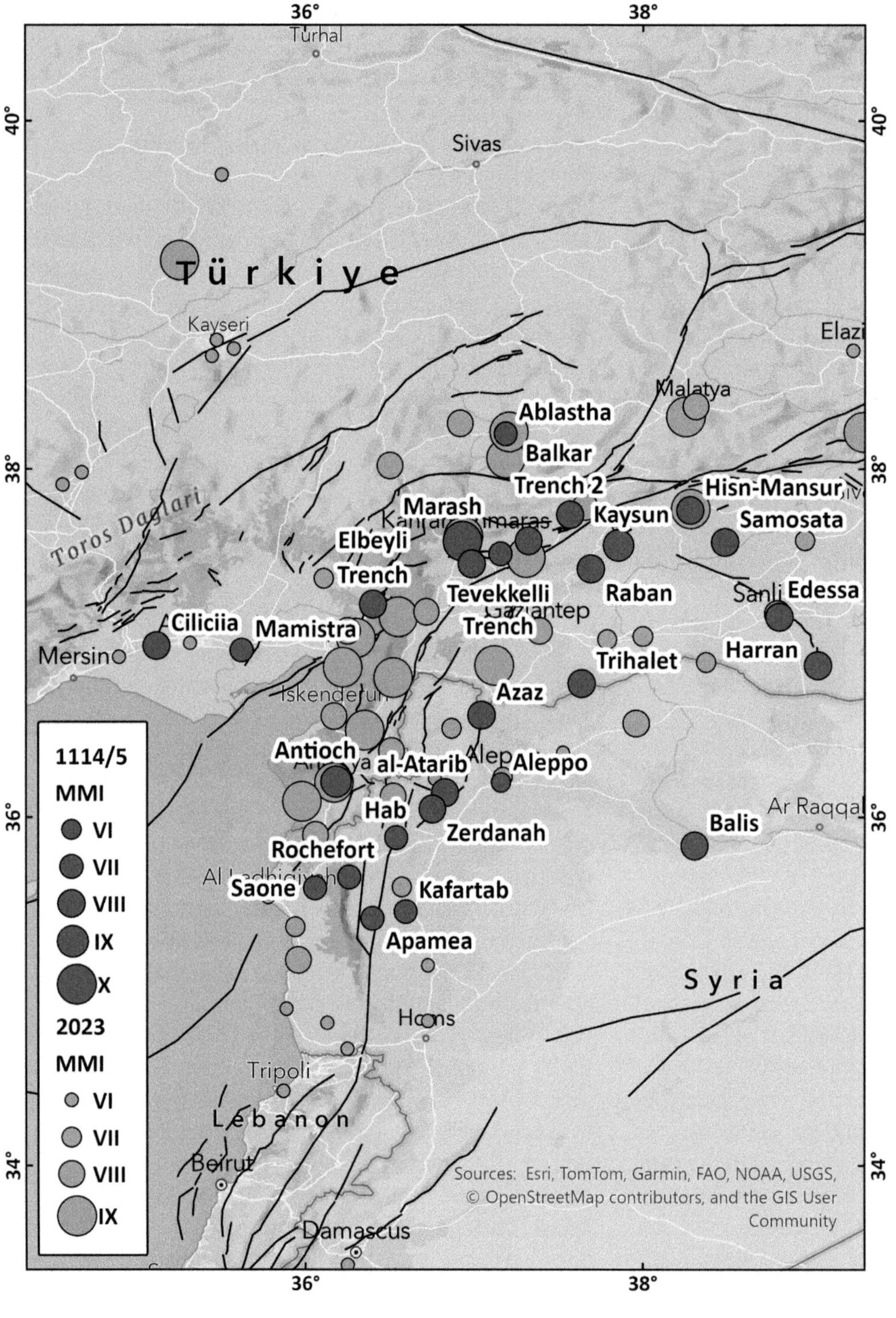

Figure 3. Interpreted IDPs of the historical 1114/5 C.E. sequence (see Tables S2 and S3) superimposed on the U.S. Geological Survey (USGS) IDPs of the 2023 Pazarcık M 7.8 and Elbistan M 7.5 earthquakes. The color version of this figure is available only in the electronic edition.

Magnitude and epicentral region

Modern catalogs and focused investigations offer differing interpretations of these earthquakes. Ambraseys and Jackson (1998) classify the third earthquake (29 November 1114) as a very large event (M ≥ 7.8). Ambraseys (2009, parametric catalog) estimated the magnitudes of the second and third earthquakes to be $M_s = 5$ and $M_s = 6.9$ (±0.3), respectively, with epicenters of 35.6° E, 37° N, and 37.2° E, 37.5° N, respectively (Fig. 3). Guidoboni and Comastri (2005), who appear to have mislocated sites from the third event into the second event and vice versa, refer to the second event (13 November 1114) as the largest event ($M_e = 7.8$, I_{max} = X). In contrast, the magnitude of the third is estimated to be $M_e = 6.3$ (I_{max} = X). They estimated the epicenter of the second and third earthquakes at 37.6° E, 37.4° N and 36.2° E, 37.2° N, respectively (Fig. 3). Sbeinati *et al.* (2005), although not decisive in the number of events, estimate magnitudes for two earthquakes in November 1114 to be M 7.4 and 7.7 with I_0 of VIII–IX and X, respectively, and identical epicenters of 38.5° E, 37.3° N. Ben-Menahem (1979) refers to two events: the first in 10 August 1114, affecting Antioch (with an accompanied tsunami) and felt in Jerusalem, with $M_L = 7.0$ and epicenter at 36.5° N, 36° E, whereas the second on 25 December 1115, in southern Türkiye and also felt in Jerusalem, with $M_L = 7.5$ and epicenter at 38.9° E, 37° N. Duman *et al.* (2020) describe two earthquakes in 1114 and 1115 but suggest they refer to the same one. In addition, they identified paleoseismic evidence that may correspond to an earthquake in 1114/1115 C.E., but the dating is roughly accurate (between ~1035 and 1215 C.E.). Carena *et al.* (2023) follow Ambraseys (2009) and refer to a single earthquake that occurred on 29 November 1114, estimating a magnitude of M_w 7.2 with five aftershocks following the main event and the Pazarcık fault as the triggering tectonic segment. Kondorskaya and Ulomov (1999) mention the 10 August 1114 earthquake with an I_{max} = X and epicenter at 38° E,

37.5° N. The Global Historical Earthquake Archive (GHEA) catalog (Albini *et al.*, 2013) includes two events that occurred in 1114: the first (M 7.4, with epicenter near Şanlurfa, east of the Euphrates valley) has been taken from Sbeinati *et al.* (2005), whereas the second (29 November 1114, M_w 6.9) has been taken from Ambraseys (2009).

Damage distribution

Modern earthquake catalogs list the resulting damage from these three events with a varying degree of discussion. Guidoboni and Comastri (2005) evaluated seismic intensities of 12 damaged and felt sites of the 1114/5 sequence on the Mercalli–Cancani–Sieberg (MCS) macroseismic scale (Sieberg, 1932; Ferrari and Guidoboni, 2000) (see Table S1, available in the supplemental material to this article). They also describe potential environmental effects in Antakya following the second earthquake. Ambraseys (2009) listed these with slightly different classifications between the resulting event sites. Although disagreeing with Guidoboni and Comastri (2005), he made no seismic intensity estimation. Sbeinati *et al.* (2005) evaluated intensities for seven localities in the European macroseismic scale (EMS-92) scale (Grünthal, 1993). However, although stating that their interpreted damage could have been the result of two plausible, separate events in November 1114 C.E., they list the damaged localities in a single list with no distinction of which locality was damaged in which event. Meghraoui *et al.* (2025) (following Sbeinati *et al.*, 2005; APAME, 2007; Ambraseys, 2009) listed 17 damaged localities associated with a single event on 29 November 1114.

Revisiting the historical sources alongside recent paleoseismic evidence yielded three lists: (1) localities damaged or felt by the 13 November earthquake (see Table S2); (2) localities damaged by the 29 November earthquake (see Table S3); and (3) debated localities for the 29 November earthquake (see Table S4). Notably, paleoseismic evidence from the Balkar trench 2, Tevekkelli trench, and the Nacar trench suggests that the Pazarcık segment ruptured during the 29 November earthquake, whereas evidence from the Elbeyli trench indicates that the Düziçi segment ruptured during the 13 November earthquake. It is also important to emphasize that none of the contemporary sources reported damage to fortifications at Apamea, Kafartab, Maarat al-Numan, Shaizar, Hab, Bourzey Castle (potentially Rochefort), or Saone during the 29 November earthquake. However, Walter the Chancellor noted that Prince Roger visited and repaired damaged structures in several castles and surrounding areas after the earthquake (Walter the Chancellor, 1999, p. 84), indicating that additional earthquake-related destruction may have occurred at these and other locations.

Constraining the Twelfth Century C.E. Historical Sequence

When comparing instrumental and pre-instrumental earthquakes, it is important to note that the epicenters and magnitudes of the latter are not calculated but rather are estimated—typically by inference from the spread and severity of the reported damage. However, in the case of a sequence of historical earthquakes, it is often difficult to determine precisely which event caused specific instances of damage. Considering the temporal proximity between the earthquakes of 1114/5, one cannot rule out potential duplication of damage on the one hand and amalgamation of several damages into one on the other hand. Therefore, our inspection of the spread of the damage was not done separately for each of the mainshocks but rather was carried out for the whole historical sequence. The same was done for the damaged localities of the 2023 Pazarcık and Elbistan earthquakes, which were grouped and examined together. If the same locality appeared in connection with two earthquakes, the entries were amalgamated, and the higher intensity value was retained. Because we only have an interpretation of damaged localities associated with the twelfth-century sequence, the examination of the 2023 sequence was carried out only on localities of MMI ≥ 6. Altogether 27 and 69 intensity data points (IDPs) were analyzed for the 1114/5 and 2023 sequences, respectively (Fig. 3).

To detect potential damage patterns with an aim to characterize seismic activity, a kernel density estimation (KDE) process (Silverman, 1986) was carried out on the two IDP datasets. KDE estimates the probability density function of the IDPs by placing a smooth kernel over each data point and adding them to create a continuous surface, allowing for the visualization of damage patterns and identifying hotspots (e.g., Amador Luna *et al.*, 2024). The density of the damage, indicating spatial severity, was evaluated as follows:

1. $\text{Kernel density} = \frac{1}{(\text{radius})^2} \sum_{i=n}^{n} \left[\frac{3}{\pi} \left(1 - \left(\frac{\text{dist}_i}{\text{radius}} \right)^2 \right)^2 \right].$
2. $\text{Radius } (h_{\text{opt}}) = (\frac{2}{3n})^{1/4} * \text{SD}.$
3. $\text{SD} = \sqrt{\frac{\sum_{i=1}^{n} Wi(Xi-X)^2}{n} + \frac{\sum_{i=1}^{n} Wi(Yi-Y)^2}{n}}.$

In which the kernel density is the value at a given location; dist_i is the distance between a given point (IDP) and the calculated density location; radius is the optimal search radius (h_{opt}); n is the number of IDPs; SD is the weighted standard distance; Wi is the weighted parameter; Xi, Yi are the coordinates of a given IDP; and X, Y are the mean coordinates of all points (all IDPs) (Zohar *et al.*, 2023). For the 2023 doublet and the 1114/5 sequence, the parameters of n, SD, and search radius (h_{opt}) are 69; 209 km; 65 km and 27; 122 km; 48 km, respectively. Naturally, the number of IDPs of the 2023 scenario is higher than that of the historical 1114/5 sequence, which results in a wider area and a larger standard distance. Yet, the central location of both datasets is relatively close (36.89° E 36.92° N versus 37.13° E 36.82° N), suggesting that the patterns of the damage distribution in both scenarios are similar. In addition, in both scenarios, one can identify two significant hotspots of damage

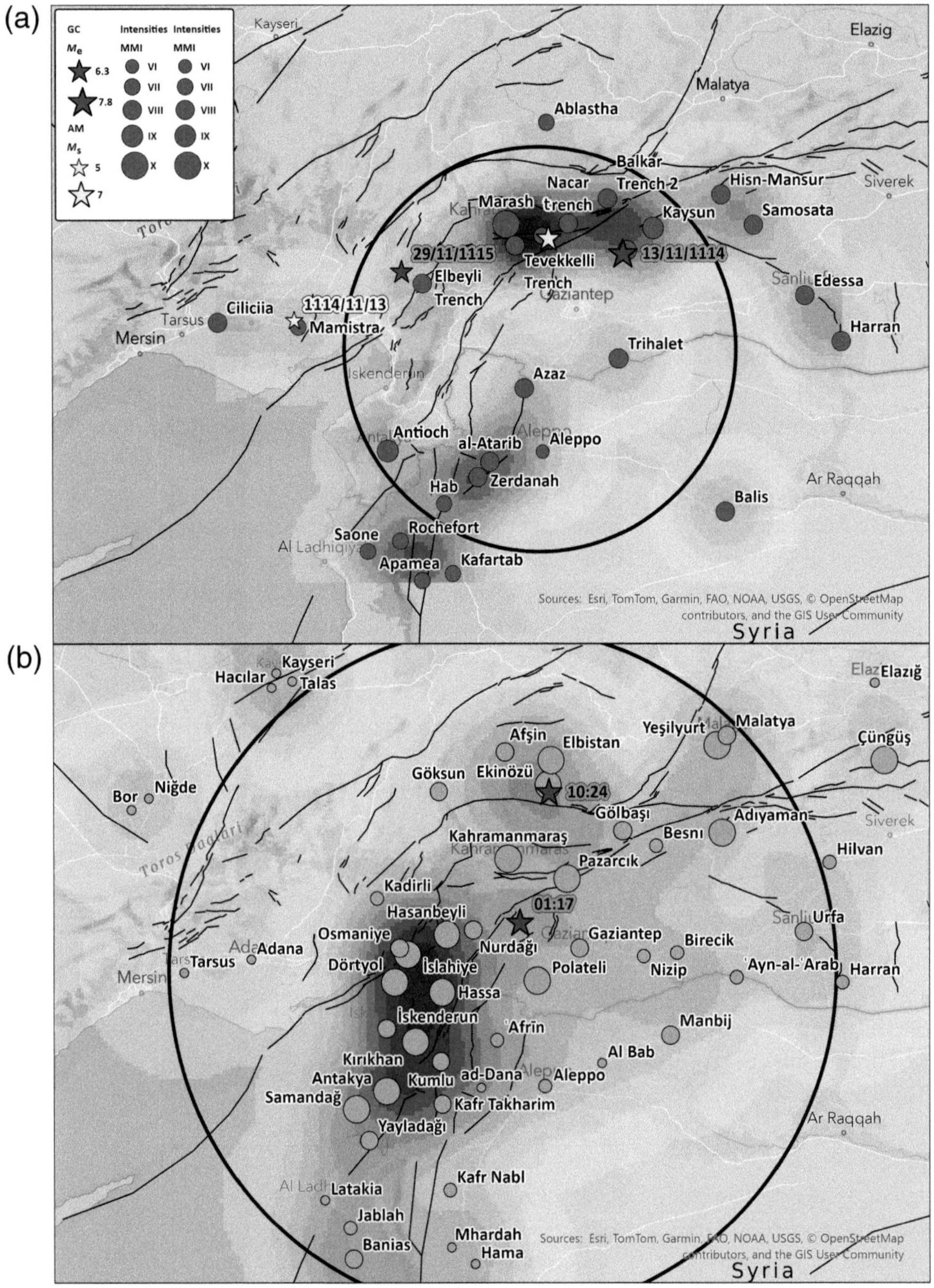

Figure 4. Standard distance and kernel density of the damage distribution of the 1114/5 C.E. and 2023 sequences: (a) IDPs (modified Mercalli intensity [MMI] scale ranging between VI and X) distribution following the 13 and 29 November earthquakes (altogether 27 IDPs without duplicate localities). (b) IDPs (MMI scale ranging between VI and IX) distribution of the M 7.8 Pazarcık (6 February 2023 01:17:35 UTC) and the M 7.5 Elbistan (6 February 2023 10:24:49 UTC) earthquake (altogether 69 IDPs with no duplicate localities). The color version of this figure is available only in the electronic edition.

spread and severity. In the 2023 doublet scenario, the northern hotspot is located close to Elbistan and Ekirozu, about 50 km north of Kahramanmaras, which is also the epicentral region of the M 7.5 Elbistan epicenter (Fig. 4). The southern hotspot, however, extends into the region between the cities Antakya, Islahiye, HasanBeyli, and Hassa. Unlike the northern one, the southern hotspot is relatively far from the epicentral region of the M 7.8 Pazarcık earthquake, some 80 km to the east. The 1114/5 sequence presents a similar dual pattern with some differences. Its northern hotspot is located in the region of Kahramanmaras, close to the epicenters evaluated by Guidoboni and Comastri (referencing 13 November 1114) and Ambraseys (2009) (referring to 29 November 1114). The southern hotspot extends between the cities Apamea and Al-Atarib, about 40 km southeast of Antakya and more than 100 km south of the epicenters evaluated by Guidoboni and Comastri (referring to 29 November 1115) and Ambraseys (2009) (referring to 13 November 1114). In other words, in both scenarios (2023 and 1114/5), the northern hotspot is located close to the epicentral region (whether calculated for the 2023 scenario or estimated for the 1114/5 scenario), whereas the southern hotspot of the 1114/5 sequence is located about 80 km south of the 2023 sequence; both hotspots are not in proximity to the epicentral region.

Comparison of the spread of the damage suggests that the magnitudes of the twelfth-century earthquakes were not substantially lower than those of the 2023 events. One might reasonably consider that poorer construction techniques and materials in the twelfth century could exaggerate the apparent severity of historical damage. However, even when the evaluated intensities are reduced by a full degree (e.g., IX and VIII become VIII and VII, respectively), the affected area remains extensive. Ambraseys (2009) assigns M 5 and 6.9 (±0.3) to the 13 and 29 November historical events, respectively, whereas Guidoboni and Comastri (2005) assign M 7.8 and 6.3 to those events, respectively. When examined and viewed alongside the 2023 damage patterns, it is reasonable to hypothesize that at least one of the 1114/5 events reached M > 7, in agreement with the recent estimates of M 6.4 and 7.7 by Stucchi *et al.* (2024).

The EAFZ is a highly active seismic region driven by the northeastward movement of the Arabian plate relative to the Anatolian plate, resulting in a horizontal slip rate of 10–11 mm/yr in the EAFZ (Cetin *et al.*, 2023). Over the past millennia, this fault system has likely generated multiple large historical earthquakes (e.g., 1269, 1513/1514, and 1544, see Stucchi *et al.*, 2024) reflecting its capacity to produce high-magnitude events (Ozkula *et al.*, 2023). In contrast to the 2023 earthquake doublet, the second event of the twelfth-century sequence appears to have been the larger of the two, as indicated by the broader geographical extent of damage aligned with the EAFZ segments. Notably, in both 2023 and 1114/5 scenarios, aftershocks occurred and persisted for several months, suggesting that the historical scenario might had a decay pattern of seismicity consistent with the modified Omori law as observed in the 2023 sequence (see Rekapalli *et al.*, 2023; Raykova *et al.*, 2024; Polat *et al.*, 2025) might have been similar in the case of the 1114/5 sequence.

The Türkiye 2023 M 7.8 Pazarcık and M 7.5 Elbistan form a doublet of two mainshocks (e.g., Chen *et al.*, 2023; Jia *et al.*, 2023, Petersen *et al.*, 2023; Yan *et al.*, 2024). Toda and Stein (2024) (after Toda *et al.*, 2023) suggest that the Pazarcık earthquake promoted the occurrence of the Elbistan earthquake through stress transfer and unclamping of its epicentral patch. This pattern is also known from other doublet cases worldwide (see examples in Toda and Stein, 2024). This notion is supported in additional studies describing the seismicity of the 2023 sequence (e.g., Okuwaki *et al.*, 2023; Ren *et al.*, 2024; Zhou *et al.*, 2025). Toward the future, Meghraoui *et al.* (2025) observed stress transfer after the 2023 sequence and accordingly suggest that the Pazarcık earthquake rupture increases potential failure along the northern Dead Sea fault.

Recently, Stucchi *et al.* (2024) suggested that the 1114/5 scenario reflects an earthquake sequence that can be considered as a predecessor of the main 2023 earthquake. As far as the 1114/5 sequence is concerned, we are aware that the 1114/5 scenario can vary between multiple patterns, including: one or more strong foreshocks and a stronger mainshock; a strong mainshock followed by one or more strong aftershocks; multiple strong events that might be classed as an earthquake swarm; or multiple earthquakes that are part of an earthquake storm. Although several studies refer to a single event in November 1114 (e.g., Duman *et al.*, 2020; Carena *et al.*, 2023), it seems that the interpretation of the historical sources and paleoseismic evidence (see Tables S2 and S3), as well as the spatial analysis (Fig. 4) suggest that at least two strong earthquakes struck southern Türkiye at the time. According to the Coulomb stress theory (King *et al.*, 1994), it is unlikely that the same fault or adjacent parallel faults with identical kinematics will generate two strong earthquakes within a short period of time. Thus, the two most plausible seismic interpretations of the 1114/5 sequence are either a foreshock–mainshock–aftershock pattern or two distinct major earthquakes rupturing different tectonic segments. Based on the discussion above, we argue that the latter scenario provides a more convincing explanation for the 1114/5 events. Nevertheless, it should be stressed that our opinion relies on an interpretation of incomplete and limited historical records.

Summary

Constraining the 1114/5 C.E. historical sequence through comparison with the February 2023 doublet provides new insights into the nature of past seismic activity in southern Türkiye. Given the limitations of historical data and the temporal proximity between the 1114/5 events, the analysis interrogated the overall damage from each sequence rather than attempting to attribute separate damage to individual events. KDE applied to IDPs reveals two consistent hotspots of severe damage: one in the north near Kahramanmaraş and Elbistan, and one in the south near Antakya, although their exact positions differ slightly between the two periods. Despite these differences, the broader spatial patterns of damage show a notable resemblance. The analysis suggests that at least one of the twelfth-century earthquakes likely exceeded magnitude 7, comparable to the 2023 events. Even when historical intensities are reduced to account for weaker construction practices, the extent of damage remains substantial.

Tectonically, the EAFZ has generated large historical earthquakes and continues to pose significant seismic risk, with a known slip rate of 10–11 mm/yr. The 2023 doublet likely involved stress transfer between the Pazarcık and Elbistan segments. Although some scholars have interpreted the 1114/5 events as a single earthquake, both paleoseismic evidence and historical records suggest a more complex sequence, possibly involving foreshocks, aftershocks, or even an earthquake storm. Coulomb stress principles imply that the twelfth-century sequence did not follow a simple mainshock–aftershock pattern but consisted of two distinct large events. The resemblance between the spatial distribution and character of the 2023 and 1114/5 sequences may imply a recurring seismic pattern, supporting the notion of the twelfth-century sequence as a plausible historical predecessor to the 2023 events. However, whether the early twelfth-century C.E. earthquakes constituted a true doublet remains uncertain because the available historical evidence is insufficient for a definitive conclusion.

Data and Resources

All data used in this article came from published sources listed in the references. Intensity data points (IDPs) and isoseismals for Figure 2 were available at https://earthquake.usgs.gov/earthquakes/eventpage/

us6000jllz/executive and https://earthquake.usgs.gov/earthquakes/eventpage/us6000jlqa/executive. The Türkiye Disaster and Emergency Management Authority (AFAD) catalog is available at https://deprem.afad.gov.tr/event-catalog. All websites were last accessed in June 2025. The supplemental material for this article includes Tables S1–S4 of damage descriptions interpretation, along with intensity evaluation.

Declaration of Competing Interests

The authors acknowledge that there are no conflicts of interest recorded.

Acknowledgments

The authors wish to acknowledge Amos Salamon from the Geological Survey of Israel for his support and insightful advice, and to the editor and anonymous reviewers for their helpful comments.

References

Abbot Anselm (1844). Sigeberti Gemblacensis Chronographia cum continuationibus [Sigebert of Gembloux's Chronographia with continuations], in *Monumenta Germaniae Historica, Scriptores*, L. C. Bethmann (Editor), Vol. 6, Hahn, Hannover, 268–535.

Albini, P., R. M. W. Musson, A. A. Gomez Capera, M. Locati, A. Rovida, M. Stucchi, and D. Viganò (2013). Global historical earthquake archive and catalogue (1000-1903), *GEM Technical Rept. 2013-01 V1.0.0*, available at https://emidius.eu/GEH/ (last accessed June 2025).

Amador Luna, D., F. M. Alonso-Chaves, and C. Fernández (2024). Kernel density estimation for the interpretation of seismic big data in tectonics using QGIS: The Türkiye–Syria earthquakes (2023), *Remote Sens.* **16,** no. 20, 3849, doi: 10.3390/rs16203849.

Ambraseys, N. N. (2005). Historical earthquakes in Jerusalem—A methodological discussion, *J. Seismol.* **9,** 329–340, doi: 10.1007/s10950-005-8183-8.

Ambraseys, N. N. (2009). *Earthquakes in the Mediterranean and Middle East. A Multidisciplinary Study of Seismicity up to 1900*, First ed., Cambridge University Press, Cambridge.

Ambraseys, N. N., and J. A. Jackson (1998). Faulting associated with historical and recent earthquakes in the eastern Mediterranean region, *Geophys. J. Int.* **133,** 390–406, doi: 10.1046/j.1365-246X.1998.00508.x.

APAME (2007). *Archeoseismology and Paleoseismology for the Protection of Cultural Heritage and Archeological Sites in the Middle East: The Impact of Large Earthquakes on the Archaeological Sites and Cultural Heritage in the Middle East (Jordan, Lebanon, Syria and Turkey*, APAME EC project—ICA-CT-2002-10024—Coordinator Mustapha Meghraoui, DG XII Brussels), available at https://cordis.europa.eu/project/id/ICA3-CT-2002-10024 (last accessed June 2025).

Arpat, E., and F. Şaroğlu (1972). The East Anatolian fault system: Thoughts on its development, *Bull. Min. Res. Explor. Inst. Türkiye* **78,** 33–39.

Bar Hebraeus (1932). *The Chronography of Gregory Abû'l Faraj, the Son of Aaron, the Hebrew Physician, Commonly Known as Bar Hebraeus: Being the First Part of His Political History of the World*, E. A. Wallis Budge (Translator), Oxford University Press, H. Milford, London.

Ben-Menahem, A. (1979). Earthquake catalog for the Middle East (92 B.C.-1980 A.D.), *Boll. Geofis. Teor. Appl.* **21,** no. 84, 245–310.

Carena, S., A. M. Friedrich, A. Verdecchia, B. Kahle, S. Rieger, and S. Kübler (2023). Identification of source faults of large earthquakes in the Turkey-Syria border region between 1000 CE and the present, and their relevance for the 2023 M_w 7.8 Pazarcık earthquake, *Tectonics* **42,** no. 12, doi: 10.1029/2023TC007890.

Cetin, K. O., M. Ilgac, G. Can, and E. Cakir (2023). *Preliminary Reconnaissance Report on February 6, 2023, Pazarcik M_w 7.7 and Elbistan M_w 7.6, Kahramanmaraş-Türkiye Earthquakes*, METU Earthquake Engineering Research Center.

Chartres, F. D. (1969). Gesta Francorum Iherusalem Peregrinantium, in *A History of the Expedition to Jerusalem*, F. Ryan (Translator), University of Tennessee Press, Knoxville, 1095–1127.

Chen, K. C., and J. H. Wang (2012). Correlations between the mainshock and the largest aftershock for Taiwan earthquakes, *Pure Appl. Geophys.* **169,** 1217–1229, doi: 10.1007/s00024-011-0352-9.

Chen, W., G. Rao, D. Kang, Z. Wan, and D. Wang (2023). Early report of the source characteristics, ground motions, and casualty estimates of the 2023 M_w 7.8 and 7.5 Turkey earthquakes, *J. Earth Sci.* **34,** no. 2, 297–303, doi: 10.1007/s12583-023-1316-6.

Chronicon ad annum 1234 (1916–1937). *Chronicon ad annum Christi 1234 pertinens*, Corpus Scriptorum Christianorum Orientalium, Scriptores Syri, J.-B. Chabot (Editor and Translator), Vols. 81 and 82, E Typographeo Reipublicae, Paris (in Latin).

Dal Zilio, L., and J.-P. Ampuero (2023). Earthquake doublet in Turkey and Syria, *Commun. Earth Environ.* **4,** no. 1, 71, doi: 10.1038/s43247-023-00747-z.

Dandolo, A. and E. Pastorello (Editors) (1938–1958). *Andreae Danduli ducis Venetiarum Chronica per extensum descripta: aa. 46–1280 d.C*, Zanichelli, Bologna (Rerum Italicarum Scriptores, Vol. 12.1) (in Latin).

Dewey, J., and P. Byerly (1969). The early history of seismometry (to 1900), *Bull. Seismol. Soc. Am.* **59,** no. 1, 183–227.

Duman, T. Y., H. Elmacı, S. Özalp, A. Kürçer, M. Kara, E. Özdemir, A. Yavuzoğlu, and Ç. Uygun Güldoğan (2020). Paleoseismology of the western Sürgü–Misis fault system: East Anatolian fault, Turkey, *Mediterranean Geosci. Rev.* **2,** no. 3, 411–437, doi: 10.1007/s42990-020-00041-6.

Emre, Ö., D. Y. Dumar, S. Özalp, F. Şaroğlu, Ş Olgun, H. Elmacı, and T. Çan (2018). Active fault database of Turkey, *Bull. Earthq. Eng.* **16,** no. 8, 3229–3275.

Estoire-Jerus (1895). *Estoire de Jerusalem et d'Antioche*, P. Riant (Editor), Vol. V, 621–648, RHC-Occ, Paris (in French).

Ferrari, G., and E. Guidoboni (2000). Seismic scenarios and assessment of intensity: Some criteria for the use of the MCS scale, *Ann. Geophys.* **43,** no. 4, 707–720.

Gomez, F., G. Karam, M. Khawlie, S. McClusky, P. Vernant, R. Reilinger, R. Jaafar, C. Tabet, K. Khair, and M. Barazangi (2007). Global Positioning System measurements of strain accumulation and slip transfer through the restraining bend along the Dead Sea fault system in Lebanon, *Geophys. J. Int.* **168,** 1021–1028, doi: 10.1111/j.1365-246X.2006.03328.x.

Grünthal, G. (1993). *European Macroseismic Scale 1992 (Updated MSK Scale)*, Conseil de l'Europe. Cahiers du Centre Europeen de Geodynamique et de Seismologie, Luxembourg.

Grünthal, G., A. Hakimhashemi, H. Schelle, C. Bosse, and R. Wahlström (2009). The long term temporal behaviour of the seismicity of the Dead Sea fault zone and its implication for time-dependent seismic hazard assessments: A report related to the DFG project Geo-DESIRE (Geoscientific Dead Sea Integrated Research Project), with participating institutions from Germany, Israel, Jordan and Palestine territories, *Scientific Technical Rept. STR 09/09*, Deutsches GeoForschungsZentrum GFZ, Potsdam, 45 pp., doi: 10.2312/GFZ.b103-09098.

Guidoboni, E., and A. Comastri (2005). *Catalogue of Earthquakes and Tsunamis in the Mediterranean Area from the 11th to the 15th Century*, INGV-SGA, Bologna.

Guidoboni, E., and G. Ferrari (1989). The inexact catalogue: The study of more than 1700 earthquakes from the XI to the XX century in Italy, *Terra Nova* **1,** no. 2, 151–162.

Gutenberg, R., and C. F. Richter (1944). Frequency of earthquakes in California, *Bull. Seismol. Soc. Am.* **34,** 185–188.

Hancilar, U., K. Sesetyan, E. Cakti, E. Safak, N. Yenihayat, F. S. Malcioglu, K. Donmez, T. Tetik, and H. Suleyman (2023). Kahramanmaraş-Gaziantep Türkiye M7.7 earthquake, 6 February 2023, (04:17 GMT+03:00) strong ground motion and building damage estimations preliminary report (v6), Boğaziçi University, Kandilli Observatory and Earthquake Research Institute, Department of Earthquake Engineering.

Jia, Z., Z. Jin, M. Marchandon, T. Ulrich, A. A. Gabriel, W. Fan, P. Shearer, X. Zou, J. Rekoske, F. Bulut, *et al.* (2023). The complex dynamics of the 2023 Kahramanmaraş, Turkey, M_w 7.8-7.7 earthquake doublet, *Science* **381,** no. 6661, 985–990, doi: 10.1126/science.adi0685.

Kagan, Y. Y., and D. D. Jackson (1999). Worldwide doublets of large shallow earthquakes, *Bull. Seismol. Soc. Am.* **89,** no. 5, 1147–1155, doi: 10.1785/BSSA0890051147.

Karabulut, H., S. E. Güvercin, J. Hollingsworth, and A. Ö. Konca (2023). Long silence on the East Anatolian fault zone (southern Turkey) ends with devastating double earthquakes (6 February 2023) over a seismic gap: Implications for the seismic potential in the eastern Mediterranean region, *J. Geol. Soc.* **180,** no. 3, doi: 10.1144/jgs2023-021.

Karcz, I. (2004). Implications of some early Jewish sources for estimates of earthquake hazard in the Holy Land, *Ann. Geophys.* **47,** nos. 2/3, 759–792.

Kaymakci, N., M. Inceöz, P. Ertepinar, and A. Koç (2010). Late Cretaceous to recent kinematics of SE Anatolia (Turkey), *Geol. Soc. London Spec. Publ.* **340,** no. 1, 409–435.

Kemal ad-Din, Ibn al-'Adīm (1884). Zubdat al-Halab min Tārīkh Halab [زبدة الحلب من تاريخ حلب, The Cream of Aleppo from the History of Aleppo], in *Recueil des historiens des croisades: Historiens orientaux*, E. Blochet (Translator), Vol. 3, Imprimerie Nationale, Paris, pp. 571–690 (in Arabic).

King, G. C. P., R. S. Stein, and J. Lin (1994). Static stress changes and the triggering of earthquakes, *Bull. Seismol. Soc. Am.* **84,** no. 3, 935–953.

Kisslinger, C. (1996). Aftershocks and fault-zone properties, *Adv. Geophys.* **38,** 1–36.

Kondorskaya, N. V., and V. I. Ulomov (1999). Special catalogue of earthquakes of the northern Eurasia from ancient times through 1995 (SECNE), available at http://www.seismo.ethz.ch/static/gshap/neurasia/nordasiacat.txt (last accessed June 2025).

Krey, A. C. (2012). *The First Crusade: The Accounts of Eye-Witnesses and Participants*, Vol. 1,. Arx Publishing, LLC.

Matthew of Edessa (1993). *Armenia and the Crusades: Tenth to Twelfth Centuries: The Chronicle of Matthew of Edessa*, A. E. Dostourian (Translator and Editor), University Press of America.

McGuire, J. J. (2008). Seismic cycles and earthquake predictability on East Pacific Rise transform faults, *Bull. Seismol. Soc. Am.* **98,** no. 3, 1067–1084, doi: 10.1785/0120070154.

Meghraoui, M., Z. Cakir, J. Kariche, R. Toussaint, F. Provost, V. Karabacak, R. Sbeinati, E. Altunel, and T. Nemer (2025). The 2023 Mw 7.8 Kahramanmaraş earthquake rupture increases potential failure along the northern Dead Sea fault, *Tectonophysics* **910,** 230799, doi: 10.1016/j.tecto.2025.230799.

Melgar, D., T. Taymaz, A. Ganas, B. W. Crowell, T. Öcalan, M. Kahraman, V. Tsironi, S. Yolsal-Çevikbilen, S. Valkaniotis, T. S. Irmak, *et al.* (2023). Sub-and super-shear ruptures during the 2023 M_w 7.8 and M_w 7.6 earthquake doublet in SE Türkiye, *Seismica* doi: 10.26443/seismica.v2i3.387.

Michael the Syrian (1899–1910). *Chronique de Michel le Syrien, patriarche jacobite d'Antioche (1166–1199)*, J.-B. Chabot (Translator and Editor), Ernest Leroux, Paris (in French).

Nalbant, S. S., J. McCloskey, S. Steacy, and A. A. Barka (2002). Stress accumulation and increased seismic risk in eastern Turkey, *Earth Planet. Sci. Lett.* **195,** nos. 3/4, 291–298, doi: 10.1016/S0012-821X(01)00592-1.

Nissen, E., J. R. Elliott, R. A. Sloan, T. J. Craig, G. J. Funning, A. Hutko, B. E. Parsons, and T. J. Wright (2016). Limitations of rupture forecasting exposed by instantaneously triggered earthquake doublet, *Nature Geosci.* **9,** no. 4, 330–336, doi: 10.1038/ngeo2653.

Okuwaki, R., Y. Yagi, T. Taymaz, and S. P. Hicks (2023). Multi-scale rupture growth with alternating directions in a complex fault network during the 2023 south-eastern Türkiye and Syria earthquake doublet, *Geophys. Res. Lett.* **50,** no. 12, e2023GL103480, doi: 10.1029/2023GL103480.

Ozkula, G., R. K. Dowell, T. Baser, J. L. Lin, O. A. Numanoglu, O. Ilhan, C. G. Olgun, C.-W. Huang, and T. D. Uludag (2023). Field reconnaissance and observations from the February 6, 2023, Turkey earthquake sequence, *Nat. Hazards* **119,** no. 1, 663–700, doi: 10.1007/s11069-023-06143-2.

Petersen, G. M., P. Büyükakpinar, F. O. Vera Sanhueza, M. Metz, S. Cesca, K. Akbayram, J. Saul, and T. Dahm (2023). The 2023 southeast Türkiye seismic sequence: Rupture of a complex fault network, *Seism. Rec.* **3,** no. 2, 134–143, doi: 10.1785/0320230008.

Polat, O., O. Calgar, and O. Serkan (2025). Seismological aspects of doublet earthquakes M_w 7.8, and M_w 7.6, 6th February 2023, Türkiye/Syria earthquake and its aftershocks: Causes and consequences, in *Seismotectonics of the East Mediterranean-Red Sea Region*, Springer, 287–307.

Raykova, P., D. Solakov, and S. Simeonova (2024). Temporal characteristics of the February 6, 2023 M_W 7. 8, Turkey earthquake aftershock sequence, *Proc. of the Bulgarian Academy of Sciences*, doi: 10.7546/CRABS.2024.03.07.

Rekapalli, R., and H. K. Gupta (2023). How long the $M_w \geq 5$ aftershocks of the 6 February 2023 M_w 7.8 Turkiye earthquake shall continue? *Nat. Hazards* **117,** no. 3, 3399–3402, doi: 10.1007/s11069-023-05953-8.

Ren, C., Z. Wang, T. Taymaz, N. Hu, H. Luo, Z. Zhao, H. Yue, X. Song, Z. Shen, H. Xu, *et al.* (2024). Super-shear triggering and cascading fault ruptures of the 2023 Kahramanmaraş, Türkiye earthquake doublet, *Science* **383,** no. 6680, 305–311, doi: 10.1126/science.adi1519.

Robert of Torigni (1889). The chronicle of Robert of Torigni, abbot of the monastery of St. Michael-in-Peril-of-the-Sea, in *Chronicles of the Reigns of Stephen, Henry II, and Richard I,* R. Howlett (Editor), Vol. 4, Her Majesty's Stationery Office, London.

Rockwell, T. (2016). Is the southern San Andreas fault really overdue for a large earthquake or just late in the cycle? *7th International INQUA Meeting on Paleoseismology, Active Tectonics and Archeoseismology (PATA),* Crestone, Colorado, 30 May–3 June 2016.

Sbeinati, M. R., R. Darawcheh, and M. Mouty (2005). The historical earthquakes of Syria: An analysis of large and moderate earthquakes from 1365 B.C. to 1900 A.D, *Ann. Geophys.* **48,** no. 3, 347–435.

Sharman, G. R., S. A. Graham, M. Grove, and J. K. Hourigan (2013). A reappraisal of the early slip history of the San Andreas fault, central California, USA, *Geology* **41,** no. 7, 727–730, doi: 10.1130/G34214.1.

Sieberg, A. (1932). Untersuchungen Uber Erbeben und Bruchschollenbau im ostlichen Mittelmeergebiet, *Denkfchriften der Medizinisch Natur-wissenschaftlichen Gesellschaft zu Jena* **18,** 159–273 (in German).

Silverman, B. W. (1986). *Density Estimation for Statistics and Data Analysis,* Vol. 26, Chapman and Hall.

Sparapet Sembat (1869). Chronique du Royaume de Petite Arménie [□?մբատ Գունդստաբլի Ժամանակագիրք, Chronicle of the Kingdom of Little Armenia], in *Recueil des historiens des croisades: Historiens arméniens,* É. Dulaurier (Translator and Editor), Vol. 1, Imprimerie Nationale, Paris, pp. 610–682 (in Armenian).

Stucchi, M., P. Albini, C. Mirto, and A. Rebez (2004). Assessing the completeness of Italian historical earthquake data, *Ann. Geophys.* **47,** nos. 2/3, 659–673.

Stucchi, M., K. Şeşetyan, V. Castelli, A. A. G. Capera, C. Meletti, and M. R. Sbeinati (2024). About the "predecessors" of the 2023 February earthquakes, Turkey, *Seismica* **2,** no. 3, doi: 10.26443/seismica.v2i3.1312.

Toda, S., and R. S. Stein (2024). The role of stress transfer in rupture nucleation and Inhibition in the 2023 Kahramanmaraş, Türkiye, sequence, and a one-year earthquake forecast, *Seismol. Res. Lett.* **95,** no. 2A, 596–606, doi: 10.1785/0220230252.

Toda, S., R. S. Stein, A. D. Özbakir, H. Gonzalez-Huizar, V. Sevilgen, G. Lotto, and S. Sevilgen (2023). Stress change calculations provide clues to aftershocks in 2023 Türkiye earthquakes, *Temblor,* doi: 10.32858/temblor.295.

Toppozada, T. R., D. M. Branum, M. S. Reichle, and C. L. Hallstrom (2002). San Andreas fault zone, California: M ≥ 5.5 earthquake history, *Bull. Seismol. Soc. Am.* **92,** no. 7, 2555–2601.

Uchida, N., and R. Bürgmann (2019). Repeating earthquakes, *Annu. Rev. Earth Planet. Sci.* **47,** 305–332, doi: 10.1146/annurev-earth-053018-060119.

Utsu, T. (2002). Statistical features of seismicity, in *International Handbook of Earthquake and Engineering Seismology,* W. Lee, H. Kanamori, P. Jennings, and C. Kisslinger (Editors), Vol. part A, pp. 719–732.

Walter the Chancellor (1999). Bella Antiochena, in *Walter the Chancellor's The Antiochene Wars: A Translation and Commentary,* T. S. Asbridge and S. B. Edgington (Editor and Translator), Routledge.

Woessner, J., and S. Wiemer (2005). Assessing the quality of earthquake catalogues: Estimating the magnitude of completeness and its uncertainty, *Bull. Seismol. Soc. Am.* **95,** no. 2, 684–698, doi: 10.1785/0120040007.

Yan, K., M. Miyajima, H. Kumsar, Ö. Aydan, R. Ulusay, Z. Tao, Y. Chen, and F. Wang (2024). Preliminary report of field reconnaissance on the 6 February 2023 Kahramanmaras earthquakes in Türkiye, *Geoenviron. Disast.* **11,** no. 1, 1–24.

Ye, L., T. Lay, H. Kanamori, Z. Zhan, and Z. Duputel (2016). Diverse rupture processes in the 2015 Peru deep earthquake doublet, *Sci. Adv.* **2,** no. 6, e1600581, doi: 10.1126/sciadv.1600581.

Zabci, C., T. Sançar, H. N. Kıray, H. S. Akyüz, S. O. Akçiz, D. Battogtokh, E. Kırkan, G. Uçarkuş, G. Sunal, M. E. Aksoy, *et al.* (2023). February 6, 2023 M_w 7.8 Pazarcık (Kahramanmarai Turkey) earthquake: A supercycle event within a complex tectonic setting, *T2B-06, AGU Fall Meeting,* San Fransisco, 11–15 December 2023.

Zhou, J., Y. Xu, Y. Zhang, W. Feng, T. Taymaz, Y.-T. Chen, C. Xu, B. Xu, R. Wang, F. Shi, Z. Shao, and Q. Huang (2025). Geometric barriers impacted rupture processes and stress releases of the 2023 Kahramanmaraş, Türkiye, earthquake doublet, *Commun. Earth Environ.-Nature* **6,** no. 56, doi: 10.1038/s43247-025-02004-x.

Zohar, M. (2020). Temporal and spatial patterns of seismic activity associated with the Dead Sea transform (DST) during the past 3000 yr, *Seismol. Res. Lett.* **91,** no. 1, 207–221, doi: 10.1785/0220190124.

Zohar, M., B. Gennosar, R. Avny, N. Tessler, and A. Gal (2023). Spatiotemporal analysis in high resolution of tweets associated with the November 2016 wildfire in Haifa (Israel), *Int. J. Disaster Risk Reduct.* 92, doi: 10.1016/j.ijdrr.2023.103720.

Manuscript received 31 July 2025
Published online 31 December 2025

Data Mine

U.S. Geological Survey Geomagnetic Variometer Data: Capitalizing on Seismic Infrastructure

Adam T. Ringler[*1], Andrew Holcomb[2], Joshua E. Rigler[3], Spencer F. Wilbur[3], Christopher Balch[4,5], Corey Beutel[6], Brendan Geels[3], Jordan A. Guerra[4,5], Alan Horton[2], Edward Kromer[2], Kristen A. Lewis[3], Jeffrey J. Love[3], Yolando Root[2], Claudia K. Rossavik[3], Nicholas Shavers[7], John Spritzer[3], Tyler Storm[1], Alexandra N. Wernle[3], and David C. Wilson[1]

Abstract

The U.S. Geological Survey's Geomagnetism Program is collaborating with the Earthquake Hazards Program and Global Seismographic Network Program to densify magnetic field observations. This collaboration focuses on the installation of magnetometers, or magnetic variometers, at existing seismic stations. Along with improving the density of space weather observations for hazard monitoring, these data can be used to correct colocated magnetic field induced noise in seismic data. Such corrections are especially useful during time periods of large magnetic storms where the magnetic field-induced instrument noise can be of similar amplitude to earthquake ground-motion records.

Cite this article as Ringler, A. T., A. Holcomb, J. E. Rigler, S. F. Wilbur, C. Balch, C. Beutel, B. Geels, J. A. Guerra, A. Horton, E. Kromer, *et al.* (2025). U.S. Geological Survey Geomagnetic Variometer Data: Capitalizing on Seismic Infrastructure, *Seismol. Res. Lett.* **97**, 2179–2190, doi: 10.1785/0220250185.

Introduction

The Natural Hazards Mission Area of the U.S. Geological Survey (USGS) conducts scientific research that can be used to help mitigate loss of life and property from natural hazards through a number of different programs. These include the Geomagnetism Program, Global Seismographic Network (GSN) Program, and Earthquake Hazards Program (EHP). Researchers collect near-real-time geophysical data which are used for characterizing Earth processes. The USGS accomplishes this by recording changes in the magnetic field with magnetometers (e.g., Love and Finn, 2017). The GSN and EHP focus on recording ground motions with force-feedback seismometers (e.g., Wilson *et al.*, 2024).

The USGS operates 14 magnetic observatories that continuously monitor vector and scalar magnetic fields on Earth's surface and deliver these data in near-real time to government, academic, and industry partners, as well as the general public. Magnetic observatories are routinely calibrated in-place using specialized surveying equipment, and according to standards established by the International Real-time Magnetic Observatory Network (INTERMAGNET; e.g., Love and Chulliat, 2013). The goal is to create accurate and precise magnetic time-series data that are capable of tracking both long timescale secular changes in Earth's internal magnetic field, as well as rapid magnetic variations on the earth's surface that are associated with electrical currents that flow in Earth's ionosphere and magnetosphere during so-called geomagnetic storms, one form of "space weather" with recognized societal impacts. Not only is there U.S. statutory support (PROSWIFT Act, 2020), but the National Oceanic and Atmospheric Administration Space Weather Prediction Center, in partnership with the USGS Geomagnetism Program, maintains a near-real-time online geoelectric field hazard map to help assess and mitigate threats to the national electrical power distribution system on days with high magnetic field activity like 22 March 2025 (refer to Fig. 1).

Magnetic observatory standards make it challenging to operate more than a relatively small number of stations. However, absolute accuracy is not strictly required for most

1. U.S. Geological Survey, Albuquerque Seismological Laboratory, Albuquerque, New Mexico, U.S.A., https://orcid.org/0000-0002-9839-4188 (ATR); 2. KBR, Contractor to the U.S. Geological Survey, Albuquerque Seismological Laboratory, Albuquerque, New Mexico, U.S.A.; 3. U.S. Geological Survey, Geomagnetism Program, Golden, Colorado, U.S.A., https://orcid.org/0000-0003-4850-3953 (JER); https://orcid.org/0000-0001-8938-1644 (BG); https://orcid.org/0000-0003-4991-3399 (KAL); https://orcid.org/0000-0003-2606-6756 (CKR); https://orcid.org/0000-0002-2147-530X (JS); 4. NOAA, Space Weather Prediction Center, Boulder, Colorado, U.S.A., https://orcid.org/0000-0002-5359-3810 (CB); https://orcid.org/0000-0001-8819-9648 (JAG); 5. University of Colorado, CIRES, Boulder, Colorado, U.S.A.; 6. Kegman, Contractor to the U.S. Geological Survey, Albuquerque Seismological Laboratory, Albuquerque, New Mexico, U.S.A.; 7. Inalab, Contractor to the U.S. Geological Survey, Geomagnetism Program, Golden, Colorado, U.S.A.

*Corresponding author: aringler@usgs.gov

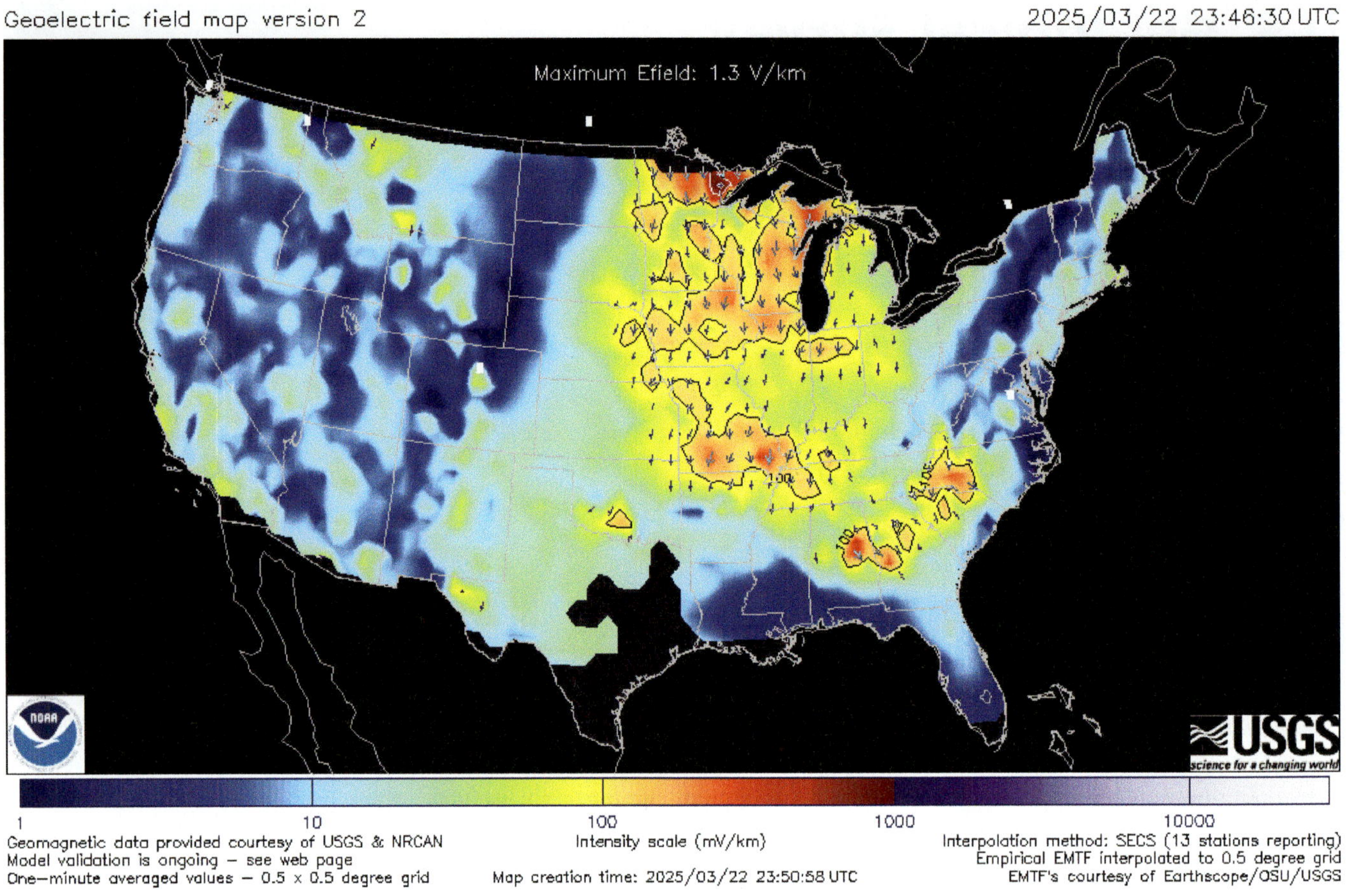

Figure 1. National Oceanic and Atmospheric Administration (NOAA) and U.S. Geological Survey (USGS) model for power grid operations for 22 March 2025. Reproduced from the website available in Data and Resources.

space weather applications. More important are continuous and near-real-time availability of data from a larger and more geographically concentrated network of geomagnetic sensors. Rigler *et al.* (2019) demonstrated that, even with sophisticated geographic interpolation, North America, and particularly the contiguous United States, was severely undersampled spatially, leading to significant uncertainty in estimated magnetic field vectors that grew quickly with distance from the magnetic observatories. To supplement magnetic observatories, the USGS began to instrument a subset of its seismic stations with commercial grade magnetometers, often described as magnetic variometers because, while their sensitivity to relative variations in the magnetic field are high, their absolute calibration is only approximate, and less applicable to many legacy geomagnetism applications like navigation. As of 2025, the locations of all North American magnetic observatories and USGS magnetic variometers, along with a color-coded distance metric to the nearest magnetometer, are shown in Figure 2.

The Albuquerque Seismological Laboratory (ASL) at the USGS manages several geophysical monitoring networks, including: the USGS portion of the GSN ("IU" network code); the U.S. National Seismic Network component of the Advanced National Seismic System ("US" network code); the Central and Eastern U.S. Network ("N4" network code); the Intermountain West Network ("IW" network code); and the New England Network ("NE" network code) (Wilson *et al.*, 2024). These stations are generally instrumented with force-feedback seismometers as well as strong-motion accelerometers. Locations of all ASL-managed seismological monitoring stations are shown in Figure 3, along with currently deployed USGS magnetometers, including both observatories and variometers.

It is known that the materials used in these instruments make them sensitive to local variations in the Earth's magnetic field (Forbriger, 2007; Forbriger *et al.*, 2010; Ringler, Anthony, *et al.*, 2020; Tape *et al.*, 2020; Diaz, 2024). Furthermore, this is complicated by the nearby conductivity at the station (Ringler *et al.*, 2024). For example, if the instruments are emplaced in a steel borehole, as compared to a nonconductive material, the situation can be further complicated. During time periods of large magnetic field variations, it is possible for the seismic data to become compromised because of the instrument noise induced by magnetic field disturbances. Another goal of deploying magnetic variometers at seismic stations is, during time periods of high-magnetic field activity, that the measurements can be used to correct for nonseismic noise coming from the sensor's sensitivity to magnetic field variations like during the Mother's Day 10 May 2024, magnetic storm (Fig. 4).

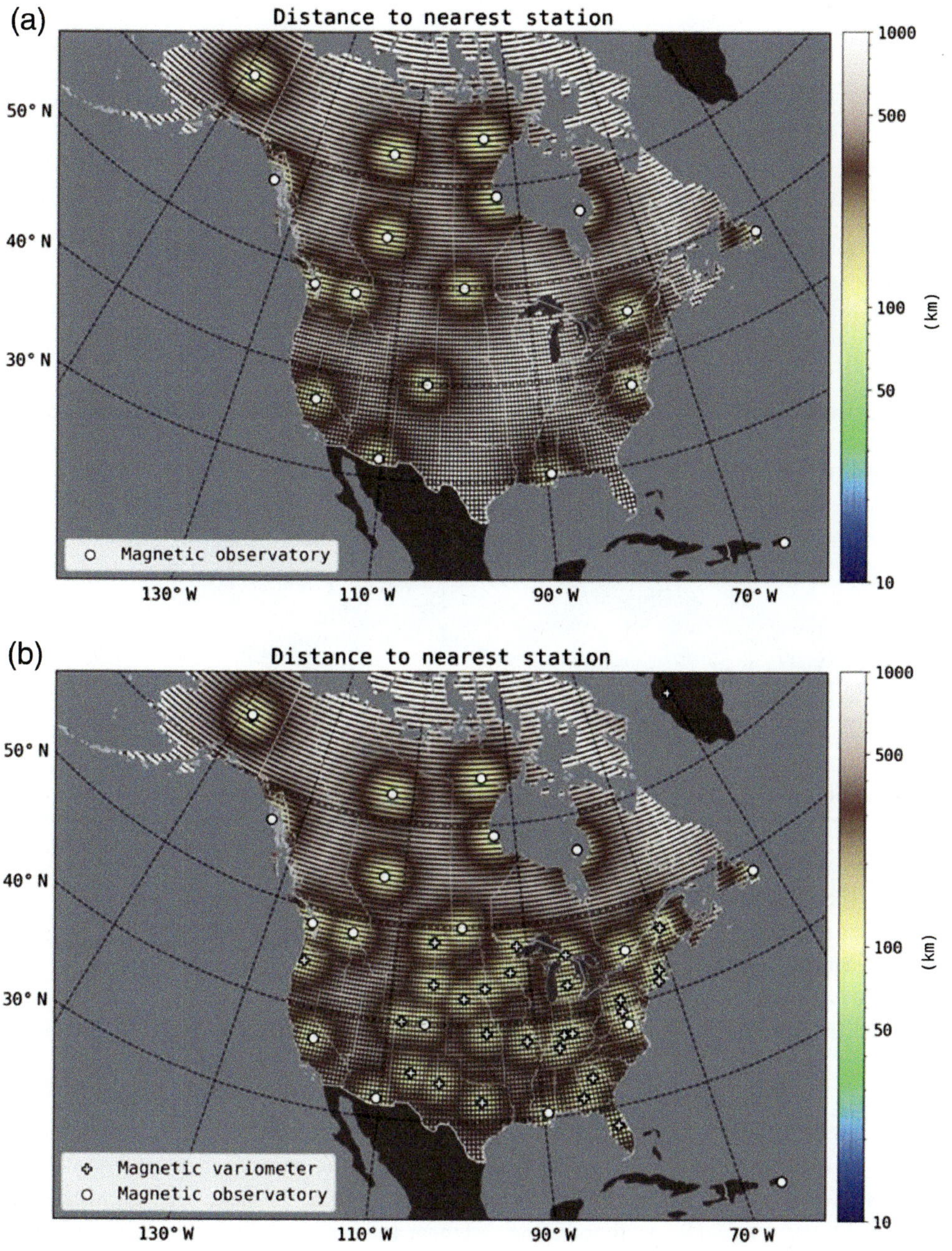

Figure 2. (a) Observatory magnetometer stations in North America operated by the USGS and National Resources Canada (black circles) with the color showing the distance to the nearest magnetometer. (b) Same as (a), but with the inclusion of the variometers introduced in this work.

respond to changes in pressure, temperature, and magnetic field variations. To shield the instruments from magnetic field variations, instruments are often surrounded by a mu-metal shield, which has been a common procedure since the start of the GSN in the late 1980s. Mu-metal shields are a closed container around the seismometer, made of a high magnetic permeability alloy, which provides a path for the magnetic field lines to go around the seismometer. Although this provides one way to reduce magnetic field contamination, it can be complicated in certain cases. The first magnetometer installed in the GSN was at QSPA (Quiet South Pole, Antarctica) near the end of 2003. These magnetometers can record rapid variations in the geomagnetic field caused by solar storms and other disturbances in the 20–800 s period band which is often used in global seismology. Classic feedback seismometers have no sensitivity at 0 Hz, sometimes referred to as "DC," because the feedback system of the instruments act as a high-pass filter. Similarly, the magnetic variometers installed at nonobservatory stations are not calibrated to account for the static or slowly varying portion of Earth's magnetic field. Therefore, they should not be relied upon to estimate things like secular variation because we have not tested for the long-term drift of the instruments.

This work documents the USGS' magnetic field monitoring densification effort. It discusses the instrumentation used, some of the differences between these and INTERMAGNET-standard observatories and the limitations of the data, and finally, the conventions used for this data, as well as some quality control methods.

Deployment and Design

The sensitivity of seismic equipment to nonseismic noise sources is well known (Forbriger, 2007). For example, seismic instruments

In 2022, the USGS added magnetometers to the existing ASL-operated seismic stations and began building several new magnetic observatories within the conterminous United States (CONUS). The current operational procedure has been to install variometers at strategic locations that would increase the densification of the USGS monitoring effort over the CONUS, and where seismic station maintenance visits were already planned. Figure 3 shows USGS variometer stations, along with magnetic observatories and ASL-operated stations that do not have variometers.

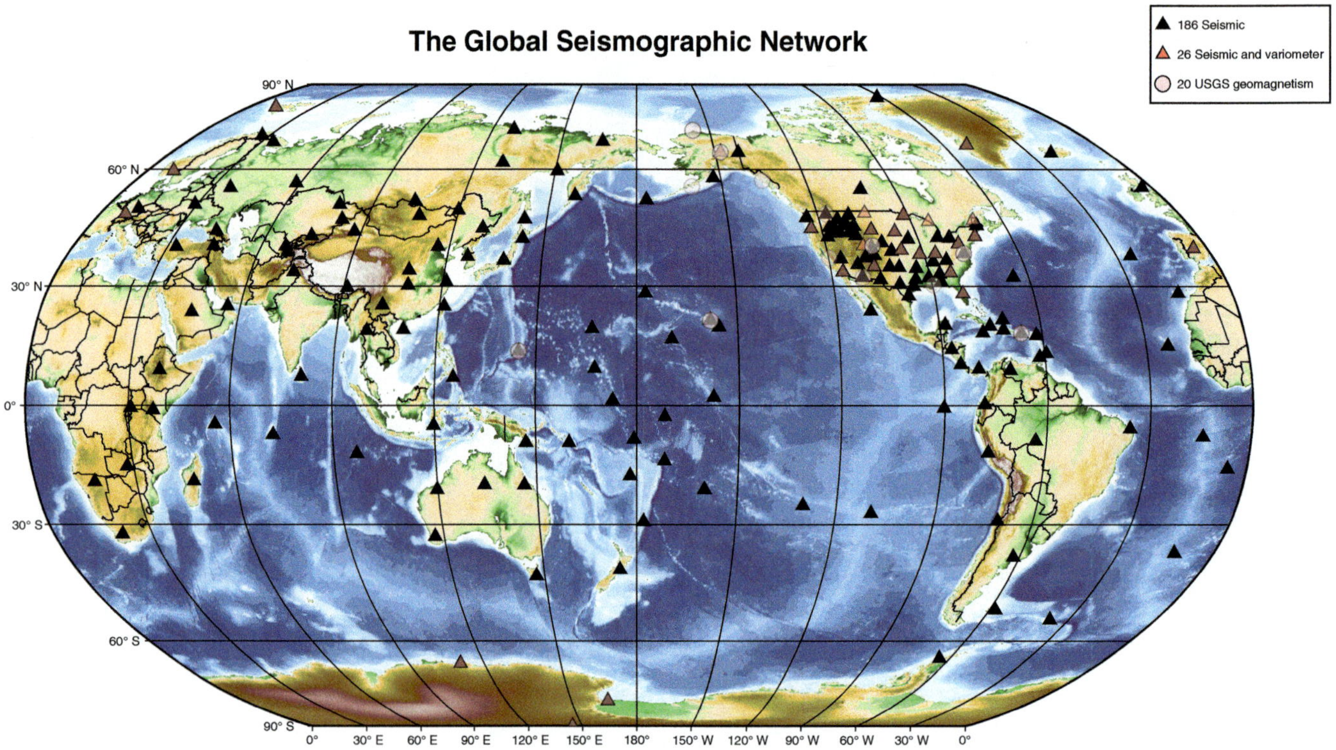

Figure 3. Map of USGS Geomagnetism observatory stations (pink circles), along with Albuquerque Seismological Laboratory (ASL)-operated seismic stations without variometers (black triangles) and with variometers (red triangles). Basemap is from Tozer *et al.* (2019).

Most ASL stations make use of six-channel Quanterra Q330 and Q330HR digitizers. At GSN stations there are often two digitizers, with the first instrument digitizing the primary broadband sensor and a strong-motion accelerometer. The second instrument digitizes the secondary broadband sensor, leaving open three channels that can be used to digitize a magnetic variometer. The ASL makes use of the Bartington Mag690 variometer. It was found in Ringler, Anthony, *et al.* (2020) that these variometers have similar noise levels to INTERMAGNET stations in the 10–1000 s period band and provide an effective way to obtain magnetic field data. This provides magnetic field data at a resolution that is sufficient to correct seismic data during time periods where the data are compromised because of magnetic field changes (Fig. 4).

Although the noise levels of these variometers are comparable to INTERMAGNET stations, the installation location within a seismic vault is not optimal. Many of these sensors are installed near various seismic equipment which produce local changes in the magnetic field (Fig. 5). This situation is unlike INTERMAGNET sites, where care is taken to avoid magnetic material, and the sensors are well isolated from local objects that could distort the magnetic field. Although reasonable effort was made to isolate magnetic variometers, no attempts were made to build new vaults or move stations to improve the data. The USGS continues to evaluate and install sensors.

Data Quality

Although magnetic variometer data do not meet INTERMAGNET's calibration standards, every attempt is made to produce low-noise, high-temporal resolution variational data. Before a variometer is installed at a station, it is colocated with our reference variometer in a "huddle test" at the ASL to ensure it is producing on-scale data with similar characteristics. When installing a magnetometer at a station, it is isolated from power cords and other sources that could change the local magnetic field. To make sure the instrument is operating and there are no orientation errors, we make use of a "screwdriver test." This involves passing a magnetized screwdriver along each of the sensitive axes of the instrument after installation (Fig. 6). The screwdriver test is similar to what is done to verify the sensitivity of an accelerometer by way of a "flip-test." For a flip-test, the accelerometer is rotated through the gravity field at the station, and it is verified that the sensor is outputting 9.8 m/s^2 in each direction. Although the screwdriver test can verify the polarity of the sensitive axes, it is unable to quantify the magnitude of the field. An example of the time-series data produced from a screwdriver test is shown in Figure 7. The small amplitude of the vertical component is caused by the physical sensor being located on the opposite side of the casing relative to the screwdriver. The screwdriver also passes by the horizontal components during the test, which is why you see the horizontal signals in Figure 7c. Although it may only be possible to verify the polarity

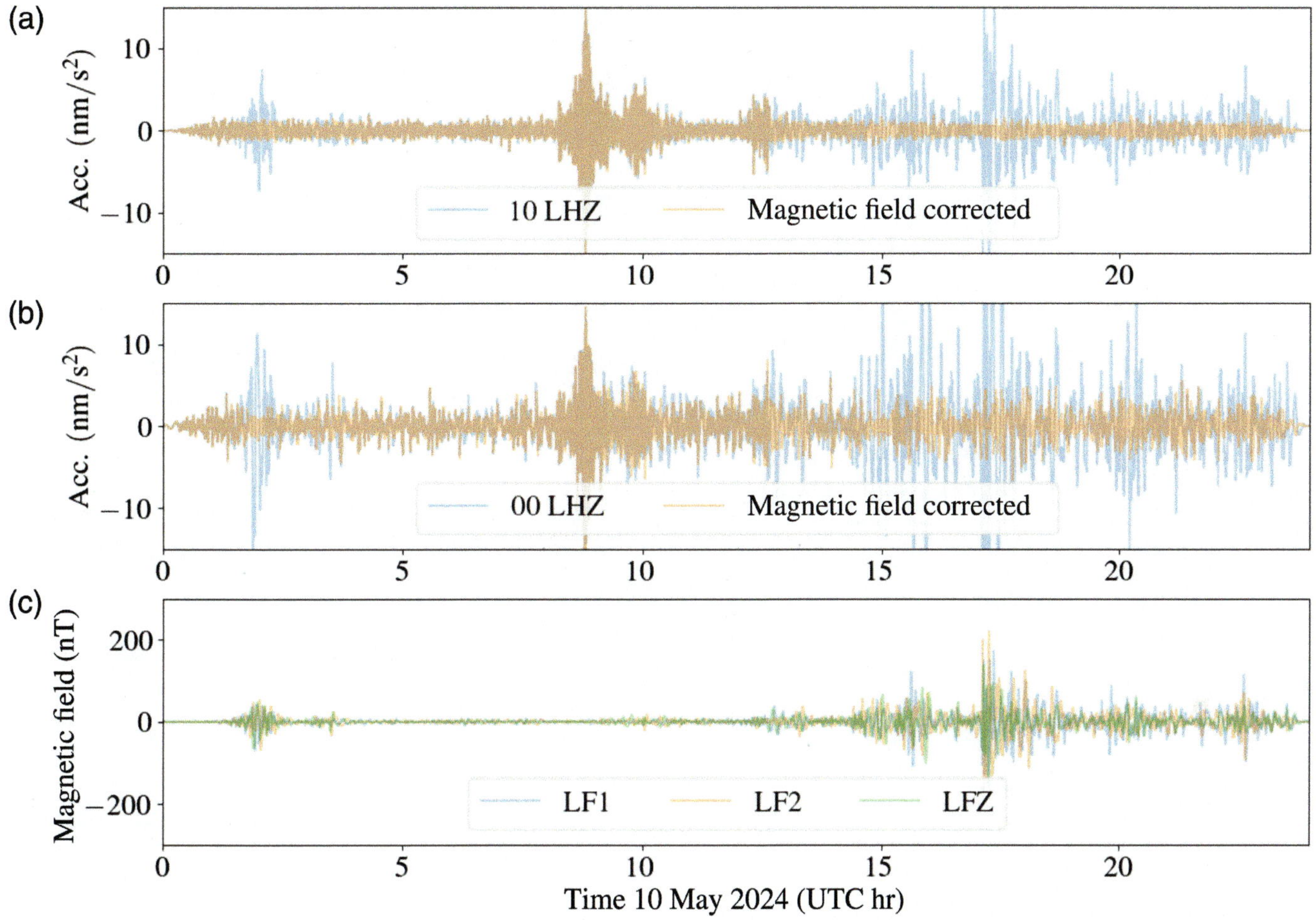

Figure 4. (a) Vertical-component secondary sensor data (blue) at USGS station QSPA (Quiet South Pole, Antarctica) from 40 to 800 s period for 10 May 2024. The same time series after correcting for the magnetic field is overlaid (orange). At ~08:00 UTC we see the **M** 5.8 Hualien City, Taiwan, earthquake. The Mother's Day solar storm can be seen starting at ~12:00 UTC. (b) Same as (a), but for the primary sensor. (c) All three variometer components at the station.

and qualitatively identify the components, this is an important test because of the difference in orientation conventions for seismic and magnetic field data. Seismologists use of a left-handed coordinate system for three-component data with the components being labeled as a north–south, east–west, and vertical component. To avoid the assumption that a station has perfect alignment, ASL publishes these three components as 1, 2, and Z. The goal is to encourage data users to make sure they have metadata that describe the orientation of the sensor instead of making an assumption of perfect north–south alignment. This can be even more important with many GSN stations making use of borehole seismometers (Ringler, Steim, *et al.*, 2020).

Seismological data are often reported in a left-handed coordinate system, with three components ordered as north–south, east–west, and vertical up. This coordinate system stems from historical instruments that were aligned to north–south and east–west directions and used a frame of reference with vertical upward motion being positive (e.g., Dewey and Byerly, 1969). In contrast, geomagnetic field data are almost always described in terms of a right-handed coordinate system, with three components ordered as east–west, north–south, and vertical down (Fig. 8). Several corrections and calibrations are applied to U.S. geomagnetism data (Rigler and Claycomb, 2020) to be able to observe things like secular variations and very slow temporal changes in the Earth's magnetic field. Unlike these data, the variometer data are presented more like seismic data. That is, the data are stored and disseminated in raw counts with no corrections being applied. To convert these counts into a physical measurement of the Earth's magnetic field (e.g., nanoTeslas) it is necessary to correct for the instrument response, which is published in the metadata for the sensor.

Although the initial huddle test, along with the screwdriver test, provide engineering functionality tests of the variometers, they provide no initial way to estimate what quality of data these stations will provide. The long wavelength features of Earth's magnetic field during solar storms allow for a comparison to nearby INTERMAGNET stations. For example, Figure 9 presents a comparison of the waveforms for seismic station WCI (Wyandotte Cave, Indiana) and USGS magnetic observatory FRD (Fredericksburg, Virginia) for 13 May 2024, which

Figure 5. (a) The seismic vault at Global Seismographic Network station SSPA (Standing Stone, Pennsylvania). (b) Close-up picture of the equipment vault. (c) Looking down into the equipment vault. The rack contains the digitizers along with the communication system used for the station. (d) Picture of the strong-motion accelerometer (left) and the variometer (right). (e) Close-up picture of the variometer as installed on a baseplate.

was shortly after the Mother's Day solar storm. These stations are ~780 km apart. Relatively similar waveforms for the north–south (Fig. 9a) and east–west (Fig. 9b) components are apparent, with correlations of 0.969 and 0.965, respectively. The low-frequency drift between the vertical components shows the waveforms are somewhat dissimilar with a correlation of 0.811. Although the correlation gives a measurement of how similar the waveforms are, it does not identify differences in timing. To estimate gross timing errors, the time-series shift that produces the highest correlation value can be estimated. For example, in Figure 9a, a shift of 9 s maximizes the correlation. The spatial difference between the station makes it so that only large timing errors (e.g., greater than 20 s) are reliable. Finally, to verify the amplitude of the waveforms the root mean square ratio between the variometer and the observatory magnetometer is examined. For example, the ratio seen in Figure 9a, between the north–south components, is 0.892, suggesting that the observatory magnetometer's waveforms are larger than the variometer. However, given the spatial difference and coarse method this suggests the variometer is producing reasonable quality magnetic field data.

Although the comparison shown in Figure 9 should be viewed as a "good" station, not all stations produce data of this quality. A similar comparison, but for a station with local magnetic field disturbances, is shown in Figure 10. Although the overall waveforms between the variometer at DWPF (Disney World Preserve, Florida) and the USGS observatory magnetometer BSL (orange; Stennis, Mississippi) is good, a large amount of high-frequency noise can be seen at DWPF. These stations are ~835 km apart. This could be coming from grounding issues in

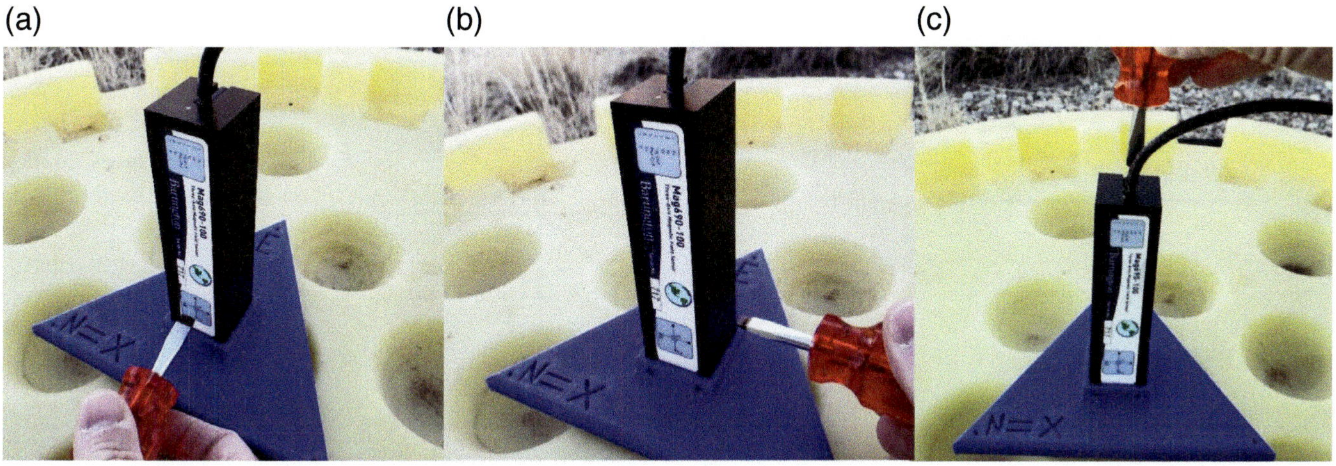

Figure 6. (a) Screwdriver test along the east–west component of the magnetometer. (b,c) Same as (a), but for the north–south and vertical components, respectively.

the vault or other local magnetic field changes caused by the equipment. To minimize such noise sources, it has been necessary to move the variometers to different locations in the vault. Although every effort is made to produce the most accurate data possible, installing the sensors in the same vault as the seismic equipment can make it difficult to avoid such situations. It can be noted that the low-frequency characteristics at DWPF track those of BSL. However, we see that the vertical components show a large shift and a negative correlation. This may be a case where the smaller vertical field combined with local disturbances are producing problematic quantitative comparisons, but the station is otherwise operating as intended.

Data Availability

All USGS magnetic variometer data are streamed in near-real time to, first, the USGS, and then are immediately retransmitted to the National Science Foundation's Data Management Center, which is an archive operated by the

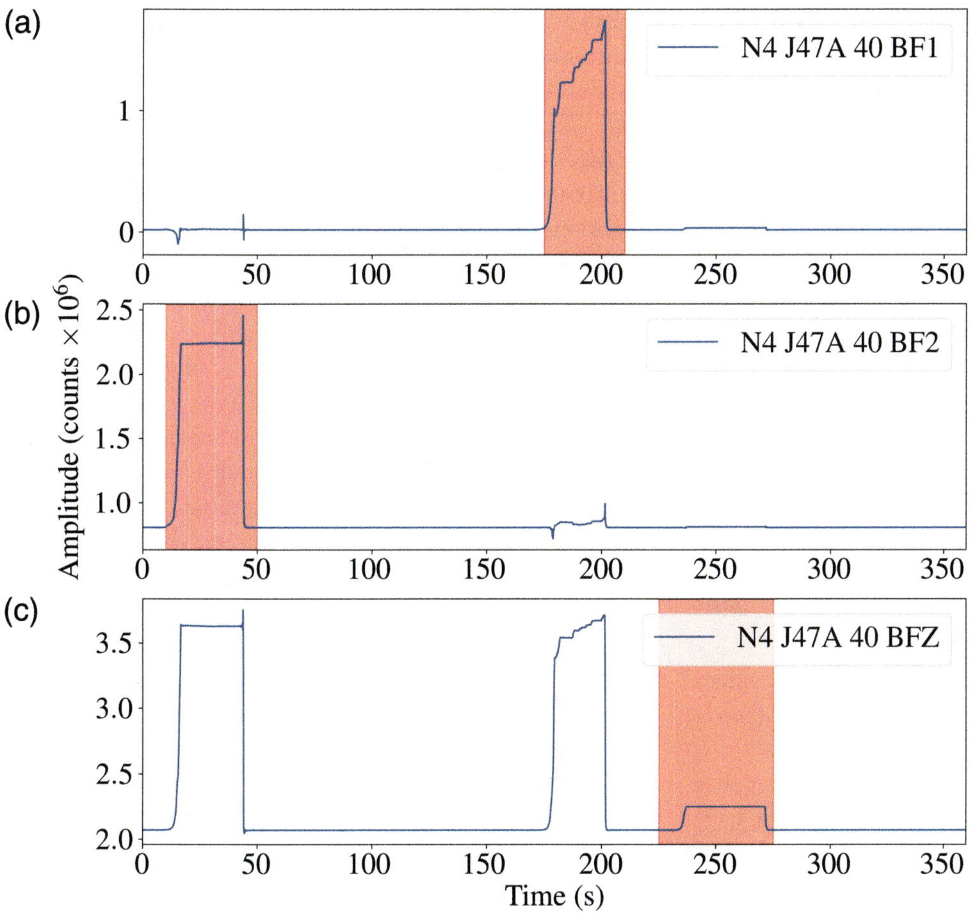

Figure 7. (a) Time-series data from a "screwdriver test" at N4 station J47A (Summer, Michigan) for the BF1 component. The blue line is the variometer data, and the red-shaded region is where the screwdriver was moved past the sensor. (b,c) Same as (a), but for the BF2 and BFZ components, respectively. Note that the amplitude of the vertical component is smaller because of where the sensor module is located inside the variometer.

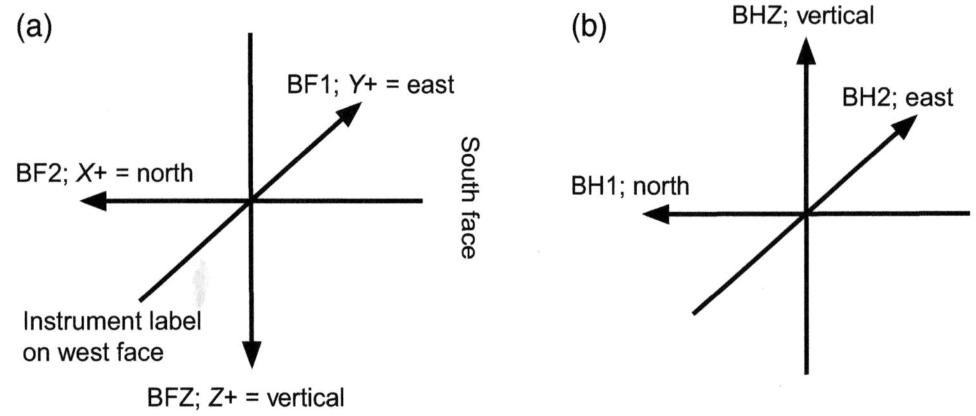

Figure 8. (a) Right-handed coordinate system and channel labeling for USGS variometers. (b) Left-handed coordinate system and channel labeling for USGS seismometers. Note that if a sensor is not oriented to north, it will be documented in the metadata.

EarthScope Consortium (formerly known as the Incorporated Research Institutions for Seismology, or IRIS). This long-term data archive can be publicly accessed through International Federation of Digital Seismograph Networks (FDSN) webservices. These data streams comprise 512-byte packets that follow the Standard for the Exchange of Earthquake Data (SEED; Ahern *et al.*, 2012; Ringler and Evans, 2015) data-only format (often referred to as "miniSEED"). Initially, only one sample per second was collected from magnetic variometers deployed at USGS seismological stations. However, because these data began to be incorporated into near-real-time applications, it became clear that this sampling frequency resulted in unacceptably long latencies. As of the end of 2024, all USGS magnetic variometer stations had been converted to collect ten samples per second. This had the added advantage of being consistent with the USGS's default observatory sampling frequency.

These magnetic data, just like their seismological counterparts, are transmitted as raw integer counts following a SEED-recommended naming convention. This convention requires: (1) a two-character network code; (2) a 3–5-character station code; (3) a three-character channel code; and (4) a two-character location code. Network codes are unique to the program or institution responsible for the data. For example, as already noted, many USGS magnetic variometers are part of the GSN, for which network code is "IU." However, ASL manages sites for additional networks at which magnetic variometers have been installed, including "US" and "N4" networks. Station codes are unique to a given site, and typically (but not always) reflect a nearby geographical point of interest. Channel codes are intended to capture in their three characters, respectively, the approximate sampling frequency, geophysical data type, and coordinate frame information. For example, one sample per second magnetic fields aligned with the vertical axis of a three-axis vector magnetometer would be "LFZ." Data collected at ten samples per second would be "BFZ." Finally, a location code is used to indicate separate sensors deployed at a given station and is especially useful if there are multiple sensors with similar channel codes. A convention that traces back to the earliest codeployed magnetic variometers assigns a location code of 40.

To convert variometer data from digital counts to magnetic field intensity, it is necessary to use the most recent metadata. Although this is obvious to most seismologists, it can be less obvious to data users in other fields where the data come already corrected for various instrumentational corrections (e.g., Global Navigation Satellite System data). At the time of this writing, seismological metadata are usually organized using either the SEED format (Ahern *et al.*, 2012) or the newer StationXML format (see Data and Resources). Metadata for both formats are available through the EarthScope Data Management Center through an FDSN webservice request, similar to how the time-series data can be retrieved, as discussed earlier. For most applications, the format and organization of these metadata are not important. There are methods to convert between the formats, and most corrections and processing can be done using outside packages such as ObsPy (Megies *et al.*, 2011) following a similar flow to that discussed in Ringler and Bastien (2020).

To facilitate access to magnetic variometer data and offer consistency to engineering and research communities more accustomed to typical magnetic observatory data, the USGS developed web-based data services that retrieve raw data and associated metadata, generate calibrated data in physical units, ensure that vector components are correctly aligned with true geographic north, east, and down, and, finally, resample to a desired cadence. Figure 11 is a sample screenshot of time series for the three vector components at one of the newer (as of early 2025) USGS magnetic variometer installations. This data visualization tool can also be used to pull digital data for each of the traces by clicking on the "Details" button, and it uses the same underlying data service as USGS magnetic observatory data.

Summary

The USGS has developed a collaborative project to make use of existing seismic infrastructure to densify our magnetic field observations using lower cost variometers. These instruments can provide low-latency data for monitoring space weather. The ferromagnetic properties of modern broadband seismometers

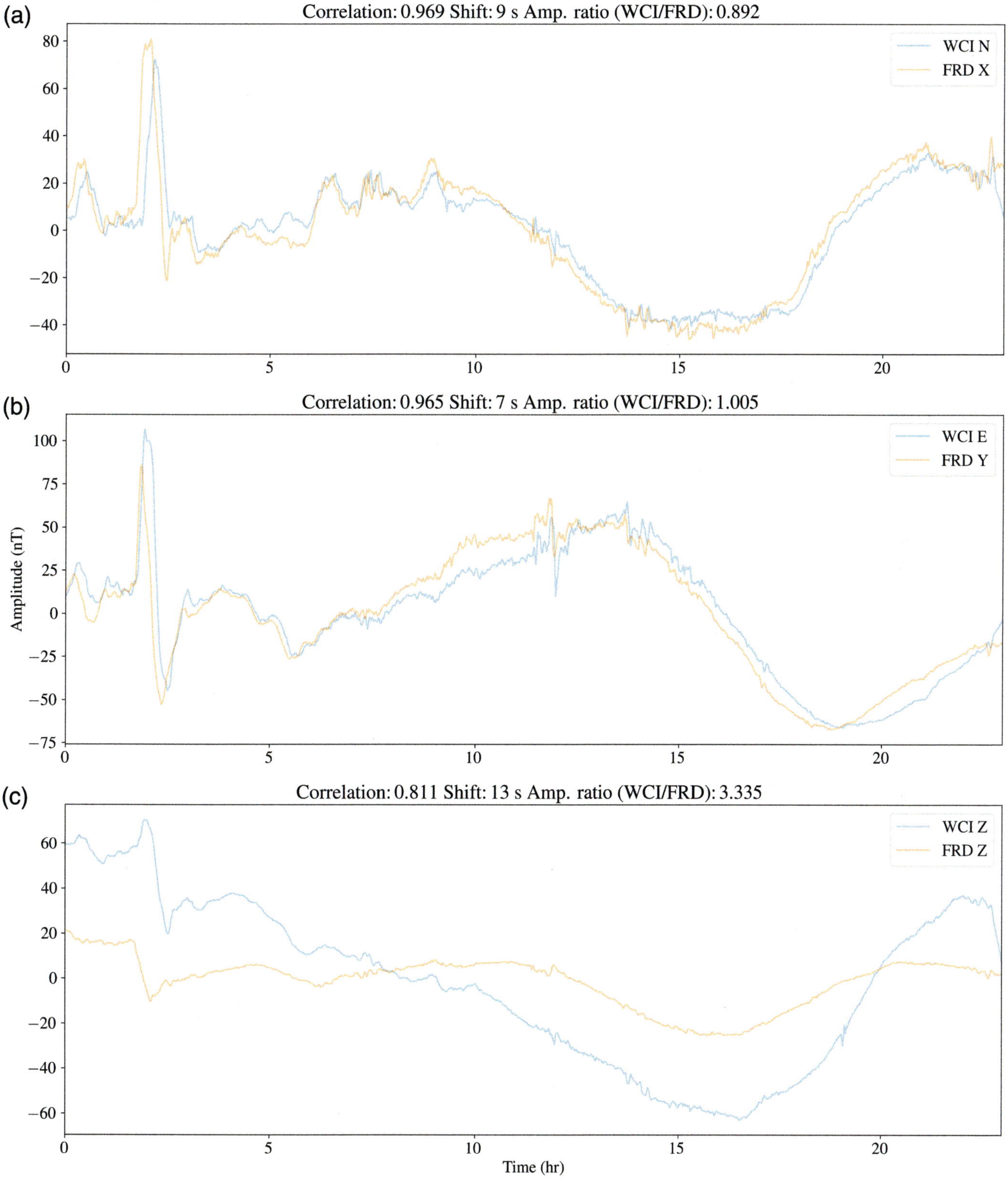

Figure 9. (a) Waveform comparison between the north–south component of the variometer installed at USGS seismic station WCI (Wyandotte Cave, Indiana) and USGS geomagnetism station FRD (Fredricksburg, Virginia) for 13 May 2024. Both components are rotated to a common frame. To quantify the comparison, we estimate the correlation (0.969) between the components, the shift at which the maximum correlation occurs (9 s), and finally the ratio of the root mean square (rms) between components (0.892). (b,c) Same as (a), but for the east–west, and vertical components, respectively.

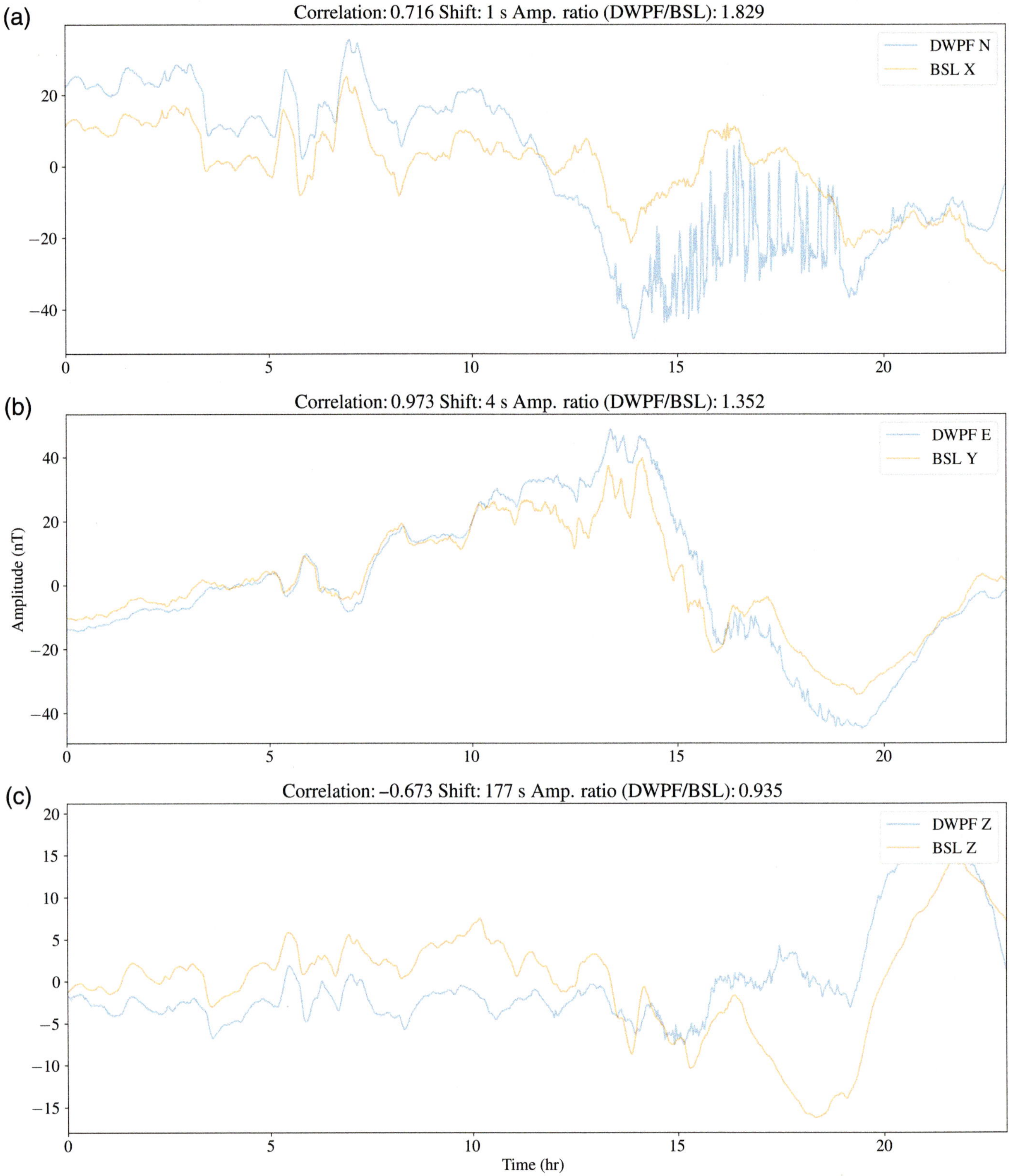

Figure 10. (a) Waveform comparison between the north–south component of the variometer installed at USGS seismic station DWPF (Disney World Preserve, Florida) and USGS geomagnetism station BSL (Stennis, Mississippi) for 26 April 2024. Both components are rotated to a common frame. To quantify the comparison, we estimate the correlation (0.716) between the components, the shift at which the maximum correlation occurs (1 s), and finally the ratio of the rms between components (1.892). (b,c) Same as (a), but for the east–west, and vertical components, respectively.

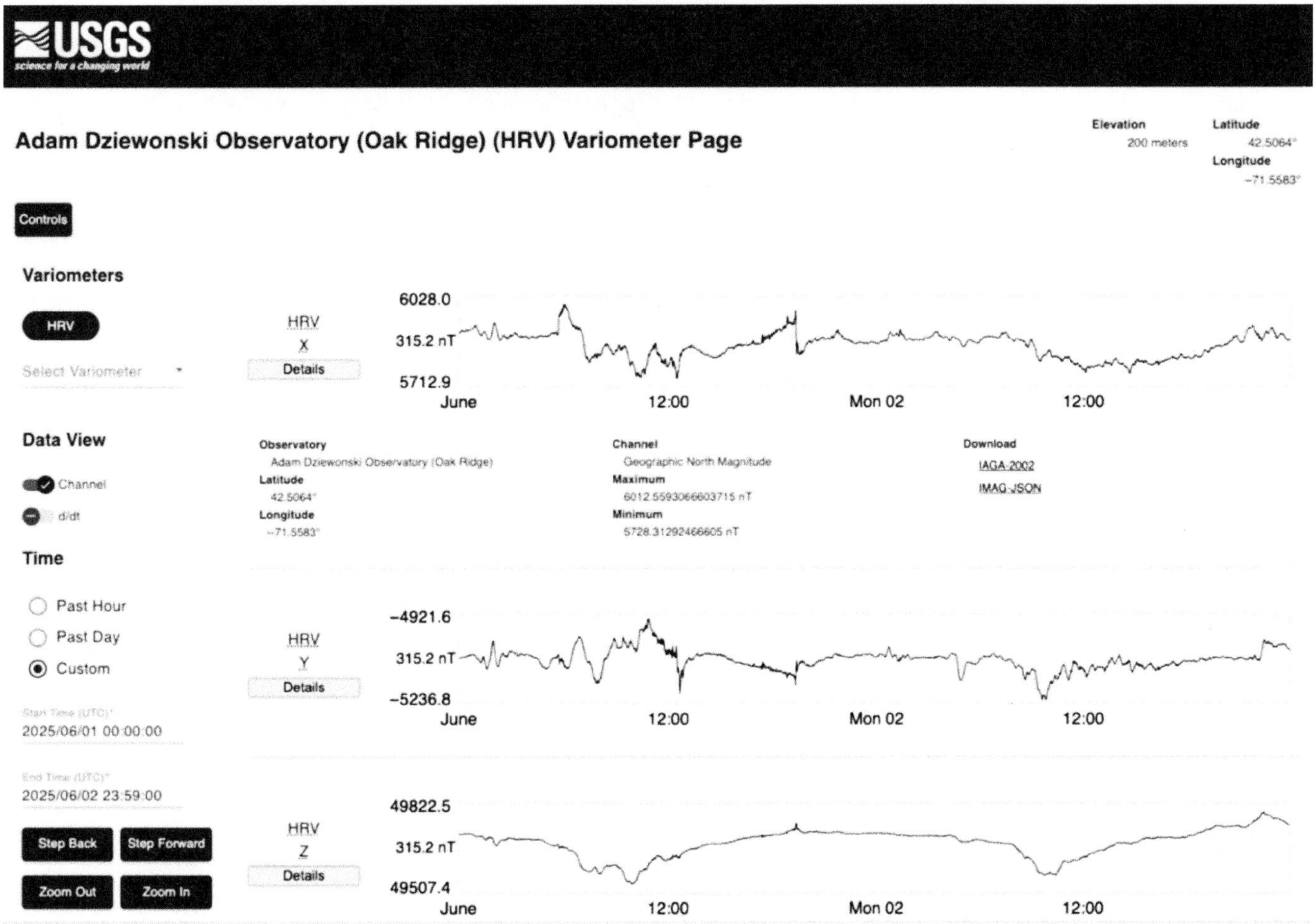

Figure 11. Example of the U.S. Geological Survey Geomagnetism Program web display for the variometer recording at the Adam Dziewonski Observatory (station code HRV) of the Global Seismographic Network. Reproduced from the website available in Data and Resources.

make them sensitive to magnetic field variations. It has been shown that by colocating a variometer near a seismometer, it is possible to correct out this unwanted magnetic field-induced noise. Large-scale magnetic storms could limit our ability to characterize seismic events and compromise seismic data during these time periods. The deployment of these sensors started in 2003 and became a formal collaboration in fiscal year 2024. By leveraging expertise and the large footprint of USGS-operated seismic stations, we have increased the number of magnetic field observations from 14 Geomagnetism Program observatories to 46 stations total recording low-latency magnetic field data.

Data and Resources

All data used in this work are freely available at EarthScope under network codes CU (Albuquerque Seismological Laboratory [ASL]/ U.S. Geological Survey [USGS], 2006), IU (ASL/USGS, 1988), IC (ASL/USGS, 1992), US (ASL/USGS, 1990), NE (ASL/USGS, 1994), N4 (ASL/USGS, 2013), IW (ASL/USGS, 2003), and NT (USGS, 1901). Magnetic data can also be obtained from INTERMAGNET: https://intermagnet.org/. Data were accessed from the National Science Foundation (NSF) SAGE data archive operated by EarthScope Consortium (NSF Award 1724509). This work makes use of the Python packages Matplotlib (Hunter, 2007), ObsPy (Megies *et al.*, 2011), and PyGMT (Dongdong *et al.*, 2025). Code for reproducing figures in this article is available at code.usgs.gov/asl/papers/ringler/geomag_vari. Seismological metadata are available at https://www.fdsn.org/xml/station/. The data to Figure 1 were available at spaceweather.gov and Figure 11 at https://geomag.usgs.gov/plots/variometer. All websites were last accessed in August 2025.

Acknowledgments

The authors thank Patrick Bastien, Jordi Diaz, Ryan Gold, Kristen Marra, Brian Shiro, and another anonymous reviewer for constructive reviews that improved the article. The authors would like to thank the field technicians that have helped in installing and servicing the magnetometers, software developers, and IT staff responsible for web-based data services and visualization tools, and administrative support staff.

Any use of trade, firm, or product names is for descriptive purposes only and does not imply endorsement by the U.S. Government.

References

Ahern, T., R. Casey, D. Barnes, R. Benson, T. Knight, and C. Trabant (2012). SEED Reference Manual, version 2.4, available at http://www.fdsn.org/seed_manual/SEEDManual_V2.4.pdf (last accessed June 2025).

Albuquerque Seismological Laboratory (ASL)/U.S. Geological Survey (USGS) (1988). Global Seismograph Network (GSN–IRIS/USGS), *International Federation of Digital Seismograph Networks, Other/Seismic Network*, doi: 10.7914/SN/IU.

ASL/USGS (1990). United States National Seismic Network, *International Federation of Digital Seismograph Networks, Other/Seismic Network*, doi: 10.7914/SN/US.

ASL/USGS (1992). New China Digital Seismograph Network, *International Federation of Digital Seismograph Networks, Other/Seismic Network*, doi: 10.7914/SN/IC.

ASL/USGS (1994). New England Seismic Network, *International Federation of Digital Seismograph Networks, Other/Seismic Network*, doi: 10.7914/SN/US.

ASL/USGS (2003). Intermountain West Seismic Network, *International Federation of Digital Seismograph Networks, Other/Seismic Network*, doi: 10.7914/SN/IW.

ASL/USGS (2006). Caribbean Network, *International Federation of Digital Seismograph Networks, Other/Seismic Network*, doi: 10.7914/SN/CU.

ASL/USGS (2013). Central and Eastern United States Network, *International Federation of Digital Seismograph Networks, Other/Seismic Network*, doi: 10.7914/SN/N4.

Dewey, J., and P. Byerly (1969). The early history of seismometry (to 1900), *Bull. Seismol. Soc. Am.* **59,** no. 1, 183–227, doi: 10.1785/BSSA0590010183.

Diaz, J. (2024). Monitoring May 2024 solar and geomagnetic storm using broadband seismometers, *Sci. Rep.* **14,** 30066, doi: 10.1038/s41598-024-81079-6.

Dongdong, T., L. Uieda, W. J. Leong, Y. Fröhlich, W. Schlitzer, M. Grund, M. Jones, L. Toney, J. Yao, J-.H. Tong, *et al.* (2025). PyGMT: A Python interface for the Generic Mapping Tools, *Zenodo*, doi: 10.5821/zenodo.14868324.

Forbriger, T. (2007). Reducing magnetic field induced noise in broadband seismic recordings, *Geophys. J. Int.* **169,** no. 1, 240–258, doi: 10.1111/j.1365-246X.2006.03295.x.

Forbriger, T., R. Widmer-Schnidrig, E. Wielandt, M. Hayman, and N. Ackerley (2010). Magnetic field background variations can limit the resolution of seismic broad-band sensors, *Geophys. J. Int.* **183,** no. 1, 303–312, doi: 10.1111/j.1365-246X.2010.04719.x.

Hunter, J. D. (2007). Matplotlib: A 2D graphics environment, *Comput. Sci. Eng.* **9,** 90–95, doi: 10.1109/MCSE.2007.55.

Love, J. J., and A. Chulliat (2013). An international network of magnetic observatories, *Eos Trans. AGU* **94,** no. 42, 373–384, doi: 10.1002/2013EO420001.

Love, J. J., and C. A. Finn (2017). Real-time geomagnetic monitoring for space weather-related applications: Opportunities and challenges, *Space Weather* **15,** no. 7, 820–827, doi: 10.1002/2017SW001665.

Megies, T., M. Beyreuther, R. Barsch, L. Krischer, and J. Wassermann (2011). ObsPy-What can it do for data centers and observatories? *Ann. Geophys.* **54,** 47–58, doi: 10.4401/ag-4838.

Rigler, J. E., and A. E. Claycomb (2020). Adjusted geomagnetic data-Theoretical basis and validation, *U.S. Geol. Surv. Open-File Rept. 2020-1053*, 26 pp., doi: 10.3133/oft20201053.

Rigler, J. E., R. A. D. Fiori, A. A. Pulkkinen, M. Wiltberger, and C. Balch (2019). Interpolating geomagnetic observations, in *Geomagnetically Induced Currents from the Sun to the Power Grid*, J. L. Gannon, A. Swidinsky, and Z. Xu (Editors), Vol. 244, American Geophysical Union, Geophysical Monograph Series, 15–41, doi: 10.1002/9781119434412.ch2.

Ringler, A. T., K. Aderhold, R. E. Anthony, R. W. Busby, A. Frassetto, T. Tanimoto, and D. C. Wilson (2024). Perspective on transportable array Alaska background noise levels, in *Tectonics and Seismic Structure of Alaska and Northwestern Canada: EarthScope and Beyond*, N. A. Ruppert, M. A. Jadamec, and J. T. Freymueller (Editors), Vol. 290, American Geophysical Union, Geophysical Monograph Series, 15–44, doi: 10.1002/9781394195947.ch2.

Ringler, A. T., and P. Bastien (2020). A brief introduction to seismic instrumentation: Where does my data come from? *Seismol. Res. Lett.* **91,** no. 2A, 1074–1083, doi: 10.1785/0220190214.

Ringler, A. T., and J. R. Evans (2015). A quick SEED tutorial, *Seismol. Res. Lett.* **86,** no. 6, 1717–1725, doi: 10.1785/0220150043.

Ringler, A. T., R. E. Anthony, D. C. Wilson, A. C. Claycomb, and J. Spritzer (2020). Magnetic field variations in Alaska: Recording space weather events on seismic stations in Alaska, *Bull. Seismol. Soc. Am.* **110,** no. 5, 2530–2540, doi: 10.1785/0120200019.

Ringler, A. T., J. Steim, D. C. Wilson, R. Widmer-Schnidrig, and R. E. Anthony (2020). Improvements in seismic resolution and current limitations in the Global Seismographic Network, *Geophys. J. Int.* **220,** no. 1, 508–521, doi: 10.1093/gji/ggz473.

Tape, C., A. T. Ringler, and D. L. Hampton (2020). Recording the Aurora at seismometers across Alaska, *Seismol. Res. Lett.* **91,** no. 6, 3039–3053, doi: 10.1785/0220200161.

Tozer, B., D. T. Sandwell, W. H. F. Smith, C. Olson, J. R. Beale, and P. Wessel (2019). Global bathymetry and topography at 15 Arc Sec: SRTM15+, *Earth Space Sci.* **6,** no. 10, 1847–1864, doi: 10.1029/2019EA000658.

USGS (1901). U.S. Geological Survey geomagnetism program, *International Federation of Digital Seismograph Networks, Other/Seismic Network*, doi: 10.7914/SN/NT.

Wilson, D. C., C. R. Hutt, L. S. Gee, A. T. Ringler, and R. E Anthony (2024). Global seismic networks operated by the U.S. Geological Survey, *Seismol. Res. Lett.* **95,** no. 3, 1578–1590, doi: 10.1785/0220230178.

Manuscript received 5 June 2025
Published online 5 November 2025

SSA News and Notes

2026 SSA Election Results

Following the 9 January **2026 SSA Board of Directors Election**, four new members will join the Board for three-year terms of service on 14 April 2026:

Aybige Akinci, *National Institute of Geophysics and Volcanology in Italy*

Esteban Chavez, *Volcanological and Seismological Observatory of Costa Rica at Universidad Nacional, Costa Rica*

Xiaowei Chen, *Texas A&M University*

Maureen Long, *Yale University*

The election was conducted by YesElections!, a third-party independent firm.

Congratulations, 2026 Honorees

At the 2026 Annual Meeting, SSA will recognize the following members for their outstanding contributions to the Society mission and to seismology, including research, mentoring, and public service.

Harry Fielding Reid Medal: Peter Shearer

Shearer, professor of geophysics at Scripps Institution of Oceanography, University of California, San Diego, is the recipient of SSA's highest honor. Recognized as one of the leading observational seismologists of his generation, he is recognized for his outstanding contributions to improving earthquake locations and other source properties and his research delineating the structure and dynamics of Earth's mantle and core. He is perhaps best known for his efforts to develop methods of precisely determining earthquake locations, which have led to further insights into fault interactions, seismic stress release, and the physics behind earthquakes.

Peter Shearer. The color version of this figure is available only in the electronic edition.

Charles F. Richter Early-Career Award: Kevin Milner

Milner, a research geophysicist at the U.S. Geological Survey's Geologic Hazards Science Center, is recognized for his wide-ranging, globally adopted research that has become central to seismic hazard analysis modeling. His contributions to seismic hazard analysis include advanced computational infrastructure open-source tool development, testing earthquake forecasting and early warning systems, quantification of epistemic uncertainty in hazard and risk models, and development of the National Seismic Hazard Model in the United States and New Zealand.

Kevin Milner. The color version of this figure is available only in the electronic edition.

Frank Press Public Service Award: Lisa Wald

Wald, retired from the U.S. Geological Survey, is recognized for her groundbreaking role at the USGS Earthquake Hazards Program in making a wealth of earthquake information available, both educational resources and real-time products, in a

Lisa Wald. The color version of this figure is available only in the electronic edition.

Ruth Harris. The color version of this figure is available only in the electronic edition.

variety of forms and through a variety of channels—including internet, text, and email—serving everyone from the general public to seismologists to governments to the media. Wald taught herself HTML in the 1990s to build earthquake.usgs.gov, ushering in the internet era for the Survey.

Distinguished Service to SSA Award: Ruth Harris

Harris, a senior research geophysicist at the U.S. Geological Survey, is recognized for her longtime service and support of the Society, including contributions made as a Board member, vice president, and SSA president. These contributions include creating the SSA Annual Meeting's Student Presentation Awards Program, supporting the development of open-access options for SSA journals and her current service as associate editor for *The Seismic Record* (*TSR*), along with her active participation on numerous SSA committees.

COSMOS/EERI/SSA Bruce Bolt Medal: Eduardo Miranda

Miranda, a professor of civil and environmental engineering at Stanford University, is recognized for developing new ground-motion models and intensity measures, refining damping modification factors and improving methods for assessing seismic demands on structures and nonstructural components. His work has shaped seismic design provisions, and he has emphasized the use of strong-motion data in a wide range of research and teaching. His many significant contributions include developments in ground-motion modeling and, more recently, ground-motion directionality.

Eduardo Miranda. The color version of this figure is available only in the electronic edition.

SSA Updates Position Statements on Hazards Monitoring and Education and Workforce Development

SSA continues to encourage U.S. Congress members to support science-driven policies that protect public safety. As part of these efforts, the Society has updated its public policy statements related to hazard monitoring and education/workforce development.

The **Statement on Monitoring Earthquakes, Tsunamis, and Other Hazards** urges Congress to support and improve observing/hazard monitoring networks as well as early warning programs and products. **The Statement on Education and Workforce Development** encourages policymakers to take steps to grow and diversify the nation's critically important pipeline of Earth sciences-focused talent.

To read the newly updated statements in full, visit seismosoc.org/us-government-relations.

SRL Welcomes First Deputy Editor-in-Chief

Hongfeng Yang has begun an editorial role that is new to him and new to our journal; He is the first deputy editor-in-chief of *Seismological Research Letters (SRL)*.

Yang, a professor in the Department of Earth and Environmental Sciences at The Chinese University of Hong Kong, joined the *SRL* editorial board as an associate editor in 2018.

"The dedication, thoughtfulness and good judgment he exercised as an associate editor will serve him well as deputy," said *SRL* Editor-in-Chief **Allison Bent**, who made Yang's appointment.

Read more about Yang at seismosoc.org/news/srl-welcomes-first-deputy-editor-in-chief.

Hongfeng Yang. The color version of this figure is available only in the electronic edition.

SSA Announces Reviewers of the Year

Norman Abrahamson (University of California, Berkeley), **Claire Doody** (Lawrence Livermore National Lab), **Daisuke Ishimura** (Chiba University), **Andrea Llenos** (U.S. Geological Survey), **Hongrui Qiu** (China University of Geosciences, Wuhan), **Vladimir Shumila** (ESG Solutions), and **Elizabeth Silber** (Sandia National Laboratory) are the 2025 recipients of SSA's Reviewer of the Year award.

Abrahamson, Llenos and Shumila were recognized for their work on behalf of the *Bulletin of the Seismological Society of America* (*BSSA*), Qiu and Doody for *Seismological Research Letters* (*SRL*), and Ishimura and Silber for *The Seismic Record* (*TSR*).

Lauded for their insightful feedback and scientific expertise, the seven individuals are essential partners in the Society's publishing program. Their volunteer hours ensure that SSA journals maintain their high quality of peer review and community prestige. But the reviewers say they have benefited as well from their experience, gaining exposure to new data and sharpening their own research and writing skills.

"While I'm contributing to the community by reviewing, the process also keeps me aware of important methodological and conceptual advances before they are published. In many cases, it saves me significant time that I would otherwise spend searching for relevant new work on my own," said Qiu. "So reviewing for *SRL* feels both meaningful and intellectually rewarding."

"Being a reviewer has helped me think critically about my own research," said Doody, "and anticipate questions and concerns a reviewer might have before I get to the stage of submitting my research."

"Understanding the reviewer's perspective has refined how I write my own papers and how I mentor my students," Ishimura agreed. "I have become more conscious of the final 'output' from the early stages of a project, allowing me to keep the eventual publication in mind throughout the entire research process."

The awardees also said spending time as a reviewer can be especially valuable for early-career researchers. "As an early-career scientist, the constructive criticism I received from reviewers was instrumental to bettering my science and helping me explore sides of my research I wouldn't have considered otherwise," Doody said, noting that reviewing "allows me to pass this benefit on to the others in the community."

Qiu decided to become a reviewer for *SRL* in part because of its excellent editorial staff. "They are outstanding scientists with strong vision and broad perspectives in our field," he said. "Knowing the people behind the journal gives me confidence in its direction and standards, and it makes me genuinely want to contribute."

These reviewers will be recognized from the podium at the 2026 Awards Ceremony.

Manuscript received 2 March 2026
Published online 15 April 2026

Corporate Members, Seismological Society of America

ExxonMobil
Sara Gates
22777 Springwoods Village Parkway
Spring, TX 77389
www.corporate.exxonmobil.com

GeoSIG Ltd
Talhan Biro
Wiesenstrasse 39
8952 Schlieren
Switzerland
www.geosig.com

Guralp Systems
James Lindsey
3 Midas House, Calleva Park Aldermaston
Berkshire RG7 8EA
United Kingdom
www.guralp.com

ISTI
Paul Friberg
5 Case Street
Saratoga Springs, NY 12866
www.isti.com

Kinemetrics, Inc.
Veronica Vera
222 Vista Avenue
Pasadena, CA 91107
www.kinemetrics.com

Lettis Consultants International, Inc.
Jeffrey Unruh
1981 N Broadway
Suite 330
Walnut Creek, CA 94596
www.lettisci.com

Moody's
Nilesh Shome
7575 Gateway Boulevard
Newark, CA 94560
www.moodys.com

Nanometrics
Alyssa Parks
250 Herzberg Road
Kanata, ON K2K 2A1
Canada
www.nanometrics.ca

Puerto Rico Strong Motion Program
Dr. José Martinez-Cruzado
Call Box 9000-Civil Engineering
Mayaguez, Puerto Rico 00681
www.prsmp.uprm.edu

Reftek Systems Inc.
Leonid Zimakov
75 MacDonald Avenue
Dartmouth, NS B3B 1T8
Canada
www.reftek.com

Seismology Research Centre
Adam Pascale
141 Palmer Street
Richmond, VIC 3121
Australia
www.src.com.au

SSA
Seismological
Society of America